AutoCAD
and its applications

by

Terence M. Shumaker
Manager
Autodesk Training Center for AutoCAD
Clackamas Community College, Oregon City, OR

David A. Madsen
Chairperson
Drafting Technology
Clackamas Community College, Oregon City, OR
Board of Directors
American Design Drafting Association

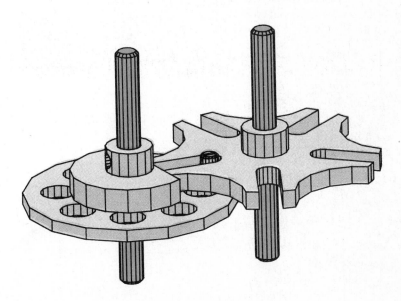

South Holland, Illinois
THE GOODHEART-WILLCOX COMPANY, INC.
Publishers

Library of Congress Catalog Card Number 92-38054
International Standard Book Number 0-87006-014-7

8 9 10   93   97 96 95 94

Library of Congress Cataloging in Publication Data

Shumaker, Terence M.
  AutoCAD and its applications release 12 / Terence M. Shumaker, David A. Madsen.

    p. cm.
  Includes index.
  ISBN 0-87006-014-7
  1. Computer graphics. 2. AutoCAD (Computer file) I. Madsen, David A. II. Title.
T385 .S46   1993
620'.0042'02855369--dc20   92-38054
                                        CIP

Software for high-resolution screen capture courtesy of Vermont Microsystems, Inc.

INTRODUCTION

AutoCAD and its Applications is a text and workbook combination that provides complete instruction in mastering AutoCAD® commands and drawing techniques. Typical applications of AutoCAD are presented with basic and design concepts. The topics are covered in an easy-to-understand sequence, and progress in a way that allows you to become comfortable with the commands as your knowledge builds from one chapter to the next. In addition, **AutoCAD and its Applications** offers the following features:

- Step-by-step use of AutoCAD's commands.
- In-depth explanations of how and why the commands function as they do.
- Examples and discussion of actual industrial practices.
- Professional tips explaining how to use AutoCAD effectively and efficiently.
- Over 200 exercises placed within the chapters. Each exercise involves several tasks to reinforce the topic just covered.
- Chapter tests allow you to review commands and key AutoCAD concepts.
- A large selection of drafting problems supplement each chapter. Problems are presented as actual plotted industrial drawings or engineering sketches.

With **AutoCAD and its Applications**, you not only learn AutoCAD commands, but also you become acquainted with:

- Office practices for firms using CAD systems.
- Preliminary planning, sketches, and drawing plan sheets.
- Linetypes and their uses.
- Drawing geometric shapes.
- Geometric constructions with AutoCAD.
- Special editing operations that increase productivity over manual drafting.
- Making multiview drawings with AutoCAD.
- Dimensioning techniques and practices, as interpreted through accepted standards.
- Drawing sectional views and designing graphic patterns.
- Designing shapes and symbols for multiple use.
- Creating symbol libraries.
- Sketching with AutoCAD.
- 3-D drawing and solid modeling with AutoCAD.
- Working with raster images, PostScript™ fonts and files, and shaded renderings.
- Database links to AutoCAD drawings and entities, and Structured Query Language (SQL).
- Plotting and printing drawings.
- Using DOS commands for system configuration and file manipulations.
- Customizing AutoCAD by creating and modifying screen and tablet menus.
- Basic AutoLISP® command.
    The most important factor in learning AutoCAD is to find a reference that:
- Answers all the questions.
- Presents the commands in an easy-to-understand, logical sequence.
- Applies AutoCAD to typical drafting and design tasks.
- Reduces the fear of using AutoCAD.

AutoCAD and its Applications does this—and even more.

Checking the AutoCAD reference manuals

No other reference should be needed when using this worktext. However, the authors have referenced the major topic areas to one of the AutoCAD reference manuals for your convenience. To the right of most major headings in this text, you will find one of the following abbreviations:

- **ARM** – AutoCAD Reference Manual
- **AMERM** – Advanced Modeling Extension Reference Manual
- **ARRM** – AutoCAD Render Reference Manual
- **ASERM** – AutoCAD SQL Extension Reference Manual
- **AEM** – AutoCAD Extras Manual
- **ACM** – AutoCAD Customization Manual
- **APRM** – AutoLISP Programmer's Reference Manual

The number to the right of each abbreviation identifies the related chapter in the AutoCAD reference manuals. For example, a reference such as "ARM 4" refers to the *AutoCAD Reference Manual*, Chapter 4. If you see the reference "APRM 1," this means that the topic is referenced to Chapter 1 of the *AutoLISP Programmer's Reference Manual*. However, due to restructuring of the AutoCAD documentation by Autodesk, these Manual references may not be directly correlated.

Introducing the AutoCAD commands

There are several ways to select AutoCAD drawing commands. The format is slightly different when entering commands on the keyboard when compared to selecting commands from the screen, pull-down, or template menus. For this reason, all AutoCAD commands and related options in this text are presented as if they were typed at the keyboard (unless otherwise specified). This allows the text to show the full command name and the prompts that appear on screen. You will note in the body of the text that the command or option is enclosed within quotation marks to make it stand out from surrounding text. (When entering these commands or options at the keyboard, do *not* type the quotation marks when entering these items.) Yet, since you are encouraged to enter commands in the most comvenient manner, other command entry methods are also presented. These include the screen menu, pull-down menus, and the AutoCAD template menu.

Commands, options, and values the user must enter are given in bold text as shown in the following example. Pressing the ENTER (RETURN) key is indicated with the ENTER symbol (↵).

    Command: **LINE** ↵
    From point: **2,2** ↵
    To point: **4,2** ↵
    To point: ↵

General input such as picking a point or selecting an object is presented in italics.

    Command: **LINE** ↵
    From point: *(pick a point)*
    To point: *(pick another point)*
    To point: ↵

Selecting commands from pull-down menus is discussed throughout the text. This is important if your computer supports this feature. The AutoCAD template is presented late in the text. This gives you the opportunity to become familiar with other input formats before using the template. Also, not everyone uses a digitizing tablet and template menu in their daily CAD endeavors.

Prerequisites

The only prerequisite to using this text is an interest in AutoCAD. **AutoCAD and its Applications** takes you through the entire AutoCAD command structure and applies AutoCAD functions to basic drafting concepts.

Flexibility in design

Flexibility is the key word when using **AutoCAD and its Applications**. This worktext is an excellent training aid for individual, as well as classroom instruction. **AutoCAD and its Applications** teaches you AutoCAD and how it applies to common drafting tasks. It is also an invaluable resource for professionals using AutoCAD. The tests and drafting problems are set up to allow an instructor to select individual or group learning goals. Several optional course syllabi are provided in the **Solution Manual** for the instructor to use or revise to suit individual classroom needs.

AutoCAD and its Applications provides several ways for you to evaluate your performance. Included are:

- **Exercises.** Each chapter is divided into short sections covering various aspects of AutoCAD. An exercise composed of several instructions is found at the end of each section. These exercises help you become acquainted with commands at your own pace.
- **Chapter tests.** Each chapter includes a written test. Questions may require you to provide the proper command, option, or response to perform a certain task.
- **Drafting problems.** A variety of drafting and design problems are presented at the end of each chapter. These are presented as "real-world" CAD drawings or engineering sketches, and like some real-world applications, may contain mistakes or inaccuracies. Always be sure to modify the drawing as needed and apply accurate dimensions to the completed drawings where required. The problems are designed to make you think, solve problems, use design techniques, research proper drawing standards, and correct errors in the drawings or engineering sketches.

── NOTE ──

Some problems presented in this text may contain errors or slight inaccuracies. This is intentional and is meant to encourage the AutoCAD user to apply appropriate techniques and standards in order to solve the problem. As in real-world applications, sketches should be considered to be preliminary layouts. Always question inaccuracies in sketches and designs, and consult the applicable standards or other resources.

In addition to the previously mentioned features, you will see a variety of notices throughout the text. They include the following:

- **Professional Tips.** These ideas and suggestions are aimed at increasing your productivity and enhancing your use of AutoCAD commands and techniques.
- **Notes.** A note alerts you to important aspects of the command or activity that is being discussed.
- **Hints.** This provides a technique for quick and efficient execution of a command or process.
- **Cautions.** A caution alerts you to potential problems if instructions or commands are used incorrectly, or if an action by the computer user could cause damage or alteration to files, directories, or disks. If you are in doubt after reading a caution, always consult your instructor or supervisor.

DISK SUPPLEMENTS

Two disk supplement packages are available for use with **AutoCAD and its Applications**. *AutoCAD Release 12 software is required for Goodheart-Willcox software to operate properly.* The Student Work Disk package contains specialized pull-down menus. The menus contain a variety of activities that are intended to be used as a supplement to the exercises and activities found in the text. The Work Disk activities correspond to Chapters 8-27 of the text. A customized ACAD.HLP file is also included in the disk package. In addition to referencing the AutoCAD reference manuals, this file also references the appropriate page number(s) for **AutoCAD and its Applications.**

The Instructor's Solution Disk package has been designed as an aid to instructors who evaluate student drawings on disk. This package enables instructors to mark errors or make comments in student drawing files. The Solution Disks contain all the necessary drawing files for use in evaluating drawings, including template drawings for correcting selected activities. In addition, the customized ACAD.HLP file previously discussed is also included. Both of these disk supplement packages can be ordered directly from the publisher at the current catalog price.

ABOUT THE AUTHORS

Terence M. Shumaker is Manager of the Autodesk Training Center for AutoCAD, and a Drafting Technology Instructor at Clackamas Community College. Terence has taught at the community college level since 1977. He has commercial experience in surveying, civil drafting, industrial piping, and technical illustration. He is the author of Goodheart-Willcox's **Process Pipe Drafting**, and co-author of **AutoCAD Essentials**.

David A. Madsen is the Chairperson of Drafting Technology and the Autodesk Training Center for AutoCAD at Clackamas Community College. In addition to community college experience, David was also a Drafting Technology instructor at Centennial High School in Gresham, Oregon. David also has extensive experience in mechanical drafting, architectural design and drafting, and construction practices. He is the author of several Goodheart-Willcox drafting and design textbooks, including **Geometric Dimensioning and Tolerancing**, and co-author of **AutoCAD Essentials**.

NOTICE TO THE USER

This worktext is designed as a complete entry-level AutoCAD teaching tool. The authors present a typical point of view. Users may find alternate and possibly better techniques for using AutoCAD. The authors and publisher accept no responsibility for any loss or damage resulting from the contents of information presented in this text.

ACKNOWLEDGEMENTS

The authors and publisher would like to thank the following individuals and companies for their assistance and contributions:

Technical assistance and contribution of materials
Margo Bilson of Willamette Industries, Inc.
Fitzgerald, Hagan, & Hackathorn
Dr. Stuart Soman of Briarcliffe College
Gil Hoellerich, Springdale, AR

Contribution of materials
Cynthia B. Clark of the American Society of Mechanical Engineers
Marty McConnell of Houston Instrument, A Summagraphics Corporation
Grace Avila, Neele Johnston, and Wayne Hodgins of Autodesk, Inc.
Dave Hall of the Harris Group, Inc.

Contribution of photographs or other technical information
Amdek Corporation
Autodesk, Inc.
CADalyst magazine
CADENCE magazine
Chris Lindner
EPCM Services Ltd.
Far Mountain Corporation
Gateway 2000
GTCO Corporation
Hewlett-Packard
Houston Instrument, A Summagraphics Corporation
IOLINE Corporation
JDL, Inc.
Jerome Hart
Jim Armstrong

Kunz Associates
Matt Slay
Mitsubishi Electronics America, Inc.
Microsoft Corporation
Mouse Systems Corporation
NEC Information Systems, Inc.
Northwest Engineering
Schuchart & Associates, Inc.
Summagraphics Corporation
The American Society of Mechanical Engineers
The Xerox Engineering Systems Company
Weiser, Inc.
Willamette Industries, Inc.

Technical assistance and reviews
Michael Jones, Instructor and Systems Manager, Autodesk Training Center for AutoCAD,
  Clackamas Community College
Kevin DeVoll, Margaret Burke
Rod Rawls for review of Chapter 34, Introduction to AutoLISP

Hardware contributions
Ann Foster of Oregon Digital for use of a Hewlett-Packard IIP Laser Printer
Brian St. Amour of Vermont Microsystems, Inc. for use of an X/Series high-resolution graphics
  card and AutoMate/PRO
Mitsubishi Electronics America, Inc. for use of a Diamond Pro 20 color monitor
Kevin Pflaum of Houston Instrument, A Summagraphics Corporation for use of a DMP series
  plotter

TRADEMARKS

CONTENTS

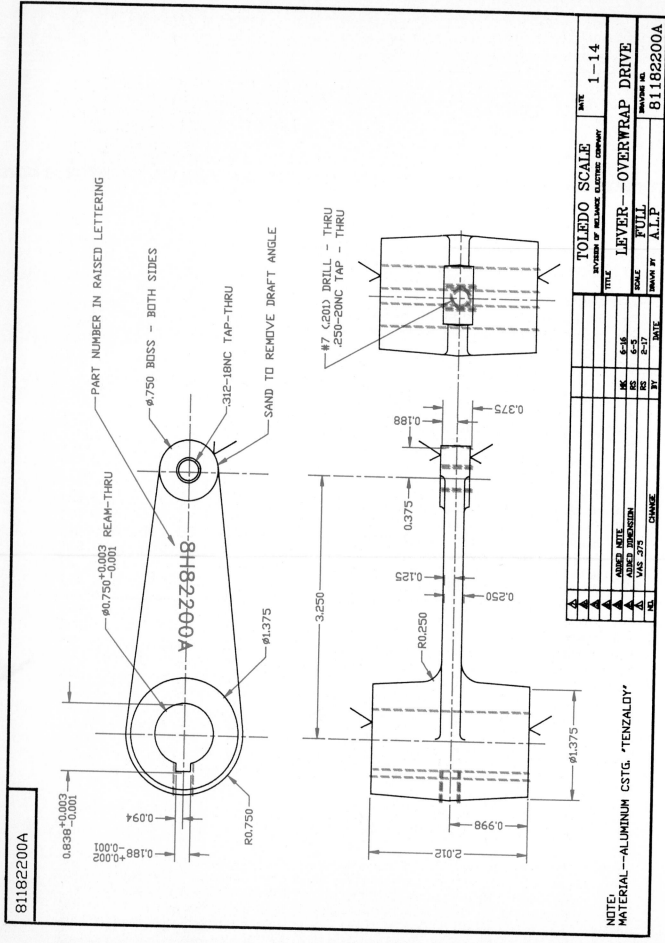

Mechanical drawing of a lever.

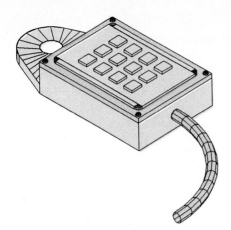

Chapter 1

INTRODUCTION TO COMPUTER-AIDED DRAFTING

Learning objectives
After completing this chapter, you will be able to:
☐ Identify the tools (equipment) used in computer-aided drafting.
☐ Describe the methods and procedures used in computer-aided drafting.
☐ Explain the value of planning and system management.
☐ Follow the basic rules of hygiene for a computer lab.

THE TOOLS OF CAD

The computer is the principal tool of the drafter's workstation. It is quickly replacing manual drafting tools such as drafting tables, pencils, scales, and templates. The drafter, designer, or engineer can create layouts and designs on a computer screen using the commands of a computer program. Points are chosen with an electronic pointing device such as a digitizer or mouse. Original drawings do not have to be copied with a blueprint machine. Instead, the CAD drafter can send the drawing data to a plotter for an inked original or to a printer for a quick check print. The final drawing is saved on magnetic media such as floppy disks, hard disks, or magnetic tape.

The AutoCAD software enables you to create your own drawing commands. This aspect of CAD is often overlooked, and is addressed in this book. You will be learning to use a new set of tools—the computer and AutoCAD. However, you will also be introduced to the methods of customization. Customization is modifying the basic program to meet your specific needs. For example, you may want to create a command to insert a specific symbol at an exact location. It is easy with AutoCAD. This skill allows you to become more productive, and prepares you to move into fields of expertise such as design, engineering, software development, animation and video production, or computer programming.

The nature of AutoCAD allows you to alter the basic program into something that is highly specialized and efficient. Along the way, however, you must pick up many new skills and ways of thinking about the drawing process.

THE NEW METHODS OF CAD

As you begin to use AutoCAD, you will encounter many new drawing methods. These require that you organize your thoughts and plan the project in order to complete the drawing productively. For example, suppose you wish to draw a symmetrical object (an object that is the same on both sides of a centerline). You should not just begin drawing shapes on one side, and then redraw them on the other side. Rather, you should select drawing commands and pick positions on the computer screen using an input device to draw one-half of the object. A special command is then used to reflect or "mirror" the shapes just drawn to complete the object. With CAD, you should never draw the same shape twice.

As you begin your CAD training, plan your drawing sessions thoroughly to organize your thoughts. Sketch the problem or design, noting size and locations of features. List the drawing commands needed in the order they are to be used. Schedule a regular time to use the computer and adhere to that time. Follow the standards set by your school or firm. These might include: specific drawing names, project planning sheets, project logs, drawing layout procedures, special title blocks, and the location where drawings are to be stored. Standards and procedures must be followed by everyone using the computers in your school or company. Confusion may result if your drawings do not have the proper name, are stored in the wrong place, or have the wrong title block.

When using AutoCAD, you will be dealing with a machine that asks questions, follows instructions promptly, and executes every command you give it. Since the computer can destroy your drawing in a fraction of a second, you should develop the habit of saving your work regularly—at least every 10 to 15 minutes. (In Release 12, the SAVETIME system variable can be set to automatically save your drawings at predetermined intervals. SAVETIME is covered in detail in Chapter 5.) Drawings may be lost due to a software error, hardware malfunction, power failure, or your own mistakes. This is not common, but you should still be prepared for such an event.

You should develop methods of managing your work. This is critical to computer drafting and is discussed throughout the text. Keep the following points in mind as you begin your AutoCAD training.

- Plan your work and organize your thoughts.
- Learn and use your classroom or office standards.
- Save your work often.

If you remember and follow these three points, your grasp of the tools and methods of CAD will be easier. In addition, your experiences with the computer will be more enjoyable.

HARDWARE

The physical pieces of equipment used in computer-aided drafting and design are referred to as *hardware*. The microcomputer is the main component. It is accompanied by several other devices called *peripherals,* Fig. 1-1. The specific components included in a CAD workstation are presented in the following discussion.

Fig. 1-1. Components of an AutoCAD workstation.   (Hewlett-Packard)

Computer

The most commonly used microcomputers for CAD in the education and industrial fields is the IBM, and other microcomputers called "IBM compatibles" or "clones." These clones must be 100% compatible with IBM models for AutoCAD to work properly. The important consideration, regardless of the brand of machine used, is that the computer has the proper components and memory. See Appendix B for the specific hardware requirements of AutoCAD.

A typical microcomputer is a rectangular-shaped metal box containing the central processing unit (CPU), memory, flexible disk drives, and hard disk drive(s).

The heart of the computer—the CPU—is a chip that handles all of the system's calculations. Several printed circuit boards called "cards," occupy the computer. These cards have a variety of integrated circuit chips and electronic components attached. Specific cards or "boards" are required for a video graphics display, the connection for a digitizer or mouse (called *serial ports*), and additional items such as extra memory for the computer.

The computer has a group of blank chips (like empty storage boxes), called *memory*. Memory is also commonly referred to as *random access memory*, or *RAM*. Random access memory refers to the ability of the computer to randomly store and search for data in this area of the memory. When the computer is turned on, the operating system (such as DOS, or the Disk Operating System) is loaded into a small portion of the computer's memory. The operating system remains there because it can be accessed faster than if it was used directly from the hard disk drive.

When AutoCAD is loaded, it is also placed into the computer's RAM. If your computer has a small amount of RAM, for example, 2MB (2 million bytes, or characters), most of the AutoCAD program can be placed in the computer's memory. Then, when you work on a drawing, some (or all) of the drawing may also initially be placed in the computer's memory. If your drawing gets too big, some of it is removed from RAM, and copied, or *paged* to the hard disk. If the "page" of your drawing or AutoCAD is needed again, it is copied back into memory. If you are quick, you may notice when this happens by looking at the flexible and hard disk lights located on the front of your computer. Watch these lights and you will begin to get a good idea of when AutoCAD accesses the flexible disk and hard disk drives.

Most computers are available with a "standard" 640K, or 640,000 bytes of memory. Remember that one byte is roughly equal to one character, such as a letter or number. Memory added to a computer above the basic 640K is called *extended memory*. In order to run AutoCAD Release 12, your computer must have at least 4MB (4 million bytes) of memory, and 8MB is recommended. The more memory a computer has, the faster it can work because it can load programs into memory and not have to work from the hard disk drive, which is much slower.

Monitor

The *monitor* is the output or display device that resembles a small TV, and usually sits atop the computer box, Fig. 1-2. Common monitor sizes are 13″ and 21″ diagonal measurement. Monitors are available in color and monochrome display. *Monochrome* refers to a single text and graphics color, most often white, amber, or green on a black background.

Display resolution determines how smooth or jagged text and objects appear on screen. Resolution is measured in *pixels*. The word "pixel" is derived from PIcture ELement. A pixel appears as a dot on the screen, but it is actually a tiny rectangle. The display of a monitor is composed of horizontal row and vertical columns of pixels. A typical display resolution is 640 x 350, meaning there are 640 dots horizontally and 350 dots vertically. High-resolution monitors may display 1024 x 768 pixels.

The resolution of your monitor is directly related to a component in the computer called a *graphics card*. The graphics card is a "board" that contains a variety of computer chips. This board is inserted in a slot inside the computer that allows the CPU of the computer to communicate with the graphics card and monitor. Graphics cards are available in three basic types:

- Color Graphics Adaptor (CGA)
- Enhanced Graphics Adaptor (EGA)
- Video Graphics Array (VGA)

EGA and VGA graphics cards are used with AutoCAD. A resolution of 640 x 350 and 16 colors are available with EGA. From 640 x 480 to 1024 x 768 resolution, and up to 256 colors is possible with VGA.

Fig. 1-2. A typical arrangement of the computer and display device.   (Mitsubishi Electronics America, Inc.)

Keyboard

If you type well, you will soon discover that the keyboard is the most used input device at your workstation. It resembles a standard typewriter keyboard but has additional keys to the left, right, and top, Fig. 1-3. The exact location and number of these keys vary from one model to another. In addition to typing commands, the keyboard can be used for entering precise coordinate values (see Chapter 5), text, and dimensions.

The keys labeled F1-F10, or F1-F12, are called *function keys*. These immediately perform commands that would otherwise have to be typed. AutoCAD uses function keys to control specific operations, many of which are discussed in Chapter 3.

Fig. 1-3. A computer keyboard. Note the two sets of function keys along the left side and top of this keyboard. Many computers have only one set of function keys.   (Gateway 2000)

Pointing devices

Another important input device is the pointer, or pointing device. A *pointing device* moves the cursor or crosshairs on the screen. With it, you can select point locations and commands from a screen or digitizer tablet menu. The most commonly used pointing devices are a multibutton *puck* or a pen-shaped *stylus*. These two devices are connected to a *digitizer tablet*. Other commonly used pointing devices include the *mouse* and *trackball*. The mouse or trackball are often suitable choices when cost and table space are concerns (since they do not require a digitizer). Each pointer functions differently, but all put information into the computer.

The digitizer tablet is the drawing board of the CAD workstation. Several examples are shown in Fig. 1-4. A plastic or paper *menu overlay* containing AutoCAD commands and/or drawing symbols can also be placed on the digitizer. Items can be selected directly from the menu without looking at the screen. Movement of the puck or stylus is recorded and displayed on the screen as the cursor position. Commands or menus can be picked on the screen by moving the pointing device to the desired item. Then press the pick button on the puck, or press down on the stylus.

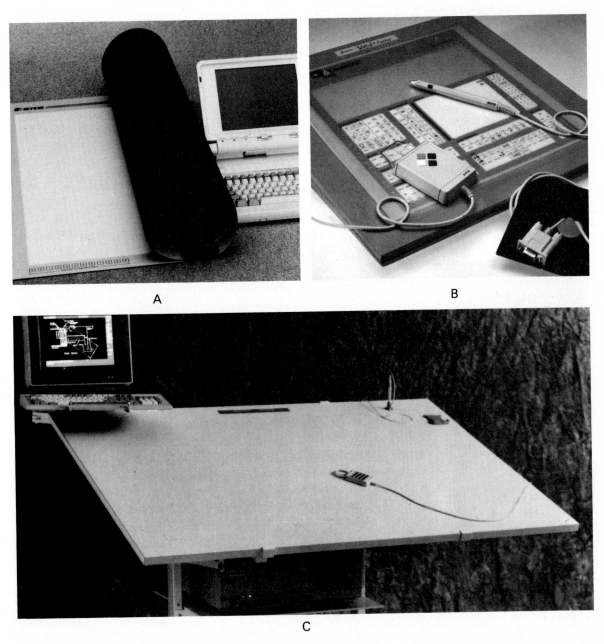

A   B

C

Fig. 1-4. A—Roll-up digitizer with laptop computer. B—A 12″ x 12″ digitizer tablet with puck and stylus. C—An adjustable table digitizer, 36″ x 48″. (GTCO Corporation)

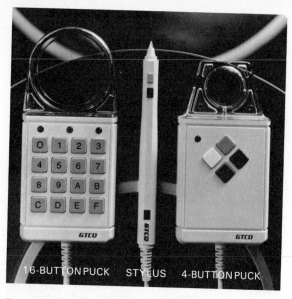

Fig. 1-5. Digitizer pucks are available with different button arrangements. The stylus resembles a pen. (GTCO Corporation)

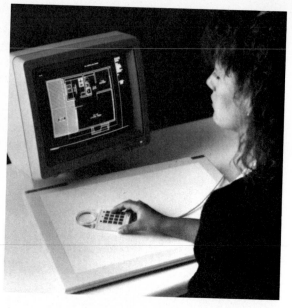

Fig. 1-6. A puck is used to select commands and points on the screen. (GTCO Corporation)

The multibutton puck, used with a digitizer tablet may have from 1 to 16 buttons. The bottom surface of the puck slides on the digitizer surface. See Fig. 1-5. A set of fine crosshairs mounted in the puck serve as the pick point for this device. When the display screen crosshairs move, they are showing the position of the puck's crosshairs on the tablet, Fig. 1-6. One button—the pick button—enters points and selects menu commands. All of the other buttons can be programmed to suit the user. This is discussed in Chapter 32.

The stylus, a pen-shaped pointer, attached to the digitizer with a wire, works in a different manner. The point of the stylus is pressed down on the surface of the digitizer. A slight click can be felt and even heard. This indicates that a point or menu item at the cursor's position on the screen has been selected. A stylus is also shown in Fig. 1-5.

The mouse is the most inexpensive pointing device because it does not require a digitizer tablet. A mouse needs only a small flat surface to operate. The mouse is available in two forms: mechanical and optical. See Fig. 1-7.

An optical mouse uses a special reflective pad with grid lines. A light shines from the mouse to the pad. The location of the mouse is shown as the crosshairs location on the screen. The optical mouse must remain on the special pad in order to work.

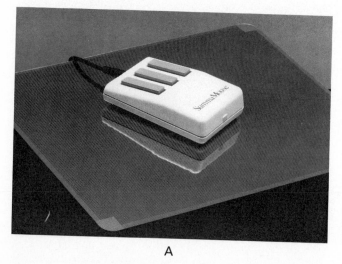

A

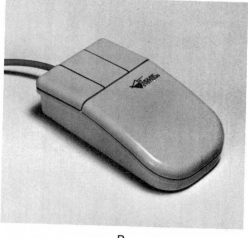

B

Fig. 1-7. A—An optical mouse. Note the reflective pad and grid lines in the pad. (Summagraphics) B—A mechanical mouse can be used on almost any surface. (Mouse Systems Corporation)

The mechanical mouse has a roller ball on the bottom. The movement of the roller on any flat surface is sent to the computer and displayed as the screen crosshairs movement. Unlike the stylus and puck, the mouse can be lifted and moved to another position without affecting the location of the screen crosshairs.

If you turn a mouse over, the roller ball is exposed. If this ball was increased in size and enlarged another inch, you would have a trackball. A trackball enables you to move the cursor on the screen by rolling a ball. A trackball requires only the amount of table space needed for it to sit on. The only part you move is the ball. There are a variety of trackballs available, but most have two or three buttons, much like a mouse. See Fig. 1-8.

Fig. 1-8. A trackball is a pointing device, which is used by rolling the ball to move the screen cursor or crosshairs. A—Desktop trackball. (Mouse Systems Corporation) B—Portable trackballs are commonly used with laptop computers. (Microsoft Corporation)

Storage devices and media

Your computer should have an arrangement of floppy and/or hard disk drives. These are the storage areas for AutoCAD and its drawings. A standard 5.25″ floppy disk holds 360,000 (360K) characters of information. A character is referred to as a *byte*. A *high-density* floppy disk holds 1.2 million bytes of information. Million is called *mega*; therefore, a high-density disk's capacity is called 1.2 megabytes, or 1.2MB. Your computer will have one or two of these floppy disk drives, Fig. 1-9. Small lights on the fronts of the disk drives indicate when they are being accessed.

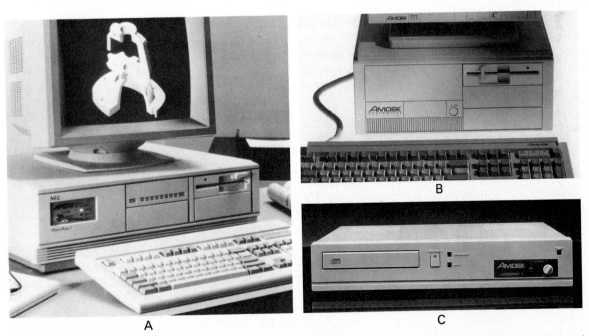

Fig. 1-9. A—Single floppy disk drive with hard disk drive to the left. Note extra compartments for additional drives. (NEC Information Systems, Inc.) B—Computer with single floppy disk drive and additional slots. (Amdek Corporation) C—Laser drive CD ROM (Read-Only Memory). (Amdek Corporation)

Many computer users prefer the 3.5″ flexible disk because of its size and the fact that the magnetic media is enclosed in a hard plastic shell, which protects it from damage. The 3.5″ disk was originally designed to fit a shirt pocket, therefore it is convenient to carry around. The 3.5″ disk can be used in either IBM/DOS compatible systems, or Apple Macintosh systems. In addition, these disks are available in either the 720K or 1.44MB formats. Most new computers are equipped with high-density disk drives, which accept either 5.25″ 1.2MB or 3.5″ 1.44MB disks. If you are using an older computer with a low-density disk drive, you will not be able to use the full storage capacity of high-density disks. Chapters 2 and 35 provide additional information about preparing disks for use.

Computer users are making increased use of the high-density compact optical digital disk (CD) for data storage. These are much like the compact audio disks. Such devices are now in use for reading CD ROM (read-only memory) disks. An example of a CD ROM drive is shown in Fig. 1-9C.

In addition to flexible disk drives, your computer also has a hard disk drive. AutoCAD requires a hard disk to operate. The hard disk is a sealed unit that contains one or more metal disks, or "platters." These disks have a much greater storage capacity than floppy disks, and are measured in megabytes. Common hard disk sizes are 40MB to 200MB. A small light on the front of the computer indicates when the hard disk drive is being accessed. Before AutoCAD can be used, it must be installed onto the hard disk drive. (See Appendix A for installation information.)

Plotter

Paper and film drawings are most often output by a plotter. A plotter uses pencil, felt tip, ballpoint, or wet ink pens to put lines on paper. These devices can plot any size drawing, and are available in a variety of sizes, Fig. 1-10. Plotting is normally done for final documents. Drafters and designers can work for a long time before they ever need to plot their work. For that, and other reasons, most schools and companies have one plotter that is shared by several workstations. The plotting routine is covered in Chapter 27.

The *electrostatic plotter*, Fig. 1-11, is increasing in popularity as its technology improves. This plotter is similar to a printer because tiny, electrically-charged wire nibs create dots on the paper. Ink adheres to these dots and then pressure or heat permanently attaches the ink to the paper. Electrostatic plotters can plot up to 600 dots per inch (dpi) in full color. This produces a high-quality printer plot. The speed of electrostatic plotters is about ten times that of standard plotters. This newer generation of plotters may eventually produce quality copies with such great speed that they will make standard plotters obsolete.

Printer

The raspy sounds of a dot matrix printer are familiar to people who have been to a store or bank. These same printers can render a quick check print of your AutoCAD drawing. Large-format dot matrix printers can produce prints up to C-size (17 x 22). However, other more quiet printing devices—ink-jet, laser, and electrostatic devices—also create high-quality prints. Using a technology similar to electrostatic plotters, laser printers plot up to 600 dpi. An assortment of printers is shown in Fig. 1-12.

Network systems

There is an increasing need for drawing symbol consistency, accurate project time accounting, instant communications between coworkers, and data security. This has led to the popularity of "network systems." A *network* is nothing more than several computers, connected by a cable, which communicate with each other. Complex networks have hundreds of computers or terminals working off of a central computer or *server*. Each workstation on the network still requires a CPU, input device, and display device. A diagram of a typical network system is shown in Fig. 1-13.

The hard disk drives in the server are normally large-capacity drives, in order to store a variety of software, and still have plenty of space for numerous files created by the computer users attached to the network. The network server can also store drawing files that may be needed by computer users in order to complete other new drawings. For example, a base drawing of the walls of a structure can be stored on the server. When a student or employee needs to work on a new drawing of the plumbing or electrical layout of the structure, they simply load the base drawing from the server into their computer and begin working. In most cases, the base drawing is preserved in its original form and a different name is given to the new drawing.

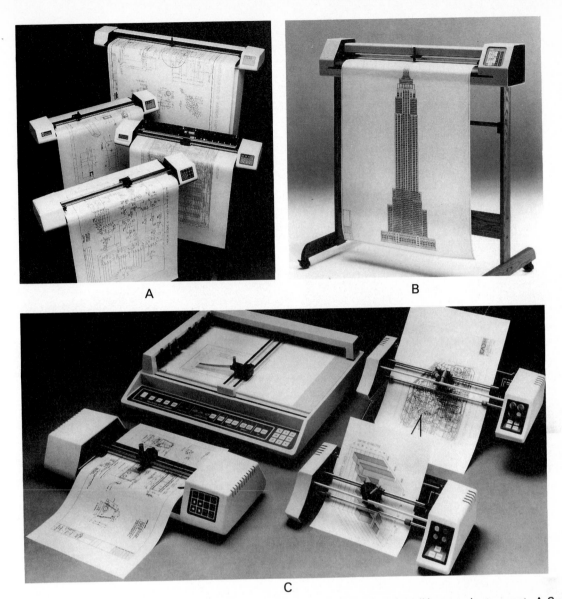

Fig. 1-10. A—Standard plotters are available in a variety of sizes and styles. (Houston Instrument, A Summagraphics Company) B—This large format (E-size) pen plotter has a wood frame. (IOLINE Corporation) C—Desktop plotters can handle A- and B-size drawings.   (Houston Instrument, A Summagraphics Company)

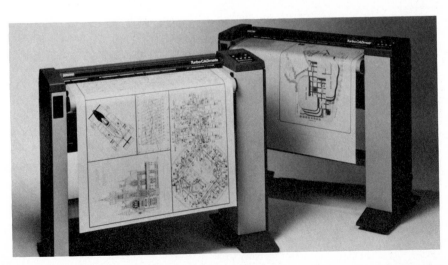

Fig. 1-11. Electrostatic plotters use a process similar to laser printers. They produce drawings about ten times as fast as pen plotters.   (The Xerox Engineering Systems Company)

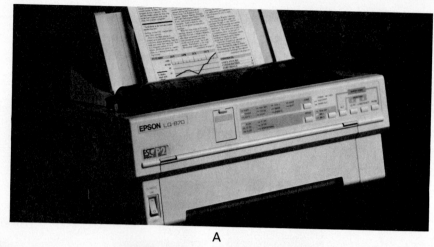

A

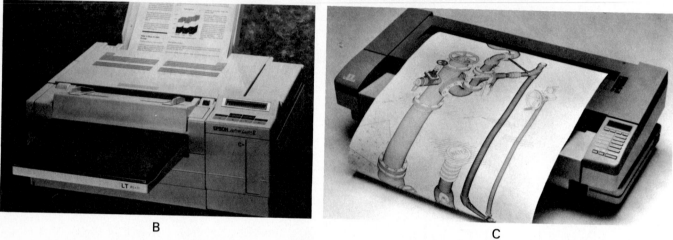

B   C

Fig. 1-12. Printers can produce quick, good-quality prints. A—24-pin dot matrix printer. (Epson) B—High-quality prints are produced by laser printers. (Epson) C—This large format (A- to D-size), thermal printer can print up to 20 colors.   (JDL, Inc.)

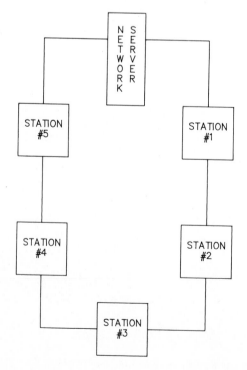

Fig. 1-13. Layout of a typical computer network system.

AutoCAD provides a facility that automatically locks a drawing when a person "checks it out" of the network. This means that only one person can work on a drawing at any given time, thus preventing several people from making different changes to the drawing.

COMPUTER DRAFTING PROCEDURES

The finished product of a CAD drafter is similar to that of a manual drafter. However, some of the thought processes and procedures used to produce the final product are different. A drawing plan must be developed in which all the aspects of the project are considered. This requires careful management of the CAD system and the creation and use of detailed standards for the planning and drawing process.

Drawing planning

Drawing planning involves looking at the entire process or project in which you as a drafter, designer, or engineer, are involved. A plan determines how a project is going to be approached. It includes the drawings to be created, how they will be titled and numbered, the information to be presented, and the types of symbols needed to show the information.

More specifically, drawing planning applies to how you create and manage a drawing or set of drawings. Drafters who begin constructing a drawing from the seat of their pants—creating symbols and naming objects, shapes, and views as they go—do not possess a good drawing plan. Those who plan, use consistent techniques, and adhere to school or company standards are developing good drawing habits.

Throughout this text you will find aids to help you develop good drawing habits. One of the first steps in developing your skills is to learn how to plan your work. The importance of planning cannot be emphasized enough. There is no substitute. Just because you are using a computer does not mean you can be sloppy and take shortcuts. Now, more than ever, there is a need for planning.

Creating and using drawing standards

Standards are guidelines for operating procedures, drawing techniques, and record keeping. Most schools and companies have established standards. It is important that standards exist and are used by all CAD personnel. Drawing standards may include:

- Methods of file storage: location and name.
- File naming conventions.
- Drawing sheet sizes and title blocks to be used.
- Drawing symbols.
- Dimensioning techniques.
- Text styles.
- Linetypes.
- Color schemes for plotting.
- File backup methods and times.

Your standards may vary in content, but the most important aspect of standards is that they are used. The more your standards are used, the more efficiently the classroom or office will run. In addition, it will be easier to manage the system and plan projects. As they are used, standards will change to reflect new methods, techniques, and symbols. All students and employees using the CAD system must be informed of changes immediately. This increases communication and maintains a high level of consistency and productivity.

Planning your work

Study the planning pyramids in Fig. 1-14. The horizontal axes of the pyramids represent the amount of time spent on the project. The vertical axes represent the life of the project. The top level is the planning stage and the bottom level is the final execution of the project. The pyramid on the right is pointed at the top and indicates a small amount of planning. As the project progresses, more and more time is devoted to planning and less time is available for other tasks. This is *not* an ideal situation. The inverted pyramid on the left shows a lot of time devoted to initial planning. As the project advances, less planning time is needed, thus freeing more time for other tasks.

Remember the message of the planning pyramids as you begin your study of AutoCAD. When you feel the need to dive blindly into a drawing or project, restrain yourself. Take the time needed for development of the project goals. Then proceed with the confidence of knowing where you are heading.

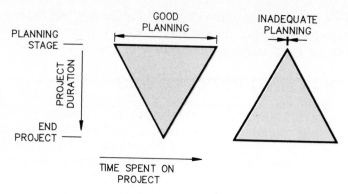

Fig. 1-14. Planning pyramids illustrate time required for well-planned and poorly-planned projects.

During your early stages of AutoCAD training, write down all of the instructions needed to construct your drawing. Do this especially for your first few assignments. This means documenting every command and every coordinate point (dimension) needed. Develop a planning sheet for your drawings or use an example shown in Chapter 6. Your time spent at the computer with AutoCAD will be more productive and enjoyable.

System management

The concepts of drawing planning and project planning are parts of system management. (See Appendix C.) System management means that the entire CAD system and related functions are governed by set guidelines. However, simply having guidelines does not mean that the system is being managed. A person or persons must see that procedures and standards are followed throughout the life of a project. If a system is not managed, it soon falls apart. A well-managed system functions smoothly.

Right now, you are probably anxious to begin learning AutoCAD and are wondering why planning, standards, and management are being discussed. It is because you are about to encounter many details, possibilities, methods, and options that you may have never dealt with before. Even if you have never drafted, a basic understanding of AutoCAD will provide you with a solid footing on which to build your experience and knowledge.

You personally may not be the ultimate manager of the CAD system. However, you still need to possess a knowledge of what is meant by system management. Therefore, it is important that you develop an early knowledge of:

- When to store drawings on floppy disks and when to store them on hard disks or other magnetic media.
- How names are assigned to drawings so other employees or your instructor understand their meaning.
- When and how to make backup copies of drawings and store them in a safe place.
- Where to physically store backup floppy disks and magnetic tapes.
- Who should have access to drawings you create.
- Who creates drawing standards and symbols.
- How symbols and standards are distributed to all CAD users.
- Who maintains the hardware and handles software upgrades.

These are just a few aspects of system management affecting your use of AutoCAD in the educational and industrial environments. Before you ever begin a drawing, you should be aware of the items listed above. Know how they relate to your standards and planning procedures because they are a part of system management.

Interactive process

A CAD drafter "interacts" with the drawing much more than a manual drafter. The CAD program asks questions, provides hints, and prompts for information that is needed to complete certain steps. The drawing taped to a drafting board just lies there. It doesn't glow, ask questions, or make demands of the drafter. CAD drafters find themselves involved in an exciting, interactive process. They communicate with the computer to create a drawing.

As you begin learning AutoCAD, you will realize that several skills are required to become a proficient CAD user. The following list provides you with some hints to help you to become comfortable with AutoCAD. They will also allow you to work quickly and efficiently. The following items are discussed in detail in later chapters.

- Plan all work with pencil and paper before using the computer.
- Check the screen menu bar to see if you are in the correct menu and are picking the right command. A command is an instruction that you give to the computer so it can perform a specific task. For example, the LINE command instructs the computer to draw a line between two points you pick.
- Check the status line at the top of the display screen to see which layer(s) and drawing aid(s) are in effect.
- Read the command line at the bottom of the display screen. Constantly check for the correct command, instructions, or proper keyboard entry of data.
- Read the command line after keyboard entry of data before pressing the ENTER or RETURN key. Backspacing to erase incorrect typing is quicker than redoing the command.
- If using a multibutton puck, develop a good hand position that allows easy movement. Your button-pressing finger should move without readjusting your grip of the puck.
- Learn the meanings of all the buttons on your puck or mouse and use them regularly.
- Watch the floppy disk and hard disk drive lights to see when the disks are being accessed. Some disk access may take a few seconds. Knowing what is happening will lessen frustration and impatience.
- Think ahead. Know your next move.
- Learn new commands every day. Don't rely on just a few that seem to work. Find commands that can speed your work and do it more efficiently.
- Save your work every 10 to 15 minutes in case a power failure or system crash deletes the drawing held in computer memory.
- If you're stumped, ask the computer for help. Use the HELP command to display valuable information about each command on the screen.

Computer lab hygiene

Computer equipment is not only costly and complex, it is sensitive. Special cautions should be taken when working with computer equipment and magnetic media.

- It is better to leave computers on all day than to turn them on and off.
- Static electricity can damage computer memory chips. Always ground yourself by stepping on antistatic mats or touching static discharge plates or a metal chair before touching computer hardware.
- Touching the display screen often can build up a static charge in your body. If you must touch the screen, ground yourself often by touching some piece of metal not connected to the computer equipment.
- Keep computers out of dusty areas and away from chalkboards.
- Keep food and drinks away from computer hardware. Coffee and soft drinks spilled in keyboards can ruin your whole day.
- Use a gentle, but firm press on keyboard keys. Avoid sharp strikes.
- Keep magnetic media (floppy disks, magnetic tape) away from magnetic fields such as radio speakers, phones, digitizer tablets, and other computer equipment.
- Store magnetic media in rooms with a moderate, even temperature. Avoid extreme temperature changes.
- Write on disk labels before attaching them to disks.
- Avoid touching the exposed portions of floppy disks and magnetic tapes.

CHAPTER TEST

Write your answers in the spaces provided.

1. How are points chosen on a screen in computer-aided drafting? _____
   _____

2. What type of machine produces an inked original drawing? _____

3. What is customization? _____
   _____

4. Why is drawing planning important? _____
   _____
   _____

5. Why should you save your work every 10 to 15 minutes? _____
   _____
   _____

6. List the seven components of a CAD workstation. _____
   _____
   _____
   _____

7. What is "drawing planning"? _____
   _____
   _____
   _____

8. What are standards? _____
   _____

9. Describe system management. _____
   _____
   _____
   _____

10. How do the CAD drafter and the computer "interact"? _____
    _____
    _____

11. Why should you read the command line at the bottom of the screen? _____
    _____
    _____

12. Why is static electricity an important concern in computer rooms? _____
    _____

PROBLEMS

1. Read through several computer magazines or AutoCAD journals and list three brand names of each piece of hardware required for a computer drafting workstation. Call or visit a local computer equipment dealer and get prices for each piece of equipment.
2. Work up an equipment proposal for the purchase of three different CAD workstation configurations that can run AutoCAD. Visit or call an Authorized AutoCAD Dealer to determine exactly what you need for each item listed below. Record prices for each piece of equipment. Write an introductory statement for each workstation proposal listing the benefits of each. The three proposals should include the following: (You may revise these lists to suit your needs.)

EQUIPMENT	PROPOSAL #1	PROPOSAL #2	PROPOSAL #3

Computer	286 type
	single 5.25″ floppy
	  disk drive
	40MB hard disk drive
	2MB RAM
	1 serial port
	math co-processor
		386 type
		single 3.5″ floppy
		  disk drive
		60MB hard disk drive
		4MB RAM
		2 serial ports
		math co-processor
			486 type
			5.25″ 1.2MB floppy
			  disk drive
			3.5″ 1.44MB floppy
			  disk drive
			100MB hard disk drive
			8 MB RAM
			2 serial ports
			math co-processor

Monitor and Graphics Card	monochrone graphics
	  card
	13″ monochrome
	  monitor
		EGA color card
		13″ color monitor
			VGA color card
			21″ color monitor

Input Device	mouse (two-button)	digitizer (11x11) with
		  4-button cursor
			digitizer (11x11) with
			  12-button cursor

Surge Protector	surge protector	surge protector with power control unit (3 switches)	surge protector with power control unit (5 switches)
Hardcopy Device	dot matrix printer (80 column, 9 pin)	B-size pen plotter (6 pens)	D-size pen plotter (8 pens and wet ink adapter)

3. Compare the following types of input devices. List the advantages and disadvantages of each. Provide general price comparisons, ease of use, space, and maintenance requirements.
   A. Mouse.
   B. Digitizer with stylus.
   C. Digitizer with multibutton puck.
   D. Keyboard.
4. Visit an AutoCAD dealer, hardware vendor, or local engineering or manufacturing firm and request a plotter demonstration. Ask questions about paper sizes, speed, pen types, price, and maintenance. Call or visit a local plotting service. Get information on their services and rates. Write a report on the uses and benefits of owning a plotter. Compare this to the benefits of using a plotting service to create final plots.
5. Write a report on the benefits of using a dot matrix printer for generating all check prints. Visit hardware vendors and research the types and sizes of printers available.
6. Write a comparative report on using dot matrix printers or pen plotters to satisfy your school or company requirements. Take into account the type of drawings you create and their uses. Determine the minimum quality print you need. Compare this to the final products produced by printers and pen plotters. Based on your needs, recommend a product and include in your recommendation the following:
   A. Price.
   B. Size.
   C. Location (where the equipment will be installed).
   D. Maintenance costs (maintenance contract, if available).
   E. Who will operate the equipment.
   F. Cost of supplies and frequency of purchase.
   G. Savings to school or company over a given period of time.

7. Interview your drafting instructors or supervisors and try to determine what type of drawing standards exist at your school or company. Write this down and keep it with you as you learn AutoCAD. Make notes as you progress through this text on how you use these standards. Also note how the standards could be changed to match the capabilities of AutoCAD.

8. Research your drafting department standards. If you do not have a copy of the standards, acquire one. If AutoCAD standards have been created, make notes as to how you can use these in your projects.

    If no standards exist in your department or company, make notes as to how you can help develop standards. Write a report on why your school or company should create CAD standards and how they would be used. Discuss who should be responsible for specific tasks. Recommend procedures, techniques, and forms if necessary. Develop this report as you progress through your AutoCAD instruction, and as you read through this book.

9. Develop a drawing planning sheet for use in your school or company. List items that you think are important for planning a CAD drawing. Make changes to this sheet as you learn more about AutoCAD.

10. Interview your instructors or supervisors to determine how CAD system management is applied in your school or company. Ask questions about the following items:
    A. Drawing storage methods.
    B. Drawing naming standards.
    C. Drawing backup procedures.
    D. Symbol creation and storage.
    E. Hardware and software maintenance and upgrades.

11. List ways in which your computer room can be made cleaner and more secure. Look for problems such as chalkboards, traffic patterns, radios, telephones, garbage cans, heating vents and elements, and locations where people drink and eat.

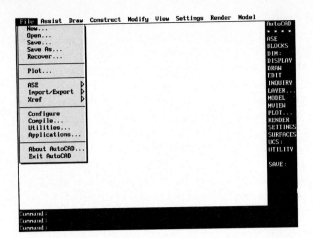

Learning objectives

After completing this chapter, you will be able to:

☐ Identify the meaning of DOS disk drive prompts.

☐ Begin the AutoCAD program from a prompt.

☐ Describe the AutoCAD screen layouts and menu structure.

☐ Describe the function of dialogue boxes.

☐ Operate the input device to select commands.

☐ Use the keyboard keys and input device buttons to select commands, enter text, and pick locations on the screen.

☐ Use the HELP command for assistance.

☐ Format a floppy diskette.

AutoCAD, like most computer software, must first be installed on the hard disk drive of your computer. The AutoCAD program is contained on several floppy disks. To install AutoCAD from floppy disks onto your hard disk drive, you use an installation program provided with the AutoCAD software. Instructions are given on-screen during the installation process to assist you in proper installation. Refer to Appendix A for installation procedures.

After the AutoCAD files have been installed on the hard disk, AutoCAD must be configured. Configuring tells AutoCAD what brand names of equipment you are using. You can select from a variety of graphics devices, printers, plotters, and pointing devices. You are also able to choose the appearance of the screen display during configuration. Installing and configuring AutoCAD are discussed in detail in Appendix A.

This chapter discusses how to get started once you have configured AutoCAD. It shows how the screen display will look when you begin a drawing. You can choose either of two different screen formats, or switch between them if you wish. You will also learn how to select commonly used commands and special functions given to keyboard keys and digitizer puck buttons.

GETTING STARTED

When you turn on your computer, the DOS software is automatically loaded. As you may recall, DOS stands for *Disk Operating System*, and is the "traffic cop" of your computer system. DOS enables the computer to work with files (including drawings), peripheral equipment, and software such as AutoCAD. See Chapter 35 for a detailed discussion of DOS and some of its functions. Some schools or companies have a menu displayed on the screen from which you can make selections. The DOS prompt might be located below this menu.

DOS prompts

A *prompt* is a statement or response issued by the computer to show that it awaits your command. The first prompt you see is a letter followed by the greater-than symbol, or *caret* (〉). These prompts are part of your DOS software and not part of AutoCAD. The prompt on your screen may be A〉, B〉, or C〉. The prompt may also display other information.

The letter indicates the DOS name of the current disk drive. If you have a dual floppy drive computer with a hard disk, the top or left floppy drive is named A: and the lower or right floppy drive is B:. The first hard disk name is C:. The colon (:) is part of the disk drive name, and must be included when you type DOS commands that require the name of the disk drive. Fig. 2-1 illustrates the names of the different drives.

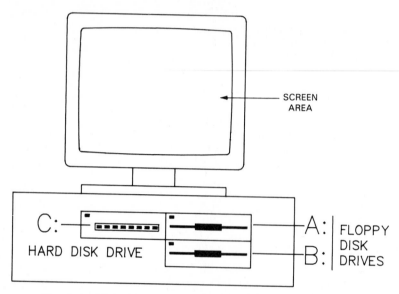

Fig. 2-1. Disk drive arrangements and their DOS names.

To run AutoCAD, the prompt must display the name of the drive that AutoCAD is stored on. This text assumes that AutoCAD is on the C: hard disk drive. The prompt that is on your screen now indicates which disk drive is current, or being looked at by the computer. You need to change drives if the display is anything other than "C〉" or "C:\〉". To change drives, type:

C: ↵

Now the display should read:

C〉 or C:\〉

If the display on the screen was already "C〉" or "C:\〉", you are ready to go.

PROFESSIONAL TIP

AutoCAD can be started automatically using a batch file. A *batch file* is a short program written using DOS commands. It performs a series of DOS commands that otherwise would have to be typed in separately. When AutoCAD is installed, it asks if you want a batch file to be automatically created. This batch file is named ACADR12.BAT, and is used to begin an AutoCAD drawing session. You can use this batch file by typing ACADR12 at the C:\〉 prompt. (You can also modify this file or create your own.) Batch files can be used to load programs and accomplish specific tasks. If your computer does not have a batch file to load AutoCAD, you might want to make one. Appendix C contains information on creating your own batch file that automatically runs AutoCAD from the DOS prompt.

Now you are ready to load AutoCAD from the hard disk into the computer's memory and begin working. First, be certain that the current directory is the one that contains AutoCAD. A directory is like a file drawer. You must be in the right drawer to access the file (AutoCAD).

In most cases, the directory name will be ACAD. Make sure ACAD is current by typing the following instructions at the DOS prompt:

C> **CD \ACAD** ↵ *(this can be in upper or lower case letters)*
C> **ACADR12** ↵

The DOS command "CD \ACAD" changes the current directory to ACAD. The command "ACADR12" loads and runs the AutoCAD program. As AutoCAD is loading into the computer's memory, a message is displayed containing copyright and release information, in addition to the Autodesk® logo. This appears briefly, and is replaced by the graphics screen and menus. You are now inside AutoCAD in what is referred to as the *drawing editor*. This is where you construct and edit drawings.

─── **NOTE** ───

If you are working on a network, and are required to "login," a small "Login to AutoCAD" dialogue box appears when you enter the drawing editor. Simply type the appropriate login name in the Name: edit box. You can save this login name by picking the "Save as default" check box, and the dialogue box will not appear the next time you enter AutoCAD. Check with your instructor or supervisor for proper login names.

AUTOCAD'S MENU STRUCTURE $\boxed{\text{ARM 2}}$

The graphics screen of AutoCAD is composed of several different menus and elements. The *screen menu* appears on the right side of the screen, whereas the *pull-down menus* are hidden behind the top line of the screen display called the *status line*. Any time you pick an item in the screen menu or pull-down menus that is followed by an ellipsis (. . .), it displays a *dialogue box*. A wide variety of the items you pick and select are found in dialogue boxes. In addition, a pick inside a dialogue box may display an *icon menu*. Each of these items is discussed in detail in this chapter. Learn the layout, appearance, and proper use of these areas, and your mastery of AutoCAD will come quickly.

Standard screen layout

The standard screen layout provides a large graphics or drawing area. The drawing area is surrounded by a screen menu on the right, status line along the top, and command line at the bottom. The graphics area is either gray or black and is bounded on two sides (right and bottom) by lines. All AutoCAD text surrounding the drawing area is white on a dark blue background in its uncustomized format. Look at your screen now and study the illustration in Fig. 2-2A.

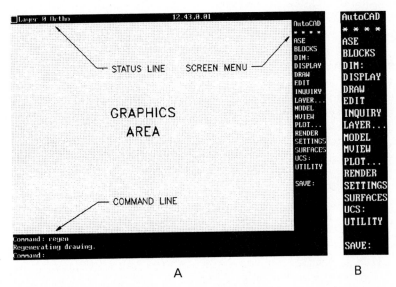

Fig. 2-2. The standard AutoCAD screen layout.

Become familiar with these unique areas of the screen and the information they provide. The list below describes the function of each area.

- **Screen menu.** The screen menu is located along the right side of the screen. Menu names and commands are displayed here. *Menu names* are not followed by punctuation, for example, DRAW. Commands and options are selected from menus by moving your cursor to highlight the item you want, and pressing the pick button of your pointing device. A *command name* is followed by a colon, for example, SAVE:. An *option* is one aspect of a command you select. Commands and options are discussed in greater detail later in this chapter. The word "AutoCAD" is shown at the top of each screen menu. Selecting "AutoCAD" returns you to the Root (beginning) Menu shown in Fig. 2-2B. Selecting the "* * * *" accesses the object snap modes discussed in Chapter 8.
- **Command line** or **prompt line.** The command line is located along the bottom of the screen. It displays the Command: prompt and reflects any entries you make. It also displays prompts that supply information to you or request values and text. Keep your eye on this line. This is where your communication with AutoCAD is shown.
- **Status line.** The status line is located along the top of the screen. It displays several items, Fig. 2-3. The first item on the left of the status line is the name of the current layer. Chapter 17 discusses layers. Next to the layer name, the words "Ortho" and "Snap" are displayed when these two toggle functions are in use. (A *toggle* function is either on or off.) These two toggle functions are discussed in Chapters 4 and 6. Farther to the right are two numbers separated by a comma. This is the X,Y coordinate display, giving your location on the drawing. The coordinate display is covered in Chapter 6. You will refer to the coordinate display often.

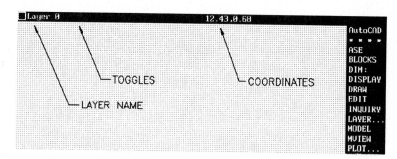

Fig. 2-3. Status line items.

Notice the commands located in the screen menu at the right side of the screen. Move your pointing device so that the items in the sidebar menu are highlighted. When an item is highlighted, it can be selected by pressing the *pick button* on your mouse or puck. With a stylus, press it until it clicks.

The first menu that AutoCAD displays is the Root Menu. It is shown in Fig. 2-4. Note the use of punctuation such as the colons and ellipsis in the menu selections. Remember, if punctuation is not used, the item is a menu name. If a colon is present, the item is a command name. If the entry is followed by an ellipsis, a dialogue box appear when picked (if the FILEDIA system variable is set to 1).

Fig. 2-4. AutoCAD Root menu.

The menu, command, and option structure of AutoCAD is a *nested* arrangement. Options nest inside a command, and commands nest inside a menu. Related commands such as drawing commands are grouped together in the DRAW menu. Fig. 2-5 shows a schematic of this concept. The actual nesting arrangement of the DRAW menu is shown in Fig. 2-6. The entire AutoCAD command structure is shown in Appendix D.

Fig. 2-5. Schematic arrangement of nested commands and options.

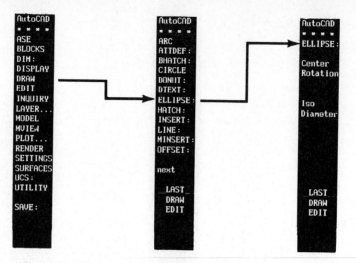

Fig. 2-6. The nesting arrangement of the DRAW menu.

Select the DRAW menu with your pointing device. The menu changes and now consists mostly of commands, Fig. 2-7. Notice that the commands are listed alphabetically. At the bottom of the menu is the following:

next
_____LAST_____
DRAW
EDIT

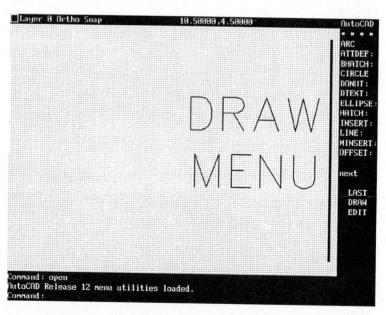

Fig. 2-7. The DRAW menu layout on the screen.

The word "next" indicates that there is another page to this menu. Some menus contain more commands than can fit on the screen at one time. These extra commands are placed on a second page. Select "next" and the second page appears. Once in the menu's second page, selecting the word "previous" takes you back to the first page of the menu. Below "next" is "LAST." Picking this takes you back to the menu that was previously displayed on screen.

The two most often used menus in AutoCAD are DRAW and EDIT. These, in addition to LAST, are displayed in every menu to allow you to access them quickly.

Two additional items are displayed on every menu at the top of the menu bar.

      AutoCAD
      * * * *

If you select "AutoCAD" from the screen menu, the Root Menu is redisplayed. This is good to remember if you get into the menus and forget how to get back. When in doubt, just pick "AutoCAD" from the top of the menu and you will be put back at the Root Menu. As previously mentioned, when the asterisks (* * * *) are picked, the object snap modes are displayed.

The remainder of the screen between the status line and the command, and to the left of the screen menu is the drawing area. Move your crosshairs around to determine the extents of this area. Note how far you must move your pointing device to locate the crosshairs on the screen.

Pull-down menus

When you move your pointing device so the crosshairs touch the status line at the top, the *menu bar* appears. Your crosshairs also change to an arrow pointer. The menu bar is composed of nine items. They are:

File   Assist   Draw   Construct   Modify   View   Settings   Render   Model

As you move the screen cursor along this row, the items are highlighted when the cursor touches them. These "items" are AutoCAD menus. Their placement enables you to quickly select a variety of commands without moving into nested screen menus. Move the cursor to highlight the "Draw" menu and press the pick button. A pull-down menu appears below Draw, Fig. 2-8A. Commands within this menu are selected by moving the cursor to highlight the command. Then press the pick button. Take note of what happens to the screen menu when a pull-down menu selection is made. In many cases, the screen menu displays the options found in the chosen command.

Several of the commands in the Draw pull-down menu have a small arrow to the right. When the arrow pointer is moved over this, a *cascading menu* appears. This menu offers you additional options for that command. See Fig. 2-8B. Each of these commands and options are discussed in the appropriate chapters. If you choose an item from a cascading menu, the menu disappears, allowing you to draw and edit as you desire. If you want to select the same item from the cascading menu again, pick the pull-down menu name twice and the same command or option will be automatically executed.

Some of the menu selections are followed by ellipsis (...). If you pick one of these items, a dialogue box is displayed. Dialogue boxes are discussed in the next section.

If you select the wrong pull-down menu, simply move the cursor to the one you want and pick it. The first menu is removed and the one you pick is displayed. The pull-down menu disappears after you pick an item in the menu, pick a point in the graphics screen, or type on the keyboard.

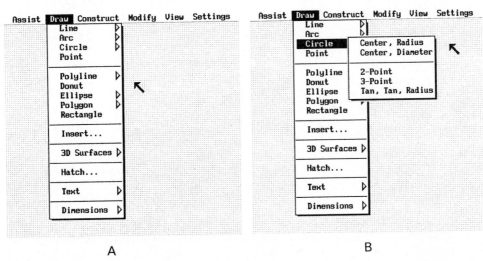

A   B

Fig. 2-8. A—AutoCAD's Draw pull-down menu. B—When the pointer is moved over an arrow in a pull-down menu, a cascading menu appears.

Dialogue boxes

One of the most important aspects of AutoCAD Release 12 is the graphical user interface (GUI). A *graphical user interface* is the manner in which information, options, and choices are displayed for you by the software. Most current versions of any software available today operate with some type of GUI. The most common aspect of the GUI is the dialogue box. The *dialogue box* is a box in which a variety of information is presented to you, and in which you can select an item by simply moving your cursor to it and picking. This process eliminates a lot of typing, thus potentially saving time and increasing productivity.

Commands and selections in the pull-down and screen menus that are followed by ellipsis (...), display a dialogue box when they are picked. A good example of a simple dialogue box is shown in Fig. 2-9. This dialogue box is displayed when you pick the New... command from the File pull-down menu. A detailed discussion of this dialogue box is included in Chapter 5.

```
┌─────────────────────────────────────────────────────┐
│                 Create New Drawing                    │
│  ┌──────────────────┐ ┌──────────────────────────┐   │
│  │   Prototype...   │ │ acad                     │   │
│  └──────────────────┘ └──────────────────────────┘   │
│  ☐ No Prototype                                       │
│  ☐ Retain as Default                                  │
│                                                        │
│  ┌──────────────────┐ ┌──────────────────────────┐   │
│  │ New Drawing Name...│ │                          │   │
│  └──────────────────┘ └──────────────────────────┘   │
│         ┌──────┐      ┌────────┐                      │
│         │  OK  │      │ Cancel │                      │
│         └──────┘      └────────┘                      │
└─────────────────────────────────────────────────────┘
```

Fig. 2-9. A dialogue box appears when you pick an item that is followed by ellipsis.

You will encounter a wide variety of dialogue boxes in your exploration of AutoCAD. Some of these dialogue boxes are very simple, while others are quite detailed. If you pick items followed by ellipsis in some dialogue boxes, a subdialogue box is then displayed. The subdialogue box will be displayed on top of the original dialogue box much like laying a sheet of paper on top of another. You must make a selection from the subdialogue box before returning to the original dialogue box.

There are standard parts to all dialogue boxes. If you take a few minutes to review them here, you will find it much easier to work with the dialogue boxes. A brief description of the dialogue box components is given here, and detailed discussions are provided in later chapters.

- **Buttons** — When you pick a button, something happens immediately. The most common buttons are OK and Cancel. Another very common button is Help. See Fig. 2-10. If a button has a dark border (such as OK in the given figure), it is the default. Pressing the ENTER key accepts the default. If a button is "grayed out," then that item is not available for selection. Buttons can also lead to other things:

    ...   The ellipsis lead to another dialogue box.
    ⟨   This symbol requires that you make a selection in the graphics screen then returns you to the dialogue box.

Fig. 2-10. When you select a button, something immediately happens. Note the dark border around the OK button; it indicates that this is the default.

- **Radio buttons** — When you press a selector button on your car radio, the station changes. Only one station can play at a time. Likewise, only one item in a group of radio buttons can be highlighted or active at one given time. See Fig. 2-11.
- **Check box** — A check box actually contains an "X" when it is active. The item represented by the "X" is either on or off. See Fig. 2-12.

Fig. 2-11. Radio buttons. Only one button in the group can be highlighted at any one given time.

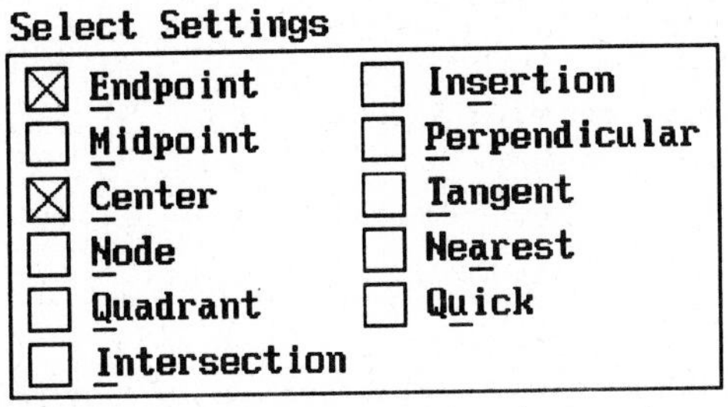

Select Settings

☒ **E**ndpoint	☐ **I**nsertion
☐ **M**idpoint	☐ **P**erpendicular
☒ **C**enter	☐ **T**angent
☐ **N**ode	☐ **N**earest
☐ **Q**uadrant	☐ **Q**uick
☐ **I**ntersection	

Fig. 2-12. Examples of check boxes. An "X" indicates which item is active.

- **List box** — This box contains a list of directories or files. You can pick from the list, or scan through it using the scroll bar. If you pick the name of a directory, it is highlighted. Press the ENTER key to see the list of files in that directory. You can also *double click* (press the pick button twice quickly) and get the same results. If you pick a file, and it is highlighted, you can pick the OK button, or press the ENTER key to select it. If you double click on the file name, it is selected and loaded automatically. See Fig. 2-13.

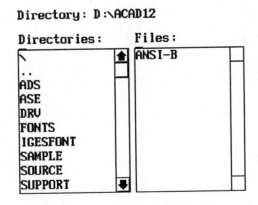

Fig. 2-13. List boxes contain a list of directories or files.

- **Popup list box** — The popup list box is similar to the standard list box, except only one item is initially shown. The remaining items are hidden until you pick the down arrow. When you pick the down arrow, the popup list pops "down" below the initial item. You can then pick from the expanded list, or use the scroll bar to find the item you need. See Fig. 2-14.
- **Edit box** — You can enter a name or single line of information using the edit box. A blinking cursor is positioned at the left of the box. You can type an entry when it is blinking, or pick a selection from the list box. If there is text in the edit box, you can edit it using

Select Filter

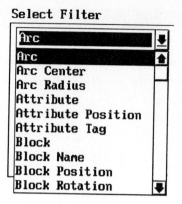

Fig. 2-14. A popup list box.

the cursor keys, HOME, END, INSERT, and DELETE keys. The HOME key moves the cursor to the extreme left end of the box. The END key moves the cursor to the end of the line. The INSERT key allows you to insert characters between existing ones. The DELETE key removes the character that is directly under the cursor. See Fig. 2-15. If the text in the edit box is highlighted, it can all be removed using the BACKSPACE key.

File:

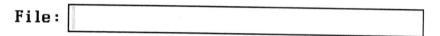

Fig. 2-15. You can enter a name or single line of information using the edit box.

- **Scroll bar** — The scroll bar can be compared to an elevator sitting next to a list of files or directories. The top arrow points to the top floor, and the bottom arrow points to the basement. The box in the middle is the elevator. If you pick the elevator and hold down the pick button, you can move the box up or down, thus displaying additional files in the upper or lower floors of your directory. Pick the blank area above the elevator box, and you scroll one page up. Pick below the elevator box, and the list scrolls down one page. If you want to scroll up or down one file at a time, simply pick the up or down arrows. See Fig. 2-16.

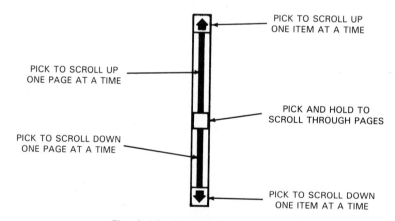

Fig. 2-16. Use of the scroll bar.

- **Label** — A label displays the value of a setting you made in another area of the dialogue box or drawing. You cannot change the label, but it changes when you alter other items. The plot area shown in Fig. 2-17 is an example of a label.
- **Image tile** — An image tile is an area of a dialogue box that displays a "picture" of the item you selected, such as a hatch style, linetype, or text font. See Fig. 2-18.
- **Alerts** — Alerts can be displayed in two forms: a note in the lower-left corner of the original dialogue box, or in a separate small dialogue box. See Fig. 2-19.

You can become efficient in your use of dialogue boxes by remembering two things: pick a *button*, and enter text in an edit box.

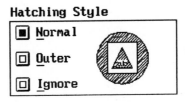

Fig. 2-17. A label displays the value of a setting.

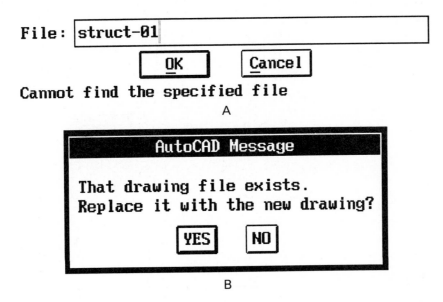

Fig. 2-18. An image tile is the part of a dialogue box in which a "picture" of the item you selected is displayed.

File: struct-01

OK   Cancel

Cannot find the specified file

A

AutoCAD Message

That drawing file exists.
Replace it with the new drawing?

YES   NO

B

Fig. 2-19. Alerts. A—Alert as a note in the corner of a dialogue box. B—Alert as a separate dialogue box.

AutoCAD tablet menu

The digitizer tablet can accept an overlay or menu that contains most all of AutoCAD's commands. Other specialized programs that operate with AutoCAD may have similar menus.

This text presents commands as if they are typed at the keyboard. If you wish to use your digitizer tablet to pick commands, the tablet must first be *configured* (arranged) before the menu can be used. (Tablet configuration is discussed in Chapter 33.) After the tablet has been configured, you can select most AutoCAD commands directly from the tablet overlay. All of the AutoCAD commands do not fit on the tablet; some must be picked from the screen. Using the tablet requires that you take your eyes off the screen and look down at the overlay. After picking a tablet command, look at the command line to be sure you picked what you wanted.

The AutoCAD tablet menu is shown in Fig. 2-20. If you plan on using a digitizer with tablet menu, take some time and study its arrangement. Become familiar with the command groups. Try to remember where each command is located. The quicker you learn the layout of the menu, the more efficient your drawing sessions will be.

ICON MENUS

An *icon* is a symbol used to graphically represent an item, such as a pattern. AutoCAD uses several menus composed of icons or patterns. Fig. 2-21 shows the icon menu for hatch patterns

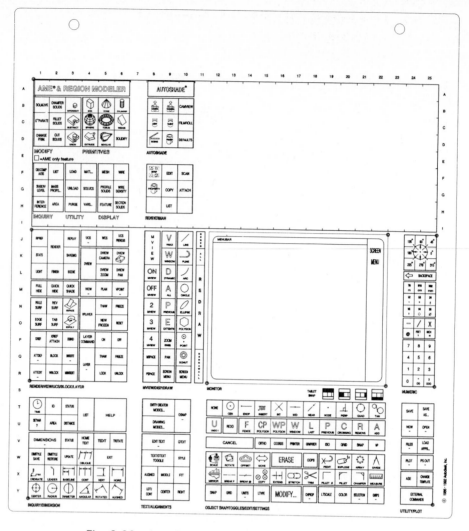

Fig. 2-20. AutoCAD tablet menu. (Autodesk, Inc.)

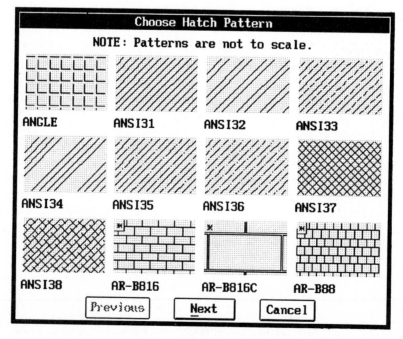

Fig. 2-21. Icon menus graphically display options or selections.

used in section views. To choose the symbol or pattern you want to use, simply pick the icon. Icon menus allow for easy selection since you can see the shape or item represented by the icon. To select an icon, move your pointing device to it and pick.

SELECTING AUTOCAD COMMANDS

Commands can be selected in AutoCAD three different ways. They can be:

- Picked after moving the pointing device to highlight a screen or pull-down menu item.
- Selected from the tablet menu.
- Typed at the keyboard.

To use the screen menu, move the pointing device to highlight the desired command and select it by pressing the pick button. You can select a command option in the same manner. An advantage of using the screen menus is that you do not have to remove your eyes from the screen, whereas you must look down to pick tablet menu commands.

On the other hand, tablet menus have advantages. They can show almost every command, including small icons that represent the command. The user does not have to page through several screen menus to find the needed command.

Typed commands do not require that you turn your eyes from the screen. There is no need to page through several menus on the screen, because the screen menu changes when a command is typed. You can learn commands quicker by typing them. Try typing commands before other selection methods are used. You will find that work progresses faster. You will also be able to concentrate on the screen for longer periods.

GETTING HELP

If you need some help with a specific command or option, use the HELP command. Whether you type "HELP" at the Command: prompt or pick "Help!" from the Assist pull-down menu, the "Help" dialogue box is displayed. See Fig. 2-22A. A list box provides a display of AutoCAD's commands. The first several pages of the listing shows all of the commands and variables in AutoCAD, as well as some basic information about point entry methods and entity selection options.

If you pick the "Next" button, the first command listed in the index is displayed in the edit box, and a short explanation is given in the file list box. Note that the name in the edit box is highlighted. If you want help on another command, simply type its name and press ENTER. If you wish to scroll through the command definitions, pick either the Next or Previous buttons.

As soon as the "Help" dialogue box is displayed, you can type the name of the command and press the ENTER key. The help file for that command is displayed. If you want to browse through the index listing, pick the Index... button. Scroll through the index until you find the command you need. Now either pick a word in the list and then pick the OK button, or double click on the word. See Fig. 2-22B.

You can also ask for help while you are working inside a command. For example, suppose you are using the ARC command and forget what type of information is required by AutoCAD for the specific prompts that are on screen. Pick "Help!" from the Assist pull-down menu. The help you need for that command is then displayed. You can accomplish the same thing by entering either an apostrophe and a question mark ('?), or an apostrophe and the word "HELP" ('HELP) at the prompt for any command. If the Command: prompt is displayed, you can omit the apostrophe and type a "?" or "HELP."

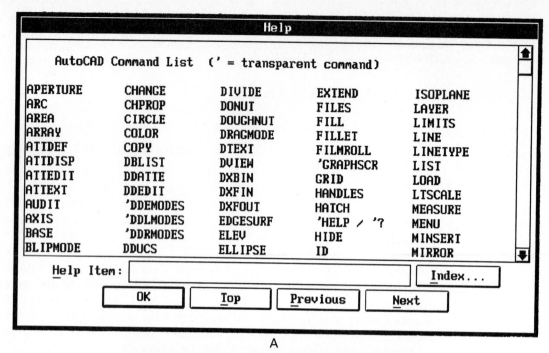

A

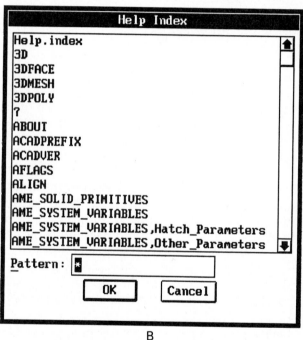

B

Fig. 2-22. Getting help while drawing. A—The ''Help'' dialogue box. B—The ''Help Index'' dialogue box is displayed by picking Index . . . from the previous dialogue box.

KEYS, BUTTONS, FUNCTIONS AND TERMINOLOGY

AutoCAD provides several ways of performing the same task. There are a variety of keys on the keyboard. Some of them you may find handy, but only if you know their meanings. Keyboard keys allow you to perform many functions. In addition, multibutton pointing devices also utilize the extra buttons for AutoCAD commands. Become familiar with the meaning of these keys and buttons.

Control keys

Most computer programs use *control key* functions to perform common tasks. Control key functions are activated by pressing and holding the CTRL key while pressing a second key. Keep the following list close at hand and try them occasionally. (If a command or key is noted as a "toggle," it is either on or off—nothing else.)

CTRL B—Snap mode (toggle).
CTRL C—Cancel.
CTRL D—Coordinate display on status line (toggle).
CTRL E—Crosshairs in isoplane positions left/top/right (toggle).
CTRL G—Grid (toggle).
CTRL H—Same as backspace.
CTRL O—Ortho mode (toggle).
CTRL Q—Echo all status listings, prompts, and keyboard inputs to an attached printer. AutoCAD DOS versions only. (toggle)
CTRL T—Tablet mode (toggle).
CTRL V—Moves through active viewports, making each one current in succession.
CTRL X—Cancels all characters on command line.

Function keys

Function keys provide instant access to commands and can be programmed to perform a series of commands. The function keys are either to the left or along the top of the keyboard, Fig. 2-23. Depending on the brand of keyboard, there will be either 10 or 12 function keys. These are numbered F1-F10 (or F1-F12). AutoCAD uses only six function keys.

F1—Flip screen from graphics to text (toggle).
F6—Coordinate display (toggle).
F7—Grid (toggle).
F8—Ortho mode (toggle).
F9—Snap mode (toggle).
F10—Tablet mode (toggle).

As you become proficient with AutoCAD, you might program the function keys to do specific tasks using other computer programs.

Fig. 2-23. The standard function keys are found along the top or side of a keyboard. In this photo, the function keys are along the side, with extra keys along the top.

Cursor keys

Cursor keys control the movement of the screen cursor (crosshairs). They are also called *arrow keys,* and are located on the right side of your keyboard, Fig. 2-24. Each of the four keys has an arrow pointing in one of the directions of the compass. Cursor keys can be used instead of a pointing device, although this method is slow and tedious.

Press one of the cursor keys one time and watch the screen. Notice the small movements of the crosshairs. The distance of this movement can be increased by pressing the PAGE UP key located near the cursor keys. Press a cursor key again. You should notice a greater movement

Fig. 2-24. The arrow keys, PAGE UP, PAGE DOWN, and INSERT keys are used to move the screen cursor and select menu items.

of the crosshairs. Press the PAGE UP key again, and then press a cursor key. The movement is much more dramatic. The amount of cursor movement can be decreased by pressing the PAGE DOWN key. Try this a few times to get the feel of it.

The keyboard can also be used to select screen menu items. Press the right arrow key until the crosshairs touch the screen menu. Additional presses of the right arrow key will not move the cursor into the menu bar. Press the INSERT key; it is near the arrow keys. One of the screen menu items highlights. Press the up or down arrow key to move around the screen menu. Pressing INSERT again or the ENTER key selects the highlighted item.

Button functions

If you are using a multibutton pointing device, you can select control key functions by pressing a single button. The meaning of the pointing device's buttons are:

    0 – Pick.
    1 – Return.
    2 – Object snap submenu displayed on screen.
    3 – Cancel.
    4 – Snap mode (toggle).
    5 – Ortho mode (toggle).
    6 – Grid (toggle).
    7 – Coordinate display (toggle).
    8 – Crosshairs isoplane positions top/left/right (toggle).
    9 – Tablet mode (toggle).

Understanding terminology

Become familiar with the following terms to help you select AutoCAD functions.
- Default – A value that is maintained by the computer until you change it.
- Select – Choose a command or option from the screen or tablet menu.
- Pick – Use the pointing device to select an item on the screen or tablet.
- Button – One of the pointing device (puck) buttons.
- Key – A key on the keyboard.
- Function key – One of the keys labeled F1-F12 along the top or side of the keyboard.
- ENTER (↵) – The ENTER or RETURN key on the keyboard.
- Command – An instruction issued to the computer.
- Option – An aspect of a command that can be selected. Displayed in lowercase letters.

FORMATTING A FLOPPY DISK

You will be saving your AutoCAD drawings on either the hard disk drive or on floppy disks. Even if you store most drawings on the hard disk drive, you will probably use floppy disks for backups. Therefore, you should learn how to prepare a floppy disk to receive drawing files. This preparation process is called *formatting*.

The formatting process is discussed in detail in Chapter 35. You should read that portion of the chapter to gain a better knowledge of the FORMAT command. The section in this chapter provides you with the basics of formatting so you can begin now to save drawings on floppy disks.

⎯⎯ CAUTION ⎯⎯

Before using the FORMAT command, check with your instructor or supervisor for information about formatting disks. Some schools and companies have special menu selections that allow you to safely format disks in the floppy disk drives.

Selecting floppy disks

Avoid buying bulk quantities of unpackaged floppy disks that are sold without dust jackets. Often these are sitting out on a store counter exposed to dust, cigarette smoke, and handling. Be safe; purchase packaged unformatted disks, keep them boxed, and store the box in a clean area. Keep disks away from extreme heat or cold and magnetic fields found around stereo speakers and ringing telephones.

A variety of disk drive configurations are now available for most new microcomputers. In some cases, you are able to specify the drive configuration that you desire when purchasing a computer. In many cases you are able to indicate whether you want a drive capable of handling double-density or high-density disks. Since there is such a variety of drive configurations, be careful when purchasing floppy disks to ensure that you have the correct disks for your computer. Check the following:

- 5.25″ vs. 3.5″
- 1.2MB vs. 1.44MB

Be sure that you purchase the proper disks for your machine.

A word about the FORMAT command

The FORMAT command is a DOS function that has caused many people grief. It is a helpful command when used properly. However, when used incorrectly, it can be a lethal weapon to floppy and hard disks. The FORMAT command erases a disk before it prepares the disk for use. Respect the FORMAT command and use it carefully.

Floppy disks are the only disks you should ever need to format. Most new floppy disks must be formatted before they can be used. The FORMAT command divides the disk into pie-shaped *sectors* and checks the disk for any bad spots. If bad spots are found, DOS marks them and informs you of their size. The bad spots are then avoided in the future. You can still use a disk with bad spots. Most of the time, the disks are in good shape. The most important thing to remember is that FORMAT's first job is to erase all information on the disk.

⎯⎯ CAUTION ⎯⎯

Always run a directory on your floppy disks before formatting them by typing "DIR A:" or "DIR B:" and pressing the ENTER key. Be sure the disk does not contain drawings or files that you need. If you must format the disk, be sure the files on it have been copied to another disk.

Using the FORMAT command

In order to use FORMAT, the DOS prompt must be displayed on the screen. It may appear as:

C:\⟩ or C⟩ or C:\ACAD⟩

You may see one of these prompts on the screen now. If you are in AutoCAD, exit the program as follows to get the DOS prompt:

Command: **QUIT** ↵

The DOS prompt returns. Now insert a blank floppy disk into the A: drive and close the lever (if equipped with one). Enter the following DOS command at the prompt. **Do not press ENTER.** Always check your entry at the prompt before continuing.

C:\\〉 **FORMAT A:** ↵

If you make a typing mistake, simply press the BACKSPACE key until the error is erased and type it over. When the entry looks exactly like the one shown above, press ENTER. The following prompt is displayed:

Insert new diskette for drive A:
and strike ENTER when ready__

Press the ENTER key. A prompt is displayed during the format process. If you are using 5.25″ 360K floppy disks, the following appears when the process is complete:

Format complete
362496 bytes total disk space
362496 bytes available on disk
Format another (Y/N)?

If you are using 5.25″ 1.2MB, 3.5″ 720K, or 3.5″ 1.44MB disks, different values than those previously shown will be displayed. Notice that DOS did not report any bad spots on the disk; therefore, the entire disk is good. You are asked if you want to format another. You should format several disks at one sitting. This saves time later when you find you need another disk. If you want to format another, simply type Y and press the ENTER key:

Format another (Y/N)? **Y** ↵
Insert new diskette for drive A:
and strike ENTER when ready__

The formatting procedure continues to cycle until you answer N or NO to the "Format another" prompt.

Once a disk is formatted, it is ready to accept AutoCAD drawing files and files from other programs. Remember, the FORMAT command has the potential to ruin your whole day if you accidentally insert a disk full of drawings to format. Use the FORMAT command carefully.

AVOIDING "DISK FULL" PROBLEMS

When you begin a new drawing, AutoCAD "looks" at the drawing file name to determine where the drawing will be stored. When you enter the drawing name, AutoCAD creates a space for it in the current directory of the active disk drive. AutoCAD does this automatically to the hard disk if you do not put a disk name in front of the file name. Suppose you give the name A:P15-5. AutoCAD creates a space on the floppy disk in the A: drive for drawing P15-5. Note that the "A:" indicates the drive, and "P15-5" is the drawing name.

Creating a drawing on a floppy disk is not the most efficient method of operating AutoCAD. This is because AutoCAD looks at the disk and then creates space for several temporary open files that it uses during a drawing session. There must be room for these open files, in addition to your drawing file, for AutoCAD to function properly. Floppy drives are slow to store and access data. In addition, limited space on the floppy disk can eventually lead to a "disk full" error, or worse a system crash. The disk full error still allows you to save the current drawing. A system crash destroys the current drawing in memory.

Creating a new drawing

It is best to begin new and edit existing drawings on the hard disk during a drawing session. If you are starting a new drawing called P15-5, begin the drawing session with the new drawing name P15-5. AutoCAD then works on the hard disk, which should have plenty of room for the temporary open files. Save the drawing as A:P15-5 to store it on a floppy, then quit without saving. This places the drawing on the floppy disk, but does not put anything on the hard disk drive.

Editing an existing drawing

If you are in training with AutoCAD, you should save all of your drawings and exercises on floppy disks, not on the hard disk drive. Keep two copies of each floppy disk. One is the original; the other is a backup copy. Each time you save a drawing on a floppy disk, save it a second time on the backup disk. This is discussed again later in the text.

When you need to edit a drawing that is on a floppy disk, select New... from the Files pull-down menu. If you want to work on drawing P15-5, enter the following in the New Drawing Name edit box and press ENTER:

P15-5 = A:P15-5 ↵

This technique instructs AutoCAD to retrieve a copy of drawing P15-5 from the floppy disk in the A: drive and begin a new drawing located on the hard disk named P15-5 using that copy. This is called the *prototype drawing method*, and preserves the original drawing. It also creates the temporary work files on the hard disk, which is where you want them—somewhere with plenty of space.

If you instruct AutoCAD to begin a new drawing by typing A:P15-5 in the New Drawing Name edit box, all of the temporary files are placed on the floppy disk. You want to avoid this situation because if AutoCAD runs out of work space on the floppy disk, the program may crash and you could lose all of your work.

Another way to use the prototype drawing method is by picking the Prototype edit box of the Create New Drawing dialogue box. The drawing name—ACAD—should be the current name in the File edit box. If you double click on the word ACAD, you can type A:P15-5 and ACAD is replaced. Now pick the New Drawing Name edit box and type P15-5. When you pick the OK button, AutoCAD gets a copy of the prototype drawing and begins a new one with the same name. This process is explained in greater detail in Chapter 5.

When you are ready to save the drawing, use the SAVEAS (SAVE AS) command. Use A:P15-5 as the drawing name. You will then get an alert message that says:

The specified file already exists.
Do you want to replace it?

Pick the YES button. Saving the drawing as A:P15-5 means you want to place the drawing on the floppy drive. (Remember you first loaded the drawing by this name from the floppy disk.) AutoCAD says that a drawing with the same name already exists on the floppy disk in that drive. By entering Y or YES, you replace the old copy with the edited (updated) version.

Use these techniques for working with drawings. You will avoid the problems associated with the "disk full" error.

CHAPTER TEST

Write your answers in the spaces provided.

1. What is the difference between installing, configuring, and loading AutoCAD? _____

_____

_____

_____

_____

_____

2. What do the following DOS prompts mean?

   A〉 _____

   B〉 _____

   C〉 _____

3. What do you type at the DOS prompt to load AutoCAD?

   C〉 _____

4. What four areas comprise the AutoCAD screen layout? _____

   _____

   _____

   _____

5. Which area displays the communications between AutoCAD and the user? _____

   _____

6. What is the difference between a command and a menu, and how is this handled in the screen menus?

   _____

   _____

   _____

7. What is an option? _____

8. Commands are listed _____ in screen menus.

9. How do you select commands that are on a second or third page of a menu? _____

   _____

10. How do you return to the Root Menu? _____

    _____

11. List the nine AutoCAD pull-down menus. _____

    _____

    _____

12. What is an icon? _____

    _____

13. What must you do to the tablet menu before it can be used? _____

    _____

14. What are the functions of the following control keys?

    A. CTRL B— _____

    B. CTRL C— _____

    C. CTRL D— _____

    D. CTRL G— _____

    E. CTRL O— _____

15. Name the function keys that execute the same task as the following control keys.

    Control Key   Function Key

    A. CTRL B _____

    B. CTRL D _____

    C. CTRL G _____

    D. CTRL O _____

    E. CTRL T _____

16. What is the difference between a "button" and a "key?" _____
    _____

17. What do you call a value that is maintained by the computer until you change it?
    _____

18. What type of pull-down menu has an arrow to the right of the item?
    _____

19. What type of menu contains a group of symbols or patterns? _____

20. The scroll bar is normally associated with what portion of the dialogue box?
    _____

PROBLEMS

1. Read the instructions in Appendix A for installing AutoCAD. Make a list of the steps required to perform the task. List the correct order in which the disks should be copied.
2. List the steps required to configure AutoCAD. (Do not list all the hardware options in the configuration routine.)
3. List the steps required to run AutoCAD and begin a new drawing named FIRST.
4. Begin AutoCAD and pick the File pull-down menu. Perform the following tasks using this menu:
   A. Open one of the drawings that are provided with AutoCAD. You may have to pick one or more of the directories to find them. (Hint: Try the SAMPLE subdirectory.)
   B. Open another drawing and do not save the previous one.
   C. Save the drawing you just opened as CH2TEST.
   D. Exit AutoCAD and do not save the changes.
5. Draw a freehand sketch of the screen display. Label each of the screen areas. To the side of the sketch, write a short description of each screen area's function.
6. Draw a freehand sketch of your keyboard by blocking each specific group of keys. Label the groups. Label the function keys, arrow keys, and control keys. To the side of your sketch write a short description of the function of each group of keys.
7. Use a C-size sheet of vellum or butcher paper for this problem. Create a freehand sketch of the screen menu layout of AutoCAD. (You will have to refer to the computer for this problem.)
   A. Write the commands for the Root Menu as they appear on the screen. Place them at the left or upper portion of the sheet.
   B. Select each menu item to display that menu on the screen.
   C. Write the commands displayed in the menu on your sketch.
   D. Draw connecting lines between menus.
   E. Use this process for all the menus in AutoCAD until you have drawn a "menu tree" or menu flow chart.

8. Draw a freehand sketch of the AutoCAD overlay menu. (Do not draw each individual box.) Block in the four menu areas and the screen area. Label each menu area that is shown in red on the template.
9. Identify the parts of the dialogue boxes shown in the following screen displays.

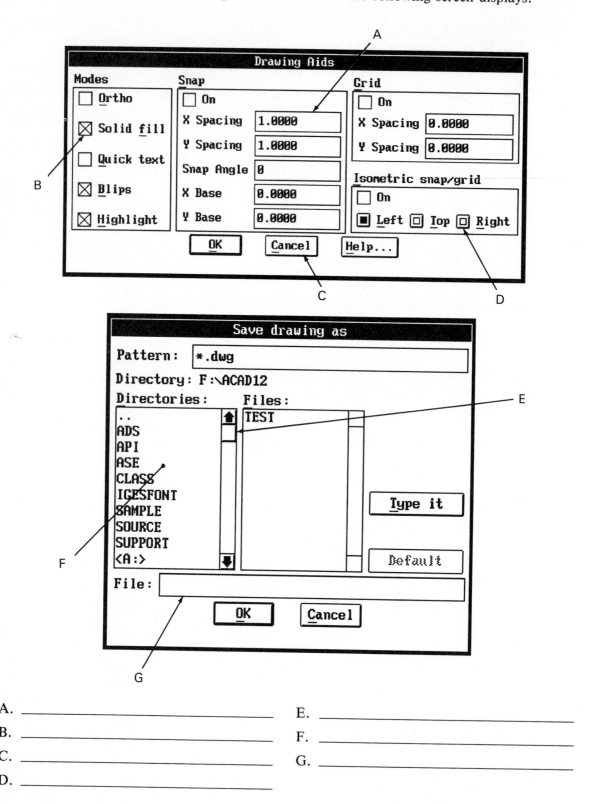

A. _____   E. _____

B. _____   F. _____

C. _____   G. _____

D. _____

Chapter 3

DRAWING SETUP

Learning objectives

After completing this chapter, you will be able to:
- ☐ Load AutoCAD and enter the drawing editor.
- ☐ Draw and erase lines.
- ☐ Use the UNITS command to establish units of measure.
- ☐ Set drawing limits.

Effective planning can greatly reduce the amount of time it takes to set up and complete a drawing. Drawing setup involves a number of factors that affect the quality and accuracy of your final drawing. Some basic planning decisions include:
- Sheet size needed to fit the drawing.
- Units of measure needed to create the drawing.
- Degree of accuracy required.
- Name of the drawing.

STARTING A DRAWING

When you turn on the computer and load AutoCAD, the standard AutoCAD screen, which was discussed in Chapter 2, is displayed. This is referred to as the *drawing editor*. See Fig. 3-1.

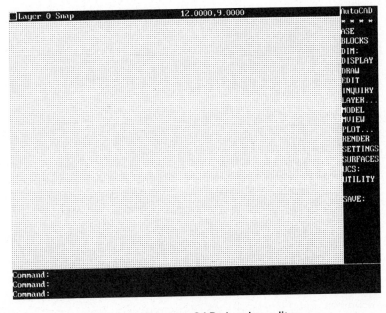

Fig. 3-1. The AutoCAD drawing editor.

Now that you are in the drawing editor, you are ready to start drawing. Notice the screen crosshairs. Move your pointing device and watch the crosshairs also move. Try doing some drawing by entering the following from the keyboard.

Command: **LINE** ⏎
From point: *(move your pointer to any desired place on the screen and pick a point)*
To point: *(move your pointer and pick another point)*
To point: *(move your pointer and pick another point)*
To point: ⏎
Command:

You should now have two lines drawn on screen. Now erase the lines as follows:

Command: **ERASE** ⏎

Notice that the crosshairs have changed to a small box called the *pick box*.

Select objects: *(move the pick box to one of the lines and pick it by pressing your pick button)*
Select objects: *(move pick box and pick the other line)*
Select objects: ⏎

Now you have erased the two lines you just drew. Look at the screen and notice some points still remain. These points are call *blips*. They are located at points that you picked when drawing. If you want to get rid of the blips, enter the following:

Command: **REDRAW** ⏎

As you can see, you can immediately start drawing as soon as you see the drawing editor. (You can also pick Redraw from the View pull-down menu for the same results.) You can continue to practice if you wish.

Even though you can begin work when the drawing editor first appears, there are a few setup tasks that make the drafting job easier and more realistic.

SETTING UP DRAWING UNITS   ARM 3

When drawing with AutoCAD, you do not have to scale a drawing. All lines, circles, and other entities are drawn and measured as full size. For example, if a part is 36 inches long, it is drawn 36 units (inches) long. Therefore, the size of the product determines the size of the drawing. Inches, millimeters, or feet can be used as the unit of measurement. The drawing may have to be scaled to fit on a given sheet size when the drawing is plotted. You can even position and plot different views of the drawing at different scales using AutoCAD's paper space capabilities. The use of paper space is explained in Chapters 9 and 27.

To set the units of measurement, pick UNITS: from the SETTINGS screen menu or type UNITS at the Command: prompt as follows:

Command: **UNITS** ⏎

The display then changes to the text screen. You are given examples showing how the units are displayed, and are then asked what type of units are desired:

Report formats:	(Examples)
1. Scientific	1.55E + 01
2. Decimal	15.50
3. Engineering	1'-3.50"
4. Architectural	1'-3 1/2"
5. Fractional	15 1/2
Enter choice, 1 to 5	⟨default⟩:

With the exception of Engineering and Architectural formats, these formats can be used with any basic unit of measurement. For example, Decimal mode is perfect for metric units as well as decimal English units. The examples given show how 15.5 drawing units are displayed in each format. The default (in brackets) shows the units currently in effect. For this example, decimal units are chosen. Enter choice "2" at the prompt and press ENTER:

Enter choice, 1 to 5 ⟨default⟩: **2** ⏎

Selecting decimal units

The American National Standard ANSI Y14.5M, *Dimensioning and Tolerancing*, specifies that decimal inch or metric units in millimeters are to be used on engineering drawings. Decimal units are used widely in mechanical drafting. Dimensions are in inches, such as 2.5 or 1.875, or in millimeters such as 25 or 30.5. Decimal units are selected by entering "2" at the prompt as previously shown.

Selecting engineering units

Engineering units are used in civil drafting. Civil drafting deals with detailed construction drawings and topographic maps for planning and constructing highways, harbors, drainage, and related projects. Engineering units are measured in feet, inches, and decimal parts of an inch, for example, 5'-6.75". Each engineering unit in AutoCAD is one inch. Respond with a "3" at the prompt for engineering units.

Selecting architectural units

Residential and commercial planning and construction drawings use architectural units. Dimensions are given in feet, inches, and fractional parts of an inch, for example, 8'-10 3/4". Enter choice "4" for architectural units.

Selecting fractional units

Units may also be fractional parts of a unit. The fractional units may take on any desired value such as inches, feet, or miles. Dimensions will be shown giving whole units and parts of a unit as a fraction, for example, 24 3/4. Enter choice "5" for fractional units.

Accuracy of decimal and fractional units

The accuracy of units is based on either the number of decimal places or the smallest fraction. When scientific, decimal, or engineering units are selected, the next prompt is:

Number of digits to right of decimal point (0 to 8) ⟨default⟩:

The default value is the number of digits previously selected. Here you make some decisions about the accuracy of the drawing display. For example, two digits is shown as 2.88, three digits 2.875, and four digits 2.8751. For mechanical drawings, three to four digits is normally adequate for inch drawings. For metric drawings, one or two place decimals are commonly used, such as 12.5 or 12.50.

When architectural or fractional units are used, the accuracy is determined by the size of the fraction's denominator. The following prompt is given:

Denominator of smallest fraction to display
(1, 2, 4, 8, 16, 32, or 64) ⟨default⟩:

Press the ENTER key to use the default value or select a new value. Selecting "16" shows parts of an inch that are displayed no smaller than 1/16-inch increments. For example, the display might read 4'-8 7/16". If "8" was chosen as the denominator, the same dimension would be rounded off to the nearest 1/8-inch increment, or 4'-8 3/8".

Measuring angles

After the accuracy of decimal or fractional units has been set, the next option determines the method of measuring angles. The screen displays:

System of angle measure:	(Examples)
1. Decimal degrees	45.0000
2. Degrees/minutes/seconds	45d0'0"
3. Grads	50.0000g
4. Radians	0.7854r
5. Surveyor's units	N 45d0'0" E
Enter choice, 1 to 5 ⟨default⟩:	

The given examples show how a 45° angle is displayed in each format. Pressing the ENTER key gives you the default value currently in effect. If the default is not appropriate, make a selection 1 through 5. The angular measurement format recommended by the American National Standards Institute is degrees (°), minutes ('), and seconds (") or decimal degrees, therefore, select "1" or "2." The next prompt requests the accuracy of angular measure:

Number of fractional places for display of angles (0 to 8) ⟨default⟩:

The degree of accuracy is determined by the drawing requirements. Two-place decimal degrees or degrees and minutes are normally adequate for mechanical drawings. Therefore, select "2." Civil (mapping) drawings often require degrees, minutes, and seconds. In this case, select "2" or "5."

Next you are asked to specify the direction for an angle of 0 degrees. In other words, where is the origin for making angular measurements? The AutoCAD default is an angle starting to the right (East) and heading in a counterclockwise direction, Fig. 3-2. If this is appropriate for your drawing, respond with "0" as follows:

Direction for angle 0:
East   3 o'clock = 0
North   12 o'clock = 90
West   9 o'clock = 180
South   6 o'clock = 270
Enter direction for angle 0 ⟨current⟩: **0** ↵

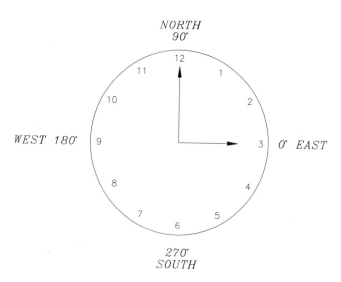

Fig. 3-2. Angle, clock, and compass orientation.

The next prompt is:

Do you want angles measured clockwise? ⟨default⟩:

The AutoCAD default is angles measured in a counterclockwise direction. To maintain this, a "NO" or "N" response is needed. If you want angles to be measured clockwise, a "YES" or "Y" response is required. Press the F1 function key to get back to the drawing editor.

Setting units using the "Units Control" dialogue box

You can also adjust drawing units in the "Units Control" dialogue box by picking Units Control... from the Settings pull-down menu. This dialogue box allows you to set units quicker and easier than the other two methods previously discussed. The "Units Control" dialogue box, Fig. 3-3, has the units set to three-place decimals, two-place decimal degrees, East angle direction, and angles measured counterclockwise. Pick Direction... to display the "Direction Control" dialogue box.

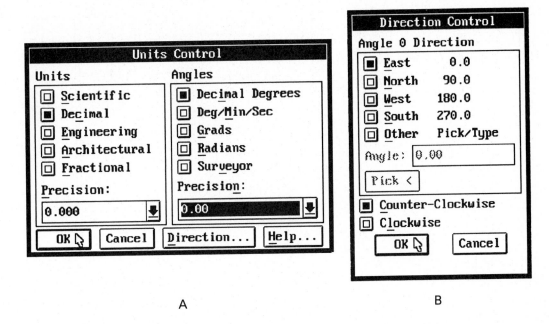

A   B

Fig. 3-3. A—The "Units Control" dialogue box. Notice the highlighted radio buttons and precision specifications. B—The "Direction Control" subdialogue box appears when you pick Direction... in the "Units Control" dialogue box.

SIZING OF THE DRAWING AREA   ARM 3

The size or limits of the AutoCAD drawing area is usually determined by:
- The actual size of the drawing.
- Space for dimensions and notes.
- Free space to avoid crowding and provide for future revisions.
- A border and title block area.

The drawing area is determined by two sets of coordinates. These coordinates are set with the LIMITS command. One set of coordinates marks the lower-left corner of your drawing area. The other set marks the upper-right corner.

It takes some practice to decide how to set the limits relative to the actual size of the object. It is always a good idea to first make a sketch of the drawing to help calculate the area needed. For example, suppose a machine part is 20 inches long and 14 inches high. An additional 4 inches around the part (2 inches on each side) is necessary for dimensions, notes, and free space. In this case, the limits should be set at 24 x 18. Suppose a house floor plan measures 68 feet by 44 feet. An additional 20 feet is needed (10 feet on each side) all around the plan for dimensions, notes, and a border. Then, the limits should be set at 88' x 64'.

Plan your drawing area in relation to sheet sizes during drawing setup or when the drawing is plotted. See Fig. 3-4. When plotting, the drawing can be made to fit the sheet or scaled as needed. AutoCAD has standard paper sizes established for plotting, or you can define your own paper size at that time. Chapter 27 covers plotting an AutoCAD drawing. The preferred method is to consider the standard drawing sheet sizes when setting the required drawing area. The screen format is much like a sheet of paper, with the length measured horizontally and the width measured vertically. This is the same as laying a sheet on a drawing board when manual drafting. Standard sheet sizes are shown in Appendix E.

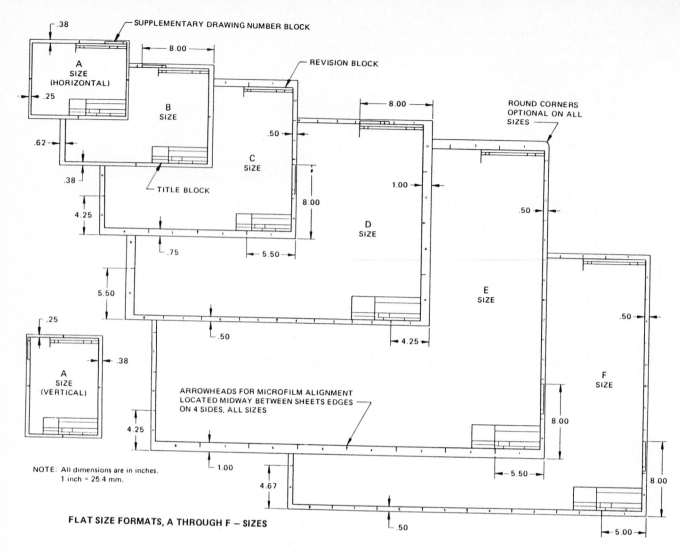

Fig. 3-4. Standard drawing sheet sizes. (ANSI Y14.1)

Setting inch limits

If the limits are based on an A-size sheet, then choose limits of 11 x 8.5 or 12 x 9. A B-size sheet is set up as 17 x 11 or 18 x 12. A C-size drawing is 22 x 17 or 24 x 18; a D-size sheet is 34 x 22 or 36 x 24.

Setting architectural limits

Most architectural floor plans are drawn at 1/4″ = 1′-0″ scale. If a C-size (22 x 17) sheet is used, then the drawing limits should be set at 88′ x 68′, where 4′ (4 units/inch) x 22 = 88′ and 4′ x 17 = 68′.

Setting metric limits

When the drawing utilizes metric units, you must convert the limits to millimeters. For example, suppose you decide to set the limits for a B-size (17 x 11) sheet and use millimeter units. Convert the limits to millimeters using the multiplication factor 25.4 mm = 1 inch. The drawing limits are 431.8 (25.4 x 17) and 279.4 (25.4 x 11). To provide limits with even units of measure, round off to the next higher whole millimeter. The limits of the metric B-size drawing are 432 x 280.

Using the LIMITS command

The LIMITS command can be accessed by picking LIMITS: from the SETTINGS screen menu, by picking Drawing Limits from the Settings pull-down menu, or by typing "LIMITS" at the Command: prompt. The following command sequence is used to set the drawing limits:

Command: **LIMITS** ⏎
Reset Model space limits:
ON/OFF/⟨Lower left corner⟩⟨current value⟩: **0,0** ⏎

This prompt sets the lower-left corner of the "sheet size" to the lower-left corner of the display screen. A response of 0,0 places the lower-left corner as shown in Fig. 3-5. The lower-left corner may be placed at any convenient location other than 0,0, however, 0,0 is common and recommended. The LIMITS command continues with a request for the upper-right corner. The AutoCAD default for upper-right corner is 12,9. This is a standard A-size sheet. The value you enter here determines the upper-right corner of the "sheet size." For example, if a 17 x 11 or B-size sheet is to be used, then the response is:

Upper right corner ⟨current⟩: **17,11** ⏎

The horizontal distance is given first, followed by a comma, and then the vertical distance is entered. See the screen display shown in Fig. 3-5.

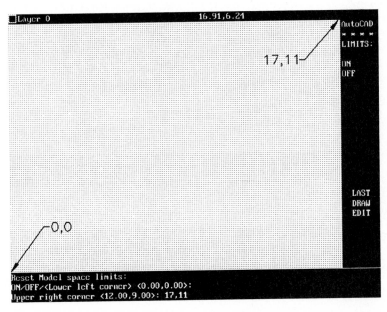

Fig. 3-5. Using the LIMITS command. In this example, the lower-left limit is 0,0 and the upper-right limit is 17,11.

If a B-size (17 x 11) architectural drawing is needed and 4 feet per inch is the scale when plotted, first set Architectural units. Then, set the limits as follows:

Command: **LIMITS** ⏎
Reset Model space limits:
ON/OFF/⟨Lower left corner⟩⟨current value⟩: **0,0** ⏎
Upper right corner ⟨current⟩: **68′,44′** ⏎

If a B-size (17 x 11) drawing is set up for millimeters, the limits are set as follows:

Command: **LIMITS** ⏎
Reset Model space limits:
ON/OFF ⟨Lower-left corner⟩⟨current value⟩: **0,0** ⏎
Upper right corner ⟨current⟩: **432,280** ⏎

Limits can be changed at any time by executing the LIMITS command. The ON/OFF portion of the first LIMITS prompt refers to a limits check. The intent of the limits is to set up a work area that confines the drawing. However, it is possible to draw outside of the limits on purpose or acccidentally. An ON response to this prompt turns the limits check on. You can still draw outside the limits area; however, if you pick or input a coordinate outside the limits, an "Outside limits" error message is shown. With limits check turned off, the "Outside limits" error is not given. If, for some reason, you draw beyond the limits you can either edit the drawing so it is within limits of increase the limits to include the extended work area.

Setting limits using the Settings pull-down menu

The drawing limits can also be changed by moving the screen cursor to the menu bar and picking Settings. When the Settings pull-down menu appears, move the cursor arrow down the menu and pick Drawing Limits. This activates the LIMITS command at which time you can type the revised limit values, if necessary.

EXERCISE 3-1

☐ Turn on your computer and load AutoCAD.
☐ Using the UNITS command, set the units to decimal with two digits to the right of the decimal point.
☐ Set the angular measure to decimal, one fractional place, 0 direction, and counterclockwise.
☐ Using the LIMITS command, set the limits to the default value of 12,9. (Set the lower-left corner at 0,0 and for the upper-right corner, press ENTER or enter 12,9.)
☐ Type SAVE at the Command: prompt. The "Save drawing as" dialogue box then appears. If you want to save the drawing in the current directory, move the cursor to the File box and type EX3-1. Pick the OK box or press the ENTER key.

   If you want to save the drawing on another drive, such as your floppy disk in the A: drive, move the cursor to the File box, and type A:EX3-1. Then, pick OK or press ENTER.
☐ Type QUIT at the Command: prompt and press ENTER if you want to exit AutoCAD.

CHAPTER TEST

Write your answers in the spaces provided.

1. The drafting table and tools of computer-aided drafting is called the _____.

2. How do you get to the standard AutoCAD screen? _____

3. When you type "UNITS" at the Command: prompt and press ENTER, what happens to the screen? _____

4. What do you do when you are finished with the UNITS command and you want to get to the standard AutoCAD screen? _____

5. The display of a measurement will change when a different number of digits to the right of the decimal point is specified. If a 1.6250 dimension is to be displayed, and the number of digits to the right of the decimal points is as follows, what will actually be displayed?

   A. One digit — _____
   B. Two digits — _____
   C. Three digits — _____
   D. Four digits — _____

6. The AutoCAD default for an angle is in a _____ direction.

7. What are the limits of an architectural drawing using a C-size (22 x 17) sheet and a scale of 4 feet per inch when plotted?

    A. Lower-left corner _____

    B. Upper-right corner_____

8. Name the five systems of units options. _____

_____

_____

9. Name the pull-down menu that contains the LIMITS command. _____

10. How do you access the "Units Control" dialogue box? _____

_____

11. Give the entries or commands needed to set the drawing units to three-digit decimal, two-place decimal degrees, East direction for angle 0, and to measure angles counterclockwise:

    Command: _____

    System of units:

    Enter choice 1 to 5 〈default〉: _____

    Number of digits to right of decimal point (0 to 8) 〈default〉: _____

    System of angular measure:

    Enter choice, 1 to 5 〈default〉: _____

    Number of fractional places for display of angles (0 to 8) 〈default〉: _____

    Enter direction for angle 0 〈current〉: _____

    Do you want angles measured clockwise? 〈current〉: _____

12. Give the commands and coordinate entries to set the drawing limits to 22 x 17:

    Command: _____

    Reset Model space limits:

    ON/OFF/〈Lower left corner〉〈current value〉: _____

    Upper right corner 〈current〉: _____

PROBLEMS

In the following problems, it is suggested that you save the drawings for future use. Saving the drawings as specified will save them to your floppy disk in the A: drive. If you prefer to save your drawings on a floppy disk in the B: drive, insert your floppy disk in the appropriate drive, and type "B:" before the file name. If in doubt, consult your instructor.

1. A. Load AutoCAD.
   B. Enter the UNITS command. Select decimal units with four digits behind the decimal. Select decimal degrees with two digits behind the decimal point and 90 (North) for direction of the 0° angle. Angles should be measured counterclockwise.
   C. Enter the UNITS command. Select architectural units with 32 as the denominator of the smallest fraction. Angles should be measured by degrees/minutes/seconds with 4 as the number of fractional places. The direction for angle 0° should be East. Angles are to be measured counterclockwise.
   D. Set the limits to correspond with a 12 x 9 (A-size) sheet. The scale to be used in calculating the limits is 1/4" = 1'-0". The lower-left corner of your drawing area should be at 0,0.
   E. Type SAVE at the Command: prompt and enter A:A12-9 to save your drawing.
   F. Type QUIT at the Command: prompt and press ENTER.

2. A. Load AutoCAD.
   B. Use the "Units Control" dialogue box. Select decimal units with three digits behind the decimal point. Select decimal degrees with two digits behind the decimal point and 90 (North) for direction of the 0° angle. Angles should be measured counterclockwise.
   C. Set the limits to correspond with a 17 x 11 (B-size) sheet (0,0; 17,11).
   D. Save the problem as A:B17-11 and quit.
3. A. Load AutoCAD.
   B. Enter the UNITS command. Select decimal units with two digits behind the decimal point. Select decimal degrees with two digits behind the decimal and 0 (East) for direction of the 0° angle. Angles should be measured counterclockwise.
   C. Set the limits to correspond with metric (millimeters) and a B-size (17 x 11) sheet. Use the formula 25.4 x inches to obtain the metric equivalents as discussed on page 3-6.
   D. Save as A:MB17-11 and quit.

Chapter 4

INTRODUCTION TO DRAWING AND DRAWING AIDS

Learning objectives

After completing this chapter, you will be able to:
☐ Set up the drawing aids in a prototype drawing, including limits, units, grid, and snap.
☐ Use the LINE command to draw several different geometric shapes.
☐ Experiment with snap grid turned on and off.

AutoCAD provides aids that help prepare the drawing layout, increase speed and efficiency, and ensure accuracy. These "drawing aids" include GRID, SNAP, and ORTHO. This chapter discusses each of these aids and how they are used to assist you when drawing lines. Drawing aids may be selected from the SETTINGS screen menu, by picking Drawing Aids in the Settings pull-down menu, or typed at the Command: prompt.

ESTABLISHING A GRID ON THE SCREEN   ARM 8

Some drafting paper used for manual drafting is printed with a grid to assist the drafter in laying out the drawing. A similar type of grid can be used in AutoCAD. The GRID command places a pattern of dots on the screen at any spacing, Fig. 4-1. The grid pattern shows only within

Fig. 4-1. Grid spacing represented by dots.

the drawing limits to help clearly define the working area. Entering the GRID command provides a prompt showing the default grid spacing and several other options. You can press ENTER to accept the default spacing value shown in brackets or enter a new value as follows:

Command: **GRID** ↵
Grid spacing(X) or ON/OFF/Snap/Aspect ⟨0⟩: **.5** ↵

The dot spacing of the grid may be set by entering a specified unit of measure such as .5. This grid is shown in Fig. 4-1. If the grid dot spacing you enter is too close to display on the screen, you will get the "Grid too dense to display" message. A larger grid spacing is required.

The grid spacing may be changed at any time. Also, the grid may be turned on (displayed) or off (not displayed) at any time by typing ON or OFF at the GRID prompt line. Other methods for turning the grid on and off include pressing CTRL G, the F7 function key, or puck button 6. When the grid is turned on after previously being off, it is set to the previous spacing.

Setting a different horizontal and vertical grid

Type "A" (for the Aspect option) at the GRID prompt line to set different values for the horizontal and vertical grid dot spacing. For example, suppose you want a horizontal grid spacing of 1 and a vertical spacing of .5. Enter the following:

Command: **GRID** ↵
Grid spacing(X) or ON/OFF/Snap/Aspect ⟨0⟩: **A** ↵
Horizontal spacing(X) ⟨0⟩: **1** ↵
Vertical spacing(X) ⟨0⟩: **.5** ↵

The Aspect option provides the grid dot spacing shown in Fig. 4-2.

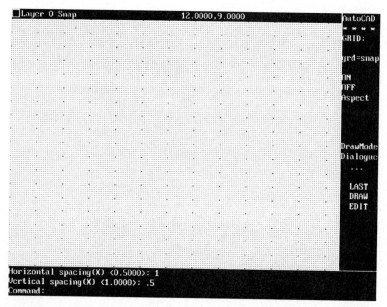

Fig. 4-2. Grid spacing using the Aspect option. Note the greater spacing in the horizontal direction.

INTRODUCTION TO DRAWING LINES

ARM 4

This section is a brief introduction to drawing lines so you can get started with AutoCAD drawing commands. It will let you see how the different drawing setup options affect the speed and accuracy of drawing lines. There are several ways to use the LINE command, but for now one method is discussed. (The LINE command is explained in detail in Chapter 6.)

Command: **LINE** ↵
From point: *(move the screen cursor to any position on the screen and pick that point)*
To point: *(move the screen cursor to another location and pick a point)*

Notice that a line has been drawn between the two points. A "rubberband" line is attached to the last point selected and the cursor. The "rubberband" shows the line's location if you picked the current cursor location. The next prompt is:

To point: *(pick the next point)*

You can continue to draw connected lines until you press the ENTER key or space bar to exit the LINE command. The following command sequence is displayed in Fig. 4-3.

Command: **LINE** ↵
From point: *(pick point number 1)*
To point: *(pick point number 2)*
To point: *(pick point number 3)*
To point: *(pick point number 4)*
To point: ↵
Command: *(meaning AutoCAD is ready for a new command)*

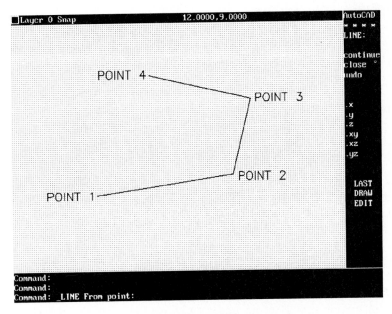

Fig. 4-3. Using the LINE command.

EXERCISE 4-1

☐ Turn on your computer and load AutoCAD to access the drawing editor.
☐ Set the grid spacing at .5.
☐ Use the LINE command to draw two sets of four connected line segments.
☐ Turn off the grid and draw two sets of three connected line segments. Notice how having the grid on provides some guidance for locating points.
☐ Type SAVE at the Command: prompt. When the "Save Drawing As:" dialogue box appears, type the file name EX4-1 to save this exercise on your hard disk, or type A:EX4-1 to save it on your floppy disk. Press ENTER or pick the OK button.
☐ Type QUIT at the Command: prompt and press ENTER if you want to exit AutoCAD.

SETTING INCREMENTS FOR CURSOR MOVEMENT $\boxed{\text{ARM 8}}$

When you move your pointing device, the cursor crosshairs move freely on the screen. Sometimes it is hard to place a point accurately. You can set up an invisible grid that allows the cursor to move only in exact increments. This is called the *snap resolution* or *snap grid*. The snap grid is different than using the GRID command. The snap grid controls the crosshair's movement; the grid is only a visual guide. However, the SNAP and GRID commands can be used together.

Properly setting the snap grid can greatly increase your drawing speed and accuracy. The SNAP command is used to set the invisible snap grid. Entering SNAP gives you the following prompt:

> Command: **SNAP** ↵
> Snap spacing or ON/OFF/Aspect/Rotate/Style ⟨current⟩:

Pressing ENTER accepts the value shown in brackets. If a new snap spacing is required, such as .25, enter the amount as shown:

> Command: **SNAP** ↵
> Snap spacing or ON/OFF/Aspect/Rotate/Style ⟨current⟩: **.25** ↵

This sets up the invisible snap spacing at .25 increments both horizontally and vertically.

The OFF selection turns snap off, but the same snap spacing is again in effect when you turn snap back on. The snap spacing may be turned on or off at any time by pressing CTRL B, function key F9, or puck button 4.

Different horizontal and vertical snap grid units

The normal application of the SNAP command is equal horizontal and vertical snap grid units. However, it is possible to set different horizontal and vertical snap grid units. This is done using the Aspect option as follows:

> Command: **SNAP** ↵
> Snap spacing or ON/OFF/Aspect/Rotate/Style ⟨current⟩: **A** ↵
> Horizontal spacing ⟨current⟩: **.5** ↵
> Vertical spacing ⟨current⟩: **.25** ↵

Rotating the snap grid

The normal snap grid pattern is horizontal rows and vertical columns. However, another option is to rotate the snap grid to an angle other than horizontal. This technique is helpful when drawing an auxiliary view that is at an angle to other views of the drawing. (Auxiliary views are discussed in Chapter 17.) When the snap grid is rotated, you are given the option of setting a new base point. The base point is the pivot around which the snap grid is rotated. The base point of a normal snap grid is the lower-left corner. It may be more convenient to set the base point at the location where you will begin the view. You will also be asked to set the rotation angle. The range is 0 to 90 or 0 to −90 degrees:

> Command: **SNAP** ↵
> Snap spacing or ON/OFF/Aspect/Rotate/Style ⟨current⟩: **R** ↵
> Base point ⟨0,0⟩: *(press ENTER or pick a new base point)*
> Rotation angle ⟨0⟩: **25** ↵

The grid automatically rotates about the base point in a counterclockwise direction when a positive rotation angle is given. It rotates clockwise if you enter a negative rotation angle. Fig. 4-4 shows the relationship between the regular and rotated snap grids. Remember, the snap grid is invisible and is shown only for illustrative purposes.

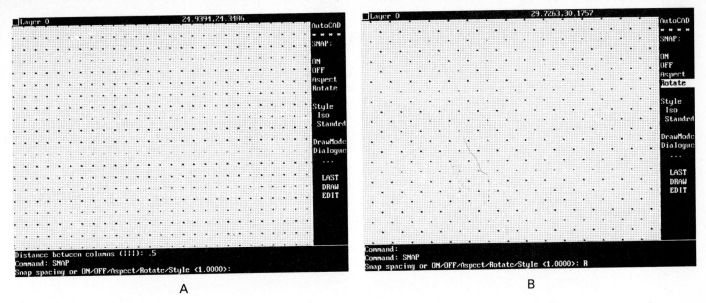

Fig. 4-4. A comparison between the invisible regular and rotated snap grids.

Setting the snap style

The Style option allows you to set the snap grid to either a standard (default) or isometric pattern. The isometric pattern is useful when doing isometric drawings, discussed in Chapter 23. If the snap grid is set to Isometric, use the Style option to return it to the Standard mode:

    Command: **SNAP** ↵
    Snap spacing or ON/OFF/Aspect/Rotate/Style ⟨current⟩: **S** ↵
    Standard/Isometric ⟨current⟩: **S** ↵

Setting the grid spacing relative to the snap spacing

The visible grid can be set to coincide with the invisible snap grid by choosing the Snap option after entering the GRID command. You may also set the dot spacing as a multiple of the snap units by entering the number of snap units between grid points. For example, 2X places grid points at every other snap unit.

    Command: **GRID** ↵
    Grid spacing(X) or ON/OFF/Snap/Aspect ⟨0⟩: **2X** ↵

Therefore, if the snap units are .25 and you specify 2X at the Grid spacing prompt, the grid point spacing will be .5 units.

EXERCISE 4-2

☐ Turn on your computer and load AutoCAD to access the drawing editor.
☐ Set the units to decimal, and two digits to the right of the decimal point.
☐ Set the angular measure to decimal, one fractional place, 0 direction, and counterclockwise.
☐ Set the limits to an A-size (12 x 9) sheet. (Lower-left corner: 0,0; upper-right corner: 12,9.)
☐ Set the grid spacing to .5.
☐ Set the snap spacing to .25.
☐ Use the LINE command to draw two sets of four connected line segments.
☐ Turn snap off and draw two sets of three connected line segments. Notice how snap on allows you to "snap" exactly at .25 intervals.
☐ Type SAVE at the Command: prompt and save the drawing as A:EX4-2, and then quit the drawing editor.

USING THE PULL-DOWN MENU TO SET
OR CHANGE THE DRAWING AIDS

The AutoCAD drawing aids may be set or changed using the Settings pull-down menu. Pick the Settings option in the menu bar, and then select Drawing Aids from the pull-down menu. The "Drawing Aids" dialogue box then appears on the screen. Typing DDRMODES at the Command: prompt also displays the same dialogue box.

Use the dialogue box to set or change the grid and snap spacing values. Other controls in the "Drawing Aids" dialogue box are discussed later. Turn snap and grid on or off by picking the On button. Enter your desired grid and snap spacing in the X/Y Spacing boxes as needed. Look at Fig. 4-5 and notice that the grid and snap are both on as indicated by the "X" in the On buttons. The grid has an equal horizontal (X) spacing and vertical (Y) spacing of 0.500 units; the snap has an equal X and Y spacing of 0.250.

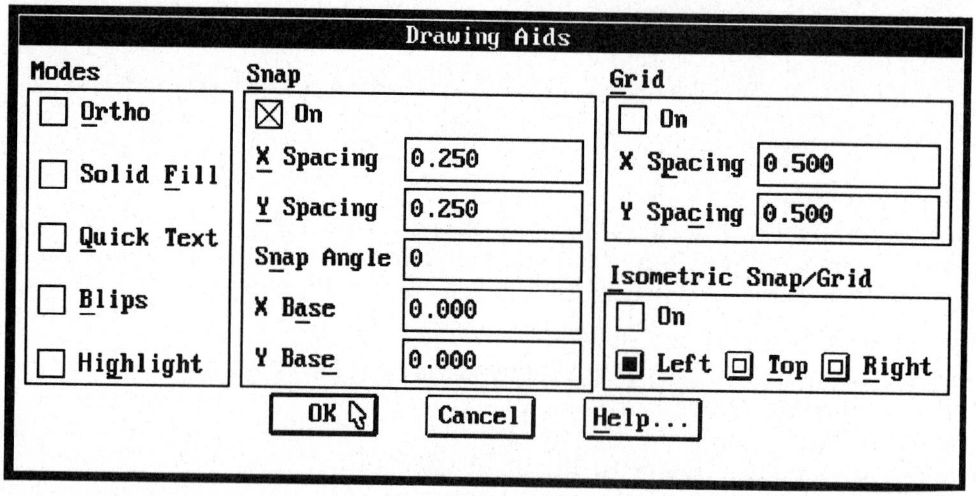

Fig. 4-5. The "Drawing Aids" dialogue box. Notice the Xs in the check boxes indicating options that are active. Also note the current snap and grid settings.

PROFESSIONAL TIP

In actual drafting practice, the SNAP and GRID commands aid in the speed and accuracy of the drawing. Thus, they are referred to as *drawing aids*. The drawing aids are usually set at different values to complement each other. For example, snap may be set at .25 and the grid at .5. With this type of format, each plays a separate role in assisting drawing layout.

FACTORS TO CONSIDER WHEN SETTING DRAWING AIDS

Factors that influence drawing aid values include:
• Drawing units. If the units are decimal inches, set the grid and snap values to standard decimal increments such as .0625, .125, .25, .5, 1; or .05, .1, .2, .5, 1. If you are using architectural units, use 1, 6, 12 inches, or 1, 2, 4, 5, 10 feet increments.
• Drawing size. A very large drawing might have a 1.00 grid spacing, while a small drawing uses a 0.5 spacing or less.
• Value of the smallest dimension. For example, if the smallest dimension is .125, then an appropriate snap value would be .125 and grid spacing .25.
• Change the values at any time. You can change the snap and grid values at any time without changing the location of points or lines already drawn. This should be done when larger or smaller values would assist you with a certain part of the drawing. For example, suppose

a few of the dimensions are in .0625 multiples, but the rest of the dimensions are .250 multiples. Change the snap spacing from .250 to .0625 when laying out smaller dimensions.
- Use the visible grid to help you place views and lay out the entire drawing. Always prepare a sketch before starting a drawing.
- Use whatever method works best and fastest for you when setting or changing the drawing aids.

EXERCISE 4-3

☐ Load AutoCAD to access the drawing editor.
☐ Set decimal units with three digits to the right of the decimal point.
☐ Set the angular measure to degrees/minutes/seconds, one fractional place, and default values for the rest of the options.
☐ Set the limits to 17,11. (Lower-left corner: 0,0; Upper-right corner: 17,11.)
☐ Set the grid spacing at .5.
☐ Set the snap spacing at .25.
☐ Use the LINE command to draw two sets of eight connected line segments.
☐ Change the snap value to .125 and the grid spacing to .25. Draw several more lines and see what happens.
☐ Change the snap value to .5 and the grid spacing to 1. Draw several more lines and observe the results.
☐ Save the drawing as A:EX4-3 and quit.

INTRODUCTION TO PROTOTYPE DRAWING 　ARM 1, 2, A

When doing manual drafting you normally begin with a sheet of drafting paper. The paper may even have a preprinted border line and title block. The title block might be labeled with the company name and address, and a place for the drawing title, part number, scale, material, and drafter's name. You tape down the sheet and add the views, dimensions, and fill in the title block information. It could be said that you began with a *prototype drawing*—the clean sheet of preprinted paper. The prototype, or drawing format, was then changed when adding the new information. The same type of process occurs when using AutoCAD. A simple prototype drawing is one set up with values for limits, grid, and snap. A complex prototype might have a border and title block, established text styles, layer names, and other drawing variables.

AutoCAD has a standard prototype drawing named ACAD which is available every time you start a new drawing. One big drawback with the ACAD prototype is that it is often too general to be used without some customization. In time you will set up a prototype for each drawing size and type. For example, there may be a border and title block format for A-, B-, and C-size drawings. There may be a different prototype for mechanical, electrical, or architectural drawings. The values for limits, units, drawing aids, and other parameters are different for each.

When you design a prototype drawing in AutoCAD, set the units, limits, snap, and grid values to your own or your company's or school's specifications. When you have all of the desired items set, save the prototype drawing with a name such as PROTODR1. A drawing name is limited to eight characters (with no spaces). To save the prototype drawing as PROTODR1, type SAVE at the Command: prompt or pick Save... from the File pull-down menu. Type the name PROTODR1 at the File box and press ENTER or pick the OK box. The prototype is now saved as PROTODR1. The prototype is ready to use anytime you need it.

When you are ready to use the prototype, turn on your computer, load AutoCAD, and pick Open... from the File pull-down menu. When you get the "Open Drawing" dialogue box, select PROTODR1 from the list of files. Now, use the prototype as the setup for doing your drawing. When finished with the drawing, pick Save As... from the File pull-down menu. Save your drawing with a new file name such as PROB4-1. By doing this, you now have the new drawing while the prototype remains as PROTODR1, to be used again. Additional prototype information is discussed in the following chapters. Saving a drawing is discussed in Chapter 5.

When you develop prototype drawings, it is a good idea to record the name of the prototype and the setup values. The following are some sample prototypes:
- A prototype for B-size mechanical drawings using inch values might be set up as:
  Name: M-IN-B (M = mechanical; IN = inches; B = B-size)
  Units: Three-place decimal, two-place decimal degrees
  Limits: 17,11
  Grid: .5
  Snap: .25

- A prototype for B-size mechanical drawings using metric values may be set up as:
  Name: M-MM-B (M = mechanical; MM = millimeters; B = B-size)
  Units: Two-place decimal, two-place decimal degrees
  Limits: 432,280
  Grid: 10
  Snap: 5

- A prototype for a C-size architectural floor plan drawing may be set up as:
  Name: ARCHFL-C (ARCH = architectural; FL = floor plan; C = C-size)
  Units: architectural, 16 fractional denominator, two-place degrees/minutes/seconds
  Limits: 88',68'
  Grid: 5
  Snap: 1

EXERCISE 4-4

□ Load AutoCAD to access the drawing editor.
□ Set the values for your prototype drawing as follows:
  □ UNITS: Three-place decimal, two-place angular decimals.
  □ LIMITS: 12,9
  □ GRID: .5
  □ SNAP: .25
□ On a piece of notebook paper, record the prototype name and all of the specifications set in this exercise. Keep this record for future reference. This is part of preparing a drawing plan sheet, discussed in detail in Chapter 6.
□ Save the drawing as PRODR1 and quit. This prototype is used in future exercises and problems. Save it a second time as A:PRODR1.

CHAPTER TEST

Write your answers in the spaces provided.

1. Give the command and value entered to set a grid spacing of .25:

   Command: _____

   Grid spacing(X) or ON/OFF/Snap/Aspect ⟨0⟩:_____

2. Give the command and value entered to set snap at .125:

   Command: _____

   Snap spacing or ON/OFF/Snap/Aspect/Rotate/Style ⟨current⟩: _____

3. Name the command used to place a pattern of dots on the screen. _____

4. Identify the pull-down menu used to select drawing aids. _____

5. How do you activate the snap grid so the screen cursor will automatically move in precise increments? _____

_____

6. How do you set different horizontal and vertical snap units? _____

_____

7. Name three ways to access the drawing aids. _____

_____

8. Name two ways to access the "Drawing Aids" dialogue box. _____

_____

_____

9. Describe a prototype drawing. _____

_____

_____

10. A drawing name is limited to _____ characters.

DRAWING PROBLEMS

1. Load AutoCAD and enter the drawing editor. Insert your floppy disk. Set up the following specifications for the new drawing:
   LIMITS: 12,9
   GRID: .5
   SNAP: .25
   UNITS: three-place decimals, two-place decimal angular, East direction for angle 0, angles measured counterclockwise.
   Save the prototype drawing as D12-9. (The D denotes decimal drawing units; the 12-9 specifies the limits.) Save the drawing a second time as A:D12-9.
2. Load AutoCAD and enter the drawing editor. Insert your floppy disk. Pick New... from the File pull-down menu. Enter A:D12-9 in the Prototype: box, and enter P4-2 in the New Drawing Name: box. Then pick OK. Turn on the grid and snap features. Draw the following objects using the LINE command so that they fit within the left half of the specified limits.
   A. Right triangle.
   B. Isosceles triangle.
   C. Rectangle.
   D. Square.
   Type "Save" and save the drawing as A:P4-2. Do not quit this drawing session, continue with Problem 3.
3. Draw the same objects specified in Problem 2 on the right side of the screen. This time, make sure the snap grid is turned off. Observe the difference between having snap on and off. Type SAVE at the Command: prompt, change the drawing name to A:P4-3, and pick OK. Then type QUIT at the Command: prompt and press ENTER twice. This saves the drawing as A:P4-3 while the prototype remains as D12-9.

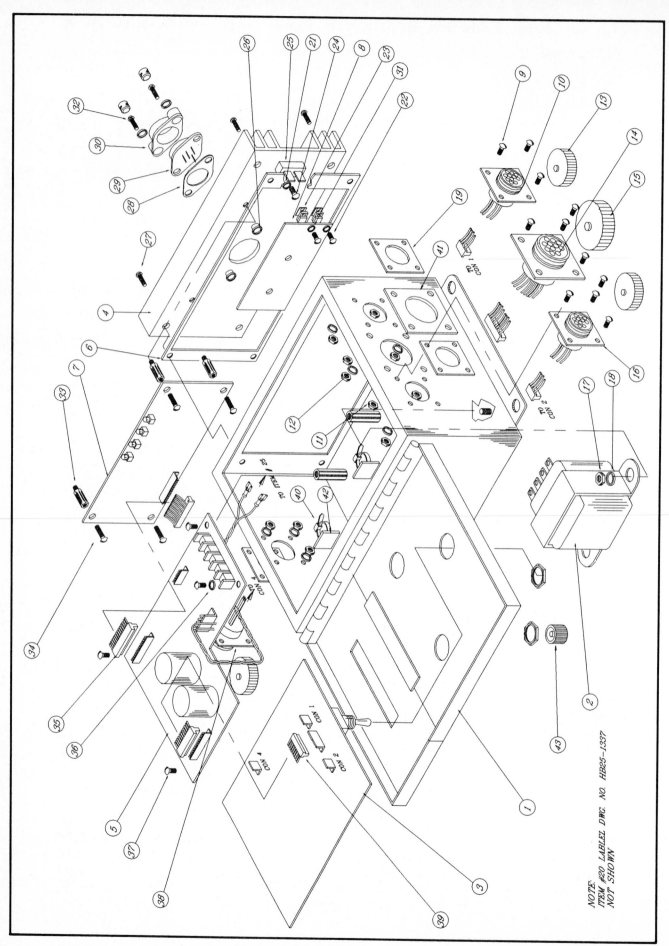

An exploded assembly drawing. (Autodesk, Inc.)

NOTE:
ITEM #20 LABLE1 DWG. NO. HB25-1337
NOT SHOWN

Chapter 5

SAVING DRAWINGS

Learning objectives

After completing this chapter, you will be able to:

☐ Open a drawing that was saved in a previous drawing session.
☐ Change the FILEDIA system variable.
☐ Save a drawing and change the drawing name.
☐ End a drawing session, saving all previous work with the current drawing name.
☐ Quit a drawing.
☐ Identify at least four ways to cancel a command.
☐ Explain the difference between the SAVE, SAVEAS, and QSAVE commands.
☐ Specify how often work should be saved, and use the SAVETIME command to automatically save your work.
☐ List two ways to move between the alphanumeric screen and the drawing editor.
☐ Explain the difference between the END and QUIT commands.

This chapter covers how to get out of a command at any time, and the methods to save or end a drawing. The commands to save or end a drawing include SAVE, SAVEAS, QSAVE, QUIT, and END. Current default values and other drawing characteristics may be displayed using the STATUS command.

CANCELING A COMMAND

It is often necessary to get out of a command. You may decide to do something else—perhaps you made an error and want to start over again. Many commands can be discontinued by pressing the ENTER key or the space bar on the keyboard. This normally exits the command and brings back a new Command: prompt. However, there are some situations where this does not work. For example, using the space bar to discontinue a command does not work when adding text. It is simply recognized as a space in the line of text. If you find that one method does not work, do not panic; try another method.

If you are entering a command and misspell it, you can backspace to remove the unwanted letters and retype the command. This can only be done if the mistake is noticed before the ENTER key is pressed. If improper information is entered, you may get an error message. When this happens, press ENTER to get back to a new Command: prompt.

You can get out of any bad command or unwanted entry by using the "CONTROL C" option. The "C" stands for cancel. Most computers have a CONTROL or CTRL key on the keyboard. Hold down the CTRL key and press the "C" key at the same time. You can use this method at any time to terminate a command.

Many drafters using a multibutton puck use button number 3 to cancel a command. The symbol "∧" stands for CONTROL. If you see the symbol "∧C" it also means CONTROL C or CANCEL. When using this method to cancel a command, the message *cancel* appears and the Command: prompt returns. You can also delete a line of input by holding down the CTRL key and pressing the "X" key. This is referred to as "CTRL X" or "∧X". A *delete* message appears and a new Command: prompt is shown. This also must be done prior to pressing the ENTER key.

There is also a Cancel option located in the Assist pull-down menu.

INTRODUCTION TO SAVING AND QUITTING A DRAWING

In Chapter 3, you were shown how to begin drawing when you access the AutoCAD drawing editor, and you also saved work or quit the drawing in the exercises and problems. The following discussion provides you with detailed information about saving and quitting a drawing.

When saving drawing files using the SAVE and SAVEAS commands, you can have dialogue boxes appear, or you can type everything at the Command: prompt. This is controlled by the FILEDIA system variable. A *system variable* is a command that lets you change the way AutoCAD works. These variables are remembered by AutoCAD and remain in effect until you change them again. There are two FILEDIA system variable options. The default is 1, which displays dialogue boxes at the appropriate times. When FILEDIA is set to 0, a dialogue box does not appear, and you must type the desired information at the prompt line. You can quickly change the FILEDIA system variable as follows:

Command: **FILEDIA** ↵
New value for FILEDIA ⟨1⟩: **0** ↵

In the following discussion, the FILEDIA variable is set to 1, unless otherwise specified.

NAMING DRAWINGS

Drawing names may be chosen to identify a product by name and number, for example VICE-101, FLPLN-92, or 6DT1005. Your school or company probably has a drawing numbering system that you can use. These drawing names should be recorded in a part numbering or drawing name log for future reference.

It is important to set up a system where you can determine the content of a drawing by the drawing number. The following rules and restrictions apply to naming a drawing:
• Drawing names contain 8 characters maximum.
• Drawing names include only letters, numbers, dashes (−), dollar signs ($), or underlines (_).
• Spaces, slashes (/ or \), periods, asterisks, or question marks cannot be used in a drawing name.

STARTING A NEW DRAWING

Once you have entered the drawing editor, you can name a new drawing, or you can use a prototype drawing that was created earlier. To do this, type NEW at the Command: prompt and press ENTER, or pick New... from the File pull-down menu, Fig. 5-1. At this time, the "Create New Drawing" dialogue box appears. See Fig. 5-2.

The New Drawing Name edit box
You enter the new drawing file name in this edit box. When you enter a new drawing named TEST and pick the OK button, AutoCAD creates a new drawing file called TEST.DWG. The drawing file name TEST is entered in Fig. 5-2.

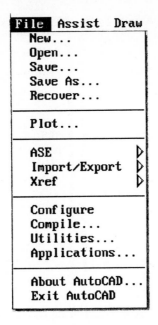

Fig. 5-1. The File pull-down menu.

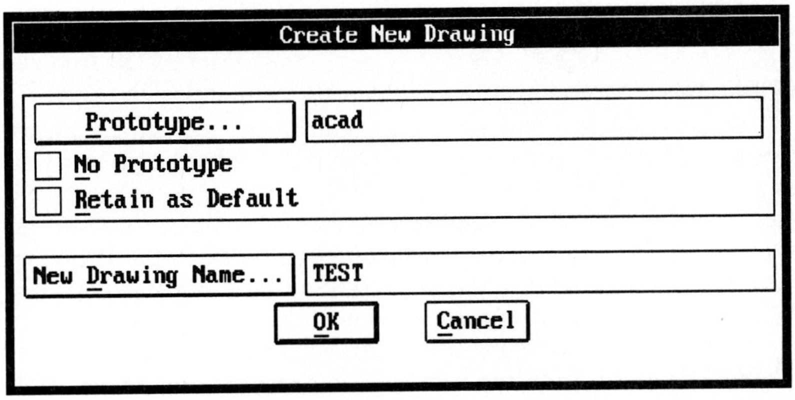

```
                    Create New Drawing

    Prototype...     acad

  [ ] No Prototype
  [ ] Retain as Default

  New Drawing Name...    TEST
                    [ OK ]   [ Cancel ]
```

Fig. 5-2. The "Create New Drawing" dialogue box. Notice the prototype is the standard ACAD prototype and the new drawing name is TEST.

The New Drawing Name button

If you want to see a list of existing drawings, pick the New Drawing Name... button. The "Create Drawing File" dialogue box is then displayed. You can pick an existing drawing name from this dialogue box. See Fig. 5-3A.

─── PROFESSIONAL TIP ───

When you enter a new drawing, AutoCAD opens the drawing file and additional temporary files to be used as extra work space. These temporary files can be compared to the scratch paper used for making sketches and calculations when doing manual drafting. In the end, all you really care about is the drawing file because everything else is a natural function of AutoCAD. However, there are two items of primary importance. First, if you enter a new drawing name as A:TEST, temporary files are made on the floppy disk in the A: drive. This may work while you have plenty of space on the floppy disk, but AutoCAD "crashes" if the disk gets full and there is no place for the temporary files to reside. With this in mind, *always* begin a new drawing on the hard disk drive where there should be plenty of room.

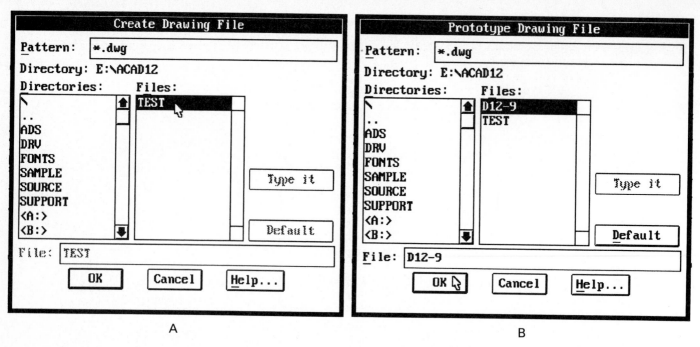

Fig. 5-3. A—The "Create Drawing File" subdialogue box. B—The "Prototype Drawing File" subdialogue box. Notice D12-9 has been picked from the Files list and is shown at the File edit box.

The Prototype edit box

As you may recall, a prototype drawing contains all of the standard elements that you need in the drawing format. These elements might be a border, title block, text style, and AutoCAD system variables set for your application. The Prototype edit box is the place where you enter the name of the prototype drawing that you want to use as the basis for your new drawing. You can also create your own prototype drawing and enter its name in the Prototype edit box. The prototype drawing in Fig. 5-2 is ACAD, which is the standard AutoCAD prototype. (All of the values of the ACAD prototype drawing are shown in Appendix E.)

In Chapter 4, you created a simple prototype drawing named D12-9 (A:D12-9 if the file is on your floppy disk). To use this prototype as the basis for a drawing named EX5-1, enter D12-9 at the Prototype edit box and the drawing name EX5-1 at the New Drawing Name edit box. Now, any work you do is saved as EX5-1 and the prototype remains unchanged and ready for use again.

─────── **PROFESSIONAL TIP** ───────

Remember, all of your work should be saved on floppy disks and not on the hard drive. Therefore, your prototype drawings are saved on a floppy disk. In order to use a prototype drawing that is saved on the floppy disk, enter the prototype drawing name in the Prototype edit box like this: A:D12-9 and then enter the new drawing name in the New Drawing Name edit box. This technique allows you to use a copy of the prototype drawing in the A: drive as the basis for a new drawing created on the hard disk drive.

The Prototype button

To see a list of the existing drawings, pick the Prototype... button to get the "Prototype Drawing File" dialogue box shown in Fig. 5-3B. Notice the D12-9 prototype in the file list (if you saved it to the hard disk drive). You can use D12-9 as your prototype by picking it and pressing ENTER, or pick the OK button. The "Prototype Drawing File" dialogue box then disappears and the D12-9 prototype is listed in the Prototype edit box of the "Create New Drawing" dialogue box. Enter a drawing name at the New Drawing Name edit box and then pick the OK button. You are then ready to start drawing.

── **PROFESSIONAL TIP** ──

An entry in a dialogue box can be approved by moving the cursor arrow to the OK action button and picking, or by simply pressing the ENTER key.

The No Prototype check box

Pick this check box if you don't want to use a prototype drawing. An X in this box sets all variables to AutoCAD default values. This is essentially how the ACAD.DWG prototype drawing was created.

The Retain as Default check box

If you pick this check box, the current prototype is kept for the next time you set up a new drawing.

EXERCISE 5-1

☐ Load AutoCAD and enter the drawing editor.
☐ Pick New . . . from the File pull-down menu and look at the "Create New Drawing" dialogue box.
☐ Pick the New Drawing Name button and see if there are any existing drawings identified in the File list. Pick the OK button.
☐ Enter a new drawing name called TEST at the New Drawing Name edit box and pick the OK button.
☐ Watch the pull-down menu disappear and the drawing editor screen appear. This means that the new drawing named TEST has set up a work space for temporary files. You are ready to begin drawing.
☐ Type QUIT at the Command: prompt.

SAVING YOUR WORK

The SAVE command allows you to protect your work by writing the existing status of your drawing to disk while remaining in the drawing editor. While working in the drawing editor, you should save your drawing every 10 to 15 minutes. This is very important! If there is a power failure, a severe editing error, or other problems, all of the work saved prior to the problem will likely be usable. If you save only once an hour, a power failure results in an hour of lost work. Type SAVE at the Command: prompt, or pick Save . . . from the File pull-down menu (if the drawing is unnamed) to display the "Save Drawing As" dialogue box shown in Fig. 5-4.

* Pattern—The file type, such as .DWG.
* Directory—The current AutoCAD directory. The directory shown in Fig. 5-4 is E:\ACAD12.
* Directories—This is a list of the current available directories and subdirectories. Notice in Fig. 5-4 the list of directories include IGESFONT, SAMPLE, SOURCE, and the various drive letters such as A: and B:.
* File—This is a list of the current files that are available for the pattern type listed. This list of drawing (.DWG) files listed in Fig. 5-4 are ACAD, D12-9, and TEST.

Enter the desired drawing name in the File edit box, pick a drawing name from the list, or pick Type it to enter the drawing name at the prompt line. Remember to change the directory to the drive and directory where you want the drawing saved. In the case of Fig. 5-4, enter A: before the file name or pick the ⟨A:⟩ if you want to save the drawing to your floppy disk in the A: drive. Pick OK or press ENTER when done. If you change your mind, pick the Cancel button.

If you are working on a drawing and then try to save it with a name that already exists, AutoCAD displays the alert box shown in Fig. 5-5. The question in the box states: "Do you want to replace it?" Pick YES if you want the existing drawing replaced with the current one. If you do not want it replaced, pick NO. Be sure to make the right choice since the existing drawing is replaced if you pick YES. Sometimes it may be appropriate to replace an existing drawing when you are changing it.

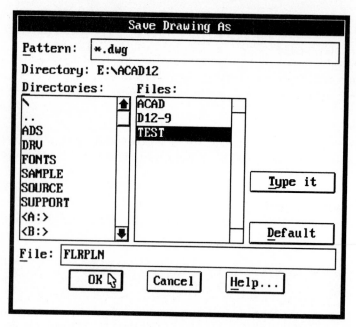

Fig. 5-4. The "Save Drawing As" dialogue box. The pattern is a .DWG (drawing) file, the current directory is ACAD12 on the E: drive, and the drawing to be saved is named FLRPLN in the File edit box.

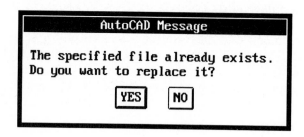

Fig. 5-5. The AutoCAD alert box appears when a drawing with the same name already exists.

PROFESSIONAL TIP

Never begin a drawing on a floppy disk when in AutoCAD. All work during your drawing session is done on the hard disk.

Save your work in two places. If anything happens to one disk, you have the other one to depend on. If you have two disk drives, backup disks may be placed in the A: and B: drives. When finished with your drawing, save it once with an A: prefix and a second time with the B: prefix. If you have only one floppy disk drive, then save your work on two separate disks in the A: drive.

SAVING YOUR WORK AUTOMATICALLY

One of the most important things to remember when working with AutoCAD is to save your drawing every 10 to 15 minutes. If something goes wrong, you will lose 10 or 15 minutes of work rather than hours. Unfortunately, most people learn this the hard way! AutoCAD provides you with an automatic work-saving tool in the SAVETIME system variable. All you need to do is decide how often you want your work saved, and enter the amount of time (in minutes) between saves. For example:

Command: **SAVETIME** ↵
New value for SAVETIME ⟨current⟩: **15** ↵

The value used for the SAVETIME variable indicates the automatic save interval. The SAVETIME timer starts as soon as a change is made to the drawing, and is reset upon use of the SAVE, QSAVE, or SAVEAS command. If you set SAVETIME to 15, work for 14 minutes, and then let the computer remain idle for 5 minutes, the automatic save will be executed when you access the next command. In this instance, an automatic save is not executed until the 19 minute interval, so be certain to manually save your drawing if you plan to be away from your computer for an extended period of time. The autosaved drawing is always saved with the name of AUTO.SV$. If you need to use the file, it can be renamed to a drawing file using the DOS RENAME command. See Chapter 35 for DOS commands.

WHERE TO SAVE THE DRAWING

When you save a drawing, it is stored in the current directory. If you have one or two floppy disk drives, you can save the drawing on your own floppy disk. To do this, place the floppy disk in the A: drive and enter the drawing name as A:NAME. The "A:" part of the name directs the drawing "NAME" to be saved on the A: drive where your floppy disk is located. Suppose you want the drawing saved on the disk in the B: drive. Place your disk in the B: drive and save the drawing as B:NAME.

It is best to do your work on the hard drive and save to a floppy disk. In fact, save your work to two floppy disks so you have a backup in case something happens to one disk. After you save your work to a floppy disk and quit the drawing session, it is best to access the hard disk when you resume your work. However, this requires that you transfer the previous work from the floppy disk to the hard disk if the drawing was not saved on the hard disk. It is easy to do if you follow these steps for an example drawing saved as A:NAME.

- Load AutoCAD and enter the drawing editor.
- Put your disk with the drawing NAME in the A: drive.
- Enter the NEW command to get the "Create New Drawing " dialogue box.
- At the New Drawing Name: edit box, type a drawing name, equal sign, and the name of the drawing on the A: drive as follows:

WORK = A:NAME

This method directs the A:NAME drawing to be copied to the hard drive with the name WORK.
- Now you are working on the hard drive. You can leave the disk in the A: drive or you can remove it.
- Save your work every 10 to 15 minutes.
- When finished for the day, save your work on the disk in the A: drive. Put the floppy disk in the A: drive (if removed) and enter the SAVEAS command.
- Change the Directory to A: and type NAME in the File box, or type A:NAME in the File box.
- The alert box shown in Fig. 5-5 is then displayed. Pick YES. This saves the work you have done on the C: drive as A:NAME.

The SAVEAS command lets you save the current drawing under a new file name. For example, if you are working on an existing drawing and make changes that you want saved with a different name, then use the SAVEAS command. This leaves the current drawing intact with the old name (before changes were made), and saves the modified drawing with the new name. When you pick Save As . . . from the File pull-down menu, or type SAVEAS at the Command: prompt, the "Save drawing as" dialogue box appears, Fig. 5-4, if the FILEDIA system variable is set to 1.

SAVING YOUR DRAWING QUICKLY

The QSAVE (Quick SAVE) command works like the SAVE command except that the drawing you are working on is automatically saved without displaying the "Save drawing as" dialogue box. If you have not used the SAVETIME command to set time intervals between automatic saves, remember to use the QSAVE command every 10 to 15 minutes to ensure your drawing is saved in the event that there is a problem with your computer.

If the drawing is not yet named, the "Save Drawing As" dialogue box is displayed. Pick a file name from the Files list box, or type the drawing name at the File edit box.

To use the QSAVE command, type QSAVE at the Command: prompt and press the ENTER key. The drawing is then saved without allowing you to change the name, directory, or drive. Picking Save . . . from the File pull-down menu activates the QSAVE command if a drawing has been named and previously saved.

EXERCISE 5-2

☐ Load AutoCAD and enter the drawing editor.
☐ Insert your floppy disk in the A: drive, and pick Save . . . from the File pull-down menu. The "Save Drawing As" dialogue box then appears.
☐ Pick ⟨A:⟩ from the Directory list and press ENTER.
☐ Pick the File box and type EX5-2.
☐ Pick the OK button.
☐ Pick Save As . . . from the File pull-down menu.
☐ Be sure C: is the current directory, then type A:EX5-2A at the File box and press ENTER. You have now saved EX5-2 and EX5-2A to the floppy disk in the A: drive.
☐ Type QUIT at the Command: prompt and press ENTER.

OPENING AN EXISTING DRAWING

An existing drawing is one that has been previously saved. You can easily access any existing drawing on the hard disk with the OPEN command. Pick Open . . . from the File pull-down menu, or type OPEN at the Command: prompt. If the drawing is on your floppy disk, use the NEW command and the prototype method discussed earlier. The "Open Drawing" dialogue box shown in Fig. 5-6 appears when you enter the OPEN command and FILEDIA is set to 1.

The "Open Drawing" dialogue box contains Directories and Files lists just as in the "Save Drawing As" dialogue box. Pick the desired directory or file from the lists for quick access, or type the file name at the File edit box. If you specify a file name that does not exist, AutoCAD provides the following alert at the bottom of the dialogue box:

Cannot find the specified file.

If this happens, be sure you have correctly entered the file name and that you are in the appropriate directory. You cannot open a drawing file that does not exist, or is not in the directory you have specified.

Look at Fig. 5-6 and notice the Select Initial View check box. When you pick this box, you are allowed to select a named view that is displayed when you open the drawing. This feature

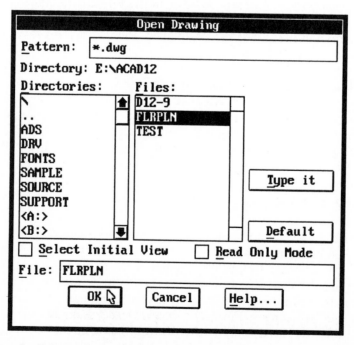

Fig. 5-6. The "Open Drawing" dialogue box. Notice the drawing FLRPLN has been picked from the Files list, and is displayed at the File edit box.

is not discussed in depth at this time, but a detailed discussion is included in Chapter 9 when you learn to establish different views of your drawing.

Refer to Fig. 5-6 again and note the Read Only Mode check box. When you pick this box, the drawing you open is available for viewing only, and any changes or modifications made to the drawing cannot be saved. This is one way to protect your drawing file from any changes made by an unauthorized user. You can also use this mode if you want to practice on your drawing without the fear of altering it.

EXERCISE 5-3

☐ Load AutoCAD and enter the drawing editor.
☐ Pick Open... from the File pull-down menu to access the "Open Drawing" dialogue box.
☐ PRODR1 and D12-9 should be in the Files list if you did Exercise 4-4 and Drawing Problem 4-1.
☐ Pick D12-9 to insert it at the File: edit box and press ENTER, or pick the OK button to open the prototype drawing D12-9.
☐ Type QUIT at the Command: prompt and press ENTER.

ENDING A DRAWING

When you have completed your drawing session, you can exit the drawing editor, save your work, and return to the operating system prompt all at once using the END command. Simply type END at the Command: prompt as follows:

Command: **END** ↵

When you enter END, the revised drawing is saved with the drawing name and a .DWG file extension. The old version is saved as a backup, with a .BAK file extension. The file extension is provided by AutoCAD. You only enter the drawing name. For example, if you work on the drawing named PROTO1 and enter END, it is saved as PROTO1.DWG. The previous version of PROTO1 is saved as PROTO1.BAK. Use the OPEN command when you want to work on PROTO1 again. AutoCAD looks for the .DWG file.

USING THE QUIT COMMAND

The QUIT command lets you exit AutoCAD if any changes you made to the drawing were saved before quitting. You can pick Exit AutoCAD from the File pull-down menu, or type "QUIT" at the Command: prompt as follows:

Command: **QUIT** ↵

If you enter QUIT before saving your work, then AutoCAD gives you a chance to decide what you want to do with unsaved work by displaying the "Drawing Modification" dialogue box shown in Fig. 5-7. Press ENTER to activate the highlighted Save Changes... button. This saves the drawing as previously named, or displays the "Save Drawing As" dialogue box if the drawing had not been previously saved. You can also pick the Discard Changes button if you plan to discard any changes made to the drawing since the previous SAVE. This is a good way to use AutoCAD for practice. Enter the QUIT command when you are done and pick the Discard Changes button. All of the practice work is gone. Pick the Cancel Command button if you decide not to quit.

If you QUIT and pick the Save Changes... button when the drawing is in Read Only Mode, then the QUIT command is automatically canceled. Use the SAVEAS command and give the drawing a new name to save these changes.

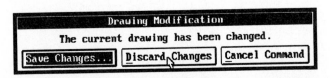

Fig. 5-7. The "Drawing Modification" dialogue box.

DETERMINING THE DRAWING STATUS

While working on a drawing you may want to refresh your memory about some of the drawing parameters, such as the limits, grid spacing, or snap value. All of the information about the drawing is displayed by typing STATUS at the Command: prompt. You can also pick STATUS: from the INQUIRY option in the Root Menu. The information displayed looks like this:

```
52 entities in DRAWING
Model space limits are X:      0.0000   Y:       0.0000   (Off) (World)
                       X:     12.0000   Y:       9.0000
Model space uses       X:      0.9600   Y:       3.5398
                       X:      6.2500   Y:       8.0400
Display shows          X:      0.0000   Y:      15.4985
                       X:      0.0000   Y:       9.4527
Insertion base is      X:     *0.0000   Y:       0.0000   Z:   0.0000
Snap resolution is     X:      0.5000   Y:       0.5000
Grid spacing is        X:      0.2500   Y:       0.2500

Current space:      Model space
Current layer:      0
Current color:      BYLAYER—7 (white)
Current linetype:   BYLAYER—CONTINUOUS
Current elevation:  0.0000 thickness:  0.0000
Fill on    Grid on   Ortho off   Qtext off   Snap on   Tablet off
Object snap modes:  None
Free disk:          14518272 bytes
Virtual memory allocated to program: 2128K
Amount of program in physical memory/Total (virtual) program size: 95%
—Press RETURN for more —
Total conventional memory: 404K       Total extended memory: 3328K
Swap file size: 388KB
Page faults: 235      Swap writes: 0      Swap reclaims: 0
Command:
```

The number of entities in a drawing refers to the total number of entites—both erased and unerased. The (Off) on the "Model space limits are" line refers to the limits check discussed in Chapter 3, and (World) means that the limits are given in World coordinates. If the message "**Over" appears to the right of "Model space uses," this indicates that the drawing extends outside the drawing limits. Free disk represents the space left on the drive containing your drawing file.

PROFESSIONAL TIP

Refer to the drawing STATUS command periodically to see how much "free disk" space is available. If this free disk space becomes dangerously low, you may be unable to complete and save the drawing. This has been known to cause severe problems. AutoCAD automatically saves your work and ends use of the drawing editor if it runs out of disk space.

EXERCISE 5-4

☐ Load AutoCAD and enter the drawing editor.
☐ Pick Open... from the File pull-down to access the "Open Drawing" dialogue box.
☐ PRODR1 and D12-9 should be in the Files list if you did Exercise 4-4 and Drawing Problem 4-1.
☐ Pick D12-9 to insert it at the File: edit box and press ENTER, or pick the OK button to open the prototype drawing D12-9.
☐ Enter the STATUS command and read all of the items displayed. Press the ENTER key to view the information on the second page.
☐ Press the F1 function key to get back to the drawing editor.
☐ Type QUIT at the Command: prompt and press ENTER.

CHAPTER TEST

Write your answers in the spaces provided.

1. Name the command used to start a new drawing. _____

2. What command saves your drawing and returns you to the operating system prompt?

   _____

3. Identify the command that you use to leave the drawing editor without saving. _____

   _____

4. What command would you use to save an existing drawing with a different name? ___

   _____

5. Identify at least four ways to cancel a command. _____

   _____

   _____

6. Explain the difference between the SAVE, END, and QUIT commands. _____

   _____

   _____

   _____

   _____

   _____

   _____

7. How do you change the name of a drawing while in the drawing editor? _____

   _____

   _____

8. How often should work be saved? _____

9. Name the command that allows you to quickly save your work without displaying the dialogue
   box. _____

10. The status of an AutoCAD drawing is currently displayed on screen. List one method to
    get back to the drawing editor. _____

    _____

11. Name the system variable that allows you to control the dialogue box display. _____

    _____

12. List the settings for the system variable described in the previous question that is used to
    achieve the following results:

    Dialogue box displayed _____

    Dialogue box not displayed _____

13. Why is it important to record drawing names in a log? _____

    _____

14. List at least three rules and restrictions for drawing names._____
_____
_____
_____
_____

15. Name the pull-down menu where the SAVE, SAVEAS, and OPEN commands are located.
_____

16. Identify two ways to exit AutoCAD without saving your work. _____
_____

17. Name the command that allows AutoCAD to automatically save your work at designated intervals. _____

18. Explain how you can get a list of existing drawing prototypes. _____
_____
_____

19. It is recommended that you resume work on the hard drive when you have saved the drawing file on a floppy disk. Name the file entry needed to transfer the drawing file named A:PROJECT to the hard disk in a file called WORK. _____

20. Why is it a good idea to save your work on two floppy disks? _____
_____
_____

DRAWING PROBLEMS

1. Enter the drawing editor and open drawing D12-9. This is the prototype that you set up in Problem 4-1. (If you did not set up this prototype, refer back to Problem 4-1 and set up the drawing now.) Draw the same objects that you drew in Problem 4-2. Use the SAVEAS command and change the file name to P5-1. This keeps the prototype unchanged for future use and saves the drawing on the hard drive as P5-1 (P = Problem, 5 = Chapter 5, 1 = Problem 1). Now, type QUIT at the Command: prompt and press ENTER.

2. Start AutoCAD and open drawing P5-1. Draw the objects in the same manner as required in Problem 4-3. Enter QUIT, press the ENTER key, and discard all changes. This procedure deletes all changes to the drawing and brings you back to the operating system prompt.

3. Start AutoCAD and open drawing P5-1. Observe that the work done in Problem 2 does not exist. This is because you used the QUIT command. Now enter END. This saves P5-1 as is and returns you to the operating system prompt.

4. Start AutoCAD and access the "Create New Drawing" dialogue box. Enter P5-4 = P5-1 at the New Drawing Name edit box. This procedure does the following:
   ☐ Creates a new drawing titled P5-4.
   ☐ Copies the drawing P5-1 to P5-4.
   ☐ When you SAVE, there is a new drawing titled P5-4. The previous drawing, P5-1, remains unchanged.
   On the right side of the screen draw a right triangle, a square, and a rectangle. Use the SNAP and GRID commands to your best advantage. Enter END to save the drawing when finished.

5. Start AutoCAD and open drawing P5-4. Enter the STATUS command and observe the drawing status. Press the F1 function key to return to the drawing editor. Draw a box around the items previously drawn. Enter the QSAVE command and press ENTER. Then, type "QUIT" and press ENTER to go back to the operating system prompt.

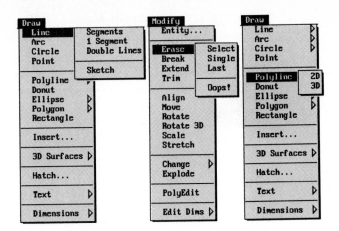

Chapter 6

DRAWING AND ERASING LINES

Learning objectives

After completing this chapter, you will be able to:

- ☐ Use the absolute, relative, and polar coordinate point entry systems.
- ☐ Use the screen cursor for point entry.
- ☐ Use the Ortho mode and coordinate display.
- ☐ Select the LINE command to draw given objects.
- ☐ Draw double lines with the DLINE command.
- ☐ Make revisions to objects using the ERASE command.
- ☐ Make selection sets using the Multiple, Window, Crossing, WPolygon, CPolygon, and Fence options.
- ☐ Use the OOPS command to bring back an entity.
- ☐ Use the PLINE command to draw given objects.
- ☐ Observe the results of using FILL on and off, and REDRAW.
- ☐ Draw given objects using the TRACE command.
- ☐ Sketch with AutoCAD.
- ☐ Use drawing plan sheets.

Drafting is a graphic language that uses lines, symbols, and words to describe products to be manufactured or constructed. Line conventions are standards based on line thickness and type, and are designed to enhance the readability of drawings. This chapter introduces line standards and shows you how to use the AutoCAD drawing editor to perform basic drafting tasks.

LINE CONVENTIONS

The American National Standards Institute (ANSI) recommends two line thicknesses to establish contrasting lines on a drawing. Lines are described as thick and thin. Thick lines are .032 in. (0.7 mm) wide and thin lines are .016 in. (0.35 mm) wide. Fig. 6-1 shows recommended line width and type as taken from ANSI Y14.2M, *Line Conventions and Lettering*.

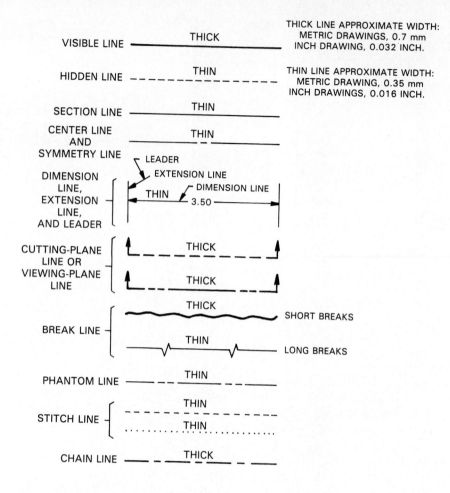

VISIBLE LINE ————————————— THICK

HIDDEN LINE – – – – – – – THIN

SECTION LINE ————————— THIN

CENTER LINE
AND ——— – ———— – ——— THIN
SYMMETRY LINE

DIMENSION
LINE,
EXTENSION
LINE,
AND LEADER

CUTTING-PLANE
LINE OR
VIEWING-PLANE
LINE

THICK LINE APPROXIMATE WIDTH:
METRIC DRAWINGS, 0.7 mm
INCH DRAWING, 0.032 INCH.

THIN LINE APPROXIMATE WIDTH:
METRIC DRAWING, 0.35 mm
INCH DRAWINGS, 0.016 INCH.

LEADER
EXTENSION LINE
DIMENSION LINE
THIN
3.50

THICK
THICK

BREAK LINE

THICK ———— SHORT BREAKS
THIN ———— LONG BREAKS

PHANTOM LINE – – – THIN – – –

STITCH LINE
THIN – – – –
THIN ·············

CHAIN LINE ——— – THICK ——— –

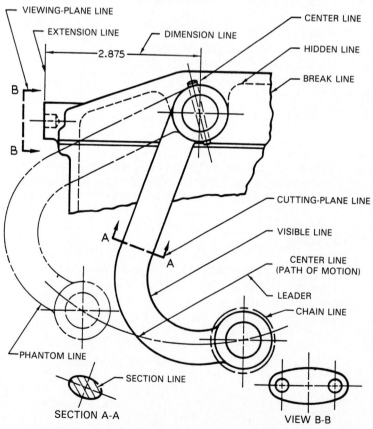

VIEWING-PLANE LINE
EXTENSION LINE
DIMENSION LINE
2.875
CENTER LINE
HIDDEN LINE
BREAK LINE

B
B

A
A

CUTTING-PLANE LINE
VISIBLE LINE
CENTER LINE
(PATH OF MOTION)
LEADER
CHAIN LINE

PHANTOM LINE

SECTION LINE

SECTION A-A

VIEW B-B

Fig. 6-1. Line conventions. (ANSI Y14.2M)

Object lines

Object lines, also called *visible lines,* are thick lines used to show the outline or contour of an object, Fig. 6-2. Object lines are the most common type of lines used on drawings.

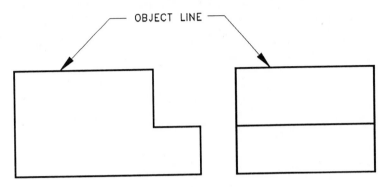

Fig. 6-2. Object line.

Hidden lines

Hidden lines, often called *dashed lines,* are used to represent invisible edges of an object, Fig. 6-3. Hidden lines are drawn thin so they clearly contrast with object lines. Properly drawn, the dashes are .125 in. (3.18 mm) long and spaced .06 in. (1.59 mm) apart. This is the recommended full size of hidden line dashes. Be careful if the drawing is to be greatly reduced or scaled down during the plotting process. Reduced dashes may appear too small.

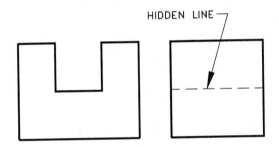

Fig. 6-3. Hidden line.

Centerlines

Centerlines locate the centers of circles and arcs, and show the axis of a cylindrical or symmetrical shape, Fig. 6-4. Centerlines are thin lines consisting of alternately spaced long and short dashes. The recommended dash lengths are .125 in. (3.18 mm) for the short dashes and .75 to 1.5 in. (19.05 to 38.1 mm) for the long dashes. These lengths can be altered depending on the size of the drawing. The dashes should be separated by spaces approximately .06 in. (1.59 mm). The small centerline dashes should cross only at the center of a circle.

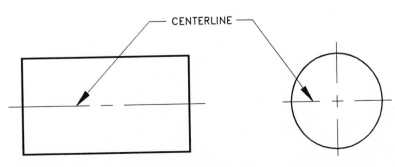

Fig. 6-4. Centerline.

Extension lines

Extension lines are thin lines used to show the extent of a dimension, Fig. 6-5. Extension lines begin a small distance from the object and extend .125 in. (3.18 mm) beyond the last dimension line. Extension lines may cross object lines, hidden lines, and centerlines, but they may not cross dimension lines. Centerlines become extension lines when they are used to show the extent of a dimension. When this is done, there is no space where the centerline joins the extension line.

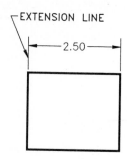

Fig. 6-5. Extension line.

Dimension lines

Dimension lines are thin lines placed between extension lines to indicate a measurement. In mechanical drafting, the dimension line is normally broken near the center for placement of the dimension numeral, Fig. 6-6. The dimension line normally remains unbroken in architectural and structural drawings. The dimension numeral is placed on top of an unbroken dimension line. Arrows terminate the ends of dimension lines, except in architectural drafting where slashes or dots are often used.

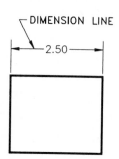

Fig. 6-6. Dimension line.

Leader lines

Leader lines are thin lines used to connect a specific note to a feature on a drawing. A leader line terminates with an arrowhead at the feature and has a small shoulder at the note, Fig. 6-7. Dimension and leader line usage is discussed in detail in Chapter 18.

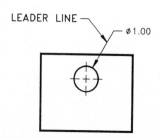

Fig. 6-7. Leader line.

Cutting-plane and viewing-plane lines

Cutting-plane lines are thick lines that identify the location of a section or view. *Viewing-plane lines* are drawn in the same style as cutting-plane lines, but identify the location of a view. Cutting-plane and viewing-plane lines may be drawn one of two ways as shown in Fig. 6-1. The use of viewing-plane and cutting-plane lines is discussed in detail in Chapters 17 and 20.

Section lines

Section lines are thin lines drawn in a sectional view to show where material has been cut away, Fig. 6-8. Section line types and applications are discussed in Chapter 20.

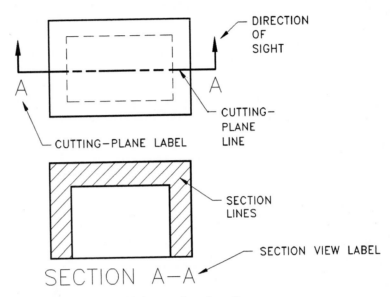

Fig. 6-8. Section lines and the cutting-plane line.

Break lines

Break lines show where a portion of an object has been removed for clarity or convenience. For example, the center portion of a very long part may be broken out so the two ends can be moved closer together for more convenient representation. There are several types of break lines shown in Fig. 6-9.

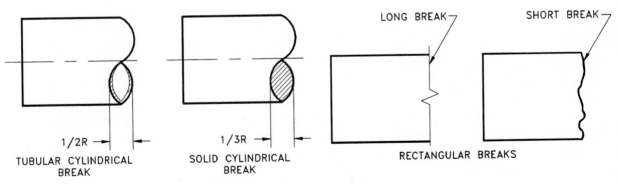

Fig. 6-9. Standard break lines.

Phantom lines

Phantom lines are thin lines with two short dashes alternately spaced with long dashes. The short dashes are .125 in. (3.18 mm) and the long dashes range from .75 to 1.5 in. (19.05 to 38.1 mm) in length depending on the size of the drawing. Spaces between dashes are .06 in. (1.59 mm). Phantom lines identify repetitive details, show alternate positions of moving parts, or locate adjacent positions of related parts, Fig. 6-10.

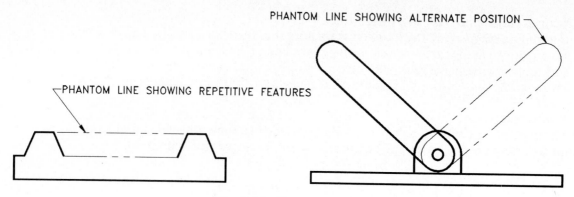

Fig. 6-10. Phantom lines.

Chain lines

Chain lines are thick lines of alternately spaced long and short dashes. They show that the portion of the surface next to the chain line has special features or receives unique treatment. See Fig. 6-11.

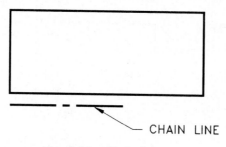

Fig. 6-11. Chain lines.

DRAWING LINES WITH AUTOCAD

ARM 5

Individual line segments are drawn between two points on the screen. This is referred to as *point entry* and is the simplest form of drafting. Enter endpoints for drawing lines after selecting the LINE command.

The command name "LINE" may be typed at the Command: prompt. It can also be selected from the DRAW screen menu or the Draw pull-down menu. When you enter the LINE command, AutoCAD asks for the "from point" and "to point" of the line. Enter these points by typing point coordinates using the keyboard or picking points by moving the crosshairs to desired locations. When you select the LINE command, a prompt asks you to select a starting point. When the first point is selected, the next point is requested. When the third "To point:" prompt is given, you may stop adding lines by pressing the ENTER key or the space bar. If you want to connect a series of lines, continue selecting as many additional points as you like. When finished, press ENTER or press the space bar to get back to the Command: prompt.

The following command sequence is for the LINE command:

> Command: **LINE** ⏎
> From point: *(select the first point)*
> To point: *(select the second point)*
> To point: *(select the third point or press ENTER to get a new Command: prompt)*
> Command: *(this appears if you press ENTER at the previous prompt)*

Responding to AutoCAD prompts with numbers

Many of the AutoCAD commands require specific types of numeric data. Each situation is explained as you learn new commands in this text. Some of AutoCAD's prompts require you to enter a number as the proper response. For example, later in this book you will learn how to divide an object into a number of equal parts using the DIVIDE command. This command requires that you specify a number of segments as follows:

Command: **DIVIDE** ↵
Select object to divide: *(pick the object)*
⟨Number of segments⟩/Block: **6** ↵

The above example illustrates the simplest form of numeric entry where any whole number may be used. Other entries require whole numbers that may be positive or negative. A number is understood to be positive without placing the plus (+) sign before the number. However, a negative number must be preceded by the minus (−) sign.

Much of your data entry is other than whole numbers. In these cases, any real number may be used and can be expressed as decimals, fractions, or scientific notation. They may be positive or negative. Here are some examples:

4.250
−6.375
1/2
1-3/4
2.5E+4 (25,000)
2.5E-4 (0.00025)

When entering fractions, the numerator and denominator must be whole numbers greater than zero such as 1/2, 3/4, or 2/3. Numbers containing fractions that are greater than one must have a dash between the whole number and the fraction, for example, 2-3/4. The dash (-) separator is needed because a space acts just like pressing ENTER, which automatically ends the input. The numerator may be larger than the denominator as in 3/2 only if a whole number is not used with the fraction.

When you enter coordinates or measurements, the value used depends on the units of measure such as feet, inches, or millimeters. Values on inch drawings are understood to be in inches without placing the inch (″) marks after the numeral. For example, 2.500 is automatically 2.500 inches. When your drawing is set up for metric values, then any entry is automatically expressed as millimeters. If you are working in an engineering or architectural environment, any value greater than one foot is expressed in inches, feet, or feet and inches. The values can be whole numbers, decimals, or fractions. For measurements in feet, the foot (′) symbol must follow the number, as in 24′. If the value is in feet and inches, there is no space between the feet and inch value. For example, 24′6 is the proper input for the value 24′-6″. If the inch part of the value contains a fraction, the inch and fractional part of an inch are separated by a dash as previously explained. For example, 24′6-1/2. Never mix feet with inches greater than one foot, for example, 24′18″ is an invalid entry. In this case, you should enter 25′6.

PROFESSIONAL TIP

Placing the inch (″) marks after an inch value at the prompt line is acceptable, but not necessary. It takes more time and reduces productivity.

POINT ENTRY METHODS

ARM 2

There are several point entry techniques for drawing lines. Being familiar and skillful with these methods is very important. It is not necessary to use only one point entry system when drawing. A combination of techniques may be used to help reduce drawing time. Each of the point entry methods uses the Cartesian, or rectangular coordinate system. The *Cartesian coordinate system* is based on selecting distances that locate a point from two intersecting axes. Each point distance is measured along a horizontal "X" axis and a vertical "Y" axis. The intersection of the axes, called the *origin,* divides the coordinate system into four quadrants. Points are located in relation to the origin where X = 0 and Y = 0, or (0,0). Fig. 6-12 shows the X,Y values of points located in the Cartesian coordinate system.

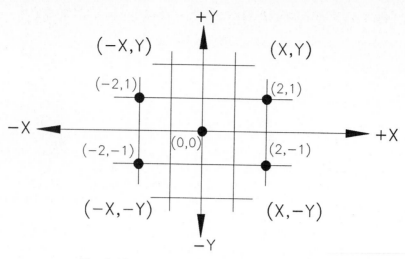

Fig. 6-12. The Cartesian coordinate system.

When using AutoCAD, the 0,0 point (origin) is usually at the lower-left corner of the drawing. This point also coincides with the lower-left corner of the drawing limits. This setup places all points in the upper-right quadrant where both X and Y coordinate values are positive, Fig. 6-13.

Methods of establishing points in the Cartesian coordinate system include absolute coordinates, relative coordinates, and polar coordinates.

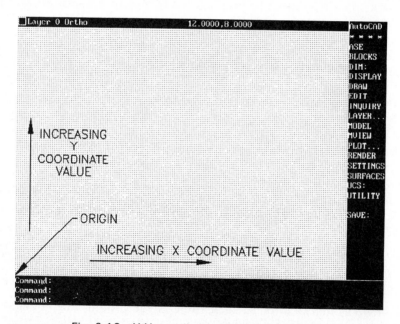

Fig. 6-13. X,Y coordinate axes on the screen.

Absolute coordinates

Points located using the absolute coordinate system are measured from the origin (0,0). For example, a point with X = 4 and Y = 2 (4,2) is measured 4 units horizontally (X) and 2 units vertically (Y) from the origin, Fig. 6-14. Notice the status line at the top right of the screen registers the location of the selected point in X and Y coordinates. This is referred to as the *coordinate display*. The coordinate display may be turned on or off by pressing CTRL D on the keyboard or puck button 7.

Remember, when the absolute coordinate system is used, each point is located from 0,0. Follow through these commands and point placements at your computer, if possible, as you refer to Fig. 6-15.

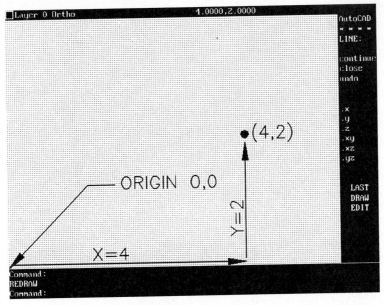

Fig. 6-14. Locating points with absolute coordinates.

Command: **LINE** ↵
From point: **4,2** ↵
To point: **7,2** ↵
To point: **7,6** ↵
To point: **4,6** ↵
To point: **4,2** ↵
To point: ↵
Command: **LINE** ↵
From point: **9,1.5** ↵
To point: **11,1.5** ↵
To point: **10,5.25** ↵
To point: **9,1.5** ↵
To point: ↵
Command:

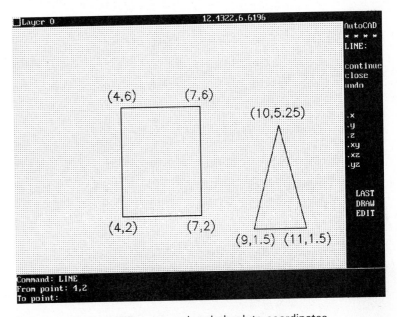

Fig. 6-15. Drawing simple shapes using the LINE command and absolute coordinates.

EXERCISE 6-1

☐ Load AutoCAD, enter the drawing editor, and open PRODR1 from Exercise 4-4, or start a new drawing and set up your own variables.
☐ Given the following absolute coordinates, use the LINE command to draw the object:

Point	Coordinates	Point	Coordinates
1	0,0	5	0,2
2	9,0	6	0,1.5
3	9.5,.5	7	.25,.5
4	9.5,2	8	0,0

☐ Save the drawing as A:EX6-1 and quit the drawing editor.

Relative coordinates

Relative coordinates are located from the previous position, rather than from the origin. The relationship of points in the Cartesian coordinate system shown in Fig. 6-12 must be clearly understood before beginning with this method. For relative coordinates, the "@" symbol must precede your entry. (This symbol is selected by holding the SHIFT key and pressing the "2" key at the top of the keyboard.) Follow through these commands and relative coordinate point placements as you refer to Fig. 6-16.

Command: **LINE** ↵
From point: **2,2** ↵
To point: **@6,0** ↵
To point: **@2,2** ↵
To point: **@0,3** ↵
To point: **@−2,2** ↵
To point: **@−6,0** ↵
To point: **@0,−7** ↵
To point: ↵
Command:

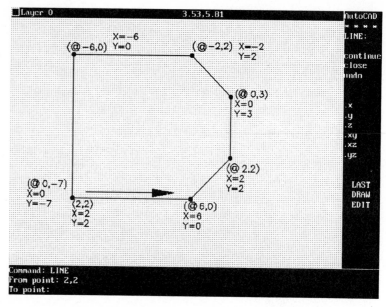

Fig. 6-16. Drawing a simple shape using the LINE command and relative coordinates.

EXERCISE 6-2

☐ Load AutoCAD, enter the drawing editor, and open PRODR1 from Exercise 4-4, or start a new drawing and set up your own variables.

☐ Use the LINE command to draw the object with the following relative coordinates:

Point	Coordinates	Point	Coordinates
1	1,1	5	@ −9.5,0
2	@ 9,0	6	@ 0,−.5
3	@ .5,.5	7	@ .25,−1
4	@ 0,1.5	8	@ −.25,−.5

☐ Save the drawing as A:EX6-2 and quit.

Polar coordinates

A point located using *polar coordinates* is based on the distance from a fixed point at a given angle. When using AutoCAD, a polar coordinate point is determined by distance and angle measured from the previous point. It is important to remember that points located using polar coordinates are always positioned relative to the *previous* point, not the origin (0,0). The angular values used for the polar coordinate format are shown in Fig. 6-17.

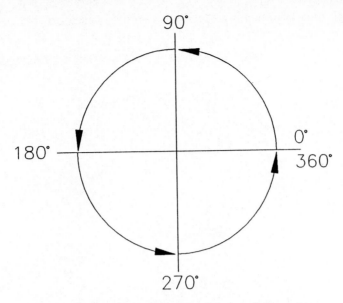

Fig. 6-17. Angles used in the polar coordinate system.

When establishing points using the polar coordinate system, AutoCAD needs a specific symbol entered. For example, if you want to locate a point 4 units from point 0,0 at a 45° angle, the following information must be typed:

Command: **LINE** ↵
From point: **0,0** ↵
To point: **@4‹45** ↵
To point: ↵

Fig. 6-18 shows the result of this command. The entry @4‹45 means the following:

@ — Tells AutoCAD to measure from the previous point. This symbol must precede all polar coordinate prompts.
4 — Denotes the distance from the previous point.
‹ — Establishes a polar or angular increment to follow.
45 — Determines the angle as 45° from 0°.

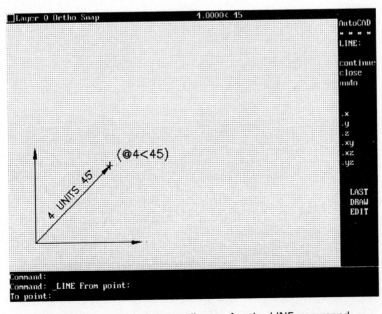

Fig. 6-18. Using polar coordinates for the LINE command.

Now, follow through these commands and polar coordinate points on your computer, if possible, as you refer to Fig. 6-19.

Command: **LINE** ↵
From point: **1,1** ↵
To point: **@4‹0** ↵
To point: **@2‹90** ↵
To point: **@4‹180** ↵
To point: **@2‹270** ↵
To point: ↵
Command: **LINE** ↵
From point: **2,6** ↵
To point: **@2.5‹0** ↵
To point: **@3‹135** ↵
To point: **2,6** ↵
To point: ↵
Command:

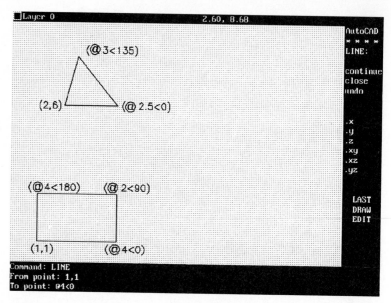

Fig. 6-19. Drawing simple shapes using polar coordinates.

EXERCISE 6-3

☐ Load AutoCAD, enter the drawing editor, and open PRODR1 from Exercise 4-4, or start a new drawing and set up your own variables.
☐ Use the LINE command to draw an object using the following polar coordinates:

Point	Coordinates
1	1,1
2	@9‹0
3	@.7‹45
4	@1.5‹90
5	@9.5‹180
6	@2‹270

☐ Save the drawing as A:EX6-3 and quit.

Picking points using the screen cursor

The cursor crosshairs may be moved to any location. Pick points at the cursor using the stylus, mouse, or puck. The GRID and SNAP modes normally should be on for precise point location. This assists in drafting presentation and maintains accuracy when using a pointing device. With snap grid on, the crosshairs move in designated increments without any guesswork.

When using a pointing device, the command sequence is the same as using coordinates except that points are picked when the crosshairs are at the desired location on the screen. After the first point is picked, the distance to the second point and the point's coordinates are displayed on the status line for reference. Also, use a visible grid and invisible snap grid for reference. For example, if the distance is 2.75, then .25 snap units and .5 grid units allow you to quickly locate the point. When picking points in this manner, there is a "rubberband" line connecting the "from point" and the crosshairs. The rubberband line moves as the crosshairs are moved. It provides a clue to where the new line will be placed. The rubberband line remains attached to the crosshairs until you complete the LINE command. See Fig. 6-20.

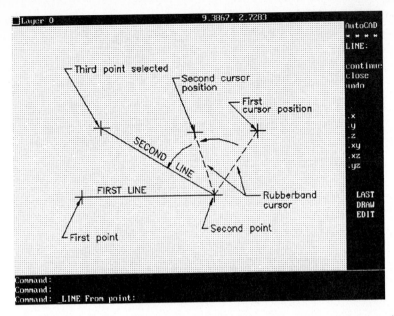

Fig. 6-20. The rubberband line is visible when using a pointing device to input points for lines.

DRAWING MULTIPLE LINES

ARM 4

The MULTIPLE command modifier is a method used to automatically repeat commands issued at the keyboard. It is available if your computer supports the AutoCAD pull-down menus. This technique may be used to draw repetitive lines, polylines, circles, arcs, ellipses, or polygons. For example, if you plan to draw several sets of line segments, type the word MULTIPLE before LINE at the Command: prompt. AutoCAD automatically repeats the LINE command until you have finished drawing all of the desired lines. You must then cancel to get back to the Command: prompt. The MULTIPLE option is used as follows:

Command: **MULTIPLE LINE** ↵
From point: *(pick the first point)*
To point: *(pick the second point)*
To point: *(pick the third point or press ENTER)*
To point: ↵
LINE From point: *(pick the first point of the next line)*
To point: *(pick the second point of the next line)*
To point: *(pick the third point or press ENTER)*
To point: ↵
LINE From point: *(pick first point of third line)*
To point: *(pick the second point of third line)*
To point: ↵
LINE From point: *(press CTRL C) *Cancel**
Command:

AutoCAD automatically reissues the LINE command so you can draw another line or lines, or press CTRL C to cancel the repeating command.

THE COORDINATE DISPLAY

ARM 9

The area above the upper-right corner of the drawing editor shows the coordinate display. The number of places to the right of the decimal point is determined by the units setting. When you begin a new drawing and before any point entry is made, the coordinate display shows the X and Y coordinates as 0.0000,0.0000. When point entries are made, the coordinate display changes to represent the location of the point relative to the origin. For example, if the first point picked is X = 4.2500, Y = 3.6250, the coordinate display reads 4.2500,3.6250. If the units are set at two places to the right of the decimal, then the reading is 4.25,3.63. Each time a new point is picked, the coordinates are updated. The coordinate display may be changed from recording the location of each point picked to a constant update as you move the cursor. By turning the coordinates on, the display then shows point location or the length and angle of a line being drawn. The coordinate display is turned on and off by pressing CTRL D, F6, or puck button 7. With coordinates on, the coordinates constantly change as the crosshairs move. There are two modes. One shows absolute coordinates and the other provides polar coordinates. A typical absolute coordinate display gives X and Y coordinates like 6.2000,5.9000. A polar coordinate display shows the distance and angle from the last point, such as 3.4000<180.

EXERCISE 6-4

☐ Load AutoCAD, enter the drawing editor, and open PRODR1 from Exercise 4-4.
☐ Draw rectangles 3 in. (76.2 mm) wide by 2 in. (50.8 mm) high using each point entry method from the following list. Experiment with the coordinate display options as you draw the rectangles.
   ☐ Absolute coordinates.
   ☐ Relative coordinates.
   ☐ Polar coordinates.
   ☐ Using the screen cursor.
☐ Use the MULTIPLE LINE command to draw several different lines or shapes. Notice the advantage of remaining in the LINE command when several different line segments or shapes must be drawn.
☐ Save the drawing as A:EX6-4 and quit.

DRAWING AT RIGHT ANGLES USING THE ORTHO COMMAND   `ARM 9`

The ORTHO command puts AutoCAD in the Ortho mode. Ortho allows lines drawn by the crosshairs movement to be only horizontal or vertical, in alignment with the current snap grid. The term *ortho* comes from "orthogonal" which means "at right angles." The Ortho mode has a special advantage when drawing rectangular shapes because all corners are guaranteed to be square. It is impossible to draw a line at an angle to the snap grid with a pointing device while Ortho is on. See Fig. 6-21. Ortho may be turned on or off by typing ORTHO at the Command: prompt, or while in another command by using function key F8, puck button 5, or CTRL O.

Command: **ORTHO** ↵
ON/OFF: **(ON** *or* **OFF** *as desired)* ↵

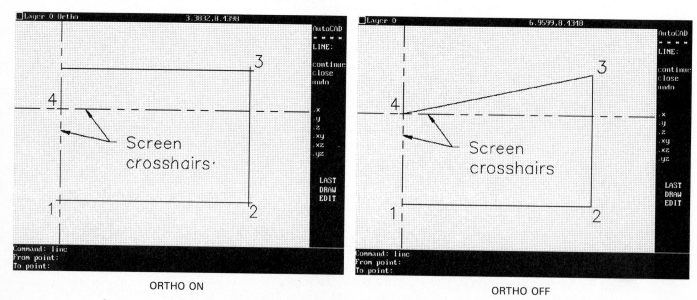

ORTHO ON   ORTHO OFF

Fig. 6-21. Angled lines cannot be drawn with Ortho mode on.

Remember, the Ortho mode is and easy to turn on or off using function key F8, puck button 5, or pressing CTRL O.

PROFESSIONAL TIP

Practice using the different point entry techniques and decide which method works best for certain situations. Keep in mind that you may mix methods to help enhance your drawing speed. For example, absolute coordinates may work best to locate an initial point or to draw a simple shape. These calculations are easy. Polar coordinates may work better to locate features in a circular pattern, or at an angular relationship. Practice with Ortho and snap settings to see the advantages and disadvantages of each. Change the snap setting at any time to assist in drawing layout accuracy. Remember, the snap grid is a drawing aid, so set the snap increment to assist in drawing accuracy.

USING THE CLOSE POLYGON OPTION

ARM 5

A *polygon* is a closed plane figure with at least three sides. A triangle or rectangle are examples of polygons. When you are drawing a polygon, the last point may automatically be connected to the first point using the Close option. This option may be picked from the LINE screen menu or by typing "CLOSE" or "C" at the prompt line. In Fig. 6-22, the last line is drawn using the Close option as follows:

Command: **LINE** ↵
From point: *(pick point 1)*
To point: *(pick point 2)*
To point: *(pick point 3)*
To point: *(pick point 4)*
To point: **C** ↵
Command:

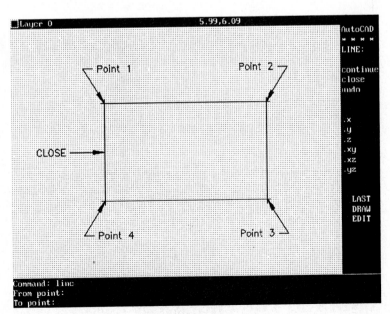

Fig. 6-22. Using the Close option.

USING THE LINE CONTINUATION OPTION

ARM 5

Suppose you draw a line, then exit the LINE command, but decide to go back and connect a new line to the end of the previous one. Go to the LINE screen menu and pick "continue." This automatically connects the next line to the last endpoint of the previous one as shown in Fig. 6-23. (The line continuation option may also be used to continue drawing arcs, as discussed in Chapter 7.) The command sequence for continuing a line looks like this:

First line:
Command: **LINE** ↵
From point: *(pick point 1)*
To point: *(pick point 2)*
To point: ↵

Next line:
Command: *(pick "continue" from the LINE screen menu)* __LINE
From point: *(AutoCAD automatically picks the last endpoint of the previous line)*
To point: *(pick point 3)*
To point: ↵
Command:

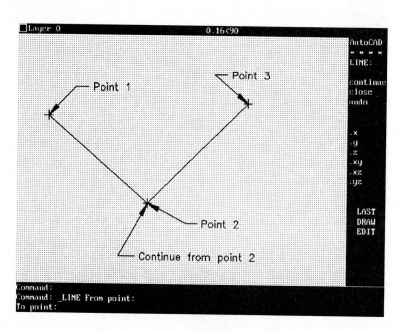

Fig. 6-23. Using the Continue option.

A quicker way to select the "continue" option is to press the space bar after entering the LINE command.

Command: **LINE** ↵
From point: *(press space bar; AutoCAD automatically picks the last endpoint of the previous line)*
To point: *(pick the next point)*
To point: ↵
Command:

UNDOING THE PREVIOUSLY DRAWN LINE

ARM 5

When drawing a series of lines, you may find that you made an error. To delete the mistake, type "U" at the prompt line and press ENTER. You can also pick "undo" from the LINE screen menu while still in the LINE command. Doing this erases the previously drawn line and allows you to continue from the previous endpoint. A series of U's followed by ENTERs may be typed to erase line segments as far back as needed. The endpoints of the removed lines remain as blips, for reference, until you enter the REDRAW or REGENERATE command, Fig. 6-24.

Command: **LINE** ↵
From point: *(pick point 1)*
To point: *(pick point 2)*
To point: *(pick point 3)*
To point: *(pick point 4)*
To point: *(pick point 5)*
To point: **U** ↵
To point: **U** ↵
To point: *(pick revised point 4)*
To point: ↵
Command:

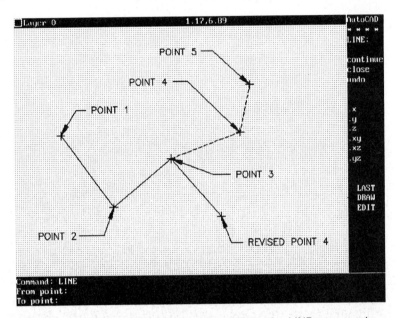

Fig. 6-24. Using the Undo option while in the LINE command.

EXERCISE 6-6

□ Load AutoCAD, enter the drawing editor, and open PRODR1, or begin a new drawing using your own variables.
□ Experiment drawing lines using the following guidelines and options:
   □ Draw two polygons using the Close option.
   □ Draw two connected lines, end the LINE command, and then select "continue" to draw additional lines.
   □ Draw eight connected lines. Then use the "undo" option to remove the last four lines while remaining in the LINE command. Finally, draw four new connected lines.
□ Save the drawing as A:EX6-6 and quit.

USING THE PULL-DOWN MENU
TO PICK THE LINE COMMAND

ARM A

You have been introduced to selecting the LINE command in the DRAW screen menu or by typing at the Command: prompt. The LINE command may also be selected from the Draw pull-down menu. After picking Line from the pull-down menu, the cascading submenu is displayed as shown in Fig. 6-25. The options in the submenu are described as follows:

- **Segments** — This option allows you to draw one or more line segments as previously described. The LINE command "From point" prompt is automatically issued. Draw as many connecting lines as you want and press ENTER to get back to the Command: prompt.
- **1 Segment** — This option allows you to draw one line segment, after which you are returned to the Command: prompt.
- **Double Lines** — This selection activates the DLINE command that allows you to draw parallel lines just as you draw single lines. This command has many options, which are discussed later.
- **Sketch** — This is a command that lets you do freehand drawing with AutoCAD. Although the command is not commonly used, it is introduced later in this chapter.

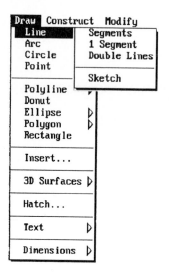

Fig. 6-25. The cascading submenu provides options for the LINE command.

PROFESSIONAL TIP

To access cascading menus, you do not actually need to pick the pull-down menu selection. Simply slide your cursor over the arrow to the right of the menu selection and the cascading menu appears. If you want to access the same option from the cascading menu again, simply double click on the item in the menu bar, and the cascading menu appears.

DRAWING DOUBLE LINES

In the previous section, you were introduced to the Double Line selection in the cascading submenu. This pick activates the DLINE, or DL command. Drawing double lines is similar to drawing single line segments. (Each segment of a double line is considered to be a separate entity.) However, instead of the "From point" and "To point" prompts, you get "start point" and "next point" prompts. You can also keep drawing several connected double lines until you end the command by pressing ENTER. For example:

Command: **DLINE** *or* **DL** ↵
Dline, Version 1.11, (c) 1990-1992 by Autodesk, Inc.
Break/Caps/Dragline/Offset/Snap/Undo/Width/⟨start point⟩: *(pick the start point)*
Arc/Break/CAps/CLose/Dragline/Snap/Undo/Width/⟨next point⟩: *(pick the next double line endpoint)*
Arc/Break/CAps/CLose/Dragline/Snap/Undo/Width/⟨next point⟩: ↵
Command:

As you can see, the DLINE command provides you with several options. The initial options are described as follows:

- **Break** — The default is on, or you may enter "OF" for off. When break is on, AutoCAD automatically breaks a line where another double line intersects, as shown in Fig. 6-26. This

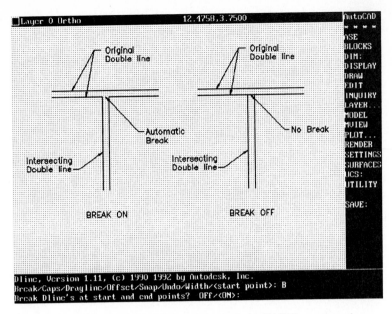

Fig. 6-26. Using the Break option of the DLINE command.

is a useful option when drawing walls that intersect in architectural floor plans. No break occurs in the intersecting line when Break is off. See Fig. 6-26.

- **Caps**—Entering "C" gives you the following prompt:

  Draw which endcaps? Both/End/None/Start/⟨Auto⟩:

This makes it possible for you to have a cap drawn between the endpoints of your double lines. Your choices are "B" for both ends capped, "E" for the last picked end to be capped, "N" for no caps, or "S" to cap the starting end of your double lines. See Fig. 6-27. The "Auto" option (the default) automatically caps both ends, providing results similar to the "Both" option.

- **Dragline**—This option controls the location on the double line where dragging occurs. When you enter "D" for Dragline, you get the following prompt:

  Set dragline position to Left/Center/Right/⟨Offset from center = 0.0000⟩:

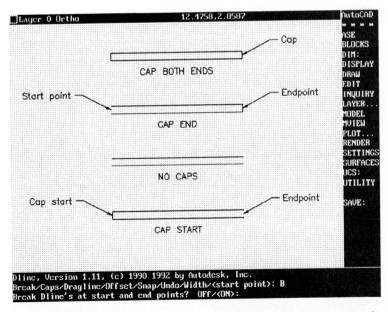

Fig. 6-27. The Caps option of the DLINE command. Note the different results obtained.

Center is the default, which drags your next double line segment from the center of the last endpoint. Enter "L" for left if you want dragging to take place from the left leg of the double line endpoint, or "R" to drag from the right leg. Fig. 6-28 illustrates the Dragline options.

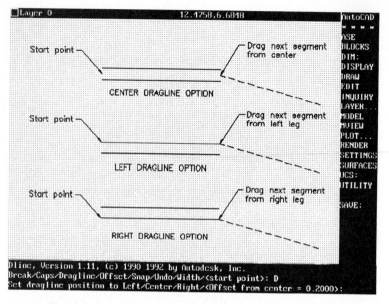

Fig. 6-28. Dragline options of the DLINE command.

- **Offset**—Enter "O" for Offset to draw a double line that is offset from any desired location on your drawing. Picking O gives you this set of prompts:

  Offset from: *(pick a desired point to begin your offset)*
  Offset toward: *(pick a point from which to locate the start point of the offset double line)*
  Enter the offset distance ⟨1.25⟩: *(press ENTER to accept the offset distance in brackets, or enter a desired value and press ENTER)*
  Arc/Break/CAps/CLose/Dragline/Snap/Undo/Width/⟨next point⟩: *(pick the next double line endpoint)*

  Fig. 6-29 shows how the Offset option works.

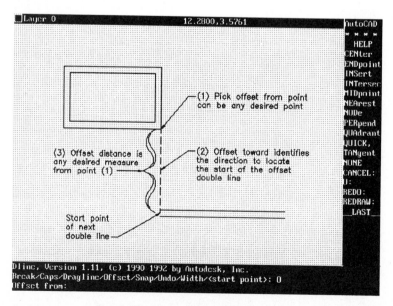

Fig. 6-29. The DLINE Offset option.

- **Snap** — The Snap option allows you to snap to an existing feature when you are within a predetermined distance from that feature. The default is on, which allows you to snap to a picked item. The double endpoints connect to a feature, and a break is made if Break is on. The Snap prompt looks like this:

Set snap size or snap On/Off. Size/OFF/⟨ON⟩:

The distance you must be from the feature is controlled by the Size suboption found in the Snap option:

Set snap size or snap On/Off. Size/OFF/⟨ON⟩: **S** ⏎
New snap size (1-10) ⟨3⟩: **8** ⏎

The snap is measured in pixels. The smaller the number, the closer you have to be to the feature for an intersection to occur, as shown in Fig. 6-30.

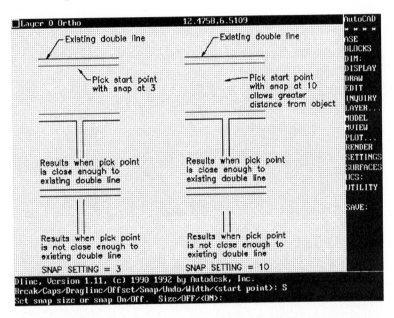

Fig. 6-30. Using the Snap option of the DLINE command.

- **Undo** — This option works only while you are in the DLINE command. Undo allows you to undo the last double line segment that was drawn, or keep using U to undo a series of double line segments in the reverse order that they were drawn. The Undo option removes existing double lines while you are in the DLINE command. Once you leave the DLINE command you can use the UNDO command to remove previously drawn double lines. Try the UNDO command by entering "U" at the Command: prompt and pressing ENTER. The last items drawn are removed in reverse order.
- **Width** — Enter "W" for Width to alter the distance between double lines. The AutoCAD default is 0.05, but you can enter any desired width like this:

New DLINE width ⟨0.05⟩: **.25** ⏎

Drawing double line arcs and closing double lines

After picking the double line start point, a new set of options is displayed, which include the Arc and CLose options:

Command: **DLINE** ⏎
Dline, Version 1.11, (c) 1990-1992 by Autodesk, Inc.
Break/Caps/Dragline/Offset/Snap/Undo/Width/⟨start point⟩: *(pick the start point)*
Arc/Break/CAps/CLose/Dragline/Snap/Undo/Width/⟨next point⟩:

Except for Arc and CLose, the other options are the same as previously discussed. The Arc option allows you to draw a double line arc alone, or at the end of a previously drawn double line. The command sequence for drawing a double line arc is as follows:

Command: **DLINE** ↵
Dline, Version 1.11, (c) 1990-1992 by Autodesk, Inc.
Break/Caps/Dragline/Offset/Snap/Undo/Width/⟨start point⟩: *(pick the start point)*
Arc/Break/CAps/CLose/Dragline/Snap/Undo/Width/⟨next point⟩: **A** ↵
Break/CAps/CEnter/CLose/Dragline/Endpoint/Line/Snap/Undo/Width/⟨second point⟩: *(pick a second point on the arc)*

Fig. 6-31 shows how double line arcs are drawn. Notice the CEnter and Endpoint options in the previous Arc prompt; these options are discussed in detail in Chapter 7. AutoCAD continues drawing connected double line arcs until you enter "L" for the Line option. After entering "L," AutoCAD changes from drawing double line arcs to drawing straight double line segments again.

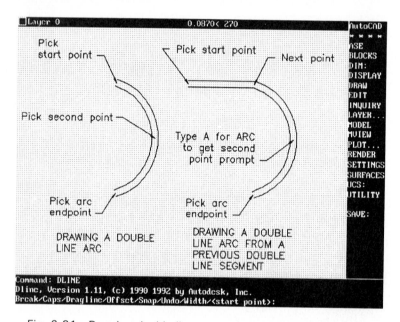

Fig. 6-31. Drawing double line arcs using the DLINE command.

The CLose option lets you close a polygon. (Remember, a polygon is a closed plane figure with three or more sides.) For example, if you are drawing a rectangular shape, all you have to do is enter "CL" and press ENTER to have the last double line segment attach itself exactly to the starting point of the first double line segment.

PROFESSIONAL TIP

If you are doing architectural drafting, the DLINE command may work well for drawing walls in floor plans. Be sure to set architectural units. A scale of 1/4″ = 1′-0″ is commonly used for floor plans. Set the double linewidth accordingly, for example, 6 in. exterior walls and 5 in. interior walls.

The Dragline option works well for connecting exterior walls to the face of studs when working around the floor plan to the left. Set Dragline to the Center option when drawing interior walls. The Break option should be on so intersecting walls break where they meet. Use the Cap option to cap the ends of stub walls. Later in this text, you will learn to use the BREAK command to break a section out of a line. This is convenient when you want to insert a door in a wall.

EXERCISE 6-7

☐ Load AutoCAD, enter the drawing editor, and open PRODR1, or begin a new drawing using your own variables.
☐ Use the DLINE option command with Width set to .25 to make a drawing similar to one shown below.

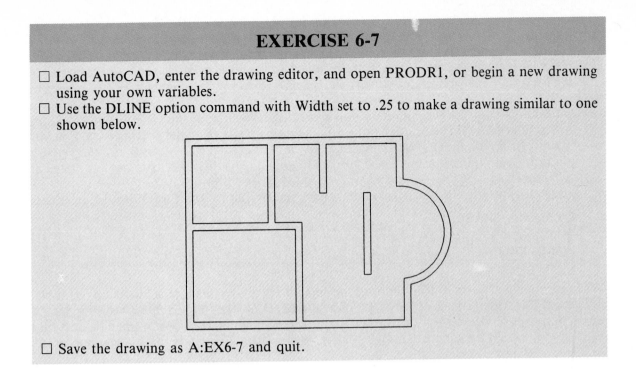

☐ Save the drawing as A:EX6-7 and quit.

INTRODUCTION TO EDITING

ARM 6

The procedure used to correct mistakes or revise an existing drawing is referred to as *editing*. There are many editing functions that help increase productivity. This discussion introduces the basic editing operations ERASE and OOPS.

When you edit a drawing, you will be selecting items when you see this prompt:

Select objects:

The items that you select are called a *selection set*. You can select one or more entities using a variety of selection set options, including Window, Crossing, WPolygon, CPolygon, and Fence. When you become familiar with the selection options, you will find that they increase your flexibility and performance. The following discussion introduces several of the selection set methods used with the ERASE command. Keep in mind, however, that these techniques may be used with any of the editing commands where the Select objects: prompt appears.

USING THE ERASE COMMAND

ARM 6

The ERASE command acts the same as using an eraser in manual drafting to remove unwanted information. However, with the ERASE command you have a second chance. If you erase the wrong item, it can be brought back using the OOPS command. Enter the ERASE command by typing "ERASE" at the Command: prompt, selecting ERASE from the EDIT screen menu, or picking Erase from the Modify pull-down menu. The next screen menu you see after selecting ERASE from the screen menu looks like this:

The commands preceded by an "E" are ERASE selection options which allow you to decide how you want to use the ERASE command. These are briefly described as follows:
- **E Last:** — Picking this automatically erases the last entity drawn. You can continue picking E Last: to erase as many entities as you want in the reverse order they were drawn.
- **E Pick:** — Use this option to have any entity on the drawing automatically erased when you pick it.
- **E Prev:** — When you erase an item you can bring it back with the OOPS command (discussed later). The E Prev: command lets you automatically erase the previous item that you brought back with the OOPS command. It may also be used to erase items that you previously put into a selection set using the SELECT command. The SELECT command is discussed in Chapter 11.

When you enter the ERASE command, a prompt is given to select an object to be erased:

    Command: **ERASE** ↵
    Select objects: *(select an object)*
    Select objects: ↵
    Command:

When you see the "Select objects:" prompt, a small box replaces the screen crosshairs. This box is referred to as the *pick box*. Move the pick box over the item to be erased and pick it. For example, suppose you draw a square and want to erase it. You must erase one line at a time because each line of the square is a single "entity." Thus, using ERASE in this manner only erases single entities.

When you pick a line to erase, the line is highlighted to acknowledge that you have chosen that entity. When this happens, the "Select objects:" prompt returns and you can select another entity to erase, Fig. 6-32. Press ENTER to complete the ERASE command and return to the Command: prompt. You can get back into the ERASE command immediately by pressing the space bar or ENTER key. This procedure, as shown in the following sequence, is an easy way to re-execute any AutoCAD command:

    Command: **ERASE** ↵
    Select objects: *(select an object)*
    Select objects: ↵
    Command: *(press ENTER or space bar)*
    ERASE
    Select objects: *(select another object to erase)*
    Select objects: ↵
    Command:

Using the Multiple selection option

When using the pick box to erase one or more items from a drawing, each picked item is highlighted before pressing ENTER to complete the ERASE command. The Multiple option allows you to pick many items on the drawing, and the items are not highlighted until you press ENTER to accept them. The command sequence is as follows:

    Command: **ERASE** ↵
    Select objects: **M** ↵
    Select objects: *(pick the items you want erased and press ENTER when finished)*
    Select objects: ↵
    Command:

PROFESSIONAL TIP

If you want to erase two intersecting lines, enter the Multiple option and pick the intersection twice. Both lines are highlighted when you press ENTER.

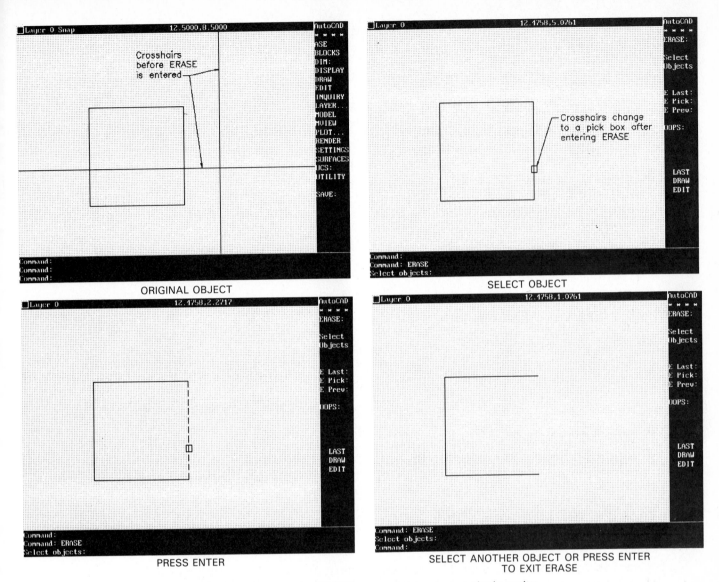

Fig. 6-32. Using the ERASE command to erase a single entity.

Using the Last selection option

The ERASE command's Last option is a handy option that saves time if you need to erase the last entity drawn. For example, suppose you draw a box using the LINE command. The ERASE command's Last option erases the last line drawn. The Last option erases entities in the reverse order in which they were drawn. The Last option may be selected by first picking Select objects from the ERASE screen menu and Last from the submenu, or by typing "L" at the prompt line as follows:

Command: **ERASE** ↵
Select objects: **L** ↵
1 found
Select objects: ↵
Command: *(press space bar or ENTER)*
Select objects: **L** ↵
1 found
Select objects: ↵
Command:

Keep in mind that using the Last option highlights the last item drawn. You must press ENTER for the object to be erased. The E Last: option, previously discussed, can only be picked from the ERASE screen menu, and it automatically erases the last item drawn without pressing ENTER.

EXERCISE 6-8

☐ Load AutoCAD, enter the drawing editor, and open PRODR1, or begin a new drawing using your own variables.

☐ Use the LINE command to draw a square similar to the "ORIGINAL OBJECT" in Fig. 6-32.

☐ Type "ERASE" at the Command: prompt and erase two of the lines.

☐ Now select E Pick: from the ERASE screen menu and pick one of the remaining lines. Erase the final line, too.

☐ Observe the difference between erasing the first two and the last two lines.

☐ Draw another square, similar to the previous one.

☐ Type "ERASE" at the Command: prompt and enter "L" at the Select objects: prompt.

☐ Press ENTER again and enter "L" to erase one more line.

☐ Pick E Last: from the ERASE screen menu twice to erase the last two lines.

☐ Observe the difference between erasing the first two and the last two lines.

☐ Type "QUIT" and exit the drawing editor without saving.

The Window selection option

The Window or "W" option can be used with several commands. This option allows you to draw a box or "window" around an object or group of objects. Everything *entirely within* the window can be erased at the same time. If portions of entities project outside the window, they will not be erased. The command sequence looks like this:

Command: **ERASE** ↵
Select objects: **W** ↵
First corner: *(select a point)*

When the First corner: prompt is shown, select a point clearly outside of the object to be erased. After you select the first point, the screen crosshairs change to a box-shaped cursor. It expands in size as you move the pointing device. The next prompt reads:

Other corner: *(pick the other corner)*
Select objects: ↵
Command:

When the Other corner: prompt is shown, move the pointing device so the box totally encloses the object or objects to be erased. Then pick the second corner, Fig. 6-33. All objects within the window become dashed. When finished, press ENTER to complete the ERASE command.

You can also automatically use the Window or Crossing selection process. However, the PICKAUTO system variable must be on. The PICKAUTO system variable controls automatic windowing when the Select objects: prompt appears. The PICKAUTO settings are: ON = 1 (default) and OFF = 0. Change the PICKAUTO setting like this:

Command: **PICKAUTO** ↵
New value for PICKAUTO ⟨0⟩: **1** ↵

Now, to use the automatic Window selection process, as follows:
• Enter the ERASE command.
• Pick a point outside and to the upper- or lower-left of the object to be erased. This is shown as the first window point in Fig. 6-33.
• Move the pointing device so the window completely encloses the object. Pick the second window point shown in Fig. 6-33. The command sequence is as follows:

Command: **ERASE** ↵
Select objects: *(pick a point outside and to the upper- or lower-left of the object)*
Other corner: *(move the cursor so the window completely encloses the object and pick)*
Select objects: ↵
Command:

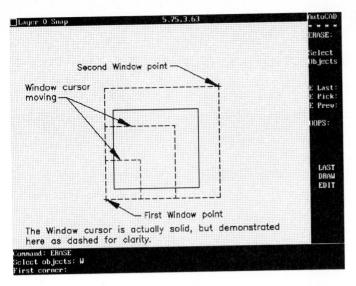
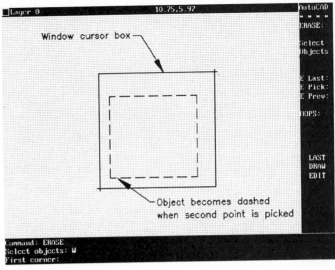

Fig. 6-33. Using the ERASE Window option.

Additional methods of selecting objects are available. However, they work better for different applications and are discussed later.

OOPS, I MADE A MISTAKE

ARM 6

The OOPS command is handy to bring back the last object you erased. If you erased several objects in the same command sequence, all are brought back to the screen. The OOPS command must be given *immediately* after making the error and prior to issuing another command. OOPS can only be used with the ERASE command. If you erased entities within a window, they could be brought back as follows:

Command: **ERASE** ↵
Select objects: **W** ↵
First corner: *(select a point)*
Other corner: *(select a point)*
Select objects: ↵
Command: **OOPS** ↵

USING THE PULL-DOWN MENU TO PICK THE ERASE COMMAND

ARM A

You have been introduced to selecting the ERASE command from the EDIT screen menu or by typing "ERASE" at the Command: prompt. You can also access the ERASE command using the pull-down menu. Move the screen cursor to the menu bar and pick Modify to access the pull-down menu. Next, move the screen cursor to Erase and access the cascading submenu. See Fig. 6-34. The following options are found in the submenu:

- **Select** — This works just like typing "ERASE" at the Command: prompt. The picked items are highlighted, and you must press ENTER when you are ready for them to be removed.
- **Single** — This option puts you into the single selection mode, which means you can pick single entities to erase, and they are automatically removed when picked. See Fig. 6-35. This option works like the E Pick: option in the ERASE screen menu.
- **Last** — This is the convenient Last option, which automatically erases the last entity that was drawn.
- **Oops!** — Pick this option if you decide you want to restore something you previously erased. Remember, this option only restores the entities deleted the last time ERASE was used.

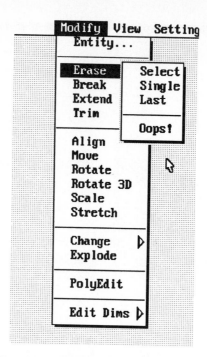

Fig. 6-34. The Modify pull-down menu.

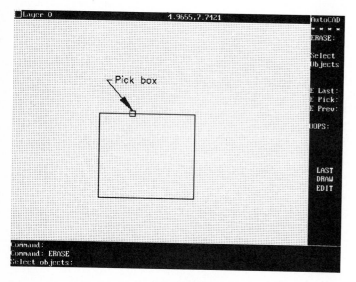

PICK ENTITY

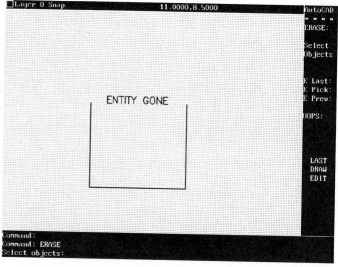

ENTITY AUTOMATICALLY ERASED

Fig. 6-35. Using the Single option for erasing.

The Crossing selection option

Another selection option called "Crossing," is similar to the Window option. Entities *entirely within and those crossing* the box are selected. Type "C" at the prompt line to initiate the Crossing option. Pick a location to the right of the object(s) to be erased. This automatically activates the first corner of the crossing box. Then move the pointing device to the left. This forms a box around the object(s) to be erased. The crossing box outline is dotted to distinguish it from the solid outline of the window box. The command sequence for the Crossing selection is:

Command: **ERASE** ↵
Select objects: **C** ↵
First corner: *(pick a point outside and to the upper- or lower-right side of the object)*
Other corner: *(move the crossing box to enclose or cross the object[s] and pick)*
Select objects: ↵
Command:

Remember, the crossing box does not have to enclose the entire object to erase it. The window box does. The crossing box must only "cross" part of the object to be erased or edited.

To automatically invoke the Crossing selection process without entering "C" at the "Select objects:" prompt, follow this procedure:

Command: **ERASE** ↵
Select objects: *(pick a point outside and to the upper- or lower-right side of the object)*
Other corner: *(move the crossing box to enclose or cross the object[s] and pick)*
Select objects: ↵
Command:

Remember, the PICKAUTO system variable must be set to 1 (on) for the automatic Window and Crossing options to work. Fig. 6-36 shows how to erase three of four lines of a rectangle using the Crossing option.

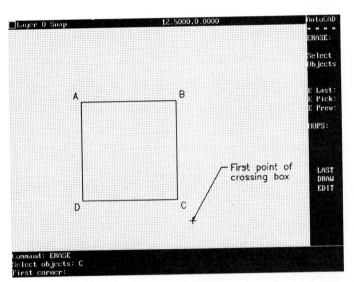

PICK FIRST POINT

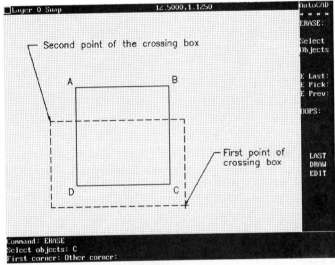

PICK SECOND POINT

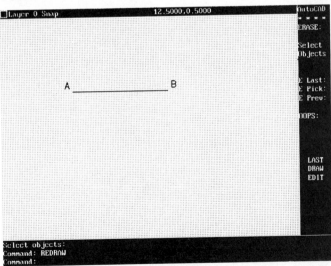

LINE NOT ENCLOSED WITHIN OR CROSSED
BY BOX REMAINS

Fig. 6-36. Using the Crossing box to erase objects.

You can use the automatic Window or Crossing selection options if PICKAUTO is 0 (off). To do this, enter "AU" for AUto at the Select objects: prompt, and then proceed as previously discussed. The command sequence looks like this:

Command: **ERASE** ↵
Select objects: **AU** ↵
Select objects: *(pick a point outside and to the upper- or lower-left side of the object for a window, or pick a point outside and to the upper- or lower-right side of the object for a crossing box)*
Other corner: *(move the cursor so the window entirely encloses the object, or move the cursor to enclose or cross the object for a crossing box)*
Select object: ↵
Command:

PROFESSIONAL TIP

Remember, you can pick any left point outside the object and then move the cursor to the right for a Window selection; the window is a solid image. Pick any right point outside the object and move the cursor to the left for a Crossing selection; the crossing box is a dashed image.

CLEANING UP THE SCREEN

ARM 7

When you draw or erase a number of objects on a drawing the screen is cluttered with small crosses or markers called *blips*. In addition, many of the grid dots may be removed. There is no problem caused by this, but it can be distracting. It is easy to clean up the screen, and restore the drawing by choosing the REDRAW command. The REDRAW command cleans the screen in the current viewport. (Viewports and the REDRAWALL command are discussed in detail in Chapter 9.) The REDRAW command can be typed at the keyboard, or selected from the DISPLAY: screen menu or View pull-down menu.

Command: **REDRAW** ↵

The screen goes blank for an instant, and the cleaned drawing and screen return.

EXERCISE 6-9

☐ Load AutoCAD, enter the drawing editor, and open PRODR1, or begin a new drawing using your own variables.
☐ Use the LINE command to draw a square similar to the "ORIGINAL OBJECT" shown in Fig. 6-32.
☐ Pick Erase from the Modify pull-down menu and use the Select, Single, and Last options to erase lines from the screen. Observe the difference between the three options.
☐ Draw another square.
☐ Type "ERASE" at the Command: prompt and use the Window selection option. Place the window around the entire square to erase it. Enter "OOPS" at the next Command: prompt to have the square reappear.
☐ Now, erase three of the four line by typing "C" at the "Select objects:" prompt. Use the Crossing selection as shown in Fig. 6-36. Enter OOPS and press ENTER to bring the three lines back on the screen.
☐ Set the PICKAUTO system variable to 1 (on).
☐ Now, enter the ERASE command and automatically erase the square using a window. Use OOPS to get the square back again.
☐ Enter the ERASE command and erase three sides of the square (as shown in Fig. 6-36) using the automatic Crossing selection.
☐ Use the REDRAW command to clean up the screen.
☐ Type "QUIT" and exit the drawing editor without saving.

Using the WPolygon selection option

The Window selection option requires that you place a rectangle completely around the entities to be erased. Sometimes it is awkward to place a rectangle around the items to erase. When this situation occurs, you can place a polygon (closed figure with three or more sides) of your own design around the objects. To use the WPolygon options, enter "WP" at the Select objects: prompt, and proceed to draw a polygon. As you pick corners, the polygon drags into place. The command sequence for erasing the four squares in the middle of Fig. 6-37 is as follows:

Command: **ERASE** ⏎
Select objects: **WP** ⏎
First polygon point: *(pick point 1)*
Undo/⟨Endpoint of line⟩: *(pick point 2)*
Undo/⟨Endpoint of line⟩: *(pick point 3)*
Undo/⟨Endpoint of line⟩: *(pick point 4)*
Undo/⟨Endpoint of line⟩: ⏎
Select objects: ⏎
Command:

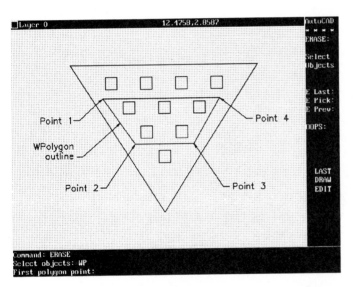
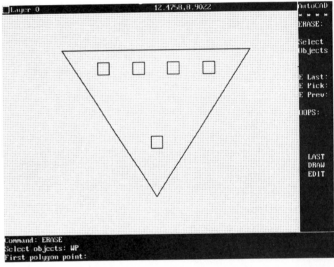

A—ORIGINAL OBJECT WITH WPOLYGON SELECTION POINTS B—OBJECT WITH ITEMS ERASED

Fig. 6-37. Using the WPolygon selection option to erase objects.

Use the Undo option by entering "U" at the Undo/⟨Endpoint of line⟩: prompt if you do not like the last polygon point you picked.

EXERCISE 6-10

☐ Load AutoCAD and open PRODR1, or start a new drawing using your own variables.
☐ Draw an object similar to the one shown in Fig. 6-37A.
☐ Use the WPolygon selection option to erase the same items as shown in the figure.
☐ Use the REDRAW command to clean up the screen.
☐ Save the drawing as A:EX6-10 and quit the drawing session.

Using the CPolygon selection option

The Crossing selection option lets you place a rectangle around or through the objects to be erased. Sometimes it is difficult to place a rectangle around or through the items to be erased without coming into contact with other entities. When you want to use the features of the Crossing selection option, but prefer to use a polygon instead of a rectangle, enter "CP" at the Select objects: prompt. Then, proceed to erase everything enclosed within or crossed by the polygon.

As you pick the points, the polygon drags into place. Note that the CPolygon is a dashed rubberband cursor, while the WPolygon is a solid rubberband cursor.

Suppose you want to erase everything inside the large triangle in Fig. 6-38A except for the top and bottom horizontal lines. The command sequence to erase these lines is as follows:

Command: **ERASE** ⏎
Select object: **CP** ⏎
First polygon point: *(pick point 1)*
Undo/⟨Endpoint of line⟩: *(pick point 2)*
Undo/⟨Endpoint of line⟩: *(pick point 3)*
Undo/⟨Endpoint of line⟩: *(pick point 4)*
Undo/⟨Endpoint of line⟩: ⏎
Select objects: ⏎
Command:

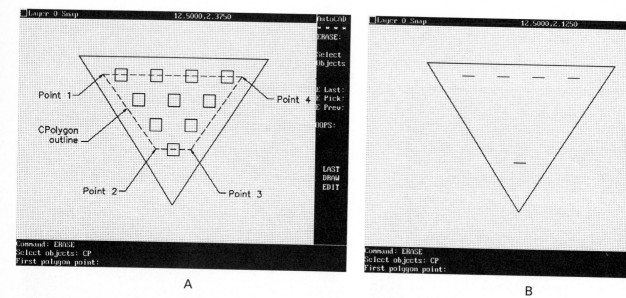

Fig. 6-38. Using the CPolygon selection option. Everything enclosed within or crossing the polygon is selected.

If you want to change the last CPolygon point you picked, enter "U" at the Undo/⟨Endpoint of line⟩: prompt.

EXERCISE 6-11

☐ Load AutoCAD and open PRODR1, or start a new drawing using your own variables.
☐ Draw an object similar to the one shown in Fig. 6-38A.
☐ Use the CPolygon selection option to erase the same items as shown in the figure.
☐ Use the REDRAW command to clean up the screen.
☐ Save the drawing as A:EX6-11 and quit.

Using the Fence selection option

Fence is another selection option used to select several objects at the same time when performing editing functions. When using the Fence option, you simply need to place a fence through the objects you want to select. Anything that the fence passes through is included in the selection set. The fence can be straight or it can stagger to pass through items as shown in Fig. 6-39. Enter "F" at the Select objects: prompt as follows:

Command: **ERASE** ↵
Select objects: **F** ↵
First fence point: *(pick the starting point of the first fence)*
Undo/⟨Endpoint of line⟩: *(pick point 2)*
Undo/⟨Endpoint of line⟩: ↵
6 found
Select objects: **F** ↵
Undo/⟨Endpoint of line⟩: *(pick point 3)*
Undo/⟨Endpoint of line⟩: *(pick point 4)*
Undo/⟨Endpoint of line⟩: *(pick point 5)*
Undo/⟨Endpoint of line⟩: *(pick point 6)*
Undo/⟨Endpoint of line⟩: *(pick point 7)*
Undo/⟨Endpoint of line⟩: *(pick point 8)*
Undo/⟨Endpoint of line⟩: ↵
6 found
Select objects: ↵
Command:

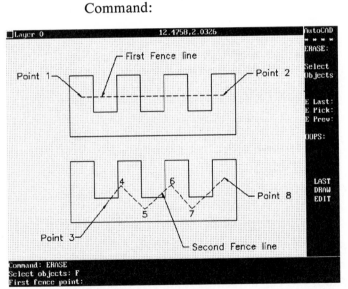

A—STRAIGHT OR STAGGERED FENCE CAN BE PLACED

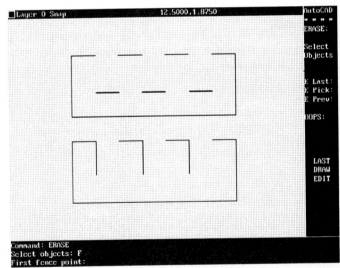

B—RESULTING DRAWING

Fig. 6-39. Using the Fence selection option to erase entities.

EXERCISE 6-12

☐ Load AutoCAD and open PRODR1, or start a new drawing using your own variables.
☐ Draw an object similar to the one shown in Fig. 6-39A.
☐ Use the Fence selection option to erase the items shown in the figure.
☐ Use the REDRAW command to clean up the drawing.
☐ Save the drawing as A:EX6-12 and quit.

Removing and adding entities to the selection set

When editing a drawing, a common mistake is to accidentally select an entity that you did not want, or not to select an entity that you want included. Do not worry; you can remove or add the entity to the selection set anytime you are at the Select objects: prompt. For example, suppose you are using the ERASE command and you selected several items to be erased. Then you decide that two of the items should not be erased. When this happens, enter "R" for Remove like this:

> Command: **ERASE** ↵
> Select objects: *(pick several items using any of the selection techniques)*
> Select objects: **R** ↵
> Remove objects: *(pick the items you want removed from the selection set)*

Now if you decide that you want to add more items to the selection set, just enter "A" for Add and pick the additional objects to be erased:

> Remove objects: **A** ↵
> Select objects: *(pick additional items to be erased)*
> Select objects: ↵
> Command:

Making a single selection

Normally, AutoCAD lets you pick as many items as you want for a selection set, and selected items are highlighted to let you know what has been picked. You also have the option of selecting an item or items and have them automatically edited without first being highlighted. To do this, enter "SI" for SIngle at the Select objects: prompt. The command sequence is as follows:

> Command: **ERASE** ↵
> Select objects: **SI** ↵
> Select objects: *(pick an individual item, or use one of the Window or Crossing options to pick several items)*

Note that the Select objects: prompt did not return after the items were picked. You can pick a group of entities using any of the Window or Crossing selection options. The entire group is automatically erased when you press ENTER or pick the second corner of a window or crossing box.

Selecting all entities on a drawing

Sometimes you may want to select every item on the drawing to erase or use with other editing functions. To do this, enter "ALL" at the Select objects: prompt as follows:

> Command: **ERASE** ↵
> Select objects: **ALL** ↵
> Select objects: ↵
> Command:

This procedure erases everything on the drawing, but you can use the Remove option at the Select objects: prompt and enter "ALL" again to remove everything from the selection set before you leave the command. If you do not leave the command, you can immediately get everything back by entering "U" for Undo at the Command: prompt.

EXERCISE 6-13

☐ Load AutoCAD and open PRODR1, or start a new drawing using your own variables.
☐ Draw an object similar to the one shown in Fig. 6-39A.
☐ Use the SI selection option to erase any single line.
☐ Use the SI selection option with a fence to erase any two lines.
☐ Experiment using the Remove and Add selection options by selecting six items to erase, remove two of the items from the selection set, and then add three different entities to the selection set.
☐ Use the REDRAW command to clean up the screen.
☐ Use the ALL selection option to erase everything from the drawing.
☐ Enter "U" at the Command: prompt to get everything back that you erased.
☐ Save the drawing as A:EX6-13 and quit.

Using the Box selection option

Another way to begin the window or crossing selection option is to type "BOX" at the "Select objects:" prompt. You are then prompted to pick the left corner of a window or right corner of a crossing box, depending on your needs. The command sequence is as follows:

Command: **ERASE** ↵
Select objects: **BOX** ↵
First corner: *(pick the left corner of the window box or the right corner of the crossing box)*
Select objects: ↵
Command:

INTRODUCTION TO LINETYPE, PLINE, AND TRACE

ARM 5

Earlier in this chapter you were introduced to line standards. AutoCAD has standard linetypes supplied with the program that may be used at any time. Standard AutoCAD linetypes are a single thickness. In order to achieve different line thicknesses, it is necessary to use the PLINE or TRACE commands. Line thickness may also be varied using different plotter pen tip widths. Draw different width lines on separate layers. Then plot with the appropriate width of pen for each layer. This is further discussed in Chapters 17 and 27.

ARM 8

AutoCAD linetypes

AutoCAD has a standard library of linetypes as shown in Fig. 6-40. The AutoCAD standard linetype library does not show a solid object line. AutoCAD refers to this line as CONTINUOUS.

Border		Divide	
Border2		Divide2	
BorderX2		DivideX2	
Center		Dot	
Center2		Dot2	
CenterX2		DotX2	
Dashdot		Hidden	
Dashdot2		Hidden2	
DashdotX2		HiddenX2	
Dashed		Phantom	
Dashed2		Phantom2	
DashedX2		PhantomX2	

Fig. 6-40. Standard AutoCAD linetype library.

The LINETYPE command allows you to change the current linetype. Individual lines or entities may be drawn with a specified linetype at any time. (Linetypes may also be set by layers. This is discussed in Chapter 17.) The LINETYPE command is found in the SETTINGS screen menu. "LINETYPE" may also be typed at the Command: prompt. If you want to look at the AutoCAD linetypes, enter "?" as follows:

Command: **LINETYPE** ↵
?/Create/Load/Set: **?** ↵

This displays the "Select Linetype File" dialogue box shown in Fig. 6-41. Notice ACAD is highlighted in the Files list and at the File edit box. Press ENTER or pick OK. An alphanumeric

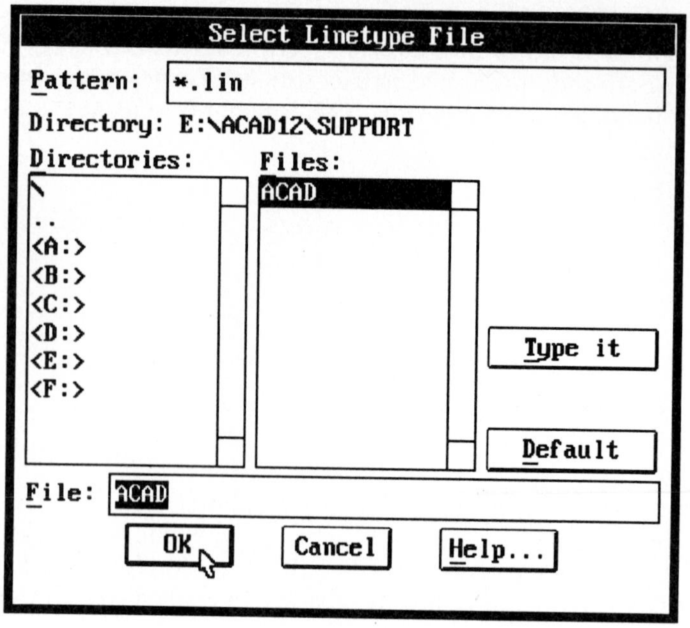

Fig. 6-41. The "Select Linetype File" dialogue box.

screen is displayed with the linetypes shown in Fig. 6-40. Look at the linetypes and press function key F1 to return to the drawing editor.

When you want to change the linetype for the next line or series of lines, use the Set option in the LINETYPE command as follows:

Command: **LINETYPE** ⏎
?/Create/Load/Set: **S** ⏎
New entity linetype (or ?) ⟨current⟩:

The current linetype is shown in brackets. The default is the solid linetype named "continuous." If you have just started using the drawing editor and have not changed the linetype, "BYLAYER" is shown in brackets. If you want to see a sample of the current linetype, type a "?". The sequence then looks like this:

New entity linetype (or ?) ⟨CONTINUOUS⟩: **?** ⏎
Linetype(s) to list ⟨*⟩: ⏎

If you want to set a new linetype, such as "dashed," for drawing the next entity or series of entities, type the linetype name:

New entity linetype (or ?) ⟨CONTINUOUS⟩: **DASHED** ⏎

The next lines are drawn as a dashed linetype until the linetype is set again. The Create and Load options are displayed with Set, and are discussed in Chapter 17.

LINETYPE can also be used as *transparent command*. This means it can be used while you are working inside another command. When the transparent command is completed, the command you were using returns. Use the transparent command by entering an apostrophe (') before the command name, for example 'LINETYPE.

EXERCISE 6-14

☐ Load AutoCAD, enter the drawing editor, and open PRODR1, or begin a new drawing using your own variables.
☐ Use the LINETYPE command to do the following:
   ☐ Look at the standard AutoCAD linetypes.
   ☐ Draw objects of your own choosing using at least six of the standard AutoCAD linetypes.
☐ Save the drawing as A:EX6-14 and quit.

INTRODUCTION TO DRAWING POLYLINES   ARM 5

PLINE is the AutoCAD command used for drawing polylines (PolyLINEs). The term *polyline* is composed of the words "poly" and "line." "Poly" means many possibilities, or more than one option. Thus, polylines are lines that may be created with many different features. Polylines have advantages over normal lines because there are an unlimited number of possibilities, including:

- Much more flexibility than lines drawn with the TRACE command (discussed later in the chapter).
- Making thick or tapered lines.
- May be used with any linetype.
- May be used to draw a filled circle or donut shape.
- Can be edited using advanced editing features.
- Closed polygons may be drawn.
- The area or perimeter of a polyline feature may be determined without extra effort.
- Arcs and straight lines of varying thicknesses may be joined as a single entity.

The PLINE command basically functions like the LINE command except that additional options are offered, and all segments of a polyline are a single entity. PLINE can be typed at the Command: prompt, picked from the DRAW screen submenu, or picked from the Draw pull-down menu:

Command: **PLINE** ↵
From point: *(select a point)*
Current line-width 0.0

The current linewidth is shown as 0.0, which produces a line of minimum width. If this linewidth is acceptable, you may begin by selecting the endpoint of a line when the following prompt appears:

Arc/Close/Halfwidth/Length/Undo/Width/⟨Endpoint of line⟩: *(select a point)*

If additional line segments are added to the first line, the endpoint of the first line automatically becomes the starting point of the next line.

Setting the polyline width

If it is necessary to change the linewidth, this may be done by selecting a "W" for Width as follows:

Arc/Close/Halfwidth/Length/Undo/Width/⟨Endpoint of line⟩: **W** ↵

When the Width option is selected, you are asked for the starting and ending widths. If a tapered line is desired follow this procedure:

Starting width ⟨0.000⟩: *(enter a width and press ENTER)*
Ending width ⟨starting width⟩: *(enter a width and press ENTER)*

The starting width that you select becomes the default for the ending width. Therefore, to keep the line the same width, press ENTER at the "Ending width" prompt. The following command sequence draws the line shown in Fig. 6-42. Notice that the start and endpoints of the line are located at the center of the line.

Command: **PLINE** ↵
From point: **4,4** ↵
Current line-width 0.0
Arc/Close/Halfwidth/Length/Undo/Width/⟨Endpoint of line⟩: **W** ↵
Starting width ⟨0.000⟩: **.25** ↵
Ending width ⟨.25⟩: ↵
Arc/Close/Halfwidth/Length/Undo/Width/⟨Endpoint of line⟩: **8,4** ↵

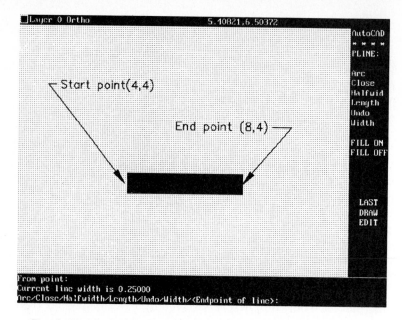

Fig. 6-42. A thick polyline drawn with the PLINE Width option.

Drawing a tapered polyline

Enter different starting and ending widths if you want to draw a tapered polyline, Fig. 6-43.

Command: **PLINE** ↵
From point: **4,4** ↵
Current line-width 0.0
Arc/Close/Halfwidth/Length/Undo/Width/⟨Endpoint of line⟩: **W** ↵
Starting width ⟨0.000⟩: **.25** ↵
Ending width ⟨.25⟩: **.5** ↵
Arc/Close/Halfwidth/Length/Undo/Width/⟨Endpoint of line⟩: **8,4** ↵

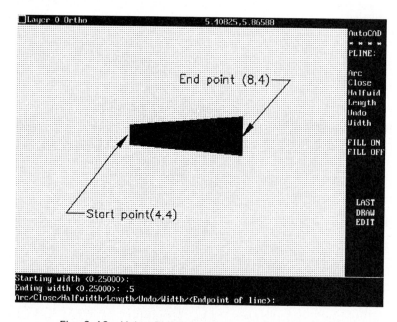

Fig. 6-43. Using PLINE to draw a wide tapered line.

If you want to draw an arrow, give 0 as the starting width and then use any desired ending width.

Using the Halfwidth option

The Halfwidth option allows you to specify the width from the center to one side. This is done by selecting the H option and then specifying the widths, Fig. 6-44:

> Arc/Close/Halfwidth/Length/Undo/Width/⟨Endpoint of line⟩: **H** ↵
> Starting half-width ⟨0.000⟩: **.25** ↵
> Ending half-width ⟨.25⟩: **.5** ↵

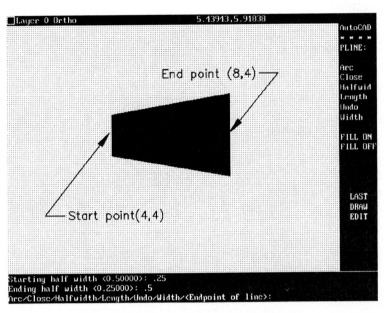

Fig. 6-44. Using the PLINE Halfwidth option.

Using the Length option

The Length option allows you to draw another polyline at the same angle as the previous polyline. Enter "L" and give the desired length. For example:

> Command: **PLINE** ↵
> From point: *(pick a starting point for polyline number 1)*
> Current line-width is 0.0000
> Arc/Close/Halfwidth/Length/Undo/Width/⟨Endpoint of line⟩: *(pick the ending point for polyline number 1)*
> Arc/Close/Halfwidth/Length/Undo/Width/⟨Endpoint of line⟩: ↵
> Command: ↵
> PLINE
> From point: *(pick a starting point for polyline number 2)*
> Current line-width is 0.0000
> Arc/Close/Halfwidth/Length/Undo/Width/⟨Endpoint of line⟩: **L** ↵
> Length of line: *(enter any desired length for polyline number 2)*
> Arc/Close/Halfwidth/Length/Undo/Width/⟨Endpoint of line⟩: ↵
> Command:

The second polyline is drawn at the same angle as the previous polyline and at the length you specify.

UNDOING PREVIOUSLY DRAWN POLYLINES | ARM 8 |

While in the PLINE command you may pick the UNDO option in the screen menu or type "U" at the prompt line and press ENTER. This erases the last polyline segment drawn. Each time you pick undo, another polyline segment is erased. A quick way to go back and correct the polyline while you remain in the PLINE command is as follows:

Command: **PLINE** ↵
From point: *(pick a starting point)*
Current line-width is 0.0000
Arc/Close/Halfwidth/Length/Undo/Width/⟨Endpoint of line⟩: *(pick the endpoint)*
Arc/Close/Halfwidth/Length/Undo/Width/⟨Endpoint of line⟩: *(pick another endpoint)*
Arc/Close/Halfwidth/Length/Undo/Width/⟨Endpoint of line⟩: *(pick another endpoint)*
Arc/Close/Halfwidth/Length/Undo/Width/⟨Endpoint of line⟩: **U** ↵
Arc/Close/Halfwidth/Length/Undo/Width/⟨Endpoint of line⟩: *(pick another endpoint or enter ''U'' again to remove an additional segment)*

After you enter "U" followed by ENTER, the last polyline segment you drew is automatically removed, but the rubberband cursor remains attached to the end of the previous polyline segment. You may now continue drawing additional polyline segments, or enter "U" again to undo more polyline segments. You can keep using Undo to remove all of the polyline segments up to the first point of the polyline. The polyline segments are removed in reverse order from which they were drawn.

The U command works in much the same way. However, the U command may be used at any time to undo any previous command. This is done by typing "U" at the Command: prompt or picking Undo from from the Assist pull-down menu. AutoCAD gives you a message telling you which command was undone:

Command: **U** ↵
LINE
Command:

In this example, the LINE command was the last command to undo. The U command is different from the UNDO command, which is discussed later in the chapter.

EXERCISE 6-15

☐ Load AutoCAD, enter the drawing editor, and open PRODR1, or begin a new drawing using your own variables.
☐ Use the PLINE command to draw several objects of your own design. Vary the width for each object.
☐ Draw three different types of arrows by specifying different starting and ending widths.
☐ Set the polyline width to .125. Draw a single polyline. Using the Length option, draw two more .125 wide polylines with a 4 unit length.
☐ Save the drawing as A:EX6-15 and quit.

DRAWING THICK LINES USING THE TRACE COMMAND | ARM 5 |

When it is necessary to draw thick lines, the TRACE command may be used instead of the PLINE command. The TRACE command is located in the DRAW screen menu or "TRACE" can be typed at the Command: prompt. All of the LINE command procedures apply to TRACE except that the linewidth is set first.

The current trace width is specified in brackets. Type ".032" if you want to specify a trace width equal to the ANSI standard width for object lines. The following command and prompts produce a six-sided object. Try using the TRACE command while responding as follows to the prompts:

```
Command: TRACE ↵
Trace width 〈current〉: .032 ↵
From point: 2,2 ↵
To point: @6,0 ↵
To point: @2,2 ↵
To point: @0,3 ↵
To point: @−2,2 ↵
To point: @−6,0 ↵
To point: @0,−7 ↵
To point: 2,2 ↵
To point: ↵
Command:
```

When you use the TRACE command, the lines are made up of *trace segments*. The previous trace segment is not drawn until the next endpoint is specified. This is because trace segment ends are mitered to fit the next segment.

EXERCISE 6-16

☐ Load AutoCAD, enter the drawing editor, and open PRODR1, or begin a new drawing using your own variables.
☐ Use the TRACE command to draw several objects of your own design. Vary the trace width for each object.
☐ Save the drawing as A:EX6-16 and quit.

USING THE UNDO AND U COMMANDS |ARM 6|

After you leave the PLINE or LINE commands, picking "undo" from the PLINE or LINE screen menu and typing "UNDO" at the Command: prompt works in a different manner. The UNDO command can be used to undo any previous command. When you select the UNDO command, the following suboptions appear:

```
Command: UNDO ↵
Auto/Back/Control/End/Group/Mark/〈number〉:
```

The default is "number." If you enter a number such as 1, the entire previous command sequence is removed. If you enter "2," the previous two command sequences are removed. You designate the number of previous command sequences you want removed. When using this command, AutoCAD tells you which previous commands were undone with a message after you press ENTER:

```
Command: UNDO ↵
Auto/Back/Control/End/Group/Mark/〈number〉: 2 ↵
PLINE LINE
Command:
```

Other options of the UNDO command are defined as follows:
• **Auto (A)**—Entering "A" gives you this prompt:

```
ON/OFF 〈current〉: (select ON or OFF)
```

With UNDO Auto turned on, any group of commands that are used to insert an item are removed together. For example, when a command contains other commands, all of the commands in that group are removed as one single command with UNDO Auto turned on. If UNDO Auto is off, each individual command in a group of commands is treated individually.
• **Back (B)**—This option undoes everything in the entire drawing. AutoCAD questions your choice with the following message:

```
This will undo everything: OK? 〈Y〉:
```

If you want everything that you have drawn to be removed, press ENTER. If not, type "N" or "NO" followed by an ENTER, or use CTRL C.

- **Control (C)**—Allows you to decide how many of the UNDO suboptions you want active. You can even disable the UNDO command altogether. When you enter "C," you get this prompt:

    All/None/One ⟨All⟩:

The control options do the following:
  - **All (A)**—Keeps the full range of UNDO options active.
  - **None (N)**—This suboption disables both the U and UNDO commands.

    Auto/Back/Control/End/Group/Mark/⟨number⟩: **C** ↵
    All/None/One ⟨All⟩: **N** ↵

  You are now unable to use either the U or UNDO commands. If you try to use UNDO, all you get is the Control options:

    Command: **UNDO** ↵
    All/None/One⟨All⟩:

  You must activate the UNDO options by pressing ENTER for All or entering "O" for the One mode. If you have U and UNDO disabled and try to use the U command, AutoCAD gives you this message:

    Command: **U** ↵
    U command disabled: Use UNDO command to turn it on

  - **One (O)**—This suboption limits UNDO to one operation only:

    Auto/Back/Control/End/Group/Mark/⟨number⟩: **C** ↵
    All/None/One ⟨All⟩: **O** ↵

  Now, when you enter the UNDO command, you get the following prompt:

    Command: **UNDO** ↵
    Control/⟨1⟩:

  You may press ENTER to undo only the previous command, or enter "C" to return to the Control options. With One active, you can remove only those items drawn with the previous command. AutoCAD acknowledges this with the message:

    Command: **UNDO** ↵
    Control/⟨1⟩: ↵
    LINE
      Everything has been undone
    Command:

PROFESSIONAL TIP

When you use the UNDO command, AutoCAD maintains an UNDO file which saves previously used UNDO commands. All UNDO entries saved before disabling UNDO with the Control None option are discarded. This frees up some disk space, and may be valuable information for you to keep in mind if you ever get close to a full disk situation. If you want to continue using U or UNDO to some extent, then you might consider using the UNDO Control One suboption. This allows you to keep using U and UNDO to a limited extent while freeing disk space holding current UNDO information.

- **End (E) and Group (G)**—These UNDO options work together to cause a group of commands to be treated as a single command. Entering the U command removes commands that follow the Group suboption but precede the End suboption. These options can be used if you can anticipate the possible removal of a consecutive group of commands. For example, if you think you may want to undo the next three commands all together, then do the following:

Command: **UNDO** ↵
Auto/Back/Control/End/Group/Mark/⟨number⟩: **G** ↵
Command: **LINE** ↵
From point: *(pick a point)*
To point: *(pick other endpoint)*
To point: ↵
Command: **PLINE** ↵
From point: *(pick one endpoint)*
Current line-width is 0.0000
Arc/Close/Halfwidth/Length/Undo/Width/⟨Endpoint of line⟩: *(pick the other endpoint of the polyline)*
Arc/Close/Halfwidth/Length/Undo/Width/⟨Endpoint of line⟩: ↵
Command: **LINE** ↵
From point: *(pick a point)*
To point: *(pick other endpoint)*
To point: ↵
Command: **UNDO** ↵
Auto/Back/Control/End/Group/Mark/⟨number⟩: **E** ↵
Command: **U** ↵

This U undoes the three commands that you executed between entering UNDO Group and UNDO End.

- **Mark (M)** — The UNDO Mark option inserts a marker in the UNDO file. The Back option allows you to delete commands "back" to the marker. For example, if you do not want any work to be undone by the UNDO Back option, then enter the Mark option following this work:

    Auto/Back/Control/End/Group/Mark/⟨number⟩: **M** ↵
    Command:

Then, use the UNDO Back option to undo everything back to the marker.

    Command: **UNDO** ↵
    Auto/Back/Control/End/Group/Mark/⟨number⟩: **B** ↵

— **PROFESSIONAL TIP** —

The UNDO Mark option can be used to assist in the design process. For example, if you are working on a project and have completed the design on a portion of the structure you can mark the spot with the Mark option and then begin work on the next design phase. If anything goes wrong with this part of the design, you can simply use UNDO Back to remove everything back to the Mark.

REDOING THE UNDONE

ARM 6

Type "REDO" or pick Redo from the Assist pull-down menu to bring back entities that were previously removed using the UNDO or U command:

    Command: **REDO** ↵

REDO does not bring back polyline segments that were removed using the Undo option within the PLINE command. Remember, REDO only works immediately after undoing something.

EXERCISE 6-17

☐ Load AutoCAD, enter the drawing editor, and open PRODR1, or begin a new drawing using your own variables.
☐ Use the PLINE command to draw the following:
  ☐ A rectangle 2 units by 4 units, 0 width.
  ☐ A rectangle 2 units by 4 units, .125 width.
  ☐ A line 6 units long with a .125 starting width and .250 ending width.
  ☐ A line 6 units long using the Halfwidth option. Starting width is .125 and ending width is .250.
☐ Use the UNDO command to remove the last three polylines.
☐ Use REDO to bring back the last removed polyline.
☐ Save the drawing as A:EX6-17 and quit.

FILLING THE PLINE AND TRACE

ARM 7

In the discussion on the PLINE and TRACE commands, the results were shown as if they were solid, or filled in. You may decide to leave traces and polylines filled in, or show an outline. This is controlled by the FILL command, Fig. 6-45. The FILL command only has ON and OFF options.

Command: **FILL** ↵
ON/OFF ⟨current⟩:

The value specified in brackets is the default, or previous setting. FILL may be turned on or off in the prototype drawing. When FILL is off, traces and polylines appear as outlines and the corners are mitered. After turning FILL off, enter "REGEN" to have the fill removed.

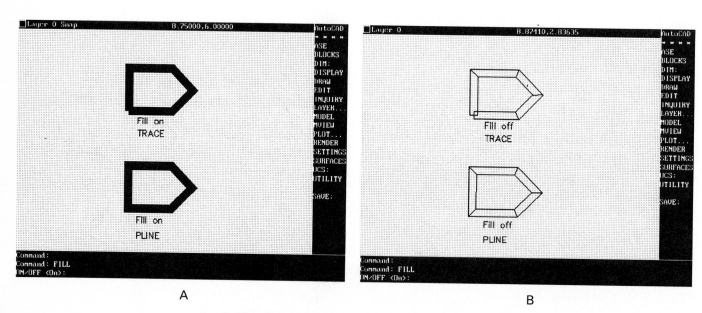

Fig. 6-45. Examples of FILL when it is turned on and off.

─── **PROFESSIONAL TIP** ───

When there are many wide polylines or traces on a drawing, it is best to have the FILL mode turned off. This saves time when redrawing, regenerating, or plotting a check copy. Turn the FILL mode on for the final drawing.

ADDING COLOR TO THE DRAWING

ARM 8

You may change the color of any part of the drawing. Whether you are drawing using a single layer or multiple layers, the color may be changed by typing "COLOR" at the Command: prompt, and entering the color name or number at the next prompt. The seven standard colors are:

- 1 – Red
- 2 – Yellow
- 3 – Green
- 4 – Cyan
- 5 – Blue
- 6 – Magenta
- 7 – White

After entering "COLOR," you are asked for the new color. Type either the color number or name as follows:

Command: **COLOR** ↵
New entity color ⟨current⟩: *(type the desired color number or name,* **5** *or* **BLUE***, for example)* ↵

COLOR is a transparent command. Enter 'COLOR to change entity color while inside another command. Additional information on color is found in Chapter 17.

EXERCISE 6-18

☐ Load AutoCAD and open PRODR1, or begin a new drawing using your own variables.
☐ Change the color to yellow. Use the TRACE command to draw a 2 unit by 4 unit rectangle with a .125 linewidth. Draw another with .25 linewidth.
☐ Change the color to blue. Use the PLINE command to draw a rectangle 2 units by 4 units with .125 linewidth. Draw another with .25 linewidth.
☐ Turn FILL off and on and observe the difference.
☐ Use the REGEN command with FILL on and off, and notice the regeneration speed in each situation. There may not be much difference with a fast computer unless the file begins to get large.
☐ Save the drawing as A:EX6-18 and quit.

SKETCHING WITH AUTOCAD

ARM 5

Earlier in this chapter, you may have noticed the SKETCH command located in the Line cascading submenu. While the SKETCH command is not commonly used, it does have value for certain applications. Sketching with AutoCAD allows you to draw as if you are sketching with pencil on paper. The SKETCH command is used when it is necessary to draw a contour that is not defined by geometric shapes or straight lines. Examples of freehand sketching with AutoCAD include:

- Contour lines on topographic maps.
- Maps of countries and states.
- Architectural landscape symbols, such as trees, bushes, and plants.
- Graphs and charts.
- Graphic design, such as found on a greeting card.
- Short breaks, such as those used in mechanical drafting.

USING THE SKETCH COMMAND

ARM 5

The SKETCH command requires the use of a pointing device. Sketching may not be done using the keyboard cursor movement keys. Before using the SKETCH command, it is best to turn SNAP and ORTHO modes off since they limit the cursor's movement to horizontal and vertical increments of the snap grid. Normally, you want total control over the cursor when sketching. The SKETCH command can be entered at the keyboard, DRAW screen menu, or Draw pull-down menu. When you enter SKETCH, AutoCAD responds with the following:

Command: **SKETCH** ↲
Record increment ⟨0.1000⟩:

The "Record increment" is the length of each sketch line element generated as you move the cursor. For example, if the record increment is 0.1 (default value), sketched images consist of 0.1 long lines. An increment setting of 1 creates sketched line segments 1 unit long. Reducing the record increment increases the accuracy of your sketched image. However, record increments less than .1 consume great amounts of computer storage. To view the chosen record increment, turn the ORTHO mode on and draw stair steps. Each horizontal and vertical element is the length of the record increment. If the SNAP mode is also on, the record increment automatically equals the snap increment. Fig. 6-46 shows a comparison of .1 and 1 record increments.

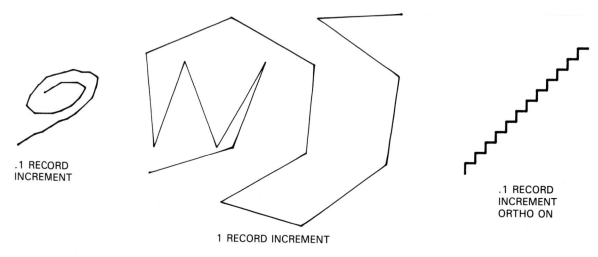

.1 RECORD INCREMENT

1 RECORD INCREMENT

.1 RECORD INCREMENT ORTHO ON

Fig. 6-46. Sketching record increments.

To set a .1 record increment, type ".1" or press ENTER to accept the default value.

Record increment ⟨0.1000⟩: ↲

AutoCAD then issues the following prompt:

Sketch. Pen eXit Quit Record Erase Connect

Once you see the "Sketch." prompt, the buttons on your puck activate the SKETCH subcommands. If you do not use a puck, the subcommands may be entered at the keyboard. Simply type the capitalized letter in each. The following list shows the puck button and keyboard letters used to access each subcommand.

Keyboard Entry	Puck Button	Subcommand Function
Pen (P)	0	Pen up, Pen down.
"." (period)	1	To draw a line from endpoint of sketched line.
Record (R)	2	Records sketched lines as permanent.
eXit (X, SPACE, or RETURN)	3	Records sketched lines and exits SKETCH command.
Quit (Q, CTRL C)	4	Removes all entities created before R or X.
Erase (E)	5	Erases selected entry prior to using R or X.
Connect (C)	6	Connects to endpoint of sketched line after a pen up has been issued.

The normal puck buttons for SNAP (4) and ORTHO (5) modes remain disabled as long as the SKETCH command is active. However, you can access ORTHO and SNAP with their function keys, F8 and F9.

Drawing sketched lines

Sketching is done with the Pen subcommand. It is similar to sketching with paper and pencil. When the pencil is "down," you are ready to draw. When the pencil is "up," you are thinking about what to draw next or moving to the next location. Type "P" to select "pen down," and sketch. Move your cursor around to create a line. Type "P" again to select pen up to stop sketching. When you type "P" or use the pick button "0," the prompt line reads:

Sketch. Pen eXit Quit Record Erase Connect . ⟨Pen down⟩ ⟨Pen up⟩

— PROFESSIONAL TIP —

If you don't consider yourself an artist, trace an existing design. Tape it to the digitizer and move the cursor along the outline of the shape with the pen down. Do not forget to select "pen up" when moving to a new sketching location.

Using the "." subcommand

To draw a straight line from the endpoint of the last sketched line to a selected point, do the following:
1. Make sure the "pen" is up.
2. Move the screen cursor to the desired point.
3. Type "." or press puck button 1.

A straight line is automatically drawn.

Using the Erase subcommand

You can erase while sketching. If you make a mistake, type "E" or press puck button 5. The pen may be up or down. If the pen is down, it is automatically raised. AutoCAD responds with the message:

Erase: Select end of delete. ⟨Pen up⟩

Move the cursor to erase any portion of the sketch, beginning from the last point. When finished, type "P" or press the pick button 0. If you decide not to erase, type "E" or press button 5. AutoCAD returns to the SKETCH command after issuing the message, "Erase aborted."

Recording sketched lines

As you sketch, the lines are displayed in color and are referred to as *temporary lines*. Temporary lines become *permanent lines* and are displayed in their final color after they are "recorded." You can record the lines and remain in the SKETCH command by typing "R" or pressing puck button 2. You may also record and exit the SKETCH command by typing "X," pressing the space bar, pressing ENTER, or using puck button 3. AutoCAD responds with a message indicating the number of lines recorded. For example, suppose you created 32 lines, the message reads: "32 lines recorded."

Quitting the SKETCH command

To get out of the SKETCH command without recording temporary lines, type "Q," press CTRL C, or press puck button 4. This removes all temporary lines and returns the Command: prompt.

Connecting the endpoint of the line

It is customary to select "pen up" to pause or to make a menu selection. When the pen is up, return to the last sketched point and resume sketching by typing "C," or pressing puck button 6. AutoCAD responds with this message:

Connect: Move to the endpoint of line.

Move the cursor to the end of the previously sketched temporary line. As soon as the crosshairs touch the previously drawn line, the pen automatically goes down and you can resume sketching.

Consuming storage space with the SKETCH command

Sketching consumes computer storage rapidly. A drawing with fine detail will quickly fill your floppy disk. Therefore, the SKETCH command should be used only when necessary. The record increment should be set as large as possible, yet still appear pleasing. In commercial applications, such as topographical maps, the storage capacity is designed to accept the required input. Fig. 6-47 shows a sketch of a rose. This drawing completely filled one double-sided, double-density floppy disk (720,000 bytes).

Fig. 6-47. A rose drawn using the SKETCH command.   (Courtesy of Susan Waterman)

EXERCISE 6-19

☐ Load AutoCAD and enter the drawing editor.
☐ Use the SKETCH command to sketch a bush, tree, or houseplant in plan (top) view.
☐ Save the drawing as A:EX6-19 and quit.

USING DRAWING PLAN SHEETS

A good work plan almost always saves drafting time in the long run. Planning should include sketches and drawing plan sheets. A rough preliminary sketch and completed drawing plan sheet help in the following ways:
- Determines the drawing layout.
- Sets the overall size or limits of the drawing by laying out the views and required free space.
- Confirms the drawing units based on the dimensions provided.
- Predetermines the point entry system and locates the points.
- Establishes the grid and snap settings.
- Presets some of the drawing variables, such as LINETYPE, FILL, and polyline width.
- Establishes how and when various activities are to be performed.
- Determines the best use of AutoCAD.
- Results in an even work load.
- Maintains maximum use of equipment.

Drawing plan sheets may range in content depending on the nature of the drafting project. One basic drawing plan sheet is shown in Fig. 6-48. Copies of plan sheets are available for duplication in the Solution Manual.

DRAWING PLANNING SHEET

The following information is to be furnished by the Assigned Project Engineer requesting design support:

PROJECT TITLE: _____

DISCIPLINE: _____

PROJECT NO. : _____   A.F.E. NO. : _____

PROJECT ENGINEER: _____   PHONE NO. : _____

CLIENT: _____

DRAWING SCOPE OF WORK: _____
_____
_____

The following information will be furnished by the assigned Lead Designer:

LEAD DESIGNER: _____   PHONE NO. : _____

DISK NAME: _____

FILE NAME: _____   DRAWING NO.: _____

DWG. GHOST (SIZE & FORMAT): _____

DRAFTER: _____   PHONE NO. : _____

DATE ASSIGNED: _____   DATE REQUIRED: _____

DATE I.F.A. : _____   DATE I.F.C. : _____

ESTIMATED M.H. : _____   ACTUAL M.H. : _____

DRAWING STANDARD: _____   MAT'L SPEC.: _____

AFFECTED TAG NO'S: REFERENCE SHEETS

_____ _____ _____   _____ _____ _____

_____ _____ _____   _____ _____ _____

Freehand sketch by drafter:

Approved by: _____   Date: _____

Fig. 6-48. A drawing plan sheet and project log combination. They are generally printed on the front and back of one piece of paper. (Courtesy of Harlton Terrie Gaines; Palmer, Alaska)

DRAWING PLANNING SHEET

Page 2 of 2

Drafters notes: ____________________

Commands used by the drafter:

Commands	Values	Commands	Values
1.		34.	
2.		35.	
3.		36.	
4.		37.	
5.		38.	
6.		39.	
7.		40.	
8.		41.	
9.		42.	
10.		43.	
11.		44.	
12.		45.	
13.		46.	
14.		47.	
15.		48.	
16.		49.	
17.		50.	
18.		51.	
19.		52.	
20.		53.	
21.		54.	
22.		55.	
23.		56.	
24.		57.	
25.		58.	
26.		59.	
27.		60.	
28.		61.	
29.		62.	
30.		63.	
31.		64.	
32.		65.	
33.		66.	

Fig. 6-48. (Continued)

CHAPTER TEST

Write your answers in the spaces provided.

1. Give the commands and entries you must use to draw a line from point A to point B, to point C, back to point A. Finally, be ready to give a new command:

   Command: _____

   From point: _____

   To point: _____

   To point: _____

   To point: _____

   To point: _____

   Command:

2. Give the commands needed to turn on the Ortho mode:

   Command: _____

   ON/OFF: _____

3. Give the command and actions needed to quickly connect a line to an existing line and then undo it because it was wrong:

   Command: _____

   From point: _____

   To point: _____

   To point: _____

   To point: _____

4. Give the command and entries needed to draw a straight .25 wide double line with caps on both ends:

   Command: _____

   Break/Caps/Dragline/Snap/Undo/Width/〈start point〉: _____

   New DLINE width 〈0.05〉: _____

   Break/Caps/Dragline/Snap/Undo/Width/〈start point〉: _____

   Draw which endcaps? Both/End/None/Start/〈Auto〉: _____

   Break/Caps/Dragline/Snap/Undo/Width/〈start point〉: _____

   Arc/Break/CAps/CLose/Dragline/Snap/Undo/Width/〈next point〉: _____

   Arc/Break/CAps/CLose/Dragline/Snap/Undo/Width/〈next point〉: _____

5. Give the command and related responses used to erase a group of objects at the same time and then bring them all back:

   Command: _____

   Select objects: _____

   First corner: _____

   Other corner: _____

   Select objects: _____

   Command: _____

6. Give the command necessary to clean the screen:

Command: _____

7. Give the commands to change the linetype from a solid line to a centerline:

Command: _____

?/Create/Load/Set: _____

New entity linetype (or ?): ⟨continuous⟩: _____

8. Give the commands to draw a polyline from point A to point B with a beginning width of .500 and an ending width of 0. Then undo the polyline because you think you made a mistake. Finally, bring it back because you realized you did not make a mistake:

Command: _____

From point: _____

Current line-width 0.0

Arc/Close/Halfwidth/Length/Undo/Width/⟨End point of line⟩: _____

Starting width ⟨0.0000⟩: _____

Ending width ⟨.500⟩: _____

Arc/Close/Halfwidth/Length/Undo/Width/⟨End point of line⟩: _____

Arc/Close/Halfwidth/Length/Undo/Width/⟨End point of line⟩: _____

Command: _____

Auto/Back/Control/End/Group/Mark/⟨number⟩: _____

Command: _____

9. Identify the following linetypes.

A. _____   A ——————————————

B. _____   B – – – – – – – – –

C. _____   C ———————— – ———————

D. _____

E. _____

F. _____

G. _____

H. _____

I. _____

J. _____

K. _____

G ————————————————

H ⌐– – – – – – – –⌐

I ———⋁——————⋁———

J —— – – —— – – ——

K ·······························

10. List two ways to discontinue drawing a line. _____
_____

11. Name four point entry systems. _____
_____
_____
_____

12. Identify three ways to turn on the coordinate display. _____
_____
_____

13. What does a coordinate display of 2.750<90 mean? _____
_____
_____

14. List four ways to turn on the Ortho mode. _____
_____
_____
_____

15. What is the purpose of the Break option in the DLINE command? _____
_____
_____

16. What is the Dragline default for drawing double lines? _____

17. How does increasing the DLINE command's Snap option influence how double lines are joined? _____
_____
_____

18. When does the DLINE command's Undo option work? _____
_____

19. How do you draw a straight double line connected to a double line arc, which is then connected to another straight double line? _____
_____
_____

20. Identify the ERASE screen menu selection that lets you automatically erase any entity on the drawing just by picking it. _____

21. How do you automatically use the Window selection method when you want to erase a group of objects? _____
_____
_____
_____

22. How do you automatically use the Crossing selection option when you want to erase three out of four lines of a square? _____

_____

_____

_____

_____

23. How does the appearance of a window and crossing box differ? _____

_____

_____

24. How does the Select option in the Erase cascading submenu work? _____

_____

_____

25. Name the command that is used to bring back the last object you erased and before you issue another command. _____

26. Name the command that is used to clean the screen of unwanted blips. _____

27. What command and option do you use if you are drawing object lines and you want to change to draw hidden lines? _____

28. How do you get an alphanumeric screen showing the AutoCAD standard linetypes?

_____

29. How do you draw a filled arrow using the PLINE command? _____

_____

30. List at least five ways to select an object to erase. _____

_____

_____

31. Name two commands that may be used to draw wide lines. _____

32. Which PLINE option allows you to specify the width from the center to one side?

_____

33. What is an advantage of leaving the FILL mode turned off?_____

_____

34. Identify at least four reasons for using a drawing plan sheet._____

_____

_____

_____

35. Explain why the SNAP and ORTHO modes should be turned off for most sketching applications. _____

_____

DRAWING PROBLEMS

1. Draw an object by connecting the following point coordinates. Save your drawing as A:P6-1.

Point	Coordinates	Point	Coordinates
1	2,2	8	@ −1.5,0
2	@ 1.5,0	9	@ 0,1.25
3	@.75⟨90	10	@ −1.25,1.25
4	@1.5⟨0	11	@ 2⟨180
5	@ 0,−.75	12	@ −1.25,−1.25
6	@ 3,0	13	@ 2.25⟨270
7	@ 1⟨90		

2. With the absolute, relative, and polar coordinate entry methods, use the digitizer, keyboard, and cursor keys to draw the following shapes. Be sure to use a drawing plan sheet. Set the limits to 22,17, units to decimal, grid to .5, and snap to .0625. Draw rectangle A three times using a different point entry system each time. Draw object B using at least two methods of coordinate entry. Do not draw dimensions. Save your drawing as A:P6-2.

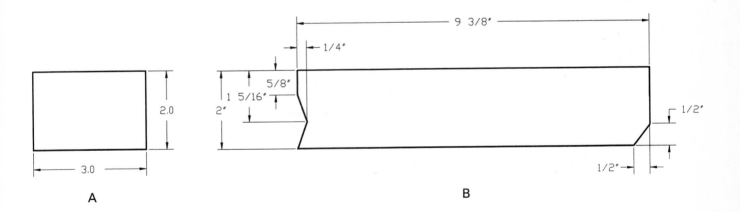

A

B

3. With the absolute, relative, and polar coordinate entry methods use the digitizer, keyboard, and cursor key to draw the following object. Use a drawing plan sheet. Set the limits to 22,17, units to decimal, grid to .25, and snap to .0625. Use the LINE command. Do not draw dimensions. Save your drawing as A:P6-3.

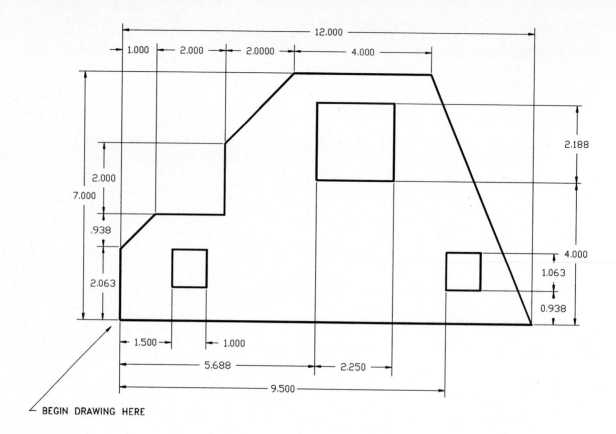

BEGIN DRAWING HERE

4. Open problem P6-3 again. This time use the PLINE command to draw the object with a .032 linewidth. Save the new drawing as A:P6-4.

5. Edit problem P6-3 so that it takes on the following changes. The dimensions shown are revisions and are not to be added. Save your drawing as A:P6-5.

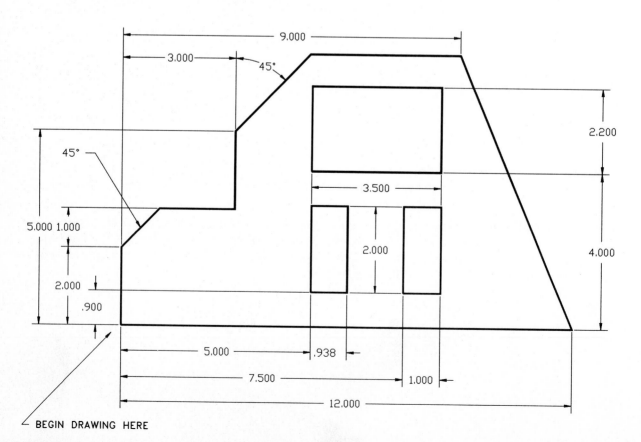

BEGIN DRAWING HERE

6. Edit drawing P6-4 so that it takes on the changes shown in problem number 5. The dimensions shown are revisions and are not to be added. Save your drawing as A:P6-6.
7. Draw the objects shown at A and B below using the following instructions:
   A. Use a drawing plan sheet.
   B. Draw each object using the LINE command.
   C. Start each object at the point shown and then discontinue the LINE command where shown.
   D. Complete each object using the Continue option.
   E. Do not draw dimensions.
   F. Save the drawings as A:P6-7.

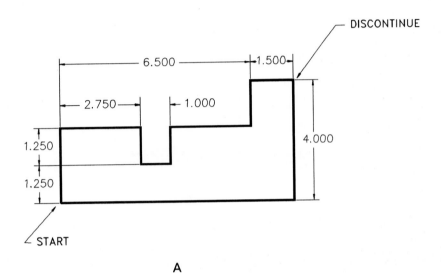

A

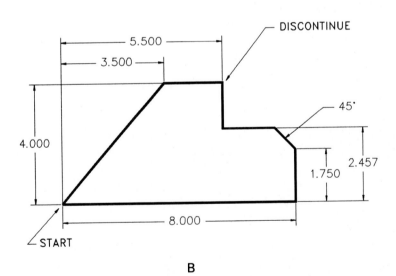

B

8. Draw the same objects shown in problem number 7 as follows:
   A. Draw the objects using the TRACE command and .25 linewidth.
   B. Draw the objects again this time using the PLINE command and .25 linewidth.
   C. Turn off the FILL mode and use the REGEN command. Then, turn on FILL and again REGEN.
   D. Observe the difference with FILL on and off.
   E. Save this drawing as A:P6-8.

9. Draw the objects shown at A and B below. Then, use the Undo option to remove object B. Use the REDO command to get object B back. Save this drawing as A:P6-9.

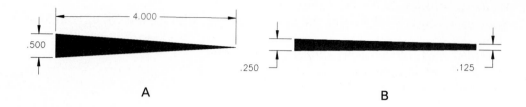

A   B

10. Draw the object shown below. Set limits at 11,8.5, decimal units, .25 grid, and .0625 snap. Save your drawing as A:P6-10.

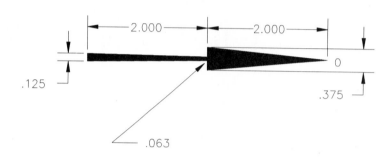

11. Draw the following objects using the DLINE command. Use the options indicated with each illustration. Set limits to 11,8.5, grid at .50, and snap at .25. Set the double line width to .125. Do not add text or dimensions to the drawings. Save the drawings as A:P6-11.

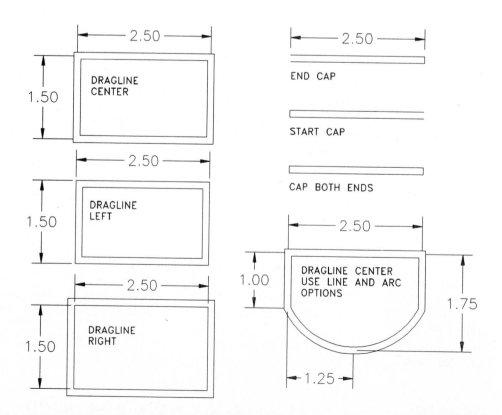

12. Draw the partial floor plan using the DLINE command. Carefully observe how the dimensions correlate with the double lines to determine your Dragline settings. Also, use the Cap and Break options appropriately. Set limits to 88',68', grid to 24, snap to 12, and use architectural units. Make all walls 6 in. thick. Do not add text or dimensions to the drawing. Save the drawing as A:P6-12.

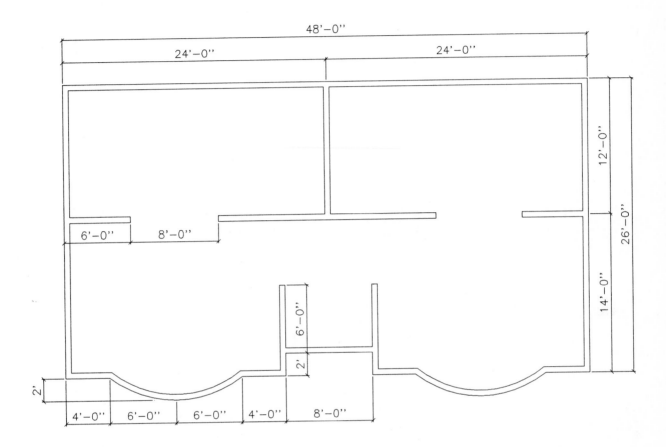

13. Use the SKETCH command to sign your name. Save the drawing as A:P6-13.
14. Use the SKETCH command to design the cover of a greeting card. Save the design as A:P6-14.
15. Find a map of your state and make a photocopy. Tape the copy to your digitizer tablet. Using the SKETCH command, do the following:
    A. Trace the outline of the map.
    B. Include all major rivers and lakes.
    Save the drawing as A:P6-15.

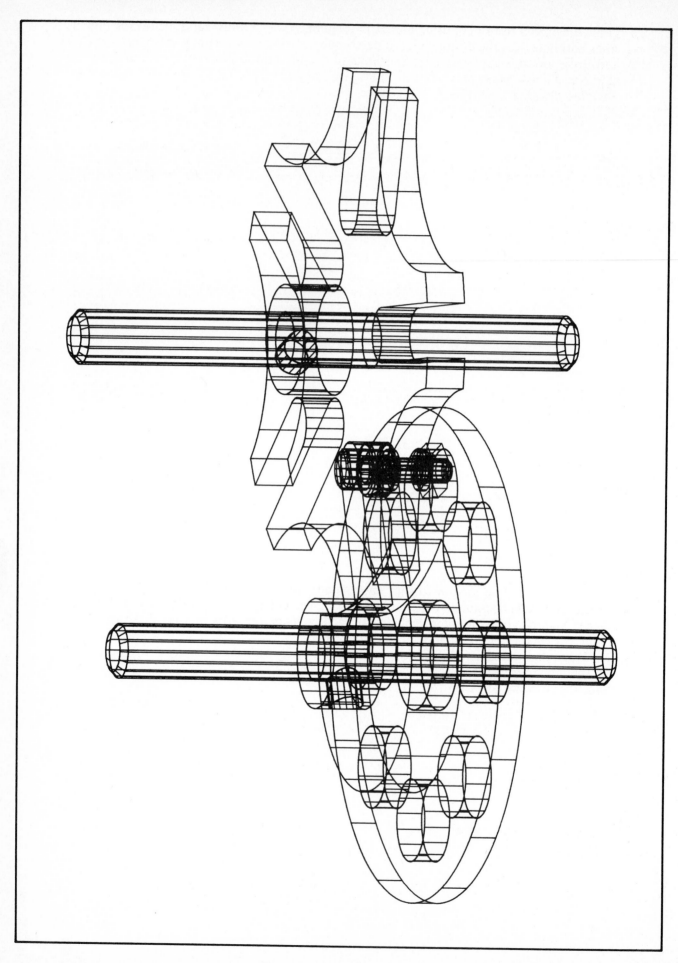

Wireframe model of a cam assembly.   (Autodesk, Inc.)

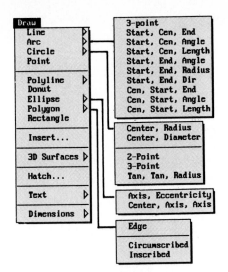

Chapter 7

DRAWING BASIC SHAPES

Learning objectives

After completing this chapter, you will be able to:
☐ Use DRAGMODE to observe an object drag into place.
☐ Draw circles using the CIRCLE command options.
☐ Identify and use the "@" symbol function.
☐ Draw arcs using the ARC command options.
☐ Draw an arc extending from a previously drawn arc.
☐ Draw an arc extending from a previously drawn line.
☐ Use the pull-down menu to draw multiple shapes.
☐ Use the ELLIPSE command to draw ellipses by various methods.
☐ Draw polygons from given information.
☐ Explain and use the MULTIPLE command modifier.
☐ Draw doughnuts.
☐ Preset polygon and doughnut specifications.

The decisions made when drawing circles and arcs with AutoCAD are similar to those required when drawing the items manually. You have options to consider. These include the center location and radius or diameter, or where the outline of the circle or arc should be located. AutoCAD provides many ways to create circles and arcs using the CIRCLE and ARC commands. AutoCAD also provides the ELLIPSE and POLYGON commands, which draw a wide variety of shapes.

WATCHING OBJECTS DRAG INTO PLACE

ARM 7

Chapter 6 showed how the LINE command displays a dashed image that is "dragged" across the screen before the second endpoint is picked. This same dashed image, called a *rubberband*, drags across the screen when drawing other entities, too. The CIRCLE, ARC, ELLIPSE, and POLYGON commands display a rubberband image to help you decide where to place the entity.

When a circle is drawn using the Center and Radius options, a dashed circle image appears on the screen. This image gets larger or smaller as you move the pointer. When the desired circle size is picked, the dragged image is replaced by a solid-line circle as shown in Fig. 7-1.

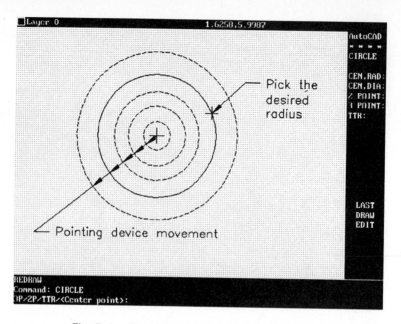

Fig. 7-1. Dragging a circle to its desired size.

The DRAGMODE may be set to be ON, OFF, or Automatic by typing DRAGMODE at the Command: prompt and pressing ENTER as follows:

Command: **DRAGMODE** ⏎
OFF/ON/Auto ⟨current⟩: *(type OFF, ON, or A and press ENTER)*

The current (default) mode is shown in brackets. Pressing the ENTER key keeps the existing status. An ON response turns DRAGMODE on. When DRAGMODE is on, dragging is permitted by entering "DRAG" at the appropriate time in the command sequence or by menu selection. When the DRAGMODE is on, you decide when to use DRAG. Selecting OFF disables the DRAGMODE, and all DRAG requests are ignored by AutoCAD. When you set DRAGMODE to AUTO by typing an "A," the drag capabilities are automatically used by AutoCAD for all commands that support dragging. Many users prefer to have the DRAGMODE set to Auto. However, some computer configurations slow down the drag process. When this occurs, you may prefer to turn DRAGMODE on and off by choice. The following command sequence shows you how to activate the DRAGMODE when in another command.

Command: **CIRCLE** ⏎
3P/2P/TTR/⟨Center point⟩: *(pick a center point)*
Diameter/⟨Radius⟩: **DRAG** ⏎ *(pick the desired radius)*

DRAWING CIRCLES

ARM 5

The CIRCLE command is located in the DRAW screen menu and the Draw pull-down menu. Picking CIRCLE displays a screen menu like this:

Drawing a circle by radius

When you select CEN,RAD: (CENter,RADius), AutoCAD asks you to first pick a center point. Then either pick the radius on the screen or type the radius value, Fig. 7-2. If the radius is picked on the screen, watch the coordinate display to locate the exact radius. CEN,RAD is also the circle command's default option. The CIRCLE command gives the following as you use the CEN,RAD option:

Command: **CIRCLE** ↵
3P/2P/TTR/⟨Center point⟩: *(select a center point)*
Diameter/⟨Radius⟩: *(drag the circle to the desired radius and pick, or type the radius size and press ENTER)*

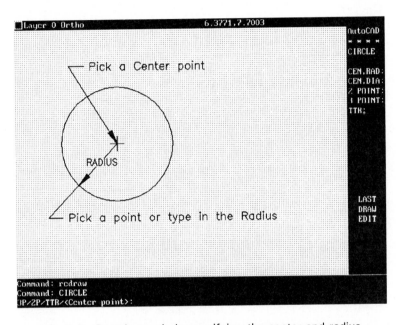

Fig. 7-2. Drawing a circle specifying the center and radius.

The radius value you enter becomes the default setting for the next time you use the CIRCLE command. Use the CIRCLERAD system variable if you want to set a radius default. This provides you with the same circle radius default value each time you use the CIRCLE command until you use a different value. The CIRCLERAD system variable works like this:

Command: **CIRCLERAD** ↵
New value for CIRCLERAD ⟨0⟩: *(set the desired default, .50 for example)*

The CIRCLE command sequence then looks like this:

Command: **CIRCLE** ↵
3P/2P/TTR/⟨Center point⟩: *(pick the center point)*
Diameter/⟨Radius⟩ ⟨.50⟩: ↵
Command:

When the CIRCLERAD system variable is set to a non-zero value, all you have to do is pick the center point of the circle and press ENTER to accept the default value. You can always enter a different radius or pick a desired radius point if you want to ignore the default value. Set CIRCLERAD to 0 if you do not want a constant radius default.

Drawing a circle by diameter

You can select the center point and the diameter of a circle by picking CEN,DIA: from the screen menu. If the CIRCLE command is typed, the Diameter option is required at the prompt line because "Radius" is the default:

Command: **CIRCLE** ↵
3P/2P/TTR/⟨Center point⟩: *(select a center point)*
Diameter/⟨Radius⟩: **D** ↵
Diameter: *(drag the circle to the desired diameter and pick, or type the diameter size and press ENTER)*

Watch the screen carefully when using the CEN,DIA: option; something a little strange happens. The pointer measures the diameter, but the circle passes midway between the center and the cursor as shown in Fig. 7-3. The CEN,DIA: option is convenient because most circle dimensions are given as diameters.

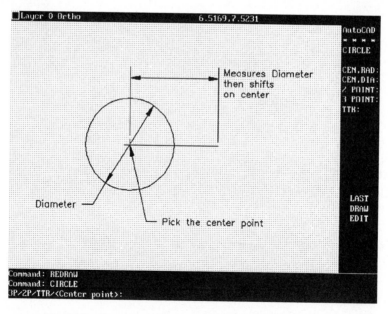

Fig. 7-3. Drawing a circle using the CEN,DIA: option.

After you draw a circle, the radius you selected becomes the default for the next circle if CIRCLERAD is set to 0. If you use the Diameter option, the previous default setting is converted to a diameter. If you use the Radius option to draw a circle after using the Diameter option, AutoCAD changes the default to a radius measurement based on the previous diameter. If you set CIRCLERAD to a value such as .50, then the default for a circle drawing with the Diameter option is automatically 1.00 (twice the radius).

Drawing a two-point circle

A two-point circle is drawn by picking two points on opposite sides of the circle, Fig. 7-4. This option is useful if the diameter of the circle is known, but the center is difficult to find.

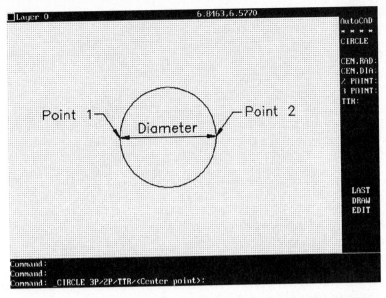

Fig. 7-4. Drawing a circle by selecting two points on the diameter.

One example is locating a circle between two lines. The command sequence for a two-point circle is as follows:

> Command: **CIRCLE** ↵
> 3P/2P/TTR/⟨Center point⟩: **2P** ↵
> First point on diameter: *(select a point)*
> Second point on diameter: *(select a point)*

If the CIRCLERAD variable is set to 0, AutoCAD uses this radius as the default for the next circle.

Drawing a three-point circle

If three points on the circumference of a circle are known, the three-point option is the best method to select. The three points may be selected in any order, Fig. 7-5. The three-point option gives the following prompts:

> Command: **CIRCLE** ↵
> 3P/2P/TTR/⟨Center point⟩: **3P** ↵
> First point: *(select a point)*
> Second point: *(select a point)*
> Third point: *(select a point)*

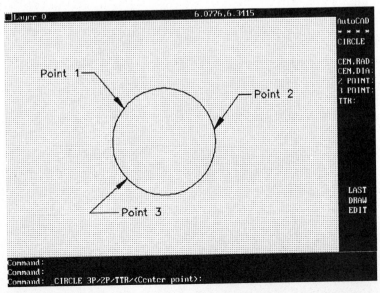

Fig. 7-5. Drawing a circle given three points on the circumference.

If CIRCLERAD is set to 0, AutoCAD automatically calculates the radius of the circle and uses this value as the default for the next circle.

Drawing a circle tangent to two entities

The term *tangent* refers to a line, circle, or arc that comes into contact with an arc or circle at only one point. That point is called the *point of tangency*. A line drawn from the circle's or arc's center to the point of tangency is perpendicular to the tangent line. Circles are tangent when they touch at only one point. A line drawn between the centers passes through the point of tangency. When it is necessary to draw a circle tangent to given lines, circles, or arcs, select the TTR: option. Then select the lines or line and arc to which the new circle will be tangent. The radius of the circle is also required. The command sequence is as follows:

Command: **CIRCLE** ↵
3P/2P/TTR/⟨Center point⟩: **TTR** ↵
Enter Tangent spec: *(pick the first line, circle, or arc)*
Enter second Tangent spec: *(pick the second line, circle, or arc)*
Radius: *(type a radius value and press ENTER)*

If the radius entered is too small, AutoCAD gives you the message: Circle does not exist. If the CIRCLERAD system variable is set to 0, the radius you use for the TTR: option becomes the default for the next circle. Two examples of the TTR option are shown in Fig. 7-6.

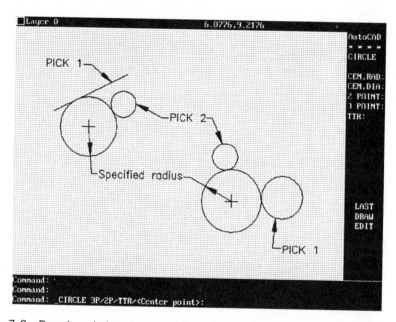

Fig. 7-6. Drawing circles tangent to two given entities using the TTR: option.

PROFESSIONAL TIP

Using the CIRCLERAD system variable to set a fixed default is helpful and saves drafting time when you plan to draw several circles with the same radius.

USING THE @ SYMBOL TO SPECIFY THE LAST COORDINATES

ARM 2

The "@" symbol may be used alone to input the same coordinates as previously selected. For example, suppose you want to draw a circle with its center at the end of a previously drawn line. Enter the "@" symbol at the "⟨Center point⟩:" prompt as follows:

> Command: **LINE** ↵
> From point: **4,4** ↵
> To point: **8,4** ↵
> To point: ↵
> Command: **CIRCLE** ↵
> 3P/2P/TTR/⟨Center point⟩: **@** ↵

The "@" symbol automatically issues the coordinate 8,4 (end of the last line) as the center of the circle. The 8,4 value is saved in the LASTPOINT system variable. The @ retrieves the LASTPOINT value.

Another application is drawing concentric circles (circles which have the same center). To do this, draw a circle using the CEN,RAD: or CEN,DIA: options. Then enter the CIRCLE command again and type "@" at the "⟨Center point⟩:" prompt. This automatically places the center of the new circle at the center of the previous circle.

EXERCISE 7-1

- ☐ Load AutoCAD and open PRODR1, or start a new drawing and set up your own variables.
- ☐ Set the CIRCLERAD system variable to 0.
- ☐ Use the CIRCLE command's CEN,RAD: option to draw a circle similar to the one shown in Fig. 7-2.
- ☐ Use the CIRCLE command's CEN,DIA: option to draw the circle shown in Fig. 7-3.
- ☐ Draw two vertical parallel lines two units apart. Then use the CIRCLE command's 2P option to draw the circle tangent to the two lines.
- ☐ Use the CIRCLE command's 3P option to draw the circle shown in Fig. 7-5.
- ☐ Use the CIRCLE command's TTR option to draw the circles shown in Fig. 7-6.
- ☐ Draw a line. Enter the CIRCLE command's CEN,RAD: option and the "@" symbol to place the circle's center at the endpoint of the line.
- ☐ Draw three concentric circles using the "@" symbol to automatically place the circles on the same center.
- ☐ Set CIRCLERAD to .5 and draw circles using each CIRCLE option to observe the difference in the prompts for the previously drawn circles.
- ☐ Save the drawing as A:EX7-1 and quit the drawing editor.

DRAWING ARCS

ARM 5

An *arc* is defined as any part of a circle or curve. Arcs are commonly dimensioned with a radius, but may be drawn by a number of different methods. The ARC command is located in the DRAW screen menu and the Draw pull-down menu. AutoCAD provides eleven methods for drawing arcs, as shown in Fig. 7-7.

The three-point option is the default if ARC is typed at the Command: prompt. The other options are given with letters that designate the option prompt sequence. Fig. 7-7 illustrates the meaning of the ARC option letters.

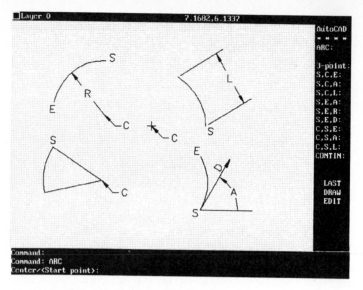

C Center of the arc as part of a circle.
S Start point. First point on the arc.
E Endpoint. Last point on the arc.
A Angle. Refers to the included angle.
R Radius of the arc.
D Direction arc is drawn.
L Length of chord. A *chord* is a line connecting the arc end points.

Fig. 7-7. Meaning of the ARC command option letters.

The last element of any arc construction option is automatically dragged into place if DRAGMODE is set to Auto.

Drawing a three-point arc

The three-point option asks for the start point, point along the arc, and then the endpoint, Fig. 7-8. The arc may be drawn clockwise or counterclockwise, and is dragged into position as the endpoint is located. The following shows the prompts of the three-point option:

Command: **ARC** ⏎
Center/⟨Start point⟩: *(select the first point on the arc)*
Center/End/⟨Second point⟩: *(select the second point on the arc)*
End point: *(select the arc's endpoint)*

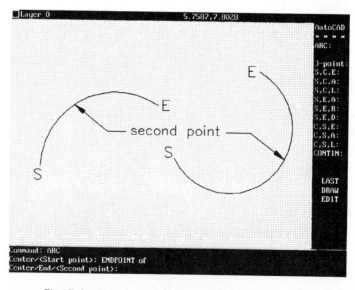

Fig. 7-8. Drawing an arc by picking three points.

Drawing an arc with the Start, Center, End (S,C,E:) option

The S,C,E: option is chosen when the start, center, and endpoints are known. Picking the start and center points establishes the arc's radius. The endpoint provides the arc length. For this reason, the arc does not pass through the endpoint unless this point is also on the radius, Fig. 7-9. The following command sequence is used and the arc is drawn counterclockwise:

Command: **ARC** ↵
Center/⟨Start point⟩: *(select the first point on the arc)*
Center/End/⟨Second point⟩: **C** ↵
Center: *(select the arc's center point)*
Angle/Length of chord/⟨End point⟩:
    (select the arc endpoint)

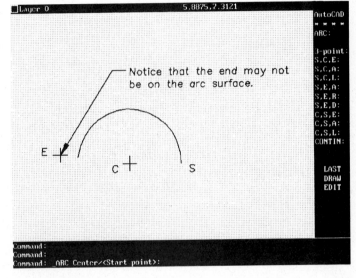

Fig. 7-9. Using the S,C,E: option.

Drawing an arc with the Start, Center, Angle (S,C,A:) option

When the arc's included angle is known, the S,C,A: option may be the best choice. The *included angle* is an angle formed between the center, and start and endpoints of the arc. The arc is drawn counterclockwise, from start to end, unless a negative angle is specified. See Fig. 7-10. The following command sequence uses the Angle option and specifies a 45° included angle:

Command: **ARC** ↵
Center/⟨Start point⟩: *(select the first point on the arc)*
Center/End/⟨Second point⟩: **C** ↵
Center: *(select the arc center point)*
Angle/Length of chord/⟨End point⟩: **A** ↵
Included angle: **45** ↵

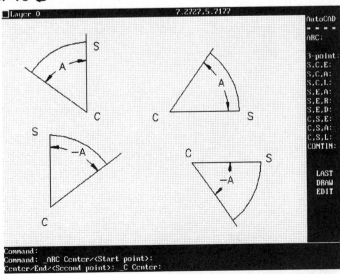

Fig. 7-10. Using the S,C,A: option to draw arcs with positive and negative angles.

Notice that "DRAG" automatically appears after the Included angle: prompt if the S,C,A: option is picked from the Arc submenu and the DRAGMODE is set to Auto. This acknowledges that drag is working.

Drawing arcs with the Start, Center, and Length of chord (S,C,L:) option
The chord length may be determined using *Chord Length Table* in Appendix I. Referring to the table, a one-unit radius arc with an included angle of 45° has a chord length of .765 units. Arcs are drawn counterclockwise; therefore, a positive chord length gives the smallest possible arc with that length. A negative chord length results in the largest possible arc. (See Fig. 7-11.) The command sequence is as follows:

Command: **ARC** ↵
Center/⟨Start point⟩: *(select the first point on the arc)*
Center/End/⟨Second point⟩: **C** ↵
Center: *(select the arc center point)*
Angle/Length of chord/⟨End point⟩: **L** ↵
Length of chord: DRAG *(type* **.765** *for the smallest arc, or* − **.765** *for the largest arc and press ENTER)*

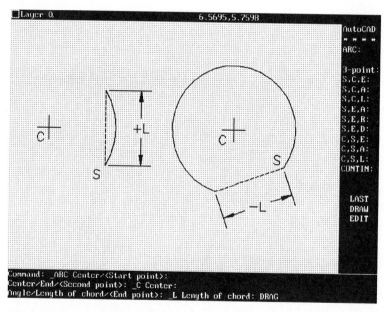

Fig. 7-11. Using the S,C,L: option with positive and negative chord lengths.

EXERCISE 7-2

☐ Load AutoCAD and open PRODR1, or start a new drawing and set up your own variables.
☐ Use the ARC command's three-point option to draw arcs similar to those shown in Fig. 7-8.
☐ Use the ARC command's S,C,E: option and draw the arc shown in Fig. 7-9.
☐ Use the ARC command's S,C,A: option and draw the arcs shown in Fig. 7-10.
☐ Use the ARC command's S,C,L: option and draw the arcs shown in Fig. 7-11.
☐ Save the drawing as A:EX7-2 and quit.

Drawing arcs using the Start, End, and Included Angle (S,E,A:) option
An arc may also be drawn by picking the start point, endpoint, and entering the included angle. A positive included angle draws the arc counterclockwise, while a negative angle produces a clockwise arc, Fig. 7-12. The command sequence is as follows:

Command: **ARC** ⏎
Center/⟨Start point⟩: *(select the first point on the arc)*
Center/End/⟨Second point⟩: **E** ⏎
End point: *(select the arc endpoint)*
Angle/Direction/Radius/⟨Center point⟩: **A** ⏎
Included angle: *(type or pick a positive or negative angle and press ENTER)*

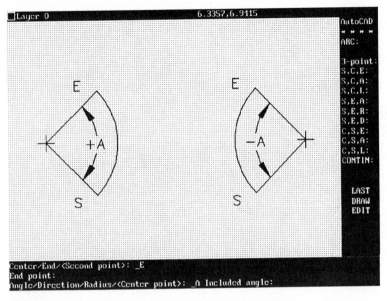

Fig. 7-12. Using the S,E,A: option.

Drawing arcs using the Start, End, Radius (S,E,R:) option

The start, end, radius method allows an arc to be drawn only counterclockwise, as are most arcs. A positive radius value results in the smallest possible arc between the two endpoints. A negative radius gives the largest arc possible, Fig. 7-13. The command sequence is as follows:

Command: **ARC** ⏎
Center/⟨Start point⟩: *(select the first point on the arc)*
Center/End/⟨Second point⟩: **E** ⏎
End point: *(select the arc endpoint)*
Angle/Direction/Radius/⟨Center point⟩: **R** ⏎
Radius: *(pick, or type a positive radius or negative radius and press ENTER)*

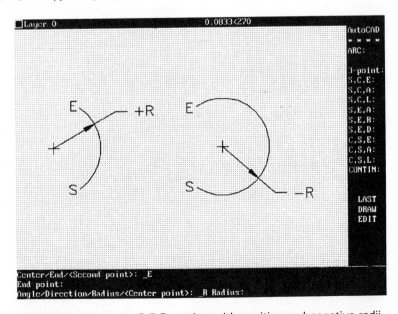

Fig. 7-13. Using the S,E,R: option with positive and negative radii.

Drawing arcs using the Start, End, starting Direction (S,E,D:) option

An arc may be drawn by picking the start point, endpoint, and entering direction of rotation in degrees. The distance between the points and the number of degrees determines the arc's location and size. The arc is started tangent to the direction specified as shown in Fig. 7-14. The command prompts for the S,E,D: option are as follows:

Command: **ARC** ↵
Center/⟨Start point⟩: *(select the first point on the arc)*
Center/End/⟨Second point⟩: **E** ↵
End point: *(select the arc endpoint)*
Angle/Direction/Radius/⟨Center point⟩: **D** ↵
Direction from start point: *(pick the direction from the start point, or type the direction in degrees and press ENTER)*

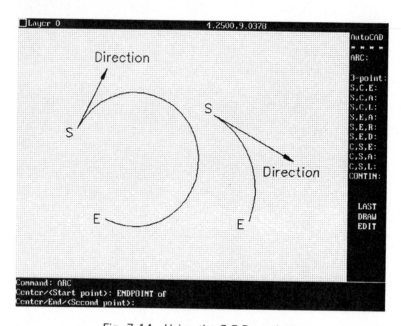

Fig. 7-14. Using the S,E,D: option.

Drawing arcs using the Center, Start, End (C,S,E:) option

The center, start, end option is a variation of the S,C,E: option. Use the C,S,E: option when it is easier to begin by locating the center. The command sequence is as follows:

Command: **ARC** ↵
Center/⟨Start point⟩: **C** ↵
Center: *(pick the center point)*
Start point: *(pick the start point)*
Angle/Length of chord/⟨End point⟩: *(pick the arc's endpoint)*

A drawing showing the use of the C,S,E: option is displayed in Fig. 7-15.

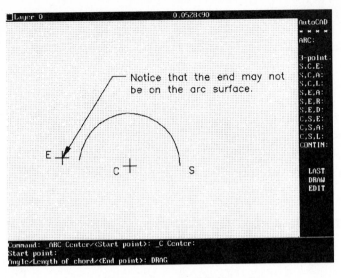

Fig. 7-15. Using the C,S,E: option.

EXERCISE 7-3

☐ Load AutoCAD and open PRODR1, or start a new drawing and set up your own variables.
☐ Use the ARC command's S,E,A: option to draw an arc similar to that shown in Fig. 7-12.
☐ Use the ARC command's S,E,R: option to draw the arc shown in Fig. 7-13.
☐ Use the ARC command's S,E,D: option to draw the arcs shown in Fig. 7-14.
☐ Use the ARC command's C,S,E: option to draw the arcs shown in Fig. 7-15.
☐ Save the drawing as A:EX7-3 and quit.

Drawing arcs using the Center, Start, Angle (C,S,A:) option

The center, start, angle option is a variation of the S,C,A: option. Use the C,S,A: option when it is easier to begin by locating the center, Fig. 7-16. The command sequence is as follows:

Command: **ARC** ⏎
Center/⟨Start point⟩: **C** ⏎
Center: *(pick the center point)*
Start point: *(pick the start point)*
Angle/Length of chord/⟨End point⟩: **A** ⏎
Included angle: *(pick the included angle or type a positive angle or negative angle and press ENTER)*

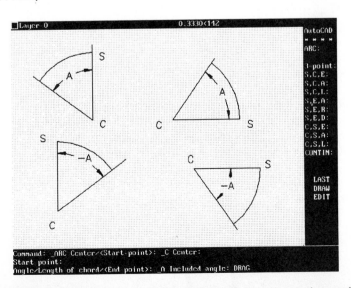

Fig. 7-16. Using the C,S,A: option with positive and negative angles.

Drawing arcs with the Center, Start, Length of chord (C,S,L:) option
The center, start, length of chord option is a variation of the S,C,L: option. Use the C,S,L: option when it is easier to begin by locating the center, Fig. 7-17. The command sequence is as follows:

> Command: **ARC** ↵
> Center/〈Start point〉: **C** ↵
> Center: *(pick the center point)*
> Start point: *(pick the start point)*
> Angle/Length of chord/〈End point〉: **L** ↵
> Length of chord: *(pick, or type the chord length and press ENTER)*

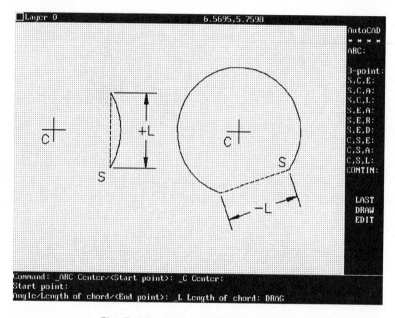

Fig. 7-17. Using the C,S,L: option.

Continuing an arc from a previously drawn arc or line
An arc may be continued from the previous arc. Press the ENTER key or space bar, or pick CONTIN from the screen menu at the "〈Start point〉:" prompt. When arcs are drawn in this manner, each consecutive arc is tangent. The start points and direction are taken from the end-point and direction of the previous arc. Figure 7-18 shows the arc continuation described below.

> Command: **ARC** ↵
> Center/〈Start point〉: *(select the first point on the arc)*
> Center/End/〈Second point〉: **E** ↵
> End point: *(select the arc's endpoint)*
> Angle/Direction/Radius/〈Center point〉: **D** ↵
> Direction from start point: *(pick, or specify the direction from the start point in degrees and press ENTER)*
> Command: ↵
> ARC Center/〈Start point〉: *(press space bar or ENTER)*
> End point: *(select the endpoint of the second arc)*
> Command: ↵
> ARC Center/〈Start point〉: *(press space bar or ENTER)*
> End point: *(select the endpoint of the third arc)*

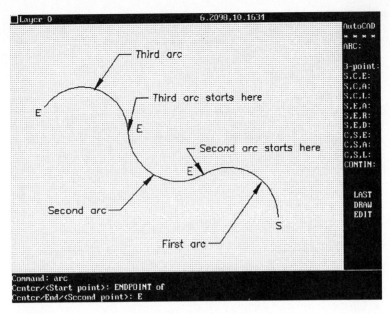

Fig. 7-18. Using the CONTIN option.

The CONTIN option may be used to quickly draw an arc tangent to the endpoint of a previously drawn line or arc, Fig. 7-19. The command sequence is as follows:

Command: **LINE** ↵
From point: *(select a point)*
To point: *(select the second point)*
To point: ↵
Command: **ARC** ↵
Center/⟨Start point⟩: *(pick CONTIN from the screen menu, press space bar, or ENTER to place start point of arc at end of previous line)*
End point: *(select the endpoint of the arc)*

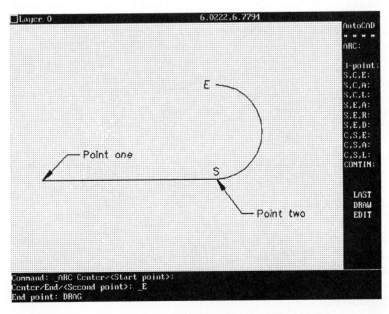

Fig. 7-19. An arc continuing from the previous line.

USING THE PULL-DOWN MENU TO DRAW CIRCLES AND ARCS

ARM A

The Draw pull-down menu displays Arc and Circle as two of the selections. Picking either of these selections displays the cascading menus shown in Fig. 7-20.

When you select Circle from the Draw pull-down menu, the Circle cascading submenu appears with the CIRCLE options listed, Fig. 7-20A. Pick the desired option and the command sequence continues as discussed earlier in this chapter.

When you pick Arc from the pull-down menu, the Arc cascading submenu with the Arc options is displayed, Fig. 7-20B.

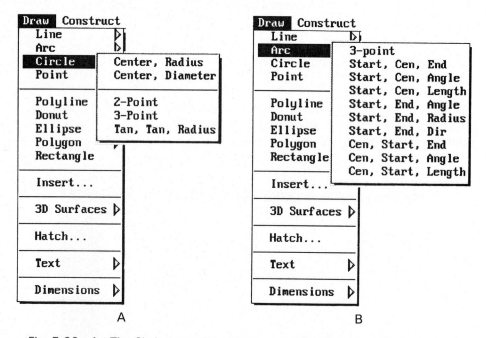

Fig. 7-20. A—The Circle cascading submenu. B—The Arc cascading submenu.

DRAWING ELLIPSES

ARM 5

When a circle is viewed at an angle, an elliptical shape is seen. For example, a 30° ellipse is created if a circle is rotated 60° from the line of sight. The parts of an ellipse are shown in Fig. 7-21.

An ellipse may be drawn using different options of the ELLIPSE command. The ELLIPSE command is found in the DRAW screen menu or the Draw pull-down menu, or can be typed at the Command: prompt:

Command: **ELLIPSE** ↵
⟨Axis endpoint 1⟩/Center: *(select an axis endpoint)*
Axis endpoint 2: *(select the other endpoint of the axis)*

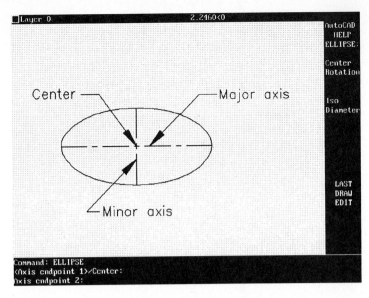

Fig. 7-21. Parts of an ellipse.

The Axis endpoints option establishes either the major or minor axis. The next prompt determines which axis is entered first, as shown in Fig. 7-22.

⟨Other axis distance⟩/Rotation: *(select a distance from the midpoint of the first axis to the end of the second axis and press ENTER)*

The ellipse is dragged by the cursor until the point is picked.

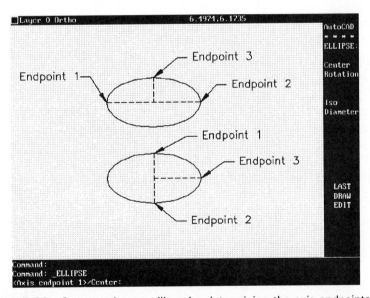

Fig. 7-22. Constructing an ellipse by determining the axis endpoints.

If you respond to the "⟨Other axis distance⟩/Rotation:" prompt with "R" for Rotation, AutoCAD assumes you have selected the major axis with the first two points. The next prompt requests the angle that the ellipse is rotated from the line of sight. The command sequence is as follows:

Command: **ELLIPSE** ⏎
⟨Axis endpoint 1⟩/Center: *(select an axis endpoint)*
Axis endpoint 2: *(select the other endpoint of the axis)*
⟨Other axis distance⟩/Rotation: **R** ⏎
Rotation around major axis: *(type a rotation angle, such as **30** and press ENTER)*

The response "30" draws an ellipse that is 30° from the line of sight. A "0" response draws a circle with both major and minor axes equal to the circle's diameter. Any angle greater than 89.4° is rejected by AutoCAD because the ellipse appears as a line. Fig. 7-23 shows the relationship between several ellipses having the same major axis length but different rotation angles.

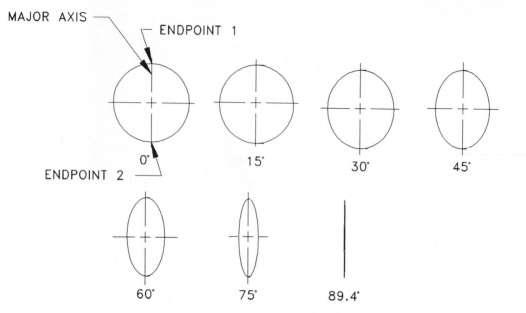

Fig. 7-23. Ellipse rotation angles.

An ellipse may also be constructed by specifying the center point and endpoints of the two axes, Fig. 7-24. Use the following command sequence:

Command: **ELLIPSE** ↵
⟨Axis endpoint 1⟩/Center: **C** ↵
Center of ellipse: *(select the ellipse center point)*
Axis endpoint: *(select the endpoint of one axis)*
⟨Other axis distance⟩/Rotation: *(select the endpoint of the other axis)*

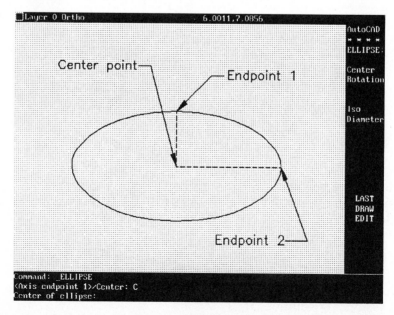

Fig. 7-24. Drawing an ellipse by picking the center and endpoints of two axes.

The rotation option may be used instead of selecting the second axis endpoint. See Fig. 7-25. The command sequence is as follows:

Command: **ELLIPSE** ↵
⟨Axis endpoint 1⟩/Center: **C** ↵
Center of ellipse: *(select the ellipse center point)*
Axis endpoint: *(select the endpoint of one axis)*
⟨Other axis distance⟩/Rotation: **R** ↵
Rotation around major axis: **30** ↵

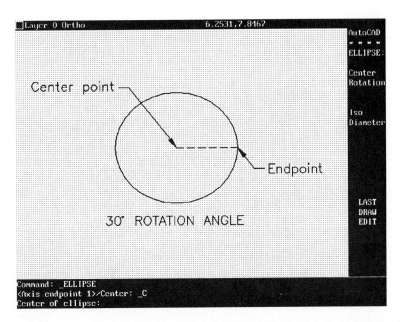

Fig. 7-25. Drawing an ellipse using the center option and the rotation angle.

EXERCISE 7-5

☐ Load AutoCAD and open PRODR1, or start a new drawing and set up your own variables.
☐ Use the ELLIPSE command's Axis endpoints option to draw the ellipse shown in Fig. 7-22.
☐ Use the ELLIPSE command's center and axis endpoints option to draw the ellipse shown in Fig. 7-24.
☐ Use the ELLIPSE command's center and rotation angle option to draw the ellipses shown in Fig. 7-25.
☐ Save the drawing as A:EX7-5 and quit.

DRAWING REGULAR POLYGONS

ARM 5

A *regular polygon* is any closed plane geometric figure with three or more equal sides and equal angles. A hexagon, for example, is a six-sided regular polygon. After drawing regular polygons using manual drafting techniques, you will be impressed with AutoCAD's POLYGON command. The command is used to draw any regular polygon with 3 to 1024 sides. A large number of sides is usually impractical; too many sides make the polygon look like a circle.

The POLYGON command is located in the DRAW screen menu and the Draw pull-down menu, and can also be accessed at the Command: prompt. It prompts for the number of sides. If you want an octagon (polygon with eight sides), enter "8" as follows:

Command: **POLYGON** ↵
Number of sides ⟨current⟩: **8** ↵

The number of sides you enter becomes the default for the next time you use the POLYGON command. Next, AutoCAD prompts for the edge or center of the polygon. If you reply by picking a point on the screen, this point becomes the center of the polygon. You are then asked if you want to have the polygon inscribed within or circumscribed outside an imaginary circle, Fig. 7-26. A polygon is *inscribed* when it is drawn inside a circle and its corners touch the circle. *Circumscribed* polygons are drawn outside of a circle where the sides of the polygon are tangent to the circle. You must specify the radius of the circle. The command continues as follows:

> Edge/⟨Center of polygon⟩: *(pick center of polygon)*
> Inscribed in circle/Circumscribed about circle (I/C): *(respond with* **I** *or* **C** *and press ENTER)*
> Radius of circle: *(type the radius, such as* **2** *and press ENTER, or pick a point on the screen at the desired distance from the center)*

The I or C option you select becomes the default for the next polygon.

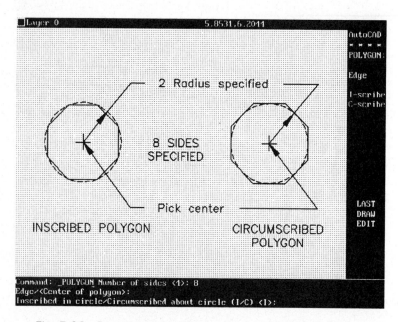

Fig. 7-26. Drawing an inscribed or a circumscribed polygon.

The "Edge/⟨Center of polygon⟩:" prompt allows you to pick the center or specify the edge. Notice that "Center of polygon" is the default. If you want to draw the polygon on an existing edge, specify the Edge option and pick edge endpoints as follows:

> Command: **POLYGON** ↵
> Number of sides: **8** ↵
> Edge/⟨Center of polygon⟩: **E** ↵
> First endpoint of edge: *(pick a point)*
> Second endpoint of edge: *(pick second point)*

After you pick the endpoints of one side, the rest of the polygon sides are drawn counterclockwise, Fig. 7-27.

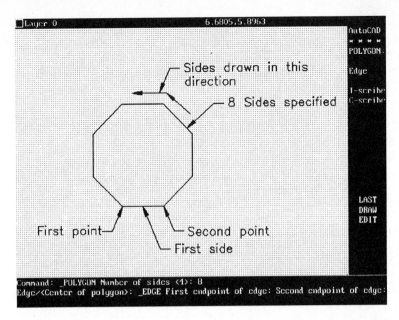

Fig. 7-27. Drawing a polygon by giving the number of sides and the length of the first side.

Ellipses and polygons are polylines, and may easily be edited using the PEDIT (Polyline EDIT) command. For example, a polygon may be given width using the Width option of the PEDIT command discussed in Chapter 16.

Hexagons (six-sided polygons) are commonly drawn as bolt heads and nuts on mechanical drawings. Keep in mind that these features are normally dimensioned across the flats. To draw a hexagon, or any polygon, dimensioned across the flats, circumscribe it. The radius you enter is equal to one-half the distance across the flats. The distance across the corners (inscribed polygon) is specified when the polygon must be confined within a circular area. One example is the boundary of a swimming pool in architectural drafting. Notice the distance across the flats and the distance across the corners in Fig. 7-28.

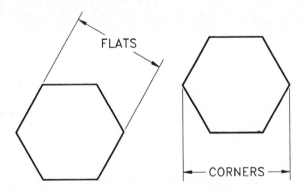

Fig. 7-28. Specifying the distance across the flats and between corners of a polygon.

Setting the Polygon SIDES default

AutoCAD allows you to set the number of polygon sides default using the POLYSIDES system variable. Set POLYSIDES like this:

Command: **POLYSIDES** ↵
New value for POLYSIDES: ⟨4⟩: **6** ↵
Command:

The value you specify for the default is used until you change the value again.

Using the pull-down menu to draw polygons

When you select Polygon from the Draw pull-down menu, the cascading submenu shown in Fig. 7-29 is displayed. Picking one of the items from the submenu automatically issues that option without needing to type at the Command: prompt. For example, if you pick Circumscribed, the C option is automatically issued:

Command: __polygon
Number of sides ⟨4⟩: **6** ⏎
Edge/⟨Center of polygon⟩: *(pick the polygon center)*
Inscribed in circle/Circumscribed about circle (I/C) ⟨I⟩: __circumscribed
Radius of circle: *(pick, or specify a radius and press ENTER)*
Command:

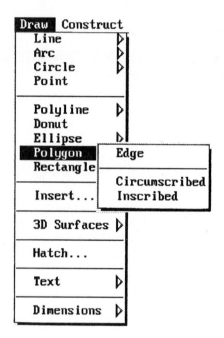

Fig. 7-29. The Polygon cascading menu.

PROFESSIONAL TIP

The MULTIPLE command modifier, introduced in Chapter 6, automatically repeats commands issued at the keyboard. It may be used to draw repetitive circles, arcs, ellipses, or polygons. For example, if you plan to draw multiple circles, do the following:

Command: **MULTIPLE CIRCLE** ⏎
3P/2P/TTR/⟨Center point⟩: *(pick the center point)*
Diameter/⟨Radius⟩: *(pick, or type the radius and press ENTER)*
CIRCLE 3P/2P/TTR/⟨Center point⟩: *(pick the center point)*
Diameter/⟨Radius⟩: *(pick, or type the radius and press ENTER)*
CIRCLE 3P/2P/TTR/⟨Center point⟩: *(continue drawing additional circles or cancel to get back to the Command: prompt)*

AutoCAD automatically re-issues the CIRCLE command. Enter CTRL C to cancel the repeating action.

DRAWING RECTANGLES

AutoCAD's RECTANGLE command allows you to easily draw rectangles; simply pick one corner, and then the opposite corner. See Fig. 7-30. RECTANGLE can be accessed from the Draw pull-down menu, or by typing "RECTANG" at the Command: prompt as follows:

Command: **RECTANG** ↵
First corner: *(pick first corner)*
Other corner: *(pick the opposite corner)*
Command:

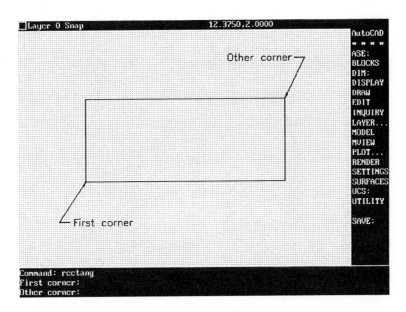

Fig. 7-30. Using the RECTANGLE command.

After the rectangle has been placed in the drawing, it is treated as one entity until it is exploded. Then the individual sides can be edited as desired. (The EXPLODE command is discussed in Chapter 16.)

EXERCISE 7-6

☐ Load AutoCAD and open PRODR1, or start a new drawing and set up your own variables.
☐ Draw a hexagon with a distance of three units across the flats. Then draw another hexagon measuring three units across the corners.
☐ Draw an octagon with a horizontal edge that is 1.75 units long.
☐ Draw a pentagon circumscribed about a circle having a 2.25 inch diameter.
☐ Draw a rectangle measuring 3 x 5 units.
☐ Save the drawing as A:EX7-6 and quit.

DRAWING DOUGHNUTS AND SOLID CIRCLES   ARM 5

AutoCAD's doughnuts are actually circular polylines. Drawing polylines was introduced in Chapter 6 and is covered in detail in Chapter 16. The DONUT command allows you to draw a thick circle. It can have any inside and outside diameter or be completely filled in, Fig. 7-31. When the FILL mode is turned off, doughnuts appear as segmented circles or concentric circles

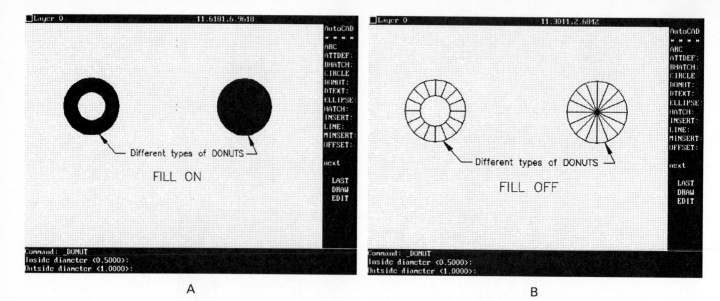

Fig. 7-31. Doughnuts having different inside and outside diameters. A—FILL mode on. B—FILL mode off.

as shown on the right in Fig. 7-31. FILL may be used transparently by entering 'FILL while inside the command. Then, simply enter ON or OFF as needed. The fill in previously drawn donuts remains on until the drawing is regenerated. The command may be issued as DOUGHNUT, or DONUT to save time:

Command: **DONUT** ↵
Inside diameter ⟨current⟩: *(specify a new inside diameter and press ENTER, or press ENTER to accept the current value)*
Outside diameter ⟨current⟩: *(specify a new outside diameter and press ENTER, or press ENTER to accept the current value)*

The previously set inside diameter is shown in brackets. A new inside diameter may be entered at this time, or press the ENTER key to keep the existing value. A "0" response to the "Inside diameter" prompt gives you a solid circle, Fig. 7-32. The next request is for a new outside diameter. Press ENTER to keep the current value. AutoCAD then asks:

Center of doughnut: *(select the doughnut center point)*

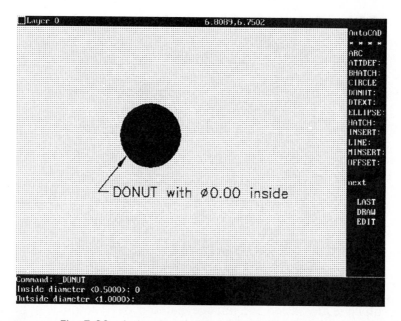

Fig. 7-32. A doughnut with a "0" inside diameter.

When a center point is picked, the doughnut is drawn with its center at that point. Next, a new "Center of doughnut" prompt is issued. You may pick another center point to draw the same size doughnut in a new location. Press ENTER if you wish to get back to the Command: prompt. The DONUT command remains active until you press ENTER or CTRL C to end it.

If you want to draw a doughnut with a .5 inside diameter and a 1.25 outside diameter, respond as follows:

> Command: **DONUT** ↵
> Inside diameter ⟨current⟩: **.5** ↵
> Outside diameter ⟨current⟩: **1.25** ↵
> Center of doughnut: *(select the donut center point)*
> Center of doughnut: *(select a center point or ENTER)*

This doughnut is shown in Fig. 7-33.

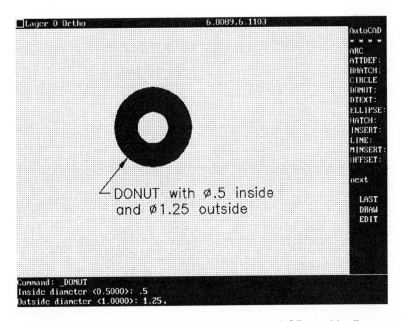

Fig. 7-33. Doughnut with .5 inside diameter and 1.25 outside diameter.

Presetting the DONUT options

AutoCAD allows you to preset the donut options so the inside and outside diameters have defaults. This saves time when you plan to draw only doughnuts with a given inside and outside diameter. To set DONUTS to automatically issue a default inside and outside diameter, use the DONUTID and DONUTOD system variables to set the inside and outside diameters respectively. The DONUTID variable can be 0 or any other value. The DONUTOD variable must be a nonzero value. If DONUTID is larger than DONUTOD, the two values are interchanged by the next command. The command sequences for DONUTID and DONUTOD variables is as follows:

> Command: **DONUTID** ↵
> New value for DONUTID ⟨⟩: **.25** ↵
> Command: **DONUTOD** ↵
> New value for DONUTOD ⟨⟩: **.75** ↵
> Command:

Now, when you type or pick the DONUT command from the screen menu or Draw pull-down menu the previously set values are the defaults.

EXERCISE 7-7

☐ Load AutoCAD and open PRODR1, or start a new drawing and set up your own variables.
☐ Draw a doughnut with a .5 inside diameter and a 1.5 outside diameter.
☐ Draw a doughnut with a 0 inside diameter and a 1.5 outside diameter.
☐ Turn the FILL mode off and type "REGEN" to see what happens to the doughnuts.
☐ Set DONUTID to .25 and DONUTOD to .75.
☐ Type "DONUT" at the Command: prompt and draw a donut using the defaults.
☐ Use a transparent FILL command ('FILL) to turn FILL on while in the DONUT command. Now, draw two more donuts.
☐ Select Donut from the Draw pull-down menu and draw three more donuts. Notice the inside and outside presets you set earlier are automatically used.
☐ Save the drawing as A:EX7-7 and quit.

CHAPTER TEST

Write your answers in the spaces provided.

1. Give the command, entries, and actions required to draw a circle with a 2.5 unit diameter:

   Command: _____

   3P/2P/TTR/⟨Center point⟩: _____

   Diameter/⟨Radius⟩: _____

   Diameter: _____

2. Give the command, entries, and actions to draw a 1.75 unit radius circle tangent to an existing line and circle:

   Command: _____

   3P/2P/TTR/⟨Center point⟩: _____

   Enter Tangent spec: _____

   Enter second Tangent spec: _____

   Radius: _____

3. Give the command, entries, and actions needed to draw a three-point arc:

   Command: _____

   Center/⟨Start point⟩: _____

   Center/End/⟨Second point⟩: _____

   End point: _____

4. Give the command, entries, and actions needed to draw an arc, beginning with the center point and having a 60° included angle:

   Command: _____

   Center/⟨Start point⟩: _____

   Center: _____

   Start point: _____

   Angle/Length of chord/⟨End point⟩: _____

   Included angle: DRAG _____

5. Give the command, entries, and actions required to draw an arc tangent to the endpoint of a previously drawn line:

    Command: _____

    Center/〈Start point〉: _____

    End point: _____

6. Give the command, entries, and actions needed to draw an ellipse with the Axis endpoint option:

    Command: _____

    〈Axis endpoint 1〉/Center: _____

    Axis endpoint 2: _____

    〈Other axis distance〉/Rotation: _____

7. Give the command, entries, and actions necessary to draw a hexagon measuring 4 inches (101.6 mm) across the flats:

    Command: _____

    Number of sides: _____

    Edge/〈Center of polygon〉: _____

    Inscribed in circle/Circumscribed about circle (I/C): _____

    Radius of circle: _____

8. Give the responses required to draw two doughnuts with a .25 inside diameter and a .75 outside diameter:

    Command: _____

    Inside diameter 〈current〉: _____

    Outside diameter 〈current〉: _____

    Center of doughnut: _____

    Center of doughnut: _____

    Center of doughnut: _____

9. Describe why the "@" symbol may be used by itself for point selection. _____

    _____

10. Define the term "included angle." _____

    _____

11. List the three input options that may be used to draw an arc tangent to the endpoint of a previously drawn arc. _____

12. Given the distance across the flats of a hexagon, would you use the I or C option to draw the hexagon? _____

    _____

13. Describe how a solid circle may be drawn. _____

    _____

14. To use the MULTIPLE command modifier to draw a series of arcs, what command will you type? _____

15. Explain how you would turn the FILL mode off while inside the DONUT command.

_____

_____

16. Name the system variable used to set the radius default value when drawing circles.

_____

17. Name the system variables used to preset the inside and outside doughnut diameters.

_____

DRAWING PROBLEMS

Load AutoCAD for each of the following problems and use the prototype PRODR1, or start a new drawing with your own variables.

1. You have just been given the sketch of a new sports car design (shown below). You are asked to create a drawing from the sketch. Use the LINE command and selected shape commands to draw the car. Do not be concerned with size and scale. Consider the commands and techniques used to draw the car, and try to minimize the number used. Save your drawing as A:P7-1 and quit.

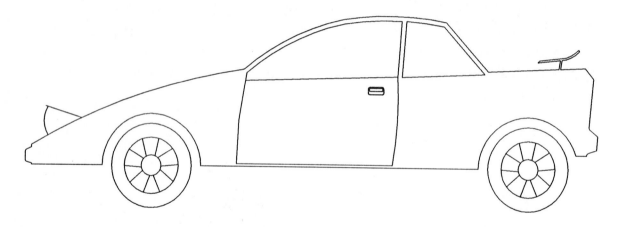

2. You have just been given the sketch of an innovative new truck design (shown below). You are asked to create a drawing from the sketch. Use the LINE and selected shape commands to draw the truck resembling the sketch. Do not be concerned with size and scale. Save your drawing as A:P7-2.

3. Use the LINE command and CIRCLE command options to draw the objects below. Do not include dimensions. Save the drawing as A:P7-3.

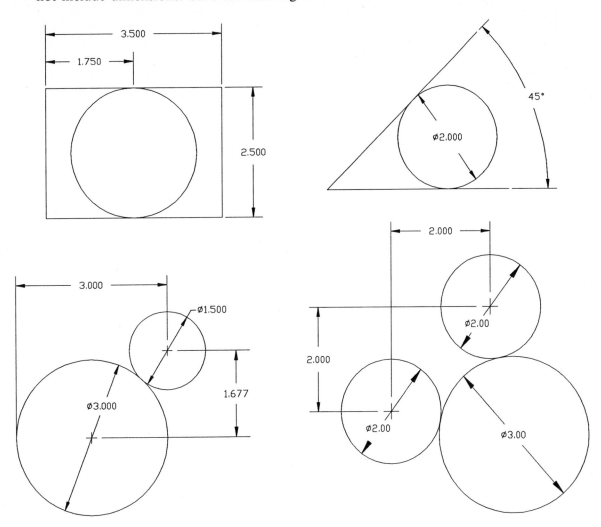

4. Use CIRCLE and ARC command options to draw the object below. Do not include dimensions. Save the drawing as A:P7-4.

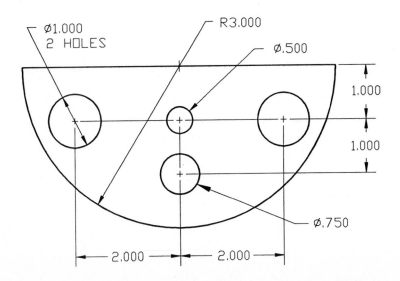

5. Select the ELLIPSE command to draw four ellipses using the following options. Then, save the drawing as A:P7-5.
    Ellipse 1: Axis endpoint 1/axis endpoint 2/other axis distance.
    Ellipse 2: Center/axis endpoint/other axis distance.
    Ellipse 3: Center/axis endpoint/rotation (use cursor and read coordinate angle display).
    Ellipse 4: Center/axis endpoint/rotation (type angle value).
6. Draw the hex head bolt pattern shown below. Do not draw dimensions. Save the drawing as A:P7-6.

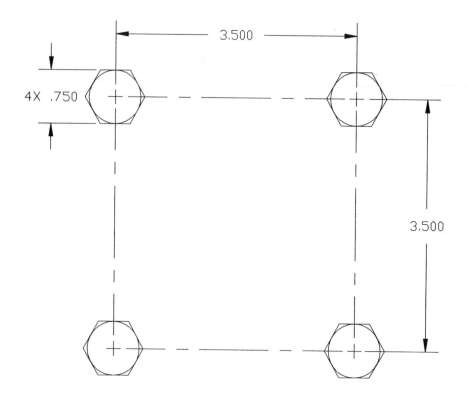

7. Use the POLYGON command to draw the three polygons shown below. Save the drawing as A:P7-7.

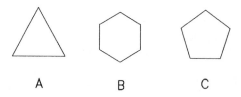

A   B   C

8. Use the DONUT command to draw the objects shown below using the following values. Save the drawing as A:P7-8.

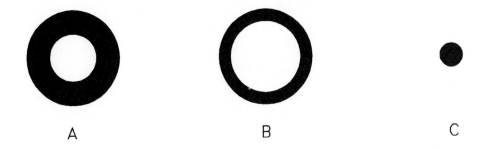

	Inner Diameter	Outer Diameter
A	.5	1.0
B	1.0	1.2
C	0	.2

A   B   C

9. Use the MULTIPLE command modifier to draw four hexagons similar to the one shown in Problem 7, Example B. Save the drawing as A:P7-9.
10. Preset the doughnut inside diameter to .25 and the outside diameter to 1.25. Turn FILL on. Use the pull-down menu selection to draw four doughnuts with these settings. Place the doughnuts 1.5 units apart in a straight horizontal line.

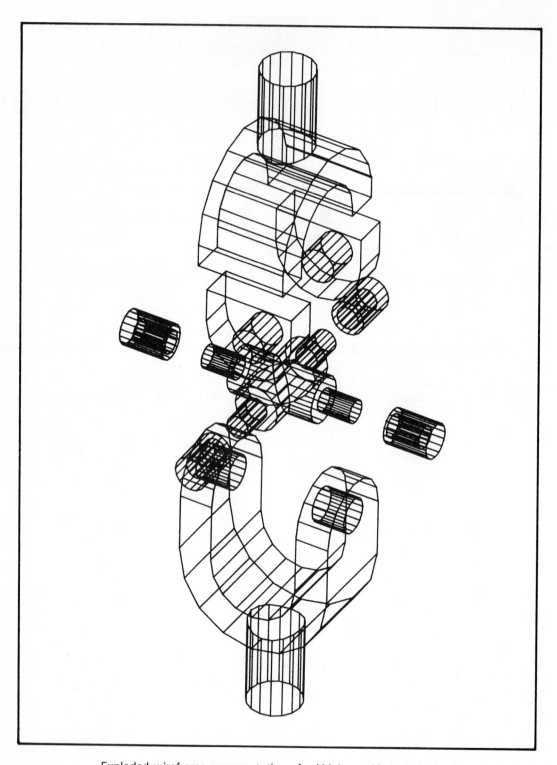

Exploded wireframe representation of a U-joint.   (Autodesk, Inc.)

```
┌─Assist──────────┐  ┌─Construct──────┐
│ Help!           │  │ Array          │
│ Cancel          │  │ Array 3D       │
│─────────────────│  │ Copy           │
│ Undo            │  │ Mirror         │
│ Redo            │  │ Mirror 3D      │
│─────────────────│  │────────────────│
│ Object Filters..│  │ Chamfer        │
│ Object Snap   ▷ │  │ Fillet         │
│─────────────────│  │────────────────│
│ Inquiry       ▷ │  │ Divide         │
│─────────────────│  │ Measure        │
│ Calculator      │  │ Offset         │
└─────────────────┘  │────────────────│
                     │ Block          │
                     └────────────────┘
```

GEOMETRIC CONSTRUCTIONS AND OBJECT SNAP

Learning objectives

After completing this chapter, you will be able to:

☐ Select the OSNAP command to set running object snaps.
☐ Use the OSNAP override.
☐ Identify three ways to discontinue a running OSNAP.
☐ List four ways to access the object snap modes.
☐ Describe the QUICK mode.
☐ Use the object snap interrupt and running modes to make several geometric constructions.
☐ Adjust the aperture size.
☐ Use the OFFSET command to draw parallel lines and curves.
☐ Divide existing objects into equal parts using the DIVIDE command.
☐ Use the MEASURE command to set designated increments on an existing object.
☐ Set point sizes and options to draw points.
☐ Use the geometry calculator to draw and edit geometric constructions.

This chapter explains how the powerful OSNAP command and its snap modes are used to perform geometric constructions. OSNAP is the command name for object snap. Object snap allows you to precisely place points on existing objects. This chapter also explains how to draw parallel lines, divide objects, and place point symbols.

SNAPPING TO SPECIFIC OBJECTS OR FEATURES   [ARM 9]

Object snap is one of the most useful tools found in AutoCAD. It increases your drafting ability, performance, and productivity. The term *object snap* refers to the cursor's ability to "snap" exactly to a specific point or place on an object. The advantage of object snap is that you do not have to pick an exact point. For example, suppose you want to place a point on the end of a line. Normally you would try to pick the endpoint, but probably miss. Using object snap, all you do is pick somewhere near the end of the line. AutoCAD automatically snaps to the exact end. There are numerous object snap modes to help simplify drawing and design.

When a point is to be picked using object snap, the screen cursor takes the shape of a box and crosshairs. This cursor box, called an *aperture,* is then used to pick the desired object. For example, suppose you want to connect a line to the end of another line. Move the aperture near the end of the line and pick. You do not have to place the aperture exactly at the endpoint. If you are drawing a line to the point of tangency on a circle, pick the "tangent" option. Then pick a point on the circle near the estimated point of tangency. See Fig. 8-1.

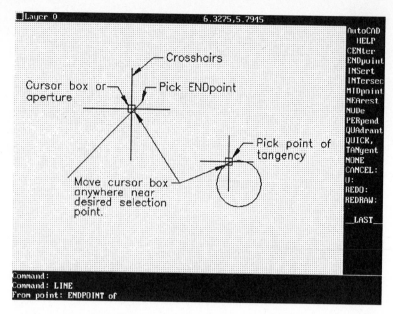

Fig. 8-1. The object snap cursor box, or aperture.

THE OBJECT SNAP MODES

ARM 9

The object snap modes determine what the aperture snaps to. Object snap modes may be typed at the prompt line or displayed by picking "* * * *" from the top of the screen menu. The OSNAP screen menu is shown in Fig. 8-1. Button number 2 of a multibutton puck or holding down the Shift key while pressing the ENTER button on puck or mouse also activates the object snap options in a cursor menu.

Object snap modes defined

Each object snap mode has a specific application. When typed at the prompt line, only the first three letters are required. The object snaps are defined as follows:

CENter	Locates the center of a circle or arc.
ENDpoint	Finds the endpoint of a line or arc.
INSert	Snaps to the insertion point on a block. See Chapter 21.
INTersection	Picks the closest intersection of two features.
MIDpoint	Locates the midpoint of a line or arc.
NEArest	Locates the point of an object nearest to the crosshairs.
NODe	Snaps to a point drawn with the POINT command.
PERpendicular	Creates a perpendicular line to one feature.
QUAdrant	Picks one of four quadrants on a circle closest to the crosshairs.
QUICK	Allows object snap to find the quickest selection for the specified OSNAP mode that is selected immediately after QUICK.
TANgent	Forms a line tangent to a picked circle or arc.
NONE	Turns running object snap off.

Using the object snap modes

Practice with the different object snap options to find which works best in various situations. Object snap may be invoked during many commands, such as LINE, CIRCLE, ARC, MOVE, COPY, and INSERT. The most common object snap uses will be discussed in detail.

Find the endpoint

Often, you need to connect a line, arc, or center point of a circle to the endpoint of an existing line or arc. Select the ENDpoint and move the aperture past the midpoint of the line or arc toward the end to be picked. To connect a line to the endpoint of existing line A in Fig. 8-2, the following command sequence is used:

Command: **LINE** ↵
From point: *(pick a point)*
To point: **END** ↵
of *(move the aperture near the end of line A and pick)*
To point: ↵
Command:

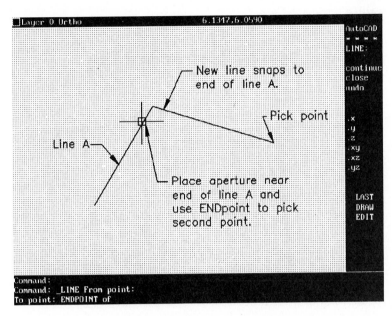

Fig. 8-2. Object snap to the endpoint of a line.

Another application is to snap an arc or line to the endpoint of an existing arc. To connect a new arc to the endpoint of existing arc A in Fig. 8-3, use the following command sequence:

Command: **ARC** ↵
Center/⟨Start point⟩: *(pick a point)*
Center/End/⟨Second point⟩: *(pick the second point)*
End point: **END** ↵
of *(move the aperture to somewhere near the end of arc A and pick)*

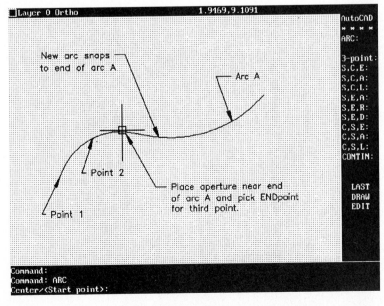

Fig. 8-3. Object snap to the endpoint of an arc.

Find the midpoint

The MIDpoint object snap mode finds and picks the midpoint of a line or arc. For example, to connect a line from any point to the midpoint of line A, shown in Fig. 8-4, use the following command sequence:

    Command: **LINE** ↵
    From point: *(pick a point)*
    To point: **MID** ↵
    of *(move aperture to anywhere on line A and pick)*

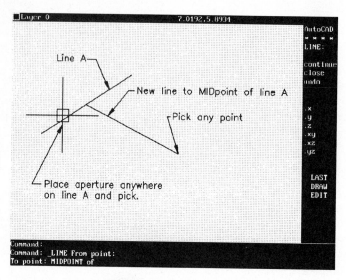

Fig. 8-4. Using object snap to locate the midpoint of a line.

EXERCISE 8-1

☐ Load AutoCAD and open PRODR1, or start a new drawing and set up your own variables.
☐ Use the ENDpoint or MIDpoint snap options to draw the object shown below. Draw line 1, then line 2 connecting to the endpoint of line 1. Draw line 3 from the endpoint of line 2 to the midpoint of line 1. Draw arc A with one end connected to the endpoint of line 1.

☐ Save the drawing as A:EX8-1 and quit.

Find the center of a circle or arc

The CENter option allows you to snap to the center point of a circle or arc. The following command sequence, as shown in Fig. 8-5, draws a line from the center of circle A to the center of circle B.

> Command: **LINE** ↵
> From point: **CEN** ↵
> of *(move aperture to anywhere on circle A and pick)*
> To point: **CEN** ↵
> of *(move aperture to anywhere on circle B and pick)*

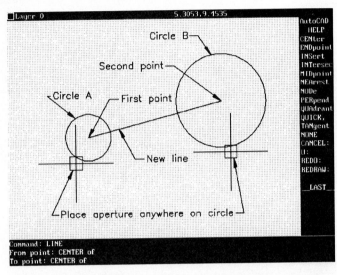

Fig. 8-5. Using object snap to find the center of a circle.

Find the quadrant of a circle or arc

A *quadrant* is a quarter section of a circle or arc. The object snap QUAdrant option finds the 0, 90, 180, and 270 degree positions on a circle or arc, Fig. 8-6.

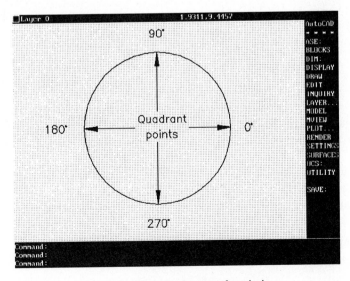

Fig. 8-6. The quadrants of a circle.

When picking quadrants, locate the aperture on the circle closest to the intended quadrant. For example, circle B in Fig. 8-7 may be drawn with its center located at one of the quadrants of circle A. The command sequence using the QUAdrant option is as follows:

Command: **CIRCLE** ↵
3P/2P/TTR/⟨Center point⟩: **QUA** ↵
of *(move the aperture to anywhere near the desired quadrant on circle A and pick)*
Diameter/⟨Radius⟩: *(pick a radius)*

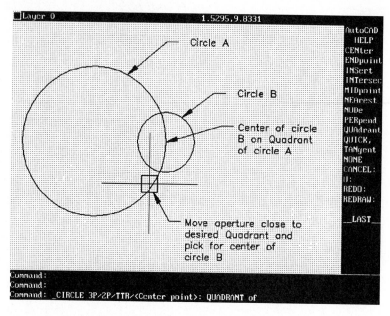

Fig. 8-7. Using object snap to locate the quadrant of a circle.

EXERCISE 8-2

☐ Load AutoCAD and open PRODR1, or start a new drawing and set up your own variables.
☐ Use the object snap center or quadrant options for the following situations:
  ☐ Draw two separate circles and refer to the one on the left as circle A and the other as circle B.
  ☐ Draw a line from the center of circle A to the 180° quadrant of circle B.
  ☐ Draw a line from the center of circle B to the 270° quadrant of circle B to the 270° of circle A, and finally to the center of circle A.
☐ Save the drawing as A:EX8-2 and quit.

Finding the intersection of lines

If it is necessary to snap to the intersection of two entities, use the INTersect option. Given line A intersecting arc A in Fig. 8-8, the method to draw another line to the point of intersection is as follows:

Command: **LINE** ↵
From point: *(pick a point)*
To point: **INT** ↵
of *(move the cursor so the intersection is somewhere inside the aperture and pick)*

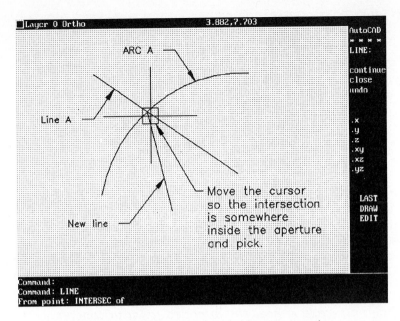

Fig. 8-8. Using the object snap intersect mode.

Drawing a perpendicular line

A typical geometric construction is to draw one line perpendicular to another. This is easily done using the object snap PERpendicular mode. For example, note line A and circle A in Fig. 8-9. A line perpendicular to line A from the center point of circle A is drawn as follows:

Command: **LINE** ↲
From point: **CEN** ↲
of *(move the aperture to any location on the circumference of the circle and pick)*
To point: **PER** ↲
to *(move the aperture to any place on line A and pick)*

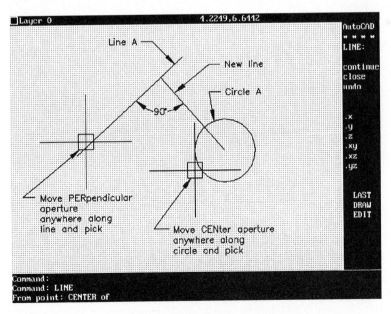

Fig. 8-9. Using the object snap perpendicular option.

EXERCISE 8-3

☐ Load AutoCAD and open PRODR1, or start a new drawing and set up your own variables.
☐ Draw a horizontal line, then draw a circle above the line. Add a new line from the circle's center, perpendicular to the first line.
☐ Draw two intersecting lines and a separate circle. Add a line from the circle's center to the intersection of the lines.
☐ Save the drawing as A:EX8-3.

Drawing a line tangent to a circle or arc

A common geometric construction is a line tangent to a circle or arc. In Chapter 6 you were shown how to draw circles tangent to lines, circles, and arcs. Now, you will use the object snap TANgent option to draw lines tangent to an existing circle or arc. Given two circles as shown in Fig. 8-10, two lines are drawn tangent to the circles. The command sequence is:

Command: **LINE** ↵
From point: **TAN** ↵
to *(pick a point on circle A near the intended point of tangency)*
To point: **TAN** ↵
to *(pick a point on circle B near the intended point of tangency)*
To point: ↵
Command: ↵
LINE From point: **TAN** ↵
to *(pick a point on circle A near the intended point of tangency)*
To point: **TAN** ↵
to *(pick a point on circle B near the intended point of tangency)*
To point: ↵
Command:

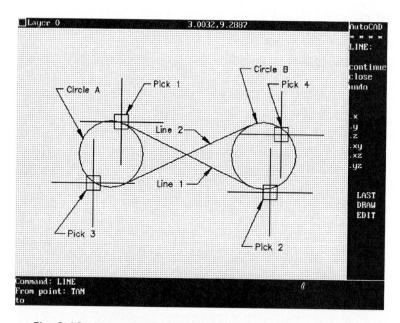

Fig. 8-10. Using object snap to draw lines tangent to circles.

EXERCISE 8-4

☐ Load AutoCAD and open PRODR1, or start a new drawing and set up your own variables.
☐ Use the object snap TANgent option to draw two circles with tangent lines similar to those shown in Fig. 8-10.
☐ Draw two lines that do not cross tangent to the same circles.
☐ Save the drawing as A:EX8-4 and quit.

Using fast object snaps

When AutoCAD draws using object snap modes, it searches for the best solution to your request. In a simple drawing, this process happens very fast. However, as your drawing becomes complex, it may take some time for the snap object to be found. You can speed up the process by selecting the object snap QUICK mode. Enter QUI, followed by a comma, and then the desired object snap option. (The QUICK mode is not effective on the object snap INTersection option.) The QUICK mode directs AutoCAD to look only for the first solution to your request, and then end the search. The only problem you may find is that the first AutoCAD selection may not be the best choice. However, in most cases the QUICK mode works to your advantage and helps increase productivity. The following command sequence shows the QUICK mode used on the example illustrated in Fig. 8-10.

Command: **LINE** ↵
From point: **QUI,TAN** ↵
to *(pick a point on circle A near the intended point of tangency)*
To point: **QUI,TAN** ↵
to *(pick a point on circle B near the intended point of tangency)*
To point: ↵
Command: ↵
LINE From point: **QUI,TAN** to *(pick a point on circle A near the intended point of tangency)*
To point: **QUI,TAN** to *(pick a point on circle B near the intended point of tangency)*

Using the cursor menu for object snaps

Button number 2 of a multibutton puck, or holding down the Shift key and pressing the ENTER button on a puck or mouse activates the object snap options in a cursor menu, which is displayed at the screen crosshairs. This feature is convenient and saves drafting time. When you need to use an object snap, simply press button 2 on the puck and the cursor menu shown in Fig. 8-11 is displayed on screen. Move the cursor arrow to the desired object snap and pick. The cursor menu disappears and the aperture is ready for you to use as you had planned.

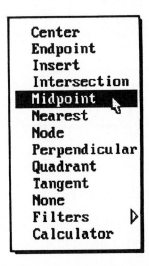

Fig. 8-11. The object snap cursor menu.

SETTING A RUNNING OBJECT SNAP

The previous discussion explained how to use object snap options by typing the first three letters, or selecting the desired mode from the screen, pull-down, or cursor menus. These are called the OSNAP *interrupt modes.* The interrupt mode works well in many situations. However, if you plan to use one object snap frequently, you can set a *running object snap.* AutoCAD automatically uses only the running object snap mode that you have selected. Set running object snaps by typing "OSNAP" at the Command: prompt or selecting it from the SETTINGS screen menu. You can also pick "Object Snap. . ." from the Settings pull-down menu to access the "Running Object Snap" dialogue box. When the command is selected, the next prompt asks: "Object snap modes." For example, if you want to set ENDpoint as the running OSNAP, type "END:"

> Command: **OSNAP** ↵
> Object snap modes: **END** ↵

If you plan to use several object snaps frequently, then set all by typing the first three letters of each, separated by commas. For example:

> Command: **OSNAP** ↵
> Object snap modes: **END,PER,TAN** ↵

Now the running object snap is set to perform endpoint, perpendicular, and tangency operations. All other object snaps are ignored unless picked from the screen menu or typed during a command.

Using the dialogue box to set running object snaps

You can also set running object snaps using the "Running Object Snap" dialogue box. Pick "Object Snap. . ." from the Settings pull-down menu or type "DDOSNAP" to access this dialogue box. Notice in Fig. 8-12 the Endpoint, Perpendicular, and Tangent running object snaps are active. You can use this dialogue box at any time to discontinue the running object snaps or to set other object snaps.

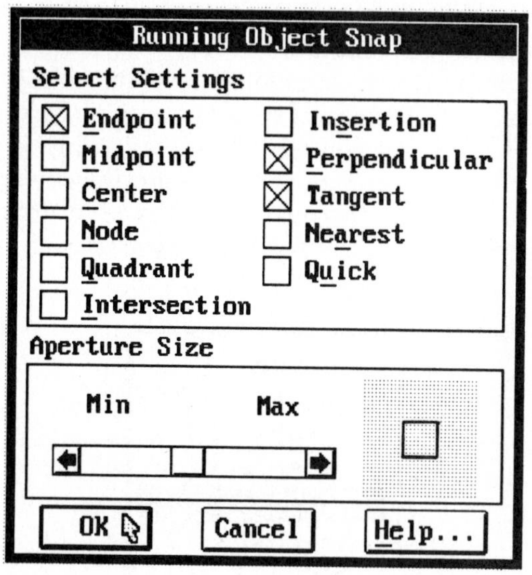

Fig. 8-12. Setting running object snap modes using the "Running Object Snap" dialogue box.

Overriding or getting out of the running OSNAP

You can temporarily override the running OSNAP by typing a different object snap request at the prompt. This is referred to as an *OSNAP override.* After the new object snap operation has been performed, the running snaps remain in effect.

The current running OSNAP may also be discontinued. Type "NONE," "OFF," or press the ENTER key as follows:

Command: **OSNAP** ↲
Object snap mode: **NONE, OFF,** or ↲

You may also remove the active checks in the "Running Object Snap" dialogue box.

── PROFESSIONAL TIP ──

Use the object snap modes not only when drawing, but also when editing. With practice, using object snaps becomes second nature. In time, your drawing productivity will increase.

CHANGING THE APERTURE SIZE

ARM 9

Earlier in this chapter, you were introduced to the aperture. It appears on the screen when you enter object snap modes or use the OSNAP command. The size of the aperture may be enlarged to provide a bigger pick area. It may also be reduced in size to provide more accurate picking of a complex detail. The size of the aperture is measured in *pixels,* short for picture elements. Pixels or picture elements are the dots that make up a display screen. The AutoCAD prototype drawing sets the aperture size at 6 pixels. If you want to change the size of the aperture, select the APERTURE command found in the SETTINGS screen menu, or type "APERTURE" at the Command: prompt. You are then asked to enter the desired aperture box size in pixels. This is limited to a number between 1 and 50 pixels. To change the aperture size to 5 pixels, do the following:

Command: **APERTURE** ↲
Object snap target height (1-50 pixels) ⟨current⟩: **5** ↲
Command:

Examples of different aperture box sizes measured in pixels are shown in Fig. 8-13.

Keep in mind that the "aperture" and the "pick box" are different. The aperture, as previously discussed, is displayed on the screen when object snap modes are used. The pick box appears on the screen for any command that activates the "Select objects:" prompt. For example, the ERASE command issues the "Select objects:" prompt.

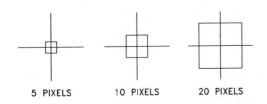

5 PIXELS   10 PIXELS   20 PIXELS

Fig. 8-13. Aperture box sizes measured in pixels.

Another easy way to change the aperture size is found in the "Running Object Snap" dialogue box. Look at Fig. 8-12 and notice the "Aperture Size" area. Move the scroll bar between "Min" and "Max" and watch the sample aperture in the image tile change size accordingly. Pick OK when the aperture is the size you want.

EXERCISE 8-6

☐ Load AutoCAD, insert your exercise floppy disk, and pick New... from the File pull-down menu. Enter A:EX8-5 in the Prototype: edit box followed by entering EX8-6 in the New Drawing Name: edit box. Pick the OK button to use EX8-5 as the prototype for EX8-6.
   ☐ Change the aperture size to 5 pixels. Draw lines to existing objects using the object snap modes of your choice.
   ☐ Change the aperture size to 20 pixels. Again draw lines to the existing objects using the object snap modes of your choice.
   ☐ Observe the difference in aperture size. Determine your personal preference between the 5 and 20 pixel sizes as compared to the AutoCAD prototype set at 10 pixels.
☐ Save the drawing as A:EX8-6 and quit.

DRAWING PARALLEL LINES AND CURVES | ARM 6 |

   If you want to draw parallel lines, or concentric circles, arcs, curves, or polylines, use the OFFSET command. OFFSET is located in the EDIT screen menu and the Construct pull-down menu. The command sequence is as follows:

     Command: **OFFSET** ↵
     Offset distance or Through 〈current〉:

In response to this prompt you may type a desired distance, or pick a point for the parallel entity to be drawn through. The last offset distance used is shown in brackets. If you want to draw two parallel circles a distance of .1 unit apart, Fig. 8-14, use the following command sequence:

     Command: **OFFSET** ↵
     Offset distance or Through 〈current〉: **.1** ↵
     Select object to offset: *(pick the object)*
     Side to offset? *(pick the side of the object for the offset to be drawn)*
     Select object to offset: *(select another object or press ENTER)*

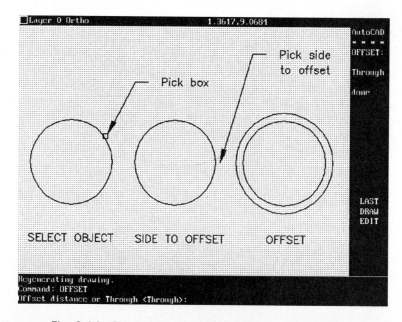

Fig. 8-14. Drawing an offset by a designated distance.

When the "Select object to offset" prompt first appears, the screen cursor turns into a pick box. After the object is picked, the screen cursor resumes the appearance of crosshairs. The Window, Crossing, and Fence options do not work with the OFFSET command.

The other option is to pick a point through which the offset is drawn. Type "T" as follows to produce the results shown in Fig. 8-15:

> Command: **OFFSET** ↵
> Offset distance or Through 〈current〉: **T** ↵
> Select object to offset: *(pick the object)*
> Through point: *(pick the point that the offset will be drawn through)*
> Select object to offset: ↵

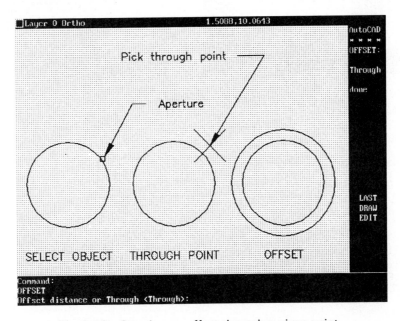

Fig. 8-15. Drawing an offset through a given point.

PROFESSIONAL TIP

Object snap modes may be used to assist in drawing an offset. For example, suppose you have a circle apart from a line, as shown in Fig. 8-16A. You want to draw another concentric circle tangent to the line as shown in Fig. 8-16B. Enter the following:

> Command: **OFFSET** ↵
> Offset distance or Through 〈current〉: **QUA** ↵
> of *(pick the existing circle)*
> Second point: **PER** ↵
> to *(pick existing line)*
> Select object to offset: *(pick existing circle)*
> Side to offset? *(pick between circle and line)*
> Select object to offset: ↵

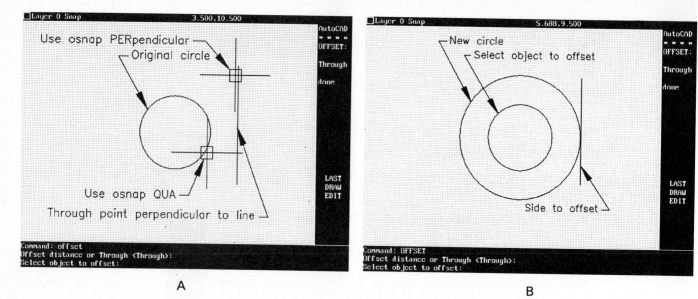

Fig. 8-16. Using object snap modes to draw an offset.

Setting the offset distance

The OFFSETDIST system variable lets you set an offset distance default. The next time you offset an entity, the preset default will appear. To enter a .2 unit offset for the default value, respond to the prompts as follows:

> Command: **OFFSETDIST** ↵
> New value for OFFSETDIST ⟨−1⟩: **.2** ↵
> Command:

A setting of −1 makes the Through option the default.

EXERCISE 8-7

☐ Load AutoCAD and open PRODR1, or start a new drawing and set up your own variables.
☐ Draw two circles and two polylines made up of line and arc segments.
☐ Use the OFFSET command to draw parallels a distance of .2 unit on the inside of one circle and one polyline.
☐ Use the OFFSET command again, this time specifying Through point on the outside of the other circle and polyline.
☐ Use the command sequence shown with Fig. 8-16 to draw a similar object.
☐ Save the drawing as A:EX8-7 and quit.

DIVIDING AN OBJECT INTO AN EQUAL NUMBER OF PARTS

| ARM 6 |

A line, circle, arc, or polyline may be divided into an equal number of segments using the DIVIDE command. The DIVIDE command is located in the EDIT screen menu and the Construct pull-down menu. Suppose you have drawn a line and want to divide it into eight equal parts. Enter the DIVIDE command and select the object to divide. Then enter the number of divisions or segments. The procedure is as follows:

> Command: **DIVIDE** ↵
> Select object to divide: *(pick the object)*
> ⟨Number of segments⟩/Block: *(enter the number of parts and press ENTER)*

After the number of segments is given, the object is divided with dots. However, the dots do not show very well. To see the divisions, the appearance of the points must be changed as shown in Fig. 8-17.

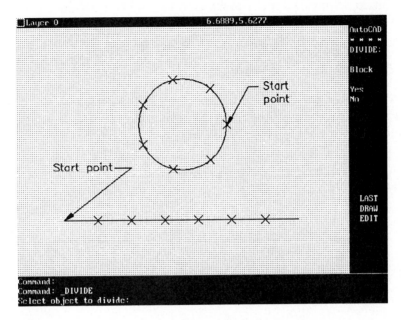

Fig. 8-17. Using the DIVIDE command.

The marks placed by the DIVIDE command are controlled by the PDMODE system variable. PDMODE is also an option of the POINT command found in the DRAW screen menu. The PDMODE can be used to establish a mark that shows on the screen. PDMODE values range from 0 to 4. The points drawn using each PDMODE value are shown in Fig. 8-18. The PDMODE default value is "0," which draws dots.

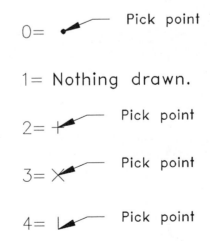

Fig. 8-18. PDMODE values and symbols.

As previously mentioned, a problem with dots when using the DIVIDE command is that they may not show up. Therefore, a different PDMODE value must be set. Use the following sequence to set one of the PDMODE values.

Command: **PDMODE** ↵
New value for PDMODE ⟨0⟩: **3** ↵

After setting a different PDMODE value, type "REGEN" at the Command: prompt. The DIVIDE points change to the current PDMODE and can be seen.

The Block option of the DIVIDE command allows you to place a block at each division point. A *block* is a previously drawn symbol or shape. To initiate the Block option, type "B" or "Block" at the prompt. You are then asked if the block is to be aligned with the object. Answer "YES" or "NO." Blocks are discussed in Chapter 21.

MEASURE AN OBJECT INTO SPECIFIED DISTANCES   ARM 6

Unlike the DIVIDE command in which a given entity is divided into a predetermined number of parts, the MEASURE command places marks a designated distance apart. The line shown in Fig. 8-19 is measured with .75 unit segments as follows:

Command: **MEASURE** ↵
Select object to measure: *(pick an object)*
⟨Segment length⟩/Block: **.75** ↵

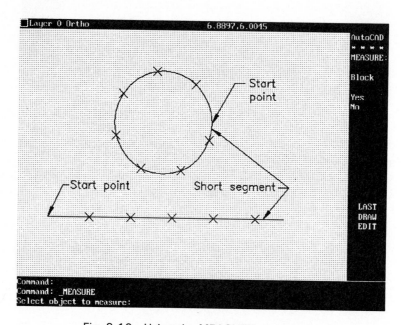

Fig. 8-19. Using the MEASURE command.

Measuring begins at the end closest to where the object is picked. All increments are equal to the entered segment length except the last segment. It may be shorter depending on the entity's length, Fig. 8-19. The PDMODE affects the marks placed on the object in the same manner that the DIVIDE command does. Blocks may be inserted at the given distances using the Block option of the MEASURE command.

EXERCISE 8-8

☐ Load AutoCAD and open PRODR1, or start a new drawing and set up your own variables.
☐ Set the PDMODE to 3 before marks are drawn in this exercise.
☐ Draw two circles of any diameter, and two lines of any length.
☐ Use the DIVIDE command to divide one circle into 10 equal parts and one line into 5 equal parts.
☐ Use the MEASURE command to divide the other circle into .5 unit parts and the other line into .75 unit parts.
☐ Draw two parallel vertical lines. Make each line 3 in. (76.2 mm) long and space them 4 in. (101.6 mm) apart. Use the DIVIDE command to divide the line on the left into 10 equal increments. Draw horizontal parallel lines from each division on the left line over to the right line. Use the OSNAP NODe and PERpendicular options to assist you.
☐ Save the drawing as A:EX8-8 and quit.

DRAWING POINTS

[ARM 5]

You can draw points anywhere on the screen using the POINT command. The POINT command is found in the DRAW screen menu and Draw pull-down menu, or can be typed at the Command: prompt. The specific type of point drawn is controlled by PDMODE discussed earlier. If you want to draw a dot (.), set the PDMODE to the default value of 0. Then proceed as follows:

Command: **POINT** ↵
Point: *(type point coordinates or pick with pointing device)*

Notice when you pick the point, it shows on the screen as a blip. The blip changes to a dot after using the REDRAW command, as shown in Fig. 8-20. If you want to change the point style to a +, x, or |, use the PDMODE command, or choose the POINT screen menu to set the PDMODE value as discussed earlier.

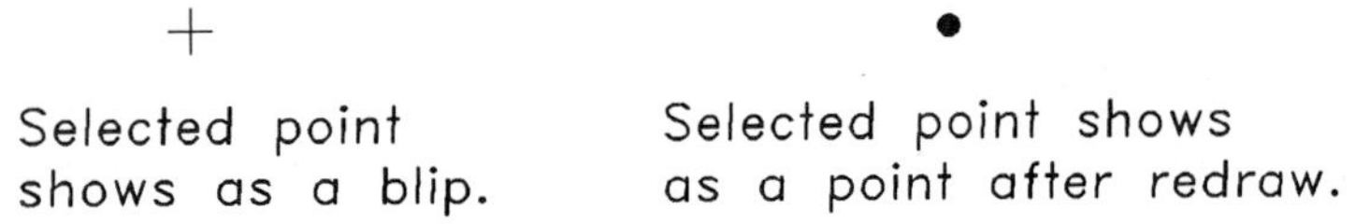

$+$ •

Selected point   Selected point shows
shows as a blip.   as a point after redraw.

Fig. 8-20. Using the POINT command.

Adding additional symbols to the point

So far you have changed the PDMODE to draw four different point types. You can draw either a circle, square, or circle and square around the selected PDMODE symbol. Do this by adding another value, Fig. 8-21. Draw a circle by adding 32 to the original PDMODE value. Add 64 to draw a square. Add 96 to draw a circle and square. For example, a point display of an X inside a circle has a PDMODE value of 35. That is the sum of the X value of 3 and the circle value of 32. If you want to draw a point with an X inside of a circle and square, enter the PDMODE value 99. Then use the POINT command as follows:

Command: **PDMODE** ↵
New value for PDMODE ⟨current⟩: **99** ↵
Command: **POINT** ↵
Point: *(pick the point)*
Command:

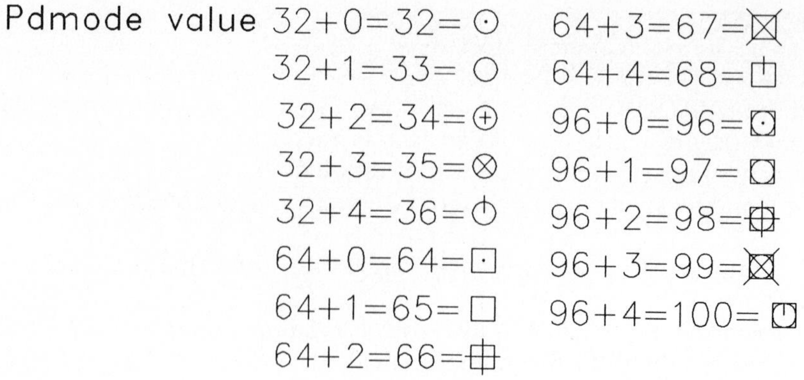

Pdmode value 32+0=32= ⊙   64+3=67=⊠
              32+1=33= ○   64+4=68=⌸
              32+2=34= ⊕   96+0=96= ⊡
              32+3=35= ⊗   96+1=97= ▢
              32+4=36= ☉   96+2=98= ⊞
              64+0=64= ⊡   96+3=99= ⊠
              64+1=65= □   96+4=100= ▢
              64+2=66= ⊕

Fig. 8-21. PDMODE values for expanded symbols.

When the PDMODE value is changed, all previously drawn points stay the same until the drawing is regenerated. After REGEN, all points take on the shape of the current value.

Changing the point size

The point size can be modified using the PDSIZE variable. You can also use the Pdsize option in the POINT submenu found in the DRAW screen menu. The default PDSIZE value of 0 displays points at the size shown in Figs. 8-18 and 8-21. If you want to draw a point with a PDSIZE of 1, use the following command sequence:

Command: **PDSIZE** ↵
New value for PDSIZE ⟨0.000⟩: **1** ↵
Command: **POINT** ↵
Point: *(pick the point)*
Command:

The point retains the set PDMODE value, but the size changes. Fig. 8-22 shows the point sizes of different PDSIZE values. Positive PDSIZE values change points in relation to different display options. For example, if the view is enlarged with the ZOOM command, the point size also increases. (Zoom is discussed in Chapter 9.) A negative PDSIZE value makes the points appear the same size no matter how much you ZOOM the drawing. Points drawn with negative PDSIZE values are shown in Fig. 8-23.

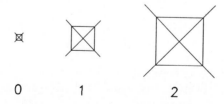

Fig. 8-22. Point sizes of different PDSIZE values.

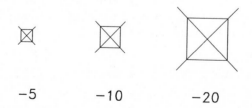

Fig. 8-23. Points drawn with negative PDSIZE values.

Using the Point Style icon menu

The "Point Style" icon menu, shown in Fig. 8-24, is accessed by selecting "Point Style..." from the Settings pull-down menu. This is convenient since it lets you see and pick the point symbols displayed as graphic images. Pick the desired style to be used next time you draw a point. Set the point size by entering a value in the "Point Size" box. Pick the "Set Size Relative to Screen" radio button if you want the point size to change in relation to different display options. Picking the "Set Size in Absolute Units" radio button makes the points appear the same size no matter what display option is used.

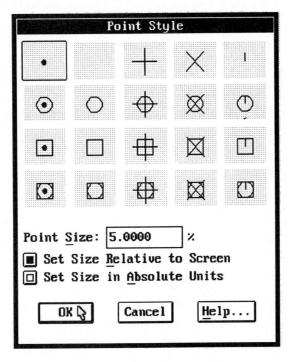

Fig. 8-24. The "Point Style" icon menu.

EXERCISE 8-9

☐ Load AutoCAD and open PRODR1, or start a new drawing and set up your own variables.
☐ Draw a point with PDMODE set to the following values: 0, 1, 2, 3, 4, 32, 33, 66, 67, 98, 99, and 100.
☐ Type "REGEN" and observe the results.
☐ Set PDMODE to a value of 35. Then draw a point using each of the following PDSIZE values: 0, 1, 2, -5, -10, and -20.
☐ Save the drawing as A:EX8-9 and quit.

USING THE CALCULATOR FOR GEOMETRIC CONSTRUCTION

AEM 4

AutoCAD's geometry calculator is a convenient tool to use when drawing and editing geometric constructions, and performing basic mathematical calculations. The geometry calculator is accessed by typing "CAL" at the Command: prompt, or by picking Calculator from the Assist pull-down menu. 'CAL can also be entered transparently when needed during any AutoCAD command. The calculator is especially helpful when entering points that are not easily located by other means, and for editing objects using mathematical calculations. You can also enter a math equation when you see the 〉〉 Expression: prompt, such as shown in the following command sequence:

>   Command: **CAL** ↵
>   〉〉 Expression: **2 + 2** ↵
>   4
>   Command:

The following discussion introduces the techniques and applications for using the geometry calculator. Additional information regarding the CAL command is found in Chapter 4 of the *AutoCAD Extras Manual*.

Making entries

Numbers are entered in the calculator in the same manner they are entered when locating coordinates on screen. (Refer to Chapter 6 for details about entering numbers.) The standard format is inches. You can use decimal inches or scientific notation. Two formats are used for entering feet and inches: feet'-inches" or feet'inches". In the following example, 5'-6" is converted to 66". The value 5'6" could also be used.

>   Command: **CAL** ↵
>   〉〉 Expression: **5'—6"** ↵
>   66.0
>   Command:

Angles are entered in decimal degrees, for example, 30d. Minutes and seconds can be omitted if their values are 0. When minutes (') and seconds (") are also included, they can be entered as 30d45'15". When *only* minutes and seconds are used, degrees are entered as 0d, for example, 0d30'10". You can also enter angles in radians by adding an "r" (3.5r), or in grads with a "g" (12.25g).

When entering coordinate values in the calculator, enclose them in square brackets ([ ]). Use the standard absolute, relative, and polar coordinate notation (discussed in Chapter 6). Absolute values are entered as [X,Y,Z], for example, [4,6,0]. Relative values are entered as [@X,Y,Z], such as [@2,4,0]. Polar values require a distance and angle value [distance〈angle,Z], for example, [6〈45d,0]. The Z value is used for 3-D applications, and may be entered as 0 or omitted for 2-D applications. Coordinate values can be added in the calculator like this:

>   Command: **CAL** ↵
>   〉〉 Expression: **[4,2,0] + [2,6,0]** ↵
>   (6.0 8.0 0.0)
>   Command:

Other mathematical functions can also be performed using the calculator. The following symbols are used in mathematical expressions:

+	Add
—	Subtract
*	Multiply
/	Divide
∧	Exponents
( )	Grouped expressions

Parentheses are used to group the symbols and values into sets. Complex mathematical expressions in which more than one set is involved are calculated beginning with the innermost grouped set. In any given set, exponents are calculated first, followed by multiplication and division, and then addition and subtraction. Calculations are then made from left to right.

EXERCISE 8-10

☐ Load AutoCAD.
☐ Use the CAL command to make the following calculations:
    A. 28.125 + 37.625 _____
    B. 16.875 − 7.375 _____
    C. 6.25 × 3.5 _____
    D. (25.75 ÷ 4) + (5.625 × 3) _____
☐ Do not save this exercise.

Additional geometric calculations

In addition to the basic math functions previously discussed, AutoCAD's CAL command also allows you to obtain information about entities or make the following calculations:

- **RXOF(P)** — Provides the X coordinate of a point.
- **RYOF(P)** — Provides the Y coordinate of a point.
- **SIN(angle)** — Sine of angle.
- **COS(angle)** — Cosine of angle.
- **TANG(angle)** — Tangent of angle.
- **ASIN(number)** — Arcsine of number between −1 and 1.
- **ACOS(number)** — Arccosine of number between −1 and 1.
- **ATAN(number)** — Arctangent of number.
- **IN(number)** — Natural log of number.
- **LOG(number)** — Base-10 logarithm of number.
- **EXP(number)** — Natural exponent of number.
- **SQR(number)** — Square of number.
- **SQRT(number)** — Square root of positive number.
- **ABS(number)** — Absolute value of number.
- **ROUND(number)** — Rounds number to nearest integer.
- **TRUNC(number)** — Provides integer part of number (portion preceding the decimal point).
- **R2D(angle)** — Converts angle in radians to degrees.
- **D2R(angle)** — Converts angle in degrees to radians.
- **CVUNIT(value,from,to)** — Converts a value from one unit of measurement to another, such as inches to millimeters, like this: CVUNIT(6,IN,MM).
- **PI** — Constant value π (3.1415926).

The CVUNIT expression can be used to convert 6 in. to millimeters as shown in the following example:

    Command: **CAL** ↵
    ⟩⟩ Expression: **CVUNIT(6,IN,MM)** ↵
    152.4
    Command:

To calculate the square root of 25, use the following procedure:

    Command: **CAL** ↵
    ⟩⟩ Expression: **SQRT(25)** ↵
    5.0
    Command:

EXERCISE 8-11

☐ Load AutoCAD.
☐ Use the CAL command to perform the following calculations:
  A. Sine of 30° _____
  B. Cosine of 18° _____
  C. Circumference of a 4 in. diameter circle. Use the formula: $C = \pi \times D$ _____
  D. Round off 9.875 to nearest integer _____
  E. Convert 18 inches to millimeters _____
  F. 23^2 _____
  G. Square root of 79 _____
☐ Do not save this drawing.

2-D entity calculations

Some functions of the geometry calculator can be used to help create or edit a drawing. The following functions involve calculations in a 2-D or XY plane environment. Additional functions are used for 3-D (XYZ) vector calculations for descriptive geometry. Chapter 4 of the *AutoCAD Extras Manual* details the use of 3-D functions.

- **CUR** — Allows you to pick a point using the cursor.
- **DEE** — Distance between two endpoints of entities. Same as DIST(END,END).
- **DIST(P1,P2)** — Distance between points 1 and 2.
- **DPL(P,P1,P2)** — Distance between point P and line with endpoints P1 and P2.
- **ILL(P1,P2,P3,P4)** — Gives the intersection between two lines, one with endpoints P1,P2 and the other with endpoints P3,P4.
- **MEE** — Gives the midpoint between two endpoints. Abbreviated version of (END + END)/2.
- **PLD(P1,P2,DIST)** — Point of line P1,P2, which is DISTance from P1.
- **PLT(P1,P2,T)** — Point on line P1,P2, defined by parameter T.
- **RAD** — Gives the radius of the circle or arc selected.
- **ROT(P,ORIGIN,ANGLE)** — Rotates point P through an angle about the origin.
- **ROT(P,P1AX,P2AX)** — Rotates point P through an angle using line with endpoints P1,P2 as the rotation axis.

To determine the length of a line, use the following command sequence:

Command: **CAL** ⏎
 ⟩⟩ Expression: **DEE** ⏎
 ⟩⟩ Select one endpoint of DEE: *(pick one end of the line)*
 ⟩⟩ Select another endpoint for DEE: *(pick the other end)*
6.30064

The radius of a circle, arc, or polyline is determined using the following procedure:

Command: **CAL** ⏎
 ⟩⟩ Expression: **RAD** ⏎
Select circle, arc, or polyline segment for RAD function: *(pick one of specified entities)*
1.06682
Command:

Using the object snap modes

The object snap modes can be used in place of point coordinates in 2-D entity calculations. This instructs AutoCAD to automatically issue the OSNAP mode you need to easily pick an exact point, thus eliminating the need for you to enter the point coordinates at the keyboard. All you need to enter are the first three letters of the object snap mode, as with any OSNAP operation. The CAL command supports the following OSNAP modes:

- ENDpoint
- INSert
- INTersection
- MIDpoint
- CENter

- NEArest
- NODe
- QUAdrant
- PERpendicular
- TANgent

Calculating the angle between lines

Some calculator functions allow you to find the angle from the X axis or between given lines. The angle is measured counterclockwise. The formulas for these functions are:

- **ANG(P1,P2)** — Provides the angle between the X axis and a line where P1 and P2 are the endpoints on the line. Use the ENDpoint object snap mode to pick the endpoints.
- **ANG(APEX,P1,P2)** — Returns the angle between lines in an XY plane. For example, if you want to find the angle between the two lines in Fig. 8-25, use the following command sequence:

Command: **CAL** ⏎
〉〉 Expression: **ANG(END,END,END)** ⏎
〉〉 Select entity for END snap: *(pick the vertex)*
〉〉 Select entity for END snap: *(pick P1)*
〉〉 Select entity for END snap: *(pick P2)*
60.5
Command:

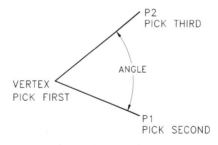

Fig. 8-25. Using the geometry calculator to determine the angle between lines in an XY plane.

The (END,END,END) notation instructs AutoCAD to issue the ENDpoint object snap mode to assist you in picking the desired points.

EXERCISE 8-12

☐ Load AutoCAD and open TITLEA.
☐ Use the LINE command to draw an angle similar to Fig. 8-25.
☐ Determine the angle formed using the CAL command.
☐ Save the drawing as A:EX8-12 and quit.

Making point calculations

You can easily calculate the distance between two points using the following command sequence:

    Command: **CAL** ↵
    ⟩⟩ Expression: **DIST(NOD,NOD)** ↵
    ⟩⟩ Select entity for NOD snap: *(pick the first point)*
    ⟩⟩ Select entity for NOD snap: *(pick the second point)*

If you want to calculate one-half the distance between any two entities, such as the endpoints of a line, follow this procedure:

    Command: **CAL** ↵
    ⟩⟩ Expression: **DIST(END,END)/2** ↵
    ⟩⟩ Select entity for END snap: *(pick the first point)*
    ⟩⟩ Select entity for END snap: *(pick the second point)*

Determining the radius of an arc or circle

Use the RAD function to determine the radius of a circle, arc, or 2-D polyline in this manner:

    Command: **CAL** ↵
    ⟩⟩ Expression: **RAD** ↵
    ⟩⟩ Select circle, arc, or polyline segment for RAD function: *(pick the circle or arc to automatically obtain the radius value)*

EXERCISE 8-13

☐ Load AutoCAD and start a new drawing.
☐ Without the assistance of either snap or grid, use the LINE command to draw a single line anywhere on the screen.
☐ Use the CAL command to determine the distance between the endpoints.
☐ Use the CAL command to determine one-half the distance between the endpoints.
☐ Draw a circle without a specified radius or diameter.
☐ Use the CAL command's RAD function to determine the radius of the circle.
☐ Save the drawing as A:EX8-13 and quit.

CALCULATOR APPLICATIONS

In some instances, using the geometry calculator to perform simple tasks that may otherwise be performed on a hand-held calculator may seem to be a poor use of time. However, the real power of AutoCAD's geometry calculator is apparent when using the calculator as part of your drawing and editing process. The following applications provide you with a few of the many tasks that can be performed using the geometry calculator.

Circular applications

You can place a circle or other entity centered inside an object such as a rectangle, Fig. 8-26, using the following calculation:

    Command: **CIRCLE** ↵
    3P/2P/TTR/⟨Center point⟩: **'CAL** ↵
    ⟩⟩ Expression: **MEE** ↵

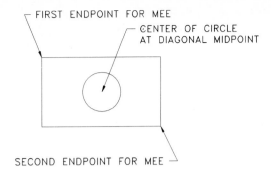

Fig. 8-26. Centering a circle within a rectangle using the CAL command.

MEE is the midpoint between two endpoints. This expression allows you to pick the opposite corners of the rectangle to get the midpoint of the diagonal, which is the center of the rectangle.

⟩⟩ Select one endpoint for MEE: *(pick one corner of the rectangle)*
⟩⟩ Select another endpoint for MEE: *(pick the opposite corner)*
Diameter/⟨Radius⟩ ⟨current⟩: *(enter a radius and press ENTER, or pick a radius)*

If you have an existing circle on a drawing, you can create another circle of equal radius using the RAD expression. The command sequence is as follows, and is shown in Fig. 8-27:

Command: **CIRCLE** ↵
3P/2P/TTR/⟨Center point⟩: *(pick a center point for the new circle)*
Diameter/⟨Radius⟩ ⟨current⟩: **'CAL** ↵
⟩⟩ Expression: **RAD** ↵
⟩⟩ Select circle, arc, or polyline segment for RAD function: *(pick the original circle)*

After you pick the original circle, a circle equal in radius to the original, is automatically drawn at the new center point. This technique is helpful if you do not know the size of the original circle.

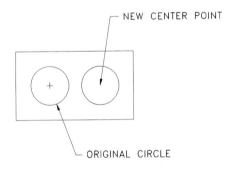

Fig. 8-27. Using the RAD function to create a circle equal in size to an existing circle.

EXERCISE 8-14

☐ Load AutoCAD and open TITLEA.
☐ Use the CAL command's MEE function to assist you in making a drawing similar to Fig. 8-26.
☐ Use the CAL command to assist you in making a drawing similar to Fig. 8-27.
☐ Save the drawing as A:EX8-14 and quit.

Calculator functions can also be combined and used productively. For example, suppose you want to draw a new circle that is 25 percent the size of the original circle, which is to be placed in a new position that also needs to be calculated. Refer to Fig. 8-28 as you follow this command sequence:

> Command: **CIRCLE** ↵
> 3P/2P/TTR/⟨Center point⟩: **'CAL** ↵
> ⟩⟩ Expression: **(MID + MID)/2** ↵
> ⟩⟩ Select entity for MID snap: *(pick line 1)*
> ⟩⟩ Select entity for MID snap: *(pick line 2)*

Now, instruct AutoCAD to calculate a new radius that is 25 percent (.25) of the size of the original circle:

> Diameter/⟨Radius⟩ ⟨current⟩: **'CAL** ↵
> ⟩⟩ Expression: **.25 * RAD** ↵
> ⟩⟩ Select circle, arc, or polyline segment for RAD function: *(pick one of the original circles)*

The new circle is automatically placed at the point specified, and at 25 percent of the size of the original circle.

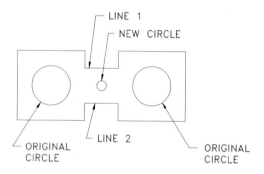

Fig. 8-28. Combining calculator functions to resize the circle and place it in a new position.

Another application of the CAL command is demonstrated in Fig. 8-29, where a new circle is 3.00 in. from an existing circle along a centerline. The new circle is 1 1/2 times (1.5X) larger than the original circle. The following command sequence can be used:

> Command: **CIRCLE** ↵
> 3P/2P/TTR/⟨Center point⟩: **'CAL** ↵
> ⟩⟩ Expression: **PLD(CEN,END,3.00)** ↵
> ⟩⟩ Select entity for CEN snap: *(pick the original circle)*
> ⟩⟩ Select entity for END snap: *(pick near the right end of the centerline)*
> Diameter/⟨Radius⟩ ⟨current⟩: **'CAL** ↵
> ⟩⟩ Expression: **1.5 * RAD** ↵
> ⟩⟩ Select circle, arc, or polyline segment for RAD function: *(pick the original circle)*

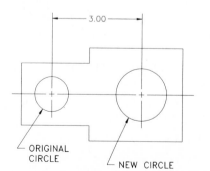

Fig. 8-29. Moving a circle along a centerline, and resizing the circle at the same time.

EXERCISE 8-15

☐ Load AutoCAD and open TITLEA.
☐ Use the CAL command to assist you in creating a drawing similar to Fig. 8-28.
☐ Use the CAL command to assist you in making a drawing similar to Fig. 8-29.
☐ Save the drawing as A:EX8-15 and quit.

Still another situation might exist where you want to draw a new circle that is .5 in. higher than one-half the distance between the center of an existing circle and the side (line) of an object. The command sequence is as follows, and is shown in Fig. 8-30:

Command: **CIRCLE** ↵
3P/2P/TTR/⟨Center point⟩: **'CAL** ↵
⟩⟩ Expression: **(CEN + MID)/2 + [0,.5]** ↵

The "(CEN + MID)/2" expression places the center point of the new circle one-half the distance between the center of the original circle and the midpoint of the line. Adding the [0,.5] locates the center point 0 units in the X direction and .5 units above (Y direction) the center point located with the "(CEN + MID)/2" expression.

⟩⟩ Select entity for CEN snap: *(pick the original circle)*
⟩⟩ Select entity for MID snap: *(pick the right line)*
Diameter/⟨Radius⟩ ⟨current⟩: **'CAL** ↵
⟩⟩ Expression: **RAD** ↵
⟩⟩ Select circle, arc, or polyline segment for RAD function: *(pick the original circle)*

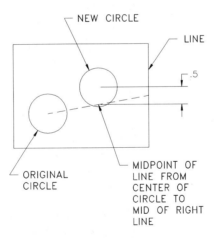

Fig. 8-30. Another example of combining calculator functions.

EXERCISE 8-16

☐ Load AutoCAD and open TITLEA.
☐ Use the CAL command to assist you in making a drawing similar to Fig. 8-30.
☐ Save the drawing as A:EX8-16 and quit.

These are only a few of the possibilities for using the CAL command. Although the examples shown here involve the CIRCLE command, similar tasks involving other commands can also be performed. More examples, related to editing drawings, are given in Chapter 11.

DRAWING WITH X AND Y FILTERS

Filters allow you to select any aspect of an entity on the screen while "filtering out" other items or features. There are many uses for filters. While a variety of applications for filters are discussed throughout this text, this discussion centers on X and Y filters—filters that let you control X and Y coordinates, respectively. (In actuality, there are X, Y, and Z coordinates, but the Z coordinate is utilized for 3-D applications. Only X and Y filters are used in the following examples.) This discussion centers around working with the LINE command to create geometric constructions with X and Y filters. When you are prompted for a point, you can respond with any combination of .X, .Y, or .XY, as needed. If AutoCAD asks you for a Z value, simply answer with a 0.

Suppose you want to construct an isosceles triangle with a given height of 4 in. on a baseline that already exists. The drawing is shown in Fig. 8-31. First, follow this command sequence to establish the base of your triangle:

    Command: **LINE** ↵
    From point: **2,2** ↵
    To point: **@3⟨90** ↵

Now, place the vertex (Y) 4 in. from the midpoint of the baseline:

    To point: **.Y** ↵
    of **MID** ↵
    of *(pick the baseline)*
    of (need XZ): **4,0** ↵

Finally, complete the triangle:

    To point: **END** ↵
    of *(pick the endpoint of the baseline)*
    To point: ↵
    Command:

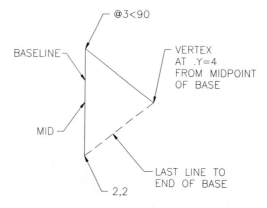

Fig. 8-31. Constructing an isosceles triangle using the geometry calculator.

Filters can also be picked from the cursor object snap menu. See Fig. 8-32.

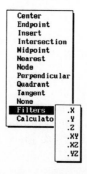

Fig. 8-32. Selecting filters from the cursor object snap menu.

EXERCISE 8-17

☐ Load AutoCAD and open TITLEA.
☐ Use the X and Y filters as previously discussed to assist you in making a drawing similar to Fig. 8-31.
☐ Save the drawing as A:EX8-17 and quit.

CHAPTER TEST

Write your answers in the spaces provided.

1. Give the command and entries needed to draw a line to the midpoint of an existing line:

   Command: _____

   From point: _____

   To point: _____ of _____

2. Give the command and entries necessary to draw a line tangent to an existing circle and perpendicular to an existing line:

   Command: _____

   From point: _____ to _____

   To point: _____ to _____

3. Give the command and entries needed to set ENDpoint, CENter, and MIDpoint as the running object snaps:

   Command: _____

   Object snap modes: _____

4. Give the command sequence required to draw a concentric circle inside an existing circle at a distance of .25:

   Command: _____

   Offset distance or Through ⟨current⟩: _____

   Select object to offset: _____

   Side of offset? _____

   Select object to offset: _____

5. Give the command and entries needed to divide a line into 24 equal parts:

   Command: _____

   Select the object to divide: _____

   ⟨Number of segments⟩/Block: _____

6. Give the command and entries used to draw a point symbol that is made up of a circle over "X":

   Command: _____

   New value for _____ ⟨0⟩: _____

   Command: _____

   Point: _____

8-29

7. Suppose after drawing the point in Question 6, you find that it is too small. Give the command and prompts needed to draw the point larger:

   Command: _____

   New value for _____ ⟨0.000⟩: _____

8. Define object snap. _____

   _____

9. What do you call the cursor box that appears on the screen when an object snap mode is selected? _____

10. List four methods to access the object snap modes. _____

    _____

    _____

11. When typed at the prompt line, which three letters are required to activate any desired object snap? _____

    _____

12. Define quadrant. _____

13. Describe the "quick mode." _____

    _____

14. Describe the OSNAP interrupt mode. _____

    _____

    _____

15. Define running object snap. _____

    _____

    _____

16. Identify two ways to set a running object snap. _____

    _____

17. How do you access the "Running Object Snap" dialogue box? _____

18. Describe the OSNAP override. _____

    _____

    _____

19. What command is used to change the aperture size? _____

20. In addition to the command identified in Question 19, what is another way to change the aperture size? _____

    _____

21. What value would you specify to make the aperture half the default value? _____

22. How is the running OSNAP discontinued? _____

    _____

    _____

23. List two ways to establish an offset distance using the OFFSET command: _____
_____

24. Name the system variable used to set the offset distance default. _____

25. The DIVIDE command is located in which screen menu? _____

26. What is the difference between the DIVIDE and MEASURE commands? _____
_____
_____

27. The object snap quick mode is not effective on which object snap option? _____

28. If you use the DIVIDE command and nothing appears to happen, what should you do?
_____
_____

29. Name the system variable used to set a point style. _____

30. Name the system variable used to set a point size. _____

31. How do you access the "Point Style" icon menu? _____
_____

32. How do you change the point size in the "Point Style" icon menu? _____

33. List the command that is used to make geometric calculations with AutoCAD. _____

34. Identify three ways the value "four feet and eight inches" can be entered in the calculator.
_____
_____

35. How is "45 degrees, 15 minutes, 30 seconds" entered in the calculator?_____

36. How are point coordinates entered in the AutoCAD calculator? _____

37. Cite the proper input for the following calculations:

    A. Sine of a 35° angle: _____

    B. Tangent of a 50° angle: _____

    C. Square root of 49: _____

    D. Convert 86 millimeters to inches: _____

    E. Area of a 6 in. diameter circle, where $A = \pi x \phi$: _____

38. Give the calculator functions used to achieve the following results:

    A. Distance between two points: _____

    B. Intersection of two lines: _____

    C. Midpoint between two endpoints: _____

    D. Radius of a circle or arc: _____

39. Define "filters." _____
_____

40. What value do you enter for Z when working with X and Y filters in a 2-D drawing?
_____

DRAWING PROBLEMS

Load AutoCAD for each of the following problems and use the PRODR1 prototype drawing, or start a new drawing with your own variables.

1. Draw the object below using the object snap modes. Save the drawing as A:P8-1 (omit dimensions).

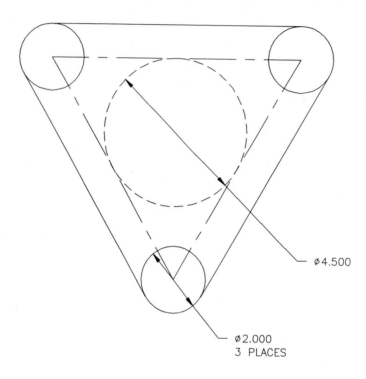

⌀4.500

⌀2.000
3 PLACES

2. Draw the object below using the object snap modes indicated. Save the drawing as A:P8-2.

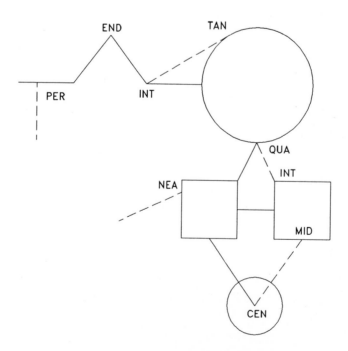

3. Draw the object below using ENDpoint, TANgent, CENter, PERpendicular, and QUAdrant running object snap modes. Save the drawing as A:P8-3.

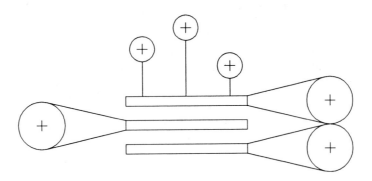

4. Draw the floor plan layout about three times the size of that shown. Use the following AutoCAD functions:
   A. Set architectural units; 48′,36′ limits; 2 ft. grid; and 6 in. snap.
   B. Use the PLINE command to draw plan A. (The LINE command may be used, but it will take longer to complete the problem.)
   C. Use the OFFSET command to draw a parallel line 6 in. on the inside of plan A. Your final drawing should look like that shown in plan B.
   D. Save the drawing as A:P8-4.

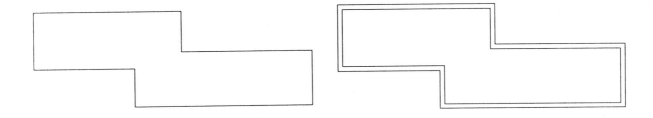

5. Create a drawing proportional, but about three times the size of the object shown below. Proceed as follows:
   A. Draw the outer circle first.
   B. Use the OFFSET command to create other concentric circles. (Try to draw the object without leaving the OFFSET command.) Select the Through option and point to the spot where you want the offset circles to be placed.
   C. Save the drawing as A:P8-5.

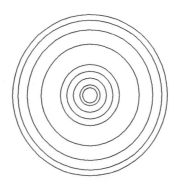

6. Draw two horizontal lines, each 8 in. (203.2 mm) long. Use the DIVIDE command to divide one of the lines into 10 equal parts. Use the MEASURE command to set off .8 in. (20.3 mm) increments on the second line. Save the drawing as A:P8-6.

7. Draw two circles, each having a 4 in. (101.6 mm) diameter. Then use the DIVIDE command to divide one of the circles into 12 equal parts. Use the MEASURE command to set off .75 in. (19.1 mm) increments on the second circle. Save the drawing as A:P8-7.

8. Draw two closed polylines each made up of line and arc segments. Then, use the DIVIDE command to divide one of the polylines into 24 equal parts. Use the MEASURE command to set off 1.5 increments on the second polyline. Save the drawing as A:P8-8.

NOTE FOR PROBLEMS 9 THROUGH 12: If several PDMODE symbols are displayed on the screen, they will all be updated to the current PDMODE value when a regeneration occurs.

9. Set the PDSIZE to 1 and draw points with each of the following PDMODEs: 0, 2, 3, and 4. Save the drawing as A:P8-9.

10. Set the PDSIZE to 2 and draw a point with each of the following PDMODEs: 32, 34, 35, 64, 65, 66, 96, 97, 98, 99, and 100. Save the drawing as A:P8-10.

11. Use the "Point Style" icon menu to draw five different point symbols. Save the drawing as A:P8-11.

12. Use the "Point Style" icon menu to change the size of each of five different point symbols. Save the drawing as A:P8-12.

13. Use the LINE command to draw the angle shown in the following illustration using the given coordinates. Use the CAL command to determine the angle, in degrees, between the lines. Save the drawing as A:P8-13.

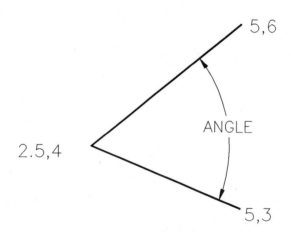

14. Draw a rectangle measuring 3.125 x 5.625. Use the CAL command to center a circle with a .75 diameter inside the rectangle. Save the drawing as A:P8-14.

15. Draw the following object. Then use the CAL command to place another circle to the left of the existing circle so the completed object is symmetrical. Do not include the dimensions. Save the drawing as A:P8-15.

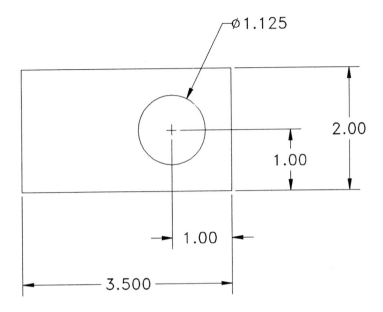

16. Draw the following object. Then use the CAL command to add another circle with a diameter which is 30 percent of the size of the existing circle. Center the new circle between the midpoints of line 1 and 2. Do not include dimensions. Save the drawing as A:P8-16.

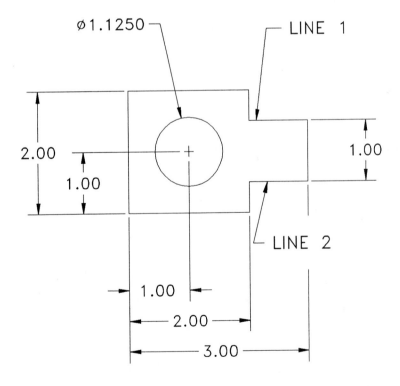

17. Draw the object shown below. Then use the CAL command to create another circle with a diameter which is 150 percent (1.5X) of the existing circle. Center the new circle 3 in. horizontally to the right of the existing circle. Do not dimension the drawing. Save the drawing as A:P8-17.

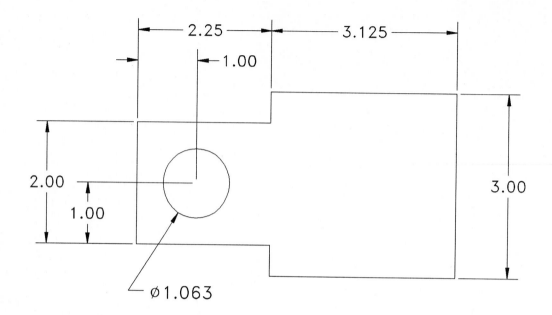

18. Draw the following object. Then use the CAL command to create another circle with the same diameter as the existing circle. Place the center of the new circle .5 in. above a point that is midway between the center of the existing circle and the midpoint of the right line of the object. Do not include dimensions. Save the drawing as A:P8-18.

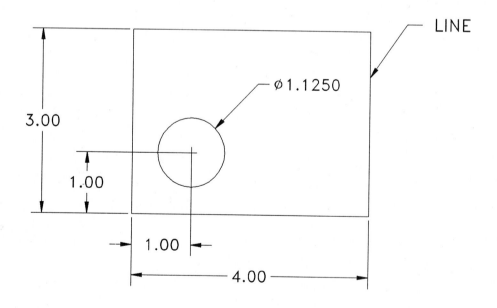

19. Use the X and Y filters to draw an isosceles triangle with a vertical baseline measuring 4.5 in. long, and a height of 5.75 in. Save the drawing as A:P8-19.

Chapter 9

DRAWING DISPLAY OPTIONS

Learning objectives

After completing this chapter, you will be able to:
- ☐ Magnify a small part of a drawing to work on details.
- ☐ Move the drawing around the screen to display portions outside the boundaries of the monitor.
- ☐ Create named views that can be recalled instantly.
- ☐ Create multiple viewports on the screen.
- ☐ Define and use model space and paper space.

You can view the exact portion of the drawing you need using AutoCAD's Display commands. The ZOOM command enables you to enlarge or reduce the amount of the drawing displayed. The portion displayed can also be moved back and forth or up and down using the PAN command. PAN can be compared to looking through a camera lens and moving the camera across the drawing. The VIEW command allows you to create and name specific views of the drawing. These views can be recalled to work on details of that view.

Specialized display functions allow you to work in "space." They are called model space and paper space, and are found by picking MVIEW in the DISPLAY screen menu, and also in the View pull-down menu. These two functions allow you to switch between the drawing and design world called *model space,* and the plotting world called *paper space.* Detailed information regarding the use of model space and paper space as related to plotting multiview drawings is provided in Chapter 27.

This chapter also discusses the differences between REDRAW and REGEN. It shows how to set the REGENAUTO and VIEWRES commands to achieve optimum display speeds and quality.

REDRAW THE SCREEN
$\boxed{\text{ARM 7}}$

The REDRAW command cleans the screen of blips that appear when a point is picked. It also fills holes left when entities are erased. REDRAW can be typed at the Command: prompt or while working inside a command.

Working inside another command

REDRAW is one of AutoCAD's transparent commands. *Transparent commands* can be used while you are working inside another command. Transparent commands include SETVAR, HELP, ZOOM, PAN, VIEW, and REDRAW. When the transparent command is completed, the command with which you were working returns. REDRAW does not prompt you; it just does its job. Select REDRAW from the screen, pull-down, or tablet menu and notice the command line displayed.

Command: 'REDRAW

The apostrophe in front of the command tells AutoCAD that this is a transparent command. All of the commands discussed in this chapter, with the exception of REGEN, VIEWRES, and VPORTS are transparent. A detailed discussion of transparent commands and how they are used is given later in the chapter.

Cleaning the screen display

REDRAW is commonly used to clean away the clutter of drawing and editing work. Most of the clutter is that of blips. A *blip* is a small cross displayed when a point is picked on the screen, Fig. 9-1. These blips are indicators of selected points and are not part of your drawing. They simply stay on the screen until it is redrawn. Using REDRAW for removing blips is fine, but it may begin to slow your drawing sessions. When you begin working on complex drawings, REDRAW takes much longer.

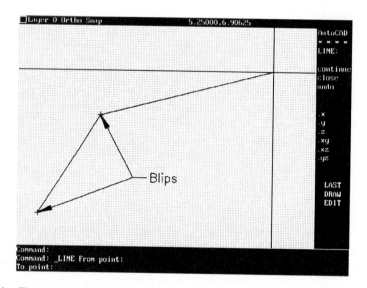

Fig. 9-1. Tiny crosshairs, or blips, show on the screen when a point is selected.

Blips remind you where points were selected, but they may be omitted. This eliminates the need to redraw as often. If you decide you do not need blips, turn them off with the BLIP-MODE command. It is found in the SETTINGS screen menu as BLIPS, or it can be typed as follows:

Command: **BLIPMODE** ↵
ON/OFF ⟨current⟩: **OFF** ↵

The blips will not show on the screen unless you access BLIPMODE again and enter "ON."

GETTING CLOSE TO YOUR WORK   ARM 7

It is doubtful whether many drafters would create drawings on a computer screen if they could not move in close to their work. This ability to "zoom in" (magnify) a drawing was an advancement that enabled designers to create the tiny circuits found in computers. The ZOOM command is a tool that you will use often because it is so helpful. It also is a transparent command and can be used while inside other commands. Ten different options allow you to use ZOOM in a variety of ways.

The ZOOM options

Entering the ZOOM command lists the options as follows:

Command: **ZOOM** ↵
All/Center/Dynamic/Extents/Left/Previous/Vmax/Window/⟨Scale(X/XP)⟩:

Brief explanations of the ZOOM options are provided below.

- **All** — Zooms to display drawing limits. If objects are beyond limits, they are included in the display.
- **Center** — Pick the center and height of the next screen display. A magnification factor instead of a height can be entered by typing a number followed by "X," such as "4X." The current value represents the height of the screen in drawing units. Entering a smaller number enlarges the image size, while a larger number reduces it. The command sequence is as follows:

  All/Center/Dynamic/Extents/Left/Previous/Vmax/Window/⟨Scale(X/XP)⟩: **C** ↵
  Center point: *(pick a center point)*
  Magnification or Height ⟨current⟩: **4X** ↵

- **Dynamic** — Allows for a graphic pan and zoom with the use of a view box that represents the screen. This option is discussed in detail later in the chapter.
- **Extents** — Zooms to extents of the drawing. This is the portion of the drawing area that has entities drawn in it.
- **Left** — Pick the lower-left corner and height of next screen display. A magnification factor instead of a height can be entered as follows:

  All/Center/Dynamic/Extents/Left/Previous/Vmax/Window/⟨Scale(X/XP)⟩: **L** ↵
  Lower left corner point: *(pick a point)*
  Magnification or Height ⟨current⟩: **3X** ↵

- **Previous** — Returns to the previous display. You can go back 10 displays in Release 12.
- **Vmax** — AutoCAD maintains a "virtual screen" composed of 4 billion pixels in each axis (X and Y). This means that each time a regeneration is required, the virtual screen is recalculated. Then, you can view any detail of your drawing that you want, within the virtual screen, and AutoCAD displays it at redraw speed. The image is redrawn (not regenerated) if the next display you request is inside the limits of the virtual screen. However, if the requested display (a small zoom window, for example) will not provide an accurate representation of the drawing entities, AutoCAD performs a regeneration. You can test Vmax by zooming in on a small detail on your drawing. You may want to do this a couple of times until AutoCAD regenerates. Then use ZOOM Vmax. The resulting display is the virtual screen.
- **Window** — Pick opposite corners of a box. Objects in the box enlarge to fill the display. The Window option is the default if you pick a point on the screen.
- **Scale(X)** — A positive number is required here to indicate the magnification factor of the original display. You can enlarge or reduce relative to the current display by typing an "X" after the scale. Type "2X" if you want the image enlarged two times. Type ".5X" if you want the image reduced by half. Typing just a number without the "X" zooms the *original* drawing. On the other hand, typing a number followed by an "X" zooms the *current view* by that scale value.
- **Scale(XP)** — This option is used in conjunction with model space and paper space, both discussed later in this chapter. Its purpose is to scale a drawing in model space relative to paper space, and is used primarily in the layout of scaled multiview drawings for plotting purposes. A detailed discussion of this option is given in Chapter 27 — Plotting and Printing a Drawing.

Enlarging with a window

The most-used ZOOM option is Window. Two opposite corners of a rectangular window enclosing the feature to be zoomed are picked. The command sequence is as follows:

  Command: **ZOOM** ↵
  All/Center/Dynamic/Extents/Left/Previous/Vmax/Window/⟨Scale(X/XP)⟩: *(pick a corner)*
  Other corner: *(pick the opposite corner)*

The first point you pick is automatically accepted as the first corner of the zoom window. After this corner is picked, a box appears attached to the crosshairs. It grows and shrinks as you move the pointing device. When the second corner is picked, the center of the window becomes the center of the new screen display. If you wish to return to the previous display, select ZOOM and use the P (Previous) option. If you want to see the entire drawing, use the A (All) option. Fig. 9-2 shows the difference between ZOOM Window and ZOOM All.

The Window option can also be selected by entering a "W" at the options prompt. This method is useful for customized applications that are designed to operate on earlier releases of AutoCAD. See Chapter 32 for information on customizing AutoCAD menus.

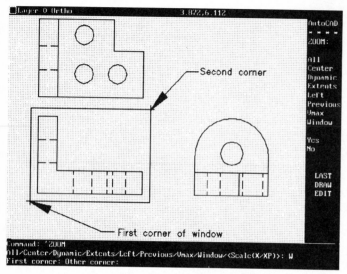

A—ZOOM WINDOW SELECTION

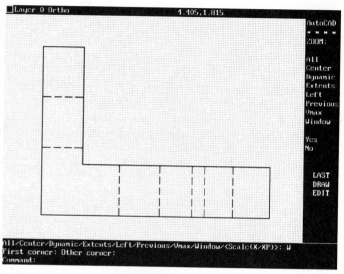

B—ZOOM WINDOW

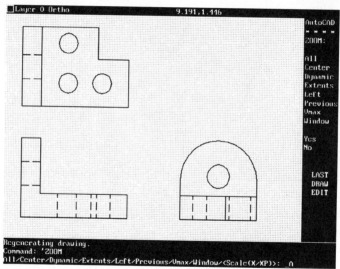

C—ZOOM ALL

Fig. 9-2. Using ZOOM Window and ZOOM All.

Accurate displays with dynamic zoom

The ZOOM Dynamic option allows you to accurately specify the portion of the drawing you want displayed. This is done by constructing a *view box*. This view box is proportional to the size of the display area. If you have zoomed in already when ZOOM Dynamic is selected, the entire drawing is displayed on the screen. To practice with this command, load any drawing into AutoCAD. Then select the ZOOM command's Dynamic option as follows:

Command: **ZOOM** ↵
All/Center/Dynamic/Extents/Left/Previous/Vmax/Window/〈Scale(X/XP)〉: **D** ↵

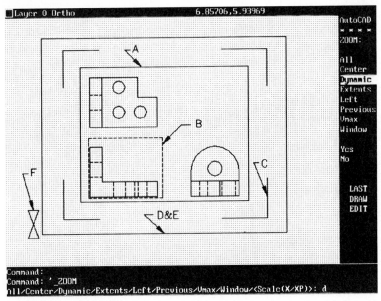

A. DRAWING EXTENTS
B. CURRENT VIEW
C. GENERATED AREA
D. and E. PANNING VIEW BOX/ZOOMING VIEW BOX
F. HOURGLASS

Fig. 9-3. Features of the ZOOM Dynamic command.

The screen is now occupied by four boxes, Fig. 9-3. A fifth box is displayed later. Each one has a specific function. The boxes and their functions are:
- **Drawing extents** — white line — This box shows the area of the drawing that is occupied by drawing features (entities). It is the same area that would be displayed with ZOOM Extents.
- **Current view** — green dotted line — This is the view that was displayed before you selected ZOOM Dynamic. It may be considerably smaller than the red corners of the generated area.
- **Generated area** — red corners — This is the most obvious box because its corners are red lines. It represents the generated area of the drawing. AutoCAD keeps a *virtual screen* of over 4 billion pixels in both the X and Y coordinate directions. (Pixels were discussed in Chapter 8.) The virtual screen is the area AutoCAD calculates with the REGEN command. Many users have screens with 640 x 480 pixels; thus, the virtual screen is much larger than the display area. This is why the generated area extends beyond the actual drawing.

  The generated area is important because it displays the portion of the drawing that can be zoomed without causing a regeneration. This means the next display is calculated at the faster redraw speed. If you select a zoom box that lies outside the generated area, a REGEN is performed, thus slowing the next display. Try to size your view and pan boxes inside the generated area.
- **Panning view box** — X in the center — The box with an X in the center is the panning view box. Move the pointing device to find the center point of the desired zoomed display. When you press the pick button, the fifth and final box appears.
- **Zooming view box** — arrow on right side — This box allows you to decrease or increase the area that you wish to zoom. Move the pointer to the right and the box increases in size. Move the pointer to the left and the box shrinks. You can also pan up or down with the zooming view box. The only restriction is that you cannot move the box to the left.

The ZOOM Dynamic command is not complete until you press ENTER. If you press the pick button to select the zooming view box, the panning view box reappears. Then you can reposition it if necessary. Press the pick button again and the zooming view box is displayed. In this manner, you can fine tune the exact display needed. This is also helpful in defining permanent views, which is discussed later in this chapter.

One final aspect of ZOOM Dynamic is the "hourglass" displayed in the lower-left corner of the screen. See Fig. 9-3. The hourglass informs you that the zooming view box is outside the generated area (red corners). AutoCAD is then forced to regenerate the drawing. The hourglass is a reminder to help you save time by avoiding unnecessary regenerations. As you adjust the view box, the hourglass may disappear. When it does, notice where the view box is located. All lines of the view box are inside the generated area. Move the view box so that one side is touching the generated area. The hourglass then reappears. If you pick that view box location, a regeneration takes place.

EXERCISE 9-1

☐ Load a drawing from a previous exercise or drawing problem.
☐ Select ZOOM Window and enlarge a portion of the drawing.
☐ Select ZOOM Window again to move in closer to a detail.
☐ Select ZOOM Vmax to show the virtual screen.
☐ Use ZOOM Previous to return to the last display.
☐ Select ZOOM Extents to show only the drawing entities.
☐ Select ZOOM All to display the entire drawing limits.
☐ Select ZOOM Dynamic. Maneuver the view box to select a portion of the drawing.
☐ Use ZOOM Dynamic to enlarge the display. Force a regeneration of the drawing by placing the view box partially outside the generated area.
☐ Save the drawing as A:EX9-1, then quit the drawing session.

CREATE YOUR OWN WORKING VIEWS $\boxed{\textbf{ARM 7}}$

On a large drawing that involves a number of separate details, using the ZOOM command can become time-consuming. Being able to specify a certain view would make better use of your time. This is possible with the VIEW command. It allows you to create named views. A view can be a portion of the drawing, such as the upper-left quadrant, or it can denote an enlarged portion. After the view is created, you can instruct AutoCAD to display it at any time.

Creating views

The VIEW command, found in the DISPLAY screen menu, has five options. Two of the options, Save and Window, allow you to create views. The Save option saves the current screen display under a name you enter. To name the view FRONT, you would follow this procedure:

    Command: VIEW ↵
    ?/Delete/Restore/Save/Window: S ↵
       View name to save: FRONT ↵

The second method of choosing a view to save is by windowing. This is much like zooming in on an area with the ZOOM Window option.

    Command: VIEW ↵
    ?/Delete/Restore/Save/Window: W ↵
       View name to save: (enter the view name and press ENTER)
    First corner: (pick one window corner)
    Other corner: (pick the second corner)

Getting information on existing views

Part of your drawing sessions should involve planning and bookkeeping activities. Keep a sheet or form containing all of the drawing variables. These might include symbols, text styles, dimensioning variables (see Chapters 18 and 19), and view names. If you do not remember the view names, list them by selecting the inquiry option (?) of the VIEW command.

    Command: VIEW ↵
    ?/Delete/Restore/Save/Window: ? ↵
       View(s) to list⟨*⟩: ↵

The alphanumeric screen appears with this display:

```
Saved views:
View name        Space
(name)           (M or P)
(name)           (M or P)
(name)           (M or P)
Command:
```

Write down these view names and keep them with the other drawing information. You can get a printout of this screen if you have a printer attached to your computer. Do so by pressing the Shift and Print Screen keys at the same time.

Recalling a saved view

A saved view can be restored to the screen at any time by selecting the Restore option of the VIEW command. Then enter the name of the view you want to display.

Command: **VIEW** ↵
?/Delete/Restore/Save/Window: **R** ↵
    View name to restore: *(type the view name and press ENTER)*

The view you enter is immediately displayed.

THE VIEW DIALOGUE BOXES

ARM 7

You can also work with views by selecting the "Set View" option in the View pull-down menu. Then pick "Named view..." from the cascading submenu to display the "View Control" dialogue box. See Fig. 9-4.

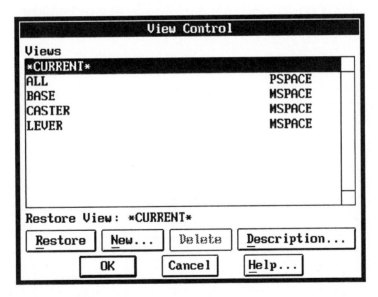

Fig. 9-4. Using the "View Control" dialogue box to work with view.

Defining views

A list of views is shown in the Views list box. If you wish to window a new view, pick the "New..." button and the "Define New View" dialogue box is displayed. See Fig. 9-5. Then pick the "Define Window" radio button. Type the name in the New Name: edit box. Pick the Window ⟨ button, and you are prompted for the first corner. Select the view window in the normal fashion. After you pick the second corner, the "Define New View" dialogue box reappears. Pick the Save View button and the "View Control" dialogue box is updated to reflect the new view.

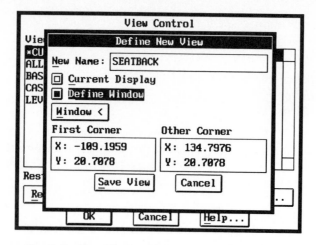

Fig. 9-5. The "Define New View" dialogue box.

NOTE

The crosshairs in a 3-D view remain on the 3-D axis until you pick the first window point, then the window is displayed. After entering a name in the New Name edit box, you must pick the Save View button, rather than pressing ENTER.

If you wish to display any of the listed views, simply pick its name from the file list, then pick the Restore button. The name of the view to be restored appears in the Restore View: label. Now, pick the OK button and the screen displays the selected view.

Saving the current display

If you want to save the current display as a view, pick the New button in the "View Control" dialogue box, then type the new name. The Current Display radio button is the default, so just pick Save View, and the view name is added to the list.

Deleting a view

If you wish to delete a view displayed in the dialogue box, first pick the view name in the list, then pick Delete. Notice that the view name is immediately removed from the list. If no view name is highlighted, the Delete button is grayed out, and thus not a valid option.

View description

You can get a detailed description of the selected view by picking the Description... button. This opens another dialogue box that provides a variety of information about the view. See Fig. 9-6. These values are discussed in Chapters 24 and 26.

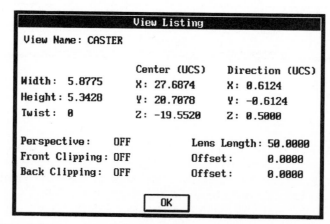

Fig. 9-6. Picking the Description... button in the "View Control" dialogue box accesses this informative dialogue box.

MOVING AROUND THE DRAWING

ARM 7

Imagine that you could put a hook in one side of the drawing and drag it across the screen. This is what the PAN command does. PAN allows you to move around the drawing without changing the magnification factor. You can then view objects which lie just outside the edges of the display screen.

Type "PAN" at the Command: prompt, or select it from the DISPLAY screen menu or View pull-down menu. AutoCAD then prompts for a point you want to drag. Pick that point. Next, you must pick where you want that point in the next display. The drawing is moved the distance between your two points, Fig. 9-7.

Command: **PAN** ↵
Displacement: *(pick the point to drag)*
     Second point: *(pick the final location of the first point)*

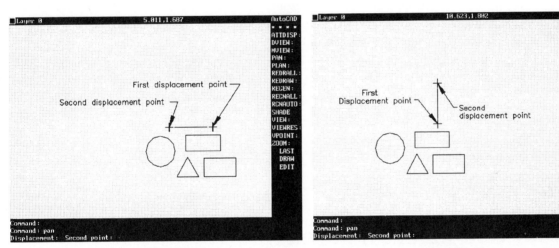

A—PAN TO THE LEFT   B—PAN UP

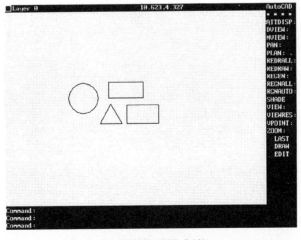

C—COMPLETED PAN

Fig. 9-7. PAN moves the drawing around the screen.

You can also enter the displacement, or the distance the drawing is to be moved by giving coordinates. See Fig. 9-8. The coordinates can be either relative or absolute. A relative displacement to move the drawing 8 units to the right and 3 units up is:

Command: **PAN** ↵
Displacement: **8,3** ↵
Second point: ↵

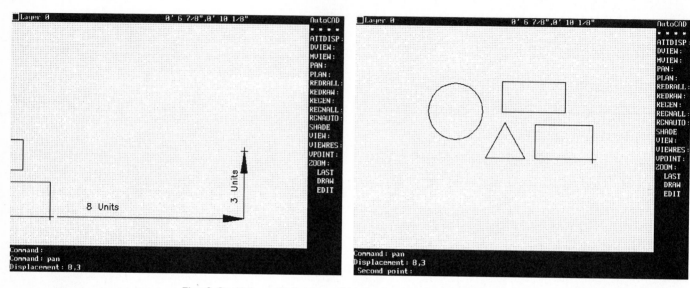

Fig. 9-8. Using relative coordinates to pan across a drawing.

Suppose the absolute coordinate location of the point you wanted to move was 4,5. Then, the absolute displacement for the above movement is calculated as 8,3 + 4,5 = 12,8 for the second point. Enter this as follows:

Command: **PAN** ↵
Displacement: **4,5** ↵
Second point: **12,8** ↵

SETTING VIEW RESOLUTION FOR QUICK DISPLAYS

ARM 7

AutoCAD allows you to save time on zooms and pans at the expense of display accuracy. On the other hand, AutoCAD provides a perfect display at the expense of zoom and pan speed. The main factor in this decision is called the view resolution. The *view resolution* refers to the number of lines used to draw circles and arcs. High resolution values display smooth circles and arcs. You can control the view resolution of circles and arcs with the VIEWRES command. It asks if you want zooms to be fast and what zoom percentage you want for circles:

Command: **VIEWRES** ↵
Do you want fast zooms? ⟨Y⟩ ↵
Enter circle zoom percent (1-20000) ⟨100⟩:

If your response to the first prompt is Yes, AutoCAD "repaints" the screen using REDRAW speed for ZOOM, PAN, or VIEW Restore. (The REDRAW speed can only be used if you do not reduce or enlarge outside of the generated areas.) After zooming in on a circle, the circle will appear less smooth.

If speed is not a concern, then answer "No" to the first prompt. This causes AutoCAD to use REGEN when any display command is issued. Circles and arcs will always appear to have the same smoothness.

The actual smoothness of circles and arcs is controlled by the circle zoom percent. It can vary between 1 and 20000. The default is 100. This produces a relatively smooth circle. A number smaller than 100 causes circles and arcs to be drawn with fewer vectors (straight lines). A number larger than 100 places more vectors in the circles, as shown in Fig. 9-9. The circle zoom percent is only used when AutoCAD is forced to do a regeneration. That is why a circle may appear to be composed of several straight sides after you zoom in on it. If you want a smooth circle, just use the REGEN command.

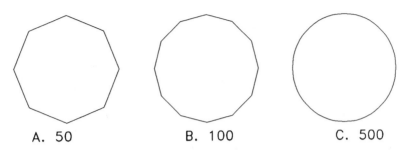

A. 50   B. 100   C. 500

Fig. 9-9. Circle smoothness at different VIEWRES values.

The VIEWRES command is a display function only and has no effect on the plotted or printed drawing. A drawing is printed or plotted using an optimum number of vectors for the size of circles and arcs. See Chapter 27 for detailed information on plotting.

— PROFESSIONAL TIP —

If you are concerned with speed, set VIEWRES for fast zooms and set the circle zoom percent to 100 or less. Circles may look like they have straight line sides, but drawing regenerations take less time.

EXERCISE 9-2

☐ Load AutoCAD and begin a new drawing named EX9-2.
☐ Draw three circles and three arcs of different sizes.
☐ Zoom in on the smallest circle using the Dynamic option. Notice the straight line segments that make up the circle.
☐ Keep zooming in on the circle edge (with ZOOM Window) until you force a regeneration. At that time, you have gone beyond the virtual screen.
☐ Set the VIEWRES command for fast zooms and a 10 percent circle zoom. ZOOM All and notice the shape of the circles and arcs after a regeneration.
☐ Select the VIEWRES command and answer "No" for fast zooms. Set circle zoom to 20 percent. Zoom in on a circle three times. Notice when regenerations are performed.
☐ Save the drawing as A:EX9-2 and quit the drawing session.

THE VIEW PULL-DOWN MENU

ARM A

Often-used display commands can be accessed by selecting View from the menu bar. The View pull-down menu with two display cascading submenus are shown in Fig. 9-10.

The View pull-down menu provides access to all of AutoCAD's display and viewing commands. Five of the selections are followed by arrows, which lead to cascading submenus that provide additional options or other commands. If the TILEMODE system variable is set to 0, and you pick the Model space, Paper space, or Mview options an error message stating: "**Command

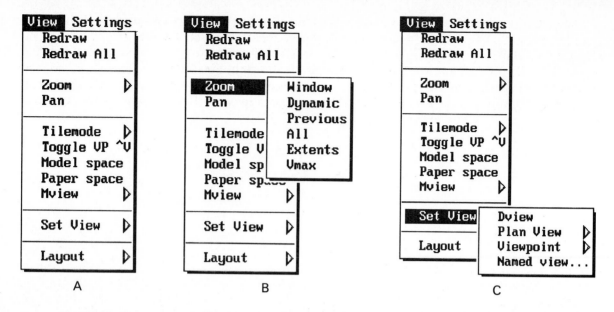

Fig. 9-10. The View pull-down menu with the "Zoom" and "Set View" cascading menus.

not allowed unless TILEMODE is set to 0" is displayed, and are not valid options. These three selections are valid when TILEMODE is set to 0. The TILEMODE system variable, model space, paper space, and the MVIEW commands are discussed later in this chapter, and in greater detail in Chapter 27.

A brief description of each of the picks in the View pull-down menu is provided here.
- **Redraw** — Redraws the screen.
- **Redraw All** — Redraws all viewports in model or paper space.
- **Zoom** — Provides access to all ZOOM command options. See Fig. 9-10B.
- **Pan** — Activates the PAN command.
- **Tilemode** — Toggles the TILEMODE system variable between 0 and 1.
- **Toggle VP** ∧V — Toggles between tiled (model space) viewports.
- **Model space** — Switches to model space if paper space is current.
- **Paper space** — Switches to paper space if model space is current.
- **Mview** — Provides access to commands that enable you to display a variety of views for 2-D or 3-D drawings.
- **Set View** — Allows you to work with views and access related dialogue boxes (previously discussed). See Fig. 9-10C.
- **Layout** — Enables you to construct layouts in model or paper space using predrawn borders and title blocks if desired.

USING TRANSPARENT DISPLAY COMMANDS   ARM 7

As mentioned earlier, certain commands can be used while you are inside another command. These commands are said to be "transparent" to the computer user. The display commands ZOOM, PAN, and VIEW are transparent. Suppose that while drawing a line, you need to place a point somewhere off the screen. One option is to cancel the LINE command. Then zoom out to see more of the drawing and select LINE again. A more efficient method is to use PAN or ZOOM while still in the LINE command. An example of drawing a line to a point off the screen is as follows:

Command: **LINE** ↵
From point: *(pick a point)*
To point: **'PAN** ↵
⟩⟩Displacement: *(pick a point to drag at edge of screen)*
⟩⟩Second point: *(pick a second point of displacement)*
Resuming LINE command.
To point: *(pick a point)*
To point: ↵

The double prompt (⟩⟩) indicates that a command has been put on "hold" while you use a transparent command. The transparent command must be completed before the original command is returned. At that time, the double prompt disappears.

The above procedure is similar when using the ZOOM and VIEW commands. An apostrophe (') is entered before the command. To connect a line to a small feature, enter 'ZOOM at the "To point:" prompt. To perform a drawing or editing function across views, enter 'VIEW. If the current display you see is not a saved view, create a view. Then you can do a transparent PAN or ZOOM to continue drawing. Finally, do a transparent 'VIEW Restore.

When trying to perform a transparent display, you may receive the following message:

**Requires a regen, cannot be transparent.
Resuming *(current)* command.

In this situation, you might try a less dramatic ZOOM, PAN, or VIEW that does not require AutoCAD to regenerate the display, or you can try ZOOM Vmax.

AutoCAD system variables can also be used in the transparent mode. Remember, when typing any transparent command, first type an apostrophe before the command name.

EXERCISE 9-3

☐ Load AutoCAD and begin a new drawing named EX9-3.
☐ Set the drawing limits at 12,9, grid spacing at .5, and snap spacing at .25.
☐ Construct the drawing shown below.

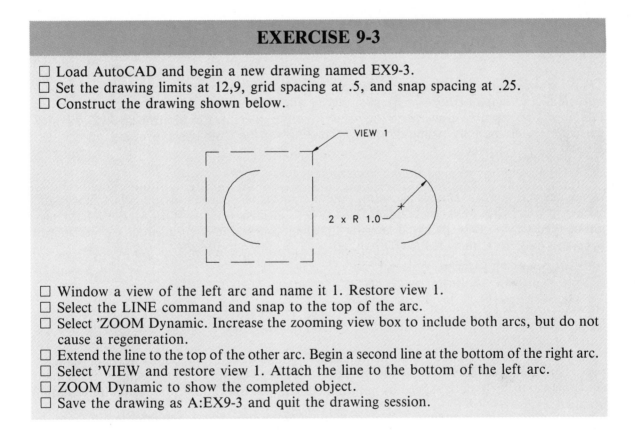

☐ Window a view of the left arc and name it 1. Restore view 1.
☐ Select the LINE command and snap to the top of the arc.
☐ Select 'ZOOM Dynamic. Increase the zooming view box to include both arcs, but do not cause a regeneration.
☐ Extend the line to the top of the other arc. Begin a second line at the bottom of the right arc.
☐ Select 'VIEW and restore view 1. Attach the line to the bottom of the left arc.
☐ ZOOM Dynamic to show the completed object.
☐ Save the drawing as A:EX9-3 and quit the drawing session.

PROFESSIONAL TIP

Although regenerations have been virtually eliminated with Release 12, they are still possible, and you should try to avoid them. They slow your work and thought processes. Try the following tips for all your new drawings:
• Set your drawing limits to include a little extra for a border.
• ZOOM All.
• Create a view named ALL (or a name of your choice) of the entire drawing area.
• Avoid using ZOOM Window, ZOOM Extents, PAN, or REGEN again.
• Create additional smaller views as you need them.
• Use ZOOM Dynamic in place of all other display commands. The hourglass in the display will appear if AutoCAD plans to regenerate the drawing.
• Use ZOOM Vmax to check the contents of the virtual screen.

MODEL SPACE AND PAPER SPACE

ARM 7

Model space can be thought of as the method and place in which you draw and design in AutoCAD. It is the "space" in which you create your drawing or model. The term "model" has more meaning when working in 3-D, but you can consider any drawing or design a model, even if it is two-dimensional. The best way to tell if you are in model space is to look at the UCS (User Coordinate System) icon. It is the symbol located in the lower-left corner of the screen, and represents the current directions of the X and Y coordinates. See Fig. 9-11. A complete discussion of User Coordinate Systems and the UCS icon is given in Chapter 24.

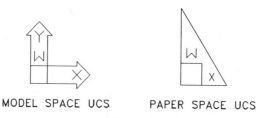

MODEL SPACE UCS   PAPER SPACE UCS

Fig. 9-11. The UCS icons for model space and paper space.

Paper space, on the other hand, is a "space" you create when you are ready to lay out a drawing or model to be plotted. Basically, you place a sheet of paper on the screen, then insert, or "reference," one or more drawings to the paper. In order to create this plotting layout, you must first enter paper space by typing "PSPACE" or "PS" at the Command: prompt.

> Command: **PS** ↵
> **Command not allowed unless TILEMODE is set to 0**

As you can see, AutoCAD does not allow you to enter paper space until you have changed the manner in which viewports are handled. This system variable is called TILEMODE. The function of tiled viewports is discussed later in this chapter, but for now, in order to enter paper space you must reset the TILEMODE value.

> Command: **TILEMODE** ↵
> New value for TILEMODE ⟨1⟩: **0** ↵

After entering the TILEMODE variable of 0 you are automatically placed in paper space. Notice the "P" that appears in the status line after the layer name and the paper space icon displayed in the lower-left corner of the screen.

Remember that you should create all your drawings and designs in model space, not in paper space. Only paper layouts for plotting purposes should be created in paper space. Therefore, you should return to model space by entering either "MSPACE" or "MS" at the Command: prompt.

> Command: **MS** ↵
> MSPACE
> There are no active Model space viewports.

Notice that you are *not* returned to model space. You must first reset the TILEMODE system variable to 1 to return to model space.

> Command: **TILEMODE** ↵
> New value for TILEMODE ⟨0⟩: **1** ↵

Do not be confused by TILEMODE, model space, and paper space. The detailed discussion in Chapter 27 will give you greater confidence. Right now, think of these terms in the following manner:

ACTIVITY	SPACE	TILEMODE
Drawing and design	Model	1
Plotting and printing layout	Paper	0

CREATING MULTIPLE VIEWPORTS $\quad$ ARM 7

Viewports are created with the VPORTS command. The screen of a DOS computer can be divided into sixteen "tiled" viewports. The edges of tiled viewports butt against one another like floor tile. The TILEMODE variable must be set to 1 or "ON" to display tiled viewports. The arrangement of the viewports can vary, as indicated by the options of the VPORTS command. The default arrangement of viewports—the 3 option—is shown in Fig. 9-12.

Command: **VPORTS** ↵
Save/Restore/Delete/Join/SIngle/?/2/⟨3⟩/4: ↵
Horizontal/Vertical/Above/Below/Left/⟨Right⟩: ↵

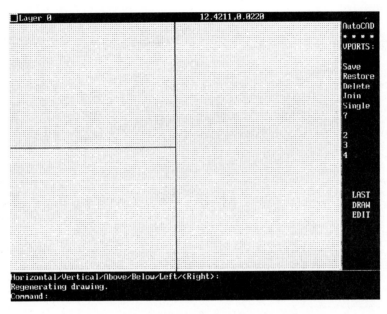

Fig. 9-12. The default arrangement of viewports.

When you accept the defaults, AutoCAD displays an arrangement of two viewports on the left side of the screen, and a large viewport on the right. The possible combinations of three viewports are shown in Fig. 9-13.

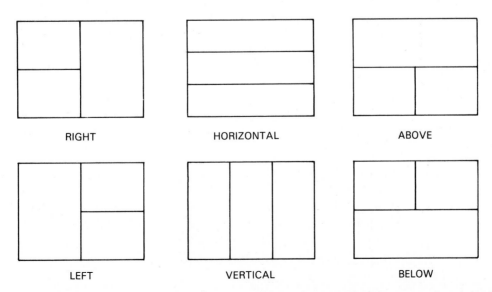

RIGHT $\qquad$ HORIZONTAL $\qquad$ ABOVE

LEFT $\qquad$ VERTICAL $\qquad$ BELOW

Fig. 9-13. A variety of viewport arrangements are possible with the VPORTS command and the 3 option.

Move the pointing device around and notice that only one viewport contains crosshairs. This is called the *active viewport*. The pointer is represented by an arrow in the others. To make a different viewport active, move the pointer into it and press the pick button. As you draw in one viewport, the image is displayed in all of them. Try drawing lines and other shapes and notice how the viewports are affected. Then use a Display command, such as ZOOM, in the current viewport and notice the results. Only the current viewport reflects the use of the ZOOM command.

Preset tiled viewport layouts can be selected from an icon menu. Pick the View pull-down menu, then select "Layout..." to display the "Tiled Viewport Layout" icon menu. You can select a pre-arranged layout by either picking the icon on the right, or by picking the written description from the list on the left. See Fig. 9-14. After you pick a layout, the icon is highlighted (as is the description). If this is the desired layout, pick OK and the screen automatically reflects your selection.

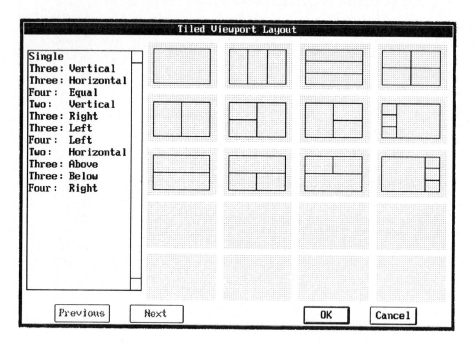

Fig. 9-14. The "Tiled Viewport Layout" icon menu.

Notice in Fig. 9-14 that there are several additional spaces in the icon menu. You can create custom viewport layouts and add them to this icon menu. See Chapter 32 for menu customization techniques.

Uses of viewports

Viewports in model space can be used for both 2-D and 3-D drawings. They are limited only by your imagination and need. See Chapter 24 for examples of the VPORTS command in 3-D. The nature of 2-D drawings, whether they are mechanical multiview, architectural construction details, or unscaled schematic drawings, lend themselves well to viewports.

━━━━━━━━━━━━━━━━ **PROFESSIONAL TIP** ━━━━━━━━━━━━━━━━

When dialogue boxes appear on screen, many times they obstruct your view of the drawing. Pick the black bar which contains the dialogue box name and hold down the pick button. You can then move the dialogue box to a new location on screen.

— **PROFESSIONAL TIP** —

Several sample drawings are included with the AutoCAD software. These files have been compressed and can only be viewed if you used the INSTALL program to copy the AutoCAD files to your hard disk. If AutoCAD was installed properly, the sample drawings should be located in the \ACAD\SAMPLE subdirectory. (The ACAD directory may be named ACAD12 or something similar.) Check with your instructor or supervisor to locate these drawings, or browse through the directories and subdirectories to determine their locations. The sample drawings include a variety of drawing and design disciplines and are excellent for testing and practice. It is suggested that you use these drawings, especially when learning the Display commands. A detailed description of the uses of VPORTS in 3-D modeling is given in Chapter 25.

EXERCISE 9-4

☐ Load AutoCAD and open the BASEPLAT drawing from your \ACAD\SAMPLE subdirectory. (BASEPLAT will reside here if AutoCAD was installed according to suggestions in the "Installation and Performance Guide.")
☐ When the drawing is displayed on the screen, you should see eight views. Zoom into various views to get familiar with the drawing.
☐ Use the VPORTS command to create the default arrangement of three viewports. (Make sure TILEMODE is set to 1.) The large viewport should be on the right.
☐ Use PAN to move the drawing up in the large viewport.
☐ In the upper-left viewport, use ZOOM Window to find Rear View, then zoom in on the note for the 13/64" DIA drill note.
☐ Zoom in on the Front View of the baseplate in the lower-left viewport (directly to the right of the Rear View). Locate the blind threaded hole in the bottom of the part and zoom in on the V-point of the hole. The point on the bottom of the hole is pointing up.
☐ While in this same viewport, use ZOOM Vmax. This displays the virtual screen for the current viewport.
☐ Quit and do not save the drawing.

INTRODUCTION TO 3-D DISPLAY COMMANDS | ARM 7 |

Three-dimensional drawing, modeling, and display is covered in detail in Chapters 25 and 26. However, a short introduction to two additional display commands will conclude the discussion of viewing drawings. The two commands are DVIEW (Dynamic VIEW), and VPOINT (ViewPOINT).

Establishing a dynamic view

When using the DVIEW command to view a 3-D drawing, you can see the object move as you perform the viewing manipulations such as rotate, turn, twist, and pan. You can rotate the "camera" (your eyes), and the "target" (focus point). Follow the given example for a brief overview of this command. Use the OPEN command and recall the SHUTTLE drawing. Again, this drawing may be in a separate subdirectory such as \ACAD\SAMPLE.

The "Open Drawing" dialogue box appears. Find SAMPLE in the Directories box and double click on it. A list of files should appear in the Files box. Pick SHUTTLE, then pick OK. The drawing that appears contains three views of the shuttle, and is displayed in a paper space layout with border and title block. Use the following commands to return the screen to a single plan view of the shuttle.

Command: **TILEMODE** ↵
New value for TILEMODE ⟨0⟩: **1** ↵
Regenerating drawing.

Now use the PLAN command to obtain the plan, or top view of the shuttle:

    Command: **PLAN** ↵

    ⟨Current UCS⟩/Ucs/World: ↵

    Regenerating drawing.

Your display should look like Fig. 9-15. Use the following commands to create viewports and a dynamic view in the large viewport.

    Command: **VPORTS** ↵

    Save/Restore/Delete/Join/SIngle/?/2/⟨3⟩/4: ↵

    Horizontal/Vertical/Above/Below/Left/⟨Right⟩: ↵

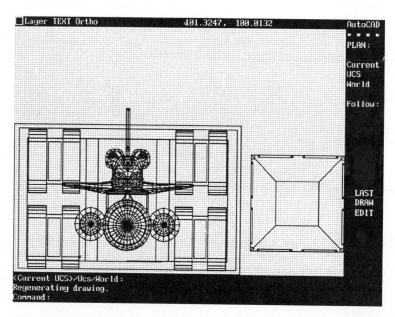

Fig. 9-15. The SHUTTLE drawing displayed in a single viewport.

Your screen should now look like the one in Fig. 9-16.

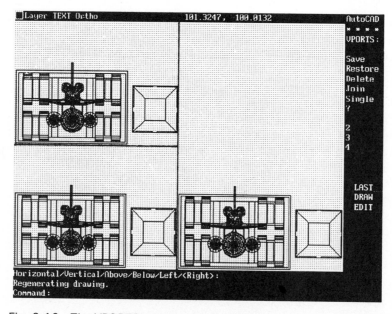

Fig. 9-16. The VPORTS command is used to display three viewports.

The DVIEW command is used next to create the 3-D view of the shuttle in the large viewport. Make the large viewport active. Instead of picking the viewport to make it active, you can press CTRL/V (hold down the CTRL key while pressing the V key) to change the active viewport. In order to speed up the DVIEW process, press ENTER at the "Select objects:" prompt. This displays a small house that requires less regeneration time. Your drawing returns to the screen at the completion of the DVIEW command, and is displayed in the same viewpoint as the house. If you want to work with your drawing on the screen using the DVIEW options, you must select it using any of the selection methods.

── NOTE ──

It is best to use the house for DVIEW purposes. If your drawing is complex, the computer slows down because it is constantly regenerating the highlighted display as the drawing is dynamically moved on the screen.

Command: **DVIEW** ↵
Select objects: ↵
CAmera/TArget/Distance/POints/PAn/Zoom/TWist/CLip/Hide/Off/Undo/⟨eXit⟩: **TA** ↵
Toggle angle in/Enter angle from XY plane ⟨−90.00⟩: **−15** ↵
Toggle angle from/Enter angle in XY plane from X axis ⟨90.00⟩: **−40** ↵
CAmera/TArget/Distance/POints/PAn/Zoom/TWist/CLip/Hide/Off/Undo/⟨eXit⟩: ↵
Command: **ZOOM** ↵
All/Center/Dynamic/Extents/Left/Previous/Vmax/Window/⟨Scale(X/XP)⟩: **E** ↵
Regenerating drawing.

Now, determine the direction in which you are viewing the shuttle. Notice in the small viewports that the bottom of the shuttle points to the bottom of the screen, or in the negative Y direction. Now look at the UCS icon in the large view. If it appears that you are looking at the top of the shuttle, you are correct. If you have trouble visualizing this, make the large viewport active, and then type "HIDE" at the Command: prompt. The screen display should look similar to Fig. 9-17.

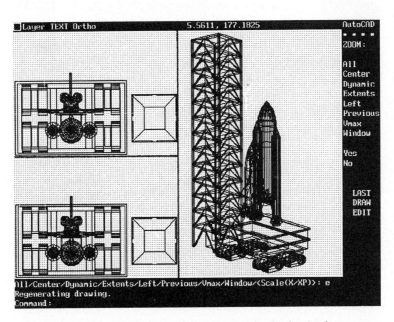

Fig. 9-17. The DVIEW command is used in the large viewport.

There are several other options and possibilities with the DVIEW command. You can create a true perspective view by specifying the distance from camera to target. In addition, you can zoom in or away from the object, or "clip" the front or rear of the screen image. Additional information regarding these options is found in Chapter 24.

Creating a 3-D viewpoint

The VPOINT command enables you to specify the direction from which you will view the object. You can enter XYZ coordinates, or you can visually determine your viewpoint using an XYZ "tripod." This introductory example uses coordinate entry to determine both viewpoints. See Chapter 24 for a discussion of the tripod method. Make the upper-left viewport active and enter the following commands:

> Command: **VPOINT** ↵
> Rotate/⟨View point⟩ ⟨0'-0″,0'-0″,0'-1″⟩: **−1,−1,1** ↵
> Regenerating drawing.

Activate the lower-left viewport and enter the following:

> Command: **VPOINT** ↵
> Rotate/⟨View point⟩ ⟨0'-0″,0'-0″,0'-1″⟩: **1,−1,1** ↵
> Regenerating drawing.

The two new displays created with VPOINT should resemble those in Fig. 9-18.

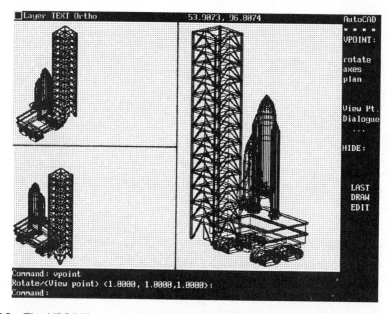

Fig. 9-18. The VPOINT command creates two different views in the small viewports.

One advantage of multiple viewports is that each viewport is a separate screen. Therefore, you can display any view of the drawing you wish in each screen. In addition, 3-D drawings can appear as either wireframe or solid. The views currently on your screen are in wireframe. The final aspect of this example illustrates these additional possibilities.

Make the lower-left viewport active and zoom in on one of the wheels of the shuttle transporter. Next, make the upper-left viewport active and zoom in on the nose of the shuttle. Now, use the HIDE command in all viewports to remove hidden lines. This process may take a few seconds depending on the speed of your computer.

> Command: **HIDE** ↵
> Regenerating drawing.
> Hiding lines: done 100%
>   Scanning xrefs...

Your screen now shows three separate 3-D views, with hidden lines removed to represent a solid. See Fig. 9-19.

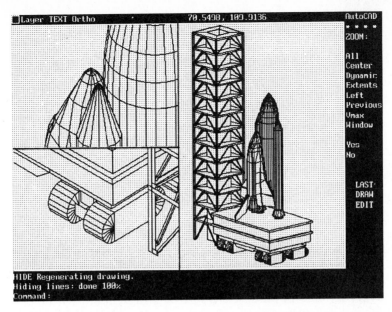

Fig. 9-19. Three separate views of the shuttle with hidden lines removed.

REDRAWING AND REGENERATING VIEWPORTS | ARM 7

Since each viewport is a separate screen, you can redraw or regenerate a single viewport at a time without affecting the others. The REGEN (REGENerate) command instructs AutoCAD to recalculate all of the entities in the drawing. This takes considerably longer than a REDRAW, especially if the drawing is large. However, a REGEN can clarify a drawing by smoothing out circles and arcs. In order to redraw all of the viewports, use the REDRAWALL command. If you need to regenerate all of the viewports, use the REGENALL command.

EXERCISE 9-5

☐ Use the display of the SHUTTLE drawing that is currently on your screen. If the display is not on your screen, refer to the previous section of this text entitled "Establishing a dynamic view," and follow the example to this point.
☐ Make the upper-left viewport active and draw some lines near the top of the shuttle. The lines should be displayed in all viewports.
☐ Make the lower-left viewport active and draw some lines by the wheel.
☐ Use the REDRAW command while the lower-left viewport is active. Notice that it is the only viewport that is redrawn.
☐ Use the REDRAWALL command.
☐ Pick the large viewport and enter the REGEN command.
☐ Use the REGENALL command. Notice how much longer it takes to perform this command than the REDRAWALL command.
☐ Save your drawing as A:EX9-5, then quit the drawing session.

Controlling automatic regeneration

When developing a drawing, you may issue a command that changes certain aspects of the entities in it. When this occurs, AutoCAD does an automatic regeneration to update the entities. This may not be of concern to you when working on small drawings, but this regeneration may take a considerable amount of time on larger and more complex drawings. In addition, it may not be necessary to have a regeneration of the drawing at all times. If this is the case, set the REGENAUTO command to off.

Command: **REGENAUTO** ↵
ON/OFF ⟨current⟩: **OFF** ↵

When REGENAUTO is off, you are given a warning if a regeneration is required:

About to regen − proceed? ⟨Y⟩

If you answer "No" to this prompt, the command you issued is not executed. The following commands may automatically cause a regeneration: ZOOM, PAN, and VIEW Restore.

MULTIPLE VIEWPORTS IN PAPER SPACE ARM 7

The viewports created with the VPORTS command in model space are called *tiled viewports* because they butt against one another. However, the viewports created in paper space are constructed with the MVIEW command, and are separate entities. You may create as many viewport entities as needed, and they can overlap. AutoCAD can only display a certain number of active viewports. A model space drawing is displayed in an active viewport. The type of operating system used by your computer and the display device determine the number of active viewports. You can check this number by entering the MAXACTVP (MAXimum ACTive ViewPorts) system variable:

Command: **MAXACTVP** ↵
New value for MAXACTVP ⟨16⟩:

The viewports created by the MVIEW command are used when laying out a multiview drawing for plotting or printing. Since these viewports are created in paper space, and they can overlap, the TILEMODE system variable must be set to 0. This places you in paper space so you can make "cutouts" or viewports in your sheet of paper with the MVIEW command. Think of the relationship of TILEMODE and viewports as follows:

ACTIVITY	SPACE	TILEMODE	COMMAND
Drawing and design	Model	1	VPORTS (tiled)
Plotting and printing layout	Paper	0	MVIEW (entities)

This procedure, and all of the options of the MVIEW command, are discussed in detail in Chapter 27.

CHAPTER TEST

Write your answers in the spaces provided.

1. What is the difference between the REDRAW and 'REDRAW commands? _____
   _____
   _____

2. What are "blips" and how does REDRAW deal with them? _____
   _____
   _____

3. Which command allows you to change the display of blips? _____

4. Give the proper command option and value to zoom in on the center of a drawing with a magnification factor of 3._____

5. What is the difference between ZOOM Extents and ZOOM All? _____
   _____
   _____

6. During the drawing process, when should you use ZOOM? _____
_____
_____

7. How many different boxes are displayed during the ZOOM Dynamic command?
_____

8. What is a "virtual screen?" _____
_____
_____
_____

9. When using the ZOOM Dynamic option, what symbol informs you that a regeneration is about to take place? _____

10. Which command and option allows you to create a view, named FULL, of the current screen display? _____

11. What option would you choose to display an existing view? _____

12. How would you obtain a listing of existing views? _____
_____

13. What is the purpose of the PAN command? _____
_____

14. How does PAN work? _____
_____

15. What is "view resolution?" _____
_____

16. What is the purpose of the VIEWRES command? _____
_____
_____

17. If you answer No to the prompt "Do you want fast zooms," what does AutoCAD do when you issue any display command? _____

18. What does the VIEWRES zoom percentage refer to? _____
_____

19. How is a transparent display command entered at the keyboard? _____
_____

20. When will AutoCAD refuse to execute a transparent display command? _____
_____

21. Explain the difference between model space and paper space. _____
_____
_____

22. What is the purpose of the TILEMODE system variable? _____
_____
_____

23. Describe the default viewport layout for the VPORTS command. _____
_____

24. What type of object does the DVIEW command use to initially establish a 3-D view?
_____

25. How do the DVIEW and VPOINT commands differ? _____
_____
_____

26. Which command regenerates all of the viewports? _____

27. What is the function of REGENAUTO? _____
_____

DRAWING PROBLEMS

1. Load a drawing from an earlier chapter. Use the following display commands and options on the drawing:
   A. ZOOM All.
   B. ZOOM Window on one detail three times.
   C. ZOOM Previous.
   D. ZOOM Extents.
   E. ZOOM Center.
   F. ZOOM Vmax.
   G. PAN in four directions.
   H. PAN diagonally.

2. Load a previous drawing that contains a large amount of detail. Use the VIEW command to create views of two areas containing detail. Also create a view that shows the entire drawing. Use the VIEW command to restore each of the views.

3. The purpose of this problem is to add six views to an existing prototype drawing that is C-size or larger. If you do not have a C-size prototype drawing, set up one for this problem. Use the following display aspects in your drawing:
   A. Create one view of the entire drawing limits and name it ALL or FULL.
   B. Window four additional views of the drawing area. Create one view for each quadrant of the drawing.
   C. Create a view of the title block.
   D. Set VIEWRES for fast zooms and a circle zoom percent of 50.
   E. Save the drawing as A:PRODRCV.

4. Load one of your B-size prototype drawings into the drawing editor. Create two views of the drawing area and one view of the title block. Set the VIEWRES for fast zooms and a circle zoom percent of 500. Save the drawing as A:PRODRBV.

5. Open the drawing named TOOLPOST. (If AutoCAD was installed properly, this drawing should be in the SAMPLE subdirectory of your AutoCAD directory.) When the drawing is displayed, perform the following:
   A. Make sure you are in paper space. Use the View command to create views of the following parts of the drawing. Name the views using the names provided in parentheses.
      • Title block (TITLE).
      • Parts list (PARTLIST).
      • Entire drawing (ALL).
      • Front view (FRONT).
      • Side view (SIDE).

B. Use the VIEW command's Restore option to check all the views you just made.

C. Restore the entire drawing with the proper view.

D. Set the TILEMODE system variable to 1. Try to restore one of your views. What happens?

E. Set TILEMODE to 0. Switch to model space by typing "MS."

F. Restore the TITLE view. Note that views created in paper space are displayed on the entire screen. Now switch to model space.

G. Create new views named FRONT and SIDE, the same as the previous views with these names.

H. Stay in model space and restore the FRONT view. Notice the difference between restoring a model space view and a paper space view.

I. Switch to paper space and restore the SIDE view. Pick the outline of the viewport when prompted to "Select Viewport for view." Notice that AutoCAD automatically switches to model space because that is where the view was created.

J. Save the drawing as A:P9-5 only if required to by your instructor.

6. Open the drawing named SEXTANT. It should be located in the \ACAD\SAMPLE subdirectory. The object is a 3-D drawing that is displayed in a perspective view. In order to use the Display commands such as ZOOM, you must first remove the perspective view.

A. Set the TILEMODE system variable to 1.

B. Type "DVIEW," then press ENTER at the "Select objects:" prompts. Your screen will go blank. Now type "OFF" and press ENTER twice to remove the perspective view and return to your drawing.

C. Then perform the following display functions on the SEXTANT drawing:

- Use ZOOM Dynamic to display the entire sextant on the screen.
- Create an arrangement of three viewports using the VPORTS command. Place the large viewport on the right.
- Use the PAN command to center the sextant in the large viewport.
- Pick the upper-left viewport and type "PLAN." This creates a top view. The PLAN command is discussed in Chapter 25.
- Pick the lower-left viewport and zoom in on the angled green box at the top of the sextant. Your display should look similar to the one shown below.
- Pick the large viewport and type "HIDE." This removes the hidden lines. Now type "SHADE." This colors in the solid faces of the object using the colors of the object. The HIDE and SHADE commands are discussed in Chapter 25.
- Use the VPORTS command to save the present configuration as THREE.
- Return the TILEMODE variable to 0.

D. Save your drawing as A:P9-6 and quit the drawing session.

E. Load AutoCAD and open P9-6 from your floppy disk using the prototype method.

F. Set TILEMODE to 1. Notice the configuration that is displayed.

G. Continue experimenting with naming views and creating other viewport configurations.

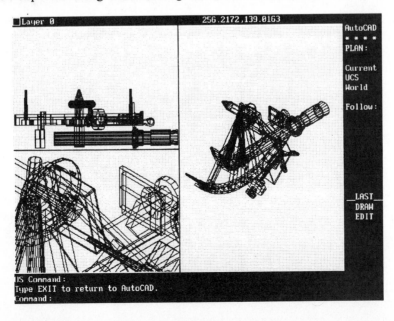

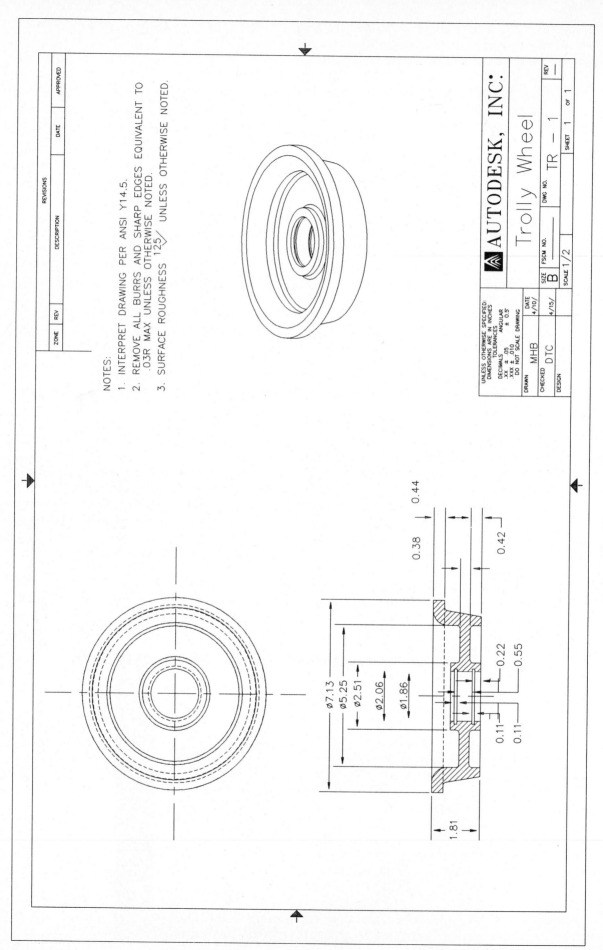

Trolley wheel drawing.   (Autodesk, Inc.)

```
Draw
  Line        ▷
  Arc         ▷
  Circle      ▷
  Point

  Polyline    ▷
  Donut
  Ellipse     ▷
  Polygon     ▷
  Rectangle

  Insert...

  3D Surfaces ▷

  Hatch...

  Text        │ Dynamic
              │ Import Text
  Dimension   │ Set Style...
              │
              │ Attributes ▷
```

PLACING TEXT ON A DRAWING

Learning objectives

After completing this chapter, you will be able to:

☐ Use the TEXT command to add words to a drawing.
☐ Change text styles using the STYLE command.
☐ Use the DTEXT command to display text on the screen while typing.
☐ Draw special symbols using control characters.
☐ Underscore and overscore text.
☐ Explain the purpose of the Quick Text mode and use the QTEXT command.
☐ Identify and use the pull-down menus for creating and drawing text.
☐ Design prototype drawings with title blocks for A-, B-, and C-size drawings.
☐ Draw objects with associated text.
☐ Edit existing text.

Words and notes on drawings have traditionally been added by hand lettering. Lettering is a slow, time-consuming task when done by hand using a pencil, pen, or a lettering device. Computer-aided drafting programs have reduced the tedious nature of adding notes to a drawing. In computer-aided drafting, lettering is referred to as *text*. There are some advantages of computer-generated text over hand-lettering techniques. Now, lettering is fast, easier to read, and follows the same consistent style. This chapter shows how text can be added by different methods. It also explains proper text presentation as interpreted from ASME Y14.2M−1992, *Line Conventions and Lettering*.

TEXT STANDARDS

Company standards often dictate how text should appear on a drawing. The minimum recommended text height on engineering drawings is 3mm (.125 in.). All dimension numerals, notes, and other text information should be the same height. Titles, subtitles, captions, revision information, and drawing numbers may be 6mm (approx. .25 in.) high. Many companies specify a 5mm (approx. .2 in.) lettering height for standard text. This text size is easy to read even after the drawing is reduced.

Vertical or inclined text may be used on a drawing depending on company preference, Fig. 10-1. One or the other is recommended; do not use both. The recommended slant for inclined text is 68° from horizontal. Computer-generated text offers a variety of styles for specific purposes, such as titles or captions.

Text on a drawing may be uppercase or lowercase letters. Most companies use uppercase letters.

Numerals in dimensions or notes are the same height as standard text, excluding titles. Most numeral dimensions on an engineering drawing are in decimal inches or millimeters. On architec-

ABC.. abc.. 123..
ABC.. abc.. 123..

Fig. 10-1. Vertical and inclined text.

tural drawings, enter dimensions as feet and inches. Fractional dimensions are not commonly used in mechanical drafting because they express a tolerance larger than the decimal equivalent. When fractions *are* used, each numeral should be the same height as the other drawing numerals. The ANSI standard recommends that the fraction bar be placed horizontally between the numerator and denominator, with full-size numerators and denominators. However, this is difficult with computer-generated text. Therefore, the fraction bar is placed diagonally. A dash or space is placed between the whole number and the fraction, Fig. 10-2. (Dimensioning is discussed in detail in Chapters 18 and 19.)

2.750 .375 (inch) 0.5 (mm)
2 3/4 or 2-3/4

Fig. 10-2. Numerals.

DETERMINING DRAWING SCALE FACTORS FOR TEXT HEIGHT

Before plotting a drawing, you should determine the scale factor. You can do this at the time of plotting, but more work is required to update text heights. Scale factors are important numbers because this value is used to ensure that the text is plotted at the proper height. The scale factor is multiplied by the desired plotted text height to get the AutoCAD text height.

The scale factor is always a reciprocal of the drawing scale. For example, if you wish to plot a drawing at a scale of 1/2″ = 1″, calculate the scale factor as follows:

    1/2″ = 1″
    .5″ = 1″
    1/.5 = 2   The scale factor is 2.

An architectural drawing that is to be plotted at a scale of 1/4″ = 1′-0″ has a scale factor calculated as follows:

    1/4″ = 1′-0″
    .25 = 12″
    12/.25 = 48   The scale factor is 48.

The scale factor of a civil engineering drawing that has a scale of 1″ = 60′ is calculated as follows:

    1″ = 60′
    1″ = (60 x 12)
    720/1 = 720   The scale factor is 720.

If your drawing is in millimeters where the scale is 1:1, the drawing scale factor may be converted to inches with the formula 1″ = 25.4 mm. Therefore, the scale factor is 25.4. When the metric drawing scale is 1:2, then the scale factor is 1″ = 50.8 (25.4 × 2). The scale factor is 50.8.

After the scale factor has been determined, you should then calculate the height of the AutoCAD text. If the text is to be plotted at 1/8″ (.125″) high, it should be drawn at that height. If the drawing scale is FULL or 1″ = 1″, then the text height is 1/8″ or .125″. However, if you are working on a civil engineering drawing with a scale of 1″ = 60′, text drawn at 1/8″ high appears as a dot. Remember that the drawing you are working on is 720 times larger than it is when plotted at the proper scale. Therefore, you must multiply the text height by the 720 scale factor to get text that appears in correct proportion on the screen. If you want 1/8″ (.125″)

high text to appear correctly on a drawing with a 1″ = 60′ scale, calculate the AutoCAD height as follows:

> 1″ = 60′
> 1″ = (60 x 12)
> 720/1 = 720   The scale factor is 720.
> text height x scale factor = scaled text height
> .125″ × 720 = 90   The proper text height is 90″.

An architectural drawing with a scale of 1/4″ = 1′-0″ has a scale factor of 48. Text that is to be 1/8″ high should be drawn 6″ high.

> 1/4″ = 1′-0″
> .25″ = 12″
> 12/.25 = 48   The scale factor is 48.
> .125 × 48 = 6   The proper text height is 6″.

Scale factors and text heights should be determined before beginning a drawing, and are best incorporated as values within your prototype drawing files.

TEXT COMPOSITION

Composition refers to the spacing, layout, and appearance of the text. With manual lettering, it is necessary to space letters freehand. This task is performed automatically with computer-generated text.

Notes should be placed horizontally on the drawing. AutoCAD automatically sets lines of text apart a distance equal to one-half the text height. This helps maintain the identity of individual notes.

Most lines of text are "left-justified." The term *justify* means to align the text to fit a given location. Left-justified text, for example, is text that is aligned along an imaginary left border. Fig. 10-3 shows minimum spacing between lines of left-justified text.

INTERPRET DIMENSIONING AND TOLERANCES
PER ANSI Y14.5M
REMOVE ALL BURRS AND SHARP EDGES

Fig. 10-3. Minimum spacing between lines of left-justified text.

USING AUTOCAD TO DRAW TEXT

ARM 5

The TEXT command places notes and other written information on a drawing. "TEXT" may be typed at the Command: prompt or picked from the DRAW screen menu. When you select or type the TEXT command, the prompt reads:

> Command: **TEXT** ↵
> Justify/Style/⟨Start point⟩:

The default option is Start point. If you want another option, type the option's first letter, such as "J" for Justify or "S" for Style, or select the option from the screen menu. The TEXT command allows you to compose the words in a variety of formats.

Selecting the Start point option

The default mode, Start point, allows you to select a point on the screen where you want the text to begin. This point becomes the lower-left corner of the text. After you pick the point, the prompt reads:

> Height ⟨0.2000⟩:

This allows you to select the text height. The default value is 0.2000. A previously selected letter height may be displayed as the current value. If you want letters that are .5 unit high, then type ".5". The next prompt is:

Rotation angle ⟨0⟩:

The default value of the rotation angle is 0. This places the text horizontally at the specified start point. Rotation angle values rotate text in a counterclockwise direction. The text pivots about the starting point, Fig. 10-4. Press ENTER for 0° rotation to place horizontal text.

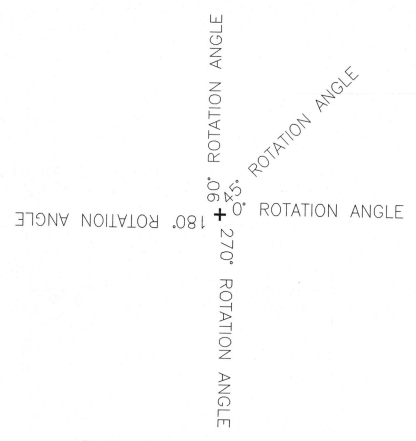

Fig. 10-4. Text using different rotation angles.

The last prompt is:

Text:

Type the desired text and press ENTER. Text added with the Start point option is left-justified. For example:

Text: **AUTOCAD LEFT-JUSTIFIED TEXT** ↵

After you type the note, press ENTER to insert the text. The information typed using the Start point option generates text as shown in Fig. 10-5. The "+" in Fig. 10-5 and future examples shows the pick point. The pick point is the point you select to locate the text.

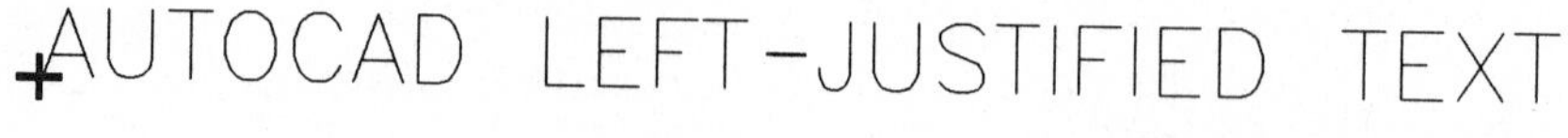

⊹AUTOCAD LEFT−JUSTIFIED TEXT

Fig. 10-5. Left-justified text using the Start point option.

Justifying your text

When you select the Justify option, you can use one of several text alignment options.

> Command: **TEXT** ↵
> Justify/Style/⟨Start point⟩: **J** ↵
> Align/Fit/Center/Middle/Right/TL/TC/TR/ML/MC/MR/BL/BC/BR:

Using the Align text option

The Align option allows you to pick two points between which the text string is confined. The beginning and endpoints may be placed horizontally or at an angle. The computer automatically adjusts the text width to fit between the points selected. One caution with this option is that the text height is also changed. This varies according to the distance between points and the number of characters. To use this option, enter "J" for Justify, and then "A" for Align as follows:

> Command: **TEXT** ↵
> Justify/Style/⟨Start point⟩: **J** ↵
> Align/Fit/Center/Middle/Right/TL/TC/TR/ML/MC/MR/BL/BC/BR: **A** ↵
> First text line point: *(pick a point)*
> Second text line point: *(pick a point)*
> Text: **AUTOCAD ALIGNED TEXT** ↵

Fig. 10-6 shows how information is aligned between the first and second points. Notice that the text is confined. The letter height and width changes in relation to the distance between points.

AUTOCAD ALIGNED TEXT

When using aligned text
the text height
is adjusted so the text
fits between
two picked points.

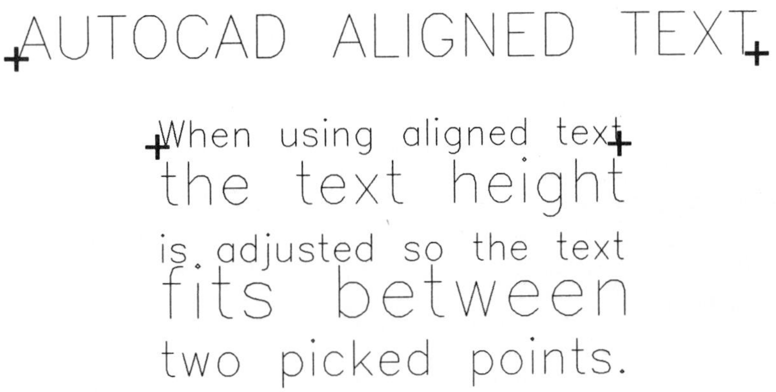

Fig. 10-6. Aligned text.

Using the Fit text option

The Fit option is similar to the Align option, except that you may select the text height. AutoCAD adjusts the letter width to fit between two given points. The height default value is .20, but you may change this.

> Command: **TEXT** ↵
> Justify/Style/⟨Start point⟩: **J** ↵
> Align/Fit/Center/Middle/Right/TL/TC/TR/ML/MC/MR/BL/BC/BR: **F** ↵
> First text line point: *(pick a point)*
> Second text line point: *(pick a point)*
> Height ⟨current⟩: **.5** ↵
> Text: **AUTOCAD FIT TEXT** ↵

Fig. 10-7 shows the note above as it appears on the screen in two different locations. Notice that the letter height remains the same, but the letter width is adjusted. In both cases, the line of text fits between the chosen points.

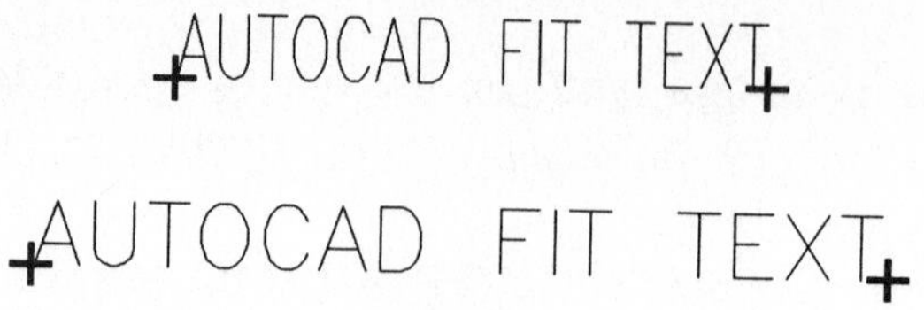

AUTOCAD FIT TEXT

AUTOCAD FIT TEXT

Fig. 10-7. Using the Fit text option.

The Center text option

The Center option allows you to select the center point for the baseline of the text. Enter the letter height and rotation angle after picking the center point. This example uses a .5 unit height and a 0° rotation angle. The prompts appear as follows:

Command: **TEXT** ⏎
Justify/Style/⟨Start point⟩: **J** ⏎
Align/Fit/Center/Middle/Right/TL/TC/TR/ML/MC/MR/BL/BC/BR: **C** ⏎
Center point: *(pick a point)*
Height ⟨current⟩: **.5** ⏎
Rotation angle ⟨0⟩: ⏎
Text: **AUTOCAD CENTERED TEXT** ⏎

Fig. 10-8 shows how the AUTOCAD CENTERED TEXT note appears.

AUTOCAD CENTERED TEXT

Fig. 10-8. Using the Center option.

Using the Middle text option

The Middle text option allows you to center text both horizontally and vertically at a given point. The letter height and rotation may be changed. The command sequence is as follows:

Command: **TEXT** ⏎
Justify/Style/⟨Start point⟩: **J** ⏎
Align/Fit/Center/Middle/Right/TL/TC/TR/ML/MC/MR/BL/BC/BR: **M** ⏎
Middle point: *(pick a point)*
Height ⟨current⟩: **.5** ⏎
Rotation angle ⟨0⟩: ⏎
Text: **AUTOCAD MIDDLE TEXT** ⏎

Fig. 10-9 shows the above note as it appears on the screen.

AUTOCAD MIDDLE TEXT

Fig. 10-9. Using the Middle text option.

The Right text option
   The Right option is similar to Start point, except text is aligned with the lower-right corner. The text is right-justified. This option also allows you to enter letter height and rotation angle. The command sequence appears as follows:

   Command: **TEXT** ↵
   Justify/Style/⟨Start point⟩: **J** ↵
   Align/Fit/Center/Middle/Right/TL/TC/TR/ML/MC/MR/BL/BC/BR: **R** ↵
   End point: *(pick a point)*
   Height ⟨current⟩: **.5** ↵
   Rotation angle ⟨0⟩: ↵
   Text: **AUTOCAD RIGHT-JUSTIFIED TEXT** ↵

Fig. 10-10 shows right-justified text.

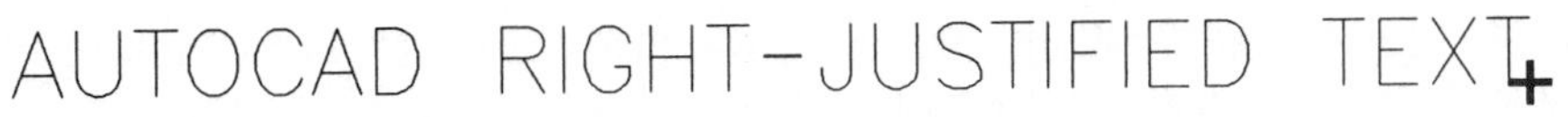

AUTOCAD RIGHT-JUSTIFIED TEXT +

Fig. 10-10. Using the Right text option.

EXERCISE 10-1

☐ Load AutoCAD.
☐ Use the TEXT command to type the following information. Each time, change the text option to obtain the format given. Use .5 letter height and 0° rotation angle.
   AUTOCAD TEXT LEFT-JUSTIFIED USING THE START POINT OPTION.
   AUTOCAD TEXT RIGHT-JUSTIFIED USING THE RIGHT OPTION.
   AUTOCAD TEXT ALIGNED USING THE ALIGN OPTION.
   AUTOCAD TEXT CENTERED USING THE CENTER OPTION.
   AUTOCAD FIT TEXT USING THE FIT OPTION.
   AUTOCAD TEXT USING THE MIDDLE OPTION.
☐ Save the drawing as A:EX10-1 and quit.

―――――――――― **PROFESSIONAL TIP** ――――――――――

   If you already know which text alignment option you want to use in your drawing, you can enter it at the Justify/Style/⟨Start point⟩ prompt without entering "J" for Justify.

Using the other text alignment options
   There are a number of text alignment options that allow you to place text on a drawing in relationship to the top, bottom, middle, left, or right side of the text. These alignment options are displayed in Fig. 10-11.

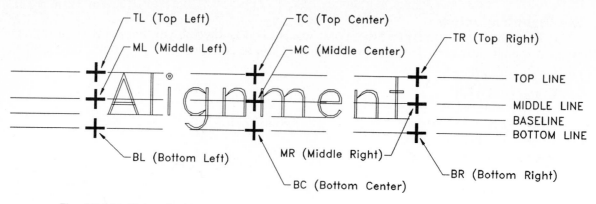

Fig. 10-11. Using the TL, TC, TR, ML, MC, MR, BL, BC, and BR text alignment options.

The alignment options displayed in Fig. 10-11 are also shown as abbreviations. Note the abbreviations shown in the illustration and those found in the TEXT prompt line.

When you select the Justify option using the prompt line or screen menu, one of several text alignment options is available to use. The command sequence for these options are similar to what was previously discussed:

Command: **TEXT** ↵
Justify/Style/⟨Start point⟩: **J** ↵
Align/Fit/Center/Middle/Right/TL/TC/TR/ML/MC/MR/BL/BC/BR:

Left-justified text

The TL option allows you to justify the text at the top left as shown in Fig. 10-12.

Command: **TEXT** ↵
Justify/Style/⟨Start point⟩: **J** ↵
Align/Fit/Center/Middle/Right/TL/TC/TR/ML/MC/MR/BL/BC/BR: **TL** ↵
Top/left point: *(pick a point)*
Height ⟨current⟩: **.5** ↵
Rotation angle ⟨0⟩: ↵
Text: **AUTOCAD TOP/LEFT TEXT** ↵

⁺AUTOCAD TOP/LEFT TEXT

Fig. 10-12. Using the TL text alignment option.

Center-justified text

The TC option allows you to justify the text at the top center as shown in Fig. 10-13.

Command: **TEXT** ↵
Justify/Style/⟨Start point⟩: **J** ↵
Align/Fit/Center/Middle/Right/TL/TC/TR/ML/MC/MR/BL/BC/BR: **TC** ↵
Top/center point: *(pick a point)*
Height ⟨current⟩: **.5** ↵
Rotation angle ⟨0⟩: ↵
Text: **AUTOCAD TOP/CENTER TEXT** ↵

AUTOCAD TOP⁺/CENTER TEXT

Fig. 10-13. Using the TC text alignment option.

Right-justified text

The TR option allows you to justify the text at the top right as shown in Fig. 10-14.

    Command: **TEXT** ↵
    Justify/Style/⟨Start point⟩: **J** ↵
    Align/Fit/Center/Middle/Right/TL/TC/TR/ML/MC/MR/BL/BC/BR: **TR** ↵
    Top/right point: *(pick a point)*
    Height ⟨current⟩: **.5** ↵
    Rotation angle ⟨0⟩: ↵
    Text: **AUTOCAD TOP/RIGHT TEXT** ↵

AUTOCAD TOP/RIGHT TEXT⁺

Fig. 10-14. Using the TR text alignment option.

In the previous discussion you have seen how the TL, TC, and TR options work. The remaining text alignment options function in the same manner. If you forget what the different abbreviations refer to, look back at Fig. 10-11 for reference.

EXERCISE 10-2

☐ Load AutoCAD.
☐ Use the TEXT command to type the following information. Each time, change the text option to obtain the format given in each statement. Use .5 letter height and 0° rotation angle.
    AUTOCAD TOP/LEFT OPTION.
    AUTOCAD TOP/CENTER OPTION.
    AUTOCAD TOP/RIGHT OPTION.
    AUTOCAD MIDDLE/LEFT OPTION.
    AUTOCAD MIDDLE/CENTER OPTION.
    AUTOCAD MIDDLE/RIGHT OPTION.
    AUTOCAD BOTTOM/LEFT OPTION.
    AUTOCAD BOTTOM/CENTER OPTION.
    AUTOCAD BOTTOM/RIGHT OPTION.
☐ Save the drawing as A:EX10-2 and quit.

MAKING MULTIPLE LINES OF TEXT   ARM 5

Lines of text may be automatically spaced, each string having the same angle, height, and alignment. Press ENTER after the first line has been entered. This brings back the Command: prompt. A second ENTER repeats the previous TEXT command. The Start point: prompt is displayed again and the previous line of text is highlighted. Press the ENTER key again to automatically justify the next line of text below the previous. The same procedure is used to continue drawing additional lines of text, Fig. 10-15. The command sequence is as follows:

    Command: **TEXT** ↵
    Justify/Style/⟨Start point⟩: *(pick the start point)*
    Height ⟨current⟩: **.5** ↵
    Rotation angle ⟨0⟩: ↵
    Text: **THIS IS THE FIRST LINE OF TEXT** ↵
    Command: ↵
    TEXT Justify/Style/⟨Start point⟩: ↵
    Text: **THIS IS THE SECOND LINE OF TEXT** ↵

Words on a drawing have traditionally been referred to as lettering. Lettering has typically been a slow, time—consuming task. Computer—aided drafting has reduced the tedious nature of preparing lettering on a drawing.

Fig. 10-15. Drawing multiple lines of text.

EXERCISE 10-3

☐ Load AutoCAD.
☐ Use the TEXT command to type the following multiple lines of text exactly as shown. Use .25 letter height and 0° rotation angle.

LETTERING HAS TYPICALLY BEEN A SLOW, TIME-CONSUMING TASK. COMPUTER-AIDED DRAFTING HAS REDUCED THE TEDIOUS NATURE OF PREPARING LETTERING ON A DRAWING. IN CAD, LETTERING IS NOW REFERRED TO AS TEXT. COMPUTER-GENERATED TEXT IS FAST, CONSIS-TENT, AND EASY TO READ.

☐ Save the drawing as A:EX10-3 and quit.

PROFESSIONAL TIP

Multiple lines of text may be placed in a box format with the Fit option. This justifies the text on the left and right. The letter height is the same for each line of text. However, the letter width is different, Fig. 10-16.

When using FIT text text height remains the same. The text width is adjusted to fit between the picked points.

Fig. 10-16. Boxing text using the Fit option.

AUTOCAD TEXT FONTS

ARM 5

A *font* is all of the uppercase and lowercase letters and numerals of a particular letter face design. The standard AutoCAD text fonts are shown in Fig. 10-17. The TXT font is the AutoCAD default when you begin a new drawing. The TXT font is rather rough in appearance and may not be the best choice for your application. On the other hand, TXT requires less time to regenerate than other fonts. The ROMANS (ROMAN Simplex) font is smoother than TXT. It closely

Fast fonts

txt   The quick brown fox jumps over the lazy dog.   ABC123

monotxt   The quick brown fox jumps over the lazy dog.   ABC123

Simplex fonts

romans   The quick brown fox jumps over the lazy dog.   ABC123

scripts   *The quick brown fox jumps over the lazy dog.   ABC123*

greeks   Τηε ϑυιχκ βροων φοξ ϑυμπσ οϵερ τηε λαζψ δογ.   ΑΒΧ123

Duplex font

romand   The quick brown fox jumps over the lazy dog.   ABC123

Complex fonts

romanc   The quick brown fox jumps over the lazy dog.   ABC123

italicc   *The quick brown fox jumps over the lazy dog.   ABC123*

scriptc   *The quick brown fox jumps over the lazy dog.   ABC123*

greekc   Τηε ϑυιχκ βροων φοξ ϑυμπσ οϵερ τηε λαζψ δογ.   ΑΒΧ123

cyrillic   Узд рфивк бсоцн еоч йфмпт охдс узд лащш гож.   АББ123

cyriltlc   Тхе цуичк брошн фож щумпс овер тхе лазй дог.   АБЧ123

Triplex fonts

romant   **The quick brown fox jumps over the lazy dog.   ABC123**

italict   ***The quick brown fox jumps over the lazy dog.   ABC123***

Gothic fonts

gothice   𝔗𝔥𝔢 𝔮𝔲𝔦𝔠𝔨 𝔟𝔯𝔬𝔴𝔫 𝔣𝔬𝔵 𝔧𝔲𝔪𝔭𝔰 𝔬𝔳𝔢𝔯 𝔱𝔥𝔢 𝔩𝔞𝔷𝔶 𝔡𝔬𝔤.   𝔄𝔅ℭ123

gothicg   𝔗𝔥𝔢 𝔮𝔲𝔦𝔠𝔨 𝔟𝔯𝔬𝔴𝔫 𝔣𝔬𝔵 𝔧𝔲𝔪𝔭𝔰 𝔬𝔳𝔢𝔯 𝔱𝔥𝔢 𝔩𝔞𝔷𝔶 𝔡𝔬𝔤.   𝔄𝔅ℭ123

gothici   𝔗𝔥𝔢 𝔮𝔲𝔦𝔠𝔨 𝔟𝔯𝔬𝔴𝔫 𝔣𝔬𝔵 𝔧𝔲𝔪𝔭𝔰 𝔬𝔳𝔢𝔯 𝔱𝔥𝔢 𝔩𝔞𝔷𝔶 𝔡𝔬𝔤.   𝔄𝔅ℭ123

Fig. 10-17. Standard AutoCAD text fonts.   (Autodesk, Inc.)

duplicates the single-stroke Gothic lettering that has long been the standard for drafting. The COMPLEX and TRIPLEX fonts are multistroke fonts for drawing titles and subtitles. The GOTHIC and ITALIC fonts are ornamental styles. In addition, AutoCAD provides several standard symbol fonts as shown in Fig. 10-18.

Several additional AutoCAD fonts provide special alphabets or symbols that you must access by typing specific keys. This method is referred to as *character mapping* for non-Romanic and symbol fonts as displayed in Fig. 10-19.

AutoCAD Release 12 also provides PostScript™ fonts for use in drawings. See Fig. 10-20. PostScript fonts are available by using the STYLE command and techniques previously discussed for the standard AutoCAD fonts. You can set a width factor or obliquing angle, but you cannot apply both options to these fonts. Additional information regarding PostScript fonts is included in Chapter 26.

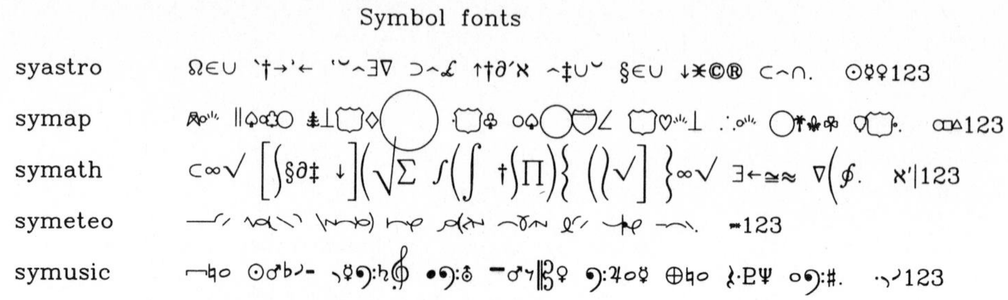

Symbol fonts

Fig. 10-18. Standard AutoCAD symbol fonts. (Autodesk, Inc.)

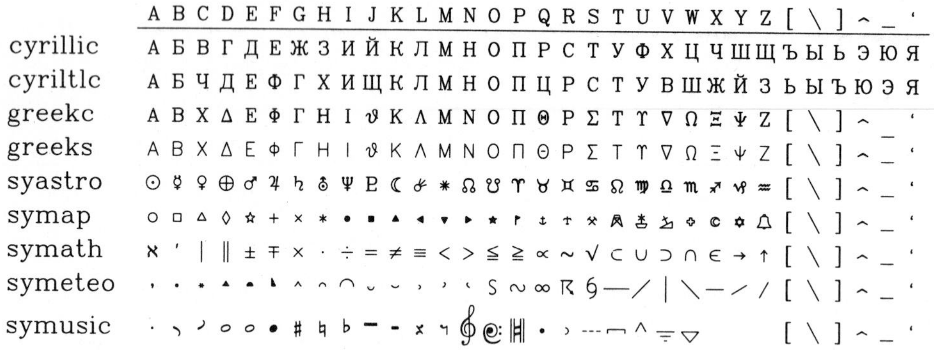

Fig. 10-19. Character mapping for non-Romanic and symbol fonts. (Autodesk, Inc.)

Fig. 10-20. AutoCAD Release 12 PostScript fonts. (Autodesk, Inc.)

SELECTING AUTOCAD TEXT STYLES

Text styles are variations of fonts. A *text style* gives height, width, obliquing angle (slant), and other features to a text font. You may have several text styles which use the same font. Text styles may be created using the STYLE command, to be discussed later. The default style name used with the TEXT command is STANDARD. If the Style option is selected, you can select another text style. The Style option is entered at the TEXT prompt line by typing "S." You can also select Style from the TEXT screen menu. The following sequence shows the TEXT command's Style option prompts:

```
Command: TEXT ↵
Justify/Style/⟨Start point⟩: S ↵
Style name (or ?) ⟨current⟩:
```

You may respond in one of the following ways:
- Press the ENTER key to activate the current style.
- Type the name of a style that was previously created using the STYLE command. If you enter a text style that was not previously created using the STYLE command, AutoCAD gives this message:

```
Unknown or invalid text style name.
Style name (or ?) ⟨current⟩:
```

- Type "?" to get a list of the available text styles. Entering "?" gives you this prompt:

```
Style name (or ?)⟨current⟩: ? ↵
Text style(s) to list ⟨*⟩:
```

You may type the specific text styles to list, or press ENTER to display all of the available text styles. The available text styles are shown on the alphanumeric screen. The style name, font file, height, width factor, obliquing angle, and generation of each are listed. Press the F1 key to return to the graphics screen.

After your response, AutoCAD displays the Start point: prompt for you to continue the TEXT command.

PROFESSIONAL TIP

The TEXT command's Style option allows you to select text styles that have already been created. The STYLE command allows you to custom design one of the standard fonts to make a new style. The Style option then allows you to select that new style to use for text added to the drawing.

MAKING FONT STYLES

ARM 5

The STYLE command is used to create and modify existing text styles or list existing styles. The prompts associated with the STYLE command are as follows:

```
Command: STYLE ↵
Text style name (or ?) ⟨current⟩: (enter text style name and press ENTER)
```

After entering the desired text style name, AutoCAD displays the "Select Font File" dialogue box shown in Fig. 10-21. If the chosen style exists, you get an "Existing style" message on the command line, and the existing font is displayed at the File: input button. You can press ENTER to keep the existing style. If the entered style is new, AutoCAD gives you a "New style" message and the default font for that style is shown in the File: input button.

In order to create or change a style, enter the style name at the Text style name: prompt, then select a font to use in one of four ways:

- Page through the list of available text fonts, move the cursor arrow to the desired font, and pick. In Fig. 10-21, the ROMANS font is picked and is shown at the input button to acknowledge its selection. Now press ENTER or pick the OK button.
- Pick the File: input button. The input button is highlighted. Then, type the font name. When ready, pick OK or press ENTER.
- Move the cursor arrow to the "Type it" button and pick. This removes the "Select Font File" dialogue box and allows you to type the desired font name:

  Font file ⟨current⟩: **ROMANS** ↵

- Pick the Default button to accept the default font style.

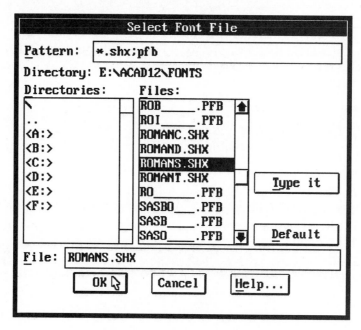

Fig. 10-21. The "Select Font File" dialogue box displays the names of fonts available to use.

No matter which entry method you use, the rest of the prompts let you establish the style characteristics.

Height ⟨default⟩: *(enter the height value,* **.25***, for example, and press ENTER)*
Width factor ⟨default⟩:*(enter the width factor,* **1***, for example and press ENTER)*
Obliquing angle ⟨default⟩: *(enter the obliquing angle,* **0***, for example and press ENTER)*
Backwards? ⟨N⟩: **Y** or **N** ↵
Upside-down? ⟨N⟩: **Y** or **N** ↵
Vertical? ⟨N⟩: **Y** or **N** ↵
ROMANS is now the current text style.

STYLE command prompts

The following discussion explains each of the STYLE command prompts.

Text style name (or ?) ⟨current⟩:

The first prompt in the STYLE command allows you to create a new style or modify an existing style. A "?" response produces a list of existing styles. Pressing the space bar or ENTER key selects the current style shown in brackets (⟨ ⟩). To create or modify an existing style, use one of the methods previously discussed. For example, suppose you want to create a ROMANS style with a height of .125. Enter the style name as ROMANS-125. The style name may contain up to 31 characters.

Font file ⟨default⟩:

This prompt appears if the FILEDIA system variable is set to 0. Type the name of the font to be used. In this example, the font you are using is ROMANS. If you respond by pressing the ENTER key, the default font shown in brackets is made current. If FILEDIA is 1, the "Select Font File" dialogue box appears. Select the desired font from the list, or enter the font file name using the procedure discussed earlier.

Height ⟨default⟩:

The Height: prompt allows you to enter a fixed character height. For example, typing ".125" draws text .125 in. high for the text style. A "0" response here gives you the opportunity to specify the text height each time you use this style. You may also press ENTER to choose the default height shown in brackets.

Width factor ⟨default⟩:

The *width factor* is a numerical value that defines the character width relative to the height. A width factor of 1 is the default. A width factor greater than 1 expands the letters. A factor less than 1 compresses the letters, Fig. 10-22.

Width Factor	Text
1	ABCDEFGHIJKLM
.5	ABCDEFGHIJKLMNOPQRSTUVWXY
1.5	ABCDEFGHI
2	ABCDEFG

Fig. 10-22. AutoCAD text width factors.

Obliquing angle ⟨default⟩:

The obliquing angle allows you to slant the letters to the right or left. A "0" response draws vertical text. A value greater than 0 slants the letters to the right. A negative angle slants the characters to the left. See Fig. 10-23.

Obliquing angle	Text
0	ABCDEFGHIJKLM
15	ABCDEFGHIJKLM
−15	ABCDEFGHIJKLM

Fig. 10-23. AutoCAD obliquing angles.

Backwards ⟨N⟩:

If you want the text to appear backwards, respond "Y" to this prompt. For text that appears normal, respond with "N." Backwards characters may be used when the text is to be printed on the back of polyester film. When the film is turned around, the image will be legible. An example of backwards text is shown in Fig. 10-24.

Fig. 10-24. Backwards text.

Upside-down? ⟨N⟩:

If you want the text to appear upside-down, respond with "Y" to this prompt. See Fig. 10-25. For text that appears normal, respond with "N."

Fig. 10-25. Upside-down text.

Vertical? ⟨N⟩:

Text is normally placed horizontally on a drawing. However, it is possible to add text in a vertical format. This application may be used for graphic designs or custom layouts. Vertical text is shown in Fig. 10-26.

Vertical text works best when the rotation angle is set at 270°. For prompts that require two points, the second point should be directly below the first. Obliquing, underscoring, or overscoring are not intended for use with the vertical format. If vertical text is desired, then a "Y" response is required. Enter an "N" for standard horizontal text.

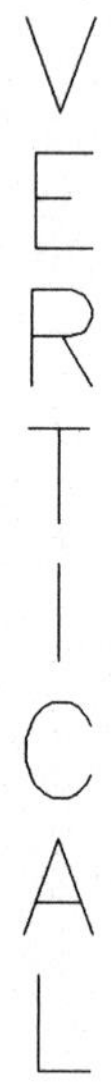

Fig. 10-26. Vertical text orientation.

CREATING A NEW TEXT STYLE

Assume that you have entered the drawing editor to begin a new drawing. Remember, the only text style available is TXT. The following command and prompts sets a new style called ROMANS-125:

Command: **STYLE** ⏎
Text style name (or ?) ⟨STANDARD⟩: **ROMANS-125** ⏎

The "Select Font File" dialogue box then appears (if FILEDIA is 1). Type "ROMANS" in the File: box and pick the extended OK box, or pick ROMANS from the list of fonts. Pick OK to close the dialogue box, and then enter the following values:

Height ⟨current⟩: **.125** ⏎
Width factor ⟨current⟩: **1** ⏎
Obliquing angle ⟨current⟩: **0** ⏎
Backwards? ⟨N⟩: ⏎
Upside-down? ⟨N⟩: ⏎
Vertical? ⟨N⟩: ⏎
ROMANS-125 is now the current text style.

Keep reference notes stating the name and features of text styles that you design. However, if you forget, enter "?" at the Text style name: prompt. A listing of created styles appears.

Using the new text style

The new text style may now be used by entering the TEXT command. Select the Start point or any of the other options. In this example, the ROMANS-125 style is now the default until you change it using the Style option. Remember, that you may use the TEXT command's Style option to select those text styles already created with the STYLE command.

——————————— PROFESSIONAL TIP ———————————

It is recommended that you use fancy text styles, such as COMPLEX and ITALIC, only on rare occasions. They require much more computer regeneration time. They also take longer to plot than TXT or SIMPLEX fonts, and make drawing files larger.

EXERCISE 10-4

☐ Load AutoCAD.
☐ Use the TEXT command to type the following information. Change the text style to represent each of the four standard AutoCAD fonts named. Use .5 unit letter height and 0° rotation angle.
   TXT—AUTOCAD'S DEFAULT TEXT FONT.
   SIMPLEX—A SMOOTH FONT OF CONVENTIONAL LETTERING STYLE.
   COMPLEX—A MULTISTROKE FONT THAT IS GOOD FOR TITLES.
   ITALIC—AN ORNAMENTAL FONT SLANTED TO THE RIGHT.
☐ Save the drawing as A:EX10-4 and quit.

Changing the format of existing styles

You can change text style without affecting existing text entities. The changes are applied only to newly added text using that style. However, you may not alter the text font or the orientation from horizontal or vertical. You can change the name of an existing text style using the RENAME command discussed in Chapter 17.

Suppose you change the values of an existing text style, including the font and orientation. *All* text items with that style are redrawn with the new values. They are displayed when the drawing is regenerated. This type of a change causes automatic regeneration if the REGENAUTO mode is on.

SELECTING TEXT FONTS
FROM THE ICON MENU

$\boxed{\textbf{ARM 3}}$

You can also select text fonts from the "Select Text Font" icon menu shown in Fig. 10-27. To access this menu, pick Text from the Draw pull-down menu and then pick Set Style... from the cascading submenu. Now, pick the icon of the desired text font, or scroll through the font file list and pick the desired text style name. When a text font style is picked, the name and icon become highlighted. Pick the OK button or press ENTER to accept the choice. Pick the Next button to view another icon menu page, and then pick Previous to return the first page. Pick Cancel if you want to exit the "Select Text Font" icon menu.

When you pick a text, the icon menu closes and the following command sequence is displayed:

Command: '__style Text style name (or ?) ⟨current⟩: romans
New style
Font file ⟨current⟩: romans Height ⟨0.000⟩:

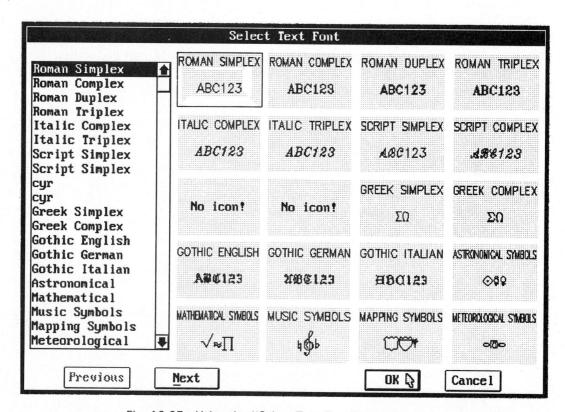

Fig. 10-27. Using the "Select Text Font" icon menu.

When this prompt appears, type the desired text height. Text is drawn at that height each time you use the TEXT or DTEXT commands. If you press ENTER at the Height: prompt, the text height is 0. Specifying a "0" text height allows you to enter the height each time the TEXT or DTEXT commands are used. This gives you more flexibility when drawing text. Additional factors are asked for with the following prompts. You may enter new values or press ENTER to keep the default value shown in brackets.

Font file ⟨current⟩: romans Height ⟨0.000⟩: **.5** ↵
   Width factor ⟨1.00⟩: ↵
Obliquing angle ⟨0⟩: ↵
Backwards? ⟨N⟩ ↵
Upside-down? ⟨N⟩ ↵
Vertical? ⟨N⟩ ↵
ROMANS is now the current text style.
Command:

The command sequence above selects ROMAN Simplex (ROMANS) as the current text font and style.

Check or change the current text style name

You can check the current text style name or change the text style to a previously set style with the TEXTSTYLE system variable like this:

Command: **TEXTSTYLE** ↵
New value for TEXTSTYLE ⟨"STANDARD"⟩: **ROMANS** ↵

Press ENTER to accept the current text style shown in brackets, or enter a new text style that was previously set using the STYLE command. If you make a mistake when typing, AutoCAD gives you an *Invalid* error message and returns you to the Command: prompt.

SPECIAL CHARACTERS

ARM 5

Many drafting applications require special symbols for text and dimensions. In order to draw symbols, AutoCAD requires a sequence of *control characters*. The *control sequence* for a symbol begins with a double percent sign (%%). The next character you enter represents the symbol. The following list gives the most used control sequences:

%%D = Draw degrees symbol (°).
%%P = Draw plus/minus tolerance symbol (±).
%%C = Draw diameter symbol (φ).
%%% = Draw a single percent symbol (%).

In order to draw the note, φ2.75, you would use the control sequence %%C2.75. The results are shown in Fig. 10-28.

$$\phi 2.75$$

Fig. 10-28. Using the control sequence %%C to create the φ (diameter) symbol.

A single percent sign may be also drawn without using the %%% control sequence; simply use the percent (%) key. However, when a percent sign must precede another control sequence, the %%% characters force a single percent sign. For example, suppose you want the note 25% ±2. You must type the following sequence: 25%%%%%P2.

Special symbols may also be drawn by entering a three-digit code between 1 and 126. These symbols and codes are given in the *AutoCAD Customization Manual*. For example, the ampersand (&) symbol is drawn by the sequence %%038. The control sequence for symbols that are often found on drawings include:

%%035 = #   %%047 = /
%%037 = %   %%060 = ⟨
%%038 = &   %%061 = =
%%040 = (%%062 = ⟩
%%041 =)   %%064 = @
%%044 = ,

Drawing underscored or overscored text

Text may be underscored (underlined) or overscored by typing a control sequence in front of the line of text. The control sequences are:

%%O = overscore
%%U = underscore

For example, to underline the note: UNDERSCORING TEXT, type the note as "%%UUNDERSCORING TEXT." The resulting text is shown in Fig. 10-29. If a line of text requires both underscoring and overscoring, the control sequence is typed as %%O%%ULINE OF TEXT.

UNDERSCORING TEXT

Fig. 10-29. The %%%U control sequence underscores text.

The %%O and %%U control codes are toggles that turn overscoring and underscoring on and off. Type "%%U" preceding a word or phrase to turn underscoring on, followed by typing "%%U" after the desired word or phrase to turn underscoring off. Any text following the second "%%U" will then appear without underscoring.

DYNAMIC TEXT—SEE THE TEXT AS YOU TYPE   `ARM 5`

The DTEXT (Dynamic TEXT) command allows you to see the text on the screen as you type. All of the options are the same as the TEXT command. DTEXT also allows you to use the backspace key to edit what has been typed on the screen. The TEXT command only lets you backspace to edit at the prompt line. Enter multiple lines of text simply by pressing ENTER at the end of each line. Press ENTER twice to exit the DTEXT command. The sequence of prompts is the same as the TEXT command, except that the Text: prompt is repeated. When the Text: prompt appears, a cursor box equal in size to the text height also appears on the screen at the text start point.

You can cancel the DTEXT command at any time by entering CTRL C. This action erases all of the text entered during the command.

A great advantage of DTEXT over TEXT is that additional lines of text can be entered. Simply press ENTER at the end of each line. The cursor box automatically moves to the start point one line below the preceding line. While in the DTEXT command, the screen crosshairs can be moved independently of the text cursor box. Selecting a new start point completes the line of text being entered and begins a new line at the selected point. Using DTEXT, multiple lines of text may be entered anywhere on the drawing without exiting the command. This saves a lot of drafting time.

A few aspects of the DTEXT command may cause you some concern at first. They are:

- When you end the DTEXT command, the entered text is erased from the screen, then regenerated.
- If you select C, M, R, TL, TC, TR, ML, MC, MR, BL, BC, or BR justification, the cursor box appears as if the text is left-justified. However, when you end the DTEXT command, the text disappears and is then regenerated with the alignment you requested.
- When you use a control code sequence for a symbol, the control code, not the symbol, is displayed. When you end the command, the text disappears and is then regenerated showing the proper symbol. For example, if the desired text is 98.6°F it first appears as typed, 98.6%%DF. However, when you end the DTEXT command, the note is redisplayed as 98.6°F.
- If you cancel the DTEXT command, all text entered while in the command is discarded. All DTEXT entries must be from the keyboard. Tablet menu picks are ignored.

```
┌──────────────── PROFESSIONAL TIP ────────────────┐
│   DTEXT is not recommended for aligned text because the text height for each line is ad- │
│  justed according to the width. Other justification options work well with the DTEXT command. │
└───────────────────────────────────────────────────┘
```

PICKING DYNAMIC FROM THE
PULL-DOWN MENU

ARM A

The Draw pull-down menu offers the DTEXT command. Pick Text from the Draw pull-down menu, and then pick Dynamic in the cascading submenu. This works the same as picking DTEXT from the screen menu. The pull-down menu provides another way to access commands. Use the method that works best and fastest for you.

EXERCISE 10-5

☐ Load AutoCAD.
☐ Use the STYLE command to create the text styles described below. Change the options as specified. Then use the DTEXT command to type the text, changing the style for each of the four standard AutoCAD fonts. Enter a .5 letter height.
    TXT—EXPAND THE WIDTH.
    ROMANS—SLANT TO THE LEFT.
    ROMANC—SLANT TO THE RIGHT.
    ITALICC—BACKWARDS.
☐ Select any four fonts from the "Select Text Font" icon menu. Customize the text fonts to your own specifications such as height, width, or slant. Type the alphabet and numerals 1-10 for each of the four styles you developed.
☐ Save the drawing as A:EX10-5 and quit.

PRESETTING TEXT HEIGHT

ARM A

If you set a text height in the STYLE command, then this value is automatically used when you use the TEXT or DTEXT commands. A default value for text height can be preset if the text height in the STYLE command is set to 0. When the text height is set to 0 in the STYLE command, then the TEXTSIZE system variable can be used to establish the text height default. The command sequence is as follows:

    Command: **TEXTSIZE** ↵
    New value for TEXTSIZE ⟨current⟩: **.125** ↵

QUICKLY REDRAWING TEXT

ARM 7

Text requires a great deal of time to regenerate, redraw, and plot. This is because each character is made up of many individual entities. The Quick Text mode makes text appear as rectangles equal to the height of each text string. This speeds regeneration and plotting time. The Quick Text mode is turned on and off with the QTEXT (Quick TEXT) command. Fig. 10-30 shows a comparison between displays when QTEXT is on and off.

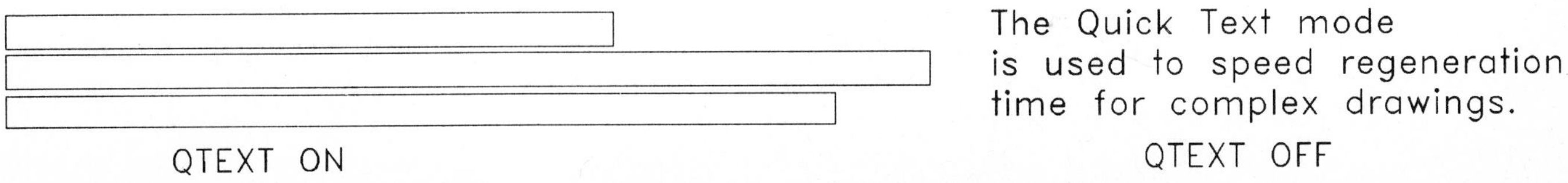

The Quick Text mode
is used to speed regeneration
time for complex drawings.

    QTEXT ON   QTEXT OFF

Fig. 10-30. Comparison of QTEXT turned on and off.

The QTEXT command is entered at the Command: prompt or picked from the SETTINGS screen menu. The options ON/OFF are shown along with the current QTEXT setting. If the last setting was off, the command line appears as follows:

Command: **QTEXT** ↵
ON/OFF 〈Off〉:

Type "ON" to quicken the redraw time. When quick text is on, new text entities first appear as text so you can check them. The text converts to the QTEXT appearance when the drawing is regenerated. If you want to review the text after QTEXT has been turned on, you need to turn QTEXT off. Follow this by the REGEN command to display the text in the normal format.

─── PROFESSIONAL TIP ───

Consider setting up QTEXT in your prototype drawing. Use QTEXT when a large amount of text or complex text begins to slow down regeneration. This helps you save valuable drafting time.

CHANGING THE LOCATION OF EXISTING TEXT $\quad$ ARM 6

Existing text can be modified or moved to a new location using the CHANGE command. Enter the CHANGE command, and follow this command sequence:

Command: **CHANGE** ↵
Select objects: *(pick text to be changed)*
Select objects: ↵
Properties/〈Change point〉: ↵
Enter text insertion point: *(pick a new text location)*
Text style: ROMANS
New style or RETURN for no change: ↵
New height 〈0.2000〉: ↵
New rotation angle 〈0〉: ↵
New text 〈selected text string〉: *(type new text or press ENTER to keep the same text)*
Command:

Fig. 10-31 shows how text can be moved.

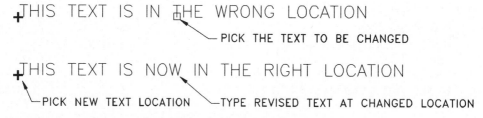

Fig. 10-31. Using the CHANGE command to move text.

If the text location is acceptable, but you want to change other characteristics of your text, simply press ENTER at the Enter text insertion point: prompt.

If you want to change the text style and already have defined an ITALICC text style, do the following:

> Properties/⟨Change point⟩: ↵
> Enter text insertion point: *(pick a new text location)*
> Text style: ROMANS
> New style or RETURN for no change: **ITALICC** ↵
> New height ⟨0.2000⟩: **.25** ↵
> New rotation angle ⟨0⟩: ↵
> New text ⟨selected text string⟩: *(type new text or press ENTER to keep the same text)*
> Command:

Fig. 10-32 shows the new text location and style.

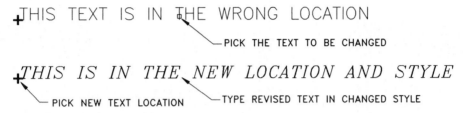

THIS TEXT IS IN THE WRONG LOCATION
⌐PICK THE TEXT TO BE CHANGED

THIS IS IN THE NEW LOCATION AND STYLE
⌐PICK NEW TEXT LOCATION   ⌐TYPE REVISED TEXT IN CHANGED STYLE

Fig. 10-32. Using the CHANGE command to relocate and change text style.

EXERCISE 10-6

☐ Load AutoCAD.
☐ Place the following text on your drawing using .25 high letters: THIS IS THE ORIGINAL TEXT.
☐ Use the CHANGE command to move and change the above text to read: THIS IS THE REVISED TEXT IN A NEW LOCATION.
☐ Use the CHANGE command to move the previous text, change its style, and reword it as follows: THIS IS THE NEW TEXT WITH CHANGED STYLE AND LOCATION.
☐ Turn QTEXT on, then off. Observe the results. Do not forget to use REGEN to change the display.
☐ Save the drawing as A:EX10-6 and quit.

ADDITIONAL TEXT TIPS

Text presentation is important on any drawing. It is a good idea to plan your drawing using rough sketches to allow room for text and notes. Some things to consider when designing the drawing layout include:
- Placement of the views.
- Arrange text to avoid crowding.
- Place related notes in groups to make the drawing easy to read.
- Place all general notes in a common location. Locate notes in the lower-left corner or above the title block when using ANSI standards. Place notes in the upper-left corner when using military standards.
- Place numbered notes away from the border so that additional notes can be added later.
- Provide extra clear space to avoid crowding and allow for future revisions.

REVISING TEXT ON THE DRAWING   **ARM 6**

AutoCAD provides the means to revise existing text. This is referred to as *text editing*. Text editing is accomplished in a dialogue box that is accessed using the DDEDIT command. DDEDIT may be typed at the Command: prompt or picked from the EDIT screen menu:

    Command: **DDEDIT** ↵
    ⟨Select a TEXT or ATTDEF object⟩/Undo: *(pick the line of text to edit)*

The default asks you to "Select a TEXT" and the screen cursor takes the shape of a pick box. Move the pick box to the desired text and pick. The "Edit Text" dialogue box is then displayed with the line of text that you picked ready for editing. Fig. 10-33 shows several lines of text and the "Edit Text" dialogue box with the first line of text displayed.

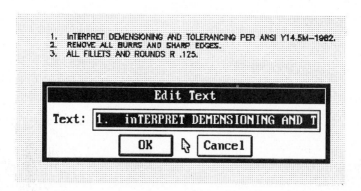

Fig. 10-33. The "Edit Text" dialogue box. The text is displayed before editing.

Notice the line of text to be edited is highlighted in the Text box. Also notice the text cursor is flashing at the end of the Text box. If you press the space bar or Backspace key, the highlighted text disappears and you can enter new text. If you make a mistake, pick Cancel and pick the desired text again. Move the cursor arrow inside the Text: box and pick to remove the highlight around the text. Use the left and right arrow keys to move through the entire line of text, and access the portion of the text that is hidden beyond the limits of the Edit box. When you are ready to edit the text, move the cursor arrow just to the right of the letters to be changed and pick. This places the text cursor in that location. Edit the line of text shown in Fig. 10-34 following this procedure:

- Notice the word "inTERPRET" should read "INTERPRET." Move the cursor arrow so it is located directly after the "n" and pick as shown in Fig. 10-34.

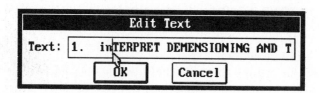

Fig. 10-34. Editing an incorrect line of text. Note the position of the text cursor.

- Backspace through the "in," removing them. Type the new "IN" as shown in Fig. 10-35.
- Notice the word "DEMENSIONING" is misspelled. Move the cursor to a position immediately behind the first "E" and pick.
- Backspace through the "E," removing it. Type the letter "I" as shown in Fig. 10-35.
- Pick OK and press ENTER to accept the text changes. The revised text is then displayed on your drawing as shown in Fig. 10-36.
- Cancel to exit the DDEDIT command, or enter "U" to undo the editing if you made a mistake.

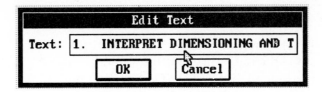

Fig. 10-35. Correcting one of the errors in the line of text.

1. INTERPRET DIMENSIONING AND TOLERANCING PER ANSI Y14.5M—1982.
2. REMOVE ALL BURRS AND SHARP EDGES.
3. ALL FILLETS AND ROUNDS R .125.

Fig. 10-36. After picking OK, the revised text is displayed on your screen.

Editing techniques

Although it is recommended that you enter text as carefully as possible initially, there will likely be times when you must revise text using the DDEDIT command. The following techniques can be used to help edit text.

- **Highlighting text in the Text: box**—Text can be highlighted by moving the cursor arrow to the desired text and picking. Hold the pick button down while you move the cursor across the text to be highlighted. Release the pick button when you have highlighted all of the intended text.
- **Removing highlighting from text in the Text: box**—When the Text box, or a portion of the text in the Text box is highlighted, pressing the space bar, the Delete key, or the Backspace key removes the highlighted text.
- **Moving around inside the Text: box**—Move the cursor arrow inside the Text: box and pick. Then use the left arrow key to move the text to the right or the right arrow key to move the text to the left. You may also pick inside the Text box, and while holding the pick button down, move the cursor arrow either to the right or left to move around.
- **Inserting text**—Type any desired text at the text cursor location. This inserts new text and shifts all existing text to the right.
- **Backspace key**—Pressing the Backspace key when text is not highlighted removes text to the left of the text cursor and moves the text to the right along with the text cursor.
- **Space bar**—Pressing the space bar when text is not highlighted moves all of the text to the right of the text cursor.
- **Left arrow**—Moves the text cursor to the left.
- **Right arrow**—Moves the text cursor to the right.
- **Control X (Ctrl X)**—Highlights the entire string of text in the Edit box.

EXERCISE 10-7

☐ Load AutoCAD.
☐ Place the following text on your drawing (incorrectly as shown) using ROMANS style and .125 text height.
    1. iNTERPRET DEMINSIONIN AND TOLERENCING PER ANSI Y14.5M.
    2. REMOVE ALL BURRS AND EDGES.
    3. ALL FILLETS AND ROUNDS ARE .125 R.
    4. FINISH ALL OVER.
☐ Use the DDEDIT command to revise the above text as follows:
    1. INTERPRET DIMENSIONING AND TOLERANCING PER ANSI Y14.5M.
    2. REMOVE ALL BURRS AND SHARP EDGES.
    3. ALL FILLETS AND ROUNDS R .125.
    4. FINISH ALL OVER 62 MICROINCHES.
☐ Save the drawing as A:EX10-7 and quit.

INSERTING TEXT FROM AN ASCII FILE

ASCII is the acronym for American Standard Code for Information Interchange. The ASCII system defines characters and symbols in a coded format. The ASCTEXT command allows you to insert ASCII text files into an AutoCAD drawing. You must enter the file extension, such as .TXT, after the file name. The command may be entered as "ASCTEXT" at the Command: prompt. You can also pick Text from the Draw pull-down menu, and then pick Import Text from the cascading submenu to access the ASCTEXT command.

If the FILEDIA system variable is set to 1, the "File to Read" dialogue box appears. Select the desired file from the Files: list and pick OK to accept your selection. If FILEDIA is set to 0, the File to read: prompt appears as follows:

> Command: **ASCTEXT** ↵
> File to read (include extension): *(enter the text file name, including the extension, and press ENTER)*

Now you pick a start point or you can justify the text with one of the options followed by the height and rotation angle:

> Start point or Center/Middle/Right/?: *(pick a start point, or select a Justify option and press ENTER)*
> Height ⟨default⟩: *(enter a height and press ENTER, or press ENTER to accept the default)*
> Rotation angle ⟨default⟩: *(enter a rotation angle and press ENTER, or press ENTER to accept the default)*

Next, you can change the text or accept it as is:

> Change text options? ⟨N⟩: *(press ENTER to accept the text, or enter Y and press ENTER to get the following prompts)*
> Distance between lines/⟨Auto⟩: *(enter a distance and press ENTER, or press ENTER to automatically space the lines of text)*
> First line to read/⟨1⟩: *(enter the first line of file to read or press ENTER for line one)*
> Number of lines to read/⟨All⟩: *(enter the number of lines to read and press ENTER, or press ENTER for all lines)*
> Underscore each line? ⟨N⟩: *(press ENTER if you do not want to underline text, or type Y and press ENTER if you want the text underlined)*
> Overscore each line? ⟨N⟩: *(press ENTER if you do not want to overscore text, or type Y and press ENTER if you want the text overscored)*
> Change text case? Upper/Lower/⟨N⟩: *(enter U for uppercase text and press ENTER, press L for lowercase text and press ENTER, or press ENTER to accept the text as is)*

You can keep the text in a single column by pressing ENTER to the next prompt, or answer "Y" to set up the text in columns:

> Set up columns? ⟨N⟩: *(press ENTER if you do not want the text in columns, or type Y and press ENTER if you want it in columns)*
> Distance between columns: *(enter a distance and press ENTER)*
> Number of lines per column: *(enter the number of lines you want in each column and press ENTER)*

AutoCAD then imports the text into the drawing after you have responded to each of the previous prompts.

── NOTE ──

Text inserted with the ASCTEXT command is given the current text style.

CHAPTER TEST

Write your answers in the spaces provided.

1. Give the command and entities required to display "IT IS FAST AND EASY TO DRAW TEXT USING AUTOCAD." The text must be .375 unit high, have the default TXT font, and fit between two points:

   Command: _____

   Justify/Style/⟨Start point⟩:_____

   Align/Fit/Center/Middle/Right/TL/TC/TR/ML/MC/MR/BL/BC/BR: _____

   First text line point: _____

   Second text line point: _____

   Height ⟨.200⟩: _____

   Text: _____

2. Give the command and entries required to create a new text style. The style should have the following specifications. Assume FILEDIA equals 0.

   • Style name: 25-TITLES.

   • Used for titles .25 inch height.

   • Double width.

   • ROMANC font.

   Command: _____

   Text style name (or ?) ⟨TXT⟩: _____

   Font file ⟨default⟩: _____

   Height ⟨current⟩: _____

   Width factor ⟨1⟩: _____

   Obliquing angle ⟨0⟩: _____

   Backwards? ⟨N⟩: _____

   Upside-down? ⟨N⟩: _____

   Vertical? ⟨N⟩: _____

   _____ is now the current text style.

3. Give the command and entries to underscore the following text and place it at a selected start point: "VERIFY ALL DIMENSIONS DURING CONSTRUCTION."

   Command: _____

   Justify/Style/⟨Start point⟩:_____

   Height ⟨0.200⟩:_____

   Rotation angle ⟨0⟩: _____

   Text: _____

4. How would you turn on the Quick Text mode if it is currently off?

   Command: _____

   ON/OFF ⟨Off⟩: _____

5. Give the letter you must enter at the TEXT prompt to place text as follows:

   A. Left-justified text: _____

   B. Right-justified text: _____

   C. Text between two points without regard for text height: _____

   D. Center the text horizontally and vertically: _____

   E. Text between two points with a fixed height: _____

   F. Center text along a baseline: _____

   G. Top and Left horizontal: _____

   H. Middle and Right horizontal: _____

   I. Bottom and Center horizontal: _____

6. List the Justify options. _____

7. How would you specify a text style with a double width factor? _____

   _____

8. How would you specify a text style with a 15° angle? _____

   _____

9. How would you specify vertical text? _____

   _____

10. How is the "Select Text Font" icon menu accessed? _____

11. Give the control sequence required to draw the following symbols and associated text:

    A. 30° _____

    B. 1.375 ± .005 _____

    C. φ24 _____

    D. Underline "NOT FOR CONSTRUCTION" _____

12. What command is used so you can see the text on the screen as it is typed? _____

13. Why use the Quick Text mode rather than have the actual text displayed on the screen?

    _____

    _____

    _____

    _____

14. Name three ways to access the DTEXT command. _____

    _____

15. When setting text height in the STYLE command, what value do you enter at the Height: prompt so text height can be altered each time the TEXT or DTEXT commands are used?

    _____

16. Give the command that lets you alter the location, style, height, and wording of existing text.

    _____

17. Identify the command used to revise existing text on the drawing by using the "Edit Text" dialogue box._____

18. List the sequence of activities required to access the "Edit Text" dialogue box.

    _____

    _____

19. When editing text, how do you remove the character located in front of the text cursor?

    _____

    _____

20. When using the "Edit Text" dialogue box, how do you move the text cursor to the left without removing text characters? _____

21. How do you remove all of the text to the right of the text cursor when editing text?

    _____

    _____

22. When editing text in the Text: box, the flashing vertical bar is called the _____.

23. Determine the AutoCAD text height for text to be plotted .188″ high using a HALF (1″ = 2″) scale. (Show your calculations.) _____

    _____

24. Determine the AutoCAD text height for text to be plotted .188″ high using a scale of 1/4″ = 1′-0″. (Show your calculations.) _____

    _____

25. What would you do if you just completed editing a line of text and discovered you made a mistake? Assume you are still in the "Edit Text" dialogue box. _____

    _____

26. Identify two ways to move around inside the Text: box of the "Edit Text" dialogue box.

    _____

    _____

    _____

    _____

27. What happens when you press the space bar or the Backspace key when the text inside the Text: box is highlighted? _____

28. What happens when you press CTRLX when using the "Edit Text" dialogue box?

    _____

    _____

29. How do you access the "Select Font File" dialogue box? _____

    _____

DRAWING PROBLEMS

1. Make three prototype drawings with borders and title blocks for your future drawings. Use the following guidelines:
   A. Prototype 1 for A-size, 8 1/2 x 11 drawings, named TITLEA.
   B. Prototype 2 for B-size, 11 x 17 drawings, named TITLEB.

C. Prototype 3 for C-size, 17 x 22 drawings, named TITLEC.
D. Set the following values for the drawing aids:
   Units = three-place decimal.
   Grid = .500.
   Snap = .250.
E. Draw a polyline border, .032 wide, 1/2 in. from the drawing limits.
F. Design a title block using created text styles. Place it in the lower-right corner of each drawing. The title block should contain the following information: company or school name, address, date, drawn by, approved by, scale, title, drawing number, material, revision number. See the following example.
G. Set a standard text style titled ROMANS-125. This style was discussed in this chapter.

SPECIFICATIONS			R -	CHANGE		DATE	ECN
			HYSTER COMPANY				
			THIS PRINT CONTAINS CONFIDENTIAL INFORMATION WHICH IS THE PROPERTY OF HYSTER COMPANY. BY ACCEPTING THIS INFORMATION THE BORROWER AGREES THAT IT WILL NOT BE USED FOR ANY PURPOSE OTHER THAN THAT FOR WHICH IT IS LOANED.				
UNLESS OTHERWISE SPECIFIED DIMENSIONS ARE IN INCHES MILLIMETERS AND TOLERANCES FOR: _____ PLACE DIMS± _____ : _____ PLACE DIMS± _____ ANGLES ± _____ ; WHOLE DIMS± _____			DR.		SCALE		DATE
			CK. MAT'L.		CK. DESIGN		REL. ON ECN
			NAME				
MODEL	DWG. FIRST USED	SIMILAR TO					
DEPT.	PROJECT	LIST DIVISION	H	PART NO.			R

2. Recall your TITLEA prototype drawing. Use the TEXT or DTEXT command to type the following information. Change the text style to represent each of the four standard AutoCAD fonts named. Use a .5 unit text height and 0° rotation angle.
   TXT—AUTOCAD'S DEFAULT TEXT FONT WHICH IS AVAILABLE FOR USE WHEN YOU BEGIN A DRAWING.
   ROMANS—SMOOTHER THAN TXT FONT AND CLOSELY DUPLICATES THE SINGLE-STROKE LETTERING THAT HAS BEEN THE STANDARD FOR DRAFTING.
   ROMANC—A MULTI-STROKE DECORATIVE FONT THAT IS GOOD FOR USE IN DRAWING TITLES.
   ITALICC—AN ORNAMENTAL FONT SLANTED TO THE RIGHT AND HAS THE SAME LETTER DESIGN AS THE COMPLEX FONT.
   Save the drawing as A:P10-2 and quit.
3. Recall your TITLEA prototype drawing. Use the STYLE command to create the following text styles. Change the options as noted in each line of text. Then use the DTEXT command to type the text, changing the text style to represent each of the four standard AutoCAD fonts named. Use a .25 unit text height.
   TXT—EXPAND THE WIDTH BY THREE.
   MONOTXT—SLANT TO THE LEFT −30°.
   ROMANS—SLANT TO THE RIGHT 30°.
   ROMAND—BACKWARDS.

ROMANC — VERTICAL.
ITALICC — UNDERSCORED AND OVERSCORED.
ROMANS — USE 16d NAILS @ 10" OC.
ROMANT — ϕ32 (812.8).
Save the drawing as A:P10-3 and quit.

4. Open drawing P10-3. Select the following fonts from the text font icon menu: SCRIPTC, ROMANT, GOTHICE, SYMAP, and SYMUSIC.

   A. Type a complete alphabet and numbers 1-10 for the text fonts, and all available symbols for the symbol fonts.

   B. Use .375 unit height with all other variables at default values.

   C. Save the drawing as A:P10-4 and quit.

5. Draw a Parts List (similar to the one shown below) connected to your A-size prototype title block.

   A. Enter "PARTS LIST" with a COMPLEX style.

   B. Enter the other information using ROMANS text and the DTEXT command. Do not exit the DTEXT command to start a new line of text.

   C. Save the drawing as A:P10-5 and quit.

3	HOLDING PINS	12
2	SIDE COVERS	3
1	MAIN HOUSING	1
KEY	DESCRIPTION	QTY

PARTS LIST

UNLESS OTHERWISE SPECIFIED
ALL DIMENSIONS IN

INCHES

AND TOLERANCES FOR:

1 PLACE DIMS: $\pm$.1
2 PLACE DIMS: $\pm$.01
3 PLACE DIMS: $\pm$.005
ANGULAR: $\pm$30'
FRACTIONAL: $\pm$.1/32
FINISH: 125μ in.

FIRST USED ON: SIMILAR TO:

JANE'S
DESIGN

DR: JANE	SCALE: FULL	DATE: XX–XX–XX	APPD:

MATERIAL:
MILD STEEL

NAME:
XXX–XXXX

B	PART NO: 123–321	REV: 0

6. Complete the following drawing.
   A. Make the symbols proportional to the ones shown. They will not necessarily be the same size.
   B. Use the DTEXT command and the variables studied in this chapter.
   C. Save the drawing as A:P10-6 and quit.

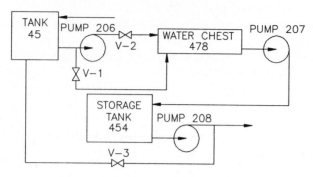

4. ALL PUMPS ON 6" THICK CONCRETE PADS.
3. ALL TANKS AND CHESTS BUILT TO CUSTOMERS SPECIFICATIONS.
2. ALL VALVES FABRIVALVE FIG. 71.
1. TEST ALL TANKS TO 175 PSI.

NOTES:

7. Complete the drawing shown below.
   A. Make the symbols proportional to the ones shown, but not necessarily the same size.
   B. Use the DTEXT command and the variables studied in this chapter.
   C. Save the drawing as A:P10-7 and quit.

GROUP DECISION MAKING PROCESS

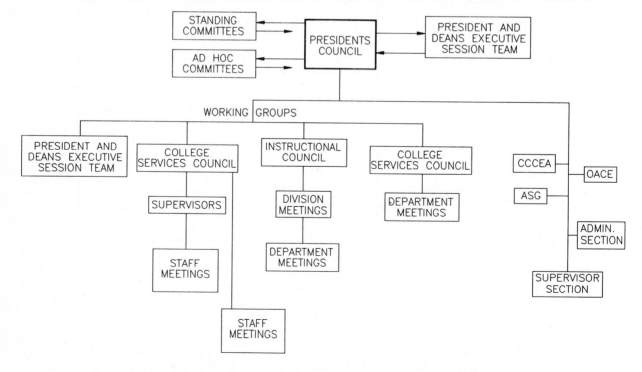

*NOTE: STANDING OR AD HOC COMMITTEES MAY BE FORMED AT ANY LEVEL.

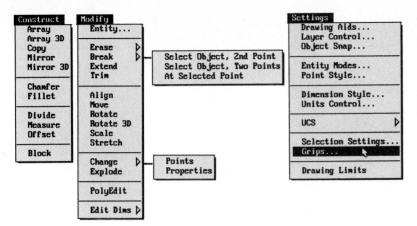

Chapter 11

BASIC EDITING COMMANDS

Learning objectives

After completing this chapter, you will be able to:

☐ Draw chamfers and angled corners with the CHAMFER command.
☐ Use the FILLET command to draw fillets, rounds, and other rounded corners.
☐ Preset chamfer and fillet specifications.
☐ Remove a portion of a line, circle, or arc using the BREAK command.
☐ Relocate an object using the MOVE command.
☐ Use the TRIM and EXTEND commands to edit an object.
☐ Use the CHANGE command to revise an existing object.
☐ Make single and multiple copies of existing objects using the COPY command.
☐ Draw a mirror image of an object.
☐ Change the angular position of an object using the ROTATE command.
☐ Use the ALIGN command to move and rotate an object simultaneously.
☐ Enlarge and reduce the size of an object using the SCALE command.
☐ Change the length and height of an object using the STRETCH command.
☐ Set the PICKAUTO, PICKFIRST, and GRIPS system variables to vary your selection techniques.
☐ Use the geometry calculator to edit drawings.

This chapter explains commands and methods for changing a drawing. Editing and modifying a drawing used to take hours or sometimes days using manual drafting techniques. AutoCAD, however, makes the same editing tasks simpler and quicker. In Chapter 6 you learned how to draw and erase lines. The ERASE command is one of the most commonly used editing commands. You also learned how to select objects to erase by picking, or by using one of the other selection techniques such as a window, crossing box, or fence. The items you selected were referred to as a *selection set*.

The same selection methods and techniques may be used for the editing commands presented in this chapter. You will learn how to easily draw angled and rounded corners. You will also learn how to copy, move, rotate, or change the scale of an existing object. These commands are found in the EDIT screen menu. You can also pick editing commands from the Modify or Construct pull-down menus. The editing commands discussed in this chapter are basically divided into two general groups—editing individual features of a drawing and editing major portions of a drawing. Commands typically used to edit individual features of a drawing are:

- CHAMFER
- FILLET
- BREAK
- TRIM
- EXTEND

11-1

Even though you can edit individual features with the following commands, they are often used to edit entire drawings or major portions of a drawing. The commands discussed in the second section of this chapter are:

- MOVE
- COPY
- ROTATE
- MIRROR

- SCALE
- STRETCH
- CHANGE

DRAWING CHAMFERS

ARM 6

A *chamfer* in mechanical drafting is a small angled surface used to relieve a sharp corner. AutoCAD defines a "chamfer" as any angled corner on the drawing. The size of a chamfer is determined by its distance from the corner. A 45° chamfer is equidistant from the corner in each direction, Fig. 11-1.

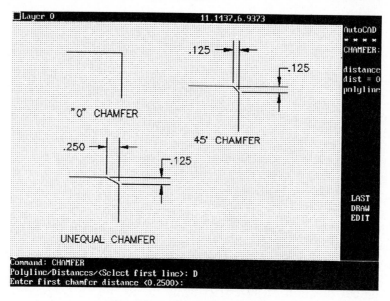

Fig. 11-1. Chamfer examples.

Chamfers may be drawn between two lines which may or may not intersect. Using the CHAMFER command, the first step is to enter the chamfer distances. This is done by typing "D" for the Distance option in the CHAMFER command. Enter the first and second chamfer distances as follows:

Command: **CHAMFER** ⏎
Polyline/Distances/⟨Select first line⟩: **D** ⏎
Enter first chamfer distance ⟨current⟩: *(specify a chamfer distance, .25 for example, and press ENTER)*
Enter second chamfer distance ⟨.25⟩: *(press ENTER for the current distance, or type a new value and press ENTER)*
Command:

The default chamfer distance is 0. This is a corner without a chamfer. After you specify new chamfer distances, they remain in effect until changed. Chamfer distances may be entered by picking two points with the pointing device; however, most drafters type in exact values.

Now you are ready to draw chamfers. Enter the CHAMFER command and select the first and second lines.

Command: **CHAMFER** ⏎
Polyline/Distances/⟨Select first line⟩: *(pick the first line)*
Select second line: *(pick the second line)*
Command:

After the lines are picked, AutoCAD automatically chamfers the corner. If you want to chamfer additional corners, press ENTER to repeat the CHAMFER command. The results of several chamfering operations are shown in Fig. 11-2.

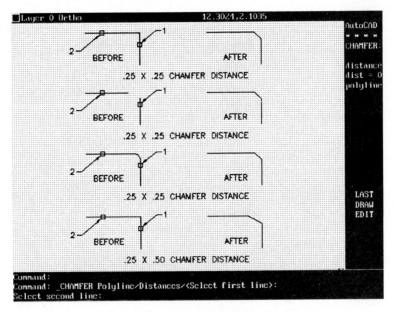

Fig. 11-2. Using the CHAMFER command.

Chamfering the corners of a polyline

All corners of a closed or open polyline may be chamfered in one task. Enter the CHAMFER command, select the Polyline option, and then select the polyline. The corners of the polyline are chamfered to the set distance values. If the polyline appears closed, but the Close option was not used, the beginning corner is not chamfered, Fig. 11-3.

Command: **CHAMFER** ↵
Polyline/Distances/⟨Select first line⟩: **P** ↵
Select polyline: *(pick the polyline)*
Command:

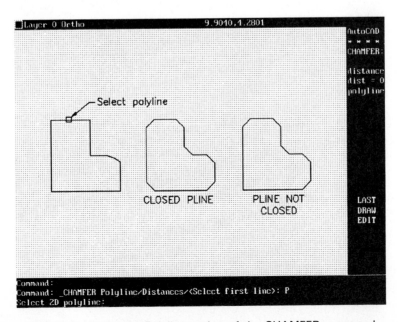

Fig. 11-3. Using the Polyline option of the CHAMFER command.

DRAWING ROUNDED CORNERS

In mechanical drafting, an inside rounded corner is called a *fillet*. An outside rounded corner is called a *round*. AutoCAD refers to all rounded corners as fillets. The FILLET command draws a rounded corner between intersecting or nonintersecting lines, circles, and arcs. Fillets are sized by radius. The radius is specified first by selecting the Radius option in the FILLET command as follows:

Command: **FILLET** ↵
Polyline/Radius/〈Select first object〉: **R** ↵
Enter fillet radius 〈current〉: *(type the fillet radius, .25 for example, and press ENTER, or press ENTER to accept the current value)*

Once the fillet radius has been given, repeat the FILLET command to fillet the objects. The command sequence shown in Fig. 11-4 is as follows:

Command: **FILLET** ↵
Polyline/Radius/〈Select first object〉: *(pick the first object to be filleted)*
Select second object: *(pick the other object to be filleted)*
Command:

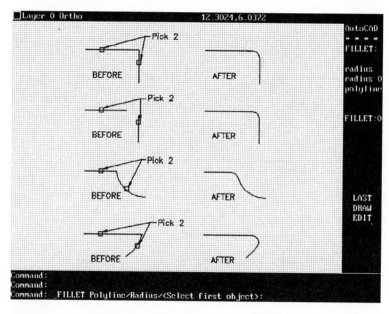

Fig. 11-4. Using the FILLET command.

Rounding the corners of a polyline

Fillets may be drawn at all corners of a polyline by selecting the Polyline option. The current fillet radius is used. The command sequence shown in Fig. 11-5 is as follows:

Command: **FILLET** ↵
Polyline/Radius/〈Select first object〉: **P** ↵
Select 2D polyline: *(pick the polyline)*

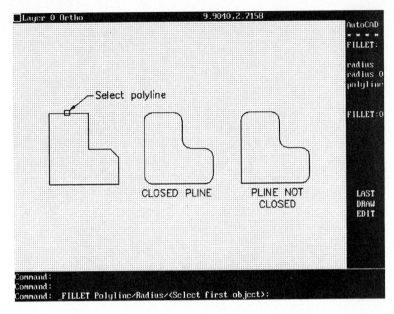

Fig. 11-5. Using the Polyline option of the FILLET command.

AutoCAD tells you how many lines were filleted. Then the Command: prompt returns. If the polyline appears closed, but the Close option was not used, the beginning corner is not filleted.

Presetting the chamfer distance and the fillet radius

AutoCAD lets you set the chamfer distance and fillet radius to a designated value. This saves time when the chamfer distance and fillet radius remains constant on your drawing. To do this, use the CHAMFERA, CHAMFERB, and FILLETRAD system variables. You can preset the chamfer distances to different or equal values. For example, if you want .125 for both chamfer distances, type the following:

> Command: **CHAMFERA** ↵
> New value for CHAMFERA ⟨current⟩: **.125** ↵
> Command: **CHAMFERB** ↵
> New value for CHAMFERB ⟨current⟩: **.125** ↵
> Command:

Now, enter "CHAMFER" at the Command: prompt and the preset values are automatically issued. The command sequence looks like this:

> Command: **CHAMFER** ↵
> Polyline/Distances/⟨Select first line⟩: *(pick the first line)*
> Select second line: *(pick the second line)*

When presetting the fillet radius, first enter "FILLETRAD" at the Command: prompt. You are then asked to enter a new value. For example, if you want .25 radius, type the following:

> Command: **FILLETRAD** ↵
> New value for FILLETRAD ⟨current⟩: **.25** ↵
> Command:

To work with the preset specifications, enter the FILLET command and the preset radius for the fillet is automatically issued. The command sequence looks like this:

> Command: **FILLET** ↵
> Polygon/Radius/⟨Select first object⟩: *(pick the first object)*
> Select second object: *(pick the second object)*
> Command:

EXERCISE 11-1

☐ Load AutoCAD and open TITLEB.
☐ Draw two 4 x 2 rectangles using the LINE command. Use the CHAMFER command on the first rectangle to chamfer two corners a distance of .125. Chamfer the other corners a distance of .25. Use the FILLET command on the second rectangle to round two corners at a .125 radius. Round the other corners at a .25 radius.
☐ Draw two more 4 x 2 rectangles using the PLINE command. Use the Close option on one but not on the other. Use the CHAMFER command on the first rectangle to chamfer all corners a distance of .25. Use the FILLET command on the second rectangle to round all corners at .25 radius. Observe what happens on the polyline rectangle that was drawn without using the Close option.
☐ Save the drawing as A:EX11-1 and quit.

PROFESSIONAL TIP

While the previous chamfer and fillet examples had mechanical applications, the CHAMFER and FILLET commands may be used in any drafting field; for example, angled or rounded corners in architectural drafting. If you are working in architectural drafting at a scale of 1/4″ = 1′-0″, be sure to set the chamfer or fillet distances in feet and/or inches accordingly.

REMOVING A SECTION FROM AN OBJECT | ARM 6 |

The BREAK command is used to remove a portion of a line, circle, arc, trace, or polyline. AutoCAD asks you to first select the object, then pick break points as follows:

Command: **BREAK** ↵
Select object: *(pick the line, circle, or arc to be broken. If a pick point is used rather than a window, that point becomes the first break point.)*

If the object you pick is a line, the pick point is your first break point. You are then asked for the second break point:

Enter second point (or F for first point): *(pick the second point, or type F and press ENTER for another first point option)*

If you pick a second break point, the line is broken between the two points, Fig. 11-6. You can also select "F" to specify a new first point:

Enter second point (or F for first point): **F** ↵
Enter first point: *(pick a new first point)*
Enter second point: *(pick the second point)*

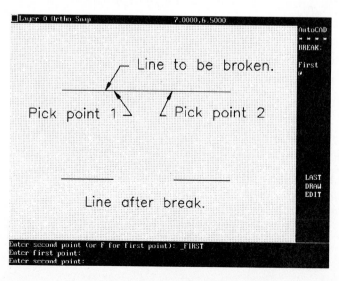

Fig. 11-6. Using the BREAK command.

When breaking arcs or circles, always work in a counterclockwise direction. Otherwise, you may break the portion of the arc or circle that you want to keep. If you want to break the end off of a line or arc, pick the first point on the line or arc. Then pick the second point slightly beyond the end to be cut off, Fig. 11-7.

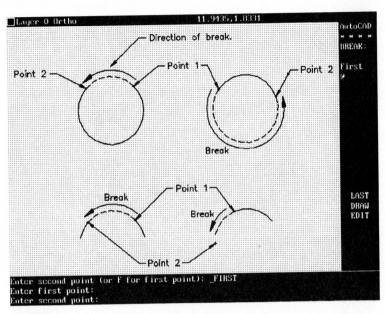

Fig. 11-7. Using the BREAK command on circles and arcs.

If you want to break a line from the point of intersection with another line, use the object snap INTersect mode as follows:

    Command: **BREAK** ⏎
    Select object: *(pick the line)*
    Enter second point (or F for first point): **INT** ⏎
    of *(move the aperture to the intersection and pick)*

The line is now broken between the first point and the point of intersection.

Using the BREAK cascading menu

The BREAK command can also be accessed from the Modify pull-down menu. When you pick Break (or slide the cursor over its arrow), a cascading submenu appears, displaying three options. The first option—Select Object, 2nd Point—allows you to pick an object, and then uses that point as the first break point. You then must pick the other break point. The second option—Select Object, Two Points—prompts you to pick both the first and second break points. The final option—At Selected Point—allows you to break an entity at any desired point. Although the break may not be visibly noticeable, when you perform further editing on the object, you will notice a difference.

TRIMMING SECTIONS OF A LINE, CIRCLE, OR ARC   ARM 6

The TRIM command prunes lines, arcs, or circles that extend beyond a desired point of intersection. The command requires that you pick a "cutting edge" and the object(s) to trim.

The *cutting edge* may be a line or corner to which the trimmed line will be cut. If two corners of an object overrun, select two cutting edges and two objects as follows: (Refer to Fig. 11-8.)

Command: **TRIM** ↵
Select cutting edge(s) . . .
Select objects: *(pick first cutting edge)*
Select objects: *(pick second cutting edge)*
Select objects: ↵
〈Select object to trim〉/Undo: *(pick the first overrun to trim)*
〈Select object to trim〉/Undo: *(pick the second overrun to trim)*
〈Select object to trim〉/Undo: ↵

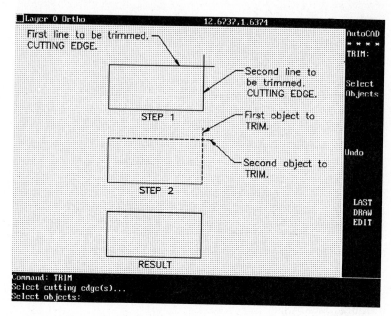

Fig. 11-8. Using the TRIM command. Note the cutting edges.

EXTENDING LINES

ARM 6

The EXTEND command can be considered the opposite of TRIM. The EXTEND command is used to lengthen lines or arcs to meet other lines, circles, or arcs. EXTEND will not work on closed lines or closed polylines since an opening does not exist. The command format is similar to TRIM. You are asked to select "boundary edges" (rather than cutting edges). *Boundary edges* are those lines, circles, or arcs that the chosen lines or arcs extend to meet. The command sequence is shown below and illustrated in Fig. 11-9:

Command: **EXTEND** ↵
Select boundary edge(s) . . .
Select objects: *(pick line to be extended)*
Select objects: *(pick a line to extend to)*
Select objects: ↵
〈Select object to extend〉/Undo: *(pick the line to be extended)*
〈Select object to extend〉/Undo: ↵

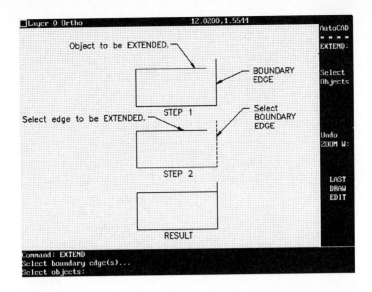

Fig. 11-9. Using the EXTEND command. Note the boundary edges.

If there is nothing for the selected line to meet, AutoCAD gives the message: "No edge in that direction" or "Entity does not intersect an edge."

CHANGING LINES AND CIRCLES

ARM 6

The endpoint location of a line or the radius of a circle may be altered using the CHANGE command. The endpoint of one or more lines may be moved by picking a new point. This new point is called the *change point*. For example, suppose a corner where two lines meet is not correct. Type "CHANGE" at the Command: prompt, or pick Change from the Modify pull-down menu. If you access the CHANGE command through the pull-down menu, a cascading submenu appears, allowing you to change properties or points. Then, use the CHANGE command to reposition the corner. At the "Change point" prompt, pick the new point. AutoCAD automatically relocates the endpoints as shown in Fig. 11-10. The command sequence is as follows:

Command: **CHANGE** ↵
Select objects: *(pick the lines individually or with a crossing box)*
Select objects: ↵
Properties/⟨Change point⟩: *(pick the new point)*

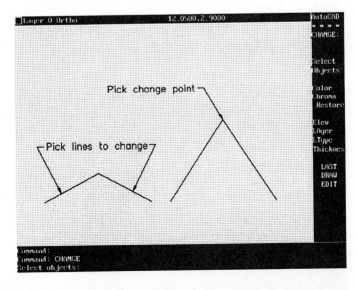

Fig. 11-10. Using the CHANGE command to relocate a corner.

The CHANGE command can also be used to revise the radius of a circle. Do this by picking a change point through which the new circle is to be drawn, Fig. 11-11.

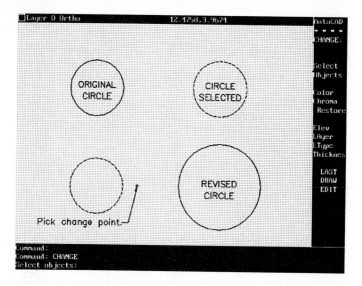

Fig. 11-11. Using the CHANGE command to revise the radius of a circle.

Using the CHANGE command to move text is discussed in Chapter 10. Changing common properties such as layer, linetype, and color is explained in Chapter 17. 3-D applications are discussed in Chapter 24.

EXERCISE 11-2

☐ Make a drawing similar to that shown below and perform the BREAK, TRIM, and EXTEND operations noted.

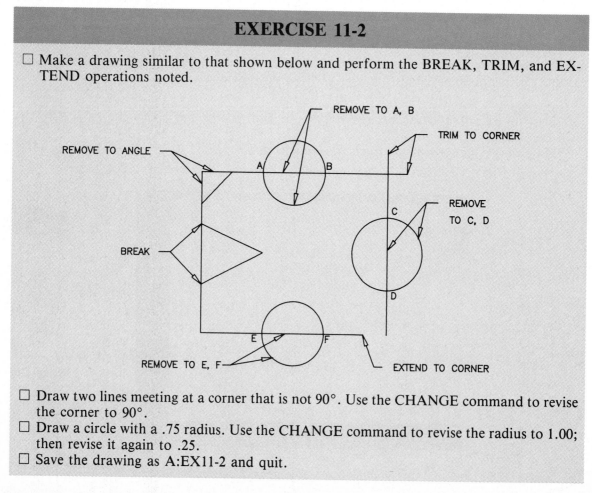

☐ Draw two lines meeting at a corner that is not 90°. Use the CHANGE command to revise the corner to 90°.
☐ Draw a circle with a .75 radius. Use the CHANGE command to revise the radius to 1.00; then revise it again to .25.
☐ Save the drawing as A:EX11-2 and quit.

MOVING AN OBJECT

ARM 6

In many situations, you may find that the location of a view or feature is not quite where you want it. This problem is easily resolved using the MOVE command. After you enter "MOVE," AutoCAD requests that you select those objects to be moved. Use any of the selection techniques: fence, window, window polygon, last, crossing, crossing polygon, or pick single items.

The next prompt requests the base point. The *base point* is any point on or adjacent to the feature. It provides a reference point. Most drafters select a point on an object, corner of a view, or center of a circle. The next prompt asks for the second point of displacement. This is the new position. All selected entities are moved the distance from the base point to the displacement point. The following MOVE command relates to the object shown in Fig. 11-12. After the base point is picked, the object is automatically dragged into position if the DRAGMODE is set to Auto.

Command: **MOVE** ↵
Select objects: *(pick individual entities or window the object to be moved)*
Select objects: ↵
Base point or displacement: *(enter coordinates or pick a point on screen)*
Second point of displacement: *(establish the new position by typing coordinates or picking a second point on screen)*

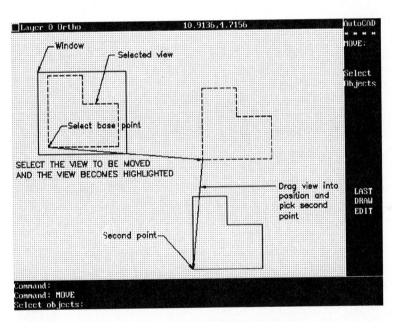

Fig. 11-12. Using the MOVE command.

COPYING OBJECTS

ARM 6

The COPY command is used to make a copy of an existing view or object. The command prompts are the same as the MOVE command. However, when a second point of displacement is picked, the original object remains and the copy is drawn. The following command sequence is shown in Fig. 11-13.

Command: **COPY** ↵
Select objects: *(pick individual entities or window the object to be moved)*
Select objects: ↵
⟨Base point or displacement⟩/Multiple: *(enter coordinates and press ENTER, or pick with the pointing device)*
Second point of displacement: *(establish the new position by typing coordinates and pressing ENTER, or pick a point on the screen)*

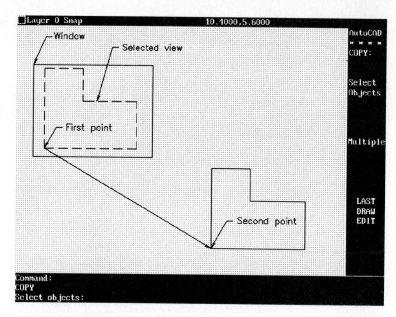

Fig. 11-13. Using the COPY command.

Making multiple copies

To make several copies of the same object, select the Multiple option of the COPY command. Type "M" or pick Multiple from the COPY screen menu. The prompt for a second point repeats. When you have made all the copies needed, press ENTER. The command sequence after you select objects continues as follows. The results are shown in Fig. 11-14.

⟨Base point or displacement⟩/Multiple: **M** ↵
Base point: *(enter coordinates and press ENTER, or pick a location with the pointing device)*
Second point of displacement: *(establish the new position by typing coordinates and pressing ENTER, or pick a location on screen)*
Second point of displacement: *(pick the second position)*
Second point of displacement: *(pick the third position)*
Second point of displacement: ↵
Command:

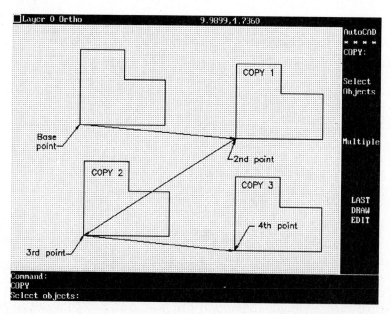

Fig. 11-14. Using the Multiple option of the COPY command.

EXERCISE 11-3

☐ Load AutoCAD and open TITLEA.
☐ Draw a square and an equilateral triangle (equal sides and angles). Use the POLYGON command.
☐ Move the square to a new location.
☐ Copy the triangle next to the new square position. Leave a small space between the two objects.
☐ Move all features to a new position in the upper-left corner of the screen.
☐ Make four copies of the square anywhere on the screen. The new copies should not touch other objects.
☐ Save the drawing as A:EX11-3 and quit.

DRAWING A MIRROR IMAGE OF AN EXISTING OBJECT

`ARM 6`

It is often necessary to draw an object, symbol, or view in a reflected, or mirrored position. The MIRROR command performs this task. Mirroring an entire drawing is common in architectural drafting when a client wants a plan drawn in reverse.

The normal mirroring operation reverses everything, including words and dimensions. However, by using the system variable MIRRTEXT, text retains its normal position. This option is discussed later in the chapter.

Selecting the mirror line

The *mirror line* is the hinge about which objects are reflected. Once you select objects to mirror, you must pick the endpoints of the mirror line. The objects, plus any space between the objects and the mirror line, are reflected, Fig. 11-15.

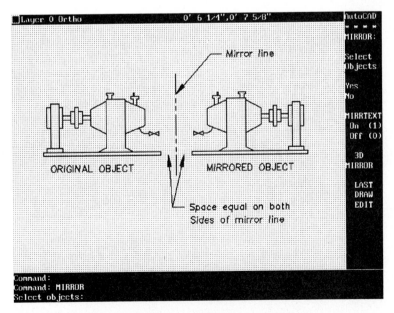

Fig. 11-15. The object is reflected about the mirror line.

The mirror line can be placed at any angle. Once you select the first endpoint, the chosen objects are displayed as they would be mirrored. Once you select the second mirror line endpoint, you can delete the original objects or make a copy. The command sequence shown in Fig. 11-16 is as follows:

Command: **MIRROR** ↵
Select objects: *(use any selection method; a window is common)*
First point of mirror line: *(pick the first endpoint on or away from the object)*
Second point of mirror line: *(pick the second endpoint)*
Delete old objects? ⟨N⟩: **Y** or ↵

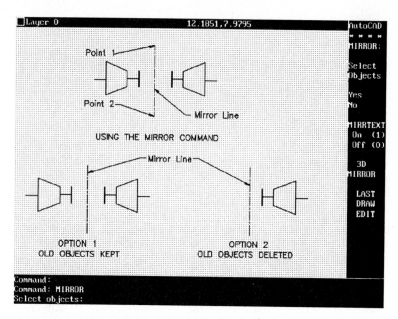

Fig. 11-16. Using the MIRROR command.

PROFESSIONAL TIP

Always use object snap to your best advantage when using editing commands. For example, suppose you want to move an object to the center point of a circle. Initiate the OSNAP CENter option as follows:

Command: **MOVE** ↵
Select objects: *(select the object to be moved)*
Base point or displacement: *(pick the base point on the object)*
Second point of displacement: **CEN** ↵
of *(snap to the center of an existing circle)*

EXERCISE 11-4

☐ Load AutoCAD and open TITLEA.
☐ Draw the half object shown below. Then complete the entire object using the **MIRROR** command. Do not dimension.

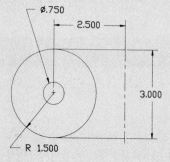

☐ Save the drawing as A:EX11-4 and quit.

MIRRORING TEXT

Normally, the MIRROR command reverses any text associated with the selected object. Backwards text is generally not acceptable. To keep the text readable, the MIRRTEXT system variable must be zero. There are two values for MIRRTEXT, Fig. 11-17.
- 1 = Default value. Text is mirrored in relation to the original object.
- 0 = Prevents text from being reversed.

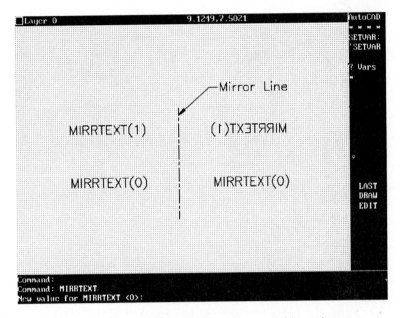

Fig. 11-17. The MIRRTEXT system variable options.

To draw a mirror image of an existing object, but leave the text readable, set the MIRRTEXT variable to 0. Then proceed to the MIRROR command. The entire command sequence is as follows:

Command: **MIRRTEXT** ↵
New value for MIRRTEXT ⟨1⟩: **0** ↵
Command: **MIRROR** ↵
Select objects: *(select objects to mirror)*
Select objects: ↵
First point of mirror line: *(pick the first mirror line point)*
Second point: *(pick the second mirror line point)*
Delete old objects? ⟨N⟩: **Y** or ↵
Command:

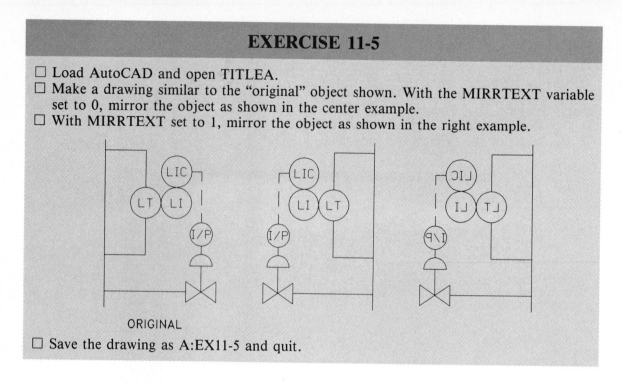

EXERCISE 11-5

☐ Load AutoCAD and open TITLEA.
☐ Make a drawing similar to the "original" object shown. With the MIRRTEXT variable set to 0, mirror the object as shown in the center example.
☐ With MIRRTEXT set to 1, mirror the object as shown in the right example.

ORIGINAL

☐ Save the drawing as A:EX11-5 and quit.

ROTATING EXISTING OBJECTS

ARM 6

Design changes often require that an object, feature, or view be rotated. For example, in an interior design the office furniture layout may have to be moved, copied, or rotated. AutoCAD allows you to easily revise the layout to obtain the final design.

Objects you select are rotated about a base point. You must pick a base point and enter the rotation angle. A negative rotation angle revolves the object clockwise, Fig. 11-18. A positive rotation angle revolves the object counterclockwise. The ROTATE command sequence appears as follows:

Command: **ROTATE** ↵
Select objects: *(use one of the selection methods, such as window)*
Select objects: ↵
Base point: *(pick the base point on or near the object, or enter coordinates and press ENTER)*
⟨Rotation angle⟩/Reference: *(type a positive or negative rotation angle and press ENTER, or pick a point on screen)*

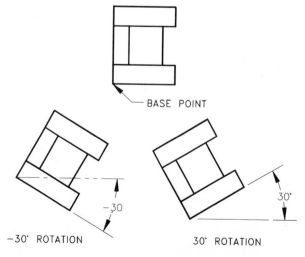

Fig. 11-18. Rotation angles.

If an object is already rotated and you want a different angle, you can do this two ways using the Reference option after selecting the object for rotation. The first method, shown in Fig. 11-19A, is to specify the existing angle followed by the proposed angle:

⟨Rotation angle⟩/Reference: **R** ↵
Reference angle ⟨0⟩: **135** ↵
New angle: **180** ↵

The other method is to pick a reference line on the object and rotate the object in relationship to the reference line as shown in Fig. 11-19B. The prompts are as follows:

⟨Rotation angle⟩/Reference: **R** ↵
Reference angle ⟨0⟩: *(pick the endpoints of a reference line that forms the existing angle)*
New angle: *(specify a new angle, such as **180**, and press ENTER)*

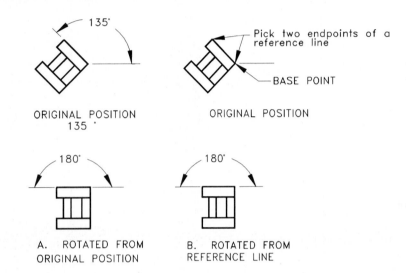

Fig. 11-19. Using the ROTATE command's Reference option.

EXERCISE 11-6

☐ Load AutoCAD and open TITLEA.
☐ Draw a 2.25 unit square with one horizontal side.
☐ Rotate the square to 75°. Then, using the Reference option, rotate the square another 45°. Finally rotate the square back to 0°.
☐ Save the drawing as A:EX11-6 and quit.

MOVING AND ROTATING AN OBJECT SIMULTANEOUSLY

AEM 5

The ALIGN command is primarily used for 3-D applications, but it has 2-D applications when you want to move and rotate an object at the same time. The command sequence asks you to select objects, and then asks for three source points and three destination points. For 2-D applications, you only need two source and two destination points. The *source points* are points on the object in its original position. The *destination points* correspond to the location where the object is to be placed. Refer to Fig. 11-20A. Press ENTER when the prompt requests the third source and destination points.

Command: **ALIGN** ↵
Select objects: *(select the desired objects)*
Select objects: ↵
1st source point: *(pick the first source point)*
1st destination point: *(pick the first destination point)*
2nd source point: *(pick the second source point)*
2nd destination point: *(pick the second destination point)*
3rd source point: ↵
⟨2d⟩ or 3d transformation: *(press ENTER to accept the 2d default)*

Fig. 11-20B shows the kitchen cabinet layout moved and rotated into the desired wall location.

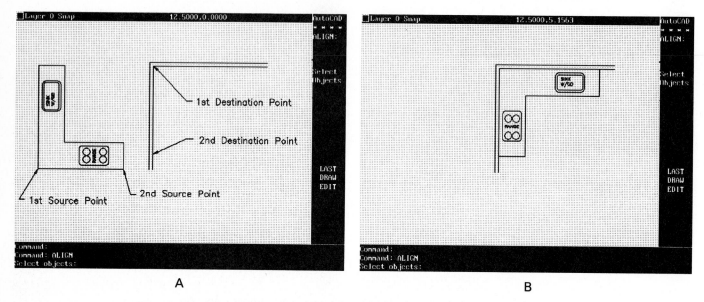

Fig. 11-20. The ALIGN command rotates and moves an object simultaneously.

EXERCISE 11-7

☐ Load AutoCAD and open TITLEA.
☐ Make a drawing similar to the following one. Do not add text or leaders.
☐ Use the ALIGN command to move and rotate part A into position with part B. S1 is the first source point and S2 is the second source point. D1 is the first destination point and D2 is the second destination point.

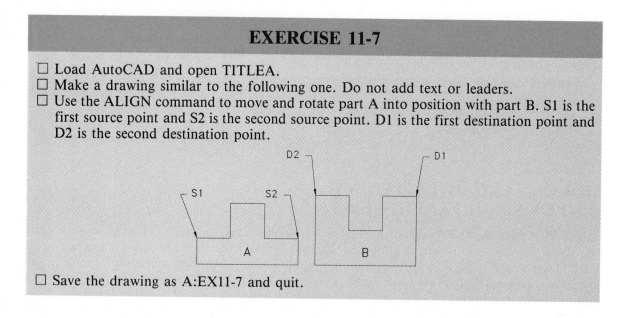

☐ Save the drawing as A:EX11-7 and quit.

CHANGING THE SIZE OF AN EXISTING OBJECT

A convenient editing command that saves hours of drafting time is the SCALE command. This command lets you change the size of an existing object or complete drawing. The SCALE command enlarges or reduces the entire object proportionately. One advantage of AutoCAD is that if the object is dimensioned, the dimensions also change to reflect the new size.

> Command: **SCALE** ↵
> Select objects: *(use any selection technique to select objects)*
> Select objects: ↵
> Base point: *(select the base point)*
> ⟨Scale factor⟩/Reference:

Scale factors

The scale factor is the default prompt. Specify the amount of enlargement or reduction in size. If you want to double the scale, type "2" at the "⟨Scale factor⟩/Reference:" prompt, Fig. 11-21. The chart in Fig. 11-22 shows sample scale factors.

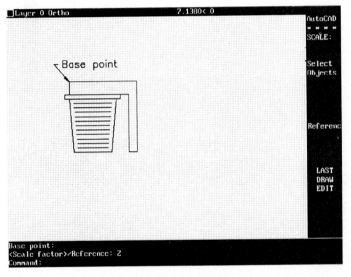

A—ORIGINAL OBJECT

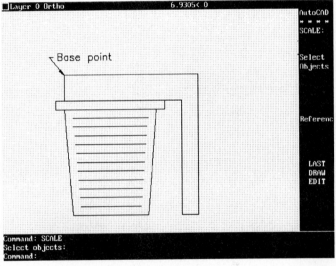

B—OBJECT AFTER BEING SCALED

Fig. 11-21. Using the SCALE command.

Scale Factor	Resulting Size
10	10 x bigger.
5	5 x bigger.
2	2 x bigger.
1	Equal to existing size.
.75	3/4 of original size.
.50	1/2 of original size.
.25	1/4 of original size.

Fig. 11-22. Scale factors and resulting sizes.

An object may also be scaled by specifying a new size in relation to an existing dimension. For example, suppose you have a shaft that is 2.50 in. long and you want to make it 3.00 in. long. Use the Reference option shown in Fig. 11-23 as follows:

〈Scale factor〉/Reference: **R** ↵
Reference length 〈1〉: **2.50** ↵
New length: **3.00** ↵

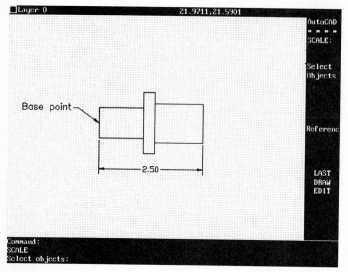
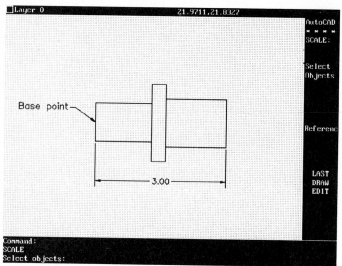

Fig. 11-23. Using the SCALE command's Reference option.

EXERCISE 11-8

☐ Load AutoCAD and open TITLEA.
☐ Draw two 2.25 in. squares each with one horizontal side.
☐ Double the size of one square.
☐ Use the Reference option to make the other square 3.25 in. along one side.
☐ Save the drawing as A:EX11-8 and quit.

PROFESSIONAL TIP

Always use the running and interrupt OSNAP modes to your best advantage when editing. For example, suppose you want to rotate an object. It may be difficult to find an exact corner without using OSNAP modes. To select the base point, use the ENDpoint or INTersect option.

STRETCHING AN OBJECT   ARM 6

The SCALE command changes the length and width of an object proportionately. The STRETCH command, on the other hand, changes only one dimension of an object or view. In mechanical drafting, it is common to increase the length of a part while leaving the diameter or width the same. In architectural design, room sizes may be stretched to increase the square footage.

When using the STRETCH command, you can select objects individually, or with the window or polygon options. For example, type "C" at the Select objects: prompt, and pick the opposite two corners of a crossing box around the objects you want to stretch.

When STRETCH is picked from the menu, it automatically uses the Crossing option at the "Select objects:" prompt. If you type the STRETCH command, the sequence looks like this:

Command: **STRETCH** ↵
Select objects to stretch by window or polygon...
Select objects: ↵
First corner: *(use a window or one of the polygon options to select the first corner of a crossing box)*
Other corner: *(pick the second corner)*
Select objects: *(pick additional objects or press ENTER)*

Select only that portion of the object to be stretched as in Fig. 11-24. If you select the entire object, the STRETCH command works like the MOVE command.

Next, you are asked to pick the base point. This is the point from which the object will be stretched. Then pick a new position for the base point. As you move the screen cursor, the object or objects are stretched or compressed. When the displayed object is stretched to the desired position, pick the new point. The command sequence after selecting objects is as follows:

Base point or displacement: *(pick the base point for the stretch to begin)*
Second point of displacement: *(pick the final location of the base point)*
Command:

The example in Fig. 11-24 shows the object being stretched. This is a common use of the STRETCH command. You may also use the STRETCH command to reduce the size of an object.

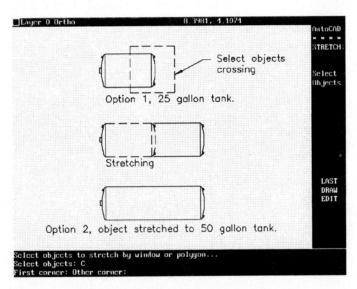

Fig. 11-24. Using the STRETCH command.

─ PROFESSIONAL TIP ─

Make sure the DRAGMODE is turned on when stretching an object; you can watch the object stretch to its new size. If the stretched object is not what you expected, cancel the command with CTRL C or puck button 3. The STRETCH command and other editing commands discussed in this chapter work well with ORTHO on. This lets you work in only horizontal and vertical directions.

EXERCISE 11-9

☐ Load AutoCAD and open TITLEB.
☐ Design and draw a cylindrical-shaped object similar to the tank in Fig. 11-24.
☐ Stretch the object to approximately twice its original length.
☐ Stretch the object to about twice its original height.
☐ Save the drawing as A:EX11-9 and quit.

SELECTING OBJECTS BEFORE EDITING

ARM A

Throughout this chapter, you have worked with the basic editing commands by entering the command name and then selecting the object to be edited. You can also set up AutoCAD to let you select the object first and then enter the desired editing command. The system variables that affect this procedure are PICKAUTO, PICKFIRST, and GRIPS. They should be set as follows:

- PICKAUTO = 1 (on). This allows you to automatically pick objects by the method used to pick and move the cursor.
- PICKFIRST = 1 (on). This system variable lets you pick the object before entering the editing command. When PICKFIRST is set to 0 (off), you must enter the command name before selecting the object. Notice the difference in the appearance of the crosshairs when PICKFIRST is on and off.
- GRIPS = 0 (off). Grips are used for automatic editing, and are discussed in detail in Chapter 12. For PICKFIRST to have its best performance, turn GRIPS off. If you are following along with this text while working at your computer, be sure to turn the GRIPS system variable back on when working in Chapter 12.

You can select objects individually or as a group at the Command: prompt. The selected entities become highlighted; then you enter the command name and proceed with the prompts as discussed in this chapter. For example, the COPY command works like this:

Command: *(select the entities to copy)*
Command: **COPY** ↵
⟨Base point or displacement⟩/Multiple: *(pick a base point)*
Second point of displacement: *(pick the final location for the copy)*
Command:

Now you have the flexibility of entering the command and then selecting the object, or selecting the object and then entering the command name. The editing commands work the same either way.

EXERCISE 11-10

☐ Load AutoCAD and open EX11-3, or start a new drawing and draw a square and triangle of any size.
☐ Set the following system variables as shown:
   PICKAUTO = 1
   PICKFIRST = 1
   GRIPS = 0
☐ Select the square; then enter the MOVE command to move it to a new position.
☐ Select the triangle; then enter the COPY command to make a copy of it.
☐ Experiment by selecting objects followed by using some of the other editing command such as ROTATE and SCALE.
☐ Erase an object by selecting the object before entering the ERASE command.
☐ Save the drawing as A:EX11-10 and quit.

EDITING WITH THE GEOMETRY CALCULATOR

In Chapter 8, you were introduced to the geometry calculator using the CAL command. This discussion shows you how to use the calculator to perform editing tasks. Review Chapter 8 before proceeding, paying special attention to the symbols, equations, and format detailed there.

Sometimes it is difficult to determine the exact position of an object you are trying to edit since the geometry does not fit into your grid and snap setup. When this occurs, it may be helpful to use the CAL command. There are an endless number of possibilities; this discussion provides you with a few of the many options.

Assume you have a drawing similar to the one shown in Fig. 11-25. You can easily locate points 1 and 2 using object snap modes; however, you cannot find the exact center between the points for the final destination of the circular object. Use the MOVE and CAL commands as follows:

Command: **MOVE** ↵
Select objects: *(select the circular object on the right)*
Select objects: ↵
Base point or displacement: *(use the OSNAP CENter option to locate the center of the circular object)*

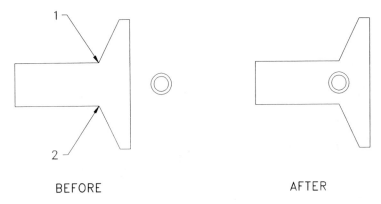

BEFORE   AFTER

Fig. 11-25. Centering an object between two endpoints using the CAL command.

Now use the CAL command to locate the center point exactly halfway between points 1 and 2:

Second point of displacement: **'CAL** ↵
⟩⟩ Expression: **(END + END)/2** ↵
⟩⟩ Select entity for END snap: *(pick point 1)*
⟩⟩ Select entity for END snap: *(pick point 2)*

The circular object automatically moves to the exact center point between points 1 and 2.

EXERCISE 11-11

☐ Load AutoCAD and open TITLEA.
☐ Create a drawing similar to the "BEFORE" example in Fig. 11-25.
☐ Use the MOVE and CAL commands to move the circular object exactly halfway between points 1 and 2. Your results should be similar to the "AFTER" example.
☐ Save the drawing as A:EX11-11 and quit.

The object at the left in Fig. 11-26 is rotated at an unknown angle. This makes it difficult to rotate the object on the right to the same angle. The objective is to rotate the object on the right so that its base is parallel with the base of the object on the left. The following command sequence accomplishes this task:

Command: **ROTATE** ↵
Select objects: *(select the horizontal object on the right)*
Select objects: ↵
Base point: *(pick point 1)*
⟨Rotation angle⟩/Reference: **'CAL** ↵
⟩⟩ Expression: **ANG(END,END)** ↵
⟩⟩ Select entity for END snap: *(pick point 2)*
⟩⟩ Select entity for END snap: *(pick point 3)*
Command:

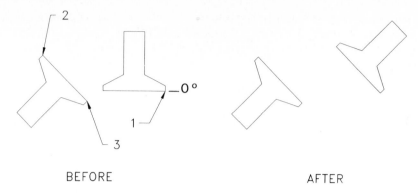

Fig. 11-26. Rotating an object so its base is parallel with an existing object.

EXERCISE 11-12

☐ Load AutoCAD and open TITLEA.
☐ Make a drawing similar to the "BEFORE" example in Fig. 11-26.
☐ Use the ROTATE and CAL commands to rotate the object on the right so that its base is parallel with the base of the object on the left. Your results should be similar to the "AFTER" example.
☐ Save the drawing as A:EX11-12 and quit.

SELECTING OBJECTS FOR FUTURE EDITING   ARM 2

The SELECT command is used to preselect an object or group of objects for future editing. It is designed to increase your productivity. Often you are working with the same set of objects, moving, copying, or scaling them. Set these aside as a selection set with the SELECT command. Then continue to perform another drawing or editing task. To return to those objects set aside, enter "P" at the Select objects: prompt. The command sequences for creating a selection set and then moving it are as follows:

Command: **SELECT** ⏎
Select objects: *(use any method to select an individual object or group of objects)*
Select objects: *(select additional objects or press ENTER)*

This sets up a selection set. Later, when you want to move these objects, use the Previous option as follows:

Command: **MOVE** ⏎
Select objects: **P** ⏎ *(this selects the object or group of objects previously selected using the SELECT command)*
Select objects: ⏎
Base point or displacement: *(pick the base point)*
Second point of displacement: *(pick the new location of the base point)*

EXERCISE 11-13

☐ Load AutoCAD and open TITLEA.
☐ Draw two circles with 1.5 in. (38.1 mm) radii spaced .25 in. (6.35 mm) apart.
☐ Use the SELECT command to select both circles for future editing.
☐ Draw at least three other small objects.
☐ Use the COPY command and the Previous option to copy the original two circles to a new location.
☐ Save the drawing as A:EX11-13 and quit.

CHAPTER TEST

Write your answers in the spaces provided.

1. Give the command and entries used to draw a 45° x .125 chamfer:

   Command: _____

   Polyline/Distances/⟨Select first line⟩: _____

   Enter first chamfer distance ⟨current⟩: _____

   Enter second chamfer distance ⟨previous⟩: _____

   Command: _____

   Polyline/Distances/⟨Select first line⟩: _____

   Select second line: _____

2. Give the command and entries required to produce .50 radius fillets on all corners of a closed polyline:

   Command: _____

   Polyline/Radius/⟨Select first object⟩: _____

   Enter fillet radius ⟨current⟩: _____

   Command: _____

   Polyline/Radius/⟨Select first object⟩: _____

   Select 2D polyline: _____

3. Give the command, entries, and actions required to move an object from position A to position B:

   Command: _____

   Select objects: _____

   Select objects: _____

   Base point or displacement:_____

   Second point of displacement: _____

4. Give the command and entries needed to make two copies of the same object:

   Command: _____

   Select objects: _____

   Select objects: _____

   ⟨Base point or displacement⟩/Multiple: _____

   Base point: _____

   Second point of displacement: _____

   Second point of displacement: _____

   Second point of displacement: _____

5. Give the command and entries necessary to draw a reverse image and then remove an existing object:

Command: _____

Select objects: _____

Select objects: _____

First point of mirror line: _____

Second point of mirror line: _____

Delete old objects? ⟨N⟩: _____

6. Give the command and entries needed to rotate an object 45° clockwise:

Command: _____

Select objects: _____

Select objects: _____

Base point: _____

⟨Rotation angle⟩/Reference: _____

7. Give the command and entries required to reduce the size of an entire drawing by one-half:

Command: _____

Select objects: _____

Select objects: _____

Base point: _____

⟨Scale factor⟩/Reference: _____

8. Give the command and entries needed to change the first break point picked to the intersection of two other lines:

Command: _____

Select object: _____

Enter second point (or F for first point): _____

Enter first point: _____

of _____

Enter second point: _____

9. Give the command sequence which revises the radius of a circle:

Command: _____

Select objects: _____

Select objects: _____

Properties/⟨Change point⟩: _____

10. Define the term "displacement" as it relates to the MOVE and COPY commands.

_____

_____

11. Explain the difference between the MOVE and COPY commands. _____

_____

_____

12. List two locations you normally choose as the base point when using the MOVE or COPY commands. _____
_____

13. Describe the purpose of the SELECT command. _____
_____

14. What is a selection set? _____
_____

15. How do you select objects for editing that have previously been picked using the SELECT command? _____
_____

16. How is the size of a fillet specified? _____

17. Identify the default selection method issued by AutoCAD for the STRETCH command.
_____

18. List two ways to cancel the STRETCH command. _____
_____

19. The EXTEND command can be considered the opposite of the _____ command.

20. Name the system variable used to preset the fillet radius. _____

21. In what direction should you pick points to break a portion out of a circle or arc?
_____

22. Name the command which trims an object to a cutting edge. _____

23. Name the command associated with boundary edges. _____

24. The MOVE, COPY, TRIM, EXTEND, and STRETCH commands are located in the _____ screen menu and the _____ or _____ pull-down menus.

25. Name the command that can be used to move and rotate an object simultaneously.
_____

26. Describe the purpose of the PICKFIRST system variable. _____
_____

DRAWING PROBLEMS

Use the TITLEA or TITLEB prototypes as appropriate for each of the following problems.

1. Draw the object shown as view A. Change the angle of the object to 45° as shown in view B. Then rotate it to a 90° rotation angle as shown in view C. Save the drawing as A:P11-1 and quit.

A   B   C

2. Draw the object shown as view A. Scale it down to 1/4 size as shown in view B. Then scale the object 10 times as shown in view C. Save the drawing as A:P11-2 and quit.

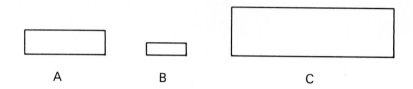

A   B   C

3. Draw object A using the LINE command, making sure that the corners overrun. Then trim the lines all at the same time. Select all four lines when asked to select cutting edges. Pick all overruns when asked to select object to trim. The object should appear as shown in view B. Save the drawing as A:P11-3 and quit.

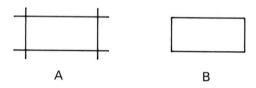

A   B

4. Draw object A using the LINE and ARC commands. Make sure that the corners overrun and the arc is centered, but does not touch the lines. Then use the TRIM, EXTEND, and MOVE commands to make the object look like the example shown in view B. Save the drawing as A:P11-4 and quit.

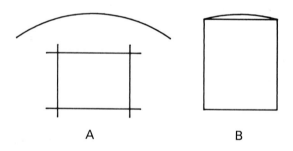

A   B

5. Open drawing P11-4 for further editing. Using the STRETCH command, change the shape to that shown in view B. Make a copy of the new revision. Change the copy to represent the example shown in view C. Save the drawing as A:P11-5 and quit.

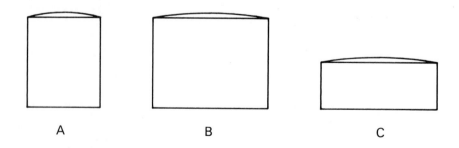

A   B   C

6. Refer to Fig. 11-24 in this chapter for this problem. Draw and make three copies of the object shown in Option 1. Stretch the first copy to twice its length as shown as Option 2. Stretch the second copy to twice its height. Double the size of the third copy using the SCALE command. Save the drawing as A:P11-6 and quit.

7. Draw objects A, B, and C shown below without dimensions. Then, move objects A, B, and C to new positions. Select a corner of object A and the center of objects B and C as the base points. Save the drawing as A:P11-7 and quit.

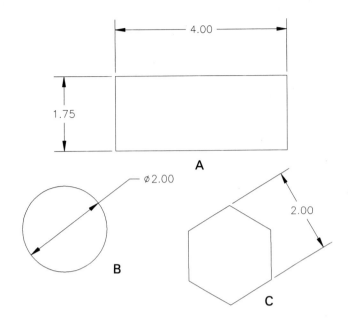

8. Draw objects A, B, and C shown in Problem 11-7 at the left side of the screen. Make a copy of object A two units to the right. Make four copies of object B three units, center-to-center, to the right using the Multiple option. Make three copies of object C three units, center-to-center, to the right. Save the drawing as A:P11-8 and, quit.

9. Draw the object shown using the ELLIPSE, COPY, and LINE commands. The rotation angle of the ellipses is 60°. Use the BREAK command when drawing and editing the lower ellipse. Save the drawing as A:P11-9 and quit.

10. Call up drawing P11-9 for further editing. Shorten the height of the object using the STRETCH command as shown below. Next, add to the object as indicated. Save the drawing as A:P11-10 and quit.

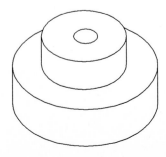

11. Draw the object shown as view A. Use the BREAK command to help change the object to the example shown as view B. Save the drawing as A:P11-11 and quit.

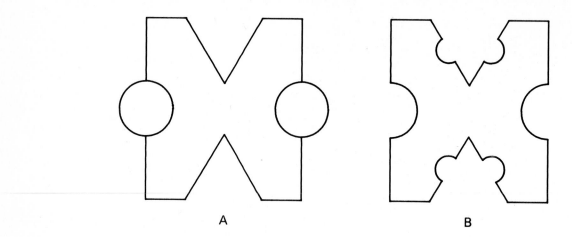

A

B

12. Draw view A, without dimensions. Use the CHAMFER and FILLET commands to your best advantage. Then draw a mirror image of it as shown in view B. Now, remove the original view and move the new view so that point 2 is at the original point 1 location. Save the drawing as A:P11-12 and quit.

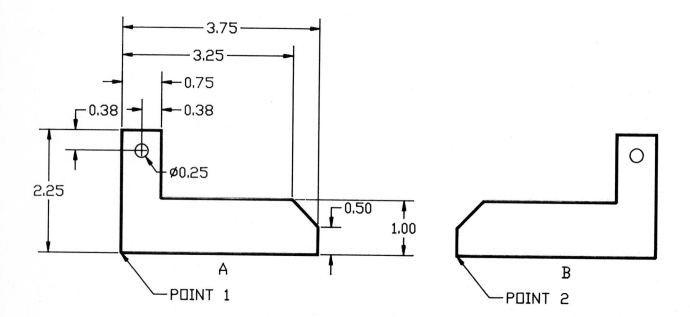

A

POINT 1

B

POINT 2

13. Draw the object shown below, without dimensions. The object is symmetrical; therefore, draw only the right half. Then mirror the left half into place. Use the CHAMFER and FILLET commands to your best advantage. Save the drawing as A:P11-13 and quit.

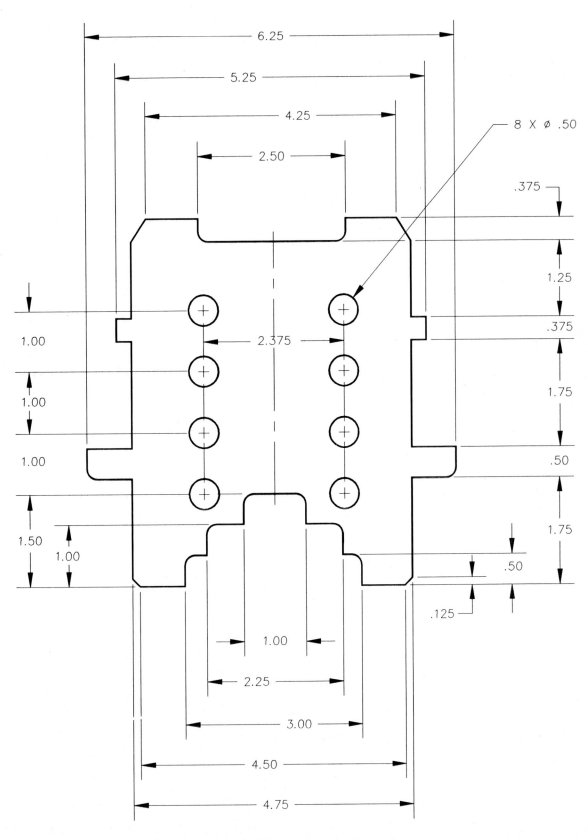

NOTE: ALL FILLETS AND ROUNDS R.125.

14. Refer to the view shown below for this problem. Plan to use the TRIM, OSNAP, and OFF-SET commands to assist you in drawing the view. Do not draw centerlines or dimensions. Save the completed drawing as A:P11-14 and quit.

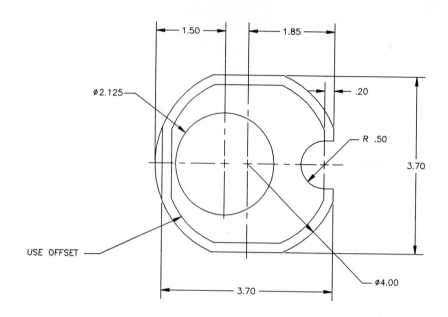

15. Draw the object shown below, without dimensions. Then mirror the right half into place. Use the CHAMFER and FILLET commands to your best advantage. Save the drawing as A:P11-15 and quit.

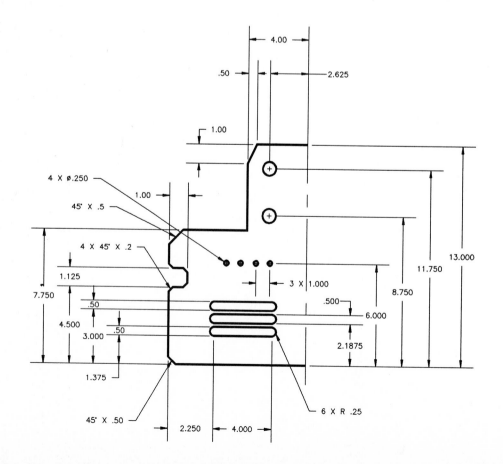

16. Redraw the objects shown below. Then mirror the drawing, but have the text remain readable. Delete the original image during the mirroring process. Save the drawing as A:P11-16 and quit.

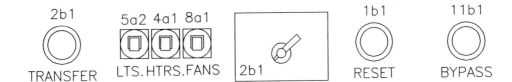

17. Draw the kitchen cabinet layout shown in view A and the partial floor plan shown at B. Make the cabinet 24 in. (609.6 mm) deep and the walls 6 in. (152.4 mm) wide. Make the sink and range proportional in size to the given illustration. Use the ALIGN command to move and rotate the cabinet layout into the wall location as shown in view C. Save the drawing as A:P11-17.

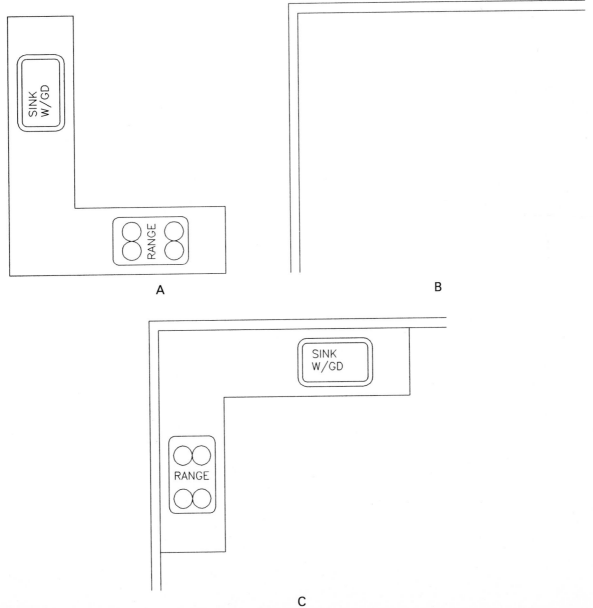

18. Draw the following objects. All rounds on the drawing are .250 unit radius. Use the CAL command to assist you in moving the circular object at the right to be centered exactly between points 1 and 2 on the object on the left. Do not dimension the drawing. Save the drawing as A:P11-18.

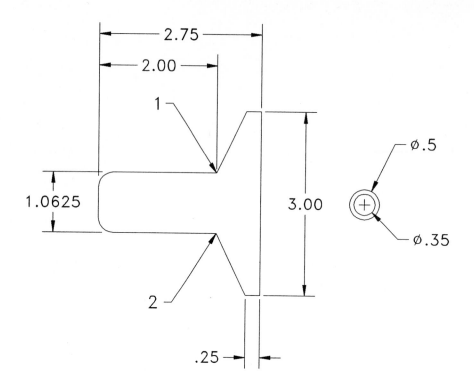

19. Open drawing P11-18. Make a copy of the object and rotate the copy to a horizontal position similar to the object shown at A below. Exact position is not critical. Rotate the original object to 225° as shown at B. Use the ROTATE, MOVE, or ALIGN commands as needed. Your objects should now look like A and B below. Use the ROTATE and CAL commands to rotate the object on the right so that the base is parallel to the base of the object on the left. Save the drawing as A:P11-19.

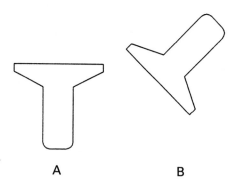

A   B

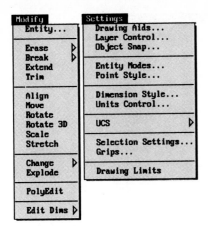

Chapter 12

AUTOMATIC EDITING

Learning objectives

After completing this chapter, you will be able to:

☐ Use grips to do automatic editing with the STRETCH, COPY, MOVE, ROTATE, SCALE, and MIRROR commands.

☐ Identify the system variables used to do automatic editing.

☐ Perform automatic editing through the "Modify" dialogue box.

☐ Change the properties of an object.

☐ Use the FILTER command to create a selection set.

In Chapter 11 you learned how to use commands that let you do a variety of drawing and editing activities with AutoCAD. These editing commands are used to give you maximum flexibility and increase productivity. The command format allowed you to enter commands such as COPY, MOVE, and SCALE before selecting objects, or you can set system variables that let you select the object before entering the command name. This chapter takes editing a step further by allowing you to select an object and automatically perform editing operations.

AUTOMATIC EDITING WITH GRIPS

"Hold," "grab," or "grasp" are all words that are synonymous with grip. In AutoCAD, *grips* are features on an entity that are highlighted with a small box. For example, the grips on a line are the ends and midpoint. When grips are used for editing, you can select an object to automatically activate the grips, and then pick any of the small boxes to perform stretch, move, rotate, scale, and mirror operations. In order for grips to work the GRIPS system variable must be on.

    Command: **GRIPS** ↵
    New value for GRIPS ⟨0⟩: **1** ↵
    Command:

When GRIPS is on there is a pickbox located at the intersection of the screen crosshairs. You can pick any entity to activate the grips. Fig. 12-1 shows what grips look like on several different entities. You can even pick text and the grip box is located at the insertion point.

    You can also control grips by picking Grips... in the Settings pull-down menu or by typing DDGRIPS. The "Grips" dialogue box shown in Fig. 12-2 is then displayed.

    Look at the "Grips" dialogue box and notice the Select Settings check boxes. Pick the Enable Grips check box to turn grips on or off. Pick the Enable Grips Within Blocks check box to have grips displayed on every entity of a block. A *block* is a special symbol designed for multiple use. (Blocks are discussed in detail in Chapter 21.) When this check box is off, the grip location for a block is at the insertion point as shown in Fig. 12-1. Grips in blocks may also be controlled

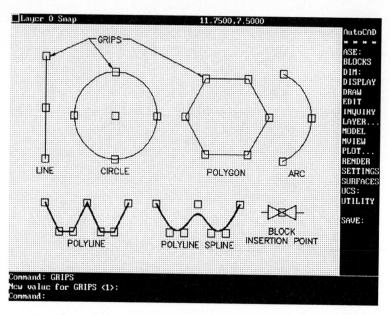

Fig. 12-1. Grips are placed at strategic locations on entities.

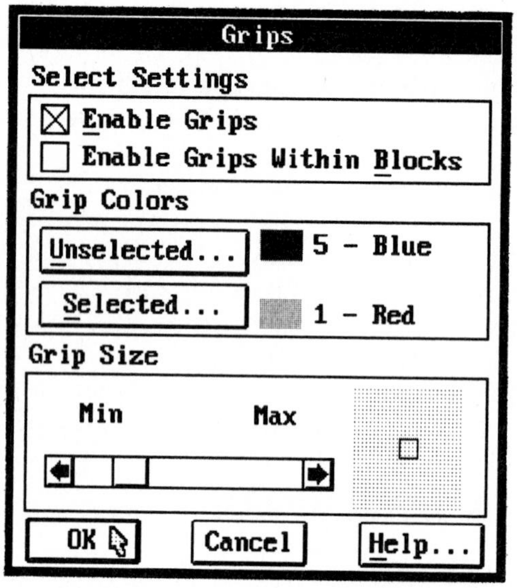

Fig. 12-2. The "Grips" dialogue box.

with the GRIPBLOCK system variable. The default for GRIPBLOCK is 0. Enter "1" and press ENTER to turn on grips within blocks.

The Grip Colors buttons allow you to change the color of grips. The grips are displayed when you first pick an entity. These are referred to as *unselected grips* because you have not yet picked a grip to perform an operation. An unselected grip is a colored square outline. Unselected grips are set to blue as default, and are considered "warm." After you pick a grip it is called a *selected grip,* and is displayed as a filled-in square as shown in Fig. 12-3. Selected grips are red by default, and are referred to as "hot." If more than one entity is selected, and they have warm grips, then they are all affected by what you do with the hot grips. Entities that have warm and hot grips are highlighted and are part of the selection set. You can remove highlighted entities from the selection set by holding down the SHIFT key and picking the entity to be removed. The highlighting goes away, but the grips remain. These are called "cold" grips. Entities with cold grips are not affected by what you do to entities with warm grips. Return the entity with cold grips to the selection set by picking it again.

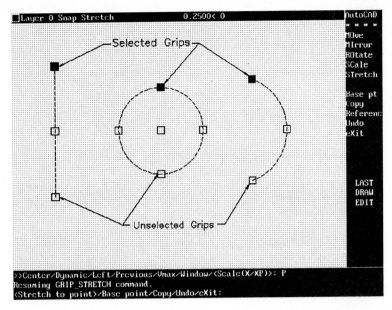

Fig. 12-3. Selected (hot) grips are filled-in squares. Unselected (warm) grips are colored outlines.

You can also control grip color with the GRIPCOLOR and GRIPHOT system variables. GRIP-COLOR controls the color of unselected (warm) grips, while GRIPHOT regulates the color of selected (hot) grips. When you enter one of these variables, simply set the color number as desired.

The Grip Size scroll bar in the "Grips" dialogue box lets you graphically change the size of the grip box. Change the grip size to whatever works best for your drawing. Very small grip boxes may be difficult to pick. However, the grips may overlap if they are too large.

If the FILEDIA system variable is 0 (off), then the grip size is given a numerical value using the GRIPSIZE system variable. To change the default of 3, enter "GRIPSIZE" at the Command: prompt and then type a desired size in pixels.

Using grips

To activate grips move the pick box to the desired entity and pick. The object is highlighted and the unselected grips are displayed. To select a grip move the pick box to the desired grip and pick it. Notice that the crosshairs "snap" to a grip. A grip becomes solid when selected. See Fig. 12-3. When you pick a grip the command line changes to this:

** STRETCH **
⟨Stretch to point⟩/Base point/Copy/Undo/eXit:

This activates the STRETCH command. All you have to do is move the cursor to make the selected object stretch as shown in Fig. 12-4. If you pick the middle grip of a line or arc, or the center grip of a circle, the object moves. These are the other options:

- **Base point**—Enter "B" and press ENTER to select an new base point for this editing command.
- **Copy**—Enter "C" and press ENTER if you want to make one or more copies of the selected object.
- **Undo**—Enter "U" and press ENTER to undo the previous operation.
- **eXit**—Enter "X" and press ENTER to exit the command. The selected grip is gone, but the unselected grips remain. You can also use CTRL C to cancel the command. Canceling twice removes the selected and the unselected grips and returns the Command: prompt.

PROFESSIONAL TIP

More than one grip can be hot at any given time. Simply hold down the Shift key and pick the grips.

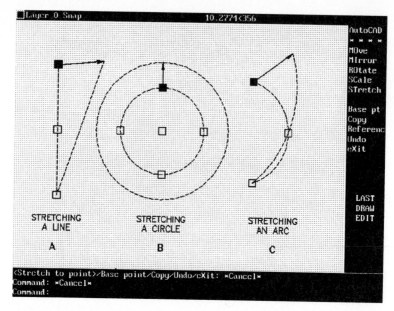

Fig. 12-4. Using the automatic STRETCH command. Note the selected grip. A—Stretching a line. B—Stretching a circle. C—Stretching an arc.

You can pick entities individually or you can use any of the selection techniques that were discussed in Chapter 6. Fig. 12-5 shows how you can stretch features of an object after selecting all of the entities. Step 1 in Fig. 12-5A illustrates stretching the first corner and Step 2 stretches the second corner. You could also make more than one grip hot at the same time by holding down the SHIFT key as you pick the grips as shown in Fig. 12-5B.

Here are some general rules and guidelines that can help make grips work for you:
- Be sure the GRIPS system variable is on.
- Pick an entity or group of entities to activate grips.
- Entities in the selection set are highlighted.
- Pick a warm grip to make it hot.
- Make more than one grip hot by holding down the SHIFT key while picking warm grips.
- If more than one entity is selected and they have warm grips, then they are all affected by the editing commands.
- Remove entities from the selection set by holding down the SHIFT key and picking them, thus making the grips cold.

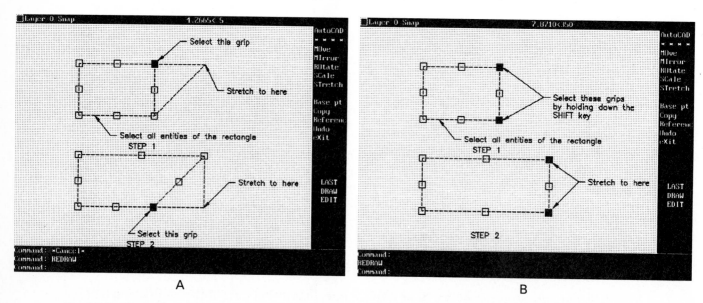

Fig. 12-5. Stretching an object. A—Select corners to stretch individually. B—Select several hot grips by holding down the SHIFT key.

- Return entities to the selection set by picking them again.
- Remove hot grips from the selection set by pressing CTRL C. Press CTRL C again to remove all grips from the selection set. If you have not yet picked a hot grip, all you have to do is press CTRL C once to remove the grips.

PROFESSIONAL TIP

When editing with grips, you can enter coordinates to help improve your accuracy. Remember that any of the coordinate entry methods discussed in Chapter 6 will work.

EXERCISE 12-1

☐ Load AutoCAD and open TITLEA.
☐ Draw a line with coordinates X=2,Y=4 and X=2,Y=7. Draw a circle with the center at X=5.5,Y=5.5, with a radius of 1.5. Finally, draw an arc with its center at X=8.5,Y=5.5, a start point of X=9.5,Y=4, and an endpoint of X=9.5,Y=7.
☐ In the space at the bottom of the screen, draw a polyline on the left similar to the one in Fig. 12-1.
☐ Make sure GRIPS are on.
☐ Experiment with the STRETCH command using grips by picking the points as follows:
    ☐ Line—Pick the ends first and then the middle to see what happens.
    ☐ Circle—Pick one of the quadrants, and the center.
    ☐ Arc—Pick the ends and the middle.
    ☐ Polyline—Pick various grips.
    ☐ Spline—Pick various grips. Editing polylines in this manner allows you to create some interesting shapes.
☐ Save the drawing as A:EX12-1 and quit.

You can also use the MOVE, ROTATE, SCALE, and MIRROR commands to automatically edit entities. All you have to do is pick the object and then select one of the grips. When you see the ** STRETCH ** command, press ENTER to get the next command option:

```
** STRETCH **
⟨Stretch to point⟩/Base point/Copy/Undo/eXit: ↵
** MOVE **
⟨Move to point⟩/Base point/Copy/Undo/eXit: ↵
** ROTATE **
⟨Rotation angle⟩/Base point/Copy/Undo/Reference/eXit: ↵
** SCALE **
⟨Scale factor⟩/Base point/Copy/Undo/Reference/eXit: ↵
** MIRROR **
⟨Second point⟩/Base point/Copy/Undo/eXit:
```

Pressing ENTER cycles through each editing command, or you can pick the desired command from the screen menu.

PROFESSIONAL TIP

When warm grips are displayed on the screen, you can also use some of the editing commands from the pull-down and screen menus, or by typing the editing command name at the Command: prompt. For example, the ERASE command can be used to clear the screen of all entities displayed with warm grips by first picking the entities and then selecting the ERASE command.

Moving an object automatically

If you want to move an object with grips, select the object, pick a grip to use as the base point, and then cycle through the commands until you get to this prompt:

    ** MOVE **
    〈Move to point〉/Base point/Copy/Undo/eXit:

The selected grip becomes the base point. Then move the object to a new point and the MOVE operation is complete as shown in Fig. 12-6. If you accidentally pick the wrong grip or decide to change the grip base point, enter "B" and press ENTER for the Base point option and pick a new one.

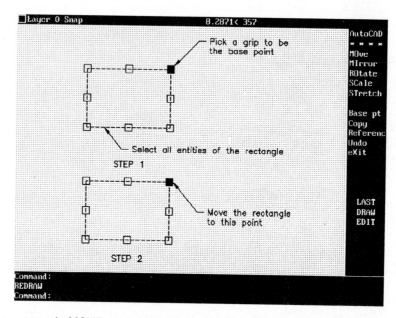

Fig. 12-6. The automatic MOVE command. The selected grip becomes the base point for the move.

EXERCISE 12-2

☐ Load AutoCAD and open TITLEA.
☐ Draw a 1.5 in. (38.1 mm) diameter circle with its center at X = 2, Y = 3.
☐ Use grips to move the circle 2 in. (50.8 mm) to the right.
☐ Save the drawing as A:EX12-2 and quit.

Copying an object automatically

The Copy option is found in each of the editing commands. When using the STRETCH command, the Copy option allows you to make multiple copies of the entity you are stretching. Holding down the SHIFT key while performing the first STRETCH operation accesses the Multiple mode. The prompt looks like this:

    ** STRETCH (multiple) **
    〈Stretch to point〉/Base point/Copy/Undo/eXit: ↵

The Copy option in the MOVE command is the true form of the COPY command. You can activate the Copy option by entering "C" for copy as follows:

    ** MOVE **
    〈Move to point〉/Base point/Copy/Undo/eXit: **C** ↵
    ** MOVE (multiple) **
    〈Move to point〉/Base point/Copy/Undo/eXit: *(make as many copies as desired and
      enter X to exit, or press CTRL C)*

Holding down the SHIFT key while performing the first MOVE operation also puts you in the Copy mode.

The Copy option works similarly in each of the editing commands. Try it with each to see what happens.

— PROFESSIONAL TIP —

When in the MOVE command's Copy option, if you make the first copy followed by holding the SHIFT key, the distance of the first copy automatically becomes the snap spacing for additional copies.

EXERCISE 12-3

☐ Load AutoCAD and open TITLEA.
☐ Use the PLINE command to draw the objects shown at A, B, C, and D below. Do not draw dimensions.

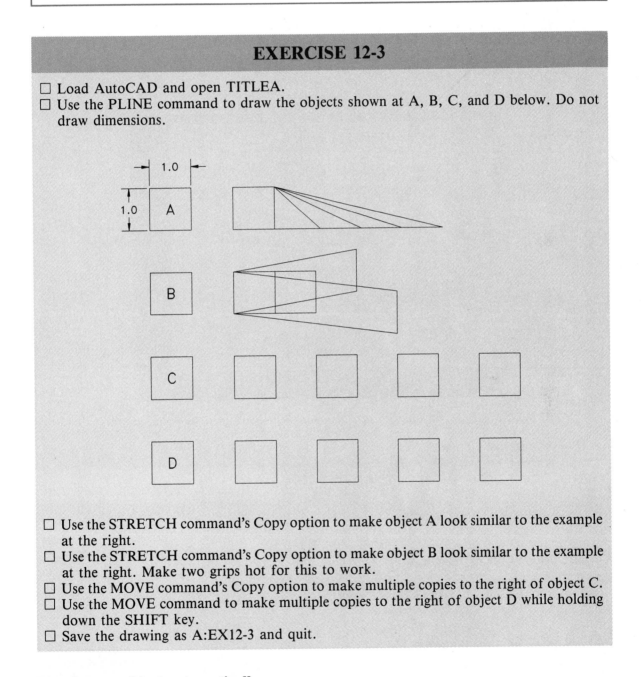

☐ Use the STRETCH command's Copy option to make object A look similar to the example at the right.
☐ Use the STRETCH command's Copy option to make object B look similar to the example at the right. Make two grips hot for this to work.
☐ Use the MOVE command's Copy option to make multiple copies to the right of object C.
☐ Use the MOVE command to make multiple copies to the right of object D while holding down the SHIFT key.
☐ Save the drawing as A:EX12-3 and quit.

Rotating an object automatically

To automatically rotate an object, select the object to be rotated, pick a grip to use as the base point, and press ENTER until you see this prompt:

    ** ROTATE **
    〈Rotation angle〉/Base point/Copy/Undo/Reference/eXit:

Now, move your pointing device and watch the object rotate. Pick the desired rotation point, or enter a rotation angle like this:

⟨Rotation angle⟩/Base point/Copy/Undo/Reference/eXit: **45** ↵

Enter "R" and press ENTER if you want to use the Reference option:

⟨Rotation angle⟩/Base point/Copy/Undo/Reference/eXit: **R** ↵

The Reference option may be used when the object is already rotated at a known angle and you want to rotate it to a new angle. The reference angle is the current angle and the new angle is the desired angle:

Reference angle ⟨0⟩: **45** ↵
** ROTATE **
⟨New angle⟩/Base point/Copy/Undo/Reference/eXit: **10** ↵

Fig. 12-7 shows the Rotation options.

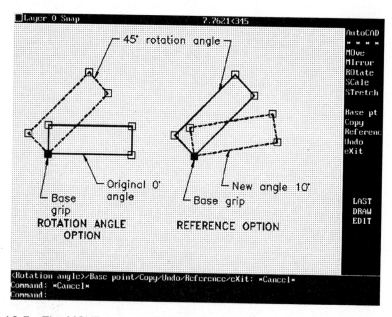

Fig. 12-7. The MOVE command's Rotation angle option and Reference option.

EXERCISE 12-4

☐ Load AutoCAD and open TITLEA.
☐ Draw a rectangle using the PLINE command similar to the one shown at the left of Fig. 12-7. Orient the long sides so they are at 0°.
☐ Use grips to rotate the object 45°.
☐ Rotate the object again to 20° using the Reference option.
☐ Save the drawing as A:EX12-4 and quit.

Scaling an object automatically

If you want to scale an object with grips, cycle through the editing options until you get this prompt:

** SCALE **
⟨Scale factor⟩/Base point/Copy/Undo/Reference/eXit:

You can move the screen cursor and pick when the object is dragged to the desired size, or enter a scale factor to automatically increase or decrease the scale of the original object. Scale factors are given on page 11-19. You can also use the Reference option if you know a current length and a desired length. Enter "R" for the Reference option:

⟨Scale factor⟩/Base point/Copy/Undo/Reference/eXit: **R** ↵
Reference length⟨⟩: **3.0** ↵
** SCALE **
⟨New length⟩/Base point/Copy/Undo/Reference/eXit: **5.25** ↵

Note that the selected base point remains in the same place when the object is scaled. Figure 12-8 shows the two Scale options.

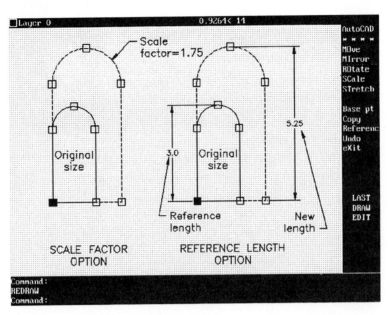

Fig. 12-8. The options for the automatic SCALE command include the Scale factor option and the Reference length option.

EXERCISE 12-5

☐ Load AutoCAD and open TITLEA.
☐ Draw an object similar to the original object at the left in Fig. 12-8.
☐ Activate grips to make a copy of the object to the right of the original.
☐ Scale the first object using a scale factor of 1.5.
☐ Use the Reference option to scale the second object to any desired height.
☐ Save the drawing as A:EX12-5 and quit.

Mirroring an object automatically

If you want to mirror an object, the selected grip becomes the first point of the mirror line. Then press ENTER to cycle through the editing commands until you get this prompt:

** MIRROR **
⟨Second point⟩/Base point/Copy/Undo/eXit:

Pick another grip or any point on the screen to be the second point of the mirror line as shown in Fig. 12-9. Unlike the MIRROR command accessed through the pull-down, screen menus, and keyboard, the automatic MIRROR command does not give you the option to delete the old objects; it does so automatically. If you want to keep the original object while mirroring, use the Copy option in the MIRROR command.

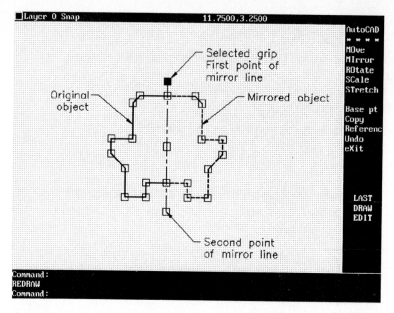

Fig. 12-9. When using the automatic MIRROR command, the selected grip becomes the first point of the mirror line. The original will be deleted.

EXERCISE 12-6

☐ Load AutoCAD and open TITLEA.
☐ Draw a shape similar to the original object in Fig. 12-9.
☐ Use grips to mirror the object along the centerline.
☐ Save the drawing as A:EX12-6 and quit.

BASIC EDITING VS. AUTOMATIC EDITING

In Chapter 11 you learned what is referred to in this text as *basic editing*. Basic editing allows you to first enter a command and then select the desired object to be edited. You could also set system variables to first select the desired objects and then enter the desired command. The automatic editing features discussed in this chapter use grips and related editing commands to edit an object automatically by picking the object first. The method you use is completely up to you. AutoCAD has given you maximum flexibility to use a variety of techniques that help you increase drafting and design productivity. You will find that certain command formats work best for you in different situations as you become an experienced AutoCAD user.

The "Entity Selection Settings" dialogue box allows you to control the manner in which you use editing commands. This dialogue box is displayed by typing "DDSELECT" at the Command: prompt, or by picking Selection Settings . . . from the Settings pull-down menu. See Fig. 12-10. These are the items found in the "Entity Selection Settings" dialogue box:

- **Noun/Verb Selection** – AutoCAD refers to Noun/Verb as the format used when you select objects and then enter the desired command. This is the technique discussed in this chapter. The pick box is displayed at the screen crosshairs. An "X" in this check box means that the Noun/Verb method is active. The PICKFIRST system variable may also be used to set the Noun/Verb selection. The opposite of the Noun/Verb selection – Verb/Noun – is the method in which you enter the command before selecting the object. The Verb/Noun method is used primarily in Chapter 11. Remove the "X" from the Noun/Verb check box to enter the command before making a selection. Some editing commands such as FILLET, CHAMFER, DIVIDE, MEASURE, OFFSET, EXTEND, TRIM, and BREAK require that you enter the command before you select the object.
- **Use Shift to Add** – When this check box is not checked (off), every entity or group of entities you select is highlighted and added to the selection set. If you pick this check box, it changes the way AutoCAD accepts entities you pick. For example, if you pick an entity it is highlighted

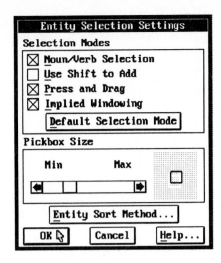

Fig. 12-10. The ''Entity Selection Settings'' dialogue box.

and added to the selection set. However, if you pick another entity, it is highlighted and the first is removed from the selection set. This means that you can only include one entity by picking, or one group of entities with a selection window, to the selection set. If you want to add more items to the selection set, you must hold down the SHIFT key as you pick them, hence the name "Use Shift to Add." Turning on the PICKADD system variable does the same thing as turning on this feature.

- **Press and Drag** — This is the same as turning on the PICKDRAG system variable. With Press and Drag on, you create a selection window by picking the first corner, and then move the puck while holding down the pick button. Release the pick button when you have the desired selection window. The default is to have "Press and Drag" turned off, which means that you have to pick both the first and second corner of the desired selection window.
- **Implied Windowing** — This option defaults to on. This means that you can automatically create a window by picking the first point, and moving the cursor to the right to pick the second point, or make a crossing box by picking the first point and moving the cursor to the left to pick the second point. This is the same as turning on the PICKAUTO system variable. This only affects selecting objects when the Select objects: prompt appears, and it does not work if PICKDRAG is on.
- **Default Selection Mode** — Picking this button sets the selection methods to the AutoCAD defaults as shown in Fig. 12-10.
- **Pickbox Size** — This scroll bar lets you adjust the size of the pick box. Watch the sample in the image tile get smaller or larger as you move the scroll bar. Stop when you have a desired size. The pick box size is also controlled by the PICKBOX system variable.
- **Entity Sort Method** — The "Entity Sort Method" subdialogue box shown in Fig. 12-11 appears when you pick this button. The check boxes in the "Entity Sort Method" subdialogue box allows you to control the order in which entities are displayed or plotted. The check boxes control these features:
  - **Object Selection** — Establishes window or crossing selections in the order they are made.
  - **Object Snap** — Issues the running object snaps in the order you establish.
  - **Redraws** — Entities are displayed in the order they were created when you use the REDRAW command.
  - **Slide Creation** — Slides are displayed in the order they were created. Creating slide shows is discussed in Chapter 29.
  - **Regens** — Entities are displayed in the order they were created when you use the REGEN command or when an automatic regeneration occurs.
  - **Plotting** — Entities are plotted in the order they were created.
  - **PostScript Output** — PostScript entities are printed in the order they were created or imported into AutoCAD.

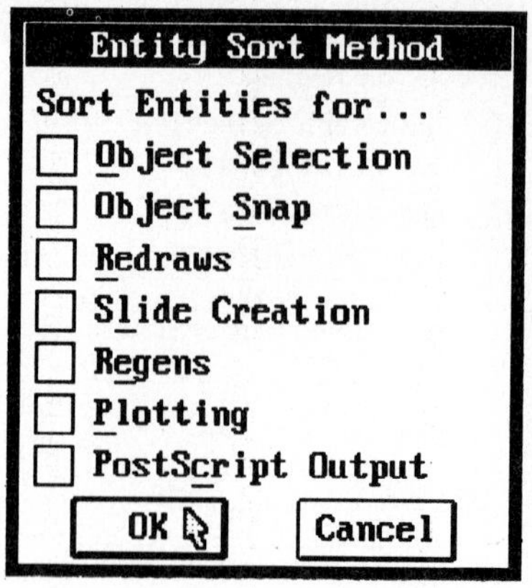

Fig. 12-11. This dialogue can be accessed by picking Entity Sort Method . . . from the "Entity Selection Settings" dialogue box.

Entity sorting is also controlled by the SORTENTS system variable where the following values duplicate the check boxes in the dialogue box:

  0 = Sorting is turned off.
  1 = Object selection sorting.
  2 = Object snap sorting.
  4 = Sorts entities in a redraw.
  8 = Slide creation sorting.
  16 = Regeneration sorting.
  32 = Plot sorting.
  64 = Sort for PostScript output.

The default, 96, specifies sorting for plotting and PostScript output.

PROFESSIONAL TIP

Notice in Fig. 12-11 that none of the check boxes are checked. Entity sorting takes time and should only be used if the drawing or application software you are using requires entity sorting. Turn the Object Selection sorting on if you want AutoCAD to find the last object drawn when selecting overlapping entities.

EXERCISE 12-7

☐ Load AutoCAD.
☐ Enter the DDSELECT command and look at the "Entity Selection Settings" dialogue box.
☐ Adjust the pick box size while watching the image tile.
☐ Pick Entity Sort Method... and see the "Entity Sort Method" subdialogue box.
☐ Cancel both dialogue boxes.
☐ Quit without saving this drawing session.

AUTOMATIC EDITING IN A DIALOGUE BOX

You can use the DDMODIFY command or pick Entity... from the Modify pull-down menu to edit an entity using the "Modify" dialogue box. You can also select DDMODIFY from the EDIT screen menu. You are first asked to select an object to modify:

  Command: **DDMODIFY** ↵
  Select object to modify: *(pick an object to modify)*

If you pick a line, you get the "Modify Line" dialogue box, or if you pick a circle you get the "Modify Circle" dialogue box shown in Fig. 12-12. The following discussion details features that are commonly found in the "Modify" dialogue box.

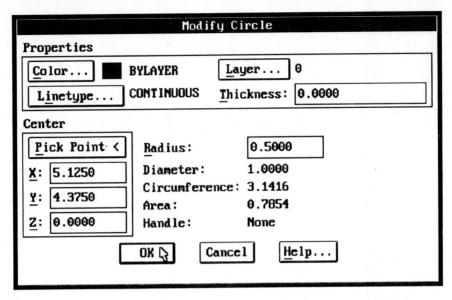

Fig. 12-12. The "Modify" dialogue boxes can be used to edit entities.

Properties

The Properties section of the "Modify" dialogue box contains several common elements. These are:
- **Color** — Pick this button to get the "Select Color" subdialogue box. This subdialogue box displays the available colors. Simply pick a desired color for this entity, or enter a color name or number in the Color: edit box.
- **Linetype** — Pick this button to see the "Select Linetype" subdialogue box. Here you can change the entity linetype by selecting one of the linetypes that has already been loaded using the LINETYPE command.
- **Layer** — Picking the Layer... button displays the "Select Layer" dialogue box where you can set the selected entity to a desired layer. Layers are discussed in Chapter 17.
- **Thickness** — This edit box lets you change the thickness of the entity. This is used in 3-D drawing, which is discussed in Chapters 24 and 25.

Changing the center point

When entities such as circles or arcs are selected using DDMODIFY, the following information is provided:
- **Pick Point <** — Pick this button to establish a new center point location. The dialogue box disappears, the graphics screen returns, and you see this prompt:

    Center point: *(pick a new center point, or enter the coordinates for a new center location and press ENTER)*

- **X:, Y:, Z:** — Use these edit boxes to change the values of the X, Y, or Z coordinates, respectively. The Z coordinate is for 3-D drawings. The center location automatically changes when you enter new values and pick the OK button.

When modifying circular entities, related information for the Diameter, Circumference, and Area appear near the center of the "Modify" dialogue box. The Radius is also given in an edit box. If you want to change the radius, double click on the Radius: edit box, enter a new value and the circle automatically changes to the new radius.

Each of the "Modify" dialogue boxes is slightly different. For example, the "Modify Line" dialogue box contains information about the line from the two endpoints, and edit boxes to change the endpoint coordinates. If you pick an entity such as a polygon you get the "Modify Polyline" dialogue box. This dialogue box contains items that allow you to automatically edit various aspects of a polyline. Remember from Chapter 7 that a polygon is a polyline.

The "Modify Text" dialogue box is an excellent way to quickly and easily edit text. To get the "Modify Text" dialogue box shown in Fig. 12-13, enter the DDMODIFY command and pick the text to be modified.

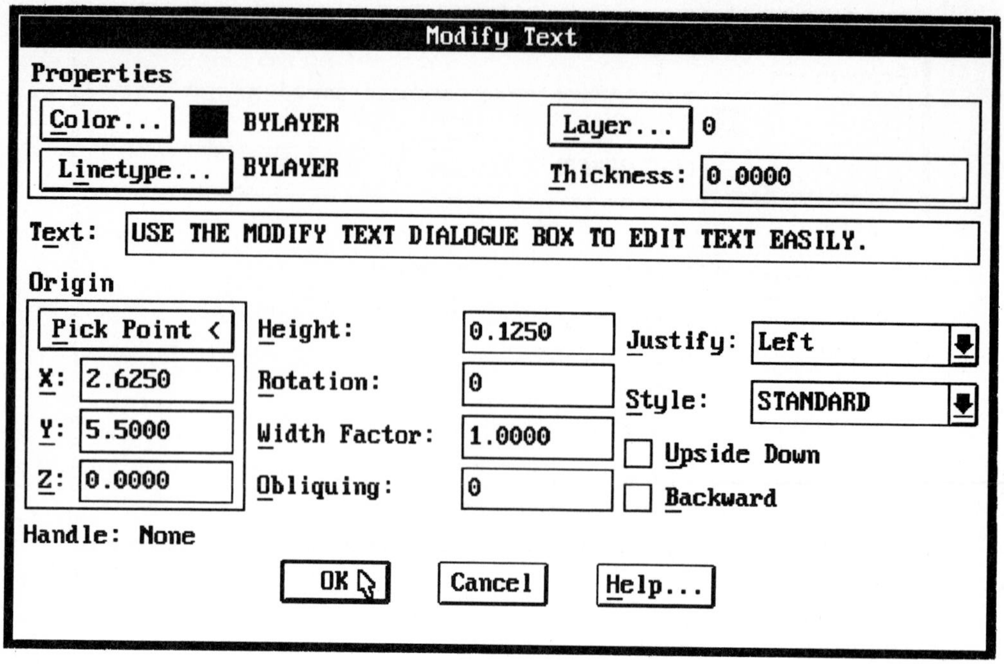

```
┌─────────────────────────────────────────────────────────────────┐
│                          Modify Text                              │
│  Properties                                                       │
│  ┌─────────┐  ██  BYLAYER          ┌─────────┐  0                 │
│  │ Color...│                       │ Layer...│                    │
│  └─────────┘                       └─────────┘                    │
│  ┌──────────┐  BYLAYER             Thickness: ┌──────────┐        │
│  │ Linetype.│                                 │ 0.0000   │        │
│  └──────────┘                                 └──────────┘        │
│                                                                   │
│  Text: ┌──────────────────────────────────────────────────────┐ │
│        │ USE THE MODIFY TEXT DIALOGUE BOX TO EDIT TEXT EASILY. │ │
│        └──────────────────────────────────────────────────────┘ │
│  Origin                                                           │
│  ┌──────────────┐  Height:  ┌────────┐  Justify: ┌──────────┐▼   │
│  │ Pick Point ‹ │           │ 0.1250 │           │ Left     │    │
│  └──────────────┘           └────────┘           └──────────┘    │
│  X: ┌────────┐  Rotation: ┌───┐         Style:   ┌──────────┐▼   │
│     │ 2.6250 │            │ 0 │                   │ STANDARD │    │
│     └────────┘            └───┘                   └──────────┘    │
│  Y: ┌────────┐  Width Factor: ┌────────┐  ☐ Upside Down          │
│     │ 5.5000 │                │ 1.0000 │                          │
│     └────────┘                └────────┘                          │
│  Z: ┌────────┐  Obliquing: ┌───┐          ☐ Backward             │
│     │ 0.0000 │             │ 0 │                                  │
│     └────────┘             └───┘                                  │
│  Handle: None                                                     │
│                                                                   │
│            ┌───────┐   ┌─────────┐   ┌─────────┐                 │
│            │ OK ⇗  │   │ Cancel  │   │ Help... │                 │
│            └───────┘   └─────────┘   └─────────┘                 │
└─────────────────────────────────────────────────────────────────┘
```

Fig. 12-13. A simple means to edit text is through the use of the "Modify Text" dialogue box.

The Properties buttons allow you to change the color, linetype, layer, and thickness. You can edit the text wording by moving the cursor to the Text: edit box and remove, add, or change the text as needed. Change the text origin by selecting the Pick Point ‹ button and picking a new point on the screen, or enter new X, Y coordinates. Automatically change the text height in the Height: edit box, or change the rotation angle, width factor, or obliquing angle by altering the values in these edit boxes. Pick the arrow at the right of the Justify box to get the justification popup list. Pick the desired justification from this list. Select a text style that has been previously loaded by picking the desired style from the Style popup list. Check either the Upside down or the Backward boxes if you want these conditions to be in effect.

EXERCISE 12-8

☐ Load AutoCAD and open TITLEA.
☐ Draw a line with endpoint coordinates $X = 2, Y = 3$ and $X = 2, Y = 6$.
☐ Draw a circle with a radius of 1.250 and a center location of $X = 6, Y = 4.5$.
☐ Use the DTEXT command with .25 in. text height and position the word "LINE" below the line and "CIRCLE" below the circle.
☐ Use the "Modify Line" dialogue box to edit the line as follows:
   ☐ Change the "from point" to $X = 6.750, Y = 3.770$.
   ☐ Change the "to point" to $X = 6.750, Y = 6.750$.
☐ Use the "Modify Circle" dialogue box to edit the circle as follows:
   ☐ Change the center location to $X = 7.125, Y = 5.25$.
   ☐ Change the radius to .375.
☐ Change the LINE label to .125 in. height and place it above the line.
☐ Change the CIRCLE label to read "Circle" and justify the middle of it with the center of the circle. Modify the text height to be .375 in.
☐ Save the drawing as A:EX12-8 and quit.

PROFESSIONAL TIP

If you are trying to pick an entity that is on top of another, AutoCAD may not pick the one you want. However, AutoCAD picks the last thing you drew if Object Selection is on in the "Entity Sort Method" dialogue box.

CHANGING THE PROPERTIES OF AN OBJECT

In Chapter 11 you learned how to make changes to an object using the CHANGE command. This is a popular command because it is easy to use and allows you to change either the location of an object or properties related to the object. The CHANGE command prompts look like this:

> Command: **CHANGE** ↵
> Select objects: *(pick the object)*
> Select objects: ↵

In Chapter 11 you used the default, Change point, to change the location of an object. You can also change properties of the feature by entering "P":

> Properties/⟨Change point⟩: **P** ↵
> Change what property (Color/Elev/Layer/LType/Thickness)?

The following properties can be changed with the CHANGE command:
- **Color** — Changes the color of the selected object.
- **Elevation** — Used to change the elevation in 3-D drawing.
- **Layer** — Changes the layer designation. Layers are discussed in Chapter 17.
- **Linetype** — Changes the current linetype of a selected object to a linetype that has been loaded using the LINETYPE command.
- **Thickness** — Used to change the thickness in 3-D drawing.

The CHPROP (CHange PROPerty) command lets you change only properties of an object. It does not allow for point change as in the CHANGE command. This is the command sequence if the FILEDIA system variable is set to 0:

> Command: **CHPROP** ↵
> Select objects: *(pick the object)*
> Select objects: ↵
> Change what property (Color/Elev/Layer/LType/Thickness)?

The change property options are the same as those discussed in the CHANGE command.

If you like to use dialogue boxes, you can change properties by entering "DDCHPROP" at the Command: prompt, or pick Change in the Modify pull-down menu and then pick Properties from the cascading submenu:

> Command: **DDCHPROP** ↵
> Select objects: *(pick the object)*
> Select objects: ↵

Now the "Change Properties" dialogue box, shown in Fig. 12-14, is displayed.

As you look at this dialogue box you can see some of the items discussed earlier. You can pick Color... to change the entity color, pick Layer... to change the layer, or pick Linetype... to change the linetype. The thickness of an object can be changed using the Thickness: edit box when performing 3-D functions.

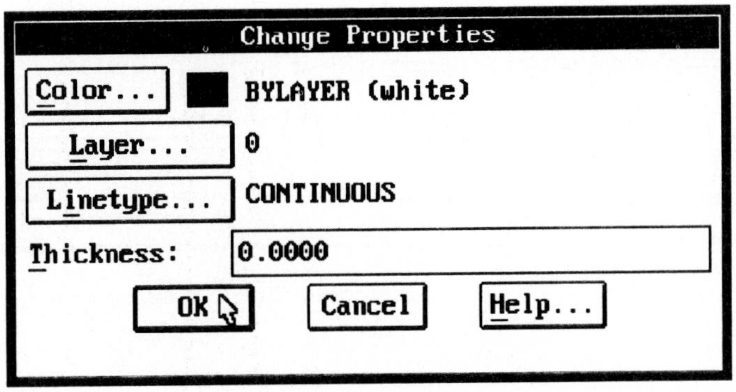

Fig. 12-14. The "Change Properties" dialogue box is accessed with the DDCHPROP command.

EXERCISE 12-9

☐ Load AutoCAD and open TITLEA.
☐ Draw a vertical line on the left side of the screen, a circle in the middle, and a hexagon on the right side.
☐ Load the CENTER, HIDDEN, and PHANTOM linetypes.
☐ Use the CHANGE command to change the linetype of the line to CENTER.
☐ Use the CHPROP command to change the circle's linetype to HIDDEN and the color to red.
☐ Enter the "Change Properties" dialogue box and change the linetype of the hexagon to PHANTOM and the color to yellow.
☐ Save the drawing as A:EX12-9 and quit.

USING FILTERS TO CREATE A SELECTION SET   AEM 4

Even though the edit commands and selection methods that you have been using provide you with maximum flexibility, there are situations, especially on complex drawings, that limit your productivity. It would be nice, in these situations, if you could develop a selection set based on only specific characteristics of the drawing, such as all circles less than $\phi 1.00$ or all text of a designated style. This is possible using filters. Filters allow you to create a selection set of only those items on the drawing that you designate.

Creating entity filters

You can create a filter list of items based on specific properties which restrict a selection set. These filter list selection sets may be used in the current drawing or in a future drawing, if needed. This is done using the FILTER command, which may be accessed by picking Object Filters... from the Assist pull-down menu or by typing "FILTER" at the Command: prompt. This command may also be accessed transparently while inside another command at a Select objects: prompt ('FILTER). These options access the "Entity Selection Filters" dialogue box shown in Fig. 12-15. You can use this dialogue box to identify filters for a variety of properties including type of entity such as line or circle, linetype, color, text style, or layer.

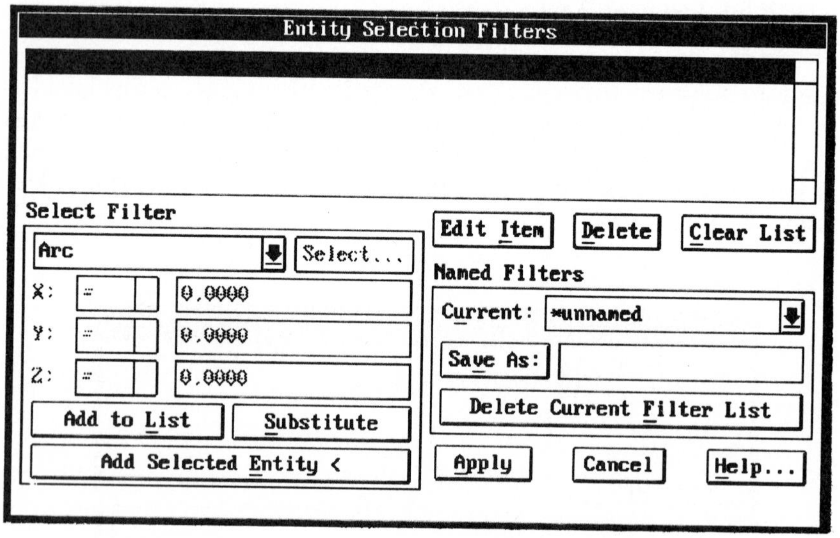

Fig. 12-15. The "Entity Selection Filters" dialogue box.

There are three major areas of the "Entity Selection Filters" dialogue box including the list box at the top of the dialogue box, the Select Filter area, and the Named Filters area. There is nothing displayed in the list box until you add something to it. This is done by picking an item from the popup list just below Select Filter. Use the scroll bar to access the desired item. For example, pick Circle as shown in Fig. 12-16. Follow this by picking the Add to List button.

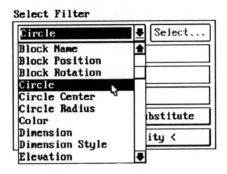

Fig. 12-16. Items picked from the popup list appear in the list box.

Now, Circle is placed in the list box. If you pick an item from the Select Filter list that has X, Y, and Z values such as Circle Center or Line Start, then the X:, Y:, and Z: coordinate popup lists and edit boxes are highlighted. Picking a coordinate popup arrow accesses the expanded popup shown in Fig. 12-17. You can change the X, Y, and Z values in the edit boxes, and you can establish relationships between the filtered items and designated units of measure. This is done by picking one of the symbols in the popup list. A description of these symbols follow:

$=$ Equals
$! =$ Not equal to
$<$ Less than
$< =$ Less than or equal to
$>$ Greater than
$> =$ Greater than or equal to
$*$ Multiply

AutoCAD refers to these symbols as *relational operators.*

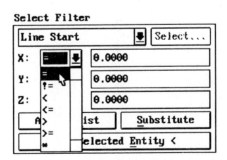

Fig. 12-17. Relation operators can be picked from the popup list.

The Select... button is only highlighted if you pick an item from the Select Filter popup list that accesses a dialogue box. For example, picking Text Style Name and then the Select button accesses the "Select Text Style Name(s)" dialogue box. This dialogue box shows you all of the currently defined text styles.

You can also add an entity from a drawing by picking the Add Selected Entity ⟨ button. This button returns you to the drawing editor and prompts with Select object:. If you pick an item such as text, the properties of this entity are displayed in the list box. Fig. 12-18 shows part of the list now present in the list box. Move the scroll bar to see all of the items listed. You can have as many items in the filter list box as you wish.

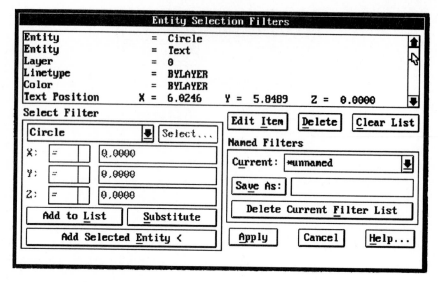

Fig. 12-18. The filters list displayed in the list box.

Now that you have a filters list you can use some of the other items in the dialogue box. For example, pick the Clear List button to get rid of everything you just put in the list. You can highlight any item in the list by moving the pointer to the item and picking it. When an item is highlighted, you can remove it from the list by selecting the Delete button. You can substitute an item in the Select Filter list with a highlighted item in the filters list by picking the Substitute button. For example, if the filter list displays "Text Style Name = ROMANS," you can change it to another existing text style (ROMANC). First, pick Text Style Name from the Select Filter popup list. Then, scroll down the list box and highlight the Text Style Name entry, followed by picking the Select... button. This accesses the "Select Text Style Name(s)" dialogue box. Pick ROMANC followed by OK to close the dialogue box. Finally, pick the Substitute button to execute the change.

If you want to edit an item in the filters list, first highlight it and then pick the Edit Item button. This places the current X, Y, and Z values of the item in the Select Filter: edit boxes for you to change as needed. Make the changes and pick the Substitute button for the alterations to take place.

The Named Filters area in Fig. 12-15 shows the Current: filter as unnamed, which is what you can expect when you start a drawing. Use the Save As: edit box to save your current filter list. Enter the desired name in the edit box followed by picking the Save As: button. This name becomes the current named filter. If there were several filter names, you could access these through the Current: popup list. You can delete the current named filter list by picking the Delete Current Filter List button.

Finally, pick the Apply button to exit the dialogue box and have the selection set filters ready for use. If AutoCAD finds a problem with your filter list, you will get a message at the bottom of the dialogue box. Pick the Cancel button if you decide not to continue with the filter list.

Using filters on a drawing

Now, try using the filtering process on the drawing shown in Fig. 12-19. Your supervisor likes the flowchart that you just finished, except you are asked to change all of the ROMANS text to ROMANC. You could use the CHANGE command and individually select each word on the chart, but you decide to use the FILTER command to make the job easier. Access the "Entity Selection Filters" dialogue box and follow these steps:

• Pick the Add Selected Entity ⟨ button. The drawing returns and you get this prompt:

Command: FILTER
Select object: *(pick one of the words in the chart such as PRESIDENT)*

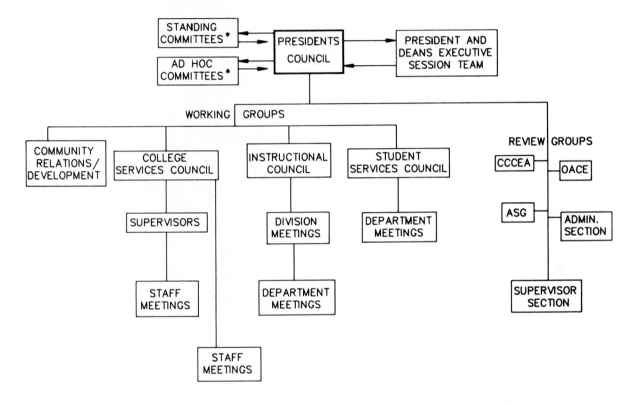

Fig. 12-19. Original flowchart requiring modification.

• The dialogue box returns and displays the characteristics of the text you picked. Highlight items such as Text Position and Text Value, and pick the Delete button for each. These filters are not needed because they limit the filter list to specific aspects of the text. See Fig. 12-20.

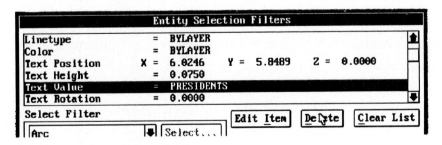

Fig. 12-20. Deleting selection filters.

- Enter a filter name such as TEXTROMANS in the Save As: edit box and then pick the Save As: button. The Current: filter name is TEXTROMANS as shown in Fig. 12-21.
- Pick the Apply button. The drawing returns and this prompt is given:

> Select object:
> Applying filter to selection.
> Select objects: *(window all of the drawing text to be included in the selection set)*
> Select objects: ⤶

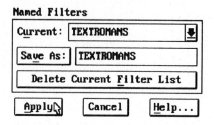

Fig. 12-21. Setting the filter name.

All of the existing ROMANS text within the flowchart is now highlighted, and you see this prompt:

> Select objects: ⤶
> 106 were filtered out.

- The highlighted text returns and the items that were previously highlighted become part of the selection set.
- Now that the desired items are part of a selection set, the next step is to access the set and change the style. Pick Applications... from the File pull-down menu to access the "Load AutoLISP and ADS File(s)" dialogue box. Now, pick the File... button to access the "Select LISP/ADS Routine" subdialogue box. Search through the directories to find the CHTEXT.LSP file. (Hint: You may want to look in the \ACAD\SUPPORT subdirectory.) Pick this file so its name appears in the File: edit box, and then pick OK. You are then returned to the "Load AutoLISP and ADS File(s)" dialogue box, with the CHTEXT.LSP file listed. Pick the Load button to load this LISP routine.
- At the Command: prompt, enter "CHT" to change all of the text to ROMANC. Enter "P" when you get the Select objects: prompt. This retrieves the selection set that was previously established with the FILTER command:

> Command: **CHT** ⤶
> Select text to change.
> Select objects: **P** ⤶
> 106 found
> Select objects: ⤶
> Height/Justification/Location/Rotation/Style/Text/Undo/Width: **S** ⤶
> New style name. ⟨ROMANS⟩: **ROMANC** ⤶
> Height/Justification/Location/Rotation/Style/Text/Undo/Width: ⤶

The revised flowchart is shown in Fig. 12-22.

GROUP DECISION MAKING PROCESS

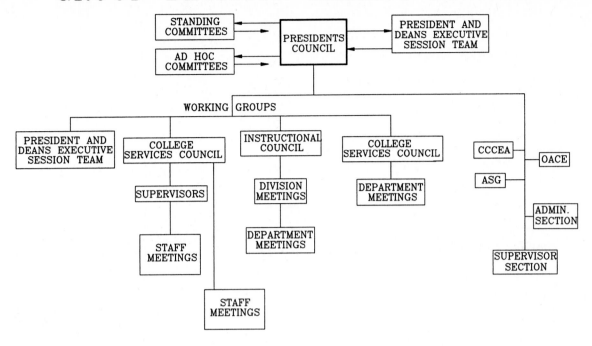

*NOTE: STANDING OR AD HOC COMMITTEES MAY BE FORMED AT ANY LEVEL.

Fig. 12-22. Revised flowchart.

CHAPTER TEST

Write your answers in the spaces provided.

1. Give the command and entries required to turn on grips:

   Command: _____

   New value for GRIPS ⟨ ⟩: _____

2. Give the prompts needed to rotate an object from an existing 60° angle to a new 25° angle:

   ⟨Rotation angle⟩/Base point/Copy/Undo/Reference/eXit: _____

   Reference angle⟨ ⟩: _____

   ⟨New angle⟩/Base point/Copy/Undo/Reference/eXit: _____

3. Give the prompts required to scale an object to become three-quarters of its original size:

   ⟨Scale factor⟩/Base point/Copy/Undo/Reference/eXit: _____

4. Name the two system variables that control the color of grips. _____

   _____

   _____

5. Name the six editing commands that can be accessed automatically. _____

   _____

   _____

6. Explain the difference between Noun/Verb selection and Verb/Noun selection. _____
   _____
   _____

7. Name the system variable that allows you to set the Noun/Verb selection. _____

8. What does "Use Shift to Add" mean? _____
   _____
   _____

9. Describe how "Press and Drag" works. _____
   _____
   _____
   _____

10. Name the system variable that is used to turn on "Press and Drag."_____

11. Name the system variable that turns on Implied Windowing. _____

12. Identify two ways to access the "Entity Selection Settings" dialogue box. _____
    _____

13. Explain two ways to change the pick box size. _____
    _____
    _____

14. Give the command sequence and explain how you would change the radius of a circle from
    1.375 to 1.875 using a dialogue box._____
    _____
    _____
    _____
    _____
    _____

15. Identify the pull-down menu and the item you pick from this menu to access the dialogue
    box described in question 14. _____
    _____

16. How would you change the linetype of an entity using the dialogue box described in ques-
    tion 14? _____
    _____
    _____
    _____

17. Name three commands that allow you to change the properties of an object. _____
    _____
    _____

18. Which of the commands in question 17 accesses the "Change Properties" dialogue box?
    _____

19. How do you access the "Change Properties" dialogue box through a pull-down menu?

_____

20. How do you change the color of an entity using the "Change Properties" dialogue box?

_____

_____

DRAWING PROBLEMS

Use prototypes TITLEA or TITLEB as appropriate for each of the following problems. Use grips and the associated editing commands or other editing techniques discussed in this chapter.

1. Draw the objects shown at A below and then use the STRETCH command to make them look like the objects at B. Do not include dimensions. Save the drawing as A:P12-1.

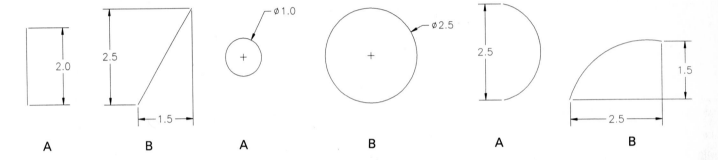

2. Draw the object shown at A below. Then using the MOVE command's Copy option, copy the object to the position shown at B. Edit object A so that it resembles example C. Edit object B so that it looks like D. Do not include dimensions. Save the drawing as A:P12-2.

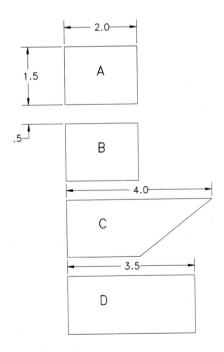

3. Draw the object shown at A below. Then copy the object, without rotating it, to a position below as indicated by the dashed lines. Then, rotate the object 45°. Copy the rotated object at B to a position below as indicated by the dashed lines. Use the Reference option to rotate the object at C to 25° as shown. Do not include dimensions. Save the drawing as A:P12-3.

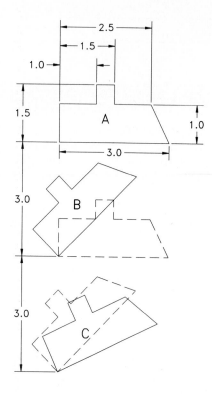

4. Draw the individual entities (vertical line, horizontal line, circle, arc, and "C" shape) at A below using the dimensions given. Then, use grips and the editing commands to create the object shown at B. Do not include dimensions. Save the drawing as A:P12-4.

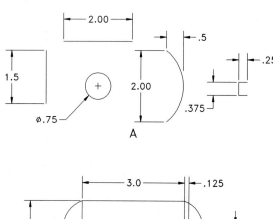

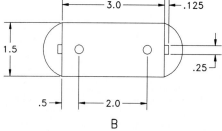

5. Use the completed drawing from Problem 12-4. Erase everything except the completed object and move it to a position similar to A below. Copy the object two times to positions B and C. Use the SCALE command to scale the object at B to fifty percent of its original size. Use the SCALE command's Reference option to enlarge the object at C from the existing 3.0 length to a 4.5 length as shown in C. Do not include dimensions. Save as A:P12-5.

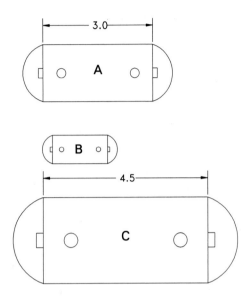

6. Draw the dimensioned partial object shown at A. Do not include dimensions. Mirror the drawing to complete the four quadrants as shown at B. Change the color of the horizontal and vertical parting lines to red. Save the drawing as A:P12-6.

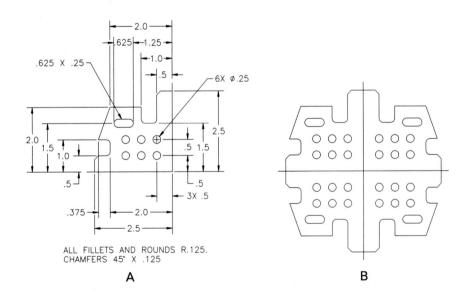

7. Load the final drawing you created in Problem 12-6. Use the "Modify Circle" dialogue box to change the circles from ⌀.25 to ⌀.125. Use the "Change Properties" dialogue box to change the linetype of the slots to PHANTOM. Be sure the linetype scale allows the linetypes to be displayed. Save the drawing as A:P12-7.

8. Use the editing commands discussed in this chapter to assist you in drawing the following object. Draw the object within the boundaries of the given dimensions. All other dimensions are flexible. Do not include dimensions in the drawing. Save the drawing as A:P12-8.

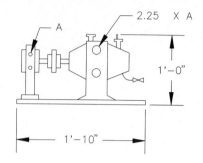

9. Draw the following object within the boundaries of the given dimensions. All other dimensions are flexible. Do not include dimensions. After drawing the object, create a catalog page as follows:
   - All labels should be ROMAND text centered directly below the view. Use a text height of .125.
   - Keep the valve the same scale as the original drawing in each additional drawing.
   - Label the existing drawing: ONE-GALLON TANK WITH HORIZONTAL VALVE.
   - Copy the original tank to a new location and scale it so that it is two times its original size. Rotate the valve 45°. Label this tank: TWO-GALLON TANK WITH 45° VALVE.
   - Copy the original tank to another location and scale it so that it is 2.5 times the size of the original. Rotate the valve 90°. Label this tank: TWO- AND ONE-HALF GALLON TANK WITH 90° VALVE.
   - Copy the two-gallon tank to a new position and scale it so that it is two times this size. Rotate the valve to 22°30'. Label this tank: FOUR-GALLON TANK WITH 22°30' VALVE.
   - Left-justify this note at the bottom of the page:
     Combinations of tank size and valve orientation are available upon request.
   - Use the "Modify Text" dialogue box to make the following changes:
   - Change all tank labels to ROMANC, .25 in. high.
   - Change the note at the bottom of the sheet to ROMANS, centered on the sheet using uppercase letters.
   Save the drawing as A:P12-9.

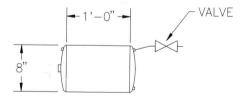

10. Open Problem 11-14 if you have already drawn it. If you have not yet drawn this object, refer to the problem on page 11-32 and draw it now. Do not include dimensions. Use the DDMODIFY command and other editing commands to change the drawing as follows:
    - Change the ϕ2.125 circle to ϕ1.50.
    - Change the R.50 dimension to R.375.
    - Change the 3.70 length to 4.80.
    Save the drawing as A:P12-10.
11. Open Problem 10-7 and use the FILTER command as discussed in this chapter. Change all text to ROMAND.

Chapter 13

CREATING MULTIPLE ENTITIES WITH ARRAY

Learning objectives

After completing this chapter, you will be able to:

☐ Create an arrangement of objects in a rectangular pattern.
☐ Create an arrangement of any objects in a circular pattern.

Some designs require a rectangular or circular pattern of the same object. For example, office desks are often arranged in rows. Suppose your design calls for five rows, each having four desks. You could create this design by drawing one desk and copying it 19 times. You might also save the desk as a block and insert it 20 times. However, both of these options are time-consuming. A quicker method is to use AutoCAD's ARRAY command. Using ARRAY, you first select the object(s) to be copied. Then enter the type of arrangement (rectangular or polar).

A *rectangular array* creates rows and columns of the selected items, and you must provide the spacing. A *polar array* constructs a circular arrangement; you must specify the number of items to array, the angle between items, and the center point of the array. Some examples are shown in Fig. 13-1.

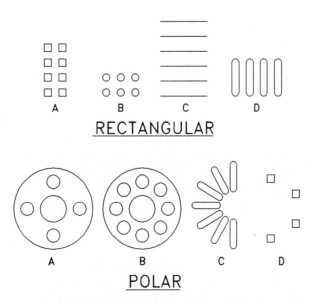

Fig. 13-1. Example arrays created with the ARRAY command.

In this chapter, you will experiment with the ARRAY command on a .5 unit square. You may want to draw this object now to use as you study the chapter.

The ARRAY command may be typed at the Command: prompt, selected from the Construct pull-down menu, or picked from the EDIT screen menu. After you enter "ARRAY," AutoCAD asks you to select objects to array. Use any selection method, such as a window. Then you must enter whether you want a rectangular or polar array. The command sequence is as follows:

Command: **ARRAY** ↵
Select objects: *(window the objects)*
Select objects: ↵
Rectangular or Polar array (R/P): *(type R or P)*

RECTANGULAR PLACEMENT OF OBJECTS ⌐ARM 6⌐

A rectangular array places objects in line along the X and Y axes. You can request a single row, a single column, or multiple rows and columns. *Rows* are horizontal and *columns* are vertical. AutoCAD reminds you of this by indicating the direction in parentheses: (---) for rows and (!!!) for columns. The following process creates a pattern having 3 rows, 3 columns, and .5 spacing between objects.

Rectangular or Polar array (R/P): **R** ↵
Number of rows (---) ⟨1⟩: **3** ↵
Number of columns (!!!) ⟨1⟩: **3** ↵
Unit cell or distance between rows (---): **1** ↵
Distance between columns (!!!): **1** ↵

The original object and resulting array are shown in Fig. 13-2. When giving the distance between rows and columns, be sure to include the width and height of the object. Fig. 13-2 shows how to calculate the distance between objects in a rectangular array.

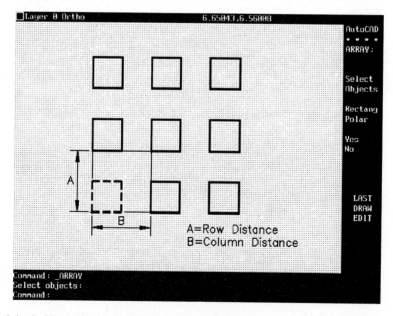

Fig. 13-2. The original object (dashed) and the created rectangular array. Note the method for determining distance between rows and columns.

AutoCAD allows you to point to the distance separating objects. It calls this measurement the *unit cell*. The unit cell distance is the same as the distance between rows and columns. However, it is entered with the pointing device, just like selecting a window. See Fig. 13-3.

Unit cell or distance between rows (---): *(pick corner)* Other corner: *(pick second corner)*

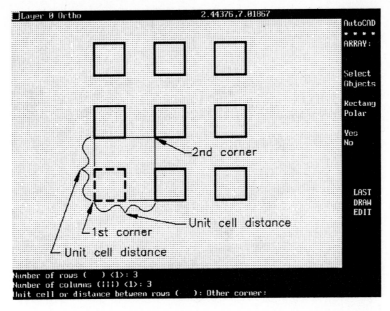

Fig. 13-3. The unit cell spacing box is the same as the distance between rows and columns.

The command is then executed. The second point's distance and direction from the first point determines the X and Y spacing for the array.

Fig. 13-4 shows how you can place arrays in four directions by entering either positive or negative row and column distance values. The dashed box is the original object. The row and column distance is one unit and the box is .5 unit square.

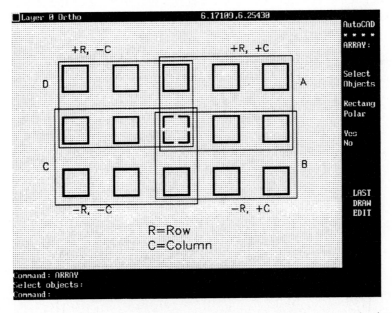

Fig. 13-4. Placing arrays in one of four directions by giving positive or negative row and column distance values.

Specifying the unit cell distance can create a quick row and column arrangement in any direction. For example, in Fig. 13-5, the second unit cell corner is picked to the left and below the first corner.

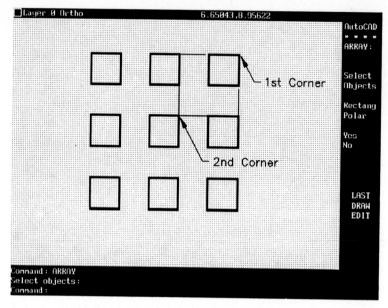

Fig. 13-5. Creating a rectangular array by picking a negative unit cell distance.

PROFESSIONAL TIP

Plan your drawing so you can array blocks. Blocks are symbols and shapes that are treated as a single entity. They are discussed in Chapter 21. Blocks save time when selecting the object. They also save drawing storage space.

A rotated rectangular array can be created. Set the snap setting to the required rotation angle before performing the array.

EXERCISE 13-1

☐ Load AutoCAD and open TITLEA, or start a new drawing and set up your own variables.
☐ Construct the Bill of Materials form shown using the LINE and ARRAY commands. Line A is arrayed in nine rows and one column. The distance between rows is given. Line B is arrayed in one row and three columns. The distance between the columns is provided.
☐ Complete the headings using the DTEXT command.
☐ Save the drawing as A:EX13-1 and quit.

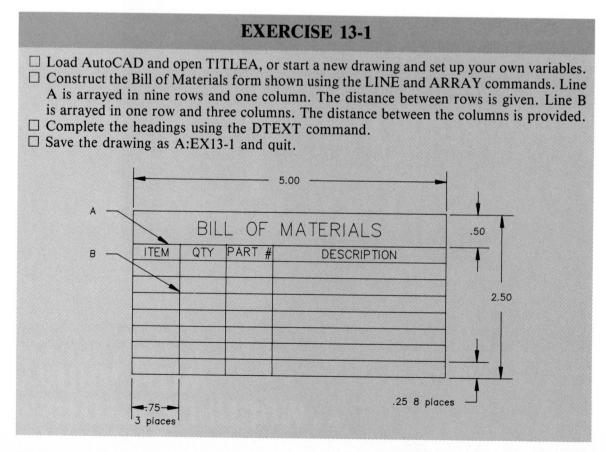

ARRANGING OBJECTS AROUND A CENTER POINT ⟨ ARM 6 ⟩

To place objects in a circular pattern, use the Polar option of the ARRAY command. At this time, erase everything on your screen except for one .5 unit square. Enter the following command sequence:

    Command: **ARRAY** ⏎
    Select objects: *(select the object using a window or other selection method)*
    Select objects: ⏎
    Rectangular or Polar array (R/P): **P** ⏎
    Center point of array: *(pick the center point)*

Next, AutoCAD requests the number of objects you want in the array. If you know the exact number needed, enter that value. If you would rather specify an angle between items, just press ENTER. In the example below, no value is given. The next prompt you see is "Angle to fill."

    Number of items: ⏎
    Angle to fill (+ = ccw, − = cw) ⟨360⟩:

Notice the letters in parentheses (+ = ccw, − = cw). You can array the object in a counterclockwise direction by entering a positive angle value. (Numbers entered without the plus sign are positive.) Objects can be arrayed clockwise by entering the minus sign before the angle value. Pressing ENTER at this prompt without entering a value copies the object through 360°. This is the default value.

The final value needed is the angular spacing between the arrayed objects.

    Angle between items: **45** ⏎

A number entered at this prompt is assumed to be the angle. This prompt is only displayed if you pressed ENTER at the "Number of items" prompt. If you specify the number of items, you are not asked for the angle between them since AutoCAD calculates it for you. The last prompt is:

    Rotate objects as they are copied? ⟨Y⟩: **N** ⏎

You can have the objects rotated as they are copied around the pivot point. This keeps the same face of the object always pointing toward the pivot point, Fig. 13-6A. If objects are not rotated as they are copied, they remain in the same orientation as the original object, Fig. 13-6B.

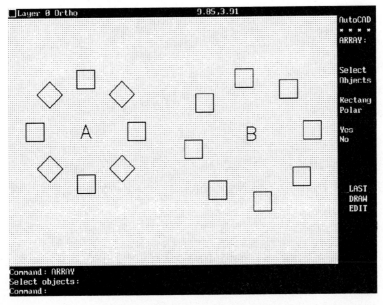

Fig. 13-6. Using polar ARRAY to rotate a box. A—The box was rotated as it was arrayed. B—The box was not rotated as it was arrayed.

EXERCISE 13-2

☐ Load AutoCAD and open the TITLEA drawing, or start a new drawing and set up your own variables.
☐ Draw a .5 radius circle near the top of the screen.
☐ Create a 360° polar array of five circles.
☐ Copy one of the circles to the side of the polar array.
☐ Create an array with the copied circle. Each circle should be 30° apart through 270°.
☐ Save the drawing as A:EX13-2 and quit.

CHAPTER TEST

Write your answers in the spaces provided.

1. What is the difference between polar and rectangular arrays? _____

_____

_____

2. What four values should you know before you create a rectangular array? _____

_____

_____

3. Define "unit cell." _____

_____

4. Suppose an object is 1.5 in. (38.1 mm) wide and you want a rectangular array with .75 in. (19.05 mm) spacing between objects. What should you specify for the distance between columns? _____

5. How do you create a rectangular array that is rotated? _____

6. What values should you know before you execute a polar array?_____

_____

_____

7. Suppose you enter a value for the "Number of items" prompt in a polar array. Which of the following values are you not required to give? Circle one.

   A. Angle to fill.

   B. Angle between items.

   C. Center point.

   D. Rotate objects as they are copied.

8. What happens to an object drawn when it is not rotated as it is arrayed? _____

_____

_____

9. How do you request a clockwise array rotation? _____

_____

DRAWING PROBLEMS

1. Draw the following object views using the dimensions given. Use ARRAY to construct the bolt hole arrangement. Place the drawing on your prototype drawing TITLEB. Do not add dimensions. Save the drawing as A:P13-1.

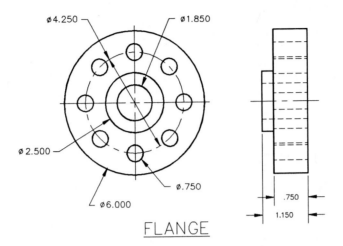

FLANGE

2. Draw the object views shown below using the dimensions given. Use ARRAY to construct the hole arrangement. Place the drawing on your prototype drawing TITLEB. Do not add dimensions. Save the drawing as A:P13-2.

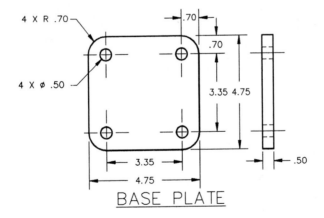

BASE PLATE

3. You have been given an engineer's sketches and notes, and asked to construct a drawing of a sprocket. Create a front and side view of the sprocket using the ARRAY command. Place the drawing on your prototype drawing TITLEB. Do not add dimensions. Save the drawing as A:P13-3 and quit.

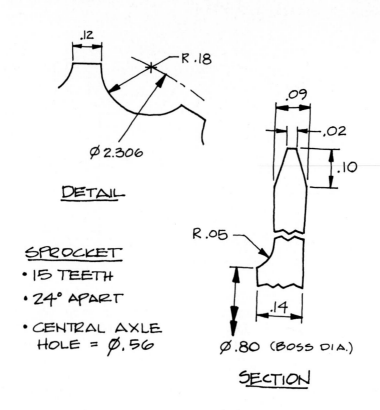

DETAIL

SPROCKET
- 15 TEETH
- 24° APART
- CENTRAL AXLE
  HOLE = ⌀.56

SECTION

4. The following engineering sketch shows a steel column arrangement on a concrete floor slab for a new building. The steel columns are represented by I-shaped symbols. The columns are arranged in "bay lines" and "column lines." The column lines are numbered 1, 2, and 3. The bay lines are labeled A through G. The width of a bay is 20'-0". Line balloons, or tags, identify bay and column lines. Draw the arrangement using ARRAY for the steel column symbols and for the tags. The following guidelines will help you.
   A. Begin a new drawing and name it P13-4.
   B. Select architectural units and 36 x 24 sheet size. Determine the scale required for this floor plan to fit on this sheet size, and determine your limits accordingly.
   C. Set the grid spacing at 2'-0" (24").
   D. Set the snap spacing at 12".
   E. Use the PLINE command to draw the steel column symbol.
   F. Do not dimension the drawing.
   G. Draw all objects to dimensions given.
   H. Place text inside the tag balloons. Set OSNAP to Center, use DTEXT, Middle, text height 6".
   I. Place a title block on the drawing.
   J. Save the drawing as A:P13-4.

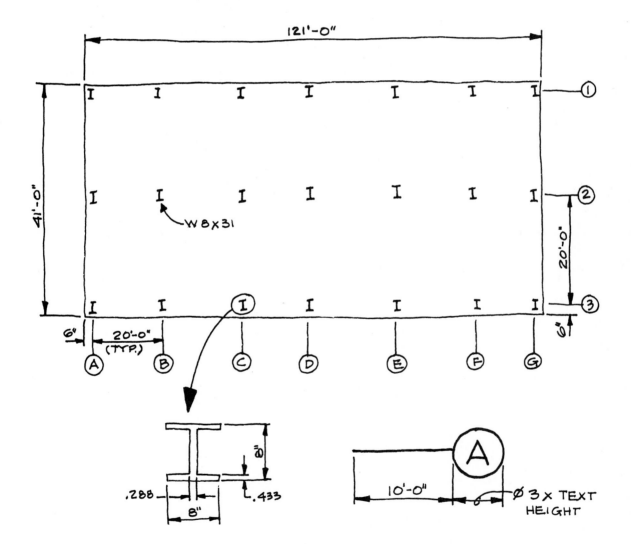

5. The engineering sketch given is a proposed office layout of desks and chairs. One desk has been shown with the layout of chair, keyboard, monitor, and tower-mounted computer (dotted lines). All of the desk workstations should have the same configuration. Exact size and locations of doors and windows is not important for this problem. Set the SAVETIME variable to save your drawing every ten minutes. Use the following guidelines to complete this problem.

A. Begin a new drawing called P13-5.
B. Choose architectural units.
C. Select an appropriate paper size. If you want to use the paper space prototype drawing for the final layout, be sure to create this drawing in model space without a border and title block.
D. Use the appropriate drawing and editing commands to complete this problem quickly and efficiently.
E. Draw the desk and computer hardware to the dimensions given.
F. Do not dimension the drawing.
G. Save the drawing as A:P13-5.

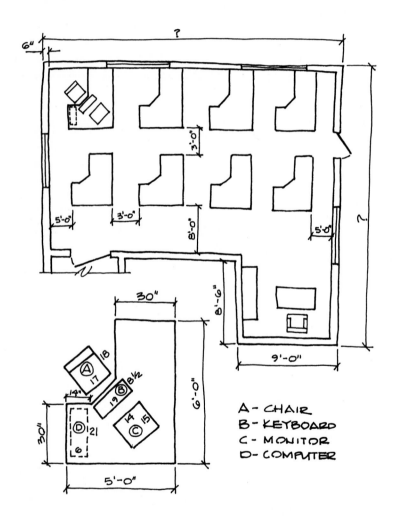

A - CHAIR
B - KEYBOARD
C - MONITOR
D - COMPUTER

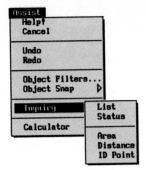

Chapter 14

OBTAINING INFORMATION ABOUT THE DRAWING

Learning objectives

After completing this chapter, you will be able to:

☐ Determine the area of an object by adding and subtracting entities.

☐ List data related to a single point, entity, group of entities, or an entire drawing.

☐ Discover the amount of time spent in a drawing session.

When working on a drawing, you may need to ask AutoCAD for information about the drawing, such as distances and areas. You can also ask AutoCAD how much time you have spent on a drawing. The commands that enable you to do this are located in the INQUIRY screen menu, the Inquiry selection of the Assist pull-down menu, or can be typed at the Command: prompt. They include AREA, DBLIST (DataBase LIST), DIST (DISTance), ID (IDentification), LIST, STATUS, and TIME. The STATUS command was discussed in Chapter 5.

FINDING THE AREA OF SHAPES AND ENTITIES   ARM 6

The most basic function of the AREA command is to find the area of any object, circle, or polyline. To select an entity for area calculation, use the Entity option as follows:

> Command: **AREA** ↵
> ⟨First point⟩/Entity/Add/Subtract: **E** ↵
> Select circle or polyline: *(pick entity)*
> Area = (n.nn), Circumference = (n.nn)

The "n" given above represents the numerical values of the area and circumference of the entity.

─────── PROFESSIONAL TIP ───────

AutoCAD gives you the area between three or more points picked on the screen, even if the three points are not connected by lines. The perimeter of the selected points is also given.

Shapes drawn with lines or polylines do not have to be closed for AutoCAD to calculate their area. AutoCAD calculates the area as if a line connected the first and last points.

To find the area of a shape created with the LINE command, pick all the vertices of that shape. See Fig. 14-1. This is the default mode of the AREA command. Set a running OSNAP such as ENDpoint or INTersection to help you pick the vertices.

Command: **AREA** ↵
⟨First point⟩/Entity/Add/Subtract: *(pick point 1)*
Next point: *(pick point 2)*
Next point: *(continue picking points until all corners of the object have been selected; then press ENTER)*
Next point: ↵
Area = (n.nn), Perimeter = (n.nn)

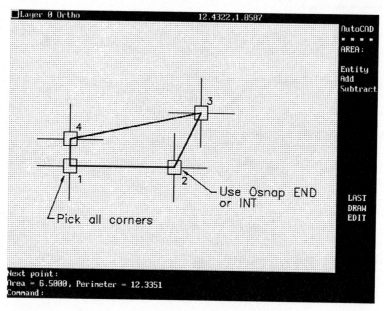

Fig. 14-1. Pick all corners to find the area of an object drawn with the LINE command.

PROFESSIONAL TIP

Calculating area, circumference, and perimeter of shapes made with the LINE command can be time-consuming. You must pick each vertex on the object. If you know you will have to calculate areas, it is best to create lines and arcs with the PLINE command. Then choose the Entity option when adding or subtracting entities.

Adding and subtracting areas

If you select the Add option, you can pick circles and entities drawn with PLINE. They are then automatically added to calculate the total area. After entities have been added, the Subtract option allows you to remove selected areas.

Once the Add option is chosen, the AREA command remains in effect until you cancel the command. You can continue to add or subtract entities and shapes using the Add and Subtract options.

The next example demonstrates using both Add and Subtract options. It also shows how entities drawn with the PLINE command are easier to pick. The object is shown in Fig. 14-2. The command sequence is as follows:

> Command: **AREA** ⏎
> ⟨First point⟩/Entity/Add/Subtract: **A** ⏎
> ⟨First point⟩/Entity/Subtract: **E** ⏎
> (ADD mode) Select circle or polyline: *(pick polyline)*
> Area = 5.51, Perimeter = 13.61
> Total area = 5.51
> (ADD mode) Select circle or polyline: ⏎
> ⟨First point⟩/Entity/Subtract: **S** ⏎
> ⟨First point⟩/Entity/Add: **E** ⏎
> (SUBTRACT mode) Select circle or polyline: *(pick first circle)*
> Area = 0.11, Circumference = 1.18
> Total area = 5.40
> (SUBTRACT mode) Select circle or polyline: *(pick second circle)*
> Area = 0.11, Circumference = 1.18
> Total area = 5.29
> (SUBTRACT mode) Select circle or polyline: ⏎
> ⟨First point⟩/Entity/Add: ⏎

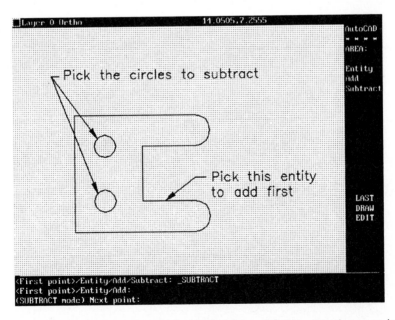

Fig. 14-2. Example of object on which AREA Add and Subtract options can be used.

The total area of the object in Fig. 14-2, subtracting the area of the two holes, is 5.29. Circumferences and perimeters are given for each object that is selected. These are not affected by the adding or subtracting functions.

Notice in the previous command sequence that if you are finished adding and wish to subtract, you must press ENTER at the (ADD mode) Select circle or polyline: prompt. The same is true if you have completed subtracting and wish to add.

EXERCISE 14-1

☐ Load AutoCAD, and begin a new drawing using the default AutoCAD drawing. Set up your own variables.

☐ Draw the objects shown. Use the size dimensions given. The exact locations of the cutout and holes are not important.

☐ Use the AREA command to calculate the area of the entire object.

☐ Use the AREA command to subtract the areas of the rectangle and two circles.

☐ List the following information:

Area of large rectangle _____

Perimeter of large rectangle _____

Perimeter of small rectangle _____

Circumference of one circle _____

Area of large rectangle minus the areas of the three shapes _____

☐ Save the drawing as A:EX14-1. This drawing is used for the next exercise.

LISTING DRAWING DATA

ARM 6

The LIST command displays data about any AutoCAD entity. Line length, circle and arc locations and radii, polyline widths, and object layers are just a few of the items AutoCAD gives you with the LIST command. You can select several objects to list.

Command: **LIST** ↵
Select objects: *(pick object(s) using any selection option)*
Select objects: ↵

When you press ENTER, the data for each of the objects picked is displayed. The information given for a line is:

```
LINE            Layer: (layer name)
                Space: Model space
   from point, X = (nn.nn)   Y = (nn.nn)   Z = (nn.nn)
     to point, X = (nn.nn)   Y = (nn.nn)   Z = (nn.nn)
Length = (nn.nn)  Angle in XY Plane = (nn.nn)
        Delta X = (nn.nn)  Delta Y =           (nn.nn)     Delta Z = (nn.nn)
```

The Delta X and Y numbers show the horizontal and vertical distance between the "from point" and the "to point" of the line. These two numbers, the length, and angle provide you with four measurements for a single line. Fig. 14-3 shows one example.

The data given by the LIST command for text and circles are as follows:

> TEXT   Layer: *(layer name)*
>   Space: Model space
>   Style = *(name)* Font file = *(name)*
>   start point, X = *(n.nn)* Y = *(n.nn)* Z = *(n.nn)*
>   height *(n.nn)*
>   text *(text label)*
>   rotation angle *(nn)*
>   width scale factor *(n.nn)*
>   obliquing angle *(nn)*
>   generation normal
>
> CIRCLE   Layer: *(layer name)*
>   Space: Model space
>   center point, X = *(nn.nn)* Y = *(n.nn)* Z = *(n..n)*
>   radius *(n.nn)*
>   circumference *(n.nn)*, Area = *(n.nn)*
>   area *(n.nn)*

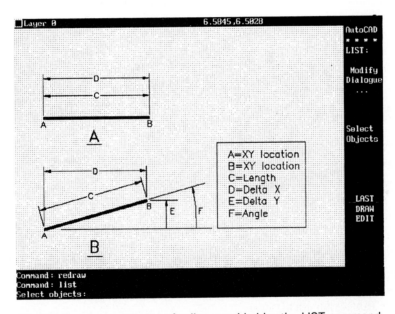

Fig. 14-3. Measurements of a line provided by the LIST command.

LISTING ALL THE DRAWING DATA ARM 6

The DBLIST (DataBase LIST) command lists all of the data about every entity in the current drawing. Information provided is in the same format as the LIST command. As soon as you enter DBLIST, the data begins to quickly scroll up the screen. The scrolling stops when a complete page has been filled with database information. Press ENTER to scroll to the end of the next page. If you find the data you need, press CTRL C to exit the DBLIST command.

FINDING THE DISTANCE BETWEEN TWO POINTS ARM 6

The DIST command finds the distance between two points. Use OSNAP modes to accurately pick locations, or make sure the two points lie on snap points. See Fig. 14-4. The DIST command provides distance and angle of the line. It also gives delta X, Y, and Z dimensions.

Command: **DIST** ↵
First point: *(select point)* Second point: *(select point)*
Distance = 2.85,   Angle in XY Plane = 353,   Angle from XY Plane = 0
Delta X = 2.83,   Delta Y = -0.37,   Delta Z = 0.000

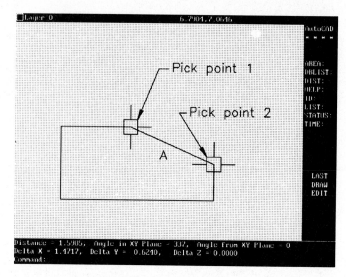

Fig. 14-4. Use OSNAP ENDpoint and DIST to find the distance between two endpoints of a line.

Delta Z refers to the third coordinate axis used in three-dimensional drawing. This value is zero unless the object was drawn with a thickness, or with 3-D drawing commands. 3-D commands are discussed in detail in Chapter 24.

IDENTIFYING A POINT LOCATION   ARM 6

The ID command gives the coordinate location of a single point on the screen. You might use it to find the endpoint of a line or the center of a circle. Simply pick the point to be identified. Use the OSNAP modes for accuracy.

Command: **ID** ↵
Point: *(select the point)*
X = (nn.nn)   Y = (nn.nn)   Z = (nn.nn)

The ID command can also help you identify a coordinate location on the screen. Enter the exact coordinate values you wish to find. Suppose you want to see where the point X = 8.75, Y = 6.44 is located. Enter these numbers at the "Point" prompt. AutoCAD responds by placing a blip (marker) at that exact location.

Command: **ID** ↵
Point: **8.75,6.44** ↵
X = 8.75   Y = 6.44   Z = 0.00

PROFESSIONAL TIP

The ID command can also be used to specify a point as the origin for relative coordinates. For example, if you wish to begin drawing a line 10'-6" on the X axis from the corner of a building, select ID and pick the corner. Next, select LINE and enter the following for the "From point" prompt:

From point: **@10'6'',0** ↵

When you use the ID command, it automatically resets the system variable called LASTPOINT to the value of the ID point. When you include the "at sign" (@), this tells AutoCAD to work from the LASTPOINT value.

EXERCISE 14-2

☐ Load AutoCAD and open EX14-1 if it is not currently on the screen.
☐ Use the LIST command to display information about one circle and one line on the drawing.
☐ Select the DBLIST command to display information about your drawing.
☐ Select DBLIST again and press CTRL C to end the listing.
☐ Use OSNAP options to find the following information:
  A. Distance between the two circle center points.
  B. Distance between the lower circle center point and the left edge of the large rectangle.
  C. Distance between the lower-left and upper-right corners of the large rectangle.
  D. ID of the center point of the upper circle.
  E. ID of the lower-left corner of the small rectangle.
  F. ID of the midpoint of the large rectangle's right side.
  G. ID of point 6,4 on your screen.
☐ Save the drawing as A:EX14-2 and quit.

CHECKING THE TIME

ARM 4

The TIME command displays the current time and time related to your drawing and drawing session. The display for the TIME command is as follows:

Current time:	2 Feb 1994 at 13:39:22.210
Times for this drawing:	
Created:	1 Feb 1994 at 10:24:48.130
Last updated:	1 Feb 1994 at 14:36:23.46
Total editing time:	0 days 01:23:57.930
Elapsed timer (on):	0 days 00:35:28.650
Next automatic save in:	0 days 01:35:26.680
Display/ON/OFF/Reset:	

There are a few things to keep in mind when checking the TIME display. First, the drawing creation time starts when you "OK" a new drawing with the NEW command, or by using the BLOCK command. (See Chapter 21.) Second, the END and SAVE commands affect the "Last updated" time. However, when QUIT is used to end a drawing session and you do not save the drawing, all time in that session is discarded. Finally, you can time a specific drawing task by using the Reset option to reset the elapsed timer.

While the TIME display is on the screen, it is static. That is, none of the times are being updated. You can request an update by choosing the Display option as follows:

Display/ON/OFF/Reset: **D** ↵

When you enter the drawing editor, the timer is on by default. If you want to stop the timer, just enter "OFF" at the prompt. If the timer is off, enter "ON" to start it again.

If the date and time are incorrect, they can be reset with the DOS commands DATE and TIME. These must be set when you are at the DOS prompt, and are discussed in Chapter 35.

EXERCISE 14-3

☐ Recall any one of your previous drawings.
☐ Select the TIME command and study the information that is displayed.
☐ If the current time and date are incorrect, inform your instructor or supervisor. Then use the DOS commands to set the correct date and time.
☐ Update the TIME display.
☐ Reset the elapsed timer.
☐ Use QUIT to exit the drawing editor without saving.

CHAPTER TEST

Write your answers in the spaces provided.

1. To add entity areas, when do you select the Add option? _____
   _____

2. When using the AREA command, explain how picking a polyline is different than picking an object drawn with the LINE command. _____
   _____

3. What information is provided by the AREA command? _____
   _____

4. What is the LIST command used for? _____
   _____

5. Describe the meaning of delta X and delta Y. _____
   _____
   _____

6. What is the function of the DBLIST command? _____
   _____

7. How do you cancel the DBLIST command? _____

8. What are the two purposes of the ID command? _____
   _____

9. What information is provided by the TIME command? _____
   _____

10. When does the drawing time start? _____
    _____

DRAWING PROBLEMS

Load AutoCAD and start a new drawing for each of the following problems. Insert your floppy disk and name the drawing as P14-(problem number).

1. Draw the object at the top of the next page using the dimensions given. Draw all of the features using PLINE and CIRCLE commands. Follow these instructions as you proceed:
   A. Check the time when you enter the drawing editor.
   B. Use the default units and limits.
   C. Set the grid spacing to .5 and snap spacing to .25.
   D. Measure the area of object A and subtract the areas of the other three features.
   E. Write your answers for the areas and perimeters in the chart provided.
   F. Use the Add, Subtract, and Entity options of AREA to find the measurements. Do not exit the AREA command. Complete all of the following calculations in one selection of AREA.
   G. Select TIME and note your time in the drawing editor: _____
   H. Save the drawing as A:P14-1.

	OBJECT A	OBJECT B	OBJECT C	OBJECT A—OBJECT B	OBJECT A—CUTOUTS AND HOLES
AREA					
PERIMETER					

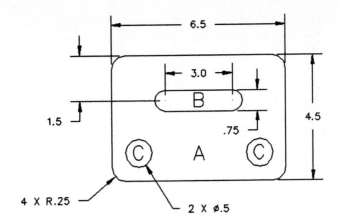

2. Draw the object shown below using the LINE command. Draw the hexagon using the POLYGON command. Use the following settings and provide all measurements listed.
   A. Set architectural units. Use 1/2 in. fractions and decimal degrees. Leave remaining units settings at default values.
   B. Set the limits to 100',80'.
   C. Set the grid spacing to 2 and snap spacing to 1.
   D. Calculate the measurements requested in the charts below.
   E. Select the DBLIST command.
   F. Select TIME and note the time in drawing editor.
   G. Save the drawing as A:P14-2.

	OBJECT A	OBJECT B	OBJECT A – OBJECT B
AREA			
PERIMETER			

	LINE CD	EC
DISTANCE		

	POINT C	POINT D	POINT F
ID			

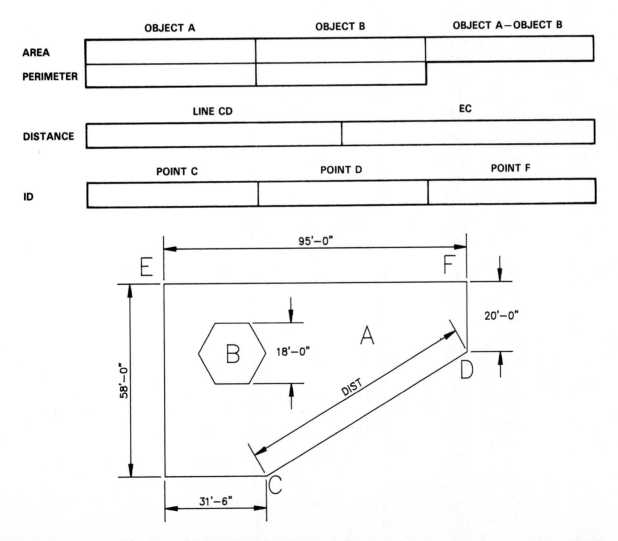

3. In this problem you will draw a piece of property in the form of a plat. A *plat* is a map of a piece of land. The lengths of the sides are measured, as well as the bearing. A *bearing* is a direction measured from the north or south to the east or west. A bearing is never greater than 90°. Refer to the drawing as you do this problem.
   A. Set units to engineering. Select four digits to right of decimal.
   B. Select surveyor's units, and four fractional places for angle display.
   C. Select East (E) for angle direction.
   D. Set the limits at 440′,340′ and Zoom All.
   E. Draw the property lines using the LINE command. Enter the distance and bearing at the "To point" prompt as follows:

   From point: *(pick a point)*
   To point: **@130′<N45dE** ↵
   To point: **@245′<S76d30′E** ↵

   F. Continue in this manner for the next two sides. When entering tenths of a foot, they must be entered as feet and inches; for example, 264.5′ should be entered as 264′6″. Convert tenths of a foot to inches by multiplying by 12. Use the Close option to draw the fifth line.
   G. Select LIST and get the bearing of the last line. _____
   H. Use the PLINE or LINE command to draw the road. It can be straight or curved. (See Chapter 16 for more information on the PLINE command.) The road should be 12 ft. wide.
   I. Use TRIM and EXTEND to clean up the ends of the road.
   J. Provide the following information:

	Areas	Perimeters
Property		
Lake		
Road		
Property-Lake		
Lake + Road		
Property-Lake and Road		

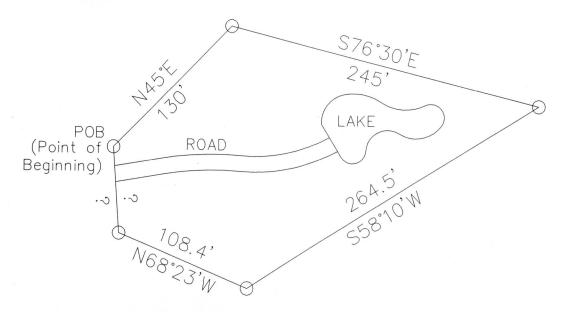

   K. Label the drawing as shown.
   L. Select TIME and note the time in drawing editor. _____
   M. Save the drawing as A:P14-3.

4. This problem requires that you create a drawing of the proposed parking lot shown below. Do not dimension the drawing.
   A. Set units to architectural.
   B. Set the limits to 400′,300′.
   C. Use the PLINE command to draw the parking lot outline.
   D. Calculate the following and record your answers:
      Area of asphalt (without landscape dividers). _____
      Area of landscape dividers (all trees and flowers). _____
      Area of landscape dividers (trees only). _____
   E. Select TIME and note the time in the drawing editor. _____
   F. Save the drawing as A:P14-4.

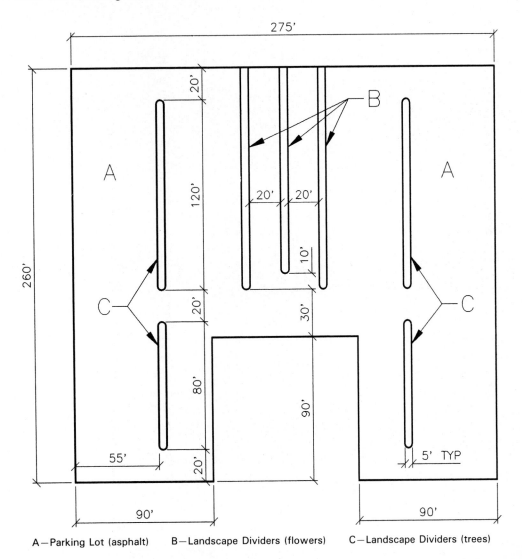

A—Parking Lot (asphalt)   B—Landscape Dividers (flowers)   C—Landscape Dividers (trees)

Exploded assembly pictorial.   (Autodesk, Inc.)

Chapter 15

WORKING WITH DRAWING FILES

Learning objectives

After completing this chapter, you will be able to:
- ☐ Explain the meaning and use of DOS file extensions.
- ☐ List any type of file using the "File Utilities" dialogue box.
- ☐ Copy, rename, and delete files using the "File Utilities" dialogue box.
- ☐ Explain the use of file locking and unlocking.

AutoCAD works with several types of computer files. These can be identified by a three-letter "file type" extension on the end of the file name. The "File Utilities" dialogue box in AutoCAD allows the user to list, copy, erase, rename, and unlock files. The file utilities are simpler than using DOS commands, discussed in Chapter 35. The menu can also be accessed during a drawing session by choosing the FILES command.

FILE NAME TYPES

ARM 4

Drawing file names can be up to eight characters long. They can contain letters, numbers, the dollar sign ($), hyphens (-), and underscores (__). When you begin a new drawing, AutoCAD adds a file "extension" to the end of the file name. This extension is ".DWG". If you began a drawing called BLDG-34, AutoCAD creates the file as BLDG-34.DWG. When you open the drawing to edit, you only have to type "BLDG-34". AutoCAD knows to look for that file, plus the .DWG extension.

After you edit the BLDG-34.DWG file and save it again, the original is converted to a backup file. Its file extension is automatically changed to .BAK (backup). AutoCAD maintains a current .DWG file and one .BAK file. If you revise the BLDG-34 drawing again, the .BAK file is erased and the previous .DWG copy becomes the backup. Only a newly revised drawing is given the .DWG file extension.

There are other extensions given to files by AutoCAD and MS-DOS. Some common file extensions are listed below. For a complete list, see Appendix C.

AutoCAD
- .BAK—Backup copy of a drawing file.
- .DCL—Dialogue Control Language description file.
- .DWG—Drawing file.
- .LIN—File containing the linetypes used by AutoCAD.
- .MNU—Menu source file.
- .PAT—Hatch patterns file.
- .PLT—Plot file.

MS-DOS
- .BAT—Batch file.
- .COM—Command file.
- .EXE—Executable file.

FILE UTILITIES DIALOGUE BOX

$\boxed{\textbf{ARM 4}}$

The "File Utilities" dialogue box contains options that allow you to perform file management functions other than creating and editing drawings. It can be accessed two ways. Either select Utilities... from the File pull-down menu, or select the FILES command from the UTILITY screen menu. Both methods display the dialogue box shown in Fig. 15-1.

Fig. 15-1. The ''File Utilities'' dialogue box.

List your drawings

It is easy to find out which drawings are stored on a particular disk. The "File Utilities" dialogue box allows you to list the drawings on any disk or directory. AutoCAD only needs to know which disk drive or directory you wish to list. Remember, if you have two floppy disk drives, the top drive is labeled "A:" and the bottom is "B:". The hard disk is named "C:". To list the drawing files on a disk in the A: drive, first insert the diskette. Then pick List files... from the "File Utilities" box.

This displays the "File List" dialogue box that is similar to the "Open Drawing" dialogue box. Notice in Fig. 15-2 that two list boxes are displayed. The box on the left contains a list of directories and disk drives, while the one on the right contains a list of files of the current pattern. The current pattern is always given in the Edit box at the top of the dialogue box.

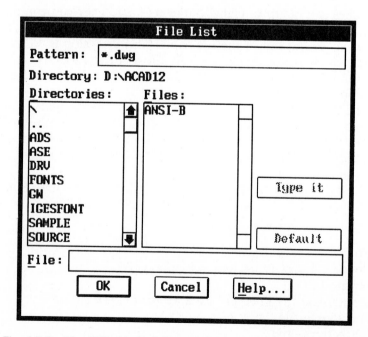

Fig. 15-2. The ''File List'' dialogue box shows directories and files.

Scroll down in the Directories list box until you see 〈A:〉. Double click on the 〈A:〉 and a list of all drawing files is shown in the Files list box. See Fig. 15-3. Use the scroll arrows to move up and down in the list. If you pick OK, the next time you use the "File Utilities" dialogue box, the A: drive will be current. If you pick Cancel, the default drive will be current.

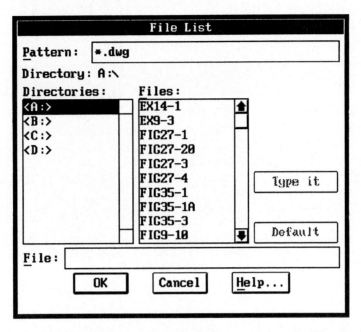

Fig. 15-3. Files on a disk or in a directory are shown in the Files list box.

PROFESSIONAL TIP

All of the file manipulation functions in the "File Utilities" dialogue box use the same basic file dialogue box. You should follow the same basic steps for all file manipulation functions. The following steps allow you to work easily with your files.

1. Pick the file command to be used.
2. Scroll (if necessary) in the Directories box to find the drive or directory you wish to work in.
3. Enter the pattern (specific file group or file type) you wish to work with in the Pattern box.
4. Select the file(s) you wish to work with.
5. Provide any final information required, such as a new name or location.

List any file type

You are not limited to listing just .DWG file types (drawing files). Suppose you need a list of all backup (.BAK) files in the \ACAD12\PROJ-01 subdirectory. Simply pick List files... from the "File Utilities" dialogue box, then pick the Pattern box.

NOTE

If you pick once in the Pattern box, you can use the cursor arrow keys, backspace, and delete keys to edit the line of text. However, if you double click in the box, the item is highlighted. Now when you type the first character, the new text replaces everything in the box.

Using one of these methods for entering information in the Pattern box, enter the following:

*.BAK

All of the files that have a .BAK file extension are listed in the Files box. The asterisk (*) used in the above entry is a DOS wild-card character. It represents any number of characters. In other words, you requested all the file names that have the .BAK extension. A detailed discussion of DOS commands is found in Chapter 35.

If you are searching for one particular file, enter that name. If the file is not on the specified drive or directory, it will not be listed.

EXERCISE 15-1

☐ Load AutoCAD, and insert a floppy disk that contains drawing files.
☐ Use the "File Utilities" dialogue box to do the following:
   A. List all .DWG files on the hard disk drive in the \ACAD directory.
   B. List all .DWG files on the floppy disk.
   C. List all files with an .EXP extension on the hard disk drive in the \ACAD directory.
   D. List all file types beginning with ACAD.
   E. List all file types beginning with ACAD and ending with any extension that begins with an "E".
☐ Exit the "File Utilities" dialogue box.

Deleting files

File deletion is a drastic measure to take with any type of file. *Before deleting a file, be sure that the file name you enter is the one you want to delete.* Select Delete file... in the "File Utilities" dialogue box. The "File(s) to Delete" dialogue box then appears.

Suppose you want to delete the drawing entitled JUNK.DWG on the disk in the A: drive. Be sure the A: drive is current. Scroll to find the file and pick it so the file name is highlighted. The selected name is displayed in the File edit box. See Fig. 15-4. If the file name displayed is correct, pick OK. Before AutoCAD deletes the file, it prompts you with an alert box as shown in Fig. 15-5.

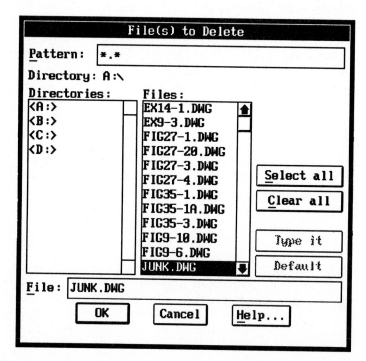

Fig. 15-4. The selected file to delete is placed in the File edit box.

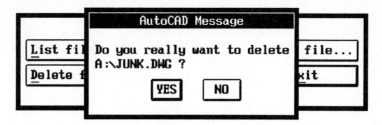

Fig. 15-5. AutoCAD alerts you before deleting a file.

PROFESSIONAL TIP

You may have noticed that many of the Edit boxes and buttons contain an uppercase, underlined letter. If you type this letter and press ENTER, that item is activated.

You can delete more than one file at a time just by picking them. After you pick the second file, no name is displayed in the File edit box. If you wish to "clean house" and delete all files on a disk or directory, simply pick the Select all button and all files are highlighted. If you do this by mistake, pick the Clear all button and all files are unselected.

If you want to delete a specific group of files, such as all drawing files that begin with "PIPE" and end with any three characters, you must first list them by typing the following in the Pattern edit box:

PIPE???.DWG

This displays only the specific files you requested. The question mark (?) is a DOS wild-card character that represents any single character. To delete the specified files, pick the Select all button, then pick OK. AutoCAD displays an alert before deleting each file.

PROFESSIONAL TIP

Users who keep their drawing files on one or more backup disks or tapes occasionally erase all .BAK files on working disks in order to make room for additional files. Do not do this unless you are sure that you have backup copies of your files elsewhere.

Remember, a question mark represents any single character. The files PIPE123.DWG and PIPEABC.DWG are selected for deletion by the previous entry. However, the file PIPE1234.DWG is not because four characters follow PIPE.

PROFESSIONAL TIP

Deleting files is dangerous. Be careful when entering the file name. Always look at the file name you typed before pressing the ENTER key.

In order to manage your files properly, a working knowledge of directories and subdirectories is important. AutoCAD displays the name of the current directory in the Directory label of many dialogue boxes. A label such as: C:\ACAD12\SAMPLE indicates that the SAMPLE subdirectory located off the ACAD12 directory on the C: drive is current. This is referred to as a *path*.

For an in-depth study of directories and DOS commands, review Chapter 35.

Changing file names

You can rename files by selecting Rename file... from the "File Utilities" dialogue box. The standard file dialogue box used for all file utility commands is displayed. This one is titled "Old File Name." Use the same method discussed previously to first select the disk drive or directory you wish to work in. Remember, you can specify the pattern of file to look for so that only specific file names are displayed. Then select the file name you wish to change from the Files list box and pick OK, or double click on the file name.

The "New File Name" dialogue box appears. You can type the new name in the File edit box and pick OK. Be sure to include the extension. A message indicates if the renaming operation was successful. If you want to put the file in another directory on the current disk drive, first pick the directory, then type the new name. This accomplishes the tasks of renaming and copying. You cannot copy from one drive to another using the Rename function.

Copying files

Copying files is similar to the functions previously discussed. When you pick Copy file... from the "File Utilities" dialogue box, the "Source File" dialogue box is displayed. Using the same procedure for all file manipulation functions, first select the disk drive and directory you wish to copy from, then select the file you wish to copy, such as P16-8.DWG, and pick OK. (You can also double click on the file name.) The "Destination File" dialogue box is then displayed. Now select the disk drive and directory in which you want the copy placed. Finally, type the full name of the file, in this case "P16-8.DWG" and press ENTER or pick OK. If you wish to change the name of the file in addition to copying it, simply type the new name in the "Destination File" dialogue box. A message is displayed indicating the file was successfully copied. See Fig. 15-6.

Fig. 15-6. The size of the copied file is indicated with a message.

— PROFESSIONAL TIP —

AutoCAD can use a .BAK file if it is renamed to a .DWG file. This may be necessary when a drawing file is accidentally erased or is unreadable because of a disk failure. It is best to copy the backup file to another disk. Then rename the backup as a drawing file. This is easily done using the Copy file... selection and ensures that you still have a backup copy.

Unlocking a file

When AutoCAD is used in a network environment, and several people have access to the same drawings, it is good practice to lock files. A locked file can be used by only one person at a time. This prevents two or more people from revising the same drawing at the same time.

File locking can be set when AutoCAD is installed, or by using the CONFIG command as follows:
- Type "CONFIG" at the Command: prompt, or pick Configure from the File pull-down menu.
- Press ENTER at the current configuration display.
- Select #7, Configure operating parameters.
- Select #12, Server authorization and file locking.
- Do not change server authorization. Answer No (N) or press ENTER at the "Do you wish to change it?" prompt.
- Answer Yes (Y) to "Do you wish to enable file-locking?" prompt.

This procedure should be used to permanently enable or disable file locking. However, to unlock one file, you should use the option in the "File Utilities" dialogue box.

One way to determine if a file is locked is by the message you get when loading a locked file. Suppose you try to load a drawing called ANSI-B. The alert message shown in Fig. 15-7 would be displayed.

Fig. 15-7. AutoCAD alerts you if you try to open a locked file.

The file (or group of files) can be unlocked by using the Unlock file... selection in the "File Utilities" dialogue box. The standard file dialogue box entitled "File(s) to Unlock" is displayed. You can list only the lock files by entering "*.DWK" in the Pattern edit box. Pick the file you need to unlock, then pick OK and the message shown in Fig. 15-8 is displayed. Pick OK if you wish to proceed with the unlocking.

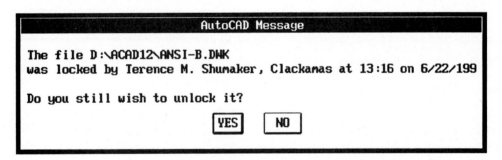

Fig. 15-8. Information is provided about the locked file and who locked it.

When file locking is enabled, AutoCAD automatically creates a small lock file with a .DWK extension. Therefore, when the ANSI-B.DWG file was loaded, a file named ANSI-B.DWK was also created. When this file was unlocked, the ANSI-B.DWK file was deleted.

─────────── **PROFESSIONAL TIP** ───────────

If your class or company works with drawings that must be accessed by more than one student or employee, it is good practice to enable file locking. Drawings such as basic site plans, floor plans, or templates or outlines that must have additional information added to them are examples of drawings that must be accessed by more than one person.

If file locking is enabled, AutoCAD creates locked versions of several file types. Keep this in mind when working with files other than drawings in the following activities:
- Configuring AutoCAD (.CFG).
- Creating plot files (.PLT) and printer plots (.LST and .PRP).
- Working with drawing interchange files (.DXF, .DXB, and .IGES).
- Customizing the AutoCAD menus (.MNX).
- Altering linetypes (.LIN), hatch patterns (.PAT), and shapes/fonts (.SHX).
- Creating slides (.SLD) and filmroll files (.FLM).
- Working with attribute extraction (.DXX and .TXT).
- Using reference drawings (.XLG).
- Converting drawing files from older versions of AutoCAD (.OLD).
- Using AutoCAD with a network password (.PWD).
- Auditing a drawing for errors (.ADT).

It is not important that you understand the meaning of all of the file types previously mentioned. As you work through this text and gain experience with AutoCAD, you will become more familiar with these activities, and the file types that are used in each.

RECOVERING A DAMAGED DRAWING |ARM 4|

A damaged drawing file is one that has been corrupted, and cannot be loaded into the AutoCAD drawing editor. Drawing files can be damaged in a number of ways. When they are damaged, it can be a frustrating experience, especially if you do not have a backup. Drawings are most often corrupted by the following actions:
- Removing a floppy disk before properly exiting AutoCAD.
- Changing floppy disks during a drawing session.
- Running out of disk space during a drawing session.
- Power failures.
- Hardware or software problems.

── NOTE ──

Never start a new drawing on the floppy disk using the following naming convention:

A:FILENAME

This can lead to "disk full" errors and damaged drawings. Always start a new drawing on the hard disk. Use a directory other than the one that holds the AutoCAD program files. Create subdirectories in the ACAD directory for your drawing and data files. For example, use the DOS commands Make Directory (MD) and Change Directory (CD) to create work space on your hard disk. If your AutoCAD directory is named ACAD, use the following commands to create a subdirectory called DWGS:

C:\〉 **CD ACAD** ↵
C:\ACAD〉 **MD DWGS** ↵

Now, you can load AutoCAD and start a new drawing called FRAMUS as follows:

New Drawing Name: **\ACAD\DWGS\FRAMUS** ↵

You have given AutoCAD a "path" to follow in order to create and store a new drawing file. You should not run out of disk space as long as there are a few megabytes of open storage space on the hard disk that contains your directory.

AutoCAD provides a method for recovering most damaged files. You can type "RECOVER" at the Command: prompt, or select Recover... from the File pull-down menu. Simply select the proper path and file and AutoCAD attempts to recover the damaged drawing. If the bad file is named \ACAD\STRUCT\SLAB for example, pick the STRUCT subdirectory, and then pick the SLAB drawing name. AutoCAD then tries to recover the damaged file. If it is successful, the file is loaded into the drawing editor, and it can be worked on in the normal fashion. If you do not save the file before exiting AutoCAD, the recovered drawing is lost.

USING THE AUDIT COMMAND $\boxed{\text{ARM 4}}$

You can perform a diagnostic check on your drawing files with the AUDIT command to check for, and correct errors. You can instruct AutoCAD to fix, or not to fix errors. A short report is generated as in the following example:

Command: **AUDIT** ↵
Fix any errors detected? ⟨N⟩ ↵
1   Blocks audited
Pass 1   145   entities audited
Pass 2   145   entities audited
Total errors found 0   fixed 0

AutoCAD automatically creates an audit report file that lists the corrections made. The report is given the same name as the drawing, but has an .ADT file extension. This file is placed in the same directory as the drawing. This is a text, or ASCII file (American Standard Code for Information Interchange), and can be listed by using the DOS command, TYPE, as follows:

Command: **TYPE** ↵
File to list: **\ACAD\DWGS\FRAMUS.ADT** ↵

The contents of the FRAMUS.ADT file are then displayed on the screen.

— NOTE —

The use of dialogue boxes is controlled by the FILEDIA system variable. If you do not want to work with the dialogue boxes, simply set the FILEDIA variable to 0. All of the file utilities discussed in this chapter are still available, but they are accessed through the File Utility Menu on a text screen. All of your entries must be typed, including all paths, file names, and file extensions.

EXERCISE 15-2

☐ Insert one of your floppy disks with drawings into the A: drive.
☐ Use the "File Utilities" dialogue box for this exercise.
☐ Copy one of your files and rename it using an ".OLD" file extension.
☐ Change the name of the file in the previous step to TEST.OLD.
☐ Copy and rename TEST.OLD to TEST-2.OLD.
☐ List all files with the .OLD extension.
☐ Delete all files with an .OLD extension.
☐ List the files on the floppy disk in the A: drive. Check to see whether there are any files with the .OLD extension.
☐ Exit the "File Utilities" dialogue menu.

CHAPTER TEST

Write your answers in the spaces provided.

1. What is a file type extension? _____

_____

2. What do the following file extension types mean:
   A. .BAK _____
   B. .LIN _____
   C. .MNU _____
   D. .PLT _____
   E. .BAT _____
   F. .EXE _____

3. Which pull-down selection leads to the "File Utilities" dialogue box? _____

4. How would you list the drawing files on the floppy disk in the A: drive? _____

_____

5. How would you list all .MNU files on the floppy disk in the B: drive? _____

_____

_____

6. How would you delete all .BAK files from the current C:\ACAD directory? The files begin
   with "PROJ2" and have three additional letters in their names. _____

_____

_____

7. What is the procedure for changing a file name? _____

_____

_____

8. What two functions can the "Rename files" option perform? _____

9. How is the "Copy files" option similar to the "Rename files" option? _____

_____

10. Which AutoCAD screen menu command gives you access to the "File Utilities" dialogue box?

_____

11. Why are files locked? _____

_____

12. What type of file is created when file locking is enabled? _____

_____

13. How can a file be unlocked? _____

_____

14. How can a damaged file be recovered? _____

_____

15. Which command allows you to run a diagnostic check of a drawing file? _____

PROBLEMS

1. Write a short report on the importance of file maintenance. Present some uses of the "File Utilities" dialogue box in file maintenance. Suggest a procedure to save drawing files and other types of files. Cover the following points in your report:
   A. Where drawing files are to be stored now: on hard disk or floppy disks.
   B. When files should be backed up.
   C. How many backups of each file should exist.
   D. Where should the original and backup disks be located.
   E. How often should .BAK files be deleted or should they be deleted at all.
   F. What file naming system should be used.
2. Make backup copies of all your diskettes. Use the "Copy File" option in the "File Utilities" dialogue box. Copy the files in two different ways.
   A. Copy all files with the .DWG extension to the new disk. Then copy all .BAK files to the new disk.
   B. Copy a second disk, or recopy the first disk.
   C. List the files on your backup disk. Be sure that files with both .DWG and .BAK extensions have been copied. Then rename all files with the .BAK extension to have an .OLD extension.
3. Get a printed listing of the files contained on one disk. Ask your instructor or supervisor for assistance if you are not familiar with the printer. See Chapter 27 for instructions on making a printout of text printed on the screen.
4. Get a printed list of all drawing files contained on your floppy disk.

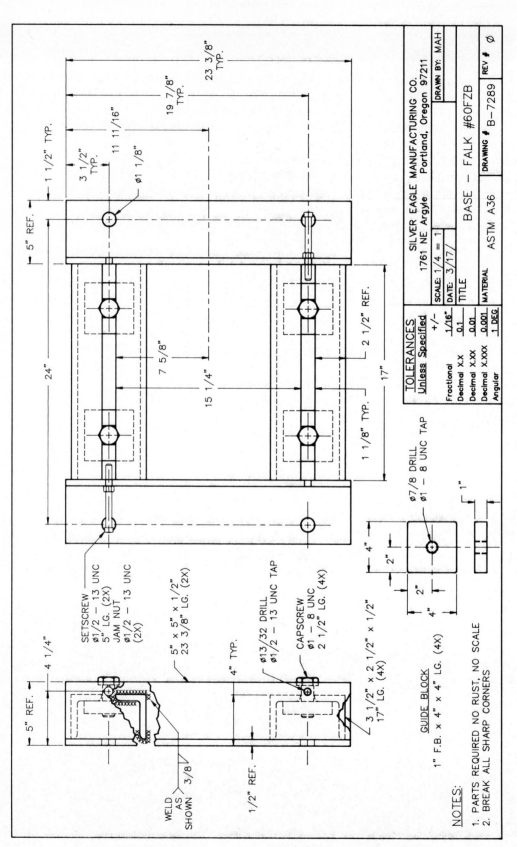

Assembly drawing. (Silver Eagle Manufacturing Co.)

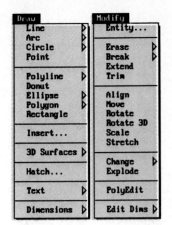

Chapter 16

DRAWING
AND EDITING
POLYLINES

Learning objectives

After completing this chapter, you will be able to:

☐ Use the PLINE command to draw given polylines.
☐ Preset the polyline width.
☐ Use the PEDIT command to make changes to existing polylines.
☐ Identify the PEDIT options.
☐ Use the EXPLODE command to remove all polyline width characteristics.
☐ Make a polyline boundary.

The PLINE command was introduced in Chapter 6 as a method to draw thick lines. As you will find, the PLINE command also draws a variety of special shapes, limited only by your imagination. The section on PLINE in Chapter 6 focused on line-related options, such as Width, Halfwidth, and Length. The editing functions were limited to ERASE and UNDO commands. This chapter covers using PLINE to make polyline arcs and advanced editing commands for polylines. The PLINE command is accessed through the DRAW screen menu, Draw pull-down menu, or by typing at the Command: prompt.

DRAWING PLINE ARCS

ARM 5

The PLINE command's Arc option functions like the ARC command except that PLINE options include Width and Halfwidth. The arc width may range from 0 up to the radius of the arc. A polyline arc with different end widths is drawn by changing the Width. The arc shown in Fig. 16-1 was drawn with this command sequence:

Command: **PLINE** ↵
From point: *(pick the first point)*
Current line-width is (status specified)
Arc/Close/Halfwidth/Length/Undo/Width/⟨Endpoint of line⟩: **W** ↵
Starting width ⟨current⟩: *(specify a starting width, such as .1, and press ENTER)*
Ending width ⟨current⟩: *(specify an ending width, such as .4, and press ENTER)*
Arc/Close/Halfwidth/Length/Undo/Width/⟨Endpoint of line⟩: **A** ↵
Angle/CEnter/CLose/Direction/Halfwidth/Line/Radius/Second pt/Undo/Width/⟨Endpoint of arc⟩: *(pick the arc endpoint)*
Angle/CEnter/CLose/Direction/Halfwidth/Line/Radius/Second pt/Undo/Width/⟨Endpoint of arc⟩: ↵

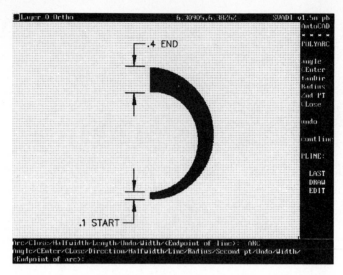

Fig. 16-1. Polyline arc with different starting and ending widths.

Drawing a continuous polyline arc

A polyline arc drawn to continue from a previous line or polyline is tangent at the last point entered. The arc's center is determined automatically unless you pick a new center. If a polyline arc is drawn before a straight polyline, the arc's direction is the same as the previous line, arc, or polyline. This may not be what you want. In this event, it may be necessary to set one of the PLINE Arc options. These include Angle, CEnter, Direction, Radius, or Second point. They work much like the ARC command options.

Specifying the included angle

The following command sequence, shown in Fig. 16-2, is used to enter the Angle option for a polyline arc:

Command: **PLINE** ↵
From point: *(pick the first point)*
Current line-width is (status specified)
Arc/Close/Halfwidth/Length/Undo/Width/⟨Endpoint of line⟩: **A** ↵
Angle/CEnter/CLose/Direction/Halfwidth/Line/Radius/Second pt/Undo/Width/⟨End-
 point of arc⟩: **A** ↵
Included angle: *(specify the included angle, such as* **60**, *and press ENTER)*
Center/Radius/⟨End point⟩: *(select the arc endpoint)*
Angle/CEnter/CLose/Direction/Halfwidth/Line/Radius/Second pt/Undo/Width/⟨End-
 point of arc⟩: ↵

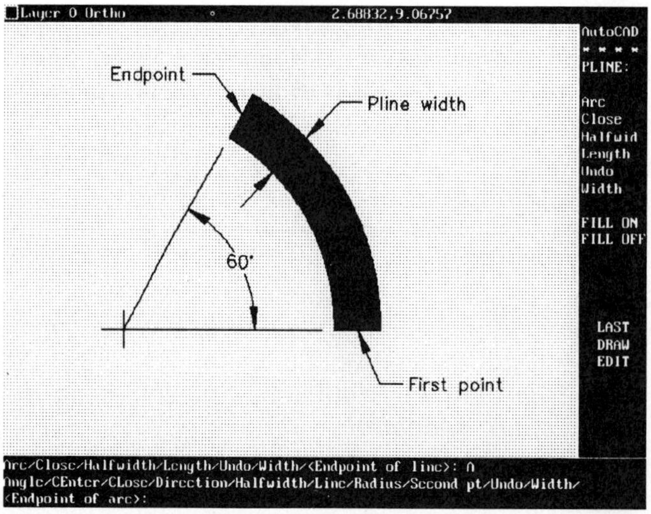

Fig. 16-2. Polyline arc with specified angle.

Selecting the CEnter option

When a polyline arc continues from a drawn item, the center point is calculated automatically. You might want to pick a center point when the polyline arc does not continue from another item. Also pick a center point if the one calculated is not suitable. The CEnter option is chosen in this manner.

Command: **PLINE** ↵
From point: *(select the first point)*
Current line-width is (status specified)
Arc/Close/Halfwidth/Length/Undo/Width/⟨Endpoint of line⟩: **A** ↵
Angle/CEnter/CLose/Direction/Halfwidth/Line/Radius/Second pt/Undo/Width/⟨Endpoint of arc⟩: **CE** ↵ *(notice that two letters, CE, are required for this option)*
Center point: *(select the arc center point)*
Angle/Length/⟨End point⟩: *(select the arc endpoint, or type A or L and press ENTER)*

If "A" was entered at the last prompt, the next request is:

Included angle: *(enter an included angle and press ENTER)*

If "L" was entered, the next prompt would have been:

Length of chord: *(select a chord length and press ENTER)*

Using the Direction option

The Direction option alters the bearing of the arc. It changes the default option of placing the polyline arc tangent to the last polyline, arc, or line. This option may also be entered when you are drawing an unconnected polyline arc. The Direction option functions much like the ARC command's Direction option. It requests the following input after "D" is typed:

Direction from start point: *(enter a direction in positive or negative degrees, or specify a point on either side of the start point)*
End point: *(select the endpoint of the arc)*

Drawing a polyline arc by radius

Polyline arcs may be drawn by giving the arc's radius. This is done by typing "R." Then respond to these prompts:

Angle/CEnter/CLose/Direction/Halfwidth/Line/Radius/Second pt/Undo/Width/⟨Endpoint of arc⟩: **R** ↵
Radius: *(enter the arc radius and press ENTER)*
Angle/⟨Endpoint⟩: *(pick the arc endpoint)*

or

Angle/⟨Endpoint⟩: **A** ↵
Included angle: *(enter the included angle of the arc and press ENTER)*
Direction of chord ⟨current⟩: *(enter chord direction and press ENTER)*

Specifying a three-point polyline arc

A three-point arc may be drawn by typing "S" for Second point. The prompts are as follows:

Angle/CEnter/CLose/Direction/Halfwidth/Line/Radius/Second pt/Undo/Width/⟨Endpoint of arc⟩: **S** ↵
Second point: *(pick the second point on the arc)*
End point: *(pick the endpoint to complete the arc)*

Using the CLose option

The CLose option adds the last segment to enclose a shape. It saves drafting time when you are drawing a polygon. This PLINE Arc option will CLose the shape with an arc, rather than a straight line. Notice that "CL" is typed at the prompt line; two letters are needed to separate this option from the CEnter option. Fig. 16-3 shows how the command sequence below encloses a shape.

Angle/CEnter/CLose/Direction/Halfwidth/Line/Radius/Second pt/Undo/Width/⟨End-point of arc⟩: **CL** ↵

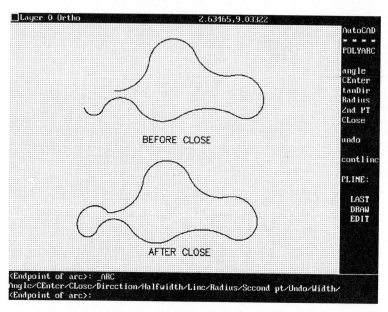

Fig. 16-3. Using the PLINE command's CLose option.

EXERCISE 16-1

☐ Open TITLEA from Problem 10-1.
☐ Draw a continuous polyline arc with at least four segments. Select the CLose option to close the polyline.
☐ Draw a polyline arc by its endpoints and a 90° included angle. Then continue from the first arc with another 90° polyline arc.
☐ Draw a polyline arc using end and center points.
☐ Choose the endpoint, center, and included angle to draw a polyline arc.
☐ Select endpoints and a positive direction to draw a polyline arc. Then see how using a negative direction affects the arc.
☐ Specify the endpoints of a 1.5 unit radius arc.
☐ Draw a polyline arc using three points.
☐ Save the drawing as A:EX16-1 and quit.

PROFESSIONAL TIP

The best way to learn and use AutoCAD's drafting tools is to practice. It is difficult for you to acquire skills unless you spend time on the computer. A successful CAD operator knows the commands and selects the best options.

REVISING POLYLINES USING THE PEDIT COMMAND $\boxed{\text{ARM 6}}$

Polylines are drawn as single segments. A polyline joined to another polyline might then be joined to a polyline arc. Even though you draw connecting segments, AutoCAD puts them all together. The result is one polyline. When editing a polyline, you must edit it as one entity or divide it into its single segments. These changes are made with the PEDIT and EXPLODE commands.

INTRODUCTION TO PEDIT $\boxed{\text{ARM 6}}$

The PEDIT command is found in the EDIT screen menu as PEDIT and in the Modify pull-down menu as PolyEdit. When either is picked, AutoCAD then allows you to pick the polylines using any of the selection options.

> Command: **PEDIT** ↵
> Select polyline: *(use one of the selection options and press ENTER when completed)*

When the Select polyline: or Select objects: prompt is issued, the screen cursor becomes a pick box. Move the cursor and pick the polyline to be changed. If the polyline is wide, place the cursor on an edge rather than in the center. You may also use the Window, Crossing, or Fence options if you need to select a group of polyline entities.

If the polyline is the last entity drawn, type "L" for Last. If the entity you pick is not a polyline, this message is displayed:

> Entity selected is not a polyline
> Do you want it to turn into one? ⟨Y⟩

A "Y" response or ENTER turns the entities into a polyline. Type "N" to leave them as is.

──── PROFESSIONAL TIP ────

Place a window around a group of connected lines and arcs and turn them into a continuous polyline using the Join option discussed later in this chapter.

REVISING A POLYLINE AS ONE UNIT $\boxed{\text{ARM 6}}$

A polyline may be edited as a single entity or it may be divided to revise each individual segment. This section shows you the options for changing the entire polyline. Note the number of options given in the prompt:

> Command: **PEDIT** ↵
> Select polyline: *(pick a polyline)*
> Close/Join/Width/Edit vertex/Fit/Spline/Decurve/Ltype gen/Undo/eXit ⟨X⟩:

The default option in brackets is "X" for exit. Pressing ENTER returns you to the Command: prompt.

Closing an open polyline or opening a closed polyline

As mentioned before, polylines may be closed with the CLose option. You might later decide to close an open polyline, or you might want to reopen a closed polyline. Both of these functions are done with the Close option of PEDIT. Type "C" at the prompt line.

If you select Close for a polyline that is already closed, AutoCAD converts the request to Open. Also, typing "O" for Open will open a closed polyline. Picking an open polyline and the Close option yields the Close prompt. Keep in mind that the Open option will not work on a polyline that was closed by drawing the closing segment. You must have entered the Close option when you closed the polyline. Fig. 16-4 shows open and closed polylines.

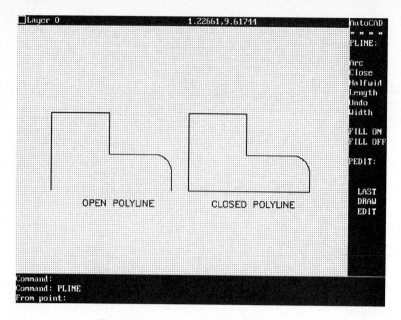

Fig. 16-4. Open and closed polylines.

Joining polylines to other polylines, lines, and arcs

Polylines, lines, and arcs may be joined together as one polyline. The Join option works only if the polyline and other entities meet exactly. They cannot cross, nor can there be spaces or breaks within the entities. These conditions are shown in Fig. 16-5. The command sequence is as follows:

Command: **PEDIT** ↵
Select polyline: *(select the original polyline)*
Close/Join/Width/Edit vertex/Fit/Spline/Decurve/Ltype gen/Undo/eXit ⟨X⟩: **J** ↵
Select objects: *(select all of the objects to be joined)*
Select objects: ↵

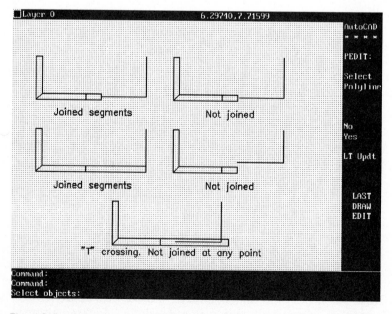

Fig. 16-5. Enlarged views of features that are joined and not joined.

Select each object to be joined or group them with the Window option. The original polyline may be included in the group or left out; it does not matter. See Fig. 16-6.

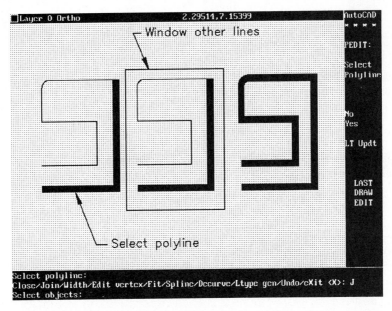

Fig. 16-6. Joining a polyline to other connected lines and arcs.

PROFESSIONAL TIP

Once items have been joined into a continuous polyline, the polyline may be closed using the Close option.

Changing the width of a polyline

The PEDIT command's Width option changes a polyline having a constant or varying width to a new width. To change a polyline from a .06 to .1 width, follow these steps:

Command: **PEDIT** ↵
Select polyline: *(pick the polyline)*
Close/Join/Width/Edit vertex/Fit/Spline/Decurve/Ltype gen/Undo/eXit ⟨X⟩: **W** ↵
Enter new width for all segments: **.1** ↵

Circles drawn with the CIRCLE command cannot be changed to polylines. Polycircles can be produced using the PLINE Arc option and drawing two 180° arcs, or by using the DONUT command. Change the width of donuts by individually picking each using the PEDIT command and Width option previously discussed. The Window, Crossing, or Fence selection will not change all donut widths at the same time. Fig. 16-7 shows an existing polyline and a new polyline using the PEDIT Width option.

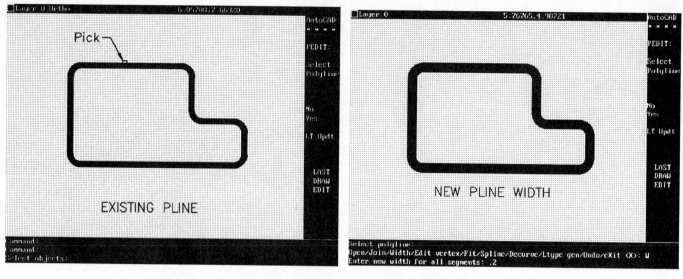

Fig. 16-7. Changing the polyline width.

EXERCISE 16-2

☐ Open TITLEB from Problem 10-1.
☐ Draw a series of connected lines and arcs. Then use the PEDIT command to change these items to a single polyline. Finally, change the width of the polyline.
☐ Draw a closed polyline. Use the Close option when drawing the final segment.
☐ Use the PEDIT command's Open option to open the previous polyline, and use Close to close it.
☐ Connect a series of lines and arcs to a polyline. Then join all items as one polyline.
☐ Draw two donuts, each with a .5 unit inside diameter and 1.0 unit outside diameter. Change the width of the donuts to .1 using the PEDIT command.
☐ Save the drawing as A:EX16-2 and quit.

Changing a polyline corner or point of tangency

Another PEDIT option is Edit vertex. When you enter "E," an "X" appears on screen at the first vertex or point of tangency. This complex PEDIT option has nine suboptions:

> Close/Join/Width/Edit vertex/Fit/Spline/Decurve/Ltype gen/Undo/eXit ⟨X⟩: **E** ↵
> Next/Previous/Break/Insert/Move/Regen/Straighten/Tangent/Width/eXit ⟨N or P⟩:

The suboptions of the Edit vertex option are defined as follows:
- **Next (N)** — Moves the screen "X" to the next vertex or point of tangency on the polyline.
- **Previous (P)** — Moves the "X" to the previous vertex or tangency on the polyline.
- **Break (B)** — Breaks a portion out of the polyline.
- **Insert (I)** — Adds a new polyline vertex.
- **Move (M)** — Moves a polyline vertex to a new location.
- **Regen (R)** — Generates the revised version of the polyline.
- **Straighten (S)** — Straightens polyline segments.
- **Tangent (T)** — Specifies tangent direction for curve fitting.
- **Width (W)** — Changes a polyline width.
- **eXit (X)** — Returns you to the PEDIT menu and command prompt.

The Next and Previous options move the "X" between the vertices or points of tangency. The current point is affected by editing functions, Fig. 16-8. If you edit the vertices of a polyline and nothing appears to happen, use the Regen option to regenerate the revised edition of the polyline.

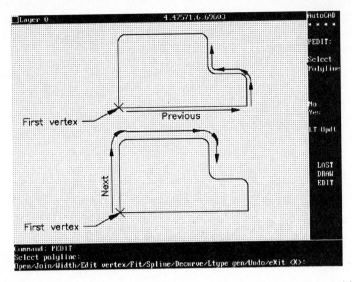

Fig. 16-8. Using the Edit vertex Next and Previous suboptions. Note the position of the "X."

Making breaks in a polyline

The Edit vertex option breaks out a portion of a polyline. Select the N or P options to move the "X" to the correct vertex. Then follow this command sequence:

Close/Join/Width/Edit vertex/Fit/Spline/Decurve/Ltype gen/Undo/eXit ⟨X⟩: **E** ↵
Next/Previous/Break/Insert/Move/Regen/Straighten/Tangent/Width/eXit ⟨N⟩: *(move the screen "X" to the desired position where you want the break to begin)*
Next/Previous/Break/Insert/Move/Regen/Straighten/Tangent/Width/eXit ⟨N⟩: **B** ↵

AutoCAD enters the point shown with an "X" as the first point to break.

Next/Previous/Go/eXit ⟨N⟩: *(move the screen "X" to the next or previous position)*

Press ENTER to move the screen "X" to the Next or Previous vertex or point. The direction depends on which option is the default shown in brackets. Typing "X" exits the option. After moving the screen "X" to the desired location, enter "G" for Go. This instructs AutoCAD to remove the portion of the polyline between the two selected points. The steps below are illustrated in Fig. 16-9.

Next/Previous/Break/Insert/Move/Regen/Straighten/Tangent/Width/eXit ⟨N or P⟩: **B** ↵
Next/Previous/Go/eXit ⟨N⟩: **P** ↵
Next/Previous/Go/eXit ⟨P⟩: ↵
Next/Previous/Go/eXit ⟨P⟩: ↵
Next/Previous/Go/eXit ⟨P⟩: **G** ↵

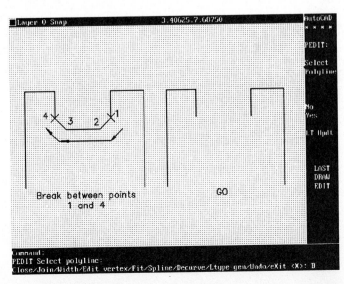

Fig. 16-9. Using Edit vertex to break out a portion of a polyline.

Insert a new vertex in a polyline

A new vertex may be added to a polyline by typing "I" for Insert. Use the Insert option only after selecting the adjacent vertex.

Close/Join/Width/Edit vertex/Fit/Spline/Decurve/Ltype gen/Undo/eXit ⟨X⟩: **E** ↵
Next/Previous/Break/Insert/Move/Regen/Straighten/Tangent/Width/eXit ⟨N⟩: *(move the "X" cursor to the desired location using N or P)*
Next/Previous/Break/Insert/Move/Regen/Straighten/Tangent/Width/eXit ⟨N⟩: **I** ↵
Enter location of new vertex: *(move the screen crosshairs to the new vertex location and pick)*

The new vertex is drawn as shown in Fig. 16-10.

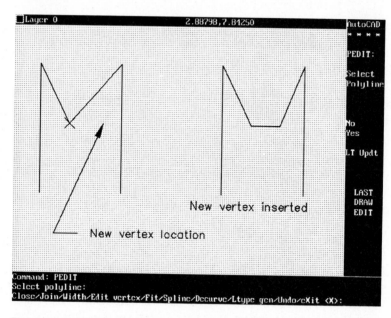

Fig. 16-10. Using the Edit vertex Insert option to add a new vertex.

Moving a polyline vertex

The Move option of Edit vertex moves a vertex. The screen "X" cursor must be placed on the point to move before you enter "M." The sequence shown in Fig. 16-11 is as follows:

Close/Join/Width/Edit vertex/Fit/Spline/Decurve/Ltype gen/Undo/eXit ⟨X⟩: **E** ↵
Next/Previous/Break/Insert/Move/Regen/Straighten/Tangent/Width/eXit ⟨N⟩: *(move the "X" cursor to the vertex to be moved, using N or P)*
Next/Previous/Break/Insert/Move/Regen/Straighten/Tangent/Width/eXit ⟨N⟩: **M** ↵
Enter new location: *(pick the new point)*

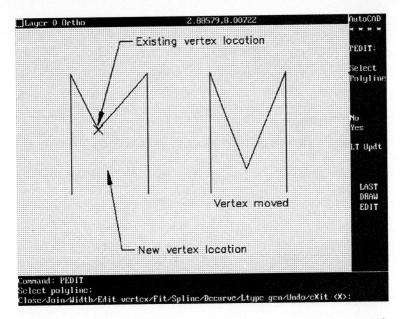

Fig. 16-11. Using the Edit vertex Move option to place a vertex in a new location.

Straightening polyline segments or arcs

You can straighten polyline segments or arcs between two points. Use the Edit vertex Straighten option as follows:

> Close/Join/Width/Edit vertex/Fit/Spline/Decurve/Ltype gen/Undo/eXit ⟨X⟩: **E** ⏎
> Next/Previous/Break/Insert/Move/Regen/Straighten/Tangent/Width/eXit ⟨N⟩: *(move the "X" cursor to the first point of the segments to be straightened)*
> Next/Previous/Break/Insert/Move/Regen/Straighten/Tangent/Width/eXit ⟨N⟩: **S** ⏎
> Next/Previous/Go/eXit/ ⟨N⟩: *(move the "X" to the last point)*
> Next/Previous/Go/eXit ⟨N⟩: **G** ⏎

If the "X" is not moved before "G" is entered, AutoCAD straightens the segment to the next vertex. This option provides a quick way to straighten an arc, Fig. 16-12.

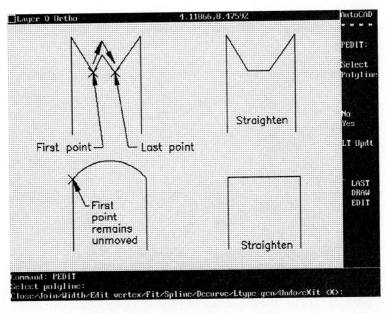

Fig. 16-12. Straightening polylines.

Changing polyline segment widths

The Edit vertex Width option is the only command that changes the starting and ending widths of an existing polyline. Move the screen "X" to the segment before the one to be altered. The command structure looks like this:

Close/Join/Width/Edit vertex/Fit/Spline/Decurve/Ltype gen/Undo/eXit ⟨X⟩: **E** ↵
Next/Previous/Break/Insert/Move/Regen/Straighten/Tangent/Width/eXit ⟨N⟩: **N** ↵
(move the "X" cursor to the segment prior to the one to be changed)
Next/Previous/Break/Insert/Move/Regen/Straighten/Tangent/Width/eXit ⟨N⟩: **W** ↵
Enter starting width ⟨current⟩: *(enter the revised starting width and press ENTER)*
Enter ending width ⟨revised start width⟩: *(enter the revised ending width and press ENTER, or press ENTER to keep the width the same as the starting width)*
Next/Previous/Break/Insert/Move/Regen/Straighten/Tangent/Width/eXit ⟨N⟩: **R** ↵

Notice that the starting width default is the current setting. The ending width default is the same as the entered starting width. When you press ENTER to complete this command, nothing happens. You select the Regen option to have AutoCAD draw the revised polyline. See Fig. 16-13.

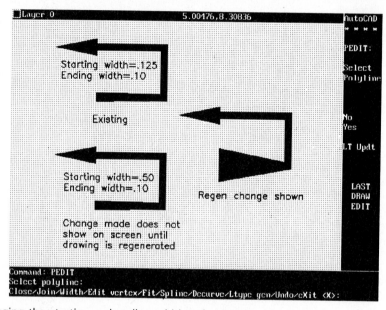

Fig. 16-13. Changing the starting and ending widths of existing polylines. Use the Regen option to display the change.

EXERCISE 16-3

☐ Open TITLEB from Problem 10-1.
☐ Draw a polyline with a series of segments. Have at least eight corners and three arcs.
☐ Enter the Edit vertex option and move the screen "X" cursor around using the Next and Previous suboptions.
☐ Break the polyline between any three points. Then Undo the breaks.
☐ Insert a new vertex in the polyline.
☐ Move one vertex of the polyline.
☐ Straighten one arc segment or at least three line segments.
☐ Change the starting and ending widths of one segment.
☐ Save the drawing as A:EX16-3 and quit.

Making a smooth curve out of polyline corners

In some situations, you may need to convert a polyline into a series of smooth curves. One example is a graph. A graph may show a series of plotted points as a smooth curve rather than straight segments. This process is called *curve fitting* and is done with the Fit suboption. The

Fit suboption constructs pairs of arcs passing through control points. You can specify control points or they may be the vertices of the polyline's corners. Many closely spaced control points produce a smooth curve. Prior to curve fitting, each vertex may be given a tangent direction. AutoCAD then fits the curve based on the tangent directions that you set. However, you do not have to enter tangent directions. Mainly, the option is used to edit vertices when Fit curve did not produce the best results.

To edit tangent directions, enter the Edit vertex option of the PEDIT command. Move the screen "X" to each vertex to be changed. Request the Tangent option and issue a tangent direction in degrees or pick a point in the expected direction. The direction you choose is indicated by an arrow placed at the vertex.

Close/Join/Width/Edit vertex/Fit/Spline/Decurve/Ltype gen/Undo/eXit/ ⟨X⟩: **E** ↵
Next/Previous/Break/Insert/Move/Regen/Straighten/Tangent/Width/eXit/ ⟨N⟩: *(move the screen "X" to the desired vertex)*
Next/Previous/Break/Insert/Move/Regen/Straighten/Tangent/Width/eXit ⟨N⟩: **T** ↵
Direction of tangent: *(specify a direction in positive or negative degrees and press ENTER, or pick a point in the desired direction)*

Once the tangent directions are given for vertices to be changed, select the Fit option. The polyline shown in Fig. 16-14 was made into a smooth curve with these steps:

Command: **PEDIT** ↵
Select polyline: *(pick the polyline to be edited)*
Close/Join/Width/Edit vertex/Fit/Spline/Decurve/Ltype gen/Undo/eXit/ ⟨X⟩: **F** ↵

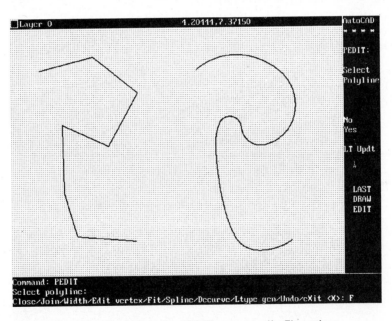

Fig. 16-14. Using the PEDIT command's Fit option.

If the result does not look like the curve you anticipated, return to the Edit vertex suboption. Make changes using PEDIT options.

Using the Spline option

With the Fit option, the curve passes through polyline vertices. The Spline option also smoothes the corners of a straight segment polyline. This option produces a different result. The curve passes through the first and last control points or vertices. However, the curve "pulls" toward the other vertices but does not pass through them. The Spline curve option is used as follows:

Command: **PEDIT** ↵
Select polyline: *(pick the polyline to be edited)*
Close/Join/Width/Edit vertex/Fit/Spline/Decurve/Ltype gen/Undo/eXit/ ⟨X⟩: **S** ↵

A comparison of the Fit and Spline options is shown in Fig. 16-15.

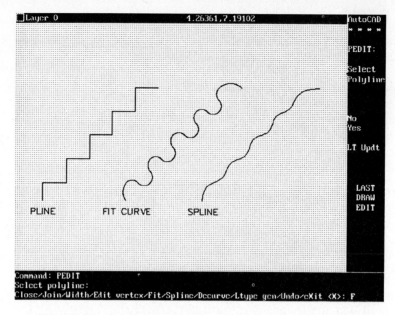

Fig. 16-15. A comparison between Fit and Spline options.

Straightening all segments of a polyline

The Decurve option returns a polyline edited with Fit or Spline options to its original form. Information entered for tangent direction is kept for future reference. The Decurve option steps below are shown in Fig. 16-16.

Command: **PEDIT** ↵
Select polyline: *(pick the polyline to be edited)*
Close/Join/Width/Edit vertex/Fit/Spline/Decurve/Ltype gen/Undo/eXit/ ⟨X⟩: **D** ↵

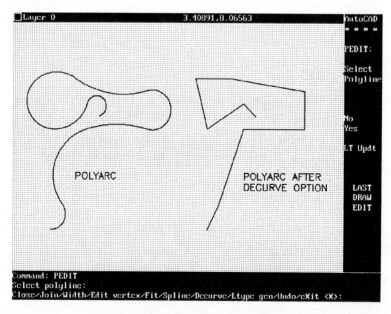

Fig. 16-16. Using the Decurve option.

PROFESSIONAL TIP

If you make a mistake, remember that the Undo option is always available. It removes the last polyline segment drawn. Entering Undo more than once removes each polyline segment in the reverse order in which they were drawn. Use the eXit option to return to the previous prompt. Undo also cancels the last PEDIT function you used.

EXERCISE 16-4

☐ Open TITLEB from Problem 10-1.
☐ Draw a polyline with at least five vertices. Smooth the polyline using the PEDIT command's Fit option.
☐ Decurve the curved polyline.
☐ Practice with Undo by first drawing a series of polyline segments. After using PEDIT to make some changes, select Undo to return to the original polyline. Finally, select Redo to work on the edited polyline again.
☐ Save the drawing as A:EX16-4 and quit.

Changing the appearance of polyline linetypes

The Ltype gen option refers to "linetype generation." This option determines how linetypes, other than continuous lines, look in relation to the vertices of a polyline. For example, when a centerline is used and Ltype gen is off, then the line has a dash at each vertex. When Ltype gen is on, the line is generated with a constant pattern in relation to the vertices. Look at the difference between Ltype gen on and off in Fig. 16-17, and also notice the effect these settings have on spline curves.

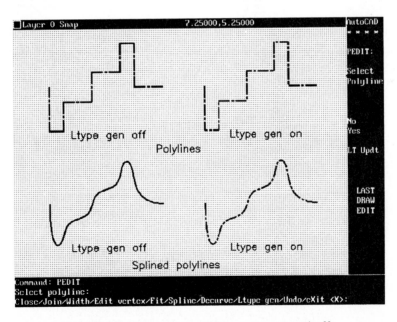

Fig. 16-17. Comparison of Ltype gen on and off.

Ltype gen is accessed by typing "L" at the prompt line, or by picking LT Updt from the screen menu. The Ltype gen option is either on or off. To turn on this option, follow these steps:

Command: **PEDIT** ↵
Select polyline: *(pick the polyline)*
Close/Join/Width/Edit vertex/Fit/Spline/Decurve/Ltype gen/Undo/eXit/ ⟨X⟩: **L** ↵
Full Pline linetype ON/OFF ⟨Off⟩: **ON** ↵

You can also change the Ltype gen value using the PLINEGEN system variable as follows:

Command: **PLINEGEN** ↵
New value for PLINEGEN ⟨0⟩: **1** ↵

Ltype gen or PLINEGEN does not affect tapered polylines.

CONVERTING A POLYLINE INTO
INDIVIDUAL LINE AND ARC SEGMENTS   ARM 6

Remember that a polyline is a single entity composed of polyline and polyline arc segments. The EXPLODE command changes the polyline to a series of lines and arcs. The EXPLODE command can be accessed from the EDIT: screen menu, Modify pull-down menu, or typed at the Command: prompt.

When a wide polyline is exploded, the resulting line or arc is redrawn along the centerline of the original polyline, Fig. 16-18. When the EXPLODE command is entered at the Command: prompt, AutoCAD makes the following request:

Command: **EXPLODE** ↵
Select objects: *(pick the polyline to be exploded)*
Select objects: ↵

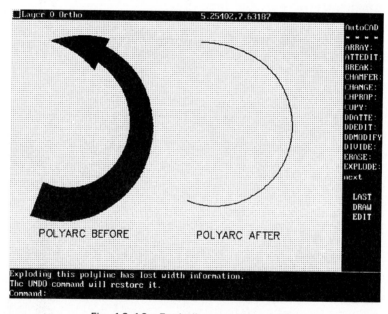

Fig. 16-18. Exploding a wide polyline.

The EXPLODE command removes all width characteristics and tangent information. However, AutoCAD gives you a chance to change your mind by offering this message:

Exploding this polyline has lost (width/tangent) information.
The UNDO command will restore it.

EXERCISE 16-5

☐ Load AutoCAD and open TITLEB.
☐ Draw a polyline of your own design. Include some width changes. Then explode it and observe what happens.
☐ Restore the exploded polyline using the UNDO command.
☐ Save the drawing as A:EX16-5 and quit.

ADDITIONAL METHODS FOR SMOOTHING POLYLINE CORNERS

Earlier in this chapter, the Fit and Spline options of the PEDIT command were discussed. With the Fit option, the resulting curve passes through the polyline vertices. The Spline option creates a curve that passes through the first and last control points, or vertices. The curve then "pulls" toward the other vertices but does not pass through them. There are two spline curve options—Quadratic and Cubic. These options create B-spline curves. The *cubic curve* is extremely smooth because the elements of the curve pass through the first and last control points, and close to intermediate control points. The *quadratic curve* is not as smooth as the cubic curve. However, it is smoother than a curve made with the Fit option. Like a cubic curve, a quadratic curve passes through the first and last control points. The remainder of the curve is tangent to the polyline segments between intermediate control points, Fig. 16-19.

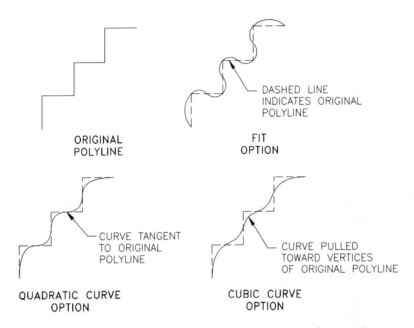

Fig. 16-19. A comparison of the Fit, Quadratic spline curve, and Cubic spline curve options.

Editing a polyline into a B-spline curve requires that you first set the SPLINETYPE system variable. If you set SPLINETYPE to 5, AutoCAD draws a quadratic curve. If you set the value to 6, AutoCAD draws a cubic curve. Set the SPLINETYPE to draw a quadratic curve as follows:

Command: **SPLINETYPE** ↵
New value for SPLINETYPE ⟨6⟩: **5** ↵

If you want to draw a cubic curve, reset SPLINETYPE to 6.

EXERCISE 16-6

☐ Draw a polyline similar to the "ORIGINAL POLYLINE" shown in Fig. 16-19.
☐ Use the COPY command to make three copies of the original polyline.
☐ Use PEDIT's Fit option to smooth the first copy.
☐ Set SPLINETYPE to 5 for a quadratic curve.
☐ Use PEDIT's Spline option to smooth the second copy.
☐ Set SPLINETYPE to 6 for a cubic curve.
☐ Use the Spline option again to smooth the third copy.
☐ Compare the original polyline with the three new curves.
☐ Save the drawing as A:EX16-6 and quit.

Another system variable, called SPLINESEGS, controls the number of line segments used to construct spline curves. The SPLINESEGS default value is 8. It allows you to create a fairly smooth spline curve with moderate regeneration time. If you decrease the value, the spline curve is less smooth. If you increase the value, the spline curve is more smooth. Although increasing the value above 8 creates a more precise spline curve, it also increases regeneration time and drawing file size. Change the SPLINESEGS variable as follows:

Command: **SPLINESEGS** ↵
New value for SPLINESEGS ⟨8⟩: **20** ↵

Fig. 16-20 shows the relationship between several SPLINESEGS values.

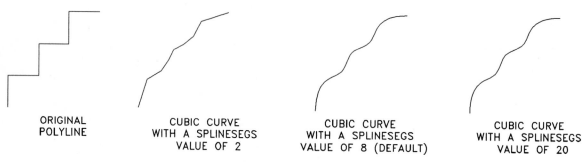

Fig. 16-20. A comparison of SPLINESEGS values.

When you pick PolyEdit from the Modify pull-down menu and select the object to edit, the first PEDIT screen menu changes to display some of the PEDIT options. Also displayed at the end of this screen menu is PolyVars (Polyline Variables). Selecting PolyVars accesses an icon menu displaying five options, including Quadratic, Cubic, and Bezier. Look at the "Polyline Variables" icon menu to see the available options. The Bezier option is discussed in Chapter 24.

EXERCISE 16-7

☐ Draw a polyline similar to the "ORIGINAL POLYLINE" shown in Fig. 16-20.
☐ Use the COPY command to make three copies of the original polyline.
☐ Set SPLINETYPE to 6 for a cubic curve.
☐ Set the SPLINESEGS system variable to 2.
☐ Use PEDIT's Spline option to smooth the first copy.
☐ Set SPLINESEGS to 8.
☐ Use the Spline option to smooth the second copy.
☐ Set SPLINESEGS to 20.
☐ Use the Spline option to smooth the third copy.
☐ Compare the original polyline and the smoothness of the three new curves.
☐ Save the drawing as A:EX16-7 and quit.

MAKING A POLYLINE BOUNDARY

When you draw an object with the LINE command, each line segment is a single entity. You can create a polyline boundary of an area made up of closed line segments. To do this, enter the BPOLY command as follows:

Command: **BPOLY** ↵

Now, the "Polyline Creation" dialogue box shown in Fig. 16-21 is displayed. Some of the items in this dialogue box (related to hatching) are discussed in detail in Chapter 20. For now, pick the Pick Points button to get this prompt:

Select internal point: *(pick a point inside a closed polygon)*
Selecting everything...
Selecting everything visible...
Analyzing selected data...
Select internal point: *(pick a point inside another closed polygon)*
Select internal point: ↵

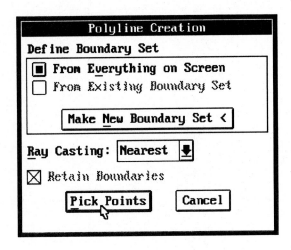

Fig. 16-21. The ''Polyline Creation'' dialogue box.

If the point you pick is inside a closed polygon, then the boundary becomes highlighted as shown in Fig. 16-22. If the area you want does not close, as shown in the lower-right example in Fig. 16-22, then you get the "Boundary Definition Error" alert box. Pick OK, close the area, and try again.

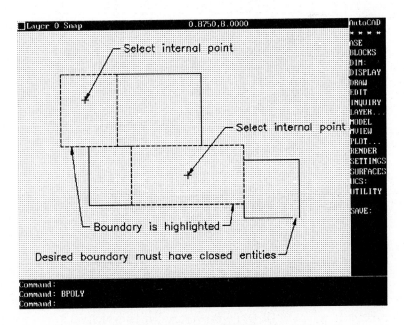

Fig. 16-22. Using the BPOLY command.

CHAPTER TEST

Write your answers in the spaces provided.

1. Give the command and entries required to make a polyline arc. It should have a starting width of 0 and ending width of .25. Draw it from a known center to an endpoint.

   Command: _____

   From point: _____

   Current line width is (status)

   Arc/Close/Halfwidth/Length/Undo/Width/⟨Endpoint of line⟩: _____

   Starting width ⟨current⟩: _____

   Ending width: _____

   Arc/Close/Halfwidth/Length/Undo/Width/⟨Endpoint of line⟩: _____

   Angle/CEnter/CLose/Directions/Halfwidth/Line/Radius/Second pt/Undo/Width/

   ⟨Endpoint of arc⟩:_____

   Angle/Length/⟨Endpoint⟩: _____

2. Give the command and entries required to turn three connected lines into a polyline:

   Command: _____

   Select polyline: _____

   Entity selected is not a polyline

   Do you want to turn it into one? ⟨Y⟩: _____

   Close/Join/Width/Edit vertex/Fit/Spline/Decurve/Ltype gen/Undo/eXit ⟨X⟩: _____

   _____

   Select objects: _____

   Select objects: _____

   2 segments added to polyline

   Close/Join/Width/Edit vertex/Fit/Spline/Decurve/Ltype gen/Undo/eXit ⟨X⟩: _____

   _____

3. Give the command and entries needed to change the width of a polyline from .1 to .25:

   Command: _____

   Select polyline: _____

   Close/Join/Width/Edit vertex/Fit/Spline/Decurve/Ltype gen/Undo/eXit ⟨X⟩: _____

   _____

   Enter new width for all segments: _____

   Close/Join/Width/Edit vertex/Fit/Spline/Decurve/Ltype gen/Undo/eXit ⟨X⟩: _____

   _____

For Questions 4 through 10, give the PEDIT Edit vertex option which relates to the definition given.

4. Moves the screen "X" to the next position. _____

5. Moves a polyline vertex to a new location. _____

6. Breaks a portion out of a polyline. _____

7. Required for AutoCAD to redraw the revised edition of a polyline. _____

8. Specifies tangent direction. _____

9. Adds a new polyline vertex. _____

10. Returns you to the PEDIT menu. _____

11. Which PEDIT option and suboption allows you to change the starting and ending widths of a polyline? _____

12. Why does nothing appear to happen after you change the starting and ending widths of a polyline? _____
_____

13. How do you change the width of a donut? _____

14. Which command will remove all width characteristics and tangency information from a polyline? _____
_____

15. What happens to the screen cursor after you select the PEDIT command? _____
_____

16. What occurs if you select Close for a polyline that is already closed? _____
_____

17. When you select the PEDIT command's Edit vertex option, where is the screen cursor "X" placed by AutoCAD? _____

18. How do you move the screen "X" to edit a different vertex? _____
_____

19. Can you use the PEDIT command's Fit option without using the Tangent option first? _____
_____

20. Explain the difference between a fit curve and spline curve. _____
_____
_____
_____

21. Explain the relationship between the Quadratic curve, Cubic curve, and Fit options.
_____
_____
_____

22. Discuss the construction of a quadratic curve. _____
_____
_____
_____

23. What SPLINETYPE setting allows you to draw a quadratic curve? _____

24. What SPLINETYPE setting allows you to draw a cubic curve? _____

25. Name the system variable that adjusts the smoothness of a spline curve. _____

26. What is the purpose of the PolyVar screen menu option in the PEDIT command?_____
_____
_____

27. Name the pull-down menu where the PolyEdit options are found. _____

28. Explain how you can adjust the way polyline linetypes are generated in the PLINE command.

_____

_____

29. Name the system variable that also allows you to alter the way polyline linetypes are generated.

_____

30. Name the command used to create a polyline boundary. _____

DRAWING PROBLEMS

Start a new drawing for the following problems. Set up your own units, limits, and other variables to suit each problem.

1. Draw the polyline shown below. Use the Line, Arc, and Close options to complete the shape. The polyline width will be 0, except at those points indicated. Save the drawing as A:P16-1.

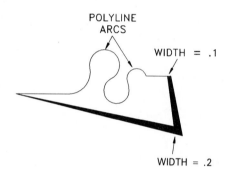

2. Draw the two curved arrows using the PLINE Arc and Width options. The arrowhead should have a starting width of 1.4 and ending width of 0. The arrow body should have a beginning width of .8 and ending width of .4. To draw the clockwise arrow, select the tanDir option of the PLINE Arc menu. Save the drawing as A:P16-2.

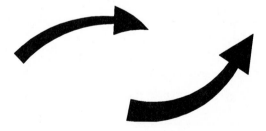

3. The object of this problem is to change the object from Problem 16-1 into a rectangle. You will be using the PEDIT options Decurve, Straighten, Width, Insert, and Move. First, open P16-1, then make a second copy of the object to edit. Save the completed drawing as A:P16-3.

4. Open P16-2 and make the following changes. Combine the two polylines using the Join option. Change the beginning width of the left arrow to 1.0 and the ending width to .2. Draw a polyline .062 wide similar to the one labeled as B. Save the drawing as A:P16-4.

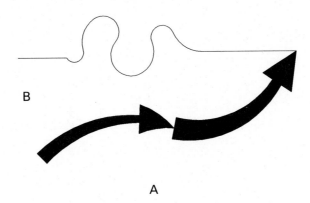

B

A

5. Draw the object shown, without dimensions, using the LINE command. Then change the object to a polyline, making the polyline .032 wide. Save the drawing as A:P16-5.

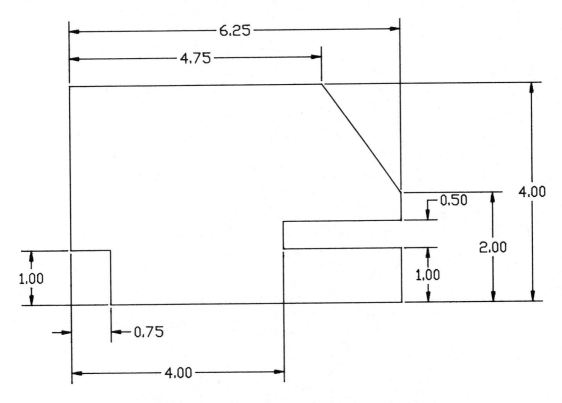

6. Load AutoCAD and open drawing P16-1. Explode the polyline and observe the results. Restore the original polyline using the UNDO command. Save the drawing as A:P16-6 and quit.

7. Draw a polyline .032 wide using the following absolute coordinates: 1, 1; 2, 1; 2,2; 3,2; 3,3; 4,3; 4,4; 5,4; 5,5; 6,5; 6,6; 7,6. Copy the polyline three times. Use the PEDIT Fit option to smooth the first copy. Use the PEDIT Spline option to smooth the second copy. Use the PEDIT Quadratic curve option to smooth the third copy. Use the PEDIT Decurve option to return one polyline to its original form. Save the drawing as A:P16-7.

8. Open drawing P12-7 for further editing. Change all of the object lines to .032 wide polylines. Then add centerlines. Save the revised version as A:P16-8.

9. Draw a patio plan similar to the example shown at A below. Use the DLINE command to draw the house walls 6 in. wide. Copy the A drawing to the positions shown at B, C, D. Your client wants to see at least four different designs. Use the Fit option at B, Spline at C, and change SPLINETYPE to create a cubic curve at D. Save the drawing as A:P16-9.

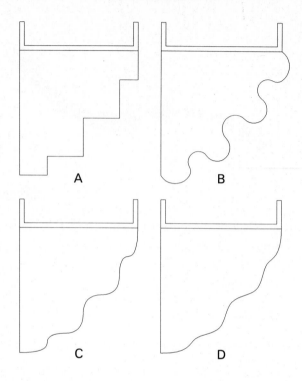

10. Open drawing P16-9 and make some new designs since your client is not satisfied with the first four proposals. This time, use the grips to edit the patio designs similar to the examples shown at A, B, C, and D below. Save the drawing as A:P16-10 and quit.

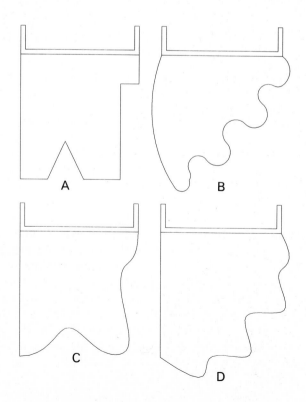

Chapter 17

MULTIVIEW DRAWINGS AND LAYERS

Learning objectives

After completing this chapter, you will be able to:

☐ Draw multiviews from given sketches.
☐ Properly draw object lines, hidden lines, and centerlines.
☐ Use the LINETYPE command to change linetypes.
☐ Change line color using the COLOR command.
☐ Use the LAYER command to draw items on separate layers.
☐ Identify guidelines for selecting the front view.
☐ Draw multiviews and associated auxiliary views from a given sketch.
☐ Use the dialogue box to edit layers.
☐ Use standard borders and title block formats provided by AutoCAD.
☐ Customize the standard title block for your company or school.

Each field of drafting has its own method to present views of a product. Architectural drafting uses floor plans (and other plan views), exterior elevations, and sections. In electronics drafting, symbols are placed in a schematic diagram to show the circuit layout. In civil drafting, contour lines are used to show the topography of the land. This chapter describes views used in mechanical drafting, called *multiviews,* based on ANSI standard Y14.3.

DRAWING MULTIVIEWS

Multiviews are made using orthographic projection. *Orthographic projection* is the projection of object features onto an imaginary plane, called a *projection plane.* The imaginary projection plane is placed parallel to the object. Thus, the line of sight is perpendicular to the object. This results in views that appear two-dimensional, Fig. 17-1.

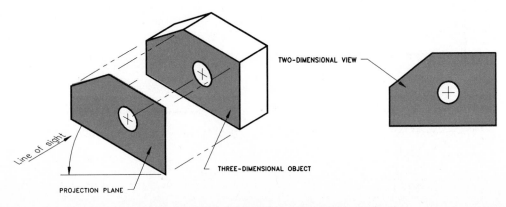

Fig. 17-1. Front view obtained by orthographic projection.

The term *multiview* refers to "many views." Six two-dimensional views completely show all sides of an object. The six views are the front, right side, left side, top, bottom, and rear. The views are placed in a standard arrangement so others can read the drawing. The front view is the central, or most important view. Other views are placed around it, Fig. 17-2.

Views are aligned, rather than scattered about the drawing. It is easy to visualize the shape by looking from one view to the next. Chapters 18 and 19 cover how this layout helps you read dimensions.

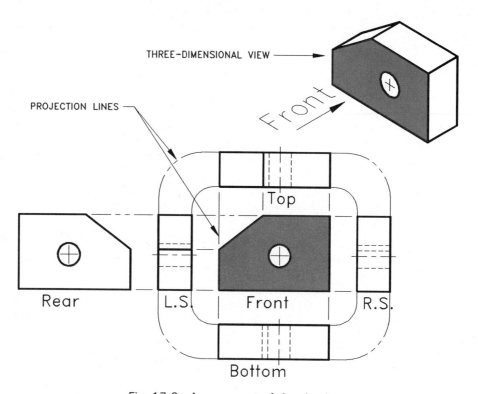

Fig. 17-2. Arrangement of the six views.

Six views are not always necessary. Actually, there are few products that require all six views. The number of views needed depends on the complexity of the object. Use only enough views to completely describe the object. Drawing too many views is time-consuming, and can clutter the drawing. In some cases, a single view may be enough to describe the object. The object shown in Fig. 17-3 needs only two views. These two views completely describe the width, height, depth, and features of the object, Fig. 17-3.

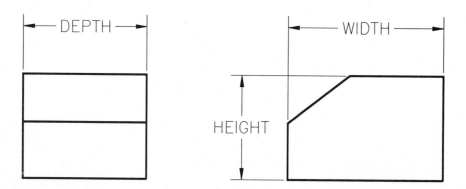

Fig. 17-3. The views you choose to describe the object should show all height, width, and depth dimensions.

Selecting the front view

The front view is usually the most important view. The following guidelines should be considered when selecting the front view:

- Look for the best shape or most contours.
- Show the most natural position of use.
- Display the most stable position.
- Provide the longest dimension.
- Contain the least hidden features.

Look at Fig. 17-4 and review the above guidelines. Do you agree with the front view chosen?

Additional views are selected relative to the front view. Choose only the number of views needed to completely describe the object's features.

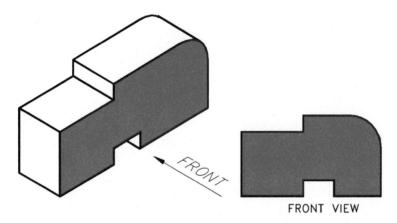

FRONT VIEW

Fig. 17-4. Selecting the front view.

Showing hidden features in multiview drawings

Hidden features are those parts of the object not visible in the view you see. A visible edge appears as a solid line when the view is drawn. A hidden edge is shown by a hidden line. Hidden lines were discussed in Chapter 6. Notice in Fig. 17-5 how hidden features are shown as hidden lines.

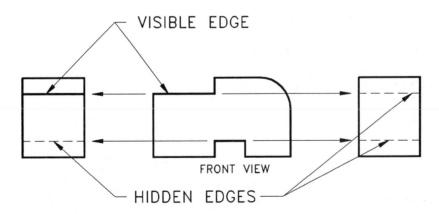

VISIBLE EDGE

FRONT VIEW

HIDDEN EDGES

Fig. 17-5. Drawing hidden features.

One-view drawings

In some instances, an object can be fully described using one view. A thin part, such as a gasket, is drawn with one view, Fig. 17-6. The thickness is given as a note in the drawing or in the title block. A cylindrical object also may be drawn with one view. The diameter dimension is given to tell that the object is round.

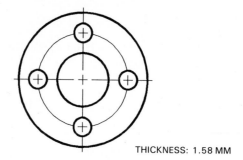

THICKNESS: 1.58 MM

Fig. 17-6. One-view drawing of a gasket.

Showing symmetry and circle centers

The centerlines of symmetrical objects and the centers of circles are shown using centerlines. For example, in one view of a cylinder, the axis is drawn as a centerline. In the other view, centerlines cross to show the center in the circular view. See Fig. 17-7. The only place that the small centerline dashes should cross is at the center of a circle.

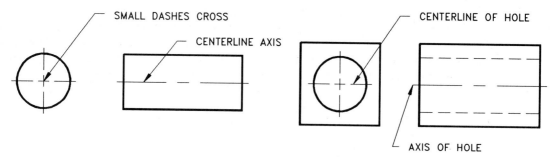

Fig. 17-7. Drawing centerlines. Left. Cylinder. Right. Round hole.

DRAWING AUXILIARY VIEWS

In most cases, an object is completely described using a combination of one or more of the six standard views. However, sometimes the multiview layout is not enough to properly identify some object surfaces. It may then be necessary to draw auxiliary views.

Auxiliary views are typically needed when a surface on the object is at an angle to the line of sight. These slanted surfaces are *foreshortened,* meaning they are shorter than the true size and shape of the surface. To show this surface in true size, an auxiliary view is needed. The reason that auxiliary views are needed is that dimensions should be placed in views showing a feature's true size and shape. Foreshortened dimensions are not recommended.

Auxiliary views are drawn by projecting perpendicular (90°) to a slanted surface. Usually, one projection line remains on the drawing. It connects the auxiliary view to the view where the slanted surface appears as a line. The resulting auxiliary view shows the surface in true size and shape. For most applications, the auxiliary view need only show the slanted surface, not the entire object. This is called a partial auxiliary view and is shown in Fig. 17-8.

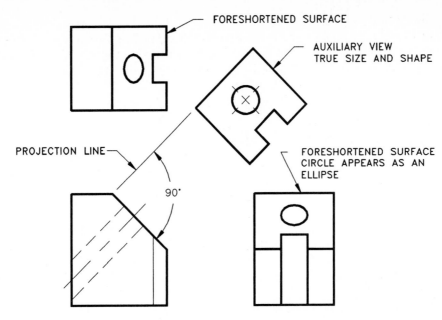

Fig. 17-8. Auxiliary views show the true size and shape of an inclined surface.

In many situations, there may not be enough room on the drawing to project directly from the slanted surface. Then, the auxiliary view is placed elsewhere, Fig. 17-9. A viewing-plane line is drawn next to the view where the slanted surface appears as a line. The viewing-plane line is capped on the ends with arrowheads. The arrowheads point toward the slanted surface. Each end is labeled with a letter such as A. The letters relate the viewing-plane line with the proper auxiliary view. A title such as "VIEW A-A" is placed under the auxiliary view. When more than one auxiliary view is drawn, labels continue with B-B through Z-Z (if necessary). The letters I, O, and Q are not used because they may be confused with numbers. An auxiliary view drawn away from the multiview retains the same angle as if it were projected directly.

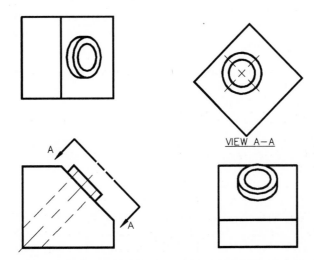

Fig. 17-9. Identifying an auxiliary view with a viewing-plane line.

Changing the snap grid rotation angle

Changing the rotation angle of your snap grid, discussed in Chapter 4, is especially useful for drawing auxiliary views. After the views have been drawn, enter the SNAP command. Then pick the base point for rotation on the line which represents the slanted surface. Then enter the snap rotation angle equal to the angle of the slanted surface. If you do not know the angle, pick points on the slanted surface to graphically show the angle. The steps are as follows:

> Command: **SNAP** ↵
> Snap spacing or ON/OFF/Aspect/Rotate/Style ⟨current⟩: **R** ↵
> Base point ⟨0,0⟩: *(pick an endpoint on the line which represents the slanted surface)*
> Rotation angle ⟨0⟩: *(enter the angle of the slanted surface or pick two points on the surface)*
> Command:

Once you have placed and rotated the snap grid, you may want to place grid points on the snap grid. Select the GRID command's Snap option. Then complete the auxiliary view as shown in Fig. 17-10A.

When you finish drawing the auxiliary view, return the snap grid rotation value to 0°.

Using the User Coordinate System for auxiliary views

All of the features on your drawing originate from the *World Coordinate System (WCS)*, which is the X, Y, and Z coordinate values measured from the origin 0,0,0. The WCS is fixed. The *User Coordinate System (UCS)*, on the other hand, can be moved to any desired orientation. The UCS is discussed in detail in Chapter 24. In general, UCS allows you to set your own coordinate origin. The WCS 0,0,0 origin has been in the lower-left corner of the screen for the drawings you have done so far. In many cases this is fine, but when drawing an auxiliary view it is best to have the measurements originate from a corner of the view. This in turn makes all auxiliary view features and the coordinate display true as measured from the corner of the view. This method makes it easier to locate and later dimension the auxiliary view features as compared with the rotated snap grid previously discussed.

First, draw the principal views such as the front, top, and right side. Then, move the UCS origin to a location that coincides with a corner of the auxiliary view using this command sequence:

> Command: **UCS** ↵
> Origin/ZAxis/3point/Entity/View/X/Y/Z/Prev/Restore/Save/Del/?/⟨World⟩: **O** ↵
> Origin point ⟨0,0,0⟩: *(pick the origin point at the desired corner of the auxiliary view as shown in Fig. 17-10B)*

Next, realign the UCS grid with the angle of the auxiliary view by adjusting the Z axis to the same angle. For example, if the auxiliary view is projected at 45° from the slanted surface in the front view, then rotate the Z axis as follows:

> Command: **UCS** ↵
> Origin/ZAxis/3point/Entity/View/X/Y/Z/Prev/Restore/Save/Del/?/⟨World⟩: **Z** ↵
> Rotation angle about Z axis ⟨0⟩: **45** ↵

If you want the UCS icon displayed at the current UCS origin, use the UCSICON command as follows:

> Command: **UCSICON** ↵
> ON/OFF/ALL/Noorigin/ORigin/ ⟨ON⟩: **OR** ↵

This automatically moves the UCS icon to the revised UCS origin at the corner of the auxiliary view as shown in Fig. 17-10C. Although this is not required, it is convenient to see the location of the UCS origin. Before you begin drawing the auxiliary view, use the UCS command's Save option to name the new UCS and save it:

> Command: **UCS** ↵
> Origin/ZAxis/3point/Entity/View/X/Y/Z/Prev/Restore/Save/Del/?/⟨World⟩: **S** ↵
> ?/Desired UCS name: **AUX** ↵

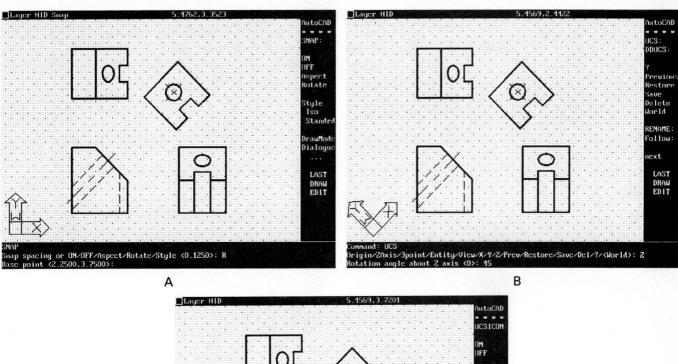

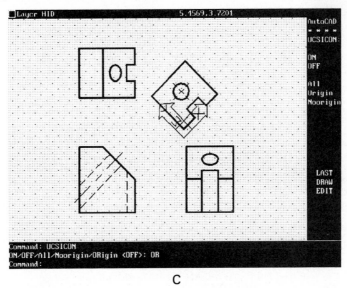

Fig. 17-10. A—Using the rotated snap grid and grid points to help draw the auxiliary view. B—Relocating the origin and rotating the Z axis of the UCS system. Notice how the position of the UCS icon has been aligned with the auxiliary view angle. C—Moving the UCS icon display to the current UCS origin at the corner of the auxiliary view.

Now, proceed by drawing the auxiliary view as shown in Fig. 17-10. When you have finished drawing the auxiliary view, use the UCS command's Previous option to move the UCS icon to its previous position:

Command: **UCS** ↵
Origin/ZAxis/3point/Entity/View/X/Y/Z/Prev/Restore/Save/Del/?/〈World〉: **P** ↵

You could also press ENTER to accept the World default and send the UCS icon display back to the WCS origin:

Command: **UCS** ↵
Origin/ZAxis/3point/Entity/View/X/Y/Z/Prev/Restore/Save/Del/?/〈World〉: ↵

── PROFESSIONAL TIP ──────

Use the orthogonal mode (ORTHO command) to help align the projected auxiliary view with the slanted surface. Also consider using the object snap modes to assist you in connecting projection lines to the exact corners or features on the slanted surface.

USING THE LINETYPE COMMAND   `ARM 8`

The lines that you have drawn so far have been solid. AutoCAD calls these lines "continuous." Continuous lines may be drawn thin using the LINE, ARC, and CIRCLE commands, or drawn thick with the TRACE or PLINE commands. Any entity is drawn with continuous lines unless you change the linetype. The LINETYPE command is found in the SETTINGS screen menu. When you enter "LINETYPE," a group of options appears. One option is a question mark (?). Typing "?" accesses the "Select Linetype File" dialogue box. ACAD should be the file name. Press ENTER for the list of AutoCAD's (ACAD) standard library of lines shown in Fig. 17-11.

    Command: **LINETYPE** ↵
    ?/Create/Load/Set: **?** ↵

NAME — SAMPLE

NAME	SAMPLE	NAME	SAMPLE
Border		Divide	
Border2		Divide2	
BorderX2		DivideX2	
Center		Dot	
Center2		Dot2	
CenterX2		DotX2	
Dashdot		Hidden	
Dashdot2		Hidden2	
DashdotX2		HiddenX2	
Dashed		Phantom	
Dashed2		Phantom2	
DashedX2		PhantomX2	

Fig. 17-11. AutoCAD's standard linetype library.

If the FILEDIA system variable is off (0), the following prompt is displayed:

    File to list ⟨ACAD⟩: ↵

If a custom linetype library such as MAPLINES has been designed, you may specify it by typing "MAPLINES" in the File: edit box, or pick it from the Files: list. The only linetypes available for your use at this point is the ACAD library. After listing the linetypes, AutoCAD returns the "?/Create/Load/Set:" prompt. Press F1 to return to the graphics screen.

Setting the linetype
When drawing views of an object, you may need to draw hidden lines and centerlines. Select the linetype using the LINETYPE command's Set option. Type "S" at the prompt. You are then asked to name the linetype:

    Command: **LINETYPE** ↵
    ?/Create/Load/Set: **S** ↵
    New entity linetype (or ?) ⟨BYLAYER⟩: **HIDDEN** ↵
    ?/Create/Load/Set:

The ?/Create/Load/Set: prompt returns; press ENTER to get the Command: prompt. Now, any lines you add are drawn with the new linetype. You must again use the Set option to draw continuous lines or set another linetype.

Loading custom linetypes

Many companies have custom linetypes. For example, cartographers may need special styles of lines to draw maps. These linetypes are usually stored in library files other than the ACAD library. To use one of these linetypes, enter "L" for the Load option and type a question mark (?) to obtain a list of linetypes. Follow these steps:

    Command: **LINETYPE** ↵
    ?/Create/Load/Set: **L** ↵
    Linetype(s) to load: **?** ↵

If FILEDIA is set to on (1), the "Select Linetype File" dialogue box is displayed. Pick MAPLINES from the Files: list, or type it in the File: edit box. If the FILEDIA variable is 0, the following prompt appears:

    Linetype(s) to load: **?** ↵
    File to search ⟨ACAD⟩: ↵

Now, suppose you want to use the PROPERTY linetype found in the MAPLINES linetype library. Enter "PROPERTY" as the name of the linetype to load and "MAPLINES" as the file to search.

If you try to load a linetype that is already loaded, such as the standard AutoCAD HIDDEN linetype, you get this message:

    Linetype HIDDEN is already loaded. Reload it? ⟨Y⟩ ↵

Press ENTER to reload the linetype, or type "N" and press ENTER if you decide not to reload it.

Creating linetypes

To create custom linetypes or modify AutoCAD standard linetypes, use the Create option.

    Command: **LINETYPE** ↵
    ?/Create/Load/Set: **C** ↵

After selecting "C," AutoCAD requests the name of the linetype to create. It also must know the file for storing the linetype. Select a linetype name which represents the line's features. For example, suppose you are designing a line having long lines which alternate between three short dashes. This linetype might be for drawing property boundaries in mapping. Call the line D3D. You can store the linetype in the ACAD default file by pressing ENTER as follows:

    Name of linetype to create: **D3D** ↵
    File for storage of linetype ⟨acad⟩: ↵ *(this prompt appears if FILEDIA is set to 0)*
    Wait, checking if linetype already defined . . .

AutoCAD first checks to see if the linetype already exists. Then you are asked for "Descriptive text." As the name implies, *descriptive text* describes the new linetype. The text should be in the format *LINETYPE-NAME [,DESCRIPTION]. The D3D linetype being created here might be described as follows:

    Descriptive text: ***D3D [,LONG AND 3 SHORT DASHES]** ↵

The Enter pattern: prompt then appears. Describe the line based on the following code:

    CODE
    A, = alignment. This instructs AutoCAD to balance out the line ends with equal beginning length segments. The "A," always begins the set of pattern code.
    – numeral = length of a space.
    + numeral = length of a dash.
    0 = dot.

Suppose the D3D linetype is designed to be drawn as:

LINE SEGMENT	LENGTH	CODE
Long dash	= 1.5 units	= 1.5
Space	= .062 units	= −.062
Short dash	= .125 units	= .125
Space	= .062 units	= −.062
Short dash	= .125 units	= .125
Space	= .062 units	= −.062
Short dash	= .125 units	= .125
Space	= .062 units	= −.062

The linetype pattern is given as follows:

Enter pattern (on text line):
A,1.5,−.062,.125,−.062,.125,−.062,.125,−.062 ↵

AutoCAD then responds with:

New definition written to file.
?/Create/Load/Set: **S** ↵

You can begin using the new linetype by responding "S" to the previous prompt. When asked for name the new linetype, enter "D3D." The new linetype, D3D is set to draw as shown in Fig. 17-12.

Fig. 17-12. The new D3D linetype.

SETTING LINETYPE USING THE PULL-DOWN MENU

The Entity Modes... selection in the Settings pull-down menu accesses the "Entity Creation Modes" dialogue box shown in Fig. 17-13. Pick the Linetype... button and the "Select Linetype"

Fig. 17-13. The "Entity Creation Modes" dialogue box.

dialogue box shown in Fig. 17-14 appears. The AutoCAD linetypes that have been loaded are displayed here. Pick the Next button if you want to see more linetypes, or pick Previous to return to the first page (if these options are available). If you want to load the DASHED linetype, pick it from the list and then pick the OK button. See Fig. 17-14.

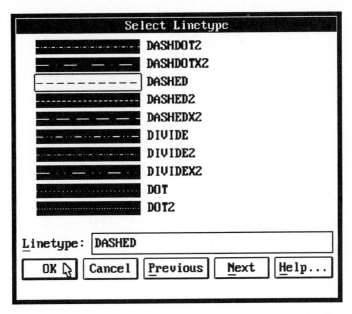

Fig. 17-14. The "Select Linetype" dialogue box displays linetypes that have been loaded.

CHANGING THE LINETYPE SCALE ARM 8

The linetype scale sets the length of dashes in linetypes having them. The default linetype scale factor is one. Any line with dashes initially assumes this factor. Fig. 17-15 shows the effects of changing the scale factor for a centerline.

You can change the scale factor to 1.5 as follows:

Command: **LTSCALE** ↵
New scale factor ⟨current⟩: **1.5** ↵

A "regenerating drawing" message appears as the linetype scale is changed for all lines on the drawing.

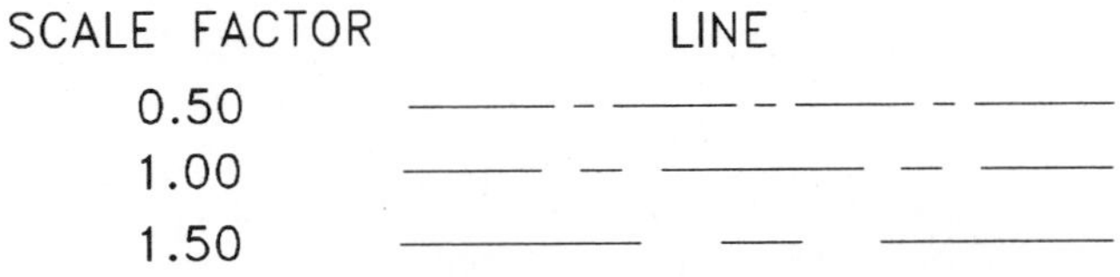

SCALE FACTOR   LINE

0.50

1.00

1.50

Fig. 17-15. A comparison of linetype scale factors.

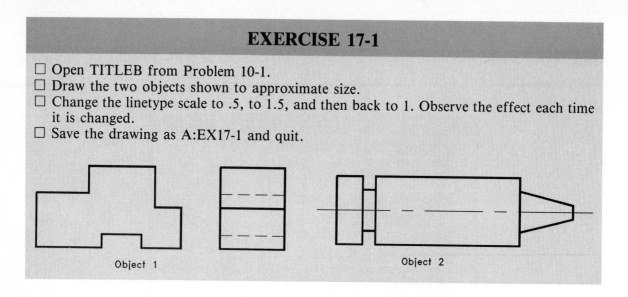

EXERCISE 17-1

☐ Open TITLEB from Problem 10-1.
☐ Draw the two objects shown to approximate size.
☐ Change the linetype scale to .5, to 1.5, and then back to 1. Observe the effect each time it is changed.
☐ Save the drawing as A:EX17-1 and quit.

Object 1

Object 2

PROFESSIONAL TIP

Changing the linetype scale affects all of the lines on the drawing. There is no standard way to change the scale of specific lines. Reset the linetype scale to obtain lines that come close to or meet your standards.

LAYERS | ARM 7 |

In manual drafting, details of a design might be separated by placing them on different sheets of media. This is called *overlay* or *pin register* drafting. Each overlay is perfectly aligned with the others. All of the layers may be reproduced together to reflect the entire design. Individual layers might also be reproduced to show specific details.

Drawing on different overlays, or *layers* as they are called with CAD, has certain benefits:
* Specific information may be grouped on separate layers. For example, the floor plan could be drawn on one layer, the electrical plan on another, and the plumbing plan on a third layer.
* Drawings may be reproduced by individual layers or combined in any desired format. For example, the floor and electrical plan are reproduced together and sent to an electrical contractor for a bid. The floor and plumbing plan are reproduced together and sent to the plumbing contractor.
* Several drafters may work on a project at the same time for a marked increase in productivity.
* Each layer may be assigned a different color to help improve clarity.
* Each layer may be plotted in a different color or pen width.
* Selected layers may be turned off, or "frozen," to decrease the clutter of information displayed on the screen, and to speed up drawing regeneration.

AutoCAD allows drafters to turn on or off any individual layer and assign colors or linetypes to layers. Changes can be made to a layer promptly, often while the client watches. These capabilities increase productivity.

Layers used in different drafting fields

In mechanical drafting, views, hidden features, dimensions, sections, notes, and symbols might be placed on separate layers. In architectural drafting, there could be over a hundred layers. These could have plans for floor, foundation, partition layout, plumbing, electrical, structural, roof drainage, reflected ceiling, heating, ventilating, and air conditioning systems. Interior designers may have floor plan, interior partition, and furniture layers. In electronics drafting, each level of a multilevel circuit board is drawn on a separate layer.

Layer colors

The number of layer colors available depends on your graphics card and monitor. A monochrome monitor displays only one color, usually white, amber, or green. Color systems usually support 8 or 16 colors. Some graphics cards offer more. Layer colors are coded by name and number. The first seven standard color numbers are as follows:

Number	Color
1	Red
2	Yellow
3	Green
4	Cyan
5	Blue
6	Magenta
7	White

Assigning colors to layers is described later in the chapter.

Setting linetype by layer

AutoCAD allows you to select a linetype for individual entities. You can also assign linetypes to layers. Any item added to a layer assumes the linetype assigned to that layer.

You may have noticed that "Layer 0" has been shown in the upper-left corner of the AutoCAD screen. Layer 0 is the AutoCAD default layer. It has a continuous linetype and white color. You can assign linetype and color to other layers as discussed later in this chapter. However, to have entities take on the layer linetype, follow this procedure:

Command: **LINETYPE** ↵
?/Create/Load/Set: **S** ↵
New entity linetype (or ?) ⟨current⟩: **BYLAYER** ↵
?/Create/Load/Set: ↵
Command:

Naming layers

Layers may be given names to reflect what is drawn on them. Layer names may have up to 31 characters and include letters, numbers, and special characters. Typical mechanical, architectural, and civil drafting layer names may be as follows:

Mechanical	Architectural	Civil
VIEWS	WALLS	PROPERTYLN
DIMENSIONS	WINDOWS	STRUCTURES
NOTES	DOORS	ROADS
HIDDEN	ELECT	WATER
SECTION	PLUMB	CONTOURS

For simple drawings, layers may be named by linetype and color. For example, the layer name OBJECT-WHITE would have white continuous lines. The linetype and layer color number, such as OBJECT-7, may also be used. Another option is to assign the linetype a numerical value. For example, object lines could be 0, hidden lines 1, and centerlines 2. If you use this method, keep a written record of the numbering system for reference.

Lastly, layers may be given more complex names. The name might include the drawing number, color code, and layer content. The name DWG100-2-DIMEN refers to drawing DWG100, color 2, and DIMENSIONS layer.

INTRODUCTION TO THE LAYER COMMAND

When a layer is *current*, it is the layer that is "currently" being used. The LAYER command is used to select a variety of options dealing with layer use. When you type "LAYER" at the Command: prompt, the response is as follows:

Command: **LAYER** ↵
?/Make/Set/New/ON/OFF/Color/Ltype/Freeze/Thaw/LOck/Unlock:

A list of LAYER command options and a brief description of each is given in Fig. 17-16.

?	Typing a "?" prompts: Layer name(s) for listing ⟨*⟩: Type a specific layer name(s) or press ENTER to get a list of all available layers. (The default means to list all layers.) The list might appear as: Layer name State Color Linetype ––––––––––––––––– ––––––– ––––––– –––––––––– 0 On 7 (white) CONTINUOUS Current layer: 0
Make	Used to create a new layer and make it current.
Set	This option sets a new current layer if the named layer exists.
New	This option creates new layers without affecting the status of the current layer.
ON	Layers turned ON are displayed and plotted.
OFF	Layers turned OFF are not displayed and are not plotted.
Color	Changes the color of specific layers, asking you for the color number or name.
Ltype	Used to change the linetype of a specific layer or layers.
Freeze	Freeze is similar to OFF in that frozen layers are invisible and are not plotted. The difference is that frozen layers are not calculated by the computer when the drawing is regenerated. Freeze layers not in use to save regeneration time on complex drawings.
Thaw	Makes frozen layers visible again.
LOck	Lock layers that you do not want edited. However, they are visible.
Unlock	Unlock locked layers. These layers are then available for drawing and editing purposes.

Fig. 17-16. LAYER command options and descriptions.

USING THE LAYER COMMAND

Most prototype drawings have layers based on linetypes. Write down the specifications for each layer color and linetype. Use one of the systems described earlier. The linetype number followed by a color number is noted as follows:

Layer Name	Linetype	Color
0-7	CONTINUOUS	WHITE
1-1	HIDDEN	RED
2-2	CENTER	YELLOW
3-3	DIMENSION	GREEN

For a complete discussion on the professional use of layers in architectural applications, refer to *Architectural AutoCAD,* published by Goodheart-Willcox.

Making new layers

The LAYER command's MAKE option is used to create a new layer, and at the same time, make the new layer current. For example, if you want to establish a new layer named JUDY and make it current, enter the following:

Command: **LAYER** ↵
?/Make/Set/New/ON/OFF/Color/Ltype/Freeze/Thaw/LOck/Unlock: **M** ↵
New current layer ⟨0⟩: **JUDY** ↵
?/Make/Set/New/ON/OFF/Color/Ltype/Freeze/Thaw/LOck/Unlock: ↵

This procedure works fine if you want to create a new layer and make it current at the same time. However, new layers are usually created prior to beginning drawing, and then made current using the Set option. To create a new layer, follow this command sequence:

Command: **LAYER** ↵
?/Make/Set/New/ON/OFF/Color/Ltype/Freeze/Thaw/LOck/Unlock: **N** ↵
New layer name(s): **ELECTRICAL** ↵
?/Make/Set/New/ON/OFF/Color/Ltype/Freeze/Thaw/LOck/Unlock: ↵

The new layer named ELECTRICAL is created and ready to use when you need it. Notice the New layer name(s): prompt is either singular or plural. This means you can enter one or more layer names at the same time. Separate each name by a comma if you are specifying more than one layer. For example:

New layer name(s): **ELECTRICAL,PLUMBING,WALLS** ↵

Setting the current layer

Layers must be created using the Make or New options before they can be set. However, once layers have been created, they can be set at any time. Layer 0 is the current layer which is set in the AutoCAD prototype drawing. If you want to make the ELECTRICAL layer (which you created earlier) current, follow this command sequence:

Command: **LAYER** ↵
?/Make/Set/New/ON/OFF/Color/Ltype/Freeze/Thaw/LOck/Unlock: **S** ↵
New current layer ⟨0⟩: **ELECTRICAL** ↵
?/Make/Set/New/ON/OFF/Color/Ltype/Freeze/Thaw/LOck/Unlock: ↵

Layer color and linetype

You can set a new layer's color and linetype, or change the color and linetype of an existing layer at any time. Use the Color and Ltype options as follows:

Command: **LAYER** ⏎
?/Make/Set/New/ON/OFF/Color/Ltype/Freeze/Thaw/LOck/Unlock: **C** ⏎
Color: **BLUE** or **5** ⏎
Layer name(s) for color 5 (blue) ⟨0⟩: **ELECTRICAL** ⏎
?/Make/Set/New/ON/OFF/Color/Ltype/Freeze/Thaw/LOck/Unlock: **L** ⏎
Linetype (or ?) ⟨CONTINUOUS⟩: **PHANTOM** ⏎
Layer name(s) for linetype PHANTOM ⟨0⟩: **ELECTRICAL** ⏎
?/Make/Set/New/ON/OFF/Color/Ltype/Freeze/Thaw/LOck/Unlock: ⏎

Putting it all together

Now, proceed by establishing the new layers 1, 2, and 3 with colors red, yellow, and green, respectively. Assign these layers the linetypes hidden, center, and continuous, respectively. Remember, you can name layers individually or enter several layer names separated by commas like this:

Command: **LAYER** ⏎
?/Make/Set/New/ON/OFF/Color/Ltype/Freeze/Thaw/LOck/Unlock: **N** ⏎
New layers name(s): **1,2,3** ⏎
?/Make/Set/New/ON/OFF/Color/Ltype/Freeze/Thaw/LOck/Unlock: **C** ⏎
Color: **1** ⏎
Layer name(s) for color 1 (red) ⟨0⟩: **1** ⏎
?/Make/Set/New/ON/OFF/Color/Ltype/Freeze/Thaw/LOck/Unlock: **C** ⏎
Color: **2** ⏎
Layer name(s) for color 2 (yellow) ⟨0⟩: **2** ⏎
?/Make/Set/New/ON/OFF/Color/Ltype/Freeze/Thaw/LOck/Unlock: **C** ⏎
Color: **3** ⏎
Layer name(s) for color 3 (green) ⟨0⟩: **3** ⏎
?/Make/Set/New/ON/OFF/Color/Ltype/Freeze/Thaw/LOck/Unlock: **L** ⏎
Linetype (or ?) ⟨CONTINUOUS⟩: **HIDDEN** ⏎
Layer name(s) for linetype HIDDEN ⟨0⟩: **1** ⏎
?/Make/Set/New/ON/OFF/Color/Ltype/Freeze/Thaw/LOck/Unlock: **L** ⏎
Linetype (or ?) ⟨CONTINUOUS⟩: **CENTER** ⏎
Layer name(s) for linetype CENTER ⟨0⟩: **2** ⏎

Layer 3 contains dimensions. Dimension lines are solid lines so it is not necessary to assign a linetype. New layers are automatically given the default linetype, continuous. After entering layer values, type "?" to request a revised layer listing:

?/Make/Set/New/ON/OFF/Color/Ltype/Freeze/Thaw/LOck/Unlock: **?** ⏎
Layer name(s) for listing⟨*⟩: ⏎

Layer name	State	Color	Linetype
0	On	7 (white)	CONTINUOUS
1	On	1 (red)	HIDDEN
2	On	2 (yellow)	CENTER
3	On	3 (green)	CONTINUOUS
ELECTRICAL	On	5 (blue)	PHANTOM
JUDY	On	7 (white)	CONTINUOUS

Current layer: 0
?/Make/Set/New/ON/OFF/Color/Ltype/Freeze/Thaw/LOck/Unlock: ⏎
Command:

Now, items added to layer 0 have white object lines. Items added to layer 1 have red hidden lines. Objects added to layer 2 have yellow centerlines. Dimensions added to layer 3 have solid green lines.

Once new layers and parameters are established, you can begin making the drawing. These steps outline the sequence for completing a mechanical drawing:
- Make a sketch and prepare a plan sheet.
- Draw all object lines.
- Use the LAYER command's Set option to select a new current layer on which to draw. At this point, select layer 1 which has the hidden linetype.
- Draw all hidden lines.
- Reset the current layer to layer 2, which has centerlines.
- Draw all center lines.
- Use the LAYER command's Set option once again to select layer 3.
- Add dimensions. (Dimensioning is discussed in Chapters 18 and 19.)
- Set the current layer as necessary when editing the drawing.

Keep records listing how you set up drawing prototypes. If your notes are not handy, list the layers, colors, and linetypes by typing "?".

EXERCISE 17-2

☐ Load AutoCAD and open PRODR1.
☐ Set up six layers, each having a different color and linetype as follows:

Layer name	Linetype	Color
0-7	Continuous	White
1-1	Hidden	Red
2-2	Center	Yellow
3-3	Continuous	Green
4-4	Phantom	Cyan
5-5	Dot	Blue

☐ Save as A:PRODR2, thus establishing a new prototype with the specified layers.
☐ Draw the objects shown below. Place objects on the layer that has their linetype. The dimension layer will not be used at this time.
☐ Save the drawing as A:EX17-2 and quit.

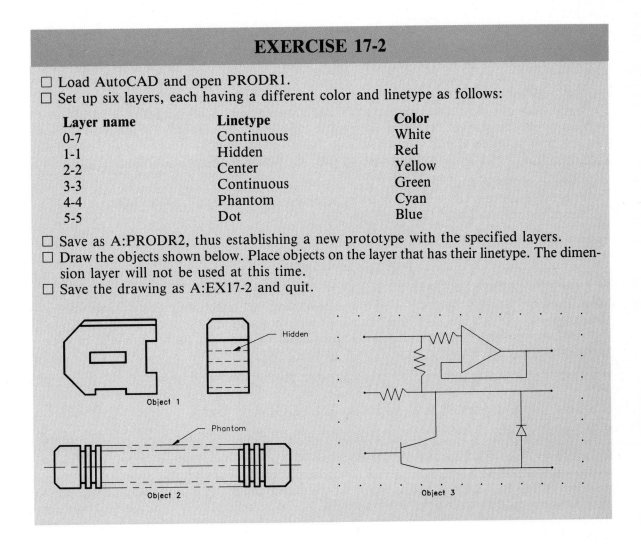

Object 1

Object 2

Object 3

Hidden

Phantom

Turning layers ON and OFF

Layers that are turned on may be displayed and plotted, but layers that are turned off may not be displayed or plotted. Even though a layer is turned off, it is still regenerated with the rest of the drawing. To turn off a layer, follow this procedure:

Command: **LAYER** ↵
?/Make/Set/New/ON/OFF/Color/Ltype/Freeze/Thaw/LOck/Unlock: **OFF** ↵
Layer name(s) to turn Off: **ELECTRICAL** ↵

This message then appears:

> Really want layer ELECTRICAL (the CURRENT layer) off? 〈N〉 ⏎

Press ENTER if you do not want the current layer turned off, or enter "Y" and press ENTER if you do want it turned off. Do not try to draw with the current layer off. Either turn it on or set another layer current. Simply use the ON option to turn layers back on.

Freezing and thawing layers

A frozen layer is similar to a layer that has been turned off, except that frozen layers are not calculated by the computer when a regeneration occurs, thus saving time. Freeze layers like this:

> Command: **LAYER** ⏎
> ?/Make/Set/New/ON/OFF/Color/Ltype/Freeze/Thaw/LOck/Unlock: **F** ⏎
> Layer name(s) to Freeze: **ELECTRICAL** ⏎

If you try to freeze the current layer, AutoCAD responds with this message:

> Cannot freeze layer ELECTRICAL. It is the CURRENT layer.

If you really want to freeze the ELECTRICAL layer, first make another layer current, and then freeze the ELECTRICAL layer. Use the Thaw option to unfreeze a frozen layer.

Locking and unlocking layers

Unlocked layers are available for you to use for drawing and editing purposes. Locked layers are visible, but they cannot be edited. Current layers can even be locked. For example, lock a layer (or several layers) if you want to be sure that no one tampers with the entities drawn on it. Lock a layer as follows. Note the use of the two-character response—LO.

> Command: **LAYER** ⏎
> ?/Make/Set/New/ON/OFF/Color/Ltype/Freeze/Thaw/LOck/Unlock: **LO** ⏎
> Layer name(s) to Lock: **ELECTRICAL** ⏎

───── PROFESSIONAL TIP ─────

Layers are meant to simplify the drafting process. They separate different details of the drawing and reduce the complexity of a displayed drawing. If you set color and linetype by layer, do not reset and mix entity linetypes and color on the same layer. Doing so can mislead you and your colleagues when trying to find certain details. Maintain accurate records of your prototype setup for future reference.

USING THE LAYER CONTROL DIALOGUE BOX   ARM 8

The LAYER command and all of its options may be used by accessing the "Layer Control" dialogue box. Type "DDLMODES" at the Command: prompt, pick Layer Control... from the Settings pull-down menu, or pick LAYER... from the Root Menu to display the dialogue box. Only layers that have been previously created are displayed. Many of the dialogue box items are grayed out until you move the arrow and pick one of the listed layers. You can pick as many layers as you want. When individual layers are picked, they become highlighted and are displayed in the edit box as shown in Fig. 17-17.

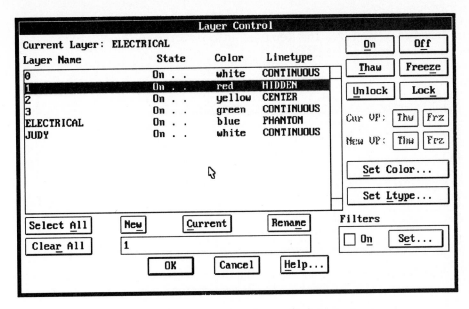

Fig. 17-17. The ''Layer Control'' dialogue box.

The Layer list

The current layer is displayed in the upper-left corner, followed by the Layer list box. Here you see the existing layer names, state, color, and linetype. (*State* means the layer status such as on, off, frozen, or locked.)

The Select and Clear buttons

Below the layer list is the Select All button, Fig. 17-18. Pick this button if you want to select all of the layers in the list. Pick the Clear All button if you want to clear the list and remove the highlighting on all items picked. You can clear individual selections by repicking highlighted layers.

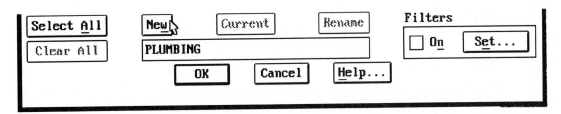

Fig. 17-18. All layers can be selected or unselected using the Select All or Clear All buttons.

The New, Current, and Rename buttons

To add a new layer to the list, first pick the edit box to activate the text cursor. Then type the new layer name, and pick the New button. The new layer name, in this case PLUMBING, is added to the list, with the color white and linetype continuous.

To make another layer current, pick a layer from the Layer list to highlight it, and then pick the Current button. You can also use the CLAYER system variable to make a layer current. Type "CLAYER" at the Command: prompt, then type the name of the existing layer you want to make current.

When you pick a layer from the Layer list, its name is displayed in the edit box. Change the layer name in the edit box and pick the Rename button. Notice in Fig. 17-19 that the PLUMB-ING layer is being renamed as PLUMB.

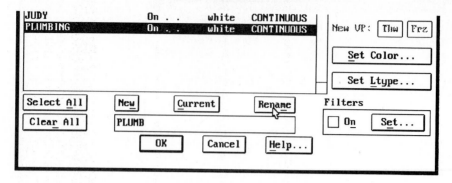

Fig. 17-19. To rename a layer, highlight the name in the Layer list box, change the name in the edit box, and then pick the Rename button.

Setting color and linetype

Note the Set Color... and Set Linetype... buttons to the right of the Layer list box. You can change the color of a selected layer by picking the Set Color... button, which displays the "Select Color" dialogue box. In this case, the new PLUMB layer color is changed to magenta.

In order for a linetype to be changed, the desired linetype must first be loaded. Pick the Set Linetype... button to access the "Select Linetype" dialogue box. Pick the DASHED line from the line list to change the PLUMB layer linetype to dashed. Notice that Fig. 17-20 displays the PLUMB layer with its color magenta and linetype dashed. Be sure to pick OK when you have completed making changes.

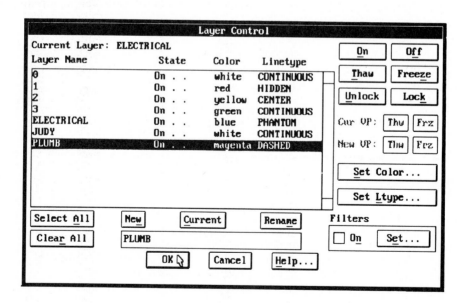

Fig. 17-20. Layer color and linetype can be changed in the "Layer Control" dialogue box.

Using the On, Off, Thaw, Freeze, Lock, and Unlock buttons

The State column in the layer list provides the status of each layer. The first column in this list is for On/Off. The second column indicates Freeze/Thaw, and the third column is for Lock/Unlock. Off, Thaw, and Unlock are shown as a period (·). Pick and highlight the desired layer in order to change the layer status. Then pick the appropriate button—On, Off, Thaw, Freeze, Lock, or Unlock—as needed. Fig. 17-21 shows the layers with their current style adjusted as desired. Remember, the current layer cannot be frozen.

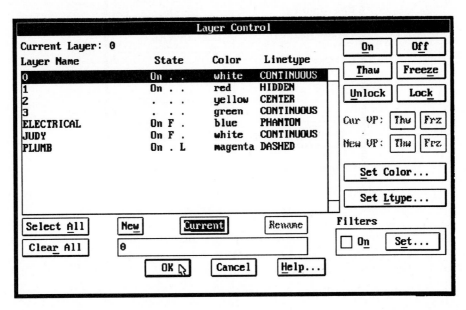

Fig. 17-21. When you highlight a layer in the Layer list box, the state of the layer can be changed.

Filtering layers

Layer filters are used to screen or "filter out" any layers that have features which you do not want displayed in the "Layer Control" dialogue box. These filters may include layer features such as name, color, or linetype. Filters may also involve the status of layers such as frozen, thawed, on, off, locked, or unlocked.

The Filters box has an On check box and a Set... button. The filters let you display only the layers you want in the Layers list box. For example, assume you are working on an electrical drawing, and want layers 0, 1, 3, and ELECTRICAL displayed. You can freeze the other layers and filter only the thawed layers. Layers can be filtered by any desired variable such as name, state, color, or linetype. To do this, pick the Set... button to get the "Set Layer Filters" dialogue box. Filter layer name, color, or linetype by entering the desired item in the related edit box. If you want to display only the ELECTRICAL layer, then filter it by listing its name as shown in Fig. 17-22. You can use the wild card (*) to list a group of similar layers if desired. For example, if you want to filter all of the WALL layers, enter "W*". This filters every layer name that

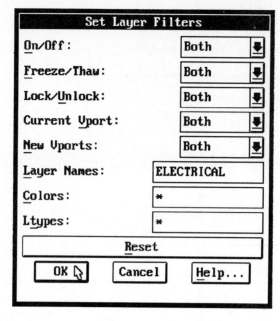

Fig. 17-22. Layers can be filtered by any desired variable using the "Set Layer Filters" dialogue box.

starts with "W". Pick one of the popup arrows in the upper right to filter either On/Off, Freeze/Thaw, Lock/Unlock, Current Viewports, or New Viewports. For example, filter all of the thawed layers by setting Thawed as shown in Fig. 17-23A. Notice in Fig. 17-23B that only the thawed layers are listed, and the filters On check box is checked. The On button is automatically checked when you pick the OK button in the "Set Layer Filters" dialogue box. However, you can turn filters on or off at any time by picking this check box.

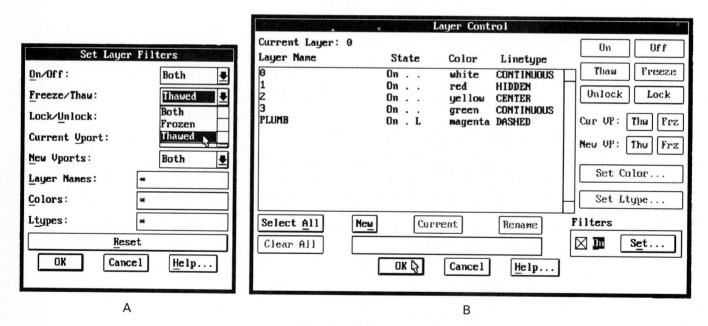

Fig. 17-23. A—Layer filters being set. B—The result of filtering layers.

CONTROLLING LAYERS IN VIEWPORTS

The preceding discussion explained that the LAYER command's Freeze/Thaw and On/Off options set the visibility of layers in all viewports (known as *global control*). For example, if you freeze a layer globally, it is invisible in all viewports. If you want to set the visibility or invisibility of layers in one viewport or a specific set of viewports, use the VPLAYER command. This flexibility allows you to create a specific layer that is visible in a designated viewport. Refer to Chapters 9 and 27 for complete discussions of viewports and Chapter 27 for the VPLAYER command.

USING ENTITY CREATION MODES

You can see the properties of current layers, or set the color, linetype, text style, or layer using the "Entity Creation Modes" dialogue box. It is accessed by picking Entity Modes... from the Settings pull-down menu, or entered by typing "DDEMODES" at the Command: prompt. Drawing entity color may be changed at any time. However, the layers must first be created and linetypes must be loaded. The changes made may not be displayed until you enter the next command. A typical "Entity Creation Modes" dialogue box is shown in Fig. 17-24. Notice that the color is currently set as BYLAYER, which is a common practice. Select a new color by picking the Color... button to access the "Select Color" dialogue box. Pick the Layer... button to make changes to the layer through the "Layer Control" dialogue box.

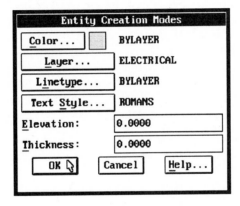

Fig. 17-24. The "Entity Creation Modes" dialogue box is used to view properties of current layers.

The Text Style... button accesses the "Select Text Style" dialogue box shown in Fig. 17-25. This is a convenient way to quickly change the text style. Simply pick one of the available styles in the list box, or type the name of a loaded text style in the Style Name: edit box. When you pick a new style, the image tile changes, displaying a sample of the selected style. You can change the sample by entering your desired text in the Sample Text: edit box. Pick the Show All... button to display the "Text Style Symbol Set" dialogue box, which shows all of the current text fonts. The current Height, Width, Obliquing angle, and Generation format are specified from your reference. The elevation and thickness items in this dialogue box refer to 3-D values (discussed in Chapter 24).

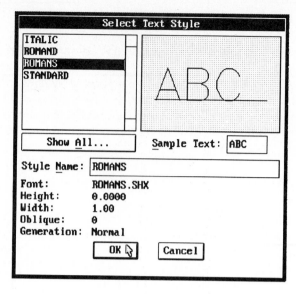

Fig. 17-25. The "Select Text Style" dialogue box is a convenient way to view and change the text style.

CHANGING LAYERS

In Chapters 6, 11, and 12, you were introduced to the CHANGE, CHPROP, and DDCHPROP commands. These commands are convenient for editing a drawing or changing a variety of properties. The CHPROP and DDCHPROP commands are the most convenient for changing layer, linetype, or color since they directly access the property options. For example, the CHPROP command's LA option moves an object or objects from one layer to another. This option only works if the intended layer has been created. When you enter "LA" and press ENTER, AutoCAD asks for the new layer. Suppose the current layer, shown in brackets, is FLPLAN. If the object should be on the ELECTRIC layer, proceed as follows:

Command: **CHPROP** ↵
Select objects: *(pick or window the object to be changed)*
Select objects: ↵
Change what property (Color/LAyer/LType/Thickness)? **LA** ↵
New layer ⟨FLPLAN⟩: **ELECTRIC** ↵
Change what property (Color/LAyer/LType/Thickness)? ↵

RENAMING LAYERS

Using the DDRENAME command, you can rename many items, including layer, linetype, and text style. This command accesses the "Rename" dialogue box shown in Fig. 17-26. Pick any of the named objects, such as Layer, to get a list of items related to the object. Notice the items in Fig. 17-26 are the layers that were previously created. To change the name of a layer, pick that layer from the Items list. Picking ELECTRICAL, for example, places it in the Old Name: edit box. Next, type the new name in the Rename To: edit box, followed by picking the Rename To: button. Finally, pick the OK button to exit the dialogue box.

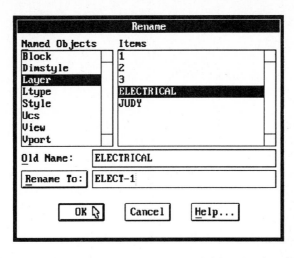

Fig. 17-26. The "Rename" dialogue box is used to rename named objects such as layers, viewports, and views.

EXERCISE 17-3

☐ Load AutoCAD, open EX17-2, and erase the drawing shown on screen.
☐ Change the layers as follows:

Layer Name	Linetype	Color
VIEW	Continuous	White
HIDDEN	Hidden	Red
CENTER	Center	Blue
CONST	Continuous	Green

☐ Omit layers 4-4 and 5-5.
☐ Save the drawing as A:EX17-3.
☐ Given the pictorial drawing and three incomplete orthographic views of the object below, draw the three orthographic views without dimensions. Add any object, hidden, or centerlines needed to complete the views. Place object lines on the VIEW layer, hidden lines on the HIDDEN layer, and centerlines on the CENTER layer. Draw construction lines on the CONST layer to help project features from one view to another. Freeze the CONST layer when you are finished.
☐ Save the drawing again as A:EX17-3 and quit the drawing session.

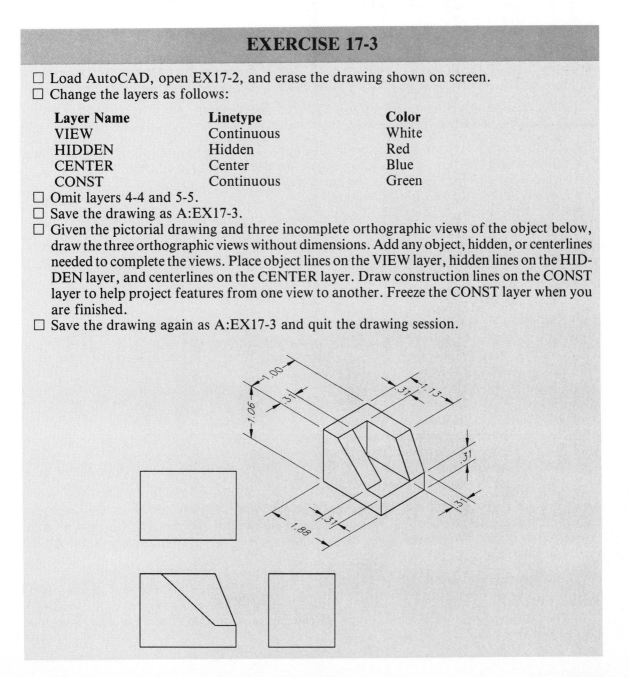

SETTING UP YOUR SHEET FOR MULTIVIEW LAYOUT

$\boxed{\textbf{AEM 2}}$

AutoCAD provides you with the MVSETUP command that allows you to insert one of several different predrawn standard border and title block formats based on ANSI, ISO, architectural, or generic layouts. The border and title block can be set up before plotting where they can be scaled, and then plotted at FULL (1:1) scale. Refer to Chapter 27 for information regarding the use of paper space viewports, and scaling a viewport.

MVSETUP is an AutoLISP routine that can be customized to insert any type of border and title block. (AutoLISP is covered in Chapter 34.) To use MVSETUP, first open a drawing that you want to display. Then, set the TILEMODE system variable to 0 to allow you to enter paper space. The following command sequence is used to change the TILEMODE variable:

Command: **TILEMODE** ↵
New value for TILEMODE ⟨1⟩: **0** ↵

Notice the paper space UCS icon is displayed and your drawing has disappeared. Next, use the MVSETUP command. You can pick MV Setup after picking Layout in the View pull-down menu, or type "MVSETUP" as follows:

Command: **MVSETUP** ↵

After the first use of MVSETUP, you can enter "MVS" as the command name. The Title block option is discussed first because it lets you establish a drawing border and title block:

Align/Create/Scale viewports/Options/Title block/Undo: **T** ↵
Delete objects/Origin/Undo/⟨Insert title block⟩: ↵

The default allows you to insert a title block. The options are detailed in the following summary:
- **Delete objects**—Allows you to select objects to delete from paper space.
- **Origin**—Permits you to relocate the sheet origin.
- **Undo**—Undoes the previous operation.
- **Insert title block**—Pressing ENTER to accept the default displays the following:
    Available title block options:
    0:      None
    1:      ISO A4 Size(mm)
    2:      ISO A3 Size(mm)
    3:      ISO A2 Size(mm)
    4:      ISO A1 Size(mm)
    5:      ISO A0 Size(mm)
    6:      ANSI-V Size(in) *(this is the vertical A-size format)*
    7:      ANSI-A Size(in)
    8:      ANSI-B Size(in)
    9:      ANSI-C Size(in)
    10:     ANSI-D Size(in)
    11:     ANSI-E Size(in)
    12:     Arch/Engineering (24 x 36in)
    13:     Generic D-size Sheet (24 x 36in)
    Add/Delete/Redisplay/⟨Number of entry to load⟩: *(type in the desired sheet size format, such as 7, and press ENTER)*

Next, you get a message that asks if you want to create a drawing with the sheet size specifications you selected. This prompt is shown only if a file named ANSI-A.DWG is not in your AutoCAD directory. For example, the previous choice was number 7, which is the ANSI-A Size (in). The following prompt is displayed:

Create a drawing named ansi-a.dwg? ⟨Y⟩: ↵

Pressing ENTER at this prompt creates a drawing file with the name shown. ANSI-A.DWG is now available to be used as a prototype for the future. AutoCAD automatically draws the border and title block shown in Fig. 17-27.

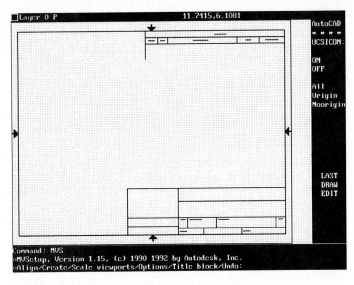

Fig. 17-27. The ANSI-A (in) border and title block arrangement with the MVSETUP command.

Now, the Create option is used to establish the viewports:

Align/Create/Scale viewports/Options/Title block/Undo: **C** ↵

Press ENTER at the following prompt to obtain a list of the viewport layout options:

Delete objects/Undo/⟨Create viewports⟩: ↵
Available Mview viewport layout options:
0:     None
1:     Single
2:     Std. Engineering
3:     Array of Viewports
Redisplay/⟨Number of entry to load⟩: **1** ↵

A single viewport works best for this application.
   The next prompt asks you to identify the boundary for the viewport by picking the opposite corners (similar to forming a window).

Bounding area for viewports. Default⟨First point⟩: *(pick a point)*
Other point: *(move the cursor and pick the second point)*

Look at Fig. 17-28. The drawing is displayed inside the viewport.

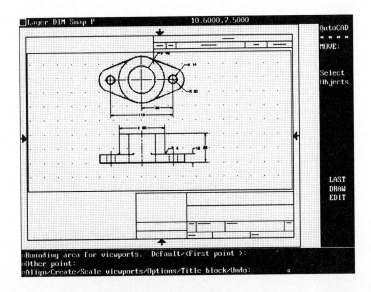

Fig. 17-28. Opening a viewport.

The Scale option is used next to scale the drawing by using a ratio of paper space to model space units. For example, 1:2 is one paper space unit for two model space units, or a one-half scale, as shown in Fig. 17-29. The defaults, used in the following example, are FULL scale, or 1:1. The drawing may not change much in size depending on the size of the viewport as demonstrated by the results in Fig. 17-28. Note the following prompts:

Align/Create/Scale viewports/Options/Title block/Undo: **S** ⏎
Select the viewports to scale:
Select objects: *(pick the viewport outline, not the drawing)*
Select objects: ⏎
Enter the ratio of paper space units to model space units...
Number of paper space units. ⟨1.0⟩: ⏎
Number of model space units. ⟨1.0⟩: ⏎
Align/Create/Scale viewports/Options/Title block/Undo: ⏎

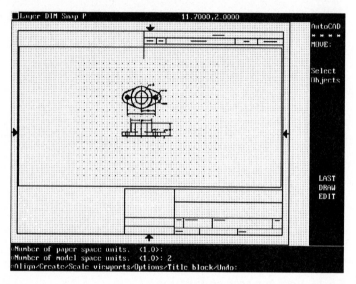

Fig. 17-29. Viewports are scaled at 1:2 with the MVSETUP command's Scale viewport option.

The viewport is an entity that may be altered in paper space using the MOVE or STRETCH commands, or with grips as needed. Part of your drawing may extend past the edge of the viewport after using the Scale option. Simply use the STRETCH command to compensate for the miscalculation. The MOVE command is used to position the drawing shown in Fig. 17-28. Note the results in Fig. 17-30A. You can also use grips to scale the viewport so the viewport borders do not overlap the title block and sheet border. To do this, pick the viewport, activate a hot grip, and press ENTER to access the SCALE command. Then enter a new scale factor like this:

** SCALE **
⟨Scale factor⟩/Base point/Copy/Undo/Reference/eXit: **.8** ⏎

The results are shown in Fig. 17-30B.

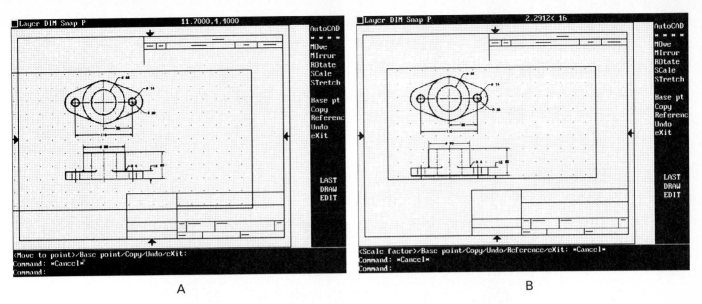

Fig. 17-30. Moving and stretching a viewport can be accomplished using grips.

Creating your own title block format

In the previous discussion, you saw how making a selection from the list of "Available title block options:" and responding with a "Y" (or pressing ENTER) to the following prompt created a drawing file with the name shown:

Create a drawing named ansi-a.dwg? 〈Y〉: ⏎

The ANSI-A.DWG is now available to be edited and customized for your own applications. Fig. 17-31A shows the ANSI-A title block and resulting customization. Fig. 17-31B shows the entire new border and title block. Now that the title block is customized for your school or company, you can rename the ANSI-A.DWG to any name you wish, such as MECH-A. When you begin a new drawing, use MECH-A as the prototype and provide a new drawing name, such as PART001, as shown in Fig. 17-32. The MECH-A format is loaded and ready for you to create the PART001 drawing, or use the MECH-A format and insert a drawing that was previously drawn. Using the MVSETUP command in this manner is very valuable because it can be used to create several prototypes for different sheet size and title block formats, and then not used again except for special needs, or used often to customize the list of drawings as explained in the next section.

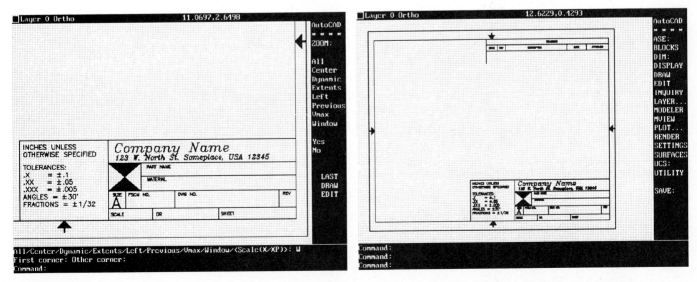

A—CUSTOMIZED TITLE BLOCK

B—CUSTOMIZED TITLE BLOCK AND BORDER

Fig. 17-31. Customizing the ANSI-A title block.

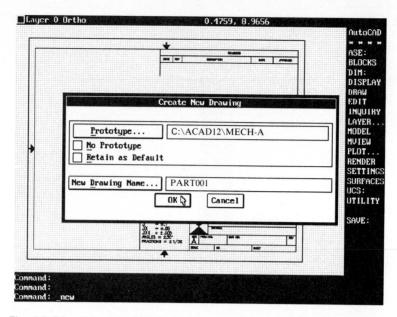

Fig. 17-32. Using the MECH-A prototype for the PART001 drawing.

Adding title blocks to the MVSETUP list

Following the list of "Available title block options" is the Add/Delete/Redisplay/⟨Number of entry to load⟩: prompt. The Add option allows you to customize the list of prototype drawings by letting you name the drawing type, size, and insert a specific drawing. The following sequence gives you an idea of how this works:

> Add/Delete/Redisplay/⟨Number of entry to load⟩: **A** ↵
> Title block description: **MECH (11 X 8.5 IN)** ↵
> Drawing to insert (without extension): **SAMPLE** ↵
> Specify default usable area? ⟨Y⟩: **N** ↵

The screen goes blank for a second and AutoCAD adds the new border and title block design to the list. A new "Available title block options:" list is displayed with your custom format listed as one of the options:

> 14. MECH (11 X 8.5 IN)
> Add/Delete/Redisplay/⟨number of entry to load⟩: *(enter a desired sheet format, such as **14**, and press ENTER)*

If you only press ENTER to this prompt, the following is displayed:

> Specify default usable area? ⟨Y⟩: ↵

Pressing only ENTER accepts the Yes default. AutoCAD then asks you to either pick diagonal corners, or you can enter the lower-left and upper-right corner block coordinates. However, the "N" response described earlier is more convenient and works well in most situations.

Additional MVSETUP options

The following descriptions outline the purpose of the MVSETUP options that were not previously discussed:

- **Align** — This option is used to align views in multiple viewports. You get these prompts when you use the Align option:

> Angled/Horizontal/Vertical alignment/Rotate view/Undo:

  - **Angled** — Used to pan a drawing in a viewport at a desired angle. The following prompts are displayed:

Base point: *(pick a point as an origin)*
Other point: *(pick a point in the viewport to be panned)*
Distance from base point: *(enter a distance and press ENTER, or pick two points to establish a distance from the base point)*
Angle from base point: *(enter an angular value and press ENTER, or pick two points representing an angle where the second point is to be positioned from the base point)*

- **Horizontal** — This option allows you to align views in horizontal viewports:

  Base point: *(pick a point as an origin)*
  Other point: *(pick a point in the viewport to be aligned)*

- **Vertical alignment** — This option allows you to align entities in vertical viewports in a manner similar to the Horizontal option.
- **Rotate view** — You can rotate a drawing in a viewport around a selected base point:

  Specify in which viewport the view is to be rotated.
  Base point: *(pick a point as the pivot point for the rotation)*
  Angle from base point: *(enter an angle and press ENTER, or pick two points representing the angle)*

- **Options** — This option lets you establish several different functions that are associated with your layout. The prompt issued with Options is:

  Set Layer/LImits/Units/Xref:

The following explanation describes these options:
- **Set Layer** — Allows you to specify an existing layer or create a new layer for your border and title block. It is a good idea to put your border and title block on a separate layer, perhaps BORDER. This gives you the flexibility to freeze, thaw, or otherwise manipulate the layer as needed. Enter "L" for layer to get this prompt:

  Layer name for title block or . for current layer: **BORDER** ↵

- **Limits** — This suboption instructs AutoCAD to reset the drawing limits so it is equal to the extents when the border is inserted. The prompt has a No default:

  Set drawing limits? ⟨N⟩: ↵

- **Units** — Allows you to specify if drawing information is to be presented in inch or millimeter values. Inch (in) units are the default. You can also enter "F" for feet, "ME" for meters, or "M" for millimeters:

  Paper space units are in Feet/Inches/MEters/Millimeters? ⟨in⟩:

- **Xref** — This option determines if the border and title block is to be inserted in the drawing or referenced to a master drawing. A referenced drawing is not added to the current drawing file, but is displayed (also referred to as *attached*). This helps to keep the file smaller. Referencing drawings is discussed in detail in Chapters 21 and 27. The default is Insert, or you can type "A" and press ENTER for Attach as follows:

  Xref Attach or Insert title block? ⟨Insert⟩: ↵

EXERCISE 17-4

☐ Use the MVSETUP command to insert the drawing from Exercise 17-3 (EX17-3) into a standard ANSI-A border and title block format.
☐ Adjust the scale and orientation as needed.
☐ Save the drawing as A:EX17-4 and quit the drawing session.

CHAPTER TEST

Write your answers in the spaces provided.

1. Give the command and entries required to display AutoCAD's standard linetypes:

   Command: _____

   ?/Create/Load/Set: _____

   File to list ⟨ACAD⟩: _____

   ?/Create/Load/Set: _____

2. Supply the command and entries needed to make CENTER the new linetype:

   Command: _____

   ?/Create/Load/Set: _____

   New entity linetype (or ?) ⟨current⟩: _____

   ?/Create/Load/Set: _____

3. Provide the command and entries that change the linetype scale to .5:

   Command: _____

   New scale factor ⟨1⟩: _____

4. Give the command and entries to create three layers named HIDDEN, CENTER, and DIMENSION. The names and associated linetypes and colors are given in the chart below.

Layer Name	Linetype	Color
HIDDEN	HIDDEN	RED
CENTER	CENTER	YELLOW
DIMENSION	CONTINUOUS	GREEN

   Command: _____

   ?/Make/Set/New/ON/OFF/Color/Ltype/Freeze/Thaw/LOck/Unlock: _____

   New layer name(s): _____

   ?/Make/Set/New/ON/OFF/Color/Ltype/Freeze/Thaw/LOck/Unlock: _____

   Color: _____

   Layer name(s) for color red ⟨0⟩: _____

   ?/Make/Set/New/ON/OFF/Color/Ltype/Freeze/Thaw/LOck/Unlock: _____

   Color: _____

   Layer name(s) for color yellow ⟨0⟩: _____

   ?/Make/Set/New/ON/OFF/Color/Ltype/Freeze/Thaw/LOck/Unlock: _____

   Color: _____

   Layer name(s) for color green ⟨0⟩: _____

   ?/Make/Set/New/ON/OFF/Color/Ltype/Freeze/Thaw/LOck/Unlock: _____

   Linetype (or ?) ⟨CONTINUOUS⟩: _____

   Layer name(s) for linetype HIDDEN ⟨0⟩: _____

   ?/Make/Set/New/ON/OFF/Color/Ltype/Freeze/Thaw/LOck/Unlock: _____

   Linetype (or ?) ⟨CONTINUOUS⟩: _____

   Layer name(s) for linetype CENTER ⟨0⟩: _____

?/Make/Set/New/ON/OFF/Color/Ltype/Freeze/Thaw/LOck/Unlock: _____

5. Supply the command and entries that change the color from yellow to magenta. Assume that you are working on a single layer.

   Command: _____

   New entity color ⟨yellow⟩: _____

6. Identify five guidelines to consider when selecting the front view:

   _____

   _____

   _____

   _____

   _____

7. Suppose the axis of a hole is perpendicular to a slanted surface. The auxiliary view shows the hole as _____.

8. The default linetype of the LINE command is _____.

9. Name at least ten of AutoCAD's standard linetypes.

   _____   _____

   _____   _____

   _____   _____

   _____   _____

   _____   _____

10. In the chart provided, list the seven standard color names and their number.

Color Name	Color Number

11. When you enter the LAYER command and select the "?" option, the prompt "Layer name(s) for listing ⟨*⟩:" appears. What does the asterisk ⟨*⟩ in default brackets mean? _____

   _____

12. Describe the LAYER command's Make option. _____

   _____

   _____

13. Describe the LAYER command's Set option. _____

   _____

14. Describe the LAYER command's New option. _____

_____

_____

15. How are the new layer names entered when creating several layers at the same time? ___

_____

16. Which pull-down menu contains the Layer Control... option? _____

17. Name the command that is typed to access the "Layer Control" dialogue box. _____

18. What condition must exist before a linetype can be chosen from the "Layer Control" dialogue

    box? _____

_____

19. How do you make another layer current in the "Layer Control" dialogue box? _____

_____

20. How do you change a layer's linetype in the "Layer Control" dialogue box? _____

_____

21. When is the "Select Color" dialogue box displayed? _____

_____

22. How do you load several linetypes at the same time? _____

_____

23. When is a linetype displayed in the "Select Linetype" dialogue box? _____

_____

24. What is the state of a layer that is not displayed on the screen and is not calculated by the

    computer when the drawing is regenerated? _____

25. Describe the purpose of locking a layer. _____

_____

_____

26. Are locked layers visible? _____

27. What should you do if you want to freeze a layer, but you get this message: "Cannot freeze

    layer PROD002. It is the CURRENT layer"? _____

_____

28. How do you select all of the layers in the "Layer Control" dialogue box list at the same time?

_____

29. When looking at the "State" column in the "Layer Control" dialogue box, how do you know

    if a layer is either Off, Thawed, or Unlocked? _____

30. Describe the purpose of layer filters. _____

_____

31. Identify two ways to access the "Entity Creation Modes" dialogue box. _____

_____

32. List at least four items that can be set using the "Entity Creation Modes" dialogue box.

_____

33. Name two commands that allow you to directly access property options for changing layer, linetype, or color. _____

34. Name the command that lets you rename layers, linetypes, and text styles. _____

35. The command that allows you to insert one of several different predrawn standard border and title block formats is _____.

36. Name the system variable that must be off (0) in order to enter paper space. _____

37. Explain the "Insert title block" default obtained after entering the Title block option in the MVS command. _____

_____

38. What happens when you press ENTER at this prompt:
Create a drawing named ansi-a.dwg?⟨Y⟩: _____

_____

39. Describe the purpose of the MVS command's Create option. _____

_____

40. How is a drawing displayed when you set the MVS command's Scale option to 1 paper space unit and 2 model space units? _____

41. What should you do if the drawing is initially displayed too far to the upper right of the sheet format when inserted in the viewport using the MVS command? _____

_____   _____

_____

42. Describe how you can customize a standard title block available in the MVS command and save it as a prototype called MECH-A. _____

_____

_____

43. How do you begin a new drawing named WALLEYE using the prototype described in question 42? _____

_____

_____

44. How do you add the custom title block name ARCH-C to the Available title block options list?

_____

_____

45. Describe the function and importance of the Set Layer suboption in the MVS command's Options selection. _____

_____

_____

DRAWING PROBLEMS

1. Draw the views necessary to describe the object completely. Draw on one layer and use the LINETYPE command to change linetypes. Do not dimension. Save your drawing as A:P17-1.

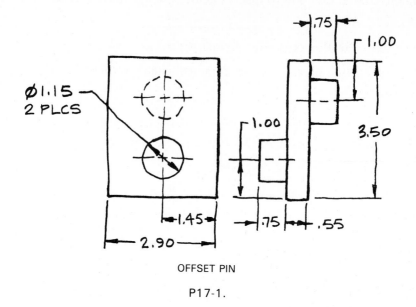

OFFSET PIN

P17-1.

2. Draw the views necessary to describe the object completely. Draw on one layer and use the LINETYPE command to change linetypes and the COLOR command to change colors. Draw object lines white, hidden lines red, and centerlines yellow. Do not dimension. Save as A:P17-2.

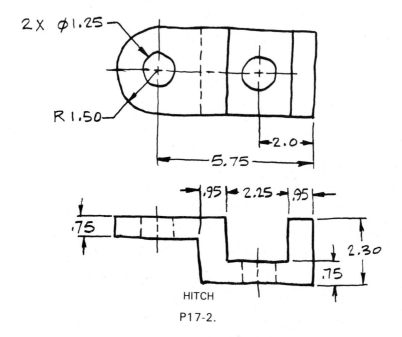

HITCH

P17-2.

3-15. Draw the views necessary to describe each object completely. Place object lines on the white layer, hidden lines on the red layer, and centerlines on the yellow layer. Do not dimension. Save each drawing on your floppy disk.

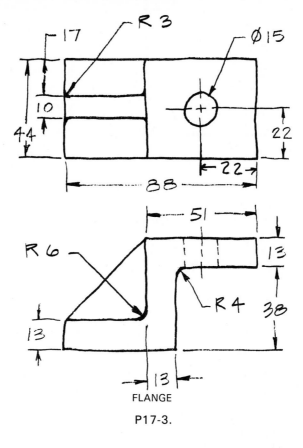

FLANGE

P17-3.

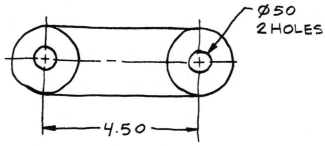

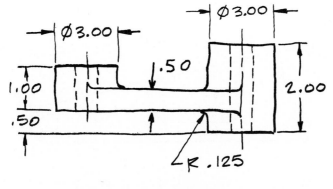

CONNECTOR

P17-4.

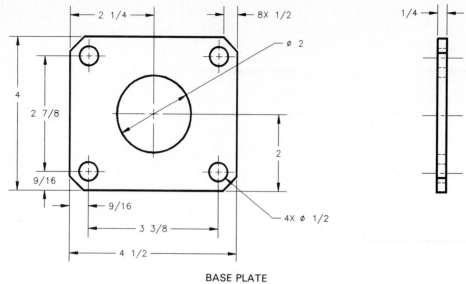

BASE PLATE

P17-5.

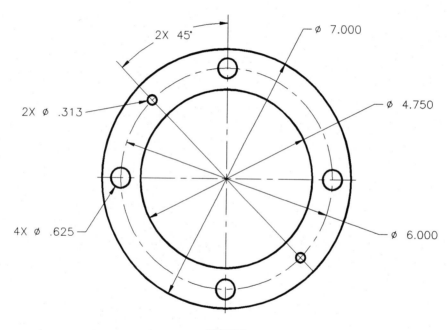

FLANGE

P17-6.

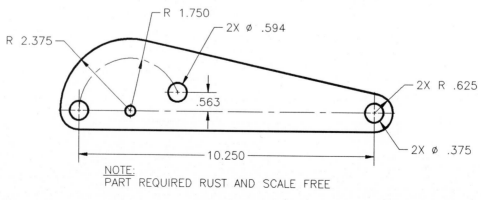

NOTE:
PART REQUIRED RUST AND SCALE FREE

TRACTION ARM

P17-7.

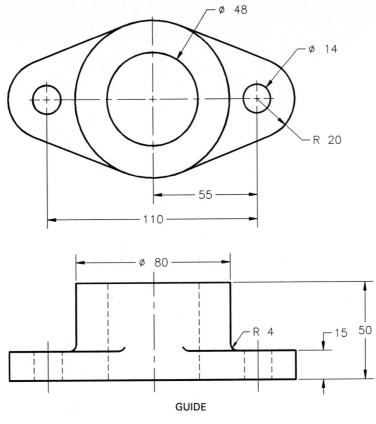

GUIDE

P17-8.

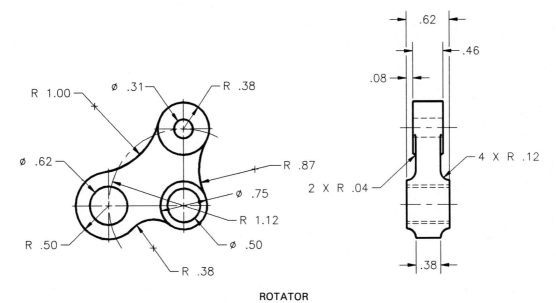

ROTATOR

P17-9.

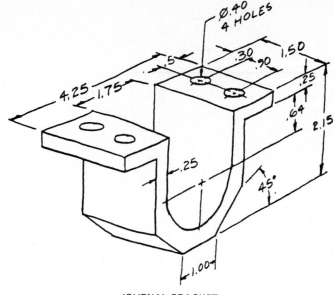

JOURNAL BRACKET

P17-10.

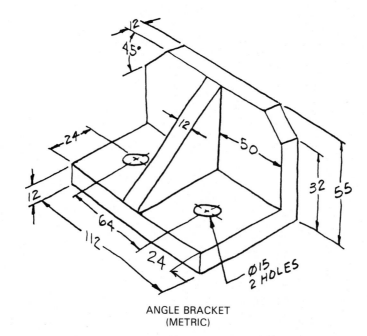

ANGLE BRACKET
(METRIC)

P17-11.

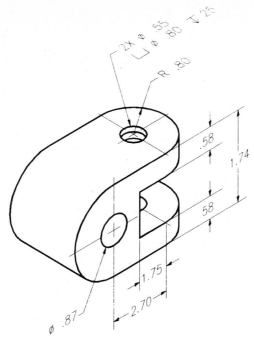

PIVOT BRACKET

P17-12.

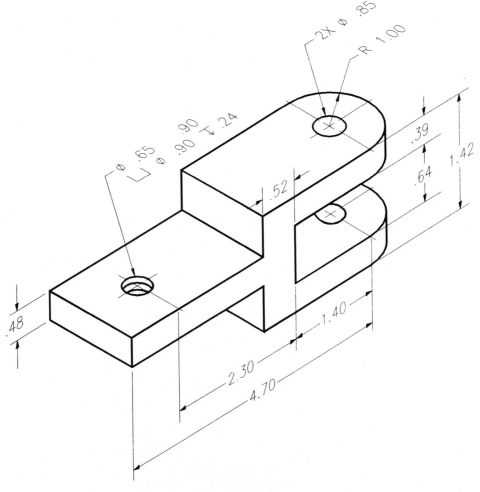

CLEVIS

P17-13.

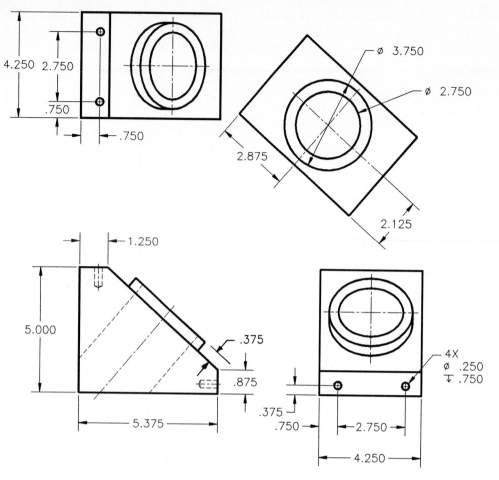

P17-14.

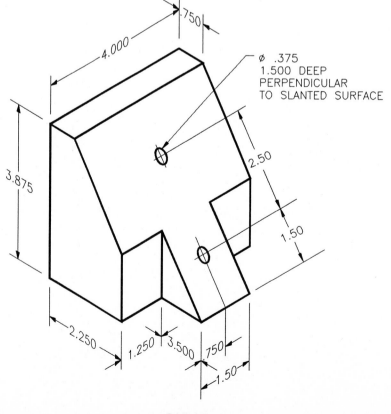

P17-15.

16. Use the MVSETUP command to customize the ANSI-A, ANSI-B, and ANSI-C title blocks for your company or school. An example is provided in Fig. 17-31, or refer to the border and title block arrangements of local industries. Be sure to include the following elements in your customized title block:
    - Company or school name, address, and telephone number.
    - Corporate logo or school mascot (if applicable).
    - Drafter's name.
    - Tolerance block for inch drawings (similar to Fig. 17-31.)
    - Sheet size.
    - Part name.
    - Material.

17. Use the MVSETUP command to customize the ISO A4, ISO A3, and ISO A2 title blocks for your company or school. Include the following items in addition to the ones listed for Problem 16.
    - Tolerance block for metric drawings. For example:
      MILLIMETERS UNLESS OTHERWISE SPECIFIED.
      TOLERANCES:
      .X   = ±.1
      .XX   = ±.05
      .XXX = ±.010

18. Use the MVSETUP command to customize architectural title blocks for your company or school. Format the design for A-, B-, and C-size sheets as needed. Refer to title blocks of local architectural firms for examples of elements in them, or use the sample below as a guide.

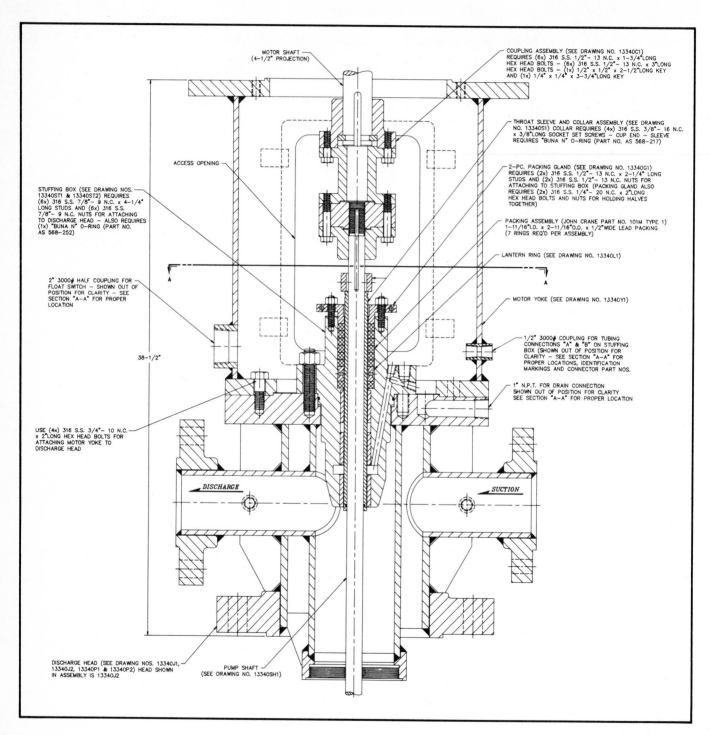

Sectional view of a pump.   (Autodesk, Inc.)

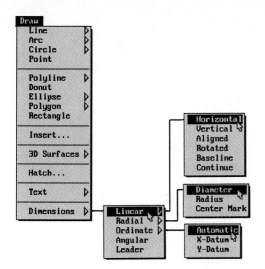

Chapter 18

BASIC DIMENSIONING

Learning objectives

After completing this chapter, you will be able to:

☐ Use the DIM and DIM1 commands to dimension given objects to ANSI standards.
☐ Identify and set variables that affect the appearance of dimensions.
☐ Add linear, angular, diameter, and radius dimensions to a drawing.
☐ Set the appropriate units and decimal places for dimension numerals.
☐ Use text size and style consistent with ANSI standards.
☐ Use the proper character codes to display symbols with dimension text.
☐ Add dimensions to a separate layer.
☐ Place general notes on drawings.
☐ Use the LEADER command to place notes.
☐ Set dimensioning variables using dialogue boxes.

Dimensions are given on product designs for manufacturing and construction to describe the size, shape, and location of features on an object or structure. The dimension may consist of numerical values, lines, symbols, and/or notes, Fig. 18-1. Each drafting field (mechanical, architectural, civil, electronics, etc.) uses a different type of dimensioning technique. Therefore, it is important for a drafter to place dimensions in accordance with company and industry standards. The standard emphasized in this text is ANSI Y14.5M, *Dimensioning and Tolerancing*. The "M" in ANSI Y14.5M means the standard is written with Metric numeric values. This text uses and discusses the correct application of both inch and metric dimensioning.

AutoCAD's dimensioning functions provide you with unlimited flexibility. Available commands allow you to dimension linear distances (HORIZONTAL, VERTICAL, or ALIGNED), circles (DIAMETER), and arcs (RADIUS). The LEADER command allows you to place a note with an arrow and leader line pointing to the feature. In addition to these commands, AutoCAD includes a number of variables that allow you to modify the appearance of dimensions. These affect the height, width, style, and spacing of individual components of a dimension.

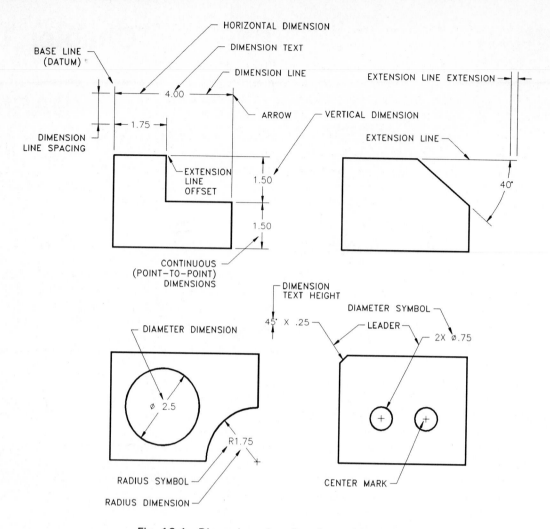

Fig. 18-1. Dimensions describe size and location.

THE AUTOCAD DIMENSIONING COMMAND $\quad$ **ARM 11**

Dimensioning is performed using the DIM command found in the Root Menu. When you select DIM:, the following options then appear:

AutoCAD
* * * *
DIM:
Aligned	(for drawing dimensions that are aligned with an object)
Angular	(dimensioning angles)
Diameter	(for dimensioning circles)
Horizntl	(making horizontal dimensions)
Leader	(draws leader lines for notes)
Ordinate	(used for arrowless dimensioning)
Radius	(dimensioning arcs)
Rotated	(for placing the dimension line at a specified angle)
Vertical	(for creating vertical dimensions)
Edit	(accesses the edit dimensions screen menu)
Dim Styl	(brings up the dimensioning style screen menu)
Dim Vars	(shows a screen menu listing the dimensioning variables)
next	(displays the next page of the DIM screen menu)
Exit	(quits the DIM command and returns to Root Menu, unless you already started a dimensioning activity)

When you pick the "next" option, the following dimensioning commands are displayed on the second page:

Baseline   (used for automatic datum dimensioning)
Continue   (used for automatic chain dimensioning)
Center   (for drawing center marks in circles and arcs)
Status   (displays all dimension variable settings)
previous   (gets you back to the first page of the DIM screen menu)

When you select DIM: from the Root Menu, the only way to return to the Command: prompt is by typing or selecting EXIT at the DIM: prompt, CTRL C, or puck button 3. If you plan to perform only one dimensioning operation, type "DIM1" at the Command: prompt. After performing the one dimensioning task, AutoCAD returns to the Command: prompt.

PROFESSIONAL TIP

The dimensioning commands can also be accessed through the Draw pull-down menu. Pick the Dimension selection, and a cascading menu appears containing these options: Linear, Radial, Ordinate, Angular, and Leader. Three of these options also have cascading menus for additional selections. As you work with dimensions, try using the pull-down cascading menus to your advantage.

INTRODUCTION TO AUTOCAD'S DIMENSIONING VARIABLES

ARM 11

AutoCAD provides options that change the appearance of dimensions. These are called *dimensioning variables,* or *dim vars* for short. All default values for dimensioning variables are set in the AutoCAD prototype drawing. To change a variable, enter "DIM" and pick Dim Vars from the screen menu, type the variable name at the Command: or Dim: prompt, or select the variable from the "Dimension Styles and Variables" dialogue box. There are three pages in the dimensioning variable screen menu. You can move from one page to another by picking "next" or "previous." Return to the DIM menu by picking DimMenu. To change a feature, pick or type the variable name. The following prompts appear when you are changing the extension line offset:

Dim: **DIMEXO** ↵
New value for DIMEXO ⟨0.0625⟩:

The default, or current value is shown in brackets. Keep this value by pressing ENTER, or type a new value and then press ENTER.

In this chapter, dimensioning variables are introduced following the sequence in which you might use them. Notice the first three letters of each variable is "dim." The remaining letters are a code giving the purpose of each variable. These codes make it easier for you to remember the content of each variable. Also notice the 41 variables are spread across three menu pages. Fig. 18-2 displays the variables in a chart with a brief description of each. Page numbers are also included in the chart indicating the page number in this text to refer to for additional information.

DIMENSIONING VARIABLES (DIM VARS)								
MENU PAGE 1			**MENU PAGE 2**			**MENU PAGE 3**		
Variable	**Meaning**	**Page**	**Variable**	**Meaning**	**Page**	**Variable**	**Meaning**	**Page**
DIMALT	ALTernate units	19-12	DIMDLE	Dimension Line Extension	18-13	DIMSHO	SHOw dragged dimensions	19-15
DIMALTD	ALTernate units Decimal places	19-12	DIMDLI	Dimension Line Increment	18-31	DIMSOXD	Suppress Outside eXtension-Dimension lines	18-47
DIMALTF	ALTernate units scale Factor	19-12	DIMEXE	EXtension line Extension	18-10	DIMTAD	Text Above Dimension line	18-12
DIMAPOST	Alternate units Text Suffix	19-12	DIMEXO	EXtension line Offset	18-10	DIMTFAC	Tolerance text scale FACtor	19-9
DIMASO	ASsOciative dimensioning	19-15	DIMGAP	dimension line GAP	18-49	DIMTIH	Text Inside extension lines, Horizontal	18-11
DIMASZ	Arrow SiZe	18-12	DIMLFAC	Length FACtor	18-51	DIMTIX	Text Inside eXtension lines	18-46
DIMBLK	arrow BLocK display	18-13	DIMLIM	LIMits tolerancing	19-9			
DIMBLK1	custom BLocK 1st extension line	18-50	DIMPOST	dimension Text suffix	19-11	DIMTM	dimension with Minus Tolerance	19-8
DIMBLK2	custom BLocK 2nd extension line	18-50	DIMRND	RouND dimension units to specified value	19-12	DIMTOFL	Text Outside, Force Line inside	18-47
DIMCEN	CENter mark size	18-33	DIMSAH	Separate custom ArrowHeads	18-50	DIMTOH	Text Outside extension line, Horizontal	18-11
DIMCLRD	CoLoR of Dimension line	18-53	DIMSCALE	overall dimension SCALE factor	18-51	DIMTOL	dimension with TOLerance	19-8
DIMCLRE	CoLoR of Extension line	18-53	DIMSE1	Suppress Extension line 1	18-11	DIMTP	dimension with Plus Tolerance	19-8
DIMCLRT	CoLoR of Text	18-53	DIMSE2	Suppress Extension line 2	18-11	DIMTSZ	Tick SiZe	18-12
						DIMTVP	Text Vertical Placement	18-47
						DIMTXT	dimension TeXT size	18-5
						DIMZIN	Zero supression in feet and INch values	18-6

Fig. 18-2. Dimensioning variables and their abbreviated meanings. The page number indicated in the right column of each menu page refers to the page number in this text.

DIMENSIONING UNITS

The standard units of measurement on engineering drawings are decimal inches and metric units (millimeters). When all dimensions are given in inches or millimeters, a general note should appear: UNLESS OTHERWISE SPECIFIED, ALL DIMENSIONS ARE IN INCHES (or MILLIMETERS). When using metric dimensions, a zero precedes the decimal point for measurements less than one millimeter. An equivalent metric measurement requires one less digit behind the decimal to maintain the same degree of accuracy, Fig. 18-3.

INCHES	MILLIMETERS
1.250	31.75
.500	12.70
.12	0.3
2.505	63.63

Fig. 18-3. Examples of decimal inch and metric dimensions. Note the zero preceding the decimal point for metric dimensions less than 1.

When dimensioning architectural or structural drawings, it is common to use feet and inches. For dimensions greater than one foot, the units are shown as FEET(')-INCHES("), such as 12'-6". Distances less than one foot are noted in inches and fractions of an inch, Fig. 18-4.

The height for dimension numerals and notes on a drawing ranges from 1/8 inch to 5/32 inch (3.2 mm to 4 mm) depending on which standards are being used. The larger text is recommended if the drawing is to be reduced. Titles and subtitles are usually 3/16 inch to 1/4 inch (4.8 mm to 6.4 mm) in height so they stand out from the rest of the drawing.

DIMENSIONS GREATER THAN ONE FOOT	8'-10 1/2" 4'-0" 24'-6"	DIMENSIONS LESS THAN ONE FOOT	0'-8" 8" 6 1/4"

Fig. 18-4. Dimension formats for the construction trades.

DIMENSIONING TEXT OPTIONS
ARM 11

When you begin a drawing, dimension text is drawn using the current text style. For example, if the text style is ROMANS with a .125 in. height, all dimension text is .125 high ROMANS. If the text height is not set, the DIMension TeXT height is controlled by the DIMTXT variable. The text style may be changed at any time without affecting previously drawn dimension text.

PROFESSIONAL TIP

The current text style plays an important role in the dimension text format. If you have a fancy style, such as ITALICC, then the dimension text is the same. Change to ROMANS if you want a more traditional look. In addition, dimension text is drawn so it is oriented horizontally. If you set the text style to a vertical format, be sure to change it to a horizontal orientation by answering "N" to the Vertical: prompt in the STYLE command before dimensioning.

DIM VARS FOR DIMENSION TEXT
ARM 11

AutoCAD gives you the flexibility to control the way the dimension text looks on your drawing. The way you set the text-related dimensioning variables may depend on your school or company standards, and on the type of drawing you are doing, such as mechanical or architectural.

Text size

Dimension text size is controlled using the DIMTXT variable. AutoCAD's DIMTXT default (.1800) is in effect until a new value is entered. To change text to the standard .125 or .166 height used by most companies, pick the "dimtxt" option from the screen menu or type it as follows:

Command: **DIMTXT** ↵
New value for DIMTXT ⟨0.1800⟩: **.125** ↵

Determining drawing scale factors for dimension text height

Before plotting a drawing, you should determine the scale factor of the drawing. You can do this at the time of plotting, but at that time more work is required to update text heights. Scale factors are important since the number is used to ensure that the text is plotted at the proper height. The scale factor is multiplied by the desired plotted text height to get the AutoCAD text height that should be used while you are drawing. After the scale factor has been determined, you should then calculate the height of the text in AutoCAD. To do this, multiply the desired text height by the scale factor to get text that appears in correct proportion on the screen.

Scale factors and dimension text heights should be determined before beginning a drawing, and are best incorporated as values within your prototype drawing files.

PROFESSIONAL TIP

If your text height was set to 0 when you used the STYLE command, then be sure the DIMTXT value is the same as the text height you specify when using the TEXT or DTEXT commands. You will get different text heights for notes and dimensions if these values are not the same, giving the drawing an "amateur" appearance.

Zero inch dimension

The DIMZIN (Zero INch) variable allows you to control the $-0''$ part of feet-inch dimensions. When architectural or fractional units are used, the DIMZIN variable controls whether the dimension includes a "0" feet or "0" inches measurement. Valid responses to this variable for architectural dimensioning are 0, 1, 2, or 3. The following chart shows the results of selecting one of the DIMZIN variables.

Value		Results	Inches		Feet and Inches	
0	(default)	Removes 0 ft. or 0 in.	1/2''	4''	2'	1'-0 1/2''
1		Includes 0 ft. and 0 in.	0'-0 1/2''	0'-4''	2'-0''	1'-0 1/2''
2		Includes 0 ft. omits 0 in.	0'-0 1/2''	0'-4''	2'	1'-0 1/2''
3		Includes 0 in. omits 0 ft.	1/2''	4''	2'-0''	1'-0 1/2''

The DIMZIN variable is convenient when doing architectural drafting. However, other settings are preferred for mechanical drafting. For example, AutoCAD places a zero in front of all decimal dimensions when DIMZIN is set to the default (0). According to ANSI standards, this is preferred for metric dimensions, but not for inch dimensions.

Metric	**Inch**
0.50	.50

In order to have AutoCAD automatically remove the 0 in front of the decimal point, set DIMZIN to 7. This is what you then get:

DIMZIN = 0	**DIMZIN = 7**
0.50	.50

It is more common to control the number of places after the decimal point with the UNITS command. However, you can have AutoCAD remove zeros after the decimal point by setting DIMZIN to 8. The results are:

DIMZIN = 0	**DIMZIN = 8**
0.50	0.5

You can even keep the zeros off the dimension before and after the decimal point with a DIMZIN setting of 15 (DIMZIN = 7 + DIMZIN = 8 = 15). You then will get the following results:

DIMZIN = 0	**DIMZIN = 15**
0.50	.5

PROFESSIONAL TIP

You can check the current status of the dimensioning variables at any time. Simply pick the Status option on the second page of the DIM: screen menu. The text screen appears, listing all dim vars and their respective values.

DIMENSION ARRANGEMENT

Dimensions are meant to communicate information about the drawing. Different industries and companies apply similar techniques for presenting dimensions. The two most-accepted arrangements of text are unidirectional and aligned.

Unidirectional dimensioning

Unidirectional dimensioning is typically used in the mechanical drafting field. The term *unidirectional* means "one direction." This system has all dimension numerals and notes placed horizontally on the drawing. They are read from the bottom of the sheet.

Unidirectional dimensions normally have arrowheads on the ends of dimension lines. The dimension numeral is usually centered in a break near the center of the dimension line, Fig. 18-5.

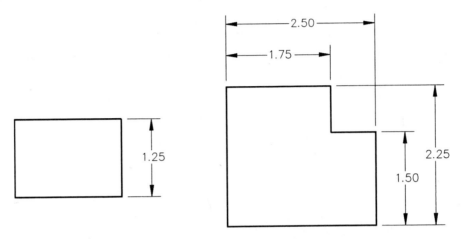

Fig. 18-5. When applying unidirectional dimensions, all dimension numerals and notes are placed horizontally on the drawing.

Aligned dimensioning

Aligned dimensions are typically placed on architectural or structural drawings. The term *aligned* means the dimension numerals are lined up with the dimension lines. The dimension numerals for horizontal dimensions read horizontally. Dimension numerals for vertical dimensions are placed so they read vertically from the right side of the sheet, Fig. 18-6. Numerals for dimensions placed at an angle read at the same angle as the dimension line. Notes are usually placed so they read horizontally.

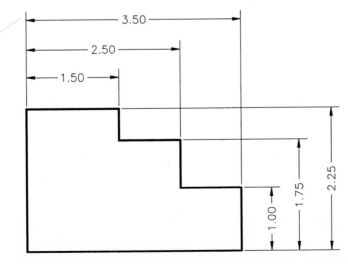

Fig. 18-6. In the aligned dimensioning system, dimension numerals for horizontal dimensions read horizontally. Dimension numerals for vertical dimensions are placed so they read from the right side of the sheet.

When using the aligned system, terminate dimension lines with tick marks, dots, or arrowheads. In architectural drafting, the dimension numeral is generally placed above the dimension line and the tick marks are used, Fig. 18-7.

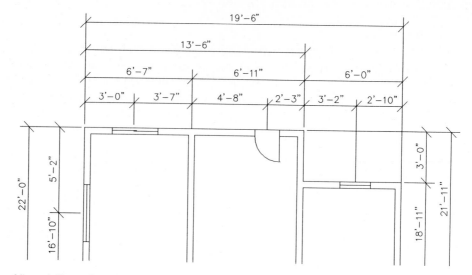

Fig. 18-7. Aligned dimensioning in architectural drafting. Notice the tick marks used in place of the arrowheads, and the placement of the dimensions above the dimension line.

PLACING HORIZONTAL AND VERTICAL DIMENSIONS

ARM 11

In most cases, dimensions measure straight distance, whether it be horizontal, vertical, or aligned with a surface. This allows you to measure the length of the object and place dimension lines, extension lines, and arrowheads automatically.

The Horizntl option of the DIM: screen menu allows you to dimension a horizontal feature. The Vertical option places dimensions for vertical features. The Aligned option aligns a dimension line with an angled surface. After entering the DIM command, entering either "HOR" or "VERT" at the Dim: prompt. This displays the following series of prompts:

Command: **DIM** ↵
Dim: **HOR** ↵
First extension line origin or RETURN to select: *(pick one end of the feature to dimension)*
Second extension line origin: *(pick the other point of the feature to dimension)*

Your picks are the extension line origins. Place the crosshairs directly on the corners where the extension lines begin; it may be helpful to use one of the object snap modes. Dimensioning standards recommend that a small space or gap be left between the object and the start of the extension line. AutoCAD does this automatically, Fig. 18-8. Do not be concerned if at first the extension lines appear to touch the object. The small spaces may not be displayed until you select REDRAW.

The next prompt in the horizontal dimension command is:

Dimension line location (Text/Angle): *(pick the dimension line location)*

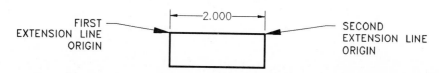

Fig. 18-8. Establishing the extension line origins. The object snap INTersection or ENDpoint options are useful in accurately locating the origins.

You can see the dimension being dragged into place. When you select the dimension line location, avoid crowding the drawing, Fig. 18-9. This is where preliminary plans and sketches help you determine proper distances.

When the dimension line location is picked, AutoCAD displays the measurement on the prompt line and allows you to change it.

Dimension text ⟨2.0000⟩: ↵

If the numeral in brackets is what you expected, press ENTER. The extension lines, dimension lines, arrowheads, and numeral are drawn as shown in Fig. 18-9. If your drawing is accurate, the dimension numeral given is the proper measurement. However, if the number shown in brackets is not correct, type a new value, or start over again and correct your drawing.

You can also alter dimension text by entering "T" for the Text option, or "A" for the Angle option when you see this prompt:

Dimension line location (Text/Angle):

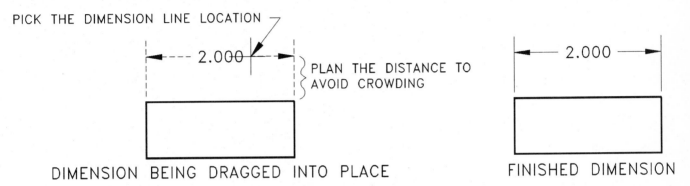

Fig. 18-9. Establishing the dimension line's location.

If you enter "T" and press ENTER, AutoCAD gives you the opportunity to provide a specified measurement or text format that you want displayed with the dimension. The value shown in brackets is the current dimension numeral. Press ENTER to accept this value, or enter a new value. For example, you can enter a numeral with parentheses, called a *reference dimension*, like the one shown in Fig. 18-10A by following this command sequence:

Dimension line location (Text/Angle): **T** ↵
Dimension text ⟨2.750⟩: **(2.750)** ↵
Dimension line location (Text/Angle): ↵

As shown in Fig. 18-10B, you can have the dimension line drawn without text by pressing the space bar followed by pressing ENTER:

Dimension line location (Text/Angle): **T** ↵
Dimension text ⟨2.750⟩: *(press the space bar once and then press ENTER)*

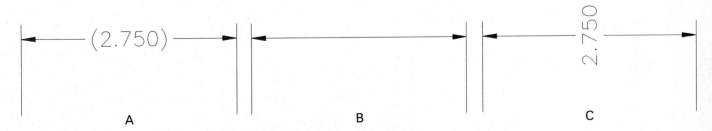

Fig. 18-10. Using the Text and Angle options. A—Entering a reference dimension. B—Press the space bar at the Dimension text: prompt to obtain a dimension line without text. C—Changing the dimension text angle using the Angle option.

The Angle option allows you to change the text angle, Fig. 18-10C. While there are not many practical applications, the Angle option works as follows:

Dimension line location (Text/Angle): **A** ↵
Enter text angle: **90** ↵
Dimension line location (Text/Angle): *(pick a point)*
Dimension text ⟨2.750⟩: ↵

The Dim: prompt is issued after each dimension is complete. If the next dimension is vertical, Fig. 18-11, the following command sequence is used:

Dim: **VERT** ↵
First extension line origin or RETURN to select: *(pick the origin of the first extension line)*
Second extension line origin: *(pick the origin of the second extension line)*
Dimension line location (Text/Angle): *(pick the dimension line location)*
Dimension text ⟨2.500⟩: ↵
Dim: *(Press CTRL C or pick Exit from the screen menu)* *CANCEL*
Command:

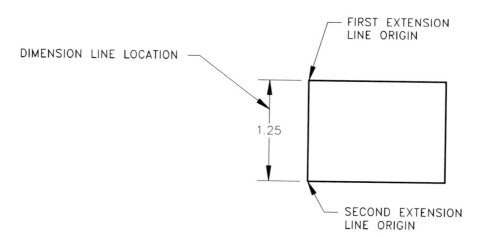

Fig. 18-11. Drawing a vertical dimension.

PROFESSIONAL TIP

Use object snap modes to your advantage when dimensioning. For example, to place exact extension line origins, use the INTersect option. This helps you find the exact corner of an object.

Setting the extension line offset

A small gap exists between the object and the start of the extension line. You can control the size of this space with DIMEXO (EXtension line Offset) variable. The default gap of 0.0625 units is the ANSI standard. Suppose you needed to change the gap to .125 units. Then use the following command sequence:

Command: **DIMEXO** ↵
Current value ⟨0.0625⟩ New value: **.125** ↵

Setting the extension line extension

Normally, extension lines extend beyond the last dimension line a short distance. In AutoCAD this is called the EXtension line Extension and is controlled by the DIMEXE variable. The default distance, 0.18, is an accepted standard. Fig. 18-12 shows the extension line extension and offset. To change the extension line extension, enter "DIMEXE" at the Dim: or Command: prompts and enter a new value.

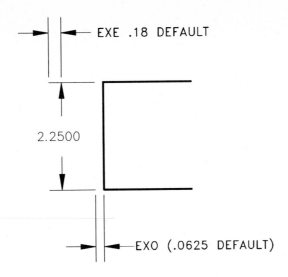

Fig. 18-12. The DIMEXE and DIMEXO variables.

Suppressing the first extension line

Normally, extension lines are placed on both ends of the dimension line. The extension lines mark those edges of the feature you are dimensioning. However, a situation where you do not want the first extension line may occur. For example, suppose the extension line coincides with another line on the object. It is then best to omit the extension line, Fig. 18-13.

The DIMSE1 dimensioning variable is used to suppress the first extension line. The variable is either on (1) or off (0). OFF (default) places the extension line on the drawing.

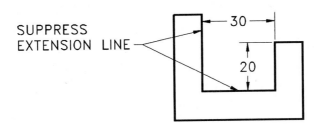

Fig. 18-13. The DIMSE1 and DIMSE2 variables are used to suppress extension lines.

Suppressing the second extension line

The DIMSE2 variable allows you to suppress the second extension line. This works the same as DIMSE1 except that the second extension line is left off the drawing. This is not a typical application and should be avoided unless absolutely necessary. Be sure to turn DIMSE1 and DIMSE2 back off before resuming normal dimensioning.

Alignment of dimension text between extension lines

When there is room, the dimension line, arrowheads, and text is placed between the extension lines. The numerals are normally placed horizontally when the DIMTIH (Text Inside Horizontal) variable is on. The DIMTIH variable is on for unidirectional dimensioning (Fig. 18-5), but off for aligned dimensioning. DIMTIH off allows the text inside extension lines to align with the dimension line angle, and the dimension numerals are placed as shown in Fig. 18-6.

Alignment of dimension text outside of extension lines

When there is not enough room between extension lines, AutoCAD automatically places the dimension lines, arrowheads, and numerals outside. In this instance, the DIMTOH (Text Outside Horizontal) variable works the same as DIMTIH. When this variable is on, text is drawn horizontally for unidirectional dimensioning. When it is off, text is drawn at the dimension line angle for aligned dimensioning, Fig. 18-14.

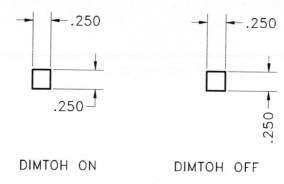

DIMTOH ON   DIMTOH OFF

Fig. 18-14. Comparison of DIMTOH on and off.

Placing the dimension text above the dimension line

In architectural drafting, the dimension numeral often appears above the dimension line. To do this, the DIMTAD (Text Above Dimension line) variable must be set to on. If it is off, the default, dimension numerals are placed in a break in the dimension line. Fig. 18-15 shows the effects of DIMTAD when turned on and off.

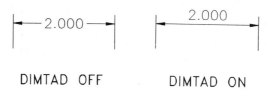

DIMTAD OFF   DIMTAD ON

Fig. 18-15. Using the DIMTAD variable.

Controlling the size of arrowheads

In mechanical drafting, dimension lines are terminated with arrowheads where they meet the extension lines. The size of arrowheads is controlled by the DIMASZ (DIMension Arrowhead SiZe) variable. The default size, 0.18 units, is used for most drawings, Fig. 18-16. To change the arrowhead size, enter the DIMASZ variable and the revised size value.

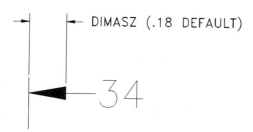

Fig. 18-16. Changing arrowhead size with the DIMASZ variable.

Drawing dimension line tick marks

The DIMTSZ (DIMension Tick SiZe) variable controls tick size. In architectural drafting, tick marks are often drawn at the ends of dimension lines. When DIMTSZ is set to 0 (default), arrowheads are drawn. If you want ticks, enter a value other than 0, such as .05. See Fig. 18-17. If a value is set for DIMTSZ, the DIMASZ value is ignored.

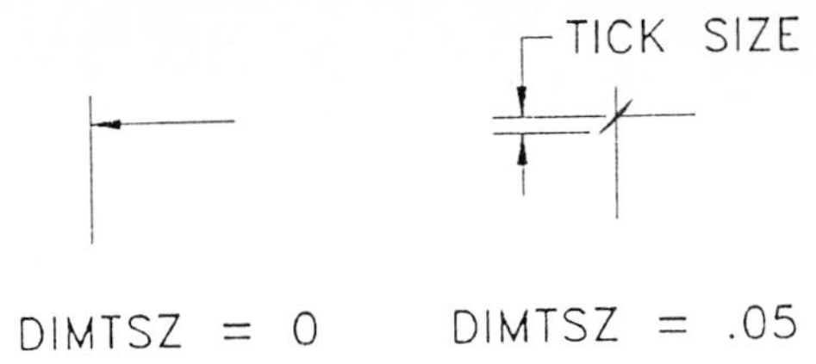

Fig. 18-17. Effects of the DIMTSZ variable.

Extending the dimension line past the extension line

Normally, dimension lines meet, but do not cross extension lines. In architectural drafting, when tick marks are used, the dimension line may extend slightly beyond the extension line depending on your school or company standard. This procedure is controlled with the DIMDLE (Dimension Line Extension) variable. When DIMDLE is set to 0 (default), there is no dimension line extension. To extend the dimension line, enter a value such as .0625. See Fig. 18-18.

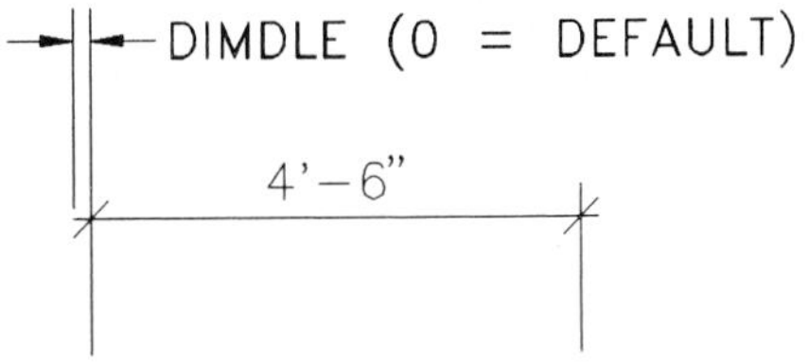

Fig. 18-18. Using the DIMDLE variable to allow the dimension line to extend past the extension line.

─── PROFESSIONAL TIP ───

It is easy to locate extension and dimension lines when grid and snap units align with the object. However, do not forget to use object snap options when it is difficult to find the extension line origins. For example, when you see the First extension line origin: prompt, type "END" and press ENTER. This issues the ENDpoint object snap option. Then pick the location where the dimension should begin. Object snap helps you save time and ensures accuracy.

Changing an arrowhead to a block

Another dimensioning variable, DIMBLK (BLocK), replaces arrowheads with a specific block. A block is an object, such as a symbol, that may be called up for use on the drawing. Blocks are discussed in Chapter 21. A block that might be used instead of an arrowhead is a custom-designed arrow or symbol. The DIMBLK default allows the standard arrowhead to be drawn.

AutoCAD has a standard block called DOT, which may be used at the ends of your dimension lines. Some architectural drafters like to use dots to terminate dimensions. The command sequence to use for dots is as follows:

    Command: **DIM** ↵
    Dim: **DIMBLK** ↵
    Current value ⟨⟩ New value: **DOT** ↵

Fig. 18-19 shows an example of the architectural dot. If the default dot is too big, make it smaller as follows:

    Command: **DIMASZ** ↵
    New value for DIMASZ ⟨0.18⟩: **.1** ↵

THE ARCHITECTURAL DOT

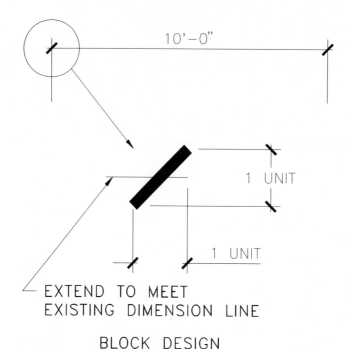

BLOCK DESIGN

Fig. 18-19. Assigning a custom block to the DIMBLK variable. A—The DIMBLK variable is set to DOT. B—Assigning the DIMBLK variable to a custom block, such as TICK1.

A common architectural arrowhead block is a bold tick mark, Fig. 18-19. To define a customized tick mark as a block, first draw the block and give it a name such as TICK1. The block should be one unit square, and you must also draw a tail to connect with the dimension line. Then set the DIMBLK variable with the block name:

    Command: **DIM** ↵
    Dim: **DIMBLK** ↵
    Current value ⟨⟩ New value: **TICK1** ↵
    Dim:

Now place a horizontal dimension using this value. The DIMASZ and DIMTSZ variables should be set to their defaults. The DIMASZ variable affects the block size.
    To disable the established DIMBLK, enter a period (.) at the New value: prompt:

    Dim: **DIMBLK** ↵
    Current value ⟨⟩ New value: **.** ↵

Additional block dimensioning variables are discussed later in this chapter. Detailed information regarding the creation and insertion of blocks is found in Chapter 21.

EXERCISE 18-1

☐ Load AutoCAD and open PRODR2.
☐ Draw the object lines of the following views on layer 0-7, and place all dimensions on layer 3-3.
☐ Use the proper dimensioning techniques and commands to dimension the objects exactly as shown.
☐ Save the drawing as A:EX18-1.

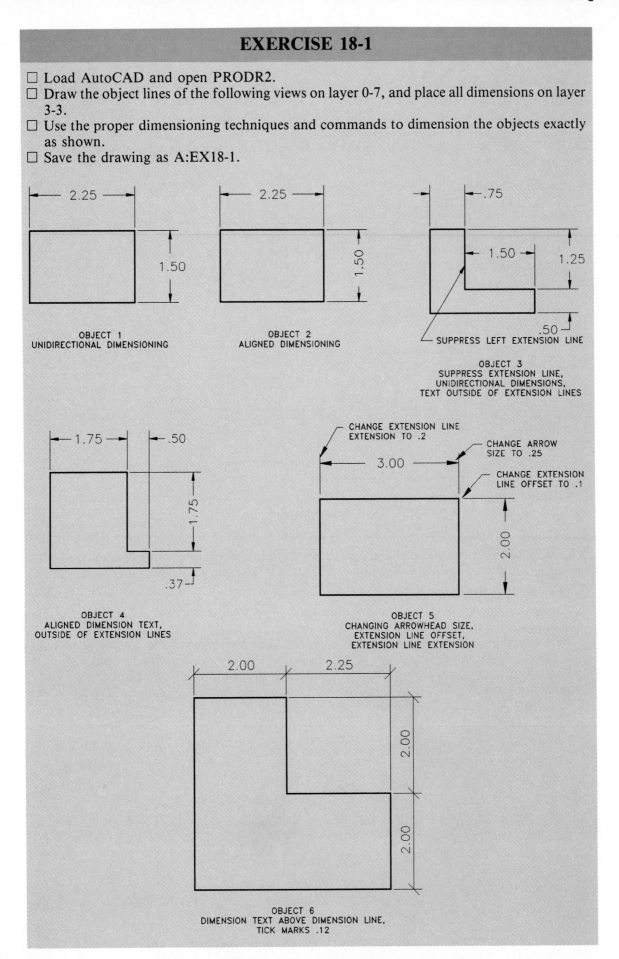

OBJECT 1
UNIDIRECTIONAL DIMENSIONING

OBJECT 2
ALIGNED DIMENSIONING

OBJECT 3
SUPPRESS EXTENSION LINE,
UNIDIRECTIONAL DIMENSIONS,
TEXT OUTSIDE OF EXTENSION LINES

OBJECT 4
ALIGNED DIMENSION TEXT,
OUTSIDE OF EXTENSION LINES

OBJECT 5
CHANGING ARROWHEAD SIZE,
EXTENSION LINE OFFSET,
EXTENSION LINE EXTENSION

OBJECT 6
DIMENSION TEXT ABOVE DIMENSION LINE,
TICK MARKS .12

DIMENSIONING ANGLED SURFACES
AND AUXILIARY VIEWS

When dimensioning a surface drawn at an angle, it may be necessary to align the dimension line with the surface. For example, auxiliary views are normally placed at an angle. In order to properly dimension these features, the DIM command's Aligned and Rotated subcommands are used. To access these options, type at the Dim: prompt, or pick Aligned or Rotated from the DIM: screen menu. The results of the ALIGNED command are shown in Fig. 18-20. The command sequence is as follows:

Command: **DIM** ↵
Dim: **ALI** or **ALIGNED** ↵
First extension line origin or RETURN to select: *(pick first extension line origin)*
Second extension line origin: *(pick second extension line origin)*
Dimension line location (Text/Angle): *(pick the dimension line location)*
Dimension text ⟨2.250⟩: ↵

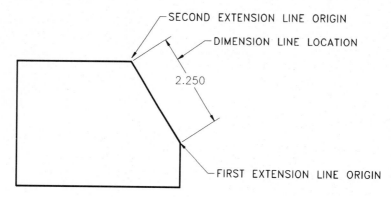

Fig. 18-20. The ALIGNED dimensioning command allows you to place dimension lines parallel to angled features.

The ROTATED command is slightly different from the other dimensioning commands. The first request is for a dimension line angle, Fig. 18-21. The remaining prompts are familiar:

Dim: **ROT** or **ROTATED** ↵
Dimension line angle ⟨0⟩: *(type the dimension line angle and press ENTER, or pick two points on the line to be dimensioned)*
First extension line origin or RETURN to select: *(pick the origin of the first extension line)*
Second extension line origin: *(pick the origin of the second extension line)*
Dimension line location (Text/Angle): *(pick the dimension line location)*
Dimension text ⟨2.000⟩: ↵

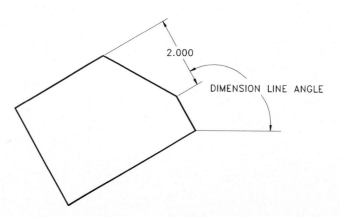

Fig. 18-21. Using the ROTATED command to dimension an angled view.

EXERCISE 18-2

☐ Open PRODR2.
☐ Draw the object lines of the following views on layer 0-7, and place all dimensions on layer 3-3.
☐ Use the proper dimensioning techniques and commands to dimension the objects exactly as shown.
☐ Save the drawing as A:EX18-2.

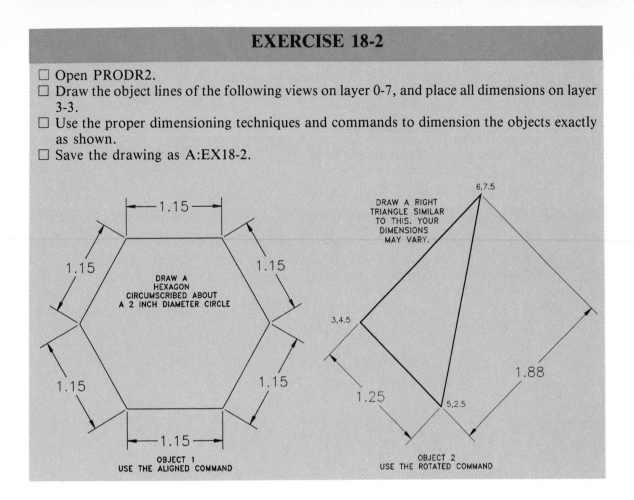

SELECTING A LINE, CIRCLE, OR ARC FOR DIMENSIONING

ARM 11

In the previous discussion, the extension line origins were picked in order to establish the extents of the dimension. Another powerful AutoCAD option allows you to pick a single line, circle, or arc to dimension. This works for the HORIZONTAL, VERTICAL, ROTATED, and ALIGNED dimensioning commands. Using the VERTICAL command as an example, this command is chosen by pressing ENTER or the space bar at the First extension line or RETURN to select: prompt. As shown in Fig. 18-22, the procedure is:

Dim: **VERT** ↵
First extension line origin or RETURN to select: ↵
Select line, arc, or circle: *(pick any line, arc, or circle on the drawing)*
Dimension line location (Text/Angle): *(pick the dimension line location)*
Dimension text ⟨1.250⟩: ↵

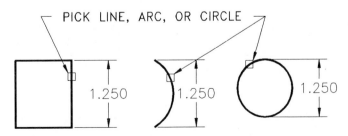

Fig. 18-22. Pressing ENTER at the First extension line origin: prompt allows you to pick the line, arc, or circle to be dimensioned.

PROFESSIONAL TIP

AutoCAD does not place a diameter symbol in front of the dimension numeral when dimensioning a circle using ENTER to select the option. You can add a diameter symbol in compliance with ANSI standards using the Text option, or by entering the "%%C" control code at the Dimension text: prompt like this:

Dimension text ⟨1.250⟩: **%%C1.250** ⏎

The resulting dimension is displayed as φ1.250.

EXERCISE 18-3

☐ Load AutoCAD and open PRODR2.
☐ Draw the following line and circle on layer 0-7, and place dimensions on layer 3-3.
☐ Dimension the objects exactly as shown.
☐ Use unidirectional dimensions.
☐ Save the drawing as A:EX18-3.

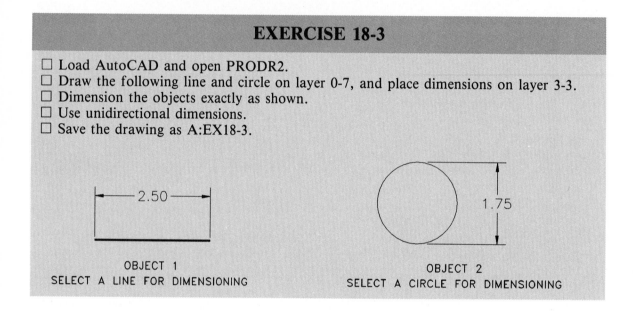

OBJECT 1
SELECT A LINE FOR DIMENSIONING

OBJECT 2
SELECT A CIRCLE FOR DIMENSIONING

DIMENSIONING ANGLES IN DEGREES ARM 11

Recommended standards for dimensioning angles are coordinate and angular dimensioning. Coordinate dimensioning of angles uses the DIM: menu's HORIZONTAL, VERTICAL, ALIGNED, or ROTATED commands. These dimensions mark the edges of the angle, Fig. 18-23.

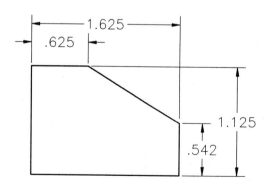

Fig. 18-23. Coordinate dimensioning of angles.

The angular method gives a dimension to one corner and the angle in degrees, Fig. 18-24. The angular method is established using the Angular option in the DIM: screen menu, or by typing "ANG" or "ANGULAR" at the Dim: prompt.

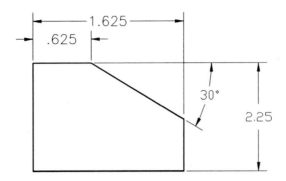

Fig. 18-24. Angular method for dimensioning angles.

Dimensioning the angle between two nonparallel lines

You can dimension the angle between two nonparallel lines. The intersection of the lines is the angle's vertex. AutoCAD automatically draws extension lines if they are needed as shown in Fig. 18-25. The command sequence is as follows:

Command: **DIM** ↵
Dim: **ANG** or **ANGULAR** ↵
Select arc, circle, line, or RETURN: *(pick one of the lines of the angle to be dimensioned)*
Second line: *(pick the second line of the angle to be dimensioned)*
Dimension arc line location (Text/Angle): *(pick the desired location of the arc-shaped dimension line)*
Dimension text ⟨45⟩: *(press ENTER to accept the text, or type in a new value and press ENTER)*
Enter text location (or RETURN): ↵

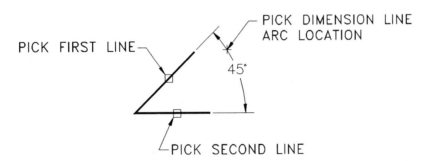

Fig. 18-25. Dimensioning angles with the text centered within the dimension line.

The last prompt asks you to enter the text location. Press ENTER to have AutoCAD draw the dimension line and center the numeral in the dimension line, Fig. 18-25. If there is not enough room between extension lines for the arrowheads and numerals, AutoCAD automatically places the arrowheads outside and the numeral inside the extension lines.

Suppose you want the text placed outside the extension lines, or you may not want the text centered. Then pick the text location yourself at the Enter text location (or RETURN): prompt. The position you pick is important. A leader is not connected to the numeral. Do not place the numeral where it could be confused with another part of the drawing. See Fig. 18-26.

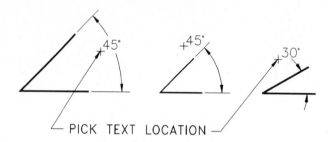

Fig. 18-26. Manually locating the angle numeral.

Placing angular dimensions on arcs

The ANGULAR command can also be used to dimension the angular relationship of an arc. When this is done, the arc's center point becomes the angle vertex and the two arc endpoints are the origin points for the extension lines as shown in Fig. 18-27. The command sequence is as follows:

Command: **DIM** ↵
Dim: **ANG** or **ANGULAR** ↵
Select arc, circle, line or RETURN: *(pick the arc)*
Dimension arc line location (Text/Angle): *(pick the desired dimension line location)*
Dimension text ⟨128⟩: ↵
Enter text location (or RETURN): *(press ENTER to accept the AutoCAD text location, or pick a desired location for the text)*

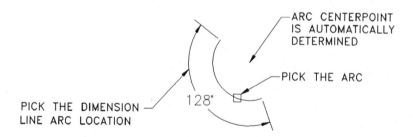

Fig. 18-27. Placing angular dimensions on arcs.

Placing angular dimensions on circles

The ANGULAR command can also be used to dimension an angular feature related to a circle. When this is done, the circle's center point becomes the angle vertex and two picked points are the origin points for the extension lines as shown in Fig. 18-28. The command sequence is as follows:

Command: **DIM** ↵
Dim: **ANG** or **ANGULAR** ↵
Select arc, circle, line, or RETURN: *(pick the circle)*

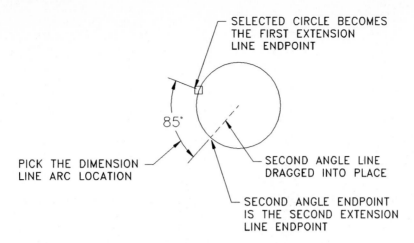

Fig. 18-28. Placing angular dimensions on circles.

The point you pick on the circle becomes the endpoint of the first extension line. You are then asked for the second angle endpoint which becomes the endpoint of the second extension line. The command sequence is as follows:

Second angle endpoint: *(pick the second point)*
Dimension arc line location (Text/Angle): *(pick the desired dimension line location)*
Dimension text ⟨85⟩: ⏎
Enter text location (or RETURN): *(press ENTER to accept the AutoCAD text location, or pick a desired location for the text)*

⎯ PROFESSIONAL TIP ⎯

The use of angular dimensioning for circles increases the number of possible solutions for a given dimensioning requirement, but the actual uses are limited. The first angle point is indicated by the point specified with the circle pick. Therefore, if this is to be an accurate point, it must coincide with a known point on the circle such as the intersection of a line and the circle using the OSNAP INTersection mode, or the quadrant of a circle using the OSNAP QUAdrant mode. One professional application may be dimensioning an angle from a quadrant point to a particular feature without having to first draw a line to dimension. This represents added convenience for specifying the angle. An additional positive aspect of this option is the ability to specify angles that exceed 180°.

Angular dimensioning through three points

You also have the flexibility to establish an angular dimension through three points. The points are the angle vertex and the two angle line endpoints. See Fig. 18-29. To do this, press ENTER after the first prompt:

Command: **DIM** ⏎
Dim: **ANG** or **ANGULAR** ⏎
Select arc, circle, line or RETURN: ⏎
Angle vertex: *(pick a vertex point)*

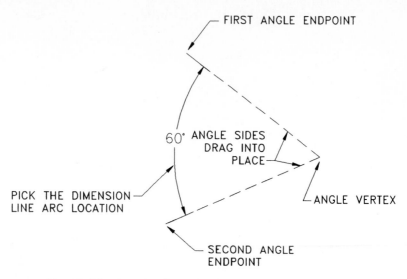

Fig. 18-29. Angular dimensioning through three points.

The side of the angle is dragged into place to assist in locating the first angle endpoint:

First angle endpoint: *(pick the first endpoint)*
Second angle endpoint: *(pick the second endpoint)*
Dimension arc line location (Text/Angle): *(pick the desired dimension line location)*
Dimension text ⟨60⟩: ↵
Enter text location (or RETURN): *(press ENTER to accept the AutoCAD text location,
  or pick a desired location for the text)*

EXERCISE 18-4

☐ Open PRODR2.
☐ Draw the object lines of the views on layer 0-7 and dimensions on layer 3-3.
☐ Use the ANGULAR command to dimension the object exactly as shown.
☐ Save the drawing as A:EX18-4.

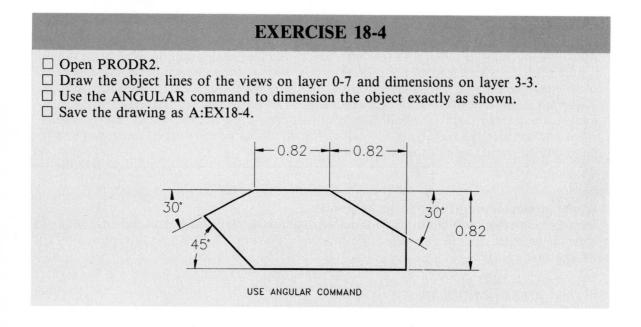

DIMENSIONING PRACTICES

Dimensioning practices often depend on product requirements, the manufacturing accuracy, standards, and tradition. Dimensional information includes size dimensions, location dimensions, and notes. Two techniques that identify size and location are chain and datum dimensioning. The method used depends on the accuracy of the product and the drafting field, such as mechanical or architectural drafting.

SIZE DIMENSIONS AND NOTES

Size dimensions provide the size of physical features. They include lines, dimension lines and numerals, or notes. Size dimensioning practices depend on the techniques used to dimension different geometric features, Fig. 18-30. A *feature* is considered any physical portion of a part or object, such as a surface, slot, hole, window, or door. Dimensioning standards are used so an object designed in one area of the country may be manufactured or built somewhere else. This discussion provides short descriptions of common features and shows recommended dimensioning techniques.

There are two types of notes on a drawing: specific notes and general notes. *Specific notes* relate to individual or specific features on the drawing. They are attached to the feature being dimensioned using a leader line. *General notes* apply to the entire drawing and are placed in the lower-left corner, upper-left corner, or above or next to the title block depending on the company practices.

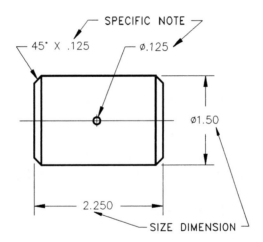

Fig. 18-30. Size dimensions and specific notes.

Dimensioning flat surfaces and architectural features

In mechanical drafting, flat surfaces are dimensioned by giving measurements for each feature. If there is an overall dimension provided, you can omit one of the dimensions because the overall dimension controls the dimension of the last feature. In architectural drafting, it is common to place all dimensions without omitting any of them. The idea is that all dimensions should be shown to help make construction easier. See Fig. 18-31.

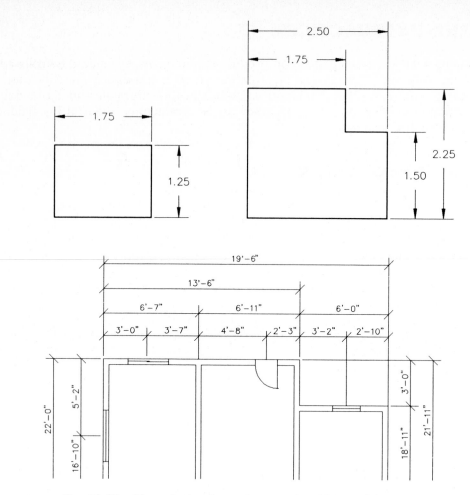

Fig. 18-31. Dimensioning flat surfaces and architectural features.

Dimensioning cylindrical shapes

The diameter and length of a cylindrical shape may be dimensioned in the view where the cylinder appears rectangular, Fig. 18-32. Using this method, both the length of the cylindrical shape and the diameter can be dimensioned in the same view. Place dimension lines far enough apart so the dimension numerals are not crowded.

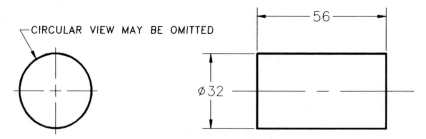

Fig. 18-32. Dimensioning cylindrical shapes.

Dimensioning square and rectangular features

Square and rectangular features are usually dimensioned in the views where the length and height are shown. The square symbol may be used preceding the dimension for the square feature, Fig. 18-33. The square symbol must be developed as a block. Blocks are discussed in Chapter 21.

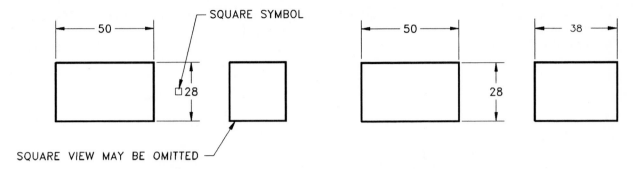

Fig. 18-33. Dimensioning square and rectangular features.

Dimensioning conical shapes

One method to dimension a conical shape is by giving the diameters at both ends and the length. See Fig. 18-34. Another method is to give the taper angle and length.

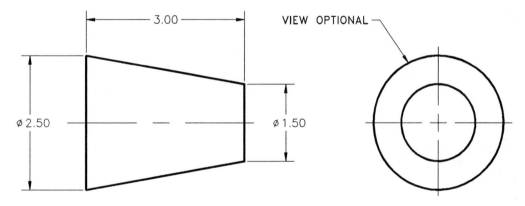

Fig. 18-34. Dimensioning conical shapes.

Dimensioning hexagons

Hexagonal shapes are dimensioned by giving the distance across the flats and the length. See Fig. 18-35.

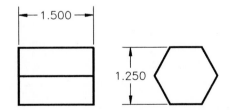

Fig. 18-35. Dimensioning hexagons.

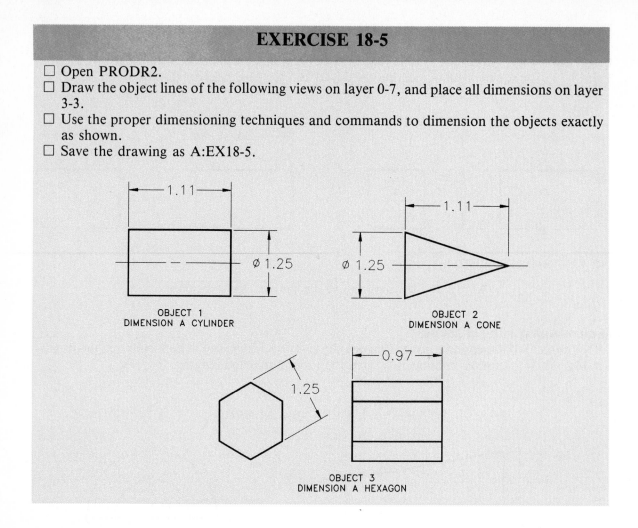

EXERCISE 18-5

☐ Open PRODR2.
☐ Draw the object lines of the following views on layer 0-7, and place all dimensions on layer 3-3.
☐ Use the proper dimensioning techniques and commands to dimension the objects exactly as shown.
☐ Save the drawing as A:EX18-5.

LOCATION DIMENSIONS

Location dimensions are used to locate features on an object; they do not provide the size. Holes and arcs are dimensioned to their centers in the view where they appear circular. Rectangular features are dimensioned to their edges, Fig. 18-36. In architectural drafting, windows and doors are dimensioned to their centers on the floor plan.

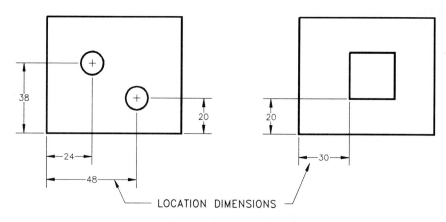

Fig. 18-36. Locating circular and rectangular features.

There are two basic location dimensioning systems: rectangular and polar coordinate dimensioning. *Rectangular coordinates* are linear dimensions used to locate features from surfaces, centerlines, or centerplanes, Fig. 18-37. AutoCAD performs this type of dimensioning using a variety of DIM subcommands. The most frequently used options are HORIZONTAL and VERTICAL subcommands, shown in Fig. 18-37.

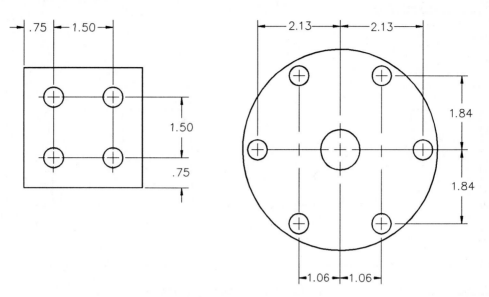

Fig. 18-37. Rectangular coordinate location dimensions.

The *polar coordinate system* uses angular dimensions to locate features from surfaces, centerlines, or centerplanes. The angular dimensions in the polar coordinate system are drawn using AutoCAD's ANGULAR command. Results of the ANGULAR command are shown in Fig. 18-38.

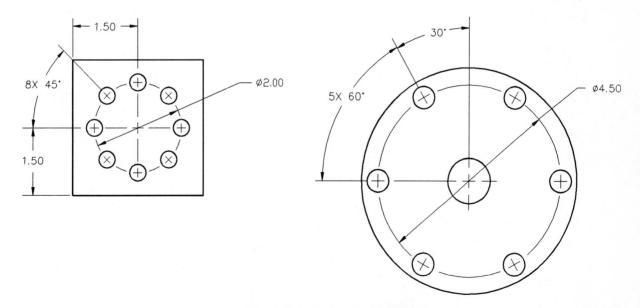

Fig. 18-38. Polar coordinate location dimensions.

CHAIN DIMENSIONING

Chain dimensioning, also called *point-to-point dimensioning*, places dimensions in a line from one feature to the next. Chain dimensioning is sometimes used in mechanical drafting. However, there is less accuracy since each dimension is dependent on other dimensions in the chain. Architectural drafting uses chain dimensioning in most applications. Fig. 18-39 shows an example of chain dimensioning.

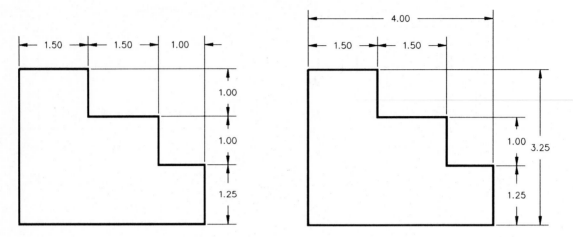

Fig. 18-39. Chain dimensioning.

DATUM DIMENSIONING

With *datum*, or *baseline dimensioning*, dimensions on an object originate from common surfaces, centerlines, or centerplanes. Datum dimensioning is commonly used in mechanical drafting because each dimension is independent of the others. This achieves more accuracy in manufacturing, Fig. 18-40.

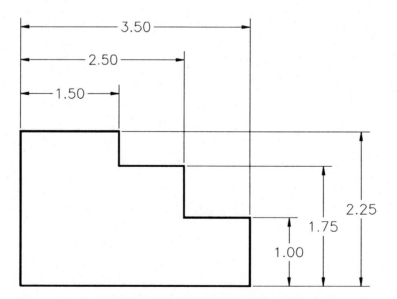

Fig. 18-40. Datum dimensioning.

MAKING DATUM AND CHAIN DIMENSIONING EASY

AutoCAD refers to datum dimensioning as "baseline" and chain dimensioning as "continue." Baseline and Continue are found on the second page of the DIM: screen menu, or may be typed as "BASE" or "CONT" at the DIM: prompt. AutoCAD automatically spaces and places the extension lines, dimension lines, arrowheads, and numerals. To use the BASELINE command, you must first place a dimension using the HORIZONTAL, VERTICAL, ALIGNED, or ROTATED subcommands. For example, to dimension a series of horizontal baseline dimensions, Fig. 18-41, use the following procedure:

> Command: **DIM** ↵
> Dim: **HORIZ** ↵
> First extension line origin or RETURN to select: *(pick the origin of the first extension line)*
> Second extension line origin: *(pick the origin of the second extension line)*
> Dimension line location (Text/Angle): *(pick the location of the first dimension line)*
> Dimension text ⟨2.000⟩: ↵
> Dim: **BASE** ↵
> Second extension line origin or RETURN to select: *(pick the origin of the next extension line)*
> Dimension text ⟨3.250⟩: ↵ *(the next dimension line is automatically spaced and drawn)*
> Dim: **BASE** ↵
> Second extension line origin or RETURN to select: *(pick the origin of the next extension line)*
> Dimension text ⟨4.375⟩: ↵ *(the next dimension line is automatically spaced and drawn)*
> Dim: *CANCEL*
> Command:

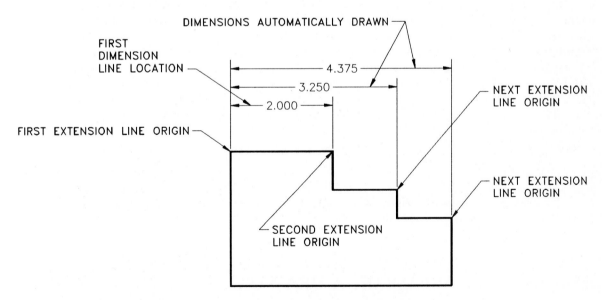

Fig. 18-41. Using BASELINE command. AutoCAD automatically spaces and places the extension lines, dimension lines, arrowheads, and numerals.

The CONTINUE command is used in the same manner as the BASELINE command. The prompts are the same. The only difference is that CONT is used at the Dim: prompt in place of BASE. The result is the chain dimensioning shown in Fig. 18-42.

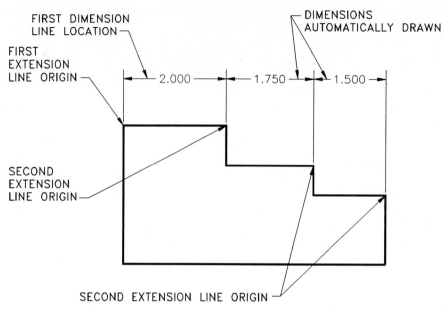

Fig. 18-42. Using the CONTINUE command.

PROFESSIONAL TIP

The preceding discussion about the BASELINE and CONTINUE commands illustrates how you can implement either datum or chain dimensioning immediately after placing your first horizontal or vertical dimension. However, you do not have to use BASELINE or CONTINUE immediately after a dimension that is to be used as a base or chained with other dimensions. You can come back later and do it. For example, you can place the first dimension for reference, and then return to work on other drawing features before you proceed with the datum or chain dimensioning. When you want to finish the datum or chain dimensioning, simply type "BASE" or "CONT" at the Dim: prompt, or pick either as needed from the screen menu. AutoCAD automatically uses the last dimension you drew as reference for the next dimensions. This is the command sequence when you pick Baseline from the screen menu:

    Command: dim
    Dim: __BASELINE
    Second extension line origin or RETURN to select: (pick the origin of the second
        extension line)

SPACING DIMENSIONS ON A DRAWING

ARM 11

The primary concern when spacing dimensions on a drawing is to avoid crowding. Begin with the smallest dimension next to the object followed by increasingly larger dimensions. Place the overall dimension last. The minimum standard for dimension line spacing recommended by ANSI is .4 inch (10 mm) away from the object. Place additional dimension lines .25 inch (6 mm) apart. However, these minimum distances are generally too close for most dimensioning. Use your own judgment. Dimension line spacing depends on:
- The size and complexity of the drawing. Complex drawings require careful consideration before dimensions are placed to avoid crowding.
- The amount of open area is important. If there is space available, use it to your best advantage to avoid crowding.

• The length of dimension numerals is important. Long numerals, such as 24.8750, require much space.

No matter what standard you use, dimension line spacing should be consistent. The drawing should look uniform. You can change dimension line spacing on different views, but keep the spacing of groups of dimension lines the same.

Setting dimension line spacing

The DIMDLI (Dimension Line Increment) variable controls the spacing between datum (baseline) dimension lines. The default spacing set in AutoCAD's prototype drawing is 0.38 units, Fig. 18-43. The 0.38 default is too close for many applications. Additional spacing, such as .50, may be specified as follows:

Command: **DIMDLI** ↵
New value for DIMDLI: **.50** ↵
Command:

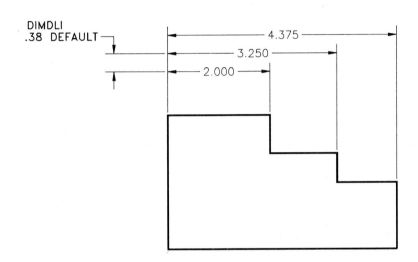

Fig. 18-43. Using the DIMDLI variable to control spacing between dimension baseline lines.

INCLUDING SYMBOLS WITH DIMENSION TEXT

ARM 5

After you select a feature to dimension, AutoCAD responds with the measurement, or dimensioning numeral. In some cases such as dimensioning radii and diameters, AutoCAD automatically places the radius (R) or diameter (ϕ) symbol before the dimension numeral when dimensioning arcs and circles. However, in other cases related to linear dimensioning this practice is not automatic. The recommended ANSI standard for a diameter dimension is to place the diameter symbol (ϕ) before the numeral. To add the diameter symbol, you must type the code followed by "⟨ ⟩." The "⟨ ⟩" tells AutoCAD to use the measurement it calculated. (See Chapter 10 for symbol codes.) You can also type the symbol code and the numeral to achieve the same result. This can be done using the Text option, or by entering the value as follows. Either of the following responses display the dimension text as ϕ1.750.

Dimension text ⟨1.750⟩: **%%C⟨ ⟩** ↵

or

Dimension text ⟨1.750⟩: **%%C1.750** ↵

Additional symbols are used in dimensions to point out certain features on the drawing. The diameter symbol (ϕ) for circles and the radius symbol (R) for arcs are easily drawn. However, additional symbols, such as "□" for a square feature can be drawn individually, but this is time-consuming. Instead, save the symbol as a block and insert it in the drawing before the dimension text. Storing and inserting blocks is discussed in Chapter 21. Symbols used often are shown in Fig. 18-44.

SYMBOL FOR:	ANSI Y14.5	ISO
DIMENSION ORIGIN	⌾→	NONE
FEATURE CONTROL FRAME	⌖ | Ø0.5Ⓜ | A | B | C	⌖ | Ø0.5Ⓜ | A | B | C
CONICAL TAPER	⌲	⌲
SLOPE	⌳	⌳
COUNTERBORE/SPOTFACE	⌴	NONE
COUNTERSINK	⌵	NONE
DEPTH/DEEP	↧	NONE
SQUARE (SHAPE)	□	□
DIMENSION NOT TO SCALE	<u>15</u>	<u>15</u>
NUMBER OF TIMES/PLACES	8X	8X
ARC LENGTH	$\frown$105	NONE
RADIUS	R	R
SPHERICAL RADIUS	SR	NONE
SPHERICAL DIAMETER	SØ	NONE

ANSI Y14.5M-1982

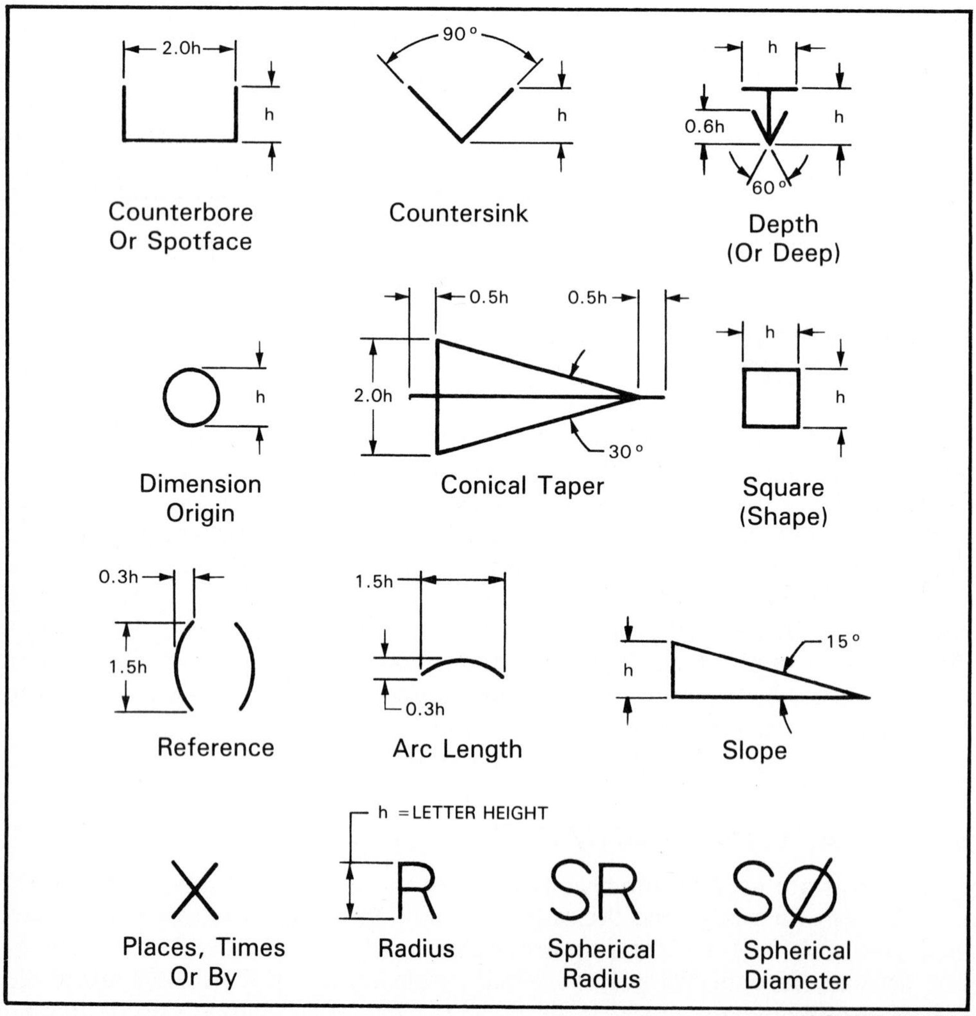

ANSI Y14.5M-1982

Fig. 18-44. Common dimensioning symbols.

ADDITIONAL SYMBOLS

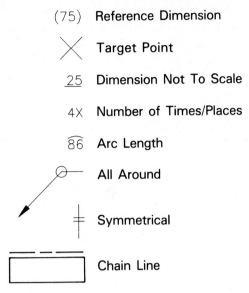

(75)   Reference Dimension

╳   Target Point

25   Dimension Not To Scale

4X   Number of Times/Places

⌒86   Arc Length

⟋⚬   All Around

╫   Symmetrical

Chain Line

Fig. 18-44. Continued.

DRAWING CENTER DASHES OR CENTERLINES IN A CIRCLE OR ARC

ARM 11

You may have noticed that circles and arcs are drawn without center dashes or centerlines. When small circles or arcs are dimensioned, the DIAMETER and RADIUS commands leave center dashes. If the dimension of a large circle crosses through the center, the dashes are left out. When you want to draw center dashes or centerlines, pick Center from the second page of the DIM: screen menu to access the Center option, or type "CEN" or "CENTER" at the Command: prompt:

> Command: **DIM** ↵
> Dim: **CEN** or **CENTER** ↵
> Select arc or circle: *(pick the arc or circle)*
> Dim:

When the circle or arc is picked, center dashes are automatically drawn. The size of the center dashes or the amount that the centerlines extend outside the circle or arc is controlled by the DIMCEN (CENterline) variable. The default provides center dashes 0.09 units long. If DIMCEN is set to 0, center dashes or centerlines are not drawn. A positive value gives center dashes. For example, the value .125 displays center dashes that are .125 units long. When decimal inch units are used, .125 is the recommended length. A negative DIMCEN value draws complete centerlines in addition to center dashes. With a negative value, centerlines extend beyond the circle or arc by the amount entered. For example, a -.125 value extends centerlines .125 unit beyond the circle or arc. See Fig. 18-45.

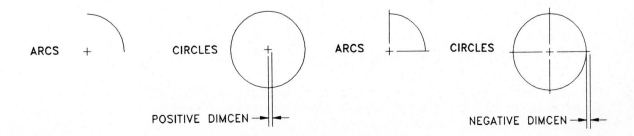

Fig. 18-45. Using the DIMCEN variable.

===== PROFESSIONAL TIP =====

The use of a negative DIMCEN value for small circles may result in placement of center dashes only. This is because AutoCAD needs room for the center dash and a space before the rest of the centerline symbol is placed. Don't be alarmed if this happens. Either try a smaller negative DIMCEN value or accept the results with the value you have set.

EXERCISE 18-6

☐ Load AutoCAD and open PRODR2.
☐ Draw circles and arcs similar to those shown in Fig. 18-45.
☐ Set the DIMCEN value to add center dashes as shown. Use positive and negative values of .125.
☐ Place center dashes on layer 3-3.
☐ Save the drawing as A:EX18-6.

DIMENSIONING CIRCLES ␣ ARM 11

Circles are normally dimensioned by giving the diameter. The ANSI standard for dimensioning arcs is to give the radius. However, AutoCAD allows you to dimension either a circle or arc with a diameter dimension. The Diameter option located in the DIM: screen menu prompts you to select the arc or circle.

Be careful when you pick the arc or circle because your pick point becomes the origin for the leader arrowhead. AutoCAD automatically establishes a leader line that points toward the circle's center as required by the ANSI standard. For this to work, the dimensioning variables DIMTIX (Text Inside eXtension lines) and DIMTOFL (Text Outside/Force Line inside) must be off. Then, after entering the dimension text, you are asked for the leader length. When you pick a desired leader length, AutoCAD automatically draws the leader line with the correct shoulder length and places the text with the ϕ symbol preceding the numeral. See Fig. 18-46A.

ANSI Y14.5M acknowledges that you can place the dimension line and text inside large circles. To do this, be sure DIMTIX is on and DIMTOFL is off. The resulting drawing is shown in Fig. 18-46B. The command sequence is as follows:

Command: **DIM** ⏎
Dim: **DIA** ⏎
Select arc or circle: *(pick the arc or circle to be dimensioned)*
Dimension text ⟨2.750⟩: ⏎
Dim:

Some drafters prefer placing the dimension line and arrowheads inside the circle and the dimension text outside. Before placing the dimensions, be sure that DIMTIX is off and DIMTOFL is on. A circle dimensioned in this manner is displayed in Fig. 18-46C. The command sequence is the same as the previous example with the addition of a leader length prompt:

Command: **DIM** ⏎
Dim: **DIA** ⏎
Select arc or circle: *(pick the arc or circle to be dimensioned)*
Dimension text ⟨1.875⟩: ⏎
Enter leader length for text: *(pick the leader length)*
Dim:

The dimensions in Fig. 18-46 show the diameter symbol in front of the dimension numeral as recommended by the ANSI Y14.5M standard. The diameter symbol "ϕ" for circles and the radius symbol "R" for arcs are placed automatically.

When this is done, a leader line points to the circle. The dimension numeral is connected to the leader. The dimension line and arrowheads are drawn inside the circle if the circle is large

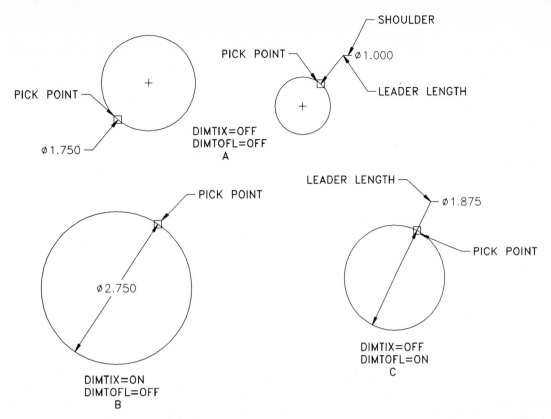

Fig. 18-46. Using the DIAMETER command. Note the DIMTIX and DIMTOFL variable settings in each example.

enough. You need to anticipate when a circle is too small. The point you pick on the circle becomes the location of the leader on the circle, as shown in Fig. 18-47. If the dimension placement is not right, type or pick UNDO and try again.

When the DIMZIN variable is set to its default (0), AutoCAD places a 0 in front of all decimal dimensions less than one, for example, 0.375. If the decimal dimension is in inches, this practice is not recommended. If the decimal dimension is metric (millimeters), then the practice is an accepted standard. Therefore, if you are using inch dimensioning, you should type the appropriate text and the Dimension text: prompt to avoid getting the 0 before the decimal point. The DIM-ZIN variable may also be used to have AutoCAD automatically remove the zero in front of decimal dimension numerals. Set DIMZIN to 4 like this:

Dim: **DIMZIN** ↵
New value for DIMZIN ⟨0⟩: **4** ↵

In the case of the dimension in Fig. 18-47, the following entry was used to get the ⌀ symbol and desired text even though the preferred method would be to set the DIMZIN variable:

Dimension text ⟨0.375⟩: **%%C.375** ↵

Remember, if the dimension placement is incorrect, just type a "U" or pick UNDO and try again.

The DIAMETER command may also be used in the same manner to apply a diameter dimension to arcs. However, it is not standard to dimension arcs by diameter.

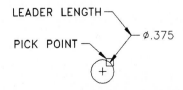

Fig. 18-47. Dimensioning very small diameters.

— PROFESSIONAL TIP —

    Dimensioning variable values can be entered at the Dim: prompt. This is convenient because you can change dimensioning variables as you work with dimensions. You can also change the dimensioning variables at any time at the Command: prompt. For example:

    Command: **DIMCEN** ↵
    New value for DIMCEN ⟨0.0900⟩: **.05** ↵

When a dimensioning variable value is an on/off toggle, enter "0" for off or "1" for on.

    Command: **DIMTIX** ↵
    New value for DIMTIX ⟨0⟩: **1** ↵

    In addition, dimensioning variables can be entered transparently at either the Command: prompt or Dim: prompt while in another command. For example:

    Command: **LINE** ↵
    From point: **'DIMASZ** ↵

    or

    Dim: **DIA** ↵
    Select arc or circle: **'DIMCEN** ↵

EXERCISE 18-7

☐ Open PRODR2.
☐ Draw the object lines of the following views on layer 0-7, and place all dimensions on layer 3-3.
☐ Use the proper dimensioning techniques and commands to dimension the objects exactly as shown.
☐ Save the drawing as A:EX18-7.

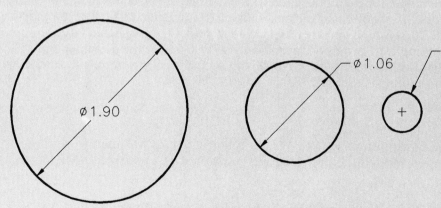

Dimensioning holes

    Holes are dimensioned in the view where they appear as circles. You should provide location dimensions to the center and a leader showing the diameter. Same size holes may be noted with one hole dimension as shown in Fig. 18-48.

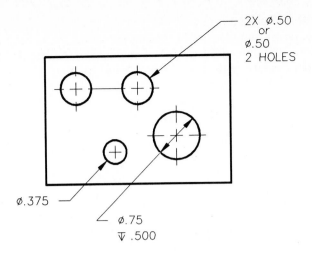

Fig. 18-48. Dimensioning holes.

Dimensioning for manufacturing processes

Manufacturing processes, such as counterbores, spotface, and countersink are dimensioned with two items. Locate the centers in the circular view. Place a leader providing machining information in a note, Fig. 18-49. A *counterbore* is a larger diameter hole machined at one end of a smaller hole. It provides a place for the head of a bolt. A *spotface* is similar to a counterbore except that it is not as deep. The spotface provides a smooth recessed surface for a washer. A *countersink* is a cone-shaped recess at one end of a hole. It provides a mating surface for a screw head of the same shape. A note for these features may be provided using words or symbols. Symbols for this type of application are discussed in Chapter 21.

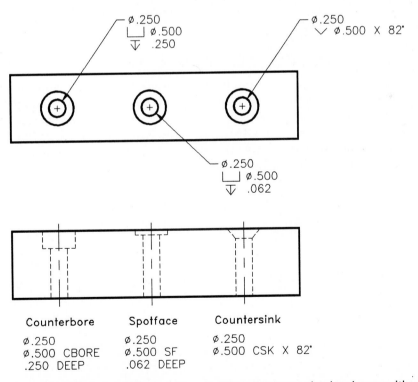

Fig. 18-49. Dimension notes for machining processes. The notes may also be shown without the counterbore, spotface, countersink, and depth symbols in note form. The respective note, when used, should be connected to the leader in place of the symbol method.

Dimensioning repetitive features

Repetitive features refer to many features having the same shape and size. When this occurs, the number of repetitions is followed by an "X", a space, and the size dimension. The dimension is then connected to the feature with a leader as shown in Fig. 18-50.

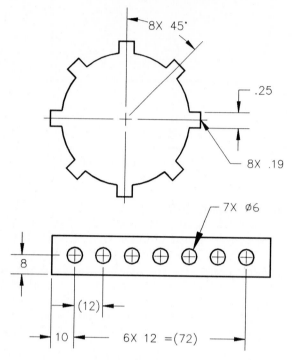

Fig. 18-50. Dimensioning repetitive features.

━ PROFESSIONAL TIP ━

The ANSI standard recommends a small space between the object and the extension line as shown in Fig. 18-1. This happens when the DIMEXO variable is set to its default or some other desired positive value. This is very useful except when providing dimensions to centerlines for the location of holes. A positive DIMEXO value leaves a space between the centerline and the beginning of the extension line as shown at A below. This is not a preferred practice. It is recommended that you change DIMEXO to 0 for these applications. See Part B in the following figure.

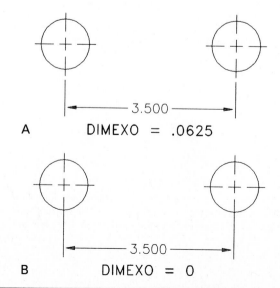

EXERCISE 18-8

☐ Load AutoCAD and open PRODR2.
☐ Draw the object lines of the following views on layer 0-7, and place all dimensions on layer 3-3.
☐ Use the proper dimensioning techniques and commands to dimension the objects exactly as they are shown.
☐ Save the drawing as A:EX18-8.

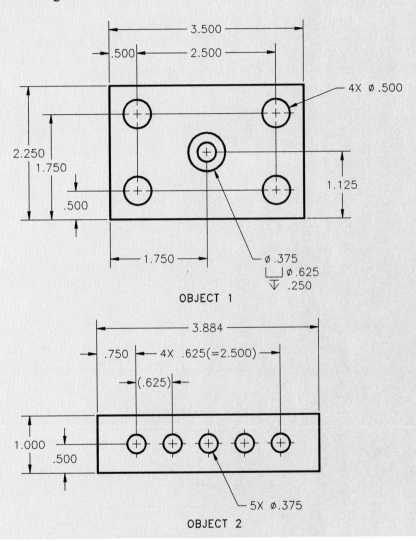

OBJECT 1

OBJECT 2

DIMENSIONING ARCS

ARM 11

The standard for dimensioning arcs is a radius dimension. The RADIUS command can be typed at the Dim: prompt, or Radius can be picked from the screen menu. The RADIUS command allows you to dimension either an arc or circle in this manner. Using this command, AutoCAD places a leader line with an arrowhead pointing at the arc. The leader line either extends away from the arc, or from the arc through the center point as with the small radii shown in Fig. 18-51A. After you enter the dimension text, AutoCAD asks you for the leader length. When you pick the leader length, AutoCAD automatically draws the proper leader shoulder and correctly places the text with the radius symbol. AutoCAD automatically adds the center dashes when the DIMCEN variable is nonzero, and when the leader is placed outside the arc, away from the center point as shown in Fig. 18-51B and E. However, even if DIMCEN is something other than zero, there is no center mark drawn when the leader line is inside the arc and passing the center point as illustrated in Fig. 18-51C, D, and F. For the leader to project away from the arc, DIMTIX and DIMTOFL must be off. When DIMTIX is off and DIMTOFL is on, the leader is drawn from the arc center with an arrowhead at the arc line and text outside the arc as shown in Fig. 18-51C. If you want to put the leader and dimension text inside the arc, set DIMTIX on and DIMTOFL off as displayed in Fig. 18-51F. The command sequence illustrated in Fig. 18-51 is as follows:

Command: **DIM** ↵
Dim: **RAD** or **RADIUS** ↵
Select arc or circle: *(pick the arc to be dimensioned)*
Dimension text ⟨current⟩: *(enter the desired value and press ENTER, or press ENTER to accept the default value)*
Enter leader length for text: *(pick the desired leader length)*
Dim:

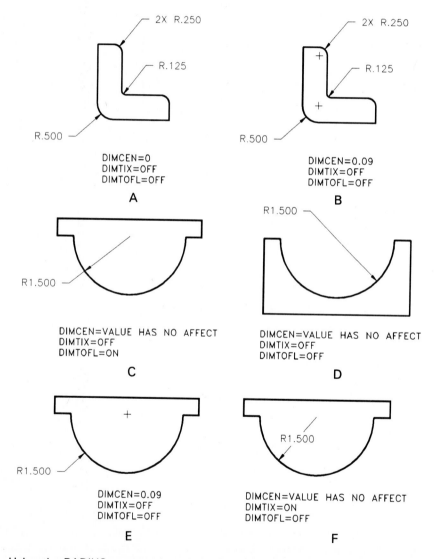

Fig. 18-51. Using the RADIUS command to dimension arcs. Note the values of the DIMCEN, DIMTIX, and DIMTOFL variables in each of the examples.

If decimal inch units are used and the value is less than 1, AutoCAD places a 0 in front of the decimal. ANSI Y14.5M recommends that a decimal inch be displayed without a 0 in front of the decimal point. Metric decimals, however, should have a 0 placed in front of the decimal point. To automatically delete the 0 in front of the decimal point, set the DIMZIN variable to 4.

Dimensioning fillets and rounds

Small arcs on the outside corners of a part are called *rounds*. Small inside arcs are called *fillets*. Rounds are used to relieve sharp corners. Fillets are designed to strengthen inside corners. Fillets and rounds may be dimensioned individually as arcs or in a general note if there are many of them on the part. When used, the general note is: ALL FILLETS AND ROUNDS R.125 UNLESS OTHERWISE SPECIFIED. See Fig. 18-52.

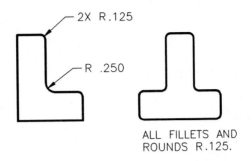

Fig. 18-52. Dimensioning fillets and rounds.

DIMENSIONING CURVES

ARM 11

When possible, curves are dimensioned as arcs. When they are not in the shape of a constant-radius arc, they should be dimensioned to points along the curve using the HORIZ or VERT commands. See Fig. 18-53.

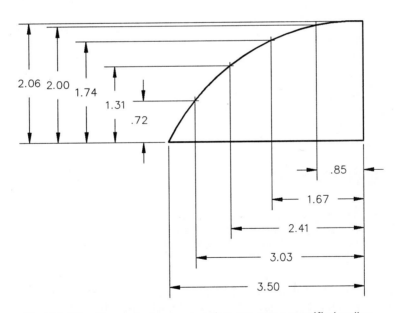

Fig. 18-53. Dimensioning curves that are not a specified radius.

Dimensioning curves with oblique extension lines

The method of dimensioning a curve shown in Fig. 18-53 is the normal practice, but in some cases, spaces may be limited and oblique extension lines are used. First, dimension the object using the VERT or HORIZ commands as appropriate, even if dimensions are crowded or overlap as shown in Fig. 18-54A. In this case, the drafter anticipated that the .150 and .340 dimensions are to be placed at an oblique angle above the view. Oblique extension lines are drawn using the OBLIQUE command or by typing "OBL" or "OBLIQUE" at the Dim: prompt. The OBLIQUE command can also be accessed through the Oblique Dimension option of the Edit Dims selection in the Modify pull-down menu. After entering "OBL", you are asked to select the objects. At this time, you select the dimensions to be drawn at the oblique angle. The .150 and .340 dimensions are selected in this case:

> Command: **DIM** ↵
> Dim: **OBL** or **OBLIQUE** ↵
> Select objects: *(pick the .150 and .340 dimensions)*
> Select objects: ↵

Next, you are asked for the obliquing angle. Careful planning is need to ensure the dimensions oblique where you want them. Obliquing angles originate from 0° East and revolve counterclockwise:

> Enter obliquing angle (RETURN for none): **135** ↵
> Dim:

The result is shown in Fig. 18-54B.

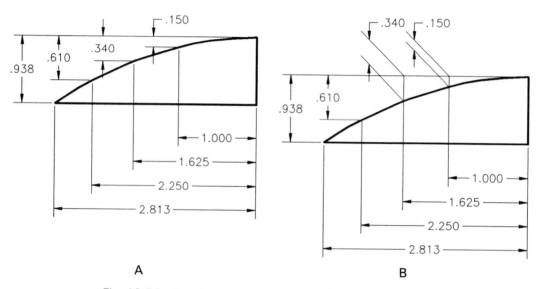

Fig. 18-54. Drawing dimensions with oblique extension lines.

DRAWING LEADER LINES   ARM 11

The Diameter and Radius options automatically place leaders on the drawing. The Leader option gives you maximum flexibility when adding leaders. The command allows you to begin and end a leader line where you desire. This command is ideal for the following situations:
- When you are working on a crowded drawing and need maximum control of dimension placement.
- Adding specific notes to the drawing.
- When a leader line must be staggered to go around other drawing features. Keep in mind that staggering leader lines is not a recommended ANSI standard.
- Where a double leader is required. Drawing two leaders from one note is not normally recommended.
- When making custom leader lines.

Use the LEADER subcommand as follows:

    Command: **DIM** ↵
    Dim: **LEADER** ↵
    Leader start: *(pick a point on the feature to be dimensioned)*

The LEADER command now acts like the LINE command. AutoCAD asks you for the end-points of the line segments. The second point determines the start of the leader shoulder. The third point is the end of the shoulder. Properly drawn leaders have one straight segment extending from the feature to the shoulder, and a horizontal shoulder about 1/4 inch (6.4 mm). You must press the ENTER key to stop drawing other leader segments. See Fig. 18-55.

    To point: *(pick the second leader point, which is usually the start of the shoulder)*
    To point: *(pick the end of the leader shoulder)*
    To point: ↵
    Dimension text ⟨measurement from the previous dimension⟩: *(change the measurement*
    if necessary, or press ENTER to accept the value)
    Dim:

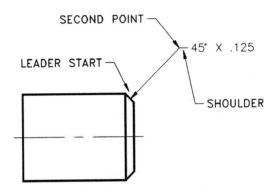

Fig. 18-55. Using the LEADER command.

The LEADER command may be used to connect notes to various features on a drawing. While single leader lines are the preferred ANSI standard, some companies allow multiple leaders, as shown in Fig. 18-56.

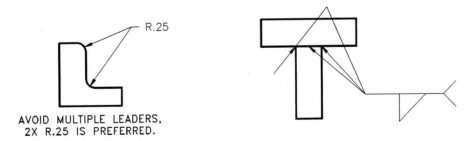

Fig. 18-56. Alternate applications of the LEADER command.

EXERCISE 18-9

☐ Load AutoCAD and open PRODR2.
☐ Draw the object lines of the views on layer 0-7 and place the dimensions on layer 3-3.
☐ Use the proper dimensioning techniques and commands to dimension the object exactly as shown.
☐ Save the drawing as A:EX18-9.

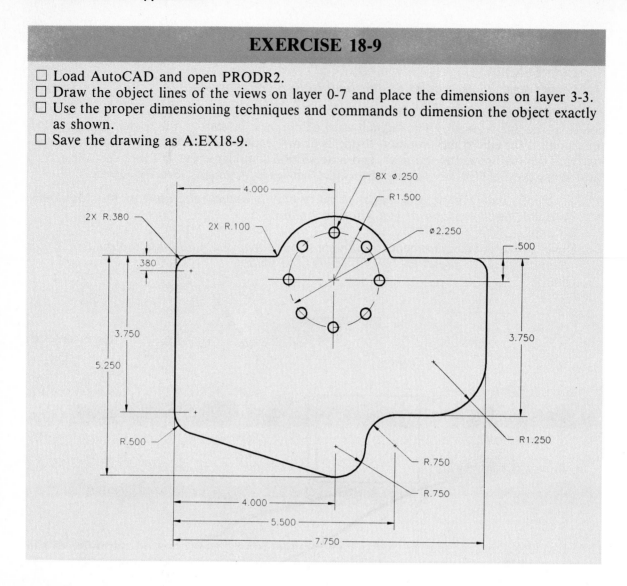

Dimensioning chamfers

A *chamfer* is an angled surface used to relieve sharp corners. The ends of bolts are commonly chamfered to allow them to engage the threaded hole better. Chamfers of 45° are dimensioned with a leader giving the angle and linear dimension, or with two linear dimensions. The LEADER command works well for this application as shown in Fig. 18-57.

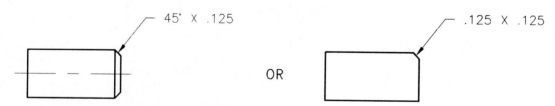

Fig. 18-57. Dimensioning 45° chamfers.

Chamfers other than 45° must have the angle and linear dimension, or two linear dimensions placed on the view, Fig. 18-58. The HORIZONTAL, VERTICAL, and ANGULAR commands are used for this purpose.

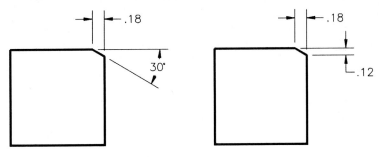

Fig. 18-58. Dimensioning chamfers that are not 45°.

PROFESSIONAL TIP

Use the object snap modes to your best advantage when dimensioning. This helps save time and increase accuracy.

EXERCISE 18-10

☐ Open PRODR2.
☐ Draw the object lines of the views on layer 0-7 and place dimensions on layer 3-3.
☐ Use the proper dimensioning techniques and commands to dimension the objects exactly as shown.
☐ Save the drawing as A:EX18-10.

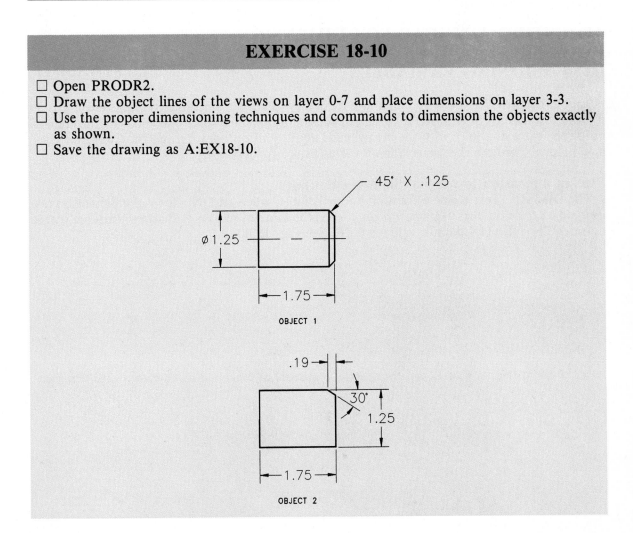

DIMENSIONING IN LIMITED SPACES

ARM 11

When space between extension lines is limited, AutoCAD places the dimension line, arrowheads, and numerals outside the extension lines. You need to plan ahead because the numeral is placed outside of the last extension line selected. See Fig. 18-59. Remember, if you do not like where the dimension is placed, enter UNDO and try again.

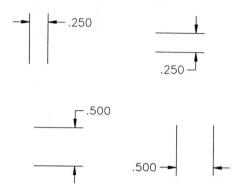

Fig. 18-59. Dimensioning in limited spaces.

ADJUSTING AUTOCAD FOR DIMENSION TEXT PLACEMENT, AND USING OTHER DIMENSIONING VARIABLES

ARM 11

AutoCAD provides you with maximum flexibility to make your dimensioning reflect proper drafting standards. For example, if you are dimensioning a limited space and you want the numeral inside the extension lines with the arrowheads and extension lines outside the extension lines, it is no problem with the dimensioning variables set appropriately.

Placing dimension text inside the extension lines

The DIMTIX (Text Inside eXtension lines) variable, when set ON, forces the dimension text inside the extension lines. This occurs only when the dimension lines and arrowheads are placed outside. The DIMTIX default value is OFF. See Fig. 18-60.

DIMTIX = OFF   DIMTIX = ON

Fig. 18-60. Using the DIMTIX variable to affect placement of dimension text between extension lines.

Drawing the dimension line between the extension lines when the text and arrowheads are outside

Some drafters prefer to place a dimension line between extension lines when the dimension text is outside. To do so, set DIMTOFL to ON and DIMTIX to OFF as shown in Fig. 18-61. The default for DIMTOFL is OFF.

Fig. 18-61. Using the DIMTOFL variable.

Placing the dimension text inside the extension lines and suppressing the dimension line

When several dimensions are adjacent, you may want to place one numeral inside the extension lines and suppress the dimension lines and arrowheads. To do this, set DIMTIX to ON and DIMSOXD to ON. The default value for each is OFF. The results are shown in Fig. 18-62.

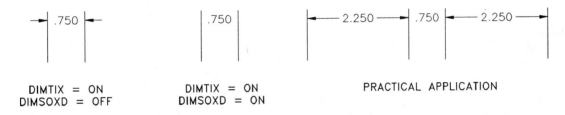

Fig. 18-62. Using the DIMSOXD variable.

Adjusting dimension text placement in relation to the dimension line

AutoCAD allows you to place the dimension text above, below, or centered within a break in the dimension line. This is called "Text Vertical Position" and is controlled by the DIMTVP variable. As shown in Fig. 18-63, DIMTVP has three settings:

- **DIMTVP = 0** (default)—Dimension text is centered within a break in dimension line. This is the normal practice for mechanical drafting.
- **DIMTVP = 1**—Dimension text is placed above the dimension line. This is common practice for architectural drafting and the construction trades.
- **DIMTVP = -1**—Dimension text is placed below the dimension line. This is an uncommon practice.

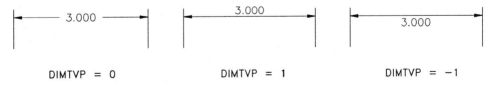

Fig. 18-63. Using the DIMTVP variable to affect vertical placement of text.

PROFESSIONAL TIP

DIMTVP can be set to any value between 1 and −1 to achieve a text location that is off-center of the dimension line, but not completely above or below it.

In addition to the dimensioning variables that control the dimension text placement, the TEDIT command lets you control the placement and orientation of an existing associative dimension. Remember, an associative dimension is a dimension drawn with DIMASO on, and all elements of the dimension act as one entity. Good dimensioning practice requires that adjacent dimension numerals be staggered rather than stacked up as shown in Fig. 18-64A. When this situation occurs, use the TEDIT command to move the dimension text into staggered positions:

> Command: **DIM** ↵
> Dim: **TEDIT** ↵
> Select dimension: *(pick the dimension to be altered)*

With DIMASO on, the text of the selected dimension automatically drags with the screen cursor. This allows you to visually see where to place the text at the next prompt:

> Enter text location (Left/Right/Home/Angle): *(pick the desired text location)*

AutoCAD automatically moves the text and re-establishes the break in the dimension line as shown in Fig. 18-64B.

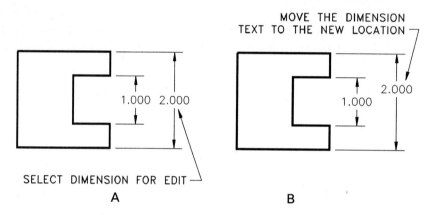

Fig. 18-64. Using the TEDIT command to stagger dimensions.

The TEDIT command also allows you to automatically move the dimension text to the left or right, place it at an angle, or move it back to the original position. This is how the text location options work:

- **Left (L)** — Moves horizontal text to the left or vertical text down.
- **Right (R)** — Moves horizontal text to the right or vertical text up.
- **Home (H)** — Moves text that had been changed previously back to its original position.
- **Angle** — Allows you to place dimension text at an angle. This works similar to the TROTATE command to be discussed later in this chapter. The text rotates around its middle point when you respond with a text angle or pick two points at the desired angle:

> Enter text location (Left/Right/Home/Angle): **A** ↵
> Text angle: **45** ↵

If you want to move text to the left, enter "L" as follows:

> Enter text location (Left/Right/Home/Angle): **L** ↵

Fig. 18-65 shows the affects of the TEDIT options.

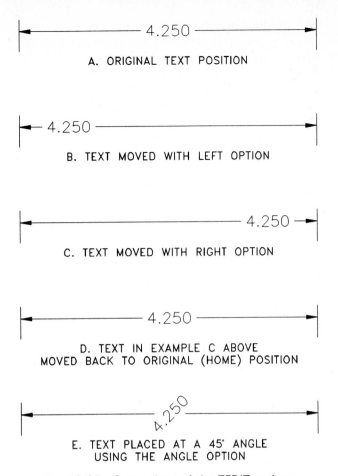

A. ORIGINAL TEXT POSITION

B. TEXT MOVED WITH LEFT OPTION

C. TEXT MOVED WITH RIGHT OPTION

D. TEXT IN EXAMPLE C ABOVE
MOVED BACK TO ORIGINAL (HOME) POSITION

E. TEXT PLACED AT A 45° ANGLE
USING THE ANGLE OPTION

Fig. 18-65. Comparison of the TEDIT options.

PROFESSIONAL TIP

The TEDIT command can also be accessed from the Modify pull-down menu. Pick Edit Dims from this menu, followed by picking Dimension Text from the cascading menu. Note the screen menu when you select one of these options. Remember, in order to reaccess the previously selected command, simply double click on the Modify pull-down menu.

Controlling the gap between the dimension line and dimension text

When the dimension line is broken for placement of the dimension text, the space between the dimension line and text is controlled by the DIMGAP variable. The default distance for DIMGAP is .09. The default gap works well in most cases. However, in some instances the dimension text may be forced outside the extension line. Closing the dimension line gap allows more text to remain between the extension lines. Fig. 18-66 shows the dimension line gap.

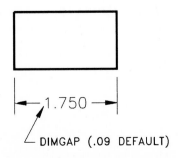

Fig. 18-66. The dimension line gap established with the DIMGAP dimensioning variable.

Drawing custom shapes at the ends of dimension lines

Creating shapes and symbols for multiple use is discussed in Chapter 21. You can place user-defined blocks rather than arrows at the ends of extension lines. The DIMBLK1 variable places a custom block at the first end of the dimension line. DIMBLK2 places a custom block at the second end of the dimension line. To place user-defined blocks at both ends of the dimension line, set DIMSAH to ON. Fig. 18-67 shows the dimension origin symbol used as a custom block at the first extension line. With DIMSAH set to ON, you can specify a custom block at both extension lines. Refer to page 18-13 for a discussion regarding the use of the DIMBLK variable.

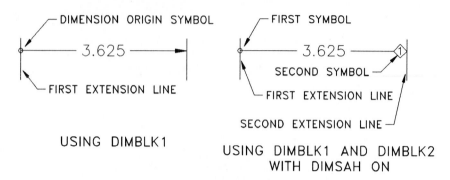

Fig. 18-67. Using the DIMBLK1, DIMBLK2, and DIMSAH variables.

USING THE UPDATE COMMAND   ARM 11

The UPDATE command changes existing dimensions to reflect the current settings for dimension variables, text style, and units settings. The only dimension options not affected by UPDATE are those drawn using the BASELINE or CONTINUE commands. For example, suppose you change the DIMDLI variable, which changes the dimension string spacing. All new dimensions drawn with the BASELINE or CONTINUE commands reflect the revised dimension line spacing. However, the UPDATE command would not alter the existing dimension line spacing. Although, if you use the DIMASZ variable to change the arrowhead size, then any dimensions picked with the UPDATE command are automatically changed to reflect the new arrowhead size. The UPDATE command works like this:

Command: **DIM** ↵
Dim: **UPDATE** ↵
Select objects: *(select dimension entities to be updated)*
Select objects: ↵
Dim:

PROFESSIONAL TIP

The Edit Dims selection in the Modify pull-down menu offers a variety of options for editing dimensions. As mentioned earlier, the TEDIT command can be accessed through this selection. In addition, the OBLIQUE and UPDATE commands are available for use.

EXERCISE 18-11

☐ With DIMTIX set to OFF, draw a .750 in. dimension as shown in Fig. 18-60.
☐ Set DIMTIX ON.
☐ Select the UPDATE command and pick the dimension again.
☐ With DIMTOFL set to OFF, draw a .750 dimension as shown in Fig. 18-61.
☐ Turn on the DIMTOFL variable.
☐ Select the UPDATE command and pick the dimension again.
☐ With DIMTIX ON and DIMSOXD OFF, draw a .750 dimension as shown in Fig. 18-62. Then draw the same dimension with DIMTIX and DIMSOXD both turned on. Finally, draw the same practical application given in Fig. 18-62 using these dimensioning variables as needed.
☐ Draw the three dimensions shown in Fig. 18-63, one with DIMTVP set to 0, the second with DIMTVP set to 1, and the third with DIMTVP set to -1.
☐ Save the drawing as A:EX18-11.

DIM VARS THAT AFFECT DIMENSION SCALES | ARM 11 |

There are two dimensioning variables that alter the dimension scales. The DIMSCALE variable is an overall scale factor that applies to all dimensioning variables that specify size, distance, or offset. When DIMSCALE is set to the default factor of 1, all dimensioning variables are displayed as set. If it is changed to 2, all variable values are doubled. See Fig. 18-68. Changing the DIMSCALE affects only future dimensions. If you are creating a drawing to be plotted at full (1:1) scale, then the DIMSCALE should equal 1. However, if the drawing is to be plotted at any other scale, the DIMSCALE should be set to the scale factor. The scale factor is the reciprocal of the drawing scale. For example, the scale factor for half scale (1:2) is 2, 1:2 is .5 = 1, and 1/.5 = 2. For the architect using a 1/4″ = 1′-0″ scale, the calculation is: .25″ = 12″, 12/.25 = 48 scale factor.

Fig. 18-68. Effects of the DIMSCALE variable.

Another dimensioning variable, DIMLFAC (Length FACtor), sets a scale factor for all linear dimensions, except angles. The default value of 1 represents a 1:1, or full scale factor. A factor of 2 multiplies dimension numerals by two as shown in Fig. 18-69.

Fig. 18-69. Using the DIMLFAC variable.

EXERCISE 18-12

☐ Load AutoCAD if the drawing editor is not currently on your screen, and open PRODR2.
☐ Set the following dimensioning values.
　☐ DIMEXE = .125
　☐ DIMEXO = .08
　☐ DIMCEN = .25
　☐ DIMDLI = .75
　☐ DIMASZ = .18
　☐ DIMGAP = .05
☐ Draw the following objects and dimension them exactly as shown.

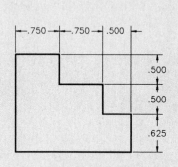

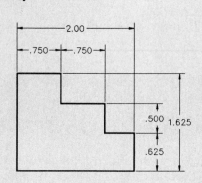

OBJECT 1　　　　　　　　　　　OBJECT 2

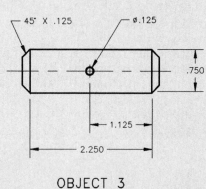

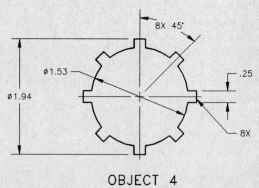

OBJECT 3　　　　　　　　　　　OBJECT 4

☐ Change the DIMSCALE variable to 2 and observe the results after using the UPDATE command and selecting all objects with a window or crossing box. Change DIMSCALE back to 1, and again use the UPDATE command.
☐ Change the DIMLFAC variable to 2 and observe the results after using the UPDATE command and selecting all objects with a window or crossing box. Change DIMLFAC back to 1 and again use the UPDATE command.
☐ Set the following new dimensioning variables:
　☐ DIMTSZ = .05
　☐ DIMTIH = OFF
　☐ DIMTOH = OFF
　☐ DIMTAD = ON
☐ Update objects 3 and 4 using the current variables.
☐ Save the drawing as A:EX18-12.

VARIABLES THAT ASSIGN COLOR TO DIMENSION COMPONENTS

There are three dimensioning variables that let you assign any valid color to dimension components. These variables are DIMCLRD, DIMCLRE, and DIMCLRT. You can set color values by number as follows:

1 = Red		5 = Blue	
2 = Yellow		6 = Magenta	
3 = Green		7 = White	
4 = Cyan			

The DIMCLRD variable is used to set the CoLoR of all Dimension lines, arrowheads, and leaders. Use the DIMCLRD variable as follows:

Command: **DIMCLRD** ⏎
New value for DIMCLRD: *(enter desired color, such as **1** for red)*

Now all new dimension lines, arrowheads, and leaders are drawn with red. Use the UPDATE command to change existing dimension colors.

The DIMCLRE variable changes the CoLoR of the Extension lines. The DIMCLRT variable is used to alter the CoLoR of the dimension Text. All three of these dimensioning variables are used in the same manner as previously described for the DIMCLRD variable.

——— PROFESSIONAL TIP ———

DIMCLRD, DIMCLRE, and DIMCLRT variables override any layer color settings. For example, even though a layer color may be yellow, the dimensions can still be different colors.

ROTATING THE DIMENSION TEXT

ARM 11

The unidirectional and aligned dimensioning systems are the standard placement of dimension text. However, AutoCAD does allow you to rotate the dimension text. First, draw the dimension in the usual way, as shown in Fig. 18-70A, and then rotate the dimension text with the TROTATE command as follows:

Command: **DIM** ⏎
Dim: **TROTATE** ⏎
Enter text angle: *(set a text angle, **45** for example)*⏎
Select objects: *(pick the dimension text to rotate)*

The selected dimension numeral is automatically rotated as shown in Fig. 18-70B.

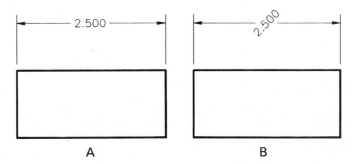

Fig. 18-70. Rotating the dimension text with the TROTATE command.

EXERCISE 18-13

☐ Open PRODR2.
☐ Practice with the DIMSCALE variable by making a drawing similar to Fig. 18-68.
☐ With DIMLFAC set at 1, draw a 3.000 inch dimension. Then change DIMLFAC to 2 and draw the dimension again to see what happens. Your drawing should look like Fig. 18-69.
☐ Draw a 1.750 dimension with the current DIMGAP setting. Then change DIMGAP and draw the dimension again to notice the difference.
☐ Set DIMCLRD to red, DIMCLRE to blue, and DIMCLRT to green. Draw the object shown in Fig. 18-70A and see what happens.
☐ Use the TROTATE command to rotate some of the dimension text on your drawing. Rotate it back if you wish.
☐ Save the drawing as A:EX18-13.

ERASING DIMENSIONS USING VARIOUS SELECTION OPTIONS

ARM 2

In Chapter 6 you were introduced to the ERASE command. There are different ways to select objects for erasure. They include Last, Previous, Window, Crossing, WPolygon, CPolygon, and Fence.

Erasing features, such as large groups of dimensions, often becomes difficult. They are very close to other parts of the drawing. It is time-consuming to erase them individually. When this situation occurs, the Crossing, CPolygon, and Fence selection options are handy. Fig. 18-71 shows a comparison between using ERASE Window and ERASE Crossing on a group of dimensions. For a review of these techniques, and the Modify pull-down menu, refer to Chapter 6.

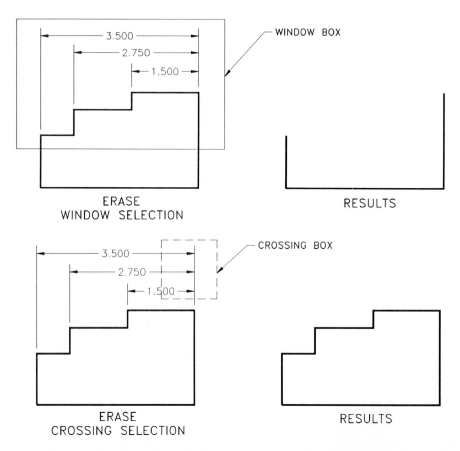

Fig. 18-71. Using the ERASE Window and Crossing options.

ALTERNATE DIMENSIONING PRACTICES

In industries where computer numerical control machining processes are used, it is becoming common to omit dimension lines. This type of dimensioning is called *arrowless*, or *tabular dimensioning*. Where changing values of a product are involved, dimensions are shown in a chart. This is referred to as *chart dimensioning.*

Arrowless dimensioning

Arrowless dimensioning is becoming popular in mechanical drafting. It is also used in electronics drafting, especially for chassis layout. This type of dimensioning has only extension lines and numerals. All dimension lines and arrowheads are omitted. Dimension numerals are aligned with the extension lines. Each dimension numeral represents a dimension originating from a common point. This starting, or "0" dimension is typically known as a *datum,* or *baseline.* Holes or other features are labeled with identification letters. Sizes are given in a table placed on the drawing as shown in Fig. 18-72.

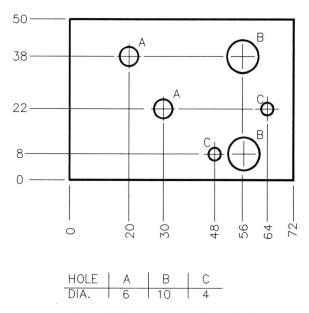

HOLE	A	B	C
DIA.	6	10	4

Fig. 18-72. Arrowless dimensioning.

Tabular dimensioning

Tabular dimensioning is a form of arrowless dimensioning where dimensions to features are shown in a table. The table gives the location of features from an X and Y axis. It also provides the depth of features from a Z axis when appropriate. Each feature is labeled with a letter or number that correlates to the table, Fig. 18-73.

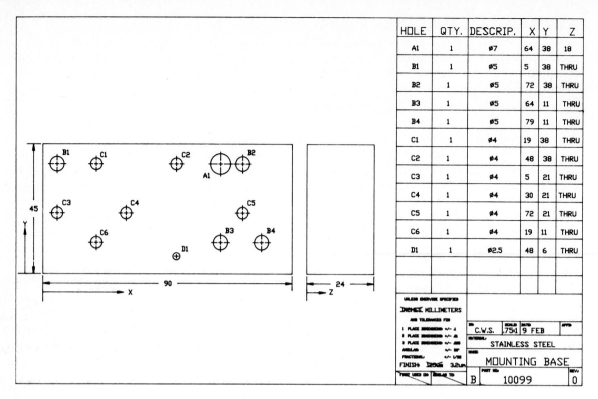

HOLE	QTY.	DESCRIP.	X	Y	Z
A1	1	⌀7	64	38	18
B1	1	⌀5	5	38	THRU
B2	1	⌀5	72	38	THRU
B3	1	⌀5	64	11	THRU
B4	1	⌀5	79	11	THRU
C1	1	⌀4	19	38	THRU
C2	1	⌀4	48	38	THRU
C3	1	⌀4	5	21	THRU
C4	1	⌀4	30	21	THRU
C5	1	⌀4	72	21	THRU
C6	1	⌀4	19	11	THRU
D1	1	⌀2.5	48	6	THRU

UNLESS OTHERWISE SPECIFIED
DIMENSIONS MILLIMETERS
AND TOLERANCES FOR

1 PLACE DIMENSIONS +/- 1	BY C.W.S.	SCALD .75:1	DATED 9 FEB	APPD
2 PLACE DIMENSIONS +/- .1			
3 PLACE DIMENSIONS +/- .005	MATERIAL STAINLESS STEEL		
ANGULAR +/- 5°			
FRACTIONAL +/- 1/32	NAME MOUNTING BASE		
FINISH 125μm 3.2μm			
FIRST USED ON / SIMILAR TO	B	PART NO. 10099	REV: 0

Fig. 18-73. Tabular dimensioning.

Chart dimensioning

Chart dimensioning may take the form of unidirectional, aligned, arrowless, or tabular dimensioning. It provides flexibility in situations where dimensions change depending on the requirements of the product. The views of the product are drawn and variable dimensions are shown with letters. The letters correlate to a chart in which the different options are shown, Fig. 18-74.

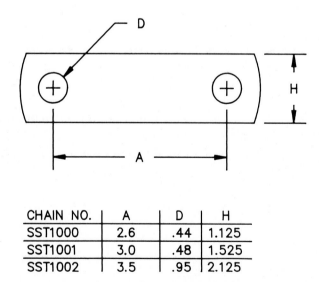

CHAIN NO.	A	D	H
SST1000	2.6	.44	1.125
SST1001	3.0	.48	1.525
SST1002	3.5	.95	2.125

Fig. 18-74. Chart dimensioning.

Ordinate dimensioning

AutoCAD refers to arrowless dimensioning as *ordinate dimensioning*. This type of dimensioning is done using the ORDINATE command found in the DIM screen menu. When using this command, AutoCAD automatically places an extension line and numeral along X and Y coordinates. Since you are working in X-Y axes it is best to have ORTHO on.

The World Coordinate System (WCS) 0,0 coordinate has been in the lower-left corner of the screen for the drawings you have already completed. In most cases, this is fine. However, when doing ordinate dimensioning it is best to have the dimensions originate from a corner of the object. The WCS is fixed; the User Coordinate System (UCS), on the other hand, can be moved to any orientation desired.

All of the ordinate dimensions originate from the current UCS origin. The UCS is discussed in detail in Chapter 24. In general, UCS allows you to set your own coordinate system. If you do this, then all of the Dimension text: prompts display the actual dimensions from the X-Y coordinates on the object. Move the UCS origin to the corner of the object using the following command sequence:

Command: **UCS** ↲
Origin/ZAxis/3point/Entity/View/X/Y/Z/Prev/Restore/Save/Del/?/⟨World⟩: **0** ↲
Origin point ⟨0,0,0⟩: *(pick the origin point at the corner of the object to be dimensioned as shown in Fig. 18-75A)*

Next, if there are circles on your drawing, use the CENTER command to place center marks in the circles as shown in Fig. 18-75B. This makes your drawing conform to ANSI standards and provides something to pick when dimensioning the circle locations. Now, you are ready to start placing the ordinate dimensions. Enter the ORDINATE command by picking from the DIM screen menu or typing at the Dim: prompt:

Command: **DIM** ↲
Dim: **ORDINATE** ↲
Select Feature: *(pick the feature to be dimensioned)*

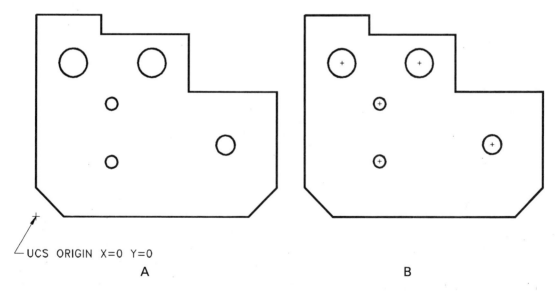

Fig. 18-75. A—Draw the object and move the UCS origin to the X-Y corner. B—Add the center marks to the circular features using the CENTER command.

When the Select Feature: prompt appears, move the screen cursor to the feature to be dimensioned. If the feature is the corner of the object, pick the corner. Use the object snaps ENDpoint or INTersect to help if needed. If the feature is a circle, pick the end of the center mark. This leaves the required space between the center mark and the extension line if the DIMEXO variable is set appropriately. Zoom in if needed and use the object snaps to help. The next prompt asks for the leader endpoint, which really refers to the extension line endpoint. You can first enter either X or Y to tell AutoCAD which axis originates the dimension:

> Leader endpoint (Xdatum/Ydatum): **X** ⏎
> Leader endpoint: *(pick the endpoint of the extension line)*

If you do not enter either X or Y to determine which axis originates the dimension, then AutoCAD makes this determination for you when you pick the leader endpoint:

> Leader endpoint (Xdatum/Ydatum): *(pick the endpoint of the extension line)*
> Dimension text: ⟨X.XXX⟩: ⏎

Fig. 18-76 shows the ordinate dimensions placed on the object. Notice the dimension text is aligned with the extension lines. Aligned dimensioning is standard with ordinate dimensioning, and is not altered by any change in the DIMTIH or DIMTOH variables. DIMTAD is off for the dimensions placed in Fig. 18-76. You can have the dimension text placed above the extension line if you turn DIMTAD on.

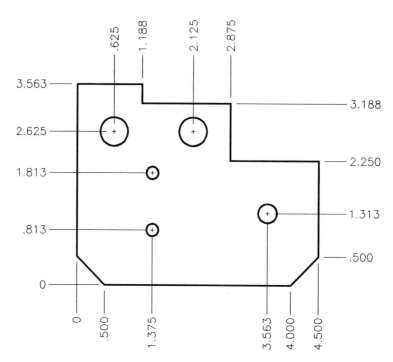

Fig. 18-76. Placing the ordinate dimensions.

Finally, complete the drawing by adding any missing lines such as centerlines or fold lines. Identify the holes with letters A, B, C (as needed), and correlate a dimensioning table as shown in Fig. 18-77.

You can leave the UCS origin at the corner of the object, or move it back to the corner of the screen (WCS) by pressing ENTER at the ⟨World⟩ default:

Command: **UCS** ↵
Origin/ZAxis/3point/Entity/View/X/Y/Z/Prev/Restore/Save/Del/?/⟨World⟩: ↵

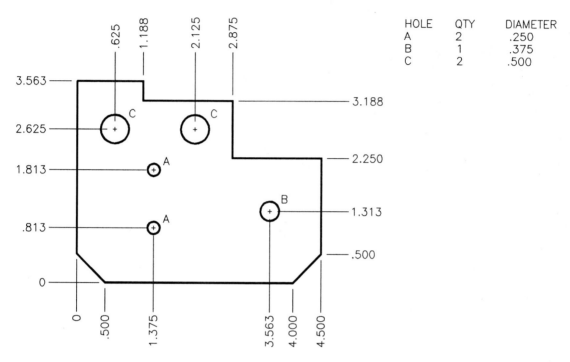

HOLE	QTY	DIAMETER
A	2	.250
B	1	.375
C	2	.500

Fig. 18-77. Completing the drawing.

PROFESSIONAL TIP

Most ordinate dimensioning tasks work best with ORTHO on. However, when you have a situation where the extension line is too close to an adjacent dimension numeral, it is best to stagger the extension line as shown in the following illustration. With ORTHO off, the extension line is automatically staggered when you pick the offset second extension line point as demonstrated.

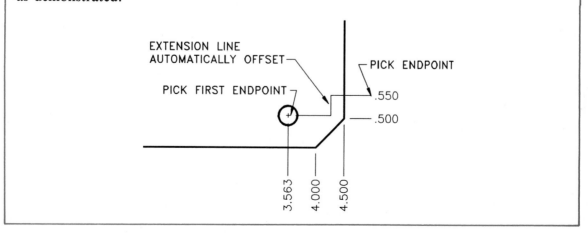

PROFESSIONAL TIP

AutoCAD's powerful ORDINATE dimensioning command allows you to quickly and accurately prepare arrowless dimensioning if you follow these steps:
- Draw the object carefully making sure that all features are accurate.
- Set the UCS origin to the X = 0, Y = 0 coordinates of the object.
- Place center marks in any circles or arcs requiring location dimensions.
- Set the units to the appropriate number of decimal places.
- Dimension the object.

EXERCISE 18-14

☐ Open PRODR2.
☐ Use ordinate dimensioning to draw and completely dimension the object shown in Fig. 18-72.
☐ Save the drawing as A:EX18-14.

THREAD DRAWINGS AND NOTES

There are many different types of thread forms. The most common forms are the Unified and metric screw threads. The parts of a screw thread are shown in Fig. 18-78.

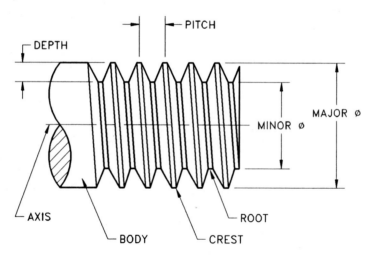

Fig. 18-78. Parts of a screw thread.

Threads are commonly shown on a drawing with a simplified representation. Thread depth is shown with a hidden line. This method is used for both external and internal threads, Fig. 18-79.

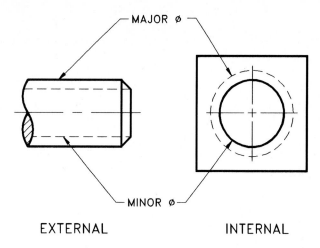

EXTERNAL   INTERNAL

Fig. 18-79. Simplified thread representations.

Showing the thread note

The view shows the reader that a thread exists, but the thread note gives exact specifications. The thread note for Unified screw threads must be given in the following order:

```
3/4  —  10UNC  —  2A
(1)     (2) (3)     (4)(5)
```

1. Major diameter of thread, given as fraction or decimal inch.
2. Number of threads per inch.
3. Thread series. UNC = Unified National Course. UNF = Unified National Fine.
4. Class of fit. 1 = large tolerance. 2 = general purpose tolerance. 3 = tight tolerance.
5. A = external thread. B = internal thread.

The thread note for metric threads is displayed in the following order:

```
M 14 X 2
(1)(2)   (3)
```

1. M = metric thread.
2. Major diameter in millimeters.
3. Pitch in millimeters.

There are too many Unified and metric screw threads to discuss here. Refer to the *Machinery's Handbook* or a comprehensive drafting text for more information.

The thread note is typically connected to the thread view with a leader, Fig. 18-80. Notice in Figs. 18-79 and 18-80 that a chamfer is often placed on the external thread. This makes it easier to enter the mating thread.

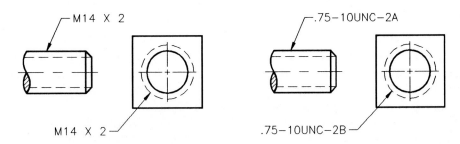

Fig. 18-80. Displaying the thread note with a leader.

EXERCISE 18-15

☐ Open drawing PRODR2.
☐ Draw a simplified representation of an external and internal Unified screw thread. Do the same for a metric screw thread.
☐ Use the LEADER command to label each view. Label the Unified screw thread as 7/8-14UNF-2 and the metric screw thread as M25X1.5.
☐ Your drawing should look similar to Fig. 18-80.
☐ Save the drawing as A:EX18-15.

USING DIALOGUE BOXES TO
CONTROL DIMENSION VARIABLES

ARM 11

Entering the dimension variables at the Command: prompt, as you have done so far, has given you an opportunity to see exactly how each variable controls the way a dimension is drawn. Now that you have used many of the dimensioning variables at the Command: prompt, take a look at how the same variables may be accessed through the "Dimension Styles and Variables" dialogue box shown in Fig. 18-81. You can access this dialogue box by entering "DDIM" at the Command: prompt, or by picking "Dimension Style..." from the Settings pull-down menu. It may be helpful to refer back to explanations and examples earlier in this chapter as you review each dimension variable in the following discussion.

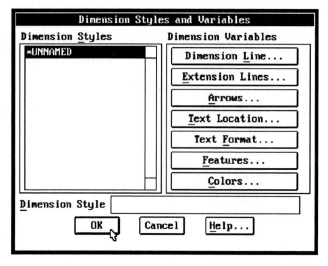

Fig. 18-81. The "Dimension Styles and Variables" dialogue box. Note the categories of dimension variables (represented by buttons) that can be set.

The Dimension Styles list box and the Dimension Style: edit box are used to select or create dimension styles. You can customize your dimensioning to correspond with specific drafting standards or office practices. This is covered in detail in Chapter 19.

The Dimension Variables buttons on the right side of the dialogue box are used to quickly adjust the dimension variables. Picking a Dimension Variable button displays a subdialogue box to control the variables associated with the name on the button.

Each of the subdialogue boxes contain these items:

- **Style** — This shows the name of the current dimension style. The dimension style identified in Fig. 18-82 is *UNNAMED, because a specific style has not been named. Chapter 19 shows you how this is done.
- **Feature Scaling** — The default is a scale factor of 1 as shown in Fig. 18-82. This edit box lets you control the DIMSCALE variable by entering a desired value.
- **Use Paper Space Scaling** — If you check this box, AutoCAD automatically calculates a scale factor between model space and paper space. This makes the DIMSCALE value 0, and the Feature Scaling: edit box is inactive because it is no longer needed.

```
┌─────────────────────────────────────────┐
│            Dimension Line                 │
│ Style: *UNNAMED                           │
│ Feature Scaling:        │1.00000   │      │
│ ☐ Use Paper Space Scaling                 │
│ Dimension Line Color: │BYBLOCK │ ▓        │
│ Dimension Line                            │
│ ┌───────────────────────────────────────┐│
│ │ ☐ Force Interior Lines                 ││
│ │ ☐ Basic Dimension                      ││
│ │ Text Gap:          │0.0900  │          ││
│ │ Baseline Increment:│0.3000  │          ││
│ └───────────────────────────────────────┘│
│   ┌─────────┐  ┌────────┐  ┌────────┐     │
│   │  OK   ▷ │  │ Cancel │  │ Help...│     │
│   └─────────┘  └────────┘  └────────┘     │
└─────────────────────────────────────────┘
```

Fig. 18-82. The "Dimension Line" subdialogue box. Note the dimension style name — in this case, *UNNAMED. Dimension styles are discussed in detail in Chapter 19.

Most of the dialogue boxes let you control color of the specific dimension feature such as dimension line, extension line, or text. This is the same as using the DIMCLRD, DIMCLRE, and DIMCLRT dimension variables. Change the color by entering a color name or number at the edit box currently labeled "BYBLOCK," or pick the color image to the right to get the "Select Color" dialogue box.

The Dimension Line... button

The "Dimension Line" subdialogue box shown in Fig. 18-82 is displayed when you pick the Dimension Line... button. The values shown in the dialogue box are defaults. Look at the "Dimension Line" box in Fig. 18-82. The first check box is "Force Interior Lines," which controls the DIMTOFL variable. The default shown, without a check, is OFF which means that dimension lines are drawn outside the extension lines when the text is placed outside. Check this box if you want to force dimension lines drawn inside the extension lines when text is placed outside. This also forces the dimension line and arrows inside a circle and arc dimension (Fig. 18-61).

The "Basic Dimension" check box allows you to place a box around the dimension numeral as shown in Fig. 18-83. AutoCAD calls this a *basic dimension*. Basic dimensions are used in Geometric Dimensioning and Tolerancing (GD&T). For a detailed study of GD&T, refer to *Geometric Dimensioning and Tolerancing* published by Goodheart-Willcox.

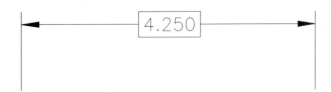

Fig. 18-83. A basic dimension is created by checking the Basic Dimensions box in the "Dimension Line" dialogue box.

The Text Gap: edit box lets you control the DIMGAP variable, which is the space between the dimension line and the numeral.

The Baseline Increment: edit box is used to change the DIMDLI variable. This is the variable that controls the distance between dimension lines when doing datum dimensioning with the BASELINE command. The default value of .38 is normally too close. The actual distance depends on your drawing, but .50 is often better.

The Extension Lines... button

The Extension Lines... button accesses the "Extension Lines" subdialogue box shown in Fig. 18-84A. The Extension Above Line: edit box controls the DIMEXE variable. This is the distance the extension line extends past the last dimension line. The .18 default is common for mechanical drawings.

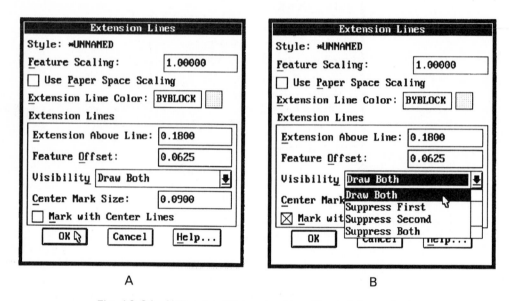

Fig. 18-84. Using the "Extension Lines" subdialogue box.

The Feature Offset: edit box is used to alter the DIMEXO variable. Some drafters prefer a gap of .0625 between the object and the start of the extension line. Change this to 0 when you are linking extension lines to centerlines.

The Visibility option has a default which lets you draw an extension line at each end of the dimension line, as specified by "Draw Both." Pick the arrow at the right for the popup list, Fig. 18-84B, which allows you to "Suppress First" extension line, "Suppress Second" extension line, or "Suppress Both" extension lines. Using this is the same as working with the DIMSE1 and DIMSE2 variables.

The Center Mark Size: edit box lets you control the way center marks or centerlines are drawn in circles and arcs when you use the DIAMETER, RADIUS, or CENTER commands. This is the same as the DIMCEN variable. The .09 default draws center marks only, such as those shown in Fig. 18-45. Pick the Mark with Center Lines check box to have center marks and centerlines drawn past the circle or arc with the CENTER, DIAMETER, and RADIUS commands.

The Arrows... button

The "Arrows" subdialogue box, shown in Fig. 18-85, is displayed when you pick the Arrows... button. The Arrow radio button is active as the DIMASZ default specified in the Arrow Size: edit box.

Pick the Tick radio button if you want to use tick marks for architectural drafting. The tick size sets DIMTSZ to the same value as in the Arrow Size: edit box, and sets DIMASZ to 0. This tick may be too big; a value such as .125 is probably better. The Tick Extension: edit box is activated at the same time in case you want to make the dimension line go past the extension line. Placing a value here controls the DIMDLE variable. (Refer back to Figs. 18-17 and 18).

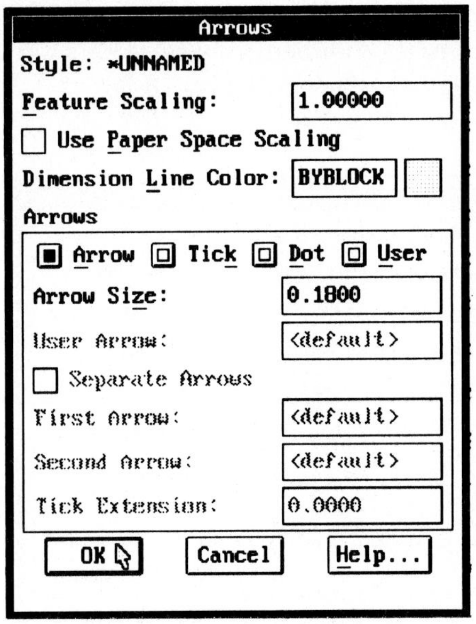

Fig. 18-85. The ''Arrows'' subdialogue box. The grayed-out options are made active when other selections are made within the dialogue box.

Pick the Dot radio button if you want dots at the ends of your dimension lines for architectural drafting. The dots you get are the same size as the value in the Arrow Size: edit box. Picking this radio button automatically makes DOT the DIMBLK value.

Notice in Fig. 18-85 that everything below the Arrow Size: edit box is inactive. The User Arrow: edit box and the Separate Arrows check box become active if you pick the User radio button. Enter a block name in the User Arrow: edit box if you want that block drawn at the ends of your dimension lines. Picking the Separate Arrows check box activates the First Arrow: and Second Arrow: edit boxes. This is used if you want a different block symbol drawn at each end of your dimension line. The DIMBLK1 and DIMBLK2 variables are controlled by this action.

EXERCISE 18-16

☐ Load AutoCAD if the drawing editor is not currently on your screen and open PRODR2.
☐ Draw a 3.000 horizontal dimension.
☐ Access the "Dimension Styles and Variables" dialogue box and pick the Dimension Line... option.
☐ Change Feature Scaling to 2 and draw the 3.000 dimension again. Observe the difference.
☐ Change Feature Scaling back to 1.
☐ Draw a .500 horizontal dimension.
☐ Check the Force Interior Lines box and draw the .500 dimension again. Observe the difference.
☐ Pick the Reference Dimension check box and draw a 3.750 horizontal dimension. Notice the box around the dimension numeral.
☐ Remove the Reference Dimension check.
☐ Access the "Extension Lines" subdialogue box and change Extension Above Line value to .125, Feature Offset to .08, and suppress both extension lines.
☐ Draw a .750 horizontal dimension, and then change the extension line visibility back to "Draw Both."
☐ Access the "Arrows" subdialogue box and pick the Tick button.
☐ Draw a 4.750 horizontal dimension.
☐ Pick the Dot radio button, and draw another 4.750 dimension.
☐ Save the drawing as A:EX18-16.

The Text Location... button

The Text Location... button in the "Dimension Styles and Variables" dialogue box accesses the "Text Location" subdialogue box shown in Fig. 18-86.

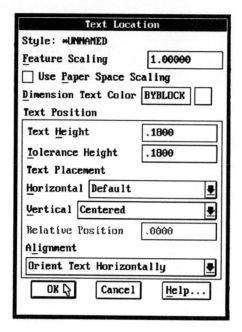

Fig. 18-86. Using the "Text Location" subdialogue box.

Change the dimension text height value in the Text Height: edit box. The .1800 default value may be used, but .125 or .160 is more common. Remember that the text height set in the STYLE command must be 0 for this text height to take effect. A preset text height in the STYLE command overrides any setting here. The text height that you use for notes on your drawing should be the same as the dimension numeral text height. The Tolerance Height: edit box is discussed in Chapter 19.

There is a popup list for Horizontal and Vertical text placement. When you pick the Horizontal popup list, the following options are available:

- **Default**—The dimension line, arrows, and numeral are placed between extension lines if there is enough room; otherwise, the dimension line, arrows, and text are placed outside the extension lines. This turns both DIMTIX and DIMSOXD off.
- **Force Text Inside**—Picking this option turns DIMTIX on and DIMSOXD off which forces AutoCAD to place the dimension text inside close extension lines and places the dimension line and arrows outside (as shown in Fig. 18-60).
- **Text, Arrows Inside**—Making this selection forces AutoCAD to place the dimension line, arrows, and text inside the extension lines. This turns DIMTIX and DIMSOXD on. One caution with this is that the dimension line and arrows are omitted if there is not enough space between the extension lines.

Picking the Vertical popup list provides you with these selections:

- **Centered**—This default centers the dimension at a break in the extension line, and turns off the DIMTAD variable.
- **Above**—Turns on DIMTAD so text is placed above the dimension line distance equal to the DIMTXT value.
- **Relative**—Picking this option activates the Relative Position: edit box, which was previously inactive, and turns off DIMTAD. "Relative" means that the dimension text is placed a distance relative to the text height from the dimension line. To determine the relative value, use the formula: Desired Distance x Text Height. For .18 text height, a relative value of .2 places the text a realistic distance above the dimension line. A break is provided if the text gets too close to the dimension line. A − .2 value places the text slightly below the dimension line. In addition, this option affects the DIMTVP variable, where DIMTVP = Relative Position ÷ Text Height. For example, .2 ÷ .18 equals a 1.1 DIMTVP value.

The Alignment selection default is text placed horizontally for unidirectional dimensioning. This is called "Orient Text Horizontally". The DIMTIH and DIMTOH variables are on. The other options are:

- **Align With Dimension Line** — Allows you to do aligned dimensioning where the text aligns with the dimension line. This turns DIMTIH and DIMTOH off.
- **Aligned When Inside Only** — Allows you to align text with the dimension line only when the text is inside the extension lines. DIMTIH is on and DIMTOH is off.
- **Aligned When Outside Only** — Allows you to align text with the dimension line only when the text is outside the extension lines. DIMTIH is off and DIMTOH is on. (Refer back to Fig. 18-14.)

The Text Format... button

The "Text Format" subdialogue box, shown in Fig. 18-87, is displayed when you pick the Text Format... button. The Basic Units options let you control the way dimension numerals are handled. The Length Scaling default is 1, which means that dimension text is displayed as its actual measurement (full size). Changing this value multiplies the measurement by the value specified. For example, if the measurement is 3.00, a value of 2 makes the text read 6.00. The value is saved as the DIMLFAC variable.

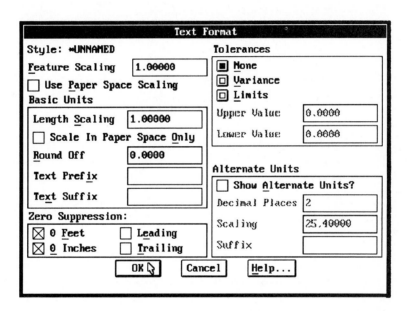

Fig. 18-87. This subdialogue box allows you to adjust the format of dimension text.

Picking the Scale In Paper Space Only check box makes the Length Scaling value apply only to dimensions drawn in paper space.

The Round Off: edit box allows you to establish how dimension numerals are rounded. The default of 0 implies that no rounding will occur. If the round off value is set to .5, numerals are rounded to the nearest .5 units. This is the same as setting the DIMRND variable (discussed in Chapter 19.) The number of digits to the right of the decimal point is controlled by the UNITS and DDUNITS commands.

The Text Prefix: and Text Suffix: edit boxes allow you to specify a prefix and/or a suffix that is added to the dimension numeral. A prefix goes before the numeral, such as SR3.75. A suffix follows the dimension numeral, for example, 3.75 MAX. These variables are controlled by DIMPOST which is discussed in detail in Chapter 19.

The Zero Suppression categories affect the DIMZIN variable. The defaults instruct AutoCAD to suppress "0 Feet" and "0 Inches" value. A feet and inches dimension that is less than one foot omits the 0′ value when the 0 Feet box is checked. An example is 8″. The same dimension would read 0′-8″ when this box is not checked. A check in the 0 Inches box removes the 0″

portion of a dimension, such as 12'. The same dimension reads 12'-0" when this box is not checked. Most architectural applications prefer a check in the 0 Feet box and no check in the 0 Inches box.

The Leading check box is not checked by default. This is for metric dimensions where numerals less than one millimeter require a 0 before the decimal point as in 0.5. Check this box when doing inch dimensioning since the ANSI standard recommends that the 0s be omitted before a decimal inch dimension, for example, .5.

A check in the Trailing check box removes all trailing zeros from a dimension numeral. For example, a dimension that would read 2.500 without a check here, reads 2.5 with a check in this box. Be careful, because trailing zeros usually have tolerance importance in mechanical drafting and should be left on the dimension. This depends on the degree of accuracy expected in a dimension tolerance.

The Tolerance area consists of radio buttons. Tolerance dimensions are discussed in Chapter 19. The None button is the default, which displays a dimension without a specified tolerance, such as 3.750.

Picking the Show Alternate Units? check box activates the Decimal Places:, Scaling:, and Suffix: edit boxes. These dimension variables are discussed in Chapter 19.

EXERCISE 18-17

☐ Open PRODR2.
☐ Draw a .500 horizontal dimension.
☐ Access the "Text Location" subdialogue box, change the text height to .125. Access the Horizontal popup list and pick the Text, Arrows Inside button. Draw the .500 dimension again.
☐ Change Horizontal back to the default.
☐ Access the "Text Format" subdialogue box, change the Length Scaling Factor to 2, and draw the .500 dimension again.
☐ Change Length Scaling Factor back to 1, pick the Leading check box, and draw the .500 dimension again.
☐ Enter "MAX" in the Text Suffix: edit box and draw the .500 dimension again.
☐ Save the drawing as A:EX18-17.

Working with all the dimension features in one dialogue box

If you pick the Features... button in the "Dimension Styles and Variables" dialogue box you get the "Features" subdialogue box shown in Fig. 18-88. As you look at this subdialogue box you might think that it looks very familiar. This is because it contains many of the features contained in the subdialogue boxes previously discussed. In fact, you can use the "Features" subdialogue box to look at and change a wide variety of dimensioning variables. Take some time comparing the "Features" subdialogue box to the "Dimension Line," "Extension Line," "Arrows," and "Text Location" subdialogue boxes.

```
┌─────────────────────────────────── Features ───────────────────────────────────┐
│                                                                                  │
│  Style: *UNNAMED                        Extension Lines                          │
│  Feature Scaling:    ┌─1.00000─┐        Extension Above Line: ┌─0.1800─┐         │
│  □ Use Paper Space Scaling              Feature Offset:       ┌─0.0625─┐         │
│  Dimension Line                         Visibility ┌─Draw Both────────▼┐         │
│  ┌────────────────────────────┐                                                 │
│  │ □ Force Interior Lines      │        Center Mark Size:     ┌─0.0900─┐         │
│  │ □ Basic Dimension           │        □ Mark with Center Lines                │
│  │ Text Gap:        ┌─0.0900─┐ │        Text Position                            │
│  │ Baseline Increment: ┌─0.3800─┐│      ┌──────────────────────────────────┐   │
│  │ Arrows                       │        │ Text Height:       ┌─0.1800─┐     │   │
│  │ ┌──────────────────────────┐ │        │ Tolerance Height:  ┌─0.1800─┐     │   │
│  │ │ ▫ Arrow ▫ Tick ▫ Dot ■ User│       │ Text Placement                    │   │
│  │ │ Arrow Size:   ┌─0.1800─┐  │ │        │ Horizontal ┌─Default─────────▼┐  │   │
│  │ │ User Arrow:   ┌─DOT────┐  │ │        │ Vertical   ┌─Centered────────▼┐  │   │
│  │ │ ⊠ Separate Arrows        │ │        │ Relative Position:  ┌─0.0000─┐  │   │
│  │ │ First Arrow:  ┌<default>┐ │ │        │ Alignment                        │   │
│  │ │ Second Arrow: ┌<default>┐ │ │        │ ┌─Orient Text Horizontally────▼┐│   │
│  │ │ Tick Extension: ┌─0.0000─┐│ │        └──────────────────────────────────┘   │
│  │ └──────────────────────────┘ │              ┌──OK ▷──┐ ┌─Cancel─┐ ┌─Help...─┐│
│  └────────────────────────────┘                                                 │
└──────────────────────────────────────────────────────────────────────────────┘
```

Fig. 18-88. The "Features" subdialogue box allows you to set many of the dimensioning variables included in other subdialogue boxes.

The Colors... button

Pick the Colors... button in the "Dimension Styles and Variables" dialogue box to access the "Colors" subdialogue box shown in Fig. 18-89. You had the opportunity to set color of individual features in previous subdialogue boxes, but this one puts them all together. The color defaults are BYBLOCK while the example in Fig. 18-89 shows specific colors selected for each feature. This was done by picking the color image to the right of each item and then changing the color in the "Select Color" dialogue box. You can also enter color numbers or names in the edit boxes if you wish. In addition to DIMSCALE, this subdialogue box controls the DIMCLRD, DIMCLRE, and DIMCLRT variables.

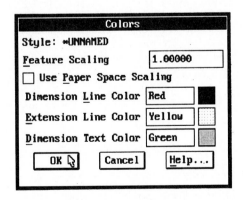

Fig. 18-89. Using the "Colors" subdialogue box. Pick the image tile to the right of any item to access the "Select Color" subdialogue box.

EXERCISE 18-18

☐ Open PRODR2.
☐ Draw a 5.750 horizontal dimension.
☐ Access the "Colors" subdialogue box, change the dimension line to red, the extension line to yellow, and the text to green.
☐ Draw the 5.750 dimension again.
☐ Save the drawing as A:EX18-18.

CHAPTER TEST

Write your answers in the spaces provided.

1. Give the command and entries required to change the dimensioning text style from TXT to ROMANS-125:

   Command: _____

   Dim: _____

   New text style ⟨TXT⟩: _____

2. If the dimension reads 2.875 and you want it to read ϕ2.875, what should you enter?

   Dimension text ⟨2.875⟩: _____

3. Give the command and entries needed to change the dimensioning text from the default size of 0.18 to .25:

   Command: _____

   Dim: _____

   Current value ⟨0.1800⟩: New value: _____

4. Give the command and entries required to dimension a 30° angle between two existing intersecting lines. Let AutoCAD center the text in the dimension line.

   Command: _____

   Dim: _____

   Select arc, circle, line, or RETURN: _____

   Second line: _____

   Dimension arc line location (Text/Angle): _____

   Dimension text ⟨30⟩: _____

   Enter text location (or RETURN): _____

5. Give the command and related responses used to dimension four holes, all having .250 inch diameter:

   Command: _____

   Dim: _____

   Select arc or circle: _____

   Dimension text ⟨0.250⟩: _____

   Enter leader length for text: _____

6. Give the command and entries required to dimension an arc. The text should read R1.750.

   Command: _____

   Dim: _____

   Select arc or circle:_____

   Dimension text ⟨1.750⟩: _____

   Enter leader length for text: _____

   Dim: _____

   Command: _____

7. Give the command and entries needed to set and draw centerlines that extend .25 unit beyond a circle's circumference:

   Command: _____

   Dim: _____

   Current value ⟨0.09⟩: New value: _____

   Dim: _____

   Select arc or circle:_____

8. Give the command and entries used to dimension a 45° X .125 chamfer:

   Command: _____

   Dim: _____

   Leader start: _____

   To point: _____

   To point: _____

   To point: _____

   Dimension text ⟨ ⟩:_____

9. Explain the difference between DIM and DIM1. _____

   _____

   _____

   _____

   _____

   _____

   _____

10. Describe the function of dimension variables. _____

    _____

    _____

    _____

11. What is the Root Menu selection used to access the dimensioning screen menu? _____

    _____

12. Identify three ways to return to the Command: prompt when in the DIM command.

_____

_____

_____

13. What are the recommended standard units of measure on engineering drawings and related documents? _____

_____

14. Name the units of measure commonly used in architectural and structural drafting, and show an example. _____

15. What is the recommended height for dimension numerals and notes on drawings? _____

16. Name the command option used to change the dimension text style. _____

17. Give the control code necessary to display the ϕ symbol. _____

18. Name the screen menu where the Horizntl, Aligned, and Rotated dimensioning commands are found. _____

19. Name the two dimensioning commands that provide linear dimensions for angled surfaces.

_____

20. Name the command used to dimension angles in degrees. _____

21. What are the two types of notes found on a drawing? _____

22. AutoCAD refers to chain dimensioning as _____ .

23. AutoCAD refers to datum dimensioning as _____ .

24. The command used to provide diameter dimensions for circles is _____ .

25. The command used to provide radius dimensions for arcs is _____ .

26. What command is used to connect specific notes to features on the object? _____

27. Identify the parts of the following Unified screw thread note:

    .625 — 11UNC — 2A

    (A)   (B) (C)   (D)(E)

    A. _____

    B. _____

    C. _____

    D. _____

    E. _____

28. Identify the parts of the following Metric screw thread note:

    M 48 X 5

    (A) (B)   (C)

    A. _____

    B. _____

    C. _____

For Questions 29-45, identify the dimensioning variable that:

29. Controls the dimension text height. _____

30. Controls the -0" part of a feet-inches dimension. _____

31. Controls the size of the gap between the object and extension line. _____

32. Controls the distance the extension line projects past the last dimension line. _____

33. Suppresses the second extension line. _____

34. Provides for aligned dimensioning of dimensions inside of extension lines. _____

35. Places dimension text above the dimension line for architectural drafting._____

36. Changes the arrowhead size. _____

37. Controls the display and size of dimension line ticks for architectural drafting. _____

38. Controls dimension line spacing. _____

39. Sets a scale factor for all linear dimensions. _____

40. Establishes center marks for circles and arcs._____

41. Sets dimension line color. _____

42. Used to change leader line color. _____

43. Sets dimension text color. _____

44. Controls extension line color. _____

45. Controls the space between the dimension line and the dimension text._____

46. Name an overall dimensioning scale factor that affects variables for sizes, distances, and offsets. _____

47. Name the dimensioning variable that, when turned on, forces dimension text inside the extension lines only when the dimension lines and arrowheads are placed outside.

_____

48. Some drafters prefer to have a dimension line drawn between extension lines when the dimension text is placed outside. Name the variable that, when turned on, achieves this task.

_____

49. What DIMTVP setting places the dimension text above the dimension line? _____

50. Where does the DIMTVP default value place dimension text? _____

_____

51. What is the function of the UPDATE command? _____

_____

52. Give an example of a proper inch and metric (millimeters) decimal numeral less than one.

_____

53. Name the dimensioning command used to place extension lines at an angle. _____

54. What command is used to do arrowless dimensioning? _____

55. Determine the AutoCAD text height for dimension text to be plotted 1/8″ (.125) high using a scale of half (1:2). (Show your calculations.) _____

_____

56. Determine the AutoCAD text height for dimension text to be plotted 1/8″ (.125) high using a scale of 1/4″ = 1′-0″. (Show your calculations.) _____

   _____

57. Name the dimensioning variable and its value which is used to draw architectural dots at the end of the dimension lines. _____

   _____

58. Name the dimensioning variable and its setting for suppressing the lead zero on decimal inch dimensions. _____

59. It is recommended that no gap exist between an extension line and a centerline when providing location dimensions to holes. Give the dimension variable and its value to use to achieve this task. _____

60. Identify two ways to access the "Dimension Styles and Variables" dialogue box. _____

   _____

61. A dimension numeral surrounded by a box is called a _____ dimension.

For Questions 62-72, identify the name of the "Dimension Styles and Variables" subdialogue boxes (excluding the "Features" subdialogue box) where the following items are found:

62. Omit leading zero in decimal dimensions. _____

63. Visiblity. _____

64. Horizontal and vertical popup lists. _____

65. Align With Dimension Line. _____

66. The Tick radio button. _____

67. Extension Above Line: edit box. _____

68. Baseline Increment: edit box. _____

69. Forces dimension text inside extension lines. _____

70. Add a prefix or suffix to dimension text. _____

71. Text Gap: edit box. _____

72. Provides dual dimensioning capabilities. _____

73. Name the "Dimension Styles and Variables" subdialogue box that contains items found in four other subdialogue boxes. _____

74. Name the subdialogue box where the color of dimension and extension lines, and dimension text may be changed. _____

DRAWING PROBLEMS

1-15. Open each of the completed drawings in Chapter 17 (P17-1 through P17-15), or start a new drawing for those drawings which were not completed. Set limits, units, dimensioning variables, and other parameters as needed. Follow these guidelines:
   A. Draw the views to exact size.
   B. Use grids, object snap modes, and the OSNAP command to your best advantage.
   C. Apply dimensions accurately using ANSI standards.
   D. Set dimensioning variables to suit the drawing.

E. Use the LAYER command to set separate layers for views and dimensions.
F. Draw object lines using .032 in. wide polylines, or use LINE and plot object lines with a wide pen.
G. Place general notes 1/2 in. from lower-left corner.
   2. REMOVE ALL BURRS AND SHARP EDGES.
   1. INTERPRET PER ANSI Y14.5M.
   NOTES:
H. Save the drawings to your floppy disk with names such as A:P18-X, where the X represents the problem number.
16. Make a drawing the same as Fig. 18-70.
17. Make a drawing the same as Fig. 18-50.
18. Make a drawing the same as Fig. 18-73.
19. Make a drawing the same as Fig. 18-73, but convert to arrowless dimensioning using AutoCAD's ORDINATE command.
20. Make a drawing the same as Fig. 18-74.
21. Make a drawing the same as Fig. 18-77.
22. Make a drawing the same as Fig. 18-80.
23. Make the drawing shown below. (If you have not yet discussed blocks, replace the depth symbol with ".375 DEEP.")

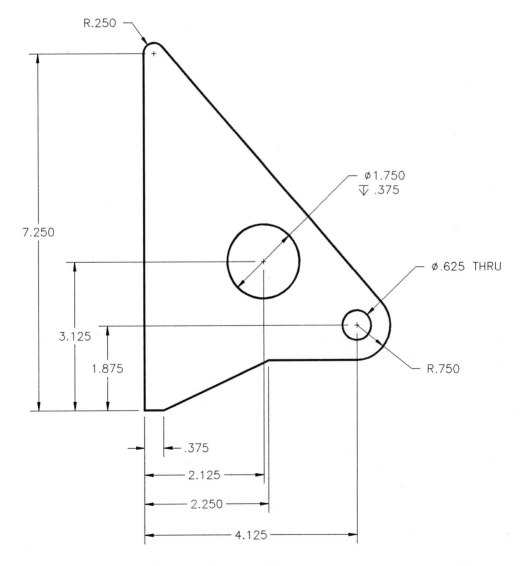

24. If you have not completed Exercise 18-9, do so now and save it as A:P18-24.

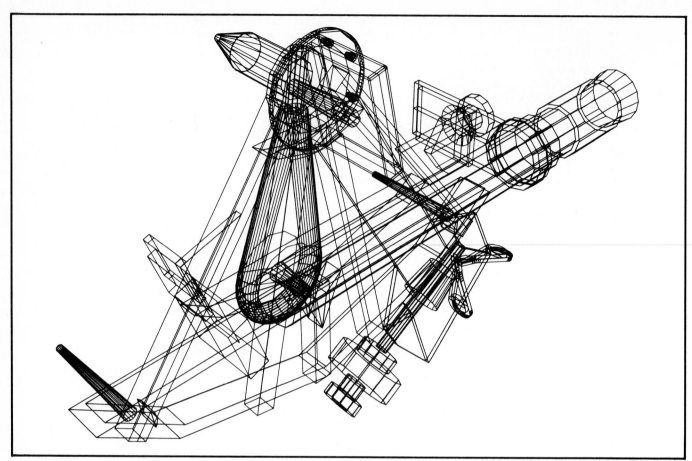

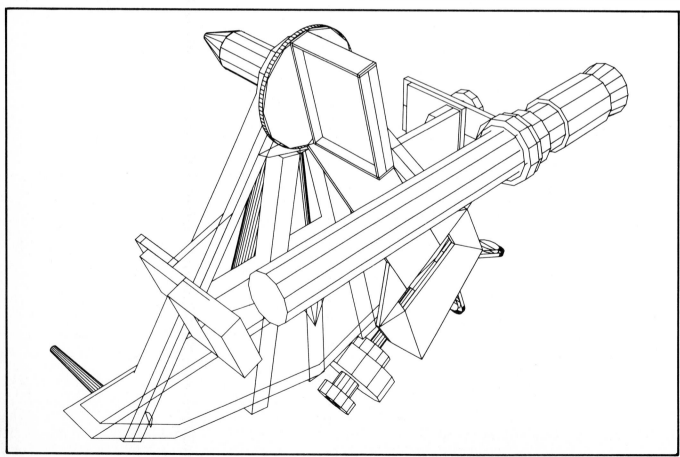

Sextant drawing before using HIDE (above), and after using HIDE.   (Autodesk, Inc.)

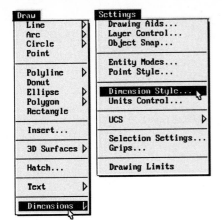

Chapter 19

ADVANCED DIMENSIONING AND TOLERANCING

Learning objectives

After completing this chapter, you will be able to:

☐ Establish AutoCAD dimensioning styles to conform with drafting standards.
☐ Override existing dimensioning variables.
☐ Prepare drawings with dimensions and tolerances from engineering sketches.
☐ Modify dimensioning variables to perform specific dimensioning and tolerancing operations.
☐ Identify and use dual dimensioning techniques.
☐ Use dimension variable icon menus.
☐ Apply associative dimensioning.
☐ Use the STRETCH, TRIM, and EXTEND commands to revise existing dimensioned objects.
☐ Make changes to existing dimension entities using the UPDATE, HOMETEXT, and NEWTEXT commands.

This chapter shows you how to establish AutoCAD dimensioning styles to conform with drafting standards. It explains tolerancing and dual dimensioning along with the AutoCAD techniques used to edit dimensions. Also introduced is associative dimensioning, a technique that allows you to revise drawings using the STRETCH, TRIM, and EXTEND commands. Changes made to an object automatically affect associated dimensions.

The number of decimal places usually reflects the accuracy of a dimension. For example, a three-place decimal dimension is more precise than a two-place decimal. Control the number of places behind the decimal point using the UNITS command. This is one setup step that you should enter on the drawing plan sheet. Another method to increase precision of a manufactured product is with specified tolerances.

CREATING AND CONTROLLING DIMENSIONING STYLE

ARM 11

AutoCAD refers to dimensioning standards as *style*. You can customize your dimensioning style to correspond to drafting standards such as ANSI, ISO (International Organization for Standardization), military (MIL), architectural, or for your own corporate or school standards. Now that you have learned basic AutoCAD dimensioning techniques and how to control the dimensioning variables, you can decide how to establish your own dimensioning styles. If you do more than one type of drafting such as mechanical and architectural, or if you create drawings for clients who require different standards such as ANSI, ISO, or MIL, then you can set up AutoCAD to assist you in preparing the type of dimensioning needed. The AutoCAD dimensioning variable that helps you identify existing dimensioning standards (styles) that you have set up is DIMSTYLE. This dimensioning variable is not listed with the other variables in the Dim Vars screen menu, because it is *read only*. This means that you cannot set DIMSTYLE as you do the other dimensioning variables. The DIMSTYLE command is found on the DIM command's screen menu as Dim Styl. Pick Dim Styl from the DIM: screen menu followed by picking Dimstyle, or type "DIMSTYLE" at the Command: or Dim: prompt:

```
Command: DIM ↵
Dim: DIMSTYLE ↵
DIMSTYLE = "*UNNAMED" (read only)
Resuming DIM command.
Dim:
```

This dimensioning variable simply tells you which dimensioning style is active. The AutoCAD default style set up in AutoCAD's prototype drawing is *UNNAMED. In other words, there is no specific style.

Creating dimension styles

Dimension styles can be created in the prototype drawing. When using this practice, you can begin a new drawing and set the dimensioning style or styles that you want used in the drawing. For example, you may typically do drawings that are either drawn to ARCH (architectural) or ANSI standards. If this is the case, then you should make a complete list of the dimensioning variables that you commonly use for each type of drafting and create dimensioning styles accordingly. Lists for ANSI or architectural styles may look like this:

ARCH	ANSI
DIMTSZ = .05	DIMASZ = .125
DIMCEN = .125	DIMTSZ = 0
DIMDLE = .1	DIMCEN = .09
DIMDLI = 6	DIMDLE = 0
DIMSCALE = 6	DIMDLI = .5
DIMTAD = ON	DIMSCALE = 1
DIMTIX = ON	DIMTAD = OFF
DIMTXT = .188	DIMTIX = OFF
	DIMTXT = .125

Any of the dimensioning variables that remain unchanged continue as AutoCAD default values. If you find that a particular dimensioning variable is not set the way you want it, then you can change it and modify the dimensioning style at any time.

Now, you are ready to create each of the dimensioning styles listed. You can start with the ARCH style by using AutoCAD to change all of the dimensioning variables that you have listed for your ARCH standard. After all of the dimensioning variables are set to your satisfaction, use the SAVE command. When used at the Dim: prompt, the SAVE command saves the current dimensioning variable settings to a dimension style and makes the new dimension style current. Type the desired dimension style:

```
Command: DIM ↵
Dim: SAVE ↵
?/Name for new dimension style: ARCH ↵
```

Now, proceed in the same manner to change the dimensioning variables reflecting your proposed ANSI style, and again use the SAVE command for the created ANSI style. Do this for any dimensioning style that you want created in your prototype drawing.

If you want to list the dimension styles created for the current drawing enter "?". List the name or names of styles you want listed to help you remember if they have been created, or press ENTER to accept the wild card ⟨*⟩ for all dimension styles:

    Command: **DIM** ⏎
    Dim: **SAVE** ⏎
    ?/Name for new dimension style: **?** ⏎
    Dimension style(s) to list ⟨*⟩: ⏎
    Named dimension styles:
      ANSI
      ARCH

The RESTORE command lets you change dimensioning variable settings by reading new settings from an existing dimension style. After typing "RES" or "RESTORE" at the Dim: prompt or picking Restore from the screen menu, the current dimension style is listed and you can press ENTER to determine the dimensioning style of any existing dimension by picking that dimension:

    Command: **DIM** ⏎
    Dim: **RES** or **RESTORE** ⏎
    Current dimension style: ARCH
    ?/Enter dimension style name or RETURN to select dimension: ⏎
    Select dimension: *(pick a dimension on the drawing)*
    Current dimension style: ARCH

Now you know that the dimension you picked was drawn using the ARCH style.

The RESTORE command lets you list the dimension styles in the current drawing by entering "?" in the same manner as described with the SAVE command.

If you want to display the difference between one of your dimension styles and the current style enter the tilde character (~) followed by the style to compare and ENTER:

    ?/Enter dimension style name or RETURN to select dimension: ~ **ANSI** ⏎

AutoCAD shows you the difference between styles on the alphanumeric screen:

    Difference between ARCH and current settings:

	ANSI	Current Setting
DIMCEN	0.0900	0.1250
DIMDLE	0.0000	0.1000
DIMDLI	0.5000	6.0000
DIMSCALE	1.0000	6.0000
DIMTAD	Off	On
DIMTIX	Off	On
DIMTSZ	0.0000	0.5000
DIMTXT	0.1250	0.1880

You can do the same thing while in the Dim: SAVE command at the ?/Name for new dimension style: prompt.

Another way to list the current dimension style and variable settings of a dimension style without changing the current settings is with the VARIABLES command. You can name a dimension style to list the variables, or pick a dimension on the screen just as with the RESTORE command:

    Command: **DIM** ⏎
    Dim: **VAR** ⏎
    Current dimension style: ARCH
    ?/Enter dimension style name or RETURN to select dimension: ⏎
    Select dimension: *(pick a dimension on the screen)*

The screen changes to an alphanumeric listing of the current dimensioning variable settings for the dimension you picked. Press ENTER to see more pages of the list, or press the F1 key to return to the graphics screen.

Use the ? option if you want to look at the dimensioning variables used in the current drawing. You can compare the current dimension style with another style by entering "~" and the style name to compare like this:

> ?/Enter dimension style name or RETURN to select dimension: ~**ANSI** ↵

The text screen then displays only the dim vars that are different between the current style and the ANSI style.

EXERCISE 19-1

☐ Design dimensioning variables that may be used for the two different dimension styles listed as follows:

	ARCH	ANSI
DIMTAD	Off	On
DIMTSZ	.05	0
DIMDLE	.08	0
DIMZIN 1	0	

☐ Save these dimension styles under the style given with each.
☐ Make one of the styles current.
☐ Use the tilde (~) to have AutoCAD show you the difference between styles.
☐ Save as A:EX19-1.

OVERRIDING EXISTING DIMENSIONING VARIABLES
ARM 11

Generally, it is appropriate to have one or more dimensioning variables set to perform specific tasks that relate to your dimensioning practices. However, situations may arise where it is necessary to alter dimensioning variables to modify one or more specific dimensions on the final drawing. For example, assume you have the DIMEXO (EXtension line Offset) variable set at .062, which conforms to ANSI standards. However, in your final drawing there are three specific dimensions that require a 0 extension line offset. You can pick these three dimensions and alter the DIMEXO variable exclusively by picking Override from the DIM: screen menu, or by typing "OVER" or "OVERRIDE" at the Dim: prompt:

> Command: **DIM** ↵
> Dim: **OVER** ↵
> Dimension variable to override: **DIMEXO** ↵
> Current value ⟨.0625⟩: New value: **0** ↵
>   Dimension variable to override: ↵
> Select objects: *(pick the specific dimensions for change)*

The DIMEXO variable automatically changes from .062 to 0 on the three selected dimensions only. If any of the dimensions you select are part of a dimension style, then AutoCAD asks you this question:

> Modify dimension style "ARCH"? ⟨N⟩:

Press ENTER to accept the No default, in which case only the dimensions selected are altered and the dimension style remains unchanged. If you want to change the related dimension style to reflect the override on all dimensions then answer "Y". AutoCAD then changes all of the dimensions on the drawing and in future uses of this dimension style.

─ **PROFESSIONAL TIP** ─

It may be better to use the DDIM command rather than the OVERRIDE command, depending on the nature of the change. In the dialogue box you can pick an existing style, change the variable, then make a new style.

EXERCISE 19-2

☐ Load AutoCAD and open PRODR2.
☐ Make a drawing similar to Fig. 18-53 with dimensioning variables set as follows:

   DIMASZ = .1
   DIMGAP = .05
   DIMDLE = .12
   DIMDLI = .5
   DIMEXO = .06

☐ Use datum (baseline) dimensioning to make your job easier.
☐ After completing the entire drawing, with the dimensioning variables set as required, use the OVERRIDE command to change only the DIMEXO variable to 0 on all dimensions except the overall dimensions.
☐ Save the drawing as A:EX19-2.

USING THE DIALOGUE BOX TO CONTROL DIMENSION STYLES

The "Dimension Style and Variables" dialogue box was introduced in Chapter 18 as an easy way to work with dimension variables. This dialogue box is also used to list, save, and restore dimension styles. The dialogue box is accessed by picking Dimension Style... from the Settings pull-down menu, or by typing "DDIM" at the Command: or Dim: prompt. The Dimension Styles list box and the Dimension Style: edit box are used to create and utilize dimension styles as discussed earlier in this chapter. Notice in Fig. 19-1 that the ANSI and ARCH dimension styles, created earlier, are in the Dimension Styles list box. The current dimension style is highlighted in the list and displayed in the edit box. Move the cursor arrow to another style name and pick it to make it current.

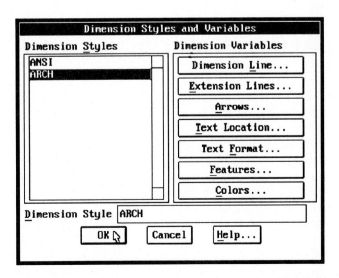

Fig. 19-1. Previously created dimension styles are shown in the Dimension Styles list box.

When you are ready to save a new dimension style, enter that style name in the edit box. For example, to save a new style named ISO, enter that name in the edit box and press ENTER. AutoCAD makes the new style a duplicate of the previous current style. AutoCAD acknowledges this with the message in the lower-left corner of the dialogue box, and the new style name is displayed in the list box as shown in Fig. 19-2.

There are many similarities between the ANSI and ISO dimension style. However, there may be times when you need to make exceptions to the standard style. In this case, while ISO is the current style, use the "Dimension Variables" subdialogue boxes to customize the ISO style to fit your needs. Pick the OK button when you are done and the ISO style becomes a unique dimension style.

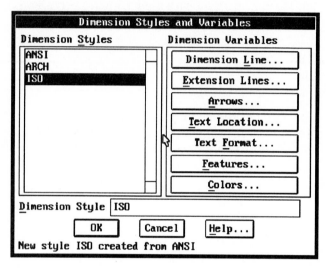

Fig. 19-2. To create a new dimension style, type the name in the Dimension Style: edit box. Note the message in the lower-left corner of the dialogue box.

PROFESSIONAL TIP

Changing any dimension variable at the Dim: prompt creates a new dimension style called *UNNAMED with the changed variable and the existing variable settings of the previously current style. You can make new dimension styles at any time by changing variables and giving the style a new name. The Save option of the DIM command creates a new style using all of the current dimension variable settings.

USING EXTERNALLY REFERENCED DIMENSION STYLES

In Chapter 17 you had a brief introduction to the XREF command. Remember, an external reference drawing is one that is not added to the current drawing, but rather "referenced" to it. This is explained in detail in Chapters 21 and 27. The Dimension Styles list box may contain externally referenced styles. These referenced styles cannot be made current, changed, or renamed. You can easily identify these names since the Xref name is given first, followed by a vertical bar, and then the dimension style name; for example: FOUNDATION|ARCH.

If you want to use an externally referenced style, simply pick the style from the list box and then change the name in the Dimension Style: edit box. Now, the new dimension style contains all the characteristics of the referenced style.

TOLERANCING

A *tolerance* is the total amount by which a specific dimension is allowed to vary. It is the difference between the maximum and minimum limits. A tolerance is not given to values that are identified as reference, maximum, minimum, or stock sizes. The tolerance may be applied to the dimension, Fig. 19-3, indicated by a general note, or identified in the drawing title block.

The dimension in Fig. 19-3 is 2.750 ± 0.005. This is referred to as *plus/minus tolerancing*. The maximum and minimum limits of the feature are then 2.755 (2.750 + .005) and 2.745 (2.750 − .005). By subtracting the lower limit from the upper limit, you find the tolerance is .010. The specified dimension, 2.750, is the value from which the limits are calculated.

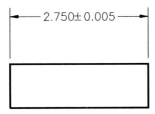

Fig. 19-3. A dimension with a plus/minus tolerance.

However, the dimension on the drawing may show only the limits, not the specified dimension, Fig. 19-4. This is referred to as *limits tolerancing*. Many companies prefer limits tolerancing over plus/minus tolerancing. Since the limits are shown, calculating them is not required.

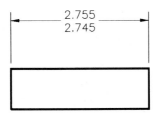

Fig. 19-4. Limits tolerancing.

A *bilateral tolerance* is permitted to vary in both directions from the specified dimension. The dimension 2.750 ± .005 is an equal bilateral tolerance. The variation from the specified dimension, 2.750, is the same in both directions. An unequal bilateral tolerance occurs when the variation is not equal. The dimension $2.750 \begin{array}{l} + .005 \\ - .003 \end{array}$ is an unequal bilateral tolerance.

A *unilateral tolerance* allows the dimension to vary in only one direction. The dimensions $2.750 \begin{array}{l} + .000 \\ - .005 \end{array}$ and $2.750 \begin{array}{l} + .005 \\ - .000 \end{array}$ are unilateral tolerances.

The tolerancing for inch and metric dimensions are shown differently on a drawing:

INCH	METRIC
1.500 ± .005	25 ± 0.05
$1.500 \begin{array}{l} + .000 \\ - .005 \end{array}$	$25 \begin{array}{l} 0 \\ - 0.05 \end{array}$
$1.500 \begin{array}{l} + .005 \\ - .000 \end{array}$	$25 \begin{array}{l} + 0.05 \\ 0 \end{array}$

Notice the 0 preceding the decimal point for metric values less than one, while the 0 is not shown for inch dimensions less than one.

DRAWING BILATERAL AND UNILATERAL
TOLERANCES WITH AUTOCAD

Three variables control how bilateral and unilateral tolerances are set up in AutoCAD: DIM-TOL, DIMTP, and DIMTM. TOL refers to TOLerance. TP is the Tolerance Plus. TM is the Tolerance Minus. The DIMTOL variable turns the tolerance option on and off. Setting DIMTOL to OFF, the dimension is shown as a numeral without tolerances. Entering "DIMTP" prompts you for the plus part of the tolerance. Entering "DIMTM" prompts you for the minus part of the tolerance. To set an equal bilateral tolerance of .001, use this procedure.

> Command: **DIM** ↵
> Dim: **DIMTOL** ↵
> Current value ⟨Off⟩ New value: **ON** ↵
> Dim: **DIMTP** ↵
> Current value ⟨0.000⟩ New value: **.001** ↵
> Dim: **DIMTM** ↵
> Current value ⟨0.000⟩ New value: **.001** ↵
> Dim:

Any dimensions drawn from now on are given the plus and minus tolerances. For example, the following command sequence is used to add the horizontal dimension in Fig. 19-5.

> Dim: **HOR** or **HORIZONTAL** ↵
> First extension line origin or RETURN to select: *(pick the first extension line origin)*
> Second extension line origin: *(pick the second extension line origin)*
> Dimension line location (Text/Angle): *(pick the dimension line location)*
> Dimension text ⟨3.625⟩: ↵

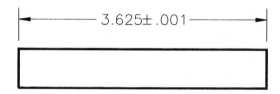

Fig. 19-5. Adding a bilateral tolerance.

Notice that AutoCAD places a 0 before the decimal point if DIMZIN = 0. In Fig. 19-5, DIMZIN was set to 4, which removes the 0 before the decimal point. If this does not suit your standard, the required dimension numeral must be typed in at the Dimension text: prompt. Enter "3.625%%P.001" to receive 3.625 ± .001.

To set an unequal bilateral tolerance, enter the appropriate values for DIMTP and DIMTM. The command sequence here adds the dimension shown in Fig. 19-6.

> Dim: **DIMTP** ↵
> Current value ⟨0.000⟩ New value: **.002** ↵
> Dim: **DIMTM** ↵
> Current value ⟨0.000⟩ New value: **.005** ↵
> Dim: **HOR** or **HORIZONTAL** ↵
> First extension line origin or RETURN to select: *(pick the first extension line origin)*
> Second extension line origin: *(pick the second extension line origin)*
> Dimension line location (Text/Angle): *(pick the dimension line location)*
> Dimension text: ⟨3.625⟩: ↵

To set a unilateral tolerance, enter 0 for either the DIMTP or DIMTM variables. Remember, TP is the tolerance plus and TM is the tolerance minus.

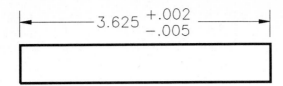

Fig. 19-6. Unequal bilateral tolerance.

── PROFESSIONAL TIP ──

The dimension text often becomes very long for dimensions having a plus/minus tolerance. Horizontal dimension text takes up more space between extension lines. Vertical dimension text requires more space between dimension lines. Allow for this space during the planning and sketching process. If you make an error when dimensioning, simply try again or move the dimension text. Remember to keep dimension lines equally spaced for a uniform appearance. The DIMDLI variable controls the dimension line spacing for baseline dimensions.

DRAWING DIMENSIONS USING LIMITS TOLERANCING

ARM 11

Limits tolerances can be drawn with AutoCAD by setting one extra variable in addition to DIMTOL, DIMTP, and DIMTM. Enter the DIMLIM variable and respond with "ON". This automatically turns DIMTOL off. Enter the DIMTP and DIMTM values if you have not already done so. AutoCAD calculates the upper and lower limits and places this as the dimension text. The sequence which follows places the dimension shown in Fig. 19-7.

Command: **DIM** ↵
Dim: **DIMLIM** ↵
Current value 〈Off〉 New value: **ON** ↵
Dim: **DIMTP** ↵
Current value 〈0.000〉 New value: **.005** ↵
Dim: **DIMTM** ↵
Current value 〈0.000〉 New value: **.005** ↵
Dim: **HOR** ↵
First extension line origin or RETURN to select: *(pick the first extension line origin)*
Second extension line origin: *(pick the second extension line origin)*
Dimension line location (Text/Angle): *(pick the dimension line location)*
Dimension text 〈3.625〉: ↵

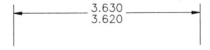

Fig. 19-7. Dimensioning with limits.

Setting the tolerance text height

You can control the text height for tolerance dimensions when DIMTOL is on and DIMTP is different than DIMTM, or DIMLIM is on and DIMTP and DIMTM are at any setting. When these conditions occur you can alter the tolerance text height with the DIMTFAC (DIMension Tolerance scale FACtor) variable. With DIMTFAC set at the default of 1, the tolerance text heights are equal to the dimension text height. This practice is consistent with the ANSI standard. However, if you want to change the text height of the tolerance to 3/4 (.75) of the normal text height, for example, then alter the DIMTFAC variable as follows:

Command: **DIM** ↵
Dim: **DIMTFAC** ↵
Current value ⟨1.000⟩ New value: **.75** ↵

Fig. 19-8 shows how changing the DIMTFAC variable affects the dimension text.

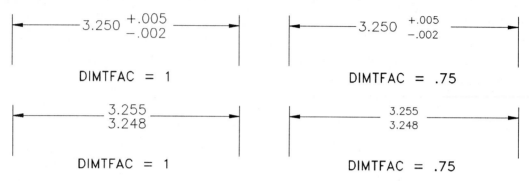

Fig. 19-8. The DIMTFAC variables.

EXERCISE 19-3

☐ Open PRODR2.
☐ Draw object lines of the views on layer 0-7. Add dimensions to layer 3-3.
☐ Set the dimensioning variables as required to obtain the tolerances shown.

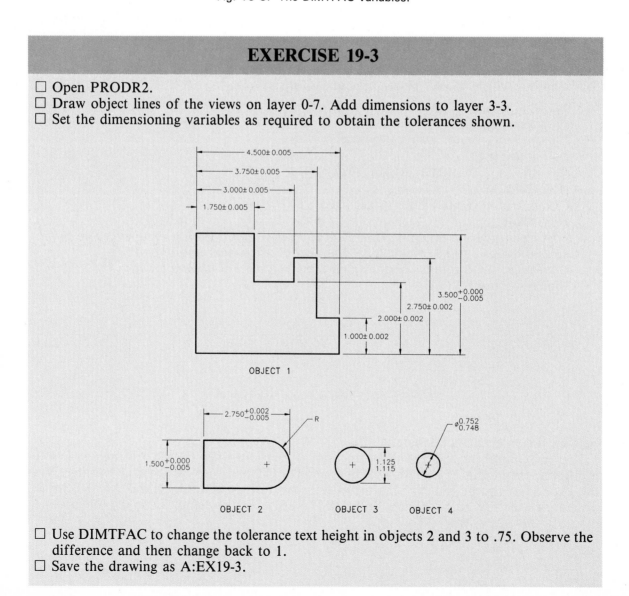

☐ Use DIMTFAC to change the tolerance text height in objects 2 and 3 to .75. Observe the difference and then change back to 1.
☐ Save the drawing as A:EX19-3.

DIMENSIONING UNITS AND DUAL DIMENSIONING   ARM 11

Dimensions in the ANSI standard Y14.5M, *Dimensioning and Tolerancing,* are given in SI (International System of Units) units. The accepted SI linear unit for engineering drawings and related documents is the millimeter. The accepted US linear unit for engineering drawings is the decimal inch. The unit of measurement chosen should be in accordance with the policy of your company or school, or the product design. When all dimensions on a drawing are given in either millimeters or inches, place this general note on the drawing: UNLESS OTHERWISE SPECIFIED, ALL DIMENSIONS ARE IN MILLIMETERS (or INCHES). The abbreviation "IN" follows all inch dimensions on a drawing dimensioned in millimeters. The abbreviation "mm" follows all millimeter dimensions on a drawing dimensioned in inches.

AutoCAD allows you to place "IN" or "mm" after any or all dimension numerals. Select DIMPOST and type "IN" or "mm" at the New value: prompt. New dimensions then carry the suffix.

Suppose only one or two dimensions need the "IN" or "mm" suffix. It may be easier to type the desired value at the Dimension text: prompt.

Dimension text: **2.75 IN** ↵

The DIMPOST default is no suffix. You can remove a suffix by typing "." at the New value: prompt of DIMPOST.

── PROFESSIONAL TIP ──

It is not a common practice to have a prefix or suffix on every dimension on the drawing. A general note usually takes care of these applications effectively. Additionally, you need to be careful when using the DIMPOST variable to set a prefix since this prefix takes the place of any standard AutoCAD prefixes such as the R symbol for radius and the ϕ symbol for diameter.

Dual dimensioning

Dual dimensioning means to place both inches and millimeters on each dimension. The current ANSI standard does not recognize dual dimensioning. Yet, a few companies prefer to use it. One technique is to show inch dimensions followed by millimeter equivalents in brackets. The opposite is millimeters followed by inch equivalents in brackets. When this is done, the general note: DIMENSIONS IN [ ] ARE MILLIMETERS, should be placed on the drawing. Another method of dual dimensioning has inch and millimeter dimensions separated by a slash. When this is done, the general note MILLIMETER/INCH or INCH/MILLIMETER should be placed on the drawing. A preferred practice is to show a table of equivalent dimensions in the upper-left corner of the drawing. This eliminates the need for dual dimensioning and cleans up the drawing. Although not a recommended ANSI standard, this method is used on dual dimensioned drawings where military standards are employed. These examples of dual dimensioning are shown in Fig. 19-9.

```
        1.250 [31.75]              1.250
                                   31.75
           IN [MM]
                                   IN/MM

        31.75 [1.250]              31.75
                                   1.250
           MM [IN]
                                   MM/IN

          BRACKET                 POSITION
          METHOD                   METHOD
```

Fig. 19-9. Dual dimensioning methods.

To convert inches to millimeters, use the formula: 25.4 × INCH = MILLIMETER. To convert millimeters to inches, use the formula: MILLIMETER ÷ 25.4 = INCH. Convert millimeters to decimal inch values with the formula: .0395 inch = 1 millimeter.

The same degree of accuracy is achieved by giving one less digit to the right of the decimal point for millimeter dimensions. The following are considered equivalent conversions:

INCH	MILLIMETER
.1	2.5
.01	0.3
.001	0.03
.0001	0.003

Using AutoCAD for dual dimensioning

AutoCAD refers to dual dimensions as "alternate" dimensions. The DIMALT, DIMALTF, and DIMALTD variables set a dual dimensioning system. The suffixes of these variables are as follows:

ALT = ALTernate units.
ALTF = ALTernate units scale Factor.
ALTD = ALTernate units Decimal places.

Select Dimaltf from the Dim vars screen menu. This allows you to set the multiplication factor. 25.4 is the DIMALTF default value for metric conversion. Next, select the DIMALTD variable. It allows you to set the number of decimal places for the conversion value. If one-place millimeters are desired, set the DIMALTD value to 1. (The default is 2.) After setting the DIMALTF and DIMALTD variables, set the DIMALT variable to ON. This places the millimeter dual dimensions in brackets after each dimension numeral, such as 2.500 [63.50].

The DIMAPOST variable places information after the alternate dimension. The normal dual dimension appears as 2.50 [63.5]. With DIMAPOST set as "mm," the same dimension reads 2.50 [63.5mm]. You can remove the suffix by typing "." at the New value: prompt. The general note discussed earlier is better for dual dimensioning. Do not confuse DIMAPOST with DIMPOST. DIMPOST sets up a dimension suffix for the non-dual dimensioning system.

Rounding dimensions

Dimension numerals may be rounded using the DIMRND variable. The DIMRND default value of 0 means no rounding takes place. Dimension numerals are given exactly as measured. IF DIMRND is set at .5, then all numerals are rounded to the nearest .5 unit. For example, 2.875 is rounded to 3.000. Rounding is seldom needed.

USING THE DIALOGUE BOX TO CONTROL TOLERANCING AND DUAL DIMENSIONING

ARM 11

The "Dimension Styles and Variables" dialogue box is a convenient way to work with dim vars since the selections indicate the function performed by the selection. The Dimension Variables buttons were discussed in detail in Chapter 18, except for a few of the tolerance-related applications.

The Text Prefix: and Text Suffix: edit boxes are found in the "Text Format" subdialogue box shown in Fig. 19-10. To access this subdialogue box, enter "DDIM" at the Command: prompt, or pick Dimension Style... from the Settings pull-down menu, and then pick the Text Format... button. These edit boxes allow you to specify a prefix and/or a suffix to accompany the dimension numeral. A *prefix*, such as "SR" (which means Spherical Radius), precedes the numeral. A *suffix* follows the dimension numeral; for example, "MAX" as in "3.75 MAX". Prefixes and suffixes are controlled by the DIMPOST variable.

Adding a specified tolerance to the dimension text

The Tolerances area of the "Text Format" subdialogue box includes several radio buttons. The None button, shown in Fig. 19-10, is the default for tolerances. The default displays a dimension without a tolerance.

Picking the Variance radio button activates the Upper Value: and Lower Value: edit boxes. Activating Variance turns on DIMTOL, turns off DIMLIM, and saves the specified upper value

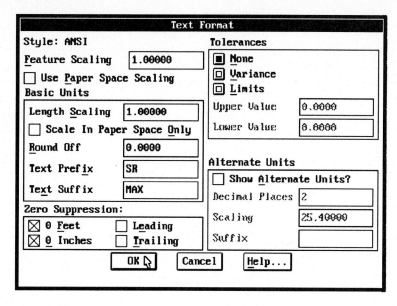

Fig. 19-10. Setting dimension prefixes and suffixes using the "Text Format" dialogue box.

in DIMTP and the lower value in DIMTM. You can specify either an equal or unequal plus/minus tolerance. An unequal plus/minus tolerance is displayed in the tolerance edit boxes. Examples of inch and metric applications are illustrated in Fig. 19-11. Be sure to pick the Leading check box in the Zero Suppression area to omit leading zeros for inch tolerances. However, turn off the Leading check box for metric dimensions.

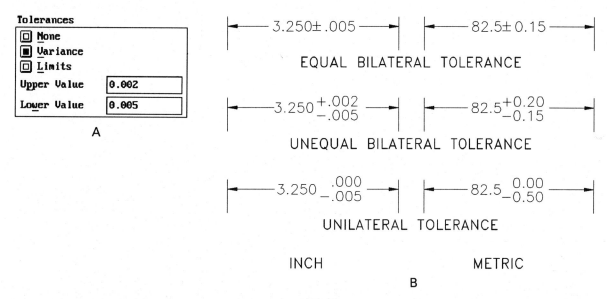

Fig. 19-11. A—Using the Variance radio button and edit boxes to set the upper and lower values. B—Effects of Variance settings.

─────────── **PROFESSIONAL TIP** ───────────

Note that the techniques used by AutoCAD to handle tolerance numerals is not exactly as preferred in the ANSI standard. For example, AutoCAD omits the + (or −) in the unilateral tolerance. This is fine for metric dimensions, but it is recommended that the + (or −) be displayed on the inch tolerance. In addition, only one zero is recommended for a metric unilateral tolerance, while AutoCAD places a number of zeros after the decimal place (equal to the number specified in the UNITS value). The following illustration shows the preferred method.

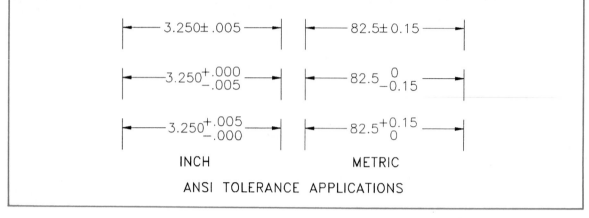

INCH   METRIC

ANSI TOLERANCE APPLICATIONS

Pick the Limits radio button if you want dimension numerals shown as a limits tolerance. A limits tolerance is one in which the plus/minus value is calculated into the dimension numeral as shown in Fig. 19-12. Note that the Upper Value: and Lower Value: edit boxes are activated when Limits is picked. The Limits selection turns on DIMLIM, turns off DIMTOL, and saves the specified upper value in DIMTP and the lower value in DIMTM.

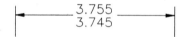

Fig. 19-12. Setting a limits tolerance.

Picking the Show Alternate Units? check box activates the Decimal Places, Scaling, and Suffix edit boxes as shown in Fig. 19-13. Alternate Units is used to display dual dimensioning as discussed earlier. This is not a recommended ANSI practice, but it is done by some companies. The practice normally displays inches followed by the metric equivalent in brackets, or vice versa; for example, "3.750[95.25]." Decimal Places is set to 2 places by default, but you can change it as needed. The Scaling: edit box is set to the metric conversion factor where INCH × 25.4 = MILLIMETER. The Suffix: edit box is used in case you want to use "mm", "IN", or the like in brackets. This is normally not necessary since a general note should accompany the drawing stating: DIMENSIONS IN [ ] ARE MILLIMETERS (or INCHES, as appropriate). Checking the Show Alternate Units? box turns on DIMALT, the decimal places are saved in the DIMALTD variable, the scale factor is saved in DIMALTF, and the suffix is stored in DIMAPOST.

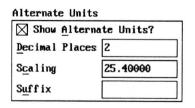

Fig. 19-13. Using the Alternate Units section of the "Text Format" subdialogue box.

EXERCISE 19-4

☐ Open PRODR2.
☐ Access the "Text Format" subdialogue box and enter "SR" in the Text Prefix edit box.
☐ Draw a 4.500 horizontal dimension and observe the results.
☐ Remove the "SR" from the Text Prefix: edit box and make the text suffix read "MAX".
☐ Draw a 4.500 horizontal dimension and observe the results.
☐ Remove "MAX" from the edit box.
☐ Enter an open parenthesis "(" in the Text Prefix: edit box, and a closing parenthesis ")" in the Text Suffix: edit box.
☐ Draw a 4.500 dimension. The parentheses indicate a reference dimension.
☐ Remove the parentheses from the edit boxes.
☐ Pick the Variance button in the "Text Format" subdialogue box, and enter a .005 upper and lower value.
☐ Draw a 4.500 dimension.
☐ Now, change the variance to show a .005 upper value and a .000 lower value. Draw another 4.500 dimension.
☐ Pick the Limits button in the "Text Format" subdialogue box, and enter a .005 upper and lower value.
☐ Draw a 4.5000 dimension.
☐ Pick the None radio button in the "Text Format" subdialogue box. Check the Show Alternate Units? box.
☐ Draw a 4.500 dimension.
☐ Save the drawing as A:EX19-4.

USING AUTOCAD'S ASSOCIATIVE DIMENSIONING ARM 11

Associative dimensioning permits dimensions to change as an object is edited. With the DIMASO variable turned on, stretching, trimming, or extending an object also changes the dimensions associated with that object. With the DIMASO variable turned off, elements of the dimension are considered separate. Thus, you could edit the dimension line, arrowheads, extension lines, and dimension numerals as individual items. With DIMASO turned on, these items act together as one entity. You could then erase the entire dimension by picking any part of the dimension. The ALIGNED, HORIZONTAL, VERTICAL, ROTATED, ANGULAR, DIAMETER, and RADIUS commands are influenced by associative dimensioning. The CENTER and LEADER commands remain as unique items and are not affected.

Another variable that works with associative dimensioning is DIMSHO. If DIMASO and DIMSHO are both on, the dimension for an object being stretched (for example) is visually recalculated as the object is dragged into position. The DIMSHO default is OFF because this function slows down the computer on complex drawings.

Revising drawings and associated dimensions

When a drawing is changed using MIRROR, ROTATE, or SCALE commands, the dimensions are also changed when DIMASO is on. Linear and Angular dimensioning options are altered by the STRETCH command. Only linear dimensions are affected by the EXTEND and TRIM commands.

Stretching an object and its dimensions

When stretching an object, select the object and dimension using the Crossing option. The command sequence shown in Fig. 19-14 is as follows:

Command: **STRETCH** ↵
Select objects to be stretched by window or polygon...
Select objects: **C** ↵
First corner: *(pick the first corner of the crossing box)*
Other corner: *(pick the second crossing box corner)*
Select objects: ↵
Base point or displacement: *(pick the base point on the object to be stretched)*
Second point of displacement: *(pick the new point to where the object is to be stretched; observe the object being dragged into position)*
Command:

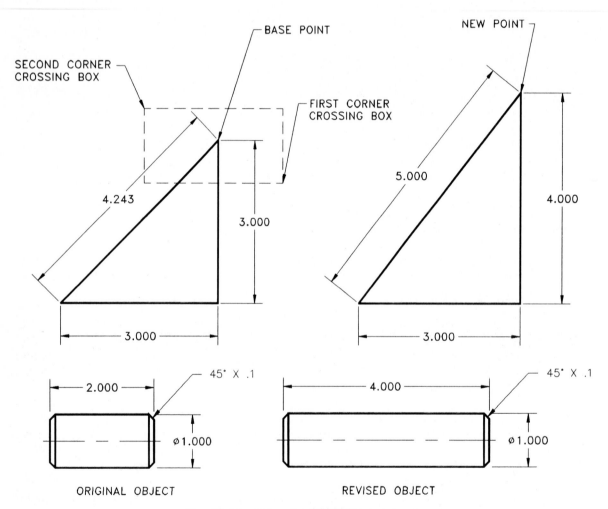

Fig. 19-14. Using the STRETCH command.

Moving a dimension numeral

The ANSI standards advise that adjacent dimensions be staggered. However, AutoCAD centers all dimension text. The STRETCH command will move dimension text within the dimension line, Fig. 19-15, as follows:

Command: **STRETCH** ↵
Select objects to be stretched by window or polygon...
Select objects: **C** ↵
First corner: Other corner: *(place the crossing box around the text to be moved)*
Select objects: ↵
Base point or displacement: *(pick the base point at the center of the existing text)*
Second point of displacement: *(pick the new point at the desired text location)*
Command:

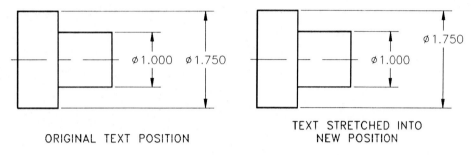

ORIGINAL TEXT POSITION

TEXT STRETCHED INTO
NEW POSITION

Fig. 19-15. Using the STRETCH command to move dimension text.

The TEDIT command also works well for this application. Try this:
Command: **DIM** ↵
Dim: **TEDIT** ↵
Select dimension: *(pick the dimension numeral to be moved)*
Enter text location (Left/Right/Home/Angle): *(move the text to a new location and pick, or use one of the available options)*
Dim:

Refer to Fig. 18-65 for a detailed discussion of all TEDIT options.
You can also add or subtract size from an object to be stretched using relative coordinates. For example, at the Second point of displacement: prompt, typing "@2,0" adds 2 units horizontally. Typing "@-1.25,0" deletes 1.25 units horizontally. Typing "@0,-.5" deletes .5 units vertically.

Trimming and extending

It is possible to extend or trim an object and related dimensions to meet another object. The TRIM and EXTEND commands were introduced in Chapter 11 to trim or extend lines of an object. The EXTEND command format is as follows:

Command: **EXTEND** ↵
Select boundary edge(s) ...
Select objects: *(pick the boundary edge)*
Select objects: ↵

The boundary edge is the line to which the desired object will extend, Fig. 19-16A. Then pick the dimension and lines to extend.

⟨Select object to extend⟩/Undo: *(pick the dimension to be extended)*
⟨Select object to extend⟩/Undo: *(pick a line to extend)*
⟨Select object to extend⟩/Undo: *(pick a line to extend)*
⟨Select object to extend⟩/Undo: ↵
Command:

Notice in Fig. 19-16C that one line of the original object remains. This line may be removed using the ERASE command.

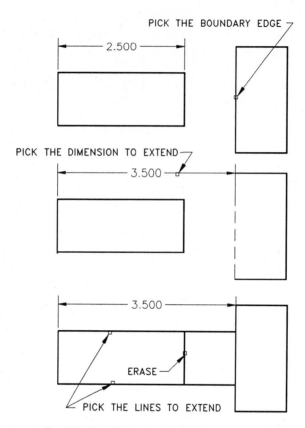

Fig. 19-16. Using the EXTEND command.

The TRIM command is the opposite of the EXTEND command. Look at Fig. 19-17. First, draw a line on the Original Object to trim to. Then, follow this TRIM command sequence:

Command: **TRIM** ↵
Select cutting edge(s)...
Select objects: *(pick cutting edges to which lines and dimensions will be shortened)*
Select objects: ↵

The location where you pick the dimension establishes the trim position the dimension takes. Pick as shown in Fig. 19-17 for the results shown.

⟨Select object to trim⟩/Undo: *(pick the dimension to be trimmed)*
⟨Select object to trim⟩/Undo: *(pick the line to be trimmed)*
⟨Select object to trim⟩/Undo: *(pick the line to be trimmed)*
⟨Select object to trim⟩/Undo: ↵
Command: **ERASE** ↵
Select objects: *(select the line on the right)*
Select objects: ↵
Command:

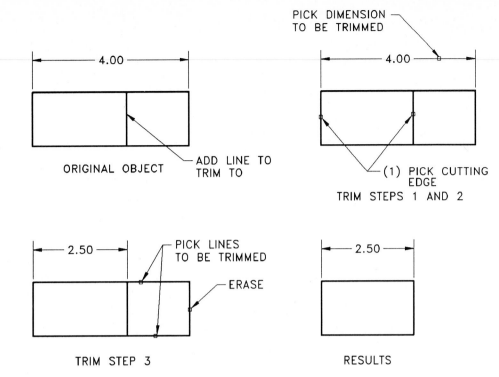

Fig. 19-17. Using the TRIM command.

─── **PROFESSIONAL TIP** ───

Be careful when editing associative dimensions to ensure that the current units setting, dimension style, and dimensioning variables are what you desire. Some editing activities cause the drawing to regenerate with the current values. The editing commands and related grip modes that affect dimensions in this manner are:
- ARRAY's Polar option.
- COPY of a polar array.
- EXTEND and TRIM of linear dimensions.
- MIRROR.
- ROTATE.
- SCALE.
- STRETCH.

MAKING CHANGES TO DIMENSIONS | ARM 11 |

The component parts of a dimension may be edited after using the EXPLODE command. Dimensions also may be changed individually or in groups using the UPDATE, HOMETEXT, or NEWTEXT commands.

Exploding an associative dimension

ARM 6

An associative dimension is treated as one entity even though it consists of extension lines, a dimension line, arrowheads, and numerals. At times it is necessary to work with the individual parts. To do this, you must break the dimension into its individual parts with the EXPLODE command as follows:

> Command: **EXPLODE** ↵
> Select objects: *(pick the dimension to be exploded)*
> Select objects: ↵
> Command:

Once exploded, the dimension is redrawn on layer 0. Then select objects to edit. For example, you can erase the text without erasing the dimension line, arrowheads, or extension lines.

Changing variables or text of existing dimensions

ARM 11

You can change the text or variables of individual dimensions or all dimensions on the drawing. The UPDATE, HOMETEXT, and NEWTEXT commands can be accessed by picking Edit from the DIM: screen menu, or by typing at the Command: prompt.

The UPDATE command updates existing dimensions with the current dimensioning variables, units, or text style. For example, the DIMASZ (arrowhead size) default value is .18. Suppose that after completing a drawing you learn the company standard requires .25 arrowheads. This is easy to fix. Select DIMASZ and enter the new value as .25. At the Dim: prompt, type "UP-DATE" and press ENTER. Then select the items to be changed by picking them individually or windowing. It is common to change the entire drawing using the window selection process. The steps are as follows:

> Command: **DIM** ↵
> Dim: **UPDATE** or **UPD** ↵
> Select objects: *(pick individual dimensions, a group of dimensions, or window the entire drawing for change)*

The entire drawing is now automatically updated with the new current variables, Fig. 19-18.

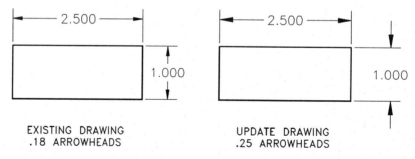

Fig. 19-18. Using the UPDATE command to change arrowhead size.

The HOMETEXT command changes the position of dimension text to its original location. For example, suppose the STRETCH or TEDIT command was used to move a dimension numeral to a new location. The HOMETEXT command moves the numeral back to the center, Fig. 19-19.

Command: **DIM** ↵
Dim: **HOMETEXT** or **HOM** ↵
Select objects: *(pick the dimension(s) to be changed)*
Select objects:
Dim:

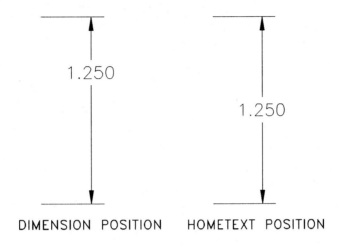

DIMENSION POSITION   HOMETEXT POSITION

Fig. 19-19. Results obtained with the HOMETEXT command.

The NEWTEXT command is used to edit dimension text. Suppose you find that a diameter symbol was left off of a dimension. Enter the NEWTEXT command, Fig. 19-20, to select and change the numeral as follows:

Command: **DIM** ↵
Dim: **NEWTEXT** or **NEW** ↵
Enter new dimension text: **%%C2.500** ↵
Select objects: *(pick the dimension to be changed)*
Select objects:
Dim:

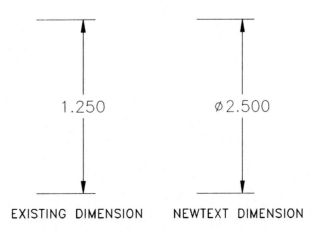

EXISTING DIMENSION   NEWTEXT DIMENSION

Fig. 19-20. Using the NEWTEXT command.

DIMENSION DEFINITION POINTS

When you draw an associative dimension, the points used to specify the dimension and the middle point of the dimension text are called *definition points*, or DEFPOINTS. When a dimension is redefined, the revised position is based on the definition points. The definition points are located on the DEFPOINTS layer which is automatically created by AutoCAD. The definition points are displayed with the dimension. The definition points are plotted only if the DEFPOINTS layer is renamed. The definition points are displayed when the dimensioning layer is on, even if the DEFPOINTS layer is off.

If you select an object for editing and wish to include the dimensions in the edit, then you must include the definition points of the dimension in the selection set. If you need to snap to a definition point only, use the Node object snap.

PAPER SPACE DIMENSIONING

Be cautious when placing associative dimensions on a drawing created in model space when you are currently in the paper space mode. These dimensions remain unchanged when you use editing commands like STRETCH, TRIM, or EXTEND, or display commands such as ZOOM or PAN in a model space viewport. To ensure that AutoCAD calculates a scale factor that is compatible between model and paper space, check the Paper Space Scaling check box in any of the subdialogue boxes accessed through the "Dimension Styles and Variables" dialogue box.

When you draw dimensions in paper space that describe something from your model space drawing, first set the Viewport option in the DIMLFAC variable while in paper space like this:

Command: **DIM** ↵
Dim: **DIMLFAC** ↵
Current value ⟨1.000⟩ New value (Viewport): **V** ↵
Select viewport to set scale: *(pick the desired viewport)*

AutoCAD automatically makes the DIMLFAC variable adjust to the zoom scale factor of the model space viewport. This does not work when dimensioning with the ORDINATE command.

EXERCISE 19-5

☐ Open EX19-3.
☐ Set the following dimensioning variable values:
   ☐ DIMEXE = .125
   ☐ DIMEXO = .08
   ☐ DIMCEN = -.25
   ☐ DIMASZ = .25
   ☐ DIMDLI = .75
   ☐ DIMTXT = .125
☐ Use the STRETCH or TEDIT command to stagger the last vertical dimension.
☐ For object 2, use the STRETCH command to make it .25 in. longer and .5 in. higher.
☐ Enter the UPDATE command to change the entire drawing to the current variables.
☐ Use the HOMETEXT command to move the staggered vertical dimension in object one back to its original position.
☐ Use the NEWTEXT command to remove the plus/minus tolerances from the horizontal dimensions on object one.
☐ Save the drawing as A:EX19-5.

CHAPTER TEST

Write your answers in the spaces provided.

1. When entered at the Dim: prompt, the _____ command saves dimensioning variable settings to a dimension style and makes the new dimension style current.

2. The _____ command lets you change dimensioning variable settings by reading new settings from an existing dimension style.

3. Give the command and responses needed to list all of the available dimension styles through the RESTORE command:

   Command: _____

   Dim: _____

       Current dimension style: ANSI

       ?/Enter dimension style name or RETURN to select dimension: _____

       Dimension style(s) to list ⟨*⟩: _____

       Named dimension styles:

4. Give the command and responses used to have AutoCAD display the difference between an existing MIL dimension style and the current dimension style:

   Command: _____

   Dim: _____

       Current dimension style: ANSI

       ?/Enter dimension style name or RETURN to select dimension: _____

5. Give the command and responses used to override the DIMEXO variable on an existing dimension from the existing setting of .06 to 0 without changing the current dimension style:

   Command: _____

   Dim: _____

   Dimension variable to override: _____

   Current value ⟨.062⟩: New value: _____

   Dimension variable to override: _____

   Select objects: _____

   Modify dimension style "ANSI"? ⟨N⟩: _____

6. Give the command and entries required to create all dimensions with a tolerance of ± .005:

   Command: _____

   Dim: _____

   Current value ⟨Off⟩ New value: _____

   Dim: _____

   Current value ⟨0.000⟩ New value: _____

   Dim: _____

   Current value ⟨0.000⟩ New value: _____

   Dim: _____

7. Give the command and entries needed to create all dimensions as limits tolerancing of ± .002:
   Command: _____
   Dim: _____
   Current value ⟨Off⟩ New value: _____
   Dim: _____
   Current value ⟨0.000⟩ New value: _____
   Dim: _____
   Current value ⟨0.000⟩ New value: _____
   Dim: _____

8. Give the command and entries that enable dual dimensioning with two decimal place millimeters in brackets:
   Command: _____
   Dim: _____
   Current value ⟨25.4⟩ New value: _____
   Dim: _____
   Current value ⟨2⟩ New value: _____
   Dim: _____
   Current value ⟨Off⟩ New value: _____
   Dim: _____

9. Give the command and entries needed to stretch an object and its dimensions:
   Command: _____
   Select objects to be stretched by window or polygon...
   Select objects: _____
   First corner: _____
   Other corner: _____
   Select objects: _____
   Base point: _____
   New point: _____

10. Give the command and entries required to split an associative dimension into its individual parts:
    Command: _____
    Select objects: _____

11. Suppose you have changed some dimensioning variables and want the new values to be revised and displayed. What command and responses should you enter?
    Command: _____
    Dim: _____
    Select objects: _____

12. Suppose you have dimension text on a drawing that reads 24. To make it read $\phi24$, what command and values should you enter?

    Command: _____

    Dim: _____

    Enter new dimension text: _____

    Select objects: _____

13. Define "tolerance." _____

    _____

14. Give an example of a bilateral tolerance. _____

15. Give an example of a unilateral tolerance. _____

16. What are the limits of the dimension 1.875 ± .002? _____

17. Give the general note that would accompany a drawing dimensioned in millimeters.

    _____

    _____

18. Give the general note used when millimeter dimensions are provided in brackets next to inch dimensions. _____

19. Name the command that can be used to list the current dimension style and variable settings of a dimension style without changing the current settings. _____

20. Name the dialogue box that allows you to work with dimension styles. _____

    _____

21. Identify at least two ways to access the dialogue box discussed in question number 20.

    _____

    _____

22. How do you save a new dimension style using the dialogue box that was accessed in question number 21? _____

    _____

23. When you save a new style in the dialogue box, it takes on the same characteristics as the previous style. How do you proceed to make the new style take on its own characteristics?

    _____

    _____

    _____

24. How do you add the suffix "MIN" to a dimension numeral by using a dialogue box?

    _____

    _____

    _____

    _____

25. Describe the procedure to use if you want dimensions displayed with plus/minus equal bilateral tolerances of ±.002 using the dialogue box. _____

_____

_____

26. Describe the procedure to use if you want dimensions displayed with limits dimensioning having a ±.005 from the specified dimension using the dialogue box. _____

_____

_____

27. Define definition points. _____

_____

_____

28. What is the importance of selecting definition points when editing an object that includes dimensions in the edit? _____

_____

_____

29. Name the object snap mode used to snap to a definition point. _____

30. Name the dimension variable to use when in paper space to make the dimension scale factor adjust to the zoom scale factor of the model space viewport. _____

For Questions 31-43, identify the dimensioning variable associated with each of the definitions.

31. Identifies the current dimension style. _____

32. Used to change the text height for tolerance dimensions without affecting the normal dimension text height. _____

33. When on, it shows a dimension numeral with tolerance. _____

34. Controls plus part of tolerance. _____

35. Controls minus part of tolerance._____

36. When on automatically calculates and displays tolerance limits. _____

37. Allows you to place a specified suffix after dimension numerals. _____

38. Automatically places millimeter dual dimensions in brackets. _____

39. Allows you to set a multiplication factor for alternate units. _____

40. Sets the number of decimal places for alternate units._____

41. Used to turn on or off associative dimensioning. _____

42. Allows dimensions to be shown as they are edited._____

43. Allows dimension numerals to be rounded as specified. _____

For Questions 44-48, name the commands that do the following:

44. Move dimension text within a dimension line. _____

45. Break an existing associative dimension into its individual parts. _____

46. Changes existing dimensions to take on current dimensioning variable values. _____

47. Changes the position of dimension text to its original location. _____

48. Used to edit existing dimension text. _____

DRAWING PROBLEMS

Set limits, units, dimensioning variables, and other parameters as needed. Follow these guidelines.

A. Draw the views to exact size.

B. Use grids, object snap options, and the OSNAP command to your best advantage.

C. Apply dimensions accurately using ANSI standards.

D. Set dimensioning variables to suit the drawing.

E. Use the LAYER command to set separate layers for views and dimensions.

F. Draw object lines using .032 in. wide polylines, or use the LINE command and plot with a wide pen.

G. Place general notes 1/2 in. from lower-left corner:

    3. UNLESS OTHERWISE SPECIFIED, ALL DIMENSIONS ARE IN MILLIMETERS (or INCHES as applicable).

    2. REMOVE ALL BURRS AND SHARP EDGES.

    1. INTERPRET PER ANSI Y14.5M.

    NOTES:

H. Save the drawings to a floppy disk as P19-(problem number).

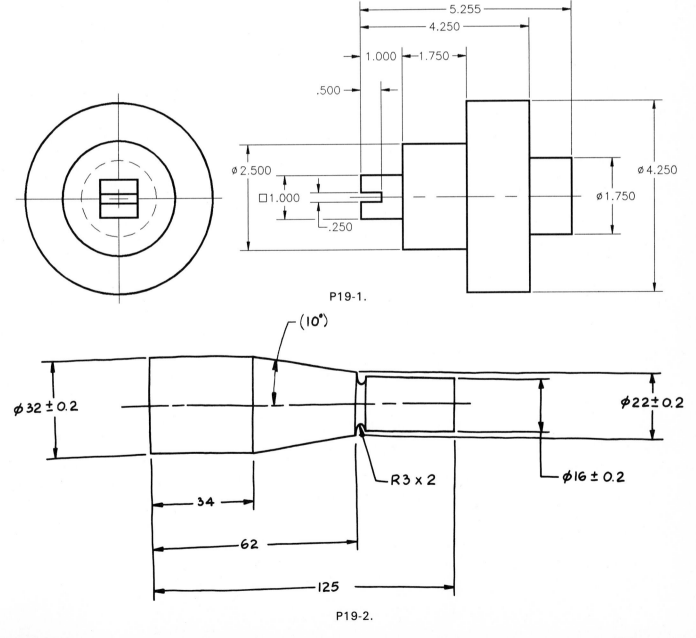

P19-1.

P19-2.

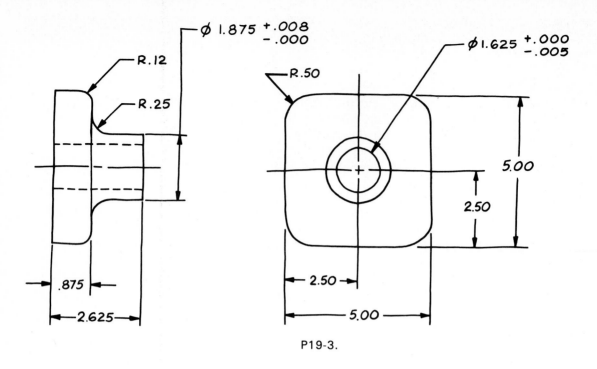

P19-3.

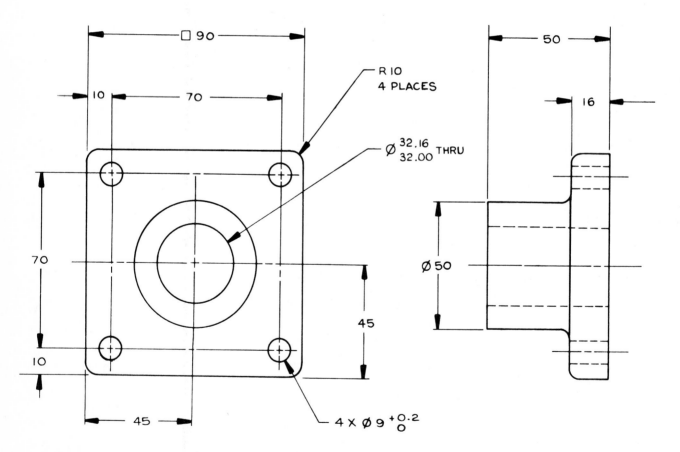

3. ROUNDS AND FILLETS R4.

2. REMOVE ALL BURRS AND SHARP EDGES.

1. INTERPRET DRAWING PER ANSI Y14.5M-1982.

NOTES:

P19-4.

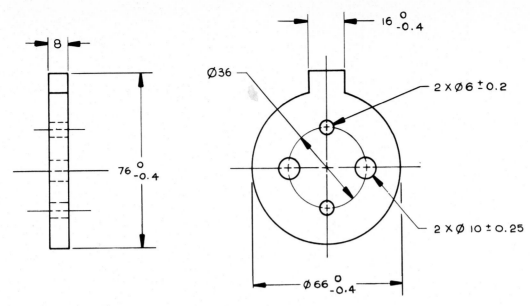

2. REMOVE ALL BURRS AND SHARP EDGES.
1. INTERPRET DRAWING PER ANSI Y14.5M-1982.
NOTES:

P19-5.

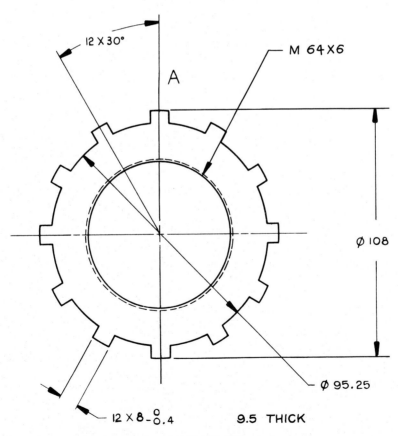

2. REMOVE ALL BURRS AND SHARP EDGES.
1. INTERPRET DRAWING PER ANSI Y14.5M-1982.
NOTES:

P19-6.

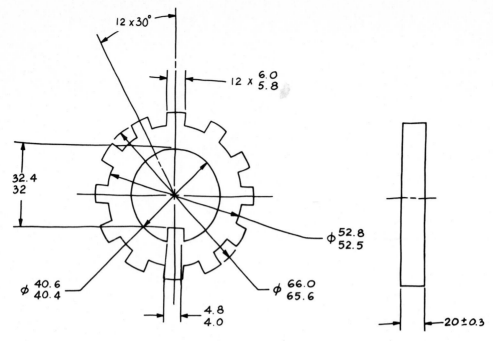

12 x 30°

12 x 6.0 / 5.8

32.4 / 32

Φ 52.8 / 52.5

Φ 40.6 / 40.4

Φ 66.0 / 65.6

4.8 / 4.0

20 ± 0.3

P19-7.

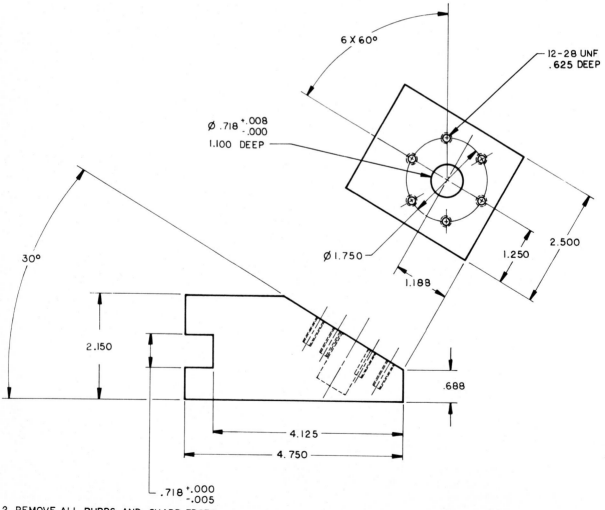

6 X 60°

12-28 UNF
.625 DEEP

Φ .718 +.008 / -.000
1.100 DEEP

Φ 1.750

Φ 1.750

1.188

1.250

2.500

30°

2.150

.688

4.125

4.750

.718 +.000 / -.005

2. REMOVE ALL BURRS AND SHARP EDGES.
1. INTERPRET DRAWING PER ANSI-Y14.5M 1982.
NOTES:

P19-8.

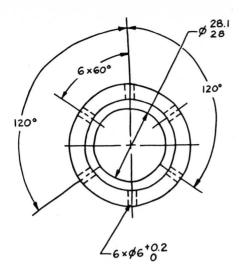

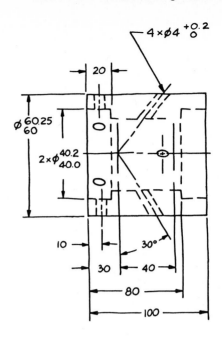

NOTE: DIMENSIONING TO
HIDDEN FEATURES IS NOT
AN ACCEPTABLE STANDARD.
THIS WILL BE CORRECTED
IN CHAPTER 20.

P19-9.

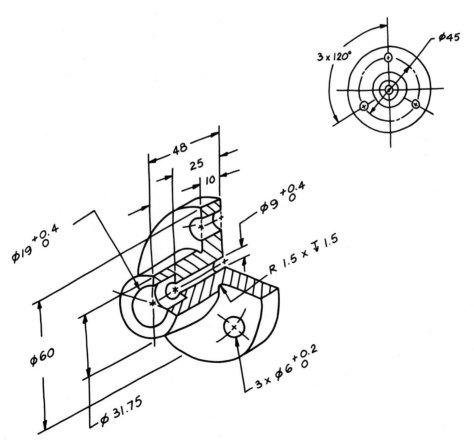

P19-10.

Ejector-locator assembly. (Autodesk, Inc.)

.500 CONSTANT FOR FINISHED FACE

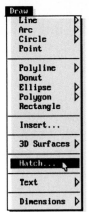

Chapter 20

DRAWING SECTIONAL VIEWS AND GRAPHIC PATTERNS

Learning objectives

After completing this chapter, you will be able to:

☐ Identify sectioning techniques.

☐ Use sections and dimensioning practices to draw objects given on engineering sketches.

☐ Draw sectional material using the HATCH, BHATCH, and SOLID commands.

☐ Prepare graphic displays, such as graphs and logos, using the HATCH and SOLID commands.

In mechanical drafting, internal features in regular multiviews appear as hidden lines. These features must be dimensioned. However, it is poor practice to dimension to hidden lines. Therefore, sectional views are used to clarify the hidden features. They show internal features as if a portion of the object is cut away. Sectional views are used in conjunction with multiviews to completely describe the exterior and interior features of an object.

When sections are drawn, a cutting-plane line placed in one of the views shows where the cut was made. The cutting-plane line is the "saw" that cuts through the object to expose internal features. The arrows on the cutting-plane line indicate the line of sight when looking at the sectional view. The cutting-plane lines are often labeled with letters which relate to the proper sectional view. This practice is necessary for drawings with multiple sections. It is optional when only one sectional view is present and its location is obvious. Section lines are used in the sectional view to show where material has been cut away, Fig. 20-1.

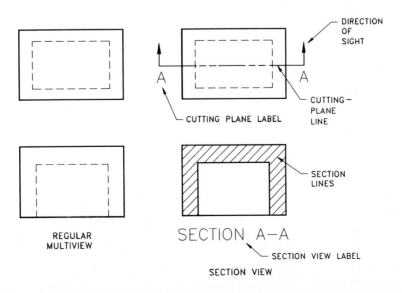

Fig. 20-1. Multiview compared to sectional view.

Sectioning is also used in other drafting fields such as architectural and structural drafting. Cross sections through buildings show the construction methods and materials, Fig. 20-2. The cutting-plane lines used in these fields are often composed of letter and number symbols. This helps coordinate the large number of sections found in a set of architectural drawings.

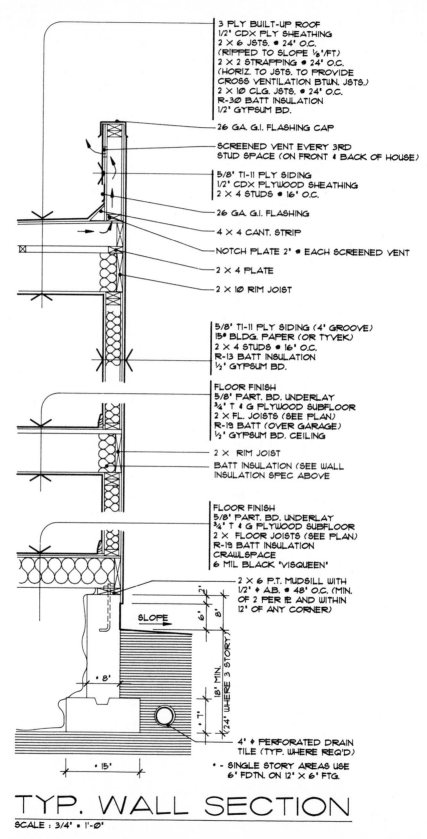

3 PLY BUILT-UP ROOF
1/2" CDX PLY SHEATHING
2 X 6 JSTS. @ 24' O.C.
(RIPPED TO SLOPE 1/8"/FT)
2 X 2 STRAPPING @ 24' O.C.
(HORIZ. TO JSTS. TO PROVIDE
CROSS VENTILATION BTWN. JSTS.)
2 X 10 CLG. JSTS. @ 24' O.C.
R-30 BATT INSULATION
1/2' GYPSUM BD.

26 GA. G.I. FLASHING CAP

SCREENED VENT EVERY 3RD
STUD SPACE (ON FRONT & BACK OF HOUSE)

5/8' TI-11 PLY SIDING
1/2' CDX PLYWOOD SHEATHING
2 X 4 STUDS @ 16' O.C.

26 GA. G.I. FLASHING

4 X 4 CANT. STRIP

NOTCH PLATE 2' @ EACH SCREENED VENT

2 X 4 PLATE

2 X 10 RIM JOIST

5/8' TI-11 PLY SIDING (4' GROOVE)
15# BLDG. PAPER (OR TYVEK)
2 X 4 STUDS @ 16' O.C.
R-13 BATT INSULATION
1/2' GYPSUM BD.

FLOOR FINISH
5/8' PART. BD. UNDERLAY
3/4' T & G PLYWOOD SUBFLOOR
2 X FL. JOISTS (SEE PLAN)
R-19 BATT (OVER GARAGE)
1/2' GYPSUM BD. CEILING

2 X RIM JOIST

BATT INSULATION (SEE WALL
INSULATION SPEC ABOVE

FLOOR FINISH
5/8' PART. BD. UNDERLAY
3/4' T & G PLYWOOD SUBFLOOR
2 X FLOOR JOISTS (SEE PLAN)
R-19 BATT INSULATION
CRAWLSPACE
6 MIL BLACK 'VISQUEEN'

2 X 6 P.T. MUDSILL WITH
1/2' Φ A.B. @ 48' O.C. (MIN.
OF 2 PER 12 AND WITHIN
12' OF ANY CORNER)

SLOPE

4' Φ PERFORATED DRAIN
TILE (TYP. WHERE REQ'D)

* - SINGLE STORY AREAS USE
6' FDTN. ON 12' X 6' FTG.

TYP. WALL SECTION

SCALE : 3/4' = 1'-0'

Fig. 20-2. Architectural sectional view. Drawing courtesy of Alan Mascord, Design Associates.

TYPES OF SECTIONS

There are many types of sections available for the drafter to use in specific situations. The section used depends on the detail to be sectioned. For example, one object may require the section be taken completely through the object. Another may only need to remove a small portion to expose the interior features.

Full sections

Full sections, such as the one shown in Fig. 20-1, are used when it is necessary to remove half of the object. In this type of section, the cutting-plane line passes completely through the object along a centerplane.

Offset sections

Offset sections are the same as full sections, except that the cutting-plane line is staggered. This allows you to cut through features that do not lie in a straight line, Fig. 20-3.

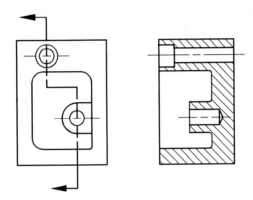

Fig. 20-3. Offset section.

Half sections

Half sections show one-quarter of the object removed. The term "half" is used because half of the view appears in section and the other half is shown as an exterior view. Half sections are commonly used on symmetrical objects. A centerline is used to separate the sectioned part of the view from the unsectioned portion. Hidden lines are normally omitted from the unsectioned side, Fig. 20-4.

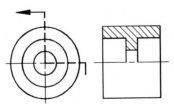

Fig. 20-4. Half section.

Aligned sections

Aligned sections are used when a feature is out of alignment with the centerplane. In this case, an offset section would distort the image. The cutting-plane line cuts through the feature to be sectioned. It is then rotated to align with the centerplane before projecting into the sectional view. See Fig. 20-5.

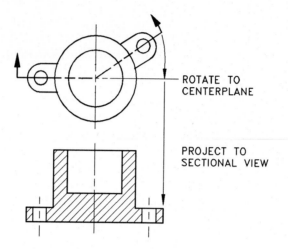

ROTATE TO
CENTERPLANE

PROJECT TO
SECTIONAL VIEW

Fig. 20-5. Aligned section.

Revolved sections

Revolved sections clarify the contour of objects that have the same shape throughout their length. The section is revolved in place within the object or part of the view may be broken away. Refer to Fig. 20-6. The advantage of breaking away part of the view is to make dimensioning easier.

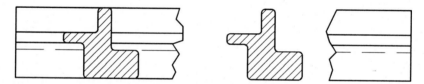

Fig. 20-6. Revolved section.

Removed sections

Removed sections serve much the same function as revolved sections. The sectional view is removed from the regular view. A cutting-plane line shows where the section was taken. When multiple removed sections are taken, the cutting planes and related views are labeled. The sectional views are placed in alphabetical order. The letters I, O, and Q are not used because they may be mistaken for numbers. Drawing only the ends of the cutting-plane lines simplifies the views. See Fig. 20-7.

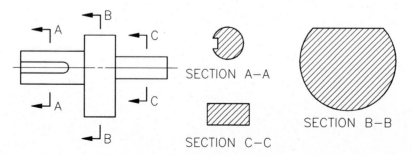

SECTION A–A

SECTION C–C

SECTION B–B

Fig. 20-7. Removed sections.

Broken-out sections

Broken-out sections show only a small portion of the view removed to clarify a hidden feature. See Fig. 20-8.

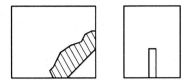

Fig. 20-8. Broken-out section.

SECTION LINE SYMBOLS

ARM A

Section lines are placed in the sectional view to show where material has been cut away. Some rules that govern section line usage are:

- Section lines are placed at 45° unless another angle is required to satisfy the following rules.
- Section lines should not be drawn parallel or perpendicular to any other adjacent lines on the drawing.
- Section lines should not cross object lines.

Section lines may be drawn using different patterns to represent the specific type of material. The equally spaced section lines shown in the preceding examples represent a general application. This is adequate in most situations. Additional patterns are not necessary if the type of material is clearly indicated in the title block. Different section line material symbols are needed when several connected parts of different materials are sectioned. AutoCAD has standard section line symbols available. These are referred to as *hatch patterns*. These symbols may be seen in the "acad.pat" file. The AutoCAD pattern labeled ANSI31 is the general section line symbol. It is also used for cast iron. The ANSI32 symbol is used for sectioning steel. Other standard AutoCAD hatch patterns are shown in Fig. 20-9. When very thin objects are sectioned, the material may be completely blackened or filled in. AutoCAD refers to this as "solid."

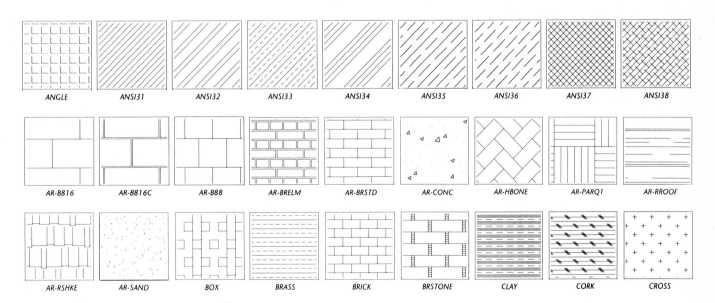

Fig. 20-9. Standard AutoCAD hatch patterns. (Autodesk, Inc.)

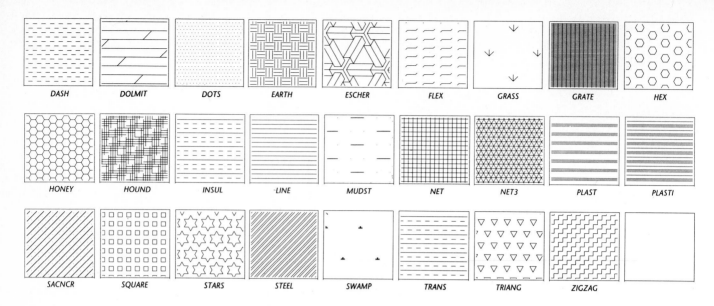

DASH   DOLMIT   DOTS   EARTH   ESCHER   FLEX   GRASS   GRATE   HEX

HONEY   HOUND   INSUL   LINE   MUDST   NET   NET3   PLAST   PLASTI

SACNCR   SQUARE   STARS   STEEL   SWAMP   TRANS   TRIANG   ZIGZAG

Fig. 20-9 Continued.

DRAWING SECTION LINES AND HATCH PATTERNS   ARM 12

The previous discussion explained the different sectioning techniques and introduced section line hatch patterns. AutoCAD hatch patterns are not limited to sectioning. They may be used as artistic patterns in a graphic layout for an advertisement or promotion. They might also be added as shading on an architectural elevation or technical illustration.

Introduction to the HATCH command

AutoCAD allows you to draw section lines or other patterns using the HATCH command. The HATCH command can be accessed by picking HATCH: from the DRAW screen menu, or by typing "HATCH" at the Command: prompt as follows:

    Command: **HATCH** ↵
    Pattern (? or name/U,style):

Typing "?" gives you this prompt:

    Pattern(s) to list ⟨*⟩:

You can type the name or names of specific hatch patterns, or press ENTER to accept the wild card ⟨*⟩ and list all the hatch patterns. AutoCAD displays the names of all standard hatch patterns each followed by a brief description. The list is three pages long so press ENTER, the space bar, or function key F1 after each page. Press flip screen, F1, when finished.

To draw a hatch pattern, type the standard pattern name, ANSI31, for example. You are then asked to define the pattern scale and angle.

    Pattern (? or name/U,style): **ANSI31** ↵
    Scale for pattern ⟨1.000⟩: ↵
    Angle for pattern ⟨0⟩: ↵

Press ENTER after each prompt to use the default value shown in brackets. The pattern scale default is 1, or full scale. If the drawn pattern is too tight or too wide, type a new scale. Fig. 20-10 shows different scale factors.

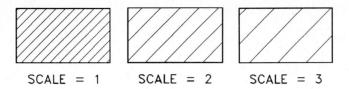

SCALE = 1   SCALE = 2   SCALE = 3

Fig. 20-10. Hatch pattern scale factors.

The default scale factor of 1 specifies one drawing unit. A relationship exists between the hatch scale in model space and paper space. This relationship is controlled by the scale factor. Respond to the scale prompt with the desired size of the pattern in model space or paper space. The hatch scale can still be specified referencing model space if desired, but it is much simpler to reference the scale to paper space. This allows the scale factor to be based on the plotted scale of the drawing. To do this, enter "XP" after the scale. The "XP" indicates relative to paper space units. Therefore, entering "1XP" as the scale factor causes AutoCAD to automatically calculate the actual scale required within model space to match the specified value of 1 in paper space:

Scale for pattern ⟨1.000⟩: **1XP** ↵

When you do this, notice that the next use of the HATCH command offers the actual pattern scale which was calculated by AutoCAD as a default. It is not necessary to reenter "1XP," since the default value shown is the model space equivalent of this already. Model space and paper space are discussed in detail in Chapter 27.

An alternate method of entering values for this prompt is by picking two points in the drawing. AutoCAD then measures the distance and uses the number of units as the scale factor. This method does not allow the XP option to be used.

PROFESSIONAL TIP

It is recommended that you enter a large scale factor when hatching big areas. This makes your section lines look neater and saves regeneration and plot time.

The pattern default angle is 0. This gives you the same pattern angle shown in Fig. 20-9. To alter the pattern angle, type a new value.

Selecting objects to be hatched

It is important to consider the boundary of the area you plan to hatch. It is easy to hatch within a circle or square. All you do is pick the circle, or window the square, when you see the Select objects: prompt. If the square was drawn as one closed polyline, then pick it as one entity. The circumference of the circle and the perimeter of the square automatically become the hatch boundary. See Fig. 20-11.

Command: **HATCH** ↵
Pattern (? or name/U,style): **ANSI31** ↵
Scale for pattern ⟨1.000⟩: ↵
Angle for pattern ⟨0⟩: ↵
Select objects: *(pick the circle)*
Select objects: **W** ↵
First corner: *(pick the first window corner)*
Other corner: *(pick the second window corner)*
Select objects: *(pick the closed polyline)*
Select objects: ↵
Command:

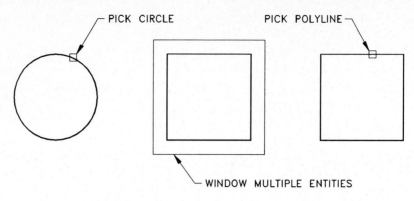

Fig. 20-11. Selecting objects to be hatched.

A problem may arise when you try to hatch an object that is composed of more than one enclosed area. If adjacent areas are drawn with interconnecting lines, the hatching may not be what you expect. The adjacent blocks in Fig. 20-12 have been drawn in different ways. The plan is to hatch only the right side of each pair of blocks. Notice how the lines were originally drawn and the effect of hatching these situations. The BHATCH command, discussed later in this chapter, makes these types of hatching easy.

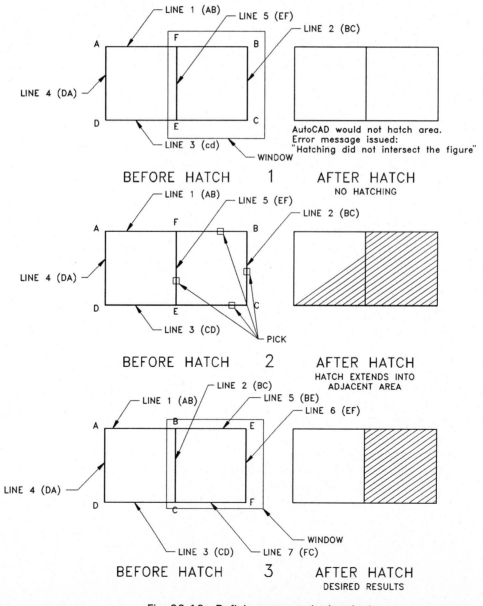

Fig. 20-12. Defining areas to be hatched.

Hatching around text

AutoCAD automatically places an imaginary box around the text in a hatch boundary. The text must also be selected as an element of the hatch boundary for this to work properly. Hatch patterns are not allowed to enter. An example is the bar graph shown in Fig. 20-13. Always place the text before hatching the area. For this to work, be sure you pick the object and the text:

Command: **HATCH** ↵
Pattern (? or name/U,style) ⟨current⟩: ↵
Scale for pattern ⟨1.000⟩: ↵
Angle for pattern ⟨0⟩: ↵
Select objects: *(pick the object to be hatched)*
Select objects: *(pick the text to be hatched around)*
Select objects: ↵

The previous example allowed you to pick the object and the text. You can also window both for this to work.

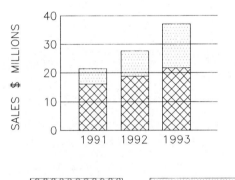

Fig. 20-13. Hatching around text.

Drawing your own simple hatch patterns

When you enter "HATCH" at the Command: prompt, one of the options is U. This allows you to provide angle, spacing, and single or double specifications for a very simple hatch pattern, Fig. 20-14. The commands are as follows:

Command: **HATCH** ↵
Pattern (? or name/U,style) ⟨current⟩: **U** ↵
Angle for crosshatch lines ⟨0⟩: *(specify angle or pick two points on the screen; press ENTER to accept the default angle)*
Spacing between lines ⟨1.000⟩: *(type in the spacing desired or pick two points on the screen to define the spacing; press ENTER to accept the default spacing)*
Double hatch area? ⟨N⟩ *(type "Y" and press ENTER for double hatch lines, or press ENTER for the single hatch default)*
Select objects: *(pick the object to be hatched)*
Select objects: ↵
Command:

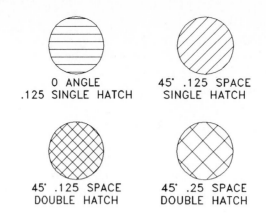

0 ANGLE
.125 SINGLE HATCH

45° .125 SPACE
SINGLE HATCH

45° .125 SPACE
DOUBLE HATCH

45° .25 SPACE
DOUBLE HATCH

Fig. 20-14. Using the HATCH command's U option.

A relationship exists between the hatch line spacing in model space and paper space. This relationship is controlled by the scale factor. If you are planning to plot a drawing at a 1/2″ = 1″ (HALF) scale then the scale factor is 2. This means that one model space unit is equal to 2 paper space units. AutoCAD automatically controls this line spacing when you enter a line spacing of 1XP:

Spacing between lines ⟨1.00⟩: **1XP** ↵

This was discussed earlier in this chapter. Model space and paper space are explained in Chapter 27.

— PROFESSIONAL TIP —

Sometimes the HATCH spacing is too wide or too close. Select ERASE Last or Undo to remove the pattern. Try a smaller or larger value.

Using the HATCH Style option

An object may have several areas enclosed within each other, Fig. 20-15. The HATCH command's Style option allows you to decide which features are to be hatched and which are not. The three style options are:

- **N**—Normal style; hatches every other feature.
- **O**—Hatches outermost feature area only.
- **I**—Ignores all interior features and hatches the entire object.

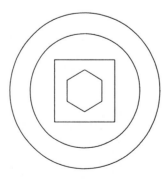

Fig. 20-15. Enclosed features.

Any one of the options may be chosen. Type the desired pattern followed by the option, and separated by a comma. For example:

Command: **HATCH** ↵
Pattern (? or name/U,style): **NET3,N** ↵
Scale for pattern ⟨1.000⟩: **2** *(for example)* ↵
Angle for pattern ⟨0⟩: ↵
Select objects: **W** ↵
First corner: *(pick first corner)*
Other corner: *(pick second corner)*
Select objects: ↵
Command:

Fig. 20-16 shows the results of using each HATCH style option on the object in Fig. 20-15.

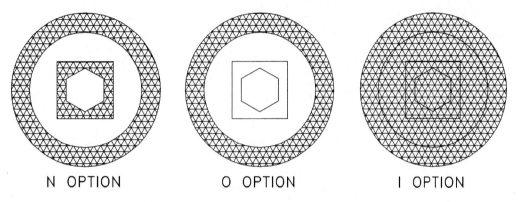

N OPTION   O OPTION   I OPTION

Fig. 20-16. Using the HATCH command's Style options.

PROFESSIONAL TIP

You can fill an area solid by specifying a dense pattern scale or close line spacing. Set the scale or line spacing equal to the width of the plotter pen. This ensures a solid fill without excessive use of plot or regeneration time. However, keep this type of application to a minimum because it slows down regeneration and plot time.

EXERCISE 20-1

☐ Load AutoCAD and open PRODR2.
☐ Draw all object lines on layer 0-7.
☐ Create a new layer for hatch lines. Set a magenta color. Name this layer HATCH-MAGENTA.
☐ Practice using the HATCH command by drawing the following objects with the specified patterns.
    ☐ Fig. 20-11. Use pattern ANSI31, scale 1, angle 0.
    ☐ Fig. 20-12. Hatch object 3 with the pattern BRASS, scale 1, angle 45.
    ☐ Fig. 20-13. Draw the "HARDWARE" and "SOFTWARE" legend boxes to practice hatching around text.
    ☐ Fig. 20-14. Set the pattern, space, and angle the same as examples.
    ☐ Fig. 20-16. Set the pattern, scale, and angle the same as examples.
☐ Save the drawing as A:EX20-1 and quit.

AUTOMATIC BOUNDARY HATCHING

So far you have seen how the HATCH command is used to place hatch patterns inside defined areas. In addition, you were cautioned about hatching adjacent areas, as demonstrated in Fig. 20-12. It is important that the hatch boundary be clearly defined, otherwise strange things could happen. The BHATCH command simplifies the confusion sometimes created with HATCH by automatically hatching any enclosed area. All you have to do with the BHATCH command is pick inside an enclosed area rather than picking the entities to be hatched as you did with the HATCH command. The BHATCH command may be typed at the Command: prompt, or may be accessed from the draw screen menu, or by picking Hatch... in the Draw pull-down menu. Entering the BHATCH command displays the "Boundary Hatch" dialogue box shown in Fig. 20-17.

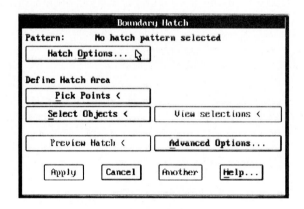

Fig. 20-17. Using the "Boundary Hatch" dialogue box.

Notice in Fig. 20-17 that the message "No hatch pattern selected" is displayed at the top of the dialogue box. The first thing to do is pick the Hatch Options...button. This allows you to establish the hatch pattern in the "Hatch Options" subdialogue box shown in Fig. 20-18.

As you look at the "Hatch Options" subdialogue box, you may note that some items are similar to those previously discussed. The Pattern Type radio buttons allow you to select either a Stored Hatch Pattern (one of AutoCAD's standard patterns), or a User-Defined Pattern (U) (a custom pattern that you design). If you pick the User-Defined Pattern (U) button, the Spacing: edit box and the Double Hatch buttons are highlighted for your use; otherwise they remain disabled.

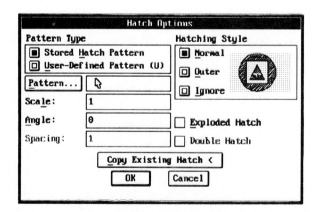

Fig. 20-18. The "Hatch Options" subdialogue box is accessed by picking Hatch Options from the previous dialogue box.

You can type a desired hatch pattern name in the Pattern: edit box or pick the Pattern button to access the "Choose Hatch Pattern" icon menu shown in Fig. 20-19. The icon menu makes it convenient to see the appearance of the standard hatch patterns. All you have to do is pick the one you want and the "Hatch Options" subdialogue box is redisplayed. Note that the pattern name is displayed in the Pattern: edit box as shown in Fig. 20-20.

You can use the Scale: and Angle: edit box of the "Hatch Options" dialogue box in Fig. 20-20 to set the values for these characteristics. The Hatching Style area has radio buttons for you to pick the desired style. Normal is the default, or pick Outer or Ignore. The image tile changes to reflect an example of the style you select. Refer to Fig. 20-16 to help you recall these options.

Normally when hatch patterns are drawn they are created as a block where all of the lines in the pattern are considered to be one unit. Picking the Exploded Hatch button makes each line within the hatch pattern an individual entity.

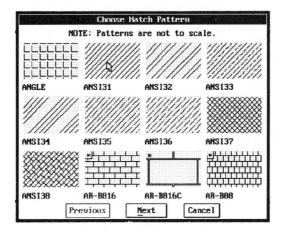

Fig. 20-19. The "Choose Hatch Pattern" icon menu.

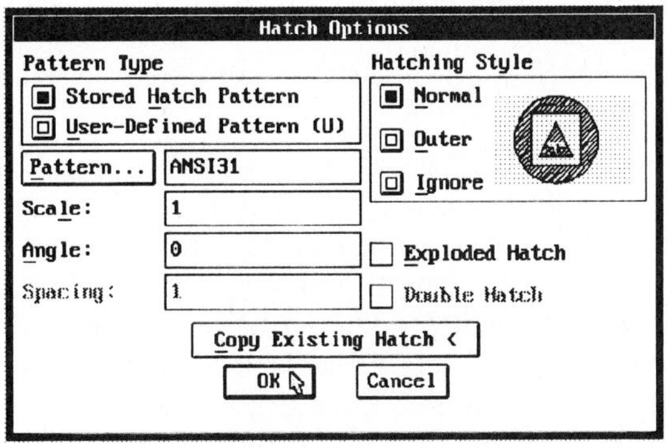

Fig. 20-20. When a hatch pattern is selected from the "Choose Hatch Pattern" icon menu, its name is displayed in the Pattern: edit box.

Drawing with BHATCH

Everything you have done so far with the BHATCH command has prepared you to draw a hatch pattern. Can you recall drawings 1 and 2 from Fig. 20-12? Remember that these drawings did not hatch as desired because the lines were not drawn in the correct order. This is not a concern with the BHATCH command. These objects are redrawn exactly as they were before hatching in Fig. 20-21. Proceed by entering the BHATCH command and click on the Pick Points 〈 button in the "Boundary Hatch" dialogue box. The drawing returns and the following prompts are displayed:

Select internal point *(pick a point inside the area to be hatched)*
Selecting everything visible...
Analyzing the selected data...
Select internal point *(pick a point inside the other area to be hatched)*
Select internal point ↵

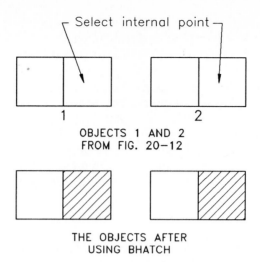

Fig. 20-21. Using the BHATCH command on simple entities. Compare these results to the ones produced when using the HATCH command in Fig. 20-12.

The "Boundary Hatch" dialogue box returns. You can pick the Apply button to have the hatch pattern drawn, or pick the Preview Hatch ⟨ button if you want to look at the hatch pattern before you apply it to the drawing. This feature allows you to make changes to the hatch pattern before it is drawn. AutoCAD temporarily places the hatch pattern on your drawing and instructs:

  Press RETURN to continue: ↵

The "Boundary Hatch" dialogue box is displayed again. Use it to change the hatch pattern as needed, preview the hatch again, or pick the Apply button to have the pattern drawn as shown in Fig. 20-21.

You can also instruct AutoCAD to let you see the boundaries of selected objects. The View selections ⟨ button becomes selectable after picking objects to be hatched. Pick this button to have the drawing with the hatch boundaries highlighted. Press ENTER at this message when you are ready:

  Press RETURN to continue: ↵

The Pick Points ⟨ button allows you to hatch an area regardless of how the closed area was drawn. Simply pick a point inside the area to be hatched.

The Select Objects ⟨ button is used when you have items such as circles, polygons, or closed polylines that you want to hatch by picking the object instead of picking inside the object. For example, if you have a casting with an internal chamber and you want to hatch only the material around the internal chamber use the Select Objects ⟨ button and pick each closed polyline as demonstrated in Fig. 20-22. You could also have used a window, crossing box, or other selection method to select both features at the same time.

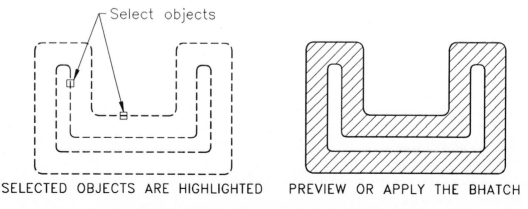

Fig. 20-22. Selecting objects for the BHATCH command.

EXERCISE 20-2

☐ Open PRODR2.
☐ Use the LINE command to draw the object to be hatched similar to the following example. The exact dimensions are up to you. Be sure each area of the object is closed, but the line sequence is up to you.
☐ Use the BHATCH command to make a full section of the object as displayed at the right. Use the ANSI31 hatch pattern.
☐ Use the PLINE command to draw an object similar to the casting shown in Fig. 20-22. Be sure to use the Close option.
☐ Use the BHATCH command's Select Objects option to section the casting as shown.
☐ Save the drawing as A:EX20-2.

OBJECT TO BE HATCHED   APPLIED HATCH

Copy an Existing Hatch

Picking the Copy Existing Hatch ⟨ button from the "Hatch Options" subdialogue box allows you to select an existing hatch in your drawing to be used as the current hatch pattern. For example, if there is a hatch pattern on your drawing that you want to use again exactly as it is, just pick the Copy Existing Hatch ⟨ button. The drawing is then displayed. Pick the pattern when you see these prompts:

Select a hatch block:
Select objects: *(pick the desired hatch pattern)*
Select objects: ↵

The name of the hatch pattern you picked is then displayed at the Pattern: edit box.

EXERCISE 20-3

☐ Open EX20-1.
☐ Enter the BHATCH command. Access the "Choose Hatch Pattern" icon menu and pick ANSI34. Notice that ANSI34 is the current pattern.
☐ Pick OK.
☐ Enter BHATCH again and pick the Copy Existing Hatch ⟨ button followed by picking an existing hatch pattern on your drawing. Notice that the name of the selected pattern becomes current.
☐ Pick Cancel to exit the dialogue box.

Correcting errors in the boundary

The BHATCH command works well unless you have an error in the hatch boundary. The most common error is a gap in the boundary. This may be very small and difficult to detect. However, AutoCAD is quick to let you know by displaying the "Boundary Definition Error" dialogue box shown in Fig. 20-23. You have the option of picking the OK button, or you can pick the Look at it button. When you pick this button, AutoCAD displays the highlighted object with a line representing the ray that found the error, but it does not necessarily point directly to the error. Fig. 20-24 shows an object where the corner does not close. The error is too small to see on the screen, but using the ZOOM command reveals the problem.

Another error message occurs when you pick a point outside the boundary area. When this happens, you get the Boundary Definition Error alert box with the message "Point is outside of boundary." All you have to do is pick OK and select a new point that is inside the boundary you want hatched.

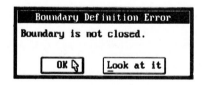

Fig. 20-23. A "Boundary Definition Error" alert box is displayed if problems occur in your hatching operation.

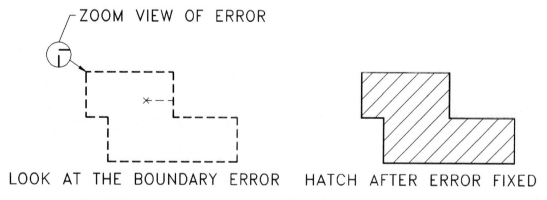

Fig. 20-24. Using the Look at it button to find the source of a hatching error.

Improving boundary hatching speed

In most situations, boundary hatching works well, and with satisfactory speed. Normally the BHATCH command evaluates the entire drawing that is visible on the screen when establishing a boundary around the internal point that you pick. This process can take some time on a large drawing. You can improve the hatching speed, or resolve other problems by picking Advanced

Options... in the "Boundary Hatch" dialogue box. This displays the "Advanced Options" sub-dialogue box shown in Fig. 20-25. Notice in the Define Boundary Set area that the From Everything on Screen radio button is active. This is the default that was previously discussed. If you want

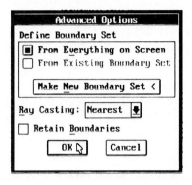

Fig. 20-25. The "Advanced Options" subdialogue box.

to limit what AutoCAD evaluates when hatching you can define the boundary area so the BHATCH command only considers a specified portion of the drawing. To do this, pick the Make New Boundary Set ⟨ button in the "Advanced Options" subdialogue box and then use a window to select the features of the object to be hatched as demonstrated in Fig. 20-26:

Command: bhatch Select entities
Select objects: *(pick the first window corner)*

Notice that the window is automatic if you move the box to the right of the first pick point.

Other corner: *(pick the second corner of the window)*
Select objects: ↵
Analyzing the selected data...

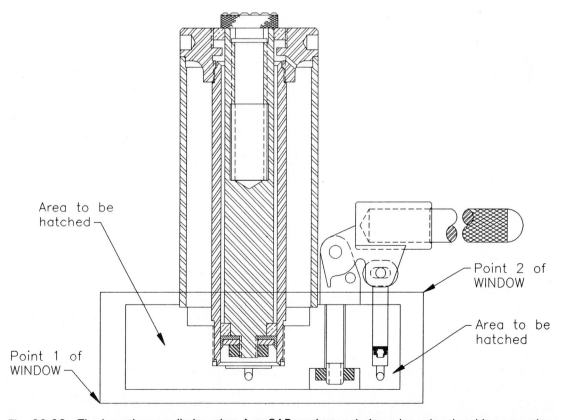

Fig. 20-26. The boundary set limits what AutoCAD evaluates during a boundary hatching operation.

Now the "Advanced Options" subdialogue box returns and the From Existing Boundary Set radio button is active as shown in Fig. 20-27. Pick the OK button and the "Boundary Hatch" dialogue box appears. Use the Pick Points ⟨ button to pick the areas to be hatched. The results are shown in Fig. 20-28.

You can make as many boundary sets as you wish; however, the last one made remains current until another is created. The Retain Boundaries check box becomes selectable as soon as a boundary set is made. Checking this box allows you to keep the boundary of a hatched area as a polyline, and continues to save these as polylines every time you create a boundary area. The default is no check in this box so the hatched boundaries are not saved as polylines.

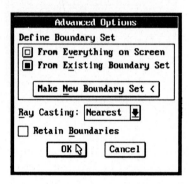

Fig. 20-27. Using the "Advanced Options" dialogue box.

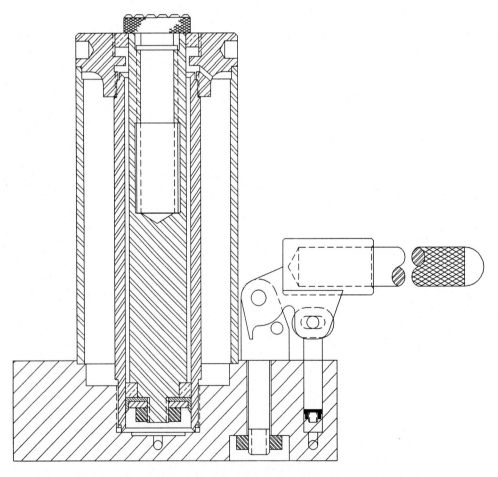

Fig. 20-28. Results of hatching after selecting a boundary set.

Directing the way AutoCAD selects a boundary for hatching

When you pick an internal point for hatching an area, AutoCAD sends an imaginary line, by default, to the nearest object and then turns left in an effort to make a boundary around the object. This is known as *ray casting*. If the first ray hits an internal area or internal text, a boundary definition error is given. For example, look at the highlighted internal area in Fig. 20-29. A Boundary Definition Error occurred because AutoCAD made a boundary around the

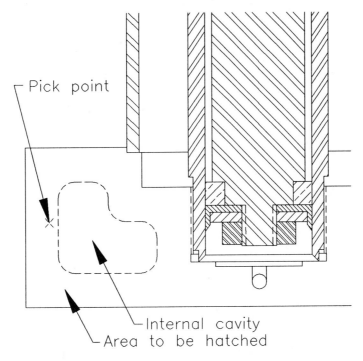

Fig. 20-29. Ray casting affects the objects selected for boundary hatching.

cavity and could not continue with the desired hatch. You can control the way AutoCAD does ray casting. Notice in Fig. 20-25 the Ray Casting: edit box specifies "Nearest." This is the default, but you can change it by picking the arrow to access the ray casting popup list. Fig. 20-30 shows the ray casting options: +X, −X, +Y, and −Y. Selecting one of these determines which way

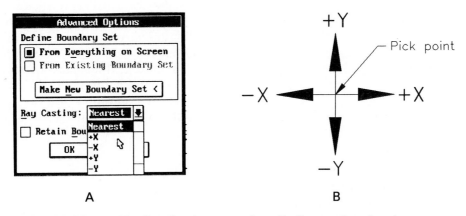

Fig. 20-30. A—The Ray Casting popup box. B—Ray casting directions.

the first ray is cast. For example, selecting a −X value for ray casting causes the same pick point in Fig. 20-29 to make the correct boundary definition. Picking this point followed by picking inside the cavity area results in the desired hatching shown in Fig. 20-31.

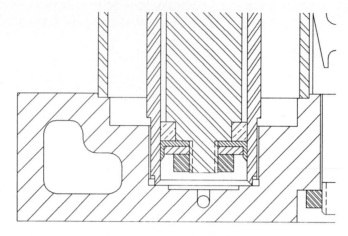

Fig. 20-31. The results of using the appropriate ray casting selection.

—— PROFESSIONAL TIP ——

There are a number of techniques that can help save you time when hatching, especially with large and complex drawings. These include the following:
• Zoom in on the area to be hatched to make it easier for you to define the boundary. When you zoom into an area to be hatched, the hatch process is much faster because AutoCAD doesn't have to search the entire drawing to find the hatch boundaries.
• Preview the hatch before you apply it. This allows you to easily make last minute adjustments.
• Turn off layers where there are lines or text that might interfere with your ability to accurately define hatch boundaries.
• Create boundary sets of small areas within a complex drawing to help save time.

DRAWING OBJECTS THAT ARE FILLED IN SOLID ARM 5

Chapter 6 introduced how polyline and trace segments may be filled solid when the Fill mode is on. They are drawn as an outline with Fill turned on. The SOLID command works in much the same manner except that it fills objects or shapes that are already drawn, or fills areas that are simply defined by points you pick. This command may be used when sectioning very thin features. Fill in the sectioned area rather than use a hatch pattern. It may also be used to accent certain features or objects on a drawing. The SOLID command is found in the DRAW screen menu, or "SOLID" can be typed at the Command: prompt. It prompts you to pick point. If the object is rectangular, pick the corners in the sequence numbered in Fig. 20-32. The command format is as follows:

Command: **SOLID** ↵
First point: *(pick point 1)*
Second point: *(pick point 2)*
Third point: *(pick point 3)*
Fourth point: *(pick point 4)*
Third point:

Fig. 20-32. Using the SOLID command.

Notice that AutoCAD prompts you for another third point after the first four. This prompt allows you to fill in additional parts of the same object, if needed. Press ENTER when you want to stop, or continue as shown in Fig. 20-33.

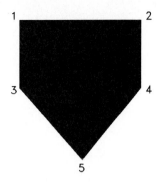

Fig. 20-33. Continued use of the SOLID command.

Different types of SOLID arrangements can be drawn by altering the numbering sequence. See Fig. 20-34. Also, the SOLID command can be used to draw shapes without prior use of the LINE or PLINE commands; simply pick the points.

Fig. 20-34. Using a different numbering sequence for the SOLID command.

PROFESSIONAL TIP

It is very difficult and time-consuming to fill a circle using the SOLID command. The best solution to this problem is to use the DOUGHNUT command and set a 0 inside diameter. You could also use the HATCH command with a dense pattern. An irregular shape such as a lake on a map may be filled in solid to denote water. This is done by drawing the outline of the lake using lines, arcs, or polylines. Then select a dense pattern. If lines and arcs are used, a window selection is best. If polylines and polyline arcs are used, pick any point on the polyline. The lake must be a full enclosure. Keep in mind that many solids and dense hatches require extensive regeneration and plot time. Make check plots with the Fill mode off.

EXERCISE 20-4

☐ Open PRODR2.
☐ Draw all object lines on layer 0-7.
☐ Create a new layer named SOLID-MAGENTA and draw all solids on this layer.
☐ Practice using the SOLID command by drawing the objects shown in Figs. 20-32, 20-33, and 20-34.
☐ Save the drawing as A:EX20-4.

CHAPTER TEST

Write your answers in the spaces provided.

1. Give the command and entries required to use the ANSI37 hatch pattern with double scale to hatch the inside of a given circle:

   Command: _____

   Pattern (? or name/U,style): _____

   Scale for pattern ⟨1.000⟩: _____

   Angle for pattern ⟨0⟩: _____

   Select objects: _____

   Select objects: _____

   Command:

2. Give the command and entries needed to draw your own hatch pattern. Set a 30° hatch angle, 1.5 spacing, and single hatch lines pattern to hatch the inside of a rectangle drawn with polylines:

   Command: _____

   Pattern (? or name/U,style): _____

   Angle for crosshatch lines ⟨0⟩: _____

   Spacing between lines ⟨1.000⟩: _____

   Double hatch area? ⟨N⟩: _____

   Select objects: _____

   Select objects: _____

   Command:

3. Given a square within a square, provide the command and entries used to hatch between the two squares (the outermost area). Use the default values of the ANSI31 hatch pattern:

   Command: _____

   Pattern (? or name/U,style): _____

   Scale for pattern ⟨1.000⟩: _____

   Angle for pattern ⟨0⟩: _____

   Select objects: _____

   First corner: _____

   Other corner:_____

   Select objects: _____

   Command:

4. Give the command and entries needed to fill in a rectangular area. Identify specific corners on the rectangle as you give the prompts. For example, specify "upper-right corner."

   Command: _____

   First point: _____

   Second point: _____

   Third point: _____

   Fourth point: _____

   Third point: _____

5. Give the command and responses to show a list and description of all the hatch patterns:

   Command: _____

   Pattern (? or name/U,style): _____

   Pattern(s) to list ⟨*⟩: _____

6. Give the command and responses used to hatch an object while providing an imaginary box around text located inside the hatch area.

   Command: _____

   Pattern (? or name/U,style) ⟨current⟩: _____

   Scale for pattern ⟨1.000⟩: _____

   Angle for pattern ⟨0⟩: _____

   Select objects: _____

   Select objects: _____

   Select objects: _____

For Questions 7-12, name the type of section identified in each of the following statements:

7. Half of the object is removed; the cutting-plane line generally cuts completely through along the centerplane. _____

8. Used primarily on symmetrical objects; the cutting-plane line cuts through one-quarter of the object. _____

9. The cutting-plane line is staggered through features that do not lie in a straight line.

   _____

10. The section is rotated in place to clarify the contour of the object. _____

11. This section is revolved and removed from the object. The location of the section is normally identified with a cutting-plane line. _____

12. Remove a small portion of the view to clarify an internal feature. _____

13. AutoCAD's standard section line symbols are called _____.

14. To use the same hatch pattern again, you must _____.

15. Give the code and results of using the three HATCH Style options:

   _____

   _____

   _____

16. In which pull-down menu is "Hatch" located? _____

17. Name the command that lets you automatically hatch an enclosed area just by picking a point inside the area. _____

18. How do you access the "Choose Hatch Pattern" icon menu? _____
_____

19. Explain how you set a hatch scale in the "Hatch Options" subdialogue box. _____
_____

20. Identify two ways to change a hatch pattern (where all elements of the hatch are one unit) so that each element is an individual entity. _____
_____

21. Explain how to use an existing hatch pattern on a drawing as the current pattern for your next hatch. _____
_____
_____

22. Describe the purpose of the Preview Hatch button found in the "Boundary Hatch" dialogue box. _____
_____
_____

23. What happens if you try to hatch an area where there is a gap in the boundary? _____
_____
_____

24. How do you limit AutoCAD hatch evaluation to a specific area of the drawing? _____
_____
_____
_____

25. Define "ray casting." _____
_____
_____

DRAWING PROBLEMS

Name each of the drawings P20-(problem number). Follow these guidelines for all of the problems.
A. Draw the views to full size.
B. Set grid, snap, limits, and units values as needed. Use object snaps to your best advantage.
C. Apply dimensions accurately following ANSI standards.
D. Set dimensioning variables to suit the drawing.
E. Use the LAYER command to set separate layers for views, dimensions, and section lines.
F. Place these general notes 1/2 in. from the lower-left corner.
    2. REMOVE ALL BURRS AND SHARP EDGES
    1. INTERPRET PER ANSI Y14.5M.
    NOTES:

1-2. Draw the full sections as indicated. For Problem 2, add the additional general note: UNLESS OTHERWISE SPECIFIED, ALL DIMENSIONS ARE IN MILLIMETERS.

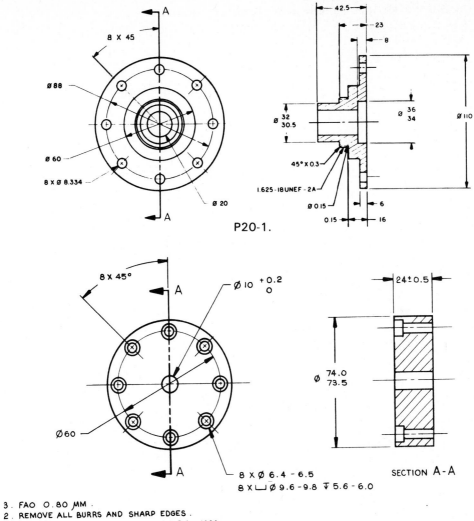

P20-1.

P20-2.

3. FAO 0.80 MM.
2. REMOVE ALL BURRS AND SHARP EDGES.
1. INTERPRET DRAWING PER ANSI Y14.5M - 1982.
NOTES:

3. Draw the half section. Add the additional notes: OIL QUENCH 40-45C, CASE HARDEN .020 DEEP, 59-60 ROCKWELL C SCALE, and MATERIAL: AISI 1018.

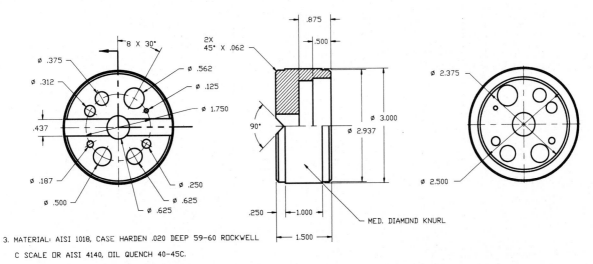

3. MATERIAL: AISI 1018, CASE HARDEN .020 DEEP 59-60 ROCKWELL
   C SCALE OR AISI 4140, OIL QUENCH 40-45C.
2. REMOVE ALL BURRS AND SHARP EDGES.
1. INTERPRET DIMENSIONS AND TOLERANCES PER ANSI Y14.5M-1982
NOTES:

P20-3.

4-5. Draw the aligned sections as indicated. Add the additional notes:
FINISH ALL OVER 1.6μM UNLESS OTHERWISE SPECIFIED and ALL DIMENSIONS
ARE IN MILLIMETERS

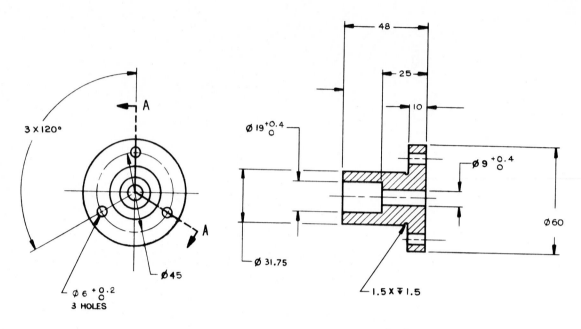

SECTION A-A

3 . FINISH ALL OVER 1.6 MM .
2 . REMOVE ALL BURRS AND SHARP EDGES .
1 . INTERPRET ALL DIMENSION AND TOLERENCE PER ANSI Y14.5M – 1982.

NOTES :

P20-4.

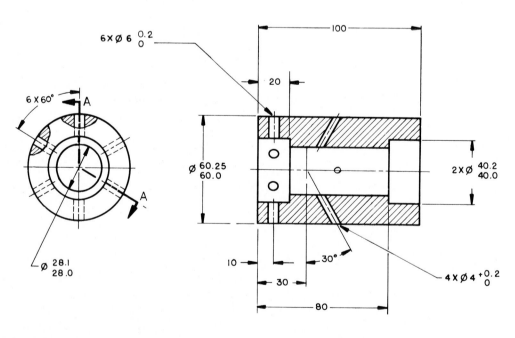

SECTION A-A

3. FINISH ALL OVER 0.25 μM.
2. REMOVE ALL BURRS AND SHARP EDGES.
1. INTERPRET DRAWING PER ANSI Y14.5M – 1982

NOTES :

P20-5.

6. Draw the offset sections.

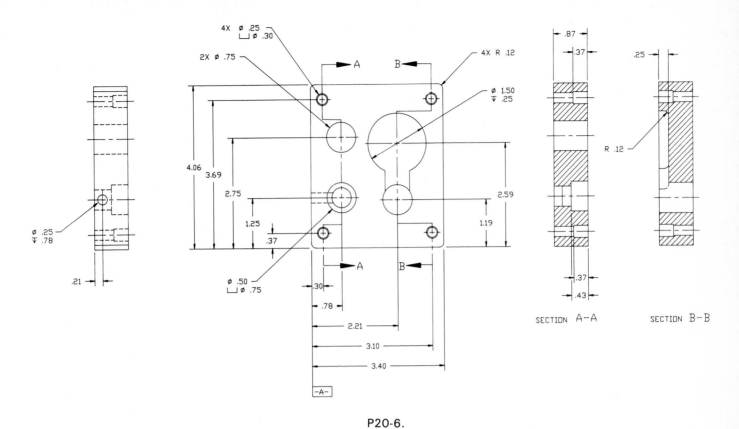

P20-6.

7. Draw the removed section and enlarged view.

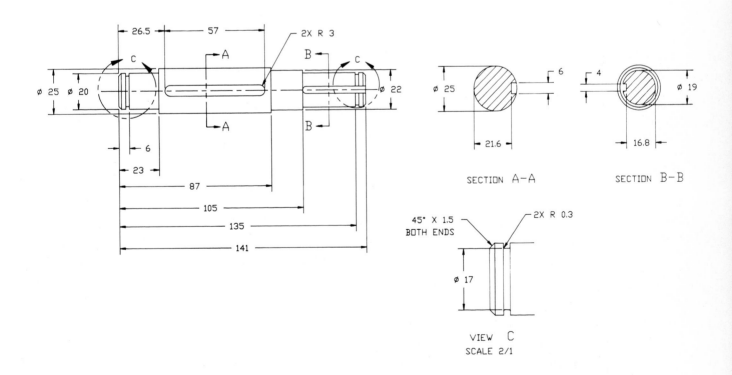

P20-7.

8. Draw the revolved section. Use the SOLID command to fill in the thin section.

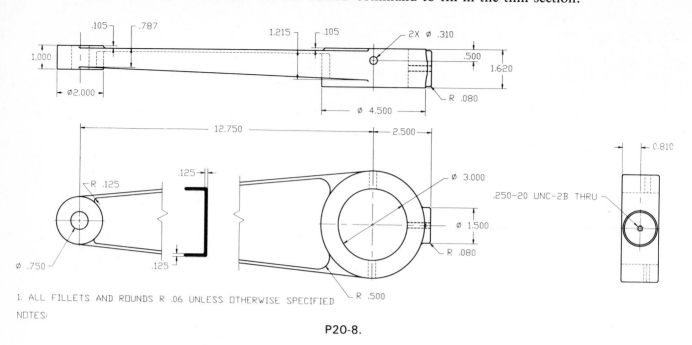

NOTES:
1. ALL FILLETS AND ROUNDS R .06 UNLESS OTHERWISE SPECIFIED

P20-8.

For Problems 9-16, use the HATCH, BHATCH, and SOLID commands as necessary. Establish appropriate grid, snap, limits, and units values.

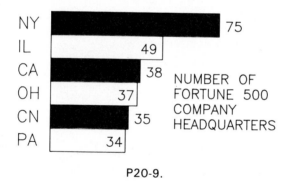

STATES WITH TOP COMPANIES

NY 75
IL 49
CA 38
OH 37
CN 35
PA 34

NUMBER OF FORTUNE 500 COMPANY HEADQUARTERS

P20-9.

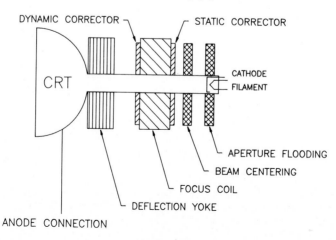

COMPONENT LAYOUT

P20-10.

SOLOMAN SHOE COMPANY

PERCENT OF TOTAL SALES EACH DIVISION

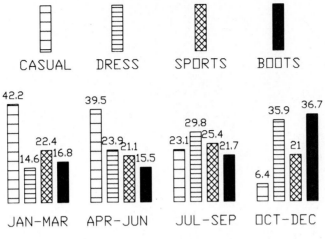

CASUAL   DRESS   SPORTS   BOOTS

P20-11.

FIVE YEAR PERFORMANCE
WHOLESALE TREES

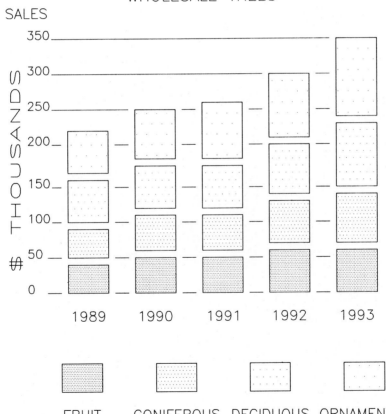

FRUIT   CONIFEROUS   DECIDUOUS   ORNAMENTAL

P20-12.

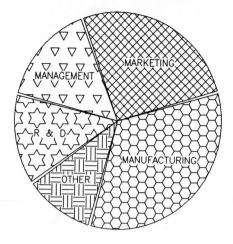

DIAL TECHNOLOGIES
EXPENSE BUDGET

P20-13.

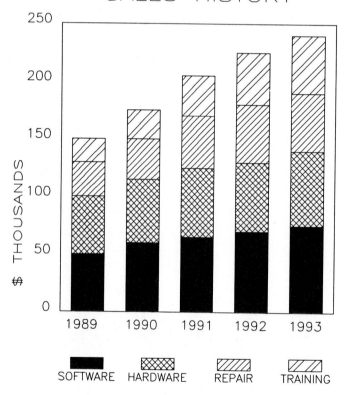

SALES HISTORY

P20-14.

P20-15.

Architectural
Design
Consultants

P20-16.

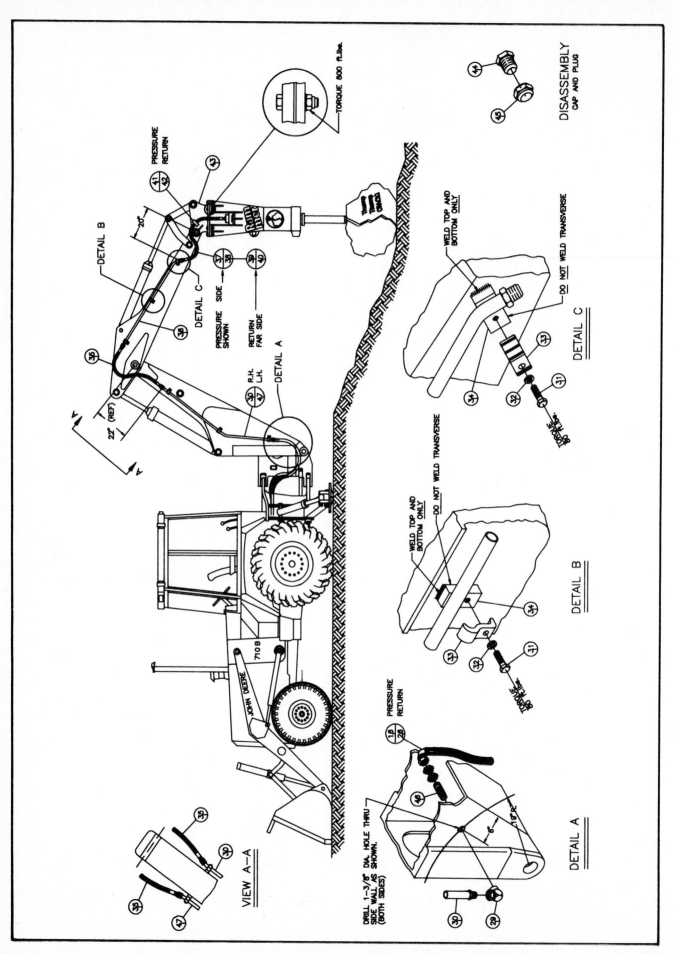

Technical illustration of a "rammer" attachment.   (Autodesk, Inc.)

Chapter 21

CREATING SYMBOLS FOR MULTIPLE USE

Learning objectives

After completing this chapter, you will be able to:
☐ Create and save blocks.
☐ Insert blocks into a drawing.
☐ Edit a block and update it in a drawing.
☐ Create, or write blocks that are saved independent of the drawing.
☐ Construct and use a symbol library of blocks.
☐ Reference existing drawings and blocks to new drawings.

One of the greatest benefits of AutoCAD is in its ability to store often-used symbols for future use. These symbols, or *blocks,* can be inserted into a drawing full size, or scaled and rotated. If a block is edited, drawings having the block can be updated to include the new version. AutoCAD has two types of blocks. A *wblock* can be used on any drawing. A *block* can be used only in the drawing in which it was created. Both types can be used to create a symbol library, which is a related group of symbols.

AutoCAD also allows you to "reference" drawings instead of inserting them into a drawing. When a drawing is referenced, it becomes part of the drawing on the screen, but its content is not added to the current drawing file. Referenced drawings and any named entities, such as blocks and layers, are referred to as *dependent symbols.* When a dependent symbol is revised, the drawing(s) it is referenced to are automatically updated the next time it is loaded into AutoCAD.

CREATING SYMBOLS AS BLOCKS ARM 10

The ability to draw and store a symbol once, and then insert it when needed, has been the greatest time-saving feature of CAD. AutoCAD provides the BLOCK command to create a symbol and keep it with a specific drawing file. A drafter can insert a predrawn block as many times as needed into any drawing. Upon insertion, the block can be scaled and rotated to meet the drawing requirements.

Constructing blocks

A block can be any shape, symbol, view, or drawing that you use more than once. Before constructing a block, review the type of drawing you are working on. (This is where a sketch of your drawing is convenient.) Look for shapes, components, notes, and assemblies that are used more than once. These can be drawn once and then saved as blocks.

Existing drawings can also be used as blocks. This can be done two different ways:
- Use the BASE command on the drawing to assign an insertion point.
- Insert the existing drawing into the drawing you are working on.

These two methods are discussed later in this chapter.

PROFESSIONAL TIP

Blocks that vary in size from one drawing to the next should be drawn to fit inside a one unit square. It does not matter if the object is measured in feet, inches, or millimeters. This makes it easy to scale the symbol when you later insert it in a drawing.

Draw a block as you would any other drawing. Use any AutoCAD commands you need. If you want the block to have the color and linetype of the layer it will be inserted on, be sure that you set layer 0 as current before you begin drawing. If you forget to do this, and draw the objects on another layer, simply use the CHANGE command to place all the objects on layer 0 before using the BLOCK command. When you finish drawing the object, decide what is the best place on the symbol to use as an insertion point. When you insert the block into a drawing, the symbol is placed with its insertion point on the screen cursor. Fig. 21-1 illustrates some common blocks and their insertion points, shown as dots.

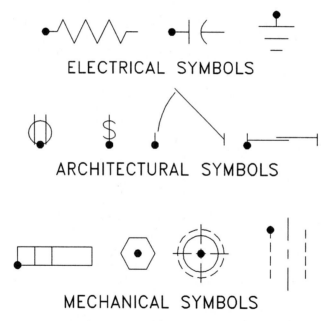

Fig. 21-1. Common symbols and their insertion points for placement on drawings.

Storing blocks

Although you may have drawn a shape, you have not created a block yet. To save your object as a block, select the BLOCK command. The BLOCK command can be accessed at the Command: prompt, picking Block from the Construct pull-down menu, or picking BLOCKS from the screen menu. Then enter the block's name and insertion point. Finally, you must select those objects on the screen that will become the block. The following procedure saves the symbol under the name PUMP.

    Command: **BLOCK** ↵
    Block name (or ?): **PUMP** ↵
    Insertion base point: *(pick an insertion point)*
    Select objects: *(select the object)*
    Select objects: ↵

The block name can be no longer than 31 characters. The insertion point should be accurate. You can type exact coordinate values of a point on the object, or use OSNAP options. Select the object with any of the selection options. Type "W" and press ENTER at the Select objects: prompt to use a window, or "F" to use a fence.

AutoCAD informs you that a block was made by removing it from the screen. It is stored as a part of the drawing file. Remember, a block can be used only in the drawing in which it was created. If you want the block to return to the screen, type "OOPS," or pick OOPS from the screen menu. The block reappears in the same position.

Check to see that the block was saved properly by selecting the BLOCK command again. At the prompt, type a question mark as follows:

Command: **BLOCK** ↵
Block name (or ?): **?** ↵
Block(s) to list ⟨*⟩:

Press ENTER to list all of the blocks in the current directory. The following information is then displayed.

Defined blocks.
  PUMP

User Blocks	External Reference	Dependent Blocks	Unnamed Blocks
1	0	0	0

This display indicates the name and number of blocks. *User blocks* are those created by you, the user. *External references* are drawings referenced with the XREF command, which is discussed later in this chapter. Blocks that reside in a referenced drawing are called *dependent blocks*. *Unnamed blocks* are entities such as associative dimensions and hatch patterns.

Step through the process of drawing a block again. Draw a one unit square and name it PLATE. See Fig. 21-2. Draw the object using the LINE command. Select the BLOCK command. Name the block PLATE. Pick the insertion point at the lower-left corner. Select the object using the Window option. Select BLOCK again and use the ? option to see that it was saved.

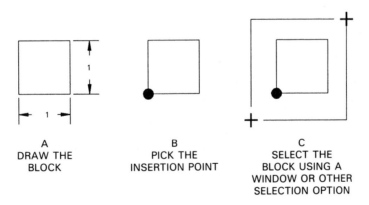

A
DRAW THE
BLOCK

B
PICK THE
INSERTION POINT

C
SELECT THE
BLOCK USING A
WINDOW OR OTHER
SELECTION OPTION

Fig. 21-2. Drawing a one unit square block.

EXERCISE 21-1

☐ Load AutoCAD and open one of your prototype drawings with decimal units to use for this exercise.
☐ Draw the circle with a one unit diameter and add centerlines on layer 0.
☐ Make a block of the circle and centerlines and name it CIRCLE.
☐ Pick the center of the circle as the insertion point.

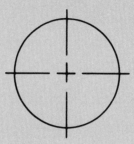

☐ Save the drawing as A:EX21-1 and quit.

PROFESSIONAL TIP

Blocks can be used when creating other blocks. Suppose you design a complex part or view that will be used repeatedly. You can insert existing blocks into the view and then save the entire object as a block. This is called *nesting;* larger blocks contain smaller blocks. The larger block must be given a different name. Proper planning and knowledge of all existing blocks can speed the drawing process and creation of complex parts.

USING BLOCKS IN A DRAWING   ARM 10

Once a block has been created, it is easy to insert it on a drawing. Before inserting a block, give some thought to the size the block should be and the rotation angle needed. Blocks are normally inserted on specific layers. Set the proper layer *before* inserting the block.

Inserting blocks

Blocks are placed on your drawing with the INSERT command. Know beforehand where the insertion point of the block will be located in the drawing. Insert the PLATE block into your drawing as follows:

Command: **INSERT** ↵
Block name (or ?): **PLATE** ↵
   Insertion point: *(pick the point)*
   X scale factor ⟨1⟩ / Corner / XYZ: *(pick a point, type a number and press ENTER, or press ENTER to accept the default)*
   Y scale factor (default = X): *(type a number and press ENTER, or press ENTER to accept the default)*
   Rotation angle ⟨0⟩: *(pick a point, or type a number and press ENTER)*

The X and Y scale factors allow you to stretch or compress the block to suit your needs. This is why it is a good idea to draw blocks to fit inside a one unit square. It makes the block easy to scale because you can type the exact number of units for the X and Y dimensions. If you want the block to be three units long and two units high, respond:

   X scale factor ⟨1⟩ / Corner / XYZ: **3** ↵
   Y scale factor (default = X): **2** ↵

Notice that the Y prompt allows you to accept the X value for Y by just pressing ENTER. The object shown in Fig. 21-3 was given several different X and Y scale factors during the INSERT command.

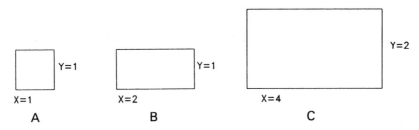

Fig. 21-3. Comparison of the PLATE block inserted using different X and Y scale factors.

Block insertion options

It is possible to obtain a mirror image of a block just by typing a negative value for the scale factor. For example, a $-1, -1$ scale factor mirrors the block to the opposite quadrant of the coordinate system, but retains the original size. Fig. 21-4 illustrates mirroring techniques; the insertion point is indicated with a dot.

An approximate dynamic scaling technique is achieved using the Corner option. You can see the block change size as you move the cursor if DRAGMODE is set to Auto. Select the Corner option at the X scale factor prompt as follows:

X scale factor ⟨1⟩ / Corner / XYZ: **C** ↵
Other corner: *(move cursor to change size and pick a point)*

A coordinate value can be typed or a point can be picked. Be sure to pick a point above and to the right of the insertion point to insert the block as drawn. Picking corner points to the left or below the insertion points will generate mirror images such as those in Fig. 21-4.

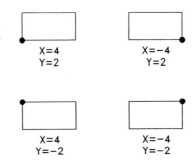

Fig. 21-4. Effects of negative scale factors on a block.

EXERCISE 21-2

☐ Open EX21-1 if it is not currently on your screen.
☐ Draw a 1 x 1 square on layer 0 and make it a block named PLATE.
☐ Insert the PLATE block into the drawing. Enter an X scale factor of 6 and a Y scale factor of 4.
☐ Insert the CIRCLE block twice into the PLATE block as shown. The small circle is one unit in diameter and the large circle is 1.5 units in diameter.

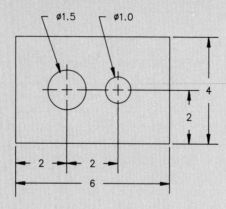

☐ Make a block of the entire drawing and name it PLATE-1. Pick the lower-left corner as the insertion point.
☐ Insert the PLATE-1 block on your drawing and enter a scale of −1, −1. Also rotate the object 45°.
☐ Save the drawing as A:EX21-2.

The effects of layers

Blocks retain the characteristics of the layer on which they are drawn. For example, suppose the CIRCLE block is drawn on layer 1 having the color red and a dashed linetype. When inserted, the block appears red and dashed, no matter what layer it is inserted on. If different colors are used in a block, they also remain the same when the block is placed on another layer.

For a block to assume the characteristics of the layer it is inserted on, it must be created on layer 0 (the default). Suppose you create the CIRCLE block on layer 0 and insert it on layer 1. The block becomes part of layer 1 and thus assumes the color and linetype of that layer.

Changing the layer and color of a block

If you insert a block on the wrong layer, select CHANGE to move it to the proper layer. Then enter the LAyer option of the CHANGE command:

Command: **CHANGE** ⏎
Select objects: *(pick the block to change)*
Select objects: ⏎
Properties/⟨Change point⟩: **P** ⏎
Change what property (Color/LAyer/LType/Thickness)? **LA** ⏎
New layer ⟨0⟩: *(enter new layer name and press ENTER)*
Change what property (Color/Elev/LAyer/LType/Thickness)? ⏎

The block is now changed to the proper layer. If the block was originally created on layer 0, it will assume the color of the new layer. If it was created on another layer, it will keep its original color.

To prevent a block from assuming a different color than the assigned layer color, set the COLOR command to BYLAYER before creating blocks:

> Command: **COLOR** ↵
> New entity color ⟨1 (red)⟩: **BYLAYER** ↵

Now any entities or blocks that are drawn assume the color of the current layer.

The same is true of the linetype of an entity. In order to avoid problems, the linetype should be set as a function of the layer rather than using the LINETYPE command. Check to be sure the LINETYPE command is set to BYLAYER.

> Command: **LINETYPE** ↵
> ?/Create/Load/Set: **S** ↵
> New entity linetype (or ?) ⟨HIDDEN⟩: **BYLAYER** ↵

All entities and blocks are drawn with the linetype of the current layer.

INSERTING MULTIPLE COPIES OF A BLOCK $\boxed{\text{ARM 10}}$

The INSERT and ARRAY features are combined in the MINSERT (Multiple INSERT) command. This method of inserting and arraying not only saves time, but also disk space.

An example of using MINSERT is to place an arrangement of desks on a drawing. Suppose you want to draw the layout shown in Fig. 21-5. Change to architectural units and set the limits to 30′,22′. Draw a rectangle 4 ft. by 3 ft. and save it as a block called DESK. The arrangement is to be three rows and four columns. Spacing between desks should be two feet horizontally and four feet vertically. Follow this sequence.

> Command: **MINSERT** ↵
> Block name (or ?): **DESK** ↵
>   Insertion point: *(pick a point)*
>   X scale factor ⟨1⟩ / Corner / XYZ: ↵
>   Y scale factor ⟨default = X⟩: ↵
>   Rotation angle ⟨0⟩: ↵
> Number of rows (---) ⟨1⟩: **3** ↵
> Number of columns (III) ⟨1⟩: **4** ↵
> Unit of cell or distance between rows (---): **7′** ↵
> Distance between columns (III): **6′** ↵

The resulting arrangement is shown in Fig. 21-5. The total pattern takes on the characteristics of a block, except that a MINSERT array cannot be exploded. If the initial block is rotated, all arrayed objects are also rotated about their insertion points.

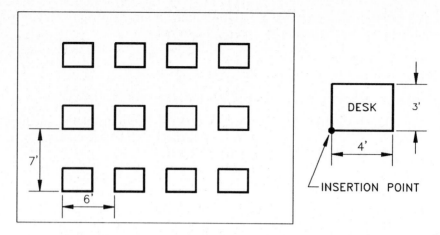

Fig. 21-5. Creating an arrangement of desks using MINSERT.

PROFESSIONAL TIP

In the previous example, if you were working with a lot of different desk sizes, a one unit square may serve your purposes better than an exact size block. To create a 5′ x 3′-6″ (60″ x 42″) desk, insert a one unit square block using INSERT or MINSERT, and enter the following for the X and Y values:

> X scale factor⟨1⟩/Corner/XYZ: **60** ↵
> Y scale factor⟨default = X⟩: **42** ↵

A one unit square block can be used in this manner for a variety of objects.

EXERCISE 21-3

☐ Load AutoCAD and start a new drawing named EX21-3. Set architectural units and 80′,60′ limits.

☐ Draw the chair shown and save it as a block named CHAIR.

☐ Use the MINSERT command twice to create the theater arrangement. The sides of the chairs should touch. Each row on either side of the aisle should have 10 chairs. The spacing between rows is 4 feet. The width of the center aisle is 5 feet.

☐ Consider where you should insert the first chair to obtain the pattern.

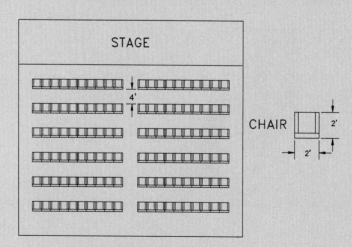

☐ Save the drawing as A:EX21-3.

Inserting entire drawings

You may construct views or entire drawings that can be used in future drawings. To be able to insert these into other drawings, set an insertion point using the BASE command.

Command: **BASE** ↵
Base point: *(pick a point)*

The base point now becomes the insertion point. The nature of the view or drawing should determine the best location for the base point. It is best to assign the origin (0,0) as the base point for entire drawings. An inserted drawing can always be moved as a whole if the location is not correct. If you insert a view that does not have a base point, the lower-left corner is used as a default base.

EXERCISE 21-4

☐ Open drawing EX21-2 if it is not already on your screen.
☐ If your drawing does not have a RED layer, make one and be sure it is current.
☐ Draw a 6 x 4 unit rectangle. Insert two CIRCLE blocks into the rectangle, both one unit in diameter. Make a new block of this drawing and name it PLATE-2.
☐ Erase the screen. Set the current layer to 0. Insert both the PLATE-1 and PLATE-2 blocks.
☐ The PLATE-2 block should appear red because it was created on the red layer. PLATE-1 should be black.
☐ Make sure RED is the current layer. Insert the PLATE-1 block into your drawing. It should appear red because it was created on layer 0 and will assume the color of the layer on which it is inserted.
☐ Enter the BASE command. Choose an insertion point below and to the left of the objects on the screen.
☐ Save the drawing as A:EX21-4.
☐ Start a new drawing named PLATES.
☐ Insert drawing EX21-4 into your new drawing. The insertion point you pick is the one established using the BASE command.
☐ Pick any editing command and select a line of one of the plates. The entire drawing should highlight since the drawing is actually one large block.
☐ Save the drawing as A:EX21-4.

Presetting block insertion variables

You can dramatically speed the insertion of blocks by presetting the scale or rotation angle. Select the INSERT command in the BLOCKS screen menu. Note the options for Scale, Rotate, and Block Name, Fig. 21-6. The preset options not only save time, but also allow you to see the scaled size and rotation angle before you pick the insertion point. This helps you determine if the scale and rotation angle are correct.

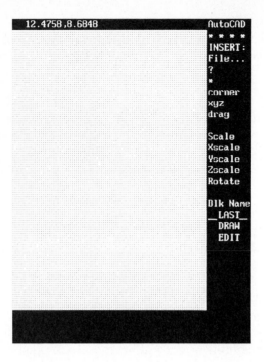

Fig. 21-6. The screen menu display of the Preset options in the INSERT command.

Preset options can be used two ways. If the S option is entered at the Insertion point: prompt, you are asked for the scale factor, then the insertion point and rotation angle. If you enter "P" and "S," a prompt requests the scale factor for insertion display purposes only. After you pick the insertion point, the normal INSERT prompts are displayed. This second method is a "temporary" preset. That difference is illustrated in the following examples. The first example inserts the block PLATE at a preset scale factor of 2.

> Command: **INSERT** ↵
> Block name (or ?) ⟨current⟩: **PLATE** ↵
>   Insertion point: **S** ↵
>   Scale factor: **2** ↵
>   Insertion point: *(pick an insertion point)*
>   Rotation angle ⟨0⟩: ↵

The next example illustrates a temporary preset of the scale factor.

> Command: **INSERT** ↵
> Block name (or ?) ⟨current⟩: **PLATE** ↵
>   Insertion point: **PS** ↵
>   Scale factor: **2** ↵
>   Insertion point: *(pick an insertion point)* X scale factor ⟨1⟩ / Corner / XYZ: ↵
>   Y scale factor (default = X): ↵
>   Rotation angle ⟨0⟩: ↵

The temporary preset allows you to see the preset scale or rotation angle as you drag the block. You can also change the scale and rotation angle by entering a value at the normal prompts. Remember to use temporary preset type "P," then the option you wish to preset at the Insertion point: prompt. For example, to temporarily set the rotation angle, enter "PR" at the Insertion point: prompt. The following list describes the functions of the preset options.

- **Scale**—Affects the overall scale of X, Y, and Z axes. Rotation angle is also requested.
- **Xscale**—Affects only the X scale. Rotation angle is also requested.
- **Yscale**—Affects only the Y scale. Rotation angle is also requested.
- **Zscale**—Affects only the Z scale. Rotation angle is also requested.
- **Rotate**—Sets the rotation angle. Prompts for X and Y scale factors.

• **Blk Name** — Activates the INSNAME system variable and requests a new value for IN-SNAME. This value is the block name you wish to insert. For example, if you will be inserting several copies of the DESK block, enter the name "DESK" at this prompt. The next time you use the INSERT command, the value "DESK" appears as the default for the block name. To specify no default block name, enter a period (.) at the INSNAME prompt. The value for INSNAME then changes each time you use the INSERT command, and allows you to enter a new block name.

USING THE INSERT DIALOGUE BOX

All of the functions of the INSERT command previously discussed can be accessed using the DDINSERT command. "DDINSERT" can be typed at the Command: prompt, or Insert... can be picked from the Draw pull-down menu. This displays the "Insert" dialogue box shown in Fig. 21-7.

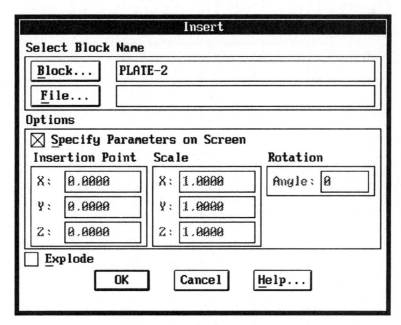

Fig. 21-7. The DDINSERT command activates the "Insert" dialogue box.

You can choose the block to insert by picking the Block... button. When you pick this box, a file list of all blocks defined in the current drawing is displayed. See Fig. 21-8. Pick the block name you wish to use and it is displayed in the Selection: edit box. If the list of block names is long, and the name you need is not displayed, you can enter the name in the Selection: box, and then pick OK.

Notice that the presets of Insertion point, Scale, and Rotation in the "Insert" dialogue box are initially grayed out. If you wish to preset the insertion point, scale, and rotation angle values, pick the "Specify Parameters on Screen" check box. Now the preset values are no longer grayed out, and can be changed in the dialogue box.

If you wish to have the block exploded upon insertion, simply pick the Explode check box to turn it on. (Editing blocks is discussed in the next section.) When you are finished, pick OK. If presets were used, look quickly because the block is immediately inserted. If presets were not used, the specified block appears on the crosshairs and the standard INSERT command prompts are issued.

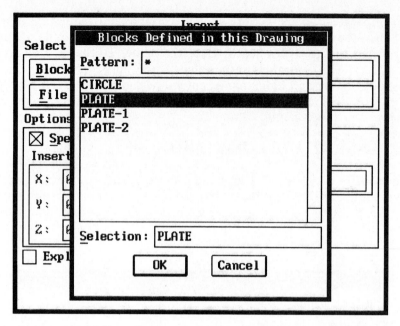

Fig. 21-8. Picking the Block . . . button displays the blocks defined in the current drawing.

EDITING BLOCKS

ARM 10

Blocks must first be broken into their original entities before they can be edited. This is especially important when an entire view or drawing has been inserted. Two methods can be used to break blocks apart. The first method—asterisk insertion—is done at the time of insertion. The second— the EXPLODE command—can be done at any time.

Breaking a block apart with asterisk insertions

A block is a single entity. Individual entities within the block, such as lines, arcs, and circles, cannot be edited. The MOVE, COPY, ROTATE, and SCALE commands affect the block as a single item.

If you plan to edit the individual items upon insertion, you can insert a block as a collection of entities. To do this, type an asterisk before the block name as follows:

Command: **INSERT** ⏎
Block name (or ?): ***PLATE-1** ⏎
   Insertion point: *(pick a point)*
   Scale factor ⟨1⟩: ⏎
   Rotation angle ⟨0⟩: ⏎

The inserted object is no longer a block. It consists of individual entities that can be edited.

Exploding the block

The EXPLODE command is used to break apart any existing block, polyline, or dimension. When the block is picked, a quick blip occurs as the block explodes.

Command: **EXPLODE** ⏎
Select objects: *(pick the block)*

The exploded block is now composed of entities that may be edited individually. To see if EXPLODE worked properly, select any edit command and then pick an entity formerly part of the block. Only that entity should highlight. If so, the block was exploded properly.

Redefining existing blocks

A situation may arise where you discover that a block must be edited. This is an easy process, even if you have placed the block on a drawing many times. To redefine an existing block, follow this procedure:

1. Insert the block to be redefined anywhere on screen.
2. Explode the block you just inserted using the EXPLODE command.
3. Edit the block as needed.
4. Recreate the block using the BLOCK command.
5. Give the block the same name it had before. Answer "Yes" to redefine the block.
6. Give the block the same insertion point as the original.
7. All insertions of the block are updated when the BLOCK command is complete.

A common mistake is to forget to use the EXPLODE command. When you try to create the block again with the same name, the following error message is displayed and the command is aborted:

> Block ⟨name⟩ references itself
> *Invalid*

This means that you are trying to recreate a block that already exists. Enter the EXPLODE command and try again.

In versions of AutoCAD prior to 2.5, the EXPLODE command does not exist. You must use the asterisk insertion method described earlier in this chapter. This method breaks the block into individual entities during insertion, allowing you to use edit commands to alter it.

Creating a block from a drawing file

You can create a block from any existing drawing. This allows you to avoid redrawing the object as a block, thus saving time. Remember, if something has already been drawn, try to use it as a block rather than redrawing it. In this case, use the INSERT command in the following manner to define a block named BOLT from an existing drawing file named FASTENER.

> Command: **INSERT** ⏎
> Block name (or ?): **BOLT = FASTENER** ⏎
>   Insertion point: *(press CTRL C)*

The drawing is not inserted on screen because the command is canceled. However, a block named BOLT is added to the drawing file and can be used like any other block.

EXERCISE 21-5

☐ Open EX21-3.
☐ Insert a block named CHAIR anywhere on the drawing.
☐ Explode the chair you just inserted.
☐ Add a feature to the chair, such as a headrest. Keep it simple.
☐ Make a block named CHAIR of the revised chair.
☐ Answer "Yes" to redefine the block, and pick the same insertion point as the original chair.
☐ When the BLOCK command is completed, all chairs should be updated to reflect the changes.
☐ Save the drawing as A:EX21-5 and quit.

MAKING PERMANENT BLOCKS

ARM 10

Symbols created with the BLOCK command can only be used in the drawing on which they were made. However, you may want to use blocks on many different drawings without having to redraw them. The WBLOCK command allows you to create a drawing file (.DWG extension) out of a block or any other shape. This symbol can then be inserted as a block in any drawing.

There are several ways to make a wblock. For the first method, open drawing EX21-1. Convert your CIRCLE block to a permanent symbol using the following procedure:

Command: **WBLOCK** ↵

The "Create Drawing File" dialogue box appears, displaying a listing of all drawing files in the current directory. Move the pointer to the File: box and type the name of the wblock, HOLE, and press ENTER. Each time you select the WBLOCK command, the "Create Drawing File" dialogue box appears, unless the FILEDIA system variable is set to the value of zero (0).

Block name: **CIRCLE** ↵

The above sequence wrote a new block, HOLE, to disk. The prompt asked for the name of an existing block, CIRCLE, to convert into a permanent symbol. Select the FILES command from the UTILITY screen menu, or type "FILES" at the Command: prompt. The "File Utilities" dialogue box appears; pick List Files... to see if HOLE.DWG is now on your disk. A wblock cannot be distinguished from standard AutoCAD drawing files because it appears in the file listing as a drawing. A wblock is a separate drawing in every way. When it is inserted into a drawing, though, it acts like a block. It is a single entity and cannot be edited unless broken into its original components.

To assign the wblock and block the same name, type an equal symbol (=) for the block name as follows:

Command: **WBLOCK** ↵
File name: **CIRCLE** ↵
Block name: = ↵

When you enter "WBLOCK," the "Create Drawing File" dialogue box appears if FILEDIA is set to 1. Pick "Type it" to obtain the previous prompts.

Making a new wblock

Suppose you want to create a wblock of a shape you just drew, but have not made a block yet. Enter the WBLOCK command, but do not supply a block name. Press ENTER instead. Then select the insertion point and the objects to be included in the wblock.

Command: **WBLOCK** ↵
File name: **DESK** ↵
Block Name: ↵
   Insertion base point: *(pick a point)*
Select objects: *(select objects to be in the wblock)*
Select objects: ↵

This sequence is exactly like that of the BLOCK command. Remember that this drawing is saved to disk not to the drawing file. Be sure to specify a path before the file name, if needed. The previous wblock would be saved in the current hard disk directory because no path was given. If you want to save the wblock on a floppy disk in the A: drive, enter the file name as "A:DESK." A wblock that is to be saved into the BLOCKS directory on the C: hard drive would be named C:\BLOCKS\DESK.

Make the entire drawing a wblock

An entire drawing can also be stored as a wblock. Type an asterisk (*) for the block name.

Command: **WBLOCK** ↵
File name: *(type a file name and press ENTER)*
Block name: * ↵

In this case, the whole drawing is saved to disk as if you used the SAVE command. The difference is that all unused blocks are deleted from the drawing. If the drawing contains any unused blocks, this method reduces the size of a drawing considerably.

─────── PROFESSIONAL TIP ───────

The WBLOCK-asterisk method is a good technique to clean your drawing of unused named entities to reduce the file size. Use this routine when you have completed a drawing and know that the unused blocks, layers, styles, and entities are no longer needed.

Inserting a wblock with the "Select Drawing File" dialogue box

When you pick INSERT from the DRAW screen menu, the next menu that is displayed contains all of the INSERT command options. The first prompt of the INSERT command requests the block name. You can enter the name of a block or wblock at this prompt because the INSERT command is used for both. If you want to look through a listing of your drawing files or wblocks, pick the File... button in the screen menu. This displays the standard "Select Drawing File" dialogue box. You can now scroll through listings in any directory and pick the file name you need.

When you pick File... from the screen menu, a tilde (~) is displayed on the prompt line. You can type this character whenever any command prompt requests a file name. One of several dialogue boxes is then displayed regardless of the FILEDIA system variable setting.

EXERCISE 21-6

☐ Open drawing EX21-2.
☐ Create a wblock called PLATE-1 using the existing block of the same name.
☐ Select UTILITY from the screen menu, and then FILES to get a listing of your .DWG files. Be sure PLATE-1.DWG is listed.
☐ Quit the drawing editor.
☐ Start a new drawing called EX21-6.
☐ Insert the PLATE-1 wblock into the drawing. Wblocks can be used on any drawing.
☐ Save the drawing as A:EX21-6 and quit.

Revising an inserted wblock or drawing

One of the basic principles of drawing, design, and engineering is that things will inevitably change. You may find that you have to revise a drawing file or wblock that has been used in other drawings. If this happens, you can quickly update any drawing in which the revised wblock is used. For example, if the drawing file named PUMP was used several times in a drawing, simply use the INSERT command, and place an equal sign (=) after the block name in the following manner to update all the PUMP symbols:

```
Command: INSERT ↵
Block name (or ?): PUMP = ↵
Block PUMP redefined
Regenerating drawing.
    Insertion point: (press CTRL C)
```

All of the PUMP symbols are automatically updated, and by canceling the command, no new symbols are added to the drawing.

Suppose you had inserted a drawing file named FASTENER into your current drawing, but gave it the block name of SCREW. Now you have decided to revise the FASTENER drawing. The SCREW block can be updated using the INSERT command as follows:

```
Command: INSERT ↵
Block name (or ?): SCREW = FASTENER ↵
Block SCREW redefined
Regenerating drawing.
    Insertion point: (press CTRL C)
```

CREATING A SYMBOL LIBRARY

As you become proficient with AutoCAD, begin to construct symbol libraries. A *symbol library* is a collection of related shapes, views, and symbols that are used repeatedly. You may eventually want to incorporate symbols into your screen and tablet menus. This is discussed in detail in Chapters 32 and 33. First, you need to know where symbols (blocks and wblocks) are stored and how they can be inserted into different drawings.

Blocks vs. wblocks

As discussed earlier, the principal difference between a block and a wblock is that a *block* is saved with the drawing in which it is created. A *wblock* is saved as an individual drawing file. This means that the block can only be used in the drawing. See Fig. 21-9. Since a wblock is a complete drawing file, it occupies considerably more disk space than a block.

If you decide to use blocks, each person in the office or class must have a copy of the drawing that contains the blocks. This is often done by creating the blocks in a prototype drawing. If wblocks are used, each student or employee must have floppy disks containing the wblocks, or the wblocks must be located on every hard disk drive if the computers are not networked.

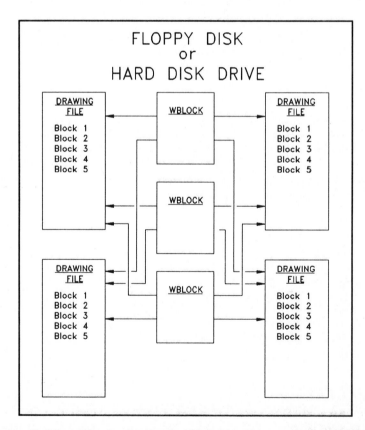

Fig. 21-9. Blocks can only be used in the drawing in which they were created. Wblocks can be inserted into any drawing.

Using floppy diskettes

Floppy diskettes are good for storing backup copies of drawing and data files. They also allow you to transport files from one workstation to another in the absence of a network. However, avoid making floppies the primary means for storage of symbols, especially if you have sufficient room on the hard disk drive. Inserting and removing floppy diskettes from a disk drive is tedious and time-consuming because it takes more time for the computer to access the floppy disks. If you must adopt this method, follow these guidelines.

- Create all symbols as wblocks.
- Assign one person to initially create the symbols for each specialty.
- Follow class or company symbol standards.
- Create a symbol library listing using a printer or plotter. Include a picture of the symbol, its insertion point, necessary information, and the disk on which it is located. See Fig. 21-10. Provide all persons who use the symbols with a copy of the listing.

PIPING FLOW DIAGRAM SYMBOLS

GATEVALVE	CHECKVALVE	GLOBEVALVE	CONTROLVALVE	SAFETYVALV-R	SAFETYVALV-L
PUMPR-TOP	PUMPR-DN	PUMPR-UP	PUMPL-UP	PUMPL-DN	PUMPL-TOP
INSTR-LOC	INSTR-PAN	TRANS	INSTR-CON	DRAIN	VENT

Fig. 21-10. Symbol library listing of piping flow diagram blocks in a prototype drawing.

- Save one group of symbols per diskette. For example, individual disks may contain the following types of symbols:
  - ✔ Electronic
  - ✔ Electrical
  - ✔ Piping
  - ✔ Mechanical
  - ✔ Structural
  - ✔ Architectural
  - ✔ Landscaping
  - ✔ Mapping
- Label floppy disks two ways:
  - ✔ Use the DOS LABEL command to assign a name to each floppy disk in the following manner:

      C:\>**LABEL A:STRUCTURAL** ↵

This gives the disk in the A: drive the name of STRUCTURAL. Eleven characters can be used for a label. Use the DOS VOL command to find out the label of a disk.

      C:\>**VOL A:** ↵

DOS responds:

      Volume in drive A is STRUCTURAL

A label can also be given to a disk when it is formatted.

  C:\>**FORMAT A:/V** ↵

The "/V" (Volume) switch activates the DOS LABEL command.

   ↙ Use stick-on floppy disk labels on all disks. Write on the label before attaching it to the disk. Use the same name as the volume label.
- Copy symbols disks and provide a copy for each workstation in the class or office.
- Keep backup copies of all symbol library disks in a secure place.
- When symbols are revised, update all copies of diskettes containing the edited symbols.
- Inform all users of any changes to symbols.

Using the hard disk drive

The hard disk drive is the best place to store symbol libraries. It is easily accessible, quicker, and more convenient to use than floppy disks. Symbols should be created with the WBLOCK command, as they were with floppy disks. The wblocks can be saved in the current directory (usually ACAD) or a subdirectory. If wblocks are stored in the ACAD directory, they are easier to enter the first time. There is less typing at the INSERT command. However, storing symbols in separate subdirectories keeps the ACAD directory uncluttered and easy to manage.

A symbol named PUMP is retrieved from the ACAD directory with the INSERT command as follows:

  Command: **INSERT** ↵
  Block name (or ?) ⟨current⟩: **PUMP** ↵

If the same symbol is stored in a subdirectory of ACAD called BLK, it is retrieved the first time as follows:

  Command: **INSERT** ↵
  Block name (or ?) ⟨current⟩: **\ACAD\BLK\PUMP** ↵

After its initial insertion, a wblock can be retrieved by just entering its file name.

Wblocks are saved on the hard disk drive using the same systematic approach as with floppy disks. These additional guidelines also apply:
- All workstations in the class or office should have directories and subdirectories with the same names.
- One person should be assigned to update and copy symbol libraries to all workstation hard drives.
- Wblocks should be copied onto each workstation's hard drive from a master floppy disk or network server.
- The master floppy disks and backup disks of the symbol libraries should be kept in separate locations.

Creating prototype symbol drawings

In addition to obtaining a printed copy, you can display all the symbols on the screen. This technique requires that you create symbols in a prototype drawing. The symbols (blocks) are then inserted into a special area of the drawing outside the drawing limits, then labeled. They can be copied from this library and placed in the drawing. An example of this arrangement was shown in Fig. 21-10. The following steps should be used to create this type of symbol library.
- Draw each symbol on layer 0 and save as a block.
- Increase the limits beyond the needed drawing area to provide space for the symbols. The amount of space required is determined by the number of symbols stored in the library.
- Draw a grid in which to place the symbols (if desired). Insert symbols inside the grid boxes.
- Make a layer named INSERT. Assign a unique color to the layer.
- Use the DONUT or POINT commands to place a dot or an "X" at the insertion point of each symbol.
- Label each symbol on the INSERT layer.
- To use a block, copy it from the library to the drawing rather than using the INSERT command.

Using prototype symbol libraries

The symbol library can be used in several different ways. Symbols can be copied directly from the library to the drawing as they are needed. You might also insert one copy of each symbol into the drawing limits when you begin. Then zoom the drawing to display only the limits. This hides the symbol library and also enlarges the view of your work. Use COPY to place symbols in your drawing. This method has limitations because you cannot scale or rotate with COPY as you can with INSERT.

Turn Quick Text mode on so that symbol labels are not recalculated when a regeneration takes place. This saves much time. Descriptive symbol names, like those in Fig. 21-10, can be replaced with numbers or letters.

The on-screen library also serves as a reference. You can check the shape, block name, or insertion point of a symbol. When using the on-screen library for this method only, create the library on layers not used in the drawing. The symbol library layers are normally frozen to speed regeneration time. To check a symbol, thaw the library layers.

— PROFESSIONAL TIP —

Create one or more views of your symbol library using the VIEW command, especially if you use them for reference purposes. It is faster to display a view than it is to use the ZOOM or PAN commands.

Copying a symbol library into a new drawing

A symbol library of blocks that are part of a prototype drawing can be copied into a new drawing file. This technique is an invisible function that transfers blocks from an existing drawing to a new drawing. The incoming blocks are not displayed, only included in the drawing file. It enables you to use blocks created on one drawing without also having to use the drawing. The process is simple. If the drawing PIPEFLOW on the disk in the A: drive contains the needed blocks, enter the following:

Command: **INSERT** ↵
Block name (or ?) ⟨current⟩: **A:PIPEFLOW** ↵
Insertion point: ∧*C*

The blocks are now included with your drawing. Check this by selecting BLOCK and the ? option.

These methods of placing symbol libraries on prototype drawings are just several possibilities. As you learn more about AutoCAD, other avenues will open. After reading Chapters 32 and 33, you will see additional possibilities. Regardless of the method chosen, it is important that you maintain consistency and adhere to standards.

Create a symbol library listing

After deciding which method of using symbols is best for you, create a symbol library listing. Distribute it to all persons who will be using the symbols. The list can be a pen or printer plot of the symbol libraries on each prototype drawing. These lists should be updated when revisions are made to symbols. A copy on 8.5 by 11 in. paper should be given to all AutoCAD users. A larger copy should be placed on a wall or bulletin board. Examples of symbol library lists used in engineering offices are shown in Fig. 21-11 and 21-12.

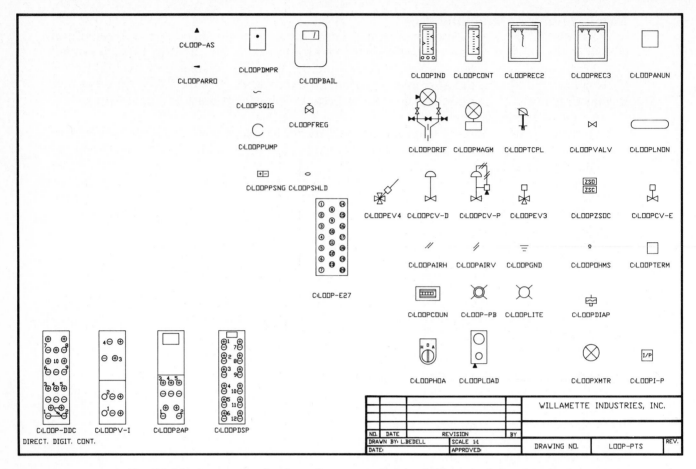

Fig. 21-11. Instrumentation loop diagram symbols. (Willamette Industries, Inc.)

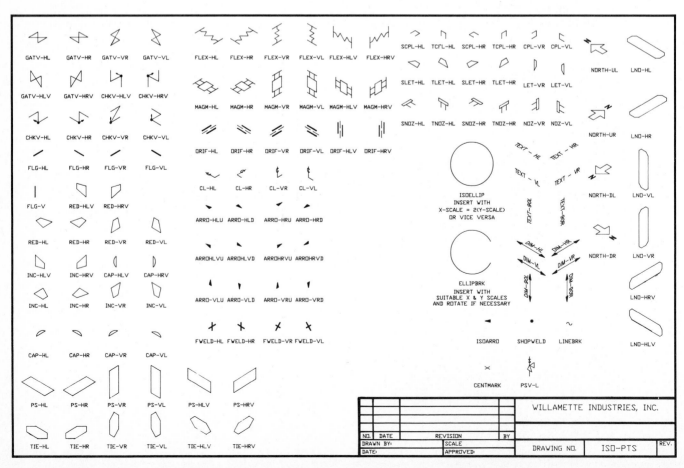

Fig. 21-12. Isometric piping symbols. (Willamette Industries, Inc.)

RENAMING BLOCKS

ARM 4

Block names can be changed with the RENAME command. It is found in the UTILITY screen menu. To change the name of the CIRCLE block to HOLE, enter the RENAME command as follows:

    Command: **RENAME** ⏎
    Block/Dimstyle/LAyer/LType/Style/Ucs/VIew/VPort: **B** ⏎
    Old block name: **CIRCLE** ⏎
    New block name: **HOLE** ⏎

The block name is changed. To check that the name was changed, select the BLOCK or INSERT command. Use the ? option to get a listing. The list will appear similar to this:

Defined blocks.	User Blocks 3
PLATE	External References 0
HOLE	Dependent Blocks 0
PLATE-1	Unnamed Blocks 0

The RENAME command in AutoCAD only works for blocks, not wblocks. To change the name of a wblock, use either the File Utilities Menu's Rename option or the DOS RENAME command. See Chapter 15 for a discussion of the "File Utilities" dialogue box, or Chapter 35 for use of the DOS RENAME command.

DELETING NAMED ENTITIES

ARM 4

Blocks are a "named entity," or object. Other such named entities are dimension styles (dimstyles), layers, linetypes, shapes, and text styles. In many drawing sessions, not all of the named entities in a drawing are used. For example, your prototype drawing may contain several layers, text styles, and blocks that are not used. Since these entities occupy drawing file space, it is good practice to delete, or "purge" the unused objects using the PURGE command. Using this command is a simple process, but it must be used as soon as you enter the AutoCAD drawing editor and before any entities are added or deleted from the drawing. You can use PURGE in the following manner to delete a block named LINESPEC:

    Command: **PURGE** ⏎
    Purge unused Blocks/Dimstyles/LAyers/LTypes/SHapes/STyles/All: **B** ⏎
    Purge block LINESPEC? ⟨N⟩ **Y** ⏎

The PURGE command individually lists all unused blocks and gives you the option to answer "YES" or "NO." Use the PURGE command in the same manner to delete any of the unused entities listed above.

A part of your efforts in file maintenance should be to remove any unused named entities from drawings that you have completed. This reduces the file size, thus creating more space on your storage media for additional files. The WBLOCK-asterisk method mentioned earlier accomplishes the same thing as the PURGE command, but does so automatically.

REFERENCE DRAWINGS

ARM 10

Any machine or electrical appliance contains a variety of subassemblies and components. These components are assembled to create the final product. The final product occupies a greater amount of space and weighs more than any of the individual parts. In the same way, a drawing composed of a variety of blocks and wblocks grows much larger and occupies more disk space than the individual symbols and components. Imagine creating a design model of an automobile by projecting numerous holograms (laser-generated 3-D pictures) onto a viewing area. The design occupies perceived space, yet weighs nothing. When the lasers are turned off, the image of the car vanishes. Yet, the individual components that were projected still exist in computer storage and can be displayed again if needed. That is the principle behind the AutoCAD reference drawing concept.

AutoCAD allows you to "reference" existing drawings to the master drawing you are currently working on. When you reference (Xref) a drawing, it is not added to the current drawing (as are wblocks), but it is displayed on the screen. This makes for much smaller files. It also allows several people in a class or office to reference the same drawing file, and always be assured that any revisions to the reference drawing will be included in the master. Reference drawings are used with the XREF command, which is found in the BLOCKS screen menu, File pull-down menu, or typed as "XREF" at the Command: prompt.

Reference drawings can be used in two basic forms:
- Constructing a drawing using predrawn symbols or details (similar to the use of blocks and wblocks).
- Laying out a drawing to be plotted, which is composed of multiple views or details, using existing drawings. This technique is discussed in detail in Chapter 27.

An important benefit of using Xrefs is that whenever the master drawing is loaded into AutoCAD, the latest version of the Xrefs are displayed. If the Xrefs are modified between the time you revise the master and the time you plot it, all of the revisions are automatically reflected. This is because AutoCAD reloads each Xref whenever the master drawing is loaded.

Other significant aspects of Xrefs is that they can be nested, and you can use as many Xrefs as needed for the drawing. This means that a detail referenced to the master drawing can be composed of smaller details that are themselves Xrefs. You can also use OSNAP options to attach entities or other Xrefs to the referenced drawing.

Using the XREF command is similar to the BLOCK or WBLOCK commands. Suppose, for example, that you want to add a standard arrangement of a pump and valves to a piping flow diagram. The pump and valve arrangement is named PUMP-VLV, and is located in the \ACAD\PIPE subdirectory. Use the Attach option of the XREF command as follows:

```
Command: XREF ↵
?/Bind/Detach/Path/Reload/⟨Attach⟩: ↵
Xref to Attach ⟨current⟩⟩: \ACAD\PIPE\PUMP-VLV ↵
Attach Xref PUMP-VLV: \acad\pipe\pump-vlv
PUMP-VLV loaded.
Insertion point: (pick an insertion point)
   X scale factor ⟨1⟩/Corner/XYZ: ↵
   Y scale factor (default = X): ↵
   Rotation angle ⟨0⟩: ↵
```

As you can see, the only outward differences between the XREF command and the BLOCK or WBLOCK commands are the options of the command. All of the commands function in a similar manner, yet it is the internal workings of the commands that are different. Remember that Xrefs are not added to the drawing file, thereby reducing the size of the master drawings.

A complete discussion of the use of Xrefs and the creation of multiview drawings for plotting is discussed in Chapter 27. It covers all of the options of the XREF command, and the manner in which they can be used to create any type of drawing that is composed of several views, details, or components of varying scales.

A brief description of each of the XREF command options is given here to provide a better understanding of their capabilities.
- **?**—Lists the Xrefs used in the current drawing.
- **Bind**—Allows you to permanently join an Xref to the master drawing. This is similar to using the WBLOCK command. It is useful if you must send a drawing file on disk to a plotting service, or give a copy of the drawing file to a client.
- **Detach**—Removes an Xref from the master drawing. It is used if you must delete a detail, view, or portion of a drawing, and wish to remove all its dependent symbols.
- **Path**—Allows you to change the location (path) of the Xref. It is convenient if you must locate the Xrefs in a different hard drive directory or disk drive.
- **Reload**—Enables you to reload any Xrefs while in AutoCAD. It is useful if you know that an Xref has been updated while you were working on your drawing.

BINDING DEPENDENT SYMBOLS TO A DRAWING   ARM 10

AutoCAD refers to *dependent symbols* as named items such as blocks, dimension styles, layers, linetypes, and text styles. If you reference a drawing, you cannot directly use any of its dependent symbols. For example, a layer that exists only on a referenced drawing cannot be made current in the master drawing in order to draw on it. It is the same for text styles. If one of the dependent symbols, such as a dimension style, or linetype, is one that you would like to use on the master drawing, you can permanently "bind," or affix any of these symbols to the master drawing. After a permanent bind is created, the dependent symbol, such as the text style, can be used on the master drawing.

When a drawing is referenced to the master, the layer names of the Xref are given the name of the referenced drawing, followed by the ¦ symbol, and then the name of the layer. This enables you to quickly identify which layers belong to the specific referenced drawing. Fig. 21-13 illustrates this technique.

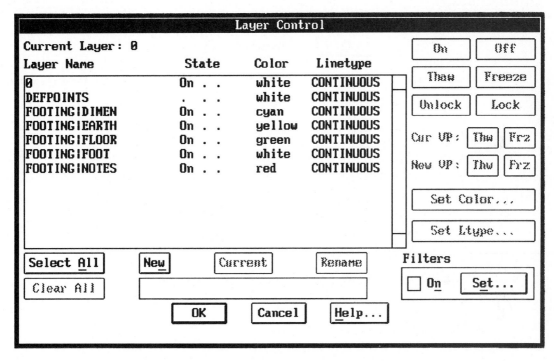

Fig. 21-13. Layer names on a referenced drawing are preceded by the Xref drawing name.

Remember, you are not allowed to draw on any layer that belongs to an Xref. If you wish to use one of these layers or any other dependent symbol in an Xref drawing, use the XBIND command. The XBIND command is also located in the BLOCKS screen menu. The command sequence is as follows:

Command: **XBIND** ↵
Block/Dimstyle/LAyer/LType/Style: **LA** ↵
Dependent layer name(s): **FOOTING¦DIMEN,FOOTING¦NOTES** ↵
   Scanning...
2 Layer(s) bound.
Command:

When a layer has been bound to the master drawing, it is renamed. The FOOTING|DIMEN layer becomes FOOTING0DIMEN. Another view of the "Layer Control" dialogue box (DDLMODES), shown in Fig. 21-14, illustrates this concept.

Keep in mind that when a dependent symbol is bound to the master drawing using XBIND, it becomes a permanent part of the drawing, thus increasing the drawing file size.

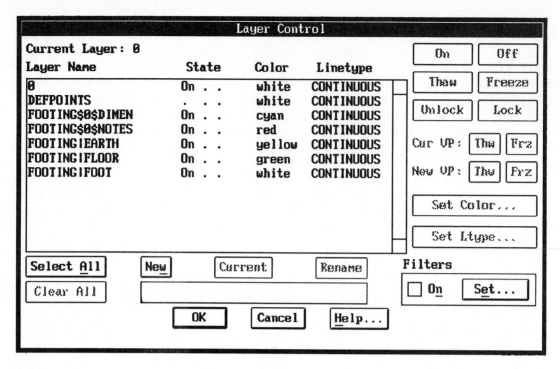

Fig. 21-14. Layers that are bound using the XBIND command are renamed. Note the use of the O.

CHAPTER TEST

Write your answers in the spaces provided.

1. Define "symbol library." _____

   _____

2. When should blocks be drawn to fit inside a one unit square? _____

   _____

3. A block name can be _____ characters long.

4. To obtain a listing of all blocks in the current drawing, you must _____

   _____

5. Describe block nesting. _____

   _____

6. How do you preset block insertion variables using a dialogue box? _____

   _____

   _____

7. Describe the effect of entering negative scale factors when inserting a block. _____

   _____

8. Why would the Corner option be used when scaling a block during insertion? _____

   _____

9. What properties do blocks drawn on a layer other than 0 assume when inserted? _____

   _____

10. Why would you draw blocks on layer 0? _____

_____

11. What are the limitations of the MINSERT command? _____

_____

12. What is the purpose of the BASE command? _____

_____

13. Explain why a drafter would choose to use preset options when inserting a block. _____

_____

14. Explain the difference between "PS" or "S" as preset options. _____

_____

_____

15. Name the two methods that break a block into its individual entities for editing. _____

_____

16. Suppose you have found that a block was incorrectly drawn. Unfortunately, you have already
    inserted the block 30 times. How can you edit all of the blocks quickly? _____

_____

17. What is the primary difference between a block and a wblock? _____

_____

_____

_____

18. The WBLOCK command asks for block name. What would you enter at the Block name:
    prompt to make a wblock out of an existing block? _____

19. What would you enter at the Block name: prompt to remove all unused blocks from a drawing?

_____

20. Suppose you revise a drawing named DESK. However, the DESK drawing had been inserted
    several times into another drawing as wblocks named DESK2. How would you update the
    DESK2 insertions? _____

_____

_____

21. Why is it best to put symbol libraries on the hard disk drive rather than floppy disks?

_____

_____

22. What would you enter at the DOS C:⟩ prompt to name a diskette located in the B: drive
    CADCLASS? _____

23. How do you request the disk-naming procedure at the DOS prompt when formatting a disk
    in the A: drive? _____

24. What advantage is offered by having a symbol library of blocks in a prototype drawing,
    rather than using wblocks? _____

_____

25. Give the command and entries needed to insert all of the blocks from a drawing named A:STRUCT-1 into the current drawing.

Command: _____

Block name (or ?) ⟨current⟩: _____

Insertion point: _____

26. What is the purpose of the PURGE command, and what conditions govern its use? ___
_____

27. What effect does the use of referenced drawings have on drawing file size? _____
_____

28. When are Xrefs updated in the master drawing? _____
_____

29. Why would you want to bind a dependent symbol to a master drawing? _____
_____

30. What does the layer name WALL0NOTES mean? _____
_____

DRAWING PROBLEMS

1. Choose one of the diagrams shown and draw it using blocks. Use the following guidelines:
   A. Start a new drawing using an A- or B-size prototype.
   B. Create a block for each different shape in the drawing.
   C. Arrows should be drawn as a block.
   D. Use a thick polyline for the flow lines.
   E. Label the drawing as shown.
   F. Place a border and title block on the drawing.
   G. Save the drawing as A:P21-1.

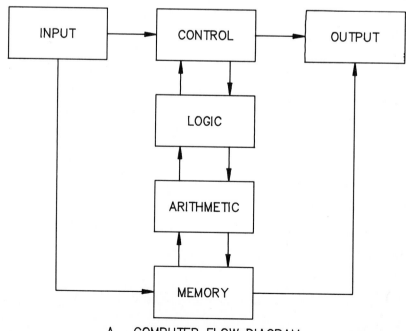

A. COMPUTER FLOW DIAGRAM

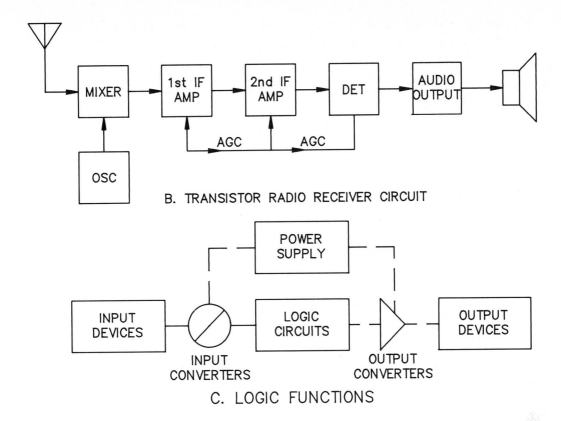

B. TRANSISTOR RADIO RECEIVER CIRCUIT

C. LOGIC FUNCTIONS

2. Create a symbol library for one of the drafting disciplines listed below on a prototype drawing. Then, after checking with your instructor, draw one problem using the library. You can use the prototype drawings in two ways:
   - Start a new drawing using a standard prototype drawing named PROTO. Name the new drawing NEWDWG.
   - Insert the prototype into the current drawing (perhaps a different size drawing) and cancel at the Insertion point: prompt.
   Specialty areas you might create symbols for include:
   - Mechanical (machine features, fasteners, tolerance symbols).
   - Architectural (doors, windows, fixtures).
   - Structural (steel shapes, bolts, standard footings).
   - Industrial piping (fittings, valves).
   - Piping Flow Diagrams (tanks, valves, pumps).
   - Electrical Schematic (resistors, capacitors, switches).
   - Electrical One-Line (transformers, switches).
   - Electronics (IC chips, test points, components).
   - Logic Diagrams (and gates, nand gates, buffers).
   - Mapping, Civil (survey markers, piping).
   - Geometric Tolerancing (feature control frames).
   Save the drawing as A:P21-2, or choose an appropriate name for the prototype, such as ARCH-PRO or ELEC-PRO.
3. Display the prototype drawing symbol library on the screen and make a print with your dot matrix or laser printer. If you are not familiar with your printer, read the first part of Chapter 27 on making quick prints. Put the printed copy of symbol library in your notebook as a reference.
4. Open Problem 4 from Chapter 13 (P13-4). Erase all copies of the symbols that were made, leaving the original intact. This includes steel column symbols and the bay and column line tags. Then follow these steps:
   A. Make a block of each of the remaining steel column and tag symbols.
   B. Use the MINSERT or ARRAY commands to place the symbols in the drawing.

C. Dimension the drawing as shown in the problem drawing of Chapter 13. Set the proper dimension variables for this type of drawing. Dimensions should be given in feet and inches. Show zero inches as follows: 20'-0".

D. Save the drawing as A:P21-4.

5. Open Problem 5 from Chapter 13 (P13-5). Erase all of the desk workstations except one. Then follow these directions:

A. Create a block of the remaining workstation.

B. Insert the block in the drawing using the MINSERT command.

C. Dimension one of the workstations as shown in the original problem.

D. Save the drawing as A:P21-5.

6-10. The following problems are presented as engineer sketches. They are not-to-scale, schematic-type drawings made using symbols. The symbols should first be drawn as blocks and then saved in a symbol library. Use one of the methods discussed in this chapter. Place a border and title block on each of the drawings.

6. This is a one-line diagram of an electrical substation. Set limits for an A- or B-size sheet. Save the drawing as A:P21-6.

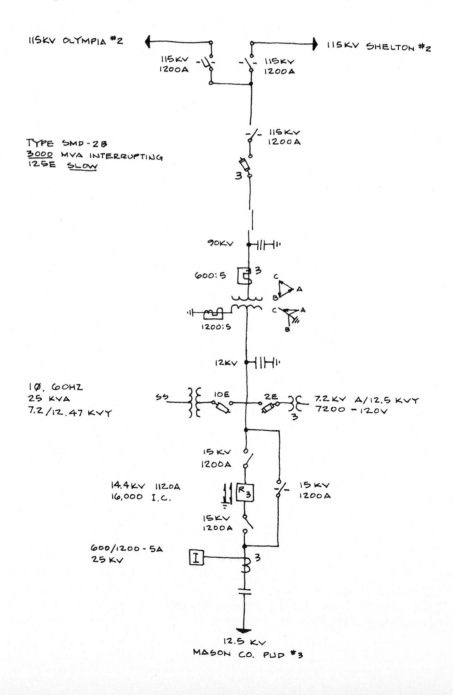

7. This is an electrical schematic of a light flasher circuit. Set limits for a B-size sheet. Align components when possible. Eliminate as many bends in the circuit lines as possible. See Appendix H for standard electronic symbols. Save the drawing as A:P21-7.

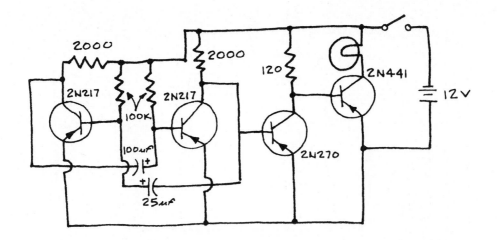

8. This is a logic diagram of a portion of a computer's internal components. Create the drawing on a C-size sheet. Save the drawing as A:P21-8.

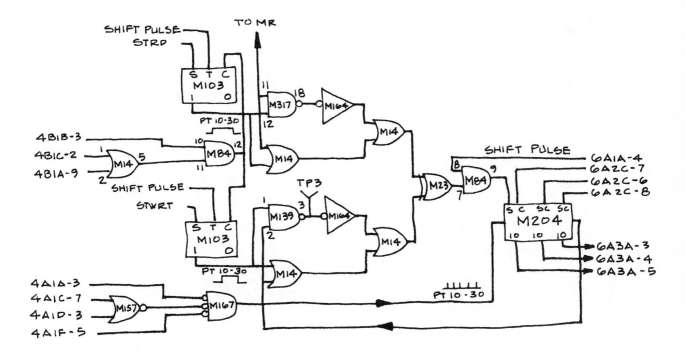

9. Draw the piping flow diagram of a cooling water system on a B-size sheet. Look closely at this drawing. Using editing commands, it may be easier than you think. Draw thick flow lines with polylines. Save the drawing as A:P21-9.

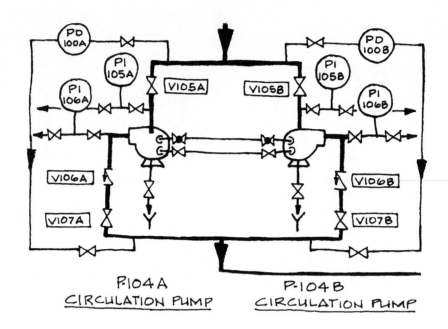

10. This piping flow diagram is part of an industrial effluent treatment system. Draw it on a C-size sheet. Eliminate as many bends in the flow lines as possible. Place arrowheads at all flow line intersections and bends. Flow lines should not run through valves or equipment. Use polylines for thick flow lines. Save the drawing as A:P21-10.

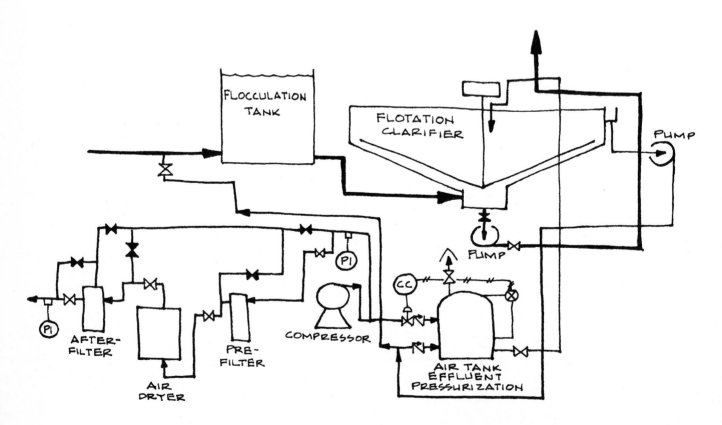

11. The general arrangement of a basement floor plan for a new building is shown here. The engineer has shown one example of each type of equipment. Use the following instructions to complete the drawing:

A. Drawing should fit on C-size sheet.

B. All text should appear 1/8″ high, except bay and column line tags, which are 3/16″ high. The text balloons for bay and column lines should be twice the diameter of the text height.

C. The column and bay line steel symbols should be 8″ x 12″.

D. The PUMP and CHILLER installations (except PUMP #5) should be located per the dimensions given for PUMP #1 and CHILLER #1. Use the dimensions shown on the sketch for other PUMP and CHILLER units.

E. TANK #2 and PUMP #5 (P-5) should be located exactly as TANK #1 and P-4, and should be the same respective sizes.

F. Tanks T-3, T-4, T-5, and T-6 are all the same size, and are aligned 12′ from column line A.

G. Plan this drawing carefully and create as many blocks or wblocks as possible to increase your productivity.

H. Save the drawing as A:P21-11.

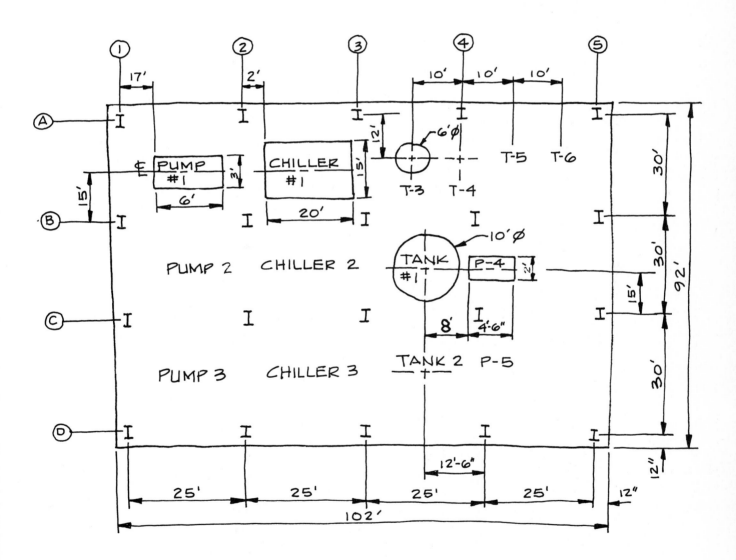

12. The drawing in Problem 21-11 (P21-11) must be revised. The engineer has provided you with a sketch of the necessary revisions. It is up to you to alter the drawing as quickly and efficiently as possible. The dimensions shown on the sketch *do not* need to be added to the drawing; they are provided for construction purposes only. Revise P21-11 so that all CHILLERS, and TANKS #3, #4, #5, and #6 reflect the changes. Save your drawing as A:P21-12.

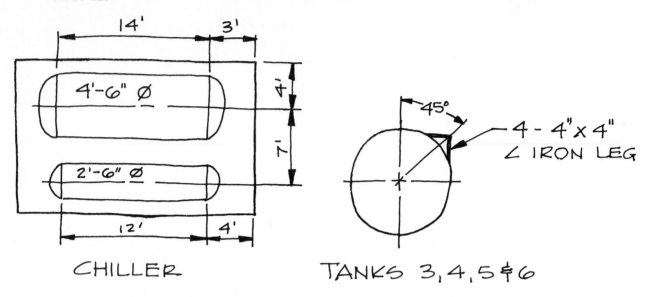

13. This drawing is an instrumentation loop diagram of software functions for the drying section of a paper machine. Each large box in the drawing represents a specific function or algorithm in the computer program. The smaller blocks on the left and right indicate different signals that are received and sent (input and output) by each function. Lay out the drawing exactly as shown on a B- or C-size sheet. Use your own title block. Save the drawing as A:P21-13.

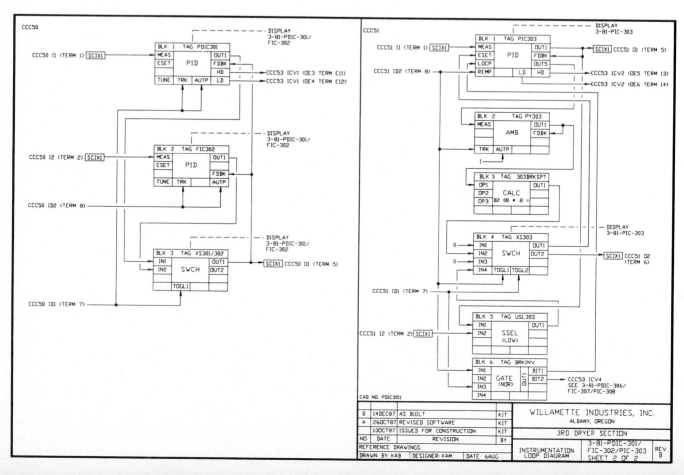

14-15. Make multiview drawings from the following engineer sketches. Add any sectioning necessary to completely describe the object. Completely dimension the drawing and apply geometric dimensioning and tolerancing symbols as shown on the sketch. Refer to Appendix H for the proper size and format of geometric dimensioning and tolerancing symbols. Be sure to include the following general notes:

> INTERPRET DIMENSIONS AND TOLERANCES PER ANSI Y14.5M-1982.
> REMOVE ALL BURRS AND SHARP EDGES.

Save the drawings as A:P21-14 and A:P21-15, respectively.

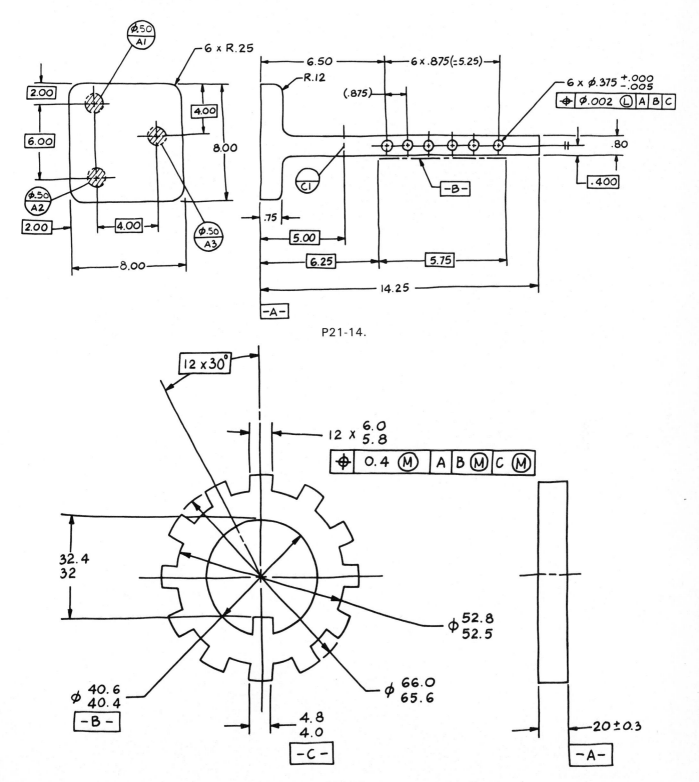

P21-14.

P21-15.

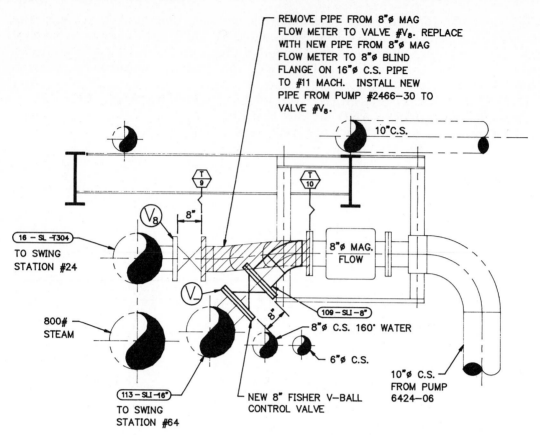

REMOVE PIPE FROM 8"∅ MAG
FLOW METER TO VALVE #V₈. REPLACE
WITH NEW PIPE FROM 8"∅ MAG
FLOW METER TO 8"∅ BLIND
FLANGE ON 16"∅ C.S. PIPE
TO #11 MACH. INSTALL NEW
PIPE FROM PUMP #2466-30 TO
VALVE #V₈.

10"C.S.

V₈

8"

16 - SL -T304
TO SWING
STATION #24

800#
STEAM

8"∅ MAG.
FLOW

8"

109 - SLI -8"

8"∅ C.S. 160° WATER

6"∅ C.S.

10"∅ C.S.
FROM PUMP
6424-06

113 - SLI -16"
TO SWING
STATION #64

NEW 8" FISHER V-BALL
CONTROL VALVE

ELEV. VIEW OF STOCK LINE CHANGE OVER @ TANK

SECTION   Ⓑ
                ⎯
(¾" = 1'-0")

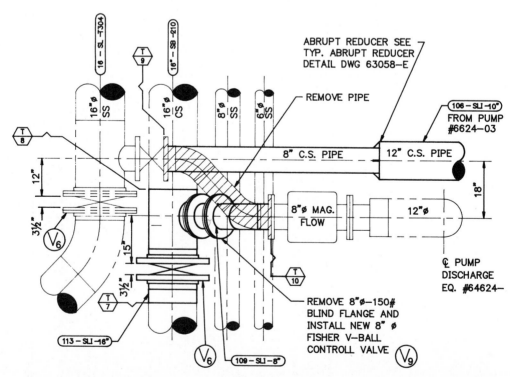

16 - SL -T304

18" - SB -210

T
9

ABRUPT REDUCER SEE
TYP. ABRUPT REDUCER
DETAIL DWG 63058-E

REMOVE PIPE

106 - SLI -10"
FROM PUMP
#6624-03

16"∅
SS

16"∅
CS

8"∅
SS

6"∅
SS

8" C.S. PIPE

12" C.S. PIPE

T
8

12"

3½"

V₆

15"

8"∅ MAG.
FLOW

12"∅

18"

₵ PUMP
DISCHARGE
EQ. #64624-

3½"

T
7

T
10

REMOVE 8"∅-150#
BLIND FLANGE AND
INSTALL NEW 8" ∅
FISHER V-BALL
CONTROLL VALVE

113 - SLI -16"

V₆

109 - SLI -8"

V₉

PLAN VIEW OF STOCK LINE CHANGE FROM STOCK TANK PUMPS

(¾" = 1'-0")

Industrial piping plans and elevation. (Jeddeloh, Hayes, Inc.)

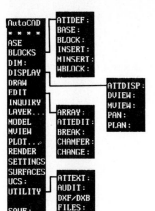

Chapter 22

ASSIGNING ATTRIBUTES AND GENERATING A BILL OF MATERIALS

Learning objectives

After completing this chapter, you will be able to:

☐ Assign visible or hidden values (attributes) to blocks.
☐ Edit attributes in existing blocks.
☐ Create a template file for the collection of block attributes.
☐ Collect attribute values in a bill of materials.

Blocks become more useful when written information is given with them. It is even more helpful to assign information that is visible (displayed) and information that is hidden. From these data, a list, much like a bill of materials, can be requested and printed.

Written or numerical values assigned to blocks are called *attributes* by AutoCAD. Attribute information can be extracted from the drawing rather than used only as text labels. Examples of blocks with attributes are shown in Fig. 22-1. The ATTDEF (ATTribute DEFined) command

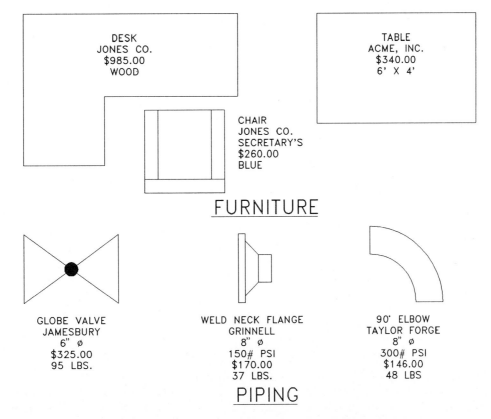

Fig. 22-1. Examples of blocks with attributes.

allows you to specify attribute text and determine how it is displayed. The ATTDISP (ATTribute DISPlay) command governs which attributes are displayed. You can selectively or collectively edit attributes using the ATTEDIT (ATTribute EDIT) command. Using the ATTEXT (ATTribute EXTract) command, you can extract any or all attributes from a drawing in a list or report form.

The creation, editing, and extraction of attributes can also be handled with dialogue boxes that are displayed with the DDATTDEF, DDATTE, and DDATTEXT commands.

ASSIGNING ATTRIBUTES TO BLOCKS ARM 10

The first step in defining block attributes is to decide what information about the block is needed. Then decide how the computer should ask you for the attribute. This might be a prompt, such as "What is the size?" The name of the object should be your first attribute. This is followed by items such as manufacturer, type, size, price, and weight. Suppose you are drawing a valve symbol for a piping flow diagram. You might want to list all product-related data. The number of attributes needed are limited only by the project requirements.

Once the symbol is completed and shown on the screen, select the ATTDEF command.

Command: **ATTDEF** ↵
Attribute modes — Invisible:N Constant:N Verify:N Preset:N
Enter (ICVP) to change, RETURN when done:

At this prompt, there are four decisions you must make. All of the options affect the attributes, and all are toggle switches. The default option is "N" for no, or normal.
- **Invisible**—Should the attribute be visible? Type "I" to make the attribute invisible. It will not be displayed when the block is inserted.
- **Constant**—Should the attribute always be the same? Typing "C" to turn on the Constant option means that all future uses of the block display the same value for the attribute. You will not be prompted for a new value.
- **Verify**—Do you want a prompt to remind you about the value you entered? When creating an attribute, you enter the attribute value at the prompt. To check that the value you entered is correct, turn Verify on.
- **Preset**—Should all attributes assume preset values and not display prompts? The Preset option creates variable attributes, but disables all attribute prompts during the insertion of a block. Default values are used instead. This works only with normal attributes. The setting does not affect dialogue box entry discussed later.

If you do not turn on any of these options, the display shows Normal. A normal display means that you will be prompted for all attributes and they will be visible. Request the Normal option by pressing ENTER. The next three prompts let you assign a value to the attribute.

Attribute tag: **TYPE** ↵
Attribute prompt: **Enter valve type:** ↵
Default attribute value: **GATE** ↵

The information needed by the ATTDEF prompts is as follows:
- **Attribute tag.** Enter the name of the attribute here. You must give a name or number. There can be any character in the tag, but blanks are not allowed.
- **Attribute prompt.** Enter the statement you want the computer to ask when this block is inserted. For example, "What is the valve size?" or "Enter valve size:" are good prompts if the attribute tag is "size." If Constant or Preset mode is set, this prompt is not displayed.
- **Default attribute value.** The entry you type here is placed in the drawing as a default when the block is inserted unless you change it at the prompt. You do not have to enter anything here. You might type a message regarding the type of information needed. The default is displayed in brackets (⟨ ⟩). You might have a message, such as "10 spaces max" or "numbers only." Only the prompt "Attribute value" is displayed if the Constant mode is set.

The remainder of the ATTDEF command is the same series of prompts found with the TEXT command. Since attributes are text, they need to be positioned and sized. The current text style is assigned unless a new one is selected. When you complete the ATTDEF command, press ENTER. A label appears on screen. This is the attribute tag. Do not be dismayed; this is the only time the tag name appears. When the block is inserted, you are asked for information that takes the place of the tag.

When you define a second attribute and reach the text positioning prompt, the previous text is highlighted. This indicates that if ENTER is pressed, the new text assumes the same justification, and is positioned directly below the highlighted text. If you prefer a different position, enter new values or pick a new point.

When you finish creating attributes, use the BLOCK or WBLOCK commands as discussed in Chapter 21. When creating the block, be sure to select the symbol (drawing) and all of the attributes that go with that block. When the block is created, it should disappear, as should all of the attributes. If attributes remain on the screen, undo and try again, making sure that all attributes are selected.

ASSIGNING ATTRIBUTES WITH A DIALOGUE BOX

All of the aspects of an attribute can be assigned on the screen in a dialogue box by using the DDATTDEF command. This command displays the "Attribute Definition" dialogue box shown in Fig. 22-2. You can also activate the DDATTDEF command by selecting AttDef Dialogue... in the ATTDEF: screen menu.

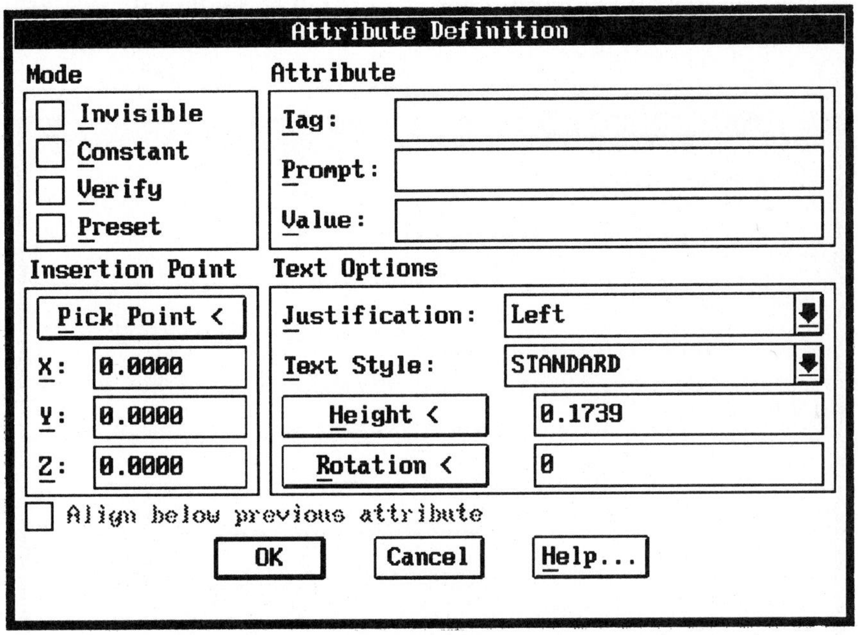

Fig. 22-2. Attributes can be assigned in the "Attribute Definition" dialogue box.

The "Attribute Definition" dialogue box is divided into four areas with the following labels: Mode, Attribute, Insertion Point, and Text Options. Each of these areas allows you to set the specific aspects of the attribute described previously. First pick any of the mode buttons you wish to set. Then, pick the Tag: edit box and enter the attribute tag. Do the same for Prompt: and Value:. If you need to change any one of these values, simply double click on the entry and type the new value. If you click once in the edit box, you can use any of the cursor keys to edit the text. Each of these edit boxes displays only 32 characters, but can contain up to 256 characters. If you type more than 32 characters, the text scrolls off the left side of the edit box. If you need to view the first part of the text, use the arrow keys to move to that position.

Notice in Fig. 22-2 that two pop-up lists (denoted by the arrow along the right of the dialogue box) enable you to select the text justification and the text style. If you wish to select centered text, just pick anywhere inside the Justification box, and a list of text alignment options is displayed. When you pick Center, the list closes and the word "Center" appears in the list box.

Similarly, if you pick inside the Text Style box, a pop-up list of all text styles in the current drawing is displayed. Pick the style you need, and it is displayed in the list box.

Note that the Pick Point, Height, and Rotation buttons are followed by the "⟨" symbol. Selecting any one of these temporarily returns you to the graphics screen and allows you to indicate to AutoCAD that value on the screen by picking points. Once the point is picked, the dialogue box returns. If everything looks good to you, pick OK and the attribute is placed on the screen. Press ENTER if you want to create another attribute. If you want the next attribute to be placed below the first with the same justification, pick the Align below previous attribute button. When you do this, the Insertion point and Text options selections are grayed out.

INSERTING BLOCKS WITH ATTRIBUTES

When you use the INSERT command to place a block in your drawing, you are prompted for additional information after the insertion point, scale factors, and rotation angle. The prompt that you entered in the ATTDEF command appears, and the default attribute value appears in brackets. Accept the default by pressing ENTER, or provide new value. Then the attribute is displayed.

Attributes can be entered using a dialogue box if the ATTDIA system variable is set to a value other than 0. After entering the rotation angle at the INSERT command, the "Enter Attributes" dialogue box appears. See Fig. 22-3. It can list up to ten attributes. If a block has more than ten attributes, you can display the next "page" of attributes by picking the Next button.

Fig. 22-3. The "Enter Attribute" dialogue box allows you to enter or change attributes when a block is inserted.

Attribute prompt suppression

Some drawings may use blocks with attributes that always retain their default values. In this case, there is no need to be prompted for the attribute values. You can turn off the attribute prompts by entering a "0" for the ATTREQ system variable.

```
Command: ATTREQ ↵
New value for ATTREQ ⟨1⟩: 0 ↵
```

Try inserting the VALVE block. Notice that none of the attribute prompts appear. The AT-TREQ value is saved with the drawing. To display attribute prompts again, change the value of ATTREQ back to 1.

— PROFESSIONAL TIP —

Part of your project and drawing planning should involve system variable settings such as ATTREQ. Setting ATTREQ to 0 before using blocks can save time in the drawing process.

EXERCISE 22-1

☐ Load AutoCAD and start a new drawing. Name the drawing EX22-1, and use an A- or B-size architectural prototype drawing.
☐ Draw the valve symbol shown below.

GATE
CRANE
6"
$365.00

☐ Select the ATTDEF command and assign the following attributes:

TAG	PROMPT	VALUE	MODE
Type	(None)	Gate	Constant
Mfgr	Enter the valve manufacturer:	Crane	Invisible
Size	Enter the size:	6''	Normal and Preset
Price	Enter the price:	$365	Invisible and Verify

☐ Select the BLOCK command. Include the valve and all of the attributes in the block and name it VALVE.
☐ Select the INSERT command to place a copy of the VALVE block on your screen. Enter new values for the attributes if you wish. You should be prompted twice for the price if the Verify option was set properly.
☐ Save the drawing as A:EX22-1

CONTROLLING THE ATTRIBUTE DISPLAY　　ARM 10

Attributes are meant to contain valuable information about the blocks in your drawings. This information is normally not displayed on the screen or during plotting. Its principal function is to generate materials lists and to speed accounting. Use the DTEXT command for specific labels. You can control the display of attributes on the screen using the ATTDISP command.

Command: **ATTDISP** ↵
Normal/ON/OFF ⟨Normal⟩:

The Normal mode displays attributes exactly as you created them. This is the default mode for ATTDISP. The ON option displays *all* attributes. The OFF position suppresses all attributes.

```
┌─────────────────── PROFESSIONAL TIP ───────────────────┐
│                                                         │
│     After attributes have been drawn, added to blocks, and checked for correctness, hide them │
│  by turning off ATTDISP. If left on, they clutter the screen and lengthen regeneration time.  │
│                                                         │
└─────────────────────────────────────────────────────────┘
```

CHANGING ATTRIBUTE VALUES   [ARM 10]

Attributes can be edited with normal editing commands before they are included in a block. Once the block is created, the attributes are part of it and must be changed using the ATTEDIT command found in the EDIT screen menu, or by typing "ATTEDIT" as follows:

    Command: **ATTEDIT** ↵
    Edit attributes one at a time? ⟨Y⟩

This prompt asks if you want to edit attributes individually. It is possible to change the same attribute on several insertions of the same block. Pressing ENTER at this prompt allows you to select any number of different attributes. AutoCAD lets you edit them all, one at a time, without leaving the ATTEDIT command. If you respond with "N" (NO), you may change specific letters, words, and values of a single attribute. This can affect all insertions of the same block. For example, suppose a block named RESISTOR was inserted on a drawing in 12 places. However, you misspelled the attribute as RESISTER. Answer "N" to the "Edit attributes one at a time" prompt. This is a "global" attribute editing method.

Each ATTEDIT technique allows you to determine the exact block and attribute specifications to edit. These prompts appear:

    Block name specification ⟨*⟩:
    Attribute tag specification ⟨*⟩:
    Attribute value specification ⟨*⟩:

To selectively edit attribute values, respond to the prompt with a name or value. Suppose you enter an attribute and receive the following message:

    0 attributes selected. *Invalid*

You have picked an attribute that was not specified. It is often quicker to press ENTER for the three specification prompts and then *pick* the attribute you need to edit.

Editing several insertions of the same attribute

A situation may occur when a block having a wrong or misspelled attribute is inserted several times. For example, in Fig. 22-4 the VALVE block was inserted three times with the manufacturer's name as CRANE. Unfortunately, the name was supposed to be POWELL. Select AT-TEDIT and respond in the following manner.

    Command: **ATTEDIT** ↵
    Edit attributes one at a time? ⟨Y⟩ **N** ↵
    Global edit of attribute values.
    Edit only attributes visible on screen? ⟨Y⟩: ↵
    Block name specification ⟨*⟩: ↵
    Attribute tag specification ⟨*⟩: ↵
    Attribute value specification ⟨*⟩: ↵
    Select attributes: *(pick CRANE on all VALVE blocks and press ENTER when completed)*
    (N) attributes selected. *(N equals the number of attributes picked)*
    String to change: **CRANE** ↵ *(words or characters to change)*
    New string: **POWELL** ↵

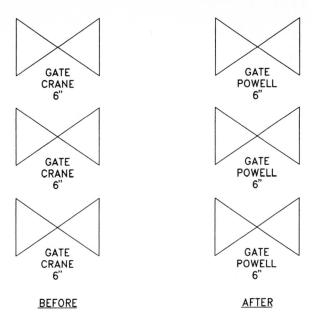

Fig. 22-4. Global editing changes the same attribute on several block insertions.

After pressing ENTER, CRANE attributes on the blocks selected are changed to read POWELL.

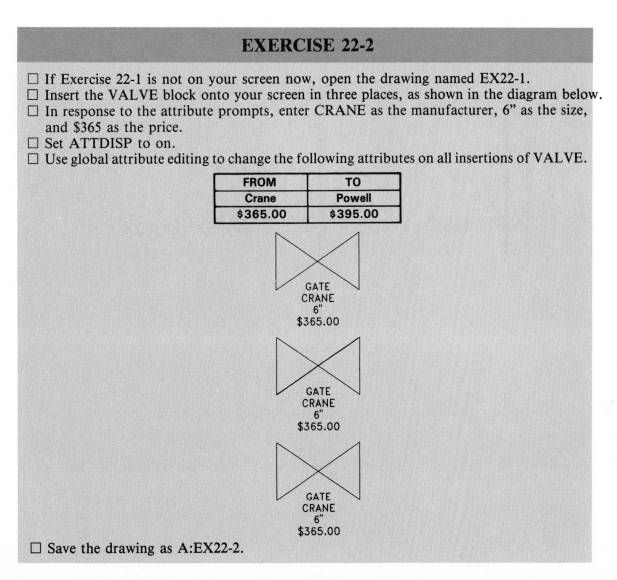

EXERCISE 22-2

☐ If Exercise 22-1 is not on your screen now, open the drawing named EX22-1.
☐ Insert the VALVE block onto your screen in three places, as shown in the diagram below.
☐ In response to the attribute prompts, enter CRANE as the manufacturer, 6" as the size, and $365 as the price.
☐ Set ATTDISP to on.
☐ Use global attribute editing to change the following attributes on all insertions of VALVE.

FROM	TO
Crane	Powell
$365.00	$395.00

☐ Save the drawing as A:EX22-2.

━━━━━━━━━━━ PROFESSIONAL TIP ━━━━━━━━━━━

When creating attributes, use care when assigning the "Constant" option. An attribute with the Constant setting cannot be changed using ATTEDIT. The block must be redefined. Assign Constant to only those attributes you know will not change.

Editing different attributes one at a time

Global editing is a more precise method of changing specific attributes and text strings. On the other hand, individual editing allows you to change any value on any attribute. Many attributes and text strings can be done without leaving the ATTEDIT command. After you answer "Y" to the Edit attributes one at a time prompt, and press ENTER for the three "specification" options, select the attributes. Press ENTER when you are finished; then this prompt appears:

> (N) attributes selected.
> Value/Position/Height/Angle/Style/Layer/Color/Next ⟨N⟩:

With this prompt, a small "X" appears at the lower-left corner of the first attribute in the last block selected. The order in which attributes were selected is shown in Fig. 22-5A. The order in which AutoCAD picks them for editing is shown in Fig. 22-5B. The "X" indicates the attribute that is being edited. The Next option is the default. Pressing ENTER causes the "X" to jump to the next attribute in sequence. The "X" does not jump to the next attribute automatically after you make a change. It remains in case you want to make more than one change to the attribute.

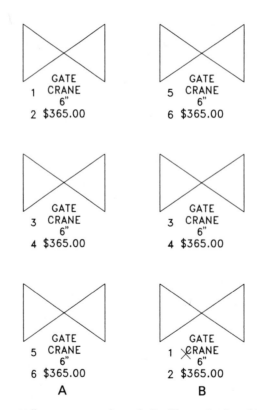

Fig. 22-5. A—The order attributes were selected. B—The order in which AutoCAD edits them.

All attribute editing options are displayed in the screen menu. Prompts for each are:
- **Value**—"Change or Replace? ⟨R⟩:" Pressing ENTER here indicates you want to replace the attribute. AutoCAD requests a new attribute value. You can change any part of the attribute by typing "C" for Change. AutoCAD responds with String to change and New string prompts. A string is any sequence of consecutive characters.
- **Position**—"Enter text insertion point:"
- **Height**—"New height ⟨0.20⟩:"

- **Angle** — "New rotation angle ⟨0⟩:"
- **Style** — "Text style: (current)
          New style or ENTER for no change:"
- **Layer** — "New layer ⟨current⟩:"
- **Color** — "New color ⟨BYLAYER⟩:"

Individual editing of attributes can be used to correct misspelled words, replace a word, or change the attribute information. Look at the attributes attached to the block in Fig. 22-6. The manufacturer was changed from POWELL to CRANE. The price was changed from $489.00 to $498.00. Suppose these are the only two attributes to be edited. The entire command sequence looks like this:

Command: **ATTEDIT** ⏎
Edit attributes one at a time? ⟨N⟩ **Y** ⏎
Select Attributes: *(select the two attributes)*
2 attributes selected. *(the ''X'' appears at POWELL, the first attribute selected)*
Value/Position/Height/Angle/Style/Layer/Color/Next ⟨N⟩: **V** ⏎
Change or Replace? ⟨R⟩: **R** ⏎
New attribute value: **CRANE**
Value/Position/Height/Angle/Style/Layer/Color/Next ⟨N⟩: ⏎ *(pressing ENTER moves the ''X'' to the next attribute, $489.00)*
Value/Position/Height/Angle/Style/Layer/Color/Next ⟨N⟩: **V** ⏎
Change or Replace? ⟨R⟩: **C** ⏎
String to change: **89** ⏎
New string: **98** ⏎
Value/Position/Height/Angle/Style/Layer/Color/Next ⟨N⟩: ⏎ *(press ENTER at this prompt to get out of the ATTEDIT command and see the final change take place)*

The completed attribute edit is shown in Fig. 22-6C.

Fig. 22-6. The attributes to be changed are indicated with an ''X.''

— PROFESSIONAL TIP —

When making blocks that contain attributes, add as many attributes you think will be needed. If you do not have values for some of them, just enter "TO COME" as the value, or enter something to remind you that information is needed. Adding an attribute to a block is much more time-consuming than changing an attribute using the ATTEDIT command.

EXERCISE 22-3

☐ Load AutoCAD and open drawing EX22-2 if it is not already on screen.
☐ Be sure there are three insertions of the VALVE block. Align them as shown in the diagram below.
☐ Set ATTDISP to on to display all attributes.
☐ Select the ATTEDIT command and choose the individual edit option.
☐ Assuming the blocks are numbered 1 to 3, top to bottom, change the individual attributes to the following values:

	1	2	3
Type	Gate	Gate	Gate
Mfgr.	Crane	Powell	Jenkins
Size	4"	8"	10"
Price	$289.00	$470.95	$685.00

☐ Connect the valves with straight lines as shown.
☐ Save the drawing as A:EX22-3.

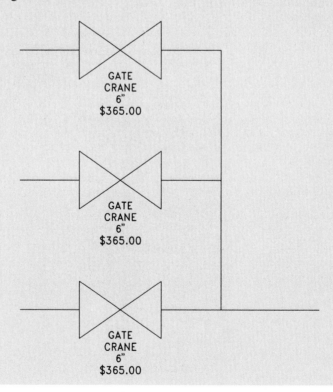

EDITING ATTRIBUTES USING A DIALOGUE BOX

The DDATTE (Dynamic Dialogue ATTribute Editing) command allows you to edit attributes in a dialogue box. You can edit single blocks or use the MULTIPLE command to edit as many block attributes as needed.

Editing attributes in a single block

If attributes in one block need editing, enter DDATTE and select the block as follows:

Command: **DDATTE** ↵
Select block: *(select block)*

The "Edit Attributes" dialogue box appears on screen, Fig. 22-7. The attributes of the selected block are listed on the left. Their current values are shown in the edit boxes on the right. Move the cursor to the value to be edited and double click so the box is highlighted, and enter the new value. Remember, that if you pick the box, you can move the cursor to the incorrect letter, then use the delete key to remove a letter, type to insert characters, or use BACKSPACE to delete. You can then pick CANCEL or OK, or you can press ENTER to move to the next attribute. If CANCEL is picked, the attribute value is left unchanged. When finished, pick OK at the bottom of the dialogue box. The attribute associated with the block is changed. If CANCEL is picked, no changes are made and the drawing is redisplayed.

```
┌─────────────────────────────────────────────────────┐
│                   Edit Attributes                     │
│ Block name: VALVE                                     │
│                                                       │
│ Enter the price:        ┌──────────────────────────┐ │
│                         │$365                      │ │
│ Enter the size:         ┌──────────────────────────┐ │
│                         │6"                        │ │
│ Enter the valve manufac ┌──────────────────────────┐ │
│                         │CRANE                     │ │
│ TYPE                    ┌──────────────────────────┐ │
│                         │GATE                      │ │
│                         ┌──────────────────────────┐ │
│                         └──────────────────────────┘ │
│                         ┌──────────────────────────┐ │
│                         └──────────────────────────┘ │
│                         ┌──────────────────────────┐ │
│                         └──────────────────────────┘ │
│                         ┌──────────────────────────┐ │
│                         └──────────────────────────┘ │
│                         ┌──────────────────────────┐ │
│                         └──────────────────────────┘ │
│                         ┌──────────────────────────┐ │
│                         └──────────────────────────┘ │
│   [ OK ]  [Cancel]  [Previous]  [Next]  [Help...]    │
└─────────────────────────────────────────────────────┘
```

Fig. 22-7. The "Edit Attributes" dialogue box displays all of the attributes assigned to the selected block.

Editing multiple blocks

The process for editing attributes in several blocks is much like that for editing single blocks. Simply add the MULTIPLE command.

Command: **MULTIPLE DDATTE** ↵
Select block: *(select the block or blocks)*

The "Edit Attributes" dialogue box appears with the existing attributes. Edit the attributes as before and select OK when finished. The next prompt appears:

DDATTE Select block: *(select block)*

This command repeats until you cancel the command.

When editing attributes using the dialogue box, keep in mind that the attribute value can have up to 256 characters. The maximum number of characters that will be displayed in the edit box is 32. The attribute prompt is limited to 23 characters in the dialogue box for display purposes only. Longer attribute prompts entered remain intact in the drawing file.

ATTRIBUTE SYSTEM VARIABLES $\boxed{\textbf{ARM 10}}$

Two system variables allow you to control whether attribute prompts are displayed. If they are, the manner in which the prompts appear can also be modified. The ATTREQ (ATTribute REQuest) variable controls the use of attribute prompting. The ATTDIA (ATTribute DIAlogue) variable determines whether normal command line prompting is used or dialogue boxes are displayed.

COLLECTING ATTRIBUTE INFORMATION $\boxed{\textbf{ARM 10}}$

AutoCAD provides a method for listing attributes associated with any specified blocks. It is helpful for tabulating block information. This method involves creating a special "template file." This file is a list of attributes that can be used in a bill of materials by third-party packages, or in databases. It is used with drawings that contain specific blocks and attributes you wish to list. Selecting ATTEXT creates an "extract file" that allows AutoCAD to find and list the attributes specified in the template file. This extract file can display the attributes on the screen or send them to a printer.

Creating a template file

You often need to be selective in the blocks and attributes that are listed. This requires guidelines for AutoCAD to use when sorting through a drawing. To pick out specific block attributes, these guidelines are in the form of a *template file*. The AutoCAD template file allows you to pick out specific items from blocks and list them. First, you have to make the template file.

The template file, a simple text file, can be made using database, word processing, or text editor programs. The text editor that resides in DOS, is discussed in Chapter 29.

In addition to listing attributes, the template file can be designed to extract block properties. Those include:

- **Level** — This refers to the nesting level of the block. If the block was nested inside another block, this number would be "2" in the extracted list.
- **Name** — Block name.
- **X** — The X coordinate location of the block insertion point.
- **Y** — The Y coordinate location of the block insertion point.
- **Layer** — Layer name.
- **Orient** — Rotation angle of the block.
- **XScale** — The X coordinate scale factor of the block.
- **YScale** — The Y coordinate scale factor of the block.

PROFESSIONAL TIP

Your application determines which properties need to be included in the template file. Template files can be created for different groups or departments of a company. The following chart lists possible attributes for a desk in the left column. Across the top are several different departments in a company. An "X" indicates which item is to be included in that department's template file.

ATTRIBUTE	SHIPPING	PURCHASING	ACCOUNTING	ENGINEERING
Manufacturer		X	X	
Size	X	X		X
Price		X	X	
Weight	X			X
Color		X		X
Material	X	X		X

The example template file shown below could be used to extract information from the piping flow diagram in Exercise 22-3.

```
BL:NAME      C010000
BL:LAYER     C005000
BL:X         N008002
BL:Y         N008002
BLANK        C004000
MFGR         C010000
SIZE         C008000
PRICE        C010000
```

You would write this file using database or text editing programs such as EDLIN or the DOS text editor. Notice that the items that are block characteristics begin with BL:. The items that are block attributes are given the name used at the Attribute tag: prompt of the ATTDEF command. The item BLANK is placed in the file to provide spacing between the Y coordinates and MFGR. Had this been omitted there would be no line space between those two items.

The numbers in the right column all begin with either C or N. The C indicates that character information is to be extracted and N represents numerical information. If a character other than a number is included in an attribute, use C instead of N. Notice that the PRICE attribute uses C. That is because the dollar symbol ($) is used in front of the price in the attribute.

The first three numbers after the C or N character indicate the number of spaces allotted for the attribute. There are ten spaces allotted for MFGR. The following three digits specify the number of decimal places in the attribute. The X and Y locations have been assigned two decimal places. This is detailed in Fig. 22-8.

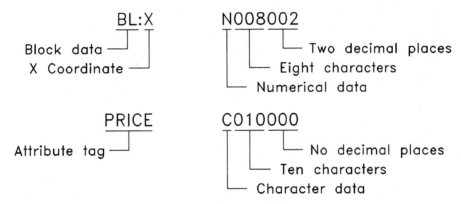

Fig. 22-8. Template file showing numerical and character entries.

EXERCISE 22-4

☐ This exercise steps you through the construction of a template file for drawing EX22-3. The DOS line editor program EDLIN can be used to create the file.

☐ Open drawing EX22-3 if it is not already on your screen.

☐ At the Command: prompt, type the following. Be sure to enter the file name correctly. EDLIN does not give you another chance to change it.

> Command: **EDIT** ⏎
> File to edit: **EX22-3.TXT** ⏎
> New file
> *

☐ You are now in the DOS EDLIN program. The asterisk (*) is the EDLIN prompt. It is displayed on the current line. Do not type it. Enter "i" at the prompt to instruct EDLIN to begin inserting new lines of text at line 1. Press ENTER at the end of each line. Enter the remainder of the file as follows. Do not put a space at the end of a line:

> *i ⏎
> 1:*BL:NAME   C010000 ⏎
> 2:*BL:LAYER   C005000 ⏎
> 3:*BL:X   N008002 ⏎
> 4:*BL:Y   N008002 ⏎
> 5:*BLANK   C004000 ⏎
> 6:*MFGR   C010000 ⏎
> 7:*SIZE   C008000 ⏎
> 8:*PRICE   C010000 ⏎
> 9:*^C
> *L ⏎

☐ Line 8 is the last line of the file. On line 9, cancel the command by pressing Ctrl/C. Enter "L" to list the file. Check it carefully for errors. Then save the file by entering:

> *E ⏎

☐ The file is automatically saved using the name you gave it at the beginning of the session.

Listing block attributes

AutoCAD provides three different formats for listing extracted information. The *DXF format* is related to programming and is the most complex. See the AutoCAD Customization Manual, Chapter 11 for a discussion of the DXF format. The other two—SDF and CDF—are formats that can be used with a variety of other programs. The *SDF (Space Delimited Format)* is the easiest for the average user to interpret. It means that the different *fields*, or groups of data are separated by spaces. The *CDF (Comma Delimited Format)* uses commas instead of spaces to separate fields.

Select the ATTEXT command found in the UTILITY screen menu. Specify the format you want or type "E" to list the attributes of specific entities. At this point, select the SDF format. The response here needs to be only the first letter.

> Command: **ATTEXT** ⏎
> CDF, SDF, or DXF Attribute extract (or Entities)? ⟨C⟩: **S** ⏎

The "Select Template File" dialogue box is then displayed. Select the file you wish to use from the Files: list box. Note in Fig. 22-9 that the file named EX22-4.TXT is selected. Pick OK, and then the "Create extract file" dialogue box appears. If you wish to have the extracted attributes saved in a file, enter a name in the File: edit box. The current drawing name is the default. Be sure the extract file name you enter is slightly different than the template file name, for example, EX22-4A.TXT. See Fig. 22-10. If you use the same name, your original template file will

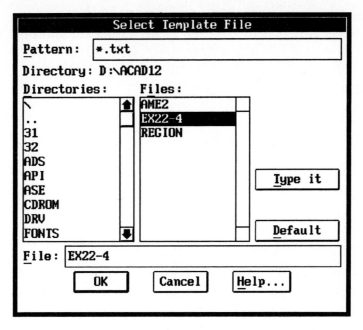

Fig. 22-9. The ''Select Template File'' dialogue box allows you to choose a file from a list box.

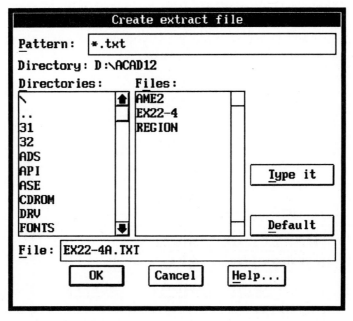

Fig. 22-10. An extract file name selected from the ''Create extract file'' dialogue box.

be deleted. Pick OK after entering the file name. If all goes well, AutoCAD prompts that you have "n records in extract file." The number of records listed in the file is based on the number of blocks that contain the attributes you were searching for.

─── **PROFESSIONAL TIP** ───

The extract file can be displayed on the text screen by using the DOS TYPE command, or can be sent to a printer with the DOS PRINT command as follows:

```
C:\ACAD12> TYPE EX22-4A.TXT ↵
C:\ACAD12> PRINT EX22-4A.TXT ↵
```

When the "Create extract file" dialogue box is on screen, you can have an immediate screen display of the extracted attributes by entering "CON" in the File edit box. You can also pick the Type it button and enter "CON" (console) or "PRN" (printer) at the Extract file name: prompt to send the contents of the extract file to the console or to the printer as follows:

Extract file name ⟨drawing name⟩: **CON** ↵

The list should be displayed as:

VALVE 0	14.50	16.00	CRANE	4″	$289.00
VALVE 0	14.50	17.50	POWELL	8″	$470.95
VALVE 0	14.50	14.40	JENKINS	10″	$685.00

If you select the CDF format at the initial ATTEXT prompt, the extract listing will look like this:

'VALVE','0',14.50,16.00,'','Crane','4''','$289.00'
'VALVE','0',14.50,17.50,'','POWELL','8''','$470.95'
'VALVE','0',14.50,14.40,'','JENKINS','10''','$685.00,

The CDF format, of the three discussed, appears the most cumbersome. Yet, it as well as SDF can be used with specific database programs such as dBASE. Decide which format is most suitable for your application.

Listing block attributes with the DDATTEXT command

The DDATTEXT command enables you to use dialogue boxes for all steps in the attribute extraction process. The "Attribute Extraction" dialogue box appears after entering the DDATT-TEXT command. See Fig. 22-11. Pick the file format, such as SDF, by selecting the appropriate radio button. If you want specific blocks in the extract file, pick the Select Objects ⟨ button, and use any selection method to pick the blocks. If you do not select objects, all blocks in the drawing (specified by the template file) will be used.

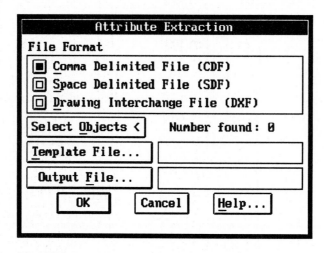

Fig. 22-11. The DDATTEXT command displays the "Attribute Extraction" dialogue box.

Pick the Template File... button to select a file name from the "Template File" dialogue box. This dialogue box is exactly the same as the one in Fig. 22-9. The output file, or extract file, can be selected by picking the Output File... button. This displays the "Output File" dialogue box, which is exactly the same the "Create extract file" dialogue box shown in Fig. 22-10.

If you want the contents of the output file displayed on the screen, type "CON" in the Output file edit box, or if you want the file sent to the printer, type "PRN."

The bill of materials listing discussed in this chapter is a basic list of each block's selected attributes. As you become familiar with AutoCAD, customize it to meet your needs. Study magazines devoted to AutoCAD and read the *AutoCAD Resource Guide*. You will find numerous software packages that generate specialized bills of materials containing quantities and totals, rather than just a list of blocks.

EXERCISE 22-5

☐ Open EX22-4 if it is not already on your screen.
☐ Select the ATTEXT command and enter SDF format.
☐ Enter the template file name as EX22-4. Enter EX22-4A for the extract file name.
☐ Select ATTEXT again and display the bill of materials on the screen.

CHAPTER TEST

Write your answers in the spaces provided.

1. Define an "attribute." _____

2. Explain the purpose of the ATTDEF command. _____

   _____

3. Define the function of the following four ATTDEF modes:

   A. Invisible — _____

   B. Constant — _____

   _____

   C. Verify — _____

   _____

   D. Preset — _____

4. What attribute information does the ATTDEF command request? _____

   _____

   _____

5. List the three options for the ATTDISP command. _____

   _____

6. What is meant by "global" attribute editing? _____

   _____

7. How does individual attribute editing differ from global editing? _____

   _____

   _____

   _____

8. Identify the purpose of the following two prompts in the global attribute editing routine.

   String to change: _____

   New string: _____

9. List the different aspects of the attribute that you can change when you edit attributes one
   at a time. _____

10. Which command allows you to use a dialogue box to create attributes? _____

11. Explain the function of the DDATTE command. _____

   _____

12. What occurs if you enter MULTIPLE DDATTE at the Command: prompt? _____
    _____

13. What purpose does the ATTREQ system variable serve? _____
    _____

14. To enter attributes using the dialogue box, you must set the ATTDIA system variable to
    _____.

15. When created, a drawing extract file is given the file extension _____.

16. The command that allows you to create the file type mentioned in Question 15 is
    _____.

17. How is character and numerical data specified in a template file? _____
    _____

18. What would you type at the Extract file name: prompt to display the extracted attributes
    on the screen? _____

19. How many characters are allowed for an attribute name in the template file? _____
    _____

20. How do you create a template file? _____
    _____

21. Define all of the aspects of each of the following template file entries.
    BL:X
    N006002
    PRICE
    C010003

22. Describe the difference between CDF and SDF attribute extract formats. _____
    _____

23. The first time you create a file using the ATTEXT command, it is given a _____
    extension.

24. Suppose you have used the ATTEXT command a second time. To display on screen the
    bill of materials, what do you enter at the following prompt?
    Extract file name ⟨drawing name⟩: _____

DRAWING PROBLEMS

1. Load AutoCAD and start a new drawing named P22-1. Draw the structural steel wide flange
   shape shown on the next page using the dimensions given. Do not dimension the drawing.
   Create attributes for the drawing using the information given. Make a block of the drawing
   and name it W12X40. Insert the block once to test the attributes.

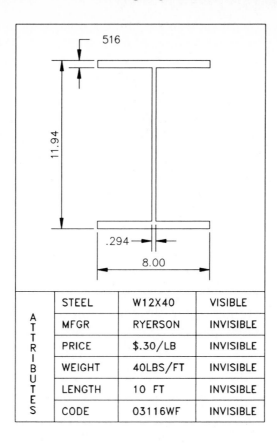

A T T R I B U T E S	STEEL	W12X40	VISIBLE
	MFGR	RYERSON	INVISIBLE
	PRICE	$.30/LB	INVISIBLE
	WEIGHT	40LBS/FT	INVISIBLE
	LENGTH	10 FT	INVISIBLE
	CODE	03116WF	INVISIBLE

2. Load the drawing in Problem 1 (P22-1) and construct the floor plan shown using the dimensions given at a scale of 1/4″ = 1′-0″. Dimension the drawing. Insert the block W12X40 six times as shown. Required attribute data is given in the chart below the drawing. Enter the appropriate information for the attributes as you are prompted for it. Note that the steel columns labeled 3 and 6 require slightly different attribute data. You can speed the drawing process by using MINSERT, ARRAY, or COPY. Save the drawing as A:P22-2.

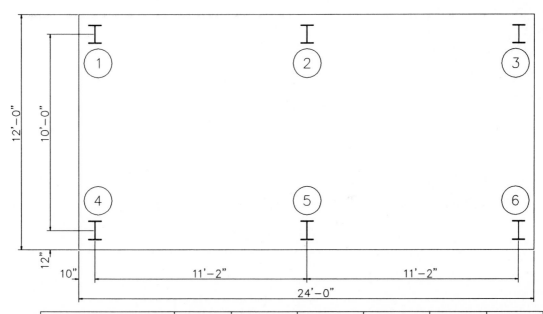

	STEEL	MFGR	PRICE	WEIGHT	LENGTH	CODE
BLOCKS 1, 2, 4 & 5	W12X40	RYERSON	$.30/LB	40LB/FT	10′	03116WF
BLOCKS 3 & 6	W12X31	RYERSON	$.29/LB	31LB/FT	8.5′	03125WF

3. Load Problem 2 (P22-2) into the drawing editor. Create a template file for use in extracting the data from structural steel blocks inserted in Problem 2. Use the following information in your template file:

ITEM	CHARACTERS	DECIMAL PLACES
Block name	8	0
Tag	8	0
Mfgr	20	0
Price	12	0
Weight	8	0
Length	6	1
Code	8	0

Use the ATTEXT command to create a listing of the attribute information. When using ATTEXT, give the extract file a slightly different name than the template file. If not, your template file will be converted into the extract file. Using a different name enables you to easily revise the template file to extract different information.

The extract file that is created from Problem 2 should appear as follows:

W12X40	RYERSON	$.30/LB	40LB/FT	10FT	03116WF
W12X40	RYERSON	$.30/LB	40LB/FT	10FT	03116WF
W12X40	RYERSON	$.30/LB	40LB/FT	10FT	03116WF
W12X40	RYERSON	$.30/LB	40LB/FT	10FT	03116WF
W12X31	RYERSON	$.29/LB	31LB/FT	8.5FT	03125WF
W12X31	RYERSON	$.29/LB	31LB/FT	8.5FT	03125WF

4. Select one of your drawings from Chapter 21 and create a bill of materials for it using the template file method and the ATTEXT command. Follow these guidelines.
   A. The template file should list all of the attributes of each block in the drawing.
   B. Use the SDF format to display the file.
   C. Display the file on the screen.

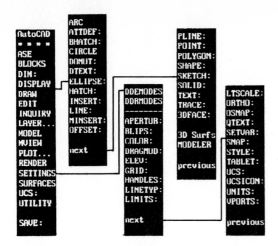

Chapter 23

ISOMETRIC DRAWING

Learning objectives

After completing this chapter, you will be able to:

☐ Understand the nature of isometric and oblique views.
☐ Set an isometric grid and construct isometric objects.
☐ Create isometric text styles.
☐ Demonstrate isometric and oblique dimensioning techniques.

Three-dimensional visualization and drawing are skills that every drafter, designer, and engineer should possess. This is especially important now that most CAD systems support 3-D modeling. However, be aware that there is a distinct difference between drawing a three-dimensional looking view and a true 3-D model. Once a 3-D model is made, it can be rotated on the display screen to view from any angle. The computer actually calculates the points, lines, and surfaces of the object in space. The topic of 3-D is presented in Chapters 24 and 25. This chapter focuses on creating three-dimensional *looking* views using two-dimensional entities and some special AutoCAD functions.

PICTORIAL DRAWING OVERVIEW

The word "pictorial" means "like a picture." It refers to any realistic form of drawing. Pictorial drawings show height, width, and depth. Several forms of pictorial drawing are used in industry today. The simplest and least realistic is *oblique*. The most realistic is *perspective. Isometric* drawing falls midway between the two in terms of realism.

Oblique drawings

An oblique drawing shows objects with one or more parallel faces having true shape and size. A scale is selected for the orthographic, or front faces. Then, an angle for the depth or receding axis is chosen. Three types of oblique drawing are used: *cavalier, cabinet*, and *general*, Fig. 23-1. They vary in the angle and scale of the receding axis. Both cavalier and cabinet drawings use an angle of 45°. The cabinet view receding axis is drawn at half scale and a cavalier's is at full scale. The general oblique is normally drawn at an angle other than 45° and at 3/4 scale.

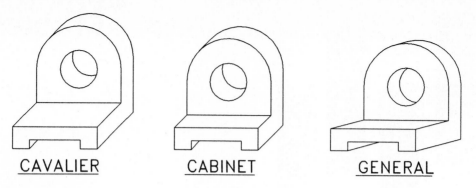

Fig. 23-1. The three types of oblique drawing differ in the scale and angle of the receding axis.

Isometric drawings

Isometric drawings are more realistic than obliques. The entire object appears to have been tilted toward or away from the viewer. The word "isometric" means equal measure. This equal measure refers to the angle between the three axes, 120°, after the object has been tilted. The tilt angle is 35°16'. This is shown in Fig. 23-2. The angle of 120° is cumbersome to measure so an angle of 30° from horizontal is used when laying out the drawing. When constructing isometric drawings, remember that lines parallel in the orthogonal views must be parallel in the isometric view.

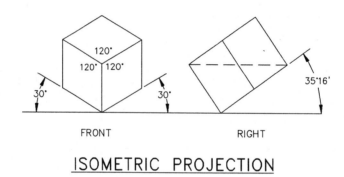

ISOMETRIC PROJECTION

Fig. 23-2. An object is tilted 35°16' to achieve an isometric view having 120° between the three axes.

The most appealing aspect of isometric drawing is that all three axis lines can be measured using the same scale. This saves time, while still producing a pleasing pictorial representation of the object. This type of drawing is produced when you use the Isometric option of the SNAP command, which is detailed later.

Closely related to isometric drawing is *dimetric* and *trimetric*. These forms of pictorial drawing differ from isometric in the scales used to measure the three axes. Dimetric drawing uses two different scales, whereas trimetric uses three scales. The use of different scales is an effort to create *foreshortening*. The length of the sides appears to recede. The relationship between isometric, dimetric, and trimetric drawings is illustrated in Fig. 23-3.

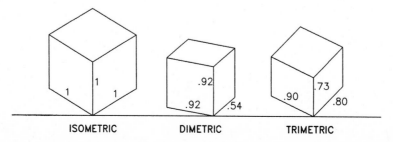

Fig. 23-3. Isometric, dimetric, and trimetric differ in the number of scales used to draw the three axes.

Perspective drawings

The most realistic form of pictorial drawing is perspective. This is done with the aid of *vanishing points*. The eye naturally sees objects in perspective. Look down a long hall and note that the wall and floor lines seem to converge at an imaginary point in the distance. That is the vanishing point. The most common types of perspective drawing are *one-point* and *two-point*. These forms of pictorial drawing are often used in architecture, and somewhat in the automotive and aircraft industries. Examples of one- and two-point perspectives are shown in Fig. 23-4.

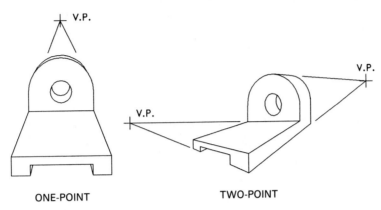

ONE-POINT   TWO-POINT

Fig. 23-4. Examples of one- and two-point perspective.

ISOMETRIC DRAWING

ARM 9

The most common method of pictorial drawing used in industry is isometric. The drawing provides a single view showing three sides that can be measured using the same scale. An isometric view has no perspective and may appear somewhat distorted. Isometric axes are drawn at 30° to horizontal, as shown in Fig. 23-5.

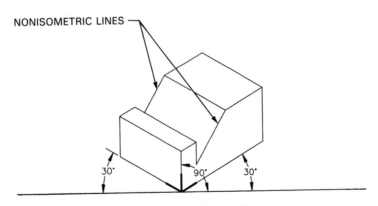

Fig. 23-5. Isometric axis layout.

The three axes shown in Fig. 23-5 represent the width, height, and depth of the object. Lines which would appear horizontal in an orthographic view are placed at a 30° angle. Lines vertical in an orthographic view are placed vertically. These are parallel to the axes. Any line parallel to the three axes can be measured and is called an *isometric line*. Lines not parallel to the axes cannot be measured and are called *nonisometric lines*. Note the two nonisometric lines in Fig. 23-5.

Circular features shown on isometric objects must be oriented properly or they will appear distorted. Fig. 23-6 shows the correct orientation of isometric circles on the three principal planes. These circles appear as ellipses on the isometric object. The small diameter of the ellipse must always align on the axis of the hole or circular feature. Notice that the centerline axes of the holes in Fig. 23-6 are parallel to one of the isometric planes.

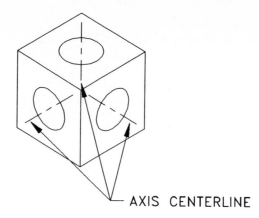

AXIS CENTERLINE

Fig. 23-6. Proper ellipse orientation on isometric planes.

A good basic rule to remember about isometric drawing is that lines parallel in an orthogonal view must be parallel in the isometric view. AutoCAD's feature makes that task, and the positioning of ellipses easy.

Setting the isometric snap

When the grid is turned on, horizontal and vertical lines of dots are displayed. To begin drawing an isometric object it is helpful to have the grid dots at an angle. The angle represents the three axis lines of the isometric layout. This is easy using the SNAP command. Enter the Style (S) option, then the Isometric (I) option. Finally, enter the vertical spacing.

> Command: **SNAP** ⏎
> Snap spacing or ON/OFF/Aspect/Rotate/Style ⟨current⟩: **S** ⏎
> Standard/Isometric ⟨S⟩: **I** ⏎
> Vertical spacing ⟨current⟩: **.25** ⏎

The grid dots on the screen change to the isometric orientation as shown in Fig. 23-7. If your grid dots are not visible, turn the grid on. Notice the crosshairs have also changed and appear

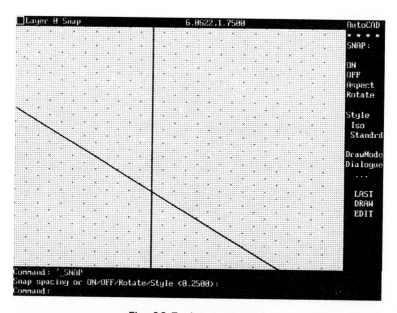

Fig. 23-7. Isometric grid.

angled. This aids you in drawing lines at the proper angles. Try drawing a four-sided surface using the LINE command. Draw it so that it appears to be the left side of a box in an isometric layout. See Fig. 23-8. To draw nonparallel surfaces, change the angle of the crosshairs to make your task easy.

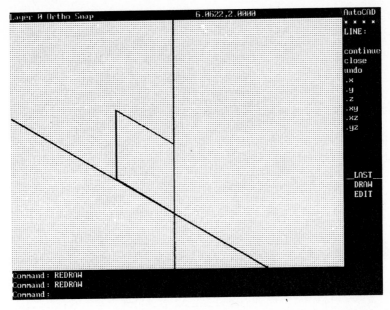

Fig. 23-8. A four-sided surface drawn with the LINE command appears to be the left side of an isometric box.

Changing the crosshairs orientation

Drawing an isometric shape is possible without ever changing the crosshairs' angle. Yet, the drawing process is easier and quicker if the angles of the crosshairs align with the axes. This is a simple task with a multibutton digitizer puck. Button 8 is a toggle for the crosshairs when the isometric snap is active. Press the button and the crosshairs immediately change to the next position. The positions are displayed on the prompt line as a reference.

Command: 〈Isoplane Left〉 〈Isoplane Top〉 〈Isoplane Right〉

The three crosshairs positions are shown in Fig. 23-9.

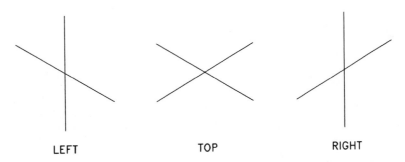

LEFT   TOP   RIGHT

Fig. 23-9. The three isometric crosshairs positions are set with the ISOPLANE command.

Another quick way to change the crosshairs' position is to use the toggle keys CTRL E. Pressing these two keys performs the same function as the puck button. The third method is to use the ISOPLANE command.

Command: **ISOPLANE** ↵
Left/Top/Right/〈Toggle〉:

Press ENTER to toggle the crosshairs to the next position. The command line displays the following message:

Current Isometric plane is: Right

You can toggle immediately to the next position by pressing ENTER at the Command: prompt and ENTER again. The prompt should now read:

Current Isometric plane is: Left

To specify the plane of orientation, type the first letter of that position:

Left/Top/Right/〈Toggle〉: **R** ↵
Current Isometric plane is: Right

The crosshairs are always in one of the isoplane positions when the isometric snap option is in effect. The one exception occurs when the Window selection option is entered for display and editing commands. The crosshairs then change to the normal vertical and horizontal positions.

Setting isometric variables with a dialogue box

You can quickly pick your isometric variables from a dialogue box. Pick Settings in the menu bar at the top of the screen. Then pick Drawing Aids. The dialogue box displayed was discussed earlier in this text. It contains the options for isometric drawing. The Isometric buttons are located at the lower right of the dialogue box. See Fig. 23-10.

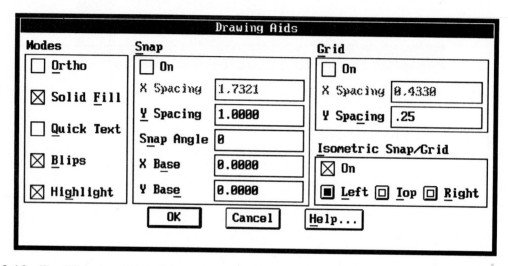

Fig. 23-10. The "Drawing Aids" dialogue box allows you to pick settings needed for isometric drawing.

To activate the isometric snap grid, pick the On check box. Notice that the X spacing for Grid and Snap are grayed out. You can only set the Y spacing for grid and snap in isometric. Three radio buttons at the lower right of the dialogue box allow you to select the isoplane orientation. Be sure to pick the On buttons for Snap and Grid if you want to turn them on. Pick OK when you have completed all of your settings.

To turn off the Isometric mode, simply select DDRMODES and pick the On check box in the isometric area. The "X" disappears, and the Isometric mode is turned off when you pick OK.

EXERCISE 23-1

☐ Start a new drawing and name it EX23-1.
☐ Set the grid spacing at .5.
☐ Set the snap style to the Isometric option. Specify .25 vertical spacing.
☐ Use the LINE command to draw the objects shown. Dimensions are given.
☐ Change the ISOPLANE orientation as needed.
☐ Save the drawing as A:EX23-1.

The isometric ellipse

Placing an isometric ellipse on an object is made easy by AutoCAD. An ellipse is positioned automatically to the current ISOPLANE setting. All you must do is pick the center point and the diameter after selecting Isocircle from the ELLIPSE command options.

Command: **ELLIPSE** ↵
⟨Axis endpoint 1⟩/Center/Isocircle: **I** ↵
Center of circle: *(pick a point)*
⟨Circle radius⟩/Diameter:

Three options are available for determining the size of the ellipse at this last prompt.
  • When DRAGMODE is on, the ellipse changes size as the cursor moves. Set the radius by picking a point.
  • Enter a numeric value and press ENTER to have AutoCAD draw the ellipse a specific radius.
  • Type "D" and you are asked for the circle's diameter. Enter a number, press ENTER, and the ellipse appears.

Always check the ISOPLANE position before locating an ellipse on your drawing. You can dynamically view the three positions that an ellipse can take. Select ELLIPSE, pick the Isocircle option, and then toggle the ISOPLANE option. See Fig. 23-11. The ellipse rotates each time you toggle the crosshairs.

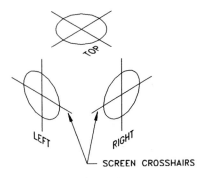

Fig. 23-11. The orientation of the isometric ellipse is determined by the ISOPLANE position.

EXERCISE 23-2

☐ Open EX23-1 if this drawing is not already on your screen.
☐ Select the ELLIPSE command to place an ellipse on the three sides of the object.
☐ Draw the ellipses in the following manner:
  1—Pick a radius of .5 using the cursor.
  2—Enter a radius of .75 at the keyboard.
  3—Type "D" and enter a diameter of .6 at the keyboard.
☐ The finished drawing should look like the example given here.
☐ Save the drawing as A:EX23-2.

Creating isometric text styles

Isometric text should appear as part of the drawing. It should not look like it was added at the last minute. Drafters and artists occasionally neglect this aspect of pictorial drawing and it shows on the final product. Text should align with the plane it applies to. This involves creating several new text styles.

Fig. 23-12 illustrates possible orientation of text on an isometric drawing. Text could be located on the object or positioned away from it as a note. These examples were done using only two text styles.

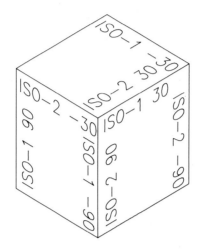

Fig. 23-12. Isometric text applications.

The text styles in Fig. 23-12 are based on styles that use a 30° or −30° obliquing angle. The labels refer to the style numbers given below. The angle shown in Fig. 23-12 indicates the rotation angle entered when using the TEXT command. The two isometric styles used are:

NAME	FONT	OBLIQUING ANGLE
ISO-1	Romans	30°
ISO-2	Romans	−30°

Find the text sample in Fig. 23-12 that says ISO-2 90. This means that the ISO-2 style was used and the text was rotated 90°. This technique can be applied to any font.

EXERCISE 23-3

☐ Load AutoCAD and open drawing EX23-1.
☐ Create one text style to label the angled (nonisometric) surface of the wedge. See the illustration.
☐ Create a second style to label the front of the wedge.
☐ Save the drawing as A:EX23-3.

Drawing solid isometric shapes

Isometric drawing can be used to produce both *wireframe* constructions and objects that appear to be solid. Wireframes are objects that you can see through, as if they were made of wire. The objects you drew in Exercise 23-1 appeared solid even though the surfaces were not colored or filled in.

Using the SOLID command, you can construct simple colored shapes that appear to be solid. Keep in mind the following points as you draw an isometric object using the SOLID command.

- The sequence of points needed to draw a rectangular shape must be correct.
- A solid fill cannot be drawn with a curved edge.
- An ellipse or circle placed on a solid surface will not open a hole in the solid shading.

The sequence you choose to pick the points is important. Fig. 23-13 shows the proper order to construct solid planes.

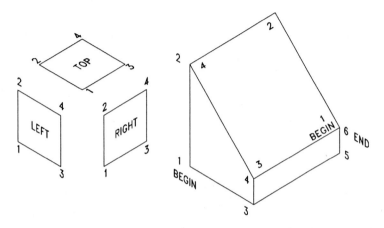

Fig. 23-13. The correct sequence of points to create solid isometric planes.

— PROFESSIONAL TIP —

Solids are drawn without the benefit of a rubberband line. Isometric snap and grids are especially helpful when creating solid surfaces.

EXERCISE 23-4

☐ Start a new drawing and name it EX23-4.
☐ Set the visible grid to .5 and isometric snap to .25.
☐ Set the colors as indicated for each side of the object. Enter the COLOR command before drawing each side with the SOLID command.
☐ Use the SOLID command to construct the object shown.
☐ Save the drawing as A:EX23-4.

ISOMETRIC DIMENSIONING

AutoCAD does not automatically dimension isometric objects. You must create isometric arrowheads and text styles. Then, manually draw the dimension lines and text as they should appear in each of the three isometric planes. This is a laborious task when compared to dimensioning two-dimensional drawings. Yet, it is much faster than manual drafting.

There are only two drawing entities you must develop in an isometric format: the arrowheads and the text styles. You have already learned how to create isometric text styles. These can be set up in an isometric prototype drawing if you draw isometrics often. The arrowheads must be drawn individually. Examples of arrows for the three isometric planes are shown in Fig. 23-14.

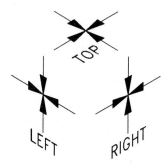

Fig. 23-14. Examples of arrowheads in each of the three isometric planes.

Arrowheads can be drawn open with the LINE command or filled in with the SOLID command. Every arrowhead does not have to be drawn individually. First, draw two isometric axes as shown in Fig. 23-15A. Then draw one arrowhead like the one shown in Fig. 23-15B. Use the MIRROR command to create additional arrows. As you create new arrows, move them to their proper plane. Save each arrowhead as a block in your isometric prototype drawing. Use block names that are easy to remember and type.

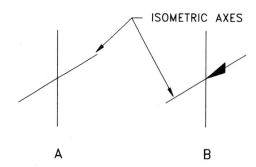

Fig. 23-15. A—Draw the two isometric axes for arrowhead placement. B—Draw the first arrowhead on one of the axis lines. Then mirror it to create others.

An important aspect of isometric dimensioning is to place dimension lines, text, and arrowheads in the proper plane. Remember these guidelines:
- The extension lines should always extend the plane being dimensioned.
- The heel of the arrowhead should always be parallel to the extension line.
- The strokes of the text that would normally be vertical should always be parallel with the extension lines or dimension lines.

These techniques, as well as a dimensioned isometric part, are shown in Fig. 23-16.

NORTHWEST/SHOALS
COMMUNITY COLLEGE

3/15/95 18:02:45   Receipt# 17174
FAR086   REGNCBS2
418-02-4067   Spring 94/95
HILL, CHRISTOPHER

BOOK STORE
DETAIL TRANSACTIONS

				Extension
AUTOCAD & ITS APPLICATIONS	1 @	35.44	Each	35.44
SUPPLIES	1 @	.97	Each	.97
SUPPLIES	1 @	13.70	Each	13.70
TOTAL TRANSACTIONS				50.11

```
PELL SUB      50.11
     TAX       4.26
PELL TOTAL    54.37
```

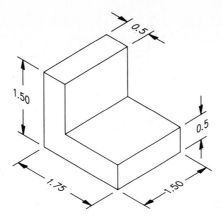

Fig. 23-16. A dimensioned isometric part. Note the text and arrowhead orientation in relation to the extension lines.

OBLIQUE DIMENSIONING

AutoCAD provides a method for semiautomatic dimensioning of oblique lines. The dimensions must already be drawn using any of the linear dimensioning commands. Fig. 23-17A illustrates an object that has been dimensioned using the ALIGNED and VERTICAL commands. The next step is to select the OBLIQUE command. OBLIQUE is a dimension editing function. Therefore, it is located in the Modify pull-down menu in the Edit dims selection. In the screen menu, pick DIM: and then Edit to locate the OBLIQUE command.

The OBLIQUE command requires that you select the dimension and enter the obliquing angle desired. It is used as follows:

Command: **DIM** ↵
Dim: **OBLIQUE** ↵
Select objects: *(pick dimension number 1)*
Enter obliquing angle (RETURN for none): **30** ↵

Fig. 23-17A shows numbers by each dimension. The following list gives the obliquing angle required for each numbered dimension in order to achieve the finished drawing shown in Fig. 23-17B.

Dimension	Obliquing angle
1	30°
2	−30°
3	30°
4	−30°
5	30°

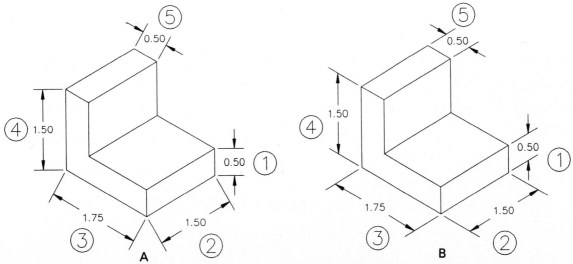

Fig. 23-17. The OBLIQUE dimensioning command requires that you select an existing dimension (shown in A) and enter the desired obliquing angle (shown in B).

This technique creates suitable dimensions for an isometric drawing, and is quicker than the previous method discussed. Bear in mind that the oblique method does not rotate the arrows so that the arrowhead heels are aligned with the extension lines, nor does it draw the dimension text aligned in the plane of the dimension.

CHAPTER TEST

Write your answers in the spaces provided.

1. The simplest form of pictorial drawing is _____.

2. How does isometric drawing differ from oblique drawing? _____

   _____

   _____

3. How do dimetric and trimetric drawings differ from isometric drawings? _____

   _____

   _____

4. The most realistic form of pictorial drawing is _____.

5. Provide the correct entries at the following prompts to set an isometric snap with a spacing

   of 0.2.

   Command: _____

   Snap spacing or ON/OFF/Aspect/Rotate/Style ⟨current⟩: _____

   Standard/Isometric ⟨S⟩: _____

   Vertical spacing ⟨current⟩: _____

6. What function does the ISOPLANE command perform? _____

   _____

   _____

7. The pull-down menu that contains the "Drawing Aids" dialogue box is _____.

8. What factor determines the orientation of an isometric ellipse? _____

   _____

9. List the three methods to define the size of an isometric ellipse. _____

   _____

   _____

10. Which aspect of the TEXT Style option allows you to create text that can be used on an

    isometric drawing? _____

11. You can create angled surfaces in an isometric drawing using the SOLID command. True

    or false? _____

12. What technique does AutoCAD provide for dimensioning isometric objects? _____

    _____

13. What value must you enter to achieve the kind of dimensioning referred to in question 12?

    _____

DRAWING PROBLEMS

1-13. Before drawing any of the objects, create an isometric prototype drawing. Then use the prototype to construct each isometric drawing. Items that should be set in the prototype include: grid spacing, snap spacing, ortho setting, and text size. Save the prototype as ISOPROTO. Use ISOPROTO as the prototype drawing for the following isometric drawings. Save the drawings as A:P23-(problem number).

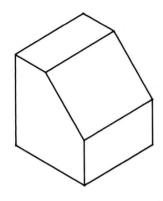

P23-1.

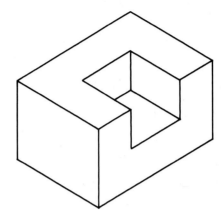

P23-4.

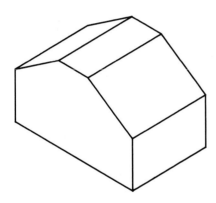

P23-2.

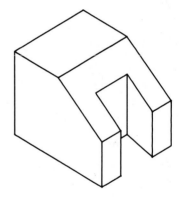

P23-5.

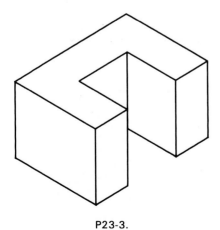

P23-3.

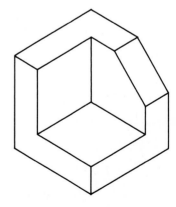

P23-6.

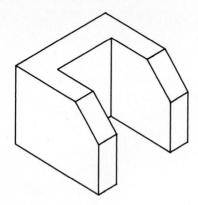

P23-7.

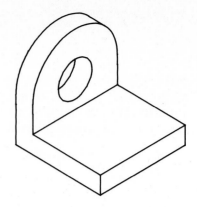

P23-11.

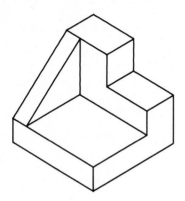

P23-8.

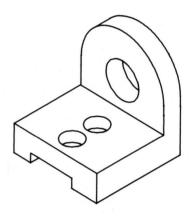

P23-12.

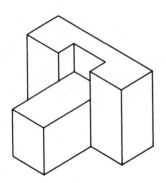

P23-9.

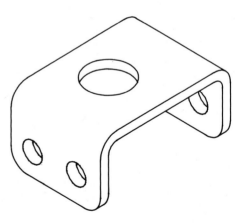

P23-13.

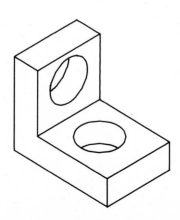

P23-10.

14-17. Create isometric drawings using the views shown.

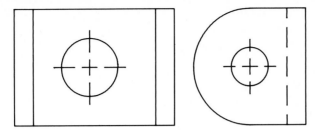

P23-14.

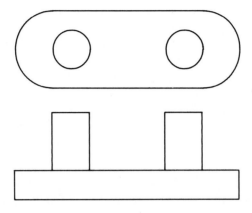

P23-15.

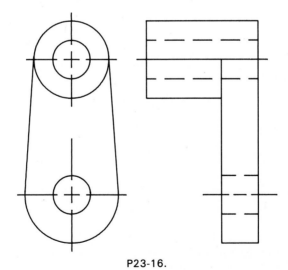

P23-16.

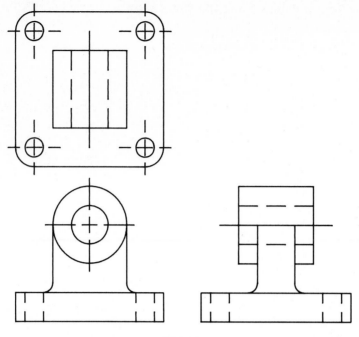

P23-17.

18. Construct a set of isometric arrowheads to use when dimensioning isometric drawings. Load your isometric prototype (ISOPROTO). Create arrowheads for each of the three isometric planes. Save each arrowhead as a block. Name them with the first letter indicating the plane: T for top, L for left, and R for right. Also number them clockwise from the top. See the example for the right isometric plane. Save the prototype again when finished.

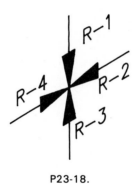

P23-18.

19. Create a set of isometric text styles like those shown in Fig. 23-12. Load your prototype drawing; make one complete set in one font. Make additional sets in other fonts if you wish. Enter a text height of 0 so that you can specify the height when placing the text. Save the prototype again when finished.
20. Begin a new drawing named P23-20 using your prototype. Select one of the following problems to dimension fully: 2, 6, 10, 11, or 12. When adding dimensions, be sure to use the proper arrowhead and text style for the plane in which you are working. Save the drawing when completed.

Chapter 24

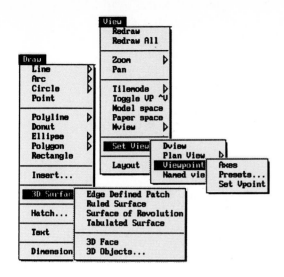

THREE-DIMENSIONAL DRAWING AND SURFACE MODELING

Learning objectives

After completing this chapter, you will be able to:

☐ Understand the nature and function of rectangular, spherical, and cylindrical 3-D coordinate systems.

☐ Understand the "right-hand rule" of 3-D visualization.

☐ Construct extruded and wireframe 3-D shapes.

☐ Display 3-D objects at any desired viewpoint.

☐ Use 3-D shapes to create a surface model design.

☐ Create a "solid-looking" model with surfacing techniques.

☐ Edit 3-D objects.

Computers are especially suited to handle information about points in space. However, in order for computer software to accept and use this information, the drafter or designer must first have good 3-D visualization skills. These skills include the ability to see an object in three dimensions, to visualize it rotating in space, and to imagine what it is like to be inside the object and look out. These skills can be obtained by using 3-D techniques to construct objects, and by trying to see two-dimensional sketches and drawings as 3-D models. This chapter discusses several aspects of 3-D drawing and visualization.

3-D COORDINATE SYSTEMS

AutoCAD allows you to enter 3-D coordinates in three different formats. Using the standard *rectangular coordinate system*, you can enter a Z value for the thickness of an object. *Spherical coordinates* are similar to longitude and latitude. You can enter a distance from the origin (the center of the earth), an angle in the XY plane (longitude), and another angle up or down from the XY plane (latitude). *Cylindrical coordinates* are similar to spherical, but instead of latitude, you can enter a Z distance. The following discussion is an introduction to the different 3-D coordinate entry systems.

Cartesian (rectangular) coordinates

A computer can draw lines because it knows the X and Y values of the endpoints. The line does not really exist in the computer, only the points do. You see one plane and two dimensions in 2-D drawing. However, when drawing in 3-D you add another plane and coordinate axis. You define the third dimension with a third coordinate measured along the Z axis. A computer can only draw lines in 3-D if it knows the X, Y, and Z coordinate values of each point on the object.

Compare the 2-D coordinate system to the 3-D system in Fig. 24-1. Note that the positive values of Z in the 3-D system come up from the drawing. Consider the surface of your screen as the new Z plane. Anything behind the screen is negative Z and anything in front of the screen is positive Z.

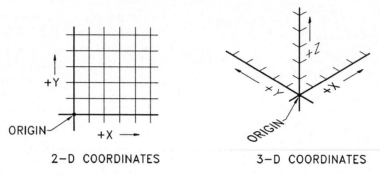

2—D COORDINATES   3—D COORDINATES

Fig. 24-1. Examples of 2-D and 3-D coordinate systems.

The shape in Fig. 24-2A is a 2-D drawing showing the top view of an object. The XY coordinate values of each point are shown, given the lower-left corner as the origin (0,0). To convert this object to its three-dimensional form, Z values are given to each vertex, or corner. Fig. 24-2B shows the object pictorially with the XYZ values of each point listed.

This same object could have been drawn using negative Z coordinates. It would extend behind the screen. Although the sign of the Z value makes no difference to AutoCAD, it is time-consuming for you to deal with negative values.

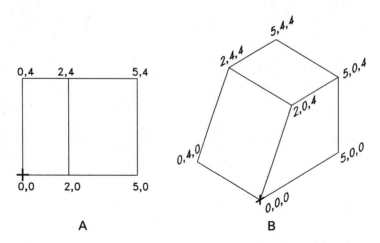

A   B

Fig. 24-2. Each corner of a 3-D object must have an XYZ value.

Study the nature of the 3-D coordinate system. Be sure you understand Z values before you begin constructing 3-D objects. It is especially important that you carefully visualize and plan your design when working with 3-D constructions.

EXERCISE 24-1

☐ Study the multiview sketch.
☐ Given the 3-D coordinate axes, freehand sketch the object pictorially.
☐ Each tick mark is one unit. Use correct dimensions as given in the multiview drawing.
☐ When you complete the freehand sketch, draw the object in AutoCAD with the LINE command by entering XYZ coordinates for each point.
☐ Save the drawing as A:EX24-1 and quit.

Spherical coordinates

Spherical coordinates are similar to locating a point on the earth using longitude and latitude. In addition, you can measure the distance from the center of the earth, or the current origin. The origin value can be the default *WCS (World Coordinate System)* or the current *UCS (User Coordinate System)*. The second value is the angle in the XY plane. You might compare this with a longitude measurement (east or west) on the earth. This is shown in Fig. 24-3A. The final part of the spherical coordinate is the angle from the XY plane. This is comparable to a measurement from the equator toward either the north pole or the south pole (latitude measurement).

The values for a spherical coordinate are entered just like polar coordinates, but with an added angle as shown in the following example:

7.5〈35〈55

This value is shown graphically in Fig. 24-3B.

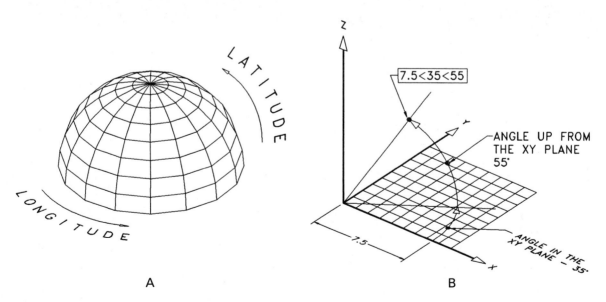

Fig. 24-3. Spherical coordinates require a distance, an angle in the XY plane, and an angle from the XY plane.

┌─────────────────────── **PROFESSIONAL TIP** ───────────────────────┐

Spherical coordinates may be especially useful in 3-D constructions for locating features on a spherical surface or model (see Chapter 25). An example might be a hole drilled into a sphere, or a feature located from a specific point on a sphere. If you are working on such a spherical object you might consider locating a UCS at the center of the sphere, then creating several different UCSs rotated at different angles on the center of the sphere.

Keep in mind that, just like rectangular coordinates, any time a location is required by an AutoCAD command, spherical coordinates may be used.

└───┘

Cylindrical coordinates

Cylindrical coordinates are based on providing coordinate locations for a cylindrical shape. The first value is the distance from the origin of the WCS or the current UCS. The second value is the angle in the XY plane. The third value is a vertical, or Z dimension. A cylindrical coordinate is entered as follows:

7.5⟨35,6.0

This is illustrated in Fig. 24-4. As with any angle or coordinate values, AutoCAD accepts negative spherical and cylindrical angles and Z coordinates.

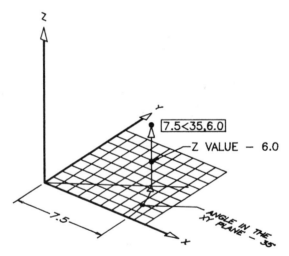

Fig. 24-4. Cylindrical coordinates require a distance from the origin, an angle in the XY plane, and a Z dimension.

CREATING EXTRUDED 3-D SHAPES   ┌──────────┐
                                            │ **ARM 8** │
                                            └──────────┘

The most shapes drawn with AutoCAD are extruded shapes. *Extruded* means that a 2-D shape is given a base elevation and a thickness. The object then rises up, or "extrudes" to its given thickness. The ELEV command, found in the SETTINGS screen menu, controls the base elevation and thickness. ELEV does not draw, it merely sets the base elevation and thickness for the next objects drawn.

The process of drawing a rectangular box four units long by three units wide by two units high begins with the ELEV command:

Command: **ELEV** ⏎
New current elevation ⟨0.00⟩: ⏎
New current thickness ⟨0.00⟩: **2** ⏎

Nothing happens on screen. Now use the LINE command to draw the top view of the rectangular box. Although it appears that you are drawing lines, you are actually drawing XY planes. Each plane has a height (the thickness) that you cannot see yet.

Before you display the 3-D construction, use the following instructions to add a hexagon and a circle as shown in Fig. 24-5. The hexagon should sit on top of the rectangle and extend three units above. The circle should appear to be a hole through the rectangle. Since the circle and rectangle have the same elevation, there is no need to use the ELEV command.

Before drawing the hexagon, set the base elevation to the top surface of the rectangle and thickness (height) of the hexagon feature using the ELEV command as follows:

> Command: **ELEV** ↵
> New current elevation ⟨0.00⟩: **2** ↵
> New current thickness ⟨2.00⟩: **3** ↵

Now, draw the hexagon. The bracketed numbers after each prompt reflect the current values. A "2" was entered for the elevation because the hexagon sits on top of the rectangle, which is two units thick. This is where the hexagon starts. The "3" is the thickness, or height of the hexagon above its starting point.

Next the elevation and thickness for the circle is set:

> Command: **ELEV** ↵
> New current elevation ⟨2.00⟩: **0** ↵
> New current thickness ⟨3.00⟩: **2** ↵

Now draw the circle to the right of the hexagon. The object is now ready to be viewed in 3-D.

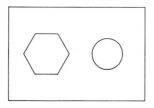

Fig. 24-5. Hexagon and circle added to rectangle.

PROFESSIONAL TIP

Keep in mind that a "hole" drawn using ELEV and CIRCLE is not really a hole to AutoCAD. It is a cylinder with solid ends. This becomes clear when you display the objects in a 3-D view with hidden lines removed.

Some 3-D drawing hints

- Erasing a line drawn with the ELEV thickness value set other than zero erases an entire plane.
- Shapes drawn using the LINE and ELEV commands are open at the top and bottom. Circles drawn with ELEV are closed at the ends.
- The PLINE and TRACE commands give thickness to lines and make them appear as walls in the 3-D view.

THE RIGHT-HAND RULE OF 3-D   `ARM 3`

The right-hand rule is a graphic representation of positive coordinate values in the three axis directions of a coordinate system. The UCS system is based on a concept of visualization called the *right-hand rule*. This requires that you use the thumb, index finger, and middle finger of your right hand and hold them open in front of you as shown in Fig. 24-6.

Although this may seem a bit unusual to do (especially if you are sitting in the middle of a school library or computer lab), it can do wonders for your understanding of the nature of the three axes. It can also help in understanding how the UCS can be rotated about each of the axis lines, or fingers.

Imagine that your thumb represents the X axis, your index finger is the Y axis, and your middle finger is the Z axis. Hold your hand directly in front of you and bend your middle finger so it is pointing directly at you. Now you see the plan view. The positive X axis is pointing to the

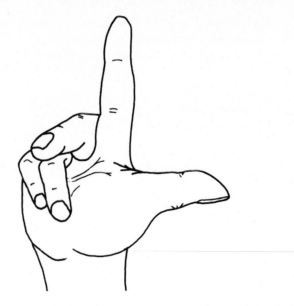

Fig. 24-6. Try positioning your hand like this to understand the relationship of the X, Y, and Z axes.

right and the positive Y axis is pointing up. The positive Z axis comes toward you, and the origin of this system is the palm of your hand.

When you use the VPOINT command (discussed later in this chapter), a tripod appears on the screen. It is composed of three axis lines—X, Y, and Z. When you see the tripod, you should be able to make the comparison with the right-hand rule. See Fig. 24-7.

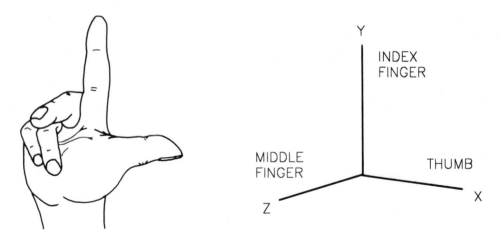

Fig. 24-7. Compare the use of three fingers on the right hand and the tripod used by AutoCAD for 3-D viewing.

Later in the chapter when the User Coordinate System (UCS) is discussed, you will discover that you can rotate a UCS to any position desired. The coordinate system rotates on one of the three axis lines, just like a wheel rotates on an axle. Therefore, if you want to rotate the X plane, keep your thumb stationary, and turn your hand toward or away from you. If you wish to rotate the Y plane, keep your index finger stationary and turn your hand to the left or right. When rotating the Z plane, you must keep your middle finger stationary and rotate your entire arm to the right or left.

If you discover that your 3-D visualization skills are weak, or that you are having trouble with the UCS method, don't be afraid to use the right-hand rule. It is a useful technique for improving your 3-D visualization skills.

DISPLAYING 3-D DRAWINGS

ARM 7

Once you draw a shape, change your point of view so that the object can be seen in three dimensions. Select the VPOINT command, found in the DISPLAY screen menu, to establish your position relative to the object, or type "VPOINT" at the Command: prompt as follows:

Command: **VPOINT** ⏎
Rotate/⟨View point⟩ ⟨0.00,0.00,1.00⟩:

The three numbers reflect the XYZ coordinates of the current viewpoint. You change these coordinates to select different viewpoints. The VPOINT values shown above represent the coordinates for the plan view. This means that you see the XY plane. Since it is difficult to visualize a numerical viewpoint, you can display a graphic representation of the XYZ axes. Then, pick the viewpoint with your pointing device. Press ENTER at the Rotate: prompt or select the Axes option from the screen menu. The screen display changes to one similar to Fig. 24-8.

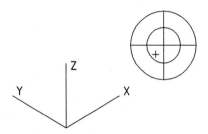

Fig. 24-8. VPOINT axes display.

As you move the pointing device, notice what happens on screen. The XYZ coordinate tripod moves and the small crosshairs above also move. The concentric circles divided into quarters represent a compass. This feature is discussed in detail after Exercise 24-2.

The easiest way to locate the viewpoint is to move the cursor while observing the XYZ axes tripod movement. Pick the location where you are satisfied with the appearance of the axes. It may take some practice. Remember that in the top or plan view, the X axis is horizontal, Y axis is vertical, and Z axis comes out of the screen. As you move the tripod, keep track of where the crosshairs are located inside the compass. Compare their position to that of the tripod. Move the tripod until it is positioned like the one given in Fig. 24-9. Press the pick button. The display should then resemble that shown in the figure.

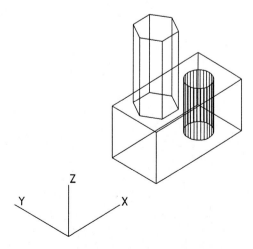

Fig. 24-9. The axes and 3-D view display.

The number of viewpoints you can select is endless. To get an idea of how the axes tripod and compass relate to the viewpoint, see the examples in Fig. 24-10. It can be hard to distinguish top from bottom in wireframe views. Therefore, the viewpoints shown in Fig. 24-10 are all from above the object and the HIDE command has been used to clarify the views. Use the VPOINT command to try each of these 3-D positions on your computer.

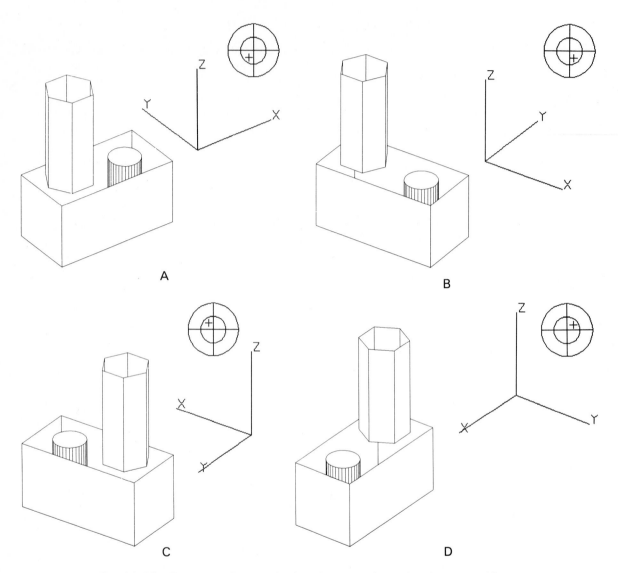

Fig. 24-10. Examples of viewpoint locations and their related axes positions.

When you are ready to return to the plan view, select the PLAN command from the DISPLAY screen menu, or type the XYZ coordinates for the plan view.

    Command: **VPOINT** ↵
    Rotate/⟨View point⟩ ⟨current⟩: **0,0,1** ↵

This returns your original top view which fills the screen. You can use the ZOOM command's All option to display the drawing limits.

Using the Rotate option

    AutoCAD allows you to enter two angles to determine the viewpoint. The angles are similar to spherical coordinates, but do not include a distance from the center point. Spherical coordinates can locate any point on, inside, or outside a sphere. The three values that comprise a spherical coordinate are shown in Fig. 24-11.

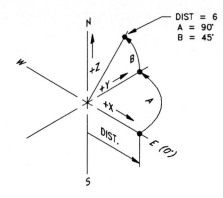

Fig. 24-11. Spherical coordinates, composed of three values, define a point on a sphere.

AutoCAD requires only the two angles when you select the Rotate option:

Command: **VPOINT** ↵
Rotate/⟨View point⟩ ⟨current⟩: **R** ↵
Enter angle in XY plane from X axis ⟨current⟩: **45** ↵
Enter angle from XY plane ⟨current⟩: **45** ↵

In Fig. 24-11, the viewpoint was moved counterclockwise 45° from the X axis and 45° from the XY plane. The resulting 3-D view is shown in Fig. 24-12.

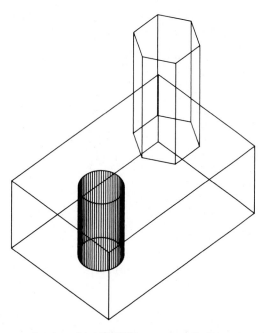

Fig. 24-12. This view was created using the VPOINT command's Rotate option. The rotation angles were 45° in the XY plane and 45° up from the XY plane.

3-D display using pull-down menus

The View pull-down menu provides a graphic means of viewpoint selection. Pick the View pull-down menu, then pick Set View. Finally pick Viewpoint. The second cascading menu displays three options: Axes, Presets..., and Set Vpoint. The Axes option displays the compass and tripod. The Set Vpoint option allows you to enter XYZ coordinates for the viewpoint. The Presets... option displays the "Viewpoint Presets" dialogue box shown in Fig. 24-13. This dialogue box enables you to graphically position your viewpoint.

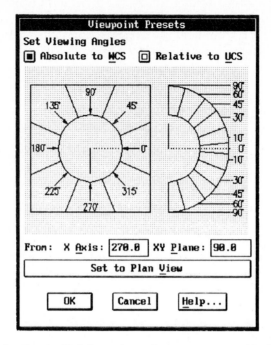

Fig. 24-13. The "Viewpoint Presets" dialogue box allows you to graphically choose your viewpoint.

The dialogue box contains two figures: a plan view on the left and an elevation view on the right. Imagine that the object on your screen is sitting inside the circle in the plan view. Your line of sight from the X axis (0°) is the line located at the 270° mark. Your line of sight *from* the XY plane is 90°, which is indicated by the black line inside the arc in the elevation view of the dialogue box.

You can achieve the same display shown in Fig. 24-12 by picking the 45° mark in the plan view and the upper 45° section (inside the large arc) in the elevation view. This display is called *absolute to the WCS* because it is based on a viewpoint from the default World Coordinate System. Notice that the Absolute to WCS radio button is active. If you pick the Relative to UCS radio button, the view will be based on the XY plane of the current User Coordinate System (UCS). User coordinate systems are discussed later in this chapter.

When you use the "Viewpoint Presets" dialogue box to set a view, the location of your pick determines the accuracy of the viewing angle. For example, if you pick a point inside the circle in the plan view on the left, you can pick any degree angle, including decimals, that you desire. Picking an angle is not accurate; therefore, if you need a specific angle it is best to enter it in the X Axis: edit box. You can select angles in 45° increments if you pick between any of the radial lines that contain the value you need. In a similar fashion, you can pick a point inside the small arc in the elevation view to select a decimal angle. However, if you need accuracy, enter the angle in the XY Plane: edit box. You can select any of the angular values listed along the right side of the dialogue box by picking inside the radial segment that applies. Pick OK when you complete your settings. You can change the current view back to a plan view if you pick the Set to Plan View button.

EXERCISE 24-2

☐ Set the grid spacing to .5 and snap spacing to .25.
☐ Set the elevation at 0 and the thickness at 2.
☐ Using the LINE command, draw a rectangle 2 x 3 units.
☐ Add a 180° arc to each end of the rectangle.
☐ Set the elevation at 2 and the thickness at 3.
☐ Draw a 1 unit diameter circle in the center of the rectangle.
☐ Use the VPOINT command to display the 3-D view of your drawing. Display it once using the axes tripod, a second time using the Rotate option, and a third time using the "Viewpoint Presets" dialogue box.
☐ Save the drawing as A:EX24-2.

Understanding the compass

After selecting the VPOINT command, you are given the chance to enter coordinate values, or to select the Axes, Rotate, or Plan options. If you select the Axes option, or press ENTER at the prompt, the compass and tripod appear. The compass, located at the upper-right corner of the screen, represents the north and south poles and the equator, Fig. 24-14. The center point of the compass is the north pole. The small circle is the equator. The large circle is the south pole. The 3-D view is controlled by the location of the tiny crosshairs when you press the pick button.

Set SNAP to on and place the small crosshairs exactly on the center of the compass. Notice the position of the tripod. The Z axis has disappeared and the X and Y axes appear to be in the plan view. If you press the pick button, the plan view displays. Now move the crosshairs into the lower-left quadrant above the equator (inside the small circle). The Y axis now points to the upper-left and the X axis points to the upper-right. See Fig. 24-14. Visualize the Z axis coming toward you out of the screen. Slowly move the crosshairs to the lower-right quadrant inside the equator. Visualize an object moving and try to determine which sides you would be seeing. Remember that all viewpoints above the equator are looking at the object from above the zero elevation plane, or the positive Z area.

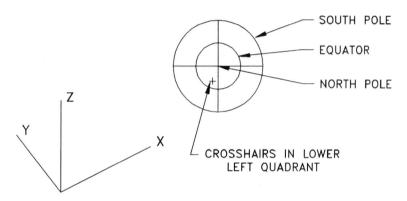

Fig. 24-14. A tripod orientation like this indicates that the crosshairs are in the lower-left quadrant of the compass above the equator.

Now move the crosshairs back to the lower-left quadrant, above the equator. Slowly drag them down toward the south pole circle. Notice that the Z axis line appears to get shorter. See Fig. 24-15. Visualize the Z axis tilting away from you into the screen. Slowly move the crosshairs around the compass, keeping them just inside the south pole. Remember, you are viewing the bottom of the object because the crosshairs are between the equator and the south pole. Thus, the viewpoint is below the zero elevation plane.

Each viewpoint has XYZ coordinates. You can enter these coordinates at the VPOINT prompt. They are based on your location in relation to the object. Fig. 24-16 provides the negative or

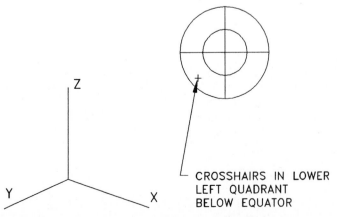

Fig. 24-15. A tripod orientation like this indicates that the crosshairs are in the lower-left quadrant of the compass below the equator.

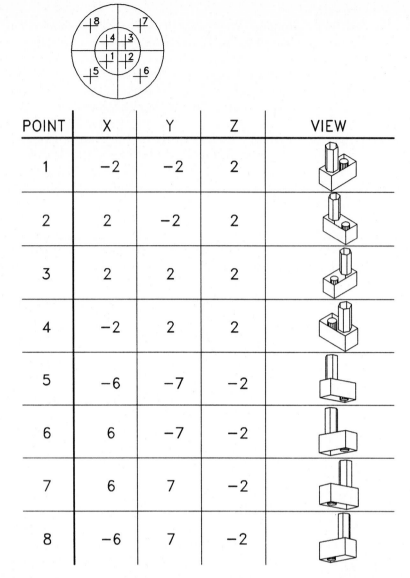

POINT	X	Y	Z	VIEW
1	−2	−2	2	
2	2	−2	2	
3	2	2	2	
4	−2	2	2	
5	−6	−7	−2	
6	6	−7	−2	
7	6	7	−2	
8	−6	7	−2	

Fig. 24-16. XYZ values for a variety of viewpoints and their compass equivalents.

positive values for each quadrant as indicated by the numbers in the compass. As an example, a reasonable viewpoint above the equator is -1.0,-1.0,1.0. That viewpoint has a crosshairs location above the equator and just inside the lower-left quadrant, and is an isometric view.

As you use the 3-D features more often, the relationship of the compass, tripod, coordinate values, and the drawing itself will become much clearer. The best way to learn is by picking viewpoints based on the position of the tripod. When you do, look at the location of the crosshairs on the compass.

Creating extruded 3-D text

Text added on the plan view is displayed in 3-D when you use the VPOINT command. However, the displayed text does not have thickness, and it always rests on the zero elevation plane. You can give text thickness and change the elevation with the CHPROP command. Select the text to change, pick the Thickness option, and enter a value.

Command: **CHPROP** ↵
Select objects: *(select the text)*
Select objects: ↵
Change what property (Color/LAyer/Ltype/Thickness)? **T** ↵
New thickness ⟨current⟩: **1.5** ↵
Change what property (Color/LAyer/Ltype/Thickness)? ↵

The selected text now has a thickness of 1.5. It is that simple. The CHPROP command does not leave the properties prompt until you press ENTER. Fig. 24-17 shows examples of 3-D text with thickness added, before and after using the HIDE command.

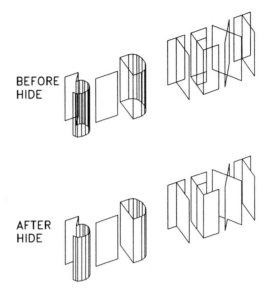

Fig. 24-17. Thickness applied to 3-D text, before and after HIDE.

Removing hidden lines in 3-D displays

The previous displays have been wireframe; every edge can be seen. This view can be confusing, especially if there are several circular features in your drawing. The best way to mask all lines that would normally be hidden is to use the HIDE command. Use HIDE only after you have selected a viewpoint to display a 3-D view.

Command: **HIDE** ↵
Regenerating drawing
Hiding lines: done 100%

The size and complexity of the drawing, and the speed of your computer, determines how long you must wait for the lines to be hidden. The final display of the object in Fig. 24-12 with hidden lines removed is shown in Fig. 24-18.

The view in Fig. 24-18 may not look quite right. You probably expected the rectangle to appear solid with a circle in the top representing a hole. Think back to the initial construction of

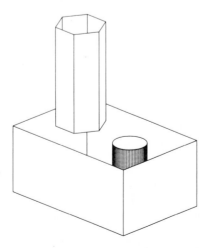

Fig. 24-18. Hidden lines removed using the HIDE command.

the rectangle. When drawn in the plan view, it consisted of four lines, or planes. It was not drawn with a top or bottom, just four sides. Then you placed a hexagon on top of the box and a cylinder inside. That is what appears in the "hidden line removed" display.

The individual features that compose the object in Fig. 24-18 are shown in Fig. 24-19. Both wireframe and hidden line views are given.

To redisplay the wireframe view, just select another viewpoint or enter "REGEN" and press ENTER. A regeneration displays all lines of the objects.

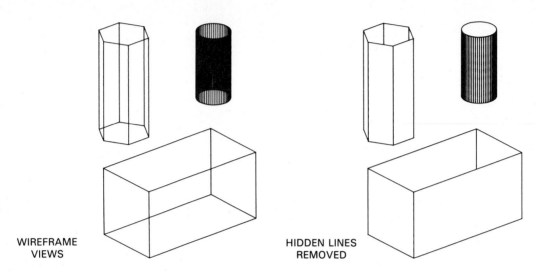

WIREFRAME VIEWS   HIDDEN LINES REMOVED

Fig. 24-19. Individual features of the object in Fig. 24-18 in both wireframe and with hidden lines removed.

Displaying hidden lines in a different color

AutoCAD allows you to display lines that have been hidden by the HIDE command. Although not used often, this technique can aid visualization. You must configure AutoCAD properly to make this function work. First, use the CONFIG command and select number 7 "Configure operating parameters." Then select number 10, "Select Release 11 hidden line removal algorithm." You are then warned that this selection is slower than Release 12. Enter "Y" if you want to use the Release 11 algorithm. Press ENTER four times to exit and save the new configuration. For each layer that may have lines hidden by the HIDE command, make a new layer of the same name but put the word "HIDDEN" in front of the name. For example, a layer named HIDDENRED is created to display lines hidden on the layer named RED.

Although helpful for simple drawings, this technique is not recommended for complex drawings, especially when objects touch. The view in Fig. 24-20 shows an object displayed using HIDE when a hidden layer was in effect. The dashed lines, which may be a different color, indicate hidden lines. They are not shown as hidden lines, but are displayed in the color assigned to the layer named HIDDENRED, and in the linetype assigned to layer RED.

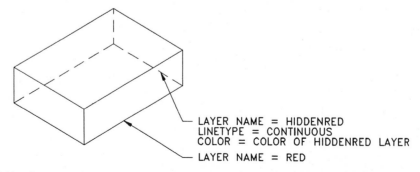

LAYER NAME = HIDDENRED
LINETYPE = CONTINUOUS
COLOR = COLOR OF HIDDENRED LAYER
LAYER NAME = RED

Fig. 24-20. Hidden lines can be placed on special layers that are displayed in a different color when HIDE is used.

HIDE and its treatment of different objects

When creating 3-D drawings, you are not limited to using just the LINE command. All of the drawing commands are available, but some are treated differently by the HIDE command.

- LINE—Treated as a vertical plane. A box made of four lines appears open at the top and bottom when HIDE is used.
- TRACE—An object drawn with the TRACE command appears to have thick walls and is open at the top and bottom. The nature of the traced line ends may create an awkward look.
- PLINE—The effect of the HIDE command on polylines is similar to that of TRACE. The width of the polyline becomes the thickness of a wall. No top or bottom is placed on the shape enclosed by the polylines.
- SOLID—A solid is treated as a plane by the HIDE command. It is given a top and bottom.

When drawn without a line thickness, objects made with these four commands may look exactly the same in the plan view. Therefore, it is important that you know the limitations of each command when constructing objects for 3-D viewing. The differences among the entities before and after using HIDE are shown in Fig. 24-21.

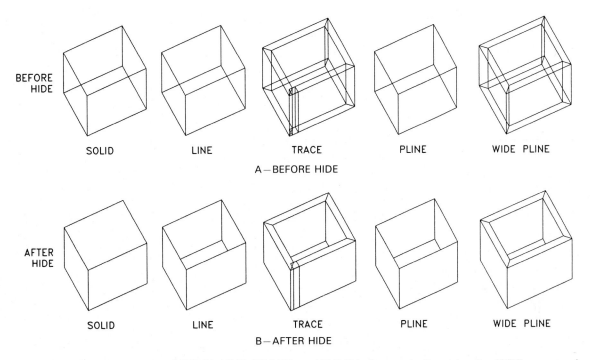

Fig. 24-21. The appearance of SOLID, LINE, TRACE, and PLINE before and after using the HIDE command.

3-D CONSTRUCTION TECHNIQUES

Three-dimensional objects can be drawn in three basic forms—wireframe, surface models, and solid models. This chapter discusses wireframes, but deals primarily with surface models. A *wireframe construction* is just that; an object that looks like it was made of wire. You can see through it. There are not a lot of practical applications for wireframe models unless you are an artist designing a new object using coat hangers. Wireframe models can be hard to visualize because it is difficult to determine the angle of view and the nature of the surfaces. Compare the two objects in Fig. 24-22.

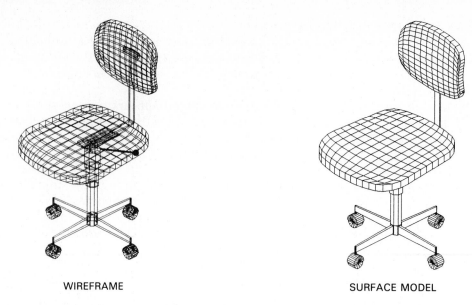

WIREFRAME   SURFACE MODEL

Fig. 24-22. The wireframe object is harder to visualize than the surface model.   (Courtesy Autodesk, Inc.)

Surface modeling, on the other hand, is much more easily visualized. It looks more like the real object. Surface models can be used to imitate solid models, and most importantly, can be used for shading and rendering models. These shaded and rendered models can then be used in any number of presentation formats including slide shows, black and white or color prints, walk-arounds or walk-through animations, or animations that are recorded to videotape. The possibilities are endless. However, remember that their usefulness is defined by the word "presentation." This means "seeing" what the model looks like while viewing it from different angles, with different lighting, shading, and surface textures.

On the other hand, *solids modeling* more closely represents designing an object using the materials from which it is to be made. This type of 3-D design involves using primitive solid shapes such as boxes, cylinders, spheres, and cones to construct an object. These shapes are added together and subtracted from each other to create a finished product. The solid model can then be shaded, rendered, and more importantly, analyzed and tested for weight, mass, surface area, moments of inertia, and centers of gravity. Some third-party programs allow you to perform finite stress analysis on the model. An introduction to the use of AutoCAD's Advanced Modeling Extension (AME) is given in Chapter 25.

Before constructing a 3-D model, you should determine the purpose of your design. What will the model be used for—presentation, or analysis and manufacturing? This helps you determine which tools you should use to construct the model. The discussions and examples in this chapter provide a view of the uses of wireframe and surface modeling.

CONSTRUCTING WIREFRAMES AND 3-D FACES $\boxed{\text{ARM 5}}$

Wireframes can be constructed using the LINE, PLINE, and 3DPOLY commands. AutoCAD provides a number of methods to use, but one particularly useful method is called "filters." A *filter* is an existing point, or vector in your drawing file. When using a filter, you instruct AutoCAD to find the coordinate values of a selected point, then you supply the missing value—X, Y, or Z, or a combination. Filters can be used when working in two-dimensional space or when using a pictorial projection resulting from the VPOINT command.

Using filters to create 3-D objects

When using LINE, you must know the XYZ coordinate values of each corner on the object. To draw an object, first decide the easiest and quickest method using the LINE command. One technique is to draw the bottom surface. Then, make a copy at the height of the object. Finally, connect the corners with lines. The filters can be used with the COPY command. From the plan view, step through the process in this manner:

    Command: **LINE** ↵
    From point: **3,3** ↵
    To point: **@4,0** ↵
    To point: *(continue picking points to construct the box)*

Next, copy the shape up to the height of 3 units.

    Command: **COPY** ↵
    Select objects: **W** ↵
    First corner: *(pick the first corner of a window)*
    Other corner: *(pick the opposite corner)*
    Select objects: ↵
    ⟨Base point or displacement⟩/Multiple: *(pick a corner of the box)*
    Second point of displacement: **.XY** ↵
    of *(pick the same corner)* (need Z): **3** ↵

    Since the shape is copied straight up, the top surface of the cube has the same XY values as the bottom surface. That is why ".XY" was entered as the second point of displacement. This filter picks up the XY values of the previous point specified and applies them to the location of the new copy. Now, all AutoCAD needs is the Z value, which it requests.

    Check your progress by looking at the object using the VPOINT command. Enter the coordinates given below. Your display should look like that in Fig. 24-23.

    Command: **VPOINT** ↵
    Enter view point ⟨current⟩: **−1,−2,0.5** ↵

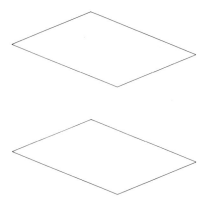

Fig. 24-23. Partially constructed box using LINE.

    Return the drawing to the plan view and finish the object using LINE command and point filters. The four remaining lines are vertical and 3 units long.

    Command: **LINE** ↵
    From point: *(pick the lower-left corner)*
    To point: **.XY** ↵
    of *(pick the lower-left corner again)* (need Z): **3** ↵
    To point: ↵

In this example, you instructed the computer to draw a line from the lower-left corner of the object to the same XY position 3 units above. The new line connects the top and bottom planes of the object. The same process can be used to draw the other three vertical lines. If you forget to enter the XY filter at the To point: prompt, AutoCAD will not ask for the Z distance. If this happens, cancel the command and start again. Use the VPOINT command again, and your drawing should look like Fig. 24-24.

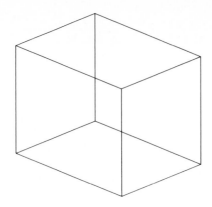

Fig. 24-24. Completed box using LINE.

PROFESSIONAL TIP

If the process of drawing Z axis lines in the plan view is difficult to visualize, there is an easier option; draw them in the pictorial view. After drawing the top and bottom faces of the box, select a viewpoint and zoom in on the object. Now use the LINE command to construct the vertical lines using OSNAP modes ENDpoint, MIDpoint, and INTersection. This method allows you to see the lines in 3-D as you draw them.

EXERCISE 24-3

☐ Set the grid spacing at .5, snap spacing at .25, and elevation at 0.
☐ Draw the object below to the dimensions indicated.
☐ Use the LINE and COPY commands to construct the object.
☐ Construct the top and bottom planes in the plan view. Connect the vertical lines in a 3-D view.
☐ Save the drawing as A:EX24-3.

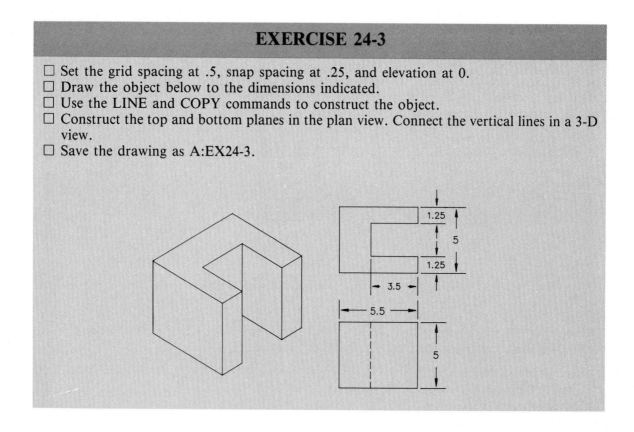

Constructing 3-D faces

Surfaces that appear solid and not wireframe are called *3-D faces*. They can be made with the 3DFACE command. Its prompt structure is similar to that of the SOLID command, but you can specify points in a clockwise or counterclockwise manner. A 3-D face must have at least three corners, but cannot have any more than four corners.

Draw the familiar box again, beginning with the bottom face, with the elevation set at 0. Then draw the top face. Draw the bottom face using the following command sequence.

Command: **3DFACE** ↵
First point: *(pick a point)*
Second point: *(pick a point)*
Third point: *(pick a point)*
Fourth point: *(pick a point)*
Third point: ↵

Notice that after you placed the fourth point, a line automatically connected the first point. A prompt then asks for the third point again if you want to continue to draw additional faces. Press ENTER to end the command.

The 3-D face can be copied using the same steps taken to copy the line surface. Remember to use XY filters for copying.

Command: **COPY** ↵
Select objects: *(pick the 3-D face)*
Select objects: ↵

Finally, the four sides of the box are drawn. First, set a viewpoint and then connect corners of each 3-D face using a running OSNAP mode of ENDpoint or INTersection.

Command: **VPOINT** ↵
Enter view point ⟨current⟩: −1,−1,1 ↵

The drawing should look like that shown in Fig. 24-25. Zoom in at this time if the view is too small.
Complete the box using the 3DFACE command and pick the points as numbered in Fig. 24-25.

Command: **OSNAP** ↵
Object snap modes: **INT** ↵
Command: **3DFACE** ↵
First point: *(pick point 1)*
Second point: *(pick point 2)*
Third point: *(pick point 3)*
Fourth point: *(pick point 4)*
Third point: ↵
Command:

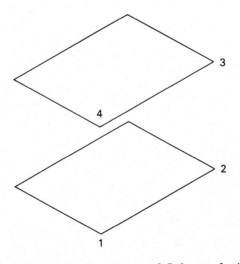

Fig. 24-25. Top and bottom 3-D faces of a box.

The first face is complete. Now draw the remaining faces in the same manner. The finished box should appear similar to that in Fig. 24-26.

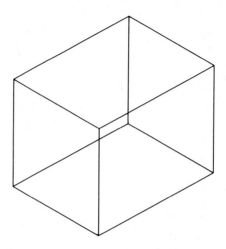

Fig. 24-26. Completed 3DFACE box.

How does a 3-D face object differ from ones drawn using the ELEV and LINE commands? For comparison, Fig. 24-27 shows boxes drawn using the ELEV, LINE, and 3DFACE commands with hidden lines removed by HIDE.

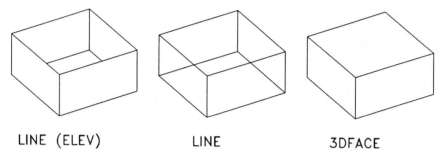

LINE (ELEV)   LINE   3DFACE

Fig. 24-27. Comparison of boxes drawn with ELEV, LINE, 3DFACE after the HIDE command was selected.

EXERCISE 24-4

☐ Set the grid spacing at .5, snap spacing at .25, and elevation at 0.
☐ Use the 3DFACE command to construct the object to the dimensions given.
☐ Draw the bottom, two end faces, and the two top angled surfaces in the plan view. Draw the front and rear V-shaped surfaces in a 3-D view. Hint: Each V-shaped end surface must be made of two 3-D faces.
☐ Use the HIDE command when you complete the object.
☐ Save the drawing as A:EX24-4.

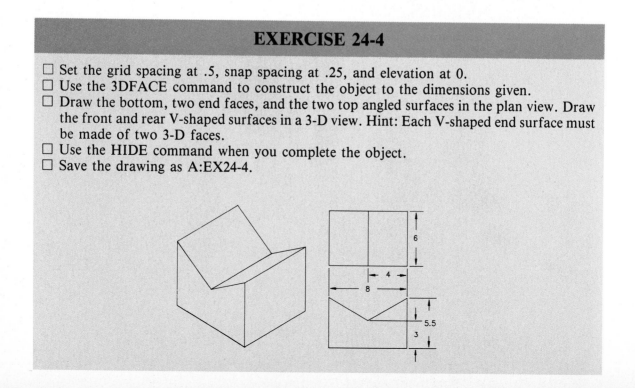

DIVIDING THE SCREEN INTO MULTIPLE VIEWPORTS

ARM 7

Viewports can be used for two different purposes. The first is to divide the screen into several separate screens for the purpose of designing a model or a layout. These different screens are created with the VPORTS command. When you use this command to create several views of a model, you are in a mode called *model space*. This is the default mode, when you enter AutoCAD. The TILEMODE system variable must be set to 1, which is the default value. You can have up to 16 viewports at a time, but this is impractical because of the small size of each viewport. An arrangement of four viewports is about the maximum number that is practical to display at one time for working purposes. This arrangement of viewports themselves cannot be plotted because they are not entities, but rather only a display function. The project and nature of the model will determine the number of viewports you need.

The second form of viewport is created in a mode called *paper space*. The MVIEW command is used to create up to sixteen active viewports. These viewports are more like "windows" cut into a sheet of paper. The viewports are entities that can be edited. You can then insert, or "reference" different scaled drawings (views), such as architectural details, or sections and details of a complex mechanical part or assembly into these windows. These viewports can be used at the end of a project when you are preparing the layout for plotting, hence the name "paper space." The TILEMODE variable must be set to 0 in order to create viewports with the MVIEW command in paper space.

NOTE

The operating system your computer uses determines the number of viewports (entities created with MVIEW) that can be active at one time. The MAXACTVP (MAXimum ACTive ViewPorts) variable retains the number of viewports that can be active at one time. Enter "MAXACTVP" at the Command: prompt to display this number.

A complete, detailed discussion of the process of creating viewports in paper space is included in Chapter 27. The following discussion covers the use of the VPORTS command in model space for the purpose of design and construction of a 3-D model.

The screen of a DOS computer can be divided into a maximum of 16 viewports. Each can show a different view of the object under construction, making it easier to construct 3-D objects. The VPORTS command, found in the SETTINGS screen menu, allows you to establish one or more viewports.

Creating viewports

Creating viewports when working in model space is similar to working with a multiview layout on a sheet of drafting vellum. Several views are on the same piece of vellum, and you can switch from one to the other simply by moving your pencil. Viewports created with the VPORTS command are similar. Using your pointing device, pick the viewport you wish to work in, and it becomes active. Although using viewports is a good method for constructing 3-D models because all views are updated as you draw, it also should not be overlooked for creating 2-D layouts.

The nature of your work determines the number of viewports you use, but keep in mind that the more viewports on your screen, the less useful they may be because of their small size. Fig. 24-28 illustrates the extremes of viewports from two, to the default arrangement of three, to the maximum of sixteen.

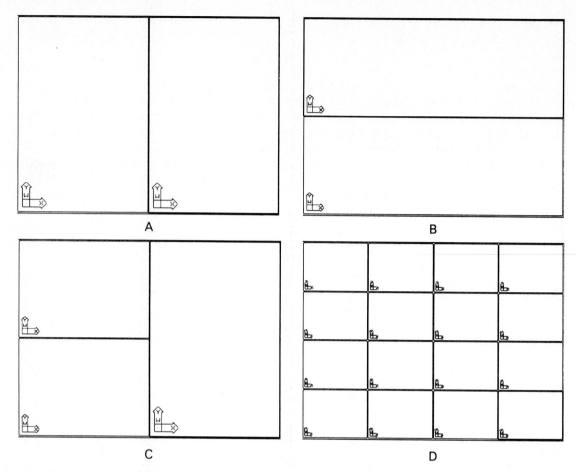

Fig. 24-28. A—The vertical arrangement of two viewports. B—Two horizontal viewports. C—The default arrangement of three viewports. D—The maximum of sixteen viewports.

You can enter a VPORTS value from 2 to 4 to create multiple views.

Command: **VPORTS** ⏎
Save/Restore/Delete/Join/SIngle/?/2/⟨3⟩/4: ⏎

Notice that "3" is the default value. After pressing ENTER in this case, the next prompt requests the type of configuration desired for three viewports.

Horizontal/Vertical/Above/Below/Left/⟨Right⟩: ⏎

Pressing ENTER defaults to the Right option. This places two viewports on the left side of the screen and a large viewport on the right. Viewports can be arranged in several ways. Selecting three viewports has the greatest number of possibilities. These options are shown in Fig. 24-29.

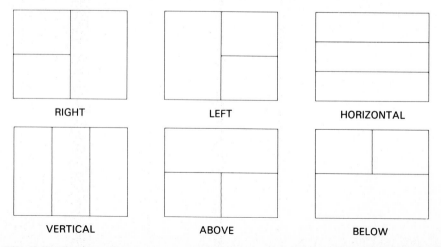

Fig. 24-29. Selecting a configuration of three viewports provides several possible arrangements.

You have probably noticed the X and Y arrow icon in the lower-left corner of the screen. If you have multiple viewports displayed, the icon appears in each view. This symbol, called the *UCS icon*, represents the orientation of the current coordinate system. The UCS icon is discussed later in the chapter.

Setting viewports with a dialogue box

A viewport layout can be quickly selected by using a dialogue box. Pick the View pull-down menu, then pick Layout at the bottom of the menu. Finally, select the Tiled Vports... option. This displays the "Tiled Viewport Layout" dialogue box shown in Fig. 24-30. You are presented with a selection of 12 viewport arrangements. You can pick either the graphic representation of the arrangement you want to use, or pick the verbal description to the left of the icons. If you pick the graphic, its verbal equivalent is highlighted, and vice versa. Pick OK when you are finished.

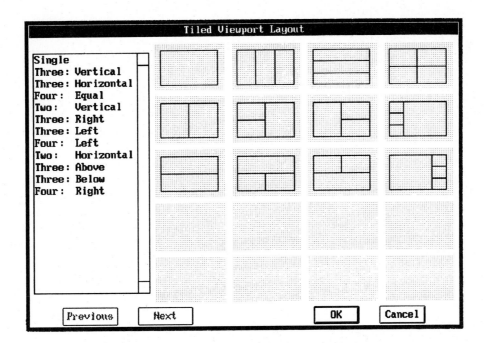

Fig. 24-30. The "Tiled Viewport Layout" dialogue box.

Notice that there are eight empty spaces for additional viewport icons. You can create your own viewport arrangements and place new icons in this menu. If you create more than twenty icons, the Previous and Next buttons allow you to see other pages of this menu. They are grayed out now because there are no other pages. Chapter 32 details the customization of icon menus.

Saving, restoring, and deleting viewports

Viewport configurations are not permanent. Once you change the configuration, only the previous one can be recalled. Although viewports are easy to create, it still saves time if you save individual configurations for later use. The Save option of the VPORTS command enables you to do just that.

Command: **VPORTS** ↵
Save/Restore/Delete/Join/SIngle/?/2/⟨3⟩/4: **S** ↵
?/Name for new viewport configuration: **FIRST** ↵

The above command sequence has saved the current viewport configuration under the name FIRST. This configuration can be recalled, or restored, at any time. If you forget the configuration names, enter a question mark when it is a valid response in a prompt as follows:

Command: **VPORTS** ⏎
Save/Restore/Delete/Join/SIngle/?/2/⟨3⟩/4: **R** ⏎
?/Name of viewport configuration to restore: **?** ⏎
Viewport configuration(s) to list ⟨*⟩: ⏎
Current configuration:
id# 8
  corners: 0.500,0.000 1.000,1.000
id# 2
  corners: 0.000,0.500 0.500,1.000
id# 5
  corners: 0.000,0.000 0.500,0.500
Configuration FIRST:
  0.500,0.000 1.000,1.000
  0.000,0.500 0.500,1.000
  0.000,0.000 0.500,0.500

The order in which the above coordinates appear may vary, but the values themselves are the same. All viewports are automatically given an identification number by AutoCAD. This number is independent of any name you might give the viewport configuration. Each viewport is also given a coordinate location, with 0.000,0.000 as the lower-left corner of the graphics area and 1.000,1.000 as the upper-right corner. Look at the coordinate locations just given for the three viewport configurations. Can you determine the layout of the viewports by reading the coordinate values? Fig. 24-31 illustrates the coordinate values of the viewport configuration saved as FIRST.

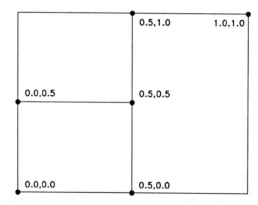

Fig. 24-31. The viewport coordinate values of the configuration named FIRST.

Unwanted viewports can be removed easily. Select the VPORTS command and then enter the Delete option.

Command: **VPORTS** ⏎
Save/Restore/Delete/Join/SIngle/?/2/⟨3⟩/4: **D** ⏎
?/Name of viewport configuration to delete: **FIRST** ⏎

If you forget the names of the viewports you have saved, enter a question mark at the prompt. At the next prompt, either type the name, or names separated by commas, that you wish to list, or press ENTER to list all viewport names.

Only one viewport is active; the cursor shows as crosshairs and a thick line surrounds the viewport. The cursor becomes an arrow when moved into inactive viewports. Any viewport can be made active. Simply move the arrow to that viewport and pick, or press CTRL V to switch viewports.

━━━ PROFESSIONAL TIP ━━━

Each viewport can have its own viewpoint, zoom scale, limits, grid spacing, and snap setting. Specify the drawing aids in all viewports of the configuration before saving it. When a viewport is restored, all settings are brought with it.

Altering the current viewport configuration

If you dislike the current viewport configuration, you can join two adjacent viewports to form a single one. This process, done with the Join option of the VPORTS command, is quicker than trying to create an entirely new configuration. The only restriction is that two viewports must form a rectangle. Fig. 24-32 illustrates viewports which can and cannot be joined. AutoCAD first prompts you for the dominant viewport. All aspects of the viewport selected as dominant—limits, grid, and snap values—are used in the new, *joined* viewport. Use the following command sequence to join two viewports:

Command: **VPORTS** ↵
Save/Restore/Delete/Join/SIngle/?/2/⟨3⟩/4: **J** ↵
Select dominant viewport ⟨current⟩: *(select the viewport or press ENTER)*
Select viewport to join: *(select the other viewport)*

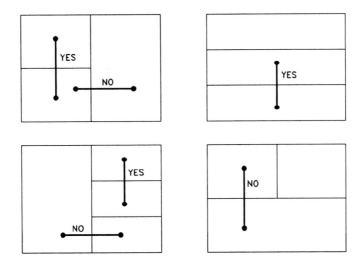

Fig. 24-32. Two viewports can be joined when they form a rectangle. All other selections are invalid.

The two viewports selected are eliminated and joined into a single viewport. If you select two viewports that do not form a rectangle, AutoCAD returns this message:

The selected viewports do not form a rectangle.
Select dominant viewport ⟨current⟩:

━━━ PROFESSIONAL TIP ━━━

Create only the number of viewports and viewport configurations needed to construct your drawing. Too many viewports on screen reduces the size of the images and may confuse you. It helps to zoom each view so that it fills the viewport.

The screen can be restored to a single viewport. Select the SIngle option of the VPORTS command as follows:

Command: **VPORTS** ↵
Save/Restore/Delete/Join/SIngle/?/2/⟨3⟩/4: **SI** ↵

EXERCISE 24-5

☐ Start a new drawing. Select the VPORTS command and create the following viewports:

NUMBER OF PORTS	CONFIGURATION	VIEWPORT NAME
1		One
2		Two
3	Vertical	Three-A
3	Above	Three-L
3	Left	Three-R
4	Right	Four

☐ List the viewports to be sure all were saved.
☐ Restore each named viewport.
☐ Restore configuration Three-A and join the two small viewports. Save the new configuration under the name TWO. Answer "YES" when asked if you want to replace the existing configuration named TWO.
☐ Restore configuration TWO. It should have two horizontal viewports.
☐ Delete configuration THREE-A.
☐ Restore configuration THREE-L. Set the grid and snap spacing in each viewport to different values. Save the configuration as THREE-L.
☐ Select the SIngle option in the VPORTS command and press ENTER.
☐ Restore configuration THREE-L. Check the drawing aids to be sure they have the same values previously set.
☐ Save your work as A:EX24-5.

Drawing in multiple viewports

If most of your work is two-dimensional drawing, viewports allow you to display a view of the entire drawing, plus views showing portions of the drawing. The function is similar to the VIEW command, but now you can have several views on screen at once. Adjust the zoom scale to a different area of the drawing in each viewport. Save the viewport configuration if you plan to continue working with it during other drawing sessions. You can create an unlimited number of viewport configurations.

The most powerful capabilities of viewports are used when constructing 3-D models. You can specify different viewpoints in each port and see the model take shape as you draw. Constructing a model is made quicker because you can switch from one viewport to another while drawing and editing the object.

The following example gives steps that can be used to construct a simple part using two viewports. A top view of the object is constructed in the left viewport and a 3-D viewpoint is established in the right viewport. The shape is drawn in the left viewport and copied up the Z axis. The connecting vertical lines are drawn in the right viewport.

Command: **VPORTS** ↵
Save/Restore/Delete/Join/SIngle/?/2/⟨3⟩/4: **2** ↵
Horizontal/⟨Vertical⟩: ↵
Command: *(make sure the right viewport is active)* **LINE** ↵
From point: **3,2** ↵
To point: **@7,0** ↵
To point: **@0,5** ↵
To point: **@−7,0** ↵
To point: **C** ↵
Command: **CIRCLE** ↵
3P/2P/TTR/⟨Center point⟩: **@3.5,−2.5** ↵
Diameter/⟨Radius⟩: **1** ↵
Command: **VPOINT** ↵
Rotate/⟨Viewpoint⟩ ⟨0.0000,0.0000,1.0000⟩: **−1,−1,1** ↵
Command: **ZOOM** ↵
All/Center/Dynamic/Extents/Left/Previous/Vmax/Window/⟨Scale(X/XP)⟩: **.9X** ↵
Command: *(press CTRL V to make the left viewport active)* **PAN** ↵
Displacement: **@** ↵
Second point: **@0,5** ↵

The screen now displays two viewports. The left viewport contains a top view of the part and the right viewport displays the part in a 3-D viewpoint, Fig. 24-33.

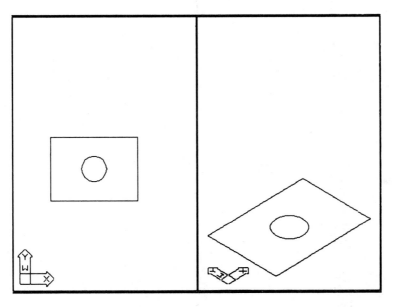

Fig. 24-33. The screen is divided into two viewports. The top view appears in the left viewport and a 3-D view appears in the right viewport.

The next step is to copy the shape in the left viewport up 2 units along the Z axis using XY filters.

Command: *(be sure the left viewport is active)* **COPY** ↵
Select objects: **W** ↵
First corner: *(pick the first corner of a window)* Other corner: *(pick the opposite corner)*
Select objects: ↵
⟨Base point or displacement⟩/Multiple: **.XY** ↵
of *(pick the lower-left corner of the object)* (need Z): **0** ↵
Second point of displacement: **.XY** ↵
of **@** ↵
(need Z): **2** ↵
Command: *(pick the right viewport to make it active)*

The screen now appears as shown in Fig. 24-34. The right viewport shows the result of the copy.

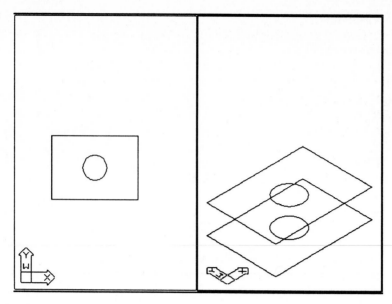

Fig. 24-34. The copied shapes appear automatically in the 3-D viewport (right).

The final step in this example is to connect the corners of the object with vertical lines. The LINE command is used with the ENDpoint running OSNAP option. Make sure the right viewport is active.

Command: **MULTIPLE LINE** ↵
From point: *(pick the corner on upper shape)*
To point: *(pick the adjacent corner on the lower shape)*
To point: ↵
Command: ↵
From point: *(continue joining corners as indicated)*

The completed object appears in Fig. 24-35.

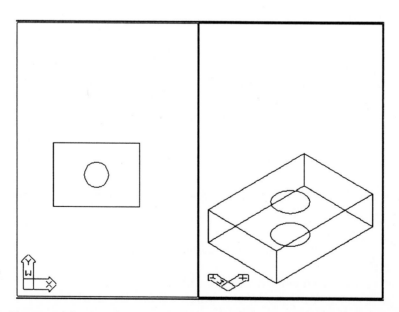

Fig. 24-35. Lines are joined to the corners of the upper and lower planes in the right viewport.

EXERCISE 24-6

☐ Start a new drawing called EX24-6.
☐ Create a viewport configuration having two views arranged horizontally and save it as TWO.
☐ Construct the object shown. Draw a top view in the upper viewport and display a 3-D view in the lower viewport. Connect edges in the lower viewport.
☐ Save the drawing as A:EX24-6.

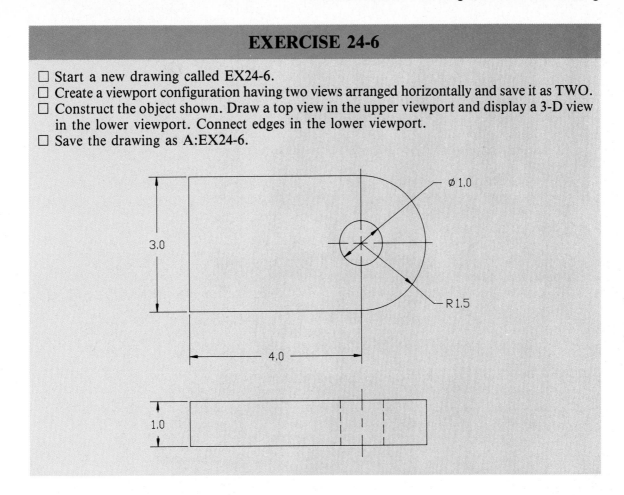

INTRODUCTION TO USER COORDINATE SYSTEMS   ARM 9

The coordinate system used in all versions of AutoCAD prior to Release 10 is fixed. It cannot be moved. All points in a drawing or on an object are defined with XYZ coordinate values measured from the origin. Since this system is fixed and universal, AutoCAD refers to it as the *World Coordinate System (WCS)*. The *User Coordinate System (UCS)*, on the other hand, can be moved to any orientation desired. You can change the position and rotation of the coordinate system to suit the shape of the object being drawn. This is done with the UCS command, found in the SETTINGS screen menu. Changes in the UCS are reflected in the orientation and placement of the UCS icon symbol, which is located in the lower-left corner of the screen.

Displaying the UCS icon

The symbol that identifies the orientation of the current origin system is called the *UCS icon*. Its default location is slightly above and to the right of the lower-left corner of the viewport. The display of this symbol is controlled by the UCSICON command. If your drawing does not require viewports and altered coordinate systems, turn the icon off.

Command: **UCSICON** ↵
ON/OFF/All/Noorigin/ORigin 〈ON〉: **OFF** ↵

The icon disappears until you turn it on again using the UCSICON command.

Changing the coordinate system

Constructing a three-dimensional object demands that you be able to visualize shapes at any angle. You will be drawing on a variety of planes to create features on angled surfaces. If you can visualize constructing features on angled planes, it is a simple process to rotate the UCSICON to match any surface of your object. The following example, constructing a wedge, illustrates this process, Fig. 24-36. The wedge has a hole a given depth in the angled surface. The first step in creating this model is to establish a viewport configuration. This example uses the default configuration of three viewports. You will better understand the concepts if you can construct the example at a workstation while you read.

Command: **VPORTS** ↵
Save/Restore/Delete/Join/SIngle/?/2/⟨3⟩/4: ↵
Horizontal/Vertical/Above/Below/Left/⟨Right⟩: ↵
Regenerating drawing.
Command: *(pick the upper-left viewport)* **LINE** ↵
From point: **3,2** ↵
To point: **@6,0** ↵
To point: **@0,5** ↵
To point: **@−6,0** ↵
To point: **C** ↵
Command: *(pick the right viewport)* **VPOINT** ↵
Rotate/⟨View point⟩ ⟨0.0000,0.0000,1.0000⟩: **1,−1,1** ↵
Command: **ZOOM** ↵
All/Center/Dynamic/Extents/Left/Previous/Vmax/Window/⟨Scale(X/XP)⟩: **.8X** ↵

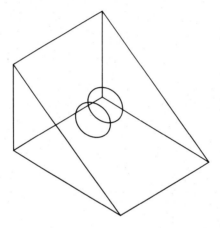

Fig. 24-36. This wedge can be constructed by changing the orientation of the coordinate system.

The screen divides into three viewports. The two left viewports contain the same shape. The right viewport displays that shape from a 3-D viewpoint. Now that the base of the wedge is constructed, draw the vertical lines. You could draw the vertical lines using XYZ filters. Yet, why not rotate the UCS to a position that allows you to draw the vertical lines as if you were drawing a front view of the wedge?

First, rotate the UCS so that the Y axis is pointing up from the bottom surface of the wedge and the X axis is pointing to the wedge tip. When this happens, the Y axis is pointing out of the screen in the two left viewports. You are looking at an edge view of the UCS. AutoCAD lets you know that you are looking at an edge view by replacing the UCS icon with a broken pencil icon, Fig. 24-37. Lines drawn in an edge view may not be what you expected, and grid, snap, and ortho do not produce the desired results. Rotate the UCS on the X axis as follows:

Command: *(pick the right viewport)* **UCS** ↵
Origin/ZAxis/3point/Entity/View/X/Y/Z/Prev/Restore/Save/Del/?/⟨World⟩: **X** ↵
Rotation angle about X axis ⟨0.0⟩: **90** ↵

The UCS icon in the right viewport changes to reflect the new UCS. The two icons in the left viewports change to the broken pencil. See Fig. 24-37.

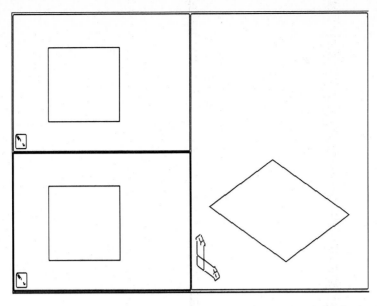

Fig. 24-37. The UCS icon is rotated 90°, and the broken pencil icons in the two left viewports indicate edge views.

The lower-left viewport should be the front, or profile view of the model. However, now it looks the same as the top view. The front view must be rotated in order to display the bottom surface of the wedge as an edge view. If this were done, the UCS icon would appear with the Y pointing up and X pointing to the right. When the UCS icon is displayed in this default manner, that view is said to be "plan" to the current UCS. In other words, your line of sight is perpendicular to the plane of the current UCS. If the lower-left viewport was a plan view of the current UCS, the vertical lines of the wedge could be drawn in true length. The PLAN command enables you to rotate a viewport to be "plan" to the current UCS.

> Command: *(pick the lower-left viewport)* **PLAN** ↵
> ⟨Current UCS⟩/Ucs/World: ↵
> Regenerating drawing

Although the view may appear to have disappeared, it has just been rotated 90° and zoomed to its extents. The bottom surface of the wedge is displayed along the bottom of the viewport. Use ZOOM and PAN commands to move the object higher into the viewport.

> Command: **ZOOM** ↵
> All/Center/Dynamic/Extents/Left/Previous/Vmax/Window/⟨Scale(X/XP)⟩: **.48X** ↵
> Command: **PAN** ↵
> Displacement: *(pick left end of line)* Second point: **@.5⟨180** ↵

The lower-left viewport should display a single horizontal line that appears to be the same length as the top view. If the line in your front view is not the same length as the top view, or is not aligned, repeat the above process until the lengths and alignment are approximate. The lower-left viewport should contain an edge view of the bottom surface of the wedge, similar to that in Fig. 24-38.

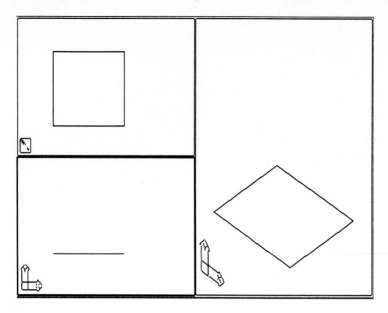

Fig. 24-38. The lower-left viewport displays an edge view of the bottom surface of the wedge and is considered "plan" to the current UCS.

The next step is to draw a vertical line from the left end of the edge in the front view. The line can then be copied in the 3-D view. Angled lines are finally drawn to the wedge point from the tops of the vertical lines.

    Command: **LINE** ↵
    From point: **END** ↵
    of *(pick the left end of the line in the lower-left viewport)*
    To point: **@0,4** ↵
    To point: **END** ↵
    of *(pick the right end of the horizontal line)*
    To point: ↵

The display should now look like that in Fig. 24-39.

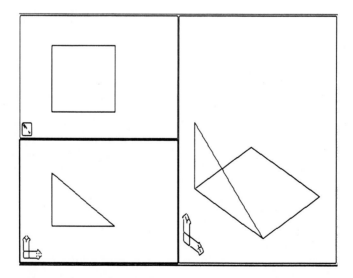

Fig. 24-39. The front surface of the wedge is added using the LINE command. It is displayed in two viewports.

The two lines just drawn represent the front face of the wedge. They are copied to the back surface, after which the upper line connecting the two surfaces is drawn. These steps can be performed in the large viewport. See Fig. 24-40.

> Command: *(pick the large viewport)* **COPY** ↵
> Select objects: *(select the vertical and angled lines)*
> Select objects: ↵
> ⟨Base point or displacement⟩/Multiple: **END** ↵
> of *(pick P1)*
> Second point of displacement: **END** ↵
> of *(pick P2)*
> Command: **LINE** ↵
> From point: **END** ↵
> of *(pick P3)*
> To point: **END** ↵
> of *(pick P4)*
> To point: ↵
> Command:

The wedge should be complete, except for the hole, and should look similar to Fig. 24-40.

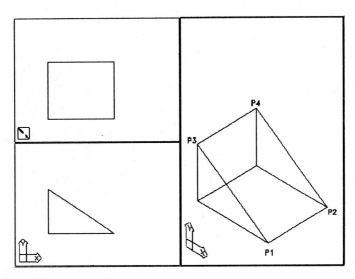

Fig. 24-40. The front face is copied to the back, and the upper connecting line is drawn in the 3-D view.

Aligning the UCS with an angled surface

The only change that has been made to the UCS in this example is to rotate the X axis 90°. Now the task at hand is to draw a circle on the angled surface. Using manual drafting techniques, an angled surface is seen in its true shape and size only when projected to an auxiliary view. An auxiliary view is nothing more than changing your line of sight perpendicular to the angled surface. This means that you see the angled surface as a "plan" view. Look at the lower-left viewport in Fig. 24-40. Notice that the UCS icon has exactly the same orientation as the vertical and horizontal lines of the wedge. The UCS and the front surface are parallel, and your line of sight is perpendicular to those planes.

The UCS in the 3-D view can be placed parallel to the angled surface of the wedge, thus making it easy to draw the circle. The orientation of the UCS must first be changed. The icon itself can then be relocated to the surface. The 3point option of the UCS command changes the UCS to any angled surface. The option requires that you locate a new origin, a point on the positive X axis, and a point on the positive Y axis. Refer to Fig. 24-41 for pick points as you read. Be sure the large viewport is active.

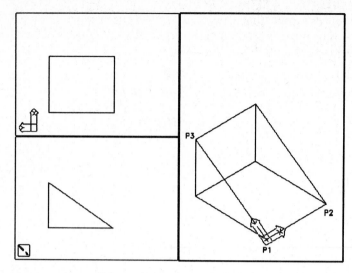

Fig. 24-41. A new UCS can be established by picking three points: P1—the origin, P2—the X axis, and P3—the Y axis.

> Command: *(pick the large viewport)* **UCS** ↵
> Origin/ZAxis/3point/Entity/View/X/Y/Z/Prev/Restore/Save/Del/?/⟨World⟩: **3** ↵
> Origin point: ⟨0,0,0⟩: **END** ↵
> of *(pick P1)*
> Point on positive portion of the X-axis ⟨10.0000,−0.0000,−2.0000⟩: **END** ↵
> of *(pick P2)*
> Point on positive-Y portion of the UCS XY plane ⟨9.0000,1.0000,−2.0000⟩: **END** ↵
> of *(pick P3)*

After you pick P3, the UCS icon changes its orientation to align with the angled surface of the wedge. However, its position at the lower-left corner of the viewport does not change. To help you visualize the drawing, consider moving the icon to the origin of the new UCS. This is done using the UCSICON command.

> Command: **UCSICON** ↵
> ON/OFF/All/Noorigin/ORigin/⟨ON⟩: **OR** ↵

The UCS icon is now located on the origin of the new User Coordinate System. Any coordinate locations you enter will be relative to the new origin. The circle can be drawn with the 3-D view in its present orientation, or you can make the view "plan" to the current UCS in order to see the angled surface in its true shape and size. This example maintains the current 3-D view.

> Command: **CIRCLE** ↵
> 3P/2P/TTR/⟨Center point⟩: **2.5,4** ↵
> Diameter/⟨Radius⟩: **.75** ↵
> Command: **COPY** ↵
> Select objects: **L** ↵
> Select objects: ↵
> ⟨Base point or displacement⟩/Multiple: **CEN** ↵
> of *(pick the circle)*
> Second point of displacement: **@0,0,−1.25** ↵

The circle appears in its correct orientation on the angled surface. The copied circle represents the bottom of the hole. The model is a wireframe. All edges and features can be seen, Fig. 24-42.

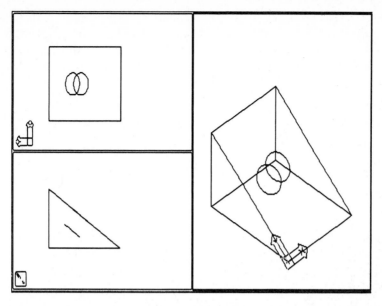

Fig. 24-42. The completed wireframe wedge shows the properly placed circles.

EXERCISE 24-7

☐ Load AutoCAD and begin a new drawing named EX24-7. Establish a three viewport configuration.

☐ Construct the object shown using the techniques discussed in this section. (Do not include dimensions.) Rotate the UCS as needed.

☐ Save the drawing as A:EX24-7.

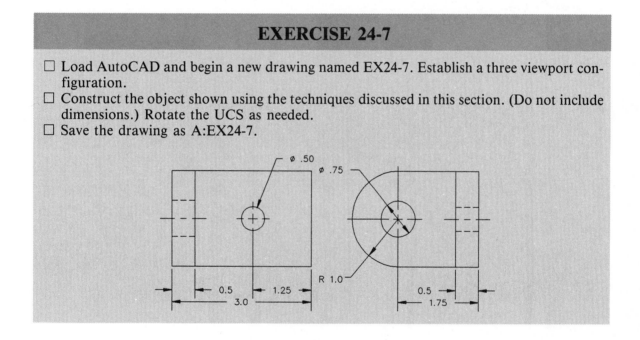

ADDITIONAL METHODS OF CHANGING THE UCS   ARM 9

The previous example illustrated two methods of changing the User Coordinate System. The first was by rotating the X axis of the UCS. The second was by picking three points on the new UCS—the origin and points on the X and Y axes. Several other options exist for altering the UCS. Their use depends on the nature of the object you are drawing. Those options include selecting a new Z axis, picking a new origin for the UCS, rotating the Y and Z axes, and setting the UCS to an existing entity.

Selecting a new Z axis

The ZAxis option of the UCS command allows you to select the origin point and a point on the positive Z axis. Once the new Z axis is defined, AutoCAD establishes the new X and Y axes. Fig. 24-43A illustrates the current UCS on the wedge model and the points required to establish a new UCS using the ZAxis option.

> Command: **UCS** ↵
> Origin/ZAxis/3point/Entity/View/X/Y/Z/Prev/Restore/Save/Del/?/⟨World⟩: **ZA** ↵
> Origin point ⟨0,0,0⟩: **END** ↵
> of *(pick P1)*
> Point on positive portion of Z-axis ⟨default value⟩: **END** ↵
> of *(pick P2)*

The UCS icon should now appear as shown in Fig. 24-43B.

The same option can be used to quickly move the UCS to the front plane of the wedge, Fig. 24-43C. Select point P2 as the origin and press ENTER to accept the default coordinates of the second prompt.

> Command: **UCS** ↵
> Origin/ZAxis/3point/Entity/View/X/Y/Z/Prev/Restore/Save/Del/?/⟨World⟩: **ZA** ↵
> Origin point ⟨0,0,0⟩: **END** ↵
> of *(pick P2)*
> Point on positive portion of Z-axis ⟨default value⟩: ↵

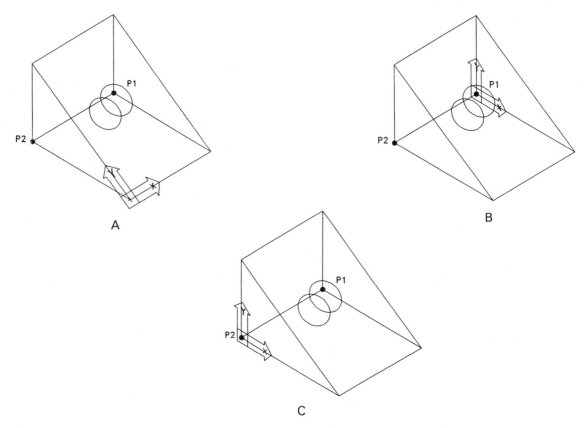

Fig. 24-43. A—The UCS command's ZAxis option requires that you select the new origin and a point on the Z axis. B—The UCS icon is located at the new origin. C—The front plane can be chosen as the origin.

Selecting a new origin

The Origin option is similar to ZAxis because it asks for a new origin point—but that is all it asks for. The UCS icon moves to the specified point and remains parallel to the current UCS. Fig. 24-44 shows how the UCS icon maintains its parallel orientation to the current UCS when moved to different origin points.

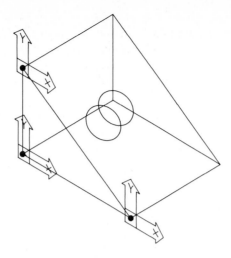

Fig. 24-44. The UCS icon remains parallel to the current UCS when you move the origin using the Origin option.

Rotating the X, Y, and Z axes

A previous example of the wedge showed how to rotate the current UCS around the X axis. The same technique is used to rotate the Y and Z axes. These options are useful when you need to rotate the UCS a given amount, such as 25°, to match the angle of a surface on a part. Fig. 24-45 shows the direction of rotation around each axis when a 90° angle is specified. You can also enter negative angles. The following sequence would be used to rotate the Z axis 90°.

Command: **UCS** ↵
Origin/ZAxis/3point/Entity/View/X/Y/Z/Prev/Restore/Save/Del/?/⟨World⟩: **Z** ↵
Rotation angle about Z axis ⟨0.0⟩: **90** ↵

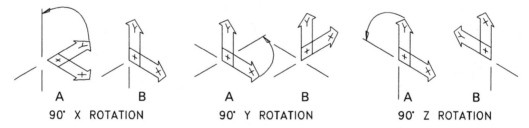

Fig. 24-45. The UCS icon can be rotated around the X, Y, and Z axes by entering a positive or negative angle.

NOTE

The rotation of X, Y, and Z axes may not seem intuitive at first. That is normal if you have not worked with this type of system before. This may be a good time to put the right-hand rule to use. Read that section of this chapter again before continuing. It is located on pages 24-5 to 24-6.

Setting the UCS to an existing entity

The UCS command's Entity option defines a new coordinate system on any entity in an AutoCAD drawing except a 3-D polyline or polygon mesh. Certain rules apply to this technique, and control the orientation of the UCS icon. For example, if you select a circle, the center point becomes the origin of the new UCS. The pick point on the circle determines the direction of the X axis. The Y axis is relative to X, and the UCS Z axis is the same as the Z axis of the entity selected. See Fig. 24-46A for selecting the circle on the wedge for the new UCS:

Command: *(pick the right viewport)* **UCS** ↵
Origin/ZAxis/3point/Entity/View/X/Y/Z/Prev/Restore/Save/Del/?/⟨World⟩: **E** ↵
Select object to align UCS: *(pick the top circle)*

The UCS icon probably looks like the one shown in Fig. 24-46A, which might not be what you expected. The rule for selecting an entity for a new UCS states that the X axis is determined by the pick point on the circle. To rotate the UCS in the current plane, so the X and Y axes are parallel with sides of the object, Fig. 24-46B, use the ZAxis option of the UCS command:

Command: **UCS** ↵
Origin/ZAxis/3point/Entity/View/X/Y/Z/Prev/Restore/Save/Del/?/⟨World⟩: **ZA** ↵
Origin point ⟨0,0,0⟩: **CEN** ↵
of *(pick the circle)*
Point on positive portion of Z-axis ⟨0.0000,0.0000,1.0000⟩: ↵

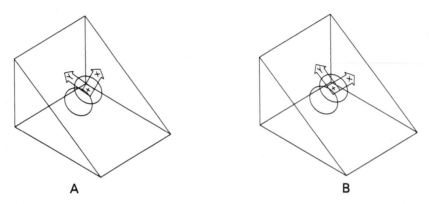

A   B

Fig. 24-46. A—The X axis of the UCS icon placed at the pick point of the circle. B—The UCS rotated parallel to the object with the ZAxis option.

Setting the UCS perpendicular to current view

You may need to add horizontal notes or labels to a 3-D drawing. This is easily done. First select the View option of the UCS command. The UCS icon rotates to a position perpendicular to the current view.

Command: **UCS** ↵
Origin/ZAxis/3point/Entity/View/X/Y/Z/Prev/Restore/Save/Del/?/⟨World⟩: **V** ↵

Any text added to the drawing now appears horizontally, Fig. 24-47.

WIREFRAME WEDGE

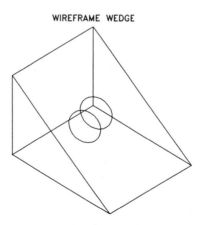

Fig. 24-47. The View option allows you to label a drawing with text that is horizontal in the current view.

Preset UCS orientations

AutoCAD offers six preset UCS orientations. Select the UCS command found in Settings pull-down menu. Then select the Presets... option. The "UCS Orientation" dialogue box shown in Fig. 24-48 is then displayed.

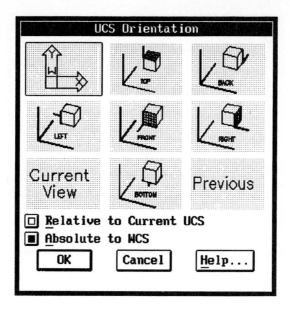

Fig. 24-48. The "UCS Orientation" dialogue box provides six preset UCS configurations.

Six icons in the dialogue box allow you to select a preset User Coordinate System. The icon at the upper left returns to the World Coordinate System. If you wish to restore the previous UCS you were working with, pick Previous in the lower-right corner. The Current View button creates a UCS that is perpendicular to the current view. The use of this feature is discussed later in the chapter. The two radio buttons in the dialogue box allow you to create a new UCS that is relative to the current UCS or absolute to the WCS.

If you have a UCS set, keep in mind that a plan view of any coordinate system can also be considered a top view. Therefore, if you select the Front icon to set a new UCS relative to the current on, you are basically rotating the UCS icon 90° around the X axis. This can be a convenient method for creating a new UCS. It is then easy to move the UCS icon to a new origin by using the Origin options of the UCS and UCSICON commands.

--- **PROFESSIONAL TIP** ---

When you select a preset UCS from the dialogue box, remember that if the World Coordinate System is current, the Absolute to WCS radio button is on by default. Therefore, any UCS icon you pick sets a new UCS based on the World Coordinate System. However, if any coordinate system other than the WCS is current when the dialogue box appears, the Relative to Current UCS radio button is the default. In this case, the icon you pick rotates the new coordinate system 90° relative to the current one. The six preset UCS selections rotate the new coordinate system 90° relative to the current one.

UCS dialogue boxes

User Coordinate Systems can be created, selected, and modified using dialogue boxes. The DDUCS (Dynamic Dialogue UCS) command activates the "UCS Control" dialogue box. You can also select the Settings pull-down menu, pick UCS, and then pick the Named UCS... option. The display is shown in Fig. 24-49.

The UCS Names area of the dialogue box contains names of all saved coordinate systems, plus *WORLD*. If other coordinate systems have been used, the word *PREVIOUS* appears in the list. The listing *NO NAME* appears if the current coordinate system has not been named. Make any of the listed coordinate systems active by picking the Current button below the list.

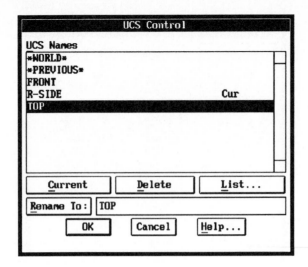

Fig. 24-49. The "UCS Control" dialogue box allows you to name, list, delete, and define User Coordinate Systems.

A list of coordinate and axis values of the current UCS can be displayed by picking List... in the "UCS Control" dialogue box. This displays the "UCS Origin Point and Axis Vectors" dialogue box shown in Fig. 24-50.

UCS Origin Point and Axis Vectors			
Name: FRONT			
Origin	**X Axis**	**Y Axis**	**Z Axis**
X=0.0000	X=1.0000	X=0.0000	X=0.0000
Y=0.0000	Y=0.0000	Y=1.0000	Y=0.0000
Z=0.0000	Z=0.0000	Z=0.0000	Z=1.0000

Fig. 24-50. The "UCS Origin Point and Axis Vectors" dialogue box displays the coordinate values of the current UCS.

Use the following steps to define and name a new User Coordinate System:
1. Pick the "UCS Orientation" dialogue box to display the preset icons.
2. Select the orientation you need and pick the OK button.
3. Select the UCS command and use the Save option to enter a name for the new UCS.

Setting an automatic plan display

Earlier in the chapter you learned how to set a viewport "plan" to the current UCS using the PLAN command. After changing the UCS, a plan view is often needed to give you a better feel for the XYZ directions. The plan view also enables you to visualize the object in a pictorial view; and, it makes it easier to decide the best viewpoint orientation to pick.

If the UCSFOLLOW system variable is set to 1, AutoCAD automatically generates a plan view in the current viewport when the UCS is changed. The default setting of UCSFOLLOW is zero (0), or off. The UCSFOLLOW variable can be set for each viewport individually. The following example sets UCSFOLLOW to 1 for the current viewport only.

Command: **UCSFOLLOW** ↵
New value for UCSFOLLOW ⟨0⟩: **1** ↵

Working with more than one UCS

You can create as many different UCSs as needed to construct your model or drawing. AutoCAD allows you to name coordinate systems for future use. Several options of the UCS command are provided so you can work with multiple coordinate systems.

- **?** — Switches the screen to text mode and displays all of the named coordinate systems. The display includes the coordinate values of the XYZ axes of each UCS, relative to the current UCS. The name of the current UCS is given first. If the current UCS does not have a name, and is different than the world UCS, "*NO NAME*" appears.
- **Previous (P)** — Allows you to display previously used coordinate systems. AutoCAD remembers ten previous systems in both model space and paper space, for a total of twenty. You can step back through them in the same manner that ZOOM Previous displays previous windows.
- **Restore (R)** — Requires the name of the UCS you wish restored. If you forget the names, enter a question mark (?) to list saved coordinate systems. Only the orientation of the UCS icon will change. The views remain the same.
- **Save (S)** — Save a UCS by entering a name having 31 characters or less. Numbers, letters, and the dollar sign ($), hyphen (-), and underscore (__) are valid.
- **Delete (D)** — Enter the name of the UCS to be deleted. You can use wild card characters and "?," or delete a list by separating the names with commas.
- **World (W)** — Resets the World Coordinate System (WCS) as the current UCS.

PROFESSIONAL TIP

Most drawings can be created using a single named UCS. This UCS is rotated and placed on any plane on which you are working. If the drawing is complex, with several planes each containing a large amount of detail, you may wish to establish a named UCS for each detailed face. Then, to work on a different plane, just restore the proper UCS. For example, when working with architectural drawings, you may wish to establish a different UCS for each floor plan and elevation view, and for roofs that require detail work.

VIEWING THREE-DIMENSIONAL MODELS | ARM 7 |

The DVIEW (Dynamic VIEW) command allows you to view models three-dimensionally and control every aspect of the display. The viewer's eye location is called the *camera,* and the focus point is the *target.* These two points form the *line of sight*, which can be adjusted to any angle. In addition, the distance from the camera to the target is adjustable in a perspective view. Moreover, the camera can be fitted with a telephoto or wide angle lens for a close-up or wide field of vision. The entire image can be panned or *twisted* (rotated) around the center point of the display. Imaginary front and back cutting planes can be established to "clip" portions of the model you do not wish to view. Hidden lines can also be removed. Since the DVIEW command is such a powerful tool, plan to test its options and experiment with the various displays you can achieve.

Test drawings for DVIEW

The DVIEW command, found in the DISPLAY screen menu, is so useful for visualization because the display moves dynamically as you alter the view. As you rotate, zoom, and pan the drawing, the view constantly changes. This process can be slow if you use the DVIEW command on a large drawing. Therefore, use a test drawing to create the view needed, then display your drawing using the new view settings.

AutoCAD has a DVIEW test drawing named DVIEWBLK. This drawing is a block in the ACAD.DWG drawing file. DVIEWBLK is a simple house with a chimney, window, and open door, Fig. 24-51. Since the drawing contains few entities, it can be rotated, zoomed, and panned quickly. When you finish using DVIEW and exit the command, the current drawing is regenerated using the display parameters just selected with DVIEWBLK.

The DVIEWBLK drawing is displayed if you press ENTER at the Select objects: prompt of the DVIEW command, or if you pick Dviewblk in the DVIEW screen menu.

Command: **DVIEW** ↵
Select objects: ↵
CAmera/TArget/Distance/POints/PAn/Zoom/TWist/CLip/Hide/Off/Undo/〈eXit〉:

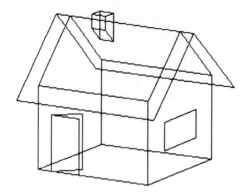

Fig. 24-51. The default DVIEWBLK drawing, a small house, helps you quickly select a viewing angle for your drawing.

A plan view of the house then appears on the screen. You may not see the entire house at first, depending on the nature of the current drawing.

PROFESSIONAL TIP

You can create your own custom block called DVIEWBLK. Draw it to fit into a one unit cube. Give the lower-left corner as the origin. Keep the drawing simple. If you work with mechanical parts, draw an object that represents a typical part. If you work with industrial piping, draw a pipe fitting. Architects can use the default DVIEWBLK. Structural designers might draw a piece of wide flange. To use your custom DVIEWBLK, select the DVIEW command and press ENTER in response to the Select objects: prompt.

View the entire drawing

When you use DVIEW on a drawing for the first time, the image may fill the entire screen. If so, zoom away in order to see the entire object.

> Command: **DVIEW** ↵
> Select objects: ↵
> CAmera/TArget/Distance/POints/PAn/Zoom/TWist/Clip/Hide/Off/Undo/⟨eXit⟩: **Z** ↵
> Adjust zoom scale factor ⟨1⟩: **.5** ↵

The entire drawing should now be centered on screen at half its original size. If not, select the Zoom option again. Enter a value less than 1.0 until the entire drawing fits within the screen borders.

Specify the camera angle

If, after selecting the DVIEW command, the drawing display is a plan view, it is best to use the CAmera option first. This option lets you locate your eye position in relation to the object.

PROFESSIONAL TIP

It often is easier to visualize your viewpoint (camera angle) first, before adjusting the view using other options. Remember that the first view displayed is a plan view.

You can move your eyes in two directions relative to object. A vertical movement is referred to as the angle *from* the XY plane, and a horizontal movement is *in* the XY plane from the X axis. A plan view is 90° from the XY plane, therefore, your line of sight is perpendicular to the XY plane of the current UCS. With the DVIEWBLK drawing on screen, a 90° camera angle places your line of sight looking down onto the roof, while a 0° camera angle places the line of sight looking into the front door.

The CAmera option of DVIEW changes the camera angle. After selecting the option, you can move the pointing device to pick the best display. The current angle (specified in the prompt) appears on the status line where the coordinates normally show. This number changes as you move the pointer. An angle value can also be entered at the keyboard.

    CAmera/TArget/Distance/POints/PAn/Zoom/TWist/CLip/Hide/Off/Undo/⟨eXit⟩: **CA** ↵
    Toggle angle in/Enter angle from XY plane ⟨90.00⟩: **15** ↵

The next prompt requests the angle of the camera in the XY plane. A 0° value results in a view looking straight down the X axis, or into the window of DVIEWBLK. As the camera moves to the right, or counterclockwise around the house, the angle increases with a positive value. A negative rotation angle moves the camera left, or clockwise, around the house.

    Toggle angle from/Enter angle in XY plane from X axis ⟨−90.00⟩: **−60** ↵

The view achieved by these vertical and horizontal angles is shown in Fig. 24-52.

    While the CAmera option prompts are on the screen, you can toggle between the horizontal and vertical angle input by using the Toggle option. If the prompt reads "Toggle angle in," you can select this option to input the angle *in* the XY plane by entering a T and pressing ENTER. Now you can enter a camera angle in the XY plane. When you use the Toggle option in this manner, the prompt changes to "Toggle angle from." This allows you to try several angles while still in the command option.

Fig. 24-52. The view achieved using a 15° value for the camera from the XY plane and a −60° value in the XY plane from the X axis.

When you first enter the CAmera option, you can move the pointing device and the object on the screen rotates in all directions. You can limit this movement to one direction by entering an angle and pressing ENTER. For example, if you enter "20" for the angle from the XY plane as follows, the object remains stationary at that angle and only moves clockwise or counterclockwise on the X axis as you move the pointing device left or right.

    Toggle angle in/Enter angle from XY plane ⟨90.00⟩: **20** ↵

In this manner, you can view the object at the vertical angle of 20° from any horizontal angle in the XY plane. You can also first enter an angle in the XY plane, such as 30, and then move the pointing device up or down to see the object rotate at this horizontal angle.

    Toggle angle from/Enter angle from XY plane ⟨90.00⟩: **30** ↵

Select the target angles

    Another way to change your view is with the TArget option. The *target* is the point at which the camera looks. The target can be rotated around the camera to any angle. A 90° vertical rotation angle would create a view opposite the side of the object shown with a 90° vertical camera angle, Fig. 24-53.

If you enter the same angles in the TArget option as were used previously in the CAmera option, the view would be from below the floor of the house, Fig. 24-54:

Command: **DVIEW** ↵
Select objects: ↵
CAmera/TArget/Distance/POints/PAn/Zoom/TWist/CLip/Hide/Off/Undo/〈eXit〉: **TA** ↵
Toggle angle in/Enter angle from XY plane 〈−90.00〉: **15** ↵
Toggle angle from/Enter angle in XY plane from X axis 〈90.00〉: **−60** ↵

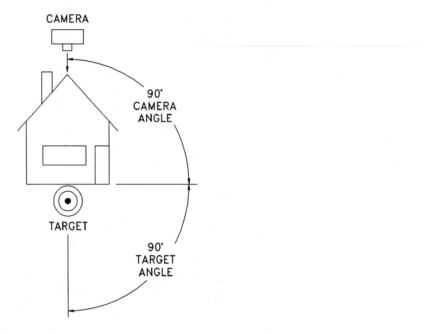

Fig. 24-53. The vertical rotation angle for the target is opposite that of the camera.

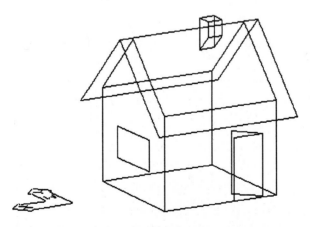

Fig. 24-54. This view from under the floor of the DVIEWBLK reflects a vertical 15° angle and a horizontal −60° angle.

Setting a distance between camera and target (perspective)

The views obtained thus far were all in a parallel projection. For a more realistic perspective display, select the Distance option. Lines in a perspective view project to vanishing points. Thus, lines farther from the camera appear to converge, or meet. AutoCAD indicates the perspective mode by placing a perspective icon in the lower-left corner on the screen. The Distance option moves the camera closer or farther from the target.

> CAmera/TArget/Distance/POints/PAn/Zoom/TWist/CLip/Hide/Off/Undo/〈eXit〉: **D** ↵
> New camera/target distance 〈1.0000〉: **50** ↵

The new view should now look like that shown in Fig. 24-55.

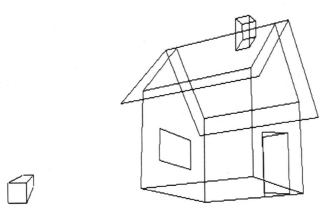

Fig. 24-55. DVIEWBLK with new Distance values. Note the perspective icon in the lower-left corner.

A slider bar appears when you select the Distance option. It is labeled from 0x to 16x. The current distance is 1x. When you move the slider bar to 9x, the camera moves away nine times the previous distance. You can pick a distance with the slider bar, by entering a distance at the keyboard, or by reading the screen display. The status line constantly displays the distance. If your drawing uses architectural units, enter a distance relative to those units to get a complete view of your drawing. For example, if the house is 40 feet wide, you may have to enter a distance greater than 40 feet to see the entire house.

Pick points for the target and camera

The POints option allows you to pick the target and camera locations using XYZ coordinates, filters, or OSNAP options. OSNAP options must be typed. When entering XYZ coordinates, consider the orientation of the current UCS, or you may get unexpected results. POints is an option best used when you have already created a display other than the initial plan view. Fig. 24-56 illustrates example target (P1) and camera (P2) pick points, and the resulting view. As you select the pick points, AutoCAD provides a rubberband line from the camera to the target to help you see the new line of sight. The command sequence to obtain the view in Fig. 24-56 is:

> Command: **DVIEW** ↵
> Select objects: ↵
> CAmera/TArget/Distance/POints/PAn/Zoom/TWist/CLip/Hide/Off/Undo/〈eXit〉: **PO** ↵
> Enter target point 〈default〉: **MID** ↵
> of *(pick P1)*
> Enter camera point 〈default〉: **END** ↵
> of *(pick P2)*

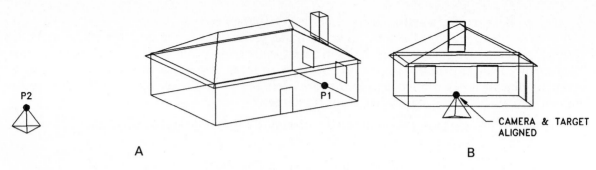

Fig. 24-56. A—The target (P1) and camera (P2) are picked using the POints option. B—The resulting pictorial view.

Notice in view B that the target and camera points are aligned. The camera point at the top of the tripod touches the target point. These two points are the line of sight. The display changes from perspective to a parallel projection to help you select camera and target points. The display then returns to perspective.

PROFESSIONAL TIP

Several DVIEW options display horizontal slider bars. Use these bars to visually set your display or read approximate values. The value to be set in the current DVIEW option replaces normal coordinate display on the status line. The diamond in the bar indicates position. Rubberband lines are anchored to a short line in the slider bar. This short line indicates the present position of the drawing. When the diamond is centered on the short line, the current dynamic position is the same as the present drawing position.

Change the position of the drawing

The PAn option of DVIEW is similar to the PAN command. It allows you to move the entire drawing in relation to the graphics display area. To see part of your drawing off the screen, use PAn as follows:

CAmera/TArget/Distance/POints/PAn/Zoom/TWist/CLip/Hide/Off/Undo/⟨eXit⟩: **PA** ↵
Displacement base point: *(pick a point to grab the image)*
Second point: *(pick the new location)*

Using a zoom lens

AutoCAD allows you to change lenses on its camera just as you would a real camera. Lens lengths are measured in millimeters. A zoom, or telephoto, lens is greater than 50 mm. It allows you to get a close-up view while not changing your distance to the object. A wide angle lens is less than 50 mm. It takes in a wider field of vision as the lens length gets smaller. You can change lenses with the Zoom option.

The Zoom option was used previously in this chapter to specify a scale factor for the DVIEWBLK drawing. If your display is not in perspective, Zoom will always request a scale factor. If the display is in perspective, Zoom allows you to adjust the lens length.

CAmera/TArget/Distance/POints/PAn/Zoom/TWist/CLip/Hide/Off/Undo/⟨eXit⟩: **Z** ↵
Adjust lens length ⟨50.000mm⟩: **28** ↵

A 28 mm lens, commonly known as a "fish-eye," creates a wide field of vision. This lens can distort the sides of your drawing depending on the current distance setting. Two views of the DVIEWBLK drawing are shown in Fig. 24-57, both using a distance of 40 feet.

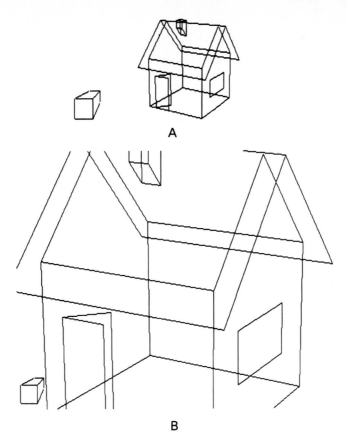

Fig. 24-57. A—A 28 mm wide angle view at a distance of 40 feet. B—A 100 mm telephoto view at a distance of 40 feet.

Rotate the drawing around a point

The TWist option allows you to rotate the drawing around the center point of the screen. When the twist, or tilt angle, is specified with the pointing device, the angle appears on the status line. A rubberband line connects the center point to the crosshairs. An exact angle, positive or negative, can be entered at the keyboard.

Clipping portions of the drawing

Portions of a drawing can be eliminated from the display by using *clipping planes*. Visualize a clipping plane as a wall, or cutting plane, that hides everything in front of or behind it. The plane is always perpendicular to your line of sight. Lines behind the back clipping plane or lines in front of the front clipping plane are removed. The CLip option lets you dynamically place a clipping plane, or enter its distance from the target. Both planes are turned on by entering a distance, or turned off by selecting the OFF option. The camera is the default position of the front plane. After being set elsewhere the front clipping plane is returned to the camera position with the Eye option.

CAmera/TArget/Distance/POints/PAn/Zoom/TWist/CLip/Hide/Off/Undo/⟨eXit⟩: **CL** ↵
Back/Front/⟨Off⟩: **B** ↵
ON/OFF/ ⟨Distance from target⟩ ⟨default distance⟩: *(enter a distance or use the slider bar to pick)*
CAmera/TArget/Distance/POints/PAn/Zoom/TWist/CLip/Hide/Off/Undo/⟨eXit⟩: **CL** ↵
Back/Front/⟨Off⟩: **F** ↵
Eye/ON/OFF/⟨Distance from target⟩ ⟨default⟩: **E** ↵

When perspective is on, the front clipping plane is automatically on. The ON/OFF options of the Front clipping plane are offered only if perspective is off. Fig. 24-58 shows a drawing with front and back clipping planes.

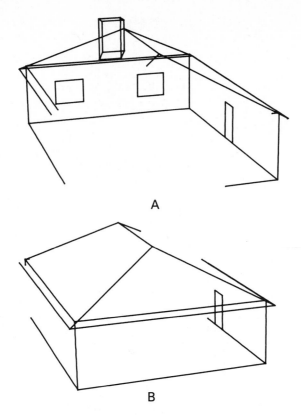

Fig. 24-58. A—Front clipping plane placed in the drawing. B—Back clipping plane placed.

Other DVIEW options

The three remaining options of DVIEW are Off, Undo, and Exit.
- **Off (O)** — Turns off perspective.
- **Undo (U)** — Enables you to undo the previous DVIEW option. Like the regular UNDO command, it lets you step back through previous DVIEW functions.
- **eXit (X)** — Exits the DVIEW command and regenerates the drawing using the last view established.

EXERCISE 24-8

☐ Begin a new drawing called EX24-8. Draw a house similar to the DVIEWBLK drawing in Fig. 24-51.
☐ Select the DVIEW command to select a camera angle. Select the Zoom option to see the entire house that you drew.
☐ Draw a small box in the center of the house.
☐ Draw another object of your choice outside the house.
☐ Use the DVIEW command's POints option to place the camera on the object outside the house and the target on a corner of the box inside the house.
☐ Select the Distance option to move farther away and then closer to the target.
☐ Zoom to a point on or near the box inside the house.
☐ Select the TArget option. Pick an angle from the XY plane near zero. Move the pointer to several positions when picking the horizontal rotation. Notice how the house moves around you. Pick a view that allows you to see the object outside the house.
☐ Use the CLip option to place a back clipping plane that hides the object outside the house.
☐ Save the drawing as A:EX24-8.

3-D OBJECTS AND CONSTRUCTIONS

AutoCAD provides a group of 3-D objects that can be constructed with a minimum amount of effort; all you need to know are the basic dimensions and the location of the object. The result is a 3-D object that is surfaced. The HIDE command makes the object appear solid, therefore, the design can be used in other presentation and animation programs such as AutoShade®, AutoFlix™, Autodesk Animator Pro™, and Autodesk 3D Studio™.

The 3-D objects provided are box, wedge, pyramid, cone, dish, dome, sphere, torus, and mesh. The box and dome are discussed later in the digitizer puck tutorial. All shapes are displayed in the "3D Objects" icon menu. This icon menu can be accessed by picking 3D Surfaces in the Draw pull-down menu and then picking the 3D Objects option. You can also type "3D" at the Command: prompt to access these shapes.

The objects are each created as a 3-D mesh, therefore, each is a single entity. If you wish to edit parts of these objects, use the EXPLODE command. After exploding, each object is composed of 3-D faces.

── NOTE ──

AutoCAD creates two types of 3-D shapes—solid primitives and surfaced wireframes. They are listed below:

Solid Primitives		**Surfaced Wireframes**		
Box	Cone	Box	Cone	Dome
Sphere	Torus	Sphere	Torus	Dish
Wedge	Cylinder	Wedge	Pyramid	Mesh

If you type the name of one of the solid primitives listed above at the Command: prompt, you will load the solid model version of that shape. If you want to use one of the surfaced wireframes listed above, pick them from the "3D Objects" icon menu, or use one of the following methods at the Command: prompt:

    Command: **3D** ↵
    Box/Cone/Dish/DOme/Mesh/Pyramid/Sphere/Torus/Wedge: **C** ↵

or

    Command: **AI_CONE** ↵

Both of these commands allow you to draw a surfaced cone. The "AI" refers to an "Autodesk Incorporated" AutoLISP command definition that is found in the 3D.LSP file. The underscore character (_) is used in the ACAD.MNU file of Release 12 to allow commands to be automatically translated in foreign language versions of AutoCAD.

Wedge

A right-angled wedge can be constructed using the WEDGE command. After you locate a corner of the wedge, enter the length, width, height, and rotation angle. AutoCAD draws the shape. The wedge and its values are shown in Fig. 24-59. Remember to access the "3D Objects" icon box and pick the wedge icon, or type the following:

    Command: **AI_WEDGE** ↵
    Corner of wedge: **6,3** ↵
    Length: **3** ↵
    Width: **2** ↵
    Height: **2** ↵
    Rotation angle about Z axis: **−15** ↵

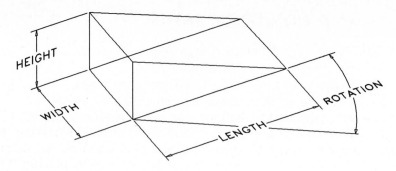

Fig. 24-59. The wedge requires a location point, length, width, height, and rotation angle.

Pyramid

The PYRAMID command allows you to draw three different shapes (shown in Fig. 24-60) and two tetrahedrons (shown in Fig. 24-61). If you wish to draw pyramids with an apex, ridge, or truncated top, first draw the four base points. Then, you are given the options of Ridge, Top, or Apex (the default). To draw the apex of a pyramid, be sure to either use XYZ filters to locate it, or enter an XYZ coordinate.

> Command: **AI_PYRAMID** ↵
> First base point: **2,6** ↵
> Second base point: **@2,0** ↵
> Third base point: **@0,2** ↵
> Tetrahedron/⟨Fourth base point⟩: **@−2,0** ↵
> Ridge/Top/⟨Apex point⟩: **.XY** ↵
> of **3,7** ↵
> (need Z): **3** ↵

The Ridge option requires two points to define the ridge. After you draw the base, select Ridge. You will notice that the last line of the pyramid that was drawn is now highlighted. This indicates that the first point of the ridge will begin perpendicular to the highlighted line. However, the first point does not have to touch the highlighted line.

> Ridge/Top/⟨Apex point⟩: **R** ↵
> First ridge point: **.XY** ↵
> of *(pick a point inside the highlighted line)*
> (need Z): **3** ↵
> Second ridge point: **.XY** ↵
> of *(pick a point inside the second highlighted line)*
> (need Z): **3** ↵

The apex and ridge pyramids are shown in Fig. 24-60.

The Top option works in a similar fashion to Ridge, but a rubberband line is attached from the first corner of the pyramid to your crosshairs when you select "T." The prompt then asks you for "First top point." Again, be sure to use filters to locate the top points. The same rubberband line is attached to each corner of the base. The top point is attached to the base along that line when the pyramid is completed. See Fig. 24-60.

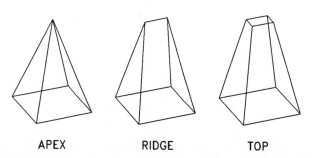

APEX   RIDGE   TOP

Fig. 24-60. The PYRAMID command allows you to create an apex, ridge, or truncated pyramid.

PROFESSIONAL TIP

Try constructing pyramids in the plan view, using XYZ coordinates or filters. Your constructions will be more accurate, and you can easily see the symmetry or asymmetry that is required.

A *tetrahedron* is a four-sided solid, all faces being triangles. A *pyramid* is a five-sided solid, four sides of which are triangles. Like the pyramid, a tetrahedron can have an apex or flattened top. The following example illustrates how to construct a tetrahedron.

> Command: **AI__PYRAMID** ↵
> First base point: **2,2** ↵
> Second base point: **@3,0** ↵
> Third base point: **@0,3** ↵
> Tetrahedron/⟨Fourth base point⟩: **T** ↵
> Top/⟨Apex point⟩: **.XY** ↵
> of *(pick P1 in the middle of the triangle)* (need Z): **3** ↵
> Command: **VPOINT** ↵
> Rotate/⟨View point⟩ ⟨default⟩: **−1,−1,1** ↵

The tetrahedron should look like the one in Fig. 24-61A. A flattened top can be given to a tetrahedron by selecting the Top option, Fig. 24-61B.

> Tetrahedron/⟨Fourth base point⟩: **T** ↵
> Top/⟨Apex point⟩: **T** ↵
> First top point: **.XY** ↵
> of *(pick P1)* (need Z): **2.5** ↵
> Second top point: **.XY** ↵
> of *(pick P2)* (need Z): **2.5** ↵
> Third top point: **.XY** ↵
> of *(pick P3)* (need Z): **2.5** ↵

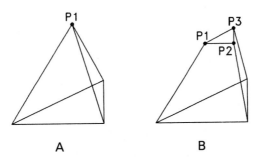

Fig. 24-61. A—Tetrahedron has four triangular sides and an apex (P1). B—A flat-topped tetrahedron showing the three pick points for the top surface.

Cone

The CONE command draws pointed and truncated cones. Two dimensions are required for the pointed cone—the base diameter and the height. The truncated cone requires an additional diameter of the top.

> Command: **AI__CONE** ↵
> Base center point: **3,3** ↵
> Diameter/⟨radius⟩ of base: **1** ↵
> Diameter/⟨radius⟩ of top ⟨0⟩: **.15** ↵
> Height: **2** ↵
> Number of segments ⟨16⟩: ↵

If you want a pointed cone, simply press ENTER at the Diameter/⟨radius⟩ of top: prompt. The two types of cones are shown in Fig. 24-62.

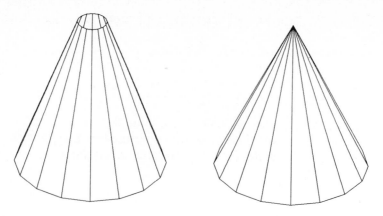

Fig. 24-62. The CONE command draws a truncated or pointed cone.

Dome and dish

Think of the dish or dome as half a sphere, or hemisphere. The top of the dome and bottom of the dish are the north and south poles respectively. The longitudinal segments run east and west around the circumference of the dome. The latitudinal segments run north and south. See Fig. 24-63. The command sequence is as follows:

Command: **AI_DOME** ↵
Center of dome: *(pick a point)*
Diameter/⟨radius⟩: **2** ↵
Number of longitudinal segments ⟨16⟩: *(enter a value or press ENTER)*
Number of latitudinal segments ⟨8⟩: *(enter a value or press ENTER)*

Fig. 24-63. Longitude runs east and west, while latitude runs north and south on the dish or dome.

Sphere

The sphere requires the same information as the dish and dome. Since the sphere is a complete globe, the default value for latitudinal segments is the same as longitudinal segments.

Torus

A *torus* looks like an inflated inner tube. Fig. 24-64 illustrates the torus radius and tube diameter. AutoCAD requires the number of segments around the torus circumference and around the tube circumference.

Command: **AI_TORUS** ↵
Center of torus: *(pick the center point)*
Diameter/⟨radius⟩ of torus: **2** ↵
Diameter/⟨radius⟩ of tube: **.5** ↵
Segments around tube circumference ⟨16⟩: ↵
Segments around torus circumference ⟨16⟩: ↵

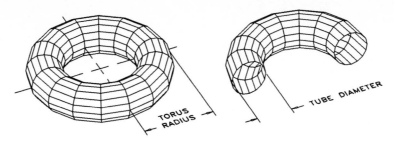

Fig. 24-64. You must specify the torus and tube radii or diameters and the number of segments around each.

Displaying a quick shaded rendering

Any solid or surfaced object in AutoCAD can be displayed with its hidden lines removed by using the HIDE command. However, you can also use the SHADE command to quickly display your drawing as a rendered solid. When you use the SHADE command, all solids and 3-D faces are shaded according to the color of the entities. This is good for visualizing the shape of objects and their relationships.

The SHADEDGE system variable controls the type of rendering the SHADE command produces. SHADEDGE has four settings:

- **0**—Edges are not highlighted and faces are shaded. This option requires a 256 color display.
- **1**—Edges are highlighted in the background color and the faces are shaded. This option also requires a 256 color display.
- **2**—Similar to hidden line removal. Edges are highlighted in the entity's color and the faces are displayed in the background color.
- **3**—Edges are highlighted and faces are shown in the entity's color. This is the default for SHADEDGE.

While using the SHADE command can help in visualization, it may also require considerable time, depending on the size of your drawing. It takes approximately twice the regeneration time to shade a drawing. It may be quicker to shade in a viewport rather than on the entire screen. The REGEN command removes the shaded image and returns the drawing to a wireframe.

Arraying 3-D objects

The 3DARRAY command lets you array an object in 3-D space. It functions much the same as the ARRAY command, but requires a third dimension. In addition to rows and columns, *levels* comprise the third dimension (Z). The command sequence is the same as the 2-D array command, with the addition of the Number of levels: prompt. The following example creates a rectangular array of a pyramid. Fig. 24-65 shows the result.

Command: **3DARRAY** ↵
Initializing... 3DARRAY loaded.
Select objects: *(pick the pyramid)*
Select objects: ↵
Rectangular or Polar array (R/P): **R** ↵
Number of rows (---) ⟨1⟩: **2** ↵
Number of columns (III) ⟨1⟩: **3** ↵
Number of levels (...) ⟨1⟩: **3** ↵
Distance between rows (---): **1.5** ↵
Distance between columns (III): **1.5** ↵
Distance between levels (...): **1.5** ↵
Command: **VPOINT** ↵
Rotate/⟨View point⟩⟨0.00,0.00,0.00⟩: **−2,−4,1** ↵
Regenerating drawing

Your drawing should look similar to Fig. 24-65.

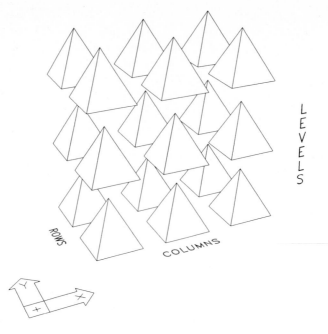

Fig. 24-65. A rectangular 3-D array is composed of rows, columns, and levels.

A 3-D polar array is similar to the 2-D version except that it needs a Z axis of rotation, Fig. 24-66. The Z axis of the 3-D polar array can be different than that of the current UCS. The command sequence is as follows:

Command: **3DARRAY** ↵
Select objects: *(pick the pyramid)*
Select objects: ↵
Rectangular or Polar array (R/P): **P** ↵
Number of items: **5** ↵
Angle to fill ⟨360⟩: **−180** ↵
Rotate objects as they are copied? ⟨Y⟩: **N** ↵
Center point of array: *(pick P1)*
Second point on axis of rotation: *(pick point on new Z axis)*

A positive number entered at the Angle to fill: prompt rotates the array counterclockwise. A negative angle rotates it clockwise. The 3-D array itself is tilted 90° to the current UCS. That is because the new Z axis defined for this 3-D array is parallel to the XY plane of the current UCS. See Fig. 24-66.

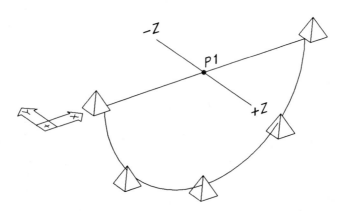

Fig. 24-66. The 3-D array can rotate about a temporary Z axis that is tilted 90° to the current UCS.

3-D polyline

A 3-D polyline is drawn using the 3DPOLY command. In addition to typing in the command, it can be picked from the cascading submenu of the Polyline option in the Draw pull-down menu, or from the 3D Surfs page of the DRAW screen menu. A 3-D polyline is similar in all ways to a regular polyline except for the addition of the third dimension. Any form of coordinate entry is valid for drawing 3-D polylines.

Command: **3DPOLY** ⏎
From point: **4,3,6** ⏎
Close/Undo/⟨Endpoint of line⟩: **@2,0,1** ⏎
Close/Undo/⟨Endpoint of line⟩: **@0,2,1** ⏎

Several 3-D polyline segments drawn together can be closed with the Close option. The Undo option allows you to remove the last segment and still remain in the command with a rubber-band line attached to the previous point.

The PEDIT command can be used to edit 3-D polylines. The Spline option of PEDIT is used to fit a B-spline curve to the 3-D polyline. Fig. 24-67 shows a regular 3-D polyline and the same polyline fit with a B-spline curve. The SPLFRAME system variable controls the display of the original polyline frame, and is either on (1) or off (0).

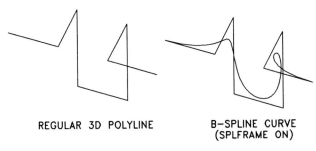

REGULAR 3D POLYLINE   B—SPLINE CURVE
(SPLFRAME ON)

Fig. 24-67. A regular 3-D polyline and the B-spline curve version after using the PEDIT command.

Invisible 3DFACE edges

The 3DFACE command allows you to remove, or hide, edges that would not normally appear as lines on a surface. This feature is handled by the Invisible option of the 3DFACE command. Simply select Invisible before picking the first point of the invisible edge. The following example illustrates how to use the Invisible option to hide edges, Fig. 24-68:

Command: **3DFACE** ⏎
First point: *(pick P1)*
Second point: *(pick P2)*
Third point: **I** ⏎ *(pick P3)*
Fourth point: *(pick P4)*
Third point: **I** ⏎ *(pick P5)*
Fourth point: *(pick P6)*
Third point: ⏎
Command: ⏎
3DFACE First point: *(pick P6)*
Second point: *(pick P7)*
Third point: *(pick P8)*
Fourth point: **I** ⏎ *(pick P5)*
Third point: ⏎

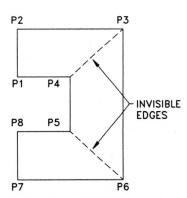

Fig. 24-68. Invisible edges can be hidden using the 3DFACE command.

Two additional options control the visibility of edges between 3-D faces. If the SPLFRAME system variable is set to 0, all invisible edges are not displayed. If SPLFRAME is set to another number, all edges are displayed. Picking either of the two selections in the 3dface option of the DRAW screen menu activates the SPLFRAME variable.

- **Showedge** — Displays all hidden edges. SPLFRAME is set to 1. Shows the following prompt:

  Invisible edges will be SHOWN after next Regeneration.

- **HideEdges** — Hides all edges drawn with the Invisible option. SPLFRAME is set to 0. Shows the following prompt:

  Invisible edges will be HIDDEN after next Regeneration.

EDITING 3-D OBJECTS | AEM 5 | | ARM 6 |

When working with objects that have been constructed using a variety of UCSs, it is important that you use the proper editing techniques and commands. If you need to trim or extend objects for example, you must first be sure that the current UCS is parallel to the entity to be edited.

The following discussion covers the use of CHPROP, GRIPS, ALIGN, ROTATE3D, and MIRROR3D with 3-D objects.

Changing properties

The CHANGE command has some limitations when the entity is not parallel to the Z axis of the User Coordinate System (UCS). If you use the CHANGE command on this type of entity, AutoCAD displays this message:

n found
n was not parallel with UCS.

To resolve this situation, you need to use the CHPROP command. This command can change any entity even if it is not parallel to the current UCS. When you enter CHPROP and select an object, AutoCAD prompts for the property to change—color, layer, linetype, or thickness:

Command: **CHPROP** ↵
Select object: *(select the object to be changed)*
Select object: ↵
Change what property (Color/LAyer/LType/Thickness)?

You do not receive the ⟨change point⟩ option as you do with the normal CHANGE command. Thus, to change text location for example, use the CHANGE command and be sure the current UCS is parallel to the entity.

Using grips to edit 3-D objects

Three-dimensional objects can be edited with commands such as COPY, MOVE, and STRETCH, or by using grips. For example, the height of a cone can be changed using the STRETCH command. The editing can be done in the plan view, but is best done in a 3-D view, where you can see the height of the cone change dynamically. See Fig. 24-69.

Command: **VPOINT** ↵
Rotate/⟨view point⟩ ⟨0.00,0.00,1.00⟩: **−1,−1,1** ↵

First pick anywhere on the cone and the grips appear, Fig. 24-69A. Next, pick the grip at the apex of the cone so it becomes hot (filled solid). The STRETCH operation can be completed as follows:

** STRETCH **
⟨Stretch to point⟩/Base point/Copy/Undo/eXit: **.XY** ↵
of *(pick the grip at the cone apex again)* (need Z): **5** ↵

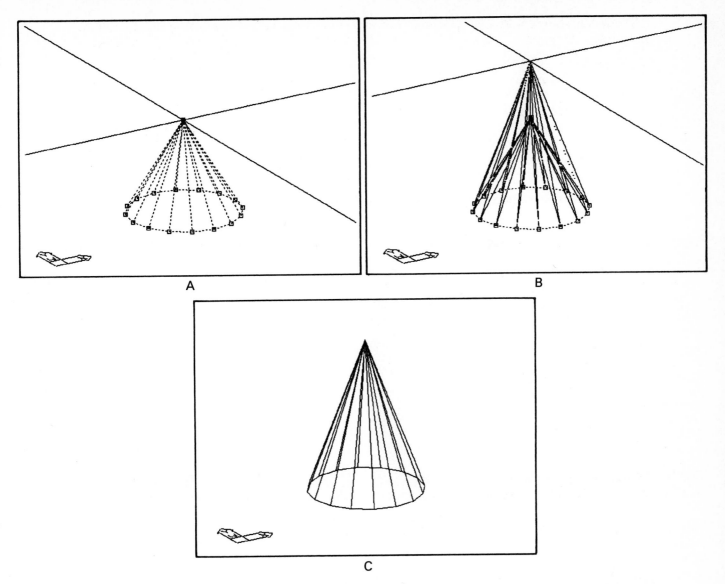

Fig. 24-69. Using grips to edit 3-D objects. A—Pick on the cone and the grips become warm. Then pick the top grip to make it hot. B—Move the top grip to the desired position. C—Final appearance of the cone with the revised height.

After you pick the apex grip to make it hot, you can move the pointing device around and see the Z dimension of the cone change. However, this is misleading. You are actually moving the apex in the XY plane, and if you pick a point, the Z value of the apex is changed to 0. Therefore, it is best to use XYZ filters to edit 3-D objects.

Aligning 3-D objects

The ALIGN command, found in the Modify pull-down menu, enables you to correct errors of 3-D construction, or quickly manipulate 3-D shapes. ALIGN requires existing points (source), and the new location of those existing points (destination).

— **NOTE** —

When working with 3-D editing commands, set the running object snap modes to enhance your accuracy and speed.

The wedge shown in Fig. 24-70A is aligned in its new position, Fig. 24-70B, using the following steps:

> Command: **OSNAP** ↵
> Object snap modes: **INT** ↵
> Command: **ALIGN** ↵
> Select objects: *(pick the wedge)*
> Select objects: ↵
> 1st source point: *(pick P1)* 1st destination point: *(pick P2)*
> 2nd source point: *(pick P3)* 2nd destination point: *(pick P4)*
> 3rd source point: *(pick P5)* 3rd destination point: *(pick P1)*

The aligned object should look like the one in Fig. 24-70B.

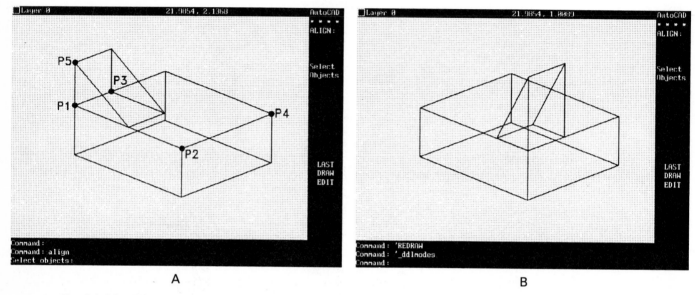

A   B

Fig. 24-70. Three-dimensional objects can be properly oriented with one another using the ALIGN command.

EXERCISE 24-9

☐ Load AutoCAD and start a new drawing.
☐ Draw a box and a wedge arranged like those shown in Fig. 24-70A.
☐ Use the ALIGN command to create the arrangement shown below.
☐ Save the drawing as A:EX24-9.

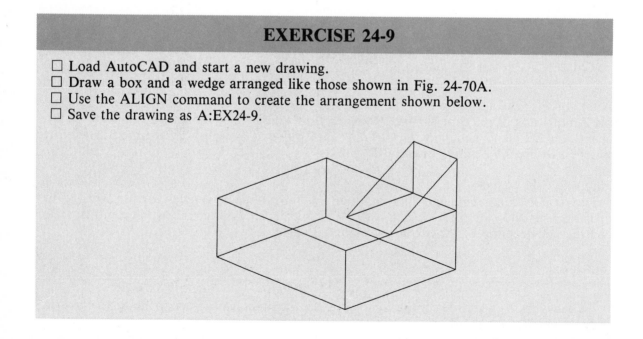

3-D rotating

The ROTATE3D command can rotate objects on any axis regardless of the current UCS. This is an extremely powerful editing and design feature of Release 12. The default option of ROTATE3D requires that you pick two points to define an axis of rotation. The second point picked determines the axis of rotation. A positive angle rotates counterclockwise on the axis when viewing it from the second point. The following example rotates the wedge -90° on the axis. See Fig. 24-71A.

Command: **ROTATE3D** ↵
Select objects: *(pick the wedge)*
Select objects: ↵
Axis by Entity/Last/View/Xaxis/Yaxis/Zaxis/⟨2points⟩: **INT** ↵
of *(pick P1)* 2nd point on axis: **INT** ↵
of *(pick P2)* ⟨Rotation angle⟩/Reference: **−90** ↵

The rotated object is shown in Fig. 24-71B.

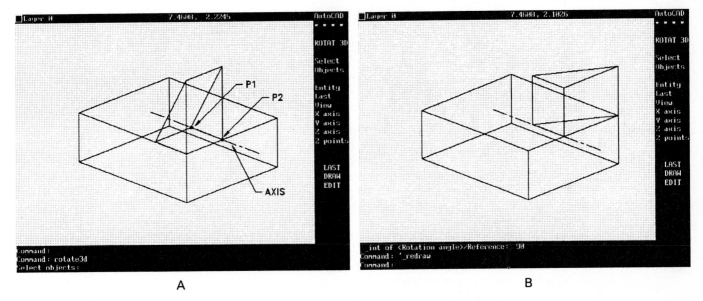

A   B

Fig. 24-71. Using the ROTATE3D command.

Several additional options of the ROTATE3D command allow you to define an axis of rotation:
- **Axis by Entity (E)** – Entities such as lines, arcs, circles, and polylines can define the axis. A line becomes the axis. The axis of a circle passes through its center, perpendicular to the plane of the circle. The axis of an arc passes through its center. A selected polyline segment, such as a line or arc, is treated as a line or an arc to determine the axis.
- **Last (L)** – Uses the last axis of rotation defined.
- **View (V)** – The viewing direction of the current viewport is aligned with the selected point to define the axis.
- **Xaxis/Yaxis/Zaxis (X, Y, or Z)** – Aligns the axis of rotation with the X, Y, or Z axis and selected point.

EXERCISE 24-10

☐ If drawing EX24-9 is not on your screen, begin a new drawing named EX24-10 and use A:EX24-9 as your prototype.
☐ Use the ROTATE3D command to rotate the wedge to the position shown below.
☐ Save the drawing as A:EX24-10.

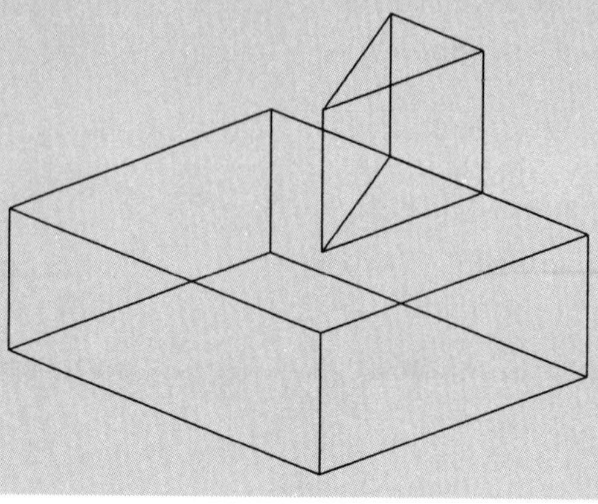

3-D mirroring

The MIRROR3D command allows you to mirror any objects on any 3-D axis, regardless of the current UCS. The default option is to define a mirror plane by picking three points on that plane, as shown in Fig. 24-72A. Object snap modes can be used to accurately define a plane.

Command: **OSNAP** ↵
Object snap modes: **MID** ↵
Command: **MIRROR3D** ↵
Select objects: *(pick the wedge)*
Select objects: ↵
Plane by Entity/Last/Zaxis/View/XY/YZ/XZ/⟨3points⟩: *(pick P1)* 2nd point on plane: *(pick P2)* 3rd point on plane: *(pick P3)*
Delete old objects? ⟨N⟩ ↵

The drawing should now look like Fig. 24-72B.

Additional options of the MIRROR3D command are similar to those of the ROTATE3D command, and allow you to define a mirror plane in several ways:
- **Plane by Entity (E)** — A circle, arc, or 2-D polyline segment can be used as the mirror line.
- **Last (L)** — Uses the last mirror plane defined.
- **Zaxis (Z)** — Pick a point on the plane and a point on the Z axis to that plane.
- **View (V)** — The viewing direction of the current viewpoint is aligned with the selected point to define the axis.
- **XY/YZ/XZ** — The mirror plane is placed in one of the three basic planes, and passing through the selected point.

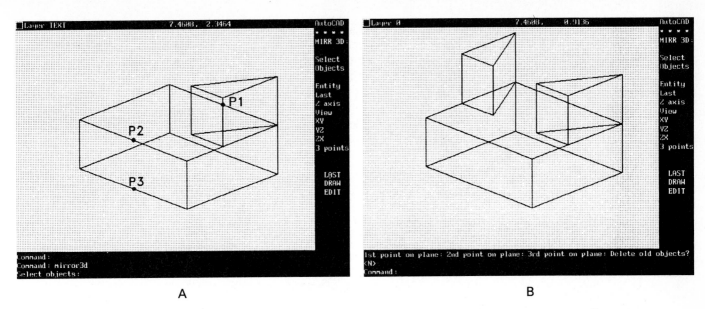

A   B

Fig. 24-72. The MIRROR3D command allows you to mirror objects on any 3-D axis, regardless
of the current UCS.

EXERCISE 24-11

☐ If drawing EX24-10 is not on your screen, begin a new drawing named EX24-11 and use
A:EX24-10 as the prototype.
☐ Use the MIRROR3D command to mirror the wedge to the position drawn below.
☐ Save the drawing as A:EX24-11.

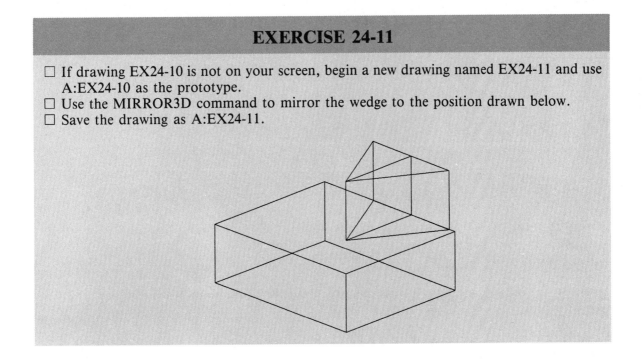

SURFACE MODELING TECHNIQUES   ARM 5

The REVSURF, EDGESURF, and RULESURF commands are covered thoroughly in the
digitizer puck tutorial at the end of this chapter. The following discussion focuses on using TAB-
SURF and REVSURF to create 3-D surface models.

AutoCAD allows you to generate surface models using a variety of techniques, each suited
to a specific situation. The RULESURF command generates a mesh of ruled surfaces between
two curves. The TABSURF command generates a tabulated surface mesh when given a curve
and a direction to extend the surface. A surface of revolution, or profile rotated around an axis,
is generated using the REVSURF command.

Constructing tabulated surfaces with TABSURF

A *tabulated surface* is like a ruled surface, but only one entity—line, arc, circle, 2-D polyline, or 3-D polyline—is needed. This entity is called the *path curve*. A second line, called the *direction vector,* indicates the direction and length of the tabulated surface. AutoCAD finds the endpoint of the direction vector closest to your pick point. It sets the direction toward the opposite end of the vector line. The tabulated surface generated follows the direction and length of the direction vector. The SURFTAB1 system variable controls the number of tabulated surfaces that are constructed. Fig. 24-73 shows the difference the pick point makes when assigning the direction.

Command: **TABSURF** ⏎
Select path curve: *(pick the curve)*
Select direction vector: *(pick correct end of vector)*

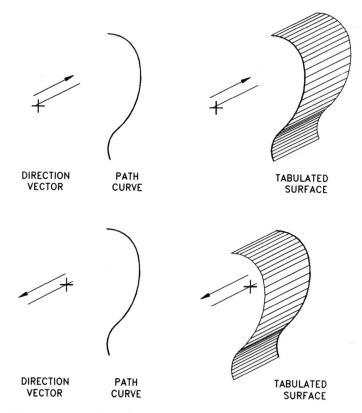

Fig. 24-73. The pick point on the direction vector determines the direction of the tabulated surface.

Construct revolved surfaces with REVSURF

The REVSURF command lets you draw a profile of a symmetrical object and then rotate that profile around an axis. This is a powerful command, and should be used by anyone who needs to draw symmetrical three-dimensional shapes. The profile, or path curve, can be drawn using lines, arcs, circles, 2-D polylines, or 3-D polylines. The rotation axis can be a line or open polyline. Notice the initial layout of the revolved surface in Fig. 24-74.

Use REVSURF in the following manner:

Command: **REVSURF** ⏎
Select path curve: *(pick the profile)*
Select axis of revolution: *(pick an axis line)*
Start angle ⟨0⟩: ⏎
Included angle (+ = ccw, − = cw) ⟨Full circle⟩: ⏎

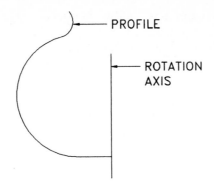

Fig. 24-74. A profile, or path curve, and rotation axis are required before a surface of revolution can be constructed.

The Start angle: prompt allows you to specify an offset angle at which the surface revolution begins. The Included angle: prompt lets you draw the complete 360° surface or just portions of the object rotated about the axis line. Fig. 24-75 shows the rotated Fig. 24-74 profile displayed with DVIEW and with hidden lines removed.

The SURFTAB1 and SURFTAB2 system variables control the mesh of a revolved surface. The SURFTAB1 value determines the number of segments in the direction of rotation around the axis. The SURFTAB2 value divides the path curve into segments of equal size.

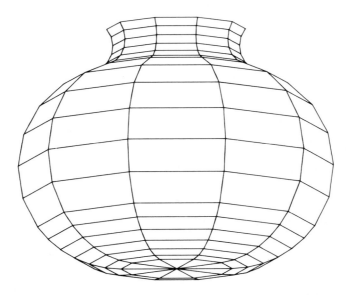

Fig. 24-75. The completed surface of revolution with hidden lines removed.

3-D MESH TECHNIQUES

AEM 2   ARM 5

AutoCAD provides three different ways to construct 3-D face meshes. These methods can be used to create meshes that cannot be constructed using any of the surfacing commands. A *3-D mesh* is a polygon mesh composed of 3-D faces. This mesh is not restricted to a single plane. A *mesh*, created with the 3D command's Mesh option, is a single flat plane composed of four sides that can have its four corners at different Z values. A *pface* is a general polygon mesh of 3-D faces. Each face can have an infinite number of vertices, and each face can occupy a different plane.

Constructing a 3-D mesh

The 3DMESH command allows you to generate a polygon mesh. The mesh must be defined in rows (N) and columns (M). Each vertex in the mesh must be given a value. You probably will not use this process often because it is tedious. However, AutoLISP programmers can create specialized meshes using this command.

A simple mesh having six faces consists of four columns and three rows. The vertices of the mesh are its definition points. A mesh can have no more than 256, and no fewer than 2 vertices in either direction. You must give AutoCAD the location of each vertex in XYZ coordinates. When prompting for coordinates, AutoCAD indicates the M and N location of the current vertex. You can think of M and N as similar to a grid of X and Y coordinates. See Fig. 24-76. The values for each vertex of the first M column must be entered. Then, AutoCAD prompts for the second and succeeding M columns.

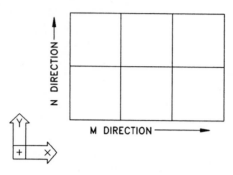

Fig. 24-76. A 3-D polygon mesh is similar to a grid of XY coordinates. M values are columns and N values are rows.

Enter the values given here to get the feel for the 3DMESH command. Use DVIEW to view the mesh from different angles. The mesh should look like that shown in Fig. 24-77.

Command: **3DMESH** ↵
Mesh M size: **4** ↵
Mesh N size: **3** ↵
Vertex (0,0): **3,2,1** ↵
Vertex (0,1): **3,3,1.5** ↵
Vertex (0,2): **3,4,1** ↵
Vertex (1,0): **4,2,.5** ↵
Vertex (1,1): **4,3,1** ↵
Vertex (1,2): **4,4,.5** ↵
Vertex (2,0): **5,2,1.5** ↵
Vertex (2,1): **5,3,1** ↵
Vertex (2,2): **5,4,1.5** ↵
Vertex (3,0): **6,2,2.5** ↵
Vertex (3,1): **6,3,2** ↵
Vertex (3,2): **6,4,2.5** ↵

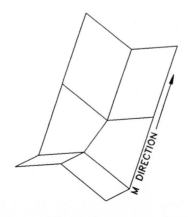

Fig. 24-77. The completed 3-D polygon mesh.

Constructing a single-plane mesh

A 3-D mesh that occupies a single plane is called *planar*. It can be composed of as few as 2, and as many as 256 vertices in either direction. Mesh directions are referred to as M and N just as with the 3DMESH command. This planar mesh is activated by picking 3D Surfaces in the Draw pull-down menu, then picking 3D Objects... from the cascading submenu. This displays the "3D Objects" icon menu, from which you can pick Mesh. You can also execute the MESH command by entering one of the following at the Command: prompt.

      Command: **AI__MESH** ↵

or

      Command: **3D** ↵
      Box/Cone/Dish/DOme/Mesh/Pyramid/Sphere/Torus/Wedge: **M** ↵

The command continues by requesting the four corners of the mesh and the number of vertices. AutoCAD highlights the M and N directions when it prompts for the mesh size.

      First corner: **4,3** ↵
      Second corner: **9,3** ↵
      Third corner: **9,8** ↵
      Fourth corner: **4,3** ↵
      Mesh M size: **10** ↵
      Mesh N size: **8** ↵

The resulting mesh is shown in Fig. 24-78.

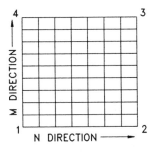

Fig. 24-78. A planar mesh can be composed of from 2 to 256 vertices in either direction.

━━━━━━━━ PROFESSIONAL TIP ━━━━━━━━

    Before constructing any of the three types of meshes, you can first draw a construction line version of the mesh. Create a layer for construction lines and give it a color. Draw the mesh with the LINE command, giving Z coordinates if needed. Label all vertices and faces for reference when drawing the mesh. Create a new layer for the final mesh using a different color. Use object snaps such as ENDpoint, INTersection, or MIDpoint, then use the appropriate command to draw the mesh, picking points on the construction line mesh. Freeze or erase the construction line layer when you are finished.

Constructing a 3-D polyface mesh

    A general polygon mesh can be constructed using the PFACE command. This creates a mesh similar to the 3DFACE command, but you do not have to pick vertices twice that join another face. You can also create faces that have an infinite number of vertices, rather than the maximum four specified by the 3DFACE command. You can use the PFACE command to construct surfaces that cannot be "faced" using any of the standard surfacing commands. This process is time-consuming, and is best suited for AutoLISP or ADS (Autodesk Development System) applications.

    The procedure for creating a PFACE mesh is to first define all of the vertices for the mesh, then assign those vertices to a face. The face is given a number, and it is composed of the vertices you assign to that face. While creating a pface, you can change the color, layer, or linetype by entering the COLOR, LAYER, or LINETYPE commands at the "Face n, vertex n" prompt. The following example creates a pface mesh consisting of two faces. See Fig. 24-79A. The first portion of the command defines all of the vertices of the two faces.

Command: **PFACE** ↵
Vertex 1: **3,3** ↵
Vertex 2: **7,3** ↵
Vertex 3: **7,6** ↵
Vertex 4: **3,6** ↵
Vertex 5: **2,7,3** ↵
Vertex 6: **2,2,3** ↵
Vertex 7: **3,3** ↵
Vertex 8: ↵

The next sequence assigns vertices to face number 1.

Face 1, vertex 1: **1** ↵
Face 1, vertex 2: **2** ↵
Face 1, vertex 3: **3** ↵
Face 1, vertex 4: **4** ↵
Face 1, vertex 5: ↵

Now you can change the color of the second face without exiting the command.

Face 2, vertex 1: **COLOR** ↵
New color ⟨BYLAYER⟩: **CYAN** ↵

The last sequence assigns vertices to face number 2.

Face 2, vertex 1: **4** ↵
Face 2, vertex 2: **5** ↵
Face 2, vertex 3: **6** ↵
Face 2, vertex 4: **1** ↵
Face 2, vertex 5: ↵
Face 3, vertex 1: ↵

Now use the VPOINT and HIDE commands to view the faces.

Command: **VPOINT** ↵
Rotate/⟨View point⟩ ⟨0.0000,0.0000,1.0000⟩: **−1,−1,.75** ↵
Command: **HIDE** ↵

The pface mesh is originally drawn as a wireframe, but after using the HIDE command, you can see the 3-D faces are evident. See Fig. 24-79B.

THINGS TO CONSIDER WHEN WORKING WITH 3-D

Working with 3-D, like working with 2-D drawings, requires careful planning to obtain the desired results efficiently. The following suggestions should be considered when working with 3-D.

Planning
- Determine the type of final drawing you need, then choose the method of 3-D construction that best suits your needs.
- Isometric is quickest and most versatile for objects needing only one pictorial view. Ellipses and arcs are easily manipulated.
- Objects and layouts that need to be viewed from different angles for design purposes are best constructed using the 3-D commands.
- Construct only the details needed for the function of the drawing. It saves space and time, and makes visualization much easier.
- Use OSNAP modes MID, END, and INT with the LINE and 3DFACE commands.
- The grid appears at the current viewpoint angle and at the current elevation.

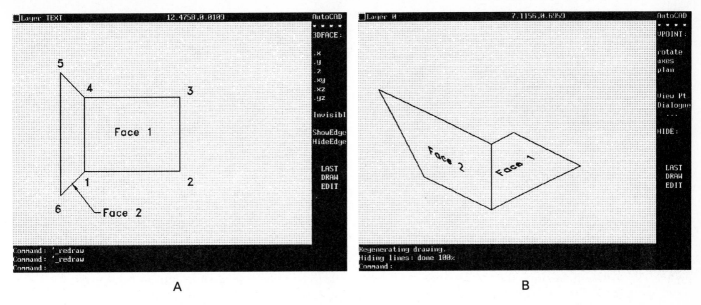

Fig. 24-79. A—Creating a pface mesh consisting of two faces. B—Appearance of the mesh after changing the viewpoint and using HIDE.

- Create layers having different colors for different entities. Turn them on and off as needed, or freeze those not being used.

Editing
- Use CHPROP to change color, layer, linetype, or thickness of 3-D objects.
- Use the STRETCH command or grips in the 3-D view to change only one dimension of the object. Use the SCALE command in the 3-D view to change the size of the entire object proportionally.
- Do as much editing as possible in a 3-D viewpoint. It is quicker and the results are seen immediately.

Displaying
- The HIDE command can help you visualize complex drawings.
- For quick viewpoints use the tablet menu RENDER/VIEW/UCS/BLOCK/LAYER section.
- Use the VIEW command to create and save 3-D views for quicker pictorial displays. This avoids having to use VPOINT or DVIEW commands.
- Freeze unwanted layers before displaying objects in 3-D and especially before using HIDE. Simply turning off layers may cause invisible entities to block out portions of other objects. This is because the computer must still regenerate layers that are off.
- Before using HIDE, zoom in on the part of a drawing to display. This saves time in regenerating the view because only the entities that are visible are regenerated.
- Objects that touch or intersect may have to be moved slightly if the display removes a line you need to see or plot.

CONSTRUCTING A SURFACE MODEL

The following discussion and tutorial illustrates how the techniques of surface modeling can be used to create an object composed of several different shapes. The model to be constructed is a twelve-button digitizer puck; a common pointing device used on a digitizer tablet. See Fig. 24-80. You will gain more experience from this example if you follow along at a workstation. It is not necessary to complete this tutorial in one drawing session. Complete what you can, save your work, and return when you have available time. If you are not able to use a computer as you read this, you will still gain good insight into the workings of surface modeling with AutoCAD.

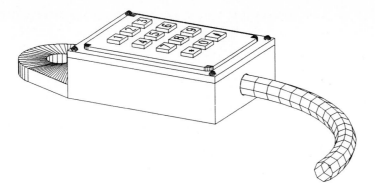

Fig. 24-80. A 3-D surface model of a twelve-button digitizer puck.

NOTE

Carefully follow the instructions in this tutorial. If you try to take shortcuts without prior knowledge of the commands, your results may not be what is shown in the tutorial. Once you have completed the tutorial, you will have greater confidence in experimenting on your own.

Drawing setup

You should plan your work carefully before beginning any 3-D drawing. Remember the basic rule for creating anything with a computer; try to draw the minimum number of elements that can be used to complete the project.

- Let the computer do as much work as possible.
- Use predrawn shapes when possible, and create blocks.
- Use editing functions to manipulate previously drawn shapes.
- Save display configurations such as views and viewports.
- As an optional step, make slides of each step of your work for later reference.

Begin your drawing by setting decimal units and limits of 18,12. Set the grid spacing to .5 and snap spacing to .25. Create the following layers and colors:

Layer Name	Color
Body	red
Body-cap	white
Face1	green
Face2	cyan
Buttons	magenta
Button1	magenta
Button2	blue
Numbers	cyan
Eyepiece	yellow
Eyesurf	yellow
Edgesurf	green
Cable	green
Screws	red
Constr	blue

Using 3-D shapes

The individual parts of the digitizer puck are shown in Fig. 24-81. The first step is to create a basic 3-D building block called BOX. This block can then be used for at least three of the parts on the puck. However, rather than drawing the BOX as a wireframe, then adding 3-D faces to it, you can use a 3-D shape called Box. Set the current layer to 0. Pick the 3D Objects... selection from the 3D Surfaces menu in the Draw pull-down menu, then pick the box shape. See Fig. 24-82.

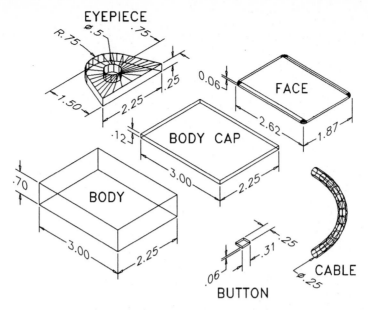

Fig. 24-81. Individual parts of the digitizer puck.

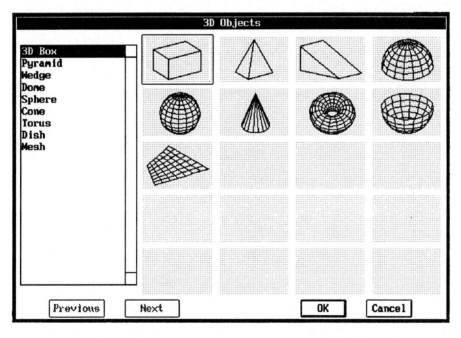

Fig. 24-82. Picking the box shape from the ''3D Objects'' icon menu.

NOTE

When you pick an object from the "3D Objects" icon menu, a file named 3D.LSP is loaded. Once this file has been loaded you can type the name of the 3-D object you wish to use at the Command: prompt, such as AI__BOX, AI__WEDGE, AI__PYRAMID, etc.

Box

The BOX command lets you construct a 3-D box or cube. You must provide the location of one corner, the box dimensions, and the rotation angle around the location point. The box rotates about the Z axis. Enter dimensions of the box at the keyboard or pick them with your pointing device.

> Command: *(pick the box in the "3D Objects" icon menu)*
> Corner of box: **3,3** ↵
> Length: **1** ↵
> Cube/⟨Width⟩: **C** ↵
> Rotation angle about Z axis: **0** ↵

If you select the Cube option, AutoCAD uses the value previously entered at the length prompt and applies it to the width and height. Fig. 24-83 shows an example of a box.

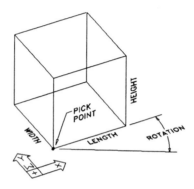

Fig. 24-83. The BOX command requires a location point, length, width, height, and rotation angle.

— PROFESSIONAL TIP —

The purpose of creating a cube exactly one-unit square is to provide a basic building block. When this cube is inserted into a drawing as a block, exact dimensions of a box or rectangle can be entered, thus creating the required shape. This basic building block can be used for anything from mechanical parts to dimensional lumber and plywood. Use your imagination.

The box is displayed in plan view after it is created. Use the VPOINT command to look at the box in 3-D.

> Command: **VPOINT** ↵
> Rotate/⟨View point⟩ ⟨0.00,0.00,0.00⟩: **−2,−2,1** ↵

The box appears to be a wireframe, but it is actually a single entity composed of 3-D faces. You can test this by exploding the box with the EXPLODE command. Use the HIDE command and you can see that it is a surface model.

Next, use the BLOCK command to make a block of the cube and name it BOX. You can do this in the 3-D display. Pick one of the corners as an insertion point as shown in Fig. 24-84 using the OSNAP command's INTersection option.

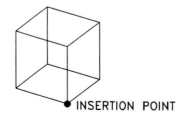

INSERTION POINT

Fig. 24-84. An insertion point is given to the box to create a block.

Inserting a 3-D block

The block can now be inserted into the drawing to create the body of the puck. Change the current layer to Body and insert the BOX block into your drawing. Return the display to the plan view and use the INSERT command as follows to insert a 3-D shape:

Command: **INSERT** ↵
Block name (or ?): **BOX** ↵
  Insertion point: *(pick a point)* X scale factor ⟨1⟩ / Corner / XYZ: **X** ↵
  X scale factor ⟨1⟩ / Corner: **2.25** ↵
  Y scale factor (default = X): **3** ↵
  Z scale factor (default = X): **.7** ↵
  Rotation angle ⟨0⟩: ↵

Now use the ZOOM command so the inserted block does not occupy the entire screen:

Command: **ZOOM** ↵
All/Center/Dynamic/Extents/Left/Previous/Vmax/Window/⟨Scale(X/XP)⟩: **.5X** ↵

The body of the puck is now in place with the required dimensions. As an alternative you can visually place and size a 3-D block using the INSERT command's Corner option. You might try it again for practice to see what the dynamic sizing of the Corner option provides.

Change the current layer to 0 and insert a copy of the BOX block. Make sure that the viewpoint previously set (−2,−2,1) is still current. This time the cube is used to create a block for the puck's buttons. Insert the block as follows:

Command: **INSERT** ↵
Block name (or ?) ⟨BOX⟩: ↵
  Insertion point: *(pick a point)* X scale factor ⟨1⟩ / Corner / XYZ: **X** ↵
  X scale factor ⟨1⟩ / Corner: **.31** ↵
  Y scale factor (default = X): **.25** ↵
  Z scale factor (default = X): **.06** ↵
  Rotation angle ⟨0⟩: ↵

Now, make a block of the box you just inserted. Name it BUTTON and give it the same insertion point as shown in Fig. 24-84. This block is used later to create an array of buttons. The next section shows how to construct a more detailed button having a curved surface.

Constructing a wireframe curved button

The following example illustrates one method for creating a wireframe model on which you can hang surface patches using the EDGESURF command. A *surface patch* is a 3-D mesh that creates a surface covering in a specified area. Begin construction of the button using the LINE command.

Command: **LINE** ↵
From point: *(pick a point)*
To point: **@.31,0** ↵
To point: **@0,.25** ↵
To point: **@−.31,0** ↵
To point: **C** ↵

This creates the base of the button. Zoom in on the object so that it nearly fills the screen. This makes it easier to draw the vertical lines of the corners. Fig. 24-85A shows what the drawing should look like. Use the LINE command to draw the corners as follows:

Command: **LINE** ↵
From point: **END** ↵
of *(pick point 1)*
To point: **@0,0,.03** ↵
To point: ↵
Command: ↵
LINE From point: **END** ↵
of *(pick point 2)*
To point: **@0,0,.06** ↵
To point: ↵

The next step is to construct an arc connecting the tops of the two vertical lines. This arc represents the curved shape of the button surface. However, in order to properly create this arc, the UCS must be changed so that the X axis is the same direction as the line between points 1 and 2. This places the new UCS in the same plane in which the arc is to be drawn. See Fig. 24-85B. Use the UCS command in the following manner:

Command: **UCS** ↵
Origin/ZAxis/3point/Entity/View/X/Y/Z/Prev/Restore/Save/Del/?/⟨World⟩: **ZA** ↵
Origin point ⟨0,0,0⟩: **END** ↵
of *(pick point 2)*
Point on positive portion of Z-axis ⟨defaults⟩: **@−1,0,0** ↵

If the UCS icon does not move to the new origin, use the UCSICON command's Origin option to move the icon.

Command: **UCSICON** ↵
ON/OFF/All/Noorigin/ORigin/⟨ON⟩: **OR** ↵

The icon moves to the new origin. The UCS icon is a good reminder of the location of the origin of the current UCS.

Now the arc can be drawn since the new UCS is parallel to the plane of the arc. Refer to Fig. 24-85C for the pick points of the arc.

Command: **ARC** ↵
Center/⟨Start point⟩: **END** ↵
of *(pick point 3)*
Center/End/⟨Second point⟩: **E** ↵
End point: **END** ↵
of *(pick point 4)*
Angle/Direction/Radius/⟨Center point⟩: **A** ↵
Included angle: **20** ↵
Command: **REGEN** ↵

The final steps in the construction of the wireframe button are to copy the two vertical lines and the arc to the opposite end of the button, and connect the top edges of the button with straight lines. Do this on your own using a running OSNAP ENDpoint. The completed drawing should look like Fig. 24-85D.

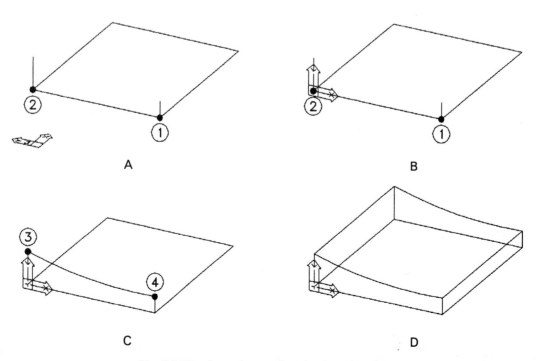

A

B

C

D

Fig. 24-85. Steps in creating the button outline.

Creating edge defined surfaces

Curved surfaces having four sides can be created using the EDGESURF command. It is located in the "3D Surfaces" option of the Draw pull-down menu as Edge Defined Patch, or in the 3D Surfs pick of the DRAW screen menu. An *edge defined patch* is actually a matrix of 3-D faces. The number of rows and columns of faces is controlled by the SURFTAB1 and SURFTAB2 system variables. Keep in mind that the greater the number of faces you have, the longer the regeneration time is, and the longer it takes to remove hidden lines using the HIDE command. Use surfaces sparingly on small objects. The following example is an illustration of how the EDGESURF command can be used. However, the first rectangular button that was created is used for the construction of the digitizer puck in this tutorial.

PROFESSIONAL TIP

When working with 3-D surfaces, try to determine the purpose of your drawing. How will you be viewing it, and what other programs will you use to shade, render, or animate the object? If you will not be looking at certain sides of an object, do not apply surfacing to those sides. Also, avoid using large values for the SURFTAB1 and SURFTAB2 variables when possible, for they represent the number of segments and 3-D faces created on a surface.

In order to create the two edge surface patches, you need to use layers Button1 and Button2 for this purpose. Select the SURFTAB1 variable and give it a value of 6. The SURFTAB2 variable should have a value of 2. Set the current layer to Button1, then create the first surface patch. The first line you pick to define the surface patch with the EDGESURF command is divided into six segments (SURFTAB1), and the second edge is divided into two (SURFTAB2). Refer to Fig. 24-86A.

Command: **EDGESURF** ↵
Select edge 1: *(pick edge 1)*
Select edge 2: *(pick edge 2)*
Select edge 3: *(pick edge 3)*
Select edge 4: *(pick edge 4)*

Next, copy the surface patch to the opposite end of the button. Your object should look like Fig. 24-86C. Now turn off layer Button1 and make layer Button2 current. This is done because if you select edge 3, for example, to create the top surface of the button, AutoCAD first finds the previous surface patch line and prompts you "Entity not usable to define surface patch." Turning off the layer where the edgesurf is located enables AutoCAD to find the original line representing that edge.

The final EDGESURF command is used on the curved top of the button. Use EDGESURF in the same manner as before. Unless you change the SURFTAB variables, the same number of segments are applied to the top of the button. SURFTAB2 is currently set to two segments, which is the minimum number allowed. To draw the final surface, be sure that the first edge you pick is one of the ends that is already surfaced. When the curved surface is completed, turn on layer Button1. The completed surface patched button is shown in Fig. 24-86D.

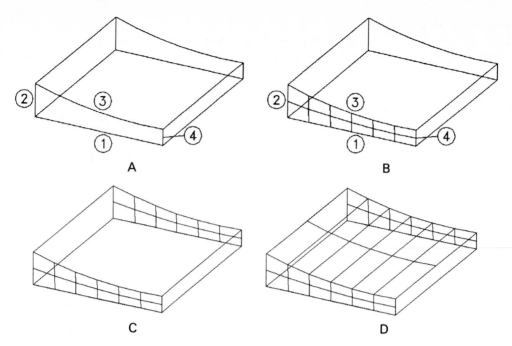

Fig. 24-86. A—Pick points for creating a surface patch with the EDGESURF command. B—An edge defined surface applied to one end. C—The surface patch copied to the opposite end. D—The completed surface patched button.

The final step in completing the surface model of this button is to use the 3DFACE command on the front and rear vertical sides. You can use the HIDE command to see that the ends are open. The 3DFACE command is best used by first setting a running OSNAP such as ENDpoint or INTersection. Then, select 3DFACE and pick the four corners of the front surface. Use the 3DFACE command in the same manner on the rear surface, then use HIDE to test your results. There is no need to use the 3DFACE command on the bottom because it will sit on another surface. See Fig. 24-87.

This shape can now be saved as a block or wblock. If you have been working along with this tutorial, save your work. You will use the blocks you have created to complete the digitizer puck later.

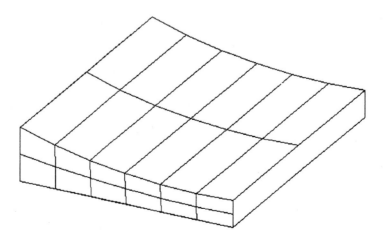

Fig. 24-87. The completed surfaced button.

Using viewports to create the face of the puck

Viewports can assist your drawing projects in various ways, and no 3-D drawing should be constructed without them. Recall the drawing of the digitizer puck if it is not currently on your screen. The body shape should be displayed. Use the UCS command to return to the World Coordinate System. Use the VPORTS command, and the default options, to display three views of the part as shown in Fig. 24-88.

Fig. 24-88. Three viewports showing the puck body.

Use the three viewports to show three different views of the part. The large view should remain the same. Create a pictorial view in the lower-left viewport and a plan view in the upper-left viewport. Pick the lower-left viewport to make it active, and then change the display as follows:

Command: **VPOINT** ⏎
Rotate/⟨View point⟩⟨0.00,0.00,0.00⟩: **−1,2,1** ⏎
Command: **PAN** ⏎
Displacement: *(pick the upper-left corner of the part)*
Second point: *(pick at the upper midpoint of the viewport)*

Use the ZOOM command to magnify this view. Use PAN again if necessary to center the object in the viewport.

Pick the upper-left viewport to make it active and create a plan view as follows:

Command: **PLAN** ⏎
⟨Current USC⟩/Ucs/World: ⏎

If the object moves to one corner of the view, use the PAN and ZOOM commands to move and enlarge the view to suit your needs.

Make the large viewport active, and use ZOOM and PAN to adjust the view to your needs. After you have adjusted all three viewports, take some time to notice the orientation of the views in relation to the UCS icon. Your ability to visualize the XYZ axes as they relate to the object you are designing, are fundamental to understanding 3-D construction and multiple view layouts. The final arrangement of the viewports should be similar to Fig. 24-89.

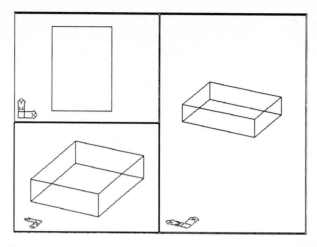

Fig. 24-89. A working arrangement of three viewports.

One of the benefits of creating a viewport arrangement like this is the ability to recall this configuration when you need it. It is easily done with the VPORTS command's Save option.

Command: **VPORTS** ↲
Save/Restore/Delete/Join/SIngle/?/2/⟨3⟩/4: **S** ↲
?/Name for new viewport configuration: **THREE** ↲

This viewport arrangement is now a named entity, just like a layer or a block, and can be recalled at any time. To see this in action, use the VPORTS command and the SIngle option to return to one viewport. Then, use VPORTS again and the Restore option. Enter the name THREE for viewport configuration to restore, and the previous arrangement is restored to the screen.

Next, you will add another part to the puck. First, set the current layer to Body-cap. Then, make the large viewport active. Insert the BOX block and attach it to the body at the insertion point shown in Fig. 24-90A. Remember that since the box you are inserting is a one unit cube, you can enter the exact dimensions of the body cap for the X,Y, and Z prompts.

Command: **INSERT** ↲
Block name (or ?): **BOX** ↲
    Insertion point: *(pick the insertion point shown in Fig. 24-90A)*
    X scale factor ⟨1⟩ / Corner / XYZ: **X** ↲
    X scale factor ⟨1⟩ / Corner: **2.25** ↲
    Y scale factor (default = X): **3** ↲
    Z scale factor (default = X): **.12** ↲
    Rotation angle ⟨0⟩: ↲

The inserted body cap is shown in Fig. 24-90B.

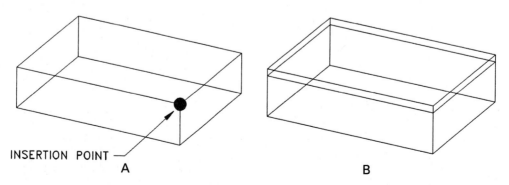

INSERTION POINT

A   B

Fig. 24-90. A—Insertion point for the body cap block. B—Cap inserted onto the body of the puck.

Using polylines in 3-D

The next part of this object to construct is the face of the puck. This part has filleted corners, so it can be constructed using a combination of polylines, ruled surfaces, and 3-D faces. Since the face is placed on top of the body cap, and you are drawing and constructing the face, it might be a good idea to create a UCS for that purpose. Be sure the large viewport is active.

Command: **UCS** ↵
Origin/ZAxis/3point/Entity/View/X/Y/Z/Prev/Restore/Save/Del/?/⟨World⟩: **O** ↵
Origin point⟨0,0,0⟩: *(pick the top of the body cap above the insertion point)*
Command: **UCSICON** ↵
ON/OFF/All/Noorigin/ORigin⟨ON⟩: **A** ↵
ON/OFF/All/Noorigin/ORigin⟨ON⟩: **OR** ↵
Command: **UCS** ↵
Origin/ZAxis/3point/Entity/View/X/Y/Z/Prev/Restore/Save/Del/?/⟨World⟩: **S** ↵
?/Desired UCS name: **FACE** ↵

The UCSICON command's All option instructs AutoCAD to execute the next option in all of the viewports. Notice that the UCS icon has moved to its new origin in all three viewports. See Fig. 24-91. In addition, the Save option is used to save the current UCS. This becomes a named entity just like the saved viewport configuration created earlier. If you change to a new UCS while working on a design, you can quickly recall a previous User Coordinate System with the UCS command's Restore option.

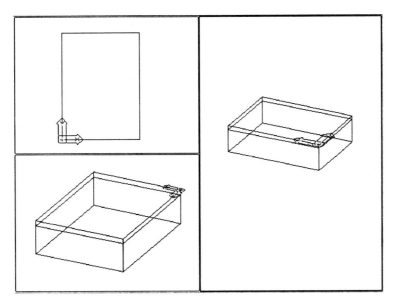

Fig. 24-91. The new UCS is reflected in all viewports.

Begin drawing the puck face by making the upper-left viewport active. Change to the layer Face1. At this point you have the option of working in the current viewport configuration, or you can return to a single viewport in order to make the object larger.

Use the PLINE command to draw the face. Be sure to use the Close option to complete the shape.

Command: **PLINE** ↵
From point: **.19,.19** ↵
Arc/Close/Halfwidth/Length/Undo/Width/⟨Endpoint of line⟩: **@1.87,0** ↵
Arc/Close/Halfwidth/Length/Undo/Width/⟨Endpoint of line⟩: **@0,2.62** ↵
Arc/Close/Halfwidth/Length/Undo/Width/⟨Endpoint of line⟩: **@1.87⟨180** ↵
Arc/Close/Halfwidth/Length/Undo/Width/⟨Endpoint of line⟩: **C** ↵

Your drawing should now look like that in Fig. 24-92.

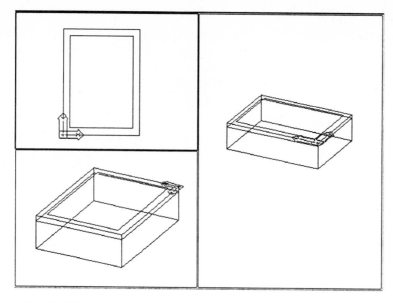

Fig. 24-92. A closed polyline is drawn for the face of the puck.

The next steps are used to enter a fillet radius for the corners of the polyline (.125 unit radius), and copy it on the Z axis the thickness of the part (.06 units). It is not important which viewport is active, but you should consider the quickest method to use. After you use the FILLET command on the polyline, use COPY as follows:

    Command: **COPY** ↵
    Select objects: **L** ↵
    1 found
    Select objects: ↵
    ⟨Base point or displacement⟩/Multiple: **@** ↵
    Second point of displacement: **@0,0,.06** ↵

The result is shown in Fig. 24-93.

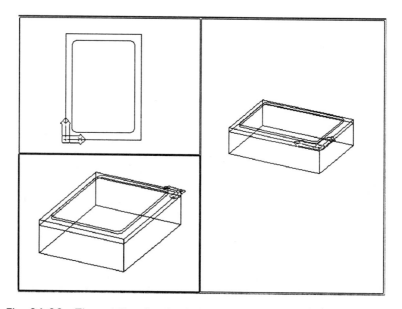

Fig. 24-93. The polyline for the face of the puck is filleted and copied.

Using RULESURF to surface fillets

A *ruled surface* is a surface between two curves that is divided into segments. The RULESURF command enables you to place surfaces between two curves, a curve and a line, a curve and a point, or a line and a point. It is useful for surfacing holes in parts, exterior fillets (rounds), interior fillets, or flat surfaces of various shapes. The number of segments created in a ruled surface is controlled by the SURFTAB1 system variable.

The RULESURF command is used on the digitizer puck to surface the round corners of the face and the top surface of the face at the corners. In order to do this efficiently, you may want to make the large viewport active and use the VPORTS command to return to a single view. Then save this viewport configuration as the name ONE. Next, zoom in on the pictorial view, then use the VIEW command to save the current display as the name ALL. Now, zoom in on the front corner (origin location) of the face and body cap. Use the VIEW command again and save this display as the name CORNER.

PROFESSIONAL TIP

Viewports and views should not be confused. *Viewports* are actually several separate screens displayed on your monitor. You can have up to sixteen viewports on a DOS computer using the VPORTS command. A *view,* on the other hand is just that; a specific view of the drawing or design. You can have as many views as you wish. In addition, you can display any named view in any one of the viewports. This makes using viewports and views much more versatile. For example, you can display different detailed views in two viewports, then begin a line in one viewport, pick another viewport, and complete the line in the second view.

You can also open a drawing in such a manner that it immediately displays a specific view. For example, if you want to display the CORNER view of the PUCK drawing, use the OPEN command and pick, or type the drawing name. Then pick the Select Initial View button, pick OK, and the "Select Initial View" dialogue box appears. Pick the view named CORNER, then pick OK. This opens the drawing named PUCK, and displays the view named CORNER.

Now that you have created additional viewport configurations and views, restore the CORNER view if it is not currently displayed. One additional item of preparation should be to place a point at the center of the radius on the top of the face. Change to the Constr layer, set the PDMODE variable to a visible symbol of your choice (such as 3), and set PDSIZE to .04. Then, use the POINT command with the OSNAP CENter option to place a point at the center of the arc as shown in Fig. 24-94A.

Use the EXPLODE command to break apart the two polylines that represent the face. This enables you to select corner arcs 1 and 2 separately with the RULESURF command as in Fig. 24-94B. Change to the Face2 layer, set SURFTAB1 to 6, and select the RULESURF command.

Command: **RULESURF** ↵
Select first defining curve: *(pick curve 1; see Fig. 24-94B)*
Select second defining curve: *(pick curve 2)*

The corner is now surfaced with six segments. See Fig. 24-94C. The SURFTAB1 variable controls the number of these segments. If you want more or less segments, you can always erase the ruled surface (it is a single entity), or just UNDO. Then, reset SURFTAB1 to the desired number of segments, and use the RULESURF command again.

The next ruled surface must be applied to the top of the face, connecting the corner arc to the point at the center of the arc. If you pick the corner of the face as the first defining curve, you may get the prompt "Entity not usable to define ruled surface." That is because you selected the previous ruled surface, not the original arc. To avoid picking the ruled surface, zoom in on the arc and the point so that your screen resembles Fig. 24-94D. Then you can more easily pick the curve. Notice that the ruled surface on the corner is composed of straight segments, whereas the corner arc is smoother. Use the RULESURF command again to pick the top curve and the center point. After the top is surfaced, you can either erase the point or turn off the Constr layer. The corner should look like Fig. 24-94E. Save your work before continuing.

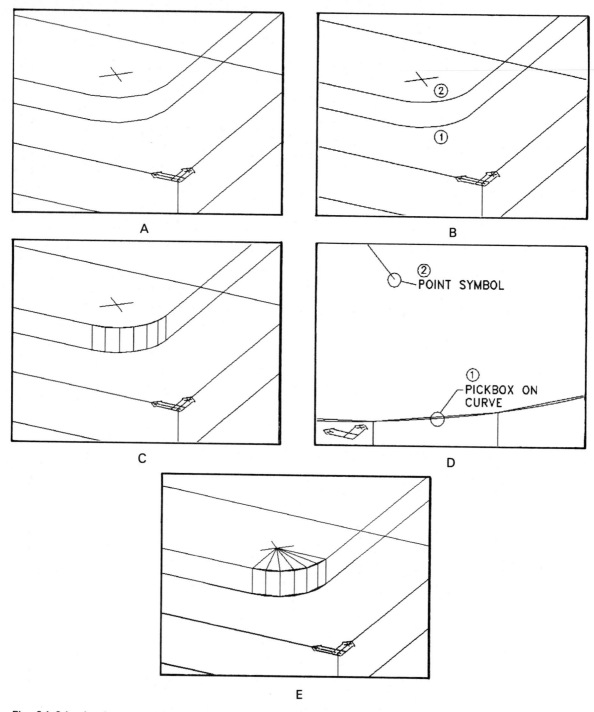

Fig. 24-94. A—A construction point is placed at the center of a face corner. B—Pick corner arcs 1 and 2 for first ruled surface. C—A ruled surface is applied to the corner. D—Zoom in on the corner to pick the arc and not the ruled surface. E—RULESURF is used to surface the top corner of the face.

EXERCISE 24-12

☐ Begin a new drawing and name it EX24-12.
☐ Draw a circle 2 in. (50.8 mm) in diameter.
☐ Copy the circle up on the Z axis four units.
☐ Use the VPOINT command to get an isometric view (-1,-1,1) of the circles.
☐ Make two copies of the circles so that your drawing looks like the following one.

☐ Set the SURFTAB1 variable to 4 and use the RULESURF command on the first set of circles.
☐ Set the SURFTAB1 variable to 8 and use the RULESURF command on the second set of circles.
☐ Set the SURFTAB1 variable to 16 and use the RULESURF command on the third set of circles.
☐ Save your drawing as A:EX24-12.

MIRROR and 3DFACE on a 3-D object

Now you can let AutoCAD duplicate the features you have just drawn. Be sure you have a single viewport and the face piece occupies most of the screen. The MIRROR command can be used to reflect the ruled surfaces at the two corners along the X or Y axes to the opposite corner. For this example, turn on ORTHO and reflect the surfaces along the Y axis 180°. Use MIDpoint to pick the mirror line. Do not delete the old objects.

Before drawing the remaining corners, there are two 3-D faces that must be constructed. To make this task a bit easier, use the VIEW command to create another view of the upper-left corner (the same one you just mirrored the ruled surfaces to). Name this view CORNER2. You might also remake the view CORNER so that it more closely matches CORNER2 in amount of detail shown. To do this, restore the CORNER view and redefine it as follows:

Command: **VIEW** ↵
?/Delete/Restore/Save/Window: **R** ↵
    View name to restore: **CORNER** ↵
Regenerating drawing.
Command: ↵
?/Delete/Restore/Save/Window: **W** ↵
    View name to save: **CORNER** ↵
First corner: *(pick first window corner)*
Other corner: *(pick second window corner)*

Next, use the VPORTS command to create a two viewport configuration and save it as TWO. Be sure the view CORNER2 is in the left viewport and use VIEW to restore the view CORNER in the right viewport. Your screen should look like Fig. 24-95.

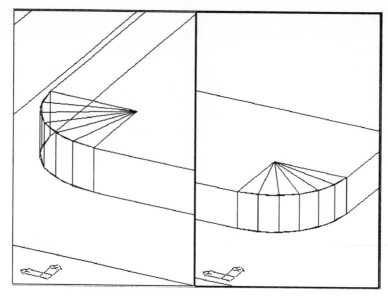

Fig. 24-95. A two viewport configuration showing two corners of the face.

Now it is an easy task to apply 3-D faces to the vertical side of the puck face and the top surface between the rule-surfaced corners. In order to see the 3-D faces as they are constructed, make the Face2 layer current. Then, set a running OSNAP of ENDpoint. When using the 3DFACE command, first draw the vertical face in the order shown in Fig. 24-96A. Pick points 1 and 2 in the right viewport, then pick points 3 and 4 in the left viewport, and press ENTER. Remember, to activate a viewport even if you are inside a command, simply move the screen cursor to the inactive viewport and pick.

NOTE

You cannot switch viewports while inside one of the following commands:

DVIEW	SNAP	VPOINT
GRID	VPLAYER	ZOOM
PAN	VPORTS	

The DVIEW command was discussed earlier in this chapter, and VPLAYER is explained in Chapter 27.

Next, draw the top face between the centers of the arcs and the edge of the previous face, using the pick points as shown in Fig. 24-96B.

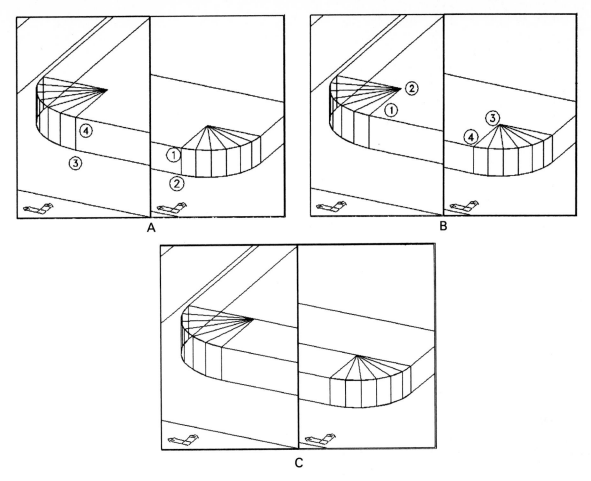

Fig. 24-96. A and B—The pick points of the areas to be 3-D faced can be selected easily using two viewports.
C—The completed 3-D faces.

The next step is to use the MIRROR command again to copy the ruled surfaces and 3-D faces to the opposite side of the face. First turn off the running OSNAP, then turn on ORTHO. When you use MIRROR, be sure to pick all of the ruled surfaces and the two 3-D faces just drawn. In order to make it easier to select the object to mirror and the mirror line, restore the viewport configuration named THREE. Then, use the VIEW command's Restore option to restore views of the corners in the two small viewports. Zoom in to pick the midpoint of line 1 in the large viewport as the first point of the mirror line, Fig. 24-97. The dots indicate the ruled surfaces and 3-D faces that must be picked.

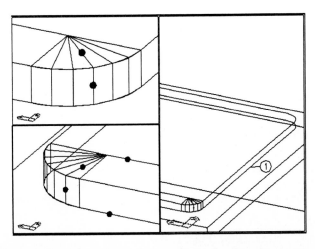

Fig. 24-97. Use viewports and views to make object selection easier. The midpoint of line 1 is picked for the mirror line. The dots indicate the ruled surfaces and 3-D faces that must be picked.

Next, you need to add the two missing 3-D faces to the narrow vertical ends of the puck face. Do this on your own. Decide if it would be quicker to draw each end separately or draw one and mirror it to the other end.

The final operation is to add one large 3-D face to the top of the puck face. It may be easier to change the viewpoint, or even return to a plan view. Set a running OSNAP, and use the 3DFACE command to pick the four corners indicated by dots in Fig. 24-98.

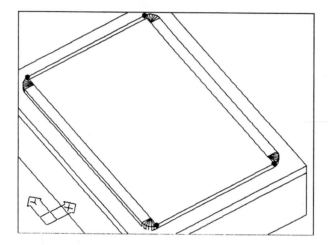

Fig. 24-98. Draw the last 3-D face by picking the four dots.

The completed face is shown in Fig. 24-99 after using HIDE command. The screen display, shown in Fig. 24-99A, may have omitted a line or two where the face rests on the body cap. This is because those two surfaces are at the same elevation and AutoCAD "thinks" some lines on the face may be hidden. The plotted version, Fig. 24-99B, shows most of the lines that are missing in the screen display.

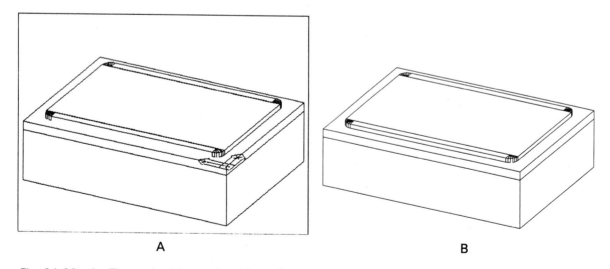

A   B

Fig. 24-99. A—The puck with completed face after using the HIDE command. B—Plotted view of the puck.

Constructing the eyepiece with RULESURF

Before drawing the eyepiece, set the current layer to Eyepiece and restore the viewport configuration named THREE. Adjust the three views using the VPOINT and PAN commands to create the arrangement shown in Fig. 24-100. This establishes a good viewport arrangement for drawing the eyepiece. Make the large viewport active and use VPOINT as follows:

Command: **VPOINT** ↵
Rotate/⟨View point⟩ ⟨0.00,0.00,0.00⟩: **−2,1.5,1**

Pick the lower left viewport, and continue as follows:

    Command: **VPOINT** ↵
    Rotate/⟨View point⟩ ⟨0.00,0.00,0.00⟩: **−1,−1,1** ↵

In order to work with the actual dimensions of the eyepiece, create a new UCS by moving the origin to the point at which the eyepiece attaches to the body. See Fig. 24-100B. Save the new UCS as EYEPIECE. Use the UCSICON command's All and Origin options to move the UCS icon to the new origin in all viewports. Save this viewport configuration as THREE, and answer "Y" to replace the existing viewport.

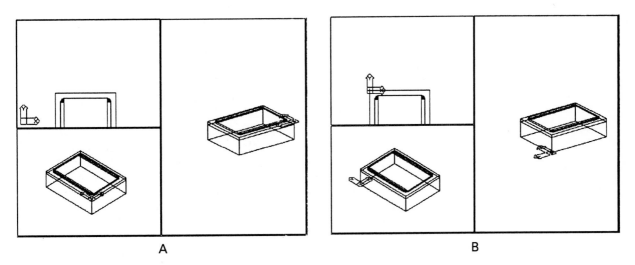

                 A   B

Fig. 24-100. A—The viewport arrangement for drawing the eyepiece. B—New UCS created for eyepiece.

To begin drawing the eyepiece, make the upper-left viewport active and return to a single viewport. Use the CIRCLE and LINE commands to draw the outline of the eyepiece. Use the TRIM command to cut away the unused portion of circle.

    Command: **CIRCLE** ↵
    3P/2P/TTR/⟨Center point⟩: **1.125,.75** ↵
    Diameter/⟨Radius⟩: **D** ↵
    Diameter: **.5** ↵
    Command: ↵
    CIRCLE 3P/2P/TTR/⟨Center point⟩: **@** ↵
    Diameter/⟨Radius⟩: **.75** ↵
    Command: **LINE** ↵
    From point: **0,0** ↵
    To point: **TAN** ↵
    to *(pick the left side of the large circle)*
    To point: ↵
    Command: ↵
    LINE From point: **2.25,0** ↵
    To point: **TAN** ↵
    to *(pick the right side of the large circle)*
    To point: ↵
    Command: **TRIM** ↵
    Select cutting edge(s)...
    Select objects: *(pick the two tangent lines)*
    Select objects: ↵
    ⟨Select object to trim⟩/Undo: *(pick the inside portion of the large circle)*
    ⟨Select object to trim⟩/Undo: ↵

Restore the viewport configuration named THREE. Use the VIEW command to window a view called EYEPIECE2 in the right viewport. Window in closely on the eyepiece. Restore this view. Your drawing should look similar to Fig. 24-101A.

Activate the right viewport and copy the eyepiece outline .25 inches on the Z axis. Draw a line connecting the two ends of the top surface of the eyepiece. The 3-D wireframe of the eyepiece is complete, as shown in Fig. 24-101B.

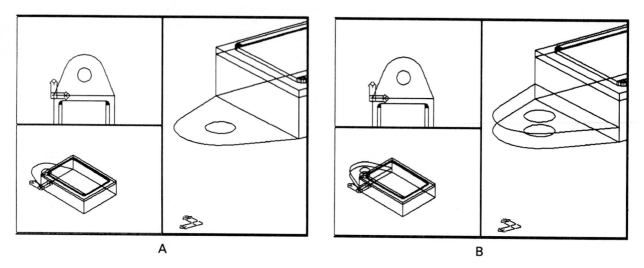

Fig. 24-101. A—Eyepiece outline added to puck body. B—Completed 3-D wireframe eyepiece.

However, before you begin surfacing, it is important to determine how to surface the top plane of the eyepiece. Remember that RULESURF requires two separate entities, one of which cannot be a closed entity such as a circle. Therefore, it is necessary to add some arcs on the circle as construction entities before surfacing. To do this set the Constr layer to current. Change the UCS origin to the top surface of the eyepiece, directly above the current origin. Zoom in on the top circle of the eyepiece. Use the ARC command's Center, Start, End option to draw three arcs using OSNAP CENter, QUAdrant, and ENDpoint as indicated in Fig. 24-102A. Then, use POINT to draw a point at the quadrant between arcs two and three. Be sure PDMODE is set to 3 and PDSIZE is set to .08.

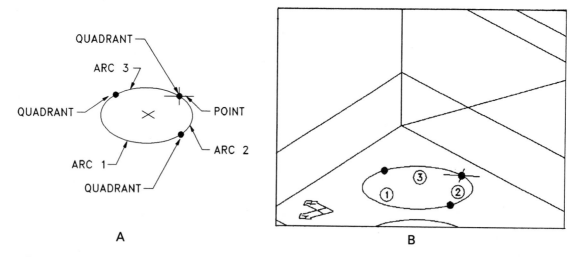

Fig. 24-102. A—Arc locations on the circle. B—The three arcs are shown in the pictorial for use in surfacing the eyepiece.

You can now use the RULESURF command to surface the entire eyepiece. Change the current layer to Eyepiece. Create four ruled surfaces on the top of the eyepiece, one for the hole, and one for the round end, for a total of six.
- The first ruled surface uses the point on the circle and the adjacent line, Fig. 24-103A.
- The second ruled surface uses arc 2 and the adjacent angled line, Fig. 24-103B.
- The third ruled surface uses arc 3 and the adjacent angled line, Fig. 24-103C.
- The fourth ruled surface uses arc 1 and the large outside arc, Fig. 24-103D.

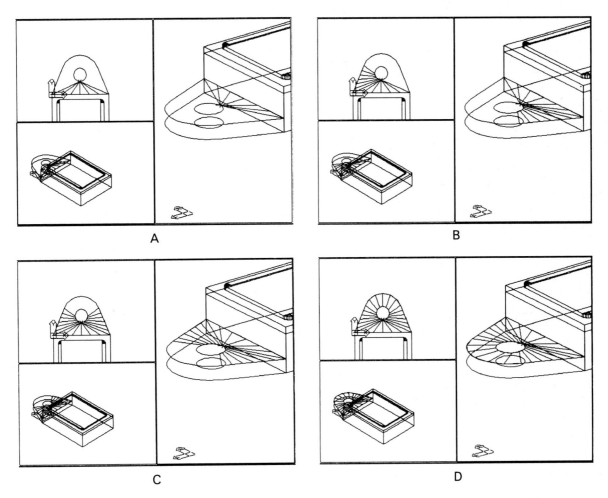

Fig. 24-103. The RULESURF command is used four times on the top surface of the eyepiece.

NOTE

Be sure to pick near the same end of both entities when using the RULESURF command. If you pick near opposite ends of the two entities, the surfacing segment lines cross over each other. For example, notice in Fig. 24-104A that the first pick is located near the far end of the line. Pick number 2 is at the near end of the arc, diagonal to pick 1, resulting in the crossed segments. Whereas in Fig. 24-104B, pick points 1 and 2 are near the same ends of the line and arc, or adjacent to each other, creating a properly ruled surface.

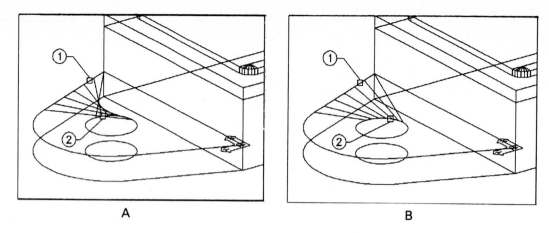

Fig. 24-104. A—Improper pick points result in an intersecting ruled surface. B—The correct pick points create a properly ruled surface.

The hole and the round end of the eyepiece must also be surfaced. Be sure to reset SURFTAB1 if you want more than six segments for the surface of the hole. A SURFTAB1 setting of 8 is used for the illustration in Fig. 24-106, but a larger value creates smoother circles. If you remember how the corners of the puck face were surfaced, this step should not pose any problems. You may have to zoom in to pick the original circle as opposed to the ruled surface. Remove the arcs from the drawing by turning off the Constr layer, because if you select an arc and a circle for the two defining curves in RULESURF, AutoCAD presents the message "Cannot mix closed and open paths." Notice how a close zoom is used to create the ruled surface in the hole in Fig. 24-105. Use the RULESURF command again to surface the curved end of the eyepiece.

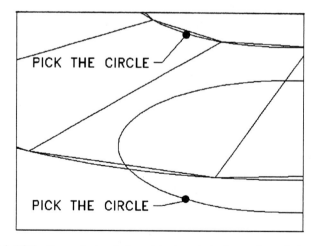

Fig. 24-105. Zoom in to distinguish the circle from the ruled surface.

The final step in construction of the eyepiece is to create a 3-D face on each vertical side. Remember your options on the vertical surfaces are to either draw two separate faces, or draw one face and mirror it. When you are finished, use the HIDE command to be sure that you have created all of the needed surfaces. See Fig. 24-106.

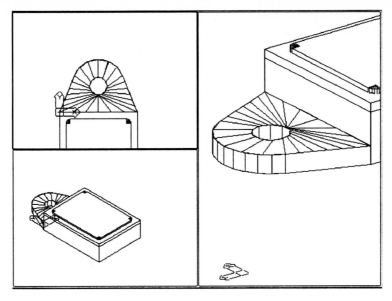

Fig. 24-106. The completed eyepiece after using the HIDE command.

Constructing a cable with REVSURF

The REVSURF (REVolved SURFace) command lets you draw symmetrical shapes that are revolved around a central axis. Two components are needed in order to draw a revolved surface. The first is the shape, or profile that is to be revolved. AutoCAD calls this profile, the *path curve*. In the case of the puck cable, the shape of the path curve is a circle. The second component needed to draw a revolved surface is a line representing the axis of rotation. The designated shape is revolved around this axis. Before using the REVSURF command, you should first determine the number of segments needed in the revolved shape (SURFTAB1), and the number of segments desired in the path curve, or shape to be revolved (SURFTAB2). For the puck cable, set SURFTAB1 to 12 and SURFTAB2 to 8. The shape can be drawn to fill any angle, including a full circle. This example uses the REVSURF command to draw a portion of the cable from the puck. The procedure you will use involves changing layers, rearranging the viewport configuration, creating a new UCS, and drawing the part as follows.

* Make the Cable layer current.
* Use the VPORTS, VPOINT, PAN, and ZOOM commands to rearrange the viewports on your screen so they resemble the arrangement in Fig. 24-107.

In order to achieve the view shown in the lower-left viewport, you need to use the UCS command to rotate the X axis 90 degrees and rotate the Y axis −90 degrees. Use the UCS command's Origin option to locate the new origin at the corner shown in Fig. 24-107.

        Command: **UCS** ↵
        Origin/ZAxis/3point/Entity/View/X/Y/Z/Prev/Restore/Save/Del/?/〈World〉: **X** ↵
        Rotation angle about X axis 〈0〉: **90** ↵
        Command: ↵
        Origin/ZAxis/3point/Entity/View/X/Y/Z/Prev/Restore/Save/Del/?/〈World〉: **Y** ↵
        Rotation angle about Y axis 〈0〉: **−90** ↵
        Command: ↵
        Origin/ZAxis/3point/Entity/View/X/Y/Z/Prev/Restore/Save/Del/?/〈World〉: **O** ↵
        Origin point 〈0,0,0〉: **END** ↵
        of *(pick the corner shown in the large viewport of Fig. 24-107)*

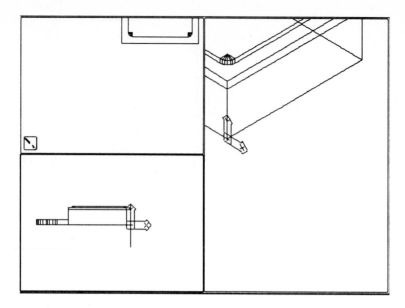

Fig. 24-107. The new viewport configuration named CABLE.

Make the lower-left viewport active, then use the PLAN command and press ENTER to make that viewport plan to the current UCS. Use the ZOOM and PAN commands to create a display similar to the one shown in Fig. 24-107. This creates a side view in the lower-left viewport. Save the new viewport configuration with the name CABLE.

Create a new UCS named CABLE in which the origin is located at the lower-left corner of the end of the puck. Use the UCS command's 3point and Save options when you are finished. See Fig. 24-108 for the pick points of the UCS.

Command: **UCS** ↵
Origin/ZAxis/3point/Entity/View/X/Y/Z/Prev/Restore/Save/Del/?/⟨World⟩: **3** ↵
Origin point ⟨0,0,0⟩: **END** ↵
of *(pick the origin shown in Fig. 24-108)*
Point on positive portion of the X-axis ⟨1.00,0.00,0.00⟩: **END** ↵
of *(pick point X)*
Point on positive-Y portion of the UCS XY plane ⟨0.00,1.00,0.00⟩: **END** ↵
of *(pick point Y)*
Command: **UCS** ↵
Origin/ZAxis/3point/Entity/View/X/Y/Z/Prev/Restore/Save/Del/?/⟨World⟩: **S** ↵
?/Desired UCS name: **CABLE** ↵

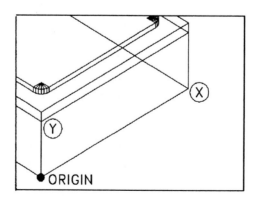

Fig. 24-108. The pick points for the new UCS named CABLE.

Pan the right viewport so the cable end of the puck is near the top of the screen. Draw a circle centered at X = 1.125, Y = .35. The diameter of the cable is .25 inch. The axis of rotation is drawn using the LINE command. Set the two SURFTAB variables and then use the REVSURF command to complete the surfacing of the cable as follows:

> Command: **LINE** ⏎
> From point: **−1.5,1,0** ⏎
> To point: **−1.5,−1,0** ⏎
> To point: ⏎
> Command: **SURFTAB1** ⏎
> New value for SURFTAB1 ⟨10⟩: **12** ⏎
> Command: **SURFTAB2** ⏎
> New value for SURFTAB2 ⟨6⟩: **8** ⏎
> Command: **REVSURF** ⏎
> Select path curve: *(pick the circle as shown in Fig. 24-109A)*
> Select axis of revolution: *(pick the line just drawn as shown in Fig. 24-109A)*
> Start angle ⟨0⟩: ⏎
> Included angle (+ = ccw, − = cw) ⟨Full circle⟩: **−90** ⏎

The completed cable is shown in Fig. 24-109B after using the HIDE command. Now, be sure to save your work.

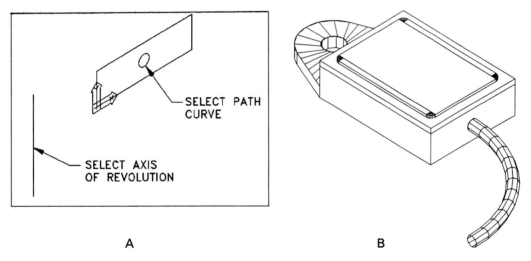

Fig. 24-109. A—Pick the path curve and axis of revolution. B—The completed cable drawn with the REVSURF command.

Create screw heads with the DOME command

The "3D Objects" icon menu in the Draw pull-down menu contains three examples of spherical shapes. The dome and the dish are simply half of a sphere. For this example, the dome can be used to represent the screw heads on the face of the puck. Fig. 24-82 shows the options in the "3D Objects" icon menu.

Set the current layer to Screws and restore the UCS named FACE. It does not matter what viewport configuration you work in. However, a single viewport zoomed in on the origin corner of the puck may be easier to work with.

— NOTE —

If you are using one of the 3-D shapes for the first time in a drawing session, you must first select either 3D Objects from the Draw pull-down menu, the "3d objects" pick from the 3D Surfs selection in the DRAW screen menu, or type "3D" at the Command: prompt. This loads the 3D Objects file, which remains active during the drawing session. After that you need only type the name of the shape you wish to draw, such as "AI__DOME."

Locate the domes in the following manner:

Command: *(pick 3D Objects . . . from the Draw pull-down menu, and then the dome from the ''3D Objects'' icon menu)*
Center of dome: **.095,.095** ↵
Diameter/(radius): **D** ↵
Diameter: **.125** ↵
Number of longitudinal segments ⟨16⟩: **8** ↵
Number of latitudinal segments ⟨8⟩: **4** ↵
Command: **ARRAY** ↵
Select objects: **L** ↵
Select objects: ↵
Rectangular or Polar array (R/P): **R** ↵
Number of rows (---) ⟨1⟩: **2** ↵
Number of columns (III) ⟨1⟩: **2** ↵
Unit cell distance between rows (---): **2.81** ↵
Distance between columns (III): **2.06** ↵

Figs. 24-110A and B show the dome detail and the array of four domes on the digitizer puck.

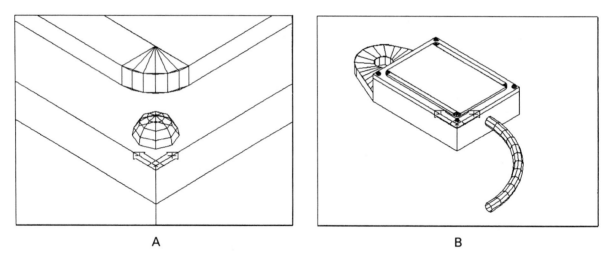

A   B

Fig. 24-110. A—The first dome is located near the origin of the UCS. B—The dome is arrayed on the puck.

Inserting the button 3-D block

The last component to be added to the puck is the group of twelve buttons. At the beginning of the tutorial, you created a block called BUTTON. You must now insert twelve buttons on the face of the puck. First, set the current layer to Buttons. Then, create a new UCS and name it BUTTON. Move the origin of the new UCS as follows:

Command: **UCS** ↵
Origin/ZAxis/3point/Entity/View/X/Y/Z/Prev/Restore/Save/Del/?/⟨World⟩: **O** ↵
Origin point ⟨0,0,0⟩: **.19,.19,.06** ↵

For the insert operation, you only need a single view of the object on the screen.

Command: **MINSERT** ↵
Block name: (or ?): **BUTTON** ↵
  Insertion point: **.3125,.5** ↵
X scale factor ⟨1⟩ / Corner / Corner / XYZ: ↵
  Y scale factor ⟨1⟩ (default = X): ↵
  Rotation angle ⟨0⟩: ↵
Number of rows (---) ⟨1⟩: **4** ↵
Number of columns (III) ⟨1⟩: **3** ↵
Unit cell or distance between rows (---): **.457** ↵
Distance between columns (III): **.457** ↵

The completed puck is shown in Fig. 24-111.

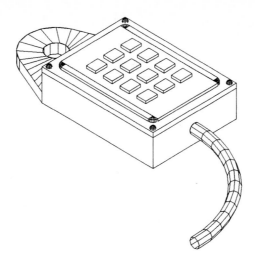

Fig. 24-111. An array of buttons completes the surface model of the digitizer puck.

— NOTE —

Determine the best method for adding numbers to the buttons. If the BUTTON block had been given an attribute, the numbers could have been added at insertion. However, the INSERT command would have to be used twelve times instead of using MINSERT. If you use DTEXT, you would first have to draw some sort of construction lines or points to define the center of the button, copy those lines to each button, then use DTEXT twelve times. What is the most efficient method?

CHAPTER TEST

Write your answers in the spaces provided.

1. When looking at the screen, in which direction does the Z coordinate project? _____

   _____

2. Explain the differences between spherical and cylindrical coordinates. _____

   _____

   _____

   _____

3. Which command allows you to give objects thickness? _____

4. If you draw a line after setting a thickness, what have you actually drawn? _____

   _____

5. What is the purpose of the right-hand rule? _____

   _____

   _____

   _____

6. What is the purpose of the VPOINT command? _____

   _____

7. The VPOINT command's Rotate option allows you to use what kind of coordinates?

_____

8. What does the small diameter circle inside the compass represent? _____

9. How do you create 3-D extruded text? _____

_____

10. What is the function of the HIDE command? _____

_____

11. To have hidden lines on the layer named DIMEN displayed in a different color, what should you do? _____

_____

12. Define "point filters." _____

_____

_____

_____

_____

13. Compare the 3DFACE and SOLID commands. _____

_____

_____

_____

_____

14. How do you select one of AutoCAD's predrawn 3-D shapes? _____

_____

_____

15. Identify the purpose of the VPORTS command. _____

_____

16. How do you name a configuration of these viewports? _____

_____

17. What is the purpose of naming a configuration of views? _____

_____

18. What is a User Coordinate System (UCS)? _____

_____

_____

19. What command controls the display of the User Coordinate System icon? _____

20. What does the broken pencil icon represent? _____

_____

21. What is the function of the UCS command's 3point option? _____

_____

_____

22. How is the UCS icon moved to the origin of the current coordinate system? _____
_____

23. When you use the Entity option of the UCS command, how does AutoCAD determine the X axis if you pick a circle for the new UCS? _____
_____

24. When would the UCS command's View option be used? _____
_____

25. How can you make sure that a view will always be plan to the current UCS? _____
_____

26. What is the total number of viewports allowed with the VPORTS command, and what is a practical number for model construction? _____
_____

27. What is the size of a basic 3-D building block and what is its purpose? _____
_____

28. Name the test drawing that can be automatically inserted for establishing a view in the DVIEW command. _____
_____

29. What DVIEW option allows you to view more or less of the drawing? _____

30. What two point options define the line of sight? _____
_____

31. Which of the two options in Question 30 should you select first when creating a 3-D view?
_____
_____

32. What does the DVIEW command's POints option allow you to do? _____
_____

33. How is a perspective view set? _____

34. When would the DVIEW command's Zoom option ask for a scale factor? When would it ask for a lens length? _____
_____
_____

35. What function does the DVIEW command's CLip option serve? _____

36. When using the 3DFACE command, when must you indicate that an edge is to be invisible?
_____
_____

37. What values does AutoCAD need to know about a 3-D Mesh? _____
_____

38. AutoCAD's surface meshing commands create what type of entities? _____

39. Which surface mesh command allows you to rotate a profile about an axis to create a symmetrical object? _____

40. What object does a TABSURF create? _____

_____

41. What do the SURFTAB1 and SURFTAB2 variables control? _____

_____

42. Name three entities that can be connected with the RULESURF command. _____

_____

43. What predrawn 3-D shapes are available? _____

_____

44. How many different types of pyramids can you draw with the PYRAMID command?

_____

45. What is the function of SPLFRAME in the 3DFACE command? _____

_____

_____

_____

46. Define "longitudinal segments" in reference to a dome or dish. _____

_____

47. What command displays a quick rendering? _____

48. What command allows you to both move and rotate an object in a 3-D drawing? _____

49. What feature do you define when using the the ROTATE3D command? _____

50. What option of the ROTATE3D command allows you to use the center axis of a circle as the feature to rotate about?_____

51. What is the default method of picking a MIRROR3D mirror plane? _____

DRAWING PROBLEMS

1. Draw Problem 12 from Chapter 23 using the ELEV command. Display the object in two different views. Use HIDE on one view. Save the drawing as A:P24-1.
2. Draw the object shown below using the ELEV command. Display the object in two different views. Use HIDE on one view. Save the drawing as A:P24-2.

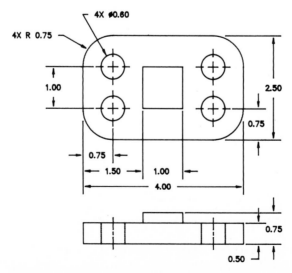

3. Choose Problem 5, 6, 7, 8, or 9 from Chapter 23 and draw it in wireframe using the LINE command. Display the drawing with VPOINT in four different views. Save the drawing as A:P24-3.

4. Load AutoCAD and open P24-3. Use the 3DFACE command to create faces on the entire part. Display the part in four different views. Save the revised drawing as A:P24-4.

5-7. Draw the objects shown below in 3-D form. Use the LINE and 3DFACE commands with the dimensions given to create the drawings. Can you create 3-D blocks for use in these drawings? Display the drawings from three different viewpoints. Select the HIDE command for one of the views. Save the drawings as A:P24-5, A:P24-6, and A:P24-7.

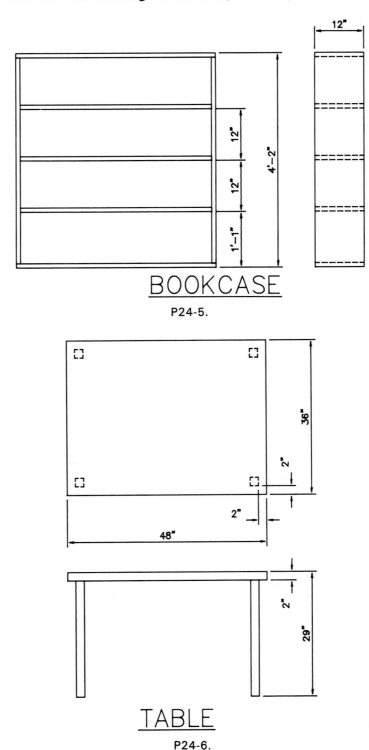

BOOKCASE

P24-5.

TABLE

P24-6.

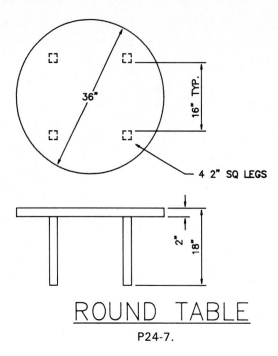

ROUND TABLE

P24-7.

8. Construct a 3-D model of the table shown.
   A. Use any 3-D construction techniques required.
   B. Use the dimensions given.
   C. Alter the design of the table to include rounded table top corners or rounded feet. Try replacing the rectangular feet shown with spheres.
   D. Use the DVIEW command to display the model.
   E. Use the HIDE command to remove hidden lines.
   F. Plot the table both in wireframe and with hidden lines removed.

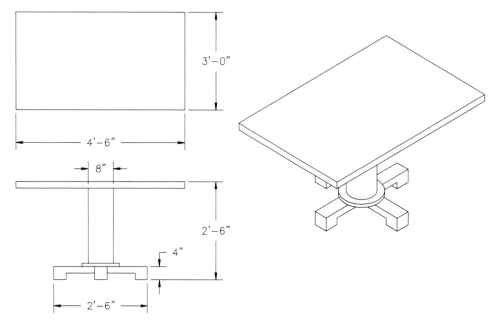

P24-8.

9-11. Problems 9 to 11 are mechanical parts. Use the following instructions to construct each drawing.
  A. Create a 3-D model.
  B. Use viewports for the model layout and work between the ports as needed.
  C. Create one viewport that is a 3-D display of the part.
  D. Do not dimension the model.
  E. Plot the finished drawings on B-size bond with felt-tip pen or make a quick print using a dot matrix printer.

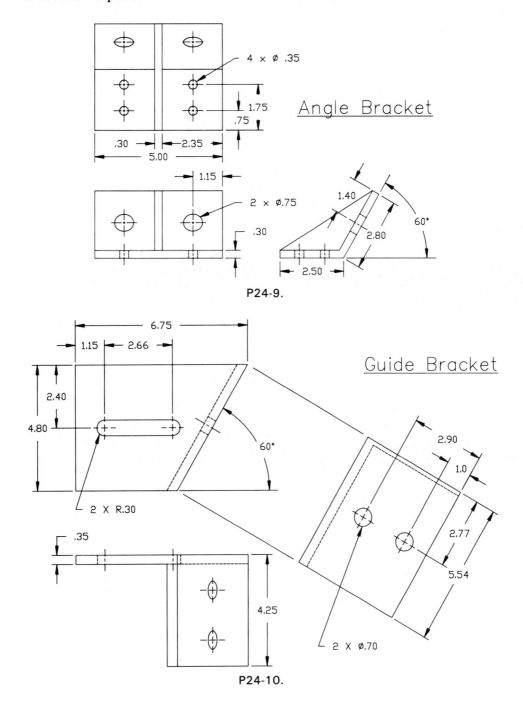

P24-9.

P24-10.

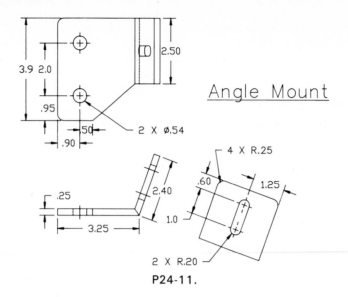

Angle Mount

P24-11.

12. Create a surface model of the half cylinder shown using the dimensions given.
   A. Use the appropriate surface modeling commands to create the model.
   B. Use the DVIEW command to view the model.
   C. Hide the hidden lines.
   D. Plot the drawing on bond or vellum twice, once as a wireframe and also with hidden lines removed.

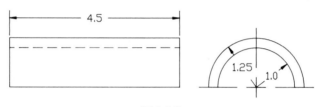

P24-12.

13. Create a surface model of the half torus shown.
   A. Use the REVSURF command to construct the model.
   B. Use the dimensions shown.
   C. Set the SURFTAB1 variable to 20.
   D. Set the SURFTAB2 variable to 10.
   E. Display the model with the DVIEW command.
   F. Use the HIDE command to remove hidden lines.
   G. Plot the finished drawing on B-size bond both as wireframe and with hidden lines removed.

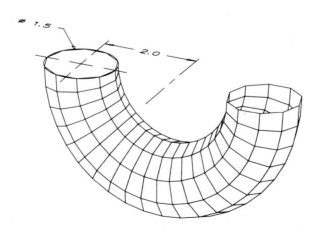

P24-13.

14. Create a surface model of a glass using the profile shown.
    A. Use the REVSURF command to construct the glass.
    B. Use the dimensions given for height and radii.
    C. Set the SURFTAB1 variable to 16.
    D. Set the SURFTAB2 variable to 8.
    E. Display the model with the DVIEW command.
    F. Use HIDE to remove hidden lines.
    G. Construct the glass a second time using different SURFTAB settings.
    H. Plot the drawing on B-size bond both as a wireframe and with hidden lines removed.

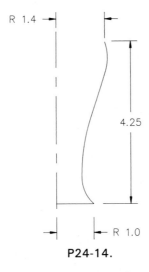

P24-14.

15-16. Draw the following objects using the REVSURF command. When using the REVSURF command, accept the default values for segments. Display the objects and use the Hide option on each one. Save the drawings as A:P24-15 and A:P24-16.

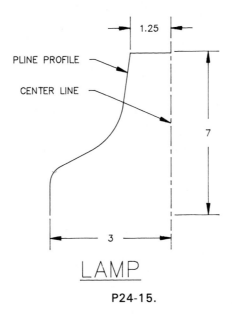

P24-15.

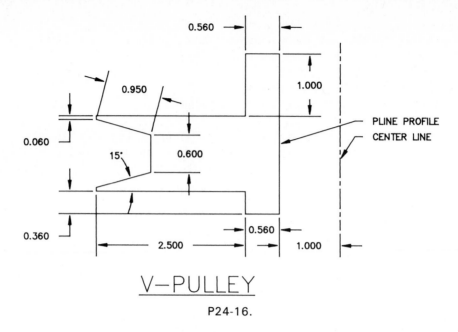

V—PULLEY

P24-16.

17-19. Problems 17 through 19 are plans of two houses and a cabin. Create a 3-D model of one of the houses using all modeling techniques covered in this chapter.
   A. Establish multiple viewports.
   B. Create named UCSs for the floor plan and the various wall elevations.
   C. Create named viewport configurations (using one viewport) of single floors or walls so you can display the working areas as large as possible on screen.
   D. Use the dimensions given or alter the room sizes and arrangements to suit your own design.
   E. Use the DVIEW command to display the house in the following ways:
   • View the house from above.
   • Zoom away from the house.
   • Zoom in on the house to view a feature up close.
   • Place the camera inside the house, looking out.
   • Use the TArget option to rotate the house around the camera.
   • Display the house in perspective.
   • Use the Hide option to remove hidden lines.
   F. Plot the model on B- or C-size bond with hidden lines removed.

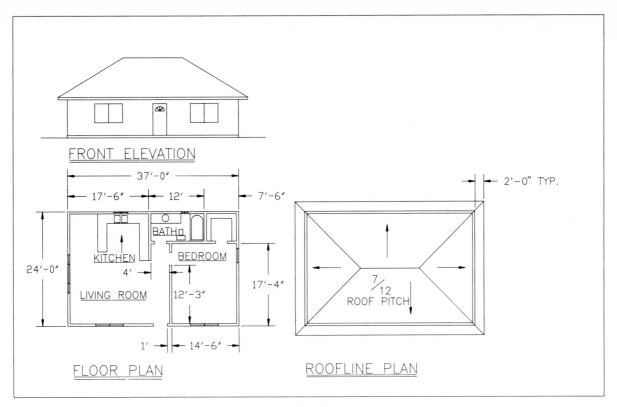

P24-17.

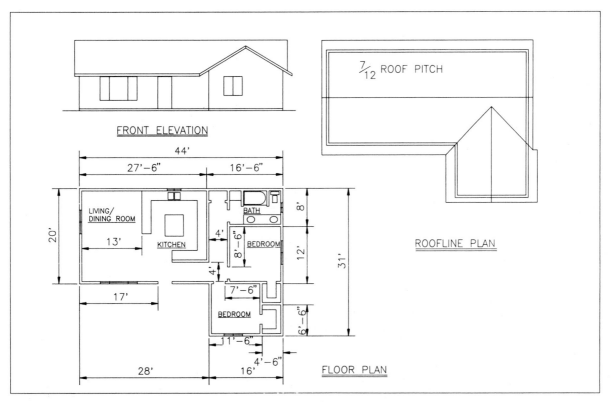

P24-18.

FLOOR PLAN

P24-19.

20. Complete the digitizer puck that was demonstrated in the tutorial.
   A. Add numbers to the buttons.
   B. Redraw as many 3-D faces as possible using the **3DFACE** Invisible option.
   C. Delete the square buttons and insert the curved buttons.
   D. Generate laser prints or pen plots on A- or B-size paper showing the view in each quadrant of the compass.

```
Model
  Extrude          Move Object
  Revolve          Change Prim.
  Solidify         Separate
  Primitives...    Cut Solids

  Union            Chamfer Solids    Variables...
  Subtract         Fillet Solids
  Intersect                          Engr Units
  Modify        ▷                    British Units
                                     CGS Units
  Setup         ▷  List Objects      SI Units
  Inquiry       ▷  Mass Property...
  Display       ▷  Area Calc.        Upgrade Vars.
  Utility       ▷  Interference      Double Prec.
                                     Script Compat.
                   Set Decomp.
                   Set Subdiv.       Mesh
                                     Wireframe
                   Material...
                   SolUCS            Set Wire Dens.

                   ASM In...         Copy Feature
                   ASM Out...        Section Solids
                   Purge Objects     Profile Solids

                   Load Modeler
                   Unload Modeler
```

INTRODUCTION TO SOLID MODELING

Learning objectives

After completing this chapter, you will be able to:

☐ Create solid primitive shapes.
☐ Create solid shapes from two-dimensional objects.
☐ Construct composite solid models.
☐ Edit solid models.
☐ Generate mass properties reports.
☐ Display solids with hidden lines removed, and as shaded renderings.
☐ Create a sectioned profile of a solid model.
☐ Construct 2-D views from a solid model.

Solid modeling is a procedure used for design and manufacturing applications. A model constructed of solid components can be studied for its composition, weight, strengths, and weaknesses. When testing and analysis of the computer-generated model is complete, the solid model data can then be used by Computer-Aided Manufacturing (CAM), and Computer Numerical Control (CNC) programs to create the finished product. This chapter introduces solid modeling methods that are a part of AutoCAD's Advanced Modeling Extension (AME), Release 2.1.

When you purchase the Advanced Modeling Extension, you are given an authorization code. The first time you load AME you are asked to enter this code. This is the only time you are asked for the code. If you did not purchase AME, you will not be able to use any of the commands in the Model pull-down or screen menus. To load AME, pick the Model pull-down menu, then pick Utility, and select Load Modeler from the cascading menu. AME can also be loaded by entering the following at the keyboard:

Command: **(XLOAD "AME")** ↵
"ame"

The following prompt is displayed when AME is loaded:

No modeler is loaded yet. Both AME and Region Modeler are available.
Autoload Region/⟨AME⟩:

At this point you can press ENTER to load the full AME program, or type "R" to load only the Region Modeler. The Region Modeler is discussed later in this chapter.

If you load a drawing that was created using AME, there is no need to load the Advanced Modeling Extension. The following prompt is displayed the first time you select an AME command:

Initializing Advanced Modeling Extension.

NOTE

Solid modeling programs require a lot of computer power, and AME 2.1 is no exception. For 100% IBM 386/486 compatible computers, the minimum amount of extended memory required is 8MB, and a minimum of 30MB of hard disk drive space for complete installation of the AutoCAD Release 12 and AME Version 2.1. The more extended memory available for the program and drawing files, the less work is required by the hard disk to page portions of the drawing to temporary files on the disk. Due to this intense memory usage by AutoCAD and AME, it is a good idea to avoid using many memory-resident programs while using AutoCAD. These programs are also known as *Terminate and Stay Resident*, or *TSR*.

MENUS AND COMMANDS

AMERM 3,4

The solid modeling package is easy to use, and the commands function the same as AutoCAD. They can be entered at the keyboard, or selected from one pull-down menu, five cascading menus (accessed through the pull-down menu), and one dialogue box. The pull-down and cascading submenus are located at the extreme right of the menu bar. All of the AME commands are located in this position. The menus and their basic functions are given in the following list. All commands in AME begin with "SOL" when typed at the Command: prompt. They are shown without the SOL prefix in the pull-down menus.

- **Model** — Commands that enable you to perform basic modeling functions such as extrusions, solidify, unions, and subtractions.
- **Primitives** — Dialogue box that enables you to construct solid primitives, both in 3-D and from existing 2-D objects. Primitives include box, sphere, wedge, cone, cylinder, and torus. Existing 2-D and 3-D shapes can be extracted, revolved, and solidified.
- **Modify** — Commands that allow you to move, change, and cut primitives and solids. These commands include chamfer, fillet, and separate.
- **Setup** — Selections that enable you to set the kind of units you will be working with and set the initial value of AME system variables.
- **Inquiry** — Commands that report on specific characteristics of the model and that set solids system variable values. These commands are list, mass properties, and area.
- **Display** — Commands that enable you to display the model in forms such as wireframe, solid, and sections. The commands include mesh and wireframe. The SHADE command (when typed at the keyboard) does not begin with SOL.
- **Utility** — These commands allow you to change the UCS, specify material, and optimize memory usage. The commands are material, UCS, and purge. The ASM in and ASM out commands allow compatibility with AutoSolid files. AutoSolid was the original AME.

The menus and commands found in the pull-down menus can be selected from the right-side screen menu also. If you pick MODEL in AutoCAD's Root Menu, the MODEL screen menu is displayed. The right-side screen menus are organized like the pull-downs and contain the same commands. All commands are preceded by "SOL."

The solid modeling menus are also represented on the tablet menu. They are provided on a separate overlay, and are grouped according to the previously discussed menus. The tablet overlay is best attached under the standard menu template. See Fig. 25-1.

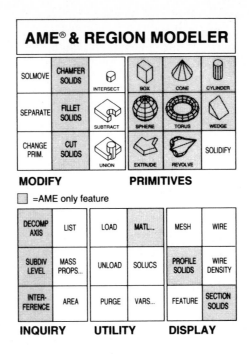

Fig. 25-1. AME tablet menu overlay.　(Courtesy Autodesk, Inc.)

CONSTRUCTING A SOLID MODEL

AMERM 5

Constructing a solid model is quite easy, and once you understand the proper sequence of commands, you will be amazed at how quickly you can construct fairly complex models. The following discussion and tutorial steps you through the construction of a solid model.

Constructing a 2-D region model

AutoCAD provides a facility for constructing a two-dimensional solid model called a *region*. A region contains all of the necessary solid model properties, except that it has no thickness. One important aspect of a region is that it can be *extruded*, or given a thickness (Z value). This means that you can convert an AutoCAD shape into a solid model in just a few steps. The following example illustrates one method that could be used to construct the base for the solid model created in this chapter.

Any AutoCAD 2-D entity can be converted to a solid model. First set your limits to 18,12, then zoom all. Now use the RECTANGLE, CIRCLE, and ARRAY commands to create the 2-D region.

```
Command: RECTANG ↵
First corner: 3,3 ↵
Other corner: 11,11 ↵
Command: CIRCLE ↵
3P/2P/TTR/〈Center point〉: 4,4 ↵
Diameter/〈Radius〉: D ↵
Diameter: .75 ↵
Command: ARRAY ↵
Select objects: L ↵
Select objects: ↵
Rectangular or Polar array (R/P) 〈R〉: ↵
Number of rows (---) 〈1〉: 2 ↵
Number of columns (|||) 〈1〉: 2 ↵
Unit cell distance between rows (---): 6 ↵
Distance between columns (|||): 6 ↵
```

This creates the AutoCAD entities that can be solidified. See Fig. 25-2. The SOLIDIFY command is used for this purpose, and it identifies the solidified object by placing the current hatch pattern inside. The default pattern, its line spacing, and angle can be changed with the SOLHPAT (SOLids Hatch PATtern), SOLHANGLE (SOLids Hatch ANGLE), and SOLHSIZE (SOLids Hatch SIZE) variables.

> Command: **SOLHPAT** ↵
> Hatch pattern ⟨U⟩: **STEEL** ↵
> Command: **SOLHANGLE** ↵
> Hatch angle ⟨0.00⟩: ↵
> Command: **SOLHSIZE** ↵
> Hatch size ⟨1.00⟩: **5** ↵

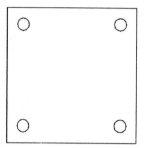

Fig. 25-2. AutoCAD entities such as rectangles and circles can be used to create 2-D solid model regions.

These variables above can also be set by entering DDSOLVAR at the Command: prompt. This displays the "AME R2.1 — System Variables" dialogue box. Then pick Hatch Parameters ... and a subdialogue allows you to enter the hatch name, angle, and size.

The region that you created will be filled with the hatch pattern for steel. To complete the 2-D region, subtract the circles (holes) from the rectangle with the SOLSUB command. You are first asked to select the "source" object. This is the object you will subtract other entities from. In this case, the source object is the rectangle, and the circles are subtracted from it to create the 2-D region.

> Command: **SOLSUB** ↵
> Source objects...
> Select objects: *(pick the rectangle)*
> Select objects: ↵

AutoCAD updates the object, then asks for objects to subtract.

> Objects to subtract from them...
> Select objects: *(pick the four circles)*
> Select objects: ↵

The 2-D region is updated to reflect the subtraction of the circles from the base. The image is redrawn showing the hatch pattern filling the rectangle, and the circles appearing as holes. See Fig. 25-3.

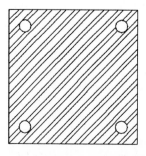

Fig. 25-3. A 2-D region with a hatch pattern applied to it.

The final step in creating a 3-D solid model from the 2-D region is to extrude the region with the SOLEXT (SOLid EXTrude) command. You can extrude an entity in a positive or negative Z direction.

> Command: **SOLEXT** ⏎
> Select regions, polylines and circles for extrusion...
> Select objects: *(pick anywhere on the region)*
> Select objects: ⏎
> Height of extrusion: **1** ⏎

At the next prompt, AutoCAD allows you to taper the extrusion by entering an angle value. Press ENTER for no extrusion in this example.

> Extrusion taper angle ⟨0⟩: ⏎

AutoCAD updates the object, and then asks if you want to extrude *loops,* which are any closed, multisegment lines. If you wanted holes of different depths, or even cylinders extending below or above the object, you could answer "YES" to this prompt. For this example, press ENTER for the default.

> Extrude loops to different heights? ⟨N⟩: ⏎

AutoCAD then prompts that it is updating the database, and computes the solid. You can use the VPOINT command to see that the object has been extruded. When you do, you will see that the holes are shown with only two lines connecting the circles. See Fig. 25-4. You can specify the number of connecting lines for better curve representation. This is discussed in the next example of solid modeling.

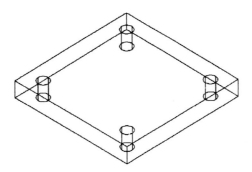

Fig. 25-4. Extruding a 2-D region.

This exercise has shown you how to develop solid models by starting with 2-D shapes called regions. These in turn can be solidified and extruded into 3-D models. The next example illustrates a method for constructing a solid model by working with 3-D shapes called "primitives." Save the current model on your screen, or erase it before you begin the next section. If you loaded only the Region Modeler, you will now need to unload the Region Modeler and load AME. Pick the Model pull-down menu, then pick Utility, and select the Unload Modeler option. Repeat the process, but pick Load Modeler and press ENTER to load AME instead of the Region Modeler. If you do not do this, then the AME commands will not function.

EXERCISE 25-1

☐ Start a new drawing and name it EX25-1.
☐ Draw a two-dimensional top view of the object using the dimensions given.
☐ Using the appropriate AME commands, create a 2-D region.
☐ Extrude the region to a 3-D solid with the given thickness.

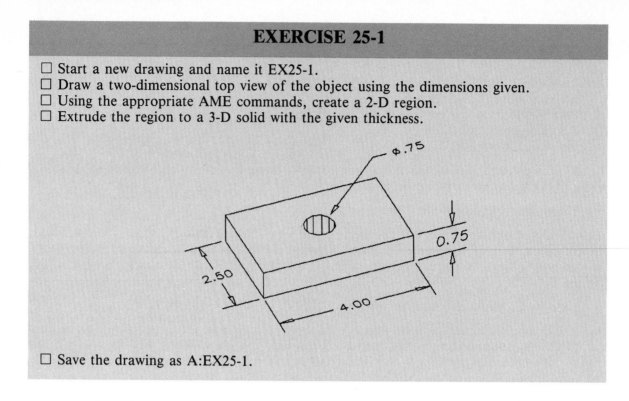

☐ Save the drawing as A:EX25-1.

Using solid primitives

For the following discussion, your task is to construct a support bracket composed of a square, one-inch thick base, and a six-inch high cylinder. A variety of solid modeling commands are used to construct the object. If you have access to a computer, use it to construct the object as you read through this discussion. Remember to save your work often.

In preparation for this design session, create the following layers:

Layer Name	Color	Linetype
OBJECT	White	Continuous
CONSTR	Blue	Continuous
VIEWPORTS	Yellow	Continuous
SECTION	Green	Continuous

The two principal solid primitives are drawn first. Set the current layer to OBJECT. Set units to two-place decimal, limits to 18,12, grid to 1, and snap to .5. Then zoom all to view the limits of the drawing. Use the SOLBOX (SOLids BOX) and SOLCYL (SOLids CYLinder) commands as follows:

Command: **SOLBOX** ↵
Baseplane/Center/Corner of box ⟨0,0,0⟩: **3,3** ↵
Cube/Length/⟨Other corner⟩: **11,11** ↵
Height: **1** ↵

Solid primitives are initially displayed as wireframes. If you do not set the wireframe density the model will not be of acceptable quality because it will not display enough "wires" connecting arcs and circles. These wires are called *tessallation lines,* and are controlled by the SOLWDENS (Wire DENSity) variable.

Command: **SOLWDENS** ↵
Wireframe mesh density (1 to 12) ⟨1⟩: **4** ↵
Command: **SOLCYL** ↵
Baseplane/Elliptical/⟨Center point⟩ ⟨0,0,0⟩: **7,7** ↵
Diameter/⟨Radius⟩: **2** ↵
Center of other end/⟨Height⟩: **6** ↵
Command: **VPOINT** ↵
Rotate/⟨View point⟩ ⟨0.00,0.00,1.00⟩: **.75,−1,.5** ↵

Use the ZOOM command and a scale factor of .9X to decrease the size of the display. Use PAN if necessary to achieve a view similar to Fig. 25-5.

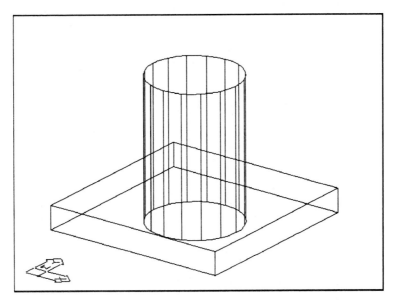

Fig. 25-5. A box and cylinder are used to begin the model.

Creating profiles with SOLREV

The internal shape of the part can be constructed by creating a profile using the LINE or PLINE commands. The SOLREV (SOLids REVolve) command can then be used to revolve the profile about an axis, thus creating a solid. The profile must be a 2-D AutoCAD object or region. Polylines to be revolved must have at least three vertices, and no more than 500, and can have no line width.

Before creating the profile, first change the UCS so it is in the same plane as the intended profile. Then construct a profile using the PLINE and LINE commands as follows:

Command: **UCS** ↵
Origin/ZAxis/3point/Entity/View/X/Y/Z/Prev/Restore/Save/Del/?/ ⟨World⟩: **X** ↵
Rotation angle about X axis ⟨0⟩: **90** ↵
Command: ↵
Origin/ZAxis/3point/Entity/View/X/Y/Z/Prev/Restore/Save/Del/?/⟨World⟩: **O** ↵
Origin point: ⟨0,0,0⟩: **CEN** ↵
of *(pick the bottom of the cylinder)*
Command: ↵
Origin/ZAxis/3point/Entity/View/X/Y/Z/Prev/Restore/Save/Del/?/⟨World⟩: **S** ↵
?/Desired UCS name: **CENTER** ↵
Command: **UCSICON** ↵
ON/OFF/All/Noorigin/ORigin ⟨ON⟩: **OR** ↵

The UCS icon should now be located at the bottom center of the cylinder, and the Y axis should be pointed up toward the top of the cylinder. Change the current layer to CONSTR, and create the profile as follows:

Command: **PLINE** ↵
From point: **0,0** ↵
Current line-width is 0.0000
Arc/Close/Halfwidth/Length/Undo/Width/⟨Endpoint of line⟩: **.75,0** ↵
Arc/Close/Halfwidth/Length/Undo/Width/⟨Endpoint of line⟩: **@0,1.5** ↵
Arc/Close/Halfwidth/Length/Undo/Width/⟨Endpoint of line⟩: **@.25,0** ↵
Arc/Close/Halfwidth/Length/Undo/Width/⟨Endpoint of line⟩: **@0,4.5** ↵
Arc/Close/Halfwidth/Length/Undo/Width/⟨Endpoint of line⟩: **@1⟨180** ↵
Arc/Close/Halfwidth/Length/Undo/Width/⟨Endpoint of line⟩: ↵

Now, use the LINE command to connect the two endpoints of the polyline. This line will be the axis of revolution in the SOLREV command. Now, set the current layer to OBJECT.

Command: **SOLREV** ↵
Select region, polyline or circle for revolution...
Select objects: *(pick the polyline)*
Select objects: ↵
Axis of revolution − Entity/X/Y/⟨Start point of axis⟩: **E** ↵
Pick entity to revolve around: *(pick the line)*
Angle of revolution ⟨full circle⟩: ↵

The new revolved solid is shown in Fig. 25-6.

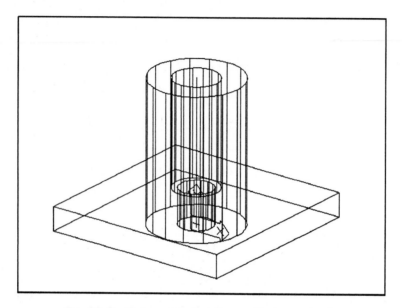

Fig. 25-6. The model after the profile is revolved.

A result of the SOLREV command is the deletion of the polyline profile entity. This is automatic if a SOLids system VARiable (SOLVAR) called SOLDELENT is set to the correct value. The SOLDELENT (SOLids DELete ENTity) variable has three options. They can be accessed by entering the variable name at the Command: prompt:

Command: **SOLDELENT** ↵
Delete the entity after extrusion, revolution, or solidification?
(1 = never, 2 = ask, 3 = always) ⟨3⟩:

The Always option (number 3) is the default because once the SOLREV command is complete, the profile entity is no longer needed. If you want AutoCAD to prompt you, enter "2" at the prompt. The next time you use the SOLREV command, the first prompt is "Delete the entities that are revolved? ⟨N⟩." You then have the option. If you want the profile entity to remain intact, enter "1" and press ENTER. AutoCAD will not prompt you.

In the previous example, the line used for the axis of revolution is not deleted, so you should erase that line when the SOLREV command is completed.

─────────── **PROFESSIONAL TIP** ───────────

If you construct profiles on a separate layer with a different color than the model, the axis lines of revolution are easier to erase when the SOLREV command is finished.

Moving solids

Rather than using the MOVE command to work with solids, the SOLMOVE (SOLids MOVE) command handles that function in a much more powerful manner. In the example of the support bracket, the cylinder just drawn must be moved up one inch so that it sits on top of the box. The SOLMOVE command displays its own Motion Coordinate System (MCS) icon. Each axis line of the icon has an arrow at its tip. The X axis has one arrow, the Y axis has two arrows, and the Z axis has three arrows.

The SOLMOVE command allows you to specify a variety of movements and rotations in one keyboard entry. Use SOLMOVE in the following manner:

> Command: **SOLMOVE** ↵
> Select objects: *(pick the cylinder and the revolved solid)*
> Select objects: ↵
> ?/⟨Motion description⟩: **TY1** ↵
> ?/⟨Motion description⟩: ↵

The motion description entered, TY1, means that the objects are to be *translated* (moved) along the Y axis one unit, hence the entry "TY1." The model before and after movement is shown in Fig. 25-7.

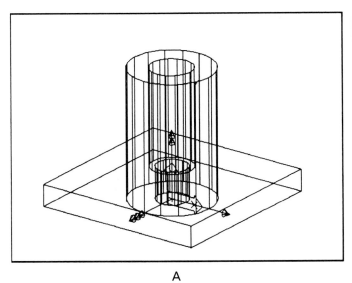
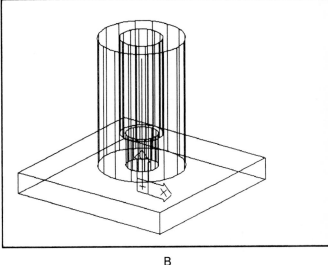

| A | B |

Fig. 25-7. A—The SOLMOVE command displays the MCS (Motion Coordinate System) icon. B—The solids after movement along the Y axis.

Converting 2-D entities into a solid model

As shown in the previous region modeler discussion, you can convert entities into solids. Another method for this process is to create the four bolt holes in the base of the support bracket in Fig. 25-8. First, draw circles and then use the CHPROP and SOLIDIFY commands to create solids. Use the UCS command to return to the World Coordinate System and proceed as follows:

> Command: **CIRCLE** ↵
> 3P/2P/TTR/⟨Center point⟩: **4,4** ↵
> Diameter/⟨Radius⟩: **D** ↵
> Diameter: **.75** ↵
> Command: **CHPROP** ↵
> Select objects: **L** ↵
> Select objects: ↵
> Change what property (Color/LAyer/LType/Thickness)?: **T** ↵
> New thickness ⟨0.00⟩: **1** ↵
> Change what property (Color/LAyer/LType/Thickness)?: ↵
> Command: **SOLIDIFY** ↵

The following prompt appears if the SOLDELENT variable is set to 2. Be sure to answer "YES."

>Delete the entities that are solidified? ⟨N⟩ **Y** ⏎
>Select objects: *(pick the extruded circle)*
>Select objects: ⏎

AutoCAD then updates its database before allowing you to proceed.

──── PROFESSIONAL TIP ────

If you do not delete the entities that are solidified at the above prompt, they may come back to haunt you later. Remember that a circle extruded into a cylinder has solid ends. If the circle that is solidified is not deleted, you will not be able to see inside of the hole later when you use the SOLMESH (SOLids MESH) and HIDE commands to display the solid.

Now that the circle has been changed into a solid primitive, you can array it around the plate.

>Command: **ARRAY** ⏎
>Select objects: **L** ⏎
>Select objects: ⏎
>Rectangular or Polar array (R/P) ⟨R⟩: ⏎
>Number of rows (---) ⟨1⟩: **2** ⏎
>Number of columns (¦¦¦) ⟨1⟩: **2** ⏎
>Unit cell distance between rows (---): **6** ⏎
>Distance between columns (¦¦¦): **6** ⏎

The cylinder is arrayed around the object and looks like Fig. 25-8.

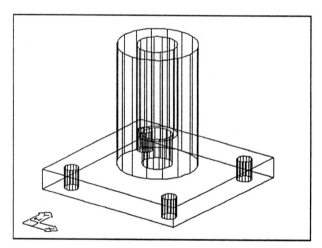

Fig. 25-8. The 2-D circle is converted to a solid and arrayed.

CREATING COMPOSITE SOLIDS
⎡ **AMERM 5** ⎤

The previous steps in the construction of the model have been creating the solid primitives from which to carve the final model. As it stands, the model in Fig. 25-8 is all solid; it has no holes in it. The next task is to create the holes in the base by subtracting the small cylinders from the base. Then, the large shape in the cylindrical part of the bracket that was created with SOLREV must be subtracted from the cylinder. Finally, the solid primitives must be joined into one part.

The commands that create composite solids are found in the Model pull-down menu or the MODEL screen menu. These commands perform *Boolean operations*. George Boole (1815-1864) was an English mathematician who developed a mathematical system in which all variables have the value of either one or zero. Boolean algebra is the basis for the mathematical calculations involved in constructing composite solids.

The SOLSUB (SOLids SUBtraction) command performs the subtraction of one solid from another. Use it on the model as follows:

Command: **SOLSUB** ↵
Source objects...
Select objects: *(pick the base solid)*
Select objects: ↵
1 solid selected.
Objects to subtract from them...
Select objects: *(pick all four small cylinders)*
Select objects: ↵

It takes several seconds for AutoCAD to process the command. You will see prompts that say "Tessellation computation begins." Tessellation lines are lines that are placed on curved surfaces to help you see the curve. Tessellations are parallel to the axis of the curve. Now, perform the next subtraction.

Command: **SOLSUB** ↵
Source objects...
Select objects: *(pick the large cylinder)*
Select objects: ↵
1 solid selected.
Objects to subtract from them...
Select objects: *(pick the revolved solid inside the cylinder)*
Select objects: ↵

Next, the two solids—the cylinder and the base—can be joined with the SOLUNION (SOLids UNION) command.

Command: **SOLUNION** ↵
Select objects: *(pick the cylinder)*
Select objects: *(pick the base)*
Select objects: ↵

Once again, AutoCAD updates its database with the new information. The model is now one composite shape. You can test this by selecting the ERASE command and picking anywhere on the model. The entire model is highlighted. Cancel the ERASE command.

Adding fillet and chamfer to a solid model

Using the SOLFILL (SOLids FILLet) and SOLCHAM (SOLids CHAMfer) commands of AME is somewhat different than using the FILLET and CHAMFER commands of AutoCAD. Whereas AutoCAD requests two intersecting lines to chamfer or fillet, AME requires an edge that is parallel to the axis of the fillet, such as a corner, and an edge to be chamfered.

The corners of the base on the solid should have one-inch radius rounds, and the intersection of the base and the cylinder should have a .25 inch fillet. You may have to do a transparent zoom ('ZOOM) to pick the back corner for filleting. Use the SOLFILL command as follows:

Command: **SOLFILL** ↵
Select edges of solids to be filleted (Press ENTER when done): *(pick the four vertical edges of the base and press ENTER when completed)*
Diameter/⟨Radius⟩ of fillet ⟨0.00⟩: **1** ↵
Command: ↵
Select edges of solids to be filleted (Press ENTER when done): *(pick the circle at the base of the cylinder and press ENTER when completed)*
Diameter/⟨Radius⟩ of fillet ⟨1.00⟩: **.25** ↵

The model should have four filleted corners and a filleted intersection of the base and cylinder as shown in Fig. 25-9.

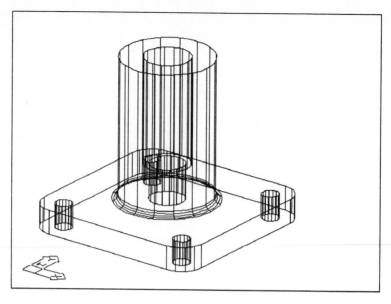

Fig. 25-9. The SOLFILL command is used to create inside or outside fillets.

PROFESSIONAL TIP

When performing a fillet between two primitives such as the cylinder and baseplate, be sure the two are joined in a union before you fillet. Otherwise, the end of the cylinder will be filleted with a rounded corner that is subtracted from the cylinder instead of added to it.

The SOLCHAM command is used to put an angled relief on edges. Use it to add a chamfer to the top of the large cylinder as follows:

Command: **SOLCHAM** ↵
Pick base surface: *(pick the top outside circle of the cylinder)*
Next/⟨OK⟩: ↵

When using the SOLCHAM command, if the wrong base surface is highlighted, you can request that the surface next to the one that is highlighted be selected by entering "N" and pressing ENTER at the previous prompt:

Pick edges of this face to be chamfered (Press ENTER when done): *(pick the top outside circle of the cylinder and press ENTER when completed)*
1 edges selected.
Enter distance along first surface ⟨0.00⟩: **.25** ↵
Enter distance along second surface ⟨0.25⟩: ↵

The chamfer on the solid is shown in Fig. 25-10.

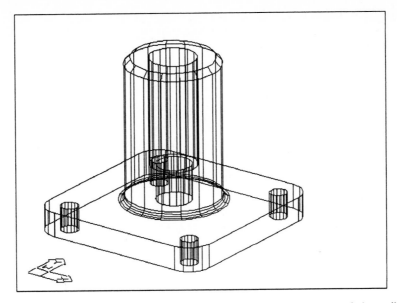

Fig. 25-10. The SOLCHAM command adds a chamfer to the top of the cylinder.

Solid model composition and analysis

A solid model can be analyzed for its physical properties. The default AME material is mild steel. It is not important that you concern yourself with the composition of the model until you are ready to perform analyses on it. At this time, you can change the material or create a material of your own. A list of available materials is included in a file named ACAD.MAT. If you want to create your own list of materials for specific applications, you can use the SOLMAT (SOLids MATerial) command and the New option to create a new material. You can then use the Save option to save the material in either the ACAD.MAT file or in a file name of your own. At this time, use the SOLMAT command to view and change materials.

> Command: **SOLMAT** ⏎
> Change/Edit/LIst/LOad/New/Remove/SAve/SEt/?/⟨eXit⟩: **?** ⏎

The "Select Material file" dialogue box is displayed, and the ACAD.MAT file is the default. Press ENTER to accept it. The following list is then displayed:

> Defined in drawing:
>   MILD-STEEL
> Defined in file:
>   ALUMINUM
>   BRASS   —   Soft Yellow Brass
>   BRONZE   —   Soft Tin Bronze
>   COPPER
>   GLASS
>   HSLA__STL   —   High Strength Low Alloy Steel
>   LEAD
>   MILD__STEEL
>   NICU   —   Monel 400
>   STAINLESS__STL   —   Austenic Stainless Steel
> Change/Edit/LIst/LOad/New/Remove/SAve/SEt/?/⟨eXit⟩: **C** ⏎
> Select objects: *(pick the model)*
> Select objects: ⏎
> New material ⟨MILD__STEEL⟩/?: **STAINLESS__STL** ⏎
> Change/Edit/LIst/LOad/New/Remove/SAve/SEt/?/⟨eXit⟩: ⏎

Now that the material has been changed to meet your needs you can request that AutoCAD perform an analysis of the model using the SOLMASSP (SOLids MASS Properties) command.

```
Command: SOLMASSP ↵
Select objects: (pick the model)
Select objects: ↵
Ray projection along X axis, level of subdivision: 3.
Mass:           1014.516 gm
Volume:         126.3408 cu cm (Err: 12.88795)
```

Bounding box:	X: 3 — 11 cm
	Y: 3 — 11 cm
	Z: 0 — 7 cm

Centroid:	X: 7 cm (Err: 0.7140662)
	Y: 7.119307 cm (Err: 0.8628214)
	Z: 1.872536 cm (Err: 0.1750455)

Moments of inertia:	X: 61926.58 gm sq cm (Err: 8342.418)
	Y: 60336.47 gm sq cm (Err: 5210.336)
	Z: 108324.4 gm sq cm (Err: 13532.01)

Products of inertia:	XY: 50558.58 gm sq cm (Err: 6127.425)
	YZ: 13292.66 gm sq cm (Err: 1392.972)
	ZX: 13298.03 gm sq cm (Err: 1243.105)

Radii of gyration:	X: 7.812842 cm
	Y: 7.711883 cm
	Z: 10.33317 cm

```
Principal moments (gm sq cm) and X-Y-Z directions about centroid:
          I: 6890.06 along [-2.372731e-14   0.7937154   -0.6082892]
          J: 7370.625 along [-1.441207e-14   0.6082892   0.7937154]
          K: 6948.996 along [1   2.759944e-14   -2.993984e-15]
Write to a file ⟨N⟩ ?
```

This data can be retained for reference by saving it to a file. The default file name is the drawing name. The file is given the extension of .MPR (Mass PRoperties), and is an ASCII text file.

The values you get in the mass properties report may vary somewhat from those shown here. That is because of the method in which AME calculates solids. Rays are fired at the solid, and both the density of the rays (SOLSUBDIV) and the direction in which they are fired (SOLDECOMP), affect the accuracy of the solid. The AME system variable SOLSUBDIV controls the number of subdivisions in a box enclosing the model. The SOLDECOMP variable specifies the direction (X, Y, or Z) in which the rays are fired. See Chapter 5 of the Advanced Modeling Extension Reference Manual for a detailed discussion of this process.

Notice in the previous report that error estimations are shown in parentheses. This error is greater on models having curved surfaces. Try different SOLSUBDIV and SOLDECOMP settings on your models to obtain the smallest error estimations. Note the different values given with the following settings.

```
SOLSUBDIV = 4                          SOLSUBDIV = 4
SOLDECOMP = Y                          SOLDECOMP = Z
Mass: 954.0873 gm                      Mass: 989.7669 gm
Volume: 118.8154 cu cm (Err: 6.290864) Volume: 123.2586 cu cm (Err: 8.585431)

SOLSUBDIV = 5                          SOLSUBDIV = 5
SOLDECOMP = Y                          SOLDECOMP = Z
Mass: 966.4481 gm                      Mass: 964.4341 gm
Volume: 120.3547 cu cm (Err: 3.133854) Volume: 120.1039 cu cm (Err: 4.224059)
```

EXERCISE 25-2

☐ Use the SOLMAT command to change the material of the support bracket to aluminum.
☐ Use the SOLMASSP command to determine the following from the support bracket:
    1. Mass: _____
    2. Volume: _____
    3. Bounding box: _____
    4. Moments of inertia: _____
☐ Save the material file as A:EX25-2.

DISPLAYING THE SOLID MODEL

Although you create a solid model and have it analyzed, it still may not look solid on the screen. In order to display the model as a solid, it is first necessary to wrap the model in a polyface mesh with the SOLMESH (SOLids MESH) command. After using this command, the curves appear to have straight segments. The straight edges are the sides of the 3-D faces.

The display of a solid model is governed by different rules than those used on an AutoCAD surface model. In order for a solid model to be shown as a solid it must first be given a *polyface (pface) mesh*. This is a mesh composed of numerous faces created with the PFACE command. However, you do not have to use this command. Instead, you can use the SOLMESH command, pick the solid to be meshed, and AME does the rest. Then, the HIDE command can be used to remove hidden lines.

    Command: **SOLMESH** ↵
    Select objects: *(pick the model)*
    Select objects: ↵

AME goes to work creating the mesh. The final operation of this command is the creation of a block. In fact, a prompt indicates just that:

    Creating block for mesh representation...

This block composed of a polyface mesh is used whenever you select the HIDE command, and is shown after using HIDE in Fig. 25-11.

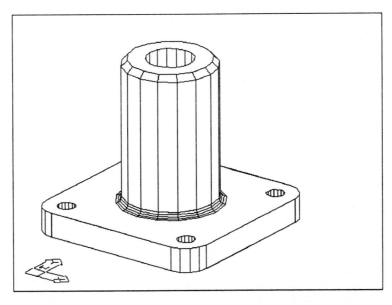

Fig. 25-11. Using the HIDE command after using SOLMESH displays a solid model.

If you wish to display the solid model as a wireframe, use the SOLWIRE (SOLids WIRE) command. Whereas the SOLMESH command creates straight segments (polyface edges) along curves, the SOLWIRE command displays the edges of the tessellation lines and pfaces as curves. A wireframe block is displayed by the SOLWIRE command.

Shading the solid model

A shaded rendering can only be achieved after the SOLMESH command has been used to create a pface mesh. After entering "SHADE" at the Command: prompt or picking Shade from the Render pull-down menu, you do not need to select objects; no prompts are given. All objects on the screen are automatically shaded. See Fig. 25-12. AutoCAD indicates the percentage of the model that is shaded. The length of time required to shade depends on the size of the drawing file, but is normally about twice the time required for a regeneration.

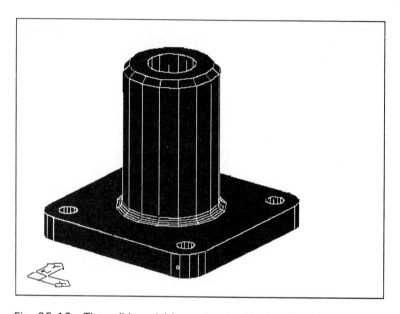

Fig. 25-12. The solid model is rendered with the SHADE command.

CREATING A SECTIONED TWO-DIMENSIONAL VIEW

One of the advantages of creating a solid model is that in addition to the benefit of having a 3-D model that can be viewed from any angle, and analyzed for specific properties, 2-D drawings and sectioned views can be constructed from it. Since AutoCAD has a complete description of the model, section views can be cut through any portion of it using the SOLSECT (SOLids SECTion) command. In order to assist in the creation of 2-D views and sections, the SOLPROF (SOLids PROFile) command is used to create a profile view of the model. Using the SOLCUT command, you can cut a solid into two separate parts. The following discussion illustrates this process using the modes of paper space and model space.

Preparing the model

AutoCAD works in two separate worlds called *model space* and *paper space*. These were discussed in Chapter 9, and are demonstrated in detail in Chapter 27. The model you just created, and all drawings that you construct, are made in model space. The standard UCS icon indicates that you are in model space. In order to prepare a model for 2-D multiview layout and dimensioning, it is necessary to move into paper space and create viewports in the paper. This discussion illustrates the use of two viewports cut into the paper of paper space. One viewport shows the front, or profile view of the model, and the second viewport shows a 3-D view.

If the model of the support bracket is not on the screen, load it into AutoCAD. The TILEMODE variable controls whether viewports are *tiled*, (butted against one another), or whether they are separate entities. The VPORTS command is used when TILEMODE is set to 1, or ON. That creates viewports that are separate screens. When TILEMODE is set to 0 or OFF, viewports are cut out of the paper, and are created with the MVIEW command. The viewports are separate entities.

If you have not done so already, create two new layers called SECTION (green), and VIEWPORTS (yellow). Set the VIEWPORTS layer as current. Prepare the drawing as follows:

Command: **TILEMODE** ↵
New value for TILEMODE ⟨1⟩: **0** ↵
Entering Paper space. Use MVIEW to insert Model space viewports.

Now, set the drawing limits to match those of the model (18,12) and then use the ZOOM command's All option.

Command: **MVIEW** ↵
ON/OFF/Hideplot/Fit/2/3/4/Restore/⟨First Point⟩: **2** ↵
Horizontal/⟨Vertical⟩: ↵
Fit/⟨First Point⟩: **F** ↵

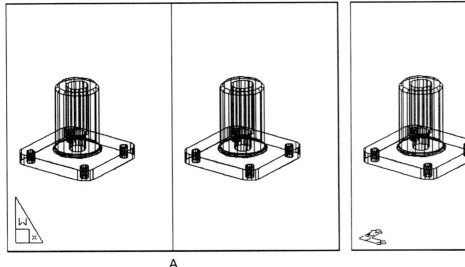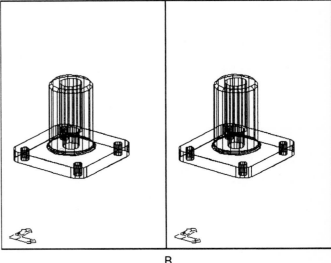

A   B

Fig. 25-13. The MVIEW command is used to create two viewports.

You just cut two viewports into a sheet of paper in paper space, Fig. 25-13A. When you return to model space by typing "MSPACE" or "MS," the model appears in each viewport as shown in Fig. 25-13B. Notice the different UCS icons.

The right view is the current viewport. Pick the left viewport to construct the front view, and show the section. The UCS must first be placed in the same plane as the section you wish cut. In this case, the UCS is to be placed in the center of the object, so the section cuts through the center of the cylinder.

Command: **UCS** ↵
Origin/ZAxis/3point/Entity/View/X/Y/Z/Prev/Restore/Save/Del/?/⟨World⟩: **O** ↵
Origin point ⟨0,0,0⟩: **7,7** ↵
Command: **UCS** ↵
Origin/ZAxis/3point/Entity/View/X/Y/Z/Prev/Restore/Save/Del/?/⟨World⟩: **X** ↵
Rotation angle about X axis ⟨0⟩: **90** ↵

— PROFESSIONAL TIP —

If you have problems determining which is positive and negative rotation around each of the three UCS axis lines, use the right-hand rule. Hold your right hand up with the three fingers (thumb, index finger, and middle finger) extended in the proper manner. See Fig. 24-7. To rotate the X axis, look at an end view of your right thumb. Now rotate your hand clockwise or counterclockwise while the thumb remains steady. A counterclockwise rotation is positive. Use the same technique for the Y axis (index finger), and the Z axis (middle finger).

Be sure the left viewport is active, and create a front view by using the PLAN command.

Command: **PLAN** ↵
⟨Current UCS⟩/Ucs/World: ↵

Adjust the size of the front view so that it occupies most of the viewport. Then use the ZOOM command's XP option as follows:

Command: **ZOOM** ↵
All/Center/Dynamic/Extents/Left/Previous/Vmax/Window/⟨Scale(X/XP)⟩: **1XP** ↵

Use the PAN command to raise the view if needed. Your screen should resemble the illustration in Fig. 25-14.

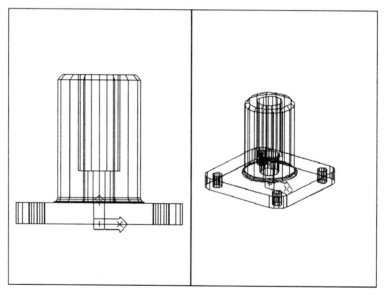

Fig. 25-14. The profile and 3-D view are created in paper space viewports.

Constructing the section

Before cutting the section, you should use the hatching variables—SOLHPAT, SOLHANGLE, and SOLHSIZE—to set the parameters for the hatching. You can set the variables by picking Hatch Parameters... in the "AME R2.1 — System Variables" dialogue box. To access this dialogue box, pick the Model pull-down menu, followed by picking the Setup option. Then select Variables... from this cascading menu. You can also type the variable names at the Command: prompt as follows:

Command: **SOLHPAT** ↵
Hatch pattern ⟨NONE⟩: **STEEL** ↵

The hatch angle can be set using the SOLHANGLE variable. Since the angle of the STEEL hatch pattern is 45°, do not adjust the hatch angle.

    Command: **SOLHANGLE** ↵
    Hatch angle ⟨0.00⟩: ↵

The size, or spacing of the pattern is controlled by a solids variable called SOLHSIZE (SOLids Hatch SIZE). The default is 1; however, it should be changed to 2 so the hatch lines are not too close together.

    Command: **SOLHSIZE** ↵
    Hatch size ⟨1.000000⟩: **2** ↵

   Set the current layer to SECTION, and then use the SOLSECT (SOLids SECTion) command as follows to create the section.

    Command: **SOLSECT** ↵
    Select objects: *(pick the model in the left viewport)*
    Select objects: ↵
    Sectioning plane by Entity/Last/Zaxis/View/XY/YZ/ZX/⟨3points⟩: **XY** ↵
    Point on XY plane ⟨0,0,0⟩: ↵

AutoCAD creates an unnamed block on the current layer that is an outline of the material that is sectioned through. You can see this outline in green on the model in both views. The block that is created is inserted at the location of the section on the current UCS. See Fig. 25-15.

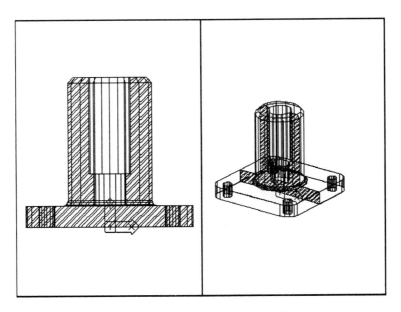

Fig. 25-15. The SOLSECT command creates a block at the location of the cross section on the current layer.

PROFESSIONAL TIP

If it seems that the AME commands are running slower and the hard disk is working harder, it may be time to use the SOLPURGE (SOLids PURGE) command. AutoCAD retains a considerable amount of information in memory related to the solids, and how the primitives are structured into unions. This is termed the *Constructive Solid Geometry tree*, or *CSG*. In addition, a variety of blocks used to define the solid for wireframe, hidden, and shaded displays are created. The SOLPURGE command enables you to remove some or all of this from memory. Use SOLPURGE as follows:

Command: **SOLPURGE** ↲
Memory/2dtree/Bfile/Pmesh/⟨Erased⟩: **M** ↲
All/⟨Select⟩: **A** ↲

This removes all information relating to solids and regions from memory. The solid information still resides in the drawing file, and if needed again by an AME command, is retrieved from the drawing file.

Creating a profile of the model

A profile of the model is needed in order to preserve some of the object lines needed for the section. If you were to freeze the OBJECT layer now, only the green lines of the section would remain. Some additional lines are required for the complete section view. The SOLPROF (SOLids PROFile) command lets you create a profile in which only the silhouette and edges of the model are visible. Be sure that the TILEMODE variable is set to 0 (OFF), and that you are working in model space. The standard UCS icon of the X and Y axes indicates that you are in model space.

Make the left viewport active and use the SOLPROF command as follows:

Command: **SOLPROF** ↲
Select objects: *(pick the solid model, not the section)*
Select objects: ↲
Updating object...
Display hidden profile lines on separate layer? ⟨Y⟩: ↲
Project profile lines onto a plane? ⟨Y⟩: ↲
Delete tangential edges? ⟨Y⟩: ↲

Nothing is visible on your screen, but if you press ENTER for the last prompt above, two separate anonymous blocks are created. One is for visible lines of the profile and the other is for hidden lines of the profile. They are both inserted over the original solid. Keep in mind that the SOLPROF command creates the profile blocks only in the current view, which means that the command is *view specific*. To experiment with this, turn off all layers except the two profiles and you will see the profile displayed in the left viewport only.

NOTE

It is important to be aware of what AutoCAD is doing at this point, and how many different lines are on the screen. The original model is visible. The section block is displayed in green. A block composed of lines representing the visible edges of the model is lying on top of the solid. If you request it at the last prompt of the SOLPROF command, another block of the hidden edges of the model in the current viewport are also part of the current display.

Access the "Layer Control" dialogue box, and look at the layer names. There should be two names that reflect the object profile.

PH-1048
PV-1048

These layers are automatically created by the SOLPROF command. PH stands for Profile Hidden, and PV for Profile Visible. The number indicates the "handle" number of the viewport the profile is located in. Your handle number will likely be different than the one shown here.

NOTE

The layer name of "PH" or "PV" is followed by the *handle* of the profile. AutoCAD assigns unique names, or entity handles, such as 1048, to every entity in your drawing if the HANDLES command has been turned on. The layer names shown above would appear as follows if the entity handle of the viewport in which the entity resides was named "1048":

PH-1048
PV-1048

For a detailed discussion of entity handles, see Chapter 8 of the *AutoCAD Reference Manual.*

While in the "Layer Control" dialogue box, notice the Cur VP: buttons. These allow you to freeze or thaw layers in the current viewport. Pick the OBJECT layer to highlight it, then pick the Frz button to the right of the Cur VP:. This freezes the solid in the current viewport. Return to the display and it should look like Fig. 25-16.

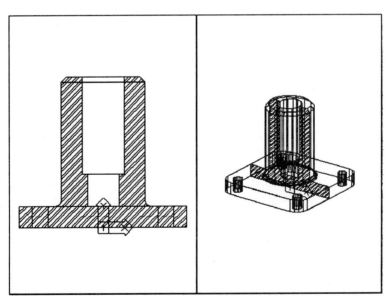

Fig. 25-16. The object lines of the solid model are frozen in the left viewport.

Fine-tuning the section view

Look at the section in Fig. 25-16 closely. You may see several lines that should not show in a proper full section. These are indicated with dots in Fig. 25-17.

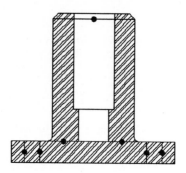

Fig. 25-17. The dots indicate lines that must be removed for the section to appear correctly.

Since the solid model layer has been frozen, the black outlines of visible and hidden edges that are displayed are the lines of the profile blocks. If you are in doubt as how to proceed, be it this model or a future project, simply freeze all layers but the two profile layers. Then you may be able to get a better idea of the lines you are working with in order to create the section view. See Fig. 25-18.

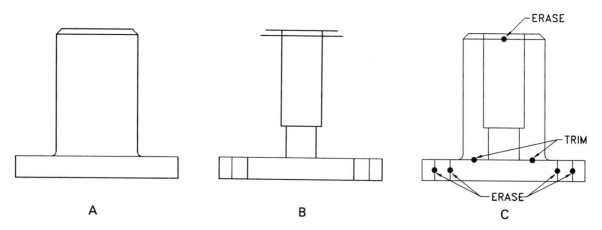

Fig. 25-18. A—The PV layer shows visible lines of the profile. B—The PH layer shows hidden lines of the profile. C—These lines should be edited to create a proper full section.

A block is a single entity, and if you tried to edit one of the lines with a dot on it, the entire profile would be affected. Instead, use the EXPLODE command and pick a line on each profile; then erase and trim the lines indicated in Fig. 25-18C. If you erase the line for the chamfer at the top of the model and redraw, the line appears again. This is because the front edge of the chamfer is on the PV layer, and the back edge of the chamfer is on the PH layer. Simply erase it a second time. When the edit is complete, turn on the SECTION layer and your drawing should look like the one shown in Fig. 25-19.

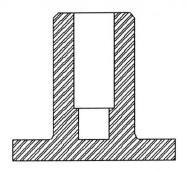

Fig. 25-19. The completed section view after removal of unwanted lines.

Cutting through a solid model

The SOLSECT command enables you to show a cutting plane in your solid model. The SOLCUT command, however, actually lets you cut through the solid and remove a portion of it. This is an excellent command to use for a variety of purposes, one of which is visualization of internal parts and features. It can also be used in conjunction with the section you just constructed to create true 3-D sections or "cutaway" views. The following example shows you how to "slice" through the previous model along the same cutting plane that you used for the section.

The SOLCUT command creates two new solids that have the same layer and color of the original solid. You can keep both new solids or only one of them. SOLCUT creates only two new solids at one time. If you want to create additional cuts, you must use the command again.

If the previous drawing is still on the screen, set the OBJECT layer as current and turn on the SECTION layer. Make the right viewport (3-D view) active.

> Command: **SOLCUT** ↵
> Select objects: *(pick the solid model)*
> Select objects: ↵
> Updating object...
> Done.
> 1 solid selected

Next, select or define the cutting plane. Since the current UCS is the same as the previous section, use the XY option to specify the current UCS, then press ENTER to accept the UCS origin as a point on the new cutting plane.

> Cutting plane by Entity/Last/Zaxis/View/XY/YZ/ZX/⟨3points⟩: **XY** ↵
> Point on XY plane ⟨0,0,0⟩: ↵

The next prompt allows you to specify which side you wish to keep. Use the Both option if you want to keep both sides, or pick the side you want to keep using one of the object snap modes.

> Both sides/⟨Point on the desired side of the plane⟩: **END** ↵
> of *(pick a point on the extreme right side of the model)*

AutoCAD calculates the new solid, then displays it as shown in Fig. 25-20. Use the SOLMESH command to create a pface mesh on the model. Then use the HIDE command to produce a realistic solid model display. Be sure to turn off the PH and PV layers before using HIDE or the profile lines will show. See Fig. 25-21.

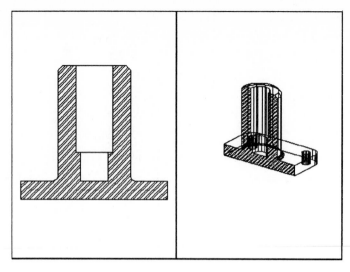

Fig. 25-20. Using the SOLCUT command.

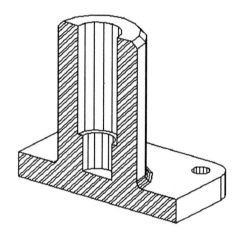

Fig. 25-21. Appearance of the solid after using the SOLMESH and HIDE commands.

USING THE SOLID MODEL

In addition to its usefulness in manufacturing, testing, stress analysis, and 3-D presentations, the solid model can be used for a variety of purposes including creating other features and shapes, and developing paper drawing layouts.

Using features of a solid model

When constructing 2-D views or entities from a solid model, you may need to use existing edges or faces to construct a new view or shape. This is possible with the SOLFEAT (SOLids FEATure) command. It allows you to select a face or an edge in any view, then the selected feature is copied to an anonymous block. The selected feature is highlighted in the color of the current layer. It can then be copied or moved to a new position.

Make the right 3-D viewport active and use SOLFEAT as follows:

> Command: **SOLFEAT** ↵
> Edge/⟨Face⟩: ↵
> All/⟨Select⟩: ↵
> Pick a face: *(pick a vertical face on the base of the solid)*
> ⟨OK⟩/Next:

If the wrong face is highlighted, such as the bottom of the solid, enter "N" (Next) at this prompt. Continue to enter "N" until the correct face is highlighted, then press ENTER.

An edge is selected in the same manner; just select the Edge option at the first prompt. Use SOLFEAT to pick the top edge of the large cylinder. After you have selected a face and an edge, use the MOVE command to move the two features to a new location.

The SOLFEAT command is best used when the solid is in a wireframe form. If the solid has been meshed, and you select a face, you are prompted to change the solid to a wireframe representation. Simply answer "YES", and proceed with the command.

Creating and using 2-D layouts

You have seen how quickly you can create a section view or a model that has been cut through. These views can then be used for 2-D layouts and dimensioned drawings. Using the techniques discussed previously, you can construct a paper space layout of two or more viewports, each containing a different view. By carefully choosing UCS planes and viewpoint rotations, you can create auxiliary and isometric views in a drawing layout. The SOLPROF, SOLSECT, and SOLCUT commands are used to construct such a drawing.

However, AME contains a supplemental program called SOLVIEW, which can automate this process. Pick Applications... from the File pull-down menu to access the "Load AutoLISP and ADS Files" dialogue box. Then select File... to access the "Select LISP/ADS Routine" subdialogue box. Locate the SOLVIEW.EXP file in one of the AutoCAD subdirectories. Pick the file name so that it shows in the File: edit box and then pick OK to return to the "Load AutoLISP and ADS Files" dialogue box. The SOLVIEW file name and directory will be shown in the list box. Then pick the Load button to load the SOLVIEW program. At the Command: prompt, type the following:

Command: **SOLVIEW** ↵

This program enables you to develop a multiview, 2-D drawing layout from a 3-D solid model. By specifying an initial view based on a UCS or the WCS, you can quickly construct several adjacent orthogonal, auxiliary, or section views. The program automatically creates layers for visible, hidden, dimension lines, and hatch patterns. After constructing the initial layout of the views, you can use the SOLDRAW command to render all of the viewports you select into their final appearance. An example of a drawing layout created with SOLVIEW and SOLDRAW is shown in Fig. 25-22. See Chapter 7 of the *AME Release 2.1 Reference Manual* for a complete discussion of these commands.

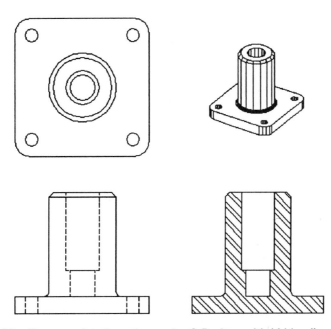

Fig. 25-22. The completed section and a 3-D view with hidden lines removed.

— **PROFESSIONAL TIP** —

The SOLVIEW and SOLDRAW commands add an extremely powerful capability to the AME program. Now you have the flexibility to produce any kind of model, paper drawing layout, technical illustration, presentation rendering, or animation from a single solid model. Consider the value, productivity, and time savings of working with solid models to produce your finished product as opposed to constructing each individual type of drawing separately. Remember: once the computer has the complete dimensional description of the part or design, the applications are limited only by your imagination.

SOLID MODELING PLANNING TIPS

As you work with solids, try to follow a logical path to the model creation using the following list.
☐ Plan the model. This includes the finished products, such as:
  • Solid model for CAD/CAM/CNC processing.
  • Shaded rendering.
  • Geometry for other presentation programs such as 3D Studio.
  • Plotted paper drawings in 2-D or 3-D, or a combination.
  • Solid model and dimensioned 2-D orthographic views.
☐ Construct the base solid primitive or use regions.
☐ Change viewpoint to suit needs of model.
☐ Construct additional solids. Use lines, circles, polylines, or arcs for special shapes or profiles.
☐ Extrude or revolve any 2-D entities, profiles, or regions.
☐ Change and create UCSs to meet needs of project.
☐ Use edit commands such as ARRAY and COPY, or utilize the editing capabilities of grips.
☐ Complete solid geometry before modifying or Boolean operations.
☐ Perform Boolean subtractions, intersections, and unions.
  • Perform as many Boolean operations at one time as possible instead of two at a time.
  • If subtraction affects two primitives, do a union of the two first.
☐ Perform additional modifications such as chamfer, fillets, and moves.
  • Carefully plan fillets and chamfers.
☐ Remember to use SOLMESH before using the HIDE or SHADE commands.
☐ Establish material type before using SOLMASSP.
☐ Use SOLPURGE to speed the design process.
As with any form of drawing and design, a little planning goes a long way.

CHAPTER TEST

Write your answers in the spaces provided.

1. How is solid modeling different from surface modeling? _____
   _____
   _____
   _____

2. What is a 2-D region? _____
   _____
   _____

3. Name three AME system variables that control the appearance of hatch patterns.
   _____

4. What is the purpose of the SOLEXT command? _____

5. Name four solid modeling primitives. _____

_____

6. What is the purpose of the SOLREV command? _____

_____

7. How can you instruct AutoCAD to prompt you before deleting an entity? _____

_____

8. What does an input of TZ-3.25 mean if entered for the SOLMOVE command?_____

_____

9. What is the difference between SOLSUB and SOLUNION? _____

_____

_____

10. What command can be used to change the material used in a solid model? _____

_____

11. Which command can give you the volume of a solid?_____

12. Which command must be used before the SHADE command can be used to render a solid?

_____

13. Name four AME commands or variables that can be used to create a section. _____

_____

14. Which command creates an outline of the solid in the current view? _____

15. When a profile is created in the current view, what layer names are created automatically?

_____

16. What command and option would you use to have AME prompt you before it deletes an
    entity used in the SOLREV command? _____

17. What command allows you to divide a model into two complete parts, and which option
    allows you to retain the halves? _____

18. What is the function of the SOLVIEW program? _____

_____

19. What command enables you to render the viewports created with the SOLVIEW program?

_____

20. How could you make a copy of a single surface on a solid model? _____

_____

DRAWING PROBLEMS

For Problems 1-17, use the dimensions from the problems in Chapter 23 to complete the following solid models.

1. Construct a solid model of P23-1.
2. Construct a solid model of P23-2.
3. Construct a solid model of P23-3.

4. Construct a solid model of P23-4.
5. Construct a solid model of P23-5.
6. Construct a solid model of P23-6.
7. Construct a solid model of P23-7.
8. Construct a solid model of P23-8.
9. Construct a solid model of P23-9.
10. Construct a solid model of P23-10.
11. Construct a solid model of P23-11.
12. Construct a solid model of P23-12.
13. Construct a solid model of P23-13.
14. Construct a solid model of P23-14.
15. Construct a solid model of P23-15.
16. Construct a solid model of P23-16.
17. Construct a solid model of P23-17.
18. Construct a solid model of P24-2. Assign the material of mild steel. Generate a mass properties report.
19. Construct a solid model of P24-9. Assign the material of aluminum. Generate a printed copy of the mass properties report. Change the material to stainless steel and generate a second printed mass properties report.
20. Construct a solid model of P20-1.
    A. Create three viewports in paper space—two side-by-side and a third in the upper-right of a B-size sheet layout.
    B. Construct a section view in the right viewport. Display a front view in the left viewport. Generate the necessary sections and profile required.
    C. Display a 3-D view in the upper-right viewport.
    D. Fully dimension the two orthographic views.
    E. Display the 3-D view in hidden and shaded format.
    F. Plot the three views with border and title block.
21. Construct a solid model of P20-2. Follow the same instructions given in Problem 25-20.
22. Construct a solid model of P20-3. Follow the same instructions given in Problem 25-20.
23. Construct a solid model of P20-4. Follow the same instructions given in Problem 25-20.
24. Construct a solid model of P20-5. Follow the same instructions given in Problem 25-20.

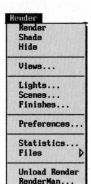

Chapter 26

INTRODUCTION TO PRESENTATION GRAPHICS AND RENDERING

Learning objectives

After completing this chapter, you will be able to:
- [ ] Import and export raster files into AutoCAD.
- [ ] Set raster file variables to create a variety of displays.
- [ ] Import and export PostScript files.
- [ ] Use PostScript fonts in AutoCAD drawings.
- [ ] Create rendered drawings using lights, views, and scenes.
- [ ] Create filmroll files for use with AutoShade and RenderMan.
- [ ] Construct AutoShade/RenderMan renderings using spotlights and surface patterns.

The fields of engineering, drafting, and design are rapidly incorporating more "presentation" quality materials and techniques into its realm. The use of these "multimedia" resources is enabling companies to not only design and manufacture, but to model, dissect, examine, test, render, shade, "walk through", animate, and export presentation-quality materials to videotape. All of these procedures can be performed on just one 2-D or 3-D model generated in AutoCAD. Now the power and productivity of a design is limited only by a company's expertise and imagination in using software to manipulate that design.

This chapter introduces you to three basic aspects of the ability of AutoCAD to work with presentation-quality graphics. This includes importing raster files into and out of AutoCAD. A *raster file* is composed of dots on the screen, or bits, and is often referred to as *bit map*. You will also learn about the use of PostScript fonts, and creating PostScript files for printing. Last, you will be introduced to the rendering capabilities of AutoCAD and AutoShade, in which you can work with lights, surface textures, and shading.

PART I—WORKING WITH RASTER FILES

AEM 2

AutoCAD drawing files are composed of vectors, which are points in space. A *vector* is defined by XYZ coordinates, and has no relation to physical pixels in your monitor other than to show the drawing at the current zoom percent. On the other hand, many illustrations created with drawing, painting, and presentation software are saved as raster files. A raster file is one in which the objects are defined by the location and color of the screen pixels, or bits. Raster files are also known as "bit map" images. There are several formats of raster files used widely for presentation graphics and desktop publishing. This section shows you how AutoCAD can work with three types of raster files, and provides you with some suggestions on their use.

Raster file types

AutoCAD enables you to work with three common types of raster files through the use of the RASTERIN.EXP ADS application.

- **.GIF (Graphics Interchange Format)**—This is a CompuServe image format. CompuServe is a computer information service accessed by phone modem, providing access to a wealth of information, products, services, forums, and ideas.
- **.PCX (Personal Computer eXchange)**—Raster file format developed by Z-Soft Corporation.
- **.TIF(F) (Tagged Image File Format)**—Developed by Aldus and Microsoft.

There are a variety of raster file formats in use. Although consistent standards are utilized in design and manufacturing industries, the computer industry is far behind in its quest for file format standardization. Software developers and hardware manufacturers are often more concerned with developing proprietary goods, rather than consistent standards. Therefore, if you have raster images that you would like to import into AutoCAD that are not one of the three listed above, there is hope. You can convert images from one format to another with screen capture and conversion software such as Pizazz Plus or Hijaak. Then use the converted images with the commands discussed next.

Inserting raster images

Three commands allow you to insert raster files into an AutoCAD drawing. They are GIFIN, PCXIN, and TIFFIN. They all work the same, and the prompt requires the complete path to the file.

> Command: **GIFIN** ↵
> GIF file name: **\ACAD12\SAMPLE\GIFS\MOUSE** ↵

There are no .GIF, .PCX, or .TIF files on the program diskettes shipped with Release 12, but there are a variety of files on the Bonus CD. You must have a CD-ROM drive to access these files. The following example shows how a GIF file is inserted.

> Insertion point⟨0,0,0⟩: *(pick a point)*
> Scale factor: **5** ↵

The insertion of the image is displayed and moved quickly because it is shown as a box with the name of the file inside. The image is inserted as a block, so you must pick the insertion point and scale factor. Then the image is displayed on the screen. See Fig. 26-1.

Fig. 26-1. A .GIF file is displayed using the GIFIN command.

Since AutoCAD does not manipulate raster files, it converts the outlines of different color raster data to solids (entities created with the SOLID command). You can see this by turning FILL off and using the REGEN command. See Fig. 26-2.

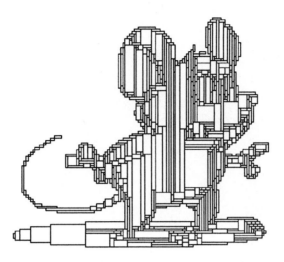

Fig. 26-2. Different raster colors are converted to solids in AutoCAD.

Raster image system variables

Six variables allow you to control the appearance of the imported raster file.

- **RIASPECT**—Controls the aspect ratio (width to height) of the image. Use this when inserting .GIF and .TIF files. Use a value of 0.8333 if your display device is using the 320 x 200 mode. The aspect ratio of Fig. 26-1 was set to 0, while Fig. 26-3 used 0.8333. Note the height difference of the character in the two figures.

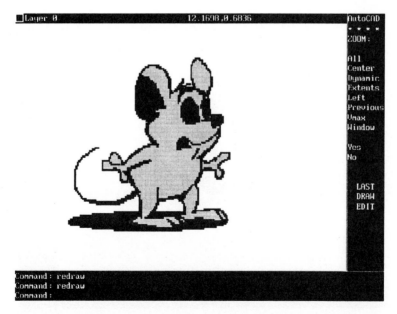

Fig. 26-3. The RIASPECT variable was set to .8333 before importing this file.

- **RIBACKG**—Controls the background color of your display device. The default is 0. RIBACKG was set to 7 in Fig. 26-4. Notice the color of the eyes.

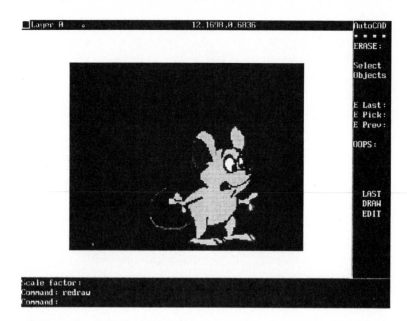

Fig. 26-4. The RIBACKG variable controls the color of the background.

- **RIEDGE**—If set to a value other than 0, edges of the image are displayed. Use this setting if you need to trace the object. The larger the setting (up to 255), the more prominent an edge must be to be displayed. The image in Fig. 26-5 is displayed with RIASPECT set to 0, and RIEDGE set to 25.

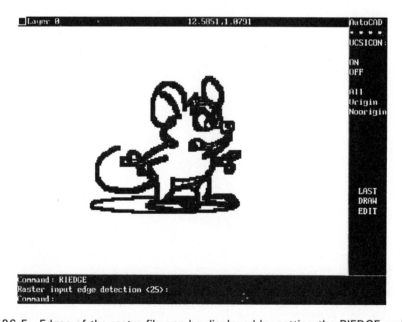

Fig. 26-5. Edges of the raster file can be displayed by setting the RIEDGE variable.

- **RIGAMUT** — Controls the range of colors used for display of the image. The default is 256. If your display device uses only 8 or 16 colors, set RIGAMUT to that value. This can create a much smaller imported file.
- **RIGREY** — Converts the imported image to a grayscale. AutoCAD has only a few gray shades, therefore, this image may not be useful other than to greatly reduce the size of the imported file.
- **RITHRESH** — Controls the display of an image based on brightness. By setting a value greater than 0, you establish a "threshold filter." Only colors with a brightness value greater than the RITHRESH setting are displayed. Colors that are dropped out are not included in the drawing. RITHRESH was set to 50 for Fig. 26-6.

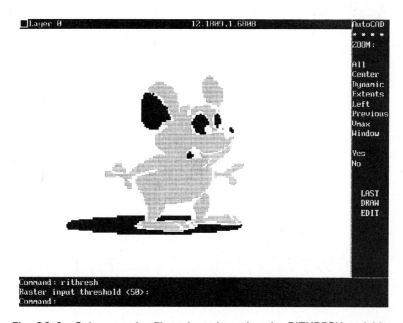

Fig. 26-6. Colors can be filtered out by using the RITHRESH variable.

———— PROFESSIONAL TIP ————

Depending on the image, it is often easier to trace a raster display by leaving RIEDGE set to 0 (OFF). As you can see when comparing Figs. 26-6 and 26-2, it may be easier to see details when the original colors are displayed.

Exporting, or saving raster files

You can save raster files in one of four formats — .TGA, .TIF, .GIF, and .RND — by using the SAVEIMG command. Pick the Render pull-down menu, followed by picking Files, and finally Save Image... from the cascading menu. This displays the "Save Image" dialogue box. This process is discussed in detail in the **Saving image files** section on page 26-31 of this chapter.

The uses of raster files in AutoCAD

The ability of Release 12 to import and export raster files can open a new range of possibilities for the drafter, engineer, and designer. AutoCAD can now use two basic file types: vector and raster. You can import a raster file, edit it, and then save it as a drawing file, or export the drawing as another raster file. The manner in which you edit the file — stretch, rotate, mirror — is up to you.

PROFESSIONAL TIP

Remember that a raster image is inserted as a block. If you explode it, the block reverts to entities created by the SOLID command. These can then be manipulated in any way you wish.

One use of raster images is sketching, or tracing. For example, you may require a line drawing of an image that is only available as a .GIF file. After importing the raster image, use the appropriate commands to sketch or trace the image. After the object is sketched, the original raster image can be deleted or frozen to produce a drawing much like Fig. 26-7A. This can be further enhanced with AutoCAD to produce any type of drawing that is required by the project. An example is shown in Fig. 26-7B.

You can also add features to raster files that may not be possible in other software you are using. For example, you can import a raster file, dimension it or annotate it, or even add special shapes to it. Then export it as the same type of file with a command such as SAVEIMG. Now you can use the revised file in the original software in which it was created. As with any creative process, let your imagination (and the job requirements) determine how you use this capability of AutoCAD.

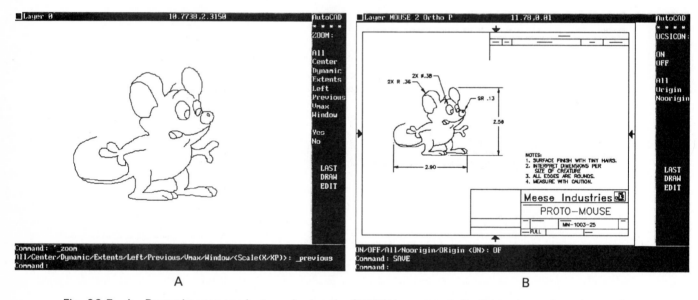

Fig. 26-7. A—Raster images can be traced using the SKETCH command. B—Raster images can be used to create any type of AutoCAD drawing.

EXERCISE 26-1

☐ Start a new drawing and name it EX26-1.
☐ Find a raster file with the extension of .GIF, .PCX, or .TIF. It can be off of the Release 12 Bonus CD, a sample file from other software, or a file down loaded from a computer bulletin board service such as CompuServe.
☐ Use the proper RASTERIN command to import the image into your drawing.
☐ Explode the image, then zoom in close to examine the entities that comprise the drawing.
☐ Make two new layers; one for the image and one called LINES.
☐ Make the LINES layer current and use commands such as SKETCH and PLINE to trace a portion of the image.
☐ Make the image layer current, freeze the LINES layer, then erase all of the entities on the image layer.
☐ Thaw the LINES layer and save the drawing as A:EX26-1.

PART II—WORKING WITH POSTSCRIPT FONTS AND FILES

PostScript is a copyrighted page description language which was developed by Adobe Systems, and is used in the desktop publishing industry. With the ability of AutoCAD to work with PostScript fonts and files and raster files such as .GIF and .TIF, you have the power to create presentation-quality graphics. AutoCAD can import and export PostScript files with the PSIN and PSOUT commands. The PSDRAG command controls the visibility of the imported image as it is being inserted with PSIN. The quality, or resolution with which the image is displayed on the screen is controlled with the PSQUALITY command, and the pattern that fills the graphics is governed by PSFILL.

Adding fill patterns to an object

Using the PSFILL command, you can add PostScript fill patterns to a closed polyline. Figure 26-8 shows the types of fill patterns available. Each pattern prompts for different values. For example, the Grayscale pattern accepts gray values from 0 to 100. To fill an area with a grayscale value of 15, enter the following:

Command: **PSFILL** ⏎
Select polyline: *(pick the polyline to be filled)*
PostScript fill pattern (. = none) ⟨.⟩/?: **GRAYSCALE** ⏎
Grayscale ⟨50⟩: **15** ⏎

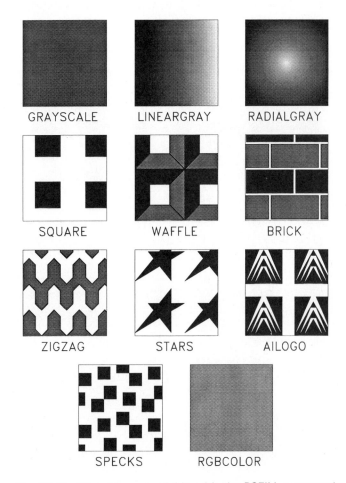

Fig. 26-8. Fill patterns available with the PSFILL command.

Nothing appears on the screen, but the pattern is included in the file and shows on the final print when you use the PSOUT command.

If you type "?" at the PostScript fill pattern: prompt, a list of available fill patterns are listed. Determine the appropriate fill pattern to use and type its name at the prompt.

When the PSOUT command is used, any PSFILL patterns are automatically surrounded by a polyline, which shows on the final print. If you do not want a polyline to surround the fill, place an asterisk (*) in front of the pattern name like this:

PostScript fill pattern (. = none) ⟨.⟩/?: ***GRAYSCALE** ↵

The fill pattern of Radialgray displays a highlight in the center of the selected polyline, and darkens toward the outer edges. You can control the brightness of the highlight (Foreground-Gray), and the darkness of the edges (BackgroundGray).

Command: **PSFILL** ↵
Select polyline: *(pick the polyline to be filled)*
PostScript fill pattern (. = none) ⟨.⟩/?: ***RADIALGRAY** ↵
Levels ⟨256⟩: ↵
ForegroundGray ⟨0⟩: ↵
BackgroundGray ⟨100⟩: ↵

The appearance of several values of Radialgray are shown in Fig. 26-9.

You can remove a fill pattern from a polyline by entering a period at the PostScript fill pattern: prompt.

PostScript fill pattern (. = none) ⟨.⟩/?: . ↵

Custom fill patterns can be added to the ACAD.PSF file by using the proper PostScript language. This is an ASCII text file and can be edited with any text editor. See the *AutoCAD Customization Manual* for the correct procedures.

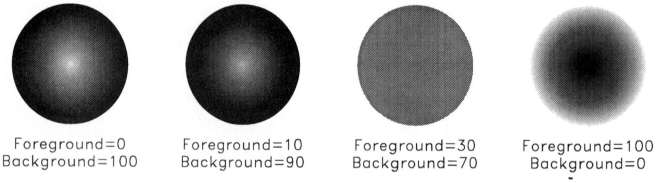

Foreground=0
Background=100

Foreground=10
Background=90

Foreground=30
Background=70

Foreground=100
Background=0

Fig. 26-9. Changing the value of the Radialgray PSFILL pattern creates different effects.

EXERCISE 26-2

☐ Begin a new drawing named EX26-2.
☐ Draw four rectangles, each measuring 1 x 2 units.
☐ Use the following PSFILL patterns to fill the rectangles.
    ☐ Lineargray—2 cycles
    ☐ Radialgray
    ☐ Waffle
    ☐ Stars—BackgroundGray = 20, ForegroundGray = 85
☐ Save the drawing as A:EX26-2.

Exporting a PostScript image

Any drawing created in AutoCAD can be converted to a PostScript file by using the PSOUT command. Normally, this command would be used if PostScript fonts or images had been added to the drawing, or if you used the PSFILL command to add patterns to closed polylines. Remember, the .EPS file can only be printed by a PostScript printer. The command prompts are as follows:

Command: **PSOUT** ↵

The "Create PostScript File" dialogue box is displayed. Enter a name and pick the OK button.

What to plot — Display, Extents, Limits, View or Window ⟨D⟩: ↵
Include a screen preview image in the file? (None/EPSI/TIFF) ⟨None⟩: ↵

A screen preview image, for use with other software such as desktop publishing programs, can be included with the file. If you respond with an "E" (EPSI file), or "T" (TIFF file), you are asked to select the image size. The default size of 128 x 128 pixels is best because it does not slow down the software into which the image is imported. The next prompt is:

Size units (Inches or Millimeters) ⟨Inches⟩: ↵
Output Inches = Drawing Units or Fit or ? ⟨Fit⟩: ↵

Enter half scale as 1 = 2. An architectural scale can be entered as 1/8″ = 1′-0″, or .125 = 12.

The next display is a list of "Standard values for output size." Several sizes are listed, and you can choose from the list and type the letter listed under the size column. You can also enter a new size:

Enter the Size or Width,Height (in Inches) ⟨USER⟩: **6,8.5** ↵

After the file has been created it can be printed by a PostScript printer at the DOS prompt as follows:

C:\ACAD12⟩ **COPY FILE.EPS LPT1** ↵

or

C:\ACAD12⟩ **PRINT FILE.EPS** ↵

Importing a PostScript image

The PSIN command enables you to import a PostScript file into AutoCAD. A PostScript file has the .EPS extension. PSIN is similar to the INSERT or GIFIN commands because all ask for an insertion point and a scale factor.

Command: **PSIN** ↵

The "Select PostScript File" dialogue box appears. Select the file and pick the OK button. It may take a few minutes to load the file, depending on its size.

Insertion point⟨0,0,0⟩: ↵
Scale factor: *(drag the image to fit and pick)*

Now you can place additional entities or text on the drawing and save it again as a PostScript file with the PSOUT command, or save it as a drawing file.

If the PSDRAG command is set to 0, only the outline of the box that represents the image is displayed when PSIN is used. If you wish to see the image as you drag it, set PSDRAG to 1.

PostScript file quality

The PSIN command renders an image according to the value of the PSQUALITY system variable. If PSQUALITY is set to 0, only a box representing the image is displayed with the file name inside. The default value is 75, which means that the image is displayed with 75 pixels per AutoCAD drawing unit. Higher quality values mean longer rendering time. A negative value such as -75 renders at the same resolution but does not fill PostScript outlines.

PROFESSIONAL TIP

When you use PSIN to import an image into AutoCAD, a file named ACADPS.EXP is used to interpret the PostScript file into a "Ghostscript" format so the entities are compatible with AutoCAD. You can then save the drawing, edit it later, or give the drawing to someone else to work with, and the ACADPS.EXP file is no longer needed. By default, ACADPS.EXP is placed in the ACAD12 directory during installation of AutoCAD.

Using PostScript fonts

A variety of PostScript fonts are included with AutoCAD. A list is shown in Fig. 26-10. These fonts are located by default in the ACAD12\FONTS subdirectory. They can only be used after the shape files are compiled. A PostScript shape file is a description of a font, and has a .PFB file extension, such as SASO____.PFB. Pick Compile... from the Files pull-down menu and the "Select Shape or Font File" dialogue box is displayed. Pick the shape file that you wish to compile from the file list and pick the OK button. It is immediately compiled, and the compiled version is given an .SHX extension.

You can use PostScript fonts exactly as you use any other AutoCAD font. Use the STYLE command, enter a style name, then pick the appropriate .SHX file from the dialogue box listing. Provide any additional style values you wish, then use the new style with the TEXT or DTEXT commands.

cibt	The quick brown fox jumped over the lazy dog.	ABC12
cobt	The quick brown fox jumped over the lazy dog.	ABC12
rom	The quick brown fox jumped over the lazy dog.	ABC12
romb	The quick brown fox jumped over the lazy dog.	ABC12
sas	The quick brown fox jumped over the lazy dog.	ABC12
sasb	The quick brown fox jumped over the lazy dog.	ABC12
saso	The quick brown fox jumped over the lazy dog.	ABC12
sasbo	The quick brown fox jumped over the lazy dog.	ABC12
te	THE QUICK BROWN FOX JUMPED OVER THE LAZY DOG.	ABC12
tel	THE QUICK BROWN FOX JUMPED OVER THE LAZY DOG.	ABC12
teb	THE QUICK BROWN FOX JUMPED OVER THE LAZY DOG.	ABC12

Fig. 26-10. PostScript fonts included with AutoCAD Release 12. (Autodesk, Inc.)

Fonts that are normally filled when printed as a PostScript file, appear only as an outline in AutoCAD and when the drawing is printed with the PLOT command. See Fig. 26-11. A PostScript print of the .EPS file shows filled fonts as solid, if the printer has that font.

Fig. 26-11. Filled PostScript fonts appear as an outline when the drawing is output with the PLOT command in AutoCAD.

NOTE

PostScript fonts must be purchased from authorized dealers, and are a copyrighted product. Like any other software, they may be used only on the machine they were purchased for.

EXERCISE 26-3

☐ Begin a new drawing and name it EX26-3.
☐ Compile the following PostScript fonts.
    ☐ TEL____.PFB
    ☐ SAS____.PFB
    ☐ ROMB____.PFB
☐ Create a style of each of the compiled fonts. The style name should be the same as the font.
☐ Write a single line of text using DTEXT with each of the styles.
☐ Plot or print the drawing.
☐ Use the PSOUT command to create a PostScript file.
☐ Print the .EPS file if you have a PostScript printer.
☐ Save the drawing as A:EX26-3.

PART III — RENDERING WITH AUTOCAD   ARRM 1

AutoCAD provides two different methods (not including AutoShade) for rendering and displaying a drawing or model. The basic command — SHADE — allows you to view a shaded image of the drawing in the current viewport. The SHADEDGE variable gives you some control of the type of display, and the SHADEDIF variable controls the intensity of the light. The AutoCAD Visualization Extension (AVE), or Render, gives you complete control over the lighting in your model. You can also specify whether the surfaces in your model are shiny or dull.

Understanding lights

The AutoCAD Visualization Extension uses three types of lighting: ambient, distant, and point light. *Ambient light* is like natural light; it is the same intensity everywhere, and faces receive the same amount of light. Ambient light cannot create highlights. You can change the intensity of ambient light, or even turn it off, but ambient light cannot be concentrated in one area. *Distant light* is a directed light source with parallel light rays, much like the sun. The intensity of distant light is the same on all objects, but the direction that it shines can be changed. The intensity of a distant light can also be changed. Distant light strikes all objects in your model on the same side. *Point light* is like a light bulb; it shines out in all directions. A point light does not cast shadows, and its intensity "falls off," or weakens over distance.

- **Angles** — AutoCAD renders the faces of a model based on the angle at which light rays strike the faces. A face that is perpendicular to light rays receives the most light. As the angle between the light rays and the face increases, the amount of light striking the face decreases. See Fig. 26-12.

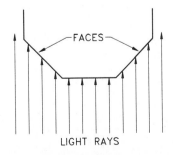

Fig. 26-12. Faces at an angle receive less light.

Point light rays radiate out from the light and can create highlights on different sides of objects. However, distant light illuminates the same side of objects because the rays are parallel. See Fig. 26-13.

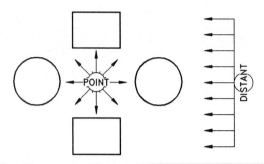

Fig. 26-13. Point light rays radiate from the source and distant light rays are parallel.

• **Reflectivity** — The brightness of reflected light from an object is actually the number of light rays that reach our eyes. Have you ever experienced the white flash of light in your eyes from a window or mirror? If so, your eyes were receiving the most light rays possible from that surface. Light rays are reflected off a surface (angle of reflection) at the same angle at which they strike it (angle of incidence). The amount of reflection, or highlight you see depends on the angle at which you view an object in relation to the angle at which the light is striking it. See Fig. 26-14.

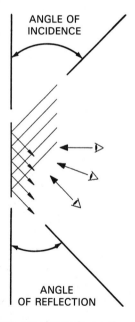

Fig. 26-14. The amount of reflection you see depends on the angle at which you view the object.

The nature of the surface greatly affects the direction in which the light is reflected. If a surface is smooth and polished, it is said to have a high *specular factor*. Smooth surfaces can also vary in the amount of polish on them. This is referred to as *roughness*, and affects the angle at which light rays are reflected.

Surfaces that are not smooth are considered to be *matte*, and thus produce *diffuse light*. When light rays hit a matte surface, they are reflected in many directions. Fig. 26-15 illustrates the difference between matte and shiny finishes.

• **Distance** — The farther an object is from a point light source, the less light that reaches it. Remember, a point light is like a light bulb. Its intensity falls off the farther an object is from the light. You can adjust this fall-off in AutoCAD Render in three different ways.

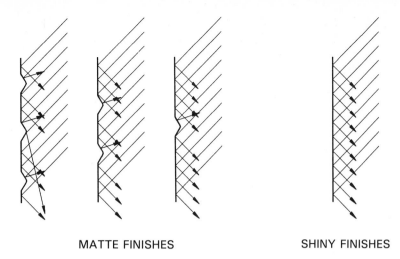

MATTE FINISHES   SHINY FINISHES

Fig. 26-15. Matte surfaces produce diffuse light, while shiny surfaces reflect light evenly.

- **None**—Applies the same light intensity regardless of distance. Basically, no fall-off is calculated.
- **Inverse Linear**—The illumination of an object decreases in inverse proportion to the distance. For example, if an object is 2 units from the light, it receives one-half (1/2) the amount of light. If the object is 4 units away, it receives one-quarter (1/4) the amount of light.
- **Inverse Square**—The illumination of an object decreases in inverse proportion to the square of the distance. For example, if an object is 2 units from the light, it receives $1/2^2$, or one-quarter (1/4) the amount of light. You can see that the light fall-off is faster with the Inverse Square option than with the Inverse Linear option.

The layout in Exercise 26-4 is used throughout the remainder of the chapter to illustrate aspects of Render, AutoShade, and RenderMan. This exercise can be completed in approximately 30 minutes, and is a quick use of 3-D shapes, user coordinate systems, and viewports. If you choose not to complete the exercise, you can use a drawing named KITCHEN2, located in the \ACAD\TUTORIAL subdirectory. You may have to adjust some of the coordinate locations for lights and cameras, but the drawing is suitable for any demonstrations of Render and AutoShade.

EXERCISE 26-4

This exercise is used in the remainder of the chapter. Construct the objects shown below to the dimensions given. Name the drawing 3DSHAPES and save as indicated.
- ☐ Begin a new drawing named 3DSHAPES using the prototype drawing method.
- ☐ Set units to architectural.
- ☐ Set limits to 24′,18′, grid to 6″, and snap to 2″. Zoom all.
- ☐ Create the following layers and colors:

Layer	Color
FLOOR-WALL	Cyan
TABLE	Red
PYRAMID	Yellow
CONE	Green
TORUS	Blue

- ☐ Make the FLOOR-WALL layer current.
- ☐ Using the 3DFACE command, draw the floor 8′ square. Draw the wall 8′ long and 6′ high You may have to change your viewpoint or UCS to draw the wall. This forms the background.

☐ Set a viewpoint of -2.5,-3,1.5.

☐ Establish a UCS at the lower-front corner of the floor. Save this UCS orientation as FLOOR.

☐ Construct the 3-D shapes using the given dimensions.

☐ Create a 1-inch cube on layer 0 with the BOX 3-D object command. Save the cube as a wblock named CUBE.

☐ Set the TABLE layer as current. Use the CUBE wblock to construct the table. Insert one cube for the first leg and enter the following values:

  Insertion point: X = 2'10"   Y = 2'
  Scale factors: X = 4   Y = 4   Z = 16
  Rotation angle = 0°

☐ Array the first leg using a unit cell distance of 24" for 2 rows and 2 columns.

☐ Use the CUBE wblock again for the table top as follows:

  Insertion point: X = 2'10"   Y = 2'   Z = 16"
  Scale factors: X = 28   Y = 28   Z = 2
  Rotation angle = 0°

☐ Establish a new UCS at the top-front of the tabletop using the Origin option, and enter the point of X = 2'10", Y = 2', Z = 18".

☐ Change the current layer to PYRAMID and select Pyramid from the "3D Objects" icon menu. Locate the first base point of the pyramid at X = 12, Y = 10, the second base point of @0,-8, third point of @8,0, and fourth point of @0,8. Give it an apex point 16,6,12. Use the ROTATE command to rotate the pyramid 45°. Use the beginning point of the pyramid as the rotation base point.

☐ Set the CONE layer as current and draw a cone at X = 8, Y = 20 with an 8" diameter and a 12" height.

☐ Set the current layer to TORUS and draw a torus located at X = 14, Y = 14, Z = 22. The torus diameter is 18" and the tube diameter is 5". Set segments to 12. The drawing should then look like the following one.

☐ Restore the UCS orientation named FLOOR.

☐ Save the drawing as 3DSHAPES and remain in the drawing editor. This exercise is used in the remainder of the chapter.

Preparing the drawing for rendering

If you are creating a drawing or model for use with Render or AutoShade, part of your planning should be to provide enough space around the model to place light icons. One technique that is useful once the drawing has been completed, is to create an arrangement of viewports using the VPORTS command. The large view can be used to see a 3-D view of the model, and the two small viewports can be used for a plan view for icon location, and a different 3-D view.

An example of this type of layout is shown in Fig. 26-16. You must use the default settings of the VPORTS command to create an arrangement of three viewports. Then, each of the two left viewports must be divided into two using the 2 option of the VPORTS command. This creates four small viewports where two were before. Now you can use the Join option of VPORTS to join the two small viewports oriented vertically in the middle of the screen. The final step is to join the large viewport with the tall thin one next to it. This gives you the arrangement shown in Fig. 26-16.

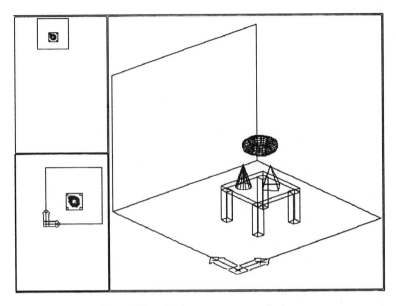

Fig. 26-16. The final arrangement of viewports.

Placing point lights in the model

You can control the amount of ambient light in your model, and place two different types of light—distant and point. After lights are placed in the model, you can fine-tune them by changing their intensities or locations. You can also turn them off if needed. The objective is to place enough lights in the model to create more than one scene, or "photo." You can select a different combination of lights for each scene.

Placing lights with the LIGHT command should be the first step in the creation of a scene for Render or AutoShade. Consider the type of lights you need for the model. There is no problem with having too many lights in the AutoCAD drawing. When you create a scene, you pick only the lights you want for that scene. After selecting LIGHTS, you must provide a name of up to eight characters for each light in the scene. Upper- or lowercase letters are valid, but light names must be different. Two types of lights are available, and their icons are shown in Fig. 26-17.

- **Point source**—Light is radiated in all directions. Intensity decreases as distance from the light increases.
- **Directed**—Parallel rays are projected in direction chosen.

Fig. 26-17. After you pick point or distant lights, their icons appear at the pick points on screen.

When placing lights in a drawing, use XYZ coordinates or filters to specify a 3-D location. Be sure the 3DSHAPES drawing shown in Fig. 26-16 is displayed on your screen. A point light is placed first. This type of light requires only a location and name with up to eight characters in the name.

The LIGHT command can be activated by picking Lights... in the Render pull-down menu. The "Lights" dialogue box is displayed as shown in Fig. 26-18. This dialogue box allows you to see a list of lights, create a new light, or pick an existing light from the model. Once a light has been selected, it can be modified or deleted. The ambient light intensity is controlled by a slider bar, or the intensity can be typed by double clicking on the value in the edit box above the slider bar. Three radio buttons give you the choice of the type of fall-off you want.

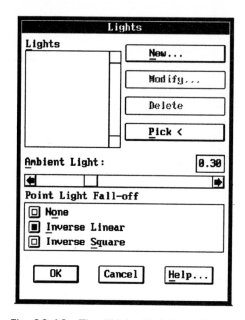

Fig. 26-18. The "Lights" dialogue box.

Pick the New... button to display the "New Light Type" subdialogue box. See Fig. 26-19. Select Point light and pick the OK button. This displays the "New Point Light" subdialogue box,

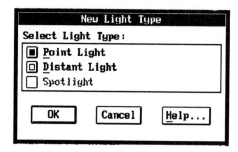

Fig. 26-19. The "New Light Type" subdialogue box.

Fig. 26-20. Enter the name "P-1" in the Light Name: edit box and pick OK. The "Lights" dialogue box returns and the name "P-1" is displayed in the Lights list box. Now, pick Modify..., and

Fig. 26-20. The "New Point Light" subdialogue box.

the "Modify Point Light" subdialogue box shown in Fig. 26-21 is displayed. Pick the Modify ‹ button and you are returned to the graphics screen. The prompt requests a light location. You can show AutoCAD the location of the light by picking, using filters, or by entering the coordinates at the keyboard as follows:

Enter light location ‹current›: **4',3'2",8'** ⏎

The dialogue box then appears. Pick OK in both dialogue boxes to complete the command and return to the graphics screen. Now, zoom all in the right viewport.

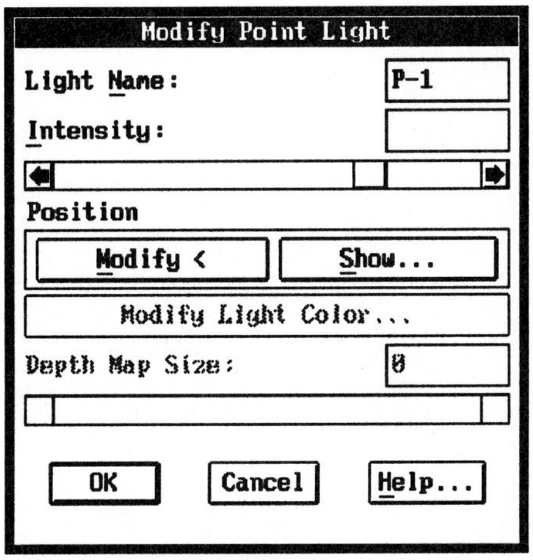

Fig. 26-21. The "Modify Point Light" subdialogue box.

Setting the icon scale

You may notice a tiny symbol directly above the torus in your model. This is the light icon, but it is much too small for viewing. You can change the scale of icons by picking Preferences... in the Render pull-down menu. Pick the Icon scale: edit box and enter "24." Pick OK to return to your model.

A symbol representing the light named P-1 appears at the specified location. Its name is written in the symbol, Fig. 26-22.

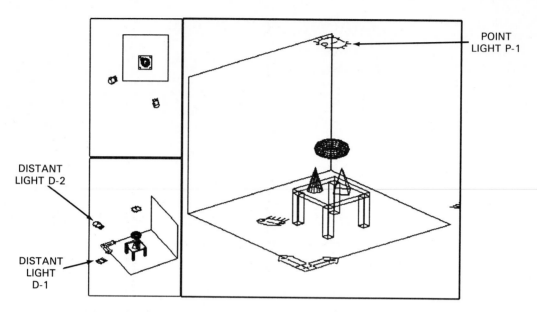

Fig. 26-22. Light icons placed in the drawing.

Placing distant lights in the model

Distant lights are placed in the same manner as point lights, but need a target as well as a location. Enter the LIGHT command or pick Lights... from the Render pull-down menu. Pick the New button, then pick the Distant Light radio button in the "New Light Type" subdialogue box. Pick OK, and the "New Distant Light" dialogue appears. Then enter the name D-1 in the Light Name: edit box. Pick Modify ⟨ and enter the following values:

Enter light target ⟨current⟩: **END** ↵
of *(pick P-1 in Fig. 26-23)*
Enter light location ⟨current⟩: **6',−4',30** ↵

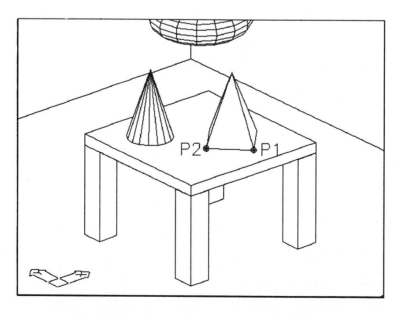

Fig. 26-23. Pick points for the distant lights.

Pick OK to return to the "Lights" dialogue box, and OK to return to the graphics screen. The distant light is placed in the drawing. You may not see it in the 3-D view, but it shows in the plan view, and possibly your other view. Place one more distant light in your model using the following information:

> **Name:** D-2
> **Light target:** Point P2, Fig. 26-23
> **Light location:** −2′,0,30

Your model should look like Fig. 26-22 when you place the second distant light.

Lights can be moved or erased using the "Lights" dialogue box by picking the Modify or Delete buttons. Before you edit a light in this manner, be sure the light name is highlighted in the Lights list box.

Rendering the model

You can request a rendering of your model at any time. If there are no lights in your model, AutoCAD places one behind your viewpoint. If you have placed lights in your model, but have not yet constructed a "scene", AutoCAD uses all of the lights and renders the current view in the active viewport.

Enter "RENDER" at the Command: prompt, or pick it from the Render pull-down menu. AutoCAD then displays the rendering of your model.

NOTE

The first time you use an AVE Render command, you are prompted to configure your rendering display device. You must know the type of graphics card that is installed in your computer in order to answer the configuration questions. You should configure for the same type of display device selected in AutoCAD's standard configuration menu. If you are using a standard VGA or SVGA card, AVE Render should be configured as follows:

> Select rendering display device:
>   1. AutoCAD's configured P386 ADI combined display/rendering driver
>   2. P386 Autodesk Device Interface rendering driver
>   3. None (Null rendering device)
> Rendering selection ⟨1⟩: ⏎
> Default ⟨1⟩ selected
> Do you want to do detailed configuration of SVADI's rendering features ⟨N⟩: ⏎
> Press RETURN to continue.
>
> Select rendering hardcopy device:
>   1. None (Null rendering device)
>   2. P386 Autodesk Device Interface rendering driver
>   3. Rendering file (256 color map)
>   4. Rendering file (continuous color)
> Rendering hardcopy selection ⟨1⟩: ⏎

If you select option 2 above and AutoCAD indicates that it cannot find the driver, enter the following:

> Enter ADI driver name: **RHEXPORT** ⏎

You can then select the kind of file you want created. If you select PostScript, the next time you render to a hardcopy device, an .EPS file is created, which you can then print on your PostScript printer.

Creating views and scenes

A *scene* consists of a view and one or more lights. A scene is like a photograph, and you can have as many scenes in a model as desired. The current view in the active viewport is used as the "camera" for the scene. You can use the VIEW, VPOINT, or DVIEW commands to set the viewpoints you want, then use the VIEW command to create named views. Create the following views using the DVIEW command. Be sure the large viewport is active.

Command: **DVIEW** ↵
Select objects: *(window the entire model)*
Select objects: ↵
*** Switching to the WCS ***
CAmera/TArget/Distance/POints/PAn/Zoom/TWist/CLip/Hide/Off/Undo/⟨eXit⟩: **PO** ↵
Enter target point ⟨current⟩: **END** ↵
of *(pick P2 in Fig. 26-23)*
Enter camera point ⟨current⟩: **8'6'',−6',4'** ↵
CAmera/TArget/Distance/POints/PAn/Zoom/TWist/CLip/Hide/Off/Undo/⟨eXit⟩: ↵

The view should look like the one shown in Fig. 26-24.

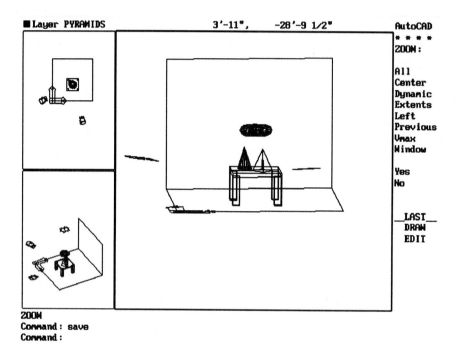

Fig. 26-24. A view created with the DVIEW command.

Now you can use the VIEW or DDVIEW commands and save this as a new view named VIEW1. Next set up a second viewpoint with the DVIEW command as follows:

Command: **DVIEW** ↵
Select objects: **P** ↵
Select objects: ↵
*** Switching to the WCS ***
CAmera/TArget/Distance/POints/PAn/Zoom/TWist/CLip/Hide/Off/Undo/⟨eXit⟩: **PO** ↵
Enter target point ⟨current⟩: **END** ↵
of *(pick top of cone)*
Enter camera point ⟨current⟩: **@−6',8'6'',5'** ↵

Now turn perspective on by setting a distance.

CAmera/TArget/Distance/POints/PAn/Zoom/TWist/CLip/Hide/Off/Undo/⟨eXit⟩: **D** ↵
New camera/target distance ⟨11′−6 1/2″⟩: **11′6″** ↵
CAmera/TArget/Distance/POints/PAn/Zoom/TWist/CLip/Hide/Off/Undo/⟨eXit⟩: ↵

Your display should look like Fig. 26-25. Create another view of the current display and name it VIEW2.

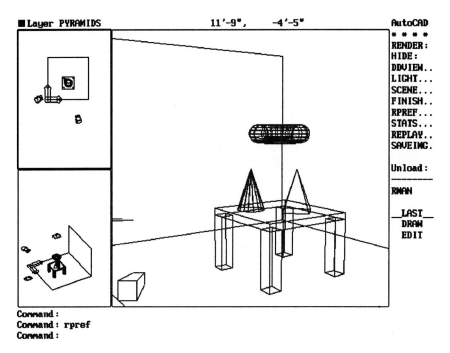

Fig. 26-25. A perspective view is created with the DVIEW command's Distance option.

Now that you have two views, make a couple of scenes by picking Scenes. . . from the Render pull-down menu. This displays the "Scenes" dialogue box. See Fig. 26-26. Pick New.. to display the "New Scene" subdialogue box. This dialogue box lists all views and lights in the drawing.

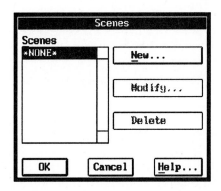

Fig. 26-26. The "Scenes" dialogue box.

Enter the scene name of FRONT in the edit box at the upper right. See Fig. 26-27. Now you need to assign a view and lights to the new scene. Pick VIEW1, then pick lights D-1 and P-1, then pick the OK button to save the scene. Pick New... again and make another scene named

Fig. 26-27. The ''New Scene'' subdialogue box lists views and lights.

SIDE. Use VIEW2 and lights D-2 and P-1. The "Scenes" dialogue box should list the two scenes as shown in Fig. 26-28. Pick OK and render the scene with the RENDER command.

The RENDER command finds the current scene, then renders the view used for that scene. Therefore, the rendering may not be the same view displayed in the active viewport.

On your own, create a third scene named SIDE-2. Use the DVIEW command to establish a new view named VIEW3 using the same target as in VIEW1. The camera location should be X = −5′, Y = −8′6″, and Z = 12′. Set the distance in DVIEW to 11′6″. Use all of the lights for scene SIDE-2.

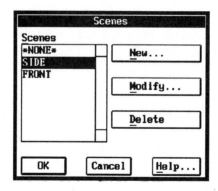

Fig. 26-28. The ''Scenes'' dialogue box displaying the SIDE and FRONT scenes.

Changing light intensities

It is best to have the full intensity of a point light strike the first object in the model. Full intensity of any light is a value of one (1). Remember that point light fall-off is based on whether you are using the Inverse Linear setting or Inverse Square setting. The top of the torus is 51 in. from the point light. Use the following calculations for each setting:
- Inverse Linear—If the point light is 51 units above the highest object (torus), it receives 1/51 of the light. Set intensity to 51 so the light intensity striking the torus has a value of 1.
- Inverse Square—Set light intensity to $1/51^2$, or 2601.

Pick Lights... in the Render pull-down menu. Set the Ambient Light intensity to 0. This allows you to see the effects of other lights. Pick P-1 in the Lights list box, then pick the Modify... button. Enter "51" in the Intensity: edit box and pick OK. Set the intensity of lights D-1 and D-2 to 1. Be sure Inverse Linear is active in the "Lights" dialogue box, and pick OK. Set the current scene to SIDE-2 by picking it in the "Scenes" dialogue box. Render the model again to see the difference. See Fig. 26-29.

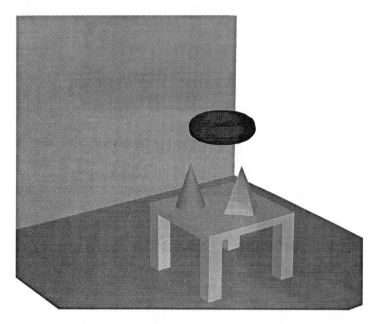

Fig. 26-29. The rendered scene after changing lights.

You can quickly examine the effects of turning on individual lights and turning off all others. Select the "Lights" dialogue box and pick each distant light—D-1 and D-2—and set each to an intensity of 0. The point light is the only one that is on. Now render the model. You will notice that the top of the table is bright and the legs have no highlight. See Fig. 26-30A. Now select Lights... and set Ambient Light to 1. Render the scene again. Notice the additional even light in the rendered scene. See Fig. 26-30B.

Try turning the point light off, and turn on only one of the distant lights at a time. First, set the intensity of light D-2 to .8, then render the model. The left sides of the objects are illuminated. Now turn off D-2, give light D-1 an intensity of 1, and render the model. The front of the objects, and the back wall are illuminated. The floor is dark because it is parallel to the light rays. Try additional combinations on your own.

A   B

Fig. 26-30. A—The scene rendered with only one point light on. B—The scene rendered with point and ambient light.

━━━ PROFESSIONAL TIP ━━━

Use the ability to change the intensity of lights often. It can quickly provide you with a variety of rendered models before you produce the final images or prints.

Creating different surface finishes

A *finish* to AutoCAD is a shiny or dull surface, or any gradation between. You can create a variety of finishes by specifying how a surface reflects light. See the section entitled **Understanding lights** earlier in this chapter. When you create a finish, it can be assigned to an entity color in your model, or to a specific AutoCAD Color Index (ACI) number. If you assign a finish to an ACI, all objects in your model with that color number are given the finish.

Create a new finish by picking Finishes from the Render pull-down menu. This displays the "Finishes" dialogue box, Fig. 26-31. Pick the New... button to display the "New Finish" dialogue

Fig. 26-31. The "Finishes" dialogue box allows you to create or modify surface finishes.

box. Enter the name of TORUS for the finish name. See Fig. 26-32. Note the default values for Ambient, Diffuse, Specular, and Roughness. Ambient light is used for general illumination

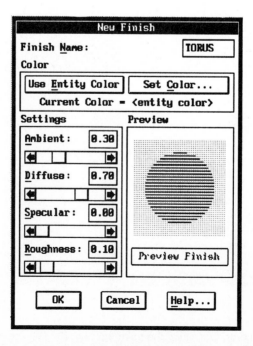

Fig. 26-32. The values of the finish are specified in the "New Finish" subdialogue box.

and contrast on all surfaces. Diffuse and Specular are percentages of the reflected light, and the sum of the two should be no greater than 1 (100%). Therefore if you decide that the specular factor should be .6, or 60%, then set the diffuse factor to .4, or 40%.

The Roughness factor determines the size of the specular reflection or highlight. The smaller the roughness number, the shinier the surface, and the smaller the area of highlight. Set the specular factor to 1, the diffuse factor to 0, and the roughness to 1.

NOTE

You can preview any finish, and see an example of it in the "New Finish" dialogue box if your graphics card supports rendering in a viewport. This is normally only possible with a high-resolution graphics card. You must first have installed the proper graphics card driver file and configured AutoCAD to work with it. If you are in doubt about the capabilities of your graphics card, see your instructor or supervisor, or check the video documentation and the *AutoCAD Interface, Installation, and Performance Guide.*

Save the finish by picking the OK button. You are then prompted for the finish location. A Surface Property Block (SPB) is placed at the UCS origin. See Fig. 26-33. You can press ENTER to leave it there, or pick a new location.

Enter New Finish location 〈current〉: *(pick a spot in the lower part of the upper-left viewport)*

Fig. 26-33. A Surface Property Block identifies a surface finish.

The "Finishes" dialogue box returns. The finish is applied to all objects in the model unless you attach it to an entity. Do this by picking the Entities 〈 button, and you are prompted:

Select objects to attach "TORUS" to: *(pick the torus)*
Select objects: ↵

You can apply the finish to all entities that have the same ACI. Do this by picking the ACI button, and the "Attach by AutoCAD Color Index" dialogue box appears. Pick the number of the color you want to apply the finish to, then pick OK. The ACI number appears to the right of the finish name in the list box. A finish with an ACI assigned to it creates a Surface Property Block with the ACI number next to it. See Fig. 26-33.

Render the model and notice the wide area of the reflection. See Fig. 26-34A. Now change the roughness to .1 and render the model again. Notice that the area of reflection is much smaller, indicating a smoother surface. See Fig. 26-34B.

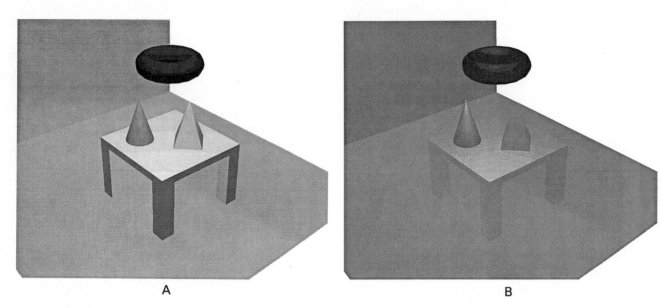

Fig. 26-34. A—Scene rendered with a large roughness value. B—Same scene rendered with a small roughness value.

If you think this is a finish you would like to use on other drawings, pick Export and it is automatically added to a file named NULLSURF.SP3. This is an ASCII (text) file that contains a list of preset finishes. You can use the preset finishes by picking Import..., which displays the dialogue box shown in Fig. 26-35. Pick the one you want to use, then pick OK. The imported finish is added to the list of finishes in the current drawing. See Fig. 26-36.

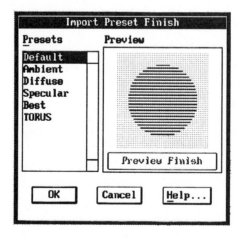

Fig. 26-35. The "Import Preset Finish" dialogue box.

Fig. 26-36. The "Finishes" dialogue box lists imported finishes.

Editing surface finishes

If you wish to delete a finish because you do not need it in this drawing, pick the finish name in the list of the "Finishes" dialogue box, and then pick the Delete box. Pick OK in the "Delete Finish" alert box, and it is deleted from the current drawing file only, not the NULLSURF.SP3 file.

You can modify the finish by picking the Modify... button in the "Finishes" dialogue box. This displays the "Modify Finish" subdialogue box, which is exactly like the "New Finish" dialogue box shown in Fig. 26-32. You can change all of the lighting factors discussed previously—ambient, diffuse, specular, and roughness. If your video card supports rendering in a viewport, you can pick the Preview Finish button to see what the new finish looks like on a sphere.

You can change the color of the finish in this dialogue box by picking the Set Color... button. This displays the "Color" dialogue box, Fig. 26-37, in which you can select the amount of red, green, and blue you want in the color. See the section entitled **Understanding color** on page

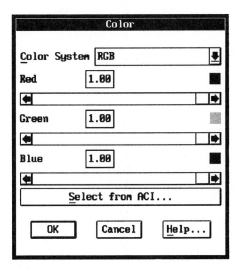

Fig. 26-37. The color can be adjusted in the "Color" dialogue box.

26-52. If you just want to select a color to use for the finish, you can pick the Select from ACI... button, which displays the "Select Color" dialogue box. See Fig. 26-38. You can pick from any of the standard colors along the top, the gray shades, or the full color palette. The color you select is displayed at the bottom. To save the changes to the finish, you must pick OK in four dialogue boxes. Then use the RENDER command to see what the new finish looks like.

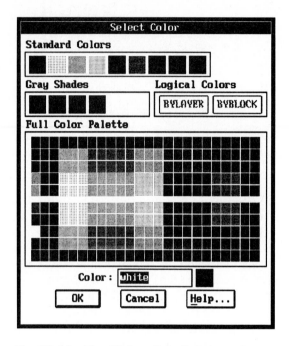

Fig. 26-38. The "Select Color" dialogue box.

Once you attach a finish to an object, it is not there forever. You can detach a finish from an entity. First pick Finishes... in the Render pull-down menu. You can select the finish by picking it in the dialogue box, or you can select the Pick 〈 button, then pick the object on the screen that is attached to the finish, such as the torus. Then pick the Entities 〈 button, and you are returned to the screen. At the prompt, use the Remove option before selecting the torus again.

Select objects to attach "TORUS" to: **R** ↵
Remove objects: ↵ *(the object is already selected, so press ENTER)*

The dialogue box returns and the finish is detached. Pick OK to complete the process.

Specifying rendering preferences
The "Preferences" dialogue box provides several options and settings. Some are only available if you are configured for a high-resolution video graphics card. The following discussion outlines the function of the items in the "Rendering Preferences" dialogue box. See Fig. 26-39.
- **Rendering Type**
  - ✔Full Render—Produces a 3-D polygon shaded image that displays the best quality image, but takes the longest to render.
  - ✔Quick Render—Quicker rendering than Full, but produces a raster image of scanned horizontal lines.
  - ✔ACAD RenderMan—Available only if RenderMan is in use.
- **Rendering Options**
  - ✔Smooth Shading—Smooths out the faces and blends colors across faces.
  - ✔Merge—Allows you to overlay images. Available only with 24-bit, full-color display devices.
  - ✔Apply Finishes—Any finishes are applied to the rendering.

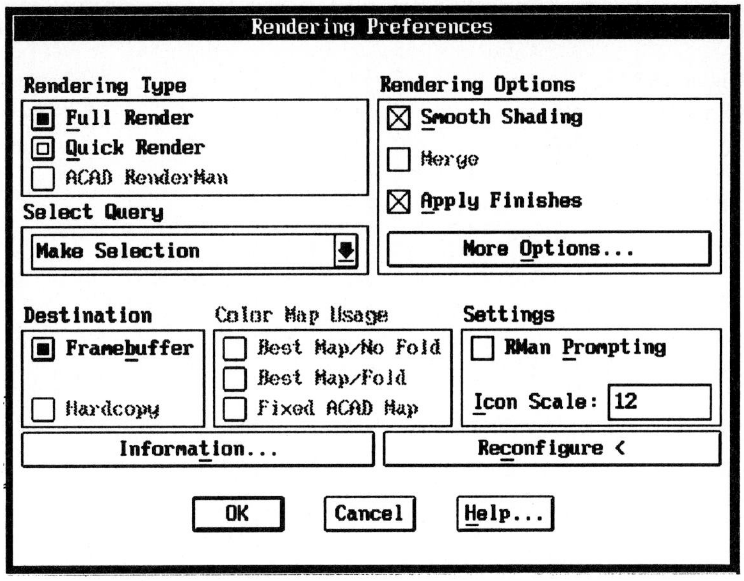

Fig. 26-39. The "Rendering Preference" dialogue box.

- **Select Query**
  Allows you to select objects to be rendered when using the RENDER command. Options are "Select All" and "Make Selection."
- **Destination**
  ✔Framebuffer—Renderings are sent to the configured display device.
  ✔Hardcopy—Renderings are sent to the configured hardcopy device, such as a PostScript printer or rendering file format, .RND.
- **Color Map Usage**
  This area is grayed-out if your graphics card does not support rendering to a viewport.
  ✔Best Map/No Fold—AutoCAD vector colors are not folded (blended) into colors 1-8. Calculates the best colors to use for rendering based on those available in your display device. The colors of entities in the other viewports may change.
  ✔Best Map/Fold—AutoCAD vector colors are folded into colors 1-8. Calculates the best colors to use for rendering based on those available in your display device. The colors of entities in the other viewports are changed to the closest color from 1-8.
  ✔Fixed ACAD Map—Uses AutoCAD's 256 colors for rendering.
- **Settings**
  ✔RMan Prompting—RenderMan prompts are enabled in the "Lights" dialogue box if this button is checked. Set this if you are using AutoShade 2 with RenderMan. Enables you to use spotlights, colored lights, and shadows.
  ✔Icon Scale—Allows you to change the size of light and finish icons.
- **Information...** —Displays the current configuration and version of AVE Render.
- **Reconfigure** ⟨—Allows you to reconfigure the rendering device. The rendering configuration is saved in a file named AVE.CFG. See the *AutoCAD Interface, Installation and Performance Guide* for information on setting the proper environment variable for this file so AutoCAD can find it.
- **More Options...** —If Full Render is selected, the dialogue box in Fig. 26-40A is displayed. If Quick Render is selected, the dialogue box in Fig. 26-40B is displayed.
  ✔Output Mode—Select whether the rendering is in color or black and white.
  ✔Separation—Only colors with an X in the check box are rendered.
  ✔Intersection—If on, AutoCAD checks for intersecting faces in the model. May slow down the rendering, but produces accurate results. The "Statistics" dialogue box reports if any faces intersect. See the next section on the "Statistics" dialogue box.
  ✔Sort by Obscuration—On by default. Ensures that faces closest to the viewpoint are rendered in front of those they obscure (hide).
  ✔Discard Back Faces—Off by default. If on, AutoCAD does not render back faces. Saves

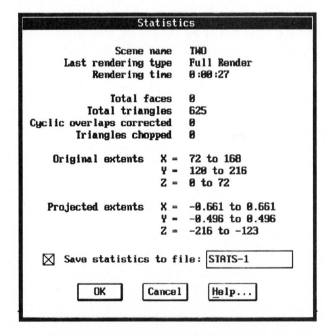

Full Render Options

Output Mode
- ■ Color
- ▢ Black and White

Separation
- ☒ Red Component
- ☒ Green Component
- ☒ Blue Component
- ☐ B&W Separations

- ☐ Intersection
- ☒ Sort by Obscuration
- ☐ Discard Back Faces
- ☒ Back Face Normal is Negative

Sort Round Off: 0.0001

Chop Round Off: 0.0001

[OK] [Cancel] [Help...]

Quick Render Options

Output Mode
- ■ Color
- ▢ Black and White

Separation
- ☒ Red Component
- ☒ Green Component
- ☒ Blue Component
- ☐ B&W Separations

- ☐ Discard Back Faces
- ☒ Back Face Normal is Negative

[OK] [Cancel] [Help...]

A   B

Fig. 26-40. A—The "Full Render Options" subdialogue. B—The "Quick Render Options" subdialogue box.

time, but may not produce the full rendering that you desire.

✓ Back Face Normal is Negative—On by default. A *normal* is a vector that projects perpendicular from a face. A negative normal projects away from the viewer, or into negative Z space. AutoCAD considers negative normals as "back faces" if this option is on.

✓ Sort Round Off—Controls the smoothness of face edges in overlapping areas.

✓ Chop Round Off—Controls the smoothness of intersecting faces.

Rendering statistics

AEM 4

The STATS command provides information about the last rendering performed. This command can be accessed from the Render pull-down menu by picking Statistics, or by typing "STATS" at the Command: prompt. See Fig. 26-41. The "Statistics" dialogue box displays information that cannot be altered, but can be saved to a file.

Statistics

Scene name TWO
Last rendering type Full Render
Rendering time 0:00:27

Total faces 0
Total triangles 625
Cyclic overlaps corrected 0
Triangles chopped 0

Original extents X = 72 to 168
                  Y = 120 to 216
                  Z = 0 to 72

Projected extents X = -0.661 to 0.661
                   Y = -0.496 to 0.496
                   Z = -216 to -123

☒ Save statistics to file: STATS-1

[OK] [Cancel] [Help...]

Fig. 26-41. The "Statistics" dialogue box.

Saving image files

A powerful aspect of AVE is the ability to save a rendered image in a variety of raster file formats. These images can then be used in virtually any other software either as they are, or by using a file conversion program. The SAVEIMG command allows you to save the rendered image in one of four different common raster formats—.TGA (default), .TIF, .GIF, or .RND. Pick Files from the Render pull-down menu, then pick Save Image to display the dialogue box, Fig. 26-42A. This dialogue box is displayed if your display device is configured to render to a separate rendering window. If you are configured to render to a viewport, the image tile on the right of the dialogue box is replaced by three radio buttons for selecting:

1. Active Viewport
2. Drawing Area
3. Full Screen.

An even more powerful aspect of the SAVEIMG command is the ability to crop the image by specifying the XY pixel values. Notice in Fig. 26-42A, the Offset and Size values. Offset is the lower-left corner of the image in pixels, and Size is the upper-right corner of the image. The default value, in this case 320 x 200, is the maximum pixel size of image you can get with your display device.

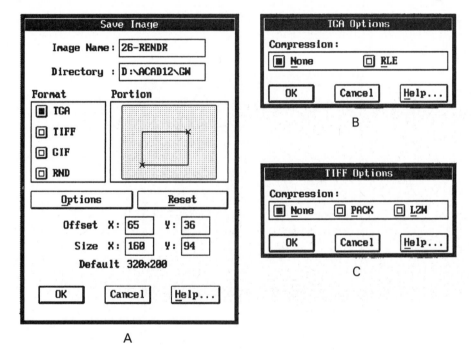

Fig. 26-42. A—The "Save Image" dialogue box. B—The "TGA Options" subdialogue box. C—The "TIFF Options" subdialogue box.

NOTE

If you are configured for a high-resolution graphics card, this may read 1161 x 932 if you have a single viewport displayed, and have the Active Viewport button selected. If you select the Full Screen button, this value may increase to 1272 x 1020.

You can crop the image by entering the appropriate offset and size values in the edit boxes, or by picking the offset and size with your pointing device inside the image tile area. The new size values are automatically displayed after you pick the second point.

━━━━━ NOTE ━━━━━

The image size represents the pixel size of the current viewport. Before saving an image, be sure that the viewport you want to save the image in is actually the current one.

Two of the file formats, .TGA and .TIF, can be saved in a compressed form. You can specify the form by picking the Options button. Depending on which file format is selected, the "TGA" or "TIFF Options" dialogue box is displayed. See Figs. 26-42B and C. The compressed form for TGA files is RLE (Run-Length-Encoded). A .TIF file can be compressed as PACK for MacIntosh, or the standard LZW format for .TIF files.

Replaying image files

Images that were saved as .TGA, .TIF, .RND, and .GIF files can be displayed on the screen with the REPLAY command. Select the type of file that can be displayed by your graphics card. You can display the entire image or a portion of it. The REPLAY command can also be accessed by picking Files from the Render pull-down menu and then picking Replay Image... from the cascading menu. This displays the "Replay" dialogue box, which is the standard directory and files list boxes. Select the directory and file you wish to display and pick the OK button. The "Image Specifications" dialogue box appears, in which you can specify the exact portion of the image you want to display. See Fig. 26-43.

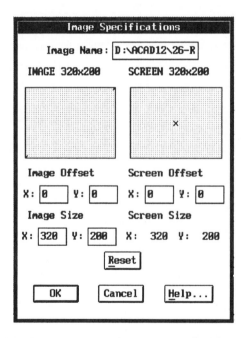

Fig. 26-43. The "Image Specifications" dialogue box.

The image tile on the left side of the dialogue box is titled IMAGE, and the size of the image is given in pixels. You can pick two points inside this tile to crop the image for display. When you do this, notice that the screen offset location of the image in the SCREEN image tile changes. You can also change the image size by entering the cropped side of the image in the Image Offset and Image Size boxes. The offset is the lower-left corner of the image and the size is the upper-right corner.

In addition to cropping the size of the image, you can place it anywhere on the screen. Do this visually by picking a point in the SCREEN image tile. This becomes the center of the image on your screen. You can accurately specify the location by entering the Screen Offset values in the boxes below the tile. Notice that the Screen Size values are not changeable. They are exactly the same as the Image Size values.

The Reset button returns all of the image and screen values to their defaults. Pick OK when you are ready to display the image.

EXERCISE 26-5

☐ Load EX26-4 into AutoCAD if it is not on your screen.
☐ Save an image of the entire model in the file format that can be displayed by your graphics card, for example, .GIF. Save it as EX26-5.
☐ Replay the image to occupy the entire screen.
☐ Replay the image again, but display only the center of the image, and locate it in the upper-right portion of the screen.

Creating a filmroll file for AutoShade Version 2

AutoShade Version 2 with RenderMan gives you the ability to control lighting, cast shadows, and apply surface textures and patterns to achieve photorealistic quality. To use AutoCAD drawings in AutoShade, you must first create a filmroll file (in AutoCAD) that contains the proper lights, camera, and scene components that are required by AutoShade.

NOTE

The following discussion assumes that AutoShade is installed in a directory named D:\SHADE2. Your version of AutoShade may be installed on the C: drive, or a hard disk partition other than D:. Check with your instructor or supervisor for its location. See the *AutoShade Installation and Performance Guide* for proper installation of this software.

The FILMROLL command translates the AutoCAD drawing to a file that AutoShade can use. Save the file in the SAMPLES subdirectory of the SHADE2 directory.

Command: **FILMROLL** ↵

The "Create Filmroll File" dialogue box appears. Enter filmroll file name as D:\SHADE2\SAMPLES\3DSHAPES and pick the OK button.

    Creating the filmroll file
    Processing face: (nnn)
    Filmroll file created

That's all there is to it. The file created is given an .FLM extension that the AutoShade program can read to create a shaded rendering.

The AutoShade program allows you to fine-tune your scene with additional settings and variables. Light locations and intensities, camera locations, and lens types can all be adjusted to suit your needs.

PART IV—INTRODUCTION TO AUTOSHADE, VERSION 2

AutoShade is a rendering program that complements AutoCAD's 3-D capabilities. Although it runs independent of AutoCAD, AutoShade uses 3-D drawings that are created with 3-D faces in AutoCAD. AutoCAD allows you to prepare a drawing with AVE. Render your model by placing lights in it and making *scenes* of the AutoCAD drawing. The drawing can then be converted into a special file called a *filmroll*. Drawings converted to filmroll files are given the file extension .FLM, and are used by AutoShade to perform the shaded rendering of the scene. The rendering is then given an .RND file extension.

Rendered 3-D drawings let you see realistic views of products or scenes in wireframe or solid shaded form. The scenes, displayed in perspective, are excellent for demonstrations, client presentations, and error-checking models.

This portion of the chapter introduces the use of lights in the layout of scenes in AutoCAD that can be used in Render and AutoShade to create shaded renderings. A wide range of light, shade, and location variables are available with lighting. Work with the examples given here and also spend some time going through the AutoShade, Version 2 Tutorial that is available with the software. This tutorial includes a variety of examples covering most of the functions of AutoShade. Consult the *AutoShade, Version 2 User's Guide* for detailed discussions of all the functions and settings in AutoShade.

The general hardware requirements for running AutoShade, Version 2 are listed below. For a detailed discussion of the specific hardware types and models, please refer to the *AutoShade, Version 2 Installation and Performance Guide*.

- 386 computer with math coprocessor.
- 4 megabytes of random-access memory (RAM), minimum. Additional memory is recommended, especially if you plan to work on large drawings.
- 20 megabyte hard disk drive minimum. The program requires 8 megabytes.
- 5.25" or 3.5" floppy disk drive.
- Video display adapter.

Optional equipment includes:
- Input device, such as mouse or digitizer tablet.
- Hardcopy output device for PostScript files.

INSTALLING AUTOSHADE

Installing AutoShade is made simple by an installation program supplied with the software. The installation procedure is discussed in the *AutoShade, Version 2 with Autodesk RenderMan Installation and Performance Guide*. This manual provides a step-by-step procedure for installing the software. It also discusses proper configuration and settings for the CONFIG.SYS and AUTOEXEC.BAT files. Please take some time to read this manual and install AutoShade properly.

NOTE

AutoShade Version 2 and RenderMan, like AutoCAD Release 12, make greater demands on the computer's memory and processing power. Therefore, it is important that you take some time to familiarize yourself with the suggested path and environment settings that are discussed in the *Installation and Performance Guide*. The settings and procedures are not difficult to understand, but if ignored, can cause problems.

If, after configuring AutoShade, you are not able to move the pointer, reconfigure the program. To do this, hold down the ALT key and type "CRASH." The DOS prompt appears. Next, change to the drive and directory in which AutoShade resides if that path is not reflected in the DOS prompt. For example, if AutoShade is located on the D: drive and the DOS prompt displays the C: drive, enter the following:

    C:\⟩ **D:** ↵
    D:\⟩ **CD SHADE2** ↵
    D:\SHADE2⟩ **SHADE —R** ↵

This instructs AutoShade to run through the configuration procedure.

Step through the configuration process again and select the correct devices. When the AutoShade main screen menu appears, move the screen pointer to the File menu and select the QUIT command.

WORKING IN AUTOSHADE

After creating a filmroll file, you must exit AutoCAD and load AutoShade at the DOS prompt as follows:

    C:\ACAD〉 **D:** ↵
    D:\〉 **CD SHADE2** ↵
    D:\SHADE2〉 **SHADE** ↵

Your exact entry will vary depending on your computer's configuration.

While in AutoShade, you can view your drawing as a plan view, wireframe, or shaded rendering. If you like a view displayed on screen, you can record it as an .RND file that can be quickly displayed later. In addition, you can make slides of any screen display or send the rendering to a printer.

The AutoShade screen layout

AutoShade contains only four pull-down menus, Fig. 26-44. The Display menu contains commands that allow you to view your drawing in plan view, wireframe, or rendered versions. You can also record images for later replay, create slides for AutoCAD, or send the rendered image to a printer. The Settings menu contains commands to select a scene, adjust camera positions and lighting intensities, and alter a variety of technical aspects of model shading and rendering. The RenderMan menu enables you to set and change lighting properties, assign surface textures and properties, and render drawings in the RenderMan format. The File menu allows you to open files, select scenes, create script files, and quit the program. It also contains information on a complex mathematical system—the Mandelbrot set. You might alter some of these variables, but most users never do.

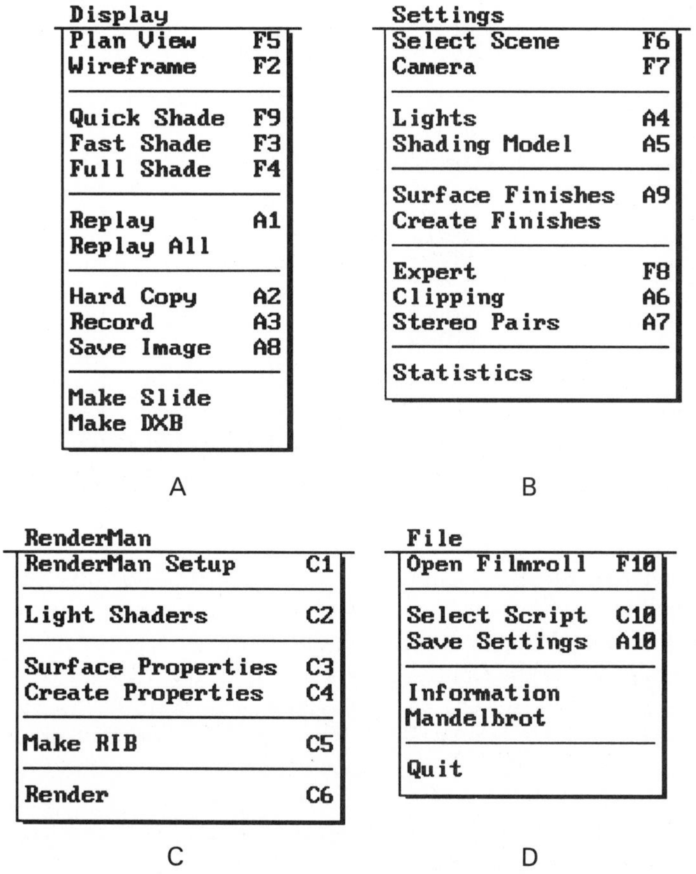

Fig. 26-44. The AutoShade pull-down layout. A—Display menu. B—Settings menu.
C—RenderMan menu. D—File menu.

The upper-right corner of the screen contains a memory meter that indicates the percentage of memory used in an operation. To the right is a clock. The bottom edge of the screen is the status line where AutoShade tells you the operations it is performing and indicates the percent of the job completed. At the extreme right of the status line is the name of the current filmroll file.

The operation of AutoShade with a mouse or digitizer is similar to using AutoCAD. Yet, if you do not have one of the supported pointing devices, you can also run AutoShade using the cursor keys. It is a bit tedious, but not difficult. The cursor (arrow) keys control the movement of the arrow pointer on the screen, and the following keys provide additional functions.

- **INSERT (INS)** — Acts like a ENTER key to select a highlighted item. Use the cursor keys to move the pointer and highlight an item, then press INSERT (INS) to select the item.
- **PAGE UP (PG UP)** — Increases the distance the screen pointer moves with one cursor key press.
- **PAGE DOWN (PG DN)** — Decreases the distance the screen pointer moves with one press of a cursor key.
- **ENTER** — Can be pressed after typing a file or scene name in a dialogue box.

Many of the items in the pull-down menus have a letter and number combination to the right of the selection. This represents one of the function keys along the top or left side of your keyboard. For example, in the Display menu, a wireframe view can be chosen by pressing function key F2. Some menu items are followed by the letter "A" and a number, such as A2. The "A" represents the ALT key on the keyboard. To select these items, hold down the ALT key and press the appropriate function key. For example, the Hard Copy command is followed by A2 in the Display menu. A hardcopy (print) of a rendering can be generated by pressing the ALT and F2 keys simultaneously.

Opening files and scenes

To work with an .FLM file created in AutoCAD, pick the File menu, then the FILMROLL command. You can also press function key F10 to open a file. The "Select Filmroll File" dialogue box appears, Fig. 26-45.

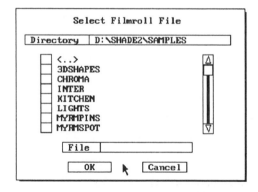

Fig. 26-45. The "Select Filmroll File" dialogue box.

The name of the current directory appears in the Directory edit box. All files with .FLM extensions are listed below it. If you wish to change directories, move the pointer to the box containing the directory name. When it highlights, enter the path name of the directory you want to look through. In order to use the filmroll file named 3DSHAPES that you created in AutoCAD, enter the name of the directory in which you saved it, for example, D:\SHADE2\SAMPLES. After typing the directory name, press ENTER or pick the OK button. Next, pick the box to the left of the file named 3DSHAPES. This name then appears in the File: edit box. Select the OK box at the bottom of the dialogue box to confirm the file choice. The status line along the bottom of the screen displays the message "Reading filmroll file." The name of the file is shown in the lower-right corner of the screen.

The "Select Scene" dialogue box is displayed next. It provides a list of the scenes in the current filmroll file. See Fig. 26-46. Pick the scene named FRONT, then pick the OK box. From this point, whatever you do in AutoShade will be applied to only the scene you selected. If you want a different scene, pick Select Scene in the Settings menu to access the "Select Scene" dialogue box.

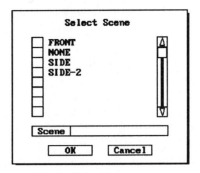

Fig. 26-46. Choose a scene from the "Select Scene" dialogue box.

Plan and wireframe views

Before proceeding with a shaded rendering, you might want to check the placement of lights and cameras in the plan view again. You might also want to see what the scene looks like again in 3-D. The preview displays of Plan View and Wireframe are found in the Display menu.

Pick Plan View, and the plan view of your drawing appears. It looks similar to the plan drawn in AutoCAD, except the symbols for lights and camera are different. The point light source resembles an asterisk, and the direct light looks like a comb, Fig. 26-47. Also note the line pointing from the camera with the arrow on the end. This is the line of sight and points to the target.

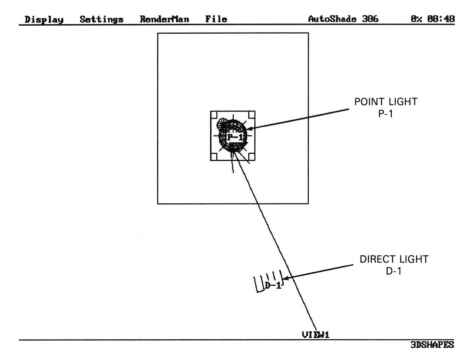

Fig. 26-47. The Plan View shows the lights, camera, and field of view for the current scene.

When the plan view displays only the one line from camera to target, the resulting 3-D display will be an orthographic view. This is probably not what you want. Change to a perspective view by selecting Expert in the Settings menu or pressing F8. Pick the box to the right of Perspective so that a check mark appears, then pick OK. See Fig. 26-48A. Select Plan View in the Display menu again and note the difference. The three lines radiating from the camera indicate that perspective is on. The two lines that angle out from the camera are the field of vision, which is controlled by the lens length of the camera. The default lens length is 50 mm, which duplicates the view from the human eye.

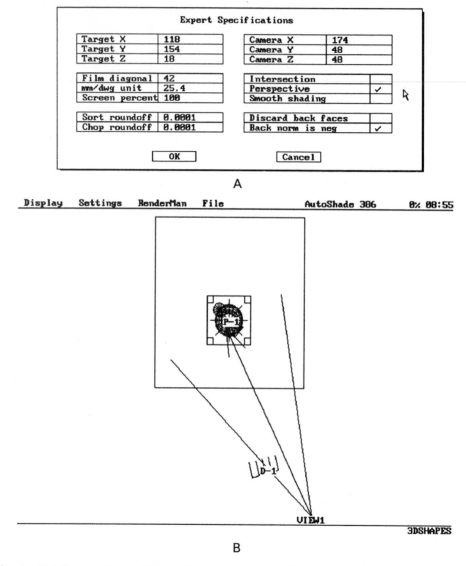

Fig. 26-48. A—Pick Perspective and OK to change to a perspective view. B—Select Plan View in the Display pull-down menu. Note the three lines that indicate perspective is ON.

A wireframe of the current view can be generated by picking the Display menu and selecting Wireframe. The resulting wireframe view of the 3DSHAPES filmroll file is shown in Fig. 26-49.

Notice in Fig. 26-49 that the left and right sides of the floor in the wireframe seem to be cut off, or "clipped." That is because left and right clip limits have been set by default. Clipping is found in the Settings menu, and is discussed later in the chapter.

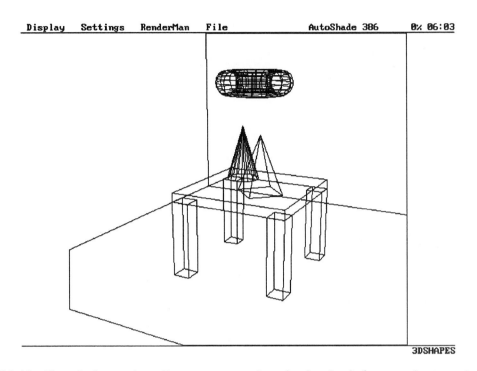

Display   Settings   RenderMan   File   AutoShade 386   0% 06:03

3DSHAPES

Fig. 26-49. The wireframe view allows you to preview the drawing before creating a rendering.

EXERCISE 26-6

☐ Load the filmroll file 3DSHAPES if it is not on your screen.
☐ Open the scene named SIDE.
☐ Display a plan view.
☐ Change the view to perspective and display another plan view.
☐ Display a wireframe view.
☐ Choose Select Scene from the Settings menu and pick the scene named SIDE-2.
☐ Display the scene in plan view. This scene should already be in perspective. How can you tell?
☐ Display a wireframe view.
☐ Quit if you are not continuing with this drawing session.

Creating shaded renderings

AutoShade provides three items in the Display menu to create shaded renderings. The Quick Shade option is the fastest method because it does not calculate polygons on the surfaces, but produces a pixel image line-by-line. It shows intersecting faces correctly, but two faces of different colors sharing the same edge may produce an improperly colored edge. Avoid using Quick Shade for hardcopy prints because it requires considerable amounts of memory and time.

The Fast Shade option generates a rendering that is sufficient for checking the lighting. However, the rendering contains errors because AutoShade does not calculate all of the hidden and overlapping surfaces. As the fast shade is generated, messages on the status line indicate what is happening. The percentage of memory used appears at the upper-right corner of the screen.

Pick the Select Scene option in the Settings menu and pick the scene named SIDE-2, if it is not displayed on your screen. Display this scene in a wireframe view. It should look similar to Fig. 26-50.

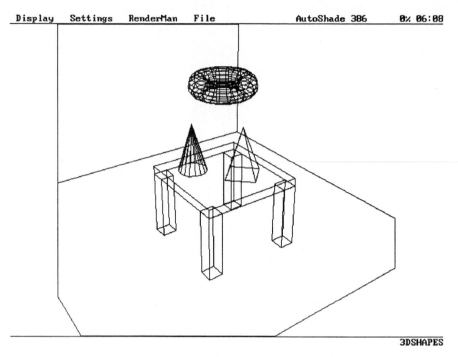

Fig. 26-50. The scene SIDE-2 displayed in wireframe.

Now test the Fast Shade option using this scene by selecting Fast Shade from the Display menu. The rendering occupies the entire screen, so to return to the menus, press key F1 or pick the left mouse button. The fast shade of the 3DSHAPES filmroll is shown in Fig. 26-51.

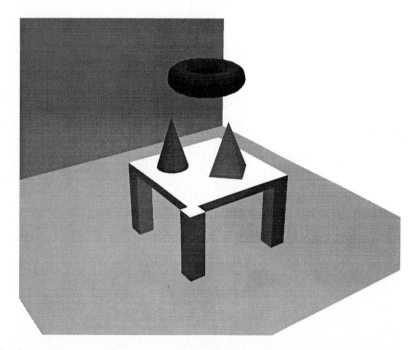

Fig. 26-51. The fast shade contains errors with overlapping surfaces, but is good for checking the lighting in a scene.

When you are ready for a final rendering, select the Display menu and pick the Full Shade option. Depending on the drawing's complexity and your computer, this may take a long time.

You can see the percentage of work that has been completed by watching the running man icon as it moves across the screen. A note under the running man says "Checking for obscuration." See Fig. 26-52. This means that AutoShade is checking for the faces to be shaded, as opposed to those that are hidden. The percentage of the drawing that has been checked is indicated to the side of this prompt. The status line indicates how many triangles must be checked. The running man gives you a graphic indicator as to the time required to complete the rendering.

Fig. 26-52. The percentage of work that has been completed is indicated by the position of the running man.

The full shade rendering contains no errors and shows all faces correctly. If your computer's graphics card and monitor display 8 or 16 colors, AutoShade creates shades of a single color with a process called *dithering*. Dithering uses a variety of patterns to indicate shades of a single color. Unless you have a monitor capable of displaying 256 colors, the quality of the full shade may not be what you expected. A full shade rendering is shown in Fig. 26-53.

Fig. 26-53. The full shaded image shows all faces correctly.

─── **PROFESSIONAL TIP** ───

If you are in doubt about the number of colors that your graphics card is capable of displaying, open the CHROMA filmroll file and perform a fast shade on SCENE1. It displays rows of boxes containing colors available with your graphics card.

Recording, saving, and printing files

You can instruct AutoShade to record (save), fast and full shade rendered images by picking the Record option in the Display menu. A check mark appears to the left of the Record option when it is picked. Notice also that the Hard Copy option is grayed out. When Record is on, a rendering file (.RND) is created instead of a hardcopy file. Nothing happens after picking Record until you select either Fast Shade or Full Shade. At that time, the "Create Rendering Replay File" dialogue box appears, Fig. 26-54. The name of the current filmroll file is given. Change it if you wish and select OK to create the file.

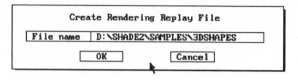

Fig. 26-54. When Record is selected, you can name the rendering file for a fast or full shaded image in the "Create Rendering Replay File" dialogue box.

The advantage of recording shaded images is that they can be replayed using the Replay or Replay All options of the Display menu. The Replay option displays a single file that you pick in the "Select Replay File" dialogue box, Fig. 26-55A, whereas the Replay All option replays all chosen file types in the selected directory. If you choose Replay All and wish to stop the replays, press CTRL C to cancel the process. AutoShade can create and display three file formats. The rendering file, .RND, is the default. Two additional files, the TGA format (.TGA extension), and the TIFF format (.TIF extension) can be displayed. See the *AutoShade User Guide* for a discussion of these two file types. The .RND file is the default selection. Pick the OK box to continue.

The "Select Replay File" dialogue box appears and lists all .RND files, Fig. 26-55B. Just pick the file you wish to view and it is displayed on screen. The display is rendered quickly because no calculations have to be performed.

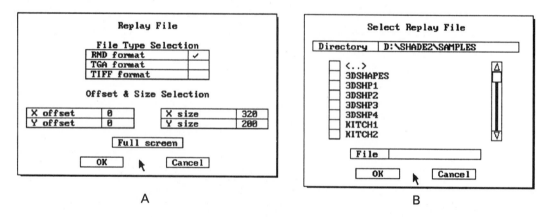

Fig. 26-55. A—The "Replay File" dialogue box allows you to pick the file format to display. B—The "Select Replay File" dialogue box provides a list of files to display.

You can make slides of any AutoShade scene, and use the slides in AutoCAD or other programs that use files having .SLD extensions. Just pick the Make Slide item in the Display menu. The "Make Slide File" dialogue box appears to request the name of the slide, Fig. 26-56. The wireframe picture that is subsequently displayed on screen is produced as a slide.

Fig. 26-56. Enter the slide file name in the "Make Slide File" dialogue box.

The Save Image option of the Display menu differs from the Record option in that you can save to one of three file types—.RND, .TGA, and .TIF—and you can specify the size of the image to save. The image size is controlled by the X and Y offset and size specifications in the "Save Image Specifications" dialogue box. See Fig. 26-57. The .TGA and .TIF file types enable you to create images for specific display devices for use in RenderMan images.

The Hard Copy option in the Display menu lets you generate a printed copy of a rendering if you have a PostScript printer configured with AutoShade. Select Hard Copy. The next time a rendering is created, it is sent to the hardcopy device. Hard Copy and Record cannot be active at the same time. If the Hard Copy option is grayed out, the device may not be configured, or Record may be active. An Encapsulated PostScript file (.EPS extension) is created, which can be printed, or used in desktop publishing programs.

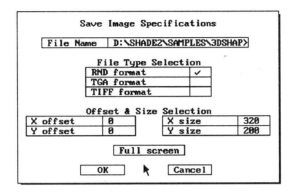

Fig. 26-57. The "Save Image Specifications" dialogue box allows you to specify image type and size to save.

EXERCISE 26-7

☐ Be sure that the 3DSHAPES filmroll file is loaded.
☐ Select the scene named FRONT.
☐ Turn on the Record option.
☐ Select Fast Shade in the Display menu. Name the file 3DSHP1.
☐ Select Full Shade, and name the file 3DSHP2.
☐ Replay the rendered files just created.
☐ Make a slide file of the wireframe. Name it 3DSHP-WF.
☐ Exit AutoShade and load AutoCAD. Display the slide 3DSHP-WF in AutoCAD.
☐ Return to AutoShade.

FINE-TUNING THE RENDERING

The Settings menu contains several options that adjust aspects of the scene to achieve different effects. Lights can be turned up or down in intensity, or set for automatic exposure, ignoring all preset lighting variables. The reflective nature of objects can be altered using shading model variables. While you cannot change the position of the lights in AutoShade, you can move the camera. New lenses can be fitted to the camera for wide angle or telephoto effects. Portions of the image can be trimmed, or *clipped*, to enhance the view or eliminate features not needed. Plus, for the adventurous person, Expert settings allow you to fine-tune the images even further.

Changing lighting variables

The most obvious aspect of lighting that you can change is its intensity. Turn the brightness up or down. The "Lights" dialogue box, Fig. 26-58, displays the name, type, and intensity value of each light in the scene. A zero turns the light off. The larger the value, the brighter the light. Use the scroll bar to see other light names when there are more than eight in the scene.

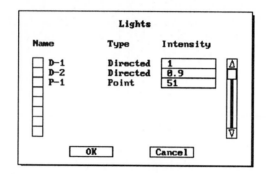

Fig. 26-58. Alter the brightness with the "Lights" dialogue box.

Changing the camera position

AVE Render does not use cameras; instead, it uses views. The location of the viewpoint is considered a "camera" location when rendering a model. The view that is selected when you make a scene becomes the "camera" for that scene. When you make a filmroll file in AutoCAD, to be used in AutoShade, there are not cameras in the scenes. AutoShade requires cameras, so it uses the view of each scene as its camera. Therefore, when you select Camera from the Settings menu, the camera name is the name of an AutoCAD view.

Camera movement can be horizontal and vertical. Positive horizontal camera rotation around the target is measured from the X axis in a counterclockwise direction in the X-Y plane. Positive vertical rotation is measured up from the X-Y plane. These two values can be changed in the "Camera Specifications" dialogue box, Fig. 26-59.

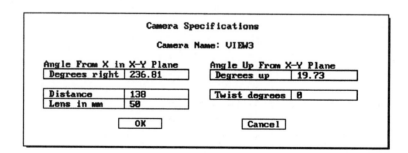

Fig. 26-59. Camera variables are changed in the "Camera Specifications" dialogue box.

This menu also allows you to change the target to camera distance and the lens length. The standard 50 mm lens produces an image like that the human eye would see. For a wider view select a wide angle lens, such as 35 mm or even 28 mm. A shorter lens length will cause more distortion around the edges of the picture. If you want a close-up view, select a telephoto lens such as 100 mm or greater. The Twist variable creates the effect of tilting the camera to one side or the other. The result of putting a 100 mm lens on the camera in scene SIDE2 is shown in the close-up of the objects in Fig. 26-60.

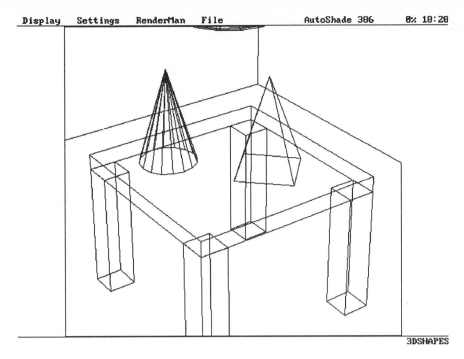

3DSHAPES

Fig. 26-60. The camera lens can be changed to telephoto to give a close-up of the model.

Shading settings

Fine control over a variety of shading factors is possible with the options in the "Shading Model" dialogue box, Fig. 26-61. The average user will not alter most of these settings since the default settings produce good renderings.

Shading Model

Ambient factor	0.3	Inverse square	0
Diffuse factor	0.7	Inverse linear	0
Specular factor	0	Inverse constant	0
Specular exponent	10	Background color	0 black

Stretch contrast	✓	Red component	✓
Z shading		Green component	✓
Black and white		Blue component	✓
Apply finishes	✓	B&W separations	

OK   Cancel

Fig. 26-61. Shading variables are controlled in the "Shading Model" dialogue box.

Whereas the light settings affect the brightness of the lights, the Shading Model options determine whether a surface has a glossy or matte finish. Factors affecting the surface finish are:

- **Ambient factor**—Controls the intensity of ambient light, or sunlight, which brightens all objects uniformly. Use settings from 0 to 1.
- **Diffuse factor**—Controls the reflected light that is diffused, or reflected in many directions. The larger the number, the more matte, or rough the objects. A value of 0 indicates a shiny surface. Use settings from 0 to 1.
- **Specular factor**—Controls the shiny nature of the surface. The higher the number, the shinier the surface. Use settings from 0 to 1. The sum of ambient, diffuse, and specular factors should not be greater than 1.
- **Specular exponent**—Controls the width of the reflected light beam. The shinier the surface, the narrower the beam. Larger numbers create narrower light beams. Use settings from 3 to 20.

All these factors are ignored if a check mark appears in the Stretch contrast box. This setting controls the *automatic exposure* of the camera. If Stretch contrast is checked, the light is adjusted automatically and AutoShade ignores the light intensity and shading model settings. If Stretch contrast is off, light intensities and shading model factors are calculated.

Several factors in the "Shading Model" dialogue box control the shading of colors relative to an object's distance from the light source. These distance factors work best for large areas containing many 3-D faces. Items that control the distance calculations in AutoShade are:

- **Inverse square**—Causes the light intensity to decrease by the square of the distance from the light source to the center of the 3-D face. The larger the number, the dimmer the light.
- **Inverse linear**—The light intensity decreases linearly from the light source to the 3-D face. Linear lighting creates brighter color shades at a distance than does the Inverse square option.
- **Inverse constant**—Creates the effect of fluorescent lighting when used with Linear lighting.
- **Z shading**—When on, all other lighting and shading factors, except Stretch contrast, are ignored. Objects farther from the camera appear darker than objects close to the camera.

PROFESSIONAL TIP

If the complexity of so many lighting variables confuses you, select the Z shading option and let AutoShade create a realistic shaded rendering for you with "automatic exposure."

Select scene SIDE-2, then select the Settings menu. Set the following values in the appropriate dialogue boxes:

Camera Specifications
- Degrees right = 205
- Lens in mm = 65
- Degrees up = 33

Lights
- Point intensity = 15
- Directed intensity = 8

Shading Model
- Ambient factor = 0.2   Specular factor = 0.5
- Diffuse factor = 0.3   Specular exponent = 10
- Stretch contrast = off   Inverse linear = 1

The lighting camera variables just discussed let you create a wide variety of scenes. Fig. 26-62 shows another view of the 3DSHAPES drawing, with changes in the camera location, lens value, and lighting variables.

Fig. 26-62. A change in camera, lighting, and shading creates a new scene.

EXERCISE 26-8

☐ Be sure the 3DSHAPES filmroll is loaded into AutoShade. Select scene FRONT.
☐ Display a plan view. Notice the camera's field of view. Turn on perspective.
☐ Turn off Stretch contrast and Z shading.
☐ Change the light intensity so the directed light is brighter than the point light.
☐ Turn Record mode on.
☐ Create a fast shade and name the file 3DFRNT-1.
☐ Change the camera location by moving it away from the object several feet.
☐ Create a fast shade and name the file 3DFRNT-2.
☐ Change the shading settings so that the ambient light is low and the surface of the object is shiny.
☐ Create a fast shade and name the file 3DFRNT-3.
☐ Turn on Stretch contrast.
☐ Create a fast shade and name the file 3DFRNT-4.
☐ Replay all of the rendering files.

Expert settings

The "Expert Specifications" dialogue box provides additional control over the nature of the drawing display. Fig. 26-63 shows some of the settings you can control as an expert:

- **Target X, Y, Z coordinates**—Controls the target location specified in the AutoCAD drawing. Any changes here will affect the camera position, and those changes are calculated by AutoShade.
- **Camera X, Y, Z, coordinates**—Controls the location of the camera. Changes here will be reflected in the "Camera Position" dialogue box and the Distance setting.
- **Intersection**—If your drawing has intersecting faces, check this box to instruct AutoShade to calculate for intersecting faces when creating a full shade.
- **Perspective**—Turns perspective on or off. If perspective is off, a parallel projection, the kind you get with the VPOINT command, is generated.
- **Smooth shading**—Smooths the rough edges and blends the colors across adjacent faces of a polygon mesh.
- **Discard back faces**—Prevents AutoShade from calculating the back faces of a solid object. Can save time, but may not show back faces that must be shown when looking through part of a solid object.
- **Back norm is neg**—AutoShade considers faces entered in a counterclockwise order to be front faces. Faces entered clockwise are considered to be back faces. If faces are entered in the opposite order, AutoShade may confuse them and the rendering will not appear correct. If this happens, check the Back norm is neg box and the order will be reversed.

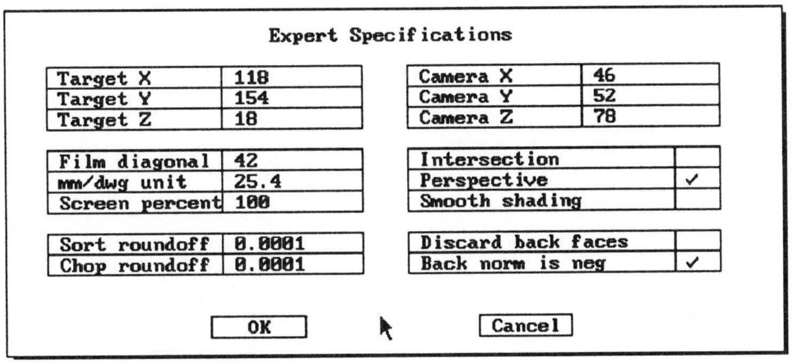

Expert Specifications

Target X	118		Camera X	46	
Target Y	154		Camera Y	52	
Target Z	18		Camera Z	78	
Film diagonal	42		Intersection		
mm/dwg unit	25.4		Perspective		✓
Screen percent	100		Smooth shading		
Sort roundoff	0.0001		Discard back faces		
Chop roundoff	0.0001		Back norm is neg		✓

OK ▸ Cancel

Fig. 26-63. The "Expert Specifications" dialogue box gives you control of a variety of AutoShade variables.

Clipping the image

You may think of *clipping* as cropping, a term used when trimming a photograph to show only desired portions. You can control the amount of image seen by using the "Clipping Specifications" dialogue box, Fig. 26-64. You can clip objects and features in front of and behind the target. You can also use top, bottom, left, and right clipping to construct a viewing frame. A check mark in the item's box indicates that it has been selected.

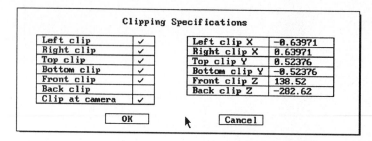

Clipping Specifications			
Left clip	✓	Left clip X	−0.63971
Right clip	✓	Right clip X	0.63971
Top clip	✓	Top clip Y	0.52376
Bottom clip	✓	Bottom clip Y	−0.52376
Front clip	✓	Front clip Z	138.52
Back clip		Back clip Z	−282.62
Clip at camera	✓		

OK   Cancel

Fig. 26-64. The "Clipping Specifications" dialogue box gives you control over the display.

The clipping values for X, Y, and Z in the right side of the dialogue box indicate distances from the target. A negative X value measures left of the target, a negative Y value measures below the target, and a negative Z value measures behind the target.

If you remember, the scenes in the filmroll file 3DSHAPES showed the effects of clipping planes, Fig. 26-65A. Test the use of clipping by selecting scene SIDE and displaying it in wireframe. Notice that the sides are all clipped. Select the Clipping option in the Settings menu and set the following values:

- Left clip X = −1.5
- Right clip X = 0.8
- Top clip Y = default
- Bottom clip Y = −0.9

Select the Wireframe option from the Display menu and the display should look like that in Fig. 26-65B.

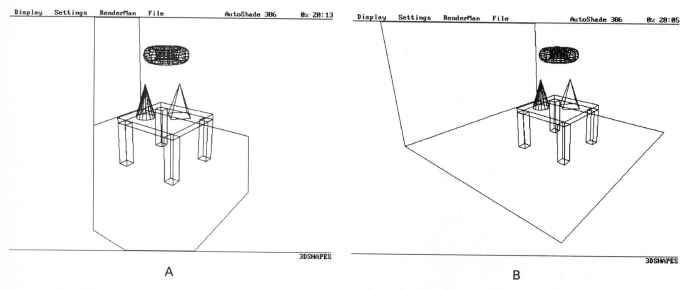

A   B

Fig. 26-65. A—The default settings show the effects of clipping planes. B—Increasing the distance of the clipping planes from the target gives a wider field of view, like a wide-angle lens.

Stereo pairs

If you have ever looked through a stereoscope or stereo viewer, you know the value of stereo photos in visualizing three-dimensional shapes. AutoShade allows you to create stereo pictures with the Stereo Pairs selection in the Settings menu. See Fig. 26-66.

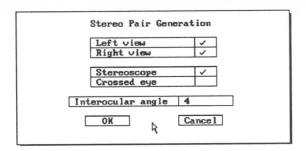

Fig. 26-66. The Left view, Right view, and Stereoscope options must be checked to view an object in three dimensions.

In order to create stereo pairs, both the Left view and Right view boxes must be checked in the "Stereo Pair Generation" dialogue box. If not, only one view is displayed. A *stereoscope display* means that the right view is calculated for the right eye and the left view is calculated for the left eye. These two images must be viewed with a stereoscope in order to see the object in 3-D. Since it is difficult to use a stereoscope on a monitor, these images are best sent to a hardcopy device. See Fig. 26-67.

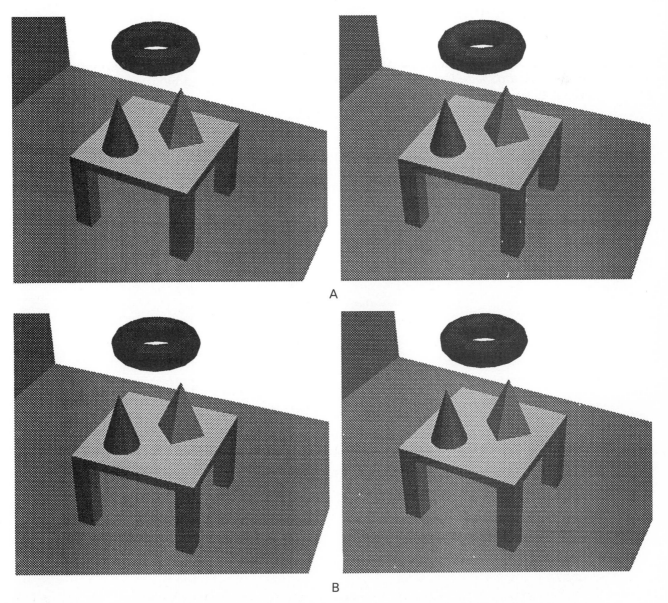

Fig. 26-67. A—These stereo images can be viewed in 3-D with a stereoscope. B—These images can be seen in 3-D using the crossed-eye technique.

The "crossed-eye" technique can be used to view the model in 3-D on the screen. If Crossed eye is selected in the "Stereo Pair Generation" dialogue box, the Stereoscope option is turned off. When one of the shading options in the Display menu is selected, two images are displayed, but the image on the left is for the right eye, and the image on the right is for the left eye. Now you can stare cross-eyed at the screen and see the model in three dimensions. Refer to the *AutoShade User Guide* for a detailed discussion of the crossed-eye fusion technique. Fig. 26-67A shows the stereo images generated for stereoscope viewing, and Fig. 26-67B shows images for crossed-eye viewing.

Settings, scripts, and statistics

One of the nice things about AutoShade is that you can change a variety of settings such as light intensity, diffuse and specular factors of surfaces, camera location and lenses, and the clipped size of the display. However, if you load another scene, all of those settings revert to defaults for the new scene. If you wish to save the settings to use again, pick the Save Settings option in the File menu. You are prompted for a file name. After entering a file name and picking OK, a script file (.SCR) is automatically created. Then, at a later date, should you wish to use that filmroll scene again with the same settings, pick the Select Script option from the File menu, then pick the desired script file from the "Select Script File" dialogue box. The script file is run, which changes the settings to reflect those in the script.

─ PROFESSIONAL TIP ─

Script files are ASCII text files and can be edited to suit your needs. They play an important part in creating renderings and AutoFlix animations (walk-throughs and kinetic motions). Refer to the *AutoShade User Guide* for a list of commands that can be used in script files to set variables.

The Statistics option of the Settings menu provides you with information about the scene. It can help you gauge the amount of memory required to render the drawing. It also displays the extents of the drawing, which may be helpful in positioning the camera. The "Statistics" dialogue box is shown in Fig. 26-68.

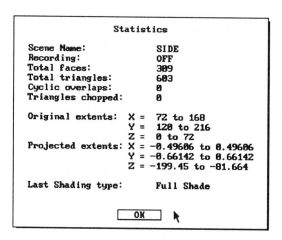

Fig. 26-68. The "Statistics" dialogue box.

EXERCISE 26-9

☐ Be sure 3DSHAPES is loaded into AutoShade.
☐ List the statistics of the current file.
☐ Turn Record mode off.
☐ Create stereo pairs of the files using a stereoscope selection. Select Full Shade.

PART V—INTRODUCTION TO RENDERMAN

The purpose of this section is to provide a brief explanation of the operation of RenderMan, and define some of the commands and options used in AutoCAD and AutoShade with Render-Man. You can create an endless variety of renderings, shadows, and lighting combinations with AutoShade and RenderMan. The best way to discover this is to create a simple drawing in AutoCAD and then experiment with the numerous possibilities available with RenderMan.

In your initial stages of experimentation with RenderMan, keep your drawings simple. When using AutoShade and RenderMan, it does not take much to create a complex rendering that can require considerable time to generate. For example, when you use lights that cast shadows, RenderMan creates numerous large shading files. If your initial drawings are small and simple, the rewards come quicker. Then, you can advance with more confidence to more complex renderings.

AutoShade by itself gives you the ability to place and control lights and cameras, and create a variety of shaded renderings, but does not allow you to change the texture or surface pattern of objects. However, with Autodesk RenderMan, AutoCAD and AutoShade have the ability to apply surface textures and patterns to the models you create. Just as you can set up a drawing in AutoCAD to be viewed and rendered in AutoShade, you can also prepare a drawing in AutoCAD with surface textures, finishes, and lights that cast shadows. A filmroll file is then created that is loaded into AutoShade. In AutoShade you create a RenderMan Interface Bytestream (.RIB) file. From the .RIB file you can then produce a final shaded rendering.

NOTE

The RenderMan module of AutoCAD and AutoShade contains a wide variety of lighting, color, and surface texture options and variables. The purpose of this discussion is to introduce the basics of a RenderMan setup to you. If you plan to work with RenderMan, it is suggested that you work the RenderMan tutorials in the AutoShade Tutorials manual. In addition, you should read the *AutoShade User Guide* for in-depth discussions of the commands and settings.

PREPARING A RENDERMAN FILMROLL IN AUTOCAD

The following discussion of RenderMan takes you through a process of applying surface properties to objects in the 3DSHAPES drawing, generating a .RIB file, and then producing a Render-Man display of the file in AutoShade. The steps involved in this process are as follows:
• Load the RenderMan routine into AutoCAD.
• Apply shaders (surface finishes) to objects in the model using the RMPROP command.
• Locate spotlights for cast shadows with the LIGHT command.
• Create new scenes.
• Specify rendering parameters by using the RMSETUP command.
• Save the filmroll file.
• Exit AutoCAD and load AutoShade.
• In AutoShade, create a .RIB file (RenderMan Interface Bytestream) and generate a rendering.
• Adjust existing shaders and lights, or apply new shaders.
• Apply texture mapping if needed.

Understanding color

A basic understanding of the nature of color will make your use of RenderMan, and other rendering and animation programs easier. The three primary colors are red, green, and blue (RGB). AutoCAD retains values called the AutoCAD Color Index (ACI), which are recognized by AutoCAD, AutoShade, and RenderMan. See Appendix B of the *AutoShade User Guide* for a list of these index numbers, and for a list of the color entities contained in the COLORS.TXT file, which is included with the software.

Color settings are given in terms of red, green, and blue, or *RGB*. A setting of 1,1,1 means an equal amount of red, green, and blue, which is white. A setting of 0,0,0 is an absence of light, which is black. The primary colors can be given as numeric values as follows:

Red   = 1,0,0
Green = 0,1,0
Blue   = 0,0,1

You may be prompted on many occasions in RenderMan, to enter a color, such as specular color, or the color of a light. The default may be 1,1,1. Remember the relationship of RGB, and refer to Appendix B of the *AutoShade User Guide* for a list of colors and their RGB values. By using color values, you can simulate colored lights shining on your objects.

Applying shaders to the AutoCAD drawing

RenderMan refers to surface patterns as either shaders or texture maps. A *shader* is a specific surface pattern that is defined in the RenderMan program. A *texture map* is a surface pattern that has been created in AutoCAD, AutoShade, or scanned and imported from another image. This discussion applies to using existing shaders.

When you work with surface patterns, or shaders, you will encounter the term "scalar." A *scalar* in RenderMan is a variable for the specific shader. For example, the wood shader asks for the following scalars:

Ka — ambient light factor
Kd — diffuse light factor
Ks — specular light factor

These terms should be familiar to you from AVE Render and AutoShade. Each shader retains different default settings for the above scalars, and some finishes require few or none of them. The cloth shader requires none of the above settings, whereas the brushed metal shader uses only Ka and Ks because its texture is not diffuse.

The wood shader requires settings called *grain, swirl,* and *swirlfreq* (swirl frequency). These are settings specific to wood and not to any other finish. Other shaders may require *specular color*. This is the color of the reflected (specular) light. Another factor is the *roughness scalar*. A higher number for this variable decreases the specular highlight on a surface.

The first step in applying surface finishes is to load a drawing into AutoCAD. If you created the 3DSHAPES drawing in the previous discussion of AutoShade, load it into AutoCAD. Check to ensure that the current UCS is located at the lower-left, or front corner of the floor. Load RenderMan by picking it from the Render pull-down menu, or entering it at the keyboard. If you load RenderMan from the keyboard, it must be entered as an AutoLISP file, and parentheses must enclose the command. See Chapter 34 for a discussion of AutoLISP. After loading RenderMan, you must use the RMPROP command to specify the shader variables.

NOTE

The RMAN.LSP file must be located in a directory that is in the search path of AutoCAD. It is best to place the file in the ACAD directory or the ACAD\SUPPORT subdirectory.

Command: **(LOAD "RMAN")**

In order for RenderMan to work properly in AutoCAD, pick Preferences in the Render pull-down menu, then pick RMan Prompting in the Settings area of the "Rendering Preferences" dialogue box. This enables the proper types of prompts for RenderMan commands.

Command: **RMPROP** ↵
Surface property name: **TABLE** ↵
AutoCAD color index/Select/〈Find〉: **S** ↵
  Select the entity whose color index is to be used: *(pick the black table)*
  Using color 7.
Air/Color/Displacement/Opaque/Project/Rate/SMooth/SUrface/Tcoord: **SU** ↵
?/Surface shader name 〈nullsurf〉: **WOOD** ↵
Searching shader file . . . done.
Enter scalar "Ka" 〈0.3〉: ↵
Enter scalar "Kd" 〈0.6〉: ↵
Enter scalar "Ks" 〈0.4〉: ↵
Enter scalar "roughness" 〈0.2〉: ↵
Enter scalar "grain" 〈5〉: **20** ↵
Enter scalar "swirl" 〈0.25〉: **1** ↵
Enter scalar "swirlfreq" 〈1〉: **4** ↵
Enter point "c0" 〈current〉: **34,24,18** ↵
Enter point "c1" 〈current〉: **34,52,18** ↵

The previous two points, c0 and c1, determine the direction of the grain.

Name/Enter color "specularcolor" 〈1,1,1〉: ↵
Name/Enter color "lightcolor" 〈0.8,0.6,0.4〉: ↵
Name/Enter color "darkcolor" 〈−1,−1,−1〉: ↵

Wood grain normally has two colors. The light and dark color variables control the hue of the two grain colors.

Write current values to preset file? Yes/〈No〉: ↵
Air/Color/Displacement/Opaque/Project/Rate/SMooth/SUrface/Tcoord: ↵
Surface property location: *(pick a location point in upper-left viewport)* ↵
Command: ↵
Surface property name: **PYRAMID** ↵
AutoCAD color index/Select/〈Find〉: **S** ↵
  Select the entity whose color index is to be used: *(pick the pyramid)*
  Using color 2.
Air/Color/Displacement/Opaque/Project/Rate/SMooth/SUrface/Tcoord: **SU** ↵
?/Surface shader name 〈nullsurf〉: **SHINYMETAL** ↵
Searching shader file . . . done.
Enter scalar "Ka" 〈0.3〉: ↵
Enter scalar "Ks" 〈1〉: ↵
Enter scalar "Kr" 〈1〉: ↵
Enter scalar "roughness" 〈1〉: ↵
Enter string "texturename": ↵
Write current values to preset file? Yes/〈No〉: ↵
Air/Color/Displacement/Opaque/Project/Rate/SMooth/SUrface/Tcoord: ↵
Surface property location: *(pick a location point in upper-left viewport)*

RenderMan shaders have now been assigned to the table and pyramid. The surface property blocks are placed in the location you specified. These blocks contain attributes for all of the variables that you entered.

The RMPROP command contains several options, and the following list provides a brief description of them.

- **Air**—Define how the light changes from the visible surface to the eye.
- **Color**—Change the reflected color of the object.

- **Displacement** — Define the variables of displacement shaders such as threads, gouges (dents in an object), and knurling. These specific shaders are identified in the *User Guide*.
- **Opaque** — Assign opacity to an object. An object that is not 100% opaque does not cast a shadow.
- **Project** — Apply a projected texture map; similar to surface patterns, but applied to any surface. For example, brick, tile, pebble, etc.
- **Rate** — Controls rendering quality. Number 1 is best; higher numbers reduce quality but decrease rendering time.
- **Smooth** — Smooths a 3-D polygon mesh instead of showing facets.
- **Surface** — The heart of RenderMan, this option allows you to specify surface finishes such as metal, wood, rubber, etc.
- **Tcoord** — Specify a texture map or surface shader that requires coordinates.

Placing spotlights in the drawing

RenderMan can create cast shadows from point, directed, and spotlights. A spotlight produces a cone of light, which you define when selecting the light. The cone of light can have an area of *fall-off*, which is a secondary cone outside the first. The area of fall-off in light intensity produces a soft edge to the spotlight. Be sure you pick ASHADE first, then RMAN because RenderMan does not recognize light commands. Place a spotlight in your drawing in the following manner:

```
Command: (LOAD "ASHADE") ↵
Command: (LOAD "RMAN") ↵
Command: LIGHT ↵
Enter light name: S-1 ↵
Point source, Directed, or Spotlight ⟨P⟩: S ↵
Enter light aim point: 42,44,30 ↵
Enter light location: 66,18,90 ↵
Light intensity ⟨1.00⟩: @ ↵
  Second point: END ↵
of (pick the top of the torus)
Name/Light color (RGB) ⟨1.000000,1.000000,1.000000⟩: ↵
Does this light cast a shadow? Yes/⟨No⟩: Y ↵
Depth map size (1-6) ⟨1⟩: 2 ↵
Cone angle ⟨10.00⟩: 20 ↵
Cone delta angle ⟨0.0⟩: 2 ↵
Beam distribution ⟨0.0⟩: ↵
```

The spotlight icon is then placed in your drawing.

Some of the terms used in the LIGHT command above are defined as follows:

- **Light intensity ⟨1.00⟩** — The "@" sign is entered to measure the distance from the spotlight to the first surface that receives full lighting. This is important because the intensity of point and spotlights have a linear *fall-off*, or decrease in intensity, so the intensity of the light should equal the distance to the first object.
- **Depth map size** — The depth map applies to cast shadows, and represents the area of the screen (in pixels) that the shadow affects. The greater the number (1-6), the longer time required to calculate shadows and generate the rendering. A setting of 1 may create a fuzzy shadow.
- **Cone delta angle** — The angle of the area of light fall-off from the edge of the cone to the edge of emitted light.
- **Beam distribution** — This is the rate of fall-off, (decrease in intensity), from the line of sight to the edge of the cone of light.

Preparing the drawing for AutoShade

After you have assigned shaders to the objects and placed spotlights in the drawing, it is necessary to make any new scenes you need. In the scenes, remember to select spotlights if needed. This is the same procedure used to create scenes in AutoShade. After creating new scenes, it is necessary to create a RenderMan setup using the RMSETUP command. A setup contains all of the default settings for the generation of the rendering. These variables can control the speed, quality, and cropped size of the RenderMan display in AutoShade. Use the defaults your first few times until you learn the function, time, and memory requirements of the various settings. Be sure that VIEW3 is displayed on your screen.

━━━━━━━━━━━ PROFESSIONAL TIP ━━━━━━━━━━━

When you are using the ASHADE.LSP and RMAN.LSP programs to prepare a drawing for rendering in AutoShade, you have access to commands that are not used with AVE Render. These commands are used specifically for drawings that will be converted to a filmroll file for use in AutoShade. The SCENE command requires that you select a camera, but cameras are only used for AutoShade. You can quickly place a camera in a perspective view with the VCAMERA command, and its location is the current viewport.

Command: **VCAMERA** ⏎
Enter camera name: **VCAM1** ⏎

The Vcamera icon can be seen in the upper-left viewport.

Command: **SCENE** ⏎
Enter scene name: **SPOT1** ⏎
Select the camera: *(pick VCAM1 in the lower-left viewport)*
Select a light: *(pick D-1)*
Select a light: *(pick P-1)*
Select a light: *(pick S-1)*
Select a light: ⏎
Enter scene location: *(pick the upper-left viewport)*
Scene SPOT1 included.

Now you need to create a RenderMan setup and place its icon in the upper-left viewport.

━━━━━━━━━━━ PROFESSIONAL TIP ━━━━━━━━━━━

More than one RenderMan setup can be created for purposes such as rough draft display, final high-quality display, file generation (PostScript printer file, for example) or experimental settings. Before rendering in AutoShade, select the setup you want displayed.

Use the RMSETUP command as follows:

Command: **RMSETUP** ⏎
RenderMan setup name: **FIRST** ⏎
Fast/Good/〈RenderMan setup options〉: ⏎
Air/Bucket/Crop/Destination/Exposure/Filter/FOrmat/Merge/Rate/Samples: ⏎
RenderMan setup location: *(pick the upper-left viewport)*

The surface finish and RMSETUP blocks are shown in Fig. 26-69.

Fig. 26-69. Surface finish and RMSETUP blocks. The number on the finish block indicates the ACI.

The final step is to create a filmroll file for use in AutoShade.

Command: **FILMROLL** ↵
Enter filmroll file name ⟨default⟩: **3DSHAPES** ↵

It is a good idea to save the drawing after completing the AutoShade and RenderMan functions since you can come back to it later and create new scenes or add lights and cameras.
The RMSETUP options are briefly defined in the following list.
- **Air** – Controls the color of light from a surface to the eye using an atmospheric shader.
- **Bucket** – The size of the screen area in pixels that is processed at one time by the renderer.
- **Crop** – Defines a specific area of the image to render.
- **Destination** – The type of output file, such as PostScript or other video display files.
- **Exposure** – Darken or lighten colors.
- **Filter** – Help correct aliasing, or the *jaggies* (stairstep lines).
- **Format** – Create .RIB, ASCII, or binary files.
- **Merge** – Controls whether the screen changes to black before a new image is displayed.
- **Rate** – Controls the quality of the display. A lower value gives you better quality.
- **Samples** – Controls aliasing by taking samples of each pixel. The more samples per pixel, the better the quality. High Samples and low Rate values produce the best quality rendering, but take the most time to render.

Creating an .RIB file and rendering the scene

After you have created scenes and made a filmroll file, exit AutoCAD and load AutoShade. Load the filmroll file 3DSHAPES and select the scene SPOT1. Preview the scene by selecting Plan View and then Wireframe. Select Fast Shade or Full Shade if you wish to view an AutoShade rendering. These displays do not show RenderMan surfaces or shadows. You first need to create an .RIB file in order to see the RenderMan properties.

Select the RenderMan menu and pick the Render option. The "Render File" dialogue box is displayed. See Fig. 26-70A. Be sure the Create new RIB first box is checked and pick OK. Pick the setup named FIRST in the "Select RenderMan Setup" dialogue box and pick OK. See Fig. 26-70B.

You may change the setup variables by picking Modify. These are the same variables found in the RMSETUP command in AutoCAD. See Fig. 26-70C. If you pick Modify, do not make

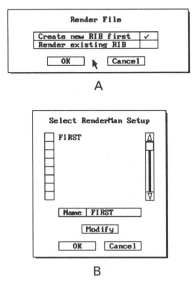

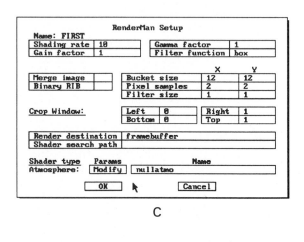

Fig. 26-70. A—The "Render File" dialogue box. B—The "Select RenderMan Setup" dialogue box. C—The "RenderMan Setup" dialogue box.

any changes. Pick OK, then pick OK again at the "Select RenderMan Setup" dialogue box. If you do not pick Modify, pick OK. The "Create RIB Specifications" dialogue box is displayed, Fig. 26-71.

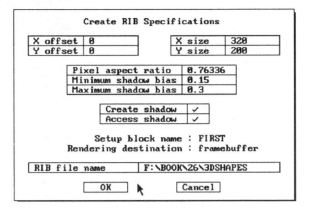

Fig. 26-71. The "Create RIB Specifications" dialogue box allows you to turn shadows on or off.

Be sure that the Create shadow and Access shadow boxes are checked, then pick OK. This begins the rendering. Since you turned off the point and directed lights, the spotlight casts shadows, and the ambient light provides an even light in the scene. See Fig. 26-72. You can change this by adjusting the lights and the Shading Model in the Settings menu.

Fig. 26-72. RenderMan enables you to create scenes with cast shadows.

You can adjust the intensity of lights by picking Light Shaders from the RenderMan menu. A light shader in RenderMan is just a light. The same lights are listed here as in the "Lights" dialogue box, with the addition of spotlights. The "Light Shaders" dialogue box is displayed. See Fig. 26-73A. Then, pick the box by the light you wish to adjust, such as a spotlight. This displays the "Light Shader Specifications" dialogue box. See Fig. 26-73B. Any aspect of the spotlight can be adjusted in this dialogue box.

In order to get a good idea of what the cast shadows look like with only directed or point lights, select Lights from the Settings menu and turn off the lights that you do not need by entering zeros in the intensity boxes. Be sure to pick Render from the RenderMan menu and Create a new .RIB file to render.

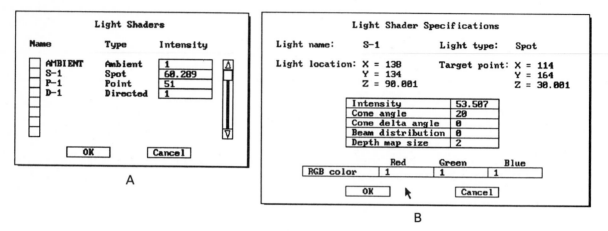

Fig. 26-73. A—Lights are listed in the "Light Shaders" dialogue box. B—Any variables of lights can be changed in the "Light Shader Specifications" dialogue box.

Changing surface properties

Surface properties that were assigned in AutoCAD can be changed in AutoShade. Pick Surface Properties in the RenderMan menu, then pick the surface name you wish to change. In this case, pick Pyramid and then pick OK. The "Surface Property Specification" dialogue box is displayed. See Fig. 26-74.

Locate the Name box for the surface shader type; it should say "shinymetal." Pick the box and the "Available Surface shaders" dialogue box appears from which you can pick the shader you want, such as granite. Be sure all your lights are turned on, then create another .RIB file. Check to ensure that shadows will not be created, then generate a new rendering.

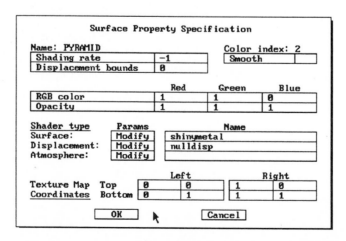

Fig. 26-74. The "Surface Property Specification" dialogue box allows you to change the surface finish in AutoShade.

Texture maps

A *texture map* is the same as a shader, but it is created as a 2-D image and saved as a .TIF file, then converted to a texture map. Consult the *User Guide* for this procedure. An example of a texture map would be a label for a can. The image can be scanned from a photograph, converted to a .TIF file, and saved as a texture. Then the pattern can be placed on any shape in the AutoShade drawing in the form of a "decal," or "projected" onto a variety of surfaces in one of three forms.

A texture map is saved with a .TEX file extension. Several sample textures are found in the subdirectory \SHADE2\TEXTURES. A texture can be specified by using the RMPROP command. You can choose between two types of textures—decal and projection. A *decal texture* is applied as the name implies, as if you are attaching a decal to a surface. It is selected by using the Tcoord option of the RMPROP command. The second type of texture, *projection*, can be applied, or projected to surfaces in three different ways—planar, cylindrical, and spherical.

- **Planar**—Projects a pattern as a flat surface.
- **Cylindrical**—Projects a cylindrical pattern.
- **Spherical**—Projects a spherical pattern.

In order to apply a texture map you must know the coordinate location of the beginning of the pattern, then the coordinate directions in which the pattern is to be applied. These textures are applied with the Project option of the RMPROP command.

RenderMan commands in AutoCAD

The following is a brief discussion of the RenderMan commands available in AutoCAD to set up a drawing for use in AutoShade with rendered surface finishes.

- **RMSETUP**—Allows you to set specific values for rendering attributes that apply to the whole drawing. These values control the speed and quality of rendering, the size of the area rendered, and the type of file to create for the rendering.
- **RMPROP**—Surface finishes and textures (properties) can be applied with this command. Use RMPROP to specify the specific shaders for each geometric entity.
- **RMATTACH**—Use this command to attach a surface finish property block that has been assigned to an existing entity. The selected entity is given the ACI of the specified surface finish. An existing surface finish can be attached to an entire layer or a single geometric entity.
- **RMEDIT**—Allows you to edit an existing surface property block. This command asks you to select a surface block to edit. Pick one of the surface finish icons, not the drawing entity.
- **RMCOPY**—You can copy an existing surface property block and redefine all aspects of the block. Then, select the entity in the drawing that you wish this adjusted finish applied to.
- **RMLIST**—Enables you to list information in the drawing that applies to RenderMan blocks. Some of this information is:
  - ✔Colors in the COLOR.TXT file.
  - ✔List shaders in the SHADER.TXT file.
  - ✔List the name and ACI of the surface property block on a selected entity.
  - ✔Find a surface property block that is attached to a layer.
  - ✔List all RenderMan surface property and finish blocks.
- **RMSCAN**—Ensures that RenderMan Prompting for commands is enabled, and that all AutoLISP routines run correctly if RenderMan setup, surface property and surface finish blocks have been edited by AutoCAD editing commands. Use RMSCAN if you perform any editing of these blocks.
- **DEFAULTS**—If you do not have RenderMan, and are working in AutoShade, you can enable RenderMan prompts for commands such as LIGHT.

PART VI—INTRODUCTION TO AUTOFLIX

AutoFlix™ is an animation program that is packaged with AutoShade. It is loaded by using the automatic installation program provided on disk 1 of the software. This program is similar to those used for AutoCAD and AutoShade. To begin installation, place disk 1 in the floppy disk drive, type "A:INSTALL" and press ENTER. Follow the instructions, and in a few minutes you will be able to experience walk-through animation of your 3-D drawings.

Take a few minutes to read through this section if you plan to use AutoFlix for animation purposes. This section contains useful definitions, guidelines, and tips for using AutoFlix, and will ensure quick success in creating animations.

The purpose of this introduction is to make you aware of the process used to create animations with AutoFlix, and to identify some of the things you should keep in mind when working with AutoFlix and AutoShade files.

The *AutoFlix User Guide* is an excellent reference, and contains eight tutorial lessons designed to step you through a variety of animation procedures. These tutorials begin with a basic walk-through in which the camera moves, and covers a variety of kinetic animations in which different parts of the drawing move. Take some time to work the lessons in the *User Guide.* They will provide you with the knowledge required to create your own exciting animations.

AutoFlix terminology

The process of animation with AutoFlix is easier if you have a basic understanding of some terms that are used in rendering and animation. A few of those terms are:
- **Model** – The 3-D AutoCAD drawing used in the animation.
- **Frame** – An individual picture; similar to a single shot on a roll of film.
- **Rendering** – A drawing that has been colored and shaded.
- **Sequential animation** – Starts at the first frame and runs to the last frame, then begins at the first frame again.
- **Palindromic animation** – Starts at the first frame and runs to the last frame, then goes from the last frame back to the first. Also referred to as "ping-pong animation."
- **Walk-through** – An animation (movie or flic) in which only the camera (your eyes) moves through the model.
- **Kinetic** – An animation in which an object in the model moves.
- **Motion path** – An open or closed polyline that defines either camera or object movement in the model.
- **Movie** – The final animation. It is either a .MOV or .FLI file.

Animation files

When you work with AutoFlix to create animations, you are actually working with three software packages: AutoCAD, AutoShade, and AutoFlix. In the animation process you use and create a variety of files, each designed for a specific purpose. The following list provides you with an overview of each file created, and its purpose.
- **.DWG** – The standard AutoCAD drawing file from which the animation is created.
- **.FLM** – Contains cameras, lights, and scenes. It is used to generate a rendered image used in the animation.
- **.SCR** – A text file that contains instructions used by AutoShade to create a rendering of each frame. Script file creation is discussed in detail in Chapter 29.
- **.MVI** – An AutoFlix file containing a list of renderings to be compiled into the movie.
- **.MOV** – The final movie. This file is read and used by the AFEGA.EXE program that is used for EGA graphics.
- **.FLI** – The final movie, or "flic," is a file that is compatible with the Autodesk Animator Pro and 3D Studio software. The .FLI file is read by the AAPLAY.EXE file used with VGA graphics.

The animation process

If you take a few minutes to plan your use of AutoFlix and establish an organized working environment, you will be surprised at how easy it is to create professional-looking animations. The following list is a condensation of the animation process, and includes several handy tips to assist you in creating movies.
1. Create the AutoCAD 3-D drawing (model).
2. Use AutoShade commands to place lights and cameras in the model.
3. Load the AutoFlix menu file at the Command: prompt to use the animation commands.

    Command: **MENU** ↵
    Menu file name or . for none ⟨current⟩: **AACAD** ↵

The AACAD.MNU file is loaded and replaces the standard AutoCAD menu on the screen. If you get an error message that states that AutoCAD cannot find the AACAD.MNU file, enter the following in response to the Menu file name: prompt (assuming AutoFlix is located in the D: drive):

Menu file name or . for none ⟨current⟩: **D:\AFLIX\AACAD** ⏎

────── PROFESSIONAL TIP ──────

You can ensure that AutoCAD always finds the AACAD.MNU file by copying it to the AutoCAD directory as follows. This example assumes the names of C:\ACAD12 for the AutoCAD directory and D:\AFLIX for the AutoFlix directory.

Command: **SH** ⏎
OS Command: **COPY D:\AFLIX\AACAD.MNU C:\ACAD12** ⏎

This example uses the SHELL command in AutoCAD, which allows you to use one operating system (OS) command while at the Command: prompt. The same function can be accomplished at a DOS prompt as follows:

C:\ACAD12⟩ **COPY D:\AFLIX\AACAD.MNU** ⏎

The AutoFlix menu file is now located in the AutoCAD directory for easy access.

---

4. Use AutoFlix commands to create motion paths for the movie. Script files are automatically created.
5. Use AutoShade to create shaded renderings of each movie frame. This is an automatic process that uses the script file (.SCR) created by AutoFlix. AutoShade renders each frame and generates a rendering file (.RND) of each frame.

────── PROFESSIONAL TIP ──────

The AutoShade rendering process can be lengthy, depending on the complexity of your drawing and the speed of your computer. This process also creates a rendering file for each frame, and possibly a filmroll (.FLM) file for each frame if you are creating kinetic animation. Therefore, if you have a 50 frame movie, one rendered frame of 40,000 bytes translates to 2,000,000 bytes, or 2MB of hard disk space! (50 x 40,000 = 2MB).

Before you begin the animation process, be sure that you have ample hard disk space for the rendering files. You can test this by entering AutoShade, turning on the record mode and creating a full shade rendering. Check the file size and multiply by the number of frames in your movie.

---

6. Create the movie file by using the appropriate command for your graphics display device. If you have EGA graphics, use the AFEGA.EXE program to create the movie (.MOV) file. If you use VGA graphics, use the FILMAKER.EXE program to generate the flic (.FLI) file. The .MOV and .FLI files are the completed animations and do not require the use of the rendering files (.RND). The .RND files can be deleted after the movie is created, thus freeing valuable hard disk space.
7. Play the .MOV file with the AFEGA command, or play the .FLI file with the AAPLAY command.

Hints for efficient movie production

During the animation process using AutoFlix, a variety of files are created and several different programs are used. Files and their sizes grow and multiply rapidly, and are directly related to the size of the original AutoCAD 3-D drawing. You may lose track of where files are located unless you practice some good planning and housekeeping. Keep in mind these hints as you begin your animations.

- What is the purpose of the animation? The answer to this should determine the amount of detail needed in the AutoCAD drawing.
- If certain sides of the 3-D model will not be seen in the animation, do not put 3-D faces or surfaces on them.
- Keep the number of 3-D faces to a minimum in the 3-D drawing. Remember, each face must be rendered by AutoShade.
- Control surface modeling detail and faces by making wise use of the AutoCAD variables SURFTAB1 and SURFTAB2.
- Place the AutoFlix and AutoShade directories in your path statement. The path statement is usually found in the AUTOEXEC.BAT file, and provides a list of places for DOS to look when searching for files. Read Chapter 35 for a discussion of DOS commands, and see Appendix C for examples of AUTOEXEC.BAT files and the proper use of the PATH command.
- If AutoShade occupies a separate directory than the AutoCAD program, copy the .SCR and .MVI files created by AutoFlix to the AutoShade directory. These are the two files that are created after instructing AutoFlix to generate a specific number of frames along a camera path.
- Delete all .RND files after the movie has been created and runs properly. If you want to save some of the files for future use, transfer them to another directory or hard drive in order to free the space for future animations.

── PROFESSIONAL TIP ──

The AutoShade directory on your hard drive is probably the one that will get the most work, so be sure that drive has plenty of space for the rendering files. The planning that has been alluded to in the previous hints, is an effort to make sure that wherever you choose to work on the hard drive to create your animation, the following files must be either located there, or be accessible by DOS from that directory.

- ☐ Script and movie instruction files—.SCR and .MVI.
- ☐ AutoShade program.
- ☐ Filmroll file (.FLM) of the 3-D drawing.
- ☐ AFEGA.EXE command.
- ☐ FILMAKER.EXE command.
- ☐ AAPLAY.EXE command.

Using animations

You may be wondering what the attraction of animations can be, especially if they can take so long to generate and must be based on first constructing a 3-D drawing. Animation is far more intuitive than two-dimensional drawing. If you have completed a project or assignment that is a 3-D model, animation is just a few steps away. Those steps also involve a couple of processes that are automatic, but they may take a long time, especially if the 3-D drawing is complex. This aspect may also seem a negative one, but remember, the computer can work while you are eating, sleeping, or performing other tasks. Let it do the drudgery overnight, and you can return to a professional animation in the morning. Try animation. It is not only a good learning and production tool, but is a lot of fun.

CHAPTER TEST

Write your answers in the spaces provided.

1. What three formats of raster images can be imported into AutoCAD? _____

_____

2. What command is used to insert a file that is in the CompuServe image format? _____

_____

3. Which raster system variable controls the width and height of the imported image? __

_____

4. Why would you set the RITHRESH variable? _____

5. After a raster image is inserted into an AutoCAD drawing, it is composed of what type of AutoCAD entity? _____

6. Name the two commands that enable you to import and export PostScript files in AutoCAD.

_____

7. When using the PSFILL command, what is the numerical value range of grays that are available? _____

8. What is the three-letter extension given to PostScript files when they are exported using the proper command? _____

9. What must you do to a PostScript font shape (.PFB) file so it can be used as AutoCAD font?

_____

_____

10. Define the following rendering terms:

Ambient light— _____

_____

Distant light— _____

_____

Point light— _____

_____

Specular factor— _____

_____

Roughness— _____

Diffuse light— _____

_____

11. What is a scene composed of in AVE Render? _____

_____

12. Which dialogue box allows you to specify the shininess and roughness of a surface? __

_____

13. What is the relationship between the numerical value or roughness and the size of the highlight on a shiny surface? _____

_____

_____

14. What command allows you to crop an image by pixels and save it as a file? What types of files can it be saved as? _____

_____

15. What is the function of the AutoShade program? _____

_____

16. What types of lights can you use in AutoShade? _____

_____

17. What is important to know about a point light and its intensity? _____

_____

18. How many cameras can be in one scene? _____

19. Which command enables you to place a camera at the current viewpoint?_____

20. What elements compose a scene? _____

21. What type of file must you load into AutoShade to create a rendering, and what is the DOS extension of this file? _____

22. Name the four pull-down menus associated with AutoShade. _____

_____

23. If you operate AutoShade with cursor keys, which key allows you to select menu items?

_____

24. Name three steps needed to select a filmroll file and scene to use in AutoShade. _____

_____

_____

_____

25. When might you want to display a plan view? _____

_____

_____

26. Why should you display a wireframe view before producing a rendering? _____

_____

_____

27. What purpose does the Fast Shade option serve? _____

_____

28. How can you gauge the time a fast shade will take? _____

_____

29. If the Record mode is on, when does it take effect? _____

_____

30. How can you list all .RND files and then select one to be displayed? _____
_____

31. Why is it wise to record renderings that you may need later? _____
_____

32. What type of display does the Make Slide option in the Display menu create? Where can it be displayed? _____
_____
_____

33. How is the Hard Copy option different from Record? _____
_____
_____

34. How are lighting and shading factors affected by the Stretch contrast setting? _____
_____

35. What feature does the Specular factor option control? _____
_____

36. What is Z shading and why is it used? _____
_____
_____
_____

37. What aspect of an AutoShade drawing do the Expert Specifications affect? _____
_____

38. How do you instruct AutoShade to search for and calculate intersecting surfaces? _____
_____
_____

39. What is the purpose of clipping? _____
_____

40. What is the difference between stereoscope display and crossed-eye display? _____
_____

41. What is the function of RenderMan? _____
_____

42. What color has the RGB numbers of 0,1,0? _____

43. What is the difference between a shader and a scalar? _____
_____
_____

44. What command allows you to assign a surface finish to an entity? _____

45. What shape of emitted light does a spotlight produce? _____

46. What is fall-off? _____

47. Why would more than one RenderMan setup be created? _____

_____

_____

48. What new blocks (icons) are inserted on the screen when producing a RenderMan scene?

_____

49. List the steps required to produce a RenderMan rendering, assuming you just entered AutoShade. _____

_____

_____

_____

50. What is a texture map, and what file extension does it have? _____

_____

_____

_____

DRAWING PROBLEMS

1. Locate some sample raster files with the extension .GIF, .PCX, or .TIF. These files can be copied from the Release 12 Bonus CD, and are often included as samples with other software. They can also be downloaded from computer bulletin boards and information services such as CompuServe. Create a subdirectory on your hard disk drive (with the permission of your instructor or supervisor) and copy the raster files to the new subdirectory. If the raster files are large, use file compression software, such as PKware, to pack the images into smaller files. Keep backup floppy disk copies of the compressed files.

2. Choose one of your smaller raster files and import it into AutoCAD using the GIFIN, PCXIN, or TIFFIN commands.
   A. Insert the image so that it fills the entire screen.
   B. Undo and insert the image again using a scale factor that fills half of the screen with the image.
   C. Set RIASPECT to a different value such as 0.8333 for a display device set to 320 x 200 mode.
   D. Create a layer named RASTER. Create a second layer named OBJECT and give it any color you like. Set the current layer to RASTER.
   E. Import the same image next to the previous one at the same scale factor.
   F. Set the current layer to OBJECT and use any AutoCAD drawing commands to trace the outline of the second raster image.
   G. Turn off the OBJECT layer and erase all of the raster image. Turn the OBJECT layer on.
   H. Save the drawing as A:P26-2.

3. This problem requires that you use AutoCAD's RASTERIN commands to import raster files, then trace objects in each file and save the objects as blocks or wblocks to be used on other drawings.
   A. Find as many raster files as you can that contain simple objects, shapes, or figures that you might use in other drawings, and save these to diskettes or a hard drive directory.
   B. Create a prototype drawing containing layers such as those in problem 2.
   C. Import each raster file into AutoCAD using the appropriate command. Set a new layer and trace the shape or objects in the files using AutoCAD drawing commands.
   D. Delete the raster information, keeping only the new lines of the traced object.
   E. Save the object as a block or wblock using an appropriate file-naming system.
   F. After all blocks have been created, insert each one into a single drawing and label each with its name. Include a path if necessary.

G. Print or plot the final drawing.

H. Save the drawing as A:P26-3.

4. In this problem, you will create a style sheet to be used for drawing standards or a presentation sheet for a detail, assembly, or pictorial drawing.

A. Begin a new drawing and name it P26-4. The drawing should be set up to A-size dimensions and the orientation should be portrait, or with the long side oriented vertically.

B. Create at least two new text styles using PostScript fonts.

C. Draw one or more closed shapes, such as rectangles. Use the PSFILL command to place a pattern of your choice inside the shapes.

D. Use the PostScript text styles to place title and related text on your drawing. See the example below. Add other graphics or text as desired.

E. Save the drawing as A:P26-4, then use the PSOUT command to save the file as P26-4.EPS.

F. Plot the drawing on a plotter or laser printer. If you have a PostScript printer, generate a printed copy of the .EPS file.

5. Begin a new drawing named P26-5 using P26-4 as the prototype.

A. Insert the blocks you created in Problem 3 into your style sheet. Arrange them in any order you wish.

B. Add any notes or explanatory text you need to identify this drawing as a sheet of library shapes. Be sure each shape is identified with its file name and location (path).

C. Print or plot the drawing.

D. Save the drawing with the current name (P26-5), then create a PSOUT file using the same name.

E. Get a PostScript print of the file.

6. In this problem, you will draw some basic 3-D shapes, place lights in the drawing, and then render it.

A. Begin a new drawing and name it P26-6.

B. Draw the following 3-D shapes using the layer names and colors as indicated.

Shape	Layer Name	Color
Box	BOX	Red
Pyramid	PYRAMID	Yellow
Wedge	WEDGE	Green
Cone	CONE	Cyan
Dome	DOME	Blue
Dish	DISH	Magenta
Sphere	SPHERE	White

   C. Draw the shapes in a circular layout as shown in the example below. Each shape should be one unit in size.

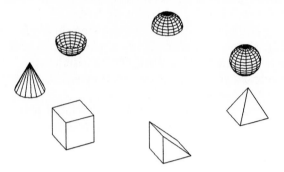

   D. Place a point light in the center of the objects, 3 units above them.

   E. Place two distant lights as shown below, having target points in the center of the objects. Light D-1 should be located at Z = 3, and light D-2 should be located at Z = 2.

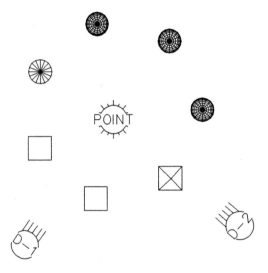

   F. Render the drawing.

   G. Save the image as a .GIF file named P26-6.

   H. Save the drawing as A:P26-6.

7. Open drawing P26-6. Generate the following scenes and renderings using the light values given. See the illustration below for view orientations.

View	Scene	Ambient	Point	D-1	D-2
View1	One	.7	2	1	1
View2	Two	.3	2	0	1
View3	Three	0	5	0	0

   A. Create a surface finish on the sphere with a specular factor of 1, diffuse factor of 0, and roughness of .1. Name it SPHERE1.

   B. Create a second surface finish for the sphere named SPHERE2 with a specular factor of .7, diffuse of .2, and roughness of.3

   C. Create a third surface finish for the sphere named SPHERE3 with a roughness of .7, specular factor of .5, and a diffuse factor of .5.

   D. Set finish SPHERE1 as current and render scene ONE.

   E. Set finish SPHERE2 as current and render scene ONE.

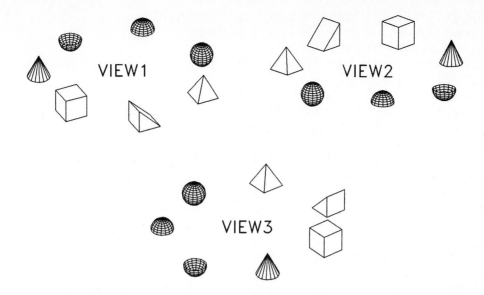

F. Set finish SPHERE3 as current and render scene ONE.

G. Save the drawing as A:P26-7. Create a filmroll file and save it as P26-7.

8. Open Problem 24-8. Place a point light directly over the table, and a distant light to one side and below the table top. Place a second distant light opposite the first, and above the table. Render the drawing using a variety of lights and intensities. Create two surface finishes for the table. One should be shiny and the other matte. Render with each surface finish. Save the drawing as P26-8.

9. Open Problem 24-9, 10, or 11. Place two point lights above the object, one to each side. Place three distant lights at positions of your choosing. Create four scenes using four different DVIEW settings. Save each DVIEW display as a VIEW. Each scene should use a different view, one point light and one or two distant lights. Render the drawing using a variety of lights and intensities. Save the drawing as P26-9.

AUTOSHADE

10. Load Problem 24-1, 2, 3, or 4 into AutoCAD. Use the following instructions to create an AutoShade filmroll file.

A. Locate a point light source (P-1) at an elevation above the object.

B. Locate two distant lights, D-1 and D-2, slightly above the elevation of the object. The horizontal angle between these two lights should be approximately 130°.

C. Create a DVIEW looking midway between the two light sources and about 8 ft. away from the object. Name the view ONE.

D. Locate a second view 6 ft. from the object and halfway between view ONE and light D-1. Name this view TWO.

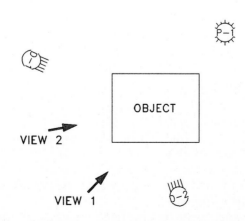

E. Create SCENE-1 to include P-1, D-1, and view ONE.
F. Create SCENE-2 to include D-1, D-2, and view TWO.
G. Save the filmroll file as P26-10.
H. Exit AutoCAD and load AutoShade. Produce a plan view and wireframe view of SCENE-1 and SCENE-2.
I. Use the Expert menu to turn the Perspective option on.
J. Set the Record mode to on and produce fast shade renderings of SCENE-1 and SCENE-2 named P26-10A and P26-10B.
K. Set the Record mode to on and create full shade renderings of SCENE-1 and SCENE-2.

11. Load the P26-10 file, SCENE-2, into AutoShade and do the following:
A. Change the camera distance to 12 feet.
B. Change the camera lens to a 135 mm.
C. Produce a plan view to see if the entire object is in the field of view. If it is not, adjust the camera lens.
D. Produce a wireframe display.
E. Create a slide of the wireframe display.
F. Turn Record mode on.
G. Generate a fast shade and a full shade. Name them P26-11A and P26-11B.
H. Change the light intensity of D-1 to be twice as bright as D-2.
I. Display a fast shade and full shade and name them P26-11C and P26-11D.
J. Use the Replay selection to view all four previous displays. Compare the lighting.

12. Load the P26-10 file, SCENE-1, into AutoShade and do the following:
A. Turn the Stretch contrast mode off.
B. Set the light intensity for D-1 to twice as bright as P-1.
C. Set the shading model factors to achieve a shiny surface.
D. Turn off the Z shading option.
E. Set the Record mode on.
F. Produce a fast shade of the drawing and name it P26-12A.
G. Reset the lighting so P-1 is twice as bright as D-1.
H. Set the shading model factors to achieve a matte surface.
I. Produce a fast shade of the drawing and name it P26-12B.
J. Use the Replay selection to view the two files again and compare the lighting.

13. Load Problem 24-17, 18, or 19 into AutoCAD and do the following:
A. Create four scenes using AutoShade commands. Two scenes should be from outside the house and two should be inside the house.
B. Each scene should have one point light and two or more distant lights.
C. Use DVIEW Zoom's wide angle lenses for the scenes inside the house.
D. Use the problem number, P26-13, as the filmroll file name.
E. Save the drawing file as P26-13A.
Exit AutoCAD and load AutoShade, and perform the following:
F. Create slides using a wireframe view of each scene.
G. Record all fast and full shaded renderings. Name them P26-13B, C, D, etc.
H. Use the Replay All selection in the Display menu to view all of the renderings created in this problem.

RENDERMAN

When working with the following problems, be sure to load the ASHADE.LSP and RMAN.LSP files before you begin working with cameras and lights. This enables you to work with the lights and cameras used by AutoShade and RenderMan.

14. Load Problem 24-2, 9, or 10 into AutoCAD. Display the drawing in the plan view.
A. Apply a surface finish of shiny metal to the object.
B. Place a spotlight in the scene, 2′ away. Place one point light directly over the part.
C. Locate a camera to achieve the best view of the part. Use the VCAMERA command.
D. Create a scene and a filmroll file.
E. Load AutoShade and create an .RIB file with cast shadows and render it.
F. Lower the intensity of the ambient and point light and create a second rendering.

15. Load Problem 24-13 into AutoCAD. Display the drawing in the plan view.
    A. Apply a surface finish of rubber to the object.
    B. Place a spotlight in the scene, 4' away. Place one point light directly over the part.
    C. Locate a camera to achieve the best view of the part, at least 10' away. Use the VCAMERA command.
    D. Create a scene and a filmroll file.
    E. Turn Record mode on.
    F. Load AutoShade and create an .RIB file with cast shadows and render it.
    G. Lower the intensity of the ambient and point light and create a second rendering.
    H. Turn off the ambient light, and generate another .RIB file.
    I. Play back the rendering files you created.

16. Load Problem 24-5, 6, 7, or 8 into AutoCAD. Display the drawing in the plan view.
    A. Create an AutoShade layout with at least two directed lights, one point light, and two spotlights. Locate one directed and one spotlight with the VLIGHT command.
    B. Create two scenes. Use the point light in both, and different directed and spotlights in each scene.
    C. In one scene, use cast shadows for both directed lights and the one spotlight. In the second scene, use cast shadows for one of the spotlights only.
    D. Locate two cameras in the scene with the VCAMERA command. Use a different camera for each scene.
    E. Assign the wood surface finish to the object. Use defaults for the wood shader. Make the scene and the filmroll file.
    F. Create an .RIB file in AutoShade without cast shadows, and one with cast shadows.
    G. Generate renderings that can be played back at a later date.
    H. If you have a PostScript printer, generate a hardcopy of the rendering.
    I. Adjust the scalars for the wood grain and swirl and create another rendering.

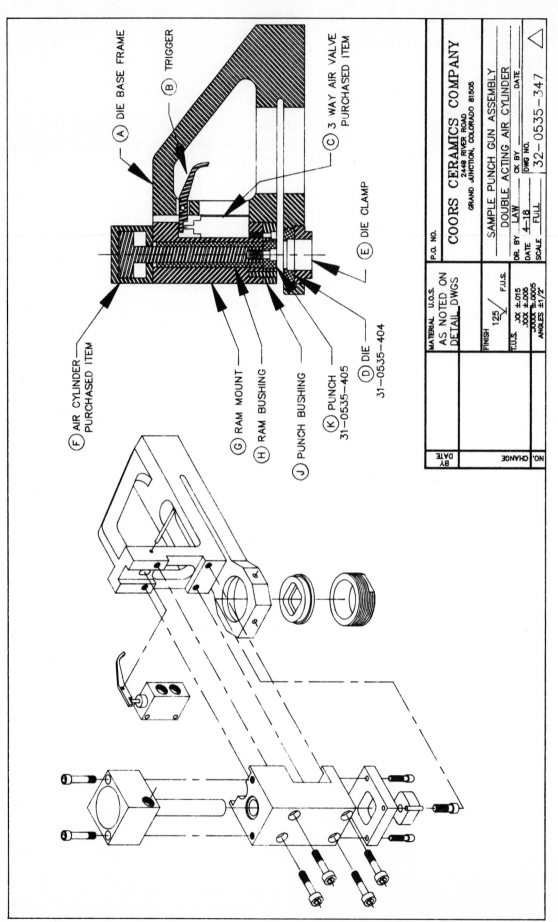

Punch gun assembly.   (Autodesk, Inc.)

Chapter 27

PLOTTING, PRINTING, AND MULTIVIEW DRAWING LAYOUT

Learning objectives

After completing this chapter, you will be able to:
- ☐ Determine the scale factor of a drawing.
- ☐ Generate a quick print of the screen display.
- ☐ Create a multiview drawing using the MVIEW, XREF, and VPLAYER commands.
- ☐ Identify options and variables found in the PLOT command.
- ☐ Print and plot a drawing.

The advent of CAD brought about two types of drawings: hardcopy and softcopy. A *hardcopy* is the paper drawing produced by a printer or pen plotter. It is called hard because it has substance and can be held and felt. *Softcopy,* on the other hand, is a screen display. It is called soft because it has no substance. If the power goes off, the softcopy drawing is gone.

AutoCAD supports two types of hardcopy devices: printers and pen plotters. Printers, usually laser or dot matrix, produce check prints, although some large-format models produce high-resolution plots. Pen plots are inked line drawings. They are high-quality drawings that can be used for check prints or final, reproducible plots on vellum and polyester film. Examples of printer and pen plots are shown in Fig. 27-1.

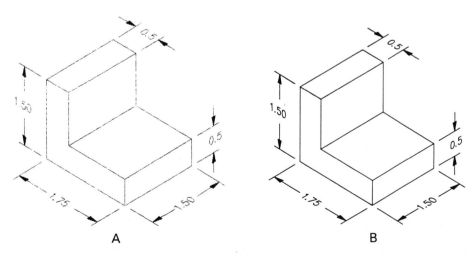

Fig. 27-1. A printer plot is used for check prints, while a pen plot is higher quality and good for final plots.

USING THE PLOT COMMAND | ARM 13 |

The PLOT command used to produce these plots is found in the File pull-down menu. PLOT is also located in the Root Menu, or may be typed at the Command: prompt. The "Plot Configuration" dialogue box is displayed when you enter the PLOT command if the CMDDIA system variable is set to 1. Plotting prompts are issued at the command line when CMDDIA is 0. To issue plot prompts at the command line, set CMDDIA to 0 like this:

Command: **CMDDIA** ⏎
New value for CMDDIA ⟨1⟩: **0** ⏎

The PLOT command asks for the part of the current drawing you want to plot, then allows you to change a variety of plotting specifications. You can choose to change the specifications or leave them as they are. When the plot is finished, AutoCAD returns you to the drawing editor.

Choose what to plot

After entering the PLOT command, decide the part of the drawing you want to plot.

Command: **PLOT** ⏎
What to plot — Display, Extents, Limits, View or Window ⟨D⟩:

Press ENTER to plot the screen display. Type the first letter of any other option to change the selection. The following describes the function of each option.
- **Display (D).** This request prints or plots the current screen display.
- **Extents (E).** The Extents option prints or plots only that area of the drawing in which objects (entities) are drawn. Before using this option, zoom the extents to include all recently edited entities to check exactly what will be plotted.
  Border lines around your drawing may be clipped off if they are at the extreme edges of the screen. This often happens because you are requesting the plotter to plot at the extreme edge of its active area.
- **Limits (L).** This option plots everything inside your drawing limits.
- **View (V).** This option plots views saved with the VIEW command. AutoCAD prompts you for the name. The view you enter does not have to be displayed on the screen.
- **Window (W).** This option allows you to pick two opposite corners of a window around the portion of the drawing to be plotted. These can be chosen with the pointing device or entered as coordinates at the keyboard. If the window is defined close to an entity, some lines may be clipped off in your plot. If this happens, adjust the window next time you plot.

--- NOTE ---

The FILEDIA system variable controls the display of any file name dialogue box regardless of the CMDDIA setting.

SETTING THE PLOT SPECIFICATIONS | ARM 13 |

After choosing the portion of the drawing to plot, you can change the default settings for the plot specifications. The first set of information is based on the type of printer or plotter you are using, and is controlled by the specification you set when configuring AutoCAD. These specifications might read like this for a laser printer:

Number of copies = 1
Resolution in dots per inch = 300
Paper tray selected is Letter
Plot device is Hewlett-Packard (PCL) LaserJet ADI 4.2 — by Autodesk
Description: (nnnn)

The next information has to do with the plot:

> Plot will NOT be written to a selected file
> Sizes are in Inches and the style is portrait
> Plot origin is at (0.00,0.00)
> Plotting area is 8.00 wide by 10.50 high (MAX size)
> Plot is NOT rotated
> Hidden lines will NOT be removed
> Plot will be scaled to fit available area
> Do you want to change anything? (No/Yes/File/Save) ⟨N⟩: ↵

These specifications may be suitable for some of your drawings. If so, press ENTER to accept the default "NO" response. AutoCAD displays a message similar to this:

> Effective plotting area: 8.00 wide by 5.77 high
> Position paper in plotter.
> Press RETURN to continue or S to Stop for hardware setup

Press ENTER to send the drawing to the printer or plotter, or enter "S" to stop. If you press ENTER, AutoCAD gives you some information about the data being sent, tells you when the plot is complete, and then issues the Command: prompt. Press the F1 key to get back to the drawing editor. Entering "S" to do hardware setup gives you this instruction:

> Do hardware setup now.
> Press RETURN to continue:

Simply press ENTER when you are ready and the drawing is sent to the printer or plotter.

Answer "Y" to the Do you want to change anything? prompt if you want to change any of the values. First you get some questions asking for changes to your printer or plotter configuration. You can respond with changes or press ENTER to keep defaults. This example shows how you would change the scale to make any size drawing fit on the paper.

> Write the plot to a file? ⟨N⟩ ↵
> Size units (Inches or Millimeters) ⟨I⟩: ↵
> Plot origin in Inches ⟨0.00,0.00⟩: ↵
>
> Standard values for plotting size
> Size   Width   Height
> MAX   8.00   10.50
> Enter the Size or Width,Height (in Inches) ⟨MAX⟩: ↵
>
> Rotate plot clockwise 0/90/180/270 degrees ⟨0⟩: ↵
> Remove hidden lines? ⟨N⟩ ↵
> Specify scale by entering:
> Plotted Inches = Drawing Units or Fit or ? ⟨1 = 1⟩: **F** ↵
> Position paper in plotter.
> Press RETURN to continue or S to Stop for hardware setup ↵

— NOTE —

> For some models of plotters, you will be prompted for a Plotter Port to Time-Out value. Accept the default value by pressing ENTER.

Additional setup for a pen plotter

After responding "Y" to change plot specifications for a pen plotter, the screen shown in Fig. 27-2 appears. Here, you can change pen numbers, linetypes, and pen speeds.

```
Enter values   blank=Next value, Cn=Color n, S=Show current values
X=Exit

Entity      Pen    Line    Pen         Entity     Pen    Line    Pen
Color       No.    Type    Speed       Color      No.    Type    Speed

1 (red)     1      0       36          9          1      0       36

2 (yellow)  2      0       36          10         2      0       36

3 (green)   3      0       36          11         3      0       36

4 (cyan)    4      0       36          12         4      0       36

5 (blue)    5      0       36          13         5      0       36

6 (magenta) 6      0       36          14         6      0       36

7 (white)   7      0       36          15         7      0       36

8           8      0       36
Line types:        0 = continuous line

                   1 = ..........................

                   2 = _____

                   3 = _ _ _ _ _ _ _ _ _ _

                   4 = _._._._._._._._._

                   5 = __ _ __ _ __ _ __ _

                   6 = ___ _ ___ _ ___ _

Do you want to change any of the above parameters? (N)
```

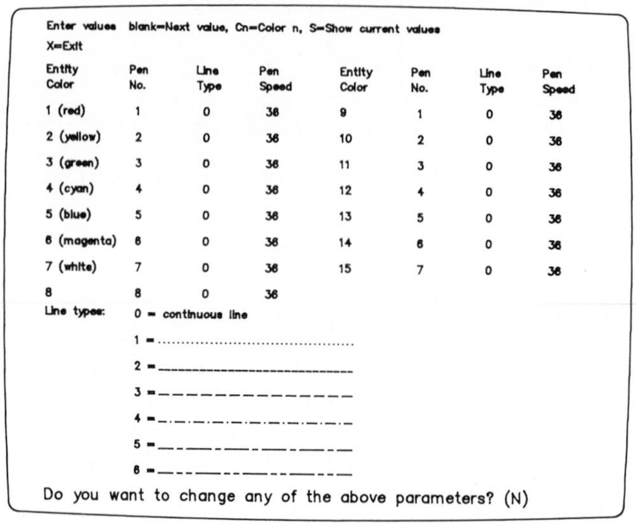

Fig. 27-2. Plot specifications, such as pen number, linetype, and pen speed, can be modified.

The possible responses, shown above in the Enter values: prompt, are defined as follows:
- **Blank (ENTER or space bar).** Uses the current value displayed in brackets and moves to the next one. AutoCAD stays in this routine until you move to the next specification by exiting.
- **Cn (color number).** You can proceed to a specific color and set that pen number by typing "Cn". The "n" represents the number of the specific color you wish to change. To assign pen number 4 to the green color, first type "C3". The screen displays the Pen number: prompt for color 3 (green). Now enter the plotter carousel or pen rack number of the green pen.
- **S (Show values).** Allows you to check the values just entered. Typing "S" displays an updated list of pen numbers, linetypes, and pen speeds.
- **X (Exit).** This completes the pen and linetype routine and moves to the next plot specification.

The display of linetypes in this prompt depends on the type of plotter you have configured. Normally, do not specify anything but a continuous linetype. Your AutoCAD drawing will already have linetypes set by the software.

Create a plot file

Some computers allow you to continue working on a drawing while another routine is being handled by the computer. This feature of some powerful computers, called *multitasking,* runs more than one program without a noticeable decline in efficiency. The PLOT command allows you to create a file that can be used in this manner. Some computer programs plot a list of files without any additional plotting information input by the user.

    Write the plot to a file? ⟨N⟩: **Y** ↵

When the scaling routine is completed (discussed in one of the following sections), you are asked to name the plot file if FILEDIA is 0. If FILEDIA is 1, the "Create Plot File" dialogue box is displayed. Here you can enter the plot file name.

    Enter file name for plot ⟨current⟩:

You either assign a different name to the plot file or accept the current name by pressing ENTER. AutoCAD assigns the plot file a .PLT extension. The file is now ready to be used by other programs. With some plotters, PLT files can be plotted directly from the DOS prompt.

    Computer network systems operating off a central server also use PLT files in a plot queue. A *plot queue* is a lineup or list of files waiting to be plotted. The PLT files can be loaded in the queue and started while users on the network continue other work.

Size of the drawing units

This prompt allows you to specify inches or millimeters.

Size units (Inches or Millimeters) 〈current〉:

The "current" size is accepted by pressing ENTER. If needed, select the other by typing "I" or "M."

Origin of the plot

The origin of a pen plotter is the lower-left corner of the paper. To begin the drawing at that point, press ENTER. The default values of the prompt should appear as shown here.

Plot origin in units 〈0.00,0.00〉:

To position your drawing away from the origin, enter the coordinate values at the prompt. Put a comma between the X and Y values. For example, to move the drawing four units to the right and three units above the plotter origin, enter:

Plot origin in units 〈0.00,0.00〉: **4,3** ↵

The origin of a printer is the upper-left corner of the paper. The coordinates above move the drawing four units to the right and three units down. The "units" in this prompt refers to the units specified in the Size units: prompt.

Size of the plot

The next prompt displays the plot sizes available from the configured plotter. You can choose one of these or enter a size of your own, as long as it is smaller than the maximum (MAX) size indicated in the list. The sizes listed will vary according to the brand and size of plotter you have.

Standard values for plotting size

Size	Width	Height
A	10.50	8.00
B	16.00	10.00
C	21.00	16.00
D	33.00	21.00
E	43.00	33.00
MAX	64.50	36.00
USER	17.00	22.00

Enter the Size or Width,Height (in units) 〈current〉:

Remember that all plotters require margins around the edges of the paper. This space allows for the plotter's grit wheels, clamps, or other holding devices. Therefore, the available size may be smaller than the standard ANSI sizes. Fig. 27-3 shows standard paper sizes and the approximate available plotting area.

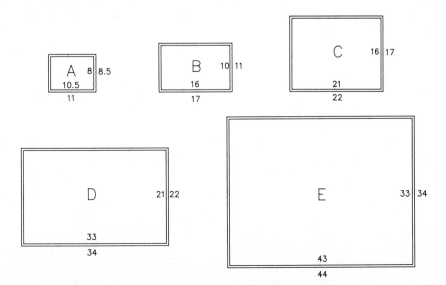

Fig. 27-3. Standard paper sizes and approximate plotting areas.

The MAX size is the largest size paper your plotter can handle. The USER values indicate the last size entered. To select a size shown on the list, type the letter. Simply press ENTER to accept the default size. For example, to use an 11 x 17 sheet of paper, the response would be:

Enter the Size or Width,Height (in units)⟨current⟩: **17,11** ↵

Be sure to enter the width (X dimension) of the paper first.

Rotate the plot

In AutoCAD, the horizontal screen measurement relates to the long side of the paper. This orientation is known as *landscape* format. However, you might create a drawing, form, or chart that must be placed in *portrait* format. The long side is positioned vertically. The next prompt allows you to make the change from landscape to portrait.

Rotate plot clockwise 0/90/180/270 degrees ⟨0⟩:

Plots can be rotated in 90 degree increments. If you type "90" the lower-left corner of your drawing is placed at the upper-left corner of the paper. Fig. 27-4 shows the effects of a 90 degree clockwise direction.

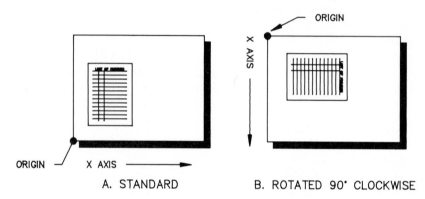

Fig. 27-4. Effects of a 90 degree clockwise rotation.

Pen width

You can increase the efficiency of AutoCAD and your plotter by knowing the widths of the pens. This value governs how many passes the pen must make when filling in polylines, trace lines, and solids. The response entered at the Pen width: prompt is measured by the units entered at the Size units: prompt.

Adjust for pen width in area fills

The Adjust area fill boundaries for pen width?: specification is one that most users seldom change. A "Y" response directs AutoCAD to move the pen inside the boundaries of filled areas one-half the pen width. Do this only if the nature of the plotted material requires extreme accuracy. Pressing ENTER instructs the plotter to place the center of the pen on the exact coordinates given.

Remove hidden lines

The hidden line removal function works the same as the HIDE command. If used with a detailed drawing, it may require a long wait on your part.

Remove hidden lines? ⟨N⟩

Answer "Y" to this prompt *only* if you must have hidden lines removed.

Determining drawing scale factors

You should have already established the scale factor of the drawing by the time you are ready to plot. However, if you haven't, it isn't too late to do so; you will have to spend some time updating dimensions and changing text styles. Scale factors are important because the number is used to ensure that text, dimension text and arrows, and tick marks are plotted or printed at the proper height. The scale factor is multiplied by the desired plotted text height to obtain the AutoCAD text height. The scale factor is also used in the DIMSCALE dimension variable.

The scale factor is always the reciprocal of the drawing scale. For example, if you wish to plot a drawing at a scale of $1/2'' = 1''$, calculate the scale factor as follows:

$1/2'' = 1''$
$.5'' = 1''$
$1/.5 = \mathbf{2}$ (The scale factor is 2.)

An architectural drawing that is to be plotted at a scale of $1/4'' = 1'\text{-}0''$ would have a scale factor calculated as follows:

$1/4'' = 1'\text{-}0''$
$.25'' = 12''$
$12/.25 = \mathbf{48}$ (The scale factor is 48.)

The scale factor of a civil engineering drawing that has a scale of $1'' = 60'$ is calculated as:

$1'' = 60'$
$1'' = (60 \times 12) = \mathbf{720}$ (The scale factor is 720.)

When the scale factor of any drawing has been determined, you should then calculate the height of the text in AutoCAD. If text height is to be plotted at $1/8''$, it should *not* be drawn at that height. For example, if you are working on a civil drawing with a scale of $1'' = 60'$ (scale factor = 720), text drawn $1/8''$ high appears as a dot. Remember, the drawing you are working on in AutoCAD is 720 times larger than it will be when you plot it at the proper scale. Therefore, you must multiply the text height by 720 in order to get text that appears in correct proportion on the screen. In this case, if you want $1/8''$ high text to appear correctly on your screen, calculate the AutoCAD height as follows:

$1/8'' \times 720$
$.125'' \times 720 = \mathbf{90}$ (The proper height of the text is 90.)

Scale factors, text heights, and DIMSCALE values should be determined *before* beginning a drawing, and are best incorporated as values within your prototype drawing files.

Scaling the plot

The final specification to set is the plot scale. Here you decide how big the drawing will be plotted.

Specify scale by entering:
Plotted units = Drawing units or Fit or ? ⟨default⟩:

Either enter a scale or instruct AutoCAD to fit the entire drawing on the paper. The Fit option can be selected by typing "F" at the prompt and pressing ENTER. No other values are needed. AutoCAD automatically adjusts your drawing to fit on the paper. You may have considerable blank space left on the paper depending on the size and proportions of your drawing.

To specify a scale you must enter a ratio of plotted units to drawing units. A mechanical drawing to be plotted at a scale of $1/2'' = 1''$ is entered as follows.

Specify scale by entering:
Plotted units = Drawing units or Fit or ? ⟨default⟩: **1/2'' = 1''** or **.5 = 1** or **1 = 2** ⏎

An architectural drawing to be plotted at 1/4" = 1'-0" is entered as follows:

Specify scale by entering:
Plotted units = Drawing units or Fit or ? ⟨default⟩: **1/4" = 1'** or **.25 = 12**

To calculate the available area on a sheet of paper at a specific scale, use this formula:

$$\frac{\text{Unit}}{\text{Scale}} \times \text{Paper size} = \text{Limits}$$

To find the limits of a B-size (17 x 11 in.) sheet of paper at 1/2" = 1" scale:

$$\frac{1}{.50} \times 17 = 17 \div .5 = 34$$

$$\frac{1}{.50} \times 11 = 11 \div .5 = 22$$

Thus the limits of a B-size sheet at the scale of 1/2" = 1" are 34,22. The same formula applies to architectural scales. The limits of a C-size architectural sheet (24 x 18 in.) at a scale of 1/4" = 1'-0" can be determined like this:

$$\frac{1'-0"}{1/4"} \times 24 = \frac{12"}{.25"} \times 24 = 48 \times 24 = 1152 \div 12 = 96 \text{ feet (X distance)}$$

Use the same formula to calculate the Y distance of the 18 in. side of the paper. The chart in Fig. 27-5 provides limits for common scales on various paper sizes for each drafting field. It also lists text height, scale factors, and linetype scales for the best linetype display.

	PAPER SIZE	APPROX DRAWING AREA	SCALE	LIMITS	PLOTTED TEXT HEIGHT (INCHES) 1/8	1/4	SCALE FACTOR	LTSCALE
MECHANICAL	11 x 8.5	9 x 7	2"=1"	4.5 x 3.5	.0625	.125	.5	.25
			3/4"=1"	12 x 9.33	.167	.33	1.33	.67
			1/2"=1"	18 x 14	.25	.5	2	1
			1/4"=1"	36 x 28	.5	1.0	4	2
	17 x 11	15 x 10	2"=1"	7.5 x 5				
			3/4"=1"	20 x 13.33				
			1/2"=1"	30 x 20				
			1/4"=1"	60 x 40				
	22 x 17	20 x 15	2"=1"	10 x 7.5				
			3/4"=1"	26.67 x 20				
			1/2"=1"	40 x 30				
			1/4"=1"	80 x 60				
	34 x 22	32 x 30	2"=1"	16 x 10				
			3/4"=1"	42.67x26.67				
			1/2"=1"	64 x 40				
			1/4"=1"	128 x 80				
	44 x 34	42 x 32	2"=1"	21 x 16				
			3/4"=1"	56 x 42.67				
			1/2"=1"	84 x 64				
			1/4"=1"	168 x 128				

Fig. 27-5. Common scales and their drawing limits.

	PAPER SIZE	APPROX DRAWING AREA	SCALE	LIMITS	PLOTTED TEXT HEIGHT (INCHES) 1/8	1/4	SCALE FACTOR	LTSCALE
ARCHITECTURAL	11 x 8.5	9 x 7	1"=1'-0"	9' x 7'	1.5	3.0	12	6
			1/2"=1'-0"	18' x 14'	3.0	6.0	24	12
			1/4"=1'-0"	36' x 28'	6.0	12.0	48	24
			1/8"=1'-0"	72' x 56'	12.0	24.0	96	48
	17 x 11	15 x 10	1"=1'-0"	15' x 10'				
			1/2"=1'-0"	30' x 20'				
			1/4"=1'-0"	60' x 40'				
			1/8"=1'-0"	120' x 80'				
	22 x 17	20 x 15	1"=1'-0"	20' x 15'				
			1/2"=1'-0"	40' x 30'				
			1/4"=1'-0"	80' x 60'				
			1/8"=1'-0"	160' x 120'				
	34 x 22	32 X 20	1"=1'-0"	32' x 20'				
			1/2"=1'-0"	64' x 40'				
			1/4"=1'-0"	128' x 80'				
			1/8"=1'-0"	256' x 160'				
	44 x 34	42 x 32	1"=1'-0"	42' x 32'				
			1/2"=1'-0"	84' x 64'				
			1/4"=1'-0"	168' x 128'				
			1/8"=1'-0"	336' x 256'				

	PAPER SIZE	APPROX DRAWING AREA	SCALE	LIMITS	PLOTTED TEXT HEIGHT (INCHES) 1/8	1/4	SCALE FACTOR	LTSCALE
CIVIL ENGINEERING	11 X 8.5	9 X 7	1" = 10'	90' x 70'	15	30	120	60
			1" = 20'	180' x 140'	30	60	240	120
			1" = 30'	270' x 210'	45	90	360	180
			1" = 50'	450' x 350'	75	150	600	300
	17 X 11	15 X 10	1" = 10'	150' x 100'				
			1" = 20'	300' x 200'				
			1" = 30'	450' x 300'				
			1" = 50'	750' x 500'				
	22 X 17	20 X 15	1" = 10'	200' x 150'				
			1" = 20'	400' x 300'				
			1" = 30'	600' x 450'				
			1" = 50'	1000'x 750'				
	34 X 22	32 X 20	1" = 10'	320' x 200'				
			1" = 20'	640' x 400'				
			1" = 30'	960' x 600'				
			1" = 50'	1600'x1000'				
	44 X 34	42 X 32	1" = 10'	420' x 320'				
			1" = 20'	840' x 640'				
			1" = 30'	1260'x 960'				
			1" = 50'	2100'x1600'				

Fig. 27-5. Continued.

Prepare the plotter

The last step you must take before plotting is to prepare the plotter. The exact procedure varies from one plotter model to the next, but the basic procedure is the same. After setting the plotter specifications, AutoCAD displays the space available for plotting:

Effective plotting area: (xx) wide by (yy) high

These are actual dimensions of the current plotting area. Then, the final prompt before plotting begins is:

Position paper in plotter.
Press RETURN to continue or S to Stop for hardware setup

Before you press ENTER, there are several items you should check.
- Plotter is plugged in.
- Plotter cable to computer is secure.
- Pen carousel is loaded and secure or pen is in plotter arm.
- Pens of proper color and thickness are in correct locations in pen carousel or rack.
- Paper is properly loaded in plotter and paper grips or clamps are in place.
- Plotter area is clear for unblocked paper movement.

PROFESSIONAL TIP

You can stop a plot in progress at any time by canceling with CTRL C. Keep in mind that it may take a while for some plotters to terminate the plot, depending on the amount of the drawing file that has already been sent to the plotter.

USING THE PLOT CONFIGURATION DIALOGUE BOX

ARM 13

The previous discussion had the CMDDIA variable set to 0 so the PLOT command settings could be issued at the keyboard. When CMDDIA is set to 1, the "Plot Configuration" dialogue box can be used. It is displayed when you pick Plot... from the File pull-down menu, PLOT in the Root Menu, or type "PLOT" at the Command: prompt. See Fig. 27-6.

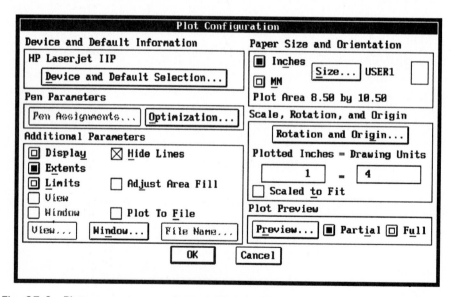

Fig. 27-6. Plot parameters can be specified in the "Plot Configuration" dialogue box.

Device and default selection

As you look at the "Plot Configuration" dialogue box, notice the Device and Default Information area in the upper-left corner. This is where AutoCAD displays information about the current configured printers and plotters. Pick the Device and Default Selection... button to access the "Device and Default Selection" subdialogue box shown in Fig. 27-7. You can use this dialogue box to review or change any of the printer or plotter specifications. The current device is highlighted in the Select Device area. When additional devices are displayed, you can make a different one current by picking it. Add printers and plotters to the list with the CONFIG command's Configure plotter option and choose the Add a plotter configuration selection.

```
╔══════════════════════════════════════════════════════╗
║          Device and Default Selection                  ║
║ Select Device                                          ║
║ Manufacturer: Hewlett-Packard (PCL) LaserJet ADI 4.2 - by Autode ║
║ Port: LPT1                                             ║
║ ┌──────────────────────────────────────────────────┐ ║
║ │ HP LaserJet IIP                                  ▓│ ║
║ │ HP Postscript IIP                                 │ ║
║ │ HP Draftpro DXL                                   │ ║
║ │                                                   │ ║
║ │                                                   │ ║
║ └──────────────────────────────────────────────────┘ ║
║ File Defaults                                          ║
║  ┌──────────────────────┐  ┌──────────────────────┐  ║
║  │ Save Defaults To File...│  │ Get Defaults From File...│  ║
║  └──────────────────────┘  └──────────────────────┘  ║
║ Device Specific Configuration                          ║
║  ┌──────────────────────┐  ┌──────────────────────┐  ║
║  │ Show Device Requirements...│  │ Change Device Requirements...│ ║
║  └──────────────────────┘  └──────────────────────┘  ║
║         ┌──────┐   ┌──────────┐                       ║
║         │  OK  │   │  Cancel  │                       ║
║         └──────┘   └──────────┘                       ║
╚══════════════════════════════════════════════════════╝
```

Fig. 27-7. Plotters and printers are listed in the "Device and Default Selection" subdialogue box.

The File Defaults area of the "Device and Default Selection" subdialogue box provides you with the Save Defaults to File... and Get Defaults from File... buttons. These are called Plot Configuration Parameters (PCP) files. You can create a PCP file for a number of purposes including:
- Make changes to plot specifications before plotting.
- Make plot files for different drawing types.
- Make a plot file for each configured plotter or printer.
- Set up a drawing to be plotted in a variety of formats.
- Give a plot file to another person or company.

Each of the values that you set in the "Plot Configuration" dialogue box is saved in the PCP file. This means that you can set values for individual prototype drawings. Then, when a prototype is used to construct a new drawing, you only have to retrieve a PCP file, then plot the drawing without making any additional changes to the plotting parameters. Pick the Save Defaults to File... button to save a PCP file. Select the directory or drive in which to save the file and enter the file name as shown in the "Save to File" subdialogue box in Fig. 27-8A. To get a previously saved PCP file, pick the Get Defaults from File... button. This displays the "Obtain from File" subdialogue box shown in Fig. 27-8B. If everything is fine with the PCP file you pick, then AutoCAD gives the message "Plot configuration updated without error" in the lower-left corner

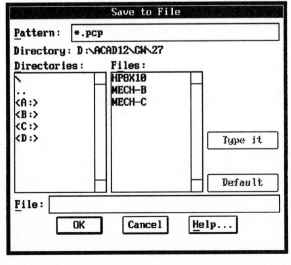

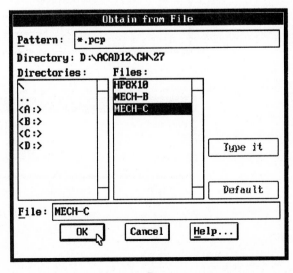

A   B

Fig. 27-8. A—The PCP (Plot Configuration Parameters) "Save to File" subdialogue box. B—Load a PCP file using the "Obtain from File" subdialogue box.

of the "Device and Default Selection" subdialogue box. If there is an error in the PCP file you select, AutoCAD issues an "Error Information on File Defaults" dialogue box. Pick the Create Error File button to make an error file (.ERR extension) that can be used to correct the PCP file.

Use the Device Specific Configuration buttons to show or change your printer or plotter settings. The Show Device Requirements... button accesses a dialogue box of the same name. Check the current device settings and pick OK when you are satisfied. See Fig. 27-9A. Make changes by picking the Change Device Requirements button. This displays the consecutive dialogue boxes shown in Fig. 27-9B through D. Change the current setting in the edit box and pick OK to continue.

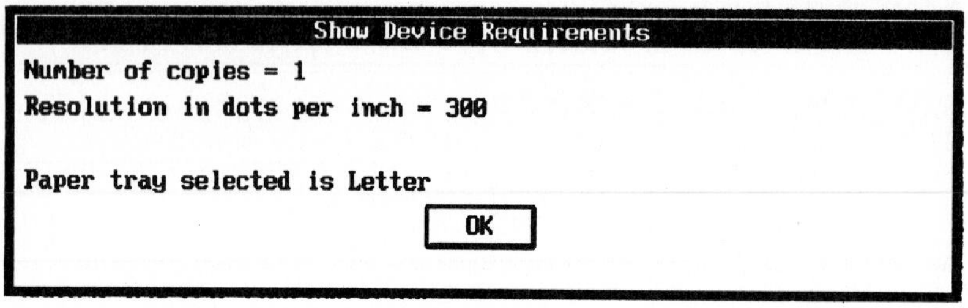

A

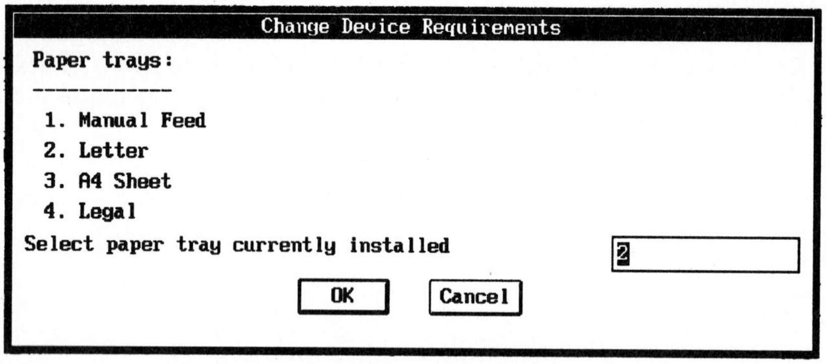

B—CHANGE THE PAPER TRAY

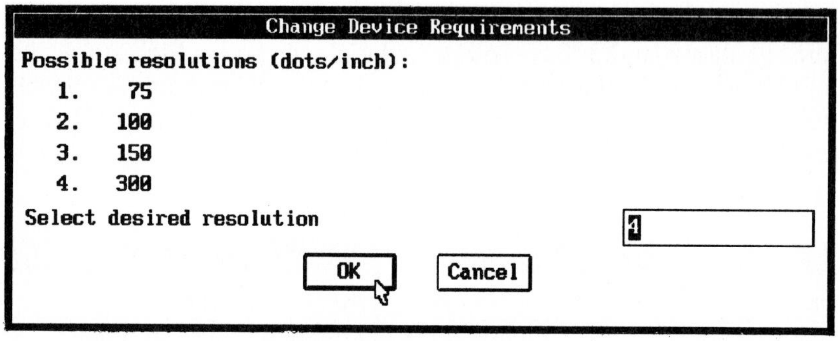

C—CHANGE THE RESOLUTION

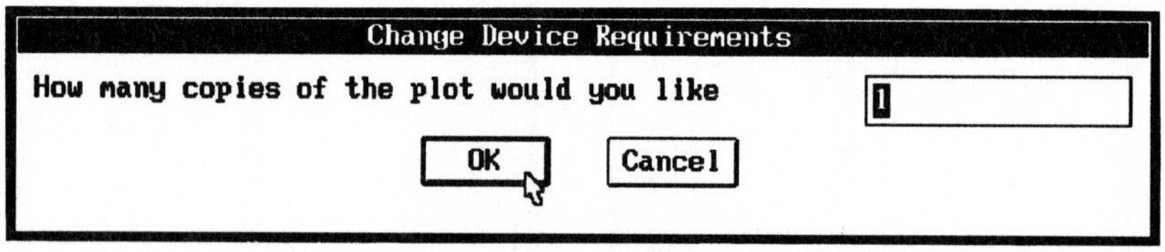

D—CHANGE THE NUMBER OF COPIES

Fig. 27-9. A—The "Show Device Requirements" subdialogue box. B-D—Device settings can be changed with the "Change Device Requirements" subdialogue boxes.

Pen parameters

The "Plot Configuration" dialogue box allows you to set pen parameters based on your drawing standards, such as line thickness or text style. To do this, pick the Pen Assignments... button to get the "Pen Assignments" subdialogue box. When you highlight a pen assignment by picking it, the values are displayed in the Modify Values edit boxes.

Make changes in the edit boxes as necessary. Pick a selection to highlight it, and its values are listed in the Modify Values area. The color listed on the left will be plotted with the pen number displayed unless you change it. If you want all lines that are red (1), yellow (2), and green (3) plotted with pen 1, be sure to pick each color and enter "1" at the Pen: edit box. Fig 27-10 shows changes made in the pen assignments 1 through 6.

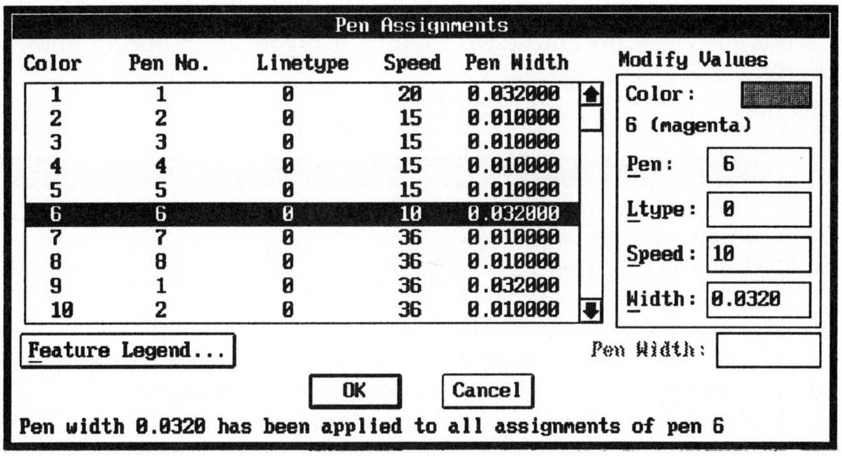

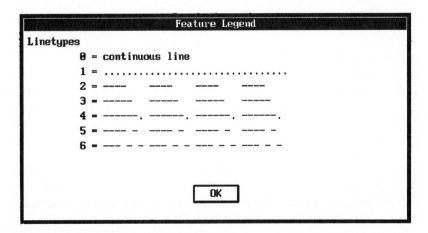

Fig. 27-10. The "Pen Assignments" subdialogue box enables you to fine-tune the plotter pen specifications.

Pick the Feature Legend... button to see a linetype display as shown in Fig. 27-11. These are linetypes that are generated by the plotter and are different from linetypes created in your drawing.

Fig. 27-11. The "Feature Legend" subdialogue box displays the linetypes generated by the plotter.

─────────────── **PROFESSIONAL TIP** ───────────────

Pen speeds should be set according to the type of paper or film, the type of pen such as liquid ink or felt tip, and the lines or text to be plotted. A fast pen speed may not draw quality lines and text. Set a slower pen speed to improve the plot quality.

The plotter-generated linetypes should remain as continuous for all AutoCAD linetypes, to ensure that the lines in your drawing are properly plotted.

The Optimization... button displays the "Optimizing Pen Motion" subdialogue box. This subdialogue box contains check boxes that let you control the efficiency of pen movement. By default, AutoCAD minimizes wasted pen motion with the check boxes picked in Fig. 27-12. Each consecutive check box increases optimization. Picking a higher level option automatically checks all previous options.

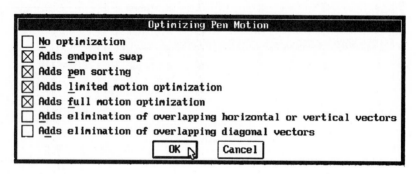

Fig. 27-12. The ''Optimizing Pen Motion'' subdialogue box.

─────────────── **PROFESSIONAL TIP** ───────────────

You need to experiment with your plotter to be sure that optimization is an asset. In most cases, it improves plot productivity, but sometimes it may cause problems such as unnecessary pen changes.

Additional parameters

Look at the Additional Parameters area in Fig. 27-6 and you can see the options for the part of the drawing to be plotted, and how it is plotted. These are Display, Extents, Limits, View, and Window, as discussed earlier in this chapter, and are shown with radio buttons. Therefore, they are either on or off. The View radio button is inactive unless a view had been previously saved using the VIEW command. Picking the View... button displays the "View Name" subdialogue box. Pick the name of the view you want plotted and then pick OK. The TILEMODE system variable must be off to plot any saved view from either model or paper space.

Picking the Window... button displays the "Window Selection" subdialogue box shown in Fig. 27-13. Enter the first corner and second corner coordinates of the desired window in the X: and Y: edit boxes. Pick the OK button to accept the coordinates. The Window radio button is then active. You can also use the Pick button in the "Window Selection" subdialogue box. This clears the dialogue boxes and displays the graphics screen. The prompt asks you to pick the window corners that surround the part of the drawing you want printed or plotted.

Command: _plot
First corner: *(pick the first window corner)*
Other corner: *(pick the second window corner)*

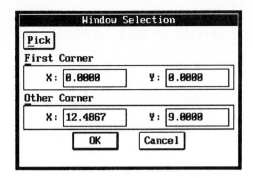

Fig. 27-13. Specify a plot window using the ''Window Selection'' subdialogue box.

The "Plot Configuration" dialogue box appears after you pick OK in the "Window Selection" subdialogue box.

The Hide Lines check box is picked if you want to plot a 3-D drawing with hidden lines removed. Note that plotting takes a little longer when removing hidden lines since AutoCAD must calculate the lines to be removed.

The Adjust Area Fill check box is activated if you want areas such as polylines and solids filled completely. These precise plots are a result of the pen being adjusted inside the boundary by one-half the pen width. When this is inactive, the pen plots at the center of the boundary, which is fine for most applications, but may be poor in printed circuit board artwork.

If you want to send the plot setup to a file, pick the Plot to File check box. This activates the File Name... button. Pick this button to get the "Create Plot File" subdialogue box. This allows you to save the plot to disk. A plot file is given a .PLT extension. Using PLT files is good practice if you have only one office or class computer connected to a plotter, or if your office or school uses a plot spooler. See Fig. 27-14. The plot spooler is cabled to a plotter and is basically a "smart" disk drive with memory. It reads the PLT file from disk and sends the drawing data to the plotter. A plot spooler removes the need of having a computer cabled to the plotter. Plot files (.PLT extension) can also be used by plot spooling software in network systems.

Fig. 27-14. A plot spooler reads PLT files from a floppy disk and sends the drawing data to the plotter.
(Far Mountain Corporation)

The upper-right area of the "Plot Configuration" dialogue box shown in Fig. 27-15 controls the paper size and orientation. This has the same application as input at the prompt line discussed earlier in this chapter. Pick either the Inches or the MM radio button to make inches or millimeters the units for all plot specifications. Pick the Size... button to access the "Paper

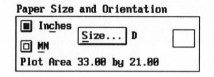

Fig. 27-15. The Paper Size and Orientation area of the "Plot Configuration" dialogue box.

Size" subdialogue box. Pick the desired standard size such as D-size as shown in Fig. 27-16, or enter your own size specifications in one of the USER Width and Height edit boxes. Also indicated is the orientation, either landscape or portrait. The orientation icon is a rectangle on

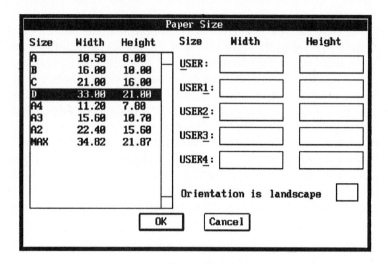

Fig. 27-16. All available sheet sizes are listed in the "Paper Size" subdialogue box.

the right side of Fig. 27-17. Fig. 27-17A shows the icon in the landscape position, while Fig. 27-17B displays the portrait orientation. This icon changes depending on the natural orientation of the paper in the current plotting device.

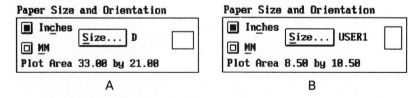

Fig. 27-17. A—The landscape sheet size icon. B—The portrait sheet size icon.

Scale, rotation, and origin

The familiar items Scale, Rotation, and Origin are found on the right side of the "Plot Configuration" dialogue box. Pick the Rotation and Origin... button to access the "Plot Rotation and Origin" subdialogue box shown in Fig. 27-18. The Plot Rotation area has radio buttons for 0, 90, 180, and 270 degree rotation settings. The Plot Origin section has edit boxes for you to specify desired X and Y plot origin settings. Pick OK when done.

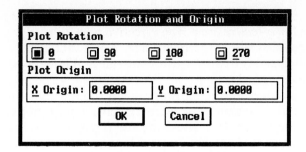

Fig. 27-18. The "Plot Rotation and Origin" subdialogue box.

The Plotted Inches = Drawing Units edit boxes (or Plotted MM = Drawing Units edit boxes if using metric units) let you set the plot scale as outlined earlier in this chapter. For example, if you are making an architectural drawing that scales 1/4″ = 1′-0″, then the scale factor is 48. For this scale factor, set the Plotted Inches to 1 and Drawing Units to 48 as shown in Fig. 27-19.

Pick the Scaled to Fit check box if you want AutoCAD to automatically adjust your drawing to fit on the paper.

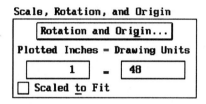

Fig. 27-19. The plotting scale is shown in the Plotted Inches = Drawing Units edit boxes.

Preview plot

This exciting feature allows you to quickly check what the plot looks like before plotting or printing. The Plot Preview area is located in the lower-right corner of the "Plot Configuration" dialogue box. It often takes a long time to plot a drawing. The Preview Plot option lets you save material and valuable plot time. The Partial and Full preview options are each controlled by a radio button.

When the Partial radio button is active and you pick the Preview button, AutoCAD quickly displays the "Preview Effective Plotting Area" subdialogue box shown in Fig. 27-20. The red

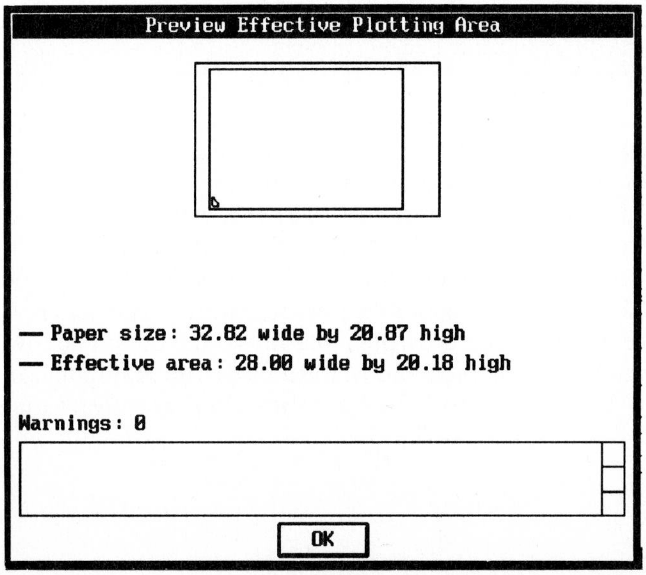

Fig. 27-20. Selecting the Preview . . . button when Partial is checked displays the "Preview Effective Plotting Area" subdialogue box.

outline is the paper size, and the paper dimensions are given below for reference. The area the image occupies is called the *effective area*. The effective area dimensions are noted and the blue outline of this area is provided within the paper size. AutoCAD displays a red and blue dashed line when the effective area and the paper size are the same. While this shows you how the drawing compares to the paper size, the final plot depends on how the printer or plotter is set up.

AutoCAD gives you messages in the Warnings box if there is something wrong with the relationship of the display and the paper. The warnings give you an opportunity to make corrections and then preview the plot again. These are the types of warnings you might expect:

- Effective area too small to display.
- Origin forced effective area off display.
- Plotting area exceeds paper maximum.

Notice the small symbol in the lower-left corner of the effective area in Fig. 27-20. This is called the *rotation icon*. The rotation icon in the lower-left corner represents the 0 default rotation angle. The icon is in the upper-left corner when the rotation is 90°, the right corner for 180° rotation, and in the lower-right corner for a 270° rotation. Fig. 27-21 clearly shows the rotation icon placement.

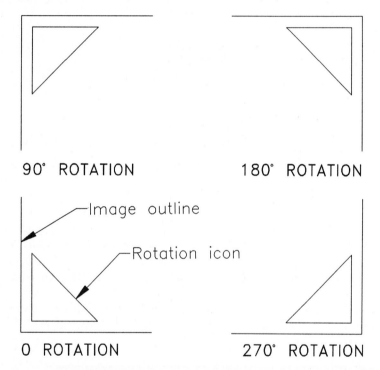

Fig. 27-21. The rotation icon as it appears in each rotation angle selection.

Pick the Full radio button followed by picking the Preview... button if you want a full preview. The Full preview takes more time, but it displays the drawing on the screen as it will actually appear on paper. This takes the same amount of time as a drawing regeneration, which means that the drawing size determines how fast this happens. AutoCAD displays a 0-100% meter in the lower-right corner of the "Plot Configuration" dialogue box as the full plot preview is generated. The graphics screen then returns with the drawing displayed inside the paper outline. At the same time, there is a "Plot Preview" dialogue box positioned near the center of the screen. See Fig. 27-22. If this dialogue obscures the drawing, just move the cursor arrow to the black title bar at the top of the dialogue box, and pick and hold to move the dialogue box to a desired location. Pick the End Preview button to return to the "Plot Configuration" dialogue box.

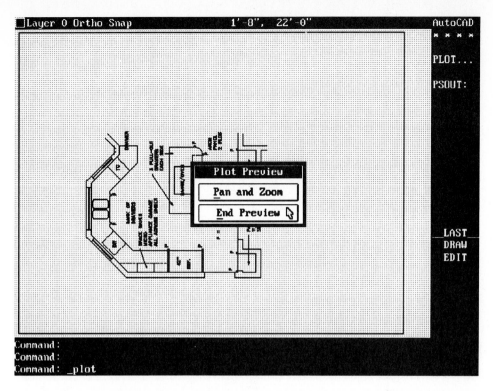

Fig. 27-22. The "Plot Preview" subdialogue box is displayed when a full preview is selected.

The Full preview also allows you to examine details on the drawing or evaluate how a multiview arrangement fits together by picking the Pan and Zoom button. When you first pick the Pan and Zoom button, you get a small view box with an X inside for panning, as shown in Fig. 27-23A. This is similar to the ZOOM command's Dynamic option discussed in Chapter 9. Move the pan view box anywhere you want. Pressing the pick button changes the image to a zoom view box. The zoom box image has an arrow on the right side as shown in Fig. 27-23B. Now you can make the zoom box bigger by moving the arrow to the right, or smaller by moving to the left. The box can be moved vertically without changing its size. Press ENTER when you have the size and position of the pan/zoom box where you want it. This re-displays the drawing

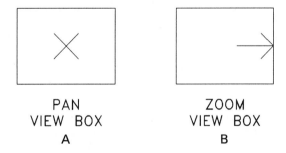

PAN
VIEW BOX
A

ZOOM
VIEW BOX
B

Fig. 27-23. The pan and zoom boxes enable you to accurately view areas of the drawing during full preview.

at the pan location and zoom scale that you selected. Fig. 27-24 shows the result of a selective pan and zoom to review some specific information on the drawing. Also notice the "Plot Preview" subdialogue box has changed and now has a Zoom Previous button. Pick this button to return to the original full preview representation, or pick End Preview to return to the "Plot Configuration" dialogue box.

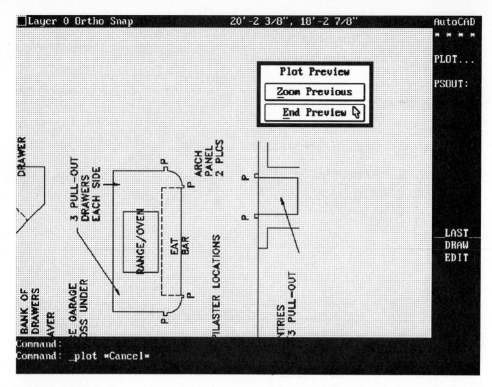

Fig. 27-24. The Zoom Previous button appears after picking a pan and zoom. Note the position of the ''Plot Preview'' subdialogue box on the screen.

INTRODUCTION TO MULTIVIEW PLOTTING

Multiview mechanical drawings and architectural construction drawings often contain sections or details of varying scales. AutoCAD allows you to lay out a multiview drawing with views of different scale and plot at full scale.

Imagine that you have manually developed three separate drawings of a house floor plan and construction details. Now, assume that you lay a C-size piece of vellum (with preprinted border and title block) on a table. Take the three drawings, each at a different scale, and arrange them on the sheet of vellum. Now, take a full-size photograph of the entire drawing. The photo contains all drawings at the proper scale, including the border and title block. Finally, remove the views from the original sheet of vellum and return them to storage. That's the concept behind multiview plotting.

THE PROCESS OF MULTIVIEW PLOTTING   ARM 7

Creating a multiview plot involves a basic understanding of two concepts — model space and paper space. The MSPACE (MS) and PSPACE (PS) commands reflect these concepts. They are found in the MVIEW screen menu, and as Model space and Paper space in the View pull-down menu. The concepts are easy to understand, especially since almost everything you draw is constructed in model space. When preparing a part for plotting, the necessary views are created in paper space. Chapter 9 includes a detailed discussion of model space and paper space.

Drawing in model space

When you begin a new drawing in AutoCAD, you are automatically in model space. This is the default setting in the ACAD.DWG file. The standard UCS icon is displayed in the lower-left corner of the screen when you are in model space. In addition, a system variable called TILEMODE controls the setting of model space and paper space. Model space default setting of TILEMODE is 1, and the paper space setting is 0. Enter the following to change the paper space:

```
Command: TILEMODE ↵
New value for TILEMODE ⟨1⟩: 0 ↵
Entering Paper space. Use MVIEW to insert Model space viewports.
Regenerating drawing.
```

Note the special paper space UCS icon resembling a triangle is displayed. See Fig. 27-25.

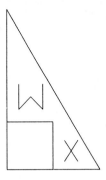

Fig. 27-25. The paper space UCS icon resembles a triangle.

─── **PROFESSIONAL TIP** ───

All system variable names can be entered at the Command: prompt.

MULTIVIEW PLOTTING OVERVIEW   ARM 13

An overview of the multiview plotting process will first be discussed to introduce the commands and options, before detailing the creation of a multiview plot. The most important visualization aspect involved in creating a multiview plot is to imagine that the sheet of paper you are creating will contain several cutouts *(viewports)*, through which you can see other drawings *(models)*. See Fig. 27-26.

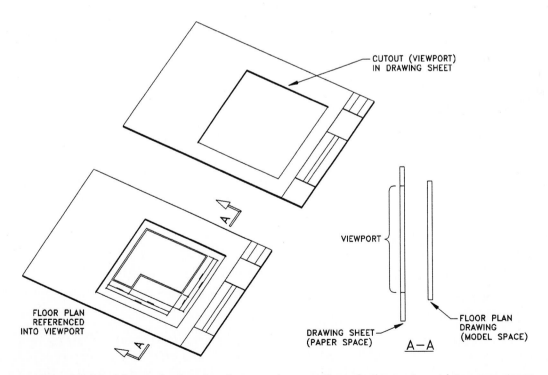

Fig. 27-26. Views of other drawings can be seen through viewports cut into paper space.

Imagine holding a sheet of paper with a border and title block in front of you. Now, use a knife to cut a rectangle out of the paper. This is a viewport. Place a print (model) of a house floor plan behind the opening. Use your knife to cut another smaller rectangular opening in the paper to the left of the first. Cut a third viewport above the second one. Find prints of a stair detail and a footing detail drawing. Place each of these behind the two new viewports. Now, take a photograph of the completed drawing. That's a simplified version of the process used to create viewports in paper space.

As you know, objects and designs should be created at full size in AutoCAD. If you are designing a machine part, you are probably using decimal units. If you are designing a house, you are using architectural units. When constructing each of these, you likely used the full dimensions of the part or house.

Now, imagine the C-size paper is hanging up in front of you, and the first viewport is cut to be 12″ wide and 10″ high. You want to display the floor plan of a house inside the opening. If you then place the full-size model of the floor plan directly behind the C-size paper, the house will extend many feet beyond the edges of the paper. How can you place the drawing within the viewport? You know that the floor plan should be displayed inside the viewport at a scale of 1/4″ = 1′-0″. The scale factor of 1/4″ = 1′-0″ is 48. Therefore, you need to move the floor plan model away from the C-size paper until it is 1/48 (reciprocal of 48) the size it is now. This is accomplished with ZOOM command's XP (Times Paper space) option discussed later. When you do that, the entire floor plan fits inside the viewport you cut. See Fig. 27-27.

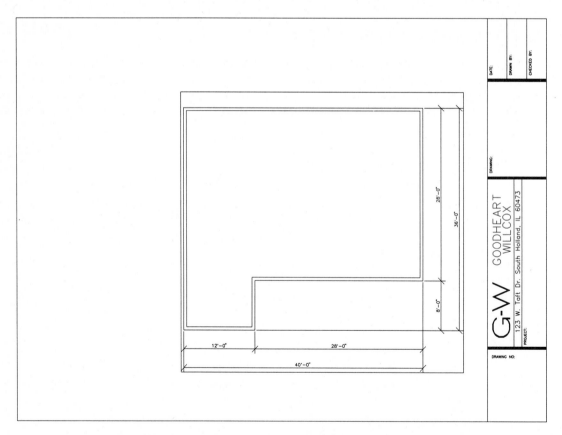

Fig. 27-27. Floor plan is placed inside a viewport.

Remember to zoom to the appropriate scale after *referencing* (inserting) a drawing into a viewport so that your multiview plots work properly. Review the brief step-by-step procedure for constructing multiview plots. The first six steps can be omitted if your prototype drawing contains these settings and entities.
- Set TILEMODE to 0 to enter paper space.
- Set UNITS to match the type of drawing you are creating.
- Set LIMITS to match paper size and plotter limits.

- Make a layer for referenced drawings.
- Create a border layer or reference a drawing that has a border and title block. You may want to use MVSETUP (discussed in Chapter 17).
- Make a layer for viewport entities, and set this viewport as the current layer.
- Enter MVIEW and make the size viewport needed.
- Change to model space.
- Use the XREF command to insert an existing drawing. Insert the drawing at 0,0 and use the remaining defaults.
- Zoom to the extents of the drawing.
- Set the scale to the appropriate value using the ZOOM command's XP option.
- Use VPLAYER (Viewpoint Layer) and either the Vpvisdflt (ViewPort VISibility DeFauLTs) or Freeze options to freeze layers of this referenced drawing in all new viewports or selected viewports.
- Return to paper space.
- Repeat the process using the MVIEW command.

CONSTRUCTING A MULTIVIEW DRAWING FOR PLOTTING

Now that you have a good idea of the multiview plotting process, the following example leads you through the details of the procedure. This example uses a house floor plan, a stair detail, and a footing detail. This drawing is not among the sample drawings furnished with the AutoCAD. Instead, the drawing is based on Exercise 27-1. Complete Exercise 27-1 before working through the example. It is composed of three simple architectural drawings.

EXERCISE 27-1

☐ If you wish to work along at your computer with the following example of multiview drawing construction, complete this exercise before reading further. It is not necessary to complete this exercise in order to understand the process discussed in the following example, but it may assist you in quickly grasping the concepts of the procedure.

☐ The three drawings shown at the top of the next page—the floor plan, stair detail, and footing detail—should be created for this exercise. They are highly simplified for the purpose of this exercise and explanation, and should not be regarded as complete representations of actual designs. Exact dimensions are not necessary, because the purpose of this exercise is to illustrate the creation of a multiview drawing. You may simplify the drawings further to speed up the exercise.

☐ Each drawing should be created, named, and stored separately with different names. Do not put a border or title block on the drawings. The names are shown in the following table.

FLOOR.DWG		STAIR.DWG		FOOTING.DWG	
Layer	Color	Layer	Color	Layer	Color
Wall	White	Wall	Yellow	Floor	Green
Dimen	Cyan	Floor	White	Foot	White
Notes	Red	Stair	Green	Dimen	Cyan
		Foot	White	Notes	Red
		Dimen	Cyan	Earth	Yellow
		Notes	Red		

☐ Use the following scales and scale factors when constructing each of the drawings.

FLOOR.DWG = 1/4″ = 1′-0″ (Scale factor = 48)
STAIR.DWG = 3/8″ = 1′-0″ (Scale factor = 32)
FOOTING.DWG = 3/4″ = 1′-0″ (Scale factor = 16)

The scale factors are important when setting the DIMSCALE dimensioning variable, and when establishing text height. Remember to multiply the plotted text height, such as .125, by the scale factor, such as 48, to get the text height to use in AutoCAD (.125 x 48 = 6). The scale factor is also used with the ZOOM XP command discussed later in the text.

☐ Save the drawings to a hard disk subdirectory, preferably not in the AutoCAD directory. Check with your instructor or supervisor before creating or using hard disk space. Save backup copies on a floppy disk.

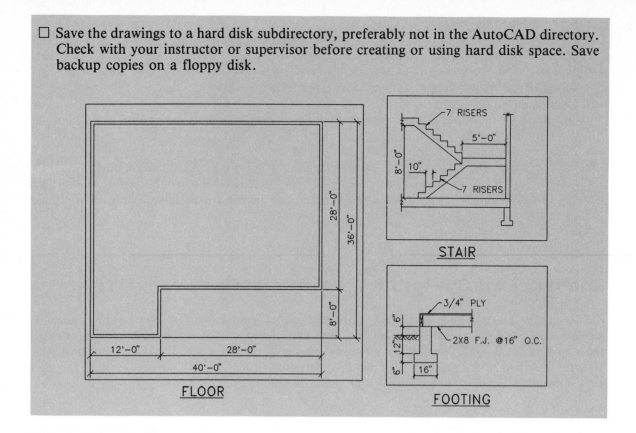

Initial drawing setup

The first aspect of drawing setup is to place a border and title block on the screen. It should be the proper size for the plot you wish to make. This can be accomplished in one of several ways, depending on the depth of your preparation. First, set TILEMODE to 0, then:
- Draw a border on a separate layer, then draw a title block.
- Draw a border and insert a predrawn title block.

or

- Insert a predrawn standard border and title block prototype containing all constant text and attributes for variable information.

The method you use is not of primary importance for this example, but it is always best to use existing borders and title blocks for reasons that are discussed later.

─────────────── PROFESSIONAL TIP ───────────────

This initial setup phase is unnecessary if your school or company uses preprinted border and title block sheets. You might use a "phantom" border and title block sheet on the screen for layout purposes, and to add additional information to the title block. This phantom information can be frozen before plotting.

When setting up a drawing, first enter paper space, then set the units and limits to match the type of drawing you are creating. Be sure that the extents of your border and title block match the maximum active plotting area, or "clip limits" of your plotter. This example uses a standard architectural C-size sheet (18 x 24), and assumes that the plotter's active area is .75″ less on all sides, for a total plotting area of 16.5″ x 22.5″.

Command: **TILEMODE** ↵
New value for TILEMODE ⟨1⟩: **0** ↵
Entering Paper space. Use MVIEW to insert Model space viewports.
Regenerating drawing.
Command: **UNITS** ↵

Use the following UNITS settings and then reply to the Command: prompts.
- Architectural.
- Denominator of smallest fraction to display = 2.
- Systems of angle measure = Decimal degrees.
- Number of fractional places for display of angles = 0.
- Direction for angle 0 = East (0).
- Angles measured counterclockwise.

Command: **LIMITS** ↵
Reset Paper space limits:
ON/OFF/⟨Lower left corner⟩ ⟨0′-0″,0′-0″⟩: ↵
Upper right corner ⟨1′-0″,0′-9″⟩: **26,20** ↵
Command: **ZOOM** ↵
All/Center/Dynamic/Extents/Left/Previous/Vmax/Window/⟨Scale(X/XP)⟩: **A** ↵
Regenerating drawing.

At this point you can set an appropriate snap grid and visible grid values. If you wish to use an existing border and title block, insert it now, and those values should already be set in the prototype drawing.

Creating new layers

The border and title block should be on a separate layer, so you may want to create a new layer, called BORDER or TITLE, and assign it a separate color. Be sure to make this new layer current before you draw the border, insert a prototype, or use MVSETUP.

One of the principle functions of this example is to use existing drawings of the house floor plan, stairs, and footing. These drawings will not become a part of our new drawing, but they will be "referenced" with the XREF command in order to save drawing file space. Therefore, you should also create a new layer for these drawings and name it XREF. Assign the XREF layer a color of 0.

The referenced drawings will fit inside viewports that are made with the MVIEW command. These viewports are rectangles and are given the entity name of Viewport. Therefore, they can be edited like any other AutoCAD entity. Create a layer called VIEWPORTS or VPORT for these entities and assign it a color.

The layers of any existing drawings that you reference (xref) into your new drawing remain intact. Therefore, you do not have to create additional layers unless you want to add information to your drawing.

If you do not have an existing C-size architectural border and title block, you can draw a border at this time. Make the BORDER layer current and draw a polyline border using the dimensions of 16.5″ x 22.5″. Draw a title block if you wish. Your screen should look similar to Fig. 27-28.

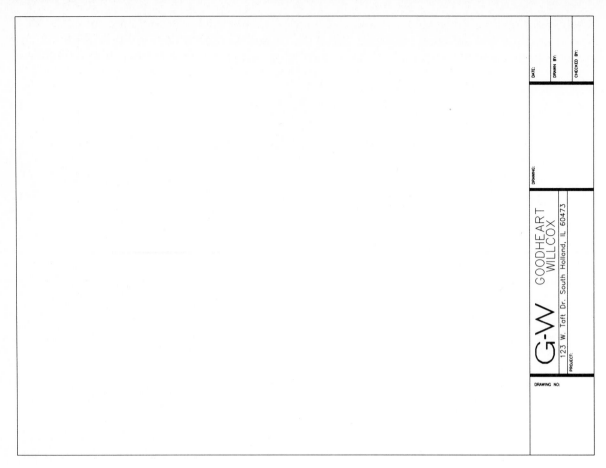

Fig. 27-28. Border and title block in paper space.

Creating a viewport

The process of creating viewports is completed in paper space because viewports are "cut" out of the paper. When creating a drawing in paper space, your screen represents a sheet of paper. You must now create an opening, called a viewport, through which you can view a model, design, or drawing. In this case, the model is a floor plan. First, cut an opening in the paper so you can see the floor plan that is behind it. Keep in mind that the sheet of paper measures 18″ x 24″ and the first viewport to be cut measures 11.5″ x 12″.

The MVIEW command is used to create the viewports. Since viewports are entities, make the VIEWPORTS layer current, so they reside on their own layer. This allows them to be frozen later to avoid being plotted. The first viewport can be located from the lower-left corner of the border by using the ID command to locate the corner. Enter the following:

> Command: **ID** ↵
> Point: **INT** ↵
> of *(pick lower-left corner of border)*
> Command: **MVIEW** ↵
> ON/OFF/Hideplot/Fit/2/3/4/Restore/⟨First Point⟩: **@7,3** ↵
> Other corner: **@12,11.5** ↵
> Regenerating drawing.

Your screen should now look like Fig. 27-29.

At this point, you can continue creating as many viewports as required. However, this example continues the process, and references a drawing into the new viewport. The other options of the MVIEW command are discussed in detail later in this chapter.

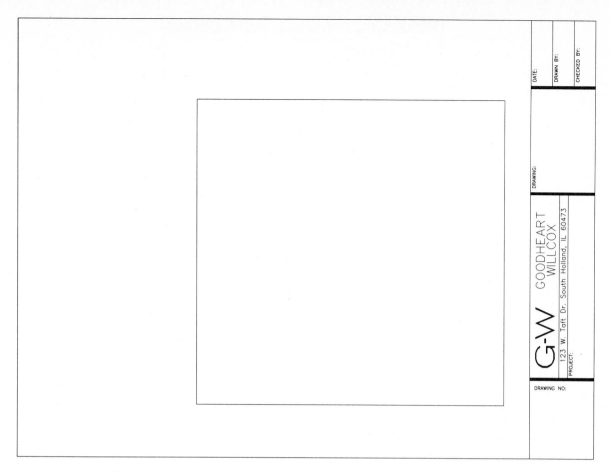

Fig. 27-29. Viewport added to the border and title block in paper space.

Placing views in the drawing

A viewport has now been created into which you can insert a view of the 2-D or 3-D model (drawing) that has been previously created. In this case, we will reference the drawing of the floor plan named FLOOR. Instead of using the INSERT command, which combines an existing drawing with the new one, use the XREF command so that AutoCAD creates a "reference" to the FLOOR drawing. This allows the size of the new drawing to remain small because the FLOOR drawing has not been combined with it.

The following procedure allows you to enter model space, reference an existing drawing to the new one, and ZOOM to see the referenced drawing.

Command: **MSPACE** ↵
Command: **LAYER** ↵
?/Make/Set/New/ON/OFF/Color/Ltype/Freeze/Thaw/LOck/Unlock: **S** ↵
New current layer ⟨VIEWPORTS⟩: **XREF** ↵
?/Make/Set/New/ON/OFF/Color/Ltype/Freeze/Thaw/LOck/Unlock: ↵
Command: **XREF** ↵
?/Bind/Detach/Path/Reload/⟨Attach⟩: ↵
Xref to Attach: ~ ↵

───────── **PROFESSIONAL TIP** ─────────

At the Xref to Attach: prompt, you can type the path to the file you wish to reference or you can type the tilde (~) symbol. When you type the tilde, the "Select File to Attach" dialogue box appears that allows you to select an existing file. See Fig. 27-30. You can scroll through the listing by using the scroll bar. If you have disabled the display of dialogue boxes by setting the FILEDIA system variable to 0, you can still force the dialogue box to appear by entering the tilde (~).

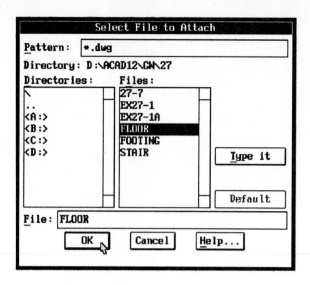

Fig. 27-30. The "Select File to Attach" dialogue box.

Select the FLOOR drawing in the dialogue box, or the file name can be typed at the Xref to Attach: prompt. The following prompt then appears:

> Insertion point: **0,0** ↵
>   X scale factor ⟨1⟩ / Corner / XYZ: ↵
>   Y scale factor (default = X): ↵
>   Rotation angle ⟨0⟩: ↵
> Command: **ZOOM** ↵
> All/Center/Dynamic/Extents/Left/Previous/Vmax/Window/⟨Scale(X/XP)⟩: **E** ↵

Your drawing should now resemble the one shown in Fig. 27-31.

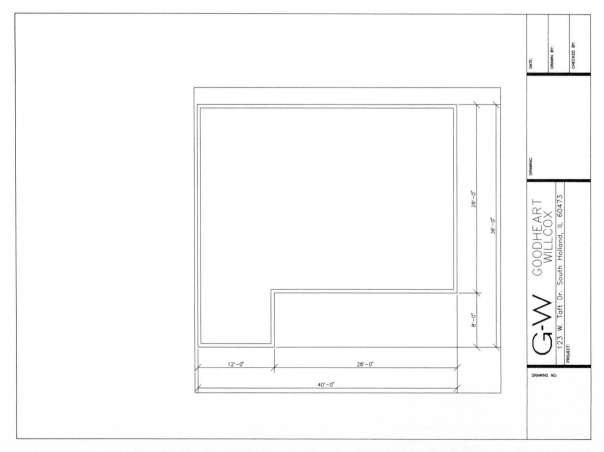

Fig. 27-31. The floor plan is referenced into the first viewport.

All of the layers on the referenced drawing are added to the new drawing. These layers can be distinguished from existing layers because the drawing name is automatically placed in front of the layer name and separated by the "|" symbol. Pick the Layer Control... selection in the Settings pull-down menu to see this layer-naming technique. See Fig. 27-32.

```
Current Layer: VIEWPORTS

Layer Name          State        Color      Linetype

0                   On . . . . white        CONTINUOUS
BLUE                On . . . . blue         CONTINUOUS
BORDER              On . . . . white        CONTINUOUS
CYAN                On . . . . cyan         CONTINUOUS
DEFPOINTS           . . . . . white         CONTINUOUS
FLOOR|DIMEN         On . . . N cyan         CONTINUOUS
FLOOR|NOTES         On . . . N red          CONTINUOUS
FLOOR|WALL          On . . . N white        CONTINUOUS
RED                 On . . . . red          CONTINUOUS
TITLETEXT           On . . . . cyan         CONTINUOUS
VIEWPORTS           On . . . . yellow       CONTINUOUS
XREF                On . . . . white        CONTINUOUS
```

Fig. 27-32. The "Layer Control" dialogue box shows the technique used for naming layers on referenced drawings.

Scaling a drawing in a viewport

When a drawing has been referenced and placed in a viewport, it is ready to be scaled. After using the ZOOM command's Extents option, the referenced drawing fills the viewport. However, this does not imply that the drawing is displayed at the correct scale.

The scale factor of each view of the multiview drawing is an important number to remember; it is the number you use to size your drawing in the viewport. The scale factor is used in conjunction with the ZOOM command's XP option (Times Paper space). Since the intended final scale of the floor plan on the plotted drawing is to be 1/4" = 1'-0", the scale factor is 48, or 1/48 of full size. A discussion of determining scale factors is given earlier in this chapter. Be sure you are still in model space, and that the crosshairs are present in the viewport where you are working. Enter the following:

Command: **ZOOM** ↵
All/Center/Dynamic/Extents/Left/Previous/Vmax/Window/⟨Scale(X/XP)⟩: **1/48XP** ↵

The drawing may not change much in size depending on the size of the viewport. Also, keep in mind that the viewport itself is an entity that can be moved or stretched if needed. Remember to change to paper space when editing the size of the viewport. If part of your drawing extends beyond the edge of the viewport after using the ZOOM command's XP option, simply use the STRETCH command to change the size of the viewport.

Controlling viewport layer visibility

If you now create another viewport using MVIEW, the floor plan will immediately fill it. This is because a viewport is just a window through which you can view a drawing or 3-D model that has been referenced to your new drawing. One way to control what is visible in subsequent viewports is to freeze all layers of the FLOOR drawing in any new viewports that are created. The VPLAYER (ViewPort LAYER) command controls the display of layers in specific viewports, whereas the LAYER command controls layers in all viewports.

The following example uses the VPLAYER command and the Vpvisdflt option to control the display of layers in new viewports.

Command: **VPLAYER** ↵
?/Freeze/Thaw/Reset/Newfrz/Vpvisdflt: **V** ↵
Layer name(s) to change default viewport visibility: **FLOOR*** ↵
Change default viewport visibility to Frozen/⟨Thawed⟩: **F** ↵
?/Freeze/Thaw/Reset/Newfrz/Vpvisdflt: ↵

The asterisk (*) after the name FLOOR instructs AutoCAD to freeze all of the layers on the FLOOR drawing in subsequent viewports. Look at the "Layer Control" dialogue box in Fig. 27-32 and note the "N" after the layer name, directly to the left of the color. This indicates the layer is frozen in a new viewport. Any layer's frozen or thawed status in a viewport can also be controlled by using the Cur VP: and the New VP: buttons on the right side of the "Layer Control" dialogue box. See Fig. 27-33B. Select one of the FLOOR layers, then pick the Thw button of the New VP: option. Notice that the "N" is removed. These buttons are the same as using the VPLAYER command.

The remaining options of the VPLAYER command are discussed later in the chapter.

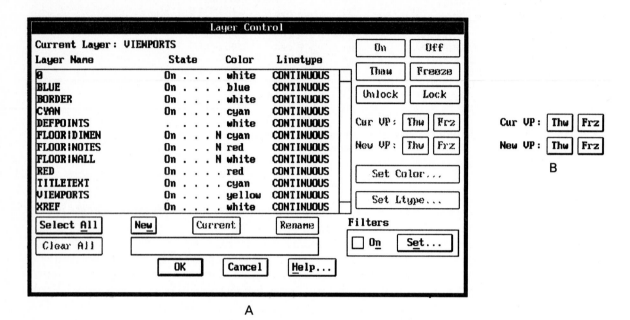

Fig. 27-33. A—The "N" to the left of the color indicates that layer is frozen in all new viewports. B—Layers can be frozen in selected viewports using the Cur VP and New VP buttons.

Creating additional viewports

The previous example of creating a viewport and referencing a drawing to it is the same process that is used to create the additional two viewports in our example. In this case, two viewports are created before using the XREF command. If you know the number, size, and location of all viewports needed on a multiview drawing, it may save time to create them all at once.

─────────── **PROFESSIONAL TIP** ───────────

If your class or company uses standard sheet layouts containing several views, create prototype drawings that contain viewports. Viewports can always be added, deleted, or resized on a drawing. Custom prototype drawings with viewports can be added to the list in the MVSETUP command.

The following command sequence resets paper space, changes the current layer to VIEWPORT, and uses the MVIEW and COPY commands to create new viewports. It then returns to model space to reference new drawings, and uses the ZOOM command to size the drawing in the viewport. The VPLAYER command is also used to control layer visibility in new viewports.

Command: **PSPACE** ↵
Command: **LAYER** ↵
?/Make/Set/New/ON/OFF/Color/Ltype/Freeze/Thaw: **S** ↵
New current layer ⟨current⟩: **VIEWPORTS** ↵
?/Make/Set/New/ON/OFF/Color/Ltype/Freeze/Thaw: ↵
Command: **MVIEW** ↵
ON/OFF/Hideplot/Fit/2/3/4/Restore/⟨First Point⟩: **.5,3** ↵ *(this is the location relative to the lower-left corner of the border)*
Other corner: **6.5,9** ↵

Be sure grips are on and pick the viewport you just drew. Copy the viewport to a position directly above the first. Next, use the grips and STRETCH command to change the height of the top viewport to 5" while keeping the width the same. The final arrangement of the three viewports is shown in Fig. 27-34.

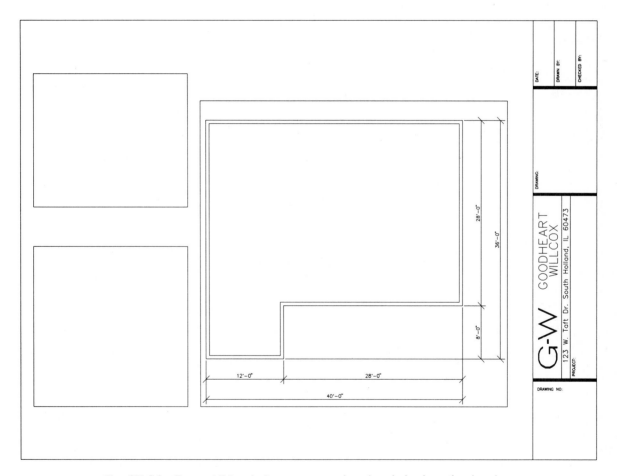

Fig. 27-34. Two additional viewports are placed and sized on the drawing.

Now that the viewports are complete, you can begin referencing the remaining two drawings. Change to model space and set the current layer to XREF. The STAIR drawing can now be referenced.

> Command: **XREF** ⏎
> ?/Bind/Detach/Path/Reload/⟨Attach⟩: ⏎
> Xref to Attach ⟨FLOOR⟩: **STAIR** ⏎

Accept the defaults for insertion of the drawing. Notice in Fig. 27-35 that the stair drawing is shown in all three viewports. The VPLAYER command must be used to freeze the stair layers in selected viewports.

> Command: **VPLAYER** ⏎
> ?/Freeze/Thaw/Reset/Newfrz/Vpvisdflt: **F** ⏎
> Layer(s) to Freeze: **STAIR*** ⏎
> All/Select/⟨Current⟩: **S** ⏎
> Switching to Paper space.
> Select objects: *(pick the outline of the first and third viewports)*
> Select objects: ⏎
> Switching to Model space.
> ?/Freeze/Thaw/Reset/Newfrz/Vpvisdflt: ⏎

Use the ZOOM command's Extents option to display the drawing completely in the lower-left viewport, then scale the drawing with ZOOM XP.

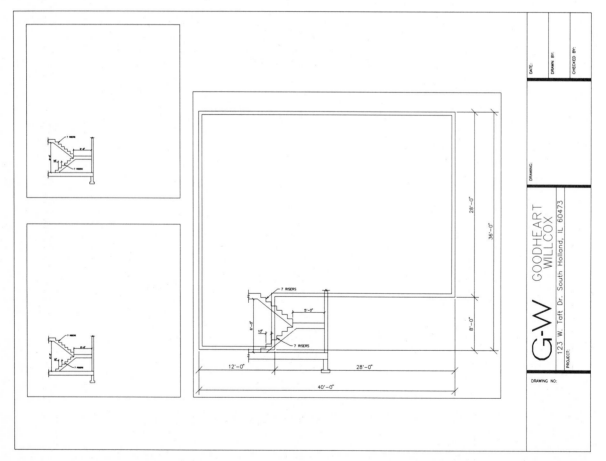

Fig. 27-35. The referenced drawing, STAIR, is displayed in all viewports. VPLAYER must be used to restrict its visibility.

NOTE

If you do not use ZOOM Extents first, your drawing may disappear after using ZOOM XP. This may occur if you pick the insertion point when using the XREF command, rather than entering 0,0 for the insertion point.

The plotted scale of the stair detail should be 3/8″ = 1′-0″. The scale factor is calculated as follows:

3/8″ = 1′-0″
.375″ = 12″
12/.375 = **32**

The scale factor is 32, but you must use the reciprocal (1/32) for the ZOOM XP command.

Command: **ZOOM** ↵
All/Center/Dynamic/Extents/Left/Previous/Vmax/Window/⟨scale⟩(X/XP)⟩: **1/32XP** ↵

Your drawing should now resemble the one shown in Fig. 27-36.

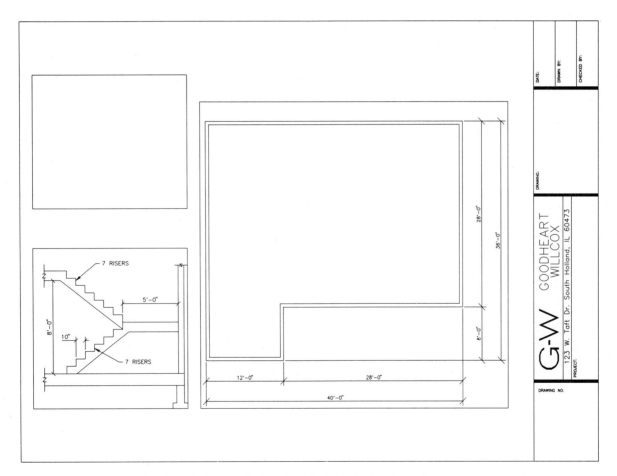

Fig. 27-36. The scaled STAIR drawing in the second viewport.

PROFESSIONAL TIP

You can use any display command inside a viewport. If a drawing is not centered after using ZOOM XP, simply use PAN to move it around. If lines of a drawing touch a viewport edge, those lines will not be visible if the viewport layer is frozen or turned off.

The final drawing can now be inserted into the last viewport. Pick the top viewport with your pointing device to make it active. Notice that the current viewport is surrounded by a white line. Crosshairs should now be displayed in the active viewport. Try to prepare the third view by following these steps.
- Model space should be active.
- The XREF layer should be current.
- XREF Attach the FOOTING drawing.
- Freeze the FOOTING layers in the other two viewports with VPLAYER.
- Zoom Extents, then ZOOM XP for proper scale. Plotted scale is to be 3/4″ = 1′-0″.
- Use the PAN command if necessary to center the drawing.

--- **NOTE** ---

Be sure to set the current layer to XREF when referencing a drawing so that the inserted drawing is not placed on another layer, such as VIEWPORTS.

When the final drawing has been referenced and scaled, your screen should look like Fig. 27-37.

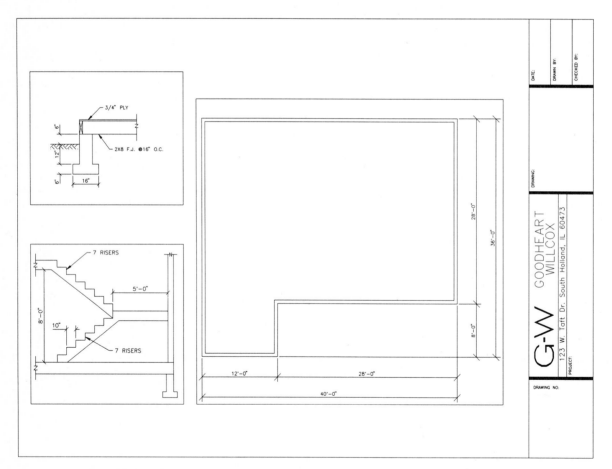

Fig. 27-37. The new drawing is completed with the referencing of the footing.

Adjusting viewport display, size, and location

If you need to adjust a drawing within a viewport, first be sure that you are in model space. Then, pick the desired viewport to make it active, and use an appropriate display command such as ZOOM Window.

The entire viewport can be moved to another location, but you must first be in paper space. Pick the viewport box and its grips appear. An object inside the viewport is not selected when picked because those objects are in model space. After selection, adjust the location of the viewports.

Remember the following when adjusting viewports:
- Model space — Adjust the display of a drawing or model inside a specific viewport.
- Paper space — Adjust the size or location of a viewport.

Adding notes and titles

There are two ways in which titles and notes can be added to a multiview drawing. The first method is to add the notations to the original drawing. In this manner, all titles and notes are referenced to the new drawing. This is the best system to use if the titles, scale label, and notes will not change.

However, titles may change. You may want to be sure that all titles of views are the same text style, or you might want to add a special symbol. This is easily completed after the drawings are referenced. The most important thing to remember is that you must be in paper space to add text. You can use new existing text styles to add titles and notes to a drawing using DTEXT.

Removing viewport outlines

The viewport outlines can be turned off for plotting purposes, as shown in Fig. 27-38. Turn off or freeze the VIEWPORTS layer as follows:

Command: **LAYER** ↵
?/Make/Set/New/ON/OFF/Color/Ltype/Freeze/Thaw: **F** ↵
Layer name(s) to Freeze: **VIEWPORTS** ↵
?/Make/Set/New/ON/OFF/Color/Ltype/Freeze/Thaw: ↵

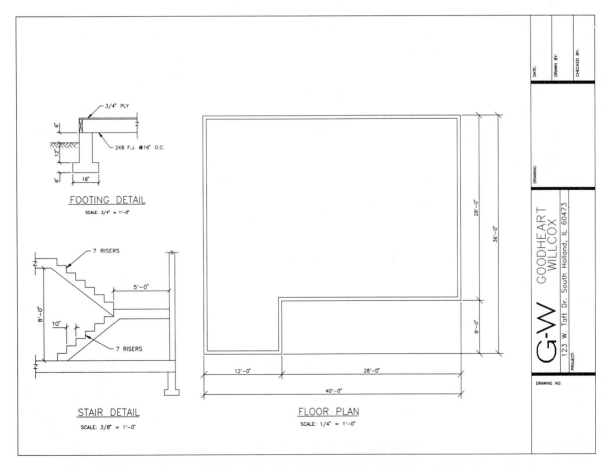

Fig. 27-38. The completed drawing with titles added and viewport outlines turned off.

━━━━━━━━━━ NOTE ━━━━━━━━━━

If you turn off the VIEWPORTS layer, and a white box still surrounds one of the views, you are probably still in model space. Remember that a white box outlines the current viewport in model space. Type "PS" to enter paper space and the outline disappears.

PLOTTING A MULTIVIEW DRAWING

You have already taken care of scaling the views when you referenced them and used the ZOOM XP command. The drawing that now appears on your screen in paper space can be plotted at full scale, 1 = 1, with the PLOT command.

━━━━━━━━━━ PROFESSIONAL TIP ━━━━━━━━━━

You may never have to specify a scale other than full (1 = 1) when plotting. Any object or design, whether 2-D or 3-D, can be referenced into a border and title block drawing, scaled with ZOOM XP, and then plotted.

MVIEW COMMAND OPTIONS   ARM 7

The primary purpose of the MVIEW command is to create viewports in paper space. If you use the MVIEW command in model space, AutoCAD changes to paper space for the rest of the command, then returns you to model space. The MVIEW command also allows you to change the size of viewports, fit them in the displayed screen area, or default to a specific value. Brief descriptions of each follow:

- **ON/OFF.** The contents of a viewport (the drawing or design in model space) can be turned on or off. If viewports are turned off, less time is required to regenerate the drawing.
- **Hideplot.** Allows you to select the viewports you wish to have hidden lines removed from when plotting in paper space. Hidden lines are removed by selecting ON, and are shown by selecting OFF.
- **Fit.** Creates a viewport to fit the current screen display. You can zoom into an area first, then use the MVIEW command's Fit option to create a viewport in the windowed area.
- **2/3/4.** AutoCAD automatically creates a configuration of 2, 3, or 4 viewports. The prompt is similar to the same option for the VPORTS command. When 2 or 3 is selected, you are prompted for specific locations and arrangements.

   2—Horizontal/⟨Vertical⟩:
   3—Horizontal/Vertical/Above/Below/Left/⟨Right⟩:

   When 4 is selected, four equal size viewports are created within a specified area.
- **Restore.** This option works if you have used the VPORTS command to create and save viewport configurations. AutoCAD asks for the configuration name, then allows you to either specify the locations and size of the viewports, or fit it into the current display.

   ?/Name of window configuration to insert ⟨default⟩: *(enter the name and press ENTER)*
   Fit/⟨First Point⟩:

   If you accept the default, you can position and size the new viewports by selecting two points to window an area in paper space. If you select Fit, the restored viewports are scaled to fit the graphics area.
- **⟨First Point⟩.** The default option allows you to select or enter the coordinates of the first corner of the viewport. Then, you are prompted for the other corner and a window is attached to the crosshairs. Pick the opposite corner and the viewport is drawn.

EXERCISE 27-2

☐ Use the prototype method to recall the border and title block drawing you used in Exercise 27-1. Name the drawing EX27-2.
☐ Create layers for referenced drawings (XREF) and viewports (VIEWPORT).
☐ Use the MVIEW 2/3/4 option to create an arrangement of three viewports on the VIEWPORT layer. Leave space in the upper-right corner for an additional viewport.
☐ Use the ZOOM command's Window option to display the open area in the upper-right corner of the drawing.
☐ Select the MVIEW command's Fit option to create a viewport in the current screen display.
☐ Reference the FLOOR drawing used in Exercise 27-1 into one of the viewports in the group of three viewports. Be sure the XREF layer is current.
☐ Turn off the contents of that viewport with the MVIEW command's OFF option.
☐ Save the drawing as A:EX27-2, then quit the drawing session.

VPLAYER COMMAND OPTIONS

| ARM 8 |

The VPLAYER (ViewPort LAYER) command controls the visibility of layers within selected viewports. This function differs from the LAYER command that controls the visibility of all layers in the drawing. The following list describes the function of each of the VPLAYER command option.

- **?** — After entering a question mark, AutoCAD prompts you to select a viewport. If you selected the upper-left viewport in Fig. 27-37, the following display appears on your screen:

        Layers currently frozen in viewport 4:
        FLOOR|WALL
        FLOOR|DIMEN
        FLOOR|NOTES
        STAIR|DIMEN
        STAIR|FLOOR
        STAIR|NOTES
        STAIR|STAIR
        STAIR|WALL
        ?/Freeze/Thaw/Reset/Newfrz/Vpvisdflt:

- **Freeze** — Enables you to selectively freeze one or more layers in any selected viewport(s).
- **Thaw** — This option allows you to thaw layers that were frozen with the Freeze option. As with the Freeze option, you can selectively thaw one or more layers in any viewport(s).
- **Reset** — Removes any viewport visibility default settings that were established with the Vpvisdflt option, and resets it to the default setting for a layer in a given viewport. This means that if you reset layers in a selected viewport, they become visible.
- **Newfrz** — Enables you to create a new frozen layer in all viewports, then you can thaw it in the viewport you wish it to be displayed in. The prompt for this option is:

        ?/Freeze/Thaw/Reset/Newfrz/Vpvisdflt: **N** ↵
        New Viewport frozen layer name(s): **WALLS** ↵
        ?/Freeze/Thaw/Reset/Newfrz/Vpvisdflt: **T** ↵

    After entering the Thaw option, you can select the viewport(s) in which you want the new layer named WALLS to be visible.

- **Vpvisdflt (ViewPort VISibility DeFauLT)** — This option enables you to control the visibility of layers in new viewports. Use this option if you do not want existing layers to be visible in new viewports.

        ?/Freeze/Thaw/Reset/Newfrz/Vpvisdflt: **V** ↵
        Layer name(s) to change default viewport visibility: *(enter layer name)*

EXERCISE 27-3

☐ Recall the drawing that you constructed in this chapter. It should contain three viewports, each containing an architectural detail.

☐ Be sure that the VIEWPORTS layer is on so that the viewport outlines are visible.

☐ List the layers currently frozen in the large viewport.

☐ Freeze the DIMEN layers in all viewports. Remember that in each viewport, the DIMEN layer name has been altered. For example, in the STAIR drawing, the layer is STAIR|DIMEN.

☐ Thaw the DIMEN layers in all viewports. Use a wild-card character (*) to thaw them all at once.

☐ Use the VPLAYER command's Reset option to remove all Vpvisdflt settings. The viewports should become crowded with multiple views. Use UNDO to remove the effects of the last command.

☐ Create a new frozen layer with the VPLAYER command's Newfrz option, and name it BOM. List the frozen layers in any of the viewports to see if BOM is frozen.

☐ Thaw BOM in the FOOTING viewport, then list the frozen layers in that viewport.

☐ Do not save your drawing.

XREF COMMAND OPTIONS

ARM 10

The XREF (eXternal REFerence) command enables you to add existing models or drawings to a new drawing without actually combining the files. AutoCAD creates a reference to an existing drawing. This allows you to keep the size of drawing files to a minimum. The following options are included when the XREF command is used.

- ?—All Xrefs in your drawing are displayed.

  Command: **XREF** ↵
  ?/Bind/Detach/Path/Reload/⟨Attach⟩: **?** ↵
  Xref(s) to list ⟨*⟩: ↵

Xref Name	Path
FLOOR	\acad12\gw\27\floor
FOOTING	\acad12\gw\27\footing
STAIR	\acad12\gw\27\stair
Total Xref(s): 3	

- **Bind**—This option permanently attaches an external reference to your drawing. It is a good idea to bind xrefs on drawings that are completed and are to be stored (archived), or drawings that are to be sent to a client, instructor, or service bureau for plotting.

- **Detach**—Referenced drawings that have been erased from your drawing, or that are no longer needed, can then be detached. AutoCAD deletes the specified xref(s) from the drawing file.

- **Path**—AutoCAD remembers the location, or "path" of a referenced drawing. If, for any reason, you must move the referenced drawings to another directory or disk drive, use the Path option to tell AutoCAD the new location. For example, if you were to relocate the FOOTING drawing to the \ACAD12\STRUCT subdirectory, use the following sequence:

  Command: **XREF** ↵
  ?/Bind/Detach/Path/Reload/⟨Attach⟩: **P** ↵
  Edit path for which Xref(s): **FOOTING** ↵
      Scanning...
  Xref name: FOOTING
  Old path: \acad12\gw\27\footing
  New path: **\ACAD12\STRUCT** ↵

- **Reload** — You can update any of the referenced drawings at any time by using the Reload option. This may be appropriate if someone in the class or office made revisions to a drawing that you referenced.

  Reload Xref FOOTING: \acad12\struct\footing

- **Attach** — This option enables you to attach an Xref to the drawing currently displayed on the screen. This is the default option and can be selected by pressing ENTER after the initial prompt is displayed.

PLOTTING HINTS

Plotting can slow down productivity in an office or a classroom if not done efficiently. Establish and adhere to a system for using the plotter. For a company, this might involve adding a special night shift that plots drawings when computer operators are not working. In a school, a student may be assigned to plot drawings, or specific times can be set aside for the task. In any situation, instruct all drafters, engineers, and other plotter users of the proper operating procedures. Post these in strategic locations.

Planning your plots

Planning is again the key word when dealing with plots. In the same way you planned the drawing, you must plan the plot. A few items to consider when planning are:
- Size and type of plotting media, such as bond paper, vellum, or polyester film.
- Type of title block.
- Location and scale of multiple views.
- Origin location.
- Scale of the drawing.
- Color, thickness, and types of pens to be used.
- Speed of pens.
- Orientation of 3-D views.
- Portion to be plotted: view, window, display, limits, or extents.

This is only a sample of decisions that should be made before you even walk up to the plotter. Remember, the plotter is the funnel through which all the drawings must go before they are evaluated, approved, and sent to production or the client. When a bottleneck develops at the plotter, production can suffer. The time savings of a CAD system can be drastically reduced.

Whether a school or business, your organization may benefit from the creation of a plotting request form. An example is shown in Fig. 27-39. This sample is used in one school's CAD lab. Its purpose is to require AutoCAD users to prepare as much as possible before thinking about a plot. Use this form or develop one of your own to increase your plotting efficiency.

——— PROFESSIONAL TIP ———

Use preprinted borders and title blocks whenever possible. Use attributes in a block for the information in the title block that will change with each drawing. This block can be inserted into any drawing or plotted separately before or after the drawing. This eliminates drawing borders and title blocks each time.

```
╔═══════════════════════════════════╗
║           PLOT REQUEST            ║
╠═══════════════════════════════════╣
```

REQUESTED BY:	DATE:
DATE REQUIRED:	

CAD STATION NUMBER:	1.	3.	5.	7.	9.
	2.	4.	6.	8.	10.

SCALE: ☐1=1 ☐1=12 ☐1=24 ☐1=32 ☐1=48
       ☐1=96 ☐FIT ☐OTHER (   )

AREA OF DWG. TO PLOT:
☐DISPLAY   ☐EXTENTS   ☐LIMITS
☐VIEW   ☐WINDOW

TYPE OF PLOT & PAPER SIZE:

CALCOMP:	☐D-SIZE ☐OTHER ( )
JDL:	☐D REDUCED TO C-SIZE
	☐B-SIZE ☐OTHER ( )
H-P:	☐D REDUCED TO B-SIZE
	☐B-SIZE ☐OTHER ( )
LASER:	☐LANDSCAPE ☐PORTRAIT

PLOT WRITTEN TO FILE:	☐NO	☐YES
PLOTTED BY:	DATE:	

Fig. 27-39. Example of a plotting request form.

Establish a plotting center

Many companies and schools have discovered the problems associated with the plotting process. One solution is the creation of a plotting center. A person or department is responsible for plotting drawings and supervising plotter use. The type of center or procedure established depends on the number of plotters available. Other factors include the number of computers serving the plotters, the numbers of computer users, office space available, and nature of the business.

The plotting center may be a special room with a dedicated computer, a terminal attached to the plotter, or a plot spooler cabled to a plotter. Disks are sent here at prearranged times or left in a "plot request" box with a plot form attached. Large companies that produce many drawings usually have a reproduction department. One or more people are responsible for making prints, copies, or photos. It is unproductive in a large office or classroom to allow all computer users to run their own plots.

Network users can operate a plotting center even more efficiently. Here plot files are created and used by a plot spooler. A plot spooler is a program that creates a plot queue (list). Plots are made as fast as paper can be loaded in the plotter. The network or spooler may also have a method for leaving instructions for the person doing the actual plotting. These instructions might replace the items that would normally be listed on a plot request form.

Establish plotting times in a classroom

In an educational environment, set a schedule for plot times. Set aside a time for plotting and have an instructor or lab assistant available to answer questions and solve problems. Options include:
- Plot at the end of the class or day.
- Plot once a week.
- Have a lab assistant make plots during the evening.
- Plot only those drawings absolutely necessary during work or class hours. This might occur during final evaluation at the end of the term. Instructors should evaluate drawings on disk whenever possible.

Eliminate unnecessary plots

A fantastic element in using computers for design and manufacturing is the elimination of paper drawings. This is a difficult concept for many people to grasp, mainly because there is "nothing" to grasp. When design data proceeds directly to manufacturing, there is no paper drawing to approve, touch, mark on, or keep lying around.

When you create plots, a bottleneck is introduced into the classroom or production environment, decreasing productivity. The easiest way to eliminate the problems associated with plotting is to eliminate plotting. Simply don't plot. Make plots *only* when absolutely necessary. This results in time and money savings. A few additional suggestions include:

- Obtain approvals of designs while the drawings are on the screen.
- Transfer files or disks for the checker's comments or supervisor's input on layout or designs.
- Create a special layer with a unique color for mark-ups. Freeze or erase this layer when finally making a plot.
- Classroom instructors should check drawings on disk at the computer screen. Use special layer for instructor comments.
- Make quick prints with a printer whenever check prints are sufficient.
- Avoid making plots for backups. Rather, save your drawing files in three different locations such as: hard disk, flexible disk at workstation, and flexible disk at another location. These may also be supplemented with a backup on tape cartridges or optical disks.

If you must plot...

Industry still exists on a paper-based system. Therefore, it is important that plotters are used efficiently—that means using the plotter only for what is required. Here are a few hints for doing just that.

- Ask yourself, "Do I *really* need a plot?" If the answer is an unqualified YES, then proceed.
- Plan your plot!
- Pick the least busy time to make the plot.
- If more than one plotter is available, use the smallest, least complex model.
- Select the smallest piece of paper possible.
- Use the lowest quality paper possible. Select bond for check plots or vellum or polyester film for final plots.
- Decide on only one color and thickness of pen to make the plot.
- Use the most inexpensive pen possible. Obtain a fiber tip or disposable pen for check plots. Choose a wet ink, steel tip pen only for final plots on vellum or polyester film.
- Enter the fastest pen speed that will still achieve quality without the pen skipping.
- Use a continuous linetype when possible. Hidden and center linetypes increase plot time significantly, and cause pen wear.

Producing quality plots

The time comes when you must plot the highest quality drawing for reproduction, evaluation, or client use. Then, use your plotter in a manner that does the job right the first time. Keep in mind these points before making that final plot.

- If you have several plotters, choose the one that will produce the quality of print you need. Select the right tool for the job.
- Choose the paper size appropriate for the drawing.
- Select the type of plotting media best suited for the application (drafting film for good reproduction; bond for check prints).
- Select the type of pen to achieve the results you need (wet ink for good reproduction; fiber or plastic tip for check prints).
- Set pen speeds slow enough to produce good lines without skipping.
- Use the proper ink for your climate.

Plotter hygiene

Computer lab hygiene, discussed in Chapter 1, extends to plotters as well. It is true that when properly maintained and cleaned, mechanical equipment works longer, more efficiently, and develops fewer problems. Here are a few suggestions for dealing with plotters and plotter supplies.

- Keep the plotter clean. Purchase a plastic or cloth dustcover if possible. Dust or vacuum it regularly. Clean the grit wheels with a stiff bristle brush (usually provided by manufacturer). Use pressurized air to clean internal parts.
- Service as soon as problems develop.
- Lock wheels on plotters that roll.
- Locate plotters out of high traffic areas. A separate room is best.
- Properly instruct all plotter users on machine operation.
- Have regular plotter operation update sessions.
- Assign people on rotating basis to regularly clean the plotter and plotting center, if a specific person is not in charge of plotting duties.
- Keep plotter supplies, paper, pens, attachments, in a storage area near the plotter.
- Adjust the humidity of the plotter room to suit the media used, or purchase plotter media that works best in the temperature and humidity of the plotter room.
- Avoid using wrinkled or creased paper or film in the plotter.

CHAPTER TEST

Write your answers in the spaces provided.

1. What command is used to generate paper copies of your drawings? _____

2. How do you get a quick print of the screen display? _____

3. What CMDDIA value is needed to issue plot prompts at the Command: line?

_____

4. List the different displays of a drawing you can select to plot in response to the What to plot: prompt._____

_____

5. To change the plotter defaults that are displayed by the PLOT command, you must

_____.

6. Define a "plot file" and explain how it is used. _____

_____

_____

7. Define a "plot queue." _____

_____

8. Explain when you would rotate a plot 90° clockwise. _____

_____

9. What would you enter at the Plot scale: prompt to make the plotted drawing twice the size of the softcopy drawing? _____

10. What would you enter at the Plot scale: prompt to enter a scale of 1/4″ = 1′-0″?

_____

11. Name the system variable that controls the display of the "Plot Configuration" dialogue box.

_____

12. How do you stop a plot in progress? _____

13. Name the pull-down menu where the PLOT command is found. _____

14. How do you add several printers or plotters to the Select Device area of the "Device and Default Selection" dialogue box? _____
_____

15. What is a PCP file? _____

16. How do you save a plot file named PLOT1 to your floppy disk?_____
_____
_____

17. How do you set pen assignments in a dialogue box? _____
_____
_____

18. Identify the two types of paper orientation. _____

19. Specify the radio button that is picked to make millimeters the units for all plot specifications.
_____

20. List an advantage of the Partial plot preview format._____

21. Enter the rotation indicated by the following rotation icon representations as presented in the partial plot preview format. _____

Image outline

Rotation icon

A. _____   B. _____   C. _____   D. _____

22. Cite at least two advantages of the Full plot preview format. _____
_____
_____

23. Identify at least one disadvantage of the Full plot preview format. _____
_____

24. Enter the name of symbols below that are used in the Pan and Zoom application of the Full plot preview format. _____

A. _____   B. _____

25. Explain the function of the Pan and Zoom boxes in the Full plot preview format.

_____

_____

_____

_____

26. Which system variable allows you to switch from model space to paper space?

_____

27. What is the function of the MVIEW command? _____

28. Why would you want to reference one drawing to another rather than insert it?

_____

29. Indicate the command, option, and value you would use to specify a scale of 1/2″ = 1′-0″ inside a viewport. _____

30. Name the command and option you would use to freeze all layers of drawings inside any new viewports. _____

31. Do you need to be in paper space or model space in order to resize a viewport?

_____

32. Why would you plot a multiview drawing at full scale (1 = 1) if it was created with MVIEW, and contained several views at different scales? _____

_____

33. Explain why you should plan your plots. _____

_____

_____

34. Provide the best method to speed up the plotting process in a classroom or company.

_____

_____

35. Quick, check prints are best generated on a _____.

36. What type of paper and pens should be used for a check plot? _____

_____

37. What type of paper and pens should be used for a final plot? _____

_____

DRAWING PROBLEMS

1. Open one of your drawings from an earlier chapter. Obtain a print of the drawing on your printer.
2. Use the same drawing from Problem 1 and generate two plots on your printer. The first should be rotated 90° and the second plot should not be rotated.
3. Open one of your dimensioned drawings from Chapter 18 or 19. Use the PLOT command to generate a B-size half-scale drawing of the limits. Use MVIEW to create viewports. Set zoom magnification appropriately.
4. Plot the same drawing used in Problem 3 on the appropriate size paper to give you a full-scale plot.

5. Plot the same drawing used in Problem 3 on B-size paper, but with a scale that will fit the entire drawing on the paper. Add a title block and border to the drawing before making the plots.

6. Open one of your drawings from Chapter 21. Plot the drawing on B-size paper using the Limits option. Use different color pens for each color in the drawing.

7. Zoom in on a portion of the drawing in Problem 6 and select the Display option. Rotate the plot 90° and fit it on the paper.

8. Using the same drawing from Problem 6, first be sure the entire drawing is displayed on the screen. Select PLOT and use the Window option. Window a detailed area of the drawing. Plot the drawing to fit the paper size chosen.

9. Plot a title block and border on a C-size sheet of paper. Put the name 3-D PLOT TEST next to Drawing Name: in the title block. Next, plot six different views of isometric or 3-D problems from Chapters 23 and 24 on a separate area of the paper.
   A. Determine the overall dimensions of the object before you plot.
   B. Determine the amount of paper space available for each object.
   C. Set the appropriate scale for each object so that it does not extend beyond the amount of space allotted to it.
   D. For 3-D objects, select the desired viewpoint before you plot.
   E. Use the appropriate plot format, such as Display, View, or Window.
   F. Use the Remove hidden lines option for one of the plots.
   G. Be sure to change the plot origin before plotting each object.

10. Open your most detailed dimensioned drawing. Generate a final plot with wet ink pens.
    A. Display the entire drawing on the screen.
    B. Load vellum or polyester film into the plotter.
    C. Insert wet ink pens into the pen holder or carousel. Use different pen widths if available.
    D. If you constructed the drawing on different layers, choose different color pens.
    E. Set pen speeds to achieve good quality lines. See the manufacturer's specifications for your particular brand of pen.
    F. Plot the drawing using the Limits or Extents option.

11. Open one of your 3-D drawings from Chapter 24. Construct a multiview layout and generate a final plot on C-size paper.
    A. Set TILEMODE to 0 and create four viewports of equal size, but separated by 1 in. of empty space.
    B. Select each viewport and display a different 3-D view of the model.
    C. Label each of the views in paper space. The label can represent the side of the object you are looking at.
    D. Plot the drawing and hide lines in two of the viewports.
    E. Save the drawing as A:P27-11.

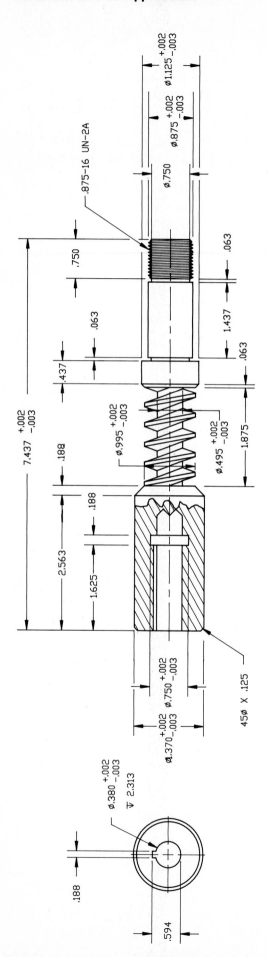

WORM GEAR DATA	
NUMBER OF THREADS	5
AXIAL PITCH	
PRESSURE ANGLE	20°
PITCH DIAMETER	.750
LEAD RIGHT HAND	.300
LEAD ANGLE	169°
ADDENDUM	.125
WHOLE DEPTH	.250
CHORDAL THICKNESS	.163
WORM GEAR PART NUMBER	1DT 1005

Detail drawing of worm gear. (Todd Given)

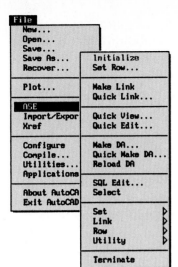

Chapter 28

INTRODUCTION TO THE AUTOCAD SQL EXTENSION (ASE)

Learning objectives

After completing this chapter, you will be able to:

☐ Define the function of a database.

☐ List the components of a database table.

☐ Describe the uses of database, SQL, and GIS applications.

☐ Load and initialize a database to work in an AutoCAD drawing.

☐ Add and edit rows to a database table using ASE.

☐ Create links between a database and an AutoCAD drawing entity.

☐ Use SQL to ask questions of the database.

☐ Add displayable attributes to the drawing.

The AutoCAD SQL (Structured Query Language) Extension, or ASE, provides a vital link between the graphical data that is created with AutoCAD and the text and numerical data generated with software called Database Management Systems (DBMS). An important aspect of any business is keeping track of inventories, clients, employees, facilities, building materials, product components, and other similar items. Most of the information we use relates to physical objects that are often represented in drawings as graphical entities. ASE enables you to relate and connect the text and numerical information (database) with the graphic information, and then ask questions about that relationship.

This chapter provides a look at the nature of information and how it is handled by database software, and by AutoCAD. For those who are unfamiliar with the terminology and structure of databases, this chapter should give you a general explanation of what they are and how the information in them is laid out. In addition, you will see how database information is used by ASE, and how you can manipulate and change that information in AutoCAD.

— **NOTE** —

After reading this chapter it is suggested that you work through the tutorials provided in the *AutoCAD SQL Extension Reference Manual*. The same drawing and database files you use in this chapter are used in the tutorials.

WHAT IS A DATABASE?

A *database* is a collection of information. "Data" is information, and a "base" is a foundation or solid component on which something rests. When you create a drawing in AutoCAD, you are, in effect, creating a database. However, when using AutoCAD, it is more graphical than textual. A common database is composed of text and numerical information. It may be as simple as a list of all the furniture in a company's offices. A *Database Management System* (DBMS) is the computer software that is used to construct, drive, and manage the databases.

A specific database, such as the inventory of furniture, is saved in a Database File with an extension of .DBF. The furniture inventory may be in a file named INVENTRY.DBF. The information in this file may be the identification number of the piece of furniture, the type, computer ID number (if it is a computer), manufacturer, office where it is located, and employee who occupies that office. When new furniture is purchased or old items are replaced, someone must revise the database using the DBMS. If the same company maintains facilities management drawings (building layouts, furniture, equipment, etc.) of their offices, the furniture may be represented in an AutoCAD drawing as blocks. These blocks must also be changed by someone else. Two databases—textural and graphical—must be maintained and updated by two or more different people. That topic is discussed later.

Let's say the company also has other database files on its employees and the computers in each office. The employee file (EMPLOYEE.DBF) contains information such as the person's office number, phone extension, type of furniture in the office, and type of computer. The computer database file (COMPUTER.DBF) may list the brand, type and speed, memory capacity, hard disk drive size, and input device.

Review the types of information found in each of these database files. Are there any items that are common to all of the three databases? Are there any relationships between the items in the three databases? Take a close look at these three database files:

INVENTRY.DBF	EMPLOYEE.DBF	COMPUTER.DBF
Inventory ID No.	*Employee ID No.*	*Computer Config. No.*
Type	Last name	CPU
Description	First name	Hard drive
Manufacturer	Title	RAM
Model	*Room No.*	Graphics
Computer Config. No.	Phone extension	Input device
Price		
Room No.		
Employee ID No.		

Note the italicized items in the three lists. These items are common to one of the other files, hence they relate to each other. If you use a basic database program, and a desk is moved to another room, its room number must be changed in the INVENTRY.DBF file. However, it also must be changed in the EMPLOYEE.DBF file. A lot of extra work is involved just to change the same piece of information twice. Since the computer has the information in one file, can't it also change it in the other?

The true power of a DBMS is in its perceived "intelligence;" in its ability to find relationships between different database files and edit them automatically. When this is possible, it means a great time-savings for employees who must maintain the database files and drawings. A database in which items in various files are interrelated is called a *relational database*. In a relational database, each file contains data designed for a specific purpose, but several files may contain data that is related to each other. If a specific item is changed in one file (such as the room number), the software automatically changes that item in all other related files.

Take a look at the contents of the three files again. What would happen if a computer with the configuration number of 3 were changed in the COMPUTER.DBF file to a number 5? Which databases would it affect? The Computer Config. No. would be changed in the INVENTRY. DBF file. That same file also contains the room number of each computer configuration number. Therefore, if you were to request the names of all employees who had a No. 5 computer configuration, how would the software find them? It would first find the Computer Config. No. in the COMPUTER.DBF file, which is also found in the INVENTRY. DBF file. The inventory file contains the room numbers in which the computer is located. The room number is also an item in the EMLOYEE.DBF file, therefore, the employee names are located.

In the previous example, you not only looked at and used the information contained in the three database files, but also asked questions, or made *queries* about the information. By giving the software one value, other values were found for you. Remember it can do this because the software is relational, and can search between files for similar information. However, the manner in which you ask questions is important, and must comply to a standard if it is to be understood by a variety of computer programs.

WHAT IS "STRUCTURED QUERY LANGUAGE"?

A *Structured Query Language* (SQL) is a computer programming format for asking questions of a database according to specific rules and syntax. The acronym SQL is often referred to as "sequel." The letters ASE refer to AutoCAD SQL Extension. The ASE syntax is derived from the ANSI X3.135 – 1989, SQL Standard.

As computer software improves and becomes more powerful, in many cases it also becomes more "intelligent." Using SQL, you can ask questions of a database, or in the case of ASE, ask questions of the drawing. SQL answers those questions, if possible, with highlighted information on the screen, or printed data. The implications of this are far-reaching, and the applications are endless.

A facilities management application of SQL

The following example uses three database files and a drawing of the office layout. Now, imagine that a new delivery of file cabinets arrives. These file cabinets are to replace a specific type that is found in only certain offices. How do you find those offices? You could open the drawing in AutoCAD and ask the database, "Which room number from the employee database file is where furniture equals file cabinet 45?" This is an example only and not the exact syntax you would use. However, the query is requesting the drawing/database to select, or highlight, all rooms that contain the Type 45 file cabinet. These are automatically listed in a dialogue box, and can be highlighted on the AutoCAD drawing. If necessary, this information—a list of office numbers—can be printed for the delivery personnel to use.

Mapping uses of SQL

The use of relational databases, intelligent drawings, and SQL has an important application in mapping. This specialized form of data is referred to as Geographic Information Systems, or GIS. A *geographic information system* is a detailed relational database of geographic entities. It is a rapidly expanding field that has applications in any field that requires the use of maps.

It is important to remember when working with any aspect of computer information, be it text, numerical, or graphic, that once the computer has the data, the manner in which that data is manipulated is up to the intelligence or creativity of the computer users. Therefore, in the near future, wider applications of GIS and SQL will be seen, thus opening broader opportunities not just for drafters, but people trained in the use of CAD software, databases, and GIS applications. Let's look at a couple of present applications of GIS and SQL.

- A forest fire is beginning to burn in steep terrain. It is hot, the forest is dry, and the fire will begin to rage out of control in the next 12 hours because strong east winds are expected. It is imperative that the Forest Service get information quickly on the following topics.
  - ✔ Topography of the terrain.
  - ✔ Roads in the area—paved, gravel, unimproved. What size vehicles will the roads support?
  - ✔ Hiking trails for fire crew use.
  - ✔ Streams: size and flow rates.
  - ✔ Lakes and ponds: quantities of water; depth; accessible by aerial tankers, helicopters, or truck.
  - ✔ Meadows, fields, and flat areas: usable for helicopters, light aircraft, staging areas, and bivouac (temporary encampment).
  - ✔ Forest cover: height, density, species composition.
  - ✔ Groundcover composition.
  - ✔ Private residences, buildings, power lines, utilities.

  This is only a sample of the type of information that could be a part of a relational database used by an agency such as the U.S. Forest Service. Using this system, an initial determination could be made that dropping water by helicopter will extinguish the blaze or retard it enough to allow a ground fire crew to surround the blaze. The query may be stated, "Show all bodies of water within a one-mile radius that are suitable for access by helicopter with a water bucket." The computer searches the database/map and then highlights all applicable bodies of water. The queries can continue from there, providing the fire managers with valuable information instantaneously.

- An emergency call has been received of a heart attack victim in a rural area. The dispatcher may need the following information:
  ✔ Exact location of the house.
  ✔ Current location of paramedic and ambulance units.
  ✔ Closest area suitable for helicopter landing if aerial transport is needed.
  ✔ Location of nearest hospital or clinic that can handle the case.

  The dispatcher can input the house location and have it displayed on the screen, then request the location of emergency response units. These can also be displayed. A call can then be made to the nearest unit to respond. A query can then be made of the system to display the quickest route to the house. This is displayed on the monitor in the ambulance. A request can also be made for alternate routes in case the primary one is blocked. The response by the paramedics can then begin. The dispatcher can also request a display of the closest helicopter access, then notify the medical flight center to be on standby. The map display and landing locations are then also displayed in the air rescue center, and flight plans can be made quickly.

Mechanical application of SQL

In addition to GIS applications, ASE has many mechanical applications, including the following:

- A routine aircraft inspection has determined that a widely used bolt is defective. It is possible that the manufacturer used inferior materials, or the manufacturing process was substandard. The information required by the maintenance crew and by management may include:
  ✔ Location of all such bolts in the aircraft.
  ✔ Other aircraft on which the bolts are used.
  ✔ Manufacturer of the bolts.
  ✔ Date of manufacture.
  ✔ Composition of materials.
  ✔ Material test results.
  ✔ Cost.
  ✔ Replacement time for all bolts.

  The maintenance supervisor may initially query the system to highlight the location of all the defective bolts, and provide a printed list of the number of bolts in the aircraft, number of bolts in inventory, and possibly alternate suppliers of the bolt. In this case, it would be important to know if the bolts in inventory were the same kind that were defective. If so, the alternate supplier could be used for replacements. This information is critical for not only safety reasons, but also economic considerations. The quicker the defective bolts can be replaced, the less downtime experienced by the aircraft.

These are just a few examples of the use of databases to obtain vital information quickly from the computer system. Now that you know what a database is, and how it can be used, it is time to look at the components of a database file and how it is structured.

DATABASE FILE STRUCTURE

The terminology used to describe the components in a database file can be confusing at first. These can also be confusing when the database is used by ASE since the appearance of database information in an AutoCAD dialogue box may not be shown as you expected. Therefore, if you are new to databases, read this section carefully. If you are familiar with database structure, you may choose to move to the next major section entitled **Getting Started With ASE**.

Sample database layouts

In its simplest form, a database is nothing more than a list of items with related information about each item. This list is most often presented in a format called a table. A *table* is an arrangement of rows (horizontal aspect) and columns (vertical aspect) of data. This format is commonly used in books and magazine articles to list a group of items and provide a variety of information about each item.

An example of a table is shown in Fig. 28-1. The row across the top of the table contains the name of each column; for example, TYPE and MFR. This column name tells you the type of information found in the column. The information shown in Fig. 28-1 is from the INVENTRY.DBF file mentioned previously. A table is normally a separate database file, such as the INVENTRY.DBF file. This file is used in the ASE tutorial, and later in this chapter.

INVENTRY.DBF

INV_ID	TYPE	DESCRIPT	MFR	MODEL	COMP_CFG	PRICE	ROOM	EMP_ID
1	Furniture	6x3 Couch	Couches are us	Lounge cat	0	800.00	101	1000
6	Furniture	Adjustable chair	Chairs R us	Comp pro	0	200.00	102	1001
45	Furniture	Two piece desk	Office Master	Desk3	0	400.00	103	1030
78	Furniture	42x18 file cabinet	Office Master	fc42x18d	0	40.00	104	1003

Fig. 28-1. A table is an arrangement of rows and columns.

Database file components

As previously mentioned, the format of a database is a table. A table consists of rows and columns. A *row* is a horizontal group of entries in a table, or the horizontal aspect of a table. Notice in Fig. 28-2 that an entry in the Inventory table begins with the INV__ID number. Eight additional items complete the data contained in the row. A row can also be referred to as a *record* or an *element*.

INVENTRY.DBF

INV_ID	TYPE	DESCRIPT	MFR	MODEL	COMP_CFG	PRICE	ROOM	EMP_ID
1	Furniture	6x3 Couch	Couches are us	Lounge cat	0	800.00	101	1000
6	Furniture	Adjustable chair	Chairs R us	Comp pro	0	200.00	102	1001
78	Furniture	42x18 file cabinet	Office Master	fc42x18d	0	40.00	104	1003

| 45 | Furniture | Two piece desk | Office Master | Desk3 | 0 | 400.00 | 103 | 1030 |

Fig. 28-2. A row is an element or entry in a table.

A *column* is a vertical aspect of the table, and contains some attribute of the row. For example, TYPE, DESCRIPT, and MFR are columns in the table. See Fig. 28-3. A column is also often referred to as a *field*, especially in the context of programming.

A table usually has a key. A *key* is one or more columns of a table used to identify a specific row in that table. A key is used as a search option and allows you to find a specific row in a table. For example, if a table contains several rows, and one of the columns is always different in each row, such as an inventory identification number, that column would be a good choice as the key. However, if more than one row could have the same value for each column, it might be a good idea to select two or more columns to be the key, called a *compound key*, in order to be more selective in your search.

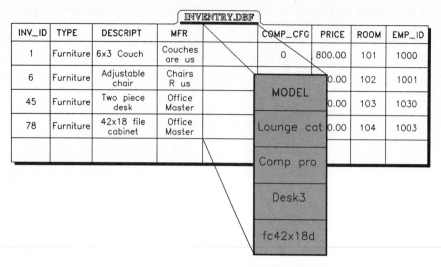

Fig. 28-3. A column contains an attribute of the row.

Database row display in ASE

As you can see in Figs. 28-1 and 28-2, a row is an element of horizontal information in the table. When you work with ASE, you are most often working with the information contained in a row. You can view it, edit it, and even link it to a graphic entity in your drawing. However, when you see a row displayed in a dialogue box in AutoCAD, it does not appear to be in the format of a row. It is actually displayed vertically in what looks like a column. See Fig. 28-4. This is an example of the "View Row" dialogue box you will be working with later. Look at the capitalized items in the list box. At first glance they may seem like different entries (rows) in a table, but they are not. They are actually column names, and the values given after the ¦ symbol are the entries in that column. Compare the information in Fig. 28-4 with that in Fig. 28-2.

This is mentioned now to try to prevent confusion when you begin working with rows in ASE. If you are still unsure of the format and layout of a table, go back over this section and study the illustrations carefully. When you understand the nature of a database table, working with ASE becomes much easier.

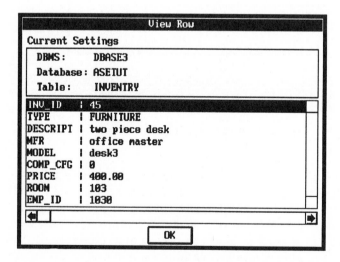

Fig. 28-4. Row attributes are listed vertically in the "View Row" dialogue box.

GETTING STARTED WITH ASE

Now that you are familiar with the meaning and structure of databases and their files, you may be developing an understanding of how the various components of databases and AutoCAD fit together. The illustration in Fig. 28-5 may help you see the relationship of the DBMS, database files, and tables.

AutoCAD must know which DBMS you are working with and where the database files are located. This information must be specified in an environment variable. Then, when you are in AutoCAD, the ASE program must be initialized before you can work with it.

If the files that are included for use with the ASE tutorial are to be used again, it is good practice to copy them to another location before working with them. The following section details backing up the database tutorial files.

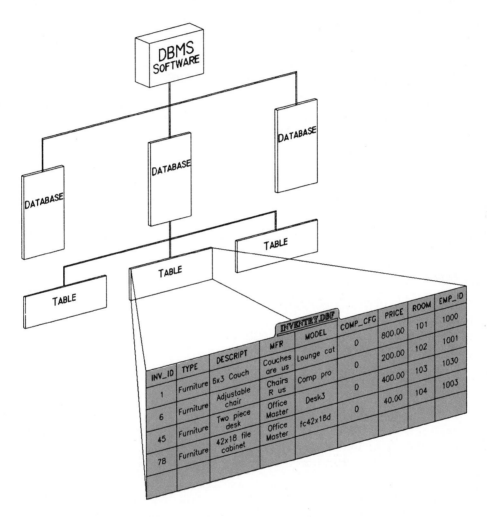

Fig. 28-5. The relationship of the DBMS, database files, and tables.

CAUTION

Always make backup copies of database files before using them with ASE. The ASE commands can alter the content of the database files.

Making backup copies of the database tutorial files

Before you begin working with ASE, you should first make copies of the files you will be using so the originals are not altered for future users or for your own exploration. You can copy the files to a separate subdirectory, or make copies of them in the directories in which they were installed. The following files are used in this text and in the *ASE Reference Manual* tutorial. The directory path in which they are installed is indicated (if installed properly).

```
\ACAD\TUTORIAL\ASETUT.DWG
\ACAD\TUTORIAL\DBF\COMPUTER.DBF
                   EMPLOYEE.DBF
                   INVENTRY.DBF
```

The following example shows you how to create a separate subdirectory for the backup files, then copy the files into it. Be sure that the DOS prompt is on your screen. This example assumes AutoCAD is located on the C: drive, and is in the directory named ACAD. If your directory is a different name, such as ACAD12, simply substitute that name for the "ACAD" shown in the examples.

```
C:\>CD ACAD\TUTORIAL ↵
C:\ACAD\TUTORIAL> MD BAK ↵
C:\ACAD\TUTORIAL> CD BAK ↵
C:\ACAD\TUTORIAL\BAK> COPY ..\ASETUT.* ↵
C:\ACAD\TUTORIAL\BAK> COPY ..\DBF\*.DBF ↵
C:\ACAD\TUTORIAL\BAK> DIR ↵
```

A listing of all files in the BAK subdirectory appears on the screen. Five files should be listed, the four listed previously and another .TXT file, which is not used in this text.

PROFESSIONAL TIP

In the two examples given here for copying files, the DOS directory alias of two periods or dots (..) is used. When you use the DIR command at the DOS prompt, the first two items listed are a dot (.) and two dots (..). The single dot is an alias for directory names. Therefore, if you issue the following command:

```
C:\> DIR *. ↵
```

You are given a listing of directory names only, and any files that have no extension characters after the name.

The two dots (..) is an alias for the parent directory of the current subdirectory. If you issue the following command:

```
C:\ACAD\TUTORIAL> CD.. ↵
C:\ACAD>
```

Notice that the command has changed directories to the "parent" of the one you were in. In this case, ACAD is the parent of TUTORIAL. As you can see, this alias can be used with other DOS commands as well.

When another person wishes to use this tutorial or the one in the Reference Manual, or if you wish to work through the tutorial from the beginning again, the five files should be copied back into the original directories as shown in this example:

```
C:\> CD \ACAD\TUTORIAL\BAK ↵
C:\ACAD\TUTORIAL\BAK> COPY *.DBF ..\DBF ↵
C:\ACAD\TUTORIAL\BAK> COPY ASETUT.* .. ↵
```

Now the original copies of the files are restored to the proper directories.

Setting the proper environment for ASE

When you load AutoCAD to work on a drawing, you are probably using a batch file. A *batch file* is a group of DOS commands assembled into a file that ends with a .BAT extension. Batch files can be used to do any number of things, and are discussed in Chapter 35 and Appendix C.

The batch file that is used to run AutoCAD (likely named ACADR12.BAT) should contain a few lines that set up an environment for the software to work in. An *environment variable* is a variable that sets a specific location in which AutoCAD can find files it needs to perform certain functions. One of the functions that AutoCAD must know before you begin working with ASE is the location of the database files. The environment variable that specifies this location is best placed in the batch file that runs AutoCAD. It must be added to the batch file using a text editor. The use of text editors is discussed in Chapter 29. The line that must be added to the batch file is:

SET ASETUT = C:\ACAD\TUTORIAL\DBF

This line must be added before the line that executes AutoCAD. If you are in doubt about how to add this to your batch file, check with your instructor or supervisor.

PROFESSIONAL TIP

The variable name that is given here, ASETUT, is actually an alias that can change. You can name it anything you wish, just remember the name. You will be asked for it when you use the ASESETDB (SET DataBase) command in AutoCAD. However, the name you use should always point to the directory that contains your database files.

Loading ASE and selecting a database

If AutoCAD and ASE were installed properly, you should have no trouble working with the examples in this text. Before you begin, the programs that run ASE must be loaded. These two files are ASE.EXP (an AutoCAD Development System [ADS] program) and ASE.LSP (an AutoLISP program). If you pick ASE from the File pull-down menu or from the screen menu, then pick Initialize, the two files are loaded automatically. You can also load them via the keyboard by entering the following:

Command: **(XLOAD "ASE")** ↵ *(this loads the ADS program)*
Command: **(LOAD "ASE")** ↵ *(this loads the LISP routine)*
Command: **ASEINIT** ↵ *(this initializes ASE)*

Next, check to be sure that the CMDDIA variable is set to 1, so that you can use dialogue boxes with ASE commands:

Command: **CMDDIA** ↵
New value for CMDDIA ⟨1⟩: ↵

NOTE

All of the ASE commands begin with the "ASE" prefix. This discussion gives you the commands to type at the Command: prompt. The commands can also be selected from the ASE pull-down and screen menus.

Now that ASE is loaded and initialized, you are ready to begin using a database file. You can work with database files in AutoCAD without loading the drawing containing links to the database. However, you first must tell AutoCAD which DBMS to use, then name the database (the environment variable you set previously), and the specific table to work in. The DBMS is specified with the ASESETDBMS command. You can set the DBMS through the set option of the ASE selection in the File pull-down menu. You can also type it at the Command: prompt as follows:

Command: **ASESETDBMS** ↵

Choose dBASE3 in the "Set DBMS Driver" dialogue box. See Fig. 28-6.

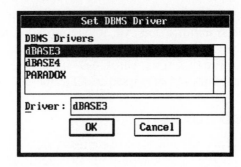

Fig. 28-6. The "Set DBMS Driver" dialogue box displays supported drivers.

Next, you must invoke the ASESETDB command to provide the name of the database to use. This is the name that is used in the SET statement in your batch file. Use the cascading menu or type as follows:

Command: **ASESETDB** ↵

The "Set Current Database" dialogue box appears. See Fig. 28-7. Enter "ASETUT" in the Database: edit box and pick OK. A username and password are requested, Fig. 28-8, but are not required. Pick OK to complete the command.

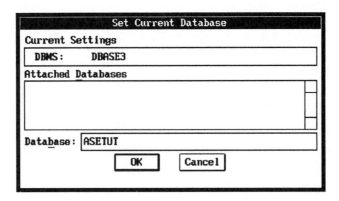

Fig. 28-7. The "Set Current Database" dialogue box.

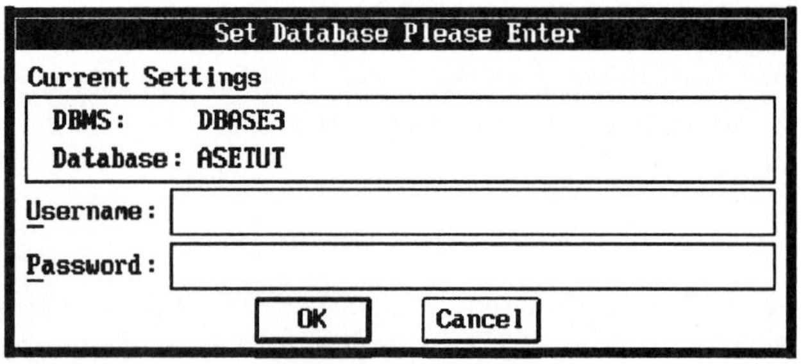

Fig. 28-8. Username and password are requested, but not required.

The last thing you need to do before you can work with individual rows in a database file is to set the specific table or .DBF file. Do this with the ASESETTABLE command by typing at the Command: prompt or by picking Table... from the cascading menu.

Command: **ASESETTABLE** ↵

The "Set Current Table" dialogue box is displayed. Enter "EMPLOYEE" in the Table: edit box and pick OK. See Fig. 28-9.

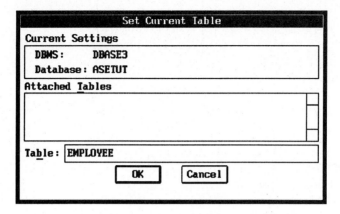

Fig. 28-9. The "Set Current Table" dialogue box.

The "Select Key Columns" dialogue box then appears. This dialogue box lists the current DBMS, database, table, and column names of the table. See Fig. 28-10. A *key value,* as mentioned previously, is one that is used to identify a row in the current table and make it accessible. In this case, the column EMP__ID is sufficient to identify the row, so either double-click on EMP__ID or press ENTER, when the selection is highlighted. Notice that On appears after EMP__ID. Pick OK.

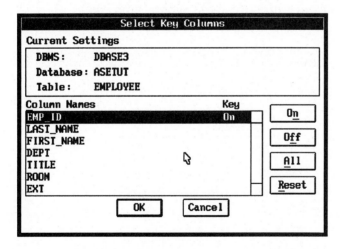

Fig. 28-10. The "Set Key Columns" dialogue box.

───────────────────────── **PROFESSIONAL TIP** ─────────────────────────

You can select more than one column name to create a *compound key.* Some database tables may have rows with the same value for one or more of the columns. If so, picking only one column for the key may retrieve more than one row when you use an SQL query. If you wish to be more selective of the row that is retrieved, pick more than one column as the key.

If you know you will need more than one table to work with on a project, it is a good idea to set them at the beginning of a drawing session, although the ASESETTABLE command can be used at any time. The last table that is set becomes the current one.

EXERCISE 28-1

☐ Use the ASESETTABLE command to set the INVENTRY table.
☐ Use the INV__ID column as the key if a key has not been set.
☐ Use ASESETTABLE again to set the COMPUTER table.
☐ Use the COMP__CFG column as the key if a key has not been set.
☐ Do *not* save the drawing.

USING SQL

Open the drawing named ASETUT located in the \ACAD\TUTORIAL subdirectory. After the drawing is loaded you need to initialize ASE. Then, select the DBMS. Use ASESETDBMS to be sure that dBASE3 is set, then use ASESETDB to see if ASETUT is the current database.

The purpose of the following example and the exercises in this chapter is to illustrate the uses of ASE in altering a database to link graphic entities with rows in a table. A new employee is going to be added to the EMPLOYEE database file (table), and this employee must be assigned to an office. However, the vacant offices must first be located. You can use SQL to ask the database to identify those offices for you. First set the current table to EMPLOYEE by using the ASESETTABLE command. Pick EMPLOYEE in the dialogue box, then pick OK. The SQL editor is then accessed with the ASESQLED command.

Command: **ASESQLED** ↵

The "SQL Editor" dialogue box is displayed. See Fig. 28-11. Enter the following in the SQL: edit box and press ENTER.

select room, emp__id from employee where emp__id = 0

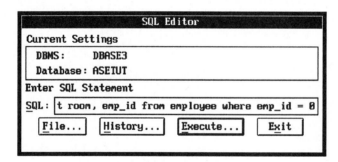

Fig. 28-11. Queries are made in the "SQL Editor" dialogue box.

The "Edit SQL Selection Set" dialogue box appears. This is discussed in detail later, but for now pick the Highlight button. Several of the room numbers have been highlighted. Zoom into one area to get a closer look. The current prompt reads:

Press ⟨enter⟩ or space bar... **'ZOOM** ↵
⟩⟩Center/Dynamic/Left/Previous/Vmax/Window/⟨Scale(X/XP)⟩: *(pick a window like the one shown in Fig. 28-12)*
Press ⟨enter⟩ or space bar... ↵

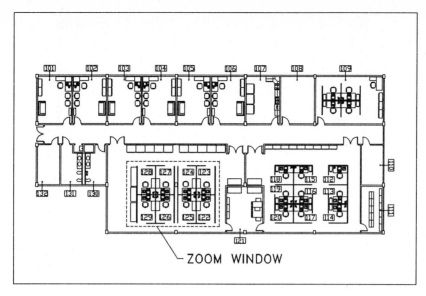

Fig. 28-12. Zoom in to see empty offices.

When the dialogue box appears, pick the Highlight button again. Notice that two rooms, 127 and 122 are highlighted. You have issued a query using SQL commands in the SQL editor, and ASE searched the database and provided you with the information.

Now, press ENTER to get the "Edit SQL Selection Set" dialogue box back and then pick the Sel. Set button. Pick Exit twice to return to the Command: prompt. You just requested ASE to create a selection set of the vacant rooms it located. Now, use an inquiry command such as LIST and use the Previous option at the Select objects: prompt. The same offices should be highlighted. Then, cancel the command. That's how easy it is to find an office for the new employee. We will place the employee in room 122.

WORKING WITH DATABASE ROWS

Most of your work in ASE will be with rows. You will either be setting, viewing, editing, displaying, or linking them to a drawing entity. Remember that a row is an entry in a database file (table) that contains several attributes. The following discussion shows you how to use rows in a variety of ways.

Setting and viewing a row

The last table to be set remains the current one. Before setting a row, be sure the correct table is current. Use the ASESETTABLE command again and be sure that the COMPUTER table is current.

The ASESETROW command enables you to set a row to use. Either pick Set Row... from the ASE cascading menu, or type it at the Command: prompt as follows:

Command: **ASESETROW** ↵

The "Set Row Options" dialogue box appears. See Fig. 28-13. It displays the current database and table settings, and provides options for selecting a row.

- **Criteria** – Using SQL syntax, you can enter search criteria. For example, if you wanted to select all of the rows having the value of "digitizer" in the INPUT column, enter the following: "input = 'digitizer' ".
- **Key** – When you used the ASESETTABLE command, you specified a key to use to set the current row in the table. Selecting the Key... button displays a dialogue box that allows you to change that key value in order to select the row to set as current.
- **Search** – Picking this button searches the entire table, loads all of the rows, and displays them in a dialogue box.
- **Graphical** – Picking this button returns to the graphics screen and asks you to select objects. Pick the entity having the row you wish to set. If the entity is linked to only one row, it is automatically set and the dialogue box is closed.

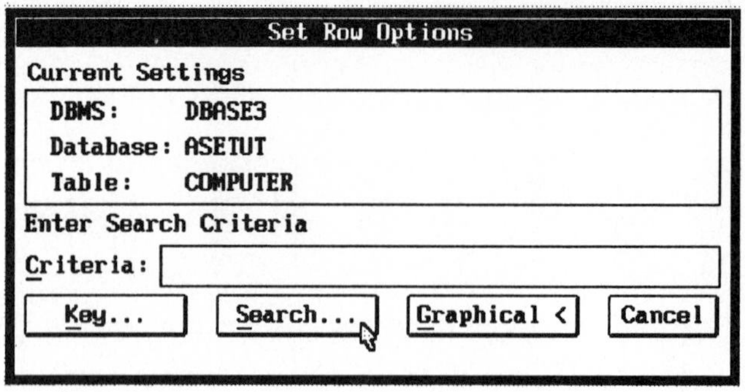

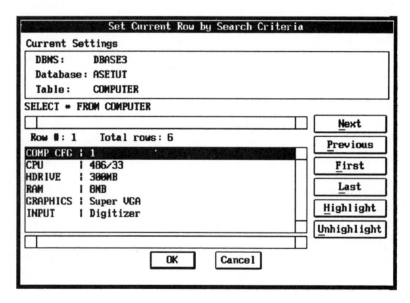

Fig. 28-13. The "Set Row Options" dialogue box.

A good way to look at all of the rows in the current table is to pick the Search... button. This displays the "Set Current Row by Search Criteria" dialogue box shown in Fig. 28-14. This dialogue box can be quite useful. It displays the current settings, an SQL select edit box, a current row and total row statement, and a list of all columns and their values in the current row. In addition, using the "scan" buttons to the right of the dialogue box, you can look through the rows by picking Next, Previous, First, and Last. If you want the current row highlighted on the screen, pick the Highlight button. The graphic screen is displayed and the entity that is linked to the current row is highlighted. Remove the highlight by picking Unhighlight. Take a moment and scan through the different rows using the buttons just mentioned.

Fig. 28-14. The "Set Current Row by Search Criteria" dialogue box.

If at any time you wish to look at a listing of the current row, use the ASEVIEWROW command, and the "View Row" dialogue box is displayed. You cannot change anything in this box, only view it. See Fig. 28-15.

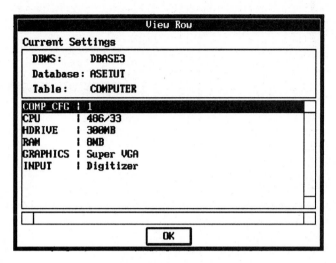

```
                        View Row
 Current Settings
 ┌──────────────────────────────────────────────┐
 │  DBMS:      DBASE3                             │
 │  Database:  ASETUT                             │
 │  Table:     COMPUTER                           │
 └──────────────────────────────────────────────┘
 ┌──────────────────────────────────────────────┐
 │COMP_CFG : 1                                  │ │
 │CPU      : 486/33                             │ │
 │HDRIVE   : 300MB                              │ │
 │RAM      : 8MB                                │ │
 │GRAPHICS : Super VGA                          │ │
 │INPUT    : Digitizer                          │ │
 │                                              │ │
 │                                              │─│
 └──────────────────────────────────────────────┘
 ┌──────────────────────────────────────────────┐
 │                                              │ │
 └──────────────────────────────────────────────┘
              ┌──────────┐
              │    OK    │
              └──────────┘
```

Fig. 28-15. The "View Row" dialogue box.

Adding a row

The "Add Row" dialogue box is displayed when you enter the ASEADDROW command. This is accessed at the Command: prompt, or by picking Add... from the Row option in the ASE cascading menu.

Command: **ASEADDROW** ↵

The values of the current row are displayed, but these are just defaults and will not be altered when you enter new values to add a row. See Fig. 28-16A. Notice that the current value for the highlighted column is displayed in the Edit: box. To add values, simply enter the new item and press ENTER. Then pick the next column by double-clicking on it. The value is displayed in the Edit: box, and you can enter the new value and press ENTER. Use the following values for creating a new row in the COMPUTER table.

Column	Value
COMP_CFG	7
CPU	486/50
HDRIVE	660MB
RAM	20MB
GRAPHICS	SVGA
INPUT	Mouse

The values in the dialogue box should look like those in Fig. 28-16B. Pick OK when you are finished.

If you wish to check to be sure the row was added, use the ASESETROW command again and pick the Search ... button. Note the number of rows now indicated. Pick Last... and the new row is displayed.

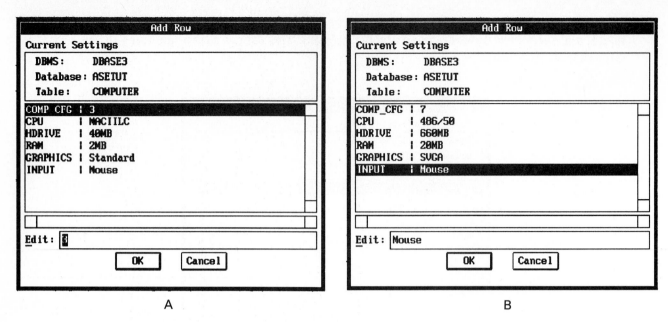

Fig. 28-16. A—The ''Add Row'' dialogue box displays the current row. B—The new row information in the ''Add Row'' dialogue box.

Editing a row

The contents of the current row can be changed at any time using the ASEEDITROW command. ASEEDITROW can be accessed through the pull-down menu or at the keyboard. You must be sure that the row you wish to edit is current. Use ASESETTABLE and ASESETROW to set the COMPUTER table and the COMP__CFG 7 row if it is not current. Now you can edit the row.

Command: **ASEEDITROW** ↵

The "Edit Row" dialogue box is displayed. Change the GRAPHICS column to TARGA, and the INPUT column to Trackball. Remember, to select an item for editing, double-click on it, then type the new value and press ENTER. The new values should look like those in Fig. 28-17. Pick OK when you are finished.

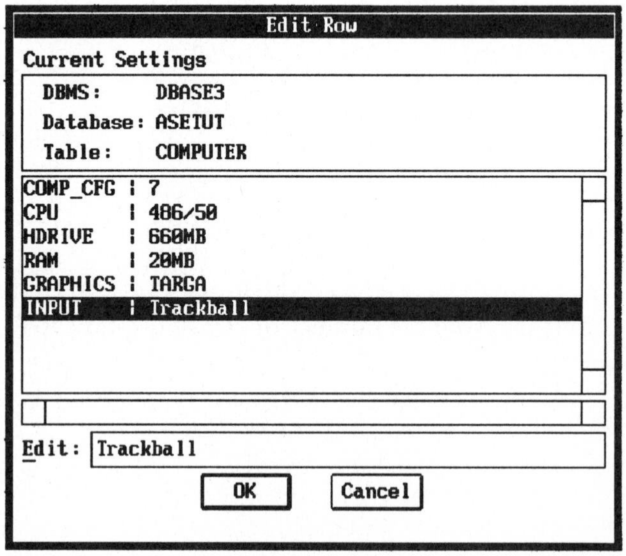

Fig. 28-17. Change row data in the ''Edit Row'' dialogue box.

EXERCISE 28-2

☐ Open the drawing ASETUT, then initialize ASE.
☐ Use the SAVEAS command and save the drawing as A:EX28-2.
☐ Add a new row to the EMPLOYEE table. Use the following information:

Column	Value
EMP_ID	1038
LAST_NAME	Desque
FIRST_NAME	Otto
DEPT	Publications
TITLE	Graphics Specialist
ROOM	122
EXT	8627

☐ View the current row to check your work.
☐ Set the INVENTRY table as current and add a new row with the following values.

Column	Value
INV_ID	215
TYPE	HARDWARE
DESCRIPT	personal inventory
MFR	Hardwire Hardware
MODEL	cpu7
COMP_CFG	7
PRICE	4900.00
ROOM	122
EMP_ID	1038

☐ View the current row to check your work.
☐ Save the drawing as A:EX28-2.

--- NOTE ---

If you leave this activity at any time, be sure to save your drawing. The next time you open the drawing, the DBMS and database are automatically set. However, you must initialize ASE again. The work you have completed to this point has altered some of the DBF files in the \ACAD\TUTORIAL\DBF subdirectory. If someone else will be working on this computer before you can return, you should copy the following files to your floppy disk or to your hard drive subdirectory.

    INVENTRY.DBF
    COMPUTER.DBF
    EMPLOYEE.DBF

When you return to complete this activity, copy these files from your floppy disk back to the \ACAD\TUTORIAL\DBF subdirectory before you begin AutoCAD.

LINKING THE DATABASE TO THE DRAWING

A *link* is a connection between a graphic entity in the AutoCAD drawing and a row, table, and database. This is one of the powerful aspects of ASE, which gives the drawing its expanded capabilities. You can select an object in the drawing, such as a computer, and have immediate access to all of the information stored in the database about that computer. Using ASE you can create links, delete, view, and edit existing links.

Viewing an existing link

Links can exist between an entity and more than one row, table, and database. If you need to determine the links that exist, use the ASEVIEWLINK command. Pick View... from the

Link cascading menu or type it at the Command: prompt as follows. However, before doing so for this activity ZOOM in on the same section of the office previously viewed.

Command: **ASEVIEWLINK** ↵
Select object: *(pick the computer in room 122)*

The "View Link" dialogue box displays the database link path and the link(s). See Fig. 28-18. If more than one link exists, they will be listed in the Values section and the buttons to the right of the dialogue box will not be grayed out. The DA Columns section is discussed later.

Note that the only link for the computer in room 122 is to the INVENTRY table. Remember this if you plan to delete this link.

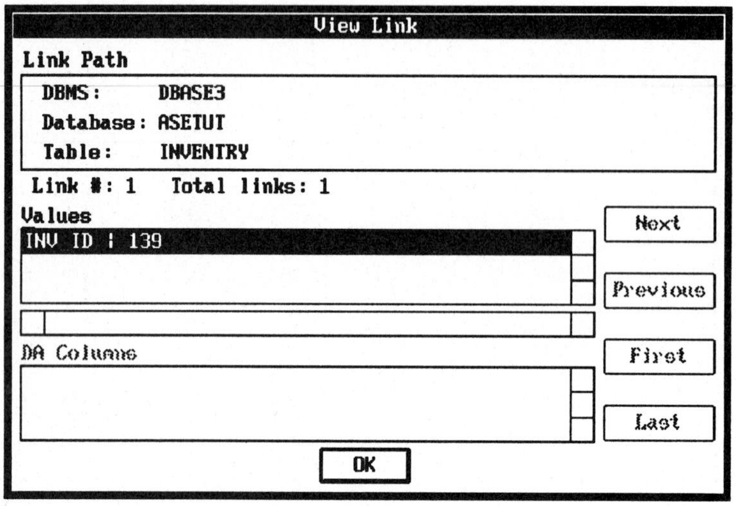

Fig. 28-18. The "View Link" dialogue box displays existing links.

Removing a link between a row and a graphic entity

As you just discovered, the computer in room 122 is currently linked to a row in the INVENTRY database file. However, the original computer is being removed and replaced by a new computer. You will want to link this computer entity in the drawing to the new row in the COMPUTER table, and the new row in the EMPLOYEE table. Therefore, you should first delete any existing links between the computer and other rows. You cannot recover a link once it is deleted, so be certain of your selection before you proceed. Use the ASEDELLINK command to remove the existing link.

Command: **ASEDELLINK** ↵
All/DBMS/dataBase/Table/⟨Row⟩:

The options allow you to delete selected links, as listed in the prompt, or all links with the All option. You know that only one link exists to the INVENTRY table, so use the Table option.

All/DBMS/dataBase/Table/⟨Row⟩: **T** ↵
Select objects: *(pick the computer in room 122)*
Select objects: ↵

An "ASE Confirmation" dialogue box appears, asking if you want to delete the linkages. Pick Yes. The linkages are then deleted.

Creating a link between a row and a graphic entity

A link can be created between a row in a table and a graphic entity with the ASEMAKELINK command. An AutoCAD entity can have links to more than one row in a table, and also to more than one table or database file. In order to make a link, you must first use ASESETTABLE. In this example, set the current table to COMPUTER. Next use ASESETROW and the Search... button to set the 486/50 computer. You may have to page through the rows using the Next button until you find it. Then pick OK. Now you can make the link.

Command: **ASEMAKELINK** ↵
Select objects: *(pick the computer in room 122)*
Select objects: ↵

The link is automatically made and the Command: prompt returns. Check the link using the ASEVIEWLINK command, and pick the computer in room 122 when asked to select objects. The "View Link" dialogue box should list "COMP__CFG ¦7" as the link. This is the key value for the COMPUTER table. Pick OK to exit the command.

The ASEQLINK (Quick LINK) command can also be used to make a link. It combines the ASESETROW and ASEMAKELINK commands. Before you use ASEQLINK, be sure that the current table is the one you want to work with.

Editing a link

You may encounter a situation in which a link exists between a row and a drawing entity, but it is no longer valid. Rather than making a new link and then deleting the old one, you can change the existing link with the ASEEDITLINK command. Use the ASEVIEWLINK command to check the link of the room 122 text label. The "View Link" dialogue box should show the value of EMP__ID¦0 as the link.

Before editing this link, check to be sure that the current table is EMPLOYEE, and the current row is set to EMP__ID ¦0. The link to the current row can be changed to another employee as follows:

Command: **ASEEDITLINK** ↵
All/DBMS/dataBase/Table/⟨Row⟩: ↵
Select object: *(pick the 122 text label)*

The "Edit Link" dialogue box appears and shows the link to the current row. See Fig. 28-19. If the link that is highlighted is the one you wish to change, pick the Proceed... button. The "Edit Link Options" dialogue box is then displayed. It is similar to the "Set Row" dialogue box,

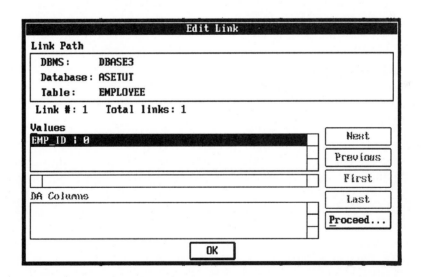

Fig. 28-19. Select the link to be changed in the "Edit Link" dialogue box.

and the remaining process is similar to setting a row. You can enter a key value, use the search function, or enter search criteria. Since you know the employee number, enter "emp__id = 1038" in the Criteria: edit box and press ENTER. See Fig. 28-20. The prompt "Only one row. Selection is automatic" is displayed on the Command: line, and the "Edit Link" dialogue box reappears. You have completed the edit, so pick the OK button. Check your work with the ASEVIEWLINK command.

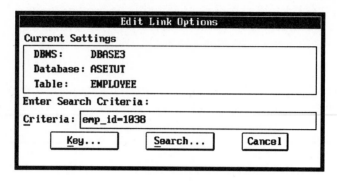

Fig. 28-20. The "Edit Link Options" dialogue box.

MAKING A DISPLAYABLE ATTRIBUTE

A *displayable attribute* is text representing values in a row that is displayed in the drawing. The text is an AutoCAD block and is composed of as many values from a row that you select. For example, you can select any of the column values of a row in the EMPLOYEE table to be displayed in that employee's office. The ASEMAKEDA (MAKE Displayable Attribute) command is used for this purpose. Before using this command, be sure the table you want to work with is current, in this case, EMPLOYEE.

Set the current row with the ASESETROW command and pick the Graphical ⟨ button. Next select the room 122 text label. Now use the ASEMAKEDA command.

Command: **ASEMAKEDA** ↵
Justify/Style/⟨Start point⟩: **109'6,42'3** ↵
Height ⟨8.0000⟩: **6** ↵
Rotation angle ⟨0⟩: ↵

The "Make Displayable Attribute" dialogue box is displayed. See Fig. 28-21A. The columns used in the current table are listed in the Table Columns area. The DA Columns area will list the column names in the order in which you select them, and will place them on your drawing in the same order. Select the column names by double-clicking. Pick FIRST__NAME, then LAST__NAME, then TITLE. Your selections should look like those in Fig. 28-21B. Pick OK when you are finished.

Notice in your drawing that "Graphics Specialist" overruns the wall. You can correct that error in several ways, but use the following steps to fix it with ASE commands.

1. Invoke the ASEEDITROW command. The "Edit Row" dialogue appears.
2. Double click on the TITLE column.
3. Change the title in the Edit: box to read "Graphic Spec." and pick OK.
4. Invoke the ASERELOADDA command. This reloads the displayable attribute according to the values in the row.
5. Select the displayable attribute you just created and press ENTER.

The displayable attribute is updated and should now reflect the revised value of the TITLE column.

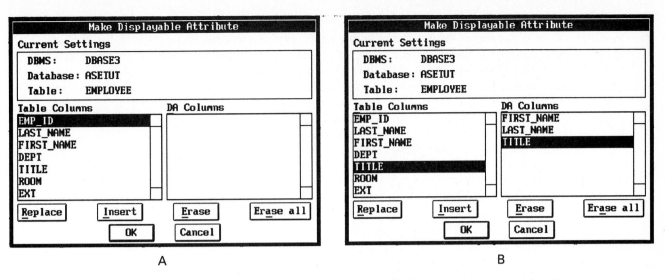

Fig. 28-21. A—The "Make Displayable Attribute" dialogue box displays the table columns. B—Selected columns are displayed in the DA Columns list box.

ASKING THE DATABASE FOR INFORMATION

Earlier in the chapter you used an SQL statement to determine where the vacant rooms were located. The command you used was ASESQLED (SQL Editor). Using the proper syntax, you can perform a number of database manipulations. Common functions are to update information in a table, and find and list data. The following example assigns all of the inventory items in room 122 to EMP_ID 1038.

Command: **ASESQLED** ↵

The "SQL Editor" dialogue box appears. Enter the following in the SQL: edit box and press ENTER.

update inventry set emp_id = 1038 where room = '122' and emp_id ⟨⟩ 1038

A message in the dialogue box indicates the number of updated rows. See Fig. 28-22.

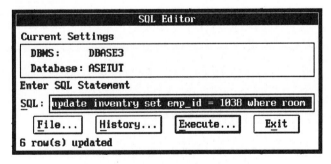

Fig. 28-22. The "SQL Editor" dialogue box.

This time you just want to list the inventory items that are located in room 122, and show the prices of each item. You are curious about the amount of money spent on Mr. Otto Desque. First, set the INVENTRY table as current. Then, use the ASESQLED command again and type the following in the SQL: edit box and press ENTER.

select inv_id, price from inventry where room = '122'

The "Edit SQL Selection Set" dialogue box is displayed and the total number of rows selected is indicated. See Fig. 28-23. As you page through the rows you will see INV__ID 139 listed. This is the original computer that was located in room 122. It has been replaced, so this computer should be reassigned to another room, such as 0, which could mean storage.

Exit from the ASESQLED dialogue boxes. Set the current row to INV__ID = 139 and then use ASEEDITROW to change the room number from 122 to 0. Then use the ASESQLED command, and enter the exact SQL command sequence you just used and press ENTER. There should be only five rows listed, and INV__ID 139 should not be one of them.

While in the "Edit SQL Selection Set" dialogue box you can page through the rows by picking the scan buttons. You can highlight or unhighlight individual items on the drawing, or pick the Sel. Set button to create a selection set of the highlighted items. The Delete button allows you to delete the selected row from the table and remove any associated links. The Edit: box displays the value of the current column. You can change this value and the table will be updated automatically if the Update button is grayed out. You can protect yourself from accidentally editing the row by picking the check box to the left of the Update button. You now must pick the Update button if you wish to revise the column value.

The ASESQLED command involves the use of the SQL programming language. It is not necessary to use or have knowledge of SQL commands in order to effectively use ASE. See Chapter 1 of the *AutoCAD SQL Extension Reference Manual* for a summary of SQL commands.

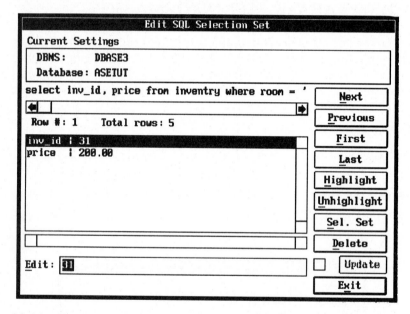

Fig. 28-23. The "Edit SQL Selection Set" dialogue box displays all selected rows.

RESOLVING DATA AND DRAWING CONFLICTS

Errors and conflicts can creep into your drawing and database files due to several factors. Persons working on the drawing may erase or alter drawing entities, and other people using the database files may delete or alter keys or rows to linked entities. In order for the drawing and database to maintain their integrity, you can use the ASEPOST command to report and fix these conflicts.

Command: **ASEPOST** ↵
Fix/⟨Report⟩: ↵

Note that the entities on your drawing are individually highlighted. If any invalid links are found they are reported, but no action is taken.

1 link(s) to rows DBASE3/ASETUT/EMPLOYEE invalid
3 link(s) to entities for DBASE3/ASETUT/EMPLOYEE invalid

You can repair and "synchronize" the drawing and databases by using the ASEPOST command's Fix option as follows:

Command: **ASEPOST** ↵
Fix/〈Report〉: **F** ↵

The "ASE Confirmation" dialogue box appears. Pick Yes and AutoCAD repairs the conflicts and indicates that the links have been "dereferenced."

— NOTE —

This chapter is intended to be an introduction to the capabilities of ASE. It is suggested that you go through the tutorials in the *AutoCAD SQL Extension Reference Manual,* and work the problems in this chapter. Begin right away to create your own small database and create a drawing that relates to it. This project should be a subject that is useful for you, and one that you can update and maintain easily. In this manner you will begin to see the value of working with a text and graphic relational database.

CHAPTER TEST

Write your answers in the spaces provided.

1. What is a database? _____

2. What is a DBMS? _____

3. A common three-letter extension of a database file is _____.

4. Define "relational database." _____

   _____

   _____

   _____

5. What does SQL stand for, and how is it pronounced? _____

   _____

6. The letters ASE stand for _____.

7. The specialized form of SQL used in mapping applications is called_____

   _____.

8. What is a database table? _____

9. What are the two principal components of a table? _____

10. The horizontal component of a table also known as a(n) _____.

11. The vertical component of a table is also known as a _____.

12. Write the proper ASE environment variable setting using the alias of DBFFILES when the

    database files are located in the directory of D:\ACAD12\DBASE. _____

    _____

13. Name the two files that must be loaded before ASE can function. _____

14. List the four commands you must use in order to select a DBMS, a database, a database

    table, and a row in the table. _____

    _____

15. What command is used to put a new row in a database table? _____

16. What command enables you to change items in a row? _____

17. Define "link." _____
    _____

18. How can you display a link you just created? _____

19. What are the options of the ASEDELLINK command? _____

20. Which command combines the ASESETROW and ASEMAKELINK commands? _____

21. Define "displayable attribute." _____
    _____

22. How do you choose the items that are to be shown in a displayable attribute? _____
    _____

23. What is the command name of the SQL editor? _____

24. Using the command in Question 23, what would you type to select and display the employee number (EMP__ID) and LAST__NAME columns of all employees who work in the DEPT of sales? Assume you are working in the EMPLOYEE.DBF file. _____
    _____

25. What is the purpose of the ASEPOST command? _____
    _____

DRAWING PROBLEMS

1. Make a copy of the ASETUT drawing and name it P28-1. Open P28-1 and set the DBMS and database used earlier in this chapter.
   A. Add the following rows to each table shown below. Use ASESQLED to find a vacant room for the new employee, and enter that number in the proper column. For any column left blank in the lists below, find the next available number in the existing tables and use that value.

   EMPLOYEE.DBF
   EMP__ID – _____
   LAST__NAME – Robinson
   FIRST__NAME – Lonnie
   DEPT – Human Resources
   TITLE – Counselor
   ROOM – _____
   EXT – _____

   INVENTRY.DBF
   INV__ID – _____
   TYPE – Laser printer
   DESCRIPT – Personal inventory
   MFR – Quasar Lasers
   MODEL – QLP-600
   COMP__CFG – 0
   PRICE – 1245.00
   ROOM – *(Lonnie's Room)*
   EMP__ID – *(Lonnie's EMP__ID)*

   B. View the new rows to check for errors.
   C. Link the new employee and the new laser printer to the room number you selected in the drawing. Save the drawing as A:P28-1.
2. Open drawing P28-1 and edit the following existing rows of the tables given.
   A. COMPUTER table: Change EMP__ID 1022's last name to Wood-Jenkins, and change her TITLE to International Sales Mgr.
   B. INVENTRY table: Change the price of INV__ID 141 to 5300.00, and change the MFR to Tradewinds Computers.
   C. COMPUTER table: Change COMP__CFG 5's RAM to 16MB, and the GRAPHICS to Metheus.
   D. View each table after completion to check for errors.

3. If you have database software, create a database for each computer in your lab named COMPUTER.DBF. Columns in the table should be:
   - COMP_ID
   - CPU
   - HDRIVE
   - INPUT
   - MFR
   - RAM
   - FDRIVE
   - GRAPHICS

   A. Before constructing the database file, make a list of each computer and record the components of each according to the requirements of the database table. Then enter all of the data at one time at the computer.

   B. Generate a printed copy when you have completed the database.

4. Construct a drawing of your computer lab. Create blocks for each workstation.

   A. Set the proper database and table in order to work with the computers in your drawing.

   B. Link each one of the computers in the drawing with the appropriate row in your database table.

   C. View the links you created to check for accuracy. Edit any links that are not correct.

   D. Create displayable attributes for each workstation. The attributes should use the COMP_ID and MFR columns.

   E. Place a label in the title block, or as a general note, referring to the database name that is linked to this drawing.

   F. Save the drawing as A:P28-4 and print or plot a copy of the drawing.

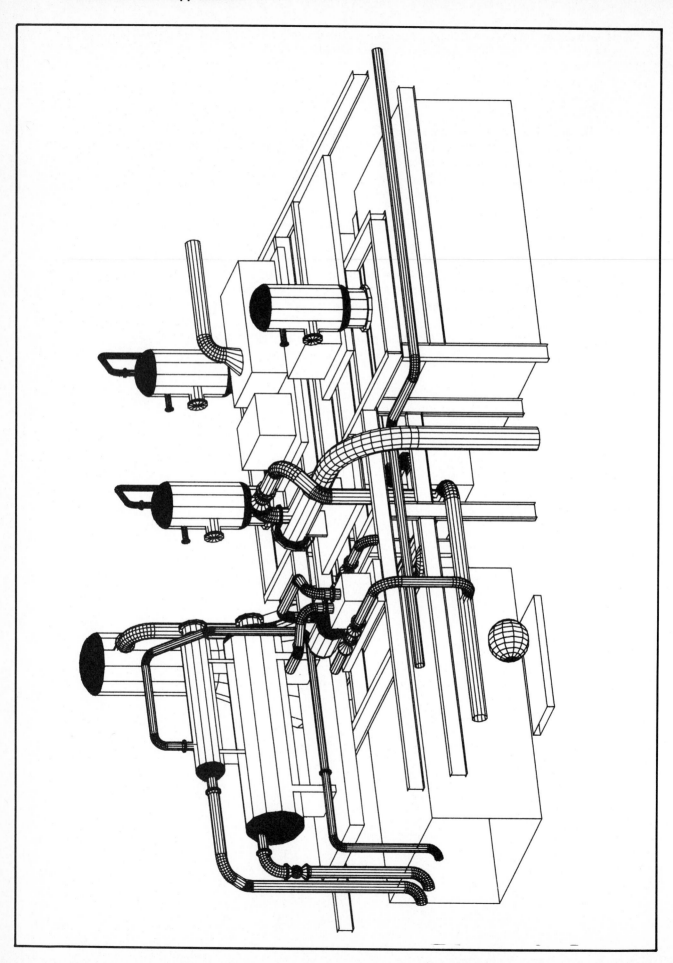

Solid model of a processing setup.   (Autodesk, Inc.)

Chapter 29

EXTERNAL COMMANDS, SCRIPT FILES, AND SLIDE SHOWS

Learning objectives

After completing this chapter, you will be able to:
- ☐ Edit the ACAD.PGP file.
- ☐ Use a text editor to create script files.
- ☐ Create a continuous slide show of existing drawings.
- ☐ Use the SLIDELIB command to create a slide library.

This chapter introduces you to the use of scripts. A *script* is a series of commands and variables listed in a text file. When the script file is activated by AutoCAD, the entire list of commands is performed without additional input from the user. One useful script is a continuous slide show. It is excellent for client presentations, demonstrations, and for grading drawings.

Word processing or text editor programs can be used to write scripts. If you are using a DOS (Disk Operating System) computer, there are three tools for writing text files: the COPY.CON command, the EDLIN line editor, and the EDIT text editor. Check for the presence of the last two files on your hard disk drive by typing the following at the DOS prompt:

> C:> **DIR \DOS\ED*.*** ↵

If EDLIN or EDIT are not listed, consult your instructor or supervisor.

— NOTE —

The EDIT text editor is a new feature of DOS Version 5.x. If you have an earlier version of DOS, this program is not available. Type "VER" at the DOS prompt to determine your DOS version.

USING TEXT EDITORS

The more experienced you become with AutoCAD, the more you will want to alter the program to suit specific needs. Most of these alterations are done with a text editor program. The EDLIN program that comes with DOS is not really powerful nor flexible enough for production work. However, it is satisfactory for creating simple files. Many AutoCAD users rely on full-fledged word processing programs to create their text files. However, the best type of text editor is a programmer's editor.

Word processors

There are hundreds of word processing programs. Two of which you might recognize are Word-Perfect and Microsoft Word. These are excellent programs when used for writing documents, but exceed what is needed to create text files for AutoCAD. If you choose to use a word processor, create the text file in "programmer's mode" or "nondocument" mode. This prevents the inclusion of special formatting codes.

PROFESSIONAL TIP

If you have used EDLIN before, you noticed that EDLIN numbers each line of the file. This is unique to EDLIN, and the numbers are not included when AutoCAD reads the file. Do not include line numbers when using a word processor or other text editor.

Programmer's text editors

There are a wide variety of text editors on the market. Inexpensive but powerful, these text editors are designed for creating the type of files needed to customize AutoCAD. Programmer's editors are recommended over word processors because of their design, size, function, ease of use, and price. If you are using DOS Version 5.x, the EDIT text editor is excellent for many of the custom files you will write for AutoCAD.

Introduction to EDLIN

The DOS text editor EDLIN is referred to as a *line editor*. This simply means that editing is done by line number. Word processors and programmer's editors, on the other hand, allow you to move around the screen easily. Since EDLIN comes with DOS, it is a popular program, especially for beginners using versions of DOS prior to Version 5.x. For this reason, all examples in this chapter and other chapters on customizing AutoCAD are written using EDLIN. If you are familiar with a word processor or text editor, feel free to use it to create the files. You can load the EDLIN program from the AutoCAD Command: prompt by typing "EDIT." Then type the name of the file to edit at the next prompt. If it is a new file the next prompt is:

        New file:
        *

Your DOS manual contains detailed instructions on using EDLIN. The most-used commands are defined in this chapter. All EDLIN commands are issued by typing a single letter. It can be lowercase or uppercase. The line numbers affected by the command are always entered before the command letter.
- **d (Delete)**—Deletes lines.
- *Line number* **(edit)**—Edits a line.
- **e (End)**—Ends editing and saves the file.
- **i (Insert)**—Inserts lines of text.
- **l (List)**—Lists lines of text.
- **p (Page)**—Pages forward 23 lines at a time.
- **q (Quit)**—Quits the editing session and does not save the file.

Delete. This command deletes a single line or multiple lines of text. To delete a single line, enter the line number followed by "d." The following example deletes line five.

        *5d ↵

A series of lines are deleted by separating the first and last lines by a comma. Lines 12 through 27 are deleted as follows:

        *12,27d ↵

Line edit. To edit a single line, enter just the line number at the EDLIN prompt (*). Suppose you wish to change line 11 of the ACAD.PGP file. Type "EDLIN ACAD.PGP" at the DOS prompt (C:\), assuming you have the appropriate path set up in the AUTOEXEC.BAT. Then, type "11." The existing line is displayed along with a blank line labeled "11" just below it. The

"ED" entered below means that you can type "ED" at the AutoCAD Command: prompt and execute the EDLIN line editor. Type the new version on the blank line as follows:

```
11:*EDIT,EDLIN,      0,File to edit: ,4
11:*ED,EDLIN,        0,File to edit: ,4 ↵
```

End. The END command quits the EDLIN program and saves the file. You are not given the opportunity to change the name of the file. Be sure to enter the proper file name when you open the file. If you enter an incorrect file name, quit the session immediately using CTRL C and try again. You might also save the file, then rename it using the DOS RENAME command or AutoCAD's File Utility menu.

Insert. Begin a file with the INSERT command as follows:

```
*i ↵
  1:*
```

Also add lines to an existing file with the INSERT command. For example, suppose you want to begin inserting lines in front of line 42. Enter the following:

```
*42i ↵
  42:*
```

The line with an asterisk appears. Enter the new line and press ENTER. You can add as many lines as you wish. They will all be listed consecutively, and will be inserted in front of the original line 42. When finished, press CTRL C.

List. The LIST command lists lines of text beginning with the line number specified. Twenty-three lines, or one screen (page), are displayed at a time. List additional pages with the PAGE command. For example, to list the file from line 46 on, enter:

```
*46l ↵
```

To return to the beginning of the file, enter:

```
*1l ↵
```

Page. The PAGE command is like LIST, but automatically lists the next 23 lines. Line numbers are not required when using PAGE.

```
*p ↵
```

Quit. The QUIT command exits the edit session without saving any of your work. It allows you to return to the edit session if you realize the file should be saved.

```
*q ↵
Abort edit (Y/N)?
```

Enter either "Y" or "N," but do not press ENTER. Doing so returns you to the DOS prompt. If you entered EDLIN by typing "EDIT" at the AutoCAD Command: prompt, pressing ENTER after entering "Y" to quit EDLIN brings you back to this prompt:

```
File to edit:
```

When you quit the session (enter "Y"), AutoCAD returns to the Command: prompt if you entered EDLIN from AutoCAD.

ADDING COMMANDS TO THE ACAD.PGP FILE   ACM 3

Since EDLIN is a DOS command, it must be entered at the DOS prompt. To create a text file named FIRST.TXT, type:

```
C:\>EDLIN FIRST.TXT ↵
New file
*
```

Enter the EDLIN command first, then the name and extension of the new file. EDLIN responds with "New file" and an asterisk, the prompt used in EDLIN in place of the drive letter displayed by DOS.

AutoCAD's external commands

Most files you create will be designed and needed while using AutoCAD. It would be time consuming to exit AutoCAD to write each text file. This is why AutoCAD provides a facility for creating your own text editing commands. These are called *external* because they request commands or programs that are not part of AutoCAD. A list of external commands is found by selecting UTILITY, found in the Root Menu. Then select the External Commands option. The following commands are shown in the screen menu:

Each of these executes a DOS command when typed at the AutoCAD Command: prompt. A file called ACAD.PGP contains instructions for their use. A .PGP file extension represents ProGram Parameters. To view this file, select TYPE.

```
Command: TYPE ↵
File to list: \ACAD12\SUPPORT\ACAD.PGP|MORE ↵
CATALOG,DIR /W,    0,File specification:  ,0
DEL,DEL,           0,File to delete:      ,4
DIR,DIR,           0,File specification:  ,0
EDIT,EDLIN,        0,File to edit:        ,4
SH,,               0,*OS Command:         ,4
SHELL,,            0,*OS Command:         ,4
TYPE,TYPE,         0,File to list:        ,0
```

The first word on each line is the command name that should be typed at AutoCAD's Command: prompt to execute the command. The second word represents the DOS command or program to be executed. Notice that typing "EDIT" at the Command: prompt runs EDLIN. A detailed explanation of the remaining information on each line is given later.

Command aliases

AutoCAD allows you to abbreviate command names. This is called a *command aliasing*. A list of existing aliases furnished with AutoCAD software can be displayed by looking at the contents of the ACAD.PGP file. You can do this by using the TYPE command, or by loading the file into EDLIN or your text editor. Scroll down to the second screen, and you will see the list of command aliases:

```
A,        *ARC
C,        *CIRCLE
CP,       *COPY
DV,       *DVIEW
E,        *ERASE
L,        *LINE
LA,       *LAYER
M,        *MOVE
MS,       *MSPACE
P,        *PAN
PS,       *PSPACE
PL,       *PLINE
R,        *REDRAW
Z,        *ZOOM
```

If you continue to scroll down into the file you will find a long list of aliases for AME commands. You can easily create your own aliases, but keep the number to a minimum if your computer does not have a lot of extra memory. Each command alias uses a small amount of memory, which reduces the amount available for drawing purposes.

If you want to add an alias for the DTEXT command, for example, enter the following below the ZOOM command in the ACAD.PGP file:

```
DT,       *DTEXT
```

Be sure to include the asterisk since it indicates to AutoCAD that this is an alias. The revised .PGP file will not work until you exit AutoCAD and re-enter the drawing editor, which reloads the ACAD.PGP file. You can also reload the ACAD.PGP file by entering the REINIT command. This displays the "Re-initialization" dialogue box. See Fig. 29-1. This box can be used if you have one of your communications ports such as COM1 configured for both a plotter and digitizer. If you physically change the cable from plotter to digitizer, pick the Digitizer box in both areas of the dialogue box, then pick OK. The digitizer will be re-initialized. In this case, you want to re-initialize the ACAD.PGP file so your new command can work. Pick the PGP file check box, then pick OK. Now you can try your new command alias.

Fig. 29-1. The "Re-initialization" dialogue box.

Creating a text editor command

You can add commands to the ACAD.PGP file list, as long as they do not have the same name as an AutoCAD command. Other utilities, such as text editors and database programs, can be added to the ACAD.PGP file. A possible addition to this file is a text editor program. To add it as another external command named TE, use EDLIN as follows:

Command: **EDIT** ↵
File to edit: **\ACAD12\SUPPORT\ACAD.PGP** ↵
End of input file *(this prompt indicates the file has been loaded)*
*8I ↵ *(list the file)*

```
        8:CATALOG,DIR /W,     0,File specification:  ,0
        9:DEL,DEL,            0,File to delete:  ,4
       10:DIR,DIR,            0,File specification:  ,0
       11:EDIT,EDLIN,         0,File to edit:  ,4
       12:SH,,                0,*OS Command:  ,4
       13:SHELL,,             0,*OS Command:  ,4
       14:TYPE,TYPE,          0,File to list:  ,0
```

Lines are added to a file using the INSERT (I) command. To begin inserting at line 15, enter "15i" at the asterisk prompt. Then type the values for the text editor.

*15i ↵ *(begin inserting at line 15)*

```
       15:*TE,TE,          0,File to edit:    ,4 ↵
       16:* ^C
```
(the spaces are used to align entries; they have no affect on the function of the item)

*e ↵ *(end and save file)*
Command:

— PROFESSIONAL TIP —

If you create a new external command in the ACAD.PGP file, be sure the name you give to execute the command or program is correct. For example, if your text editor is named Boris' Easy Editor, check the program disk or the documentation for the name of the executable file. In this case the executable file might be named BEE.EXE. Therefore, the line in the ACAD.PGP file to run this program may look like this:

```
    BE,BEE,         0,File to edit: ,4
```

The parts of the ACAD.PGP file entry are defined as follows. Each is separated by a comma.
- TE—The command to be typed at the AutoCAD Command: prompt.
- TE—The command or program name executed after the external command name is typed. This is the file name entered at DOS to run the text editor.
- 0—Previous versions of AutoCAD require a specified memory reserve for the command to function. Release 12 handles this automatically, but a 0 is still required for proper operation.
- File to edit:—The prompt that you want to appear after the command is typed.
- 4—A code that determines the type of screen mode to display when the command has completed. To return to graphics mode, put the number "4" in this location. Enter "0" here to have AutoCAD remain in the text mode.

If you are using DOS Version 5.x, you can quickly modify the PGP file to enable you to use the EDIT text editor from the AutoCAD Command: prompt, instead of EDLIN. Alter the ACAD.PGP file in the following manner:

Command: **EDIT** ↵
File to edit: **\ACAD12\SUPPORT\ACAD.PGP** ↵
End of input file
*11 ↵

```
       11:*EDIT,EDLIN,       0,File to edit:  ,4 ↵
       11:*EDIT,EDIT,        0,File to edit:  ,4 ↵
```
*e ↵ *(end and save the file)*
Command:

If you try using the new commands now, they will not work. This is because AutoCAD is still using the original version of the ACAD.PGP file. Use REINIT command before the TE and EDIT commands function properly.

EXERCISE 29-1

☐ Enter the AutoCAD drawing editor.
☐ Use the EDIT external command found in the UTILITY menu to edit the ACAD.PGP file.
☐ Create a new command named DIRDWG that lists only DWG files on the A: drive. The DOS command to use (if you haven't already devised it) is DIR A:*.DWG.
☐ The new command does not need a prompt. Therefore, place two commas after the 0 memory value.
☐ The line should end with 0 so that the screen remains in text mode.
☐ Save the file and use the REINIT command.
☐ Test the new command.

CREATING SCRIPT FILES TO AUTOMATE AUTOCAD

$\boxed{\text{ACM 7}}$

A *script file* is a list of commands that AutoCAD performs in sequence without input from the user. A script's principal function is to present slide shows. However, they can also be used for specific functions such as plotting a drawing with the correct PLOT command values and settings. A good working knowledge of AutoCAD commands and options is needed before you can confidently create a script file.

When writing a script file, put just one command or option per line in the text file. This makes the file easier to fix if the script does not work properly. A RETURN is specified by pressing ENTER after typing a command. If the next option of a command is a default value to be accepted, press ENTER again. This leaves a blank line in the script file, which represents pressing ENTER.

The following example shows how a script file can be used to plot a drawing. At your computer, enter these files with EDLIN or your favorite text editor. The file extension of the script name must be .SCR. Also, place the file in the ACAD directory of the hard disk. This occurs automatically if you enter "EDIT" at the Command: prompt to run the text editor. If the file is written outside AutoCAD, enter the file name as C:\ACAD\filename.SCR.

A drawing plotting script

In Chapter 27, you learned that you can save plotter settings for a specific drawing in the form of a PCP file. This eliminates setting all of the plot values each time you plot the same drawing. You can automate this process by including all of the plot values in a script file. If you have drawings that will always be plotted with the same settings, use script files to plot them.

The following script plots a C-size drawing. The contents of the script file are shown in the left column, and a description of each line is given to the right. This script file is named ARCH24-C.SCR. The "ARCH" indicates an architectural drawing, the "24" is the scale factor, and "C" is the paper size.

─── NOTE ───

When writing a script file, it is important to include every keystroke that is required to accomplish the task at the keyboard. It is also important to know how many plotters and printers are configured in AutoCAD, and how they are listed when using the PLOT command at the Command: line.

cmddia	*(executes CMDDIA system variable)*
0	*(disables the "Plot Configuration" dialogue box)*
plot	*(executes PLOT command)*
E	*(what to plot—extents)*
Y	*("Y" to change plot settings)*
Y	*("Y" to change plotters)*
3	*(description #3 for HP DraftPro)*
E	*(what to plot—extents)*
Y	*("Y" to change plot settings)*
N	*("N"—not to change plotters)*
60	*(number of seconds to wait for plotter port)*
Y	*("Y" to change plot parameters)*
C1	*(specify color number 1)*
1	*(pen 1 for color 1)*
0	*(linetype 0 for color 1)*
15	*(pen speed for color 1)*
0.010	*(pen width for color 1)*
C2	*(specify color 2)*
2	*(pen 2 for color 2)*
0	*(linetype 0 for color 2)*
15	*(pen speed for color 2)*
0.010	*(pen width for color 2)*
C3	*(specify color 3)*
3	*(pen 3 for color 3)*
0	*(linetype 0 for color 3)*
15	*(pen speed for color 3)*
0.010	*(pen width for color 3)*
C4	*(specify color 4)*
4	*(pen 4 for color 4)*
0	*(linetype 0 for color 4)*
15	*(pen speed for color 4)*
0.010	*(pen width for color 4)*
X	*(exit parameter settings)*
N	*(do not write plot file)*
I	*(size units in inches)*
0,0	*(plot origin)*
C	*(paper size)*
0	*(plot rotation angle)*
N	*(do not adjust for pen width)*
N	*(do not remove hidden lines)*
1 = 24	*(drawing scale)*

CAUTION

A single incorrect entry in a script file can cause it to malfunction. Test the keystrokes at the keyboard before you write the script file, and record them for future reference. When writing a script for plotting purposes, this is an important step. Plotters and printers have different settings, and thus have different prompts in the PLOT command. Always step through the PLOT command and specify the plotter or printer you wish to use before writing the script file.

PROFESSIONAL TIP

Avoid pressing the space bar at the end of a line in the script file. This adds a space, and can cause the script to crash. Plus, finding spaces in a script file can be tedious work.

At the Command: prompt, type "SCRIPT" and then select the file name ARCH24-C from the "Select Script File" dialogue box. See Fig. 29-2. Then sit back and watch the script run.

Command: **SCRIPT** ↵

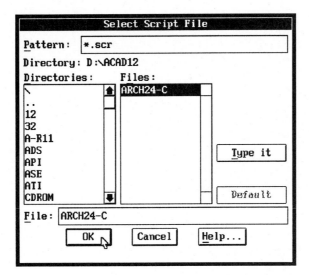

Fig. 29-2. The ''Select Script File'' dialogue box.

All of the commands, options, and text screens associated with the commands in the script are displayed in rapid succession on the screen. If the script stops before completing, a problem has occurred. Flip the screen to text mode (F1) to determine the last command executed. Return to your text editor and correct the problem. Most often, there are too many or too few RETURNs. Another problem is spaces at the end of a line. If you suspect these errors, retype the line.

Running a script from the DOS prompt

A script file can be run from the DOS prompt by entering a drawing name and script name after typing "ACADR12".

C:\〉 **ACADR12 FLRPLAN2 ARCH24-C** ↵

In this case, AutoCAD is executed by ACAD and the FLRPLAN2 drawing file is opened. Then, the ARCH24-C script is run. This is enabled by a line in the batch file that runs AutoCAD. A *batch file* executes a group of DOS command automatically. The file that loads AutoCAD is automatically created when AutoCAD is installed. The default name of this file is ACADR12.BAT. Find this file, or find the batch file that runs AutoCAD in your computer and use the TYPE command to list it. Find the following line:

ACAD %1 %2

In DOS terminology, the two percent symbols are called replaceable parameters. A *replaceable parameter* is a symbol that holds a place for a command or file name that is entered at the DOS prompt. The first percent symbol holds a place for the first command or name that is entered after the initial command. The second percent symbol holds a place for the second command or name entered after the initial command. Therefore, if your batch file that runs AutoCAD is named ACADR12.BAT, you can type the following at the DOS prompt:

C:\〉 **ACADR12 FLRPLAN2 ARCH24-C** ↵

DOS finds the batch file named ACADR12 and runs it. When the line "ACAD %1 %2" is encountered, DOS looks back at the initial command to find a substitute for %1. In this case, it finds FLRPLAN2, which for AutoCAD, is a drawing name to open. Then DOS substitutes ARCH24-C for the %2, which AutoCAD interprets as a script file name and runs it.

EXERCISE 29-2

☐ Begin a new drawing named SCRPTEST.
☐ Use the DTEXT command to write your name in the lower-right corner.
☐ Save the drawing.
☐ Use your text editor and write a script file named TEST.SCR. The script file should do the following:
    ☐ Draw a circle at coordinates 4,4 with a radius of 1.
    ☐ Change the color to green.
    ☐ Draw a donut centered on the circle with an inside diameter of 2.5 and an outside diameter of 2.8.
☐ Save the script file and exit AutoCAD if you are not currently at a DOS prompt.
☐ Use your batch file to load AutoCAD, open the SCRPTEST drawing, and run the TEST.SCR file.
☐ If the script file does not run to completion, use your text editor to correct it. Exit AutoCAD and run the script file again until it works.

SLIDES AND SLIDE SHOWS   ARM 11

A *slide* in AutoCAD, similar to a slide in photography, is a snapshot of the screen display. Because of its nature, it cannot be edited or plotted. Slides can be viewed one at a time or as a continuous show. This is why slides are excellent for demonstrations, presentations, displays, and grading procedures.

Students and prospective employees can create an impressive portfolio using a slide show. A *slide show* is a group of slides that are displayed at preset intervals. The slide show is controlled by a script file—a list of commands similar to the previous script examples. Each slide is displayed for a specific length of time. The show can be continuous or a single pass.

Making and viewing slides

Creating slides is easy. First display the drawing for which you need a slide. You might display the entire drawing or zoom to a specific area or feature. AutoCAD creates a slide of the current screen display, no questions asked. Make as many slides of one drawing as you want. For each, select the MSLIDE command and provide a file name for the slide. Do not enter a file type, as AutoCAD automatically attaches an .SLD file extension. If FILEDIA is set to 1, a dialogue box appears after entering "MSLIDE". Use the MSLIDE command as follows:

    Command: **MSLIDE** ↵

The "Create Slide File" dialogue box is displayed. This is the standard file dialogue box. Pick the drive and directory in which the file is to be stored, then enter the name in the File: edit box, and pick the OK button.

Slide names should follow a pattern. Suppose you are making slides for a class called CAD1. File names such as CAD1SLD1 and CAD1SLD2 are appropriate. If working on project #4305 for the Weyerhauser Company, you might name the slide to reflect the client name or project number, such as WEYERSL1 or 4305SLD1. Slide names can use the full eight characters allowed by DOS. This lets DOS manipulate files easier, as you will discover in Chapter 35.

Viewing a slide is as simple as making one. The VSLIDE command asks for the slide file name. Do not enter the .SLD file extension because AutoCAD knows it is looking for a slide.

    Command: **VSLIDE** ↵

The "Select Slide File" dialogue box appears. Pick the slide you want to display and pick OK.

Keep the ACAD directory free of drawing, slide, and AutoLISP files. This speeds the computer's access to AutoCAD files. Create a separate hard disk directory for slides or save slides on a floppy disk. See Chapter 35. If using floppy disks, be sure to give the appropriate file name when creating slides. A file name of CAD1SLD1 is entered to place a slide on a floppy disk in the A: disk drive.

    Command: **MSLIDE** ↵
    Slide file: **A:CAD1SLD1** ↵

EXERCISE 29-3

☐ Load any one of your drawings into the drawing editor.
☐ Create a slide of the entire drawing, using an appropriate file name.
☐ Make slides of two more drawings. Use similar naming techniques.
☐ View each of the slides as they are created.
☐ These slides are required to complete the next exercise.

Writing a slide show script file

A slide show script file contains only two or three commands. This depends on whether it is a single pass or continuous show. The RSCRIPT (Repeat SCRIPT) command is used at the end of a continuous script file. Any slide file can be displayed for up to 33 seconds using the DELAY command. Delays are given in milliseconds. A delay of four seconds is written as DELAY 4000. The next slide is "preloaded" into computer memory for quick display by placing an asterisk before the slide name. A slide is displayed with the VSLIDE command.

A slide show begins with the creation of a script file using a text editor. The following script uses four slides. Each appears for three seconds and the script repeats. Notice that the next slide is preloaded while the previous one is viewed. The file, SHOW.SCR, is created as follows:

    Command: **EDIT** ↵
    File to edit: **SHOW.SCR** ↵
    New file
    *I ↵
                1:*VSLIDE CAD1SLD1 ↵   *(if you use a text editor other than EDLIN,*
                2:*VSLIDE *CAD1SLD2 ↵   *do not place an asterisk at the begin-*
                3:*DELAY 3000 ↵   *ning of each line; it is an EDLIN prompt)*
                4:*VSLIDE ↵
                5:*VSLIDE *CAD1SLD3 ↵
                6:*DELAY 3000 ↵
                7:*VSLIDE ↵
                8:*VSLIDE *CAD1SLD4 ↵
                9:*DELAY 3000 ↵
               10:*VSLIDE ↵
               11:*DELAY 3000 ↵
               12:*RSCRIPT ↵
               13:*^C
    *I ↵ *(list file to check for errors)*
    *e ↵ *(end and save the file)*

When using slide files on diskettes, include the disk drive path in front of the file name, such as A:CAD1SLD2. Use this method with each VSLIDE command.

Viewing the slide show

A slide show is started with the SCRIPT command as follows:

    Command: **SCRIPT** ↵
    Script file: **SHOW** ↵

The show begins and the commands in the script file are displayed at the Command: prompt as the slides appear. To stop the show, press the BACKSPACE key. You can then work on a drawing, use DOS commands, or work with a text editor on another script file. When finished, resume the slide show where it left off by typing RESUME. Any script file can be interrupted and restarted in this manner.

Your slide show may run into a bug and not finish the first time through. This is not unusual, so do not panic. Take the following steps to "debug," or correct, problems in your script file.

- Run the script to see where it crashes (quits working).
- Check the command line for the last command that was executed.
- Look for error messages, such as:
  - "Can't open slide file xxxxx" (incorrect slide file name).
  - "xxxxx Unknown command" (command spelled incorrectly or a space left at the end of the line).
  - "Requires an integer value" (delay value not all numerical characters. Possibly a space at the end of the line).
- Correct the problem in the script file.
- Test the script.

The most common errors are misspelled commands and spaces at the end of lines. If you suspect there is a space at the end of a line, it is best to retype the line. Retype line 4 as follows:

> ***4** ↵ *(to edit line 4)*
>   4:*VSLIDE ↵
>   4:***VSLIDE** ↵
>   *

If you use a text editor, it is easy to see if a space exists. The flashing cursor, when placed at the end of a line, does not rest on the last character. This feature is not possible with EDLIN.

EXERCISE 29-4

☐ Create a script file named EX29-4. Use EDLIN or your own text editor. It is not necessary to be in the AutoCAD drawing editor to create the script file.
☐ Include the three slides created in Exercise 29-3. If these slides have not been created, make slides of any three of your drawings.
☐ Delay each slide for two seconds.
☐ Make the show run continuously.
☐ Run the slide show. Correct any errors and run it again until it recycles without failing.

CREATING AND USING SLIDE LIBRARIES   ARM 14

A *slide library* is a list of slide files that can be used not only for slide shows, but also for constructing icon menus. Icon menus are groups of slides displayed in a dialogue box. Examples are the hatch patterns displayed after selecting Hatch from the Draw pull-down menu. Constructing icon menus is discussed in Chapter 32.

Creating the slide library

To create the slide library, you must use a utility program, called SLIDELIB.EXE, that operates from the DOS prompt. By default, the SLIDELIB.EXE utility is installed in the ACAD\ SUPPORT subdirectory. Be sure to include this path when using the utility. SLIDE.EXE can be used to create slide libraries one of two ways. The first method involves listing the slides and their directory location after entering the SLIDELIB command. For example, suppose you have four slides of pipe fittings in the PIPE subdirectory of ACAD. List these in a slide library called PIPE in the following manner:

> Command: **SH** ↵
> OS Command: **\ACAD12\SUPPORT\SLIDELIB PIPE** ↵
> SLIDELIB 1.2 (3/8/89)
> (C) Copyright 1987-89 Autodesk, Inc.
>   All Rights Reserved
> **\ACAD\PIPE\90ELBOW** ↵
> **\ACAD\PIPE\45ELBOW** ↵
> **\ACAD\PIPE\TEE** ↵
> **\ACAD\PIPE\CAP** ↵
> ↵
> ↵
> Command:

After entering the last slide, press ENTER three times to end the SLIDELIB command. The new slide library file is saved as PIPE.SLB.

The second way to use SLIDELIB is to first create a list of the slides you will eventually want in the library. Do this with a text editor. This method allows you to accumulate slides over a period of time. Then, when you are finally ready to create the slide library, the list is prepared. A list of those same pipe fittings slides would be listed in EDLIN as follows:

> Command: **EDIT** ↵
> File to edit: **PIPE.TXT** ↵
> New file
> ***i** ↵
>   1:***90ELBOW** ↵
>   2:***45ELBOW** ↵
>   3:***TEE** ↵
>   4:***CAP** ↵
>   5:*∧**C**
> ***e** ↵

After completing the list of slides to include, use the SLIDELIB command. The SLIDELIB command needs to find the PIPE.TXT file and use it to create a slide library file called PIPE.SLB. This can all be handled with one entry at the DOS prompt.

> Command: **SH** ↵
> OS Command: **SLIDELIB PIPE ⟨PIPE.TXT** ↵
> SLIDELIB 1.0 (7/29/87)
> (C) Copyright 1987 Autodesk, Inc.
>   All Rights Reserved
> Command:

The SLIDELIB command automatically creates a file called PIPE.SLB using the information it found in the PIPE.TXT file. The reverse caret (⟨) instructs the SLIDELIB program to use the contents of PIPE.TXT to create the PIPE.SLB file. To see the results, obtain a directory listing of all SLB files and look for PIPE.SLB.

Viewing slide library slides

The VSLIDE command also is used to view slides contained in a slide library. Provide the library name plus the slide name in parentheses as follows:

> Command: **VSLIDE** ↵
> Slide file: *(pick Type it in the dialogue box, and enter ''PIPE(90ELBOW)'' in the edit box)*

To remove the slide from the screen to display the previous drawing, enter "REDRAW."

Making a slide show using the slide library

The advantage of using a slide library for a slide show is that you do not need to preload slides. A slide show of the four slides in the PIPE.SLB file would appear as follows:

    VSLIDE PIPE(90ELBOW)
    DELAY 1000
    VSLIDE PIPE(45ELBOW)
    DELAY 1000
    VSLIDE PIPE(TEE)
    DELAY 1000
    VSLIDE PIPE(CAP)
    DELAY 1000
    REDRAW

The REDRAW command at the end of the slide show clears the screen and replaces the previous display. An RSCRIPT command instead of REDRAW repeats the show continuously.

CHAPTER TEST

Write your answers in the spaces provided.

1. EDLIN is_____.

2. What precautions should you take when using a word processor to create text files for AutoCAD? _____

_____

3. Explain why EDLIN is called a "line editor."_____

_____

4. To delete line number 46 in a file when using EDLIN enter _____.

5. When using EDLIN, enter _____ to delete lines 27 through 59.

6. What function does the EDLIN command END perform? _____

_____

7. To begin a new file in EDLIN, enter _____

_____

8. An EDLIN command that lists 23 lines at a time is _____.

9. The EDLIN command QUIT saves your file. True or false? _____

10. Describe external commands. _____

_____

11. Commands located in the ACAD.PGP file are executed by _____.

12. Name the parts of a command listing found in the ACAD.PGP file. _____

_____

_____

13. What is a command alias, and how would you write one for the POLYGON command?

_____

14. Define "script file." _____

_____

15. Why is it a good idea to put one command on each line of a script file? _____

_____

16. List two common reasons why a script file might not work. _____

_____

17. The commands that allow you to make and view slides are _____ and

_____.

18. The file extension that AutoCAD assigns slides is _____.

19. Explain why it is a good idea to keep slide files in a separate directory and not in the ACAD

directory. _____

_____

20. List the three commands that are included when writing a slide show. _____

_____

21. To stop a slide show press the _____ key.

22. To begin a slide show that has been stopped, _____.

23. Briefly explain the two methods used to create a SLIDELIB file._____

_____

_____

_____

24. Suppose you want to view a slide named VIEW1 that is in a slide library file called VIEWS.

How must you enter its name at the Slide file: prompt?

Slide file: _____

25. What is the principal difference between a slide show script file written for a slide library

and one simply written for a group of slides? _____

_____

DRAWING PROBLEMS

1. If you use a text editor or word processor other than EDLIN, create a new command in the ACAD.PGP file that loads the text editor. Set the screen mode to return to the graphics display.

2. Create a new command for the ACAD.PGP file that generates a directory listing of all your slide files. Be sure to specify the directory path that contains the slides. For example, if your slides are kept on a floppy disk, the DOS command to execute is: DIR A:*.SLD. Set the screen mode to remain in the text display.

3. Write a script file called NOTES.SCR that does the following:
   A. Executes the TEXT command.
   B. Selects the Style option.
   C. Enters a style name.
   D. Selects the lastpoint using the "@" symbol.
   E. Enters a text height of .25.
   F. Enters a rotation angle of 0.
   G. Inserts the text: "NOTES:".
   H. Selects the TEXT command again.
   I. Enters location coordinates for first note.

    J. Enters a text height of .125.

    K. Enters a rotation angle of 0.

    L. Inserts the text: "1. Interpret dimensions and tolerances per ANSI Y14.5."

    M. Enters an ENTER keystroke.

    N. Inserts the text: "2. Remove all burrs and sharp edges."

    O. Enters ENTER twice to exit the command.

Immediately before this script file is used, select the ID command and pick the point where you want the notes to begin. That point will be the "lastpoint" used in the script file for the location of the word "NOTES:". The script file when executed should draw the following:

NOTES:

1. Interpret dimensions and tolerances per ANSI Y14.5.

2. Remove all burrs and sharp edges.

4. Create a slide show of your best AutoCAD drawings. This slide show should be considered as part of your portfolio for potential employers. Place all of the slides and the script file on a floppy disk. Make three copies of the portfolio disk: a 5.25″ 360K floppy disk, a 5.25″ high-density floppy disk, and a 3.5″ microdisk. Since employers may have different machines, be prepared. Keep the following guidelines in mind:

    A. Do not delay slides longer than 5 seconds. You can always press the BACKSPACE key to view a slide longer.

    B. One view of a drawing is sufficient unless the drawing is complex. If so, make additional slides of the drawing's details.

    C. Create a cover slide, or title page slide that gives your name.

    D. Create an ending slide that says "THE END."

5. Create a slide show that illustrates specific types of drawings. For example, you might make a slide show for dimensioned mechanical drawings or for electrical drawings. These specialized slide shows in your portfolio are useful if you apply for a job in a specific discipline. Store all slide shows on the same disk. Identify slide shows by their content as follows:

MECH.SCR — Mechanical

ARCH.SCR — Architectural

PIPE.SCR — Piping

STRUCT.SCR — Structural

ELECT.SCR — Electrical or Electronics

MAP.SCR — Mapping

CIVIL.SCR — Civil

6. Create a script file to plot your most frequently used drawing. Use the following guidelines to write the script:

    A. Run a trial plot of the drawing first. Record all of the keystrokes required to plot the drawing correctly.

    B. Check the results of the trial plot to be sure that the use of pens and the location of the drawing on the paper is correct.

    C. Write the script file using the exact keystrokes you recorded.

    D. Test the script and note where problems occur.

    E. Fix the problems in the script file and test the script until it runs properly.

    F. Run the script file from the DOS prompt so the drawing is loaded and plotted from one entry.

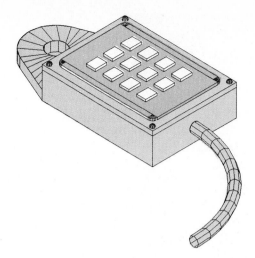

Chapter 30

DIGITIZING
EXISTING
DRAWINGS

Learning objectives

After completing this chapter, you will be able to:

☐ Describe the digitizer and the digitizing process.

☐ Digitize existing drawings into AutoCAD.

☐ Define scanning and discuss the advantages and disadvantages of scanning over manually digitizing a drawing.

Digitizing is the process of transferring information from a digitizing tablet into the computer. You might send commands to the computer by digitizing a command cell on the menu overlay. A *digitizing tablet,* or *digitizer,* also is used to convert existing paper drawings into AutoCAD drawing files. Digitizers range in size from 6 in. square to 44 x 60 in. Many schools and industries use 12 in. square digitizers to input commands from standard and custom tablet menus. Most companies do not have the time to convert existing drawings to CAD because they rely on the CAD system for new product drawings. Therefore, an increasing number of businesses digitize existing drawings for other companies. These commercial operations use larger digitizers so that D- and E-size drawings can be digitized.

Another way to convert existing drawings to CAD files is with a scanner. It sends a light or camera over the drawing to transfer the image to the computer. This technique is called *scanning.*

THE DIGITIZER

A digitizer consists of a plastic surface, called a *tablet,* and a pointing device for picking locations on the tablet. The digitizer provides extremely accurate location in the form of XY coordinates. Fig. 30-1 shows a digitizer and pointing device with a 12 in. x 12 in. digitizer.

DIGITIZING AN EXISTING DRAWING   ARM 4

When a company begins converting to CAD, the normal procedure is to have a manual drafting group and a CAD group. Selected new drawings are done on the computer. This situation may continue until the full capabilities of CAD are realized. Manual drafters remain important because older drawings are often revised in the original format. There comes a time when a company must make a decision to convert existing paper drawings to CAD drawing files. This problem is not confined to paper drawings. Sometimes it is necessary to convert one type of computer-generated drawing to another CAD system. This might be done with a translation program.

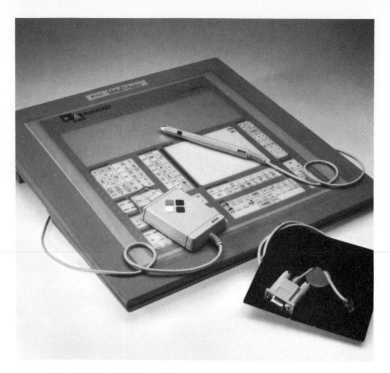

Fig. 30-1. A 12 x 12 digitizer with pointing device.

However, in some situations the only solution is to redraw the existing drawings with AutoCAD. However, time is usually saved by digitizing the existing drawing, depending on the type of drawing. A digitizer large enough to accommodate the largest drawings is best, yet large drawings can be digitized on small digitizers. The process consists of a combination of digitized points and AutoCAD drawing and editing commands. Also plan to use SNAP, ORTHO, and OSNAP modes to your best advantage.

Configuring the tablet

Before digitizing a drawing, you must configure the tablet even if it was previously configured for another application. This is done to utilize the maximum area on the tablet. To configure the tablet, select TABLET from the SETTINGS screen menu and then pick Config, or type "TABLET" at the Command: prompt, followed by "CFG" at the Option: prompt as follows:

> Command: **TABLET** ↵
> Option (ON/OFF/CAL/CFG): **CFG** ↵

Next, AutoCAD asks for the number of tablet menus. Since the entire tablet is used when digitizing an existing drawing, there are no menu areas. Type "0" and press ENTER. When asked if you want to respecify the screen pointing area, answer "Y." Then pick the lower-left corner followed by the upper-right corner. If your digitizer has proximity lights, watch them as you do this. One of the lights is on when the puck is in the screen pointing area, and off when the puck leaves the area. Move the pointing device slowly to the extreme corners until you find the location where the light comes on. This will help you gain use of the entire screen pointing areas when digitizing. See Fig. 30-2. The prompt sequence is as follows:

> Enter number of tablet menus desired (0-4) ⟨ ⟩: **0** ↵
> Do you want to respecify the screen pointing area? ⟨N⟩: **Y** ↵
> Digitize lower-left corner of screen pointing area: *(pick the lower-left corner of the pointing area)*
> Digitize the upper-right corner of screen pointing area: *(pick the upper-right corner of the pointing area)*
> Command:

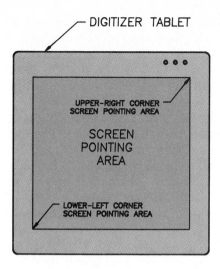

Fig. 30-2. Respecifying the screen pointing area.

Preparing the drawing and calibrating the tablet

The next step, calibrating the tablet, aligns the drawing to be digitized with the tablet. Attach the drawing to the tablet using drafting tape. The drawing does not have to be exactly square on the screen pointing area, but it should be flat. Fig. 30-3 shows a plot plan attached to the digitizer tablet.

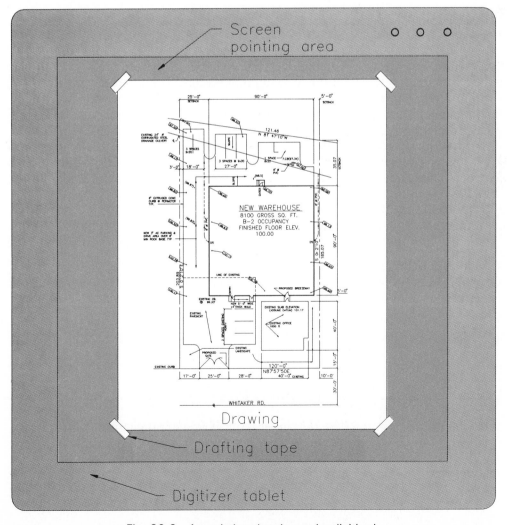

Fig. 30-3. An existing drawing to be digitized.

The number of points that you digitize when calibrating the drawing to the tablet determines how accurately the existing drawing coordinates are transferred to the computer. This is called *transformation*. AutoCAD allows you to enter two coordinates, which is referred to as *orthogonal transformation*. Two points work well if the existing drawing is dimensionally accurate. A dimensionally accurate drawing normally has stable length and width measurements, and angles are not distorted.

Digitizing three points for calibration is called *affine*. This is necessary when lines are generally parallel, but the horizontal dimensions are stretched in relationship to the vertical dimensions. The calibration of three points provides accuracy by triangulation of three points.

When the existing drawing has stretched or has been distorted to the point where parallel lines tend to converge, then the calibration of four points may be necessary. This is referred to as *projective calibration*.

Digitizing more than four points is referred to as *multiple-point transformation*. AutoCAD mathematically calculates the relationship between the points with increased accuracy, which is proportional to the number of points digitized. However, nine points are usually the maximum number of points needed since additional points tend to slow down the transformation process without improving the accuracy.

PROFESSIONAL TIP

When selecting points for calibration, choose locations that are as accurate as possible. For example, in mapping applications, pick property corners or bench marks. In mechanical drafting, use datums on the drawing. Select points that are distributed in a wide area around the drawing. In addition, the points should be in a triangular relationship rather than in a straight line.

When attaching a drawing to the digitizer, use the following guidelines:
- Set the limits to correlate with the drawing dimensions. The limits for the drawing in Fig. 30-3 should relate to the overall dimensions of the plot, plus space for notes. The plot is approximately 120′ x 200′. Allowing an additional 40′ in the horizontal and vertical directions for dimensions and notes makes the limits 160′ x 240′, or 1920″ x 2880″.
- Set the drawing units to correspond with the type of drawing you are transferring. The drawing in Fig. 30-3 is a surveyed plot plan where engineering units are used, angles are measured in degrees/minutes/seconds, the direction of angle 0 is North 90d, and angles are measured clockwise.
- Set the grid and snap to a convenient value. A 20′ (240 in.) value works well for the plot plan.
- The property lines on the plot plan are based on a survey and are probably accurate. With this in mind, use the UCS command to set the origin to one of the property corners:

Command: **UCS** ↵
Origin/ZAxis/3point/Entity/View/X/Y/Z/Prev/Restore/Del/?/⟨World⟩: **O** ↵
Origin point: ⟨0,0,0⟩: *(pick the lower-left property line corner)*

This establishes the property corner at a 0,0 origin for convenience in locating other property corner points.

PROFESSIONAL TIP

Be sure to look straight down on the target point if you are digitizing points using a puck with crosshairs. Looking at an angle through the puck viewing glass results in inaccuracies when picking points.

Now you are ready to calibrate the tablet. The orthogonal, or two-point calibration is used on the plot plan because the existing drawing was done with ink on polyester film and there is very good accuracy. To do this, enter the TABLET command and respond with "CAL" for calibrate. At this point, the tablet mode is turned on and the screen cursor no longer appears.

Command: **TABLET** ↵
Option (ON/OFF/CAL/CFG): **CAL** ↵

AutoCAD then requests that you digitize two points on the drawing and give the coordinates of each point. These two points may be anywhere, but usually are the endpoints of a vertical line. Drafters often pick two points on the left side of the object such as the west property line on a plot plan. This begins the orientation of the digitizer in relation to the object as you work from left to right. AutoCAD next asks for the exact coordinates of the two points. Look at the existing drawing in Fig. 30-4 to be digitized as you follow these prompts:

Digitize first known point: *(pick the lower-left property corner where you set the UCS origin)*
Enter coordinates for first point: *(enter 0,0 to coincide with the UCS origin)*
Digitize second known point: *(pick the North end of the west property line)*

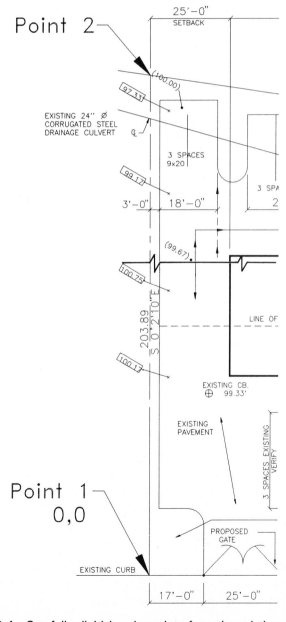

Fig. 30-4. Carefully digitizing the points from the existing drawing.

Enter the length of the property line relative to the first point (X = 0, Y = 203.89′ or 2446.68″) when entering the coordinates for the second point:

    Enter coordinates for the second point: **0,2446.68** ↵

Pressing ENTER for the third point request automatically makes AutoCAD use the orthogonal transformation format:

    Digitize third known point: ↵

    Enter the TABLET command and turn the tablet on now that the existing drawing has been calibrated to the digitizer:

    Command: **TABLET** ↵
    Option (ON/OFF/CAL/CFG): **ON** ↵

The screen cursor returns for you to use AutoCAD commands to draw lines and other features. Use the LINE command to draw the property boundaries by picking each property corner when you see the "From point" and "To point" prompts. Use the Close option for the last line. The resulting property boundaries are shown in Fig. 30-5.

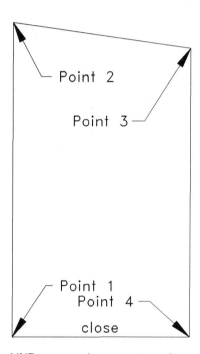

Fig. 30-5. Use the LINE command to construct the property boundaries.

    Proceed by digitizing the buildings, roads, walkways, utilities, and other features using AutoCAD commands such as LINE, PLINE, ARC, or CIRCLE. Use the DIM command to dimension the plot plan, and use the DTEXT command to add notes. The finished drawing is shown in Fig. 30-6.

    When the tablet mode is on, the screen menu is disabled. Commands may only be input from the keyboard. To use the screen menu, turn the tablet mode off by entering "OFF" at the TABLET command's Option prompt. You can also press function key F10. Turning the tablet off allows you to use the screen cursor. The command sequence is as follows:

    Command: **TABLET** ↵
    Option (ON/OFF/CAL/CFG): **OFF** ↵

    Configuring the tablet to menu areas of the AutoCAD template is discussed in Chapter 33. The tablet may also be turned on and off using the TABMODE system variable, or by pressing CTRL T. When using TABMODE, 0 is off and 1 is on.

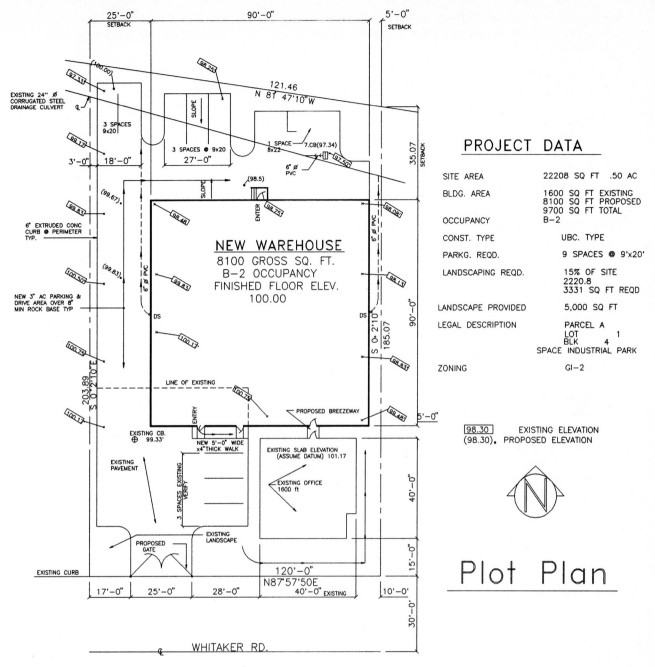

Fig. 30-6. Completed drawing.

PROFESSIONAL TIP

Remember, when digitizing an existing drawing, use the SNAP and ORTHO commands to your advantage. Also be careful when you pick points on the existing drawing. Place the digitizing tablet at a convenient angle. Look directly into the crosshairs of the puck.

The plot plan example in the previous discussion used two calibration points. The existing drawing was very accurate, allowing for two-point calibration to be successfully used. However, three or more points may be digitized to help provide greater accuracy. The same example may have been used to continue calibrating a third point. The third point would be another property line corner, forming a triangular relationship between the points. Simply press ENTER when you have picked three calibration points. When three points are digitized, AutoCAD calculates the relationship between orthogonal, affine, and projective transformation types. When AutoCAD is finished making the calculations, a table is displayed on the text screen, providing you with this information:

3 calibration points

Transformation type:	Orthogonal	Affine	Projective
Outcome of fit:	success	exact	impossible
RMS error:	6.324		
Standard deviation:	2.941		
Largest residual:	9.726		
At point:	2		
Second largest residual:	8.975		
At point:	1		

These elements can be interpreted as follows:
- **Outcome of fit**

    success—AutoCAD was successful in calibrating the points, and this is the only category that gives the calculation results.

    exact—There were exactly enough points for AutoCAD to complete the transformation.

    impossible—AutoCAD was not given enough points to provide a projective transformation.

    failure—If this message is displayed, there may have been enough points, but AutoCAD was unable to complete a transformation.

    canceled—Can happen in a projective transformation.
- **RMS Error**—RMS means Root Mean Square, which is a calculation of the accuracy of your calibration points.
- **Standard deviation**—This indicates how much difference there is between the accuracy of points. If this value is near zero, then the points have nearly the same degree of accuracy.
- **Largest residual**—Estimates the worst error you might have in the digitized points, and tells you which point this occurs across from the At point: specification.
- **Second largest residual**—Gives the next least accurate calculation at the point specified.

When you pick more than three points, a successful calibration reports back to you in all three types of transformation with a table similar to this:

7 calibration points

Transformation type:	Orthogonal	Affine	Projective
Outcome of fit:	success	success	success
RMS error:	6.324	5.852	2.602
Standard deviation:	2.941	2.469	0.508
Largest residual:	9.726	8.984	4.7634
At point:	3	3	3
Second largest residual:	8.975	8.233	4.012
At point:	5	5	5

Digitizing large drawings

Companies with many large drawings to digitize typically invest in a table-size digitizer. The photographs in Fig. 1-4 show a variety of digitizer sizes and pointing devices, including a table-size digitizer.

The drawing you plan to digitize may be too large for your tablet. Then you must divide the drawing into sections that fit the tablet area. Establish the coordinates of the boundaries for each section. A large drawing is divided into four sections as shown in Fig. 30-7. The coordinates of each section are labeled and shown with dots for reference.

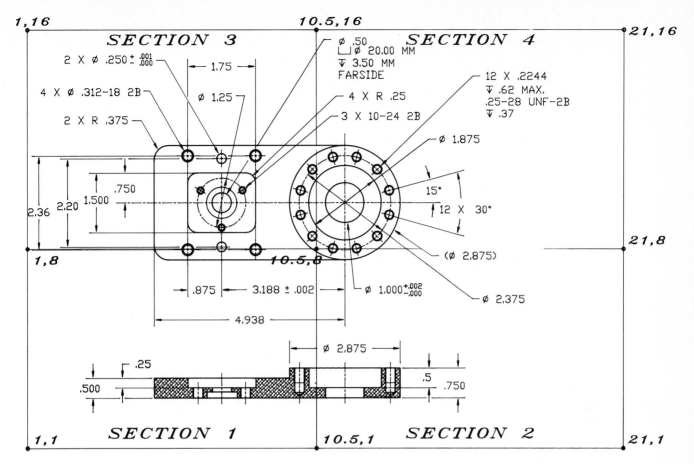

Fig. 30-7. Dividing a large drawing into sections for digitizing.

Next, tape the portion labeled as SECTION 1 to the tablet and calibrate the tablet to the coordinates 1,1 and 1,8. Digitize the portion of the object shown as SECTION 1, Fig. 30-8.

Proceed by placing the portion of the drawing labeled as SECTION 2 on the digitizer. Calibrate the tablet to the coordinates 10.5,1 and 10.5,8. Digitize the portion of the object shown as SECTION 2. See Fig. 30-9.

Proceed by moving SECTION 3 of the drawing into place on the digitizer. Calibrate the tablet to the coordinates 1,8 and 1,16. Digitize the portion of the object shown as SECTION 3.

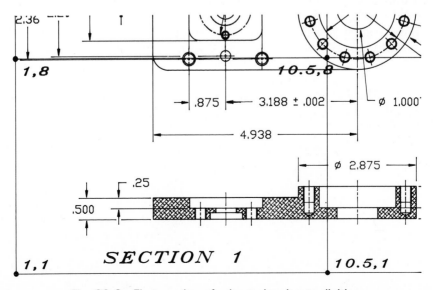

Fig. 30-8. First section of a large drawing to digitize.

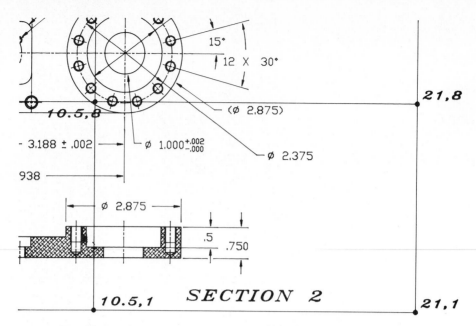

Fig. 30-9. The second section of a large drawing to be digitized.

Proceed by moving SECTION 4 into place on the digitizer. Calibrate the tablet to the coordinates 10.5,8 and 10.5,16. Digitize the portion of the object shown as SECTION 4. The entire drawing has now been digitized.

OPTICAL SCANNING OF EXISTING DRAWINGS

Scanning is a method of automatically digitizing existing drawings to become computer drawings. Scanners work much the same way as taking a photograph of the drawing. One advantage of scanning over manually digitizing drawings is that the entire drawing — including dimensions, symbols, and text — is transferred to the computer. A disadvantage is that some drawings, when scanned, require much editing to make them presentable. The scanning process picks up images from the drawing. What appears to be a dimension, for example, is only a graphic representation of the dimension, it is not an "entity." If you want the dimensional information to be technically accurate, the dimensions must be edited and redrawn.

After the drawing is scanned, the image is sent to a raster converter that translates information to digital or vector format. A *raster* is an electron beam that generates a matrix of pixels. As you learned previously, pixels make up the drawing image on the display screen. A raster editor is then used to display the images for changes.

Companies using scanners can, in many cases, reproduce existing drawings more efficiently than companies that manually digitize existing drawings. When an existing drawing has been transferred to the computer, it becomes an AutoCAD drawing that may be edited as necessary.

Houston Instrument has an optical scanning accessory that attaches to their DMP-60 series of drafting plotters. This system provides an easy-to-use, cost-effective way to enter drawings up to 36 x 48 in. into the computer system. The scanning accessory automatically scans drawings from paper, vellum, film, or blueline prints and converts the hardcopy image into a raster data file. An example of this product in operation is shown in Fig. 30-10.

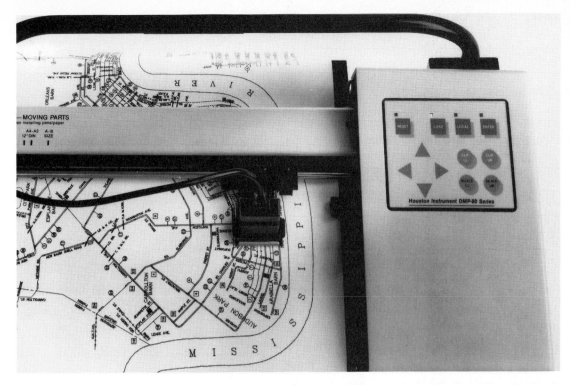

Fig. 30-10. Optical scanner in operation.   (Houston Instrument, A Summagraphics Corporation)

CHAPTER TEST

Write your answers on a separate sheet of paper.

1. Give the command and related entries to configure the tablet so that the entire area is available as the screen pointing area:

   Command: _____

   Option (ON/OFF/CAL/CFG): _____

   Enter number of tablet menus desired (0-4) ⟨ ⟩: _____

   Do you want to respecify the screen pointing area? ⟨N⟩: _____

   Digitize lower-left corner of screen pointing area: _____

   _____

   Digitize upper-right corner of screen pointing area: _____

   _____

2. Give the command and related entries needed to calibrate an existing drawing for digitizing using orthogonal transformation:

   Command: _____

   Option (ON/OFF/CAL/CFG): _____

   Digitize first known point: _____

   Enter coordinates for first point: _____

   Digitize second known point: _____

   Enter coordinates for second point: _____

   Digitize third known point: _____

3. Explain why commands must be typed at the keyboard when the tablet mode is on.

_____

_____

4. List at least three methods to turn the tablet mode on and off. _____

_____

5. Describe the function of a digitizer. _____

_____

_____

_____

6. List the four types of transformation and give the number of points required to digitize each.

_____

_____

7. Why is it generally never necessary to digitize more than nine points? _____

_____

8. List at least three things to consider when digitizing points for drawing transformation.

_____

_____

_____

9. Explain the relationship of the limits, units, grid, and snap to digitizing an existing drawing.

_____

_____

10. Why is it important to look straight down into the puck crosshairs when digitizing points?

_____

_____

11. Define the following terms related to digitizing three or more points when transferring an existing drawing.

Outcome of fit:

A. success — _____

B. exact — _____

_____

C. impossible — _____

_____

D. largest residual — _____

_____

12. How are sections of a drawing coordinated when a large drawing is digitized? _____

_____

13. Define "scanning." _____

_____

14. List an advantage and a disadvantage of scanning over digitizing drawings. _____

_____

_____

_____

_____

DRAWING PROBLEMS

1. Make a photocopy of the drawing in Fig. 30-6 or 30-7. Use the process for digitizing an existing drawing to convert the drawing to AutoCAD.
2. Make a photocopy of one or more of the drawing problems listed below. Use the process for digitizing an existing drawing to convert the drawings to AutoCAD:
   Chapter 6, Problems 2, 3, and 5.
   Chapter 7, Problem 4.
   Chapter 16, Problem 5.
   Chapter 17, Problems 5, 8, and 14.
   Chapter 18, Problem 23.
3. Obtain an existing industrial or class drawing which was created using manual techniques. Use the process for digitizing an existing drawing to convert it to AutoCAD.

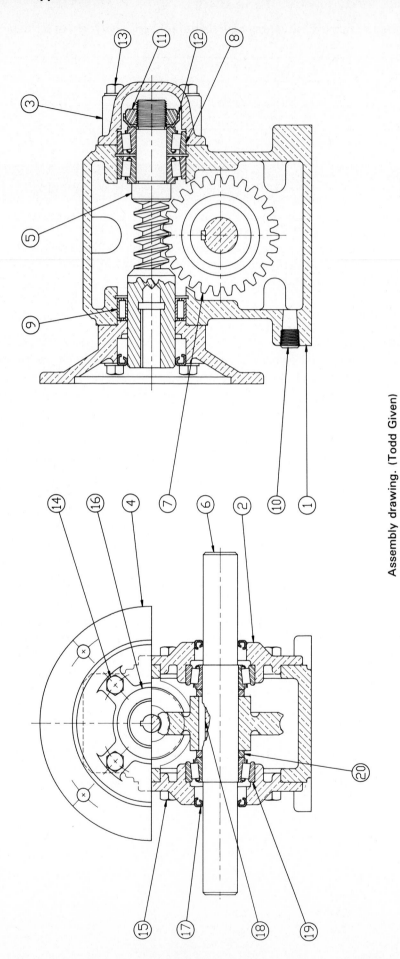

Assembly drawing. (Todd Given)

Chapter 31

CONVERTING DRAWINGS TO DXF AND IGES FORMAT

Learning objectives

After completing this chapter, you will be able to:
☐ Understand the uses of the DXF and IGES drawing interchange standards.
☐ Use the DXFOUT command to convert an AutoCAD drawing file to DXF format.
☐ Use the DXFIN command to import a drawing file.
☐ Convert an AutoCAD drawing file to IGES format.
☐ Create an AutoCAD drawing from an IGES file.

Standardization is an elusive concept in the computer industry. Yet, efforts have been made to allow CAD users to translate files among different programs. AutoCAD users may wish to work on a drawing using another CAD program, such as MicroStation or CADKEY. For this purpose, Autodesk, Inc. created the DXF (Drawing interchange File) file format. This format has become the accepted standard for microcomputer CAD programs. The standard for translating files between microcomputer CAD programs and minicomputer or mainframe CAD systems is the IGES (Initial Graphics Exchange Specification) format. For a detailed description of DXF file format, see Chapter 11 of the *AutoCAD Customization Manual*.

AUTOCAD'S DXF FILE FORMAT   ACM 11

Files prepared using the DXF format are standard ASCII code. (ASCII stands for American National Standard Code for Information Interchange.) This means that the information contained in the file can be read by any computer.

Unfortunately computer translations, as with spoken languages, often lose something in the translation. The problem is not the ASCII code, but rather the way in which CAD systems create entities, layers, and other drawing characteristics. For example, AutoCAD allows layer names; other programs use numbers. Even if layer numbers are used in AutoCAD, they may not translate to be the same number in another program. AutoCAD has polylines and other programs do not. AutoCAD's blocks may become individual entities in other programs.

This may seem like a roadblock to drawing file translation, but often creates only minor problems, depending on the drawings and the systems involved. These problems may soon be eliminated. The field of microcomputer CAD (microCAD) is still young. Companies are beginning to realize the importance of standardization. The ability to translate files will become an even more valuable tool in the near future.

Creating a DXFOUT file

The DXFOUT command creates a .DXF file extension ASCII drawing file from an AutoCAD drawing. To test the use of the DXFOUT command, begin a new drawing and name it DXFTEST. Draw a single line on your screen using the LINE command. The DXF commands are located in the UTILITY screen menu, or by picking Import/Export in the File pull-down menu. You can also enter the DXFOUT command at the Command: prompt as follows:

Command: **DXFOUT** ↵

The "Create DXF File" dialogue appears on the screen if the FILEDIA system variable is set at 1. Notice the file name default is the same as the drawing name. Look at the Pattern: edit box and notice that the file has a .DXF extension. Pick the OK button to accept the file name.

AutoCAD then asks you to indicate the degree of accuracy you want for numeric values. The choices range between 0 and 16 decimal places. In this example, the default accuracy of six decimal places is accepted by pressing ENTER. The DXF file is created and stored on disk.

Enter decimal places of accuracy (0 to 16)/Entities/Binary ⟨6⟩: ↵
Command:

The Entities option allows you to select specific shapes or entities for inclusion in the DXF file. If you use this option, only the entities that you pick are placed in the file. When you pick the specific entities, AutoCAD asks for the desired accuracy as before:

Enter decimal places of accuracy (0 to 16)/Binary ⟨6⟩: ↵

Check to be sure that it was created by listing files as follows:

Command: **DIR** ↵
File specification: ***.DXF** ↵

This entry indicates that you want to see a list of all files with a .DXF extension.

When using the DXFOUT command, you can specify a file name other than the default. If you do this, the .DXF extension is not used, because it is assumed by AutoCAD. Be careful, any DXF file with the same name is deleted if FILEDIA is 0 and a dialogue box does not appear. When the "Create DXF File" dialogue appears, enter the desired file name. If there is a file with that name, AutoCAD displays an alert box with the warning "The specified file already exists. Do you want to replace it?" Pick the OK button to replace the file, or Cancel.

After using the DXFOUT command to create the DXF file, use the SAVEAS command to save your drawing file. The "Save Drawing As" dialogue box appears. Accept the file name DXFTEST by picking the OK button. Notice the pattern extension is .DWG. Now quit the drawing editor.

Binary DXF file

The standard DXF file is in ASCII format, but you also have the option of creating a binary form of the DXF file. A *binary code* is one composed of data in the form of bits having a value of either 1 or 0. This type of file can be up to 25% smaller than an ASCII file, and it is just as accurate. The binary file is given the same extension of .DXF. It can be read quicker than an ASCII file, and AutoCAD can create it and load it using the DXFOUT and DXFIN command. Since DXF files are so much smaller than drawing files, and binary files are even smaller, using the DXFOUT command's Binary option may be a good practice if you must provide interchange files to a co-worker or client who works with Release 10 or more recent versions of AutoCAD.

Contents of an ASCII DXF file

You do not need to understand the contents of a DXF file to successfully translate drawings. Yet, when customizing or programming AutoCAD and using AutoLISP, you will use information like that found in a DXF file. The contents of a DXF file is arranged into four sections.

*   **Header**—Every drawing variable and its value is listed in this section.
*   **Tables**—Named items, such as layers, linetypes, styles, and views, are found in this section.
*   **Blocks**—All entities and their values that comprise blocks are listed in this section.
*   **Entities**—Entities used in the drawing are located here.

You can display the contents of a DXF file with the TYPE command at the Command: prompt:

Command: **TYPE** ↵
File to list: **DXFTEST.DXF** ↵

After pressing ENTER, press CTRL S to stop the file from scrolling. The first part of the file looks like this:

```
        0
SECTION
        2
HEADER
        9
$ACADVER
        1
AC1004
        9
$INSBASE
       10
      0.0
       20
      0.0
        9
$EXTMIN
       10
      4.0
       20
      5.0
        9
$EXTMAX
       10
```

These items are all part of the header. Press CTRL S again and let the file scroll to the end. The last items displayed are:

```
BLOCKS
        0
ENDSEC
        0
SECTION
        2
ENTITIES
        0
LINE
        8
0
       10
      4.0
       20
      5.0
       11
      7.0
       21
      5.0
        0
ENDSEC
        0
EOF
```

This last portion of the file indicates that there are no blocks in the drawing. The only entity used is a line.

Creating a DXFIN file

The DXFIN command allows you to create an AutoCAD drawing file (.DWG extension) from a DXF file. It is important that you begin a new drawing in AutoCAD first. Do not add entities or make setup steps. If you use an old drawing, only the entities of the DXF file are inserted. The layers, blocks, and other drawing definitions of the old drawing will override those of the DXF file.

Begin a new drawing and name it DXFTEST1. Select the DXFIN command and enter the file name DXFTEST at the File: edit box in the dialogue box. Then, pick OK or press ENTER. The dialogue box disappears and the drawing is regenerated.

Command: **DXFIN** ↵
Regenerating drawing.
Command:

The line should appear on the screen as it was in the original DXFTEST drawing. The new drawing, DXFTEST1, with the inserted DXF file, is not listed as a .DWG file until you save it.

DXF applications

There are several applications where you will want to convert an AutoCAD file to DXF format. The most common application is translating drawings between CAD systems. Numerical control (NC) programs such as SmartCAM™ and NCProgrammer™ use DXF files. The file is used to translate the shape and features of a machine part to code that can be used for lathes, milling machines, and drill presses. Desktop publishing programs like Ventura Publisher and Pagemaker use DXF files to translate drawings into images that can be inserted into a page layout. Programs that perform stress analysis and calculations often rely on DXF drawings.

Importing a scanned file

Scanning programs create a DXB (Drawing interchange Binary) file after scanning an existing paper drawing with a camera or plotter-mounted scanner. A plotter-mounted scanner is shown in Fig. 31-1. The created file consists of binary code—a computer code composed of combinations of the numbers 1 and 0. The DXBIN command converts this code to drawing data to become an AutoCAD drawing file with a .DWG extension. The command is used as follows:

Command: **DXBIN** ↵

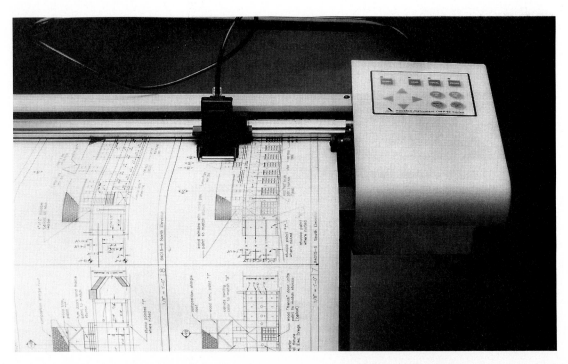

Fig. 31-1. This scanner is attached to a large format plotter and is capable of detecting lines as fine as 0.007 inch. (Houston Instrument, A Summagraphics Corporation)

The FILEDIA system variable determines what you see on the screen. If FILEDIA is 1, the file dialogue box automatically appears. If FILEDIA is 0, the file dialogue box is replaced with a file name prompt. When the "Select DXB File" dialogue box appears, accept the default file name, or enter the file name of a specific scanned drawing and pick the OK button or press ENTER. The following prompt then appears if the file dialogue box is inactive:

DXB file: *(enter file name)*

The drawing file created can then be edited using typical AutoCAD commands.

THE IGES FILE FORMAT | ACM 11 |

Drawings translated to IGES format suffer the same pitfalls as DXF conversions; something is always left out in the translation. When an AutoCAD drawing is converted using the IGESOUT command, the attribute definitions are not translated. Solid fills are also lost. There is an IGESFONT subdirectory created when you install AutoCAD. For a detailed description of IGES translations, see Chapter 11 of the *AutoCAD Customization Manual*.

In spite of these limitations, the IGES translation ability may still be valuable. It is often used by companies and schools having different CAD systems. It is also the primary translation between microcomputer and minicomputer or mainframe CAD programs.

Creating an IGESOUT file

The IGESOUT command converts an AutoCAD drawing file to an IGES file having an .IGS extension. To experiment, open the DXFTEST drawing. Use the IGESOUT command as follows:

Command: **IGESOUT** ↵

The "Create IGES File" dialogue box appears. Pick OK or ENTER to accept the file name shown at the File: edit box. The file name should be the same as the drawing name, but it now has an .IGS extension. You get the following prompt if the file dialogue box is inactive. Keep in mind that you can enter a specific file name at the File: edit box, but if the file already exists AutoCAD gives this warning: "The specified file already exists. Do you want to replace it?" Pick the OK button to replace the file, or Cancel. Be careful; any file with the same name is deleted if FILEDIA is 0 and no dialogue box appears.

File name ⟨dxftest⟩: **IGESTEST** ↵

Once the IGS file is created, check for it by using the DIR command:

Command: **DIR** ↵
File specification: ***.IGS** ↵

Compare this to the listings of the DXFTEST.DWG and DXFTEST.DXF files:

DXFTEST	DXF	5398
DXFTEST	DWG	3328
IGESTEST	IGS	902

Note the size of the file. The IGES format file is the smallest and the DXF file is the largest. Remember that IGES translation strips most attribute data from a drawing.

Before continuing, save the drawing and quit the drawing editor.

Creating an IGESIN file

The IGESIN command enables you to convert IGES drawings from other CAD systems into AutoCAD drawing files. The same restrictions apply here as with DXF files. Begin a new drawing and do not add anything to the drawing until the translation is complete. Use the IGESTEST.IGS file you just created for this example. First begin a new drawing named IGESTEST. Then proceed as follows.

Command: **IGESIN** ↵

When the "Select IGES File" dialogue box appears, enter the name of the IGES file, IGESTEST, that you created earlier. Then, pick the OK buttons.

Regenerating drawing.

You should see the familiar line appear on the screen again once the translation is complete. Obtain a directory listing of this new drawing to see the file size. Some additional IGES information has been added to it. Use the TYPE command to view the contents of the IGESTEST.IGS file.

LOCATING ERRORS IN A TRANSFERRED FILE   ARM 4

AutoCAD generally does not check a DXF file for errors, but this function can be performed if you desire. In order for this to happen, instruct AutoCAD to automatically list errors in the file before you transfer a DXF file. Use the following steps:

Command: **CONFIG** ↵

• Press ENTER until the Configuration menu is displayed.
• Select "7. Configure operating parameters" from the Configuration menu.
• Select "9. Automatic Audit after IGESIN, DXFIN, or DXBIN" from the Configure operating parameters menu.
• Answer "Y" to this question:

Do you want an automatic audit after IGESIN, DXFIN or DXBIN? ⟨N⟩: **Y** ↵

• The automatic audit is ready to be performed. Press ENTER until you get back to the Configuration menu.
• Be sure to press ENTER to update the configuration.

The automatic auditing process does not correct errors in the file. Errors must be corrected by editing the DXF file or by using the AUDIT command while working on the drawing. This powerful command lists errors and fixes them. If you want to list any errors when in the drawing editor, press ENTER as follows:

Command: **AUDIT** ↵
Fix any errors detected? ⟨N⟩: ↵

Any errors are listed for your reference, but they are not fixed. To fix errors in the transferred drawing, answer "Y" as follows:

Command: **AUDIT** ↵
Fix any errors detected? ⟨N⟩: **Y** ↵

AutoCAD displays the errors and notifies you that they are fixed like this:

3 Blocks audited
Pass 29   entities audited
Pass 14   entities audited
total errors found 2 fixed 2

CHAPTER TEST

Write your answers in the spaces provided.

1. Explain why drawing file translations are needed. _____

_____

2. Define the following abbreviations.

DXF – _____

DXB — _____

IGES — _____

3. What is the purpose of the DXFOUT command? _____

_____

_____

4. When would you use the DXFIN command? _____

_____

5. Provide the input required to get a listing of all DXF files, assuming you are at the Command: prompt.

Command: _____

File specification: _____

6. List the four sections contained in a DXF file. _____

_____

7. Suppose you plan to import a DXF file. What setup steps must you perform to the new drawing before importing the DXF file? _____

_____

8. List programs that can use DXF files. _____

_____

_____

9. When would you use the DXBIN command? _____

_____

10. Describe some limitations of the IGES file translation method. _____

_____

_____

11. When would you create an IGESOUT file? _____

_____

12. Which file type is larger: DWG, DXF, or IGS? _____

13. Explain the purpose of the IGESIN command? _____

_____

14. Which file type is a true industry standard: IGS or DXF? _____

15. What FILEDIA system variable value must be used to ensure that a file dialogue box appears when needed? _____

16. Does AutoCAD automatically list errors in a transferred DXF file? _____

_____

17. Does the automatic auditing process correct errors in a file? _____

18. Describe the function of the AUDIT command when used to correct errors in a transferred file.

_____

DRAWING PROBLEMS

1. Load one of your simple drawings into the AutoCAD drawing editor. Create a DXF file of the drawing. Generate a printed copy of the contents of the DXF file.
2. The purpose of this drawing is to create entities and generate a DXF file. Then, edit the DXF file with a text editor and use the DXFIN command to view the revised drawing. You must refer to Chapter 11 of the *AutoCAD Customization Manual* to complete this problem. Use the following steps:
   A. Begin a new drawing and name it P31-2.
   B. Draw circle A at 4,4 with a 1 in. radius.
   C. Draw circle B at a distance of 3,0 from circle A with radius of .5.
   D. Save the drawing.
   E. Make a DXF file of the drawing using the name of the drawing.
   F. Load the DXF file into your text editor and make the following changes to circles. They are listed in the ENTITIES section of the DXF file. Use a Search function of your text editor to find this section.
      • Change the radius of circle B to 2.
      • Change the location of the circle A to 4,2.
   G. Save the DXF file.
   H. Begin a new drawing named P31-2A. Use the DXFIN command to load the P31-2.DWG file. Do you notice any changes? Save the drawing.

   Problems 3 and 4 require that you have access to another microCAD program or a program that is designed to work with AutoCAD output. Another school or company in your area may have one such program with which you can exchange files.
3. Load one of your drawings that contains layers, blocks, and a variety of entities into AutoCAD. Create a DXF file of the drawing. Import the file into another program that can accept DXF file translations. Compare the new drawings with the AutoCAD version. Look especially at layers, block definitions, and entities such as polylines.
4. Obtain a DXF file from another microCAD or CAD/CAM program. Use the DXFIN command to convert it to an AutoCAD drawing file. Compare the new AutoCAD drawing with the original version.
5. This problem requires that you have access to a large-scale CAD system, such as Intergraph. Follow the same procedures as stated in Problems 3 and 4, but use the IGESIN and IGESOUT commands to import and export files. Try to pinpoint exactly what does not translate between AutoCAD and the large-scale system.
6. If you have access to a scanner, create a DXB file from an old, hand-drawn print. Import the DXB file using the DXBIN command. Compare the new AutoCAD drawing with the original.
7. Use one of the previous problems to fix errors that may exist in the transferred file using the AUDIT command.

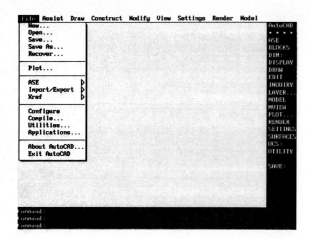

Chapter 32

CUSTOMIZING AUTOCAD'S SCREEN MENUS

Learning objectives

After completing this chapter, you will be able to:
☐ Understand the structure of button, screen, pull-down, and icon menus.
☐ Create a variety of button menus.
☐ Customize existing screen menus and create new ones.
☐ Create single or multiple page pull-down menus.
☐ Use the SLIDELIB facility to create icon menus.
☐ Construct icon menus using existing blocks or newly-drawn shapes.

One of the most attractive aspects of AutoCAD is that its menus can be customized to suit specific needs. Users can add special commands to the standard menus or create their own menu system from scratch. Existing commands can be used in a macro. A *macro* is a function that combines the capabilities of existing commands and options.

All of the aspects of the menu system can be changed. This includes the cursor button functions, standard screen menus, pull-down menus, and icon menus. Study this chapter carefully to create your own menus. The results will be a greater understanding of AutoCAD, and an increase in performance and productivity.

AUTOCAD'S MENU STRUCTURE

Before constructing your own menus, look at AutoCAD's standard menu structure to get a feel for the layout. A few minutes spent browsing through AutoCAD's menu file will give you a better understanding of the tools and techniques you can use to build custom menus. The basic components of a menu are the main sections, submenus, item titles, and command codes.

─────────────── PROFESSIONAL TIP ───────────────

Since the ACAD.MNU file is so large, it is not productive or efficient to customize it using EDLIN. Therefore, it is suggested that you use a programmer's text editor or the DOS text editor for menu customization. The text editor you use should have "search" and "find" functions so you can navigate quickly through large file like the ACAD.MNU file.

It must be assumed, for Chapters 32 to 34, that you are familiar with the use of a programmer's text editor or a word processor program. Since EDLIN will only accept limited amounts of information, it is to your benefit to avoid using it when customizing the ACAD.MNU file or any other large ASCII file. Therefore, when mention is made of scrolling or paging through a file such as ACAD.MNU, you must be familiar with the command or keys in your text editor that allow you to perform such functions.

———— PROFESSIONAL TIP ————

Before beginning any serious work with AutoCAD's menus, it may be a good idea to make a printout of portions of the ACAD.MNU file. It is a large file; therefore, print only the portions of the menu that you need. This is possible in most text editors or word processors by first defining a "block" of text, and then printing the block.

It is beneficial to have a printed copy of the menu with you as you are creating new commands or macros, because you can see how existing commands are put together and how the menu codes are used without having to stare at the computer screen.

Menu section labels

As you look through the menu file, notice the menu section headings. Major menu headings are identified by three asterisks (***) in front of the name. The major headings are:

```
***BUTTONS
***AUX1
***POP (0 through 16)
***ICON
***SCREEN
***TABLET1
***TABLET2
***TABLET3
***TABLET4
```

In this chapter, you are working with button, pull-down, icon, and screen menus. Tablet menus are discussed in Chapter 33. The AUX1 menu is used for a system mouse that comes with computers such as Macintosh or SPARCstation.

There are a variety of different screen submenus in AutoCAD. These are listed with two asterisks (**) in front of the name. You will be working mostly with submenus, so keep this in mind.

A look at the menu layout

The AutoCAD menu file is found in two forms. The menu that you will be customizing is the ACAD.MNU file. This is an ASCII text file that can be edited with any text editor or word processor. When you load AutoCAD and enter the drawing editor, AutoCAD searches for the ACAD.MNX file. This is a compiled version used by AutoCAD. Whenever you revise the ACAD.MNU file, AutoCAD recompiles it to a new ACAD.MNX version when you use the MENU command, or when you enter the drawing editor.

Before beginning any editing of the ACAD.MNU file, take a few minutes to look at it and notice how it is laid out, and what the main headings represent. Load the ACAD.MNU file into your text editor and locate the line that says ***BUTTONS1. Scroll down in the file until this line is at the top of your screen. The following portion of the menu should be displayed:

```
***BUTTONS1
;
$p0 = *
^C^C
^B
^O
^G
^D
^E
^T
```

```
***BUTTONS2
$p0 = *

***AUX1
;
$p0 = *
^C^C
^B
^O
^G
^D
^E
^T
```

This is the first page of the ACAD.MNU file. The first line, ***BUTTONS1, is the beginning of the button menu. Next, find the ***SCREEN section. The entire file has more than 6200 lines. You will have to page down several times until you find the screen section headings. The items that follow ***BUTTONS1 are specific assignments to the buttons on your pointing device. The items following ***SCREEN are assigned positions on the standard screen menu.

Page back up to the ***BUTTONS1 heading, and then scroll down until you see the ***POP1 heading. This is the first pull-down menu, and appears on the left end of the menu bar at the top of your screen in AutoCAD. Notice that the first word on each line is enclosed in square brackets ([ ]). Any word or characters appearing inside these brackets is displayed in the pull-down menu on the screen in AutoCAD.

PROFESSIONAL TIP

The ACAD.MNU file can be accessed from the DOS prompt or from the Command: prompt in AutoCAD. Edit the ACAD.PGP file to include a command that loads your text editor while in AutoCAD. Refer to Chapter 29 for specific instructions.

AutoCAD uses all available memory in a computer. If you are using memory-resident programs in addition to AutoCAD, be sure to read Chapter 4 of the *AutoCAD Interface, Installation and Performance Guide* for specific information on memory management. If you run your text editor from the Command: prompt as a "shelled" program, AutoCAD reserves approximately 450K of memory.

Menu item titles

Learn to use the "search" function of your text editor or word processor right away. This function is extremely useful in moving around in your file in order to find or change text. Use the search function, or the PAGE DOWN key to find the **ED menu. Remember, the two asterisks represent a subheading under a major section. The **ED menu is the first page of the EDIT screen menu.

The appearance of the commands listed on the screen menu in AutoCAD are compared to their appearance in the ACAD.MNU file in the following list. The first page of the EDIT menu as seen in AutoCAD is shown on the left, and the same page as it appears in the ACAD.MNU file is shown on the right.

SCREEN MENU	ACAD.MNU FILE
AutoCAD	
* * * *	**ED 3
ARRAY:	[ARRAY:]^C^C__ARRAY
ATTEDIT:	[ATTEDIT:]^C^C__ATTEDIT
BREAK:	[BREAK:]$S = X $S = BREAKO ^C^C__BREAK
CHAMFER:	[CHAMFER:]^C^C__CHAMFER
CHANGE:	[CHANGE:]^C^C__CHANGE
CHPROP:	[CHPROP:]^C^C__CHPROP
COPY:	[COPY:]^C^C__COPY
DDATTE:	DDATTE:]^C^C__DDATTE
DDEDIT:	[DDEDIT:]^C^C__DDEDIT
DDMODIFY:	[DDMODFY:]^C^CDDMODIFY
DIVIDE:	[DIVIDE:]^C^C__DIVIDE
ERASE:	[ERASE:]^C^C__ERASE
EXPLODE:	[EXPLODE:]^C^C__EXPLODE
next	[next]$S = X $S = ED2
___LAST___	
DRAW	
EDIT	

Notice that the command name is exactly the same in the menu and in its file listing inside brackets ([ ]). A screen menu name can be up to eight characters long. The first eight characters inside the brackets are displayed on the screen. You can have longer names and descriptions inside the brackets. However, only the first eight characters are displayed. The characters to the right of the closing bracket are the command codes. Fig. 32-1 shows the difference between title information and command code. Any text after the eighth character can be reminder information, or comments for you.

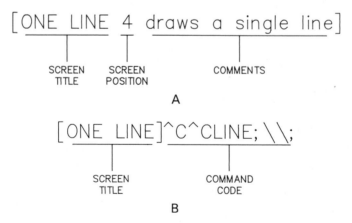

Fig. 32-1. A—Information that can be included inside the title brackets. B—Information outside the brackets is processed by AutoCAD.

MENU COMMAND CODES AND SYNTAX

When paging through the menu file, you probably noticed several characters and symbols that did not seem to make much sense, such as "$S = X" and "\." These are menu codes, and have explicit functions in the meaning of the menu. You will be using these codes to create menus. The characters listed here can be used for button and screen menus. Special characters that are used in pull-down menus are described later.

Character	Function
***	Major menu sections. Must be placed directly in front of the name of the section, for example: ***SCREEN.
**	Submenu section. Appears in front of the submenu name. The EDIT menu example shown in the previous section shows the name of **ED. This is the name of the first page of the EDIT menu.
[ ]	The name of a menu item is enclosed in brackets. Only the first eight characters inside the brackets are displayed on the side screen menu in AutoCAD.
$S =	This indicates that another screen menu is to be displayed and enables AutoCAD to move between submenus. Find these in the EDIT menu discussed previously. Other similar codes are $B (BUTTONS), $T (TABLET), $I (ICON), $P (PULL-DOWN or POP), and $A (AUXILIARY). Notice in the previous EDIT menu that almost all commands have "$S = X" immediately after the command name in brackets. This means that a screen menu named "X" is displayed first, then the next screen menu is displayed. This is creating a "menu stack," and is discussed later in the chapter.
^C^C	This cancels any current command. If you are in a transparent or DIM: command, two ^Cs are needed to get you out. Placing this in front of your commands ensures that you begin the new command cleanly by canceling any command you are in.
;	The semicolon represents pressing an ENTER.
\	The backslash represents information that must be typed at the keyboard or entered with the pointing device.
+	The plus symbol is placed at the end of a long menu line and tells AutoCAD that there is more of this code sequence on the next line.
=*	The current cursor, pull-down, or icon menu is displayed.
(space)	A blank space between items is the same as pressing ENTER or the SPACE bar.
*^C^C	Creates a repetitive command.
si	Specifies immediate action on a single item. Placed at the end of the macro; for example: Erase;si

CREATING BUTTON MENUS

ACM 6

Button menus control the functions of the pointing device buttons. If using a stylus or a mouse with only one or two buttons, you will not be using button menus. If you have a pointing device with two or more buttons, you can alter the functions of the buttons to suit your needs. This can add to your drawing productivity and speed the access of commonly used commands.

Standard button menu layout

The main button menu that comes with AutoCAD is named BUTTONS1, and is arranged for a cursor with nine programmable buttons. The button menu is the first section listed in the ACAD.MNU file. A list of the button menu and its functions is shown in the following chart:

MENU FILE LISTING	BUTTON NUMBER AND FUNCTION
***BUTTONS1	Menu name
;	#1—Return
$p0 = *	#2—Displays cursor object snap menu
^C^C	#3—Cancel
^B	#4—Snap on/off toggle
^O	#5—Ortho on/off toggle
^G	#6—Grid on/off toggle
^D	#7—Coordinate display toggle
^E	#8—Isoplane crosshair display
^T	#9—Tablet on/off toggle
	#0—Pick button—non-programmable

Additional button menus

You can have instant access to four button menus named BUTTONS1 through BUTTONS4. Each of these menus can be accessed with a keyboard and cursor button pick combination as shown here:

Action	Button Menu
Pick	BUTTONS1
Shift + Pick	BUTTONS2
CTRL + Pick	BUTTONS3
CTRL + Shift + Pick	BUTTONS4

Each of these button menus can contain any commands you need. For example, you may place a variety of display commands in the BUTTONS2 menu. To access these commands, simply hold down the SHIFT key on the keyboard and press the pick button on your cursor. The buttons are reconfigured. Use the key and pick combination between menus.

Make a copy of the ACAD.MNU before changing it

Before you edit the ACAD.MNU file, check with your instructor or supervisor to find out what procedures should be used. It makes sense to first copy the ACAD.MNU file to your own subdirectory or floppy disk. Then experiment and make changes to your copy. This protects the original program copy. It also prevents undue frustration for students or employees who find that the revised menu does not function properly.

To avoid confusing ACAD.MNU with your menu, name the new copy MYMENU.MNU. You might also use your first name, such as NANCY.MNU. This distinguishes it from all others.

── PROFESSIONAL TIP ──

The prerequisite for creating AutoCAD menus is to know the commands and how they work. Know the command options, when they can be used, and how they are used. Always plan your commands and macros in the following manner:
- Write out what you want the command or macro to do.
- Write the macro as it will appear in the menu file using command codes.
- Check the written macro to be sure it has the proper commands, options, and syntax.
- Add the macro to the menu file.
- Test the macro.

Replacing button menu items

The process of replacing button menu items is the same as editing a line in a text file. For example, replace the existing button commands shown below with the new commands indicated. Place a double cancel before each command. This cancels the current command when you pick a button.

EXISTING	NEW
#5 Ortho	LINE
#6 Grid	ERASE
#7 Coords	CIRCLE
#8 Isoplane	ARC

When you have finished editing, the new button menu should look like this:

```
***BUTTONS1
;
$p1 = *
∧C∧C
∧B
∧C∧CLINE
∧C∧CERASE
∧C∧CCIRCLE
∧C∧CARC
∧T
```

Before testing the new menu, you must reload it with the MENU command, otherwise AutoCAD will work with the old copy. The MENU command brings the new version into memory. If your file is MYMENU.MNU, load it as follows:

Command: **MENU** ↲
Menu file name or . for none ⟨ACAD⟩: **MYMENU** ↲

Providing for user input

An important aspect of menu customization is having a good grasp of AutoCAD's commands and options. Most commands require some form of user input by picking a location of the screen or entering values at the keyboard and pressing ENTER. The final action of any user input is using a button pick or pressing ENTER. The symbol that is used for user input is the backslash (\). A second important aspect of menu customization is inserting RETURNs, or when the ENTER key is pressed. This is handled with the semicolon (;).

When a command is listed in a menu file, AutoCAD automatically inserts a blank after it, which is interpreted as a RETURN. The following command would execute the LINE command and prompt for the "From point":

LINE

If the command is followed by a semicolon, backslash, or plus sign, AutoCAD does not insert a blank, therefore, a RETURN is not issued. If you want to allow for user input, and then provide a RETURN, you should end the line with a semicolon:

LINE;\\;

If placed in a BUTTONS menu, this executes the LINE command, picks the "From point" at the crosshairs location, pauses for one user input for the "To point," then provides a RETURN. This draws a single line and ends the LINE command without the user pressing ENTER.

The button menu can do additional things with the user input symbol. If a backslash is provided after the command, the coordinates of the crosshairs on the screen are recorded when the pick button is pressed. Therefore, the following button command accepts the location of the crosshairs as the "From point" for the LINE command when the button is pressed, and the prompt that is displayed is the "To point."

LINE;\

This instant input can be used for other applications such as object snaps. For example, the following command, placed in a button menu, tries to instantly find the object snap on an entity at the crosshair location when the button is picked.

ERASE;\

Adding new button menus

You are not limited to the four button menus mentioned previously. You can create as many as needed. However, one of the buttons should get from one menu to the other. Here are a few things to keep in mind when creating new button menus:

- There is no screen display of button names. Use brackets in your menu file to contain button labels or numbers. AutoCAD does not act on anything inside brackets. For example:

```
***BUTTONS1
[5]^C^CLINE
[6]^C^CERASE
[7]^C^CCIRCLE
[8]^C^CARC
```

- The letter "B" is used to call button menu names. Therefore, the code of $B= is used to call up other button submenus, just as $S= is used to call other screen submenus. For example, you could specify button 9 in the ***BUTTONS1 menu to call up submenu B1 as follows:

```
[9]$B=B1
```

When this button is pressed, submenu B1 is activated and the buttons change to reflect the new menu.

- A button menu selection can also call up a screen menu in the same manner. For example, button 9 could call up the OSNAP screen menu in addition to changing the button submenu to B1. (You will alter the OSNAP screen menu for using buttons in one of the chapter problems.) The entry in the menu file would look like this:

```
[9]$B=B1 $S=OSNAPB
```

- A button menu selection can display a pull-down menu as follows:

```
$P6=*
```

The P6 calls for pull-down menu 6 (the Modify pull-down menu), and the =* displays it on screen.

- A space is not required after the button submenu in the file to separate it from other menus.

The following example shows revisions to the BUTTONS1 menu. It includes a selection for button 9 that switches to the B1 button menu and also displays the OSNAPB screen menu. The B1 menu provides eight object snap options, and button 9 returns to the BUTTONS1 menu and displays the S screen menu.

```
***BUTTONS1
[1];
[2]$p0=*
[3]^C^C
[4]^B
[5]^C^CLINE
[6]^C^CERASE
[7]^C^CCIRCLE
[8]^C^CARC
[9]$B=B1 $S=OSNAPB
**B1
[1]ENDpoint
[2]INTersect
[3]MIDpoint
[4]PERpendicular
[5]CENter
[6]TANgent
[7]QUAdrant
[8]NEArest
[9]$B=BUTTONS1 $S=S
```

EXERCISE 32-1

☐ Copy the ACAD.MNU file into your subdirectory or onto a floppy disk. Change the name of the file to MYMENU.MNU or use your name.
☐ Create a button submenu named **B2.
☐ Include three drawing commands and three editing commands.

CREATING STANDARD SCREEN MENUS

ACM 6

Standard screen menus are located along the right side of the screen. They are created with the same techniques used for button menus. Screen menus are more versatile than button menus because you can see the command titles. The positions of commands along the screen menu are referred to as *screenboxes*. The number of boxes available to you depends on your display device. You can find out how many boxes are available using the SCREENBOXES variable as follows:

Command: **SCREENBOXES** ↵
SCREENBOXES = 26(read only)

Most people rarely use all of the commands found in AutoCAD's screen menus. In time, you will find which commands you use most often, and those you seldom use. At this stage, begin to develop ideas on what the menu structure should look like. Then start constructing custom menus, even though you may not completely know what to include. Menus are easy to change, and can be revised as many times as needed.

─ **PROFESSIONAL TIP** ─

Develop a plan for your menus, but build them over time. Create one command or macro and then test it. It is much easier to create one macro and test it than to create an entire untested menu. Building menus a small portion at a time is also more efficient. It can be done as you work or study, or when you have a spare minute.

Parts of a screen menu item

A screen menu item is composed of the command name and the command code. The command name is enclosed in brackets. The code is a combination of commands, options, and characters that instruct AutoCAD to perform a function or series of functions. Take a closer look at the example in Fig. 32-2. It is the same one that was introduced in Fig. 32-1. The individual parts of the macro are:

• Brackets ([ ]) enclose the screen title. The first eight characters inside the brackets are displayed on the screen.
• The command name (ONE LINE) is displayed on the screen. Try to give descriptive names to your commands so they indicate what the command does.
• The double cancel (∧C∧C) cancels out any command that you are working with.
• AutoCAD commands determine what function the macro performs (LINE).
• A RETURN (;) represents pressing the ENTER key after typing "LINE" at the keyboard.
• The two backslashes (\\) represent user input for the "From point" and "To point" of the line. Remember, one backslash indicates a value entered at the keyboard, or a selection made with the pointing device.
• A final RETURN (;) represents pressing the ENTER key to end the LINE command.

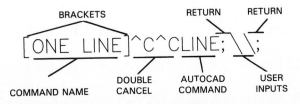

Fig. 32-2. Components of a screen menu item.

As you can see, you need to know exactly the commands, prompts, options, and entries required to perform AutoCAD functions before you can modify or create screen menus. Look at the next menu item and try to determine what it is doing.

    [ERASE —1]^C^CERASE;\;

The title should give you a clue. It erases a single entity. The ERASE command is followed by a RETURN, which is followed by a single backslash. This allows one pick on the screen. The second RETURN completes the command. Here is another one.

    [EXTEND 1]^C^CEXTEND;\;\;

This macro issues the EXTEND command, then allows for one user input to pick a boundary edge. Then a RETURN is entered and one additional user input is allowed for the object to extend. After one object is picked, the last RETURN completes the command automatically.

    Look at one more menu item that combines two commands. What function do you think this macro performs?

    [LINE T]^C^CLINE;\\;;MID;\\;

Notice that the first half of the item is exactly the same as the macro shown in Fig. 32-2. It draws a single line. The RETURN just before MID selects the LINE command again. "MID;" specifies an OSNAP mode for the From point: prompt. The first backslash lets you pick the line on which the midpoint is needed. The second backslash is the "To point." The final RETURN ends the command.

PROFESSIONAL TIP

When writing menu commands and macros, write them as if you are entering the commands and options at the keyboard. Use the semicolon (;) for the ENTER key. Use first letters where appropriate for command options.

Constructing menu commands

When you think of a useful command or function to include in a menu, the first step is to write it out in longhand. This gives you a clear picture of the scope of the command. The second step is to list the keyboard steps required to execute the new function. Third, write out the menu item as it should appear in the menu file. The following examples each utilize this three-step process:

Example 1
  1. Make a command called ERASE L to erase the last entity drawn.
  2. ERASE ↵
     LAST ↵
  3. [ERASE L]^C^CERASE;L

Example 2
  1. Make a command called ERASE 1 that erases one entity and returns to the Command: prompt.
  2. ERASE ↵
     SELECT ENTITY ↵
  3. [ERASE 1]^C^CERASE;\;

Example 3
  1. Make a command called ZOOM W that zooms a window without the user having to pick the Window option.
  2. ZOOM ↵
     WINDOW ↵
     SELECT FIRST CORNER
     SELECT SECOND CORNER
  3. [ZOOM W]^C^CZOOM;W

Example 4
  1. Make a command called ZOOM P that zooms to the previous display.
  2. ZOOM ↵
     PREVIOUS ↵
  3. [ZOOM P]^C^CZOOM;P

Example 5
1. Make a command that draws as many circles as needed.
2. MULTIPLE CIRCLE ↵
3. [M CIRCLE]^C^CMULTIPLE CIRCLE   or   *^C^CCIRCLE

These examples should give you the feel for the process used when creating menu items. The command items can now be written to a menu file and tested. Before doing this, though, take a look at two more examples that are a little more involved.

Example 6
1. Create a new command called 25FILLET that can set a .25 fillet radius on a polyline without restarting the 25FILLET command.
2. FILLET ↵
   RADIUS ↵
   .25 ↵
   FILLET ↵
   POLYLINE ↵
   SELECT 2D POLYLINE ↵
3. [25FILLET]^C^CFILLET;R;.25;;P;\

Example 7
1. Create a new command called DWG AIDS that sets the grid to .5 and turns it on, sets the snap grid to .25 and turns it on, and turns Ortho on.
2. GRID ↵
   .5 ↵
   SNAP ↵
   .25 ↵
   ORTHO ↵
   ON ↵
3. [DWG AIDS]^C^CGRID;.5;;ON;SNAP;.25;;ON;^O

Adding macros to the menu file

The next step is to add the new macros to the menu file and then test them. But where in the menu file can they be written? Create a new submenu after the **S menu. Load your copy of the ACAD.MNU file into your text editor and search to find the following:

    ***SCREEN
    **S

Listed below the **S is AutoCAD's familiar Root Menu. Find the last command in that menu, which is SAVE. Just below SAVE is the beginning of another submenu. It will probably be labeled **HEADER. You want to begin writing your new submenu on the line above **HEADER. The first screen menu listed in the ACAD.MNU file is displayed when you enter the drawing editor. (If you insert your submenu in front of the **S menu, yours will be the first displayed when AutoCAD enters the drawing editor.)

Name this first submenu TEST. Type the entries in your text editor exactly as they are shown below. Be sure to press ENTER at the end of each line. Your first entries in this menu should look like the following:

    **TEST 3 *(begins the menu on the third line from the top of the screen)*
    [TEST]
    [MENU]
    [ERASE L]^C^CERASE;L
    [ERASE 1]^C^CERASE;\;
    [ZOOM W]^C^CZOOM;W
    [ZOOM P]^C^CZOOM;P
    [M CIRCLE]^C^CMULTIPLE CIRCLE
    [25FILLET]^C^CFILLET;R;.25;;P;\
    [DWG AIDS]^C^CGRID;.5;;ON;SNAP;.25;;ON;^O

Long menu items

If the menu item you write occupies more than one line, instruct AutoCAD that there is more to the item. Type a plus (+) symbol at the end of the line. Do not put spaces in front of or behind the mark. Use the long-line technique to create a command that does the following:

- ZOOM All.
- Set LIMITS to 0,0 and 20,12.
- Set SNAP to 0.25.
- Set GRID to 0.50.
- Draw a PLINE border from 1.5,.5. The border should be 17 x 11 in.
- Set the MIRRTEXT to zero.
- Set the APERTURE to 3.
- Set the ORTHOMODE to on.
- ZOOM Extents.

The item name and code for this macro is written as follows:

```
[B-11x17]^C^CZOOM;A;LIMITS;;18,12;SNAP;.25;GRID;.5;PLINE;1.5,.5; +
17.5,.5;17.5,11.5;1.5,11.5;C;MIRRTEXT;0;APERTURE;3;ORTHO; +
ON;ZOOM;E
```

Place your menu in the root menu

You have created your first screen menu, but how do you access it from the Root Menu of AutoCAD? There is nothing in the Root Menu that calls the TEST menu. You need to add that item to the Root Menu now. Look again at the **S menu and notice that only 20 lines are occupied with commands inside brackets. You can insert your menu name on the line after SAVE. Insert the following item on the line after the SAVE command.

```
[TEST]$S = X $S = TEST
```

Do not press ENTER at the end of the line or you will insert an additional line in the menu. This could push the last menu item off the screen if your monitor displays only 21 lines in the menu area.

The menu stack

The items you entered above do two things. The first part, $S = X, calls the **X submenu and lays it over the **S menu. The second part, $S = TEST, calls your submenu, TEST, and lays it over the **X menu. This has now created a menu "stack." When viewed from the side, it looks like a "stack" of pancakes. See Fig. 32-3.

Fig. 32-3. A menu stack is created as additional menus are called upon.

The **X menu plays an important role in the stack. Find the **X menu in the ACAD.MNU file and display the entire menu on the screen. It is composed of 23 lines. The first 15 lines are blank, and the next three are:

```
[___LAST___]$S =  $S =
[    DRAW    ]^C^C$S = X $S = DR
[    EDIT     ]^C^C$S = X $S = ED
```

These should look familiar to you because they are displayed at the bottom of the screen on all AutoCAD menus. In addition, at the top of each screen menu is the following:

```
AutoCAD
* * * *
```

These two items are the first two listed in the **S menu. They always show through from the bottom of the stack. The three menus you are working with now are shown in Fig. 32-4 as they appear on the screen.

```
**S                    **X              **TEST

AutoCAD
* * * *
ASE                                     TEST
BLOCKS                                   MENU
DIM:                                    ERASE L
DISPLAY                                 ERASE 1
DRAW                                    ZOOM W
EDIT                                    ZOOM P
INQUIRY                                 M CIRCLE
LAYER...                                25 FILLET
MODEL                                   DWG AIDS
MVIEW
PLOT...
RENDER
SETTINGS
SURFACES
UCS:
UTILITY                 ___LAST___
                        DRAW
SAVE:                   EDIT
```

Fig. 32-4. The three menus—**S, **X, and **TEST—as they appear on the screen.

Now try to visualize these three menus—**S, **X, and **TEST—stacked on top of each other. This is illustrated in Fig. 32-5, which shows the stack as a plan (top) and elevation (side) view. Notice which items on the **S menu show through, and which items on the **X menu show through. Your menu, TEST, contains only commands that you create. It allows the top two lines of the **S menu to show through. This is because the menu heading you gave, **TEST 3, means to skip to the third line and write the first command. There is no need to add calls for LAST, DRAW, EDIT, AutoCAD, and OSNAP to your menus. These are picked from the menus lower on the stack.

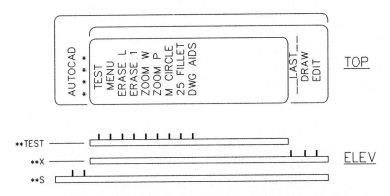

Fig. 32-5. The menu stack is shown in plan and elevation view. This illustrates how items from previous menus can show through and be used with the current menu.

One last thing about the stack. In the ACAD.MNU file, scroll to the **X menu on your screen, if it is not there already. Notice the listing for the LAST command:

[___LAST___]$S= $S=

The $S= code without a menu name represents a call for the last menu. To return to the Root Menu from your submenu, two menu overlays must be removed from the stack. The entry shown above removes two menus. If the following code was used, what would happen?

[___LAST___]$S=

This entry would remove only one menu from the stack. The **X menu, a blank screen except for the LAST, DRAW, and EDIT selections, would appear. You would have to select LAST again to return to the Root Menu. In order to see the last menu that was displayed, you must remove two menus from the stack, the current one, and the **X menu. AutoCAD allows up to eight menus on a stack.

Using variables and control characters

AutoCAD system variables and control characters can be used in screen menus. They might be included to increase the speed and usefulness of your menu commands. Become familiar with these variables so you can make use of them in your menus. The control characters you can use are:

- ^B—Snap ON/OFF toggle
- ^C—Cancel
- ^D—Coords ON/OFF toggle
- ^E—Isoplane ON/OFF toggle
- ^G—Grid ON/OFF toggle
- ^H—Issues a backspace
- ^I—Issues a Tab key
- ^M—Issues a ↵
- ^O—Ortho ON/OFF toggle
- ^P—MENUECHO variable ON/OFF toggle
- ^Q—Prompts, inputs, and status listing echoed to printer
- ^T—Tablet on/off toggle
- ^V—Switches current viewport

EXERCISE 32-2

☐ Use the three-step process to write the menu items given below.
☐ Use the spaces provided to write the macros.
   ☐ [GRID]—Turn the snap and grid on or off. _____
   ☐ [TEXT-S.1]—Set the snap at .1 and select the TEXT command. _____
   ☐ [MIRROR]—Turn the MIRRTEXT variable off and select the MIRROR command's Window option. Do not delete the old object. This command should return the user to Command: prompt. _____
   ☐ [BREAK @]—Break a single line into two parts. _____
   ☐ [CHMFER.5]—Set a chamfer distance of .5 and allow two lines to be picked. ___

PULL-DOWN MENUS

The names of the nine standard pull-down menus appear at the top of the screen in the menu bar. They are selected by placing the crosshairs at the top of the screen, highlighting the item you want, and pressing the pick button. Pull-down menus are referred to as "POP" menus in the ACAD.MNU file. They are listed as POP0 through POP9. POP0 is the cursor menu. When the cursor menu is active, the pull-down menus are not available. A few things to remember about pull-down menus are:

- You can have from 1 to 16 pull-down menus.
- The name of the pull-down menu, or "header," can be up to 14 characters long. Headers should be less than five characters if all 16 POP menus are used.
- Menu item labels can be any length. The menu is as wide as its longest label.
- There can be at least 21 items listed in the menu, including the header.
- Each menu can have multiple cascading submenus.
- A pull-down menu, plus its cascading submenus, can have up to 999 items.
- The cursor menu, plus its cascading submenus, can have up to 499 items.

Pull-down menu structure and codes

Pull-down menus look the same as screen menus. Furthermore, the same codes that are used in writing screen menus are used for pull-down menus. The primary difference between pull-down menus and screen menus is the sequence of characters or *syntax* used for cascading submenus. This is best seen by loading your copy of the ACAD.MNU into your text editor. Page through the menu until you find the headings for POP menus. Look for the ***POP5 heading. This is the Modify menu. The first 14 lines are shown below.

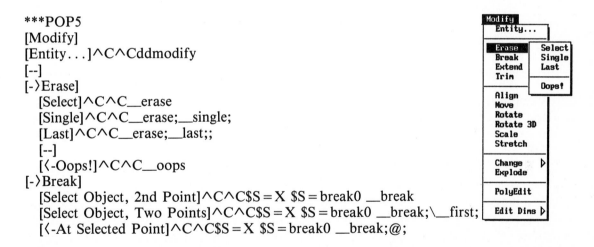

```
***POP5
[Modify]
[Entity...]^C^Cddmodify
[--]
[->Erase]
   [Select]^C^C_erase
   [Single]^C^C_erase;_single;
   [Last]^C^C_erase;_last;;
   [--]
   [<-Oops!]^C^C_oops
[->Break]
   [Select Object, 2nd Point]^C^C$S=X $S=break0 _break
   [Select Object, Two Points]^C^C$S=X $S=break0 _break;\_first;
   [<-At Selected Point]^C^C$S=X $S=break0 _break;@;
```

Compare the appearance of the menu file syntax on the left and the display of the pull-down menu on the right in the previous example. A few new menu syntax characters are found in this menu, and are explained below. These characters provide a separator line, and indicate where cascading submenus begin and end.

Character	Function
[--]	Two hyphens used to insert a separator line across the pull-down menu.
->	Indicates this item has a cascading submenu.
<-	Indicates this is the last item in the submenu.
<-<-	Indicates this item is the last item in the submenu, and the last item of the previous menu (parent menu).

You can see an example of the <-<- characters by searching the ACAD.MNU file for the ***POP7 menu. Scroll down to the following item:

[->UCS]

This line open a submenu that contains two additional submenus:

[->Axis]
[->Icon]

You could say that the [UCS] menu is the "parent" of [Axis] and [Icon]. Now notice the last line of the [Icon] submenu:

   [⟨-⟨-Origin]

The ⟨-⟨- characters indicate that this item is the last of the submenu and the last of the parent menu.

———— PROFESSIONAL TIP ————

Notice in the Modify pull-down menu listing that indentation has been used to indicate cascading submenus. Indenting is not necessary to write a valid menu file, but it gives the file an appearance that is similar to the actual submenus and makes the file easier to read and understand.

Marking menu items

Menu items can be marked with a check mark (✓), or other character of your choosing, or they can be grayed out. The following characters are used for these purposes:

Character	Function
[--]	Two hyphens are used to insert a separator line across a pull-down menu. The line is automatically drawn to fit the width of the pull-down menu.
[~]	The tilde grays out any characters that follow.
[!c]	An exclamation point indicates that a character is used to mark a menu item. Another character must follow the exclamation point. The "c" shown here represents any character.
!.	The combination of an exclamation point and a period places a check mark (✓) before the menu item.

———— PROFESSIONAL TIP ————

A pull-down menu item can be as long as needed, but should be within reason for ease of reading. The pull-down menu width is automatically created to fit the width of the longest item. Separator lines, indicated by the [--] symbols, are also drawn the width of the pull-down menu.

When these marking characters are used in a menu, they mark an item permanently. This may be desirable for the separator line and for graying out specific items, but a check mark is often related to an item that is toggled on or off. Look at the following example menu file and its equivalent pull-down menu.

```
***POP1
[Test]
[!. Checkmark]
[--]
[!X Check & Character]
[--]
[~ Gray text]
[~!X Gray Character]
[~!. Gray Checkmark]
```

Creating "smart" pull-down menu items
ACM 6,8

A common example of placing a check mark by any item is to indicate that it has been selected, or that it is on. You can add this capability to your pull-down menus by using a new "string expression language" called DIESEL. A *string* is simply a group of characters that can be input from the keyboard or from the value of a system variable. The language called *DIESEL (Direct Interpretively Evaluated String Expression Language)* uses a string for its input, and provides a string for output. In other words, you give DIESEL a value, and it gives something back to you.

An excellent example of how DIESEL can be used in menu items is with a check mark. For example, you may want to put the SNAP command in a pull-down menu, and indicate it is on with a check mark. Use the following line in your menu:

[$(if,$(getvar,orthomode),!.)Ortho]^O

The first $ sign signals the pull-down menu to evaluate a DIESEL macro. This macro gets the value (getvar) of the ORTHOMODE system variable, and places the check mark by the item if the value is 1 or on. Notice that the AutoCAD command being executed is ORTHO, ^O.

The following examples shows how two DIESEL additions to the previous Test menu look in the menu file and the pull-down menu. The pull-down menu shows that ORTHO is on.

```
***POP1
[Test]
[$(if,$(getvar,orthomode),!.)Ortho]^O
[$(if,$(getvar,snapmode),!.)Snap]^B
[!. Checkmark]
[--]
[!X Check & Character]
[--]
[~ Gray text]
[~!X Gray Character]
[~!. Gray Checkmark]
```

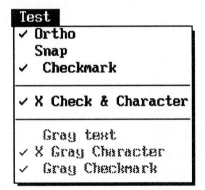

The use of DIESEL expressions in your menus can enhance their power and make them more "intelligent." See Chapters 6 and 8 of the *AutoCAD Customization Manual* for a complete discussion of the DIESEL language. A second example of using DIESEL is shown in the next section.

Referencing other pull-down menus

A pick on one menu can activate, or "reference" a pull-down or cursor menu. A menu pick can also gray out or place a marking character by another pull-down menu item. The following character codes are used for these purposes:

Character	Function
$pn =	Activates another pull-down menu, where "n" is the number of the menu.
$pn = *	Activates and displays another pull-down menu.
$pn.1 =	References a specific item number on another pull-down menu.

When referencing other pull-down menus with the above characters, you can combine the marking symbols to add "gray out," or place check marks or other characters. Study the following menu item examples. The first example activates POP3 and displays it.

$p3 = *

The next menu item places a check mark on item 7 of POP4.

$p4.7 = !.

— NOTE —

Menu item numbering begins with the first line of the pull-down menu below the title and continues to the bottom of the file. AutoCAD numbers items consecutively through all submenus without considering submenu levels.

Now, study these menu item examples. The first entry grays out item 3 of POP4.

$p4.3 = ~

The following menu item places an X by item 2 of POP7 and grays it out.

$p7.2 = !X ~

The next menu item removes all marks and gray-out from item 2 of POP7.

$p7.2 =

The following examples show how these techniques can be combined in a macro.

[Insert desk]^C^Cinsert;desk;\\\\\$p2 = *
[Setup .5]^C^Cgrid;.5;snap;.25;$p2.1 = !. $p2.2 = !. ~
[Defaults]^C^Cgrid;off;snap;off;$p2.1 = $p2.2 =

Customizing the status line

ACM 8

The left side of the status line can be altered to display almost any information that you desire. However, you are limited to the number of characters your display device provides before the coordinate display on the status line, up to 255 characters. The customizable area of the status line is called the *mode status line*. The variable that controls this display is MODEMACRO. Enter the following at the Command: prompt:

Command: **MODEMACRO** ↵
New value for MODEMACRO, or . for none⟨""⟩: **This is a test** ↵

Notice the change in the status line. You can display any text you wish, but it must be entered at the Command: prompt using MODEMACRO each time you want to change it. Return the status line to its default display by entering a period (.) at the MODEMACRO prompt.

New value for MODEMACRO, or . for none⟨""⟩: . ↵

The value of the MODEMACRO variable is in displaying useful information for the user. Try the following examples:

Command: **MODEMACRO** ↵
New value for MODEMACRO, or . for none⟨""⟩: **$(GETVAR,DWGNAME)** ↵

This displays the current drawing name in the mode status line. The next example displays an additional item.

Command: **MODEMACRO** ↵
New value for MODEMACRO, or . for none⟨""⟩: **$(GETVAR,DWGNAME) Layer:**
$(GETVAR,CLAYER) ↵

This entry displays the current drawing name and the current layer.

The more automatic you can make these settings, the more useful they become. It is not productive to type a mode setting each time you need it. However, one method of providing several different mode settings is to place them in a menu. For example, you can create items in a pull-down menu as follows:

[Dwg name/layer]modemacro;$(getvar,dwgname) Layer: $(getvar,clayer);
[Layer/snap]modemacro;Layer: $(getvar,clayer) Snap: $(getvar,snapunit);

A group of selections such as these may be useful, but they must be picked from the menu before being displayed.

┌─────────────────── PROFESSIONAL TIP ───────────────────┐

The MODEMACRO variable can be displayed automatically by using the AutoLISP language to create a function that is activated when AutoCAD is loaded. See Chapter 34 for an introduction to AutoLISP. AutoLISP is a programming language that can be used to create special programs and functions that can increase your productivity with AutoCAD. See Chapter 8 of the *AutoCAD Customization Manual* for a discussion of MODEMACRO settings in AutoLISP files.

└───┘

Creating a new pull-down menu

Scroll through your copy of the ACAD.MNU file until you find the ***icon menu. It is located after the last line of pull-down menu, P9.

```
[<-Unload Modeler]^C^CP(ai_unloadame) ^P
***icon
**poly
```

If you want to add a tenth pull-down menu, it should be inserted before the ***icon section. Move the cursor to the line before the ***icon section and begin inserting there. Be sure to leave an empty line between pull-down menus.

Always test each item of a new menu to make sure they all work properly. Remember, when you return to the drawing editor, you must use the MENU command to reload the revised menu. If you neglect to do this, you will be working with the old version of the menu.

Command: **MENU** ↵
Menu file name or . for none ⟨current⟩: **MENUNAME** ↵

Sample menu items

The following examples show how AutoCAD commands and options can be used to create pull-down or screen menu items. They are listed using the three-step process:
- Step 1 is a verbal description of the macro.
- Step 2 lists the keyboard strokes required for the macro.
- Step 3 gives the actual macro as it appears in the menu file.

Example 1

1. This HEXAGON command should be repeated and should display the polygon screen menu. It should select the POLYGON command and request a six-sided polygon inscribed in a circle.
2. POLYGON ↵
   6 ↵
   SELECT CENTER ↵
   I ↵
3. [Hexagon]*^C^C$S = X $S = polygon polygon 6 \I

As mentioned earlier, you can indicate a RETURN in a command or macro by using either a space or a semicolon. Look closely at the italicized portions of the following two commands. Both commands perform the same function.

[Hexagon]*^C^C$S = X $S = polygon *polygon 6 \I*
[Hexagon]*^C^C$S = X $S = polygon *polygon;6;\I*

The first example uses spaces and the second example has semicolons to represent pressing the ENTER key. The technique you use is a matter of personal preference.

——— PROFESSIONAL TIP ———

Some people prefer to use the semicolon for a RETURN to clearly indicate that a RETURN has been inserted. Whereas, when using spaces, an extra space can slip into a menu item and go unnoticed until the item is tested.

Example 2

1. This DOT command should draw a solid dot, .1 inch in diameter. Use the DONUT command. The inside diameter is 0 (zero) and the outside diameter is .1.
2. DONUT ↵
   0 ↵
   .1 ↵
3. [Dot]^C^Cdonut;0;.1

Example 3

1. This X-POINT command displays the POINT screen menu and draws an "X" at the pick point. The command should be repeated.
2. PDMODE ↵
   3 ↵
   POINT ↵
   Pick the point
3. [X-Point]*^C^C$S = X $S = point ;pdmode;3;point

Example 4

1. This macro named "Notation" could be used by a drawing checker or instructor. It allows them to circle features on a drawing or design that requires editing, and then add a leader and text. It first sets the color to red, then draws a circle, snaps a leader to the nearest point that is picked on the circle, and prompts for the text. User input for text is provided, then a cancel returns the Command: prompt and the color is set to white (7).
2. COLOR ↵
   RED ↵
   CIRCLE ↵
   Pick center point
   Pick radius
   DIM ↵
   LEADER ↵
   NEA ↵
   Pick a point on the circle
   Pick end of leader ↵
   Press ENTER for automatic shoulder
   Enter text ↵
3. [Notation]^C^Ccolor;red;circle;\\dim;lea;nea;\\;\^Ccolor;7

Example 5

1. A repeating command named "Multisquare," which draws one inch squares oriented at a 0° horizontal angle.
2. RECTANG ↵
   @1,1 ↵
3. [Multisquare]*^C^Crectang;\@1,1

☐ Use your text editor and create a new file named EX32-3.MNU. Put the following commands in a ***POP1 menu.

   ☐ [Copy M] – Make multiple copies. Allow two picks.

   ☐ [Rotate45] – Rotate an object 45° counterclockwise. Should be an automatic command.

   ☐ [Fillet .5] – A repeating command that applies a .5 fillet.

☐ All commands should display their screen submenus.

☐ Use the spaces below to write out the commands before you enter them in the computer.

   [COPY M] – _____

   [ROTATE45] – _____

   [FILLET .5] – _____

Some notes about pull-down menus

Here are a few more things to keep in mind when developing pull-down menus.

• If the first line of a pull-down menu (the title line) is blank, that menu is not displayed in the menu bar, and all menus to the right are moved left to take its place.

• Pull-down menus are disabled during the following commands:

   DTEXT, after the rotation angle is entered

   SKETCH, after the record increment is set

   VPOINT, during use of the tripod and compass

   ZOOM Dynamic

   DVIEW

• Pull-down menus that are taller than the screen display are truncated to fit on the screen.

• The cursor menu is named POP0, and can contain items that reference other pull-down and screen menus.

• The menu bar is not active while the cursor menu is displayed.

ICON MENUS

Icon menus contain graphic symbols displayed in dialogue boxes. They appear when you select some items from the pull-down menu bar, such as 3D Objects... from the Draw pull-down menu. See Fig. 32-6. The display is composed of several small boxes. Each box contains a small drawing. These displays are slides. The slides are saved in a file that is created with the SLIDELIB.EXE

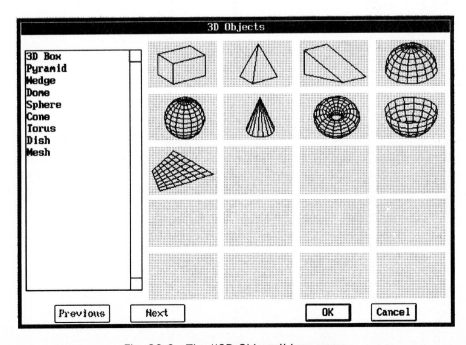

Fig. 32-6. The "3D Objects" icon menu.

program. This program creates a file with an .SLB extension. The slides in this file become an icon menu by entering them as menu items in the ACAD.MNU file. Chapter 29 discusses the use of SLIDELIB.EXE.

The addition of icon menus can enhance the operation of AutoCAD. However, you must create icons using certain guidelines:

- Keep symbols simple. The icon menu display can be a simplified version of the actual symbol. This saves display time and storage space.
- When making slides, fill the screen with the image. Center long items on the screen using PAN. This centers them in the icon box and fills the box with the image.
- Use icon menus for graphic symbols only. Do not clutter your program with icon menus of text information. This slows the system down and is not a good use of the icon menu.
- AutoCAD does not display solid filled areas in icon menus. If you use fills such as arrowheads, turn off the fill to see how the slide will look in the icon menu.
- A maximum of 20 slides can be displayed in one icon menu. The names of the icons are automatically displayed in a list box to the left of the icons. Icon names (up to 17 characters) are displayed in the list box.
- If you have more than 20 slides in an icon menu, AutoCAD creates additional "pages," each containing a Next and a Previous button for changing pages. The OK and Cancel buttons are automatically provided in the icon menu.
- If an item label in an icon menu has a space before the first character, no icon is displayed for that label, but the label name is shown, and is indented in the list box. This item in the menu file can be used to execute other commands or call other icon menus.

Making symbols and slides for the icon menu

Icon menus can be used for a variety of purposes, but they are most commonly used to display blocks or wblocks. Regardless of the types of symbols used, follow these steps when making slides and icon menus.

1. Draw the symbol or block.
2. Center the drawing on the display screen. When the drawing appears in the icon menu, it is displayed in a box with a 1.5:1 ratio of width to height. With your drawing on the screen, set TILEMODE = 0, then create a 3 x 2 viewport. Now, ZOOM Extents and then switch back to model space. The drawing is now at the correct ratio.
3. Make a slide of the symbol using the MSLIDE command.
4. Write the SLIDELIB file.
5. Write the icon menu file and test it.

Draw the three shapes shown in Fig. 32-7. They represent a table, desk, and chair. Draw them any size you wish. Save each one as a block, and name them TABLE, DESK, and CHAIR. Do not include text or attributes.

Fig. 32-7. These objects are to be saved as blocks and used in an icon menu file.

Now, insert into the current drawing, copies of all of the blocks you plan to include in the icon menu; in this example, one TABLE, DESK, and CHAIR. Do not scale or rotate the blocks. Use the MSLIDE command to make a slide of each one of the blocks, centering the slide as previously discussed. Make slides of each of the blocks in the same manner. Give the slides the same name as the block. This completes the second step. Now you will use the SLIDELIB program to make the slide file.

Using the SLIDELIB program for an icon menu

The SLIDELIB.EXE program operates in DOS and allows you to create a list of slide (.SLD extension) files. This list of slides can then be used for slide shows and icon menus. Since you may be using this command frequently, it is a good idea to add SLIDELIB to your ACAD.PGP file. Use your text editor to add the following line to the ACAD.PGP file:

```
SLIDELIB,SLIDELIB,          0,Slide library name: ,4
```

This new ACAD.PGP command cannot be used until you exit AutoCAD and begin a new drawing, or use the REINIT command.

If you choose not to add SLIDELIB to your ACAD.PGP file, you must use the SHELL command. Then enter SLIDELIB at the OS prompt and provide a file name for the slide library. The creation of a slide file called FITTINGS begins as follows:

```
Command: SHELL ↵
OS Command: ↵
C:\ACAD⟩ SLIDELIB FITTINGS ↵
```

The use of SLIDELIB after this is the same for both methods.

Assuming that SLIDELIB is specified in the PGP file, you can create the slide file of the three blocks as follows. Name the library FURNITUR.

```
Command: SLIDELIB ↵
Slide library name: FURNITUR ↵
SLIDELIB 1.2 (3/8/89)
(c) Copyright 1987-89 Autodesk, Inc.
   All Rights Reserved
TABLE ↵
CHAIR ↵
DESK ↵
↵
↵
```

The third ENTER after the last slide name exits the SLIDELIB program. Check to see that the slide file was created by listing all files with the .SLB extensions. It should be listed as FURNITUR.SLB.

A second method of creating a slide library involves using an existing list of slides in a text file. This method is useful if you add slide names to a text file (.TXT) as the slides are made. The method was discussed in Chapter 29.

Creating an icon menu file listing

Load your copy of the ACAD.MNU into the text editor and page through the file until you find the ***icon section. You can insert your new icon menu between any of the existing ones. Be sure to leave a space between the previous and next menus.

Now begin a menu called "furniture" below the last icon heading, **vporti. Move the cursor to the blank line between the last icon menu and the **Comment line and begin inserting the new icon menu entries. The first item in the menu is used as the title. If you neglect to put a title here, the first line of the menu, whatever it is, will be used as the title. Your new menu should look exactly like the following:

```
**furniture
[Select Furniture]
[furnitur(table)]^C^Cinsert;table
[furnitur(desk)]^C^Cinsert;desk
[furnitur(chair)]^C^Cinsert;chair
[ Plants]$I = plants $I = *
```

Notice the space in the last entry, [Plants], after the left bracket. This technique is used to specify a label in the icon menu. Instead of displaying a box with a symbol, this label is shown indented in the list box of the icon menu. An icon is not displayed for this item, but it can be used to execute other commands, or as in this case, display another icon menu. These are called "branching" icon menus. In this example, the Plants icon menu may show icons of several types of plants. Using this technique you can have as many branching icon menus as needed. However, keep the branches and levels realistic and understandable.

The new icon menu is still not usable because there is no selection that calls this menu to the screen. A good place to put the call for this icon menu is the Draw or Construct pull-down menus. Insert the following line at a convenient location in the pull-down menu:

[Furniture]$I = furniture $I = *

The first part of this entry, "$I = furniture," calls the new furniture icon menu. The second part, "$I = *," displays the furniture menu and makes the items selectable. Now your new menu should work.

Save the file and use the MENU command to reload the menu. Test all the items in the menu and correct any problems. The new icon menu should look like the one in Fig. 32-8.

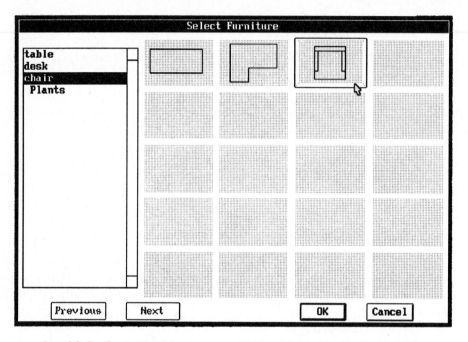

Fig. 32-8. Customized icon menu utilizing objects previously created.

NOTE

AutoCAD has two files that control the function of your screen and tablet menus. They are the ACAD.MNU and ACAD.MNL. The ACAD.MNL file is composed of AutoLISP routines, and must be located in the same directory as the ACAD.MNU file. By default, these two files are installed in the \ACAD\SUPPORT subdirectory. Do not delete or move the ACAD.MNL file.

The ACAD.MNL file contains AutoLISP code that would otherwise lengthen and complicate the ACAD.MNU file. If you wish to add menu items that utilize AutoLISP, consider adding the AutoLISP code to the ACAD.MNL file. See Chapter 34 for a discussion of the basic AutoLISP commands.

EXERCISE 32-4

☐ Using your text editor, create an icon menu named EX32-4 using three blocks that you have on file.

☐ Plan this menu so that you can add to it in the future.

☐ Remember to include an entry in the Draw pull-down menu that calls the new icon menu.

┌─────────────────────────── PROFESSIONAL TIP ───────────────────────────┐
│   │
│   Your primary goal in developing menus is to eliminate extra steps required to perform a │
│ function. The end result is that you can execute a thought or idea with one pick, rather than │
│ labor through a series of commands and options.   │
│   │
└──┘

CHAPTER TEST

Write your answers in the spaces provided.

1. The name and extension of the file that contains all of the menus for AutoCAD is ___
   _____ .

2. List the names of the major sections in AutoCAD's default menu. _____
   _____

3. How many different button menus can you have? _____
   _____

4. What kind of symbol is used to indicate a screen submenu? _____

5. Describe the function of each of the following screen menu commands:
   A. [Layer:]$S = X $S = LAYER ^C^CLAYER − _____
   _____
   _____

   B. [Copy W]^C^CCOPY;W;\\ − _____
   _____
   _____

   C. [CHANGE 1]^C^CCHANGE;\;− _____
   _____
   _____

6. Give the function of the following menu command codes:
   [Brackets] − _____
   Semicolon (;) − _____
   Backslash (\) − _____
   _____
   Plus sign (+) − _____
   Single (si) − _____

7. How many button menus can be accessed with combinations of key and button picks?
   _____

8. How would the following button menu command function?
   Erase;\ − _____

9. What system variable gives you the number of screen menu items you can have? _____
   _____

10. How many items can a pull-down menu contain? _____

AutoCAD and Its Applications

11. Define the following pull-down menu characters.

 -〉 _____

 〈- _____

 〈-〈- _____

 _____

12. Provide the character(s) required to perform the following functions:

 A. Insert a separator line across the pull-down menu. _____

 B. Gray out characters. _____

 C. Place a check mark before the menu item. _____

13. Define a macro. _____

 _____

14. List the three steps you should use when creating a new menu command.

 A. _____

 B. _____

 C. _____

15. Suppose you add a new menu to the ACAD.MNU file. How does the new menu get displayed

 on the screen? _____

 _____

16. Define a menu stack. _____

 _____

17. What code is used to make pull-down menus display and be selectable? _____

18. Describe the uses of the following menu codes:

 Asterisk (*)— _____

 [--]— _____

 _____

 Tilde (~)— _____

19. Name two ways to represent a RETURN in a menu item. _____

 _____

20. How many pull-down menus can be displayed on one screen? _____

21. If 10 pull-down menus are used, the maximum length of a pull-down menu heading should be

 _____.

22. How wide is a pull-down menu? _____

23. What is the function of the following DIESEL expression?

 [$(if,$(getvar,snapmode),!.)Snap]^B— _____

 _____

24. What is the function of the following menu item characters?

 $p3 = * _____

 $p4.1 = ~ _____

 $p6.7 = !. _____

32-26

25. Provide the input to dislay the label "Layer:" and the current drawing name on the mode status line.

    New value for MODEMACRO, or . for none⟨""⟩: _____

26. How many items can be listed in a pull-down menu? _____

27. The command used to create the slide file that is used for an icon menu is _____.

28. What is the first line of an icon menu called? _____

29. Interpret the following menu item:

    *^C^Crectang;\@1,1 − _____

    _____

30. List the steps required in the creation of an icon menu.

    A. _____

    B. _____

    C. _____

    D. _____

    E. _____

31. Why is it a good idea to make a copy of the ACAD.MNU file before you begin experimenting

    or customizing? _____

    _____

DRAWING PROBLEMS

1. Begin an entirely new AutoCAD menu composed of a general button section and an OSNAP button menu and screen menu. Name the menu P32-1.MNU. Plan your menu items before you begin. The main button menu (***BUTTONS1) should have the following items:

BUTTON #	FUNCTION
1	Select text and allow user to reword.
2	Cancel last and activate the LINE command.
3	Cancel last and activate the CIRCLE command.
4	ZOOM dynamic.
5	Leave blank.
6	Erase one object and end the ERASE command.
7	Cancel last and ZOOM window.
8	Enter (Return).
9	Cancel last and ZOOM previous.

The **BUTTONS2 menu is an OSNAP interrupt menu. All OSNAP items should activate the OSNAP mode and select a point when the button is pressed. The **BUTTONS2 menu should contain the following items:

BUTTON #	FUNCTION
1	ENDpoint
2	INTersect
3	PERpendicular
4	MIDpoint
5	CENter
6	TANgent
7	QUAdrant
8	Return to main button and screen menus.
9	NODE

Write the menus in small segments and be sure to test all items. Generate a printed copy of the menu file.

2. Add the menu given below to the P32-1.MNU file you created in Problem 1. The section name should be ***SCREEN. The main menu name should be **S. Plan all of your menu items before entering them in the text editor. The following items should be included.

POSITION	MENU ITEMS
1	Menu title [H O M E].
2	Cancel and ARC.
3	Cancel and POLYGON.
4	Cancel and PLINE.
5	Cancel and LIST.
6	Cancel and DIST.
7	Cancel and SCALE.
8	Cancel and OFFSET.
9	Cancel and ROTATE.
10	Cancel and STRETCH.
11	Blank.
12	Cancel and ZOOM.
13	Blank
14	Rotate crosshair axis to user specified angle. Allow user to set base point and leave snap on.
15	Reset crosshair axis to zero and turn snap off.
16	Allow user to pick multiple objects and change all to a new layer.
17	Select text string and allow user to input new height.

Test all menu items to ensure that they are working properly before going to the next problem. Generate a printed copy of the menu file.

3. Add the following screen menu to your P32-1.MNU file. This is an editing menu and should be named **EDIT. At position 18 in your main screen menu (see Problem 2), add an item that calls the EDIT menu. Place the following items in the EDIT menu:

POSITION	MENU ITEM	
1	[ERASE-W]	Erase with fence option.
2	[COPY-WP]	Copy with window polygon option.
3	[MOVE-W]	Move with window option.
4	[BREAK-F]	Activate BREAK, allow user to select object, then pick first and second points without entering "F."
5	[CHANGE-1]	Activate CHANGE, select object, and stop for user input.
6	[REWORD-M]	Allow user to reword one to four lines of text without restarting the command.
7	[O-FILLET]	Select two lines and clean up corners with zero radius fillet. Allow selection of one to five clean-ups without restarting the command.
8	[O-BREAK]	Select line or arc and split into two parts.
9	[O-CORNER]	Select two intersecting lines at the intersection. Clean up corner using two picks.

Generate a printed copy of the menu file.

4. Add an item to the main button menu at button 5 that calls the **BUTTONS2 menu and a new screen menu called **OSNAP. The line should read:

    [5]$B = BUTTONS $S = OSNAP

The new **OSNAP screen menu should contain the following items:

POSITION	MENU ITEM	
1	[BUTTONS]	Label
2	[1 = Endpt]	Show button assignment and activate normal OSNAP if picked from screen.
3	[2 = Inter]	Show button assignment and activate normal OSNAP if picked from screen.
4	[3 = Perp]	Show button assignment and activate normal OSNAP if picked from screen.
5	[4 = Middle]	Show button assignment and activate normal OSNAP if picked from screen.
6	[5 = Center]	Show button assignment and activate normal OSNAP if picked from screen.
7	[6 = Tangnt]	Show button assignment and activate normal OSNAP if picked from screen.
8	[7 = Quad]	Show button assignment and activate normal OSNAP if picked from screen.
9	[8-HOME]	Page back to main button and screen menus.
10	[9 = Node]	Show button assignment and activate normal OSNAP if picked from screen.
11	[Nearest]	Activate Nearest OSNAP from screen.
12	[Insert]	Activate Insert OSNAP from screen.

   Generate a printed copy of the menu file.
5. Alter the **OSNAPB menu in your copy of the ACAD.MNU file. Make it function with a button menu in the same manner as given in Problem 4. If you have not added a **BUTTONS2 menu to your ACAD.MNU file (explained earlier in this chapter), do so for this problem.
6. Create a dimensioning pull-down menu. Place as many dimensioning commands as you need in the menu. Use cascading submenus if necessary. One or more of the submenus should be dimensioning variables.
7. Create a 3-D pull-down menu. Add it to your copy of ACAD.MNU. The contents of the menu should include the following:
     Elev
     3Dobjects
     3Dsurfaces
     3Dface
     VPoint
     VPorts
     Dview
     Hide
     Filters
8. Construct an icon menu of a symbol library that you created in Chapter 21. This menu can be selected from the Draw pull-down menu or from a new pull-down menu. Use as many icons as needed.

DARLEY CHAMPION
(18HP) 500GPM

96.00 MAX

NOTES:
1) TANK CAPACITY IS 1800
   U.S. GALLONS.
2) COMPATIBLE WITH VARIOUS
   CHASSIS.

56.25

18.000
MAX.

156.25

2.50

DUMP WATER VALVE
2000 GALLONS PER MINUTE

19.000 × 36.000
OPENING SIZE
BOTH SIDES

CLOSED SIZE: 11'3" × 30" × 7"
2100 GALLON CAPACITY
PORTABLE TANK

CA = 102.00

Technical specifications for a fire engine.   (Jim Armstrong)

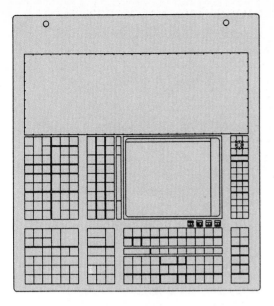

Chapter 33

CUSTOMIZING AUTOCAD'S TABLET MENU

Learning objectives

After completing this chapter, you will be able to:
☐ Configure and use the AutoCAD tablet menu template.
☐ Customize the AutoCAD tablet menu.
☐ Create a new tablet menu.

If you have a digitizer, the AutoCAD standard tablet menu is an alternative to keyboard entry or picking screen commands. The tablet menu template is a thick piece of plastic that measures 11 x 12 in. Printed on it are most of the commands available in AutoCAD. Some commands are accompanied by small symbols, or icons, that indicate the function of the command. The menu is helpful because it provides a clear display of various AutoCAD commands.

Like the screen menus, the tablet menu can be customized. Notice the empty spaces on it, Fig. 33-1, at the top. This space is available for adding commands or symbols, to aid in the picking and inserting functions. You can have several overlays for this area.

You do not have to use the template supplied with AutoCAD. Most people discover that many of the AutoCAD commands are not used for specific types of drawings, so they construct their own tablet menus. This is similar to creating screen menus, but there are different techniques involved when making tablet menus.

USING THE AUTOCAD TABLET MENU

To use a tablet menu, the digitizer must first be configured for the specific menu you have. When you initially configure AutoCAD to recognize a digitizer, the entire surface of the tablet represents the screen pointing area. The TABLET command allows you to configure the digitizer to recognize the menu. This includes telling AutoCAD the exact layout of the menu areas and the size and position of the screen pointing area.

Tablet menu layout

The AutoCAD tablet menu presents commands in related groups. See Fig. 33-1. Notice the headings below each menu area.

Item	Group
A	Monitor
B	User area
C	MVIEW/DISPLAY/DRAW
D	OBJECT SNAP/TOGGLES/EDIT/SETTINGS
E	NUMERIC
F	TEXT/ALIGNMENTS
G	INQUIRY/DIMENSION
H	RENDER/VIEW/UCS/BLOCK/LAYER
I	UTILITY/PLOT
J	AME & REGION MODELER
K	AUTOSHADE

Find the Change Template command in the UTILITY/PLOT section in the lower-right corner of the template. This command changes the meaning of the digitizer to recognize additional third-party software packages or your own custom menu. Each third-party package must work with AutoCAD, and must be installed on your hard disk drive for this command to work.

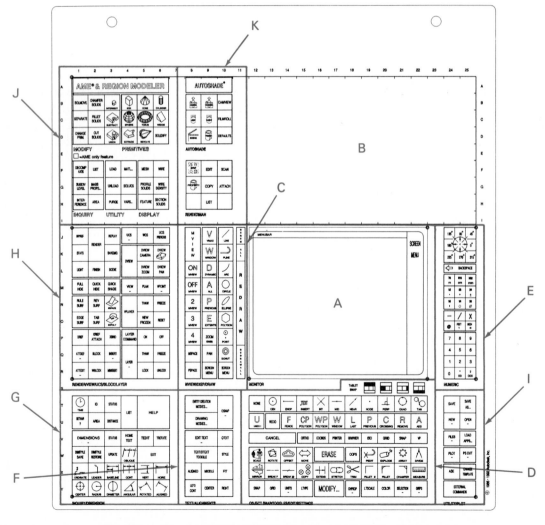

Fig. 33-1. The AutoCAD tablet menu template. (Autodesk, Inc.)

In order for the Change Template command to work, you must set an environment variable called ACADALTMENU. This variable must be set in a batch file before loading AutoCAD. For example, if you have an alternate menu called PIPING.MNU located in the C:\CADPIPE subdirectory, add the following statement to a batch file before AutoCAD is loaded:

SET ACADALTMENU = C:\CADPIPE\PIPING.MNU

Now, when you pick Change Template it looks for a value in the ACADALTMENU environment variable and loads the menu. Keep in mind that the alternate menu can be an entirely new menu composed of button, screen, pull-downs, icons, and tablet menus.

Configuring the tablet menu

The TABLET command allows you to tell AutoCAD the layout of the tablet menu. It prompts for three corners of each menu area and the number of columns and rows in each area. The screen pointing area is defined by picking two opposite corners. Three corners of each menu area are marked with small donuts. As you read the following example, look at Fig. 33-2. It illustrates how the standard AutoCAD tablet menu is configured and shows the donuts marking menu area corners.

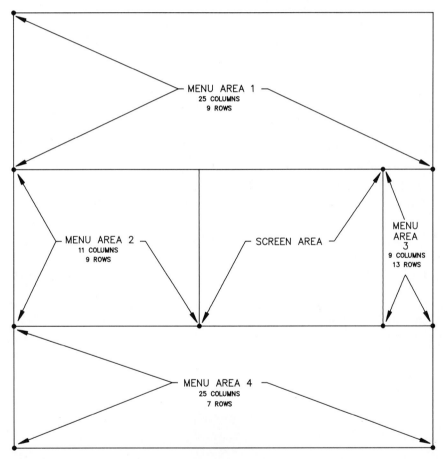

Fig. 33-2. Small donuts mark the corners of the menu areas on the AutoCAD template. (Autodesk, Inc.)

Command: **TABLET** ⏎
Option (ON/OFF/CAL/CFG): **CFG** ⏎
Enter number of tablet menus desired (0-4) ⟨4⟩: ⏎
Do you want to realign tablet menu areas? ⟨N⟩ **Y** ⏎
Digitize upper left corner of menu area 1: *(pick the donut at the upper left corner)*
Digitize lower left corner of menu area 1: *(pick the point)*
Digitize lower right corner of menu area 1: *(pick the point)*
Enter the number of columns for menu area 1: **25** ⏎
Enter the number of rows for menu area 1: **9** ⏎

You have now given AutoCAD the location of menu area 1 and specified the number of boxes that are available. The command continues with menu area 2:

Digitize upper left corner of menu area 2: *(pick the point)*
Digitize lower left corner of menu area 2: *(pick the point)*
Digitize lower right corner of menu area 2: *(pick the point)*
Enter the number of columns for menu area 2: **11** ⏎
Enter the number of rows for menu area 2: **9** ⏎
Digitize upper left corner of menu area 3: *(pick the point)*
Digitize lower left corner of menu area 3: *(pick the point)*
Digitize lower right corner of menu area 3: *(pick the point)*
Enter the number of columns for menu area 3: **9** ⏎
Enter the number of rows for menu area 3: **13** ⏎
Digitize upper left corner of menu area 4: *(pick the point)*
Digitize lower left corner of menu area 4: *(pick the point)*
Digitize lower right corner of menu area 4: *(pick the point)*
Enter the number of columns for menu area 4: **25** ⏎
Enter the number of rows for menu area 4: **7** ⏎

Next, you must locate opposite corners of the screen pointing area:

Do you want to respecify the screen pointing area? ⟨N⟩ **Y** ⏎
Digitize lower left corner of screen pointing area: *(pick donut at lower left corner of screen area)*
Digitize upper right corner of screen pointing area: *(pick upper right corner)*
Command:

The tablet configuration is saved in the ACAD.CFG file, which is in your ACAD directory. The system reads this file when loading AutoCAD to determine what kind of equipment you are using. It also determines which menu is current. Use this same process when configuring the tablet for your custom menus.

Configuring the AutoCAD template is made quicker by selecting the TABLET command from the screen menu. Pick SETTINGS in the Root Menu, then pick TABLET. The screen menu in Fig. 33-3 is displayed.

Fig. 33-3. Select Re-Cfg from the TABLET screen menu to configure the tablet menu.

Select the Re-Cfg option from the menu. The configuration prompts appear as shown earlier, but you do not have to enter the number of columns and rows. The Re-Cfg option assumes you are reconfiguring the AutoCAD template. Therefore, it only requires the locations of the menu areas and the screen pointing area. Use this option when you wish to return to the standard AutoCAD template after using a custom menu.

Swapping template areas

Look at the digitizer template below the monitor area and you can see the "Tablet swap" icons. These four picks allow you to swap each of the four tablet areas. The black area of each icon indicates the area that is swapped when the icon is picked. In addition, a prompt on the monitor indicates the type of swap. For example, if you pick area 1, the AME and AutoShade commands are removed and the entire area is available for custom commands. Customizing this area is discussed later. In addition, the number 1 is placed below the word AutoCAD in the screen menu, in the position of the first asterisk. The following list indicates the area swapped, the prompt, and the number placed in the line of asterisks in the screen menu.

- Area 1 prompt:
  Alternate tablet area 1 loaded.
  This area is for your personal applications and menu items.
  1 * * *
- Area 2 prompt:
  Alternate tablet area 2 loaded.
  Zoom and other commands issue CTRL Cs: VPOINT and DVIEW in current UCS mode.
  * 2 * *
- Area 3 prompt:
  Alternate tablet area 3 loaded.
  Select Metric units from the Numeric menu.
  * * 3 *
- Area 4 prompt:
  Alternate tablet area 4 loaded.
  Object snap modes issue running modes: commands repeat.
  * * * 4

Any of the areas can be swapped back to the default menu by just picking the icon again. Also, all swapped areas can be reset to defaults by picking "AutoCAD" at the top of the screen menu. You can have more than one swapped menu at a time. For example, if areas 2 and 4 are swapped, the asterisk line reads:

* 2 * 4

You will always know if you are working with a swapped menu because one or more numbers are displayed on the asterisk line below AutoCAD in the screen menu.

The prompt that is issued after picking a swap icon can be shortened or eliminated if you decide that you do not need to see it. Use the EXPERT system variable to change the prompt. A value of 0 for EXPERT displays the entire prompt. A value of 1 to 3 displays only the first part of the prompt:

Alternate tablet area 3 loaded.

A value of 4 for the EXPERT variable displays no prompt when a swap icon is picked. A value of 3 displays an abbreviated prompt. Set the variable as follows:

Command: **EXPERT** ↵
New value for EXPERT ⟨0⟩: **3** ↵

CUSTOMIZING THE AUTOCAD
TABLET MENU

| ARM A | ACM 6 |

The empty upper portion of the AutoCAD tablet menu was left blank for users to customize. This is menu area 1. It contains 225 boxes that can be programmed for additional commands, macros, scripts, or blocks. It is a good place to locate often-used symbols and shapes. An overlay containing block names and drawings can be plotted and slipped under the plastic template. Several overlays can be added for different disciplines, and can be structured to operate in different ways.

Plan the template

Before adding items to the AutoCAD template, take time to think about what the template should include. Ask yourself the following questions:
- What kinds of drawings will the template be used for?
- What kind of symbols should be placed in a template?
- What additional commands or macros should be in the template?
- Should the symbols be stored as blocks or wblocks?
- Which symbols and blocks are used most often?
- If the symbols are blocks, should they be in a prototype drawing?

After answering these questions, you will be able to lay out a quality template. The next step is to draw the overlay.

Draw the menu overlay

Part of your plan should be drawing or sketching the menu area. The quickest way to make an accurate drawing is to plot menu area 1 of the AutoCAD template. There is such a drawing, called TABLETAC.DWG, furnished with the software. It is located in the \ACAD\SAMPLE subdirectory. The following steps should be used to create the drawing of menu area 1:
- Open the drawing file named TABLETAC. Enter the file name \ACAD\SAMPLE\ TABLETAC, or pick it from the dialogue box.
- ZOOM Window around menu area 1. See Fig. 33-4.

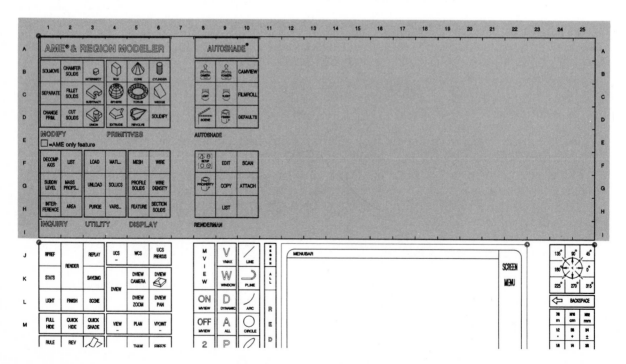

Fig. 33-4. Menu area 1 is located at the top of the AutoCAD template. It contains an invisible grid of 225 boxes inside the menu area border.

- Freeze all layers except:
  0
  OUTLINES
  PLINES
- Make a new layer named AREA1, and give it the color cyan.
- Use PLINE to trace over the outline of AREA1.
- Draw a vertical line between tick marks on the right or left side and array it in 24 columns with a spacing of .4020.
- Draw a horizontal line between tick marks at the top or bottom and array 8 rows with a spacing of .4020.
- Erase the remaining black lines in the menu. See Fig. 33-5.
- Plot the menu on B size or larger paper. A plot using 1.5 = 1 or 2 = 1 scale provides a larger drawing which is easier to work with for initial menu design purposes.
- Erase all unnecessary layers.
- Save the drawing as TABAREA1 for future use.

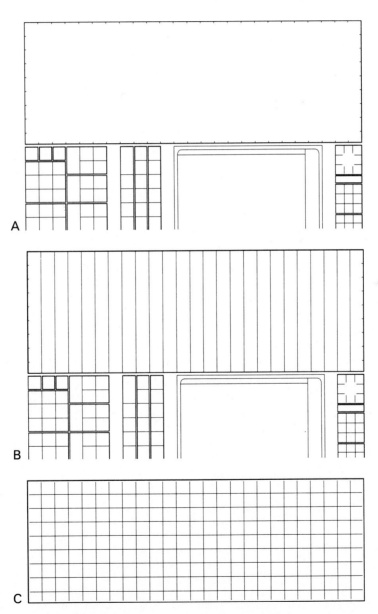

Fig. 33-5.   A—The TABLETAC drawing in its unedited form. B—Tablet menu area 1 after drawing vertical lines.
C—Completed tablet menu area 1.

Make several copies of your drawing. Pencil in command and symbol names you want. Try more than one arrangement based on some of the considerations previously mentioned. Keep in mind the purpose of the template you are making. Symbols that are used frequently should be placed along the outer edges for quick selection.

Complete the menu drawing

The next step in creating your customized AutoCAD template is to draw the symbols in the menu. This should be relatively easy. Symbols should already be in the form of blocks. They can now be inserted into the boxes of the menu. You will have to scale the symbols down to make them fit. The menu should now resemble that shown in Fig. 33-6. These symbols were inserted from the symbols library prototype drawing created in Chapter 21.

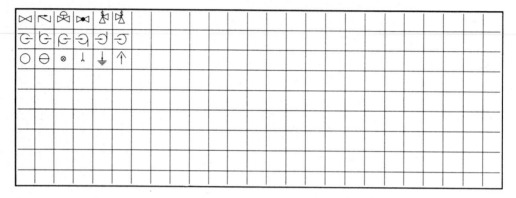

Fig. 33-6. Symbols (blocks) are inserted into the boxes of the menu.

The menu area can be modified to suit your needs. The symbols shown in Fig. 33-7 are used for isometric process piping drawings.

After drawing the menu, plot it at full scale (1 = 1). Use vellum or polyester film and wet ink. Use black rather than colored ink. This produces a good-quality plot, clearly seen when slipped under the AutoCAD template.

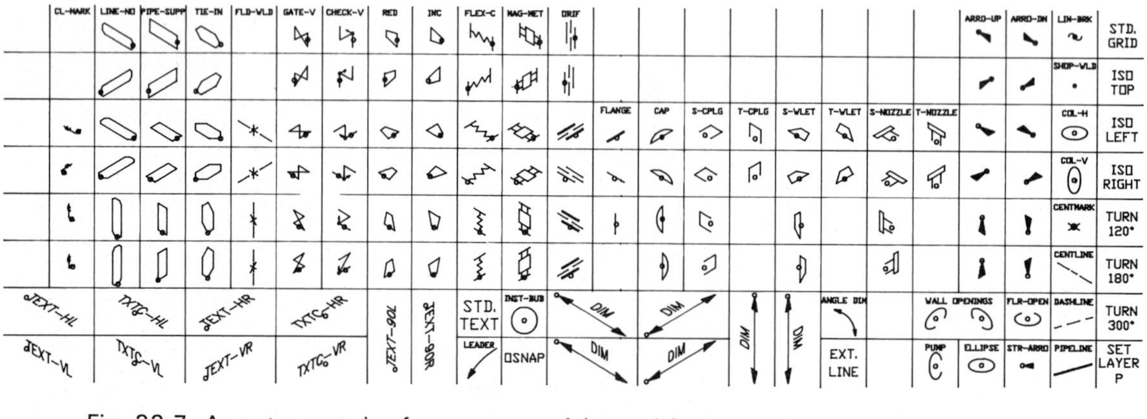

Fig. 33-7. A custom overlay for menu area 1 is used for isometric process piping drawings.
(Willamette Industries, Inc.)

PROFESSIONAL TIP

When developing your custom tablet menu for area 1, decide if you will be needing the AME and AutoShade commands located there. If so, locate your menu commands and symbols to the right of these two menus. If you will not be needing AME and AutoShade, pick the swap icon for area 1 and the menu is now free for your use.

EXERCISE 33-1

☐ Open the TABLETAC drawing.
☐ Edit the drawing as shown in the previous discussion to create a tablet menu area 1 with boxes.
☐ Save the drawing of menu area 1 as A:EX33-1.
☐ Insert two blocks of your choice into the first two boxes of the menu area.
☐ Scale the blocks so they fit in the boxes.
☐ Save the drawing as A:EX33-1 and quit.

Write the menu file

The final step in customizing the AutoCAD template is to write the code in the ***TABLET1 section of the menu file. Load the ACAD.MNU file into your text editor and find the section label ***TABLET1. It should look like the following:

```
***TABLET1
[A-1]
[A-2]
[A-3]
[A-4]
[A-5]
```

Look at the tablet menu in Fig. 33-4 and notice the row and column numbers and letters along the top and sides of the tablet. These correspond to the numbers in brackets in the ACAD.MNU file under the ***TABLET headings. Each row contains 25 boxes numbered from left to right. There are 225 boxes in all. Therefore, box number 70 would also be C-20.

The left portion of tablet area 1 contains the AME and AutoShade menus. These occupy columns 1 through 10. Now look at the ACAD.MNU file and you can see that beginning with row B, the first ten columns are filled with command codes. That leaves you with columns 11 through 25 in rows B through H. All of row A is available should you need it, even though headings show on the tablet menu. Row I columns 1-7 and 11-25 are also open for your use.

If you will not be using AME and AutoSHADE, you can delete all of the command code in this section, thus freeing more space for your own custom menu. If you want to use all of the boxes in tablet area 1, and preserve the AME and AutoShade commands, you can place your custom menu in the ***TABLET1ALT section. Use the Search or Find capabilities of your text editor to find this section. This area is completely empty and available for you to use. Should you choose to use this area, be sure to pick the tablet swap icon for menu area 1 when you are ready to use your custom commands.

Notice in Fig. 33-6 that the symbols placed in the menu occupy the first six boxes of each row. The first box of each row is labeled [A-1], [B-1], and [C-1] respectively.

The code can be entered in two ways. It can replace the box numbers listed in the menu file, or it can be entered after the box numbers. The latter method is recommended because it provides you with reference numbers for the tablet box. There are no screen labels for tablet menus. Thus, anything inside brackets is not displayed, nor is it read by AutoCAD. This means that the notations inside the brackets can be left as helpful reminders.

Before making changes to the menu, make a copy of the ACAD.MNU file. Then load your copy of ACAD.MNU into the text editor. The following example shows what the first six columns of rows A, B, and C for the menu in Fig. 33-6 look like after writing the items in the ***TABLET1ALT section.

```
***TABLET1ALT
[A-1]^C^Cinsert;gatevalve
[A-2]^C^Cinsert;checkvalve
[A-3]^C^Cinsert;controlvalve
[A-4]^C^Cinsert;globevalve
[A-5]^C^Cinsert;safetyvalv-r
[A-6]^C^Cinsert;safetyvalv-l

[B-1]^C^Cinsert;pumpr-top
[B-2]^C^Cinsert;pumpr-up
[B-3]^C^Cinsert;pumpr-dn
[B-4]^C^Cinsert;pumpl-dn
[B-5]^C^Cinsert;pumpl-up
[B-6]^C^Cinsert;pumpl-top

[C-1]^C^Cinsert;instr-loc
[C-2]^C^Cinsert;instr-pan
[C-3]^C^Cinsert;trans
[C-4]^C^Cinsert;instr-con
[C-5]^C^Cinsert;drain
[C-6]^C^Cinsert;vent
```

After you edit or create a new menu in this maner, save the menu file and then exit the text editor. Use the MENU command to load your copy of the ACAD.MNU file. If your menu file is in a subdirectory, be sure to enter the proper path to the file. Pick tablet swap icon 1 to use your menu. If you will be editing your menu a lot, consider making a menu pick on the screen that automatically loads the menu file as follows:

```
[LOADMENU]^C^Cmenu;/cadpipe/piping
```

Alternate ways to use the menu

The method just discussed uses blocks that have been saved in a prototype drawing. In order to use the blocks, the prototype must first be inserted into the current drawing. Or, the new drawing must be started using the prototype method. For example, suppose the piping flow diagram symbols are saved in a prototype drawing called PIPEFLOW. You may want to begin a new drawing with the name of PROJ2-05. You can use the symbols if you enter the following drawing file names for the prototype drawing method:

Prototype: PIPEFLOW
New drawing name: **PROJ2-05** ↵

This loads the PIPEFLOW drawing into the computer and gives it the name of PROJ2-05. All of the blocks in the PIPEFLOW drawing can be picked from your new tablet menu.

There is yet another method to use the blocks located in another drawing. Select the INSERT command. (Consider putting an insertion command on your tablet menu.) You can insert one drawing into another, but only the named items, such as blocks, views, and layers are inserted.

Command: **INSERT** ↵
Block name (or ?): **PIPEFLOW** ↵
Insertion point: ^**C**

Remember to cancel the INSERT command at the Insertion point: prompt. Wait for all of the named items to be inserted into the drawing first.

The "insert prototype drawing" pick in your tablet menu file can be written as follows:

```
^C^CINSERT PIPEFLOW ^C
```

This does the same thing as entering the prototype drawing name to begin a new drawing. However, it takes less time because you do not have to type in any command names or drawing files.

A third way to use the menu is to use all wblocks. This method does not require using symbol drawings. The wblocks can be on the hard disk or floppy disks. The use of wblocks as opposed to blocks was discussed in Chapter 21. Remember that symbols stored as wblocks require more disk storage space. Disk access time also is often slower.

PROFESSIONAL TIP

Do not bypass evaluating your present use of blocks and wblocks when making or modifying tablet menus. If you have an efficient method, take into account your current method of symbol creation, storage, and usage when developing tablet menus for symbols. If symbol drawings (prototypes) are working best for your application, develop your tablet menu around these, or if wblocks are used in your school or company, the menus should access these.

DESIGNING A NEW TABLET MENU

It is often said that using a tablet menu is inefficient. The most common complaint is that a tablet menu requires you to remove your eyes from the screen to find a tablet command. On the other hand, there are advantages of tablet menus over screen menus.
- Screen menus must be "paged" or "cascaded" when looking for a command. Flipping through pages of screen menus and submenus slows down the design and drawing process.
- A tablet menu provides immediate access to all commands. If necessary, it can be paged for additional commands and symbols.
- Available tablet commands can be chosen with only one pick of the input device.
- Graphic symbols on the template make it easy to identify commands.
- Numerous commands can be printed on a tablet menu. This enables users to select commands that they might seldom select if using just screen menus.

Any technique that increases your efficiency and productivity should be investigated and incorporated as part of your operating procedures. You will find that making custom tablet menus is one such procedure. They can be used alone, or together with screen menus. A tablet menu pick can display a specialized screen menu or can load new tablet menus. After gaining experience and confidence in your menu-creating abilities, you will become aware of the value of tablet menus.

Plan your new tablet menu
Planning was discussed as it applied to customizing the AutoCAD menu. It is doubly important when developing new tablet menus. The creation of a tablet menu should not be the first thing you do when customizing AutoCAD. There are several important preliminary steps that should be taken before designing a menu.
- List the commands that you use most often in school or work.
- Develop macros that automate your CAD work as much as possible.
- List the different types of symbol overlays you may need.
- List each group of symbols used in order of most often used to least often used.

PROFESSIONAL TIP

When designing macros, think of the commands and functions you use most often. Automate these first. Keep in mind that your goal is to create a drawing or design. This requires knowledge of the specific discipline. You want to spend more time using your knowledge and skills rather than picking the proper succession of AutoCAD commands and options. Therefore, for each function that you automate, reduce the number of picks required to complete the function. In doing so, your time spent at the computer will be more productive.

After listing the items previously mentioned, begin the process of creating commands, macros, and menus.

- Develop and test individual macros in a screen menu or tablet menu.
- Determine major groups of commands and macros based on their frequency of use.
- Design the tablet menu layout. With a pencil, draw it larger than actual size. This gives you room for lettering and sketches. You can have up to four menu areas and a screen pointing area. Some common layouts are shown in Fig. 33-8.
- Draw the basic menu layout with AutoCAD. This should be a preliminary test menu. Do not add text or graphics yet. Pencil in commands on a plotted copy of the menu.
- Write the code for the menu and test each function for convenience and ease of use.
- Add text and graphics to the menu, then plot it. Later revise the menu as needed to make it more efficient.

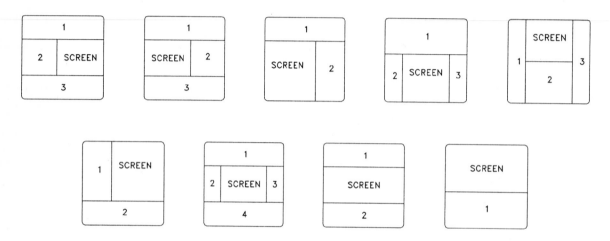

Fig. 33-8. Some common tablet menu layouts.

PROFESSIONAL TIP

Tablet menus can get dirty and smudged with use. Plot the final copy on single matte polyester film (emulsion on one side only). Use the following process to plot the menu:
- Display the menu drawing on the screen.
- Mirror the menu and delete the original. Be sure that the MIRRTEXT variable is set to 1 (ON). The menu should appear reversed.
- Plot the menu full size using wet ink.
- Punch registration holes in the top of the menu to match those in the AutoCAD template.
- Trim the menu and attach it to your digitizer. The inked side should be facing the digitizer surface.

This process creates a template where the inked menu is protected. If single matte film is used, a smooth surface is provided for the digitizer puck to slide on.

Creating a menu definition file

The process of developing your own menu is much the same as customizing the AutoCAD template. Of course, it takes longer because you are creating the entire menu. But do not let this bother you. Autodesk has developed a menu definition and compiling process that can dramatically speed up the process of creating menus. This capability is available in the \ACAD\ SAMPLE subdirectory.

A menu definition file is a preliminary menu file in which macros can be created to represent frequently used functions. In addition, a command located in several boxes of the menu can be defined once using a multiple line definition. The menu definition file is created with a file extension of .MND. If you are developing a menu named TEST, name the file TEST.MND.

The definition file must be compiled to become a menu file before it can be used by AutoCAD. This is done with the MC.EXE program. The relationship between the MC.EXE, .MND, .MNU, and .MNX files is shown in Fig. 33-9. The .MND file is written first. Then the MC.EXE program, run from DOS, compiles the .MND file into an .MNU file. AutoCAD then reads the .MNU file and further compiles it into an .MNX file. This is the version used for drawing.

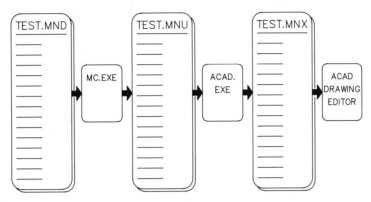

Fig. 33-9. The .MND file must be compiled twice before it can be used by AutoCAD for drawing purposes.

Creating menu definition file macros

A menu definition file is a preliminary file that can be constructed with the aid of macros. For example, suppose several commands in your menu use "∧C∧C." You can define that function at the beginning of the menu as any word or character. The menu definition macro must be listed at the beginning of the file before the first menu section. If you assign the letter "C" to the double cancel, it would be written as:

{C} = ∧C∧C

Put this in the menu file immediately after the section heading. Anything inside the braces represents the macro given after the equals sign. Place a {C} in your menu where you need a ∧C∧C in the compiled .MNU file.

Defining multiple lines

The menu definition file also allows you to specify multiple lines (template boxes) that have the same command. For example, suppose menu boxes 5, 6, 30, and 31 should have the 'REDRAW command. This can be written as:

⟨5,6,30,31⟩'REDRAW

This is interpreted by the MC.EXE program to mean that menu boxes 5, 6, 30, and 31 are assigned the 'REDRAW command. Multiple definitions such as this must be entered immediately below the menu heading.

***TABLET1
⟨5,6,30,31⟩'REDRAW

This ability to specify multiple line definitions is especially useful for tablet menus. There may be several boxes on the template that represent the same thing. Look at the Inquiry area of the

AutoCAD template and notice the HELP box. See Fig. 33-10. AutoCAD does not see this as one large box because tablet menu area 4 is divided into 175 equal size boxes. The HELP command on the template is located across four boxes. Therefore, four lines in the menu file must have the HELP command.

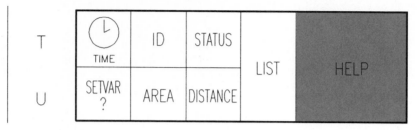

Fig. 33-10. The HELP box on the AutoCAD template is actually composed of four smaller boxes.

Load ACAD.MNU into your text editor and page to the ***TABLET4 section. You should notice 25 lines on which there is just a semicolon (;). These specify the blank, gray space above tablet menu area 4. All of the gray spaces on the tablet produce a RETURN when picked. Now scroll down two pages until you find two lines that read 'HELP. These are boxes 30 and 31 in menu area 4. Scroll down until you find the next two 'HELP commands. They are in boxes 55 and 56 in menu area 4. These four boxes would be defined at the beginning of the MND file as:

```
***TABLET4
⟨30,31,55,56⟩'HELP
```

A sample tablet menu

An example of a custom menu is shown in Fig. 33-11. It is similar to the AutoCAD template, but contains fewer boxes. The template shows a grid of numbers along the top and letters down the left side. These locations are used in the menu file for reference at the beginning of each line of code:

```
***TABLET1
[A-1]
[A-2]
[A-3]
```

Anything inside brackets in a tablet menu section is not displayed, and does not affect the menu code. It is only a helpful reference. The same notation is used in the ACAD.MNU. It indicates the tablet section and box number within that section.

━━━━━━━ PROFESSIONAL TIP ━━━━━━━

When creating a tablet or screen menu, provide a reference number in brackets for each menu entry. This immediately tells you the template box, grid location, or screen menu line on which you are working. Numbers used in tablet menus are not displayed on the screen. Numbers in screen menus must be after the eighth space in the command name, otherwise, they are displayed on the screen.

A line referenced by a multiple line definition in the .MND file should not have numbers or letters in brackets on it. If it does, it will cause an error when MC.EXE compiles the menu.

In Fig. 33-11, notice that commands used often, such as RETURN, REDRAW, ACADMENU (loads the AutoCAD menu), DIM VARS, and EXIT (from the dimension menu) are placed inside large boxes. This allows you to pick them quickly.

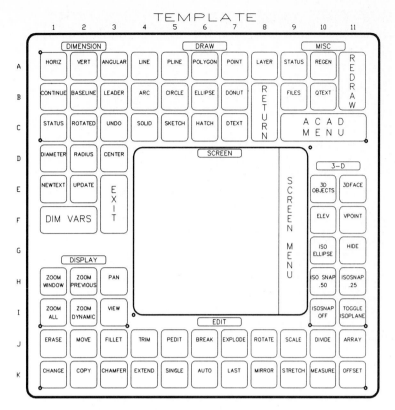

Fig. 33-11. A sample custom menu layout.

The code for this menu can be written as an .MNU file or .MND file. Remember, the menu definition (.MND) file involves less typing if you use its macro functions. Both versions are given here for comparison. As you look through the following files, compare the entries to the appropriate template boxes in Fig. 33-11. Also note the codes located at the beginning of the menu, and the box numbers left blank in the .MND file. The blank lines indicate that the function of the boxes were defined in one of the multiple line codes at the beginning of the tablet section. The grid locations of each menu item are indicated in brackets for quick identification. The button menu given is that for a 12 button cursor.

If you plan to try this menu, enter the code with your text editor. Assign the name MENU1.MND.

MENU1.MND	MENU1.MNU
***BUTTONS	***BUTTONS
;	
'REDRAW	'REDRAW
^C	^C
^B	^B
^O	^O
^G	^G
^D	^D
^E	^E
^T	^T
{D}=^C^Cdim	
{C}=^C^C	
{MA}=^C^Cmenu;acad	
{DV}=^C^Cdim $s=var1	
***TABLET1	***TABLET1
⟨11,22⟩redraw	
⟨19,29⟩'	
[A-1]{D};horiz	[A-1]^C^Cdim;horiz
[A-2]{D};vert	[A-2]^C^Cdim;vert
[A-3]{D};angular	[A-3]^C^Cdim;angular

MENU1.MND	MENU1.MNU
[A-4]{C}line	[A-4]^C^Cline
[A-5]{C}pline	[A-5]^C^Cpline
[A-6]{C}polygon	[A-6]^C^Cpolygon
[A-7]{C}line;\\	[A-7]^C^Cline;\\
[A-8]{C}point	[A-8]^C^Cpoint
[A-9]{C}status	[A-9]^C^Cstatus
[A-10]{C}regen	[A-10]^C^Cregen
	[A-11]'redraw
[B-1]{D};continue	[B-1]^C^Cdim;continue
[B-2]{D};baseline	[B-2]^C^Cdim;baseline
[B-3]{D};leader	[B-3]^C^Cdim;leader
[B-4]{C}arc	[B-4]^C^Carc
[B-5]{C}circle	[B-5]^C^Ccircle
[B-6]{C}ellipse	[B-6]^C^Cellipse
[B-7]{C}donut	[B-7]^C^Cdonut
	[B-8];
[B-9]{C}files	[B-9]^C^Cfiles
[B-10]{C}qtext	[B-10]^C^Cqtext
	[B-11]
[C-1]{D};status	[C-1]^C^Cdim;status
[C-2]{D};rotated	[C-2]^C^Cdim;rotated
[C-3]{D};undo	[C-3]^C^Cdim;undo
[C-4]{C}solid	[C-4]^C^Csolid
[C-5]{C}sketch	[C-5]^C^Csketch
[C-6]{C}hatch	[C-6]^C^Chatch
[C-7]{C}dtext	[C-7]^C^Cdtext
	[C-8]
[C-9]{MA}	[C-9]^C^Cmenu;acad
[C-10]{MA}	[C-10]^C^Cmenu;acad
[C-11]{MA}	[C-11]^C^Cmenu;acad
***TABLET2	***TABLET 2
[D-1]{D};diameter	[D-1]^C^Cdim;diameter
[D-2]{D};radius	[D-2]^C^Cdim;radius
[D-3]{D};center	[D-3]^C^Cdim;center
[E-1]{D};newtext	[E-1]^C^Cdim;newtext
[E-2]{D};update	[E-2]^C^Cdim;update
[E-3]exit	[E-3]exit
[F-1]{DV}	[F-1]^C^Cdim $s=var1
[F-2]{DV}	[F-2]^C^Cdim $s=var1
[F-3]exit	[F-3]exit
[G-1]	[G-1]
[G-2]	[G-2]
[G-3]	[G-3]
[H-1]'zoom;w	[H-1]'zoom;w
[H-2]'zoom;p	[H-2]'zoom;p
[H-3]'pan	[H-3]'pan
[I-1]'zoom;a	[I-1]'zoom;a
[I-2]'zoom;d	[I-2]'zoom;d
[I-3]{C}view	[I-3]^C^Cview
***TABLET3	***TABLET 3
[D-10]	[D-10]
[D-11]	[D-11]
[E-10]$i=3dobjects $i=*	[E-10]$i=3dobjects $i=*
[E-11]{C}3dface	[E-11]^C^C3dface
[F-10]{C}elev	[F-10]^C^Celev
[F-11]{C}vpoint;;	[F-11]^C^Cvpoint;;
[G-10]{C}ellipse i	[G-10]^C^Cellipse;i
[G-11]{C}hide	[G-11]^C^Chide
[H-10]{C}snap;s;i;5	[H-10]^C^Csnap;s;i;5
[H-11]{C}snap;s;i;.25	[H-11]^C^Csnap;s;i;.25
[I-10]{C}snap;s;s;;	[I-10]^C^Csnap;s;s;;
[I-11]^E	[I-11]^E
***TABLET4	***TABLET 4
[J-1]{C}erase	[J-1]^C^Cerase
[J-2]{C}move	[J-2]^C^Cmove
[J-3]{C}fillet	[J-3]^C^Cfillet
[J-4]{C}trim	[J-4]^C^Ctrim
[J-5]{C}pedit	[J-5]^C^Cpedit
[J-6]{C}break	[J-6]^C^Cbreak
[J-7]{C}explode	[J-7]^C^Cexplode
[J-8]{C}rotate	[J-8]^C^Crotate
[J-9]{C}scale	[J-9]^C^Cscale

MENU1.MND	MENU1.MNU
[J-10]{C}divide	[J-10]^C^Cdivide
[J-11]{C}array	[J-11]^C^Carray
[K-1]{C}change	[K-1]^C^Cchange
[K-2]{C}copy	[K-2]^C^Ccopy
[K-3]{C}chamfer	[K-3]^C^Cchamfer
[K-4]{C}extend	[K-4]^C^Cextend
[K-5]single	[K-5]single
[K-6]auto	[K-6]auto
[K-7]last	[K-7]last
[K-8]{C}mirror	[K-8]^C^Cmirror
[K-9]{C}stretch	[K-9]^C^Cstretch
[K-10]{C}measure	[K-10]^C^Cmeasure
[K-11]{C}offset	[K-11]^C^Coffset

After creating the menu definition file, you must compile it with MC.EXE program. The program is found in the ACAD\SAMPLE subdirectory. Both the MC.EXE file and your .MND file should be in the same directory, or you must provide a path for MC to find your definition file. If you are not in AutoCAD, but the DOS prompt is displayed, be sure the ACAD\SAMPLE subdirectory is current.

The MC.EXE program can now be run to compile the MENU1.MND file and create a file named MENU1.MNU. Run MC.EXE as follows:

Command: **SHELL** ⏎
OS Command: **MC MENU1** ⏎
AutoCAD Menu Compiler 2.5 (8/1/89)
Copyright/(c)/1985-89 Throoput, Ltd.
Command:

When the Command: prompt returns, the .MNU file has been created. You can check by getting a directory of all .MNU file extensions as follows:

Command: **DIR** ⏎
File specification: ***.MNU** ⏎

The new menu cannot be used until it is loaded into AutoCAD using the MENU command. This command automatically looks for a .MNU file extension, so you need only enter the menu name.

Command: **MENU** ⏎
Menu file name or . for none ⟨current⟩: **MENU1** ⏎
Compiling menu C:\ACAD\MENU1.mnu ...
Command:

The compiled version of the menu file has an .MNX extension. AutoCAD looks for the latest version of the compiled menu file when you begin a new drawing. If there is no such file, AutoCAD compiles the menu file again.

— PROFESSIONAL TIP —

The name of the particular menu you use to construct a drawing is saved in the drawing file. If you use different menus, be sure that they are in the same directory as the drawings, or use the proper path when loading the menu. This path is saved with the drawing file. If AutoCAD cannot find a menu, the following message appears if FILEDIA is set to 0:

"MENU1.mnu": Can't open file
Enter another menu file name (or RETURN for none):

At this time you can enter the proper path to the menu, or enter the name of another menu.

After loading your new menu, select the TABLET command and configure the new template. If you select the TABLET command from the screen menu, do not pick the Re-Cfg option. This starts the configuration routine for the ACAD tablet menu. Instead, use the Config option. The process of configuring the new template is much the same as was done when customizing the AutoCAD template.

The configure routine asks the number of tablet menus desired. The MENU1 template requires four. You are then asked if you want to realign tablet menu areas. Answer "Y" (Yes). Now digitize the upper-left, lower-left, and lower-right corners of each of the four tablet menu areas. When prompted, provide the number of columns and rows in each area. The corners of MENU1 are shown in Fig. 33-12. The columns and rows in each area are given in the following chart:

Menu Area	Columns	Rows
1	11	3
2	3	6
3	2	6
4	11	2

The final prompt in the configure process asks you to specify the lower-left and upper-right corners of the screen pointing area. These are also shown in Fig. 33-12.

Test all of the menu items to be sure they function properly. Correct any mistakes you find. You may encounter one shortcoming if you select the ACAD MENU item in menu area 1. The AutoCAD menu will be loaded, but how do you get back to the MENU1 template? There must be a call, or item in the AutoCAD menu, that loads the MENU1 template. Load the ACAD.MNU file into your text editor and add the following line to the **S menu, or to a pull-down menu:

[MENU1]^C^Cmenu;menu1

If you insert this entry between two existing items, do not press ENTER. Othewise you will insert a blank line into the menu.

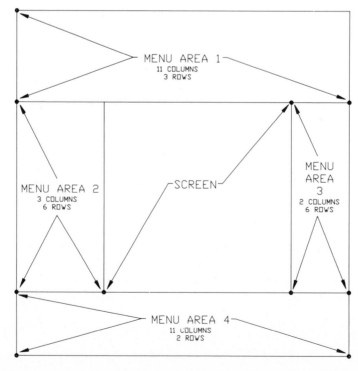

Fig. 33-12. Digitize the corners of the tablet menu areas indicated here. Also pick the lower-left and upper-right corners of the screen pointing area to properly configure the template.

7. Describe how the tablet menu area 1 boxes are numbered in the ACAD.MNU file. ___
   _____

8. Explain why it is a good idea to leave the box numbers in the menu file. _____
   _____

9. List two advantages of using tablet menus instead of screen menus. _____
   _____
   _____

10. Which commands should you automate first when designing a screen or tablet menu?
    _____

11. Define a menu definition file. _____
    _____
    _____
    _____
    _____
    _____

12. The extension of the menu file AutoCAD uses for drawing purposes is _____.

13. How would a custom macro that represents REDRAW be shown in an .MND file? ___
    _____

14. Suppose boxes 25, 50, 75, and 100 are to be used for the REDRAW command. How would
    they be listed in the .MND file as a multiple line function?_____

15. Give the advantage of creating an .MND file instead of an .MNU file. _____
    _____
    _____
    _____

16. Explain the purpose of the MC.EXE program. _____
    _____

17. How do you combine different menus to form a larger menu? _____
    _____
    _____

18. Why is it a good idea to combine screen menus with a tablet menu? _____
    _____
    _____

DRAWING PROBLEMS

1. Add ten new commands or macros to the user area of the AutoCAD template. Follow these
   guidelines:
   A. Place the commands along the bottom line (I) of the template. They should occupy boxes
      I-1 through I-10.
   B. Plot a copy of the menu area 1 grid and sketch the commands in the boxes.
   C. Sketch graphic symbols to represent the commands.
   D. Draw the command text and graphics in a copy of the menu area 1 grid.
   E. Plot a final copy of the overlay on vellum or polyester film.
   F. Make a copy of the ACAD.MNU file and write the code for the new commands in it.

2. Create a menu overlay for the user area of the AutoCAD template. It should contain graphic symbols for one of the following drafting disciplines:
   - Architectural
   - Structural
   - HVAC
   - Mechanical (Fasteners, machining symbols, tolerance symbols, etc.)
   - Industrial Piping
   - Electrical
   - Electronics
   A. Use existing blocks that you have on file, or create new ones.
   B. Provide a tablet pick that allows you to insert all symbols into a drawing without inserting the additional prototype drawing data.
   C. Provide a tablet pick that calls the AutoCAD menu.
3. Redesign the user area of the AutoCAD template so that it contains a complete selection of dimensioning commands, options, and variables. Follow these guidelines:
   A. Use the standard 225 boxes or change the numbers of boxes to suit your needs.
   B. Provide access to dimensioning icon menus.
   C. Design a special section for dimensioning variables. Draw a small graphic symbol for each variable and place in the menu box.
   D. Plot a menu overlay of vellum or polyester film that can be slipped under the AutoCAD template.
4. Design a new tablet menu that occupies only the lower half of your digitizer. Follow these guidelines:
   A. The menu should contain a screen pointing area and two menu areas.
   B. Design the menu so it can work with the AutoCAD screen menus.
   C. Provide an area of symbols (blocks) and an area for special commands that you have created.
   D. Make a drawing of the new tablet overlay and plot it on vellum or polyester film. Plot the overlay as a mirror image of the original as discussed earlier in this chapter.
5. Design a new tablet menu that occupies the entire active area of your digitizer. Follow these guidelines:
   A. Provide four menu areas and a screen pointing area.
   B. Provide access to the AutoCAD menu.
   C. Include custom commands you have created, plus an area for symbols. Allow the user to change the symbols section of the menu to a different set of drawing symbols.
   D. Draw an overlay for the new tablet menu. Draw two separate, smaller overlays for the two sets of drawing symbols.
   E. Draw graphic symbols to represent commands and place them in the menu overlay.
   F. Insert scaled-down copies of blocks into the symbol overlays of the menu.
   G. Plot test copies of the template and two symbol overlays and use them for several days.
   H. Plot a final copy of the template on vellum or polyester film using the mirror image technique discussed in this chapter.
6. Design a custom tablet overlay for a specific drafting field, such as electronics, piping, or mapping. Follow these guidelines:
   A. Create as many menu areas as you need, between one and four.
   B. Provide space for a complete selection of symbols. These should reflect the type of drawing for which you will be designing the template.
   C. Place only those commands on the template that you will use often for this type of drawing.
   D. Place commands used less frequently in special screen menus. These should be accessed from the template.
   E. Provide the ability to load a variety of prototype drawings from the template.
   F. Create menu selections that allow you to do the following:
      - Edit a file using the operating system (DOS, UNIX, etc.) text editor.
      - Edit a file using your text editor or word processor.
      - Edit the menu template file that you design for this problem.
      - Exit to DOS.
      - List all drawing files in your active subdirectories.
   G. Plot the template overlay on vellum or film using the mirroring technique.

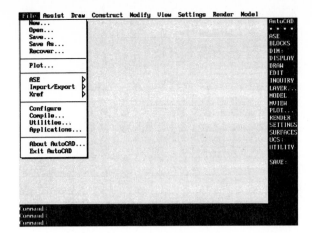

Chapter 34

INTRODUCTION TO AUTOLISP

Learning objectives

After completing this chapter, you will be able to:
- ☐ Locate, load, and run existing AutoLISP programs.
- ☐ Use basic AutoLISP commands.
- ☐ Write screen and tablet menu macros using AutoLISP.
- ☐ Write basic AutoLISP programs.

AutoLISP is a dialect of the LISP programming language. LISP, which stands for LISt Processing, is a high level language used in artificial intelligence (AI). The AutoLISP dialect, or "interpreter," was specially designed by Autodesk for use with AutoCAD. It has special graphic features designed to work within the AutoCAD drawing editor. Overall, it is a flexible language that allows the programmer to create commands and functions that can greatly increase productivity and drawing efficiency.

AutoLISP can be utilized in several ways. It resides in AutoCAD and is therefore available at the Command: prompt. When AutoLISP commands and functions are issued inside parentheses, the AutoLISP program goes to work. AutoLISP functions incorporated into screen and tablet menu items are executed with a single pick. AutoLISP programs can also be saved as .LSP files and then "loaded" into AutoCAD at the Command: prompt. Frequently used AutoLISP programs can be included in a file called ACAD.LSP that is automatically loaded with AutoCAD. The programs in the ACAD.LSP file can then be used at any time without going through the "load" procedure.

The benefits of AutoLISP are endless. A wealth of third-party software (add-on programs that enhance AutoCAD) uses AutoLISP to create special shapes, symbols, and functions. Persons with a good knowledge of AutoLISP can create new commands and programs to satisfy specific needs. In reading this chapter, you will be able to add greater capabilities to your screen and tablet macros. Examples of these new functions might include:
- Automatically creating shapes with text placed inside.
- Drawing parallel lines by specifying beginning and end points.
- Creating multiple lines of text in a preset style at a specific height and spacing.
- Deleting specific layers or changing selected entities to a new layer.

Even though you may not need, or want, to learn programming, knowing basic AutoLISP gives you a feel for how AutoCAD works. Read through this chapter slowly while you are at a computer. Type all of the examples and exercises as you read them. This is the best way to get a feel for AutoLISP.

The references given in this chapter, such as APRM 4, refer to the *AutoLISP Programmer's Reference Manual.*

FINDING, STORING, AND USING AUTOLISP PROGRAMS

Most AutoLISP programs are separate files located in the default AutoCAD directory or a subdirectory for .LSP files. A program must first be loaded into AutoCAD before it can be used. Once loaded, entering the command or function name invokes the program.

Locating standard AutoLISP files

A variety of AutoLISP programs are supplied with the AutoCAD software. If you installed the program according to instructions in the *Interface, Installation and Performance Guide*, you should have LISP files located in at least two of the following directories:

```
\ACAD
\ACAD\SUPPORT
\ACAD\SAMPLE
```

The standard support LISP files are located in the \ACAD or \ACAD\SUPPORT directory. Use the DIR command and get a listing of just the .LSP files in this directory as follows:

Command: **DIR** ↵
File specification: **\ACAD\SUPPORT*.LSP /P** ↵

```
Directory of C:\ACAD\SUPPORT
Volume in drive C is MS-DOS 5
Volume Serial Number is 1627-8B24
3D       LSP     21569  05-26-92   4:38p
3DARRAY  LSP      8358  05-23-92   7:34p
ACADR12  LSP     12560  06-15-92  10:52a
AI_UTILS LSP     14383  09-08-92  11:00a
APPLOAD  LSP     12664  06-09-92  12:19a
ASCOMMON LSP     44186  05-31-92   7:09p
ASCTEXT  LSP     12623  06-09-92  12:19a
ASE      LSP      3300  06-01-92   7:53a
CHTEXT   LSP     23516  05-18-92   2:25p
DDATTDEF LSP     18691  05-27-92  11:33a
DDATTEXT LSP     12107  06-12-92   6:25p
DDCHPROP LSP     30879  05-27-92  12:24p
DDGRIPS  LSP      9436  05-27-92  11:35a
DDINSERT LSP     23724  05-31-92   3:39p
DDMODIFY LSP     83016  06-14-92   1:20p
DDOSNAP  LSP      7485  05-27-92  11:28a
DDPTYPE  LSP      6012  05-27-92  11:42a
DDRENAME LSP     18021  05-27-92  11:32a
DDSELECT LSP      8916  05-27-92  11:36a
DDSOLPRM LSP      8615  06-17-92   8:13p
DDUCSP   LSP      7659  06-09-92  12:19a
DDUNITS  LSP     16146  06-01-92  12:59p
DDVIEW   LSP     24778  06-16-92   4:12p
DDVPOINT LSP     15584  06-15-92   3:13p
DLINE    LSP     68403  05-31-92   9:58a
FILTER   LSP     74223  06-13-92   7:24p
MVSETUP  LSP    114723  06-01-92   2:44p
PLUD     LSP      3653  04-13-92   7:17p
PTEXT    LSP     64985  05-18-92   2:25p
RMAN_DCL LSP      3203  04-21-92   4:55p

       30 file(s)        773418 bytes
                       136245504 bytes free
```

A brief description of a few of these routines is given below. Many of the support AutoLISP files work automatically when you make the appropriate AutoCAD menu selection.
- 3D — This routine is activated when you select the 3D objects... option of the 3D Surfaces selection in the Draw pull-down menu. It allows you to draw polymesh shapes such as a box, wedge, torus, sphere, and pyramid.
- 3DARRAY — An arrangement of rows, columns and levels of an object is possible with this routine. See Chapter 24 for a detailed explanation.
- ASCTEXT — This program allows you to directly import text from a file into the drawing editor of AutoCAD.
- CHTEXT — Allows you to globally change text properties such as height, justification, location, rotation, style, text, and width.

Supplied AutoLISP files

Additional AutoLISP programs are supplied with AutoCAD. These are copied to the \ACAD\SAMPLE subdirectory when AutoCAD is installed. Use the DIR command again to get a listing of only the .LSP files in that directory, but this time in a wide format as follows:

Command: **DIR** ↵
File specification: **\ACAD\SAMPLE*.LSP /W** ↵

ALIAS	LSP	ATTREDEF	LSP	AVE_XMPL	LSP	BMAKE	LSP	CHROMA	LSP
CL	LSP	DDTYPE	LSP	DELLAYER	LSP	DLGTEST	LSP	EDGE	LSP
EP	LSP	FACT	LSP	FCOPY	LSP	FPLOT	LSP	FPRINT	LSP
GP	LSP	HOLE	LSP	JULIAN	LSP	MFACE	LSP	PROJECT	LSP
RPOLY	LSP	SOLMAINT	LSP	SPIRAL	LSP	SQR	LSP	STLSUP	LSP
TABLES	LSP	WBLKSOL	LSP	XDATA	LSP	XPLODE	LSP	XREFCLIP	LSP

These program files must be loaded by the operator in order to use them. This can be done by selecting Applications... from the File pull-down menu. Select the File... option from the "Load AutoLISP and ADS Files" dialogue box, and use the file dialogue box to select the file you want to load. Then, pick the Load button to load the desired program file.

AutoLISP files that are used by AutoCAD should reside in a directory that is specified in the ACAD environment setting. It is good practice to keep the main \ACAD directory free of nonessential files, and this is true of .LSP files. However, do not remove files from the directory that the AutoCAD installation program put them in unless you add the new directory's name to the ACAD environment setting. You can check the directories in the ACAD setting by listing the contents of the batch file that runs AutoCAD. Look for a line similar to the following:

SET ACAD = C:\ACAD;C:\ACAD\SUPPORT;C:\ACAD\FONTS;C:\ACAD\ADS

This assumes that your AutoCAD program is in the \ACAD directory. If this line does not exist in your batch file, you should add one. See Appendix C for more information on batch files and environment settings.

The appearance of an AutoLISP file

AutoLISP programs are best created using a programmer's editor or text editor. They are text files, but different in appearance from any other type of file you have worked with in this text. To view any type of ASCII file, use the DOS command TYPE. Enter the command, the file name, and file extension. For example, find the location of the FCOPY.LSP file. It should be in the \ACAD\SAMPLE directory.

Command: **TYPE** ↵
File to list: **\ACAD\SAMPLE\FCOPY.LSP¦MORE** ↵ *(Scroll to "Main Program" area.)*

```
(defun fcopy (in out / ifp ofp 1)
    (cond ((null (setq ifp (open in "r")))      ; try to open in for reading
        (princ "Can't open ")                   ; if nil print error message
        (princ in)
        (princ " for reading.")
    )
    (if ifp
        (progn
            (setq ofp (open out "w"))            ; else open out for writing
            (while (setq 1 (read-line ifp))      ; read each line from in
                (write-line 1 ofp)               ; and write it to out
            )
            (close ofp)                          ; close both files
            (close ifp)
        )
    )
    )
    (princ)
)
```

Notice that several lines of the program begin with a semicolon (;) and a brief explanation of the line follows. The semicolon indicates that everything that follows on that line is a remark and is not evaluated by AutoLISP. This is how explanations, definitions, programmers' names, and copyrights are noted.

Notice that AutoLISP statements (except remarks) are enclosed in parentheses. This is true of the statements in an AutoLISP file, a menu macro, and an AutoLISP command entered at the Command: prompt.

EXERCISE 34-1

☐ Use the TYPE command to display the first portion of the ASCTEXT.LSP file.
☐ Provide the following information about the file:

☐ Copyright holder's name: _____

☐ Year of copyright: _____

☐ Brief explanation of its function: _____

_____

LOADING AND USING AUTOLISP PROGRAMS   AEM 1

AutoLISP programs must first be loaded into AutoCAD before they can be used. This can be done using the dialogue box as explained previously in this chapter, or a program can be loaded at AutoCAD's Command: prompt by using the AutoLISP LOAD function. Remember to enclose AutoLISP commands and functions in parentheses. When loading an AutoLISP file, it is not necessary to include the extension .LSP. Also, the file name must be enclosed in quotation marks.

Begin a new drawing called LISPTEST. You will use this drawing to experiment with two AutoLISP programs. If you must quit before completing this section, save the drawing.

A program that deletes a layer

The DELLAYER program erases entities on a layer. To use the DELLAYER.LSP program or any Auto LISP program, enter the following format at the AutoCAD Command: prompt:

Command: **(LOAD ''/ACAD/SAMPLE/DELLAYER'')** ↵
C:DELLAYER
Command:

AutoCAD responds with the name of the loaded program. If preceded by "C:," you can enter the program name just as you would any AutoCAD command. The "C:" indicates that DELLAYER is now a legal command. Before you delete entities on a specified layer, set up the current drawing as follows:
 • Make three layers named 1, 2, and 3.
 • Assign each layer a different color.
 • Draw two lines on layer 1, two arcs on layer 2, and two circles on layer 3.
Now enter the DELLAYER command at the prompt:

Command: **DELLAYER** ↵
Layer to delete? *(enter layer name to delete)* ↵

All of the entities on the specified layer are deleted. (This command provides a quick, selective edit of your drawing.)

```
┌──────────────────── PROFESSIONAL TIP ────────────────────┐
│                                                           │
│   Certain types of drawings may require you to use construction lines, projection lines, or │
│ guidelines which are not a permanent part of the drawing. You may want to create a layer │
│ named CONST on which you can place reference lines, ticks, and points. When finished with │
│ the entities, use DELLAYER to eliminate all of the entities on the CONST layer. │
│                                                           │
└───────────────────────────────────────────────────────────┘
```

Changing all aspects of text

The CHTEXT.LSP file is a combination of the CHANGE and DDEDIT commands. All aspects of the text can be changed, and the text itself can be changed in a dialogue box. Load the CHTEXT.LSP file, and remember to include the quotation marks around the path and name of the LISP program.

Command: **(LOAD ''/ACAD/SUPPORT/CHTEXT'')** ↵
     c:CHText loaded. Start command with CHT.
Command: **CHT** ↵
Change text, Version 1.02, (c) 1990-1991 by Autodesk, Inc.
Select text to change.
Select objects: *(pick a text entity)*
1 found
Select objects: ↵
1 text entities found.
Height/Justification/Location/Rotation/Style/Text/Undo/Width:

At this point, you can pick any option you need to change the text. The Text option allows you to change the text itself, and this can be done on the prompt line or in a dialogue box. If you want to have this routine accessible as a menu selection, insert the following code into the appropriate menu section (such as tablet or pull-down menu):

[CHTEXT]^C^C(if (not C:CHT) (load "/ACAD/SUPPORT/CHTEXT")) ;CHT

BASIC AUTOLISP FUNCTIONS | APRM 4 |

The best way to get started with AutoLISP is to enter the commands and functions and see what they do. The following discussion includes basic AutoLISP functions that are the foundation for all AutoLISP programs. Practice using the commands as you read. Then begin using them in menus and macros. Practice using AutoLISP for at least 30 minutes, twice a week.

AutoLISP math functions

You can perform arithmetic calculations using AutoLISP. Calculations are given as either real numbers or integers. A real number is any number that contains a decimal. AutoLISP keeps 16 decimal place accuracy. An integer is any number that does not contain a decimal. Note the following examples:

4	integer	0.4	real	25	integer	378	integer
4.0	real	0.25	real	25.0	real	378.002	real

Arithmetic calculations, as well as all AutoLISP commands, are given inside parentheses. The first item inside the left parenthesis is the math function. The following functions are allowed:

SYMBOL	FUNCTION
+	Returns the sum of all numbers.
−	The second number is subtracted from the first and the difference is returned.
*	Returns the product of all numbers.
/	The first number is divided by the second and the quotient is returned.

When data is "returned" by AutoLISP, it is displayed at the command line.

The examples below illustrate math functions entered at the Command: prompt. Enter data in the following order: beginning parenthesis, math function, space, first number, and spaces between following numbers. Close the statement with a parenthesis. If you leave out a parenthesis, AutoLISP reminds you as follows:

Command: (+ 2 4 ↵
1⟩

The "1⟩" indicates that you are missing one closing parenthesis. Enter the missing parenthesis and the function is completed.

1⟩) ↵
6
Command:

Enter the following examples at your keyboard:

Command: (+ 6 2) ↵
8
Command: (+ 6.0 2) ↵
8.0
Command: (– 15 9) ↵
6
Command: (* 4 6) ↵
24
Command: (/ 12 3) ↵
4
Command: (/ 12 3.2) ↵
3.75
Command: (/ 15 6) ↵
2

The answer "2" is returned for the last function. The actual answer should be a decimal. However, only an integer was given because only integers were used in the calculation. To obtain a real number answer, give at least one real number in the equation.

Command: (/ 15.0 6) ↵
2.5

If using numbers less than zero, give a zero before the decimal or you will receive an error message.

Command: (+ .5 6) ↵
error: invalid dotted pair
⟩*Cancel*

The correct entry is

Command: (+ 0.5 6) ↵
6.5

EXERCISE 34-2

□ Solve the following equations by entering the AutoLISP functions and numbers at the Command: prompt. Write down the equation you used.

A. 57 + 12 _____

B. 86.4 + 16 _____

C. 24 + 12 + 8 + 35 _____

D. 8 − 3 _____

E. 29 − 17 _____

F. 89.16 − 14.6 _____

G. 8 × 4 _____

H. 16 × 5 × 35 _____

I. 7.3 × 22 _____

J. 45 / 9 _____

K. 60 / 2 / 2 _____

L. 76 / 27.3 _____

Multiple calculations can be done on a single line if the functions and numbers are "nested" properly. All left parentheses must have closing right parentheses. Additional math functions must be enclosed in their own set of parentheses. AutoLISP evaluates the nested function first, then applies the result to the beginning function. This is shown in the following examples:

Command: **(+ 24 (* 5 4))** ↵
44
Command: **(* 12 (/ 60 20))** ↵
36
Command: **(/ 39 (* 1.6 11))** ↵
2.2159
Command: **(− 67. (−14. (+3.2 6)))** ↵
62.2

EXERCISE 34-3

□ Use the proper AutoLISP format to solve the following problems. Write the AutoLISP notations and answers in the space provided.

A. 56.3 + (12 / 3) _____

B. 23 − (17.65 / 4) _____

C. 14 × (12 / 3.6) _____

D. 47 / (31 − 16.4) _____

E. 257 / (34 − 3.6) _____

F. 123.65 + 84 − 43.8 _____

G. 16 × (46 − 23) _____

Storing values using variables

The most frequent AutoLISP function is SETQ. An acronym for SET Quote, SETQ allows you to create a variable, assign it a value, and store it. Once a variable is set, AutoLISP returns the value. Variables must begin with a letter and can be any combination of letters and numbers. They may not contain the following symbols:

( ) parentheses
. period
' apostrophe
" quotation marks
; semicolon

The following examples show legal and illegal variable names. Notice that the statement must be placed inside parentheses.

Command: **(setq a 5)** ↵
5
Command: **(setq 5 a)** ↵
error: bad argument type
(SETQ 5 A)

AutoLISP lets you know if something does not work. In the previous example, a number was entered as a variable name, which is illegal. AutoLISP displays the point at which the error was found. The error "bad argument type" refers to the item after the SETQ function name, the "5." The first item after a function is called an *argument*. An AutoLISP statement that has a function, argument, and options is called an *expression*. Look at another example:

Command: **(setq point1 6)** ↵
6

If you do not remember the value of a variable, confirm it by entering an exclamation mark (!) and the variable name:

Command: **!a** ↵
5
Command: **!point1** ↵
6

Variables can be given as the result of a mathematical calculation.

Command: **(setq b (− a 1))** ↵
4
Command: **(setq c (− a b))** ↵
1
Command: **(setq d (* (+ a b) 2))** ↵
18

Look closely at the example illustrated in Fig. 34-1. Find the three separate expressions inside parentheses. AutoLISP evaluates expression 3 first. The result is applied to expression 2, which is then evaluated. The result of expression 2 is applied to 1. The final evaluation determines the value of variable "d."

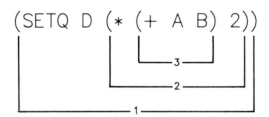

Fig. 34-1. Each AutoLISP expression is enclosed with parentheses.

EXERCISE 34-4

☐ In the spaces provided, write the AutoLISP expressions in the proper format. After writing the expression, enter it into the computer to test your solution.

A. Assign the value of 4 to the variable ONE. _____

B. Assign the value of 3 + 2 to the variable TWO. _____

C. Assign the value of ONE + TWO to the variable THREE. _____

D. Assign the value of THREE + (TWO − ONE) to the variable FOUR. _____

_____

Assigning input to variables

Variables can be assigned point coordinates by picking a point on the screen or entering the values at the keyboard. In this case, AutoLISP needs to be instructed to get the value from an input device using the GETPOINT function. GETPOINT looks for a coordinate pair (X,Y) that is entered at the keyboard or picked with the pointing device. For example:

Command: **(setq pt1 (getpoint))** ↵

After pressing ENTER nothing happens—no readout appears on the command line. AutoLISP is waiting for you to enter a value to be assigned to the variable, pt1. Pick a point on the screen. That number is displayed on the command line as shown below. If you know the (X,Y) coordinates to be assigned the variable, enter them at the keyboard.

Command: **(setq pt1 (getpoint))** ↵
9.5,6.3 ↵

An example of how closely AutoCAD and AutoLISP work together follows. First enter the two variables given below. Then select the LINE command and use AutoLISP notation to return the values of p1 and p2 as the "from point" and "to point."

Command: **(setq p1 (getpoint))** ↵
2,2
Command: **(setq p2 (getpoint))** ↵
6.25,2
Command: **line** ↵
From point: **!p1** ↵
To point: **!p2** ↵
To point: ↵

AutoCAD uses the values you assigned to p1 and p2 for the points. You will later see how to add AutoCAD commands, such as LINE, to LISP expressions and avoid exiting AutoLISP to complete the function.

When developing AutoLISP routines, you may need to assign a variable the length of a line or the distance between two points. The GETPOINT function will not work for this because it only retrieves one point. The GETDIST function allows you to assign distance to a variable.

Command: **(setq lgth (getdist))** ↵ *(pick the first point)*
Second point: *(pick the point)* 8.35

When picking the points, use OSNAP options for accuracy if the points are on existing entities. The distance between the two points appears and is assigned to the variable. In this example, 8.35 was assigned to the variable, LGTH. Confirm the variable:

Command: **!lgth** ↵
8.35

Remember the difference between GETPOINT and GETDIST functions. This is important when deciding the type of information required for a variable.

A function similar to GETDIST, DISTANCE, does not require picking two points. Similar to the DISTANCE command in AutoCAD, it measures the distance between two existing points. It can be used to return a distance or assign a distance to a variable.

Command: **(distance p1 p2)** ↵
4.25
Command: **(setq d1 (distance p1 p2))** ↵
4.25

The first example above returned only the distance between p1 and p2. The second example applied the distance to the variable d1. Check this by asking AutoLISP to return the value of "d1":

Command: **!d1** ↵
4.25

EXERCISE 34-5

☐ Use the proper AutoLISP format to write the following expressions. Use the spaces provided to write the code. Test all of the exercise examples by entering them in the computer.

A. Assign a point picked on the screen to the variable "pnt1." _____

B. Assign a point picked on the screen to the variable "pnt2." _____

C. Create the variable "dis" and assign it the distance between "pnt1" and "pnt2." ___

_____

D. Draw a line between "pnt1" and "pnt2."

_____

_____

_____

E. Use the AutoLISP DISTANCE command to return the distance between "pnt1" and "pnt2." _____

Issuing prompts and getting text

Variables can be given values other than numbers. You may need to assign a word or line of text to a variable. Use the SETQ command and enclose the word(s) in quotation marks as follows:

Command: **(setq w "What next?")** ↵
"What next?"

You can also allow a user to assign a word or line of text to a variable. This is done in the same manner as the GETPOINT function, but the GETSTRING function is used instead.

Command: **(setq e (getstring))** ↵

Nothing is displayed on the command line because AutoLISP is waiting for a "string" of characters. You can enter as many characters (numbers and letters) as you wish. Once you press the space bar, the string is entered and displayed.

To allow for spaces in the response, enter a letter or number after the GETSTRING function.

> Command: **(setq e (getstring 4))** ↵
> **hi there** ↵
> "hi there"
> Command:

Confirm the value of the new variable.

> Command: **!e** ↵
> "hi there"

So far you know what AutoLISP needs because you have been reading about it and trying it on the computer. Yet, under normal circumstances, a person using an AutoLISP program needs to be prompted for information. For example, suppose you want a prompt to appear asking the user to pick a point. This is done in conjunction with the GETPOINT function. Enter the following:

> Command: **(setq p1 (getpoint ''Pick a point: ''))** ↵
> Pick a point:

Now the user knows what the computer needs.

The same technique can be used when assigning a distance to a variable. Place the prompt in quotation marks and leave a space before the ending quotes.

> Command: **(setq g (getdist ''What is the distance? ''))** ↵
> What is the distance?

The GETSTRING function may also require a prompt to make it look like an AutoCAD command. Remember to use a number or letter after the function to allow for spaces between words. The letter "T" is used, but the number 6 would achieve the same result.

> Command: **(setq s (getstring T ''Enter text: ''))** ↵
> Enter text: **Using the ''T'' allows spaces between words.** ↵

The PROMPT function is used just to display a message. It has no value and is not assigned to a variable. AutoLISP indicates this by printing "nil" after the prompt.

> Command: **(prompt ''Select an object: '')** ↵
> Select an object: nil

You can use prompts in AutoLISP programs to provide information or prompt the user.

EXERCISE 34-6

☐ Use the proper AutoLISP format to write the following expressions. Use the spaces provided to write the code. Test all of the exercise examples by entering them in the computer.

A. Assign the word "Void" to the variable "vo." _____

B. Assign the text "Enter text height" to the variable "te." _____

C. Create the variable "jp" as a point that is picked on the screen. Issue the prompt "Pick a point:." _____

D. Create the variable "kp" as a point that is picked on the screen, and issue the prompt "Pick a point:." _____

E. Set the distance between points "jp" and "kp" to the variable, "lp." _____

F. Issue a prompt that says "This is only an exercise." _____

A quick review

Before applying these newly learned commands to an AutoLISP program, take a few minutes to review the following list. They are used in the next section.

- (+, −, *, /) Math functions—Must be the first part of an expression. Example: (+ 6 8).
- (SETQ) SET Quote—The command that allows a value to be assigned to a variable. Example: (setq city "San Francisco") sets the value of San Francisco to the variable, city.
- (!)—Returns the value of a variable. Example: (!city) returns "San Francisco."
- (GETPOINT) Get Point—Gets a point entered at the keyboard or pointing device. Can be applied to a variable. Example: (setq a (getpoint)) assigns a point to the variable, a.
- (GETDIST) Get Distance—Gets a distance from two points entered at the keyboard or picked with the pointing device. Can be applied to a variable, and a prompt is allowed. Example: (setq d2 (getdist "Pick two points: ")) gets a distance and assigns it to the variable, d2.
- (DISTANCE) Distance—Returns a distance between two existing points. Example: (distance p1 p2) returns the distance between p1 and p2. Can also assign the distance to a variable. Example: (setq d (distance p1 p2)).
- (GETSTRING) Get String—Returns a word or group of characters. No spaces are allowed. Example: (getstring) waits for a string of characters and displays the string when ENTER or the space bar is pressed. Can be assigned to a variable. Spaces are allowed in the string if a letter or number follows the GETSTRING function. Example: (setq t (getstring T "Enter text: ")) assigns the text entered to the variable, t.
- (PROMPT) Prompt—Allows a prompt to be issued in a program. Example: (prompt "Select an entity: ") returns the prompt "Select an entity: ".

Using AutoCAD commands in AutoLISP

Earlier you saw how the LINE command can be combined with AutoLISP statements to draw a line. This combination is allowed when writing menu macros, but is not possible when developing a LISP program. To incorporate AutoCAD commands into an AutoLISP program, the COMMAND function is used. For example, draw a line in the following manner:

```
Command: (command "line") ↵
line From point nil
From point: (pick the "from" point)
To point: (pick the "to" point)
To point: ↵
```

Notice how this sequence automatically puts you in the LINE command. Also notice how it is executed in AutoLISP. The LINE command, like any AutoCAD command or option in AutoLISP, is enclosed in quotes. Try another one:

```
Command: (command "circle") ↵
circle 3P/2P/TTR/⟨Center point⟩: nil
3P/2P/TTR/⟨Center point⟩:
```

The next section shows you how to incorporate all of the previously discussed functions into a program.

CREATING AUTOLISP PROGRAMS   APRM 2

When entering AutoLISP commands at the Command: prompt, you can only enter one line at a time. After you press ENTER, AutoLISP goes to work. The line of code is evaluated and, if correct, the function is performed. Unfortunately, the line of code you entered is gone. It is not stored anywhere. The only data saved are variables, and even those disappear if you quit the drawing editor.

To save AutoLISP programs create them as an ASCII text file using a word processor or text editor. Although EDLIN can be used, it is not designed for the task of programming. If you plan on developing menus and AutoLISP programs, invest in a good text editor.

Load your text editor and begin a new file named FIRST.LSP. Enter the following lines of AutoLISP code exactly as they appear. Be sure to press ENTER after each line. Save the file and exit the text editor when finished.

```
(defun first ( )
(prompt "This is my first AutoLISP program. ")
)
```

Now examine the lines of the program.

```
(defun first ( )
```

The first line uses the DEFUN command. This stands for DEfine FUNction and allows you to define a word that activates the AutoLISP program. This command begins most AutoLISP programs. The second word, first, is the name of the new function. The parentheses ( ) indicate that there are no defined variables in the program.

```
(prompt "This is my first AutoLISP program. ")
```

The second line begins with the PROMPT command and the text string prompt follows. The string is in quotes and a space precedes the closing quote. Parentheses enclose the entire line. The last line of the program is a single closing parenthesis. Can you find the matching left parenthesis? It is the first one in the program.

The correct use of parentheses is critical to the operation of your programs. Therefore, remember to place them in the proper locations. A technique that helps to solve this problem is indenting. Look at the FIRST.LSP program as written in its indented format:

```
(defun first ( )
    (prompt "This is my first AutoLISP program. ")
)
```

This allows you to easily see all closing parentheses.

Exit the text editor and return to the drawing editor. Be sure to save FIRST.LSP. Run the program now to see if it works. Load AutoLISP programs at the Command: prompt by entering LOAD and the file name inside parentheses. Also enclose the file name with quotes. Load the FIRST.LSP program as follows:

```
Command: (load "first") ↵
first
Command: (first) ↵
This is my first AutoLISP program. nil
Command:
```

The name returned after entering LOAD is the name assigned the program with DEFUN. This name is then types (in parentheses) to run the program, and display your prompt.

The next program combines an AutoCAD command with AutoLISP to draw a line between two points. Enter your text editor and name the file LINE1.LSP. Enter the code exactly as it appears below.

```
(defun line1 (/ p1 p2)
    (graphscr)
    (setq p1 (getpoint "Enter first point: "))
    (setq p2 (getpoint "Enter second point: "))
    (command "line" p1 p2)
)
```

Take a close look at each line of the program.

```
(defun line1 (/ p1 p2)
```

The word "line1" is the defined function of the program. The program has two variables, p1 and p2. The "/" indicates that the variables will only be available for use inside this program. Once the program is completed, the variables are removed. This kind of variable is called "local" because it can only be used by the program for which it is defined.

```
(graphscr)
```

The GRAPHSCR command resets the screen to the graphics mode. This is a good function to place at the beginning of your programs to switch the monitor from text to graphics.

```
(setq p1 (getpoint "Enter first point: "))
(setq p2 (getpoint "Enter second point: "))
```

These two lines allow the user to pick or enter points for variables p1 and p2. The values are supplied by the GETPOINT function. A prompt is provided with each.

```
(command "line" p1 p2)
```

This expression executes AutoCAD's LINE command. AutoLISP retrieves the value for "p1" and uses it for the "From point" of the line. The value of "p2" is returned and used for the "To point."

The last line of the program is the closing parenthesis for the first function, "defun."

When finished, save the file and return to the Command: prompt. Load and run the program to see how it works. The following sequence of prompts should appear.

```
Command: (load "line1") ↵
line1
Command: (line1) ↵
Enter first point: (pick first point)   Enter second point: (pick second point)
line From point:
To point:
To point: nil
To point:
```

Notice two things about the program. First, the prompt for the second point is on the same line as the first prompt. It might be better to have this prompt begin on a new line for clarity. Second, the LINE command does not end. There is still a rubberband line attached to the cursor. The program should be changed to end the line.

Load the LINE1.LSP file into your text editor again and add the following items that are in bold face:

```
(defun line1 (p1 p2)
   (graphscr)
   (setq p1 (getpoint "Enter first point: ")) (terpri)
   (setq p2 (getpoint "Enter second point: ")) (terpri)
   (command "line" p1 p2 "")
)
```

Two prompts that follow each other in a program are displayed on the same line unless you instruct AutoLISP to terminate the line. This is done with the "terpri" command, placed at the end of the line that contains the prompt, or text string, in quotes. A line can also be terminated by using the "\n" statement in front of the prompt. The "\n" is common usage, and is quicker to type. Use it as follows:

```
(setq p1 (getpoint "\nEnter first point: "))
```

Notice also that a double quote has been added after p2 in the last line of the program. This indicates a RETURN. The semicolon (;) cannot be used for a RETURN as it is used in screen and tablet macros. This is because it represents a remark in AutoLISP. Anything after a semicolon is ignored. The RETURN (" ") should now end the LINE command.

Load and run the program again. The sequence of prompts should look like the following:

Command: **(load "line1")** ⏎
line
Command: **(line1)** ⏎
Enter first point: *(pick the first point)*
Enter second point: *(pick the second point)*
line From point:
To point:
To point:
Command: nil
Command:

— PROFESSIONAL TIP —

Design your AutoLISP programs to closely resemble the way AutoCAD works. For example, it is clearer to show back-to-back prompts on separate lines. Use the "terpri" command for this.

EXERCISE 34-7

☐ Write an AutoLISP program that places the word "NOTES:" at a location that you pick on the screen. Name the file EX34-7.LSP.
☐ Write a description of the program in longhand first.
☐ Write each line of code in the space provided.
☐ Write the program with your text editor and test it.
☐ The lines of your program should include the following:
   ☐ A remark line containing the author, date, and name of the file.
   ☐ The function defined is "notes" and has two local variables, p1 and t.
   ☐ The graphics screen should be activated.
   ☐ Set the p1 variable. Provide a prompt for entering the text location.
   ☐ Give the variable, t, the value, "NOTES:."
   ☐ Execute the TEXT command to do the following: Use p1 as the text location; enter text height of 0.25"; rotation angle of 0; and use the variable t as the text.
☐ Write the program on the lines below.

_____

_____

_____

_____

_____

_____

GETTING DEEPER INTO AUTOLISP $\quad$ APRM 2

As you practice with AutoLISP, you will develop ideas for programs that require additional commands and functions. Some of these programs may require that the user pick two corners using the Window option to select entities. Another program may use existing points to draw a shape. You may also need to locate a point using polar coordinate notation, or determine the angle of a line. All of these can be AutoLISP programs.

Getting additional input

The GETREAL command allows you to enter a real number at the keyboard. Remember, a real number is more accurate than an integer because it has a decimal value. The command works with numbers at the unit level—you cannot respond with a value of feet and inches. The command waits for user input. It issues a prompt if one is provided. It then returns the real number. It can be used to set the value of a variable as follows:

Command: **(setq x (getreal "Enter number: "))** ↵
Enter number: **34** ↵
34.0

The GETCORNER command allows you to pick the opposite corner of a rectangle. It functions like placing a window around entities in a drawing. An existing point serves as the first corner. When positioning the opposite corner, a rubberband box appears on the crosshairs, similar to the window box. The command can also be used to set the value of a variable. The second corner can be picked with the pointing device or entered at the keyboard. To find the second corner, the first point must have been chosen. An example use of GETCORNER follows:

Command: **(setq pt1 (getpoint "\nPick a point: "))** ↵
Pick a point: *(pick the point)*
Command: **(setq pt2 (getcorner pt1 "\nPick the second corner: "))** ↵
Pick the second corner: *(pick the corner)*

Notice the placement of "pt1" before GETPOINT. Point "pt1" becomes the base point for locating "pt2". This example has located two points, or corners that can be used to construct an angled line, rectangle, or other shape. It can also be applied to other functions.

Using the values of system variables

AutoCAD's system variables can be accessed with AutoLISP GETVAR and SETVAR commands. An application may require you to store the value of a system variable, change the variable for your program, then reset it to its original value. This is possible with GETVAR and SETVAR. The GETVAR command is commonly used to see the value of a variable.

Command: **(setq v1 (getvar "textsize"))** ↵
0.125
Command: **(setq v2 (getvar "filletrad"))** ↵
0.0

The SETVAR command is used to change a system variable. Assign the value to a variable as follows:

Command: **(setq v3 (setvar "textsize" 0.25))** ↵
0.25
Command: **(setq v4 (setvar "filletrad" 0.25))** ↵
0.25

Suppose you need to save a current system variable, reset the variable, and then reset the variable to its original value after the command is executed. For example, the GETVAR command can be used to supply a value to a new variable as shown in the previous "textsize" example. When the program is complete, the SETVAR command is used to reset the textsize to its original value as follows:

Command: **(setvar "textsize" v1)** ↵
0.125

This returns the value of "textsize" to the variable, v1, which is the default, 0.125.

EXERCISE 34-8

☐ In the spaces provided, write the following expressions in longhand using proper AutoLISP format. Enter the expressions into your computer to see if they work.

  ☐ Get the current aperture size and set it to the variable, "aper." _____

  ☐ Set the variable aper4 to the aperture size of four pixels. _____

  ☐ Use the LINE command and an OSNAP setting to connect the line with other entities on the screen. _____

  ☐ Reset the aperture to the original setting using AutoLISP commands and the variables previously set. _____

☐ Add the following capabilities to the EX34-7.LSP file that you created in the previous exercise:

  ☐ Create a variable, "v1," to hold the current textsize. Insert this line after the "defun" line. _____

  ☐ At the end of the program, insert a line that resets the textsize to its original size. _____

Working with lists

AutoLISP processes lists. For example, a list is created when you pick a point on the screen in response to the GETPOINT command. The list is composed of three numbers, the X, Y, and Z coordinate values. You can tell it is a list because AutoLISP returns the numbers enclosed in parentheses. A number entered in response to the GETREAL command returns as just a real number not enclosed in parentheses. This is because a single number is not a list. The following expression returns a list:

  Command: **(setq p1 (getpoint "Enter point: "))** ↵
  Enter point: *(pick a point)*
  (5.5 2.75 0.0)

The individual values in a list are called *elements,* and can be used in an AutoLISP program to create new points to draw shapes. To retrieve the first element of a list (the X coordinate in the above example), use the CAR function. The variable "p1" in the example above is composed of the list (5.5 2.75 0.0). Thus, 5.5 should be the CAR. Enter the following:

  Command: **(car p1)** ↵
  5.5

The second element of a list, the Y coordinate, is retrieved with the CADR function. Find the CADR of "p1" by entering:

  Command: **(cadr p1)** ↵
  2.75

You can create a new list of two coordinates by selecting values from existing points using the CAR and CADR functions. This is done with the LIST function. Values returned by the list function are placed inside parentheses. The coordinates of p1 can be combined with the coordinates of a second point, p2, to form a third point, p3. Study the following example, and the illustration in Fig. 34-2.

  Command: **(setq p2 (getcorner "Enter second point: " p1))** ↵
  (6.0 4.5)
  Command: **(setq p3 (list (car p2)(cadr p1)))** ↵
  (6.0 2.75)

+ P2
X = 6.0 (CAR)
Y = 4.5 (CADR)

+ P1
X = 2.0 (CAR)
Y = 2.75 (CADR)

+ P3
X = 6.0 (CAR P2)
Y = 2.75 (CADR P1)

Fig. 34-2. Point p3 has been created using the CAR of p2 and the CAR of p1.

In AutoLISP, a function is followed by an *argument*. An argument is a value passed to a function for evaluation by AutoLISP. An expression must be composed of one function and at least one argument. Therefore, the functions CAR and CADR must be separated because they are two different expressions, combined to make a list. Examine Fig. 34-3. The CAR value of p2 is to be the X value of p3, so it is given first. The CADR of p1 is placed second because it is to be the Y value of p3. Notice the number of closing parentheses at the end of the expression.

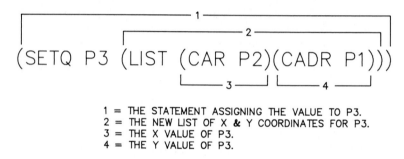

1 = THE STATEMENT ASSIGNING THE VALUE TO P3.
2 = THE NEW LIST OF X & Y COORDINATES FOR P3.
3 = THE X VALUE OF P3.
4 = THE Y VALUE OF P3.

Fig. 34-3. The CAR and CADR of two existing points, p1 and p2, are used to create a third point, p3.

So what can you do with these three points? A good start is to draw lines through them. Use the COMMAND function as follows:

Command: **(command "line" p1 p2 p3 "c")** ↵

A line should be drawn automatically from p1 to p2 to p3 and back to p1.

The CAR and CADR allow you to work with 2-D coordinates. A special function, CADDR, allows you to get the Z value of a 3-D coordinate. It returns the third element of a list. Enter the following at your keyboard:

Command: **(setq b (list 3 4 6))** ↵
(3 4 6)

You have created a list of three elements, or coordinate values. The third element is the Z coordinate. Retrieve that value with the CADDR function, which looks for the third element of a list.

Command: **(caddr b)** ↵
6

Since 6 is a single value, not a list, it is not enclosed in parentheses. Now use CAR and CADR to find the other two elements of the list:

Command: **(car b)** ↵
3
Command: **(cadr b)** ↵
4

Try these examples before you read on. Enter them at the Command: prompt exactly as shown here and press ENTER at the end of each line.

```
(setq a1 (getpoint "Enter point: "))
(setq b1 (getpoint "Enter point: "))
(setq c1 (list (car a1)(cadr b1)))
(car a1)
(cadr a1)
(car b1)
(cadr b1)
(setq c1 (list (car a1)(cadr b1)(car b1)))
!c1
(car c1)
(cadr c1)
(caddr c1)
```

The last function to discuss in basic list manipulations is the CDR function. It allows you to retrieve the second and remaining elements of a list. Therefore, suppose the list (3 4 6) is assigned to variable b (done earlier in this section). The CDR function should return the list (4 6). Try it:

Command: **(cdr b)** ↵
(4 6)

This is now a separate list that can be manipulated with CAR and CADR just like a 2-D coodinate list. Study Fig. 34-4 and the following examples:

Command: **(car (cdr b))** ↵
4
Command: **(cadr (cdr b))** ↵
6

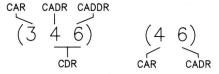

Fig. 34-4. The CDR consists of the second and remaining elements of a list.

The first example was asking for the first element (CAR) of the list (4 6). It originally was the last two elements (CDR) of the list for variable, b. In the second example, the second element (CADR) of the list (4 6) was returned.

The four functions used to manipulate lists—CAR, CADR, CADDR, and CDR—may seem confusing at first. Reading or saying two or more of them together seems like a tongue twister. Practice using them and discover how they work. Practice with a list of numbers, coordinate values, or text strings. Remember, text strings must be enclosed in quotes. Try the following examples to see what happens. Enter the following expressions at the Command: prompt exactly as shown and press ENTER at the end of each line.

```
(setq notes (list "do" "re" "mi"))
(car notes)
(cadr notes)
(caddr notes)
(cdr notes)
(setq last (cdr notes))
(car (cdr notes))
(cadr (cdr notes))
(car last)
(cadr last)
```

Review of list-making functions
- (CAR) – Returns the first element of a list.
- (CADR) – Returns the second element of a list.
- (CADDR) – Returns the third element of a list.
- (CDR) – Returns the second and remaining elements of a list. Because the CDR function returns more than one element, the values it returns are always placed in a list.
- (LIST) – Creates a list of all values entered after the function LIST.

EXERCISE 34-9

☐ Write an AutoLISP program that draws a right triangle. The 90° angle can be on either the left or right side.

☐ Write the program in proper AutoLISP format. Then use your text editor to write it to a file named EX34-9.LSP.

☐ Use the following items in writing the program:
  - ☐ Define the function as "triangle."
  - ☐ Turn the graphics screen mode on.
  - ☐ Set the variable p1 as the first point of the triangle. Use a prompt.
  - ☐ Set the variable p2 as the endpoint of the hypotenuse (getcorner). Place the prompt on the next line.
  - ☐ Set the variable p3 to the X coordinate of p2 and the Y coordinate of p1.
  - ☐ Draw a line through all three points and close the triangle.

☐ Before saving the program, check for matching parentheses and quotes. Save the program and test it.

POLAR COORDINATES AND ANGLES

APRM 2

The ability to work with angles is vital if you plan to do much AutoLISP programming. Four functions, ANGLE, POLAR, GETANGLE, and GETORIENT allow you to use angles. AutoLISP works with these commands using the *radian* system of angle measurement.

Measuring an angle
The ANGLE function is used to calculate the angle between two given points. The value of the angle is given in radians. Radian angle measurement is a system in which 180° equals 3.14159 or "pi" (π). AutoLISP functions use radians for angular measurement, but AutoCAD commands use degrees. Therefore, to use an angle in an AutoCAD command, it must first be converted to degrees. Conversely, an angle to be used by AutoLISP must be converted to radians. The following two expressions handle those conversions.
- To convert degrees to radians:
  (* pi (/ ad 180.0))   (ad = angle in degrees)
- To convert radians to degrees:
  (/ (* ar 180.0) pi)   (ar = angle in radians)

The following example illustrates how the angle between two points can be set to a variable, then converted to degrees.

```
Command: (setq p1 (getpoint "Enter first point: ")) ↵
Enter first point: (1.75 5.25) ↵
Command: (setq p2 (getpoint "Enter second point: ")) ↵
Enter second point: (6.75 7.25) ↵
Command: (setq ar (angle p1 p2) ↵
0.380506
```

The angle has been given in radians (0.380506) and now must be converted to degrees:

Command: **(/ (* ar 180.0) pi)** ↵
21.80141

The value, 21.80141, is the angle in degrees between p1 and p2.

The following list gives common angles, their values in radians, and the AutoLISP expressions that determine the radian value.

Angle/Degrees	Radians	AutoLISP Expression
0.0	0.0	
30.0	0.523599	(/ pi 6)
45.0	0.785398	(/ pi 4)
60.0	1.0472	(/ pi 3)
90.0	1.5708	(/ pi 2)
135.0	2.35619	(+ (/ pi 4)(/ pi 2))
180.0	3.14159	pi
270.0	4.71239	(+ pi (/ pi 2))
360.0	6.28319	(* pi 2)

EXERCISE 34-10

☐ Using AutoLISP expressions, locate the endpoints of a line and store each endpoint as a variable.
☐ Use GETANGLE to find the angle of the line.
☐ Use the proper formula to convert the radian value to degrees.
☐ Use the proper formula to convert the degree value back to radians.

Getting angular input

The GETANGLE command is for angle value input from the user. It is used to set a variable that can be used in another command. The GETANGLE function automatically issues the prompt "Second point:" and cannot use the TERPRI, or \n function. If you use TERPRI, a nil value will be given for the angle. The following example illustrates how you can set a variable to an angle input by the user:

Command: **(setq a (getangle "Pick first point: "))** ↵
Pick first point: *(pick first point)* Second point: *(pick point)*
2.35619

The angle value is given in radians. It is converted to degrees using the conversion technique shown here:

Command: **(/ (* a 180.0) pi)** ↵
135.0
Command: **!a** ↵
2.35619

Notice that the radian value is returned, even after the conversion to degrees. This is because the conversion did not set the angle value to a variable. Make the value permanent by assigning it to a variable using the following expression:

Command: **(setq a (/ (* a 180.0) pi))** ↵
135.0
Command: **!a** ↵
135.0

The variable angle, a, now has a value of 135°.

An important point to remember is that GETANGLE uses the current ANGBASE (angle 0 direction) and ANGDIR (clockwise or counterclockwise) system variables. Therefore, if you have angles set to be measured from north (ANGBASE = 90°), angles picked with GETANGLE will be measured from north. If the ANGDIR variable is set to measure angles clockwise, GETANGLE will accept input of clockwise values, but returns counterclockwise values.

A companion command to GETANGLE is GETORIENT. It is used in exactly the same manner, but always measures angles counterclockwise from east (0°).

EXERCISE 34-11

☐ Use GETANGLE to assign an angle to the variable, "ang1."
☐ Convert the radian value to degrees using AutoLISP expressions.
☐ Convert the degree value back to radians using AutoLISP expressions.
☐ Use GETORIENT to find the angle in radians of any two points.
☐ Reset ANGBASE to 90.
☐ Use GETORIENT to find the angle of the two points chosen previously.
☐ Use GETANGLE to find the angle of the two points chosen previously.
☐ Compare the difference. Why is the GETANGLE value different?

Using polar coordinates

The POLAR command allows you to specify a point that is located at a set angle and distance relative to another point. Two variables must first be set for POLAR to work properly: the point from which you are locating a new point and the distance between the two points. Suppose you want to specify a point p1, then locate another point, p2, at a specific distance and angle from p1. Enter the following expressions and see what happens:

Command: **(setq p1 (getpoint "Enter point: "))** ↵
Enter point: *(pick point)* (4.0 4.5)
Command: **(setq d (getdist p1 "Enter distance: "))** ↵
Enter distance: *(pick distance or enter at keyboard)* 3.0
Command: **(setq a (dtr 60))** ↵
1.0472

In this expression, the angle 60° is used, but AutoLISP need radians. Therefore the DTR function (presented in the next section) is used to evaluate 60°. The resulting angle, 1.047198, is saved as variable "a." A line can now be drawn from p1 using the POLAR command as follows:

Command: **(setq p2 (polar p1 a d))** ↵
(5.5 7.09807)
Command: **(command "line" p1 p2 " ")** ↵

A line is drawn at an angle of 60°. If not, retype the expressions.

EXERCISE 34-12

☐ Write a program to draw a right triangle. (See EX34-9.) However, use POLAR instead of LIST commands. Name the file EX34-12.LSP.
☐ Write the AutoLISP expessions for the program in the proper format.
☐ Enter the program in your computer when you have finished writing it.
☐ Use the following items in the program:
   ☐ Define a function called "polartri."
   ☐ Set a variable p1 as the first corner of the triangle.
   ☐ Set a variable d as the length of one side.
   ☐ Set a variable p2, 0° from p1 at a distance of d.
   ☐ Set a variable p3, 90° from p2 at a distance of d.
   ☐ Use the LINE command to draw the triangle.

SAVING OFTEN-USED FUNCTIONS IN ACAD.LSP

Certain AutoLISP programs are used quite frequently. It is a hassle to load these programs individually when needed. Instead, you can place often-used AutoLISP functions in a common file, ACAD.LSP, which is loaded each time you run AutoCAD. Two programs that should be entered into ACAD.LSP are the angle/radian conversion formulas.

Before you create the ACAD.LSP file, check to see if it already exists in the ACAD directory. (Use DIR\ACAD*.LSP.) Then, either load the existing file into your text editor or begin a new text file called ACAD.LSP. Enter the following programs exactly as they appear here:

```
; Converts degrees to radians
(vmon)
(defun dtr (a)
   (* pi (/ a 180.0))
)
; Converts radians to degrees
(defun rtd (a)
    (/ (* 180.0) pi)
)
```

The line that reads "(vmon)" at the beginning of the file is not needed with AutoCAD Release 12, but is still supported for compatability with earlier versions. It helps to eliminate errors that occur from a lack of memory.

Any program added to the ACAD.LSP file must be loaded into AutoCAD using parentheses. This is because AutoCAD is working with the old version of the file. To use the updated version of ACAD.LSP, quit the drawing editor and then return to AutoCAD.

CREATING DIALOGUE BOXES

$\boxed{\text{ACM 9}}$

As you become proficient with AutoLISP, you will want to create applications that appear to be a "seamless" extension of AutoCAD commands. Using simple techniques of providing prompts for the user that resemble AutoCAD's is a good start. However, using the Dialogue Control Language (DCL), you can construct your own dialogue boxes for use with your customized menus and AutoLISP programs.

All of the features of dialogue boxes are available for you to use with DCL. The process of constructing a dialogue box begins with writing a file using your text editor. This file has a .DCL extension. The file is composed of a structured organization of DCL commands and syntax. In addition, you must write a companion AutoLISP file that controls its DCL counterpart. For example, if you write a file named SETUP.DCL, you must also write an AutoLISP file named SETUP.LSP. The .LSP file contains functions that allows it to handle the dialogue box.

The use of dialogue boxes in your customized menus and applications can give them a more professional and consistent appearance. A detailed description of dialogue box construction is given in Chapter 9 of the *AutoCAD Customization Manual*.

SOLUTIONS TO CHAPTER EXERCISES

Compare these solutions to your versions of the AutoLISP exercises given in this chapter. If your program works, but looks different from those given here, do not immediately change it. There are several ways to program the same function. If it works, do not fix it.

Exercise 34-7

```
;   Author, date, file name EX34-7.LSP
(defun notes (/ t p1)
   (graphscr)
   (setq p1 (getpoint "Enter text location: ")) (terpri)
   (setq t "NOTES:")
   (command "text" p1 0.25 0 t)
)
```

Exercise 34-9

```
;Draws a right triangle given the length of a side
(defun triangle (/ p1 p2 p3)
  (graphscr)
  (setq p1 (getpoint "Enter point: ")) (terpri)
  (setq p2 (getcorner p1 "Pick endpoint of hypotenuse: ")) (terpri)
  (setq p3 (list (car p2)(cadr p1)))
  (command "line" p1 p2 p3 "c")
)
```

Exercise 34-12

```
;   Draws a triangle using POLAR
(defun triangle2 (/ p1 p2 p3 d)
  (graphscr)
  (setq p1 (getpoint "Pick a point: ")) (terpri)
  (setq d (getdist p1 "Enter length of a side: ")) (terpri)
  (setq p2 (polar p1 0.0 d))
  (setq p3 (polar p2 (dtr 90) d))
  (command "line" p1 p2 p3 "c")
)
```

SAMPLE AUTOLISP PROGRAMS

One of the best ways to become familiar with AutoLISP is to enter expressions and programs on your computer. Look for programs in books or magazines that you read. Get a feel for how the functions and arguments go together and how they work in AutoCAD. Make a habit of reading through one of the AutoCAD journals. Copy AutoLISP routines printed in them and refer regularly to the *AutoLISP Programmer's Reference Manual*.

The following programs are provided for you to copy and add to your ACAD.LSP file or to your menus. Practice for a few minutes a couple of times a week. You will begin to better understand and utilize AutoLISP. Train yourself to learn a new function every week. Before long, you will be writing your own useful programs.

Erase the entire screen

This program sets two variables to the minimum and maximum screen limits. It then erases everything within those limits and redraws the screen. Name this program ZAP.LSP.

```
; Erases entire limits
(defun C:ZAP ( )
  (setq min (getvar "limmin"))
  (setq max (getvar "limmax"))
  (command "erase" "c" min max "")
  (command "redraw")
)
```

Set the current layer

This program asks for the user to point to a linetype or color of the layer to be set current. The program finds the layer of the entity picked and sets the layer as current.

```
;Author    : Margo K. Bilson
;Company : Williamette Industries, Inc., Portland, OR
(defun C:SETLAYER (/ E)
  (setq E (entsel "\nPoint to linetype and\or color..."))
  (setq E (entget (car E)))
  (setq L (cdr (assoc '8 E)))
  (command "layer" "s" L "")
)
```

Inserting centerlines on circles

This program works with a block composed of equal length, vertical and horizontal centerlines which intersect at the midpoint. This type of centerline mark is used on circles (holes) and circular features. Draw the lines each 1 in. long. Then, when the block is inserted, it can be scaled easily. For example, suppose you need to put centerlines in a 3 in. circle, with .25 in. extensions beyond the circle. The X and Y scale factors will be 3.5. This allows for .25 in. on each side. Name the program CENL1.LSP.

```
;Author       : Matt Slay
;Address      : 2475 Pinson Highway, Tarrant, Alabama 35217
;Phone        : (555) 555-2304
(defun C:CENL1 ( )
   (command "insert" "cenl1" (getpoint)
      (getpoint) "" "")
)
```

Clean overlapping corners

This program allows you to trim the overlapping ends of intersecting lines. You are requested to pick the two lines that intersect and overlap. The program does the rest. Name the program TRIMENDS.LSP.

```
;Author       : George Head
;Printed in the January, 1988 issue of "Cadence" magazine
(defun C:CLEANC (/ o1 p1 p2)
   (setq o1 (getvar "osmode"))
   (setvar "osmode" 512)
   (command "fillet" "r" 0)
   (setq p1 (getpoint "\nPick a line "))
   (setq p2 (getpoint "\nPick other line "))
   (command "fillet" p1 p2)
   (setvar "osmode" o1)
)
```

Calculate the length of lines

This program calculates the length of all lines on a specified layer. It can be used for estimating and material takeoffs. This program works only with lines, not with polylines. Name the program LINEAR.LSP. After loading it into the AutoCAD drawing editor, respond to the first prompt by entering the name of the layer that contains the lines you wish to total. The answer is given in current drawing units.

```
;Author       : Joe Pucilowski
;Company      : Joseph & Associates
;Address      : 7809A River Resort Lane, Tampa, FL 33617-8059
;Phone        : (555) 555-3587
;Date         : 9/19/xx
;Note         : This program figures the total number of linear units (feet, inches, etc.) of
               LINEs on a specific layer.
;Revised      : 10/8/xx by Rod Rawls
;
(defun C:LINEAR ( )
   (setq TOTAL      0
         E          (entnext)
         NUMLIN     0
         LAYPIK     (strcase
                        (getstring "\nAdd up lines on layer: ")
                    )
   )
   (if (tblsearch "LAYER" LAYPIK)
```

```
(progn
  (while E
    (set ENTTYP (cdr (assoc 0 (setq EG (entget E))))
          LAYNAM (cdr (assoc 8 EG??
    )
    (if
      (and
        (equal ENTTYP "LINE")
        (equal LAYNAM LAYPIK)
      )
      (progn
        (setq LINLEN (distance (cdr (assoc 10 EG)) (cdr (assoc 11 EG)))
              TOTAL (+ TOTAL LINLEN)
              NUMLIN (1+ NUMLIN)
        )
      )
    )
    (setq E (entnext E))
  )
  (princ
    (strcat "\nFound "
            (itoa NUMLIN)
            " lines on layer <"
            LAYPIK
            "> with a total of "
            (rtos TOTAL)
            " linear units."
    )
  )
)
(princ "\nLayer does not exist.")
)
(princ)
)
```

Easy grid rotation

This program, titled S.LSP, rotates the grid to the angle of any picked line. The second routine, SS.LSP, returns the grid to zero rotation. These programs work with AutoCAD versions later than 2.18.

```
;Author    : Eben Kunz
;Company : Kunz Associates Architects
;Address   : 38 Greenwich Park, Boston, MA 02118
;Phone     : (555) 555-1482
;
(defun C:S (/ pt1 pt2)
  (setvar "orthomode" 0)
  (setq pt1 (osnap (getpoint "\nPick line to match new Grid angle: \n") "nea"))
  (setq pt2 (osnap pt1 "end"))
  (command "snap" "r" pt1 pt2)
  (setvar "snapmode" 0)
)
(defun C:SS ()
  (prompt "\nReturn Grid to zero.")
  (command "snap" "r" "" 0.0)
  (setvar "snapmode" 0)
)
```

Move to current layer
This simple program quickly changes selected entities to the current layer. It works on versions 2.5 and later.

```
;Author    : Bill Fane
;Company : Weiser, Inc.
;Address   : 6700 Beresford St., Burnaby, B.C., Canada, V5E 1Y2
;
(defun C:CL (/ things)
   (setq things (ssget))
   (command "change" things "" "p" "1a"
      (getvar "clayer") "" )
)
```

Change to selected layer
This routine, for versions 2.5 and later, allows you to move entities to a layer by picking an entity on the destination layer.

```
;Author    : Sheldon McCarthy
;Company : EPCM Services Ltd.
;Address   : 2404 Haines Road, Mississauga, Ontario, Canada L4Y 4B8
;Phone     : (555) 555-3388
;
(defun C:LA ( )
   (setq la (cdr (assoc 8 (entget (car (entsel "Entity on destination layer:"))))))
   (prompt "Select objects to change:")
   (ssget)
   (command "change" "p" "" "1" la)
)
```

Change text quickly
This program for versions 2.5 and later, enables you to change the content of a line of text. It eliminates pressing ENTER several times inside the CHANGE command.

```
;Author    : Chris Lindner
;Address   : 274 Marconi Blvd., Columbus, OH 43215
;
(defun C:TEDIT ( )
   (setq p (ssget))
   (if p
     (progn
     (setq L 0)
   (setq n (sslength p))
   (while (< L n)
     (if ( = "test" (cdr (assoc 0
        (setq e (entget (ssname p L))))))
      (progn
      (setq s (cdr (setq as
        (assoc 1 e))))
      (prompt "\nOld text: ")
      (princ s)
      (setq ns
        (getstring t "\nNew text: "))
      (setq e (subst (cons 1 ns) as e))
      (entmod e)
      )
    )
   (setq L (1 + L))
    )
  ))
)
```

CHAPTER TEST

Write your answers in the spaces provided.

1. The extension used for AutoLISP files is _____.

2. Why is it a good idea to make a separate subdirectory for LISP files? _____

   _____

   _____

3. A remark is indicated in an AutoLISP file with _____.

4. When in the drawing editor, how would you load an AutoLISP file named CHGTEXT.LSP?

   _____

   _____

5. Define an integer. _____

6. Define a real number._____

7. Write the following arithmetic expressions in the proper AutoLISP format.

   A. 23 + 54   _____

   B. 12.45 + 6.28 _____

   C. 56 − 34   _____

   D. 23.004 − 7.008_____

   E. 16 × 4.6 _____

   F. 7.25 × 10.30 _____

   G. 45 / 23   _____

   H. 147 / 29.6   _____

   I. 53 + (12 × 3.8) _____

   J. 567 / (34 − 14) _____

8. Explain the purpose of the SETQ function. _____

   _____

9. Write the proper AutoLISP notation to assign the value of (67 − 34.5) to the variable, num1.

   _____

10. What does the GETPOINT function allow you to do? _____

    _____

11. Write the proper AutoLISP notation to assign the values of X = 3.5 and Y = 5.25 to the

    variable, pt1._____

12. The AutoLISP function that allows you to get the measurement between two points is

    _____.

13. The AutoLISP function that allows you to find the length of a line is_____.

14. Explain the purpose of the GETSTRING function. _____

    _____

15. Write the proper AutoLISP notation for assigning the string "This is a test:" to the variable, txt.

    _____

16. How do you allow spaces in a string of text when using the GETSTRING function? ___
_____

17. Write the proper AutoLISP notation for using the PLINE command. _____

18. How must an AutoCAD command be handled in an AutoLISP expression? _____
_____

19. Define a function. _____

20. Define an argument. _____
_____

21. The name of the AutoLISP function which describes the name of a function in a program is
_____.

22. Describe why lines are indented in an AutoLISP program. _____
_____

23. Explain the purpose of the TERPRI function. _____
_____

24. The command that allows you to retrieve a decimal number is _____.

25. Which two commands allow you to work with system variables? _____

26. Define the following AutoLISP functions:

    A. car — _____

    B. cadr — _____

    C. cdr — _____

    D. caddr — _____

    E. list — _____

27. Write the proper AutoLISP notation to return the last two numbers of the list (4 7 3).
_____

28. Write an expression to set a variable, a, to the result of Question 27. _____

29. Write an expression to select the second element of the list that was returned in Question 28.
_____

30. Compare and contrast the GETANGLE and GETORIENT functions. _____
_____
_____

31. Write an expression to set the angle between points p3 and p4 to the variable, a. _____
_____

32. What system of angle measurement does AutoLISP use? _____

33. The name of the function that converts degrees to the system mentioned in Question 32 is
_____ .

34. What is the value of 270° in the angular system AutoLISP uses? _____

35. Explain the purpose of the POLAR function. _____
_____

DRAWING PROBLEMS

1. Add the following capabilities to the right triangle function developed in Exercise 34-9.
   A. Use GETDIST instead of GETCORNER.
   B. Allow the angle of the hypotenuse to be picked.
   C. Allow the length of a side to be picked.

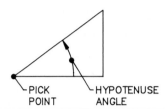

2. Create an AutoLISP program similar to that in Problem 1, but it should draw an equilateral triangle (equal angles and equal sides). Use the POLAR function.

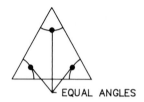

3. Write a program to draw a rectangle. Use only the GETPOINT function to set opposite corners of the rectangle. Follow these guidelines:
   A. Set p1 as the first corner.
   B. Set p3 as the opposite corner.
   C. Set points p2 and p4 using the list functions of AutoLISP.
   D. Use the LINE command to draw the rectangle.

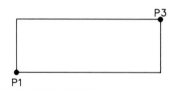

4. Revise the program in Problem 3 to draw a rectangle using the GETCORNER function to find the second corner.
5. Create an AutoLISP command to draw a square. Follow these guidelines:
   A. Set a variable for the length of one side.
   B. Set the variable, p1, as the lower-left corner of the square.
   C. Use the LINE command to draw the square.

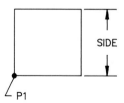

6. Revise the program in Problem 5 to draw a square using the PLINE command.

7. Use the program in Problem 6 to create a new command that draws a square and allows you to change the line thickness.
   A. Use either PLINE or POLYGON commands to draw the square.
   B. Set a variable to get the line thickness input by the user.

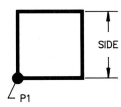

8. Add a "Fillet 0" command to your EDIT screen menu. Use menu code and AutoLISP expressions to create the command. Follow these guidelines:
   A. Get the current fillet radius and assign it to an AutoLISP variable.
   B. Set the fillet radius to "0."
   C. Select two lines and enter a "0" fillet.
   D. Reset the fillet radius to the original value.
9. Add a DISTANCE command to any screen menu area. Use menu code and AutoLISP expressions to do the following:
   A. Get desired unit precision from user and store it as a variable.
   B. Store current unit precision as an AutoLISP variable.
   C. Set unit precision with a user variable.
   D. Reset unit precision to the original value.
10. Write an AutoLISP program to draw parallel rectangles.
   A. Use the rectangle program in Problem 3, but replace LINE with the PLINE command.
   B. Get user offset distance for the inside rectangle.
   C. Use the OFFSET command to draw the parallel rectangle inside the original.

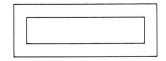

11. Write a program to draw a rectangle and place a circle having a user-specified diameter in the center of the rectangle.
   A. Incorporate the rectangle program in Problem 3.
   B. Use the ANGLE, POLAR, and DISTANCE functions to find the center point of the rectangle.
   C. Request the user to enter the diameter.
   D. Draw a circle at the center point of the rectangle.

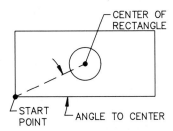

12. Write a program to draw a leader with a diameter dimension having plus and minus tolerances.
   A. Prompt for and allow user to set DIMTP and DIMTM system variables.
   B. Activate the DIM command and turn DIMTOL to "on."
   C. Activate the DIAMETER command, select the circle, and CANCEL.
   D. Start the leader from the "Lastpoint" and allow two leader picks.

E. End the leader and accept default dimension text.
F. Turn tolerancing off and exit the DIM command.

13. Write a program to draw a leader with a bubble attached to the end.
    A. Get the start point of the leader and set it to p1.
    B. Get the end point of the leader and set it to p2.
    C. Ask the user for text height and set it to a variable.
    D. Ask for the text string (maximum of two characters) and set it to a variable.
    E. Calculate the circle diameter 2.5 or 3 times the text height and set it to a variable.
    F. Set the circle centerpoint, p3, to a value relative to p2 using "polar."
    G. Activate the DIM1 command and draw a leader from p1 to p2.
    H. Erase the "last" portion of the leader.
    I. Draw a circle at p3.
    J. Draw text in the center of the circle using the appropriate option in the TEXT command.

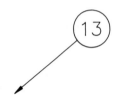

14. Develop a program that writes a line of text and places a box around it.
    A. Ask the user for the text height and set it to variable, thgt.
    B. Ask for the lower-left corner to start box.
    C. Ask for the text string from the user.
    D. Set string length to variable lg1. Use the STRLEN function.
    E. Set the X length of the box to: (lg1 * thgt).
    F. Set the Y length to: (3 * thgt).
    G. Draw box to X and Y lengths.
    H. Calculate center of the box, and set it to variable cen1.
    I. Draw the text string inside the box. Use the "M" justification option from point cen1.

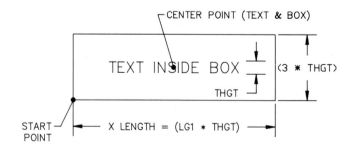

(STRLEN) example:
```
(setq text (getstring T "Enter Text:"))
(setq lg1 (strlen text))
```

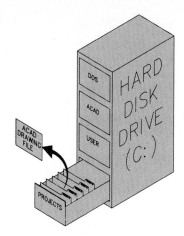

Chapter 35

USING DOS COMMANDS

Learning objectives

After completing this chapter, you will be able to:
- ☐ Format, label, and examine the contents of floppy disks.
- ☐ List, erase, rename, and copy files on floppy and hard disks.
- ☐ Create, remove, and move files between directories and subdirectories.
- ☐ Set the date and time in your computer.
- ☐ Change the DOS prompt.
- ☐ Reclaim deleted files using the DOS 5.0 UNDELETE command.
- ☐ Examine the contents of files.

The Disk Operating System (DOS) is a program that handles the movement of files in your computer. It is basically the traffic cop, or system manager, that enables AutoCAD to work with your computer, and the computer to work with attached equipment. DOS is the first program installed onto your hard disk drive when you purchase a computer. It manages your disk drives and files much like you use a filing cabinet. You might even think of the hard disk drive as one large filing cabinet.

There are two types of DOS commands: internal and external. Internal commands reside in the computer's memory once DOS is loaded. (DOS is loaded when the computer is turned on, or booted.) *Internal commands* are the most used functions of DOS. They perform file manipulations, such as listing, deleting, renaming, and copying files on or between disks. *External commands* are DOS files that are actually individual programs. These must be run from the DOS prompt, just as you might run AutoCAD, because they do not reside in memory.

DISK DRIVE NAMES

Disk drives have names, as discussed in Chapter 2. When you turn the computer on (before loading AutoCAD), the following DOS prompt appears:

C⟩

This is the basic DOS prompt, and means that the hard disk drive is current. Your computer may show something different, such as:

C:\⟩

If it does, do not worry. Your computer has been set to display the current directory as part of the prompt. This is discussed in the next section.

If you want to make the A: drive current, insert a disk in the A: drive and type:

C⟩ **A:** ↵

The prompt changes to reflect the new current drive:

A⟩

If your computer has a second flexible disk drive, access it in the same manner. Be sure a disk is in the B: drive, and type:

A⟩ **B:** ↵

Again, the prompt changes.

B⟩

Remember the difference between a DOS prompt and a disk drive name. A DOS prompt is followed by a caret (⟩), and a disk drive name is followed by a colon (:).

A⟩ = prompt
A: = drive name

When you wish to change drives (at the DOS prompt) be sure to type the colon after the drive letter before pressing ENTER. You can get back to the hard disk drive by entering:

B⟩ **C:** ↵
C⟩

The prompt again indicates the hard disk drive is current.

————— NOTE —————

If you get the error message:

Not ready error reading drive A:
Abort, Retry, Fail?

it means that there is no disk in the drive you are trying to access. Insert a disk in the drive and type "R," but do not press ENTER.

DIRECTORIES AND PATH NAMES

Before you begin working with files and disks, there is one important concept to learn: directories. Think of your hard disk drive as one big filing cabinet. It would be a mess if you dumped all of your files and records into a filing cabinet without drawers or file folders. Rather, the drawers and folders help you to organize your materials. The same is true with your hard disk. See Fig. 35-1. You divide the hard disk (file cabinet) into directories (drawers). Here you might store the AutoCAD main program files. You can then further divide the directories into subdirectories (file folders). These subdirectories—possibly named ELEC (electrical), STRUCT (structural), etc.—hold individual drawing files.

When working with files, you need to specify where a file is located. For example, suppose you want to delete the file TEST1.DWG on drive A:. You would enter:

C⟩ **DEL A:TEST1.DWG** ↵

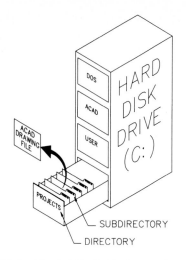

Fig. 35-1. Hard disk divided into directories.

The A: is needed to tell DOS you want to delete the file located on the disk in the A: drive. How then do you delete a file that is located in the ELEC subdirectory of the ACAD directory on your hard disk? Here, you need to specify a "path" for the DOS command to follow to find your file. Look at Fig. 35-2. Suppose you want to delete the drawing PROJECT1.DWG located in the STRUCT subdirectory of the ACAD directory on drive C: (the hard disk). You would enter:

C〉 **DEL \ACAD\STRUCT\PROJECT1.DWG** ↵

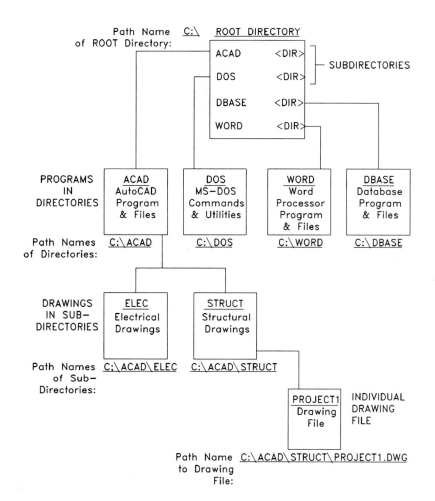

Fig. 35-2. Using a path to find files.

You do not need to include the drive name (C:) because the hard disk drive is already current (C). The first backslash (\) means to begin the path at the root directory. The second backslash means that you are digging deeper by entering a subdirectory. The final backslash separates the subdirectory from the file you wish to delete. You must enter the full file name and its extension, if it has one.

SETTING YOUR OWN PROMPTS

The normal DOS prompt, C), does not show what directory or subdirectory you are in. You can have the prompt do so by using the PROMPT command as follows:

C⟩ **PROMPT PG** ↵
C:\ACAD⟩

The prompt now shows that you are in the ACAD directory.

You can make the prompt read other things too. When creating a new prompt, be sure to use the dollar ($) symbol before items of the prompt. The following symbols may be used with the PROMPT command.

Prompt	Description
$Q	= (equal sign)
$R	$ (dollar sign)
$T	Current time
$D	Current date
$P	Current drive and path
$V	DOS version
$N	Current drive
$G	⟩ (greater than symbol, or caret)
$L	⟨ (less than symbol)
$B	Displays the ¦ (pipe symbol)
$_	Prompt moves to the next line (linefeed)
$E	ASCII escape code
$H	Enters a backspace (to delete a character)

Try some of these at your computer. The following example sets the DOS prompt to display the message READY:

C⟩ **PROMPT READY** ↵
READY

READY is now the prompt. Notice that it was entered as uppercase and is displayed as uppercase. The PROMPT command is sensitive to uppercase and lowercase letters. Change the prompt to lowercase and add the caret (⟩) after "ready" in the following manner:

READY **PROMPT ready$G** ↵
ready ⟩

Adding the "$g" after "ready" displays the caret. Display the date in brackets, current drive and directory, and caret as follows:

ready⟩ **PROMPT LD$G PG** ↵
⟨Fri 1-1-93⟩ C:\⟩

You can create any short message you wish using the PROMPT command, but most people want the current directory displayed.

WORKING WITH DISKS

Before your floppy disks can become small filing cabinets, they must be prepared. This involves *formatting* and *labeling*. Disks can then be used for file storage.

Preparing a disk for use

Before a disk can be used by the computer, it must be formatted. This divides the disk into pie-shaped *sectors,* checks it for defects, and gives a file location directory. This is all accomplished with the FORMAT command. The DOS external command that handles this is FORMAT.COM. If FORMAT.COM is listed, it is installed on the hard disk in the DOS directory. To format a floppy disk, insert it in drive A: and type the following:

> C:\〉 **CD DOS** ↵ *(change the directory to DOS)*
> C:\DOS〉 **FORMAT A:** ↵ *(run the FORMAT command on the disk in drive A:)*

You then get this prompt:

> Insert new diskette for drive A:
> and strike ENTER when ready...

When the disk has been formatted, you get a message indicating the disk space and the opportunity to format another disk:

> Format complete
>   1213952 bytes total disk space
>   1213952 bytes available on disk
> Format another (Y/N)?

Enter "Y" to format another disk or "N" and press ENTER to get back to the DOS prompt. Your prompts may vary slightly depending on the version of DOS being used.

Formatting different sizes of disks

Most floppy disk drives are high-density drives. A *high-density disk* has smaller particles of magnetic material, and thus can have more tracks on it. When you format high-density disks, either 5.25″ or 3.5″, in a high-density drive, the only thing you have to type is:

> C:\〉 **FORMAT A:** ↵

or

> C:\〉 **FORMAT B:** ↵

The two standard sizes of floppy disks are 5.25″ and 3.5″. The following chart provides you with the most commonly used disk sizes and capacities. The third column in the chart indicates the FORMAT command syntax to use when formatting the disk in a high-density drive.

Disk	Capacity	Format Syntax (for A: or B:)
5.25″	360K	Format A: /F:360
5.25″	1.2MB	Format A:
3.5″	720K	Format B: /F:720
3.5″	1.44MB	Format B:

You may want to create a *system* disk in addition to formatting. This procedure puts two hidden files and the COMMAND.COM file on the disk, which can then be used to boot the computer. The COMMAND.COM file contains *internal* commands such as DIR, COPY, RENAME, and others discussed in the following sections. Create a system disk in drive B: as follows:

> C:\〉 **FORMAT B: /S** ↵

PROFESSIONAL TIP

The FORMAT command, in addition to preparing a new disk, will erase any data on a previously formatted disk. It will also erase your entire hard disk. Therefore, take two precautions. First, make sure you are inserting a new, blank floppy. Then, read the command you type several times and make sure it reads "FORMAT A:." Many hard disks have been accidentally erased because the C: drive was specified when the FORMAT command was issued. Newer versions of DOS provide a warning if the hard disk is about to be formatted.

Recovering a formatted disk　　　　　　　　　　　　　　　　　　$\boxed{\textbf{DOS 5.0}}$

The FORMAT command doesn't really erase the data on your disk; it simply deletes the information in its file directory. This list is called the *File Allocation Table*, or *FAT*, for short. It's like throwing away your phone book. All the people and houses are still in town, but to find one, you have to drive all over town looking for the street and address. It's the same with DOS. If you format a disk safely, as previously described, the files are still on the disk! DOS can find all the files again, but it just has to drive all over the disk to locate them because it no longer has a phone book, or file directory (FAT).

Using the FORMAT command as previously described conducts a "safe" format. You can specifically instruct DOS to perform this type of format by using the "quick" switch. This option can only be used on disks that have been previously formatted. A "quick format" does not create sectors or check for bad spots, it simply deletes the File Allocation Table. Use the "quick" switch as follows:

　　　　C:/⟩ **FORMAT A: /Q** ↵

If you format a disk that contains files you need, you can recover from that mistake by using the UNFORMAT command. This command attempts to rebuild the file directory on the floppy disk.

　　　　C:/⟩ **UNFORMAT A:** ↵

Follow the instructions displayed on screen, and be prepared to wait awhile.

You can provide greater insurance for your disks, and the data on them, if you do the following:
* Label your disks with the adhesive labels that come with them.
* Label your disks using DOS as described later on this page.
* Use the write-protect tabs to protect data. See page 35-7.
* Use the MIRROR command in DOS to provide extra protection for your files. Information pertaining to the DOS MIRROR command is found in the DOS manual.

The format of no return

You can unconditionally format a disk from which you will not be able to recover information. This option erases everything on the disk, and the UNFORMAT command cannot recover the lost data. Use this option only if you wish to format disks for security purposes.

　　　　C:/⟩ **FORMAT A: /U** ↵

Be sure you want to perform this type of formatting; DOS does not ask whether you are "really sure."

Giving your disk a name

You can assign a name to your disk by using the *volume* parameter as follows:

　　　　C:\DOS⟩ **FORMAT A: /V** ↵

When the format is complete, you are prompted for a volume label. This label can be up to 11 characters long. Get in the habit of naming your disks. The label is the first item displayed in a directory listing of a disk. Also write the disk name on the adhesive label that comes with the disk before attaching it to the disk. Attempting to write on the label after attaching it to the disk may damage the disk.

If you forget to label a disk when formatting, use the LABEL command to name the disk. Enter LABEL in the following manner to name a backup disk of chapter problems:

　　　　C:\⟩ **LABEL A:PROBLEM-BAK** ↵

Giving your disk a checkup

You can get a quick examination of a disk by using the CHKDSK (CHecK DiSK) command. Insert the disk in drive A: and type:

　　　　C:\DOS⟩**CHKDSK A:** ↵

The computer then gives you a short report on the status of the disk. It looks similar to this:

```
362496 bytes total disk space
  7168 bytes in 7 directories
200704 bytes in 69 user files
154624 bytes available on disk


655360 bytes total memory
607344 bytes free
```

Again, the information that appears on screen may differ slightly from what is shown here, depending on the version of DOS you are using.

Most computer programs create open files to use while they are working. AutoCAD is no exception. When you exit the program properly, the open files are closed and put away. Some files are just closed and tossed out. However, if you exit the program improperly, reset the computer while in a program, or the computer crashes, those open files are left "hanging" and can no longer be used. These files are referred to as "lost clusters" or "lost chains." They are disk units that cannot be used, but they are occupying space on the disk. You can use the CHKDSK command to find these lost clusters as follows:

> C:\〉 **CHKDSK /F** ↵
> 49 lost allocation units found in 1 chains
> Convert lost chains to files (Y/N)?

If you answer "N" to this prompt, DOS fixes the disk and recovers the lost chains. If you answer "Y," the files DOS creates are given names such as FILE0001.CHK, and are placed in the root directory. In most cases, these files cannot be viewed, so you might as well delete them as follows:

> C:\〉 **DEL *.CHK** ↵

— NOTE —

Floppy disks can collect lost clusters if you open AutoCAD drawings on the floppy, or if you remove or insert disks at the wrong time while AutoCAD is in session. Lost clusters can also accumulate on your disk as a result of program or system crashes. Therefore, use the CHKDSK command regularly on your floppy disks like this:

> C:\〉 **CHKDSK A: /F** ↵

Protecting your disks

Dust, heat, cold, magnets, cigarette smoke, and coffee do great damage to your disks. Placing your disk on or near the digitizer tablet or any other electrical or magnetic device can quickly ruin your files. A ringing telephone can even be a dangerous enemy of the disk because of its magnetic field. Beyond physical damage, you or someone else could write over the files on a disk or put files on the wrong disk, making them difficult or impossible to find.

The easiest way to protect the data on your floppy disk from accidental erasure by formatting, saving, or copying files, is to use the *write-protect tab*. For 5.25″ disks, the write-protect tab is a small, rectangular adhesive-backed piece that is placed over the write-protect notch. See Fig. 35-3. A 3.5″ disk uses a small, sliding tab located on the bottom side of the disk. Notice in Fig. 35-3 that the write-protect tab is in effect when it is moved toward the edge of the disk. Use the point of a pen or your fingernail to slide the tab.

When the tab is covering the notch, or moved to the write-protect position, you cannot format, save, or copy files to that disk, but the files can be read from it. Trying to format or save to the disk gives you a write-protect error in DOS. If you must use the disk for writing or formatting purposes, simply remove the tab or move it to the appropriate position.

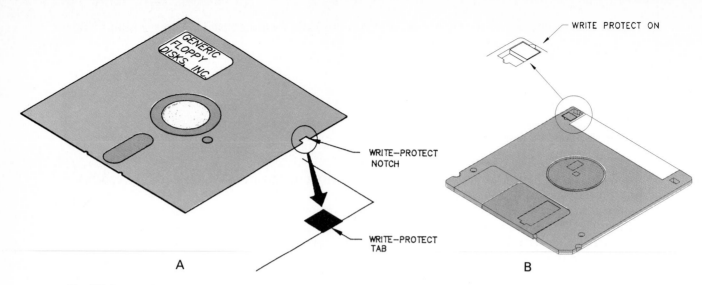

Fig. 35-3. A—Protect your 5.25″ disks by placing a write-protect tab over the notch on the disk. B—On a 3.5″ disk, move the write-protect tab to the "Read Only" position.

WORKING WITH FILES

The most-used DOS commands are DIR (Directory), DELETE, RENAME, and COPY. When using these commands with individual files, always give the path (if necessary) and include the file extension. Omitting the file extension at the end of the file name may cause an error to occur later.

File types

When using DOS to perform manipulations, remember file types, or extensions. A *file extension* is a three-letter combination that represents a specific type of file. AutoCAD recognizes several different file extensions. The most common ones are listed here.

File Extension	Description
.DWG	Latest version of a drawing file.
.BAK	Backup file—Previous version of a DWG file.
.MNU	Menu file—Contains AutoCAD screen and tablet menu commands.
.HLP	Help file—Contains help for AutoCAD commands.
.SCR	Script file—A file that automatically executes several AutoCAD commands.
.SLD	Slide file—A screen display of an AutoCAD drawing file.
.DXF	Drawing interchange file—Used to convert from one CAD system to another.

Some common DOS file extensions are:

File Extension	Description
.COM	Command file—A DOS external command.
.BAT	Batch file—An external DOS program that accomplishes specific tasks.
.TXT	Text file—A file composed of text.
.EXE	Executable file—An external command that is executed when its name is entered at the DOS prompt.
.SYS	System file—Contains information about your hardware.

Listing your files

The DIR command provides a view inside your diskette or any directory on the hard disk. It can give you several kinds of information, such as:
- Drawing names
- Number of files
- File size
- Space left on the disk

If your computer is on, be sure the DOS prompt A⟩ is on the screen. Insert a diskette in drive A: and list its contents as follows:

A⟩ **DIR** ↵

On the screen should be a listing of the disk's contents. The information you see is the volume label (name of the diskette), directory name, file name, file type (indicated by a three-letter extension), size of file in bytes, and the date and time it was last revised. A sample directory listing is shown in Fig. 35-4.

```
Volume in drive A is VIRUS CHECK
Directory of A:\

REGISTER  DOC      4884  12-23-91   3:08p
SCAN      EXE     65936  01-29-92  10:39a
VALIDATE  COM      6537  10-31-89   4:16p
VALIDATE  DOC      3131  01-29-92  10:15a
VIRLIST   TXT     40740  01-23-92   7:09p
CLEAN     EXE     84526  01-24-92  12:12p
CLEAN86   DOC     16540  01-24-92   3:45p
README    1ST      4207  08-22-91   2:31p
SCAN      PIF       545  10-15-91  11:41a
SCAN86    DOC     36893  01-29-92  12:36p
SCANHLP   HLP     53754  01-29-92   2:21p
VSHIELD   EXE     37559  01-29-92  10:44a
VSHIELD1  EXE     11323  02-14-91   3:26p
VSHLD86   DOC     32254  01-29-92  12:53p
WINSTALL  EXE     13201  10-15-91  11:41a
WSCAN     EXE     65099  01-29-92   2:09p
       16 file(s)      477129 bytes
                       732160 bytes free
```

Fig. 35-4. An example of the information provided by the DIR command.

If your disk contains many files, they may begin to scroll off the screen. Stop the scrolling by pressing the CTRL and S keys at the same time (CTRL S). To begin scrolling again, press any key. Press CTRL C to cancel the scrolling.

To prevent scrolling of large directories, specify a pause that shows a screen or "page" at a time.

C⟩ **DIR /P** ↵ *(uppercase or lowercase letters are acceptable)*

Press any key to continue the scroll to the next page.

It is often not necessary to see all the information about the files. A "wide" display gives you only the file name and extension. It packs five columns of files on the screen.

C⟩ **DIR /W** ↵

If the disk or directory contains numerous files, even a wide display may scroll off the screen. If that happens, combine the "page" and "wide" formats like this:

C⟩ **DIR /P/W** ↵

A page at a time is displayed in the wide format.

--- NOTE ---

The DIR command has a variety of switches that are activated with the forward slash (/). These allow you to display and sort files and directory information in a variety of ways. Check your DOS manual for detailed instructions.

Special characters

When working with files, you may want to limit your commands and requests to specific files and file types. A couple of DOS characters come in handy for this.

      *   Wild-card—Can be used as a substitute for any number of characters.

      ?   A substitute for any single character.

Try getting a listing of specific file types. For example, to list all files with a .DWG extension on drive C: in the ACAD directory, enter:

    C> **DIR \ACAD*.DWG** ↵

You should have a listing of just drawing files (.DWG extension). If the list scrolled off the screen, how do you stop the scroll to display one screen at a time?

Try the same thing, only this time obtain a listing of all BAK files on the disk in the A: drive. (You can request a directory listing of any drive no matter which drive is current.) For example, try this:

    C> **DIR A:*.BAK** ↵

Even though drive C: is current, a listing of all .BAK files on the disk in drive A: appears. That is because you provided DOS with a "path" to the files you need to see. The "A:" pointed DOS to the disk on which the files were located.

The wild-card character (?) enables you to pick out files that may have similar characters. For example, suppose you have created several electrical drawings. The file names all begin with "ELEC-" and then have three additional numbers, such as ELEC-100, ELEC-101, etc. The files are located on the disk in the B: drive. To obtain a listing, enter:

    C> **DIR B:ELEC-???.DWG** ↵

This lists only the drawing files that begin with "ELEC-" and have any three additional characters.

Finally, list all files that begin with "ELEC-", have three additional characters, and have any extension.

    C> **DIR B:ELEC-???.*** ↵

Suppose you knew there were over 70 possible files with that combination. How would you prevent them from scrolling off the screen? Try using the "p" switch to pause scrolling.

    C> **DIR B:ELEC-???.* /P** ↵

──── PROFESSIONAL TIP ────

Always enter a space after a DOS command. Omitting the space can result in a "Bad command" message.

EXERCISE 35-1

☐ Use the PROMPT command to set your DOS prompt to reflect the current drive and directory.

☐ Insert one of your disks in the A: drive.

☐ Make the C: drive current (show on the DOS prompt).

☐ Change the directory so the A: drive is current.

☐ Obtain a directory of all files on the A: drive.

☐ Obtain a directory listing of just the .DWG files on the A: drive.

☐ Change the directory to make the C: drive current.

☐ List all the files on drive C: in a wide format.

☐ List all the files on drive C: in a page format.

Erasing files

When it comes time to clean out your file drawers, you will want to use the DELETE (DEL) command. This command eliminates files, no questions asked. Always double-check the file name you enter before pressing ENTER. To delete a drawing file named JUNK on the C: drive, enter:

> C⟩ **DEL JUNK.DWG** ⏎

— PROFESSIONAL TIP —

When deleting files, it is a good practice to first change the DOS prompt to reflect the drive or directory in which you are doing the erasing. For example, suppose you plan to delete a drawing file named TEST on drive A:. The current prompt reflects the C: drive. Enter the following:

> C⟩ **A:** ⏎
> A⟩ **DEL TEST.DWG** ⏎

This prevents erasing files on the wrong drive.

You can erase entire groups of files by including wild-card characters. The asterisk (*) and question mark (?) can be used with several DOS commands. To delete all .BAK files on the A: drive, enter:

> A⟩ **DEL *.BAK** ⏎

You can even erase all files within a directory or on a disk. This is a highly destructive procedure, but one you eventually might want to do. Enter the following:

> A⟩ **DEL *.*** ⏎

At first, nothing happens. A prompt is displayed and asks you:

> Are you sure (Y/N)?

If there is any doubt in your mind, type "N" and press ENTER. If you are sure, type "Y" and press ENTER. If you answer "Y," all the files in the current directory of that disk are gone.

Retrieving deleted files

DOS 5.0

Files that have been deleted can be retrieved using the UNDELETE command. Use this command as soon after deleting as possible because new files that are saved to this disk may take residence in the space that the deleted file occupies. If you can't remember what the deleted file name(s) was, DOS gives you a good idea if you type the following:

> C:\⟩ **UNDELETE A: /LIST** ⏎

A display similar to that in Fig. 35-5 appears.

```
Directory: A:\
File Specifications: *.*

        Deletion-tracking file not found.

        MS-DOS directory contains     2 deleted files.
        Of those,    2 files may be recovered.

Using the MS-DOS directory.

        ?5-5        TXT        235 10-17-92 10:59a   ...A
        ?CAN        EXE      65936  1-29-92 10:39a   ...A
```

Fig. 35-5. Naming scheme for files that are undeleted.

If you don't care about the name of the file(s), but simply want it back, enter the following:

    C:\〉 **UNDELETE A:*.* /ALL** ↲

DOS finds all undeleted files, as best it can, and puts a number symbol (#) in place of the first character of each file. For example, the two deleted files in Fig. 35-5 are given the following names after undeleting them:

    #5-5.TXT
    #CAN.EXE

You can return each file name to its original name (or any other desired name) by using the RENAME command, which is discussed next.

Renaming files

When you wish to change the name of a file, use the RENAME (REN) command. For example, to rename a file called FLOTSAM.DWG to JETSAM.DWG, enter the following:

    A〉 **REN FLOTSAM.DWG JETSAM.DWG** ↲

Note that the current name is given first, then a space, then the new name. Do not forget the file extensions. To see if the change has been made, list the directory.

Copying files

To copy files for backup purposes, use the COPY command. Give the source file first, the destination second, and remember the file extensions. Copy the ACAD.DWG file from the C: drive to a diskette in the A: drive.

    C〉 **COPY ACAD.DWG A:** ↲
      1 File(s) copied

DOS lets you know that the file has been copied. Notice that a file name was not used for the destination. If the name is to remain the same, it does not need to be typed. You can copy and rename at the same time with the COPY command. To do this, type a new name after the destination drive. For example, to copy the C:ACAD.DWG file to a disk in the A: drive and rename it TEST.DWG, do the following:

    C〉 **COPY ACAD.DWG A:TEST.DWG** ↲
      1 File(s) copied

Now the drawing has been both copied and renamed using just the COPY command.

Copying entire disks

You can copy the entire contents of one disk to another using the DISKCOPY command. Keep in mind that the *source* disk is the original you want copied. The *target* disk is the destination of the copied files. Type the following, regardless of the number of floppy drives included in your computer's configuration:

    C:\DOS〉 **DISKCOPY A: B:** ↲

A single-disk drive computer prompts for the source disk to be inserted into drive A:. It reads the disk and then asks for the target disk to be inserted into drive B:. Since DOS is using the one drive as both drive A: and B:, remove the source disk and insert the target disk. A dual-disk drive computer prompts for the source and target disks to be inserted into drives A: and B: respectively. Once the copy is made, a prompt asks if you wish to copy more disks. Answer "Y" or "N" as appropriate and press ENTER.

CAUTION

There is no need to spend time formatting a disk before making a disk copy, since the DISKCOPY command not only copies, it erases! The target disk is formatted before any copying is done. Therefore, be certain your target disk is not one that already has files on it; unless, of course, you want to delete all the files on that disk.

The DISKCOPY command, as discussed previously, when used on a dual-disk drive machine only works if both disk drives are the same size. If you have an A: drive for 5.25″, 1.2MB floppy disks, and a B: drive for 3.5″, 1.44MB disks, then the two formats are incompatible. There are a couple of ways to copy disks in this situation. The first method allows you to copy disks in only one of the two disk drives. To do this, instruct DOS to copy disks in the A: drive only like this:

    C:\DOS⟩ **DISKCOPY A: A:** ↵

You can copy disks in the B: drive only like this:

    C:\DOS⟩ **DISKCOPY B: B:** ↵

The other method that allows you to copy from the 5.25″ disk format to the 3.5″ disk without formatting the target disk is this DOS command:

    C:\DOS⟩ **COPY A:*.* B:** ↵

PROFESSIONAL TIP

It is good practice to have backup copies of all of your flexible disks. These copies should be labeled as "backups" and stored separate from your work disks. Set up a routine in which you regularly back up the disks or individual files as you revise and add to them.

EXERCISE 35-2

☐ Choose a drawing file on your diskette to copy.
☐ Copy the file to the C: drive.
☐ List only DWG files on the C: drive to be sure it is there.
☐ Change the name of the drawing file on the C: drive to TRIAL.BAK.
☐ List only BAK files on the C: drive to see that the file was renamed.
☐ Erase TRIAL.BAK from the C: drive.
☐ Use DISKCOPY to copy one of your floppy disks.

WORKING WITH DIRECTORIES

A consistent method of file storage is one of the most important aspects of computer system management. Directories and subdirectories should reflect the nature of your work, whether it be in school or industry. Everyone who uses the files should know the system and method of creating and naming directories.

The filing cabinet of the hard disk is called the *root directory* and is indicated with a backslash by DOS. All other programs and subdirectories are accessed by first going through the root directory. A prompt set to reflect the current drive and directory should now look like that shown below when the root directory is current.

    C:\⟩

If your prompt does not look like this, use the PROMPT command to change it.

    C⟩ **PROMPT PG** ↵
    C:\⟩

The prompt indicates the C: drive is active and the root directory is current. This is a handy prompt to use because you always know what directory is current.

Making a directory

Creating your own directories on the hard drive or on a flexible disk is easy. Just use the MD (Make Directory) command. Before making directories on the hard disk, obtain permission from your instructor or supervisor. Otherwise, use a floppy diskette and change the current drive to A:. Keep in mind that directory names are governed by the same restrictions that apply to file names.

Using the MD command, create a directory called PROJ-001 as follows:

    C:\⟩ **MD \PROJ-001** ↵

That is it. The new directory is made. You can now create subdirectories under PROJ-001 if they are required. To do so, you must specify the *path* of the new subdirectory. Make two subdirectories and call them ELEC and STRUCT.

    C:\⟩ **MD \PROJ-001\ELEC** ↵
    C:\⟩ **MD \PROJ-001\STRUCT** ↵

Now you have two new subdirectories under the PROJ-001 directory. Obtain a directory listing to be sure they are there.

    C:\⟩ **DIR** ↵

How many of your new directories do you see? Why are the ELEC and STRUCT directories not listed? You will not be able to see them listed until the PROJ-001 directory is current. This requires that you change from one directory to make another directory current.

Changing the current directory

You can be in one directory and manipulate files in another just by specifying the proper path. However, it is much safer to change over to the directory in which you plan to work. Move to another existing directory with the CD (Change Directory) command. To change from the root directory to the PROJ-001 directory, enter:

    C:\⟩ **CD \PROJ-001** ↵
    C:\PROJ-001⟩

Now the DOS prompt has changed to reflect the new current directory. Now list the files.

    C:\PROJ-001⟩ **DIR** ↵

You should see the two directories ELEC and STRUCT, indicated by the ⟨DIR⟩ that follows. There are no files listed unless you have added some.

You can change to the ELEC or STRUCT directories using the same command.

    C:\PROJ-001⟩ **CD ELEC** ↵
    C:\PROJ-001\ELEC⟩

The prompt reflects the new current directory. Notice the path. In order to have the prompt display the root directory again, type:

    C:\PROJ-001\ELEC⟩ **CD ** ↵
    C:\⟩

Remove a directory

A directory can be removed from the disk with the RD (Remove Directory) command. There are two restrictions: you cannot remove a directory that contains files or subdirectories, and you cannot remove a directory that is current. First, delete the files from the directory you want to remove. To delete all files from the ELEC subdirectory, first use the CD command to make ELEC current:

> C:\〉 **CD \PROJ-001\ELEC** ↵
> C:\PROJ-001\ELEC〉 **DEL *.*** ↵
> Are you sure (Y/N)? **Y** ↵

All files are deleted. Now you must get out of the ELEC subdirectory in order to remove it.

> C:\PROJ-001\ELEC〉 **CD \PROJ-001** ↵
> C:\PROJ-001〉 **RD ELEC** ↵
> C:\PROJ-001〉

You can check to be sure the ELEC directory is gone by getting a directory listing.

Any subdirectory can be removed from the root directory as long as the proper path is specified, and that the subdirectory is empty.

> C:\〉 **RD \PROJ-001\STRUCT** ↵

The STRUCT directory is now deleted. List the PROJ-001 directory to check.

EXERCISE 35-3

- ☐ Insert one of your disks in the A: drive.
- ☐ Change directory so the A: drive is current.
- ☐ Make a directory called CLASSES, and another called PROJECTS.
- ☐ Make two subdirectories in the CLASSES directory called CAD-I and CAD-II.
- ☐ Make two subdirectories in the PROJECTS directory called P-100 and P-200.
- ☐ List the directories to see that all new directories were properly created.
- ☐ Copy a group of drawing files from the hard disk to one of the subdirectories under either CLASSES or PROJECTS.
- ☐ List this directory to view the contents.
- ☐ Make the subdirectory that contains the copied files current.
- ☐ Delete all files from the current subdirectory.
- ☐ Remove the current subdirectory.
- ☐ Remove all the directories created in this exercise.

MISCELLANEOUS COMMANDS

The DOS program contains more commands than can be discussed in this text. Most AutoCAD users will not use these additional commands. Consult your DOS manual for a detailed discussion of other commands if extensive DOS programming is required.

There are several commands that are useful when creating text or batch files. These commands let you set the date and time, create a text file, and display any file on the screen.

Setting the date and time

The DATE and TIME commands allow you to set the date and time and ask the computer for the date and time. Enter the following:

> C:\〉 **DATE** ↵
> Current date is Fri 1-01-1993
> Enter new date (mm-dd-yy):

If you just wanted to know the date, press ENTER now and the DOS prompt returns. If you need to reset the date for any reason, enter it in the following manner:

Enter new date (mm-dd-yy): **1-04-93** ↵
C:\〉

If you enter the date incorrectly, the "Invalid date" error message appears and a prompt asks you to enter the new date again.

The TIME command is used in the same manner:

C:\〉 **TIME** ↵
Current time is 8:37:12.82a
Enter new time:

Press ENTER if you are just checking the time. Notice that the time is given in hundredths of a second. When entering a new time, only the hour and minute is needed, and if it is A.M. or P.M.:

Enter new time: **7:37a** ↵
C:\〉

Some users make the date and/or the time part of the DOS prompt. Enter the following to make the date part of the prompt:

C:\〉 **PROMPT $P DG** ↵
C:\ Mon 1-04-1993〉

Notice that a space was left after the "$P" in the prompt entry. This adds a space after the current directory in the new prompt. The time can be added to the prompt in the same manner:

C:\ Mon 1-04-93〉 **PROMPT $P TG** ↵
C:\ 7:46:58.04〉

The time displayed reflects the last time you pressed ENTER. To know the current time, press ENTER.

C:\ 7:46:58.04〉 ↵
C:\ 7:47:05.89〉

PROFESSIONAL TIP

Include DATE and TIME in the AUTOEXEC.BAT file if your computer does not have a clock, or if the battery in your computer is not functioning. It is important that the internal clock is working, especially if you customize the screen and tablet menus. AutoCAD uses the menu file with the latest date and time.

Writing quick files

The COPY CON (COPY CONsole) command allows you to create small text or batch files without using a text editor program, such as EDLIN. Files created using COPY CON cannot be edited; therefore, make them short. If you discover a mistake in a file, you must rewrite it using the COPY CON command, or edit it with a text editor. Create a short batch file to clear the screen and display the date and time:

C:\〉 **COPY CON TEST.BAT** ↵
CLS ↵
ECHO OFF ↵
DATE ↵
TIME ↵

Press function key F6 to end the file. This displays a "∧Z," which terminates the file. Then press ENTER. A message appears indicating the file has been copied. You can test the file by entering "TEST" at the DOS prompt:

C:\〉 **TEST** ↵

The file runs and the screen clears. The date prompt appears, allowing you to change the date. After pressing ENTER, the time prompt appears. When you press ENTER a second time, the DOS prompt returns.

Try entering this short batch file from within AutoCAD using the COPY CON command.

```
Command: SHELL ↵
OS Command: ↵
C:\ACAD>> COPY CON TEST.BAT ↵
CLS ↵                        (clear the screen)
ECHO OFF ↵                   (do not display DOS commands)
DIR A:*.DWG ↵                (list all .DWG files in drive A:)
PAUSE ↵                      (pause to read the list)
CD \ACAD\SAMPLE ↵            (change directory to \ACAD\SAMPLE)
DIR *.DWG ↵                  (list all .DWG files in the \ACAD\SAMPLE subdirectory)
PAUSE ↵                      (pause to read the list)
CLS ↵                        (clear the screen)
CD..                         (change to the previous or "parent" directory)
```
(Press key F6 and ENTER)

Execute this file by typing "TEST" at the DOS prompt. When this is completed, type "EXIT" to return to the drawing editor.

Displaying the contents of files

The TYPE command allows you to see the data a file contains. Enter the TYPE command at the DOS prompt, followed by the name and extension of the file to display. Display the contents of your AUTOEXEC.BAT file by entering:

```
C:\> TYPE AUTOEXEC.BAT ↵
```

The contents of the entire file scroll up the screen. The DOS prompt then returns. If the file is long, the screen display does not automatically stop when the first page scrolls. Stop the file by entering CTRL S, then press CTRL S to start the scroll again. This requires quick fingers and a measured eye to stop the scroll exactly where you want to look at the file.

A more precise method of displaying only one screen at a time is the MORE command. It allows only one screen display at a time to scroll by. To see the next screen, press any key. You are using two commands in one entry, so you must use the *pipe* symbol (|) before the MORE command. This is a vertical bar (|), or two short vertical dashes (¦), usually located on the backslash key (\). Use SHIFT to activate this symbol. The pipe symbol takes output from one command (file) and sends it to another. In this case, it takes the output of the TYPE command (a continuous list) and sends it to the MORE command (breaks the list into separate pages).

Try this with the ACAD.MNU file. First change directory to ACAD. Then use the TYPE and MORE commands:

```
C:\> CD \ACAD\SUPPORT
C:\ACAD\SUPPORT> TYPE ACAD.MNU|MORE ↵
```

When one page scrolls by, the following prompt appears at the bottom of the screen:

```
–More–
```

Press any key and the next page appears. The ACAD.MNU file is long. When you have seen enough, press CTRL C to cancel the command.

--- **NOTE** ---

Most computer programs come with files such as README.DOC, READ.ME, or README.NOW. Anytime you see one of these file, especially if you have just installed new software or received files via a modem, you should read them first. These files are usually ASCII files, so they can be displayed without using special software. Use the TYPE command to view these files:

```
C:\> TYPE README.DOC|MORE ↵
```

In addition, many of the files that come with software or *shareware* (software that is free or available for a nominal fee), are registration forms or instruction manuals. These usually have a .DOC file extension. They can be printed like this:

C:\⟩ **PRINT REGISTER.DOC** ⏎

Before initiating this command, be sure to have paper in your printer.

EXERCISE 35-4

☐ Using the COPY CON command write a batch file named EX35-4.BAT that does the following:
  ☐ Clears the screen.
  ☐ Turns the screen echo off.
  ☐ Sets the prompt to display the current directory, the words "hi there," and the caret (⟩).
  ☐ Sets the date.
  ☐ Sets the time.
  ☐ Changes the current directory to ACAD.
☐ Use the TYPE command to list the file.
☐ Run the file by entering EX35-4 at the DOS prompt.

CHAPTER TEST

Write your answers in the spaces provided.

1. List the names of the first two floppy disk drives and the hard disk drive. _____

_____

2. What does the C⟩ prompt indicate?

_____

3. What command would you enter at the DOS prompt so that the prompt reads "OK⟩"?

C⟩ _____

4. The name of the DOS command that lets you prepare a floppy disk for use is _____.

5. What command allows you to recover a disk that has been prepared with the command in

Question 4? _____

6. What would you enter at the DOS prompt to prepare and assign a name to a floppy disk

in the A: drive?

C⟩ _____

7. Explain the function of the CHKDSK command. _____

_____

_____

8. Describe how you can protect your floppy disks from having data written to them accidentally.

_____

9. Define a BAT file. _____

10. Provide the correct DOS command to list the directory of drive A: in a wide format displayed

one page at a time.

C:\⟩_____

11. Explain what the following command would accomplish.

    C:\\〉 DIR B:ARCH-???.DWG_____

    _____

12. Given the following DOS prompt, provide the command that would erase the file named STRUCT05.BAK from the disk in the B: drive.

    C:\\〉_____

13. Explain how the COPY and RENAME commands are similar. _____

    _____

14. What two commands enable you to remove files and then recover them again? _____

    _____

15. The DISKCOPY command can be used with single-disk drive computer. True or false?

    _____

16. Why should you exercise caution when using the DISKCOPY command? _____

    _____

17. Given the prompt below, provide the command to make a directory called DRAWINGS on the disk in the A: drive.

    C:\\〉_____

18. Name two restrictions when using the RD command._____

    _____

    _____

19. Explain why it is important that AutoCAD have the current date and time. _____

    _____

20. List the proper DOS entry to begin writing a small batch file called FIRST, without using a text editor such as EDLIN.

    C:\\〉_____

21. Explain how you would display a long file on the A: drive named MYFIRST.BAT, one page at a time.

    C:\\〉_____

22. Provide complete, but brief explanations of the following DOS commands:

    A. PROMPT LDPG — _____

    _____

    B. FORMAT B: /F:720 /V — _____

    C. CHKDSK B: /F — _____

    D. DIR D:\TEST*.DWG /W — _____

    _____

    E. DEL ARCH???.DWG — _____

    _____

    F. UNDELETE A:*.BAK /LIST — _____

    _____

G. REN TOAD.BAK NEWT.DWG – _____

H. MD \BAT\UTIL – _____

PROBLEMS

───── NOTE ─────

Have the permission of your instructor or supervisor before making or removing directories, formatting disks, deleting files, writing batch files, or using any DOS command that may alter the structure of the hard disk files and directories.

1. This problem involves making new subdirectories and copying drawing files to them. In addition, you will list the contents of the subdirectories.
   A. Make your own subdirectory of the ACAD directory. Name it using your initials.
   B. Make the subdirectory current.
   C. Copy all of your drawing files from one floppy disk to the subdirectory.
   D. Make a subdirectory within your new directory and name it BAK.
   E. Make the BAK subdirectory current.
   F. Copy all of your BAK files into the BAK subdirectory.
   G. List the files in each new subdirectory.
   H. Generate a printed copy of each directory listing.
2. Make a new subdirectory of the directory you created for Problem 1. Name the new subdirectory TEST.
   A. Copy the contents of the BAK subdirectory into TEST.
   B. List the contents of the TEST subdirectory.
   C. Rename one of the files in the TEST subdirectory HEY.YOU.
   D. List the contents of the TEST subdirectory.
   E. Copy the HEY.YOU file to the BAK subdirectory and rename it WHO.ME.
   F. List the contents of the BAK subdirectory.
   G. Copy WHO.ME to one of your floppy disks and name it YES.YOU.
   H. Delete the three files you just created.
   I. Make the BAK subdirectory current. Delete the entire contents of the BAK subdirectory.
   J. Remove the BAK subdirectory.
3. Format four disks in a row without exiting the FORMAT command. Provide names for the disks as they are formatted by using the proper FORMAT option.
4. List the contents of one of your newly formatted diskettes. Use the CHKDSK command on your old diskettes. (If there are any lost clusters, do not convert them to files.)
5. Use a text editor or the COPY CON command to write a batch file called CHECK.BAT that does the following:
   A. Clears the screen.
   B. Turns the display of DOS commands off.
   C. Lists all files on the disk.
   D. Pauses to view the files.
   E. Checks the disk in drive A:.
   F. Clears the screen.
6. Use a text editor or the COPY CON command to write a batch file called DELBAK.BAT that does the following:
   A. Clears the screen.
   B. Turns the display of DOS commands off.
   C. Changes the current drive to A:.
   D. Lists the contents of the disk.
   E. Pauses.
   F. Deletes all BAK files.
   G. Changes the current disk to C:.
   H. Clears the screen.

INSTALLING AND CONFIGURING AUTOCAD

Before you can use AutoCAD, it must be loaded onto the hard disk and then configured to work with your specific hardware. When AutoCAD is installed on the hard disk, you begin the continuous process of disk and system management. This involves creating storage space for files and maintaining them. The configuration procedure should have to be used only once, unless equipment is upgraded or new peripherals are added. To use two or more different menu systems, you can duplicate and alter AutoCAD's standard configuration file, ACAD.CFG.

LOADING AUTOCAD ONTO THE HARD DISK

Before loading AutoCAD, follow these preparation and setup steps:
• Determine the hard disk drive to install AutoCAD on.
• Make backup copies of the AutoCAD diskettes.
• Label the backup disks.
These steps require only a few minutes and can prevent problems later.

Making backup copies of the AutoCAD disks

Always make backup copies of original disks before loading the software onto the hard disk. Be sure you have the correct number of blank disks before starting to copy the AutoCAD disks. Attach labels to the blank disks that contain the disk name, number, and AutoCAD serial number. Enter the DISKCOPY command at the DOS prompt. This program prepares the blank disk (formats) and then copies onto it the contents of the original. DISKCOPY can be used with a single- or dual-disk drive computer if both drives are the same type. For a two-drive system, enter:

 C⟩ **DISKCOPY A: B:** ↵
 Insert SOURCE disk in drive A:
 Insert TARGET disk in drive B:
 Press any key when ready...

Insert the AutoCAD Disk 1 into drive A: and the blank "target" disk into drive B:. Press a key and the copy begins. If you have only one disk drive, enter "DISKCOPY A: A:" and insert the source disk in drive A:. You are prompted to insert the target disk into drive A:. When the copy is complete, you are asked if you want to copy another diskette. Answer "Y" and continue the process above until all of the disks have been copied.

 Copy another diskette (Y/N)? **Y** ↵

When you finish copying the disks, return the originals to the slipcase and store them in a safe place. Use the backup copies for loading AutoCAD, and any other future needs.

Installing AutoCAD onto the hard disk

Installing AutoCAD on a hard disk is a simple process, but it does require that you are somewhat prepared before beginning. First, be sure that you have enough physical hard disk space for the program files. Approximate storage areas required for some of the files are given below.

Files	Disk Space
Executable/Support files	11.2MB
Bonus/Sample files	3.3MB
Support Source files	.5MB
IGES Font files	114K
Tutorial files	260K
ADS files	2MB
Render files	1.2MB
SQL Extension files	1.3MB
Advanced Modeling Extension files	5.1MB
Complete installation	25MB

In an effort to run smoothly through the installation process, know the following information before starting.
- Disk drive on which to install AutoCAD. _____
- Portion of the AutoCAD files to install. See previous list. _____
- Dealer's name. _____
- Dealer's telephone number. _____
- Did you purchase AME 2.1? _____

After you have created backup disks of all of the AutoCAD program disks, you are ready to install the software. Insert Disk #1, Executables 1, into the disk drive and enter the following at the DOS prompt:

C:\\> **A:INSTALL** ↵

The installation program begins and provides you with information on the install process, and prompts you for the previously listed items. You are asked for specific information that becomes a permanent part of the Executable disk. This is both a security measure, and enables AutoCAD to display the name and phone number of your dealer in the "About AutoCAD" dialogue box. The screen that prompts for this information is shown in Fig. A-1.

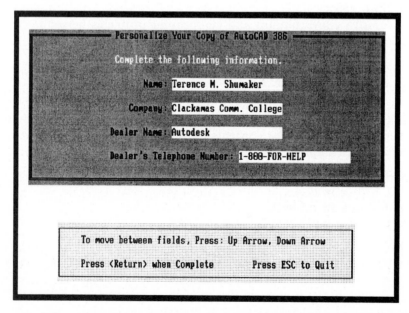

Fig. A-1. The personal data entered at this screen becomes a permanent part of the Executables 1 disk.

After entering the required information, you are given a chance to change your mind or correct anything you entered, and you are warned that the data entered becomes permanent. See Fig. A-2.

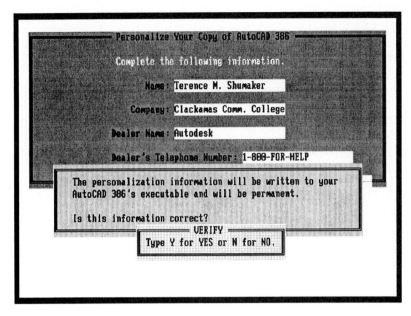

Fig. A-2. You can correct personal data at this screen by typing "N" for No before it becomes permanent.

After verifying your personal data, you are informed of the language version that is to be installed, then provided with some information and instructions for installation. Then, a list of the parts of AutoCAD that you can install is displayed. See Fig. A-3.

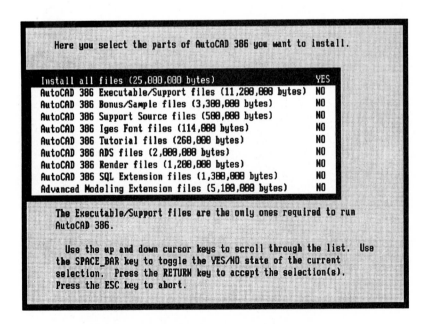

Fig. A-3. Choose the files to install from this list.

The next decision you have to make is how much of the program you want to install on the hard disk. Check the appropriate boxes for the portions of AutoCAD you need.
- If you will be using AutoCAD and its associated drawing and LISP routines, install the following:
  - ☐ Executable/Support files
  - ☐ Bonus/Sample files
  - ☐ Support Source files
- If you will be using solid modeling (AME), install the following:
  - ☐ Advanced Modeling Extension files
- If you will be working the AutoCAD tutorials, install the following:
  - ☐ Tutorial files
- If you will be working with renderings and raster files, install the following:
  - ☐ Render files
- If you will be working with databases and SQL, install the following:
  - ☐ SQL Extension files
- If you will be programming with the AutoCAD Development System (ADS), install the following:
  - ☐ ADS files
- If you will be exchanging drawing files in the international IGES format (Initial Graphics Exchange Specification), install the following:
  - ☐ IGES Font files
- If you are unsure about the applications that will be needed, install everything. Just remember, you'll need about 25 megabytes of storage space. Fig. A-3 shows the program file selections that are displayed on the screen.

Next, you are asked for the disk drive in which you want AutoCAD installed. You are shown a list of all hard disk drive names in your computer. Use the arrow keys to scroll up or down to highlight your choice, then press ENTER to select it. See Fig. A-4.

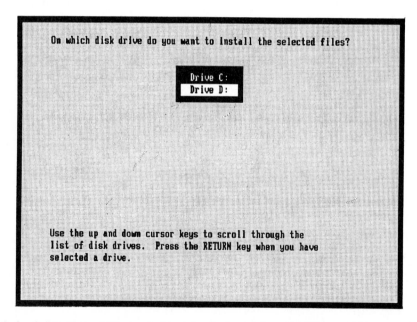

Fig. A-4. A list of available hard drives is displayed from which to make your choice.

Next, you are allowed to name the directory for the AutoCAD files and a directory for the support files. As mentioned above, it is suggested that you have the support files placed in a subdirectory of \ACAD such as \ACAD\SUPPORT. If the directory that you specify for the AutoCAD files already exists, you will be informed and given a chance to name another directory.

After that, the automatic installation process takes over, and it is just a matter of removing and inserting the proper disks when you are prompted to do so. This may take ten to thirty minutes depending on the portions of the program you are installing. You are ready to configure AutoCAD upon completion of the installation.

The installation program provides a startup batch file named ACADR12.BAT, if you wish to use it. This is a simple batch file, but it sets three important environment variables needed for efficient operation of AutoCAD. It is suggested that you have this file installed if you do not have a batch file to execute AutoCAD. This file can be edited later to suit your application. See Appendix C for examples of this and other batch files.

CONFIGURING AUTOCAD

The configuration process allows you to tell AutoCAD the specific brands and styles of equipment you are using. Before you begin, make a list of the following pieces of equipment that comprise your workstation:

Video Display _____

Input Device (Digitizer or Mouse) _____

  Size _____

  Number of buttons_____

Plotter _____

Printer _____

Once you have a list of your equipment, the configuring process should go quickly. Make the ACAD directory current with the Change Directory (CD) command.

    C:\〉 **CD ACAD** ↵
    C:\ACAD〉

Remember, if you did not change the prompt's appearance using PROMPT, the display will not show the current directory:

    C〉 **CD ACAD** ↵
    C〉

Start AutoCAD by entering "ACAD" at the prompt, or "ACADR12" if you are using the suggested startup batch file.

    C:\ACAD〉 **ACADR12** ↵

If AutoCAD has not yet been configured, it will proceed past the copyright notice and display a message saying "AutoCAD is not yet configured". You are then instructed:

You must specify the devices to which AutoCAD will interface.
Press ENTER to continue:

You are then presented with a list of the following video display selections.

Available video displays:
1. Null display
2. 8514/A ADI 4.2 Display and Rendering - by Panacea for Autodesk
3. ADI display v4.0
4. ADI display v4.1
5. Compaq Portable III Plasma Display 〈obsolete〉
6. Hercules Graphics Card 〈obsolete〉
7. IBM Enhanced Graphics Adapter 〈obsolete〉
8. IBM Video Graphics Array ADI 4.2 - by Autodesk
9. SVADI Super VGA ADI 4.2 - by Autodesk
10. Targa+ ADI v4.2 Display and Rendering - by Autodesk
11. VESA Super VGA ADI v4.2 Display and Rendering - by Autodesk
12. XGA ADI 4.2 Display and Rendering - by Panacea for Autodesk

Make the appropriate selection and then be prepared to answer the following questions:
- Do you want to correct the aspect ratio of the graphics screen? _____
- Do you want a status line? _____
- Do you want a command prompt area? _____
- Do you want a screen menu area? _____

Depending on the type of display devices that you may select, you may be asked different questions regarding detailed configurations or specific screen color settings. Consult your video card documentation for instructions.

After configuring your video display, you are asked to choose a digitizer. This is actually referring to the pointing device since you can select pointing devices other than digitizers. You are given the following list:

Available digitizers:
1. None
2. ADI digitizer (Real Mode)
3. Calcomp 2500 and 9100 Series ADI 4.2 - by Autodesk
4. GTCO Digi-Pad (Types 5 and 5A) ⟨obsolete⟩ ADI 4.2 - by Autodesk
5. Hitachi HICOMSCAN HDG Series ADI 4.2 - by Autodesk
6. Kurta IS/1, Series I ⟨obsolete⟩ ADI 4.2 - by Autodesk
7. Kurta XLC, Series II and III ⟨obsolete⟩, IS/3 ADI 4.2 - by Autodesk
8. Logitech 3-D mouse ADI 4.2 - by Autodesk
9. Logitech Logimouse ADI 4.2 - by Autodesk
10. Microsoft Mouse Driver ADI 4.2 - by Autodesk
11. Numonics 2200 ⟨obsolete⟩ ADI 4.2 - by Autodesk
12. Summagraphics MM Series v2.0, ADI 4.2 - by Autodesk
13. Summagraphics MicroGrid v1.0 (Series II or later) ADI 4.2 - by Autodesk
Select device number or ? to repeat list ⟨1⟩: *(enter your selection and press ENTER)*

You are next asked a variety of questions regarding digitizer size, number of buttons, mouse scaling parameters, etc., depending on which pointing device you selected.

The configuration process continues, presenting available plotters and printers. Choose the appropriate hardware and answer the ensuing questions. After the printer or plotter is configured, you are required to provide the following information:
- Default login name—The default name is the one entered when AutoCAD was installed.
- Maximum number of users for this package
- Run the executable from a read-only directory? (Y/N)
- Password, or enter a period (.) for none
- Enable file locking? (Y/N)

After answering these questions, the screen displays the current AutoCAD configuration. This is only a display; you cannot change anything here. If you wish to change something, you can do so at the Configuration menu after pressing ENTER, or you can use the CONFIG command when you are in AutoCAD.

Press ENTER to continue:

Pressing ENTER displays the Configuration menu. Correct any configuration errors or add a piece of equipment that you may have forgotten.

Configuration menu
0. Exit to drawing editor
1. Show current configuration
2. Allow detailed configuration

3. Configure video display
4. Configure digitizer
5. Configure plotter
6. Configure system console
7. Configure operating parameters
Enter selection ⟨0⟩: ↵

Press ENTER if you do not wish to configure any additional equipment or change the hardware you chose. Be sure to press ENTER at the following prompt, or enter "Y", to save the configuration file:

> If you answer N to the following question, all configuration
> changes you have just made will be discarded.
> Keep configuration changes? ⟨Y⟩ ⤶

The AutoCAD drawing editor then appears, and you can begin a drawing session. Test the equipment you configured and reconfigure those which do not operate properly.

When you enter the AutoCAD drawing editor, if you have a digitizer, notice that the entire surface of the digitizer tablet represents the screen. The tablet menu will not work until you use the TABLET command to configure it. This is explained in detail in Chapter 33. After the tablet is configured, this information is added to the ACAD.CFG file, which is saved in the \ACAD directory.

ALTERNATE CONFIGURATIONS

The ACAD.CFG file contains all of the information needed to allow AutoCAD to work with the equipment you specified during configuration. It also includes information about the screen and tablet menus, and additional system variable settings. As you gain experience with AutoCAD, you will use additional configurations of tablet and screen menus, and possibly different input devices. Creating and maintaining multiple configuration files is discussed in Appendix C, Hard Disk Management. If you plan to work with projects that require different menus, become familiar with multiple configuration techniques. These eliminate the need to reconfigure the tablet and load new menus each time you begin a new project or work on a different drawing.

Portion of a sectional drawing for a centrifugal casting machine. (Applied Technical Support, Inc.)

Appendix B

SYSTEM REQUIREMENTS FOR AUTOCAD RELEASE 12

AutoCAD is the industry-standard design and drafting software for desktop computers and workstations. One reason for AutoCAD's popularity over the years has been its consistent technical superiority.

This Appendix lists the system requirements for AutoCAD Release 12 and outlines the hardware, software, and data exchange options available for this latest AutoCAD release. It is intended to be used as a guide for configuring the AutoCAD system that best meets your needs. Your local authorized AutoCAD dealer will provide you with detailed information about system configuration options and assist you in selecting the platform, peripherals, and companion programs that are right for you.

SOFTWARE AND HARDWARE

The following software and hardware, unless noted as optional, is required to run AutoCAD Release 12.
- DOS operating system, Version 3.3 or later.
- Microsoft Windows, Version 3.1 or later (optional).
- Compaq Deskpro® 386, 386SX, IBM® PS/2® models 70, 80, Hewlett-Packard® 386 systems, or a true 386-compatible computer. The 486 is also supported because it is 386-compatible.
- 387 or 487 math coprocessor. On the 486DX, the 487 coprocessor is an integral part of the chip.
- Minimum of 8 megabytes of random-access memory (RAM) recommended. AutoCAD can access up to 4 gigabytes of memory or page out to an equivalent disk space.
- Hard disk with approximately 26 megabytes of free disk space to install all AutoCAD files. A minimum of 11.2MB is required to run the Executable and Support files.
- A 5.25", 1.2 megabyte floppy drive or a 3.5", 1.44 megabyte floppy drive.
- A video display and adapter. See accompanying peripheral chart.
- Digitizing tablet or mouse. See accompanying peripheral chart.
- Plotter or printer (optional). See accompanying peripheral chart.
- Asynchronous communications adapter (serial port—required for digitizers and some plotters).

Device	Model
Video Displays	Protected-mode ADI version 4.2 and previous
	Real-mode ADI version 4.1 and 4.0 or earlier
	COMPAQ Portable III Plasma Display (obsolete) †
	Hercules Graphics Card™ (obsolete) †
	XGA Display Adapter
	8514/A
	IBM Enhanced Graphics Adapter (obsolete) †
	TARGA+
	Video Graphics Array (VGA) and Super VGA (SVGA)
	VESA-compliant display
	Null display †
Digitizers	Null digitizer (none) †
	Protected-mode ADI version 4.2 and previous
	Real-mode ADI version 4.0 and 4.1 or earlier
	CalComp 2500 Series Tablet
	CalComp 9100 Series Tablets
	GTCO Digi-Pad 5 Tablets (obsolete)
	Hitachi® HICOMSCAN HDG Series Tablet
	Kurta® Tablet, IS/ONE® (Series I is obsolete)
	Kurta Tablet, XLC (Series III is obsolete)
	Kurta Tablet, Series II (obsolete)
	Kurta Tablet, IS/THREE™
	Logitech Logimouse
	Microsoft Mouse (Mouse Systems Mouse and IBM PS/2 Mouse supported with this driver)
	Numonics 2200 Series Tablet (obsolete)
	Summagraphics® SummaSketch® MM Series Tablet
	Summagraphics MicroGrid Tablet (series II or later)

Device	Model
Plotters	Null plotter (none) †
	Protected-mode ADI version 4.2 and previous
	Real-mode ADI version 4.0 and 4.1 or earlier
	AutoCAD file formats
	CalComp Colormaster Plotters
	CalComp DrawingMaster Plotters
	CalComp Electrostatic Plotters
	CalComp Pen Plotters
	Canon Laser Beam Printer
	Epson® Printers
	Hewlett-Packard HP-GL™ and HP-GL/2™ Plotters
	Hewlett-Packard LaserJet® (PCL)
	Hewlett-Packard PaintJet (PCL)
	Houston Instrument DMP Series
	IBM 7300 Series
	IBM Graphics Printer
	IBM ProPrinter
	JDL-750 Printer (obsolete)
	NEC Pinwriter P5, P5XL, and P9XL (obsolete)
	PostScript Laser Printer
	Raster file formats

† internal driver

SEE WIRING DIAGRAM

BACKHOE VALVE BANK

SUPPLY TEST PORT

RETURN TEST PORT

RETURN

PRESSURE

BOLT OR WELD HOSE BRACKET (21) AS SHOWN.

IN

REG

POSITION 90° FITTINGS SO THAT INLET AND PRESSURE HOSES WILL CLEAR TOP OF SWING CYLINDERS.

REAR DIFFERENTIAL HOUSING

Application kit illustration for a backhoe valve bank. (Autodesk, Inc.)

Appendix C

HARD DISK AND SYSTEM MANAGEMENT

Any business — be it a bakery or engineering firm — relies on structure, organization, and standard procedures. A business lacking in one of these areas does not operate efficiently. The widespread use of computers in business and industry has introduced another facet to business operations. Computer systems can be used within the company structure for organization and procedure; or computers can contain the structure and organize procedures. In either case, the method in which computer systems are managed greatly affects the operation of the entire company.

Effective management of an AutoCAD system in a school or business means paying careful attention to the following items:
- The structure and makeup of the hard disk.
- The location of all files and drawings.
- Storage procedures for student/employee drawing files.
- Drawing file backup procedures.
- The kind of prototype drawings used for specific projects.
- The location and use of symbol libraries and reference drawings.
- The location and use of special screen and tablet menus.
- Drawing naming procedures.
- Drawing file creation procedures.
- Creation and distribution of new symbols and menus.
- Timely updating of software and hardware.
- Hardware maintenance.

Effective procedures and management techniques must be practiced by all students or employees. In addition, look for ways that the standards can be improved and revised for greater efficiency. Read the section in Chapter 1 on system management and the section in Chapter 21 on creating and using symbol libraries.

DOS HARD DISK STRUCTURE

The hard disk drive is the heart of the AutoCAD computer system. It is the storage center for AutoCAD and other programs you use. In addition, it may hold hundreds of additional files, including drawings, menus, AutoLISP programs, slides, scripts, and text files. The manner in which you work with the hard disk and arrange its contents can affect your productivity and efficiency at the computer. Take some time to learn the nature of the hard disk drive.

The root directory and its contents

The root directory is the trunk of the hard disk tree from which every other directory, sub-directory, and file branches. After your computer is installed, the root directory contains only a DOS directory. See C-1. No other programs are on the hard disk. In addition to the DOS directory, two files occupy the root directory, COMMAND.COM and AUTOEXEC.BAT. A third file, CONFIG.SYS, should be placed in the root directory when AutoCAD is installed.

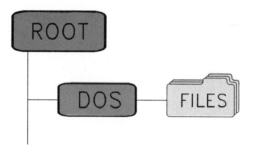

Fig. C-1. The root directory contains only the DOS directory when the computer is installed.

Before a program is installed on the hard disk, a directory should first be created. The program files are copied into that directory. Program files should not be placed in the root directory. A common name for the AutoCAD directory is ACAD, and all AutoCAD files reside in it. After AutoCAD is installed, the structure of the hard disk resembles Fig. C-2.

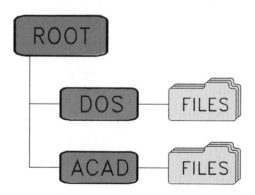

Fig. C-2. AutoCAD files are stored in the ACAD directory.

Keep the number of files stored in the ACAD directory to a minimum. Only essential files for operating AutoCAD need be in the ACAD directory. If this directory is kept clean and organized, less time is required by the hard disk to search the directory looking for files. Files that should be kept in the ACAD directory are shown as DOS file extensions in Fig. C-3.

The files that reside in the \ACAD directory after the software is installed, are the only ones that need to be there. Any files that you create should be stored in subdirectories. See Chapter 35 for information on creating directories and subdirectories.

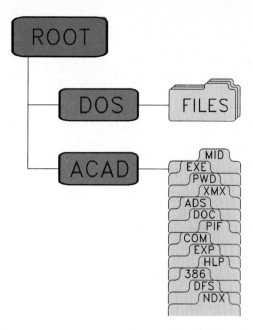

Fig. C-3. The only files that should be stored in the ACAD directory have these file extensions.

Designing and building a hard disk tree

When you install AutoCAD using the INSTALL program provided on the disks, several subdirectories are automatically created depending on which files you instruct AutoCAD to install. These subdirectories are created so that the ACAD directory is not filled with files it does not need. Take some time to look at the contents of these subdirectories and notice the files that are stored there.

PROFESSIONAL TIP

If you are responsible for hard disk organization and management in your school or company, it is a good idea to keep a printed copy of the contents of each subdirectory. Get a print of each directory and subdirectory immediately after installing the software. Periodically check the contents of each directory and look for unnecessary files. Compare the contents with your printed list. Then, delete all unnecessary files.

You can automate this process with a batch file. This file can delete all file types, such as .DWG, that are not supposed to be in the directory. See the next section for batch file examples and instructions.

After installing the software, you will be faced with other decisions about where to store new files that must go on the hard disk. Only you can decide which files should be saved on the hard disk and where they are to be saved. Regardless of the decisions you make, they should be based on careful consideration of the following:

Questions to ask
- Are the computers used for training or production?
- Will the computers be used for demonstrations?
- Will the system hardware be upgraded often?
- How often will drawings be saved to the hard disk?
- How many drawings, from how many users, are to be saved on the hard disk?
- Will custom menus and AutoLISP be used?
- Will users have their own subdirectories?

Points to consider
- Load new software in its own directory.
- Store nonessential files in subdirectories of the parent software directory.
- Use short names or abbreviations for directory names.
- If you have multiple hard drives, leave an empty buffer of at least five megabytes per hard drive for work space.
- If users have their own subdirectory, encourage them to work in it, not in the program directory.

When you answer these questions, and keep these points in mind, you can better estimate what to store on the hard disk and how it should be structured.

Regardless of what you store on the hard disk, have a plan for it. Drawings should not be saved in the ACAD directory. Users should not be allowed to save files in the root directory. Decide on the nature of the hard disk structure and then stick to it. Make sure that all users are informed by documenting and distributing standard procedures to all who use the system. Place copies of procedures at each workstation.

Files to be used in conjunction with AutoCAD should be located in subdirectories of the ACAD directory. Possible subdirectories include drawings, AutoLISP files, drivers, slides, and user directories. Within each of these subdirectories reside the individual files. This is clearly illustrated in Fig. C-4. The subdirectories of \ACAD in Fig. C-4 are some of those that are automatically created when AutoCAD is installed. For example, only drawing files should be in the DRAWINGS subdirectory, and only LISP files should be in the LISP subdirectory.

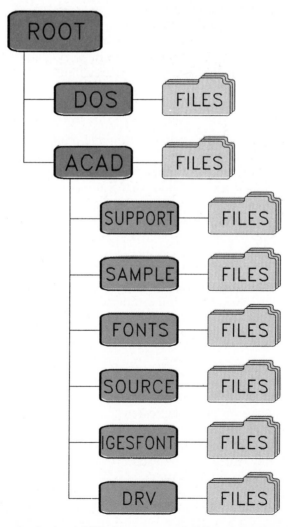

Fig. C-4. Specific subdirectories in the ACAD directory are for files that are used with AutoCAD, and are automatically created when AutoCAD is installed.

Your hard disk planning should take into account future software. New programs should be stored in their own directories on the hard disk, and managed in the same fashion as the AutoCAD files. The structure of a well-planned and closely managed hard disk should appear like that shown in Fig. C-5.

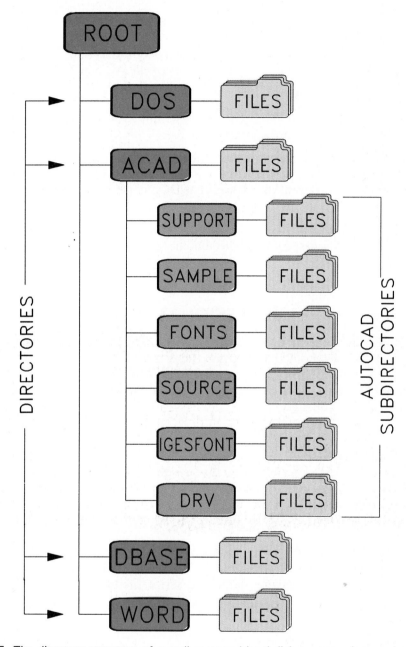

Fig. C-5. The directory structure of a well-managed hard disk appears clean and organized.

USING BATCH FILES FOR AUTOCAD EFFICIENCY

After turning on your system, the computer checks itself, and the COMMAND.COM file (the DOS command interpreter) searches for a file named AUTOEXEC.BAT. If found, this file is executed. The AUTOEXEC.BAT file may simply set the date and time, or establish operating parameters for the entire drawing session. It can also automatically run other batch files.

A batch file (.BAT file extension) is a short DOS program that processes a group of commands. Batch files can be used to display menu selections, perform disk checking functions, and call other programs. Periodic use of special batch files can allow the user to accomplish tasks such as cleaning unwanted files from directories, formatting disks, displaying directory contents, and giving the disk a checkup.

────── PROFESSIONAL TIP ──────

One of your goals should be to work toward automating as many of the routine functions as possible. Use batch files to help achieve this goal in preliminary setup functions.

AUTOEXEC.BAT files

The AUTOEXEC.BAT file is one of several files needed in the root directory. The computer first looks to this file when turned on. List the contents of the AUTOEXEC.BAT file as follows:

    C:\〉 **TYPE AUTOEXEC.BAT** ↵

You may not understand the contents of the file now, but soon you will be writing your own. Several commands you may see in the file are:

- CLS—Clears the screen of everything except the DOS prompt.
- ECHO OFF—Turns off the display of DOS commands when the batch file is run.
- PATH—Indicates the different directories that DOS can search through to find batch files and commands.
- SET—Enables you to set specific values and functions.

These commands are discussed later with batch files. For now, take a look at sample AUTOEXEC.BAT files.

────── PROFESSIONAL TIP ──────

When experimenting with new AUTOEXEC.BAT files, give them names other than AUTOEXEC.BAT. Names should indicate that the files are preliminary. Typical names might be AUTOTEST.BAT, BATTEST1.BAT, or BATTEST2.BAT. When you develop a file to replace the old AUTOEXEC.BAT file, rename the original AUTOEXEC.OLD, and rename the new one AUTOEXEC.BAT.

AutoCAD's default batch file

When you install AutoCAD, you are asked if you want a batch file automatically created that is named ACADR12.BAT. If you are not sure about constructing batch files, and the settings and commands that they should contain, it is a good idea to let AutoCAD create this batch file for you. Later, when you learn more about batch files, you can easily edit the default file, or even create a new one.

The file named ACADR12.BAT provides AutoCAD with locations for support files and its configuration file. Then, it changes to the directory containing AutoCAD, executes the program, and also allows you to enter a drawing name and script file to run.

```
SET ACAD = C:\ACAD\SUPPORT;C:\ACAD\FONTS;C:\ACAD\ADS;C:\ACAD
 \SAMPLE
SET ACADCFG = C:\ACAD
SET ACADDRV = C:\ACAD\DRV
C:\ACAD\ACAD %1 %2
```

The last line loads AutoCAD and allows you to enter a drawing name to begin or edit (%1), and executes a script file that has already been written (%2). The script file can perform any additional operations you desire. The following is an example of a simple setup script file.

SETUP.SCR

VIEW	*(executes the VIEW command)*
R	*(selects the Restore option of VIEW)*
TBLOCK	*(restores the view named TBLOCK)*

In order to run the ACADR12.BAT file to load an existing prototype drawing named PIPEPROT, enter the following at the DOS prompt.

C:\⟩ **ACADR12 PIPEPROT SETUP** ↵

This not only runs the ACADR12 batch file, but loads the PIPEPROT drawing and displays the view of the title block as specified in the file SETUP.SCR.

In the next three sample batch files, notice that the ACADR12.BAT file is called at the end of each file. This is a good example of how one batch file can run another.

Batch file 1

Batch files can be written using the COPY CON command in DOS, EDLIN, or a text editor such as the DOS 5.0 EDIT text editor. A text editor gives you the greatest flexibility in creating and editing batch files. Enter the lines given here exactly as shown, pressing ENTER at the end of each line.

This first batch file allows the user to set the date and time. Then it clears the screen, changes to the ACAD directory, and executes AutoCAD. Give this file the name ACADBAT1.BAT.

```
DATE
TIME
CLS
CD\ACAD
ACADR12
```

Run this program by entering the filename at the DOS prompt:

C:\⟩ **ACADBAT1** ↵

Batch files can be executed by entering the name without the file extension ".BAT."

As the batch file begins, the DATE and TIME prompts appear and ask for the date and time. The commands appear only because the DOS command ECHO is ON. All commands in the batch file are displayed on the screen. You can prevent displaying these commands by inserting ECHO OFF at the start of your batch file. Notice also that the batch file does not begin with a CLS (Clear screen) command. Any text left on the screen from previous computer self-checks, DOS commands, or batch files still shows. Finally, the last line in the ACADBAT1.BAT file runs the ACADR12.BAT file in order to properly load AutoCAD. This file and the ACADR12 file can easily be combined into one file and function exactly the same. When you exit AutoCAD, the DOS prompt does not reflect the current directory. Revise this batch file as shown below to incorporate the items just discussed. Comments are contained inside parentheses; do not type them.

```
ECHO OFF        (turns off the display of DOS commands)
CLS             (clears the screen)
PROMPT $P$G     (sets DOS prompt to reflect current directory)
DATE
TIME
CLS
CD\ACAD
ACADR12
```

Run this file and compare it to the previous version. The DATE and TIME commands do not have to be included in the AUTOEXEC.BAT file if your computer has an internal clock and battery backup.

Batch file 2

This batch file is a bit more specific in its instructions. The function of the file is to set the operating *environment* for AutoCAD, and then execute the program. The environment is modified by the values given in the SET and PATH commands. The PATH provides a route for DOS to use when searching for files. Name this file ACADBAT2.BAT.

```
ECHO OFF
CLS
PROMPT $P$G
PATH = C:\;\DOS;\ACAD
SET ACADALTMENU = C:\CADPIPE\PIPING
SET ACADPAGEDIR = C:\TEMP
ACADR12
CD\
```

This batch file is a little more involved than the previous one. It contains three new lines that should be examined closer.

- PATH = C:\;\DOS\ACAD – The PATH is the route DOS uses to search for programs, commands, and batch files. The path is most often different direcoties, which are separated by a semicolon (;). In this example, DOS first searches through the root directory, then the DOS directory, and finally the ACAD directory.
- SET ACADALTMENU = C:\CADPIPE\PIPING – This environment variable specifies the locatioin of the alternate menu that is used when the CHANGE TEMPLATE command is picked on the tablet menu. See Chapter 33 for a discussion of this process.
- SET ACADPAGEDIR = C:\TEMP – This environment variable provides a location for "pages" of a drawing file that is being worked on. AutoCAD divides drawings into pages and places these pages in memory. If the allotted memory space fills, the "pager" removes the least recently accessed page and places it as a file in the current directory. If the ACADPAGEDIR variable has been set prior to entering AutoCAD, the page file is placed in the location specified by the variable, in this case, the C:\TEMP directory.

PROFESSIONAL TIP

AutoCAD contains several *environment variables* that enable you to fine-tune the operating environment in which AutoCAD is placed. An environment variable generally specifies an exact value for a specific aspect of AutoCAD's operation. Since AutoCAD requires considerable memory and can be tailored to suit any user, it is important that you become familiar with some of the settings that can make the program work efficiently for you. Read the *Interface, Installation and Performance Guide* and the *AutoLISP Programmer's Reference Manual* for specific information on environment variables and memory management. Using some of these variables in your batch files can enhance the operation of the software and hardware.

The previous batch file is typical of AUTOEXEC.BAT files used on AutoCAD systems. You can add a variety of functions to the AUTOEXEC.BAT file, such as displaying a menu or maintaining the hard disk.

MENU SELECTIONS

New computer users should not be required to deal with the step-by-step functions of DOS and AutoCAD. Therefore, the goal of designing menus is to automate tasks as much as possible. The repetitive functions of commands should be transparent, so that the user can spend more productive time working with drawing and design. With batch files, you can automate execution of programs and DOS functions.

A good menu displays a list of program options. This allows the user to enter a number in response to a list of programs. An example of such a menu is shown below.

AutoCAD Training Center
MAIN MENU
1. AutoCAD
2. AutoShade
3. ASG Architectural
4. AutoSketch
5. Dbase
6. Text Editor
7. Utilities Menu
TYPE THE NUMBER OF YOUR CHOICE AND PRESS ENTER

The user merely decides which program to use, types a number, and presses ENTER. The program automatically loads. This removes many possible errors and frustrations from novice users trying to enter the exact directory and file names.

NOTE TO INSTRUCTORS AND TRAINERS

People learning AutoCAD, or any computer program for the first time, should be taught that specific program only. Do not request that they wade through the many details of entering DOS commands. That can come later. Make the entrance into AutoCAD as smooth as possible. Menus help avoid some of those problems.

The menu screen just shown is not a batch file. It is a text file (.TXT) called by the AUTOEXEC.BAT file. The menu, possibly named MENU.TXT, is written with a text editor exactly as you see it. Each of the selections in the menu execute their own batch file. An example of an AUTOEXEC.BAT file that calls the above menu is as follows:

```
ECHO OFF
CLS
PROMPT $P$G
PATH = C:\;\DOS;\BAT;\ACAD;\ASG;\SKETCH;\DBASE;\TE
CD BAT
TYPE MENU.TXT
```

PROFESSIONAL TIP

Create a new directory called BAT if you will be using batch and text files in menus and other applications. This helps keep the root directory clean.

This AUTOEXEC.BAT file is brief because additional values that must be set for individual programs are specified in the batch files for those programs. Notice that the PATH command lists several new directories. Each program should have its own directory. The last line displays the MENU.TXT file using the TYPE command.

The individual selections in the Main Menu must now be established as batch files. Since the user enters a number in response to the menu selections, the names of batch files must correspond to numbers. For example, the batch file to run AutoCAD must be 1.BAT. The batch file that calls the Utilities Menu must be 7.BAT. An example of 1.BAT is shown as follows:

```
ECHO OFF
CLS
SET ACAD = C:\ACAD\SUPPORT;C:\ACAD\FONTS;C:\ACAD\ADS;C:\ACAD\SAMPLE
SET ACADCFG = C:\ACAD
SET ACADDRV = C:\ACAD\DRV
SET ACADPAGEDIR = C:\TEMP
CD \ACAD\ACAD %1 %2
CLS
CD\BAT
TYPE MENU.TXT
```

This batch file does not have to set the PATH because that was taken care of by the AUTOEXEC.BAT file. Notice also that when the user exits AutoCAD, the current directory is changed to BAT, and the Main Menu is redisplayed.

The Utilities Menu can contain disk functions that enable you to perform hard disk organizing, floppy disk formatting, and other tasks. The batch file 7.BAT calls the Utilities Menu and should appear like this:

```
ECHO OFF
CLS
TYPE UTIL.TXT
```

This short batch file displays the Utilities Menu, which is also a .TXT file, the same as MENU.TXT. The UTIL.TXT file looks like this:

AutoCAD Training Center
UTILITIES MENU

```
M.  Return to Main Menu
F.  Format a diskette in drive A:
O.  Organize the hard disk
S.  Shut the system down
    TYPE THE LETTER OF YOUR CHOICE AND PRESS ENTER
```

The functions shown above are just a few possibilities that you might choose. Letters are used instead of numbers because batch files in the Main Menu use numbers. Keep in mind that menus should not contain an overwhelming number of selections.

The individual batch files that perform the functions listed in the menu above are given as follows:

F. Format a diskette in drive A:

It is wise to have this command in a menu, especially in a training environment. (The mere sound of the word FORMAT sends shivers down the spine of instructors and managers. Many users have accidentally erased the hard disk with FORMAT.) When this menu selection is made, the user can format a disk *only* in drive A:. This file can be made safer by renaming the FORMAT.COM command and using the new name in the batch file. The batch file is named F.BAT to correspond to the menu selection.

```
ECHO OFF
CLS
FORMAT A:/F:360/V
CLS
TYPE UTIL.TXT
```

Quick and easy. The user never sees the commands. After entering "F," and pressing ENTER, insert a diskette in drive A: when the computer prompts, and press ENTER. The formatting is performed by line 3 in the batch file. Look at the line closely. The FORMAT command is applied to drive A: only. The /F:360 indicates that the disk is to be formatted as a 360K disk. The "/V" allows the user to assign the disk a volume name. To format a 1.2MB disk, use FORMAT A:/V.

C. Organize the hard disk

Through normal use of a computer, the hard disk drive begins to fragment files because it does not put data back where it found them. Over several weeks, accessing data on the hard disk slows down as the drive must search far and wide to find all parts of a single file. This can be remedied by any number of commercially available disk organizing programs. Computers that are used every day should have their hard disks organized at least once a month, and preferably once a week. One such program, VOPT, is called by the following batch file, named O.BAT.

```
ECHO OFF
CLS
CD\VOPT
VOPT
CD\BAT
TYPE UTIL.TXT
```

Notice again that programs have their own directories on the hard disk. Therefore, the CD \VOPT command must be given to access the VOPT program. The last line displays the Utilities Menu again.

S. Shut the system down

The DOS command RETRACT moves the read/write heads away from the hard disk platters. This is a preventative measure in case the computer is bumped or jarred. If the read/write heads were not retracted, they could crash into the disk surface and damage the data and possibly the disk itself. Newer computers perform this function automatically when the power is turned off.

An additional part of this batch file includes the DOS command CHKDSK, used to check a disk for lost clusters and bad spots. The lost clusters, which are data somehow separated from a file, can be reclaimed using the "/F" parameter after the CHKDSK command. Lost clusters are converted to files with a .CHK extension if the user answers YES to the CHKDSK prompt. The files should be deleted. This is handled by line 4 of the S.BAT file shown below.

```
ECHO OFF
CLS
CHKDSK C:/F
DEL *.CHK
RETRACT
```

ENSURING EFFICIENT OPERATION

AutoCAD and DOS require a certain amount of reserve memory for efficient operation. AutoCAD opens several files at once, and DOS needs space for input/output operation. To have adequate memory, these parameters must be entered in the CONFIG.SYS file, which the computer looks for when turned on.

The CONFIG.SYS file is a text file that should reside in the root directory. When the computer is booted, DOS reads the CONFIG.SYS file, reserves the amount of memory specified, then runs the AUTOEXEC.BAT file. The contents of the CONFIG.SYS file, normally just two lines of text, can be written using COPY CON, EDLIN, or your text editor. A sample CONFIG.SYS file is as follows:

```
BUFFERS=20
FILES=40
```

The "BUFFERS=20" line states that 20 input/output buffers are reserved for DOS. Each buffer is approximately 520 bytes, or about one-half K of memory. If the CONFIG.SYS file does not exist, DOS sets the default number of two buffers. The more buffers available, the more efficiently the computer and your programs can run because disk access is reduced. Too many buffers can increase the time DOS spends searching the buffers for data. A value between 10 and 20 is recommended. DOS allows up to 99 buffers. AutoCAD 386 contains a DOS extender to handle memory, so the setting for buffers is not important for its operation.

The "FILES = 40" line sets the number of open files allowed. AutoCAD opens several files during operation. These include overlays, text fonts, slides, and AutoLISP programs. If too few files are specified by CONFIG.SYS, AutoCAD must temporarily close some open files in order to open others. This can detract from performance of the software. The default value for open files is eight, but should be set to at least 40 for AutoCAD to run efficiently.

SETTING A HEALTHY ENVIRONMENT

Several commands found in the AUTOEXEC.BAT file form what is called the *environment*. The environment is a source of information that programs refer to for specific instructions. The DOS commands that comprise the environment are PATH and SET. The form of these commands is an equation, such as:

    PATH = C:\;\DOS;\ACAD

This instruction occupies "environment space." If you include too many environment instructions in your AUTOEXEC.BAT and CONFIG.SYS files, the error message "Out of environment space" may appear. This can be remedied by including the following command in the CONFIG.SYS file:

    SHELL = COMMAND.COM /P /E:256

This entry uses the DOS SHELL command, and instructs the COMMAND.COM program to operate as it normally does (/P), but increase the environment space to 256 bytes of memory (/E:256). See your DOS manual for further discussion of the SHELL command. The CONFIG.SYS file should now appear like this:

    BUFFERS = 20
    FILES = 20
    SHELL = COMMAND.COM /P /E:256

ESTABLISHING MULTIPLE CONFIGURATIONS

When configured, AutoCAD is set up to operate with certain pieces of equipment, using a specific tablet menu and screen menu. These parameters are all stored in the ACAD.CFG file. Some schools and companies may need to change from a digitizer to a mouse, or switch tablet menus for certain applications. It is time consuming and frustrating to reconfigure AutoCAD each time hardware or menus are switched. This can be avoided by having multiple configurations.

Assessing the need
How do you know if you need multiple configurations? If you answer YES to any of the following questions, multiple configurations will help:
- Do you occasionally switch between different pieces of computer hardware?
- Do you use a mouse for certain applications and a digitizer tablet for others?
- Do you use more than one tablet menu?

Creating batch files for multiple configurations
Multiple configurations can be established through the use of batch files. Two methods can be used to execute the batch files.
1. At the DOS prompt, the user enters the name of a batch file and directory. The configuration specified in that batch file is loaded by AutoCAD. The current directory is set to the one entered after the batch file name. When the SAVE command is entered, the drawing is automatically placed in the current directory.
2. The user chooses a menu selection that executes a batch file. The batch file sets a current directory, searches for a specific configuration, and loads it with AutoCAD.

Method one

With the first method, the user enters the batch file name followed by the name of the directory that contains the desired configuration. The DOS variable "%1" allows you to provide for user input. This variable is used in the following batch file named STRUCT-1.BAT to specify a directory:

```
ECHO OFF
CLS
CD\%1
SET ACAD=C:\ACAD;C:\ACAD\SUPPORT;C:\ACAD\FONTS;C:\ACAD\ADS;C:
 \ACAD\SAMPLE
SET ACADCFG=C:\STRUCT
SET ACADDRV=C:\ACAD\DRV
SET ACADPAGEDIR=C:\TEMP
ACAD
CD\
```

Look closely at the following three lines in this batch file.
- CD\%1 — Changes the current directory to one specified by the user. The "%1" variable is assigned to the first group of characters entered after the batch file name. For example, this batch file is executed by entering STRUCT-1 at the DOS prompt. If a directory name is given after the batch file name, DOS uses the directory name as the "%1" variable. Then DOS sets the current directory to the one entered by the user.

  C:\〉 **STRUCT-1 PROJ-005** ↵

  This sets the current directory to PROJ-005.
- SET ACAD=C:\ACAD;C:\ACAD\SUPPORT;C:\ACAD\FONTS;\C:\ACAD\ADS;C: \ACAD\SAMPLE — This tells AutoCAD to look in the four specified directories for AutoCAD and related files such as hatch patterns, .PGP files, shape files for text fonts, LISP routines, and prototype drawings.
- SET ACADCFG=C:\STRUCT — This instructs AutoCAD to look in the STRUCT directory to find the configuration file, ACAD.CFG. This line is important because it allows you to use alternate configurations.

  The batch file shown above, STRUCT-1.BAT, should be duplicated if additional configurations are required. Be sure to create separate directories for each project, or configuration. Specify each configuration location with the "SET ACADCFG=" statement.

NOTE

The first time you run a batch file that specifies a new directory containing an alternate configuration, AutoCAD requires that you go through the configuration routine. After that, AutoCAD loads each time using the configuration found in the directory specified in the batch file.

Method two

Menus allow users to select exactly what they want to do, without entering DOS commands or specifying directories. It is an efficient method, and maintains consistency in the office or classroom while at the same time eliminating time-wasting errors. The menu system is appropriate where several classes or projects require different configurations. The configurations may be alternative default drawings or prototype drawings. Each prototype drawing might contain a different menu. Thus, with one pick, the user can access a specific project directory and use a prototype drawing that contains the proper menu. One such menu is shown below.

AutoCAD Training Center
PROJECTS MENU

1. AutoCAD Standard Menu
2. Mechanical
3. Structural
4. Piping
5. Electrical
6. Return to MAIN MENU
TYPE THE NUMBER OF YOUR CHOICE AND PRESS ENTER

This menu could be used with the Main Menu discussed earlier in this Appendix. The batch file for the selection 1 in the Main Menu, AutoCAD should look like this:

```
ECHO OFF
CLS
TYPE PROJ.TXT
```

The PROJ.TXT file would be a text file that looks exactly like the Projects menu.

PROFESSIONAL TIP

When using more than one menu, you cannot use the same numbers for menu selections if the batch files reside in the same directory. If numbers are used in the Main Menu, continue with higher numbers in the Projects Menu, or use letters instead. A second solution is to create a new directory for batch and text files relating to the Projects Menu. Then, the numbers for the menu items can duplicate those in the Main Menu. For example, the batch file for the selection 1, AutoCAD, in the Main Menu might read:

```
ECHO OFF
CLS
CD\BAT2
TYPE PROJ.TXT
```

In this case, the directory must be changed to BAT2 where the files for the Project Menu are stored.

With method two, batch files in the Project Menu are the same as those in method one except for the directory names. The batch file must specify the name of the current directory. An example of the batch file for the selection 4, Piping, is given. It must be understood that each of the projects has its own directory on the hard disk.

```
ECHO OFF
CLS
CD\PIPE\DWG
SET ACAD=C:\ACAD;C:\ACAD\SUPPORT;C:\ACAD\FONTS;C:\ACAD\ADS;C:
  \ACAD\SAMPLE
SET ACADCFG=C:\PIPE
SET ACADPAGEDIR=C:\TEMP
ACAD
CD\BAT
TYPE MENU.TXT
```

With this batch file, the user does not need to specify a path when saving an AutoCAD drawing. The drawing is saved in the current directory specified in the batch file.

USEFUL BATCH FILES

With a little time and experimenting, you will find that batch files have a variety of applications. These functions can be executed by entering the name of the batch file or by accessing batch files from a menu. Set aside a few minutes each day to develop useful batch files for your applications. The reward is a smooth-functioning system that removes the routine nature of many tasks.

The following examples will help you get started. Enter them exactly as given with your text editor. Remember, batch files are executed by entering the name of the file at the DOS prompt. Adding the .BAT extension is not required to run the file.

Looking through several directories

This file is useful in training situations when the instructor or trainer needs to check whether students have saved their required exercises, problems, or drawings. The batch file searches the selected directories and lists files. You can specify certain file types, or display the entire contents of a directory. Any number of directories can be included in this file. The batch file name might be LOOK.BAT. Alternative B allows you to enter specific directory names after typing LOOK.BAT.

```
A.  ECHO OFF              B.  ECHO OFF
    CLS                       CLS
    CD \DIR-1                 CD \%1
    DIR *.DWG/P               DIR *.DWG/P
    PAUSE                     PAUSE
    CD \DIR-2                 CD \%2
    DIR*.DWG/P                DIR *.DWG/P
    PAUSE                     PAUSE
    CD \                      CD \
```

Delete backup files from a drawing directory

As drawings are edited and resaved, a collection of .BAK files begins to accumulate. If you regularly backup the drawing files on separate disks, these files are not needed. To reclaim valuable space on the hard disk, use this batch file, possibly named DELBAK.BAT.

```
ECHO OFF
CLS
CD\PROJ-002
DEL *.BAK
CD\
```

Delete drawings that do not belong

Try to keep the ACAD directory free of nonessential files. Create subdirectories for .DWG, .LSP, and .SLD files. Yet nonessential files have a way of creeping into the most guarded directories, especially in an instructional environment. A handy batch file is one that can delete those wayward files and leave the essential ones intact. The following batch file deletes all .DWG files in the \ACAD directory. (Make sure needed drawings are stored in their directory.) The file name might be ACADPURG.BAT or DELDWG.BAT.

```
ECHO OFF
CLS
CD \ACAD
DEL *.DWG
DIR/P
PAUSE
CD\
```

MANAGING THE AUTOCAD SYSTEM

One of your goals as an AutoCAD user should be to keep the computer system as efficient as possible. This means being organized and knowledgeable of school or company standards. Also know who has the authority to manage the system, and follow the system manager's guidelines.

If you are the system manager, develop standards and procedures, relay these to system users, and distribute up-to-date documentation, symbol libraries, menus, and standards. Revise standards as needed and distribute these to all users. In addition, handle software updates in a consistent and timely manner and make the maintenance of hardware a priority.

The system manager

One or two people, depending on the size of the department or company, should be assigned as system manager. The manager has control over all functions of the computer system, preventing inconsistencies in procedure, drawing format, and file storage caused by lack of organization and structure. The manager is responsible for the following:

- Scheduling computer use.
- Structure of the hard disk directories.
- Appearance and function of start-up menus.
- Drawing naming techniques.
- File storage procedures.
- File backup procedures.
- Drawing file access.
- Creation of symbol libraries.
- Development of written standards.
- Distribution of standards to users.
- Upgrading software and hardware.
- Hardware hygiene and maintenance.

When tasks are delegated, such as the creation of symbol library shapes, be sure to include accurate sketches or drawings. Check and approve final drawings before distributing them to users.

Developing operating standards and procedures

The crux of system management is that everyone performs their job using the same procedures, symbols, and drawing techniques. When this happens, the details of drawing and designing are transparent because they are established routines. A department that operates smoothly is probably using standards such as the following:

- File naming conventions.
- Methods of file storage: location and name.
- Drawing sheet sizes and title blocks to be used.
- Prototype drawings.
- Creation of blocks and symbols.
- Dimensioning techniques.
- Use of dimensioning variables.
- Use of layers and colors.
- Text styles.
- Line types.
- Color schemes for plotting.
- Creation of screen and tablet menus.
- File backup methods and times.

Take the time initially to study the needs of your school or company. Meet with other department managers and users to determine the nature of their drawings. Always gain input from people who use the system and avoid making blanket decisions on your own. When needs have been established, develop a plan for implementing the required standards and procedures. Assign specific tasks to students or employees. Assemble the materials as they are completed and distribute the documentation and procedures to all users.

When developing procedures, begin with start-up procedures and work through the drawing process. Develop prototype drawings for specific types of projects first. The final aspects of system development should be screen and tablet menus and AutoLISP programs.

File maintenance

The integrity of files must be protected by all who work with the system. Procedures for file maintenance must be documented. Files of every type, including .DWG, .SLD, .BAT, .LSP, .MNU, and .BAK must have a secure storage area. This can be hard disk directories, floppy disks or magnetic tape storage areas, kept clean of nonessential files. File maintenance procedures should include the following:

• Location of essential AutoCAD files.
• Location of backup AutoCAD files.
• Print the contents of all hard disk directories for each workstation.
• Location and contents of all prototype drawings, supplemented with printed listings.
• Location and contents of all batch files and associated menus.
• Location of all user files including drawings, slides, and text files.
• Proper creation of drawings using prototypes, layers, dimensioning techniques, linetypes, text styles, and symbols.
• Storage and backup methods for drawing files.
• Storage of printed or plotted copies of all drawing files.

Symbol libraries and menus

The development of symbol libraries and menus is a primary concern of managing an AutoCAD system. Symbols must be consistent and up-to-date. Menus must also be consistent throughout the department or company. A vital aspect of maintaining standards and consistency is a facility for updating symbol libraries and menus. This task should be given to certain students or employees and the results distributed to all users. Maintaining symbol libraries and menus includes the following:

• Standards for drawing symbols.
• System for naming symbols (blocks).
• System for block storage.
• Post a printed or plotted copy of all symbol libraries, their names and locations.
• Creation and maintenance of custom screen and tablet menus.
• Use of custom menus by specific departments.
• Revisions to custom menus.
• Upgrading of menus on all hard disks.

Maintaining the software

Software upgrades and releases are issued regularly. If you purchase upgrades, converting to the new version should be smooth and have little, if any, affect on production. Establish a procedure for upgrading all computers in the classroom or office. Inform all users of changes by providing a printed listing of new features. Offer training sessions on the new release if necessary. Make backup copies of the new software and store the originals in a safe place.

Maintain the management system

All systems require continuous maintenance to function efficiently. Enable users to contribute to the function of the system. Foster creativity by inviting suggestions from users. Meet with users and managers on a regular basis to learn what is functioning well and what is not. Remember, the system will function efficiently if a majority of those using it enjoy working with the system, and are encouraged to contribute to its growth and development.

System management references

A variety of books are available that discuss system management. One of these books, *Architectural AutoCAD* by David A. Madsen and E. Henry Fitzgibbon, discuss system management in an architectural environment. Even though architecture is the focus of this book, many of the concepts can be applied to other disciplines.

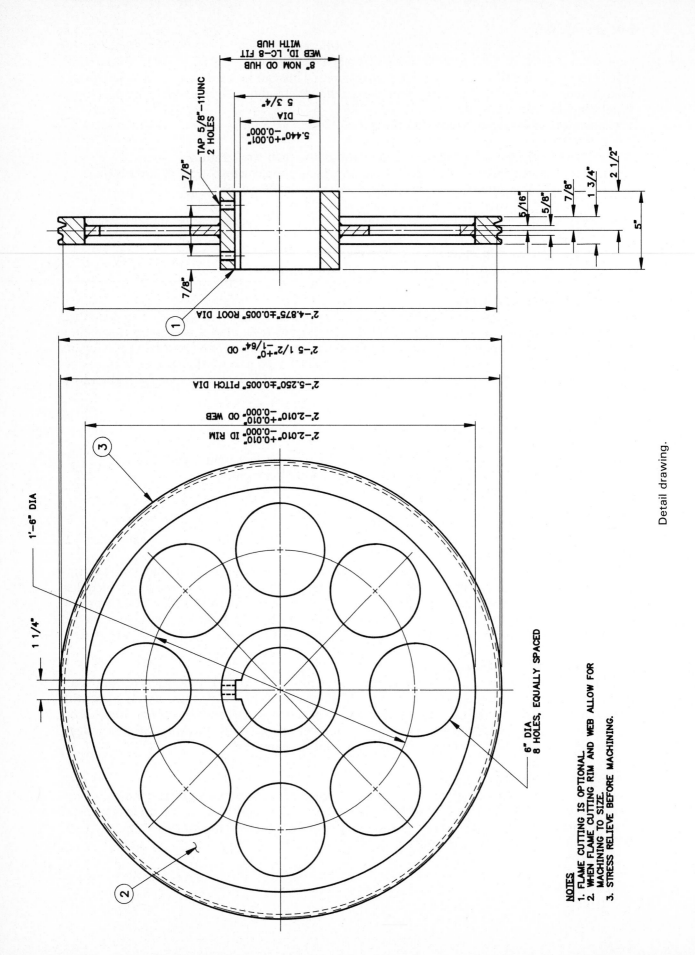

Detail drawing.

Appendix D

AUTOCAD MENU TREE

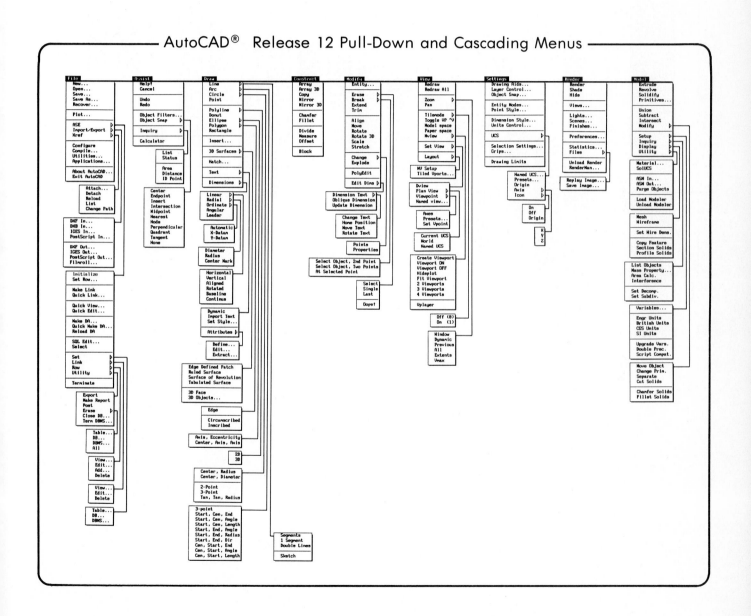

AutoCAD® Release 12 Pull-Down and Cascading Menus

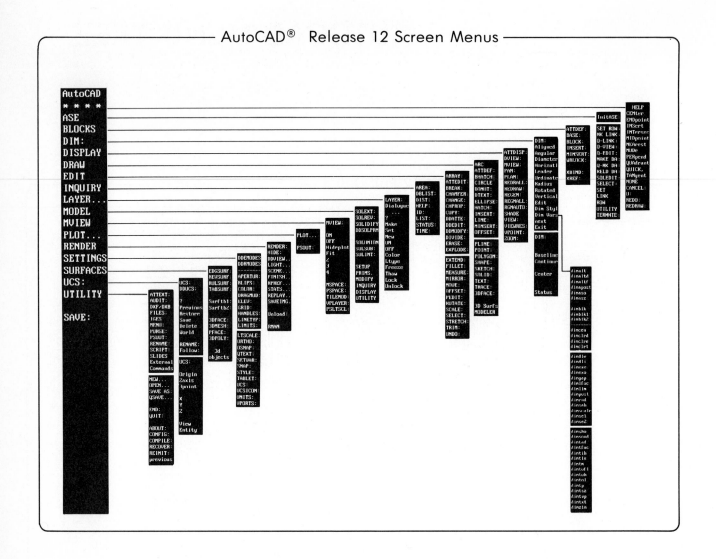

AutoCAD® Release 12 Screen Menus

AUTOCAD PROTOTYPE DRAWING DEFAULTS, PROTOTYPE DRAWING SHEET SIZE AND SCALE PARAMETERS

VALUE	DEFAULT SETTING
Attributes	Visiblity controlled individually, entry of values during DDINSERT or INSERT permitted (using prompts rather than a dialogue box)
BASE	Insertion base point (0.0,0.0,0.0)
BLIPMODE	On
CHAMFER	Distance 0.0
COLOR	Current entity color BYLAYER
DIM variables	

DIMALT	Off	DIMDLI	0.3800	DIMSTYLE	*UNNAMED
DIMALTD	2	DIMEXE	0.1800	DIMTAD	Off
DIMALTF	25.4	DIMEXO	0.0625	DIMTFAC	1.0000
DIMAPOST	None	DIMGAP	0.0900	DIMTIH	On
DIMASO	On	DIMLFAC	1.0000	DIMTIX	Off
DIMASZ	0.18	DIMLIM	Off	DIMTM	0.0000
DIMBLK	None	DIMPOST	None	DIMTOFL	Off
DIMBLK1	None	DIMRND	0.0000	DIMTOH	On
DIMBLK2	None	DIMSAH	Off	DIMTOL	Off
DIMCEN	0.0900	DIMSCALE	1.0000	DIMTP	0.0000
DIMCLRD	BYBLOCK	DIMSE1	Off	DIMTSZ	0.0000
DIMCLRE	BYBLOCK	DIMSE2	Off	DIMTVP	0.0000
DIMCLRT	BYBLOCK	DIMSHO	On	DIMTXT	0.1800
DIMDLE	0.0000	DIMSOXD	Off	DIMZIN	0

DRAGMODE	Auto
ELEVATION	Elevation 0.0, thickness 0.0
FILL	On
FILLET	Radius 0.0
GRID	Off, spacing (0.0, 0.0)
HANDLES	Off
Highlighting	Enabled
ISOPLANE	Left

LAYER	Current/only layer is 0, On, with color 7 (white) and linetype CONTINUOUS
LIMITS	Off, drawing limits (0.0, 0.0) to (12.0, 9.0)
LINETYPE	Current entity linetype BYLAYER, no loaded linetypes other than CONTINUOUS
LTSCALE	1.0
MENU	*acad*
MIRROR	Text mirrored same as other entities
ORTHO	Off
OSNAP	None
PLINE	Line-width 0.0
POINT	Display mode 0, size 0.00
QTEXT	Off
REGENAUTO	On
SKETCH	Record increment 0.10, producing lines
SHADE	Rendering type 3, percent diffuse reflection 70
SNAP	Off, spacing (1.0, 1.0)
SNAP/GRID	Standard style, base point (0.0, 0.0), rotation 0.0 degrees
Space	Model
Spline curves	Frame off, segments 8, spline type = cubic
STYLE	Only defined text style is STANDARD, using font txt with variable height, width factor 1.0, horizontal orientation, and no special modes
Surfaces	6 tabulations in M and N directions, 6 segments for smoothing in U and V directions, smooth surface type = cubic B-spline
TABLET	Off
TEXT	Style STANDARD, height 0.20, rotation 0.0 degrees
TILEMODE	On
TIME	User elapsed timer on
TRACE	Width 0.05
UCS	Current UCS same as World, origin at World (0,0,0), auto plan view off, coordinate system icon on (at origin)
UNITS (linear)	Decimal, 4 decimal places
UNITS (angular)	Decimal degrees, 0 decimal places, angle 0 direction is to the right, angles increase counterclockwise
Viewing modes	One active viewport, plan view, perspective off, target point (0,0,0), front and back clipping off, lens length 50 mm, twist angle 0.0, fast zoom on, circle zoom percent 100, WORLDVIEW 0. The default for WORLDVIEW is 1.
ZOOM	To drawing limits

In addition to the previous prototype drawing settings, the following settings are stored as part of the AutoCAD configuration. AutoCAD retains the last value set for future drawing sessions.

AUDITCTL	Creation of the audit report file (file type *.adt)* disabled
Dragging control	DRAGP1 10, DRAGP2 25
Entity selection	PICKADD 1, PICKBOX 3 pixels, PICKFIRST 1
Grips	On, one grip for Blocks, height 3 pixels, color blue, selected color red
MENUCTL	Enables page switching on the screen menu
Object Selection	Pick box size 3 pixels, PICKAUTO 1, PICKDRAG 0
Object snap	Aperture size 10 pixels
PLOT	CMDDIA on (1)
dialogue boxes	
PostScript	PSQUALITY 75 pixels, no name assigned to the prologue section of *acad.psf*
SAVEFILE	As configured
SAVETIME	Automatic save every 2 hours (120 minutes)
SORTENTS	Entity sort operations disabled except for plotting and PostScript output
Sorting	On, 200 symbols maximum
Standard file	FILEDIA on (1)
dialogue boxes	
TREEDEPTH	Database spatial index setting 3020
XREFCTL	No external reference log files (file type *.log)* written

PROTOTYPE DRAWING SHEET SIZE PARAMETERS

DRAWING SCALE	"D" SIZE (34"x22") DRAWING LIMITS	"C" SIZE (22"x17") DRAWING LIMITS	"B" SIZE (17"x11") DRAWING LIMITS
1"=1"	34,22	22,17	17,11
1/2"=1"	68,44	44,34	34,22
1/4"=1"	136,88	88,68	68,44
1/8"=1"	272,176	176,136	136,88
1"=1'-0"	408,264	264,204	204,132
3/4"=1'-0"	544,352	352,272	272,176
1/2"=1'-0"	816,528	528,408	408,264
3/8"=1'-0"	1088,704	704,544	544,352
1/4"=1'-0"	1632,1056	1056,816	816,528
3/16"=1'-0"	2176,1408	1408,1088	1088,704
1/8"=1'-0"	3264,2112	2112,1632	1632,1056
3/32"=1'-0"	4352,2816	2816,2176	2176,1408
1/16"=1'-0"	6528,4224	4224,3264	3264,2112

PROTOTYPE DRAWING SCALE PARAMETERS

DRAWING SCALE	DIMENSION SCALE (DIMSCALE)	LINETYPE SCALE (LTSCALE)	INSERTION SCALE OF BORDER & PARTS LIST BLOCKS
1"=1"	1	.5	1=1
1/2"=1"	2	1	1=2
1/4"=1"	4	2	1=4
1/8"=1"	8	4	1=8
1"=1'-0"	12	6	1=12
3/4"=1'-0"	16	8	1=16
1/2"=1'-0"	24	12	1=24
3/8"=1'-0"	32	16	1=32
1/4"=1'-0"	48	24	1=48
3/16"=1'-0"	64	32	1=64
1/8"=1'-0"	96	48	1=96
3/32"=1'-0"	128	64	1=128
1/16"=1'-0"	192	96	1=192

Courtesy of Leonard Billings

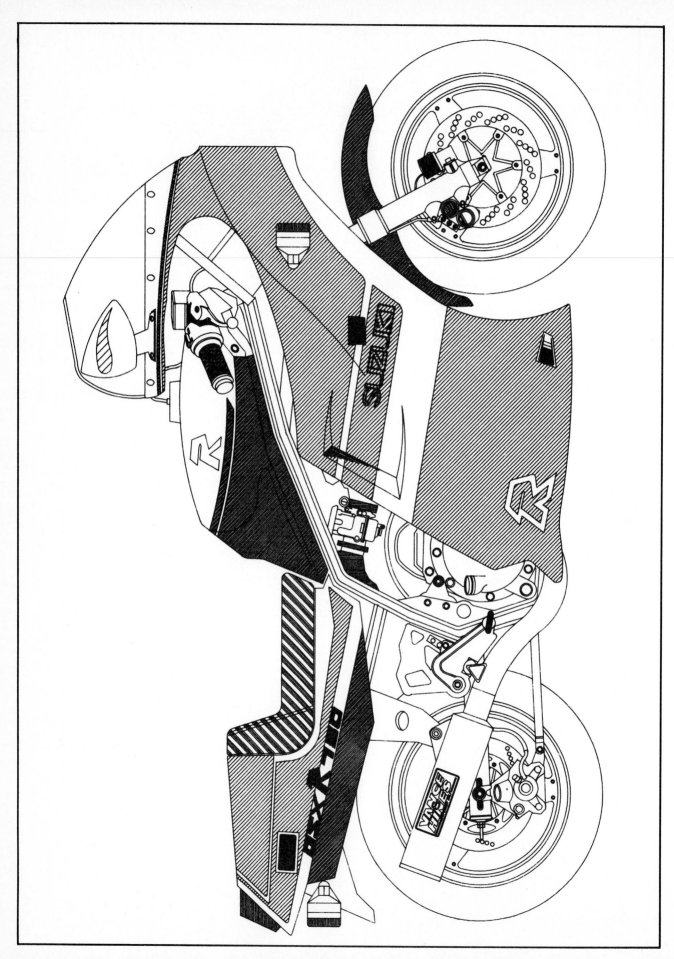

Presentation drawing. (Autodesk, Inc.)

SAMPLE TABLET
MENUS

The tablet menu templates illustrated here show how the AutoCAD menu template can be altered to suit the needs of a company or individual. The menu shown in Fig. F-1 is used for

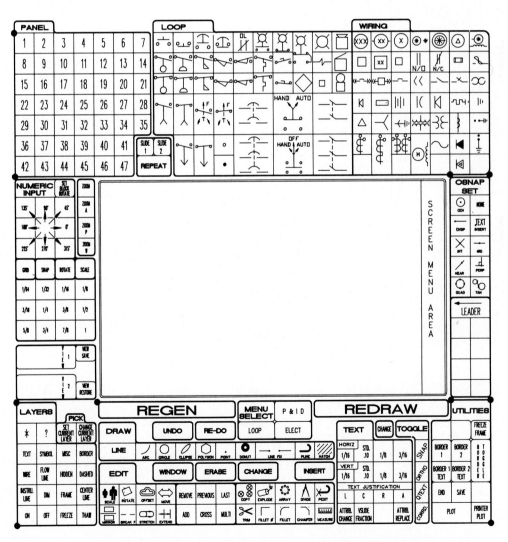

Fig. F-1. Tablet menu for electrical loop and wiring diagrams.
(Fitzgerald, Hagan & Hackathorn, Inc., Norwest Engineering)

creating electrical loop and wiring diagrams. Look closely at some of the special commands. Also note that different menus can be called from this template.

The tablet menu template shown in Fig. F-2 was developed specifically for isometric piping drawings. All symbols are displayed in an orderly manner at the top of the menu. Note the section at the left of the screen area for isometric text.

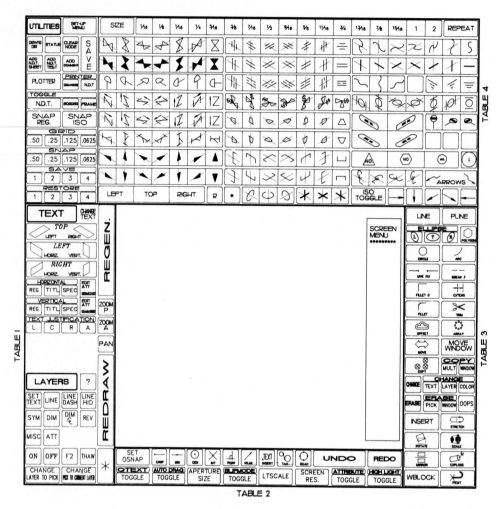

Fig. F-2. Tablet menu template for isometric piping symbols.
(Fitzgerald, Hagan & Hackathorn, Inc., Norwest Engineering)

The tablet menu template shown in Fig. F-3 was created for instrumentation loop diagrams. This menu does not have the detail as those shown earlier, but still reflects the needs of the individual using it. Notice the conversion chart on the right side of the template. Also note the cursor button references inside the screen area.

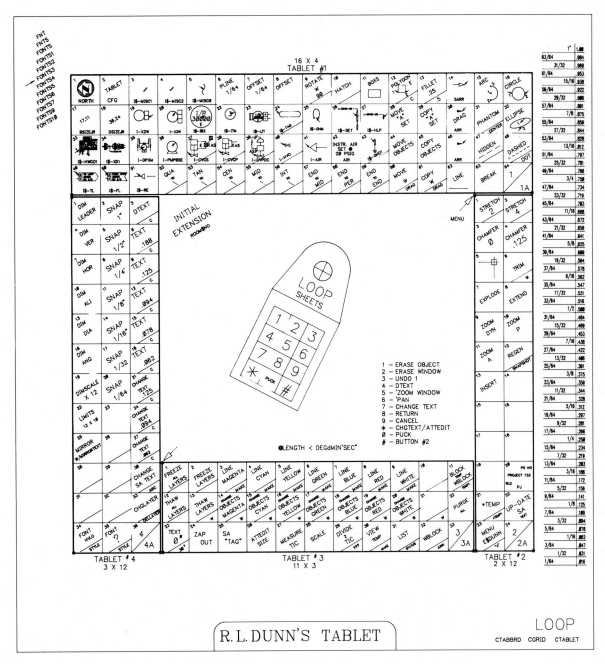

Fig. F-3. Tablet menu template for instrumentation loop diagrams.
(Courtesy R.L. Dunn, Harris Group, Inc.)

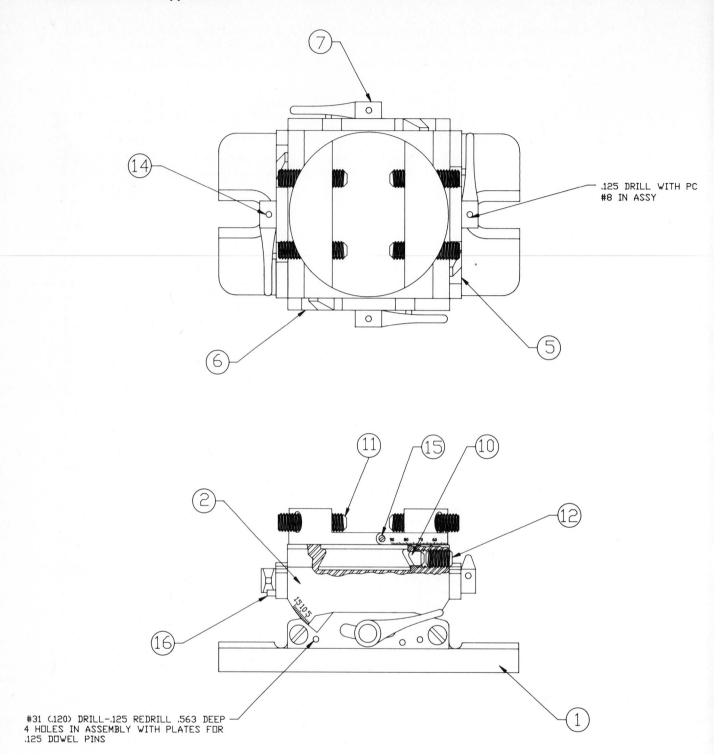

Assembly drawing. (David Torvend)

.125 DRILL WITH PC
#8 IN ASSY

#31 (.120) DRILL-.125 REDRILL .563 DEEP
4 HOLES IN ASSEMBLY WITH PLATES FOR
.125 DOWEL PINS

Appendix G

ANSI STANDARDS DOCUMENTS

CHARTS AND GRAPHS (Y15)

ANSI Y15.1M-1979, Illustrations for Publication and Projection
ANSI Y15.2M-1979, Time Series Charts
ANSI Y15.3M-1979, Process Charts

DRAFTING MANUAL (Y14)

ANSI Y14.1-1980, Drawing Sheet Size and Format
ANSI Y14.2M-1979, Line Conventions and Lettering
ANSI Y14.3-1975 (R1980), Multi and Sectional View Drawings
ANSI Y14.4-1957, Pictorial Drawings
ANSI Y14.5-1982, Dimensioning and Tolerancing
ANSI Y14.6-1978, Screw Thread Representation
ANSI Y14.6aM-1981, Screw Thread Representation (Metric Supplement to Y14.6-1978)
ANSI Y14.7.1-1971, Gear Drawing Standards—Part 1—for Spur, Helical, Double Helical, and Rack (Partial Revision of Y14.7-1958)
ANSI Y14.7.2-1978, Gear and Spline Drawing Standards—Part 1—Bevel and Hypoid Gears (Partial Revision of Y14.7-1958)
ANSI Y14.9-1958, Forgings
ANSI Y14.13M-1981, Mechanical Spring Representation
ANSI Y14.15-1966 (R1973), Electrical and Electronics Diagrams, Including Supplements Y14.15a-1971 and Y14.15b-1973
ANSI Y14.17-1966 (R1974), Fluid Power Diagrams
ANSI Y14.26M-1981, Digital Representation for Communication of Product Definition Data
ANSI Y14.26.3-1975, Dictionary of Terms for Computer-Aided Preparation of Product Definition Data (Including Engineering Drawings)
ANSI Y14.32.1-1974, Chassis Frames—Passenger Car and Light Truck—Ground Vehicle practices
ANSI Y14.34M-1982, Parts Lists, Data Lists, and Index Lists
ANSI Y14.36-1978, Surface Texture Symbols
ANSI Y14 Report No. 1, Digital Representation of Physical Object Shapes
ANSI Y14 Report No. 2, Guidelines for Documenting of Computer Systems Used in Computer-Aided Preparation of Product Definition Data—User Instructions
ANSI Y14 Report No. 3, Guidelines for Documenting of Computer Systems Used in Computer-Aided Preparation of Product Definition Data—Design Requirements

GRAPHIC SYMBOLS (Y32)

ANSI Y32.4-1977, Plumbing Fixture Diagrams Used in Architectural and Building Construction
ANSI Y32.7-1972 (R1979), Railroad Maps and Profiles
ANSI Y32.9-1972, Electrical Wiring and Layout Diagrams Used in Architecture and Building
ANSI Y32.10-1967 (R1979), Fluid Power Diagrams
ANSI Y32.11-1961, Process Flow Diagrams in the Petroleum and Chemical Industries
ANSI Y32.18-1972 (R1978), Mechanical and Acoustical Elements as Used in Schematic Diagrams
ANSI Z32.2.3-1949 (R1953), Pipe Fittings, Valves, and Piping
ANSI Z32.2.4-1949 (R1953), Heating, Ventilating, and Air Conditioning
ANSI Z32.2.6-1950 (R1953), Heat/Power Apparatus
ANSI/AWA A2.4-79, Welding and Nondestructive Testing, Including Brazing
ANSI/IEEE 91-1982, Logic Diagrams (Two-State Devices)
ANSI/IEEE 200-1975, Reference Designations for Electrical and Electronics Parts and Equipments
ANSI/IEEE 315-1975, Electrical and Electronics Diagrams (Including Reference Designation Class Designation Letters)
ANSI/IEEE 623-1976, Grid and Mapping Used in Cable Television Systems
ANSI/ISA S5.1-1973 (R1981), Instrumentation Symbols and Identification
ANSI/NFPA 172-1980, Fire-Protection Symbols for Architectural and Engineering Drawings
ANSI/NFPA 174-1980, Fire-Protection Symbols for Risk Analysis Diagrams
ANSI/NFPA 178-1980, Fire Fighting Operations

LETTER SYMBOLS (Y10)

ANSI Y1.1-1972, Abbreviations for Use on Drawings and in Text
ANSI Y10.1-1972, Glossary of Terms Concerning Letter Symbols
ANSI Y10.2-1958 Hydraulics
ANSI Y10.3-1968, Quantities Used in Mechanics of Solids
ANSI Y10.4-1982, Heat and Thermodynamics
ANSI Y10.5-1968, Quantities Used in Electrical Science and Electrical Engineering
ANSI Y10.7-1954, Aeronautical Sciences
ANSI Y10.8-1962, Structural Analysis
ANSI Y10.10-1953, Meteorology
ANSI Y10.11-1953, Acoustics
ANSI Y10.12-1955, Chemical Engineering
ANSI Y10.14-1959, Rocket Propulsion
ANSI Y10.15-1958, Petroleum Reservoir Engineering
ANSI Y10.16-1964, Shell Theory
ANSI Y10.17-1961, Greek Symbols for Math
ANSI Y10.18-1967, Illuminating Engineering
ANSI Y10.20-1975, Technology Math Signs
ANSI/IEEE 260-1978, Units of Measurement

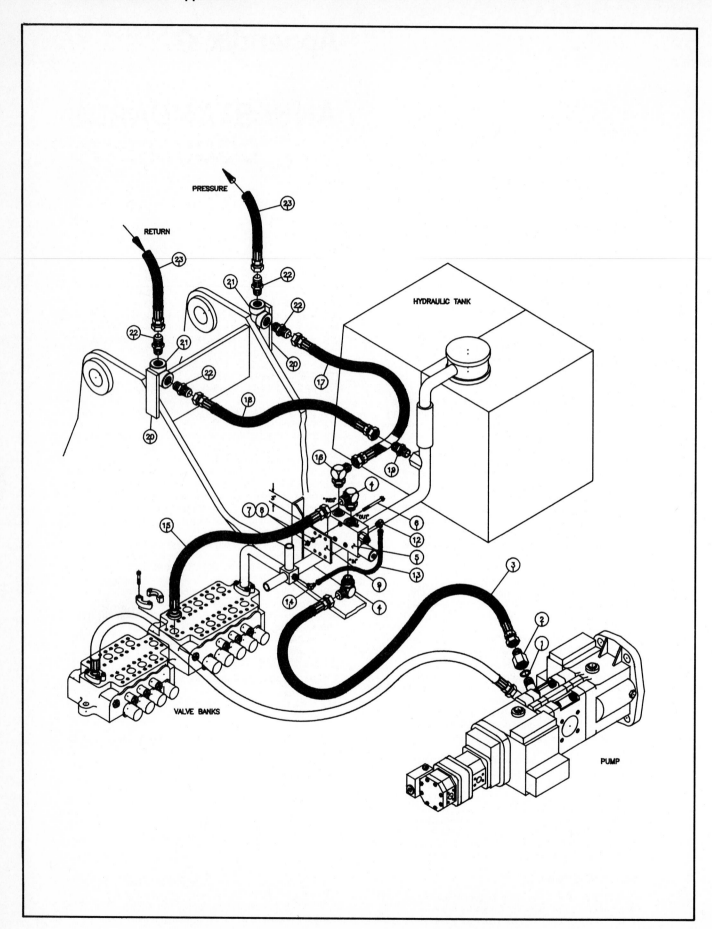

Application illustration for a hydraulic sysem.   (Autodesk, Inc.)

Appendix H

DRAFTING SYMBOLS

STANDARD DIMENSIONING SYMBOLS

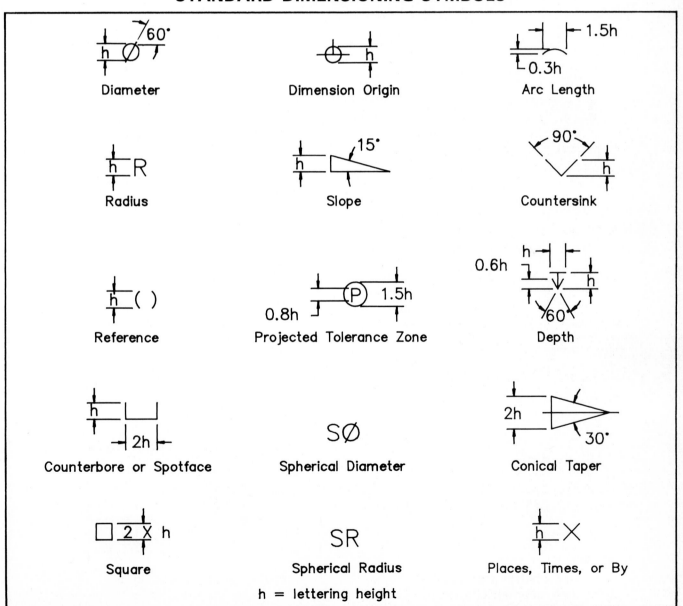

Diameter	Dimension Origin	Arc Length
Radius	Slope	Countersink
Reference	Projected Tolerance Zone	Depth
Counterbore or Spotface	Spherical Diameter	Conical Taper
Square	Spherical Radius	Places, Times, or By

h = lettering height

GEOMETRIC DIMENSIONING AND TOLERANCING SYMBOLS

Additional GD&T information is found in *Geometric Dimensioning and Tolerancing* by David A. Madsen, and is available through Goodheart-Willcox.

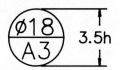

Datum Target Symbol

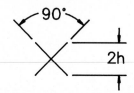

Datum Target Point

Datum Target Line

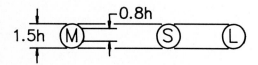

Ⓜ MMC, Maximum Material Condition
Ⓢ RFS, Regardless of Feature Size
Ⓛ LMC, Least Material Condition

Material Condition Symbols

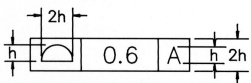

Profile of a surface symbol in a feature control frame.

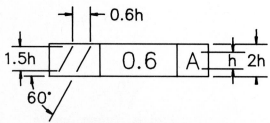

Feature control frame with parallelism geometric tolerance.

Datum Target Area

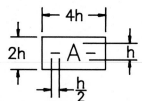

Datum Feature Symbol

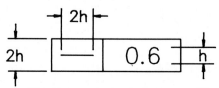

Feature control frame with straightness geometric characteristic symbol.

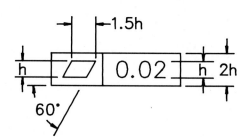

Flatness feature control frame.

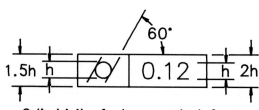

Cylindricity feature control frame.

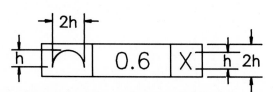

Profile of a surface in a feature control frame.

h = lettering height

GEOMETRIC DIMENSIONING AND TOLERANCING SYMBOLS, Cont.

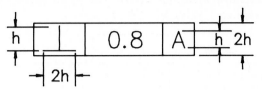

Perpendicularity feature control frame

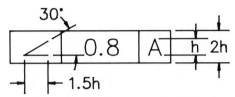

Angularity feature control frame.

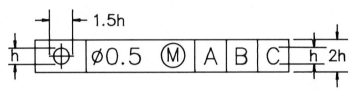

Position tolerance in a feature control frame.

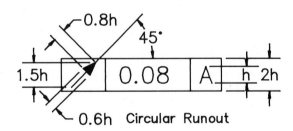

Circular Runout

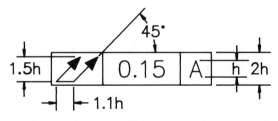

Total Runout

Symbols may be drawn open or filled in
where the symbols are produced on a
CADD system the open arrow is prefered.

h = lettering height

COMMON SINGLE LINE PIPE FITTING SYMBOLS

Additional pipe drafting information is found in *Process Pipe Drafting* by Terence M. Schumaker, and is available through Goodheart-Willcox.

Name	Screwed			Buttwelded		
	left side	front	right side	left side	front	right side
90° Elbow						
45° Elbow						
Tee						
45° Lateral						
Cross						
Cap						
Concentric Reducer						
Eccentric Reducer						
Union						
Coupling						

COMMON SYMBOLS FOR ELECTRONIC DIAGRAMS

Amplifier		Triode with directly heated cathode and envelope connection to base terminal		Fluorescent, 2-terminal lamp	
Antenna, general				Incandescent lamp	
Antenna, dipole		Pentode using elongated envelope		Microphone	
Antenna, dipole				Receiver, earphone	
Antenna, counterpoise		Twin triode using elongated envelope		Resistor, general	
Battery, long line positive				Resistor, adjustable	
Multicell battery		Voltage regulator, also, glow lamp		Resistor, variable	
Capacitor, general					
Capacitor, variable		Phototube		Transformer, general	
Capacitor, polarized					
Circuit breaker		Inductor, winding, reactor, general		Transformer, magnetic core,	
Ground		Magnetic core inductor		Shielded transformer, magnetic core	
Chassis ground		Adjustable inductor			
Connectors, jack and plug				Auto-transformer, adjustable	
Engaged connectors		Balast lamp			

COMMON ARCHITECTURAL SYMBOLS

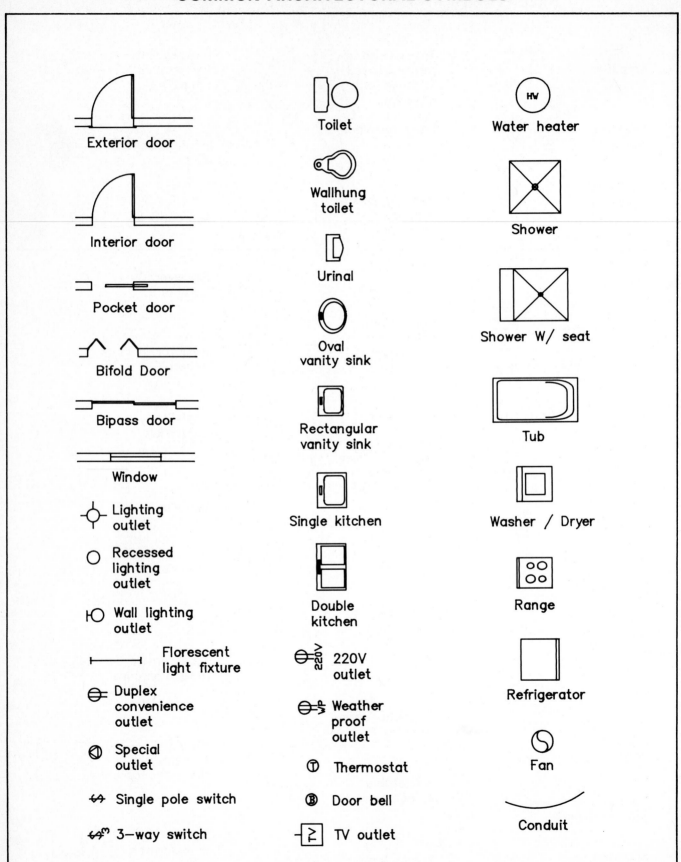

Exterior door

Interior door

Pocket door

Bifold Door

Bipass door

Window

Lighting outlet

Recessed lighting outlet

Wall lighting outlet

Florescent light fixture

Duplex convenience outlet

Special outlet

Single pole switch

3—way switch

Toilet

Wallhung toilet

Urinal

Oval vanity sink

Rectangular vanity sink

Single kitchen

Double kitchen

220V outlet

Weather proof outlet

Thermostat

Door bell

TV outlet

Water heater

Shower

Shower W/ seat

Tub

Washer / Dryer

Range

Refrigerator

Fan

Conduit

METRIC CONVERSION CHART

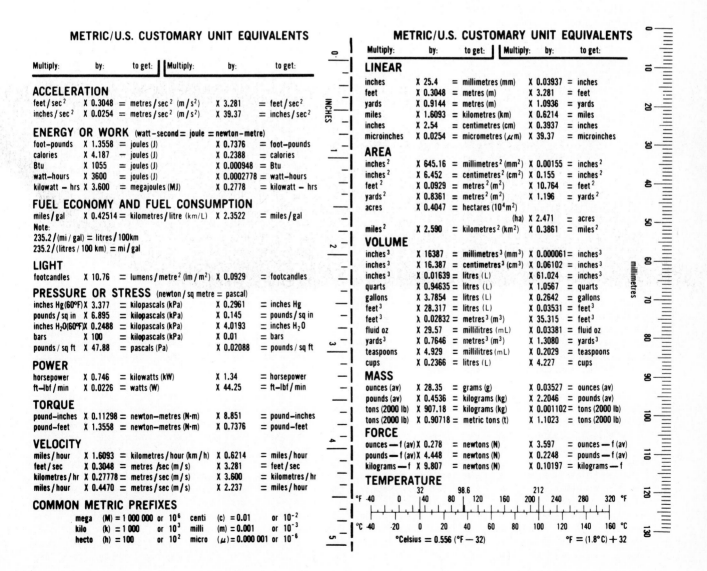

METRIC/U.S. CUSTOMARY UNIT EQUIVALENTS

Multiply:	by:	to get:	Multiply:	by:	to get:
ACCELERATION					
feet/sec^2	X 0.3048	= metres/sec^2 (m/s^2)	X 3.281	= feet/sec^2	
inches/sec^2	X 0.0254	= metres/sec^2 (m/s^2)	X 39.37	= inches/sec^2	
ENERGY OR WORK (watt−second = joule = newton−metre)					
foot-pounds	X 1.3558	= joules (J)	X 0.7376	= foot−pounds	
calories	X 4.187	= joules (J)	X 0.2388	= calories	
Btu	X 1055	= joules (J)	X 0.000948	= Btu	
watt-hours	X 3600	= joules (J)	X 0.0002778	= watt−hours	
kilowatt − hrs	X 3.600	= megajoules (MJ)	X 0.2778	= kilowatt − hrs	
FUEL ECONOMY AND FUEL CONSUMPTION					
miles/gal	X 0.42514	= kilometres/litre (km/L)	X 2.3522	= miles/gal	
Note:					
235.2/(mi/gal) = litres/100km					
235.2/(litres/100 km) = mi/gal					
LIGHT					
footcandles	X 10.76	= lumens/metre^2 (lm/m^2)	X 0.0929	= footcandles	
PRESSURE OR STRESS (newton/sq metre = pascal)					
inches Hg(60°F)	X 3.377	= kilopascals (kPa)	X 0.2961	= inches Hg	
pounds/sq in	X 6.895	= kilopascals (kPa)	X 0.145	= pounds/sq in	
inches H$_2$O(60°F)	X 0.2488	= kilopascals (kPa)	X 4.0193	= inches H$_2$O	
bars	X 100	= kilopascals (kPa)	X 0.01	= bars	
pounds/sq ft	X 47.88	= pascals (Pa)	X 0.02088	= pounds/sq ft	
POWER					
horsepower	X 0.746	= kilowatts (kW)	X 1.34	= horsepower	
ft−lbf/min	X 0.0226	= watts (W)	X 44.25	= ft−lbf/min	
TORQUE					
pound−inches	X 0.11298	= newton−metres (N·m)	X 8.851	= pound−inches	
pound−feet	X 1.3558	= newton−metres (N·m)	X 0.7376	= pound−feet	
VELOCITY					
miles/hour	X 1.6093	= kilometres/hour (km/h)	X 0.6214	= miles/hour	
feet/sec	X 0.3048	= metres/sec (m/s)	X 3.281	= feet/sec	
kilometres/hr	X 0.27778	= metres/sec (m/s)	X 3.600	= kilometres/hr	
miles/hour	X 0.4470	= metres/sec (m/s)	X 2.237	= miles/hour	

COMMON METRIC PREFIXES

mega	(M) = 1 000 000	or 10^6	centi	(c) = 0.01	or 10^{-2}
kilo	(k) = 1 000	or 10^3	milli	(m) = 0.001	or 10^{-3}
hecto	(h) = 100	or 10^2	micro	(μ) = 0.000 001	or 10^{-6}

METRIC/U.S. CUSTOMARY UNIT EQUIVALENTS

Multiply:	by:	to get:	Multiply:	by:	to get:
LINEAR					
inches	X 25.4	= millimetres (mm)	X 0.03937	= inches	
feet	X 0.3048	= metres (m)	X 3.281	= feet	
yards	X 0.9144	= metres (m)	X 1.0936	= yards	
miles	X 1.6093	= kilometres (km)	X 0.6214	= miles	
inches	X 2.54	= centimetres (cm)	X 0.3937	= inches	
microinches	X 0.0254	= micrometres (μm)	X 39.37	= microinches	
AREA					
inches^2	X 645.16	= millimetres^2 (mm^2)	X 0.00155	= inches^2	
inches^2	X 6.452	= centimetres^2 (cm^2)	X 0.155	= inches^2	
feet^2	X 0.0929	= metres^2 (m^2)	X 10.764	= feet^2	
yards^2	X 0.8361	= metres^2 (m^2)	X 1.196	= yards^2	
acres	X 0.4047	= hectares (10^{4}m^2)			
		(ha)	X 2.471	= acres	
miles^2	X 2.590	= kilometres^2 (km^2)	X 0.3861	= miles^2	
VOLUME					
inches^3	X 16387	= millimetres^3 (mm^3)	X 0.000061	= inches^3	
inches^3	X 16.387	= centimetres^3 (cm^3)	X 0.06102	= inches^3	
inches^3	X 0.01639	= litres (L)	X 61.024	= inches^3	
quarts	X 0.94635	= litres (L)	X 1.0567	= quarts	
gallons	X 3.7854	= litres (L)	X 0.2642	= gallons	
feet^3	X 28.317	= litres (L)	X 0.03531	= feet^3	
feet^3	λ 0.02832	= metres^3 (m^3)	X 35.315	= feet^3	
fluid oz	X 29.57	= millilitres (mL)	X 0.03381	= fluid oz	
yards^3	X 0.7646	= metres^3 (m^3)	X 1.3080	= yards^3	
teaspoons	X 4.929	= millilitres (mL)	X 0.2029	= teaspoons	
cups	X 0.2366	= litres (L)	X 4.227	= cups	
MASS					
ounces (av)	X 28.35	= grams (g)	X 0.03527	= ounces (av)	
pounds (av)	X 0.4536	= kilograms (kg)	X 2.2046	= pounds (av)	
tons (2000 lb)	X 907.18	= kilograms (kg)	X 0.001102	= tons (2000 lb)	
tons (2000 lb)	X 0.90718	= metric tons (t)	X 1.1023	= tons (2000 lb)	
FORCE					
ounces −f (av)	X 0.278	= newtons (N)	X 3.597	= ounces − f (av)	
pounds −f (av)	X 4.448	= newtons (N)	X 0.2248	= pounds − f (av)	
kilograms −f	X 9.807	= newtons (N)	X 0.10197	= kilograms − f	

TEMPERATURE

°Celsius = 0.556 (°F − 32)   °F = (1.8°C) + 32

SEGMENTS OF CIRCLES

Length of arc (l = radians), height of segment (h), length of chord (c), and area of segment (A) for angles from 1 to 180 degrees and radius = 1. For other radii, multiply the values given for distance by the radius, and the values given for area by r^2, the square of the radius. The values in the table can be used for U.S. customary or metric units.

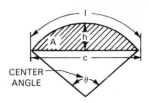

Center Angle θ, Degrees	l	h	c	Area of Segment A	Center Angle θ, Degrees	l	h	c	Area of Segment A	Center Angle θ, Degrees	l	h	c	Area of Segment A	Center Angle θ, Degrees	l	h	c	Area of Segment A
1	0.01745	0.00004	0.01745	0.00000	46	0.803	0.0795	0.781	0.04176	91	1.588	0.2991	1.427	0.2942	136	2.374	0.6254	1.854	0.8395
2	0.03491	0.00015	0.03490	0.00000	47	0.820	0.0829	0.797	0.04448	92	1.606	0.3053	1.439	0.3032	137	2.391	0.6335	1.861	0.8546
3	0.05236	0.00034	0.05235	0.00001	48	0.838	0.0865	0.813	0.04731	93	1.623	0.3116	1.451	0.3123	138	2.409	0.6416	1.867	0.8697
4	0.06981	0.00061	0.06980	0.00003	49	0.855	0.0900	0.829	0.05025	94	1.641	0.3180	1.463	0.3215	139	2.426	0.6498	1.873	0.8850
5	0.08727	0.00095	0.08724	0.00006	50	0.873	0.0937	0.845	0.05331	95	1.658	0.3244	1.475	0.3309	140	2.443	0.6580	1.879	0.9003
6	0.10472	0.00137	0.10467	0.00010	51	0.890	0.0974	0.861	0.05649	96	1.676	0.3309	1.486	0.3405	141	2.461	0.6662	1.885	0.9158
7	0.12217	0.00187	0.12210	0.00015	52	0.908	0.1012	0.877	0.05978	97	1.693	0.3374	1.498	0.3502	142	2.478	0.6744	1.891	0.9314
8	0.13963	0.00244	0.13951	0.00023	53	0.925	0.1051	0.892	0.06319	98	1.710	0.3439	1.509	0.3601	143	2.496	0.6827	1.897	0.9470
9	0.15708	0.00308	0.15692	0.00032	54	0.942	0.1090	0.908	0.06673	99	1.728	0.3506	1.521	0.3701	144	2.513	0.6910	1.902	0.9627
10	0.17453	0.00381	0.17431	0.00044	55	0.960	0.1130	0.923	0.07039	100	1.745	0.3572	1.532	0.3803	145	2.531	0.6993	1.907	0.9786
11	0.19199	0.00460	0.19169	0.00059	56	0.977	0.1171	0.939	0.07417	101	1.763	0.3639	1.543	0.3906	146	2.548	0.7076	1.913	0.9945
12	0.20944	0.00548	0.20906	0.00076	57	0.995	0.1212	0.954	0.07808	102	1.780	0.3707	1.554	0.4010	147	2.566	0.7160	1.918	1.0105
13	0.22689	0.00643	0.22641	0.00097	58	1.012	0.1254	0.970	0.08212	103	1.798	0.3775	1.565	0.4117	148	2.583	0.7244	1.923	1.0266
14	0.24435	0.00745	0.24374	0.00121	59	1.030	0.1296	0.985	0.08629	104	1.815	0.3843	1.576	0.4224	149	2.601	0.7328	1.927	1.0428
15	0.26180	0.00856	0.26105	0.00149	60	1.047	0.1340	1.000	0.09059	105	1.833	0.3912	1.587	0.4333	150	2.618	0.7412	1.932	1.0590
16	0.27925	0.00973	0.27835	0.00181	61	1.065	0.1384	1.015	0.09502	106	1.850	0.3982	1.597	0.4444	151	2.635	0.7496	1.936	1.0753
17	0.29671	0.01098	0.29562	0.00217	62	1.082	0.1428	1.030	0.09958	107	1.868	0.4052	1.608	0.4556	152	2.653	0.7581	1.941	1.0917
18	0.31416	0.01231	0.31287	0.00257	63	1.100	0.1474	1.045	0.10428	108	1.885	0.4122	1.618	0.4669	153	2.670	0.7666	1.945	1.1082
19	0.33161	0.01371	0.33010	0.00302	64	1.117	0.1520	1.060	0.10911	109	1.902	0.4193	1.628	0.4784	154	2.688	0.7750	1.949	1.1247
20	0.34907	0.01519	0.34730	0.00352	65	1.134	0.1566	1.075	0.11408	110	1.920	0.4264	1.638	0.4901	155	2.705	0.7836	1.953	1.1413
21	0.36652	0.01675	0.36447	0.00408	66	1.152	0.1613	1.089	0.11919	111	1.937	0.4336	1.648	0.5019	156	2.723	0.7921	1.956	1.1580
22	0.38397	0.01837	0.38162	0.00468	67	1.169	0.1661	1.104	0.12443	112	1.955	0.4408	1.658	0.5138	157	2.740	0.8006	1.960	1.1747
23	0.40143	0.02008	0.39874	0.00535	68	1.187	0.1710	1.118	0.12982	113	1.972	0.4481	1.668	0.5259	158	2.758	0.8092	1.963	1.1915
24	0.41888	0.02185	0.41582	0.00607	69	1.204	0.1759	1.133	0.13535	114	1.990	0.4554	1.677	0.5381	159	2.775	0.8178	1.967	1.2084
25	0.43633	0.02370	0.43288	0.00686	70	1.222	0.1808	1.147	0.14102	115	2.007	0.4627	1.687	0.5504	160	2.793	0.8264	1.970	1.2253
26	0.45379	0.02563	0.44990	0.00771	71	1.239	0.1859	1.161	0.14683	116	2.025	0.4701	1.696	0.5629	161	2.810	0.8350	1.973	1.2422
27	0.47124	0.02763	0.46689	0.00862	72	1.257	0.1910	1.176	0.15279	117	2.042	0.4775	1.705	0.5755	162	2.827	0.8436	1.975	1.2592
28	0.48869	0.02970	0.48384	0.00961	73	1.274	0.1961	1.190	0.15889	118	2.059	0.4850	1.714	0.5883	163	2.845	0.8522	1.978	1.2763
29	0.50615	0.03185	0.50076	0.01067	74	1.292	0.2014	1.204	0.16514	119	2.077	0.4925	1.723	0.6012	164	2.862	0.8608	1.981	1.2934
30	0.52360	0.03407	0.51764	0.01180	75	1.309	0.2066	1.218	0.17154	120	2.094	0.5000	1.732	0.6142	165	2.880	0.8695	1.983	1.3105
31	0.54105	0.03637	0.53448	0.01301	76	1.326	0.2120	1.231	0.17808	121	2.112	0.5076	1.741	0.6273	166	2.897	0.8781	1.985	1.3277
32	0.55851	0.03874	0.55127	0.01429	77	1.344	0.2174	1.245	0.18477	122	2.129	0.5152	1.749	0.6406	167	2.915	0.8868	1.987	1.3449
33	0.57596	0.04118	0.56803	0.01566	78	1.361	0.2229	1.259	0.19160	123	2.147	0.5228	1.758	0.6540	168	2.932	0.8955	1.989	1.3621
34	0.59341	0.04370	0.58474	0.01711	79	1.379	0.2284	1.272	0.19859	124	2.164	0.5305	1.766	0.6676	169	2.950	0.9042	1.991	1.3794
35	0.61087	0.04628	0.60141	0.01864	80	1.396	0.2340	1.286	0.20573	125	2.182	0.5383	1.774	0.6813	170	2.967	0.9128	1.992	1.3967
36	0.62832	0.04894	0.61803	0.02027	81	1.414	0.2396	1.299	0.21301	126	2.199	0.5460	1.782	0.6950	171	2.985	0.9215	1.994	1.4140
37	0.64577	0.05168	0.63461	0.02198	82	1.431	0.2453	1.312	0.22045	127	2.217	0.5538	1.790	0.7090	172	3.002	0.9302	1.995	1.4314
38	0.66323	0.05448	0.65114	0.02378	83	1.449	0.2510	1.325	0.22804	128	2.234	0.5616	1.798	0.7230	173	3.019	0.9390	1.996	1.4488
39	0.68068	0.05736	0.66761	0.02568	84	1.466	0.2569	1.338	0.23578	129	2.251	0.5695	1.805	0.7372	174	3.037	0.9477	1.997	1.4662
40	0.69813	0.06031	0.68404	0.02767	85	1.484	0.2627	1.351	0.24367	130	2.269	0.5774	1.813	0.7514	175	3.054	0.9564	1.998	1.4836
41	0.71558	0.06333	0.70041	0.02976	86	1.501	0.2686	1.364	0.25171	131	2.286	0.5853	1.820	0.7658	176	3.072	0.9651	1.999	1.5010
42	0.73304	0.06642	0.71674	0.03195	87	1.518	0.2746	1.377	0.25990	132	2.304	0.5933	1.827	0.7803	177	3.089	0.9738	1.999	1.5184
43	0.75049	0.06958	0.73300	0.03425	88	1.536	0.2807	1.389	0.26825	133	2.321	0.6013	1.834	0.7950	178	3.107	0.9825	2.000	1.5359
44	0.76794	0.07282	0.74921	0.03664	89	1.553	0.2867	1.402	0.27675	134	2.339	0.6093	1.841	0.8097	179	3.124	0.9913	2.000	1.5533
45	0.78540	0.07612	0.76537	0.03915	90	1.571	0.2929	1.414	0.28540	135	2.356	0.6173	1.848	0.8245	180	3.142	1.0000	2.000	1.5708

INDEX

AutoCAD and Its Applications

More Valuable Resources from Goodheart-Willcox

AutoLISP Programming   *Rawls and Hagen*

AutoLISP® is a version of the LISP programming language, which has many functions specific to AutoCAD. **AutoLISP Programming** covers functions included in AutoCAD Release 2.18 through 12, including ANGTOF, NENTSELP, TEXTBOX, and ALERT. **AutoLISP Programming** offers the following advantages over other AutoLISP books:

* Begins at a level that is understandable to the novice AutoCAD user.
* Progresses in a step-by-step manner, describing how to create useful and productive routines and programs with AutoLISP.
* Provides Exercises within the chapters to provide immediate reinforcement of the concepts previously covered.
* Designed to stress that the true effectiveness of AutoLISP comes not from being taught how the programming language works or how to build a program, but from learning how to direct one's skills with problem-solving techniques.

AutoCAD Essentials   *Shumaker and Madsen*

AutoCAD Essentials is designed to help students understand the fundamentals of AutoCAD. Basic commands and techniques are presented with common drafting practices and standards to help students learn drafting and AutoCAD at the same time. The content of **AutoCAD Essentials** is based on Releases 10 and 11. Release 11 information is clearly marked with a vertical color bar in the margin.

AutoCAD Essentials is intended to be used in a first year CAD course. Features built into the text include:

* Objectives at the beginning of each chapter.
* Tutorials to allow students to get their ''feet wet'' right away.
* Over 100 activities interspersed throughout the chapters.
* Helpful Hints to make the students' learning experience enjoyable.
* Review Questions provide a comprehensive review of the chapters.
* Problems allow students to practice their newly learned skills.

AutoCAD and its Applications – Release 10   *Shumaker and Madsen*

This edition of **AutoCAD and its Applications** is designed to help you master AutoCAD Release 10. This write-in text is not just another version of the reference manual. It is a comprehensive, easy-to-understand guide that shows how to apply AutoCAD® functions to typical drafting and graphic design tasks. The topics progress from simple to complex and are suitable for both novices and practicing professionals. Each new chapter builds on the previous one. A step-by-step approach is used to eliminate the anxieties often associated with learning AutoCAD. In addition, **AutoCAD and its Applications** offers the following features:

* Over 150 drawing exercises are placed within chapters after important sections. These provide hands-on experience while breaking the material into small learning segments.
* End-of-chapter drawing problems are given as actual industrial prints or engineering sketches. These require that you apply all skills learned through the current chapter.
* Text covers versions of AutoCAD through Release 10; topics keyed to AutoCAD Reference Manual.

AutoCAD and its Applications – Release 11 *Shumaker and Madsen*

The Release 11 edition of **AutoCAD and its Applications** includes all of the features that made the Release 10 edition one of the most widely acclaimed books in the AutoCAD educational market. ''Screen captures'' depicting the actual appearance of the screen displays have been integrated throughout the text for maximum educational transfer. In addition to topics addressed in the Release 10 edition, new topics include (but are not limited to) the following:

- Expanded dimensioning capabilities.
- New drawing and plotting modes—model space and paper space.
- XReferencing details and other drawing components into a master drawing.
- Introduction to the Advanced Modeling Extension (AME).
- Surface Modeling tutorial.
- Introduction to AutoShade® and Autodesk RenderMan®.
- Solid Modeling tutorial.

Architectural AutoCAD *Madsen and Fitzgibbon*

Architectural AutoCAD is a text/workbook combination that provides complete instruction for mastering AutoCAD AEC® commands. It also introduces professional architectural management and project planning concepts. Topics are covered in an easy-to-learn sequence that allow the student to become comfortable with commands as knowledge builds from one chapter to the next. Applications include residential, multifamily, and commercial structures.

AutoSketch for Drafting and Design *Duelm*

An innovative text which discusses the application of AutoSketch®, Versions 3 and 2.0 in typical drafting and design tasks. In addition to completely describing the AutoSketch software, the text also covers the hardware, practices, and technical language of computer-aided drafting and design. This text is a valuable resource for anyone interested in using AutoSketch for drawing, design, and technical illustration.

For additional information about any of these books, or any other Goodheart-Willcox books, please call (708) 333-7200.